T0180500

Lecture Notes in Computer Science   10290

Commenced Publication in 1973
Founding and Former Series Editors:
Gerhard Goos, Juris Hartmanis, and Jan van Leeuwen

Editorial Board

More information about this series at http://www.springer.com/series/7409

Aaron Marcus · Wentao Wang (Eds.)

Design, User Experience, and Usability

Understanding Users and Contexts

6th International Conference, DUXU 2017
Held as Part of HCI International 2017
Vancouver, BC, Canada, July 9–14, 2017
Proceedings, Part III

 Springer

Editors
Aaron Marcus
Aaron Marcus and Associates, Inc.
Berkeley, CA
USA

Wentao Wang
Baidu, Inc.
Beijing
China

ISSN 0302-9743   ISSN 1611-3349   (electronic)
Lecture Notes in Computer Science
ISBN 978-3-319-58639-7   ISBN 978-3-319-58640-3   (eBook)
DOI 10.1007/978-3-319-58640-3

Library of Congress Control Number: 2017939729

LNCS Sublibrary: SL3 – Information Systems and Applications, incl. Internet/Web, and HCI

Printed on acid-free paper

This Springer imprint is published by Springer Nature
The registered company is Springer International Publishing AG
The registered company address is: Gewerbestrasse 11, 6330 Cham, Switzerland

Foreword

The 19th International Conference on Human–Computer Interaction, HCI International 2017, was held in Vancouver, Canada, during July 9–14, 2017. The event incorporated the 15 conferences/thematic areas listed on the following page.

A total of 4,340 individuals from academia, research institutes, industry, and governmental agencies from 70 countries submitted contributions, and 1,228 papers have been included in the proceedings. These papers address the latest research and development efforts and highlight the human aspects of design and use of computing systems. The papers thoroughly cover the entire field of human–computer interaction, addressing major advances in knowledge and effective use of computers in a variety of application areas. The volumes constituting the full set of the conference proceedings are listed on the following pages.

I would like to thank the program board chairs and the members of the program boards of all thematic areas and affiliated conferences for their contribution to the highest scientific quality and the overall success of the HCI International 2017 conference.

This conference would not have been possible without the continuous and unwavering support and advice of the founder, Conference General Chair Emeritus and Conference Scientific Advisor Prof. Gavriel Salvendy. For his outstanding efforts, I would like to express my appreciation to the communications chair and editor of *HCI International News*, Dr. Abbas Moallem.

April 2017   Constantine Stephanidis

HCI International 2017 Thematic Areas and Affiliated Conferences

Thematic areas:

- Human–Computer Interaction (HCI 2017)
- Human Interface and the Management of Information (HIMI 2017)

Affiliated conferences:

- 17th International Conference on Engineering Psychology and Cognitive Ergonomics (EPCE 2017)
- 11th International Conference on Universal Access in Human–Computer Interaction (UAHCI 2017)
- 9th International Conference on Virtual, Augmented and Mixed Reality (VAMR 2017)
- 9th International Conference on Cross-Cultural Design (CCD 2017)
- 9th International Conference on Social Computing and Social Media (SCSM 2017)
- 11th International Conference on Augmented Cognition (AC 2017)
- 8th International Conference on Digital Human Modeling and Applications in Health, Safety, Ergonomics and Risk Management (DHM 2017)
- 6th International Conference on Design, User Experience and Usability (DUXU 2017)
- 5th International Conference on Distributed, Ambient and Pervasive Interactions (DAPI 2017)
- 5th International Conference on Human Aspects of Information Security, Privacy and Trust (HAS 2017)
- 4th International Conference on HCI in Business, Government and Organizations (HCIBGO 2017)
- 4th International Conference on Learning and Collaboration Technologies (LCT 2017)
- Third International Conference on Human Aspects of IT for the Aged Population (ITAP 2017)

Conference Proceedings Volumes Full List

Design, User Experience and Usability

Program Board Chair(s): **Aaron Marcus, USA, and Wentao Wang, P.R. China**

- Sisira Adikari, Australia
- Claire Ancient, UK
- Jan Brejcha, Czech Republic
- Hashim Iqbal Chunpir, Germany
- Silvia de los Rios Perez, Spain
- Marc Fabri, UK
- Patricia Flanagan, Australia
- Nouf Khashman, Qatar
- Tom MacTavish, USA
- Judith A. Moldenhauer, USA
- Francisco Rebelo, Portugal
- Kerem Rizvanoglu, Turkey
- Christine Riedmann-Streitz, Germany
- Patricia Search, USA
- Carla Galvão Spinillo, Brazil
- Marcelo Márcio Soares, Brazil
- Virginia Tiradentes Souto, Brazil

The full list with the Program Board Chairs and the members of the Program Boards of all thematic areas and affiliated conferences is available online at:

http://www.hci.international/board-members-2017.php

HCI International 2018

The 20th International Conference on Human–Computer Interaction, HCI International 2018, will be held jointly with the affiliated conferences in Las Vegas, NV, USA, at Caesars Palace, July 15–20, 2018. It will cover a broad spectrum of themes related to human–computer interaction, including theoretical issues, methods, tools, processes, and case studies in HCI design, as well as novel interaction techniques, interfaces, and applications. The proceedings will be published by Springer. More information is available on the conference website: http://2018.hci.international/.

General Chair
Prof. Constantine Stephanidis
University of Crete and ICS-FORTH
Heraklion, Crete, Greece
E-mail: general_chair@hcii2018.org

http://2018.hci.international/

Contents – Part III

DUXU Practice and Case Studies

Contents – Part I

Aesthetics and Perception in Design

User Experience Evaluation Methods and Tools

User Centered Design in the Software Development Lifecycle

Contents – Part II

Mobile DUXU

Designing the Playing Experience

Designing the Virtual, Augmented and Tangible Experience

Information Design

An Interactive Behavior-Based Hierarchical Design Method for Form Hints

Cao Huai and Zhou Qi[✉]

School of Mechanical Science and Engineering,
Huazhong University of Science and Technology, Wuhan,
People's Republic of China
caohuai@hust.edu.cn, 384415003@qq.com

Abstract. A form prompt message refers to the prompt message generated when a user accesses to a form. At present, the research on the approach to design the form prompt message is not perfect. Therefore, this paper provides a method to design the form prompt message based on behavior path. The first part of the paper combs through the existing interactive behaviors and the basic theories of prompt message design, then analyzes the interaction among behavior and path, hint and memory load, and plans a hierarchical model of interactive behavior combined with the existing GOMS model. Moreover, this paper discusses the influence of the importance, frequency and circumstance property on evaluating the priority of prompt message, and sorts out a hierarchy diagram of form prompt message based on interactive behavior. Finally, experiments are carried out with this approach to verify the validity of the hierarchy design approach presented in this paper.

Keywords: Prompt message · Hierarchy design · Interactive behavior · Path

1 Introduction

Jared• M• Spoor, the founder of User Interface Engineering (UIE), once said: "Identifying the subtle points of form design may bring dramatic influence to online experience (and baseline) and the whole. Once you learn to control these subtle points, you may become a top master-hand" [1]. A form prompt message is generated during the user access, which is the subtle point mentioned by Jared• M• Spoor. When users meet some difficulties in visiting forms, the prompt message will provide users with some necessary hints and guidance. But in the meanwhile, in case of a large form experience load, the prompt message may degrade the user experience with the form.

In recent years, the theory of prompt message design is improved gradually; and the ideological level of design is also enhanced gradually. But meanwhile, enterprises and design researchers have not reached a consensus on the definition of form prompt message. In a book named Web Form Design: Filling in the Blanks, Luque • Wroblewski, a famous user experience designer of Google, interpreted the prompt message as: help text as well as error and success messages. Help text refers to the words helping users fill in the form successfully; error message is to inform users of their failure to continue filling in the form and of other solutions; and success message

A. Marcus and W. Wang (Eds.): DUXU 2017, Part III, LNCS 10290, pp. 3–15, 2017.
DOI: 10.1007/978-3-319-58640-3_1

is to inform users of their success in completing the form. In a book named About Face 3: The Essentials of Interaction Design, Cooper et al. [3] interpreted the prompt message as: dialog box—a dialog box for error, warning and confirmation. Xiong [4] described the prompt message as a supplement function helping users complete interactive behaviors in the access process, and the prompt message is generally a feedback of interactive behaviors. They think that the prompt message is a feedback of user behavior; and the form of feedback is diversified, i.e., help texts also can be error messages and dialog boxes, etc.

In the existing literatures, the research on the approach to design form becomes increasingly richer; however, there is deficient in research on prompt message design approach. And at present, the research mainly focuses on the fields such as cognitive psychology, behavioral psychology and ergonomics. Rasmussen [5] summarized three modes of interactive behaviors in information design, among which, Rules Based Behavior (RBB) mode means dividing all behaviors into several steps, which will be executed step by step. This mode provides guidance for this paper to analyze interactive behavior path. Raskin [6] put forward Goals, Operators, Methods and Selectors (GOMS) keystroke mode. Figure 1 shows a simple calculation method to quantify interface efficiency, which helps this paper quickly quantify the user's behavior path. Wei [7] thinks that combing through information hierarchy and establishing a suitable information architecture are extremely important to applications. Furthermore, Cao Ruping et al. also discussed the approach to design information hierarchy with visual elements. All these theories are beneficial to the development of researches in this field (Table 1).

Table 1. GOMS keystroke mode

Name (tag)	(Keying) K	(Pointing) P	(Homeing) H	(Mentally preparing) M	(Responding) R
Average time (S)	0.2 s	1.1 s	0.4 s	1.35 s	
Implication	The time required to tap a key on the keyboard or mouse	The time that the user (with the mouse) points to a position on the display	The time it takes a user to move his hand from the keyboard to the graphical input device (mouse), or from the graphical input device to the keyboard	The user to enter the next step required for mental preparation time	The time the user waits for the computer to respond to the input

This paper solves two difficulties: the first one is to extract the path of user's interactive behavior and put forward a hierarchy mode of interactive behavior based on the existing GOMS Keystroke mode; and the second one is to divide the priority of information and present a hierarchy diagram of form prompt message. And then the designer obtains a result by quantitative grading.

This paper creatively puts forward an approach to guide designers to design form prompt message.

2 Problem Definition

Form has various types. In the time dimension, users take several seconds or hours to complete a form; in the information dimension, users usually fill in information on several items to several papers. The current design methods mainly aim at simple forms requiring less time and information. However, the methods are not properly applied in complex forms. Complex forms have a large amount of information with a number of prompt messages, which increase the cognitive difficulty for users. The version of form upgrades rapidly. Influenced by design cost, etc., enterprises usually make minor modifications, making it difficult to form the design specification of form prompt message. As shown in Fig. 1, Facebook Advertisement Management Form, we mark all prompt messages in grey including icons, links, help texts, etc. All these prompt messages are stiffly presented on forms, which not only distract user's attention but also reduce the availability of form.

Fig. 1. Facebook advertisement management form

3 Interaction Behavior

Interactive design focuses on not only behavior design, but also the way how behaviors relate to content and form [9]. The decision logic of interactive design mainly adopts behavior logic [10]. Good behaviors shall be designed as considerate as a person, so do prompt messages. Consideration has been given a series of features which will be analyzed in the following aspects:

3.1   Behavior Path

A considerate prompt message is timely. We always hear some users complain like "why not tell me earlier" when they are filling in forms. In practice, we find out that many prompt messages are not designed correspondingly for a certain behavior, which usually appear earlier or later, disturb user's focus and even arouse user's negative emotion. To make prompt messages timely, users' behaviors have to be made clear.

Form is usually composed of elements such as label, input box, text, drop-down menu, check box and radio box, etc. Based on GOMS keystroke mode theory, the interactive behaviors of these elements are broken down into single actions whose integration is user's behavior path. Label and text message mainly involve user's eye movement and reading behavior, which are not mentioned in this paper. From Table 2: Behavior Path of Each Element in Form, we can clearly see the behavior path of each element. Only when the prompt message is arranged after a correct subaction based on the path can the prompt message be timely.

Table 2. Behavior path of each element in form

Element	Sample	Path
Label	昵称	
Input box		M+H+P+nK
Text	修改原因： 请在此填写修改原因	M+H+P+nK
Drop-down menu	公历 ▾ 公历 农历	M+H+P+K+P+K
Radio box	详细信息 ☑ 籍贯 ☐ 性别 ☐ 生日 ☑ 身份证 ☑ 学历 ☑ 电话	n(M+H+P+K)
Check box	◉ 男 ○ 女	M+H+P+K

3.2   Hint

On one hand, the usability of a product is reflected in whether the product adequately guides and hints user's behavior; on the other hand, it is reflected in whether the path for setting product functions is direct and short enough. When users judge that task completion needs a relatively short operation path, the task will have a better guidance [11].

The research shows that the majority of users hate filling out forms. The limitation of existing technology leads to a result that users are usually forced to complete forms. Therefore, it is really necessary to relieve the strained relation between users and forms. In emotional design, Norman [12] mentioned that users like to communicate with people rather than machine. Interactive design adopts enlightening information related to target user's behavior and habit [13]. Once this kind of enlightening information is associated with behavior, it not only enables the experience more humanized but also reduces the perceived gap among users and makes the design closer to user's habit.

In addition to this, this design can also establish and convey the relationship among elements; and location also hints the ordinal relation between elements. In the course of interactive design, the more important the function is, the briefer the operation path shall be adopted preferentially [11]. Briefer operation path is to hint users: we think this function is more useful compared with other ones. Replacing functions with prompt messages means that the core information has higher priority and shorter operation path. In man-machine interface design, we always use similar philosophies, because the delivery of information is in rhythm. Rhythm not only helps users to memorize but also hints them the priority of information.

3.3   Memory Load

In form interaction, users may face a situation that a pop-up window appears in another pop-up window, and a new page jumps to another page successively. This may make users lost in the process of interaction, which is the result of the continuous growth of memory load [15]. Through the analysis of Sects. 3.1 and 3.2, the relation between information and behavior path becomes clearer. We think that behavior path is the basis for division of prompt message hierarchy. Information with higher priority shall be arranged before the path. Hierarchy will be produced according to the number of subaction in the path. Therefore, the prompt message shall be arranged more logically. However, many daily behaviors are "habitual behaviors" cultivated by practicing and learning repeatedly, and also "automatic behaviors" without concentration [16], which are the function of subconscious memory and can dramatically reduce the memory load in interactive design. We deem that user's memory space is limited; the more the hierarchies are, the larger memory space is occupied; the heavier the user's memory load is, the higher the error rate of automatic behavior will be. To ensure the stability of form interaction, we put forward that the number of hierarchies must be balanced with the memory load produced. Hierarchy is not infinite; and we consider that 3 to 5 levels are the best.

Summary: This chapter extracts the path of form interactive behavior, puts forward the concept of hierarchy division based on path, discusses that enlightening elements can make hierarchy division more reasonably and rigorously comes up an idea that the number of hierarchy shall be limited. We make Fig. 2 to help you understand the hierarchy more intuitively. Taking the input box of the form for example, the space between every two subactions is for the prompt message. In a path, the earlier a subaction appears, the higher the hierarchy the prompt message has.

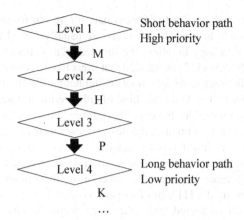

Fig. 2. Hierarchy of behavior path of input box. Level 1 is the highest hierarchy

4 Prompt Message Hierarchy

From the perspective of function, the form prompt message mainly falls into reminder message, guiding message, interpreting message and feedback message. As for the rule based on behavior, prompt messages for content and interface are consistent and have one-to-one mapping [17]. Since the designer must consciously analyze the priority of information sources [8], we put forward the following three criteria for analysis.

- Importance

Generally, the more important the information is, the more quickly the user shall be informed. When users advertise on Tencent social advertisement platform, the prompt message they first notice is the balance of account, because in case of insufficient money logically set for the product, the user will fail to do the advertisement. This prompt message can effectively avoid the user's invalid operation. Unlike Tencent, Google advertisement platform does not have this prompt message. Google users always find that the form cannot be completed during the creation, and then they have to give up filling out the form for topping up. Obviously, in doing an advertisement, the balance of account directly determines whether the task can be completed successfully. This prompt message, which has a great influence on the result of behavior, is fairly significant. We consider that the importance of a prompt message shall be measured in accordance with the result of user's behavior. The more probably the prompt message helps the user to complete the task, the more important the prompt message is; and vice versa.

- Frequency of use

Every user has a distinct cognition of information; and information also has memorability and learnability. When filling out a form, we may have access to interpreting prompt messages. Generally, the cost of cognizing these prompt messages is quite low, which means that users can easily understand and memorize them after reading once or several times. And afterwards, these messages will become a "useless decoration" to disturb users. Almost all forms have the problems above; therefore, the designer shall reasonably judge the use frequency of each prompt message so as to determine their priorities.

- Circumstances

If we do not understand the circumstance, many behaviors in our life will be difficult to understand [18]. Forms shall be designed so that users are provided with the appropriate help information based on the practical circumstance [9]. When filling out forms, we may also encounter a situation where a feedback prompt message may appear if we input an unqualified character. This feedback prompt message must appear in the current circumstance, which is a fixed logic hierarchy. We define the situation above as the prompt with strong circumstance. The stronger the circumstance the prompt message has, the more specific the problem is. We can judge the circumstance of a prompt message by its impact scope and accurately arrange the hierarchy of the prompt message, so as not to affect the user experience.

Summary: This chapter explicitly analyzes three criteria of dividing the priority of prompt messages: the more important the prompt message is, the higher the priority the prompt message has; the higher the frequency of use is, the higher the priority the prompt message has; and the stronger the circumstance the prompt message has, the higher the priority the prompt message has; and vice versa. Combined with the result in Sect. 3, we propose to design the model based on the prompt message hierarchy of the behavior path, as shown in Fig. 3. The higher the priority the prompt message has, the shorter the user's behavior path is; and vice versa.

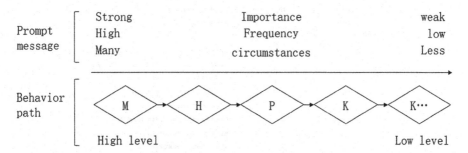

Fig. 3. Hierarchy design method model of prompt message. The higher the priority the prompt message has, the shorter the operation path the user needs.

5 Experiment and Practice

5.1 Experiment 1

To test the validity of the approach to design the prompt message hierarchy based on the behavior path, we design the following experiment.

- Preparation and process of experiment

(1) Testee group

College student, the aborigines of the Internet, not only have a deep understanding of the Internet, but also can clearly and accurately express their thoughts. Therefore, the testee group is determined to be college students aged between 18 and 27.

(2) Testee form design

Since some information frequently appears in a form, the cryptomnesia formed will lead to a result that users easily neglect these information, such as name. Users know how to fill out them without knowing their prompt messages. Therefore, when designing the form, some information that is unfamiliar to college students is selected to raise users' concern, ensuring the feasibility of the experiment.

(3) Test task

This experiment requires testees to complete Form 1 (Fig. 4) and Form 2 (Fig. 5) designed by us. The two forms have the same content. However, all prompt messages in Form 1 are presented directly based on hierarchy while the prompt messages in Form 2 are presented in sequence based on behavior.

Fig. 4. Form 1

- Planning and implementation of experiment

(1) This test involves 30 testees who are divided into group A and B; and each group includes 15 testees. The two forms have the same content, and the first completion

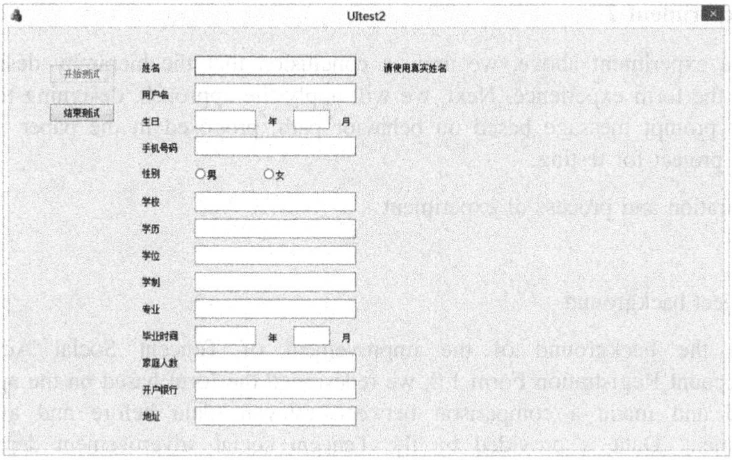

Fig. 5. Form 2

produces memory and affects the test result. Therefore, we asked group A to fill out Form 1 before Form 2 and group B to fill out Form 2 before Form 1. At the meantime, we recorded the time that testees spent on filling out the form.

(2) After the testees completed the form, we interviewed them and recorded their experience.

- Analysis of experimental results

As shown in Table 3, the average time to complete the two forms and the subjective satisfaction proportion of the two forms were obtained based on the data statistics of experiment. Based on the experimental result, we found out that Form 1 has a higher completion efficiency than Form 2; moreover, the majority of testees think that the experience of filling out Form 2 is much better than that of Form 1; and they also consider that the design of Form 2 makes them become more focused during the completion, the attention paid on the prompt message in Form 2 is higher and Form 2 also has a lower error rate.

Table 3. Summary of experimental results

Sample	Form 1	Form 2
Average time to complete (s)	102	83
Subjective satisfaction proportion	15.6%	28.1%

In the experiment, there are still some irresistible factors affecting the experimental results; for example, the testees have different cognitions to the same prompt message. Even though the experiment is not absolutely precise, we can also achieve the objective of the experiment.

5.2 Experiment 2

From the experiment above, we draw a conclusion that the hierarchy design can improve the form experience. Next, we will apply the approach, designing the hierarchy of prompt message based on behavior path, proposed in the paper into the practical project for testing.

- Preparation and process of experiment

(1) Project background

With the background of the improvement of Tencent Social Advertisement_Account Registration Form 1.0, we redesigned the form based on the approach proposed and made a comparison between relevant data before and after the improvement. Data is provided by the Tencent social advertisement department (Table 4).

Table 4. Hierarchies of prompt messages in tencent social Advertisement_Account form

Sample	Importance (1–5)	Frequency (1–5)	Properties and circumstances (1–5)	Total	Hierarchy	Behavior path
4	1	1	1	3	**Level 3**	M + H + P + K + R
1	2	1	1	4		
2	2	1	1	4		
8	2	1	1	4		
9	5	1	1	6	**Level 2**	M + H + P
5	4	2	1	7		
6	4	2	1	7		
11	3	2	3	8		
3	5	2	3	10	**Level 3**	M
7	5	2	3	10		
10	3	4	5	11		

(2) Optimal design of Tencent Social Advertisement_Account Registration Form 1.0

We first numbered the prompt messages in the original form, as shown in Fig. 6. Then we graded the prompt messages according to the three criteria for determining the priority of prompt from 1 to 5 points and recorded the data. After sorting out the grades, we divided the hierarchy based on behavior path; the result is given in Fig. 4. Finally, we designed Tencent Social Advertisement_Account Registration Form 2.0, as shown in Fig. 7.

Fig. 6. Serial numbers of prompt messages in tencent social Advertisement_Account form

Fig. 7. Tencent social Advertisement_Account registration form 2.0

- Planning and implementation of experiment

The new form has been put into use for 3 months; meanwhile we record the change of relevant data.

- Analysis of experimental results

The experimental result has been demonstrated in Figs. 8 and 9. The rate of submitting form is improved from 16.8% to 21.5% in the process of improvement. At meantime, in the process of scheme review, most designers and experts express that the redesigned Tencent social advertisement form becomes clearer visually; users also feedback that they fill out forms more efficiently, which signifies a better user experience.

时间	进入编辑页面		提交			提交成功			提交失败		
	PV	UV	PV	UV	提交率	PV	UV	成功率	PV	UV	失败率
2015.12.25–12.31	5879	3787	1418	635	16.8%	1046	607	95.6%	372	107	16.9%
2016.01.22–01.28	5056	3231	1080	559	17.3%	835	532	95.2%	245	87	15.6%
2016.01.29–02.04	4817	2474	666	324	13.1%	463	301	92.9%	203	72	22.2%
2016.02.19–02.25	7682	4034	1767	760	18.8%	1339	732	96.3%	428	127	16.7%
2016.02.26–03.03	6980	4475	1544	1044	23.3%	1402	1019	97.6%	142	68	6.5%
2016.03.04–03.10	7588	4930	1531	1059	21.5%	1400	1022	96.5%	131	62	5.9%

Fig. 8.

渠道	统计周期	用户数			占比	
		注册用户	信息补全	有效用户	信息补全率	有效用户率
官网自助	3.4-3.10	6175	664	263	10.75%	4.26%
	2.26-3.3	6008	652	284	10.85%	4.73%
	2.19-2.25	5461	448	219	8.20%	4.01%
	2.18-2.25	6309	522	269	8.27%	4.26%
	1.29-2.4	3515	199	88	5.66%	2.50%
	1.22-1.28	4358	306	151	7.02%	3.46%
	12.25-12.31	5015	342	185	6.82%	3.69%
	12.18-12.24	5393	463	250	8.59%	4.64%

Fig. 9.

6 Conclusions and Extension

This paper proposes an approach to design the form prompt message. As mentioned above, in form interaction, each interactive behavior relates to the next development. The approach to design the hierarchy of form prompt message based on user's behavior path is effective, but this approach is not the only way to design prompt messages. This approach is only a strategy to improve user experience in design, which can help the interaction designer to design more logic form prompt messages and guide users to complete the form more effectively. This approach can help the designer to set the criteria for interactive design and control the design experience of products more easily.

The discussion on form prompt messages in this paper inevitably has limitations, but the approach and thought of hierarchy design are also of significance to other fields. I hope this paper can enlighten today's designers and a more complete knowledge system is available in the future to help designers.

References

1. Wroblewski, L.: Web Form Design: Filling the Blanks, p. XVIII. Tsinghua University Press, Beijing (2010). Translated by, Lu, Y., Gao, Y.-B.
2. Wroblewski, L.: Web Form Design: Filling the Blanks, pp. 107–140. Tsinghua University Press, Beijing (2010). Translated by, Lu, Y., Gao, Y.-B.
3. Cooper, A., Riemann, R., Cronin, D.: About Face 3: The Essentials of Interaction Design, pp. 388–421. Electronics Industry Press, Beijing (2008). Translated by, Liu, S.-T.
4. Xiong, K.-J.: Study on the prompting information in web design. Beauty Times (02) 2015
5. Rasmussen, J.: Skill, rules and knowledge; signs and symbols and other distinctions in human performance models. IEEE Trans. Syst. Man Cybern SMC 13(3), 257–266 (1983)
6. Raskin, J.: The Humane Interface: New Directions for Designing Interactive Systems, vol. 10, no. 3, pp. 299–302. Addison-Wesley Professional, Boston (2000)
7. Wei, Y.-L.: Mobile tablet application information architecture based on card sorting study. Hunan University (2013)
8. Cao, L.-P.: Study on information level in advertising design. Design (11) (2015)
9. Cooper, A., Riemann, R., Cronin, D.: About Face 3: The Essentials of Interaction Design, p. XIII. Electronics Industry Press, Beijing (2008). Translated by, Liu, S.-T.
10. Xing, X.-Y.: Interaction design: from physical logic to behavioral logic. Art Des. (01) 2015
11. Liao, W.-J., Xiao, Y.-Q.: The optimal interaction path and user behavior guidance in design. Youth (03) 2014
12. Norman, D.A.: Emotional Design. Electronic Industry Press, Beijing (2005)
13. Fu, J.: Inspiration of Interaction Design Based on Subconscious and Behavior. Hunan University (2013)
14. Cooper, A., Riemann, R., Cronin, D.: About Face 3: The Essentials of Interaction Design, pp. 224–225. Electronics Industry Press, Beijing (2008). Translated by, Liu, S.-T.
15. Miller, G.A.: The magical number seven, plus or minus two: some limits on our capacity for processing information. Psychol. Rev. 63(2), 81 (1956)
16. Fu, J., Zhao, J.-H., Tan, H.: Inspiration of interaction design based on subconscious and behavior. Packag. Eng. (01) (2013)
17. Lu, X.-B.: Interactive design method in information design. Sci. Technol. Rev. (13) (2007)
18. Hinman, R.: The Mobile Frontier: A Guide for Designing Mobile Experiences. Tsinghua University Press, Beijing (2013). Translated by, Xiong, Z.-C., Li, M.-M.

Usability Modeling of Academic Search User Interface

Tsangyao Chen[✉] and Melissa Gross

Florida State University, Tallahassee, USA
tc16k@my.fsu.edu, mgross@fsu.edu

Abstract. Usability is a core concept in HCI and is a common quality attribute for the design and evaluation of interactive systems. However, usability is a fluid construct and requires context-specific frameworks to be clearly defined and operationalized. Academic search user interfaces (SUIs) include the search portals of academic and research libraries, digital data repositories, academic data aggregators, and commercial publishers. In addition to information lookup, academic SUIs serve scientific information seeking in learning, exploration, and problem-solving.

Researchers in library and information science (LIS) have intensively studied information seeking behavior. In recent years, exploratory search has gained attention from LIS researchers and experimental SUI features are prototyped to support information seeking. In the meantime, many academic and research libraries have conducted usability evaluation and adopted discovery systems as part of SUIs. However, there is a lack of context-specific usability models for guiding academic SUI implementation and evaluation.

This study takes the perspectives of information seeking tasks and usability contextualization to propose a formative conceptual framework of academic SUI usability. Information seeking tasks from information seeking and behavior models are integrated based on the exploratory search paradigm. Information seeking tasks are mapped to the layered usability construct to shows how academic information seeking tasks may be supported to achieve high usability. Future studies should focus on developing contextualized academic SUI usability models with measurement metrics to guide the empirical implementation and evaluation of academic SUIs.

Keywords: Usability · Search user interface (SUI) · Academic search · Conceptual modeling · Information seeking

1 Introduction

Searching for information has become an increasingly important human activity in the modern world. As the explosion of information has become commonplace for knowledge workers, search has been widely used to ease the stress of information overload. Contemporary search happens in many different types of data collections: general Web search, image collections, ecommerce sites, government data, health and medical databases, and digital libraries and archives. While many see the search engine Google as the synonym of search, Amazon users would understand that it takes more

© Springer International Publishing AG 2017
A. Marcus and W. Wang (Eds.): DUXU 2017, Part III, LNCS 10290, pp. 16–30, 2017.
DOI: 10.1007/978-3-319-58640-3_2

than an omnibox to identify one suitable product from the enormous online store. Faceting, sorting, checking rankings, reading reviews, comparing product details are among the common techniques an online shopper engages in an ecommerce environment. General purpose search user interfaces (SUIs), therefore, do not satisfy all search needs [1]. In other words, specialized SUIs are necessary when the information seeking needs and contexts go beyond a general Web search.

Academic search SUIs include the search portals of academic and research libraries, digital data repositories, academic data aggregators, and publishers. The design of SUIs is important to information seeking activities and could influence information seeking behavior. For example, a simplistic design such as Google Search requires users to issue longer queries to compensate for the lack of a functional faceting mechanism; ineffective SUIs could waste the cognitive resources of the information seeker [2]. For academic information seekers, the use of Google Search is convenient but at the cost of search result quality [3].

Due to the intensive use of information in scientific activities, library and information science (LIS) researchers have long been interested in the information seeking and retrieval behavior of scholars. However, although scientific researchers spend much of their time in information seeking [4], how academic SUIs could better support scientific information seeking remains under-studied. As Bates [5] has pointed out, "[t]o optimize information search, … various design layers need to be recognized, understood, and designed for in an interface that nonetheless feels simple and natural to the end user." Other researchers have also framed search as "data exploration for knowledge building" [6] to call for the design of future search interfaces.

As a core concept of human-computer interaction (HCI), usability has been used as an attribute for quality measurement of interactive systems. To achieve scientific understanding and better user experience of academic SUIs, usability evaluation has received attention among LIS researchers and professionals. According to a survey, 85% of academic libraries of the Association of Research Libraries (ARL) have conducted usability testing on their websites or OPAC [7]. However, usability is a fluid concept and the variation in perspective has led to different usability conceptualizations and evaluation approaches, which makes usability difficult to operationalize in practice. As a result, many usability measurement studies fall short in validity and reliability [8, 9].

The lack of consensus in usability conceptualization has also caused usability evaluation studies in digital libraries and discovery tools to be mostly ad hoc. In order to create academic SUIs with high usability, a clearly articulated conceptual framework of usability is critical for the design and evaluation of academic SUIs. Such a framework should bring the scientific information seeking knowledge together with contextualized usability conceptualization to further conceptual development and empirical examination of academic SUIs.

Conceptual models are critical for theory-informed design. Researchers have adopted models to guide the design of SUI. Jackson et al. [10] designed an exploratory search interface to support scholarly activities in searching an Internet archive (webarchive.ca) following Shneiderman's [11] visual information seeking mantra as a design principle and the chess analogy of Hearst et al. [12] as a task model. Many recent prototyped experimental SUI features have been developed under the exploratory search paradigm [13–15]. The development of contextualized usability models for academic SUI would therefore provide guidance for the design and evaluation of SUIs for academic search.

A major difference between academic SUIs and general interactive systems is that academic SUIs take content, rather than the system's functional features, as the purpose of the interaction. Content relevance hence becomes a key criterion of successful retrieval. In addition, the design of academic SUIs is further complicated by the huge volume and idiosyncratic essence of content used by users from various disciplines. Researchers [16] have therefore called for the study of the work needs, patterns, and workflow of researchers in order to integrate internal and external content with search services. As Shneiderman and Plaisant [17] point out, "[t]he conversion of information needs … to interface actions is a large cognitive step." The objective of this study, therefore, is to explore the issue of contextualized academic SUI usability modeling through the perspectives of academic information seeking tasks and contextualized usability factors.

2   Literature Analysis

While LIS researchers have intensively studied the information seeking behavior of scientists, research issues related to HCI have received relatively little attention from information retrieval researchers [18]. Pettigrew and McKechnie [19], after a content analysis of six major information science journals, found that HCI represents only 2% of the published articles. Many usability evaluation studies on academic and research library websites have also placed less attention to usability concepts and specific SUI features. As Bates [5] pointed out, interface design specific to searching is an under-studied and promising research area in information seeking and HCI.

2.1   Usability

Usability as a quality attribute of interactive systems has critical implications for the implementation and evaluation of information systems. However, the lack of a clear definition of usability as a conceptual construct has led to problems in the principled design and measurement of interactive systems. This predicament is shown by the popularity of the term user experience (UX) as both a displacement and synonym of usability to denote the broader aspects of human experience with products and services. The conceptual evolution and overlapping are evidenced by the rebranding of the Usability Professional Association as User Experience Professional Experience in 2012 and the inclusion of the subtitle of "improving the user experience" in the U.S. government usability website (www.usability.gov) [20]. In many cases, the terms usability, user experience, and human-centered design have been used commonly without carrying specific meanings [21].

One reason for the lack of conceptual clarity in usability is that the evolvement of context has changed the nature of interaction that usability as an academic term once meant. For example, usability was discussed in a time when "[m]ost computer software in use today is unnecessarily difficult to understand, hard to learn, and complicated to use" [22]. Users, instead of systems, were once the target of improvement in that "[u]sability depends heavily on users' abilities to map their goals onto a system's capabilities" [23]. The commonly referenced ISO 9241-11:1998 was conceived when "evaluation of usability by user based measurement of effectiveness, efficiency, and satisfaction, as this was a convincing way of demonstrating the existence of usability problems to system developers" [24]. When these contexts no longer hold true, reconceptualization or creation of new concepts become necessary. That is the reason why the new ISO usability guidelines are incorporating UX perspectives under the satisfaction aspect in the coming new revision [24].

Usability Frameworks. General usability frameworks such as ISO standard 9241-11 [25] and Nielsen's heuristic evaluation [26] are commonly used in conducting empirical usability design and evaluation. It should be noted that these models are often defined with different factors. The ISO standard 9241-11 defines usability with three factors of (1) effectiveness, (2) efficiency, and (3) satisfaction; while Nielsen [27] defines usability with five quality components of (1) learnability, (2) efficiency, (3) memorability, (4) errors, and (5) satisfaction. Research reviews have thus pointed out the lack of consensus in the definition of usability [9, 28, 29].

Among the attempts to clarify the concept of usability, Alonso-Ríos et al. [30] proposed a usability taxonomy with six factors of (1) knowability, (2) operability, (3) efficiency, (4) robustness, (5) safety, and (6) subjective satisfaction with sub-attributes discussed under each factor. Similarly, Seffah et al. [31] reviewed various usability standards and models, and proposed a Quality in Use Integrated Measurement (QUIM) model with ten factors (efficiency, effectiveness, productivity, satisfaction, learnability, safety, trustfulness, accessibility, universality, and usefulness), 26 sub-factors, and measurement metrics.

The existence of multiple definitions with varied factors has evidenced usability as a multi-dimensional concept [32]. What troubles a unified definition of usability is that the included factors are related to each other [31, 33] and thus making analysis difficult. A solution for conceptual clarification is to specify the use context of the usability framework. In fact, this emphasis on context is addressed in the ISO 9241-11 standards by defining usability as the "[e]xtent to which a product can be used by specified users to achieve specified goals with effectiveness, efficiency, and satisfaction in a specified context of use" [25].

Contextualizing Usability. Fidel [34] discussed the design of context-specific information systems and suggested that a context-specific system serves a particular community of users and its design may rely on the use of a context-general system. The efforts to address the issue of usability in context can be seen in the specialized models, metrics, and instruments developed for measuring usability in various fields. The Questionnaire for User Interface Satisfaction [35, 36] is a usability scale for interface measurement and has aspects of screen and terminology specifically as factors. To ease the difficulty in usability implementation and the dependency on evaluator expertise, Lin et al. [37] developed a comprehensive index of software interface usability based on human information processing theory. Eight factors (compatibility, consistency, flexibility, learnability, minimal action, minimal memory load, perceptual limitation, and user guidance) are indexed and the resulting Purdue Usability Testing Questionnaire (PUTQ) contains 100 questions.

Many contextualized usability models and measurement instruments are based on the ISO 2941-11 model's factors of effectiveness, efficiency, and satisfaction. Some models are also informed by theories, while most are based on literature review and domain features. Evaluation tools are often based on the developed models containing metrics and/or questionnaires. Usability contextualization is emphasized by researchers [38, 39]. As Bevan and Macleod [22] state: "[t]he ideal way to specify and measure usability would be to specify the features and attributes required to make a product usable, and measure whether they are present in the implemented product" thus enabling quality to be designed into a product. They also suggest that usability can only be measured empirically "by assessing effectiveness, efficiency, and satisfaction with which representative users carry out representative tasks in representative environments" [22].

2.2   Academic Information Seeking

Among the academic SUIs, the library websites of academic and research universities are studied more than publishers, aggregators, and academic databases. Broadly speaking, the websites of academic and research libraries are academic SUIs since the central function of a library website is content discovery and delivery. Academic searchers engage in scientific problem-solving with browsing and search activities. The process of academic information seeking is therefore usually complicated, longitudinal, and exploratory in nature.

As Shneiderman and Plaisant [17] point out, the weaknesses of traditional search interfaces include "difficulty in repeating searches across multiple databases, weak methods for discovering where to narrow broad searches, poor integration with other tools." Contemporary academic SUIs have made progress in the capacity of combining content sources through federated search and discovery tools, although tool integration has not been greatly improved and academic library websites are still often complicated and low in usability due to the issue of resource management [40, 41]. As Web search engines have gradually evolved from keyword matching and Boolean search to semantic search, the representation of search results has also progressed from "search for links" to "search for information;" yet the topic of academic search continues to be under-studied [42].

Nel and Fourie [4], for example, found that about one-third of veterinary researchers spend more than 50% of their research time on information seeking and that they rely on electronic journal articles, scientific databases, and internet search tools as their sources of information. These scientific information needs should cause researchers to primarily rely on academic SUIs. However, according to a large-scale survey on researcher information behavior, a new generation of researchers across disciplines have a strong preference for using Google/Google Scholar for information seeking [43]. While academic SUIs and Google Search should complement each other, academic SUI's would satisfy the information needs of scientists more if they offered better usability.

Information Seeking Tasks. LIS researchers have investigated the information behavior of scientists and developed influential descriptive models of the information seeking processes. Wilson [44] reviewed information seeking models and indicated that the models are at different levels of information behavior, information-seeking behavior, and information search behavior. Descriptive models such as Wilson's [44] model of information behavior provide overarching descriptions of information behavior; Ingwersen's [45] cognitive model of IR interaction is a high-level overview of information retrieval; whereas Saracevic's [46] stratified model of IR interaction analyzes the information retrieval process from the interface perspective. Such models provide a basis for understanding academic searchers and their interaction with academic SUIs.

Due to the complexity in information needs and content, academic SUIs are less studied and most library website usability evaluation studies are ad hoc in nature. This complexity is evident in the question raised by Bates [47] of "how much and what type of activity the user should be able to direct the system to do at once." Although Bates [48] has proposed the embedment of search tasks in SUI to support academic search, embedding tasks in SUI is difficult. As Shneiderman and Plaisant [17] explain, "[t]he conversion of information needs ... to interface actions is a large cognitive step."

Järvelin and Ingwersen [49] propose that information seeking and retrieval research should pay more attention to tasks and their contexts, which include information retrieval, information seeking, and work task contexts. Bates [48] emphasizes the importance of information seeking tasks in academic search by discussing the embedment of six scholarly browsing techniques that are commonly used by scientists in SUIs: footnote chasing, citation searching, journal run, area scanning, subject searching, and author searching. These browsing techniques are partially supported in existing SUIs, but not fully developed and integrated to support academic search.

Researchers have described the behavioral tasks of academic searchers from experience and empirical studies and formulated these tasks in information seeking models. These models offer components at the task level in addition to conceptual and procedural descriptions. For example, Kuhlthau [50] proposed the six-stage model of Information Search Process with specific tasks (task initiation, topic selection, prefocus exploration, focus formulation, information collection, and search closure). Ellis [51] identified six behavioral characteristics of scholarly information seeking: starting, chaining, browsing, differentiating, monitoring, and extracting. Bates [48] used the metaphor of berrypicking to describe the evolving nature of academic search and suggested six common browsing techniques to be supported by SUIs. Belkin's [52] model of the standard view of information retrieval illustrates information seeking behavior as an interaction between information need and text with four tasks of comparison, retrieve texts, judgment, and modification. Shneiderman et al. [53] also propose an SUI model with four phases: formulation, action, review of results, and refinement. These models offer task descriptions grounded in the information seeking and retrieval practice of academic searchers and are thus critical to the conceptualization of academic SUI usability.

Prior studies in information seeking models and tasks have been used as lens for further understanding of information seeking behavior and tasks of scientists. Al-Suqri

[54] integrated the work of Ellis [51], Kuhlthau [55], and Wilson [44] to propose an information seeking behavior model and verified the model elements through a qualitative study. Following the grounded theory approach of Ellis [56], Moral et al. [57] analyzed data collected from one focus group and eight interviews with computer science researchers in a modeling study. An information-seeking process model was developed from the 169 derived concepts with eight information seeking purposes: (1) obtain relevant information about a topic, (2) elaborate a state-of-the-art, (3) find again a forgotten reference, (4) update a bibliography, (5) find a specific information, (6) find a reference for a citation, (7) browse a document collection, and (8) incorporate a set of documents into an existing local collection. Also, in the information seeking task sub-model, five first-level tasks are identified: exploration, reading, filtering, single information-seeking, and chained information-seeking [57].

Exploratory Search. Early research in search has characterized scientific information seeking as exploratory browsing and search. The exploratory nature of information seeking behavior is discussed by Bates [48] as "berrypicking," depicting information seeking as evolving with iteration of browsing and retrieval tasks through feedback and query refining. The resurgence of exploratory search since the mid-2000's [58, 59] has brought attention to the exploratory nature of search and its importance in the design of SUI features in support of academic search tasks.

Exploratory search is one approach to dealing with the complexity of search, which traditional search systems are not built to support [60]. As empirical study has shown, exploratory search can be characterized by the use of short queries, maximum scroll depth, and long task completion time [61]. Marchionini [62] differentiated lookup from browsing and proposed the two features of learning and investigation in exploratory search. The idea that exploratory search is closely related to learning and problem solving [62, 63] has enriched exploratory search as a field of study and demonstrated the uniqueness of academic search. Such extended definition of exploratory search is therefore widely used by contemporary exploratory search researchers. Many of the exploratory search feature prototyped therefore conceptually follow the processes of lookup, learn, and investigate.

With the evolution of technology and data science, exploratory search researchers are able to prototype SUI features to support learning and investigation. For example, temporal presentation of single search query results [15], temporal comparison of multiple entities [10], overview of searched area topic flows [14], comparative overviewing of query result documents [14, 15], and spatial presentation of query results [13, 64]. At task level, these developments echo Shneiderman's [11] proposal of visual data types and information retrieval tasks (overview, zoom, filter, details-on-demand, relate, history, and extract). In addition to learning and investigation, the exploratory search prototypes have also given much management capacity to the academic searcher; for example, displaying documents collected in session for document management and search trail for query management [15]. Contemporary academic search, therefore, can contain the four processes of lookup, learn, investigate, and manage within one SUI (Fig. 1).

Fig. 1. Processes of contemporary exploratory search in an academic SUI

Discovery Tools. In recent years, discovery tools have become increasingly dominant in academic and research libraries [65] for the integration of information resources across institutional repositories, subscribed commercial publication databases, open access resources, aggregation services, and Web resources. Discovery tools offer a Google-like simplistic search interface and attempt to address the issue of a growing volume and complexity of data. As libraries gradually adopt discovery tools, research has shown that users favor the Google-type single search box feature although usability and content integration are still major problems [66]. Hanrath and Kottman [67] also point out that existing discovery tools lack sufficient integration between the discovery tool interface and content providers such as publishers and content aggregators.

Academic search tasks are in the middle ground of the search activity levels of move, tactic, stratagem, and strategy as Bates [47] proposed. These search tasks are seen in both research lines of information seeking modeling and exploratory search and could serve as the foundation for usability modeling of academic SUI. With the strength to search across information resources with a single search interface, discovery tools have the potential to serve as contextualized academic SUIs if the academic search tasks are embedded through implementation of exploratory search features.

2.3   Academic SUI Usability

While there is a lack of research in the conceptualization of academic SUI usability, usability studies of digital libraries may inform the design of academic SUIs. Usability has received attention from digital library researchers because content and usability are important for users when evaluating digital libraries [68]. In the context of digital library research, researchers have defined usability as "a system has visible working functionality familiar to its users, maximum readability, and useful content that is supported by its environment and aligned with context of use" [69]. Tsakonas et al. [70] proposed a contextualized digital library interaction model, in which usability and usefulness are placed at the same conceptual level (Fig. 2). Usability in this model is defined as the interaction between user and system, and usefulness is defined as the interaction between user and content. Such conceptualization reflects the unique importance of content in digital library context. Content is therefore unique in the usability conceptualization of academic SUI.

Jeng [72] reviewed usability definitions and proposed a digital library usability model to add learnability to the ISO factors of effectiveness, efficiency, and satisfaction. Similarly, also based on the ISO 2941-11 usability factors and Nielsen [73], Joo and

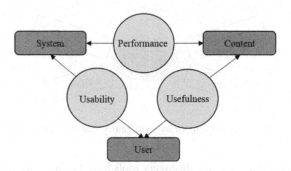

Fig. 2. Associations in the interaction triptych framework [70, 71]

Lee [74] developed a model for digital library usability evaluation to include the four dimensions of efficiency, effectiveness, satisfaction, and learnability. A study [69] to survey and contrast usability definitions between library researchers and practitioners found 11 attributes of usability in a library context. As researchers [29] indicated after reviewing the digital library evaluation models, the major challenge in usability evaluation in digital libraries remains to find consensus on the definition of usability. This definition issue is complicated by the finding that there is a correlation relationship among the digital library usability factors [71, 72] as general usability frameworks. This phenomenon of a lack of consensus in definition demonstrates the need for contextualized efforts to define and develop usability models for academic SUI.

3   A Formative Model

As Fidel [34] discussed, formative models describe the required context under which a desired behavior happens. A conceptualization of usability for academic SUI, therefore needs to describe the conditions under which information seeking tasks would be better supported before metrics can be specified. Information seeking tasks are grounded in information seeking and behavior models and can be integrated into the exploratory search processes to map with related usability constructs.

Given the complicated nature of usability, it is not surprising that researchers have not been able to reach consensus on the academic SUI usability factors. Some research has, however, approached the issue of user interface usability from a different perspective. Parush [75], in discussing conceptual models and design for interactive systems, proposed five human factors to assess the implications of conceptual models: (1) mental models and understanding, (2) location awareness, (3) visual search effectiveness, (4) operational load, and (5) working memory load. These factors seem to be appropriate in intermediating between the user tasks and usability factors given that they are human behavioral performance constructs and can also be interpreted as usability evidenced through interaction.

Due to the lack of clearly defined usability factors in academic SUI, this study takes the layered architect approach of Folmer and Bosch [28] by including levels of related usability factors and indicators to form a framework of usability. The layered elements are organized to demonstrate the rough relationships between the layers without specific matches among the elements. Based on the above analysis of literature, the proposed framework puts together a formative model of academic SUI by mapping the academic search tasks of users and the usability constructs to indicate the specific conditions to be achieved in order to effectively support the academic searcher. This mapping has led to the academic SUI usability framework depicted in Table 1.

The matching of the information seeking tasks involves identifying and interpreting the information seeking tasks from prior studies. For example, the "Details-on-demand" in Shneiderman [11], which focuses on selected items for details, is similar to Reading in the Prefocus stage of Kulthau [50], in which reading is "Reading to become informed," and associated with the strategy of "Reading to learn about topic" (p. 238) after locating relevant information. They are therefore grouped under the task of

Table 1. Conceptual mapping of task-usability for academic SUI

Process	Task[b]	Usability[a]				
		Effectiveness efficiency satisfaction learnability usefulness				
		Control/flexibility error management aesthetic design memorability user characteristics				
		Mental models and understanding	Location awareness	Visual search effectiveness	Operational load	Working memory load
Lookup	Querying (2, 4, 5, 8, 9)				v	
	Viewing (4, 6, 7, 8, 9, 10)	v		v		
	Retrieving (2, 4, 6, 7, 10)				v	
	Filtering (1, 3, 4, 6, 7, 8, 9)				v	v
Learn	Skimming (5, 11)	v	v	v		
	Reading (2, 7, 11)	v		v		
	Comparing (4, 5, 6, 10)	v		v		v
	Annotating (2)	v			v	v
Explore	Browsing (1, 2, 3, 6, 7, 8, 9, 10, 11)	v	v	v		
	Chaining (1, 3)		v	v		
	Subject search (1)	v			v	
Manage	Collecting (2, 6, 7, 9, 10, 11)				v	v
	Organizing (11)	v	v	v		
	Monitoring (3, 5, 9, 10)				v	v

[a]ISO [25]; Tsakonas et al. [70]; Jeng [72]; Joo and Lee [74]; Chen et al. [69]; Parush [75]
[b]1. Bates [48]; 2. Kuhlthau [50, 55]; 3. Ellis [51]; 4. Belkin [52]; 5. Marchionini [62]; 6. Shneiderman [11]; 7. Moral et al. [57]; 8. Xie and Cool [76]; 9. Xie et al. [77]; 10. Al-Suqri [54]; 11. Palmer et al. [78]

Reading. The task Browsing is taken broadly to mean going through resources such as scanning topic or spatial areas, online collections, or lists of resources. This broad definition approach follows Ellis [51], although similar activities and behavior are sometimes termed exploration.

The information seeking tasks are generally grouped into the category of lookup, learn, explore, and manage. This category roughly matches the search activities of lookup, learn, and investigate of Marchionini [62] and Kuhlthau's [55] description of actions in the Information Search Process model: seeking background information, seeking relevant information, and seeking relevant/focused information. The process of Manage is added due to the user capacity offered by contemporary search systems. Especially with the recent features in exploratory search SUI prototypes, the process of Manage is thereby added as an extension of information seeking processes.

4 Conclusion

The development of a context-specific usability framework through identification of user information seeking tasks and integration of usability constructs is the focus of this study. This study stipulates the relationship between the information-seeking tasks and the usability constructs in the academic SUI context to reveal how scientific infor-mation seeking behavior could be supported in the SUI to achieve high usability. As Shneiderman and Plaisant [17] have indicated, there is a huge gap between information needs and interface actions. Well-developed usability conceptual frameworks, how-ever, would guide the implementation of academic SUIs and their empirical validation for validity and reliability.

Usability is a broad field of study significant to research and design in the industry. This study aims at the conceptualization of a contextualized usability framework grounded in the existing knowledge of information seeking tasks and usability. This framework may be further refined and developed into context-specific usability models of and evaluation tools for academic SUIs. The architect approach to model usability in the context of academic SUI is pragmatic in generally presenting the usability con-structs. Future studies should further clarify usability factors and indicators according to context.

A number of SUI features unseen in the traditional information seeking models are supported in recent exploratory SUI prototypes and more innovative features could be developed in the future [6]. These tasks especially enhance the exploration and man-agement processes in academic search and are mostly open-ended tasks at a higher cognitive level, which would trigger the next browsing and search moves. In contrast to general search, in which search is meant to satisfy the information needs of the searcher, future academic SUIs could include more personalization and collaborative academic information management features to facilitate the learning and investigation tasks. Development of strategic SUI features such as collaboration, recommendation, and adaptation and their corresponding usability constructs are also needed for future academic SUIs.

As Galitz [79] indicated, interface design must start with knowing the user. Ethnographic studies may provide new understanding of representative user tasks and information seeking scenarios when the academic search context has undergone changes with the adoption of discovery systems and development of exploratory search research. A desired development may be to integrate the SUI features developed in the exploratory search prototypes into existing discovery systems for empirical evaluation and improvement. Meanwhile, such implementations would be better if guided by clearly contextualized academic SUI usability models.

References

1. Swanson, T.A., Green, J.: Why we are not Google: lessons from a library web site usability study. J. Acad. Librariansh. **37**, 222–229 (2011)
2. Gooding, P.: Exploring the information behaviour of users of Welsh Newspapers Online through web log analysis. J. Doc. **72**, 232–246 (2016)
3. Kroll, S., Forsman, R.: A Slice of Research Life: Information Support for Research in the United States. OCLC Research, Dublin (2010)
4. Nel, M.A., Fourie, I.: Information behavior and expectations of veterinary researchers and their requirements for academic library services. J. Acad. Librariansh. **42**, 44–54 (2016)
5. Bates, M.J.: Many paths to theory: the creative process in the information sciences. In: Sonnenwald, D.H. (ed.) Theory Development in the Information Sciences, pp. 21–49. University of Texas Press, Austin (2016)
6. Wilson, M.L., Kules, B., Schraefel, M.C., Shneiderman, B.: From keyword search to exploration: designing future search interfaces for the web. Found. Trends® Web Sci. **2**, 1–97 (2010)
7. Chen, Y.-H., Germain, C.A., Yang, H.: An exploration into the practices of library web usability in ARL academic libraries. J. Am. Soc. Inf. Sci. Technol. **60**, 953–968 (2009)
8. Faulkner, L.: Beyond the five-user assumption: benefits of increased sample sizes in usability testing. Behav. Res. Methods Instrum. Comput. **35**, 379–383 (2003)
9. Hornbæk, K.: Current practice in measuring usability: challenges to usability studies and research. Int. J. Hum.-Comput. Stud. **64**, 79–102 (2006)
10. Jackson, A., Lin, J., Milligan, I., Ruest, N.: Desiderata for exploratory search interfaces to web archives in support of scholarly activities. Presented at the (2016)
11. Shneiderman, B.: The eyes have it: a task by data type taxonomy for information visualizations. In: Proceedings IEEE Symposium on Visual Languages, pp. 336–343. IEEE Computer Society, Boulder (1996)
12. Hearst, M.A., Smalley, P., Chandler, C.: Faceted metadata for information architecture and search. In: CHI Course for CHI. ACM, Montréal (2006)
13. Glowacka, D., Ruotsalo, T., Konuyshkova, K., Kaski, S., Jacucci, G.: Directing exploratory search: reinforcement learning from user interactions with keywords. In: Proceedings of the 2013 International Conference on Intelligent User Interfaces, pp. 117–128. ACM (2013)
14. Medlar, A., Ilves, K., Wang, P., Buntine, W., Glowacka, D.: PULP: a system for exploratory search of scientific literature. In: Proceedings of the 39th International ACM SIGIR Conference on Research and Development in Information Retrieval, pp. 1133–1136. ACM, New York (2016)

15. Singh, J., Nejdl, W., Anand, A.: Expedition: a time-aware exploratory search system designed for scholars. In: Proceedings of the 39th International ACM SIGIR Conference on Research and Development in Information Retrieval, pp. 1105–1108. ACM, New York (2016)

16. Bourg, C., Coleman, R., Erway, R.: Support for the Research Process: An Academic Library Manifesto. OCLC Research, Dublin (2009)

17. Shneiderman, B., Plaisant, C.: Designing the User Interface: Strategies for Effective Human-Computer Interaction. Pearson Education, Inc., Upper Saddle River (2005)

18. Ahmed, S.M.Z., McKnight, C., Oppenheim, C.: A review of research on human-computer interfaces for online information retrieval systems. Electron. Libr. 27, 96–116 (2009)

19. Pettigrew, K.E., McKechnie, L.E.F.: The use of theory in information science research. J. Am. Soc. Inf. Sci. Technol. 52, 62–73 (2001)

20. U.S. Department of Health and Human Services. https://www.usability.gov/

21. Merholz, P.: Peter in conversation with Don Norman about UX & innovation (2007). http://adaptivepath.org/ideas/e000862/

22. Bevan, N., Macleod, M.: Usability measurement in context. Behav. Inf. Technol. 13, 132–145 (1994)

23. Borgman, C.L.: Designing digital libraries for usability. In: Bishop, A.P., House, N.A.V., Buttenfield, B.P. (eds.) Digital Library Use: Social Practice in Design and Evaluation, pp. 85–118. The MIT Press, Cambridge (2003)

24. Bevan, N., Carter, J., Harker, S.: ISO 9241-11 revised: what have we learnt about usability since 1998? In: Kurosu, M. (ed.) HCI 2015. LNCS, vol. 9169, pp. 143–151. Springer, Cham (2015). doi:10.1007/978-3-319-20901-2_13

25. International Standards Organization: ISO 9241-11:1998(en), Ergonomic requirements for office work with visual display terminals (VDTs) — Part 11: Guidance on usability. https://www.iso.org/obp/ui/#iso:std:iso:9241:-11:ed-1:v1:en

26. Nielsen, J.: Heuristic evaluation. In: Nielsen, J., Mack, R.L. (eds.) Usability Inspection Methods, pp. 25–62. Wiley, New York (1994)

27. Nielsen, J.: Usability 101: Introduction to Usability. https://www.nngroup.com/articles/usability-101-introduction-to-usability/

28. Folmer, E., Bosch, J.: Architecting for usability: a survey. J. Syst. Softw. 70, 61–78 (2004)

29. Heradio, R., Fernandez-Amoros, D., Javier Cabrerizo, F., Herrera-Viedma, E.: A review of quality evaluation of digital libraries based on users' perceptions. J. Inf. Sci. 38, 269–283 (2012)

30. Alonso-Ríos, D., Vázquez-García, A., Mosqueira-Rey, E., Moret-Bonillo, V.: Usability: a critical analysis and a taxonomy. Int. J. Hum.-Comput. Interact. 26, 53–74 (2009)

31. Seffah, A., Donyaee, M., Kline, R.B., Padda, H.K.: Usability measurement and metrics: a consolidated model. Softw. Qual. J. 14, 159–178 (2006)

32. Alshamari, M., Mayhew, P.: Technical review: current issues of usability testing. IETE Tech. Rev. 26, 402–406 (2009)

33. Hornbæk, K., Law, E.L.-C.: Meta-analysis of correlations among usability measures. In: Proceedings of the SIGCHI Conference on Human Factors in Computing Systems, pp. 617–626. ACM (2007)

34. Fidel, R.: Human Information Interaction: An Ecological Approach to Information Behavior. MIT Press, Cambridge (2012)

35. Chin, J.P., Diehl, V.A., Norman, K.L.: Development of an instrument measuring user satisfaction of the human-computer interface. In: Proceedings of the SIGCHI Conference on Human Factors in Computing Systems, pp. 213–218. ACM, New York (1988)

36. Perlman, G.: Questionnaire for User Interface Satisfaction. http://garyperlman.com/quest/quest.cgi?form=QUIS

37. Lin, H.X., Choong, Y.Y., Salvendy, G.: A proposed index of usability: a method for comparing the relative usability of different software systems. Behav. Inf. Technol. **16**, 267–277 (1997)
38. Brooke, J.: SUS: a quick and dirty usability scale. In: Jordan, P.W., Thomas, B., Weerdmeester, B.A., McClelland, I.L. (eds.) Usability Evaluation in Industry, pp. 189–194. Taylor & Francis, Milton Park (1996)
39. Vilar, P.: Information behaviour of scholars. Libellarium J. Hist. Writ. **7**, 17–39 (2015)
40. Pennington, B.: ERM UX: electronic resources management and the user experience. Ser. Rev. **41**, 194–198 (2015)
41. Teague-Rector, S., Ballard, A., Pauley, S.K.: The North Carolina State University libraries search experience: usability testing tabbed search interfaces for academic libraries. J. Web Librariansh. **5**, 80–95 (2011)
42. Khabsa, M., Wu, Z., Giles, C.L.: Towards better understanding of academic search. Presented at the (2016)
43. Carpenter, J., Wetheridge, L., Tanner, S.: Researchers of tomorrow: the research behaviour of Generation Y docotral students. British Library and Joint Information Systems Committee (JISC) of the Higher Education Funding Council (HEFCE) (2012)
44. Wilson, T.D.: Models in information behaviour research. J. Doc. **55**, 249–270 (1999)
45. Ingwersen, P.: Cognitive perspectives of information retrieval interaction: elements of a cognitive IR theory. J. Doc. **52**, 3–50 (1996)
46. Saracevic, T.: The stratified model of information retrieval interaction: extension and applications. In: Proceedings of the Annual Meeting-American Society for Information Science, pp. 313–327. Learned Information (Europe) Ltd. (1997)
47. Bates, M.J.: Where should the person stop and the information search interface start? Inf. Process. Manag. **26**, 575–591 (1990)
48. Bates, M.J.: The design of browsing and berrypicking techniques for the online search interface. Online Rev. **13**, 407–524 (1989)
49. Järvelin, K., Ingwersen, P.: Information seeking research needs extension towards tasks and technology. Inf. Res. Int. Electron. J. **10**, paper 212 (2004)
50. Kuhlthau, C.C.: Developing a model of the library search process: cognitive and affective aspects. Res. Q. **28**, 232–242 (1988)
51. Ellis, D.: A behavioural model for information retrieval system design. J. Inf. Sci. **15**, 237–247 (1989)
52. Belkin, N.J.: Interaction with texts: Information retrieval as information seeking behavior. Inf. Retr. **93**, 55–66 (1993)
53. Shneiderman, B., Byrd, D., Croft, W.B.: Clarifying search: a user-interface framework for text searches. D-Lib Mag. **3**, 18–20 (1997)
54. Al-Suqri, M.N.: Information-seeking behavior of social science scholars in developing countries: a proposed model. Int. Inf. Libr. Rev. **43**, 1–14 (2011)
55. Kuhlthau, C.C.: Inside the search process: Information seeking from the user's perspective. J. Am. Soc. Inf. Sci. **42**, 361 (1991)
56. Ellis, D.: A behavioural approach to information retrieval system design. J. Doc. **45**, 171–212 (1989)
57. Moral, C., De Antonio, A., Ferre, X.: A visual UML-based conceptual model of information-seeking by computer science researchers. Inf. Process. Manag. **53**, 963–988 (2016)
58. White, R.W., Kules, B., Bederson, B.: Exploratory search interfaces: categorization, clustering and beyond: report on the XSI 2005 workshop at the human-computer interaction laboratory, University of Maryland. In: ACM SIGIR Forum, pp. 52–56. ACM (2005)

59. Wilson, M.L.: Search User Interface Design. Morgan & Claypool Publishers, San Rafael (2011)
60. Ahn, J., Brusilovsky, P.: Adaptive visualization for exploratory information retrieval. Inf. Process. Manag. **49**, 1139–1164 (2013)
61. Athukorala, K., Głowacka, D., Jacucci, G., Oulasvirta, A., Vreeken, J.: Is exploratory search different? A comparison of information search behavior for exploratory and lookup tasks. J. Assoc. Inf. Sci. Technol. **67**, 2635–2651 (2016)
62. Marchionini, G.: Exploratory search: from finding to understanding. Commun. ACM **49**, 41–46 (2006)
63. Marchionini, G.: Information Seeking in Electronic Environments. Cambridge University Press, Cambridge (1995)
64. Roux, C.: Using spatialisation to support exploratory search behaviour (2016)
65. Wells, D.: Library discovery systems and their users: a case study from Curtin University library. Aust. Acad. Res. Libr. **47**, 92–105 (2016)
66. Niu, X., Zhang, T., Chen, H.: Study of user search activities with two discovery tools at an academic library. Int. J. Hum.-Comput. Interact. **30**, 422–433 (2014)
67. Hanrath, S., Kottman, M.: Use and usability of a discovery tool in an academic library. J. Web Librariansh. **9**, 1–21 (2015)
68. Xie, I.: Evaluation of digital libraries: criteria and problems from users perspectives. Libr. Inf. Sci. Res. **28**, 433–452 (2006)
69. Chen, Y.-H., Germain, C.A., Rorissa, A.: Defining usability: how library practice differs from published research. Portal-Libr. Acad. **11**, 599–628 (2011)
70. Tsakonas, G., Kapidakis, S., Papatheodorou, C.: Evaluation of user interaction in digital libraries. In: Notes of the DELOS WP7 Workshop on the Evaluation of Digital Libraries, Padua, Italy. Citeseer (2004)
71. Tsakonas, G., Papatheodorou, C.: Analysing and evaluating usefulness and usability in electronic information services. J. Inf. Sci. **32**, 400–419 (2006)
72. Jeng, J.: Usability assessment of academic digital libraries: effectiveness, efficiency, satisfaction, and learnability. Libri **55**, 96–121 (2005)
73. Nielsen, J.: Usability Engineering. AP Professional, Boston (1993)
74. Joo, S., Lee, J.Y.: Measuring the usability of academic digital libraries: instrument development and validation. Electron. Libr. **29**, 523–537 (2011)
75. Parush, A.: Conceptual Design for Interactive Systems: Designing for Performance and User Experience. Morgan Kaufmann/Elsevier, Amsterdam (2015)
76. Xie, I., Cool, C.: Understanding help seeking within the context of searching digital libraries. J. Am. Soc. Inf. Sci. Technol. **60**, 477–494 (2009)
77. Xie, I., Joo, S., Bennett-Kapusniak, R.: User involvement and system support in applying search tactics. J. Assoc. Inf. Sci. Technol. **68**, 1165–1185 (2016)
78. Palmer, C.L., Teffeau, L.C., Pirmann, C.M.: Scholarly Information Practices in the Online Environment: Themes from the Literature and Implications for Library Service Development. OCLC Research, Dublin (2009)
79. Galitz, W.O.: The Essential Guide to User Interface Design: An Introduction to GUI Design Principles and Techniques. Wiley, Indianapolis (2007)

The Influence of Task-Oriented Human-Machine Interface Design on Usability Objectives

Julia N. Czerniak$^{(\boxtimes)}$, Christopher Brandl, and Alexander Mertens

Institute of Industrial Engineering and Ergonomics,
RWTH Aachen University, Aachen, Germany
{j.czerniak,c.brandl,a.mertens}@iaw.rwth-aachen.de

Abstract. Modern machine tools have become highly automated versatile production systems, often showing deficits in intuitive control opportunities. To match human-machine interfaces to increasing functionality requirements, the software complexity can be reduced by task-oriented human-machine interface design. Content of this paper is the evaluation of task-orientation and its influence on usability dimensions in a field and laboratory investigation. For this purpose, a function-oriented software for cutting machines, currently used in production, was compared to a task-oriented prototype by means of the IsoMetrics^S. Results show an effect of task-orientation on conformity with user expectations and learnability in the laboratory study. Furthermore performance measurement shows that task-orientation leads to decreasing execution times.

Keywords: Human-machine interaction · Interface design · IsoMetrics^S · Machine tool controlling · Task-oriented HMI · Usability

1 Introduction

Technological advantages lead to tremendous changes in the production industry. Modern machine tools have been developing to exceedingly automated production systems with highly complex functionality due to the increasing demand for high production rates and quality. However, the human-machine interface is not adapted to these circumstances yet, resulting in a lack of intuitive controlling features, causing high levels of mental strain for the operator [1]. Mental strain can be summarized as the intensity of cognitive processing amongst all stages of human information processing during informational operations. According to the stress-strain concept it is defined as a working person's subjective psychic reaction towards a given amount of stress. The quantity of stress hereby depends on several objective influence variables such as working and environment conditions. The reaction's extend and the resulting user performance on the other hand are dependent on internal and external factors of the individual, and thus vary amongst different individuals [2]. In this context overstraining tasks lead to the same consequences for performance as subchallenging operations [3]. These circumstances point out the necessity for more intuitive human-machine interaction concepts regarding increasing complexity of production systems, respective machine tool controlling.

© Springer International Publishing AG 2017
A. Marcus and W. Wang (Eds.): DUXU 2017, Part III, LNCS 10290, pp. 31–41, 2017.
DOI: 10.1007/978-3-319-58640-3_3

This can be realized by adjusting the human-machine interface. Technical principles for human-machine interaction design are given by ergonomic requirements, for instance formulated in different parts of the European standard "Ergonomics of human-system interaction", representing usability guidelines for product designers. The standard is based on legal requirements of the European Commission regulated in the machine directive 2006/42/EC, which is to be implemented in law by every European State [4]. The standard DIN EN ISO 9241-210 (2011) describes the steps of the user-centered design process for interactive systems. According to this approach, usability just like accessibility of products, are dependent on the context of use, specifically on user requirements, task to be completed and environment requirements [5]. Since actual standards already deal with ergonomic information display, as well as information input, recommendations for interface design have already been implemented in several technical systems. Moreover, research about information perception has been comprehensively conducted within the last decades in numerous eye tracking studies prove. However, less effort has been spend regarding the implementation of central cognitive processes as a design dimension of HMI.

To include the user's mental strain into HMI-design, a deeper knowledge of human information processing is required. In this regard three phases of information processing exist. The first phase is given by early processes including information perception. The perceived information is further processed by central cognition processes; before it becomes translated into a motoric reaction during the phase of late processes [6]. To support the machine operator within these processes, information is to be organized that perception, speed and ease of comprehension is optimized to guarantee that the operator perceives essential information and is able to intuitively translate decisions into actions [7]. Following this approach, information corresponding to human mental models can be processed easiest. A mental model is a mind construct, representing a reduced reflection of a part of reality in someone's head. However, current navigation structures of machine tool interfaces are structured function-oriented, whereas human mental models tend to be task-oriented [8]. Therefore the function-oriented model must be transferred into a task-oriented model for every single operation. Designing an interface with a task-oriented navigation structure, would be more suitable to mental operating models, reducing mental strain. In addition, the software of current HMIs has been mapping the ever-increasing machine complexity, leading to depth and complex hierarchical navigation structures [9].

To study these effects, we investigated a preliminary laboratory study in prior research that showed effects of task-oriented HMI design on performance and errors [10]. Based on these findings, we implemented a field study to test results in real working conditions. Using the example of a cutting machine, the human-machine interface was analyzed. Regarding to ergonomic requirements we formulated design recommendations according to task-orientation. On this basis a software prototype for cutting machine interfaces was developed. This paper deals with a field and a laboratory control investigation, evaluating the prototype according to relevant usability objectives for software dialogues [11].

2 Method

An actual cutting machine controlling software was analyzed by usability experts and machine manufacturers as model case. In a first step the navigation hierarchy was visualized in a tree structure. The navigation tree contained up to 10 hierarchy levels arranged by functions. In the next step, the graphical user interface (GUI) was observed according to ergonomic principles. Moreover operators were interviewed concerning the actual interface. Finally, we summarized results to design recommendations for programming a task-oriented prototype [5]. For the evaluation, we conducted a field study in a company of a machine tool manufacturer with a cutting machine, as well as a laboratory study in order to identify results, caused by side effects of the field environment. Both software versions were tested with one of the most commonly operated workflow "Cut foam block manually" in industry applications. This standard workflow (see Fig. 1) consists of short, non-complex substeps to guarantee comparability of the setup and to maintain a more standardized evaluation.

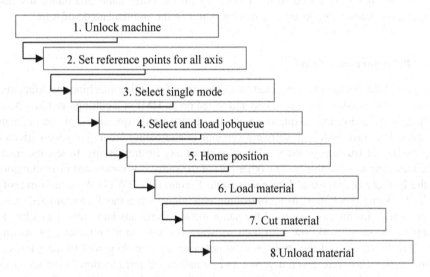

Fig. 1. Standard workflow "Cut foam block manually"

The main objective was to test the task-oriented HMI prototype compared to the actually used function-oriented HMI. Therefore usability was tested for both versions with the IsoMetrics[S] questionnaire [12], based on Standard DIN EN ISO 9241-110 [11]. We concentrated on a single workflow that did not imply any tasks, which neither demanded individual adaption of the GUI nor triggered error situations. Thus, we eliminated these dimensions from the questionnaire. Results for each objective were analyzed by mean and standard deviation and compared within the two HMI software versions. Furthermore we tested subjective mental strain with the Rating Scale of

Mental Effort (RSME) [13]. The RSME is a discrete scale with values from zero "no strain at all" to 150 "unbearable strain". Thereby lower levels of subjective mental strain implicate a better support of the human-machine interaction, and thus indicate a better usability. Participants were shown the RSME scale after each condition and we asked to answer their stress experience spontaneously.

2.1 Participants

The study was divided into two parts, a field study in a cutting machine company, and a laboratory study as reference group. For the field study 8 participants (aged between 26 and 65 years) with an average age of 43.25 years were tested. Seven of the tested participants were male, only one participant was female. The same number of persons participated in the laboratory study. In this study the average age of participants was 25.75 and the number of male and female participants was both four.

All participants in the field study were employees of the cutting machine company and therefore had good knowledge on cutting machines and software on average. Participants that were tested in the laboratory on the other hand predominantly had neither good knowledge in cutting machines nor in the implemented software.

2.2 Procedure and Task

One part of the study was conducted in a company of a cutting machine manufacturer. Both software versions were installed and tested on an HMI of a cutting machine. After a short introduction and a questionnaire for demographic questions, all participants completed the task with both software versions in alternating order. They were given a step-by-step instruction of the workflow, without any further details, to test the interface according to its usability. The other part of the study was conducted in a laboratory of the Institute of Industrial Engineering and Ergonomics RWTH Aachen University under the same conditions, as a controlling condition with a more standardized study environment. In this case we used the same software versions and participants had to complete the same workflow with both software versions on a computer representing the HMI. In this part of the study, we did not connect a machine tool to the interface. Thus, participants were given a verbal and picture-based introduction to the scenario. The task to fulfil was the workflow for cutting a foam block manually (see Fig. 1). The starting task was permuted between condition 1 and 2 for each participant.

In condition 1 we used the actual software version on the HMI (see Fig. 2). The graphical user interface screen is organized as follows: a wide work area that displays the cutting job in progress is arranged centered. Top left the position of all axises is displayed, as well as the machine's lock status and work mode. Center left the job queues can be modified, loaded and started. At the bottom a navigation tool bar is located, which can be switched and changes as a whole, when different operations are needed.

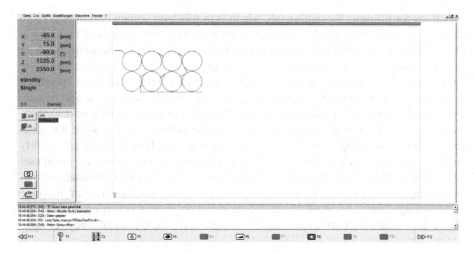

Fig. 2. Screenshot of the actual software version for cutting machines

In condition 2 the newly developed software prototype was installed (see Fig. 3). The HMI prototype was designed with task-oriented menu structuring and user centered design elements. In addition buttons were arranged according to their relevance regarding the workflow. As visible in the screenshot, similar to the actual GUI, a wide centered work area is located, visualizing the loaded cutting job. Information about axis values is rearranged top right. Top left position now implies relevant task-oriented

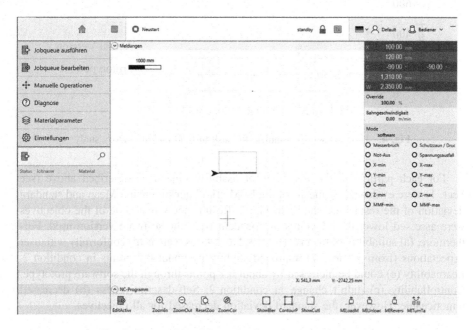

Fig. 3. Screenshot of the task-oriented software prototype

operations for fulfilling the cutting job, which is to take into account this area as more attentive for western people that are used to left-to-right and top-to-bottom reading [8]. For the same reason, buttons for often needed or rather critical operations, such as "home positioning", "start/stop process", "lock/unlock machine", "machine mode" or "start process" are located top center, unlike the actual HMI, where some operations could not be seen constantly, when navigating through the tool bar at the bottom. User specific options, for example language or user group are located next to these on top right. Instead of the operation tool bar at the bottom, the prototype has some general functions arranged on this position on the screen. Here the user can modify display parameters, such as zoom in and out to take into account individual visual user abilities, as well as general operations independent from the actual job load, such as "load/unload material". Furthermore, the prototype GUI visualizes relevant machine errors through circuit symbols, I/O-coded, in red if an error is occurring on the right hand side, for an easier error handling (not of relevance for the actual study set up).

3   Results

Figure 4 shows that execution time for completing the workflow in both studies was lower when using the prototype than using the actual software version. Furthermore, process times in the field study were longer in general, as expected due to machine operations in the field study.

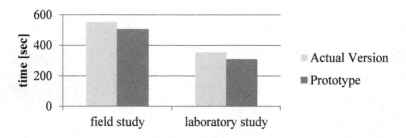

Fig. 4. Time needed to complete the task in field and alboratory study

For each participant the five relevant usability objectives described above (see Sect. 1) were evaluated by means of the IsoMetrics^S questionnaire. Mean and standard deviation of the results are shown in Fig. 5. Results show that none of the objectives were assessed lower than 3 points independent from the software version used. Furthermore, (a) suitability of the task (from 3.2 to 3.4), as well as (d) conformity with user expectations (from 3.5 to 3.7) improved slightly by about 0.2 points in condition 2. Learnability (e) could be increased by about 0.7 points through the software prototype. Controllability (c) didn't change in condition 2. Self-descriptiveness (b) decreased unnoticeable. However, the standard deviation decreased for all objectives.

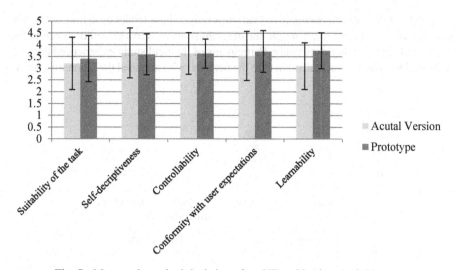

Fig. 5. Mean and standard deviation of usability objectives in field study

In the laboratory control group, results occurred to be more clearly (see Fig. 6). In this condition the minimum was about 1.1 points and thus lower than in the field study. Moreover the mean over all objectives had a wider range up to 3.94. The graph does not show a difference in suitability of the task (a), self-descriptiveness (b) or controllability (c) between the two conditions. For conformity with user expectations (d) and learnability (e) on the other hand, results show a clear improvement of 2.8 points for (d) and 1.7 points for (e). Similar to the field study, the standard deviation decreased for all objectives, except for learnability.

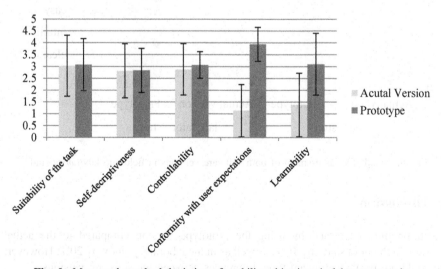

Fig. 6. Mean and standard deviation of usability objectives in laboratory study

Results of the subjective cognitive load show only a slight tendency to lower values in both conditions (see Fig. 7). Though, the diagram shows a remarkable difference in the values for field and laboratory study. Participants of the field study experienced the task by about 35% lower in mental strain than the persons, who attended the laboratory study.

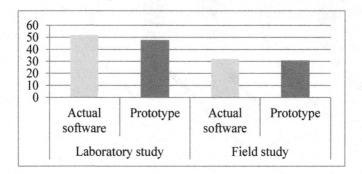

Fig. 7. Mean of RSME values when using actual software version and prototype in laboratory and field study

Qualitative assessment of participants shows that more than half of the participants found it easier, more intuitive and clearly to work with the prototype version in both studies (see Fig. 8).

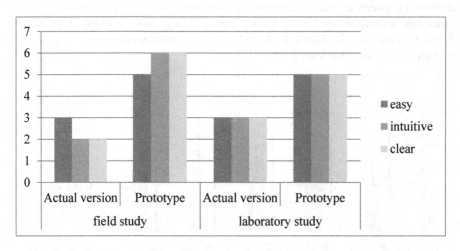

Fig. 8. Qualitative assessment of both software versions in field and laboratory study

4 Discussion

Execution time decreased by using the prototype version compared to the actual software in the field study by 10%, as well as in the laboratory study by 20%. However, we could not prove significant time differences between the software versions.

Results of the field study show that both software versions meet usability objectives exclusively with values above the mean (3) on the five point scale applied for the questionnaire. However, findings do not explicitly show an improvement of usability objectives due to task-orientation of the human-machine interface for the prototype version in condition 2. Regarding the software prototype only "task suitability", "conformity with user expectations" and "suitability for learning" show a tendency to higher values compared to the actual software version. The participant's knowledge with respect to the machine and actual software, the small sample size and furthermore, influence factors in the machine hall, e.g. external distractions from other workers or commonly occurring noises could be a possible explanation for these findings, since results in the laboratory study were more definite. Values of standard deviation were lower in the prototype condition, than in the actual software version tested in condition 1 for all usability dimensions. Based on this, results for the prototype usability are more consistent over all participants. This allows a more reliable interpretation, also indicating potential for more efficient process scheduling in production planning by means of task-oriented machine tool HMIs.

Results for the laboratory study point out this fact: the dimensions "conformity with user expectations", as well as "suitability for learning" show decisive differences by means of task-oriented human-machine interface design. For both dimensions participants rated the actual software version only with 1 of 5 points on average. According to correspondence with the tested usability objective the value is equivalent to disagreement. The prototype version on the other hand, was rated with higher values above mean regarding these objectives. Participants agreed to the prototype's conformity with user expectations by valuing with 4 of 5 points.

However, findings for task suitability, self-descriptiveness and controllability are less conclusive. For these usability objectives no change can be observed. Regarding the purpose for the same task of both software versions, it seems appropriate, that quantitative results for task suitability are similar. Moreover, neither "self-descriptiveness", nor "controllability" is affected by ergonomic improvements considered in the prototype software design, according to the participant's impressions. The value was near average of 3 for both versions. Self-descriptiveness is an indication for intuitive software handling, which becomes especially obvious for novices, who are dependent on self-descriptiveness, if they are not further assisted. The fact that all laboratory participants were novices, who were indifferent about the quality of self-descriptiveness of the prototype with no difference to the actual software version, clearly shows the ergonomic potential that is not exploited yet. In addition, controllability principally requires system knowledge, as well as understanding of tasks, processes and consequences. Hence, lack of experience with machine tool interfaces, and thus a missing mental model of controlling operations can be regarded as reasonable to explain the findings. The assumption about a lack of expertise of persons attending the lab study becomes more probable according to this observed little deviation from the mean. As controllability was rated nearly equal for both software versions, participants seem to have experienced similar challenges interacting with, respectively controlling both systems. Inappropriate mental models definitely contain potential to positively influence the discussed effect, since it is the most dominant common factor within the group, though unproven yet. To concern the probable correlation, and to validate this hypothesis, future studies are required.

In contrast to the questionnaire results for usability objectives, we found a clearer qualitative evaluation in the interview results. Using the prototype version was perceived as easier and more intuitive, furthermore this version was perceived as clearlier arranged by more than half of all participants, even in the field study, where differences did not show up between both software versions.

Results of the subjective cognitive load do not differ between both software versions, what could be originated in the standardized workflow task with short term subtasks that do not lead to high strain levels independent of the implemented software. Obviously knowledge about cutting machines and software has an influence on subjective mental strain, because novices had a higher subjective cognitive load than experienced participants for both software versions.

The main limitation of the study is the small sample size of 8 resulting from the effort of conducting the study during business hours in the machine hall and therefore limited access to employees. To better compare results, we tested the same number of persons in the laboratory study, which leads to unclear finding, difficult to interpret.

5   Summary and Conclusion

This paper deals with a field study about usability of task-oriented cutting machine HMIs. Prior research has already shown the benefit of task-oriented human-machine interfaces for a more intuitive interaction by reducing complexity and supporting human mental models [1]. However, these works did not study the influence of task-orientation on usability objectives. A better usability is one factor that can improve strain level by providing less stress while interacting with the system itself. After our findings in the explorative preliminary study, this study can be seen as a pursuing study built upon our explorative preliminary study [11] to gain first important findings of the impact of task-oriented HMI design on usability objectives in real working conditions. In this study we tested effects among two groups of participants. Participants in the field study were employees, familiar with the current software, whereas participants in the lab study were novices.

The results of the IsoMetrics[S] revealed that task-oriented HMI did not have an effect for skilled workers, who are accustomed to the actual software, since none of the usability objectives showed an improvement for the prototype compared to the actual version. Longtime trained mental models for the actual software version could be seen as an explanation. The findings are different, however, when regarding the novices. In this case results show a usability improvement according to "conformity with user expectations" and "suitability for learning", which proves that the prototype HMI had a more intuitive navigation structure, is easier to learn for unskilled workers and, therefore, reduces initial training and execution time. Regarding results for the standard deviation, however, results were spread more evenly for both groups for the prototype version, confirming the quality of the discussed results. Nevertheless, results mostly valued above mean by three points rating and still reveal potential for improvement for the prototype version. This should be considered for future work. The study design aimed at standardized conditions and time efficiency to save field resources. Thus, very short workflow subtasks did not lead to real stress situations for the participants. Further studies therefore should extend procedure time to evaluate effects on mental strain with clearer results.

Acknowledgements. The Research is funded by the German Federal Ministry of Education and Research (BMBF), Project: MaxiMMI, according to Grant No. 16SV6237, supervised by the VDI/VDE Innovation + Technik GmbH. The authors would like to express their gratitude for the support given.

References

1. Herfs, W., Kolster, D., Lohse, W.: Handlungsorientiertes Werkzeugmaschinen-HMI. atp Edit. **55**(11), 32–41 (2013)
2. Rohmert, W.: Das Belastungs-Beanspruchungs-Konzept. Z. für Arbeitswissenschaft **38**(4), 193–200 (1984)
3. Kantowitz, B.H., Campbell, J.L.: Pilot workload and flightdeck automation. In: Parasuraman, R., Mouloua, M. (eds.) Automation and Human Performance. Theory and Applications, pp. 135–136. Lawrence Erlbaum Associates, Mahwah (1996)
4. Machine Directive 2006/42/EC: Of the European Parliament and of the Council of 17 May 2006 on machinery, and amending Directive 95/16/EC (recast), Appendix I, pp. 29–63 (2006)
5. DIN EN ISO 9241-210: Ergonomics of human-system interaction - Part 210: Human-centered design for interactive systems (ISO 9241-210:2010) German version EN ISO 9241-210:2010 (2010)
6. Luczak, H.: Untersuchungen informatorischer Belastung und Beanspruchung des Menschen. VDI-Z. **10**(2), 13–18 (1975)
7. Schlick, C., Bruder, R., Luczak, H.: Arbeitswissenschaft. vollst. überarb. und erw, vol. 3. Springer, Heidelberg (2010)
8. Rudlof, C.: Handbuch Software-Ergonomie – Usability Engineering, pp. 27–62. Unfallkasse Post und Telekom, Tübingen (2006)
9. Herfs, W., Kolster, D., Lohse, W.: Handlungsorientierte Werkzeugmaschinen-HMI. Vernetzte Apps steigern die Benutzerfreundlichkeit der Maschinen. atp Edit. Automatisierungstechnische Prax. **55**(11), 32–41 (2013)
10. Czerniak, J.N., Hellig, T., Kiehn, A., Brandl, C., Mertens, A., Schlick, C.M.: Analysis of different types of navigational structures for machine tool controlling. In: Kurosu, M. (ed.) HCI 2016. LNCS, vol. 9733, pp. 494–504. Springer, Cham (2016). doi:10.1007/978-3-319-39513-5_46
11. DIN EN ISO 9241-110: Ergonomics of human-system interaction – Part 110: Dialogue principles (ISO 9241-110:2006); German version EN ISO 9241-110:2006 (2006)
12. Gedia et al.: The IsoMetrics Manual Version 1.15. The section "Arbeits- & Organisationspsychologie" and "Methodenlehre" of the University Osnabrück (1998)
13. Zijlstra, F., van Doorn, L.: The construction of a scale to measure subjective effort. Technical report. Delft University of Technology (1985)

ViVid: A Video Feature Visualization Engine

Jianyu Fan[1(✉)], Philippe Pasquier[1], Luciane Maria Fadel[2],
and Jim Bizzocchi[1]

[1] Simon Fraser University, Vancouver, Canada
{jianyuf,phillipe.pasquier,jimbiz}@sfu.ca
[2] Federal University of Santa Catarina, Florianópolis, Brazil
liefadel@gmail.com

Abstract. Video editors are facing the challenge of montage editing when dealing with massive amount of video shots. The major problem is selecting the feature they want to use for building repetition patterns in montage editing. It is time-consuming when testing various features for repetitions and watching videos one by one. A visualization tool for video features could be useful for assisting montage editing. Such a visualization tool is not currently available. We present the design of ViVid, an interactive system for visualizing video features for particular target videos. ViVid is a generic tool for computer-assisted montage and for the design of generative video arts, which could take advantage of the information of video features for rendering the piece. The system computes sand visualizes the color information, motion and texture information data. Instead of visualizing original feature data frame by frame, we re-arranged the data and used both statistics of video feature data and frame level data to represent the video. The system uses dashboards to visualize multiple dimensional data in multiple views. We used the project of Seasons as a case study for testing the tool. Our feasibility study shows that users are satisfied with the visualization tool.

Keywords: Video features · Data visualization

1 Research Topic

Generative video refers to creating videos using generating systems [1]. Potentially, multiple results can be produced, because a generative video is built using montage editing to connect shots and transitions that are drawn from a database. We present the design of the ViVid, which is a generic system for video feature visualization. We present a case study about "Seasons[1]", a generative media project, which uses a variety of computational processes to build the audio-visual output. "The system for Seasons builds video sequencing and transitions based on procedural rules and video metatags. Simultaneously, the system composes and mixes music and soundscape tracks that incorporate both semantic and affective elements of the video into their own aesthetic rules." [2].

---

[1] Seasons is a generative video from Simon Fraser University Generative Media Project coordinated by Jim Bizzocchi, Arne Eigenfeldt, Philippe Pasquier, and Miles Thorogood.

© Springer International Publishing AG 2017
A. Marcus and W. Wang (Eds.): DUXU 2017, Part III, LNCS 10290, pp. 42–53, 2017.
DOI: 10.1007/978-3-319-58640-3_4

2 Film Editing

In film editing, there are two techniques widely used. The first is continuity editing, which uses sequences of shots to create a sense of real-time and mask the time and space. For example, a filmmaker wants a scene in which a person is cutting trees. The first shot shows the entire tree. When the person is about to cut the tree, the shot turns to the middle view. It becomes the close view when the axe is on the tree. This three-shot sequence is an example of continuity editing.

Another widely used technique is Montage editing. A "montage sequence" is a short segment in a film in which narrative information is presented in a condensed fashion" [3]. It has been used in various genres, such as science fiction, silent film, propaganda, sports, commercials, and city films. In the movie 2001: A Space Odyssey, the director depicted the development of a man evolved from apes to humans. For each shot, the creature evolves to a higher stage. This montage sequencing is based on the concept of evolution and time.

In the silent film, Battleship Potemkin, which is directed by Sergei Eisenstein, the montage theory was tested. Different types of montages were used, such as metric montage, rhythmic montage, tonal montage, over-tonal montage and intellectual montage, [4].

- Metric: The length of video segments follows the number of frames
- Rhythmic: The length of the shot suggests a pattern and the cutting points create visual continuity
- Tonal: Each shot reflects certain emotions to enhance the emotional experience in the viewers
- Overtonal: It is a combination of metric, rhythmic, and tonal montage
- Intellectual: It uses a combination of shots that are not from the original film to create new meanings

As for Olympic propaganda films, directors not only used sequences of shots of different athletes to show the diversity of the Olympic games, but also used the different stage of competitions to tell audiences the opening of the Olympic game. They used the concept of sport, development, and emotion, to build their sequences. This is an example of Overtonal montage.

Motion is widely used in the montage sequencing. In the city documentary Berlin Symphony of a Great City, the director used a sequence of shots containing objects moving in the same direction to indicate the train is coming to Berlin. This is an example of Rhythmic montage.

Other features have been used in montage editing include color, shape, texture, scale, photographic, focus, visual complexity, motion intensity, content, and emotion. Our system can be an assistant tool for selecting features and videos for montage editing.

2.1 Video Data

We extracted video feature data of the Seasons' video database. Original videos have the resolution of 1920 × 1080, which cause a massive amount of computation

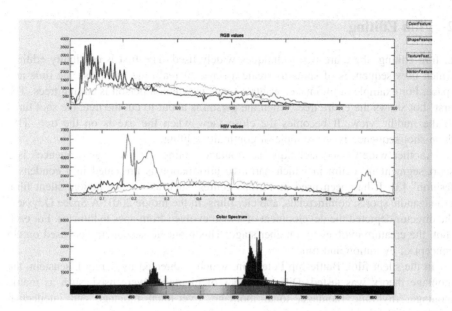

Fig. 1. A simple visualization of original color feature data of a target video (Color figure online)

regarding feature extraction and data visualization. We lower the resolution of video and extract features. Since there are many dimensions in video features, we separate video features into three categories including color, motion, and texture features. We used Matlab[2] to extract RGB and HSV values as color features, which are represented as a 2D chart, where the horizontal axis shows the frames and the vertical axis shows the value, as shown in Fig. 1. Matlab also extracts optical flows as motion features and represents this feature in each frame using directional lines as shown in Fig. 2.

We argue that these forms of visualization are not intuitive for users. To address this problem we selected only hue, saturation, and brightness, which we believe are more related to human perception of colors. Also, we rearrange the original video feature data for better visualization. It is hard to visualize each feature dimension frame by frame in real time. Therefore, we use probabilistic distribution to represent hue, saturation, and brightness. For motion features, we calculated the motion intensity value, motion direction value per frame and overall motion direction of the entire video. The motion intensity data is frame level data. That is also the case of texture feature visualization, which was represented using entropy and contrast. For texture features, we used entropy and contrast.

With both frame level feature data and statistics feature data of the entire video, users can have a macro view of the whole video that saves more time and has the micro observation of details of features. All the video features are extracted by using Matlab.

---

[2] Matlab is a developed by Mathworks.

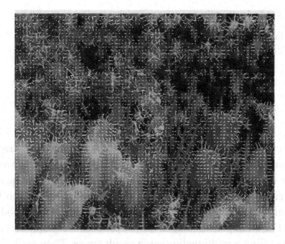

Fig. 2. Simple visualization of original motion feature data of a video (optical flow) (Color figure online)

We rearrange the original video feature data by using multi-view and representing each feature based on its probability distribution.

3 Method

We adopted the design science research, which is a method that addresses the development of an artifact while enables the researcher to learn a certain phenomenon [5]. Vaishnavi and Kuechler [6] suggested the design cycle used in this paper, which is composed of the following process steps: awareness of the problem; suggestion; development; evaluation; and conclusion.

The first step of the method involves the understanding the problem and the definition of the performance for the system. To do that, we adopted a systematic literature review. During the suggestion phase, we suggested a tool built based on multidimensional views of the multimodal data. The ViVid engine was developed based on bar charts visualization of saturation and brightness, radar visualizations for hue and overall motion direction, line graph visualization for motion intensity, pointer visualization for motion direction every frame, and bar charts visualization of contrast and entropy. The usability evaluation phase was conducted with montage editors, and the analysis of the results is written in the conclusion phase.

3.1 Related Works

The systematic literature review was performed in electronic databases: ACM library and Science Direct. As inclusion criteria, we opted only full papers published in the last five years. The keywords were chosen based on previous literature review and were defined as: Data visualization "AND" video feature, multiple windows "AND"

Table 1. Distribution of papers after applying the filters

Database	Data visualization "AND" video feature	Selected for reading	Multiple window visualization	Selected for reading
Science direct	41	2	75	0
ACM library	96	5	41	1
Total	137	7	116	1

visualization, which should appear in papers' title, keywords or abstract. In addition, only Arts and Humanities, Computer Science and Design sources were considered. Table 1 shows the quantity of papers found in each database and the quantity of papers selected for full reading after analyzing their abstract and relevance to this paper.

The problem of visualizing data extracted from videos is understood as visualizing multimodal data. For example, Rashid et al. [7] proposed a graph-based approach for visualizing and exploring a multimedia search result space. They explored the idea that each media can be accessed through different modalities (i.e., visual, acoustic or textual) depending on the considered low-level features or on the available metadata extracted from or associated with it. Their interface is composed of five panels: one for input and is a text window (query); one for the result of the query, which is also a text window; the next panel shows thumbnails of all media objects contained in the retrieved documents; for the media selected is possible to listen, watch or view; and finally a graph panel represents the selected media objects and its semantically related media objects. Multiple views are also used by Chandrasegaran et al. [8] to create a visual analytics framework named VizScribe that employs multiple coordinated multiple views that enable the viewing of multimodal data, such as audio, video, and text. Their interface layout is divided into two main sections: temporal view (time-series data) and transcript view (text). These data are displayed as interactive timeline views, such as video progress, transcript visualization, and sketch timeline. Video data is designed to answer the question: "what was happening when…?". The temporal view pane thus includes a video playback interface, with time encoded as a progress bar spanning the width of the pane.

Different signals and rates can also be synchronously visualized, played and re-arranged using the web interface by Mayor et al. [9]. They created the repoVizz, an integrated online system capable of structural formatting and remote storage, browsing, exchange, annotation, and visualization of synchronous multimodal, time-aligned data (audio, video, motion capture, physiological signals, extracted descriptors, annotations, etc.).

Other approaches to visualize video data take advantage of the data available from image domain. Liu and Shi [10] represented each frame by high-level attributes rather than visual features. They proposed a novel sequence for sequence architecture by using a pre-learnt image-captioning model to generate for video-description. Video sequencing can also be seen as synthesized visual storyline. Chen et al. [11] used clustering and automatic storyline extraction to generate these storylines. Video sequencing is a problem of detecting screen shot boundaries, which divides a video into groups with spatio-temporal similarities. Bhattacharya et al. [12] proposed a method to detect these boundaries and to generate video storyboards using the local features as well as the global features presented in the scene. Their method reserves the continuity by ensuring at least one frame from each shot avoiding scene kipping.

The content of a video can also be detected in real time. Tanase et al. [13] created the IMOTION, which is an interactive video retrieval system that offers a sketch-based user interface. The system recognizes in real-time the user's sketch and makes suggestions based both on the visual appearance of the sketch and semantic content.

4 Design Strategy

Based on the literature review, and given the multi-dimensional video feature data, we suggested multidimensional views and balanced spatial and temporal benefits using multiple views. ViVid is a tool created based on bar charts visualization of saturation and brightness, radar visualizations for hue and overall motion direction, line graph visualization for motion intensity, pointer visualization for motion direction every frame, and bar charts visualization of contrast and entropy. We listed the features that we used below.

- Color: Red, Green, Blue, Hue, Saturation, and Brightness.
- Motion: Motion Intensity, Motion Direction.
- Texture: Entropy, Contrast.

The background color is set to white so that it contrasts sufficiently with the object. As for each graph, we utilize different colors because they correspond to different meanings in the data [14]. We adjust the size of each graph so that viewers can observe both details and macro information. We use perceptual techniques to focus user attention. For example, we select the color that has highest hue value within the hue wheel as the color for making saturation bar chart, brightness bar chart and motion direction radar graph. This also keeps views and state of multiple views consistent. For motion direction, we use the same dataset but different encoding including frame level motion direction visualization and overall motion direction visualization. Users have the freedom to control the tool, load database, load target video, play and pause the video and visualization. The video feature extraction is implement in Matlab. The ViVid system is implemented in Java.

4.1 Color Feature Visualization Interface

When a user clicks the "Color" button on the left corner, the interface will appear. Figure 3 shows the result. The video player will play the video frame by frame (2 frame per second in the target video). Color feature is represented using hue, saturation and brightness features.

Hue is defined as "the degree to which a stimulus can be described as similar to or different from stimuli that are described as: red, orange, yellow, green, blue, violet" [15]. Because the hue is usually described using a wheel, for hue value visualization, we adopted a radar graph to visualization overall hue value, which is the average of

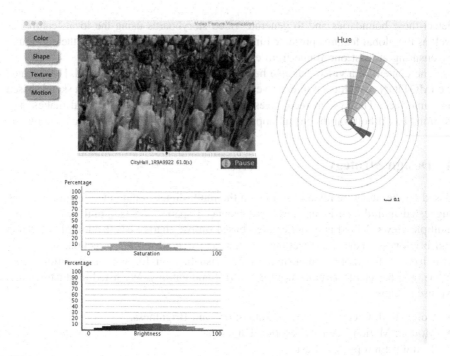

Fig. 3. Interface of color feature visualization (Color figure online)

every frame of a target video. We separated the hue wheel into 24 parts. In each part, we use inner circles to represent the number of pixels that have corresponding hue value. The highest value is normalized to 1. Between each circle in the concentric circle, the distance is 0.1. In Fig. 3, we can see that the highest hue value is light green, which is 1. The same normalization process is used to other values such as saturation, brightness, and motion direction. Once the system has found the highest hue value, it extracts the saturation and brightness values for this specific color. This brings users a consistent feeling of color style when watching the video and the visualization together. We normalized the biggest value of hue to 1 and made the visualization within a circle that is not big. Though it makes that the small hue value hard to be observed, it provides a better layout for users.

Saturation is the level of colorfulness, which also represents the level of purity of the color. The higher saturation value indicates less missing of colors. If we mix more colors together, the purity will decrease, and the picture will turn gray. We define the range of saturation value between 0 and 100 and separate the level of saturation into 16 parts, which is not too dense or sparse. The horizontal axis corresponds to each level of saturation, and the vertical axis represents the percentage of pixels that have the corresponding saturation value.

Brightness feature represents the level of a source appears to be radiating or reflecting light, which is the perception elicited by the luminance of a visual target [16]. Similar to saturation, we separated the brightness value into 16 parts. The horizontal axis corresponds to each level of brightness, and the vertical axis represents the percentage of pixels that have the corresponding brightness value.

4.2   Motion Feature Visualization Interface

While the color feature is presented based on its statistics and distribution, motion feature is visualized based on each frame. We use real-time data to visualize the motion intensity and motion direction per frame. In addition, we used the statistics of motion direction to represent the overall motion direction of the video.

Motion Intensity is the level of motion between frames within the video. We used a timeline based line graph visualization for motion intensity [15]. This allows the viewers to observe the motion intensity and its variation within the video. The timeline of the video player is horizontally aligned with the timeline of the motion intensity graph. The vertical axis indicates how intense the motion is. We separate the vertical axis into four sections, including low motion, medium motion, high motion and super high motion; each section is highlighted by an individual color. Rule of the separating point is based on the multiple observations of visualization of many videos. The horizontal axis represents time (Fig. 4).

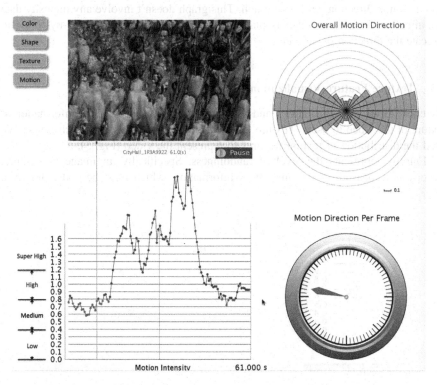

Fig. 4. Interface of motion feature visualization (Color figure online)

The bottom right corner shows the duration of the video. Since we want the user to compare the image of the frame and the feature of the frame at the same time, we used a pointer to connect the timeline with the horizontal axis of the motion intensity line graph. Each dot on line graph is corresponding to the time point of the video player. We enable the user to pause the player so that the user can view the feature data and image carefully. In the original data extracted by Matlab, we have optical flow vector of every moving point. To make a trade off and provide more useful information to users, we use statistics of the motion data of both frame-by-frame and overall video.

The motion direction can be defined using 360°. Therefore, we use the radar visualization for overall motion direction data, which is the average of every frame in a video. We separate 360° into 24 parts. We detect optical flow vectors and obtain its absolute value and its angle. Then we accumulate the optical flow vector value in each direction among 24 parts frame by frame and obtain the average motion direction value for an entire target video. In each part, we use the length of the radius of an arc to represent the number of pixels that moves toward the corresponding direction. When considering the absolute value, values of certain parts will be high and take space. Therefore, the biggest value of the motion direction is normalized to 1 to save space. Though it makes that the small hue value hard to be observed, it provides a better layout for users.

Because the user needs to observe the arc of motion direction within the video, we added motion direction per frame graph. This graph doesn't involve any intensity data but direction. When the video is playing, the pointer will move frame-by-frame to indicate the direction of the video.

4.3 Texture Feature Visualization Interface

We chose to visualize the entropy and the contrast feature to provide the information of texture of the video to users. Texture feature visualization is based on each frame. We used the distribution of texture features to represent the video (Fig. 5).

Entropy represents the level of randomness. Specifically, in image processing, entropy is a measure of the amount of information, which must be coded for by a

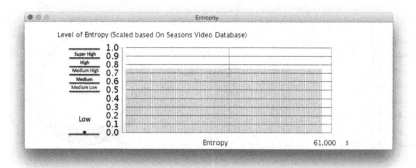

Fig. 5. Visualization of the entropy feature (Color figure online)

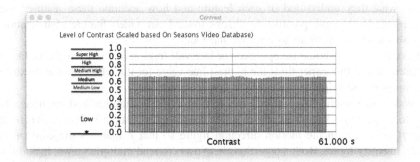

Fig. 6. Visualization of the contrast feature (Color figure online)

compression algorithm. If the image has higher entropy, such as an image of flowers, it contains more information. Low entropy images, such as those containing a white wall, have less information. Therefore, the high entropy images cannot be compressed as much as low entropy images. Similar to motion intensity, we used timeline based line graph visualization for entropy, which allows the visualization of this evolving entity over time. This allows the viewers to observe the change of entropy. The timeline of the video player corresponds to the timeline of the entropy graph. The vertical axis indicates how high the level of entropy is. We separate the vertical axis into six sections, including low, medium-low, medium, medium-high, high and super high; each section is highlighted by an individual color. The idea of the design is similar to the motion intensity (Fig. 6).

Contrast indicates how distinguishable regarding color that objects are within an image. This property is determined by the difference of color between the objects within an image. Similar to the design of visualization of Entropy, we used timeline based line graph visualization.

5   Usage, Feasibility Study and Considerations

The ViVid engine was built to help editors during the montage phase of a video. Thus, the system extracts and presents hue, saturation, brightness, motion direction and texture of a shot using multiple views. The interface was designed to focus attention on these data. The ViVid engine was used for the creation of the automatic music video generation system, DJ-MVP [17]. The systems used a color heuristic method for video selection. The target video segment is either closest or the furthest in the HSV color space to the previous video segment. This mechanism enabled the generative video to become more diverse regarding color. Examples can be found online.[3]

To evaluate the system, we conducted a feasibility study to understand how intuitive the interface is perceived by the users. The study was carried out at Simon Fraser University, and the system was presented using a 60" TV. Eight people were asked to

---

[3] https://vimeo.com/channels/djmvp.

discuss what they understood of each feature and how accurate these features were represented. Users gave positive feedbacks toward our video feature visualizations. They also made suggestions to improve the tool.

First, the system should accept frame or intervals (regions) or any length. So far, the tool presented in this paper finds the highest hue value for the whole shot and extracts the saturation and brightness values for this specific color.

Second, it is useful to normalize the vertical axis of saturation and brightness bar chart to make three visualizations of HSV consistent. Third, we should change the color of the arrow in the motion direction figure so that it matches the color in the motion intensity figure. Both suggestions help users to read multiple views. In addition, these perceptual cues make the relationship among views more clearly to the user.

Fourth, the interface should represent hue, saturation, and brightness divided into more than 24 parts to make the visualization more precise. This suggestion might increase cognitive attention demanded to perceive the information. Ideally, the information extracted should provide users a stable context of analysis without adding complexity. Thus, providing more detailed information might be an option provided by the system, while the default could remain as 24.

In addition, to obtain a clear understanding of each feature and the visualization tool, users recommend us to give a detailed explanation of each feature in the interface. These explanations would be useful when learning about the interface. All these feedbacks will be considered in further development of the tool.

Acknowledgement. We would like to acknowledge the Social Sciences and Humanities Research Council of Canada and Ministry of Education CAPES Brazil for their ongoing financial support. And we would like to thank the reviewers, who through their thoughtful comments have been assisting with this publication.

References

1. Galanter, P.: What is generative art? Complexity theory as a context for art theory. Digit. Creat. (2009)
2. Bizzocchi, J.: Ambient Video (2012). https://ambientvideo.org/seasons/
3. Eisenstein, S.: Film Form: Essays in Film Theory. Harcourt Brace and Company, New York (1949)
4. Walid, M.: Eisenstein and Montage: Battleship Potemkin, essay. https://www.academia.edu/7875638/Eisenstein_and_Montage_Battleship_Potemkin
5. Bunge, M.: Philosophical inputs and outputs of technology. In: Doner, D. (ed.) The History and Philosophy of Technology. University of Illinois, Champaign (1979)
6. Vaishnavi, V., Kuechler, W.: Design Research in Information Systems (2011). http://desrist.org/design-research-in-informationsystems
7. Rashid, U., Viviani, M., Pasi, G.: A graph-based approach for visualizing and exploring a multimedia search result space. Inf. Sci. **370–371**(20), 303–322 (2016)
8. Chandrasegaran, S., Badam, S.K., Kisselburgh, L., Peppler, K., Elmqvist, N., Ramani, K.: VizScribe: a visual analytics approach to understand designer behavior. Int. J. Hum.-Comput. Stud. **100**, 66–80 (2016)

9. Mayor, O., Llimona, Q., Marchini, M., Papiotis, P., Maestre, E:. repoVizz: a framework for remote storage, browsing, annotation, and exchange of multi-modal data. In: Proceedings of the 21st ACM International Conference on Multimedia, MM 2013, October 2013

10. Liu, Y., Shi, Z.: Boosting video description generation by explicitly translating from frame-level captions. In: Proceedings of the 2016 ACM on Multimedia Conference, MM 2016, September 2016

11. Chen, T., Lu, A., Hu, S.: Visual storylines: semantic visualization of movie sequence. Comput. Graph. **36**(4), 241–249 (2012)

12. Bhattacharya, S., Gupta, S., Venkatesh, K.S.: Video shot detection & story board generation using video decompositio. In: Proceedings of the Sixth International Conference on Computer and Communication Technology, ICCCT 2015, September 2015

13. Tanase, C., Giangreco, I., Rossetto, L., Schuldt, H., Seddati, O., Dupont, S., Altiok, O.C., Sezgin, M.: Semantic sketch-based video retrieval with autocompletion. In: Companion Publication of the 21st International Conference on Intelligent User Interfaces, IUI 2016 Companion, March 2016

14. Few, S.: Practical Rules for Using Color in Charts, Perceptual Edge Visual Business Intelligence Newsletter February (2008)

15. Van Wijk, J.J.: Cluster and calendar based visualization of time series data. In: Proceedings of INFOVIS 1999, pp. 4–9 (1999)

16. Vadivel, A., Sural, S., Majumdar, A.K.: Robust histogram generation from the HSV space based on visual colour perception. Int. J. Sig. Imaging Syst. Eng. InderScience **1**(3/4), 245–254 (2008)

17. Fan, J., Li, W., Bizzocchi, J., Bizzocchi, J., Pasquier, P.: DJ-MVP: an automatic music video producer. In: Proceedings of the Advances in Computer Entertainment Technology Conference, ACE 2016, November 2016

Comparison of Circle and Dodecagon Clock Designs for Visualizing 24-Hour Cyclical Data

Chen Guo, Shuang Wei, Mingran Li, Zhenyu Cheryl Qian,
and Yingjie Victor Chen[✉]

Purdue University, IN West Lafayette, USA
{guo171, wei93, li1940, qianz, victorchen}@purdue.edu

Abstract. Radial visualization is an important technique to depict serial periodic data. Circle clock design is intuitive to encode 24-hour cyclical data. However, the biggest limitation of the design is the accuracy of reading time points on circle. Dodecagon is another way to represent time series data. We empirically evaluated the effectiveness of circle and dodecagon clock design in perceiving specific points in time. A post-testing interview was also conducted to understand participants' strategies to read the times. Results show that dodecagon is more accurate than circle in terms of reading time points. Dodecagon was voted as a powerful approach to read the time points and circle was regarded as a better beautiful visualization method.

Keywords: Quantitative evaluation · Time series data · Radial designs

1 Introduction

Visualizing human mobility patterns has been a hot research topic with widespread applications in information visualization domain. Time series data are sets of values taken by a variable changing over time. Representing and analyzing the hourly trends in time series data is one of the most important research problems in this field. The primary role of time series visualization is typically to convey temporal information easily and accurately to users and help detect patterns and trends in the data. Circular layout has been widely used to encode time series and identify cyclic patterns in a day. Due to the traditional clock metaphor, it is intuitive to comprehend temporal information from a circular layout.

Circle design uses circular layout to encode temporal data with periodic structures in a compact way. It is particularly effective to model cyclic behaviors. Recently, many researchers have paid attention to the benefits and drawbacks of circle design, however, few work have presented effective strategies to improve circular diagrams with respect to answer times quickly and accurately. The accuracy of reading time points is the biggest limitation of circle clock design. Therefore, Guo et al. [1] proposed to use dodecagon instead of circle to visualize 24-hour cyclical data. 24 h are equally divided into 12 segments on the dodecagon. The segments enable users to recognize time values based on the positions of time points and lengths of lines.

This paper is mainly focused on the legibility of circle and dodecagon clock designs. Researchers conducted an experiment to compare the time and accuracy of

© Springer International Publishing AG 2017
A. Marcus and W. Wang (Eds.): DUXU 2017, Part III, LNCS 10290, pp. 54–62, 2017.
DOI: 10.1007/978-3-319-58640-3_5

these two different designs on identifying time values in a circular layout. We then discuss the implications of the experimental results and contribute a discussion on metaphoric glyph designs that will help to further our understanding of visualization designs for serial periodic data.

2 Related Work

Radial visualization is used to describe any interactive system that lays out data with an elliptical style [2]. Radial visualization contains many forms such as pie charts, star plots, sociograms, and polar plots. Concentric Circles Technique was used to visualize periodic patterns [3]. A set of concentric circles were arranged to reflect quantitative histories. Some researchers presented a spiral data layout to map serial periodic data and each period filled one lap of the spiral [4]. The Event Tunnel system adopted a disconnected ring pattern to visualize event streams. Each unit of time was encoded as a ring and multiple rings were stacked as a cylindrical tunnel to represent sequences of events. Calendar based visualization has been proposed to identify patterns and trends in daily, weekly, or yearly data [5]. A fisheye calendar interface was designed to visualize more complex tasks with longer time periods [6].

Moreover, techniques such as Ringmaps [7], Spiral Graph [8], SpiraClock [9], and ClockMap [10] map time series in a 24-hour clock. The 24-hour clock metaphor is an intuitive approach to represent 24-hour cyclical data; however, it also has its disadvantages. A big limitation of the clock design is the accuracy of recognizing the time points and time intervals. The quality of data reading from radial visualization is determined by angles' reading and relevance accuracy. Pie chart is much better to estimate the proportions of the whole when providing at least five anchors – 0%, 25%, 50%, 75%, and 100% [11]. Making comparison of visual elements by angles and areas is less effective and accurate than by line lengths [12]. Furthermore, anchors usually provide natural references to facilitate the estimation of numerical values [13, 14]. As a result, tick marks, labels, axis lines and gridlines are usually added to facilitate value reading. These features maximize the data-ink ratio without changing the core meaning of a graph [15].

The goal of data visualization is to help users understand insights in the way of being graphical, readable and notable. The accuracy of reading quantitative information depends on visualization methods. The most effective parameter of perceptual tasks in visualization is position, then line length, angle, area, and volume [16]. Perceptual tasks require not only being more accurate but also being faster. Preattentive processing is regarded as one of the most common tests on the aspect of speed in perceptual level of visualization [11]. However, previous studies on preattentive processing do not necessarily apply to polygon shape recognitions.

Additionally, researchers have investigated different techniques to evaluate radial visualizations. Some researchers conducted a controlled experiment to compare the Radar chart with flower charts and concentric radial space filling circles for composite indicator visualization [17]. The circles method was inferior for trend identification and item comparison. Researchers found that Start Glyph and Clock Glyph were better than Line Glyph in terms of detecting a particular temporal location [18]. They also stated that the clock metaphor increased users' chronological orientation [18]. Participants argued that the clock metaphor may help them locate certain points in time on radial glyphs. Another work evaluated different data glyph designs based on a systematic review of research papers and indicated the usefulness of metaphoric glyph designs [19]. However, the past studies about metaphoric design were limited because of the type of metaphors and type of data.

3   Circle and Dodecagon Clock Designs

The daily routine is a continuous cycle of everyday lives. Everyone has to live on the 24-hour daily circle. The activity patterns vary at different times; however, it can show remarkable similarities across different people. One of the advantages of radial visualization is to simply gain insights in the relations and make comparisons through the circular layout. Many researches employ the clock metaphor to depict the time series data since it is tempting to use analogies to visualize the cyclical nature of daily time. A circular layout looks aesthetically appealing to visualize 24-hour cyclical data. 24-hour circle typically shows 24 h clockwise, with midnight at the top, 6:00 o'clock at the right, 12:00 o'clock at the bottom, and 18:00 o'clock at the left (Fig. 1 left). The time point is encoded as an orange dot located on the circle (Fig. 1 left). We can estimate the time on the circle is between 2 am and 4 am in Fig. 1.

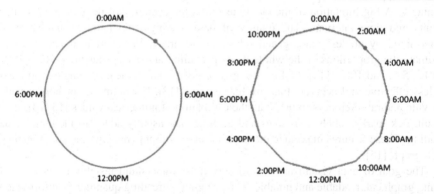

Fig. 1. Left: 24-hour circle clock design. Right: 24-hour dodecagon clock design. The time data is located on the two shapes as an orange dot. (Color figure online)

However, 24-hour circle clock design may not be the most appropriate and accurate way to perceive specific points in time. It is hard to recognize the position of the data point on the circle. Due to the limitation of 24-hour circle, Guo et al. [1] suggested to use dodecagon to represent a 24-hour clock. The 24 h are equally divided into 12 segments on the dodecagon. Each segment represents 2 h (Fig. 1 right). It enables audiences to estimate time based on positions and lengths of lines. The time point is also represented as an orange dot on the dodecagon. We can easily tell it is about 2:30 am to 3 am.

According to Tufte's design principles [15], visualization design should reduce non-data ink, avoid redundancy, and reduce ambiguity. Clock metaphor is closely related to serial periodic data. Nevertheless, few studies have been conducted to compare the effectiveness of metaphoric data glyph designs and generate design suggestions for clock metaphor approaches. As a result, we conducted an experiment to compare the time and accuracy of circle and dodecagon clock designs.

4 Experiment

4.1 Objectives and Research Questions

The goal of this experiment is to compare the visualization effectiveness of circle and dodecagon on identifying time values with 24-hour clock metaphor. The objective is to understand if dodecagon outperforms circle in regards to fewer errors and less completion time. The hypothesis is as follows:

H_1: With respect to 24-hour clock metaphor graphs, dodecagon would result in more accurate time reading than circle.

H_2: With respect to 24-hour clock metaphor graphs, dodecagon would result in faster time reading than circle.

4.2 Design and Tasks

We set up an experiment to measure completion time and errors of identifying time values with dodecagon or circle. Subjects were required to complete the task shown in Fig. 2.

The task used a one-way ANOVA to compare the legibility of circle and dodecagon. The within-subjects design required participants to do 24 tests in the two different conditions – circle and dodecagon. We ran a series of two independent questions 12 times. All the time points for each question were generated randomly. Participants were required to read the time points as accurately and quickly as possible. Figure 2a shows an example of the first round of tasks. We used red color to encode the time. In particular, we asked the users to answer the following question for the presented graph:

- Please identify the time of the red dot and pick the related hours and minutes on the next page.

The survey notified subjects of how many questions were left after each round. We recorded the user's answers, the correctness of the answers, and the completion time. There was no time limit for answering each question. Participants were instructed to glance at the diagram, click on the next button, and choose the correct answer from a drop down list of hours (0–23) and a drop down list of minutes (0–59) in the next page. Both the perceived hours and minutes were logged. The reading time was recorded after the next button was clicked. Participants were not allowed to go back to review the graph or modify the submitted result.

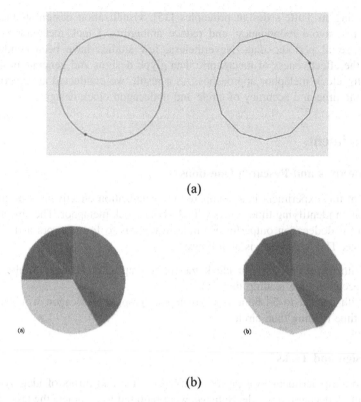

(a)

(b)

Fig. 2. Screenshots of the task. (a) Task: identify the time of the red dot on the dodecagon or the circle; (b) Images for the post-testing interview. (Color figure online)

4.3   Post-testing Interview

At the end of the survey, we conducted a short interview with participants. We showed participants two images and asked them to pick which one they prefer, circle or dodecagon, in terms of aesthetic and legibility (Fig. 2b). Their strategies to read the times and comments to the designs were documented.

4.4   Participants and Instruments

We recruited participants who were not aware of the experimenter's hypothesis in order to minimize the possibility of demand characteristics. There were 55 persons (39 males, 16 females) who participated voluntarily with age between 15 and 45 years. Except for one participant, all were from our university and had a broad range of academic backgrounds – 23 Computer Graphics Technology graduate students, 13 undergraduate Engineering students, five Art and Design graduate students, and other undergraduate and graduate students from Building Construction Management, Chemistry, Aviation Technology, Audiology, and Linguistics.

The study was conducted in a laboratory environment where researchers were able to provide detailed instructions. Participants used a mouse to perform the tasks on a computer with 24 inch LED monitor and 1600 * 900 pixel resolution. The average duration of the survey was about 15 min per participant.

4.5 Results

We eliminated data of seven participants who withdrew from studies before they finished it. We ended up with 48 remaining participants (13 females, 35 males) with a mix of different backgrounds. The total trails for the task were 1152. The overall average error across variations was 26.20 min with the standard error 1.22 min for the circle, and 16.13 min with the standard error 1.22 min for the dodecagon. ANOVA showed that there was a significant effect of the shape on errors ($F (1, 1151) = 43.03$; $p < .0001$). A noticeable mean difference was visible across the two shapes with $p < .0001$. A closer pairwise comparisons showed that dodecagon was significantly more accurate than circle ($p < .0001$). Therefore, we can conclude that H1 is accepted and there was a significant mean difference between circle and dodecagon in respect of time reading errors. There was a high probability that dodecagon was more accurate for reading compared with circle.

The results also show that dodecagon may perform slightly better with the average completion time of 12.68 s and the standard deviation of 13.45 s. The mean completion time for circle is 14.22 s and the standard deviation is 17.62 s. However, ANOVA didn't show that there was a significant effect of the completion time on errors ($F (1, 1151) = 1.04$; $p = .3730$). The F Value and p-value, respectively, tested the null hypothesis that the completion time did not explain a significant proportion of the shape variance. Therefore, we can conclude that there was not a significant mean difference between circle and dodecagon with respect to reading speed. There was a comparatively small probability that dodecagon would result in faster time reading than circle.

The interview result showed that 66% of the participants preferred circle in terms of aesthetics, while 34% chose dodecagon. 82% of the participants chose dodecagon in terms of legibility, while 18% preferred circle. Thus, dodecagon was voted as a powerful approach to read the time points and circle was regarded as a better beautiful visualization method.

5 Discussion

5.1 Participant Feedback

After the survey, participants provided comments on their reading strategy. Most of them identified the time points based on adding up intervals or counting lines on the dodecagon. At first they counted how many sides the figure had and related the vertices to the hour markings on the clock to help them get a reference. Thus, they were able to use percentage of the line in between the two vertices as the percentage of minutes have transpired in that hour.

As we can see, it was easier to tell what time value fell where on the polygons because people can use each point to signify the hour. However, it was very interesting to notice that many participants always defaulted to the thinking that the glyph started in AM. They used the bottom of the glyph as 6:00 o'clock and the far left was 9:00 o'clock and the far right was 3:00 o'clock. Although we told the participants that one circle or one dodecagon represented 24-hour a day, they still mentally marked 12 and 6 as being the top and bottom vertices instead of using 0 and 12. Here we borrowed a term called anchoring from psychology to describe people's intuitive estimation [20]. Anchoring refers to the cognitive bias that influence the way human beings intuitively make decisions. Human have a tendency to use the initial piece of information to interpret information. 12-hour time and clock are commonly used in daily life. Since people rely heavily on the initial time information stored in their brain, it would be difficult for them to convert it into 24-hour format.

Except for the time used in the military and hospital, the 12-hour clock rule is much more common in the U.S. and Canada. The infoVis researches using 12-hour clock consider that it matches people's mental model of analog clock and makes it easier to decode time with the spatial layout. But the 12-hour approach needs to draw two circles on the clock to represent one day, and confusion will take place. Some researches insist on the 24-hour approach since there is no need to specify the time is AM or PM. Furthermore, this approach can reduce non-data ink, avoid redundancy, and reduce ambiguity. The pros and cons of both approaches point to the need for further research to compare their effectiveness.

5.2   Design Suggestions for Visualizing 24-Hour Cyclical Data

We provided two design options and conducted an empirical study to evaluate their performances. Our study showed that dodecagon is more accurate than circle in terms of reading time points on the shapes. Participants were significantly more confident with the dodecagon clock designs. Our feedback also shows that circle is more appealing to audiences but its legibility is low. Although 12-hour clock metaphor matches human's mental model of analog clock, we still suggest to use 24-hour clock because 12-hour clock increases the cognitive load of the design by adding another circle in the graph. All in all, using dodecagon to represent 24-hour cyclical data is the most appropriate and accurate way to visualize 24-hour cyclical data.

5.3   Limitations and Challenges

In the visual context, clustered shapes are very common to describe the distribution of the data. By dividing data into groups, humans are capable to identify daily routines or abnormal events in serial periodical data. The first limitation of the study is that it doesn't consider the other design parameters such as clustered glyphs, glyph sizes, widths, and line spacing. In order to inform more completed visualization design, we need to evaluate tasks including selecting similar time on clustered diagrams, reading time points on diagrams with different sizes, choosing preferable diagrams with different line widths and line spacing, and picking center points of circle and dodecagon.

The second limitation is related to bias pattern in proportion judgment. Spence [21] found there was a four-cycle pattern that produced a pattern of overestimation and underestimation of proposition with pie charts and stacked bar graphs. It stated that with tick marks at .25 intervals, a bias cycle occurred around different proportions. People have the tendency to overestimate proportions less than .25 as well as those between .50 and .75. On the contrary, proportions between .25 and .50 as well as greater than .75 were intent to be underestimated. In our test, we didn't consider these bias patterns. Either the quadrant angles or the points on the edges of the polygon provided reference for participants and helped them perceive the time more accurately. So there may be fewer errors around the 0:00, 6:00, 12:00 and 18:00 clock position. If the position of the time point was closer to the tick mark position, the error may become very small.

6   Conclusion

This paper presented two visual designs to support the 24-hour cyclical data visualization. We compared the effectiveness of the two different shapes – circle and dodecagon through the empirical study. The results of the study indicate that dodecagon outweighs circle with respect to accuracy and speed. Although we were able to demonstrate the effectives of the two shapes on reading time points, we found that people used different strategies to comprehend the information. We are interested in how different strategies would influence their performance. People may use different strategies to read time points and time intervals, thus it is necessary to measure the effectiveness of reading time intervals on circles and dodecagons. Our future study will focus on testing people's performance on identifying time intervals and then compare the results with our current work. In this way, we are able to provide more accurate, faster, and appealing visualization to improve the radial time series visualization.

References

1. Guo, C., Xu, S., Yu, J., Zhang, H., Wang, Q., Xia, J., Zhang, J., Chen, Y.V., Qian, Z.C., Wang, C., Ebert, D.: Dodeca-rings map: interactively finding patterns and events in large geo-temporal data. In: 2014 IEEE Conference on Visual Analytics Science and Technology (VAST), pp. 353–354 (2014)
2. Draper, G., Livnat, Y., Riesenfeld, R.F.: A survey of radial methods for information visualization. IEEE Trans. Vis. Comput. Graph. 15, 759–776 (2009)
3. Daassi, C., Dumas, M., Fauvet, M.-C., Nigay, L., Scholl, P.-C.: Visual Exploration of Temporal Object Databases (2000)
4. Carlis, J.V., Konstan, J.A.: Interactive visualization of serial periodic data. In: Proceedings of the 11th Annual ACM Symposium on User Interface Software and Technology, pp. 29–38. ACM, New York (1998)
5. Wijk, J.J.V., Selow, E.R.V.: Cluster and calendar based visualization of time series data. In: 1999 IEEE Symposium on Information Visualization, (Info Vis 1999) Proceedings, pp. 4–9, 140 (1999)

6. Bederson, B.B., Clamage, A., Czerwinski, M.P., Robertson, G.G.: DateLens: a fisheye calendar interface for PDAs. ACM Trans. Comput.-Hum. Interact. **11**, 90–119 (2004)

7. Zhao, J., Forer, P., Harvey, A.S.: Activities, ringmaps and geovisualization of large human movement fields. Inf. Vis. **7**, 198–209 (2008)

8. Weber, M., Alexa, M., Müller, W.: Visualizing time-series on spirals. In: Proceedings of the IEEE Symposium on Information Visualization 2001 (INFOVIS 2001), p. 7. IEEE Computer Society, Washington, DC (2001)

9. Dragicevic, P., Huot, S.: SpiraClock: a continuous and non-intrusive display for upcoming events. In: Extended Abstracts of Chi 2002, pp. 604–605 (2002)

10. Fischer, F., Fuchs, J., Mansmann, F.: ClockMap : enhancing circular treemaps with temporal glyphs for time-series data. Presented at the EuroVis (2012)

11. Zwislocki, J.: Sensory Neuroscience: Four Laws of Psychophysics. Springer Science & Business Media, Heidelberg (2009)

12. Cleveland, W.S., McGill, R.: An experiment in graphical perception. Int. J. Man-Mach. Stud. **25**, 491–500 (1986)

13. Hollands, J.G., Dyre, B.P.: Bias in proportion judgments: the cyclical power model. Psychol. Rev. **107**, 500–524 (2000)

14. Simkin, D., Hastie, R.: An information-processing analysis of graph perception. J. Am. Stat. Assoc. **82**, 454–465 (1987)

15. Tufte, E.R.: The Visual Display of Quantitative Information. Graphics Press, Cheshire (2001)

16. Cleveland, W.S., McGill, R.: Graphical perception: theory, experimentation, and application to the development of graphical methods. J. Am. Stat. Assoc. **79**, 531–554 (1984)

17. Albo, Y., Lanir, J., Bak, P., Rafaeli, S.: Off the radar: comparative evaluation of radial visualization solutions for composite indicators. IEEE Trans. Vis. Comput. Graph. **22**, 569–578 (2016)

18. Fuchs, J., Fischer, F., Mansmann, F., Bertini, E., Isenberg, P.: Evaluation of alternative glyph designs for time series data in a small multiple setting. In: Proceedings of the SIGCHI Conference on Human Factors in Computing Systems, pp. 3237–3246. ACM, New York (2013)

19. Fuchs, J., Isenberg, P., Bezerianos, A., Keim, D.: A systematic review of experimental studies on data glyphs. IEEE Trans. Vis. Comput. Graph. **PP**, 1 (2016)

20. Vessey, I.: Cognitive fit: a theory-based analysis of the graphs versus tables literature*. Decis. Sci. **22**, 219–240 (1991)

21. Spence, I., Krizel, P.: Children's perception of proportion in graphs. Child Dev. **65**, 1193–1213 (1994)

Design of Tooltips for Data Fields

A Field Experiment of Logging Use of Tooltips and Data Correctness

Helene Isaksen[1], Mari Iversen[1(✉)], Jens Kaasbøll[1], and Chipo Kanjo[2]

[1] University of Oslo, Oslo, Norway
{helenis,mariive,jensj}@ifi.uio.no
[2] University of Malawi, Zomba, Malawi
chipo.kanjo@gmail.com

Abstract. Many health professionals in developing countries carry out tasks which require a higher level of education than they have. To help such undereducated health workers filling correct data in patient information systems, data fields were furnished with tooltips for guiding users. In a previous study with questionnaires and interviews, health workers preferred tooltip contents being normal values of the data with medical explanation as the second best. The experiment reported in this paper set out to test these content alternatives and also aimed at finding health workers' use of tooltips and possible effects on data correctness. In order to resemble the work setting, each of the 15 undereducated health workers participating was given a tablet PC with the patient information system and booklet of 22 cases to be entered over a period of two weeks. They were given a one hour introduction to the system. Their use of the tablet was recorded, and after completing, the participants were interviewed. The health workers opened tooltips frequently for the first cases, and thereafter the use dropped. Reasons given were that they learnt the data field during the first cases, and thereafter they did not need the tooltips so often. The number of correct data entries increased over time. The group with medical explanation tooltips performed better than the group with normal value tooltips, thus the preferred tooltip in the questionnaire gave a lower performance than the second alternative. While the experiment demonstrated that tooltips improved performance, it did not quantify the effect.

Keywords: Usability evaluation · Field experiment · Logging use · Learnability · Context-sensitive help · Tooltip contents · Normal data values · Formal definitions · Data quality

1 Introduction

Health workers in developing countries are often assigned tasks meant for those of higher cadres. As an example, undereducated staff have to do the tasks of nurses [5]. Doing work-related tasks beyond one's competence may lead to wrong data capturing and may cause fatal decision making. Training and follow ups of undereducated are often unsuccessful due to lack of supporting staff and funding. In addition, IT systems

© Springer International Publishing AG 2017
A. Marcus and W. Wang (Eds.): DUXU 2017, Part III, LNCS 10290, pp. 63–78, 2017.
DOI: 10.1007/978-3-319-58640-3_6

are often designed for expert users, thus there is a need for providing information health workers can look up and use themselves.

There are several methods to provide additional information for users. These include users looking up information online, from external sources or by including inline information in the system. Adding inline additional information may be a solution, however, this research aim to test different content types for additional information, and to find the most effective type. Tooltips are the most common ones and have been shown several times to be effective [1, 4, 7]. Due to limitations in the software used for the experiment, textual tooltips are the basis for our research.

Our definition of tooltips is information that can be viewed when the user push a button. The information will disappear from the screen when a button is pushed, or when the user start or finish entering data into the field. The goal for tooltips, in our case, are for the users of the system to understand the medical terms and enter correct information.

Little previous research has addressed the identification of the most effective tooltips in terms of correctness of data entry. Some research has considered user-preference of expression format for tooltips. Petrie et al. [7] identified four expression formats for tooltips and asked their participants to rate the different formats based on satisfaction, understandability and preference, however the research did not opt to find the most effective tooltips. One of the end goals for tooltips are for the user to use the system effectively, therefore, a decreasing usage of help commands or tooltips is seen as a sign of system learnability [6]. Dai et al. [1] developed a software consisting of step-by-step instructions for carrying out tasks. However, these instructions would not function with tooltips, as tooltips are unsuitable for displaying sequences of instructions, since they disappear once a single task is finished. Isaksen et al. [5] conducted a survey of preferences of content types of tooltips by lower cadre health workers. The health workers preferred tooltips expressed as normal values of the data to be entered. However, their study did not explore if the tooltips actually led to more correct data entry. Their findings constitute a basis for our study.

The objectives for this research is to compare two content types for tooltips and find out whether there is a difference between them in terms of correctness of data entry. We also wish to see if the tooltips actually affect the correctness. Our research is, therefore, an experiment to find out how often the users use the tooltips, and if they can be seen as successful. By successful tooltip, we mean that they have opened the tooltip, and that they enter the correct data.

2 Tooltip Contents

Through interviews with professionals within Antenatal care (ANC) systems, Isaksen et al. [5] identified four content types for tooltips for medical terms. These content types were normal values, the formal definition, treatment, and procedure to find measurements. They found that normal values were the most preferred among health workers of different cadres, with formal definitions as the runner up. Therefore, this study will focus on these two alternatives.

Tooltips containing formal definitions, or explanations, explain medical terms. An example from the study is "Occurs when the woman has hypertension and proteinuria. It can happen at any point after week 20 of pregnancy.", which is the explanation of pre-eclampsia.

Normal values in the tooltips provide either a range of normal values or signs of the given condition. For example, pre-eclampsia has the following normal value tooltips: "Signs: Diastolic blood pressure above 90 and protein in urine.".

Below are some examples from the experiment, showing both versions of the tooltip (Table 1).

Table 1. Examples of the two content types

Data element	Normal value	Explanation
Pre-eclampsia	Signs: diastolic blood pressure above 90 and protein in urine	Occurs when the woman has hypertension and proteinuria. It can happen at any point after week 20 of pregnancy
Diastolic blood pressure	Diastolic blood pressure should be between 60 and 80	Diastolic blood pressure is the minimum blood pressure
Fundal height	Normal fundal height measurement: 20 weeks = 17–20 cm 28 weeks = 25.5–28.5 cm 36 weeks = 33–35 cm 40 weeks = 36–38 cm	Measurement from the public bone to the top of the uterus. This is done to assess how far into the pregnancy the woman is

3 Technology Description

In order to conduct the experiment, we utilized a generic software package called District Health Information System 2 (DHIS2). The DHIS2 package can either be run through a web browser or through Android apps. For our study the Tracker Capture (TC) android app was used for hosting the testing program. The TC enables the end users to track people or objects over a period of time, and follow up each individual case. The TC can be tailored in the web version for different purposes, and one can create specific programs. For our research the two first authors created two shortened antenatal care programs, and added data elements, skip logics, tooltips and options sets. The data elements were chosen based on Malawian health passports. The programs used exactly the same data elements and order, but the tooltips had different content types.

In Malawian health passports, blood pressure is registered in a single field, labeled either "Blood pressure" or just "BP", and is not marked diastolic and systolic. Therefore, we wanted to check the participants' ability to cope with unusual order of data fields, and chose to list diastolic and systolic in the opposite order of how one usually writes them (see Fig. 1).

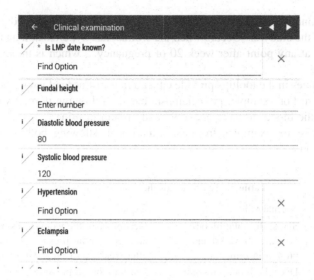

Fig. 1. Example of diastolic and systolic data elements in Tracker Capture

The data elements were assigned to stages, like "Previous pregnancies" and "First antenatal care visit", and categories, like "Family history" and "Clinical examination". "Previous pregnancies" stood out by being the only one which contained checkboxes for different data elements. This was done for the program to resemble the health passports, where information is entered for all previous pregnancies in one page, rather than separate pages for each pregnancy (Fig. 2).

In order to register the informant's behavior in the system, an analytic tool called UXcam was utilized. UXcam is a tool used for improving user experiences in applications, through screen recordings, emphasizing the touches on the screen. The recordings are stored on UXcam's server and are accessible through their web page. The tool was added to the TC code, enabling us to watch and analyze the informants behavior on the screen. The tablets could be traced by the tablet's own ID, as well as the profession of the participant using the tablet. This gave us an impression of their progress throughout the experiment. However, there were risks using this additional software, as we were dependent on the participants being connected to internet when doing their tasks. UXcam is only able to send recordings if connected to the internet, meaning we were at risk of not getting all of the recordings. Thus we equipped each of the tablets with sim cards and preloaded internet bundles. To ensure that the internet bundle was only used for the experiment, an app called "Applocker" was installed, blocking the usage of all other applications.

For the study, 30 tablets were bought, one for each participant. The two first authors installed the TC on all the tablets, making sure the system was running.

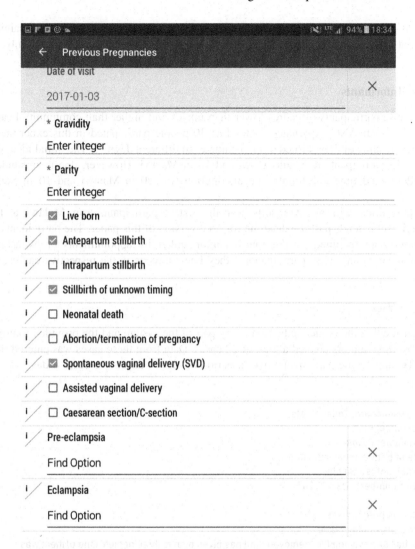

Fig. 2. Here is "Live born", "Antepartum stillbirth", Stillbirth of unknown timing" and Spontaneous vaginal delivery (SVD)" checked, meaning that the woman has experienced these in her previous pregnancies.

4   Method

In order to get a better understanding of the health worker's use of the tooltips, we decided to carry out an experiment. We chose to conduct the experiment in natural settings, as this could introduce issues which the participants would not encounter in a lab [2]. It was also important to test over time, in order to see their evolvement. We also wanted to see if they learned anything from the tooltips.

As mentioned, the tablets contained either a program with tooltips containing normal values, or explanations, and these were given to the participants randomly.

4.1 Informants

We chose participants of cadres lower than nurses and higher than community health workers, with ANC experience. A total of 30 people participated in this experiment, however, some of them turned out to be nurses of different degrees. The initial idea was to do 15 participants in South Africa and 15 in Malawi. However, due to misunderstandings and time constraints, the distribution was 20 in Malawi and 10 in South Africa.

This article will include results from the first 15 participants from Malawi, as the experiment extends past the deadline for final version of this paper. The participants in Malawi were recruited by the fourth author, either by appointments or by asking acquaintances and other participants if they knew anyone in the respective cadres.

4.2 Cases

To ensure that the participants used every part of the system and the provided tooltips, the two first authors created a total of 22 cases. Data from these cases was entered into the TC app by the participants over a period of eleven days, two cases a day.

Enrollment date: Today's date
First name: Pika
Last name: Chula
Date of birth: 14th march 1985
Marital status: Single
Mobile number: 123 123 245

Previous pregnancies:
Date of visit: today's date
Pika has had two embryos removed, and has given birth to three babies. One of them was delivered through an incision in the abdomen, but, unfortunately, died before the onset of labour. Pika doesn't remember much of it because she was in a coma. The two other were born in normal manners.

First visit:
Date of visit: today's date
Pika's father react to blinking lights and often get seizures, while her mother has a disorder of metabolism which makes her drink a lot of water and produce large amounts of urine. Pika herself often experience difficulties breathing due to spasms in the bronchi of the lungs, and is in addition allergic to antibiotics in general. She cannot remember her LMP, but her fundal height is 25 cm, her blood pressure is 120/90 and she has protein in her urine. She has been given malaria prophylaxis and iron supplements.

Fig. 3. An example of a case from the booklet

The cases contained information about fictive pregnant women, often quite sick and having lost multiple children. However, it was not written straightforward, but was instead disguised as symptoms, or resembling the information the participants could find in the tooltips. Examples are ".. lost the child in week 38, before the onset of labour", which indicates an antepartum stillbirth, or ".. has abnormally high blood pressure and protein in the urine", which indicate pre-eclampsia.

Several of the cases contained similar information, and these were distributed evenly over the period. This was to see is the participants learned the different expressions from one day to another (Fig. 3).

4.3   Introducing the Experiment

The experiment started with a brief introduction about who we were, where we came from, and that we wanted to work on improving the usability of a system. We did not inform them about the testing of the tooltips, to make sure we wouldn't affect the results. We then introduced them to the tablets and the TC, explaining what the application did, using a modified question suggestion approach [5]. This included making them aware of the tooltips, informing them that they could use these if they were in doubt regarding what information to enter. We also presented them with the same example case, similar to the next 22 cases they would solve.

The participants in Malawi were situated in groups of three, four or five people, enabling them to cooperate and discuss the matter as they would have in a normal work situation. This also gave us the opportunity to observe what each of them did, and to evaluate their technical skills. The observation enabled us to adapt the information given during the introduction, and to give proper follow-up on each participant. Also, a lot of the explaining of the different elements and tasks was repeated in Chichewa, the local language, by the fourth author. This seemed to increase their understanding of the experiment, the tasks and other unfamiliar expressions. At the end of the introduction they were given the same questionnaire as Isaksen et al. used, capturing the preference of content types for tooltips.

4.4   The Booklets

For this experiment we created a booklet containing information about us, the experiment and 22 cases with tasks for each day. Diaries are used to collect data about user behavior and activities over a longer period of time, and may provide a contextual understanding of the usage of the system [3]. Thus, the booklets were inspired by a diary technique, where the task section would function as a diary. Here, the participants could write down when and where they entered the case, how they felt using the system, what data elements they used and thoughts on the cases. The goal of this was to make them reflect on their case, and to make it easier for them to discuss their thoughts and ideas during the post-interview. The participants were given the booklets after going through the example case.

The booklet also contained information about who we were, and what they were supposed to do. Email contact information was also given in the booklet, allowing for the participants to contact us if they had any questions. In addition, they were also given a phone number to the fourth author, who functioned as a local contact, in case of urgent questions.

4.5   The Post-interviews

After approximately two weeks we asked the participants for a semi-structured interview, aiming to get a better understanding of their use of the tooltips and general thoughts of the entire experience. The questions focused on opinions on the information in the tooltips, and whether they opened the tooltips before or after data entry, and why they did so.

We also collected the booklet and had the participants do the aforementioned questionnaire again to see whether the opinion remained the same or changed. In addition, an online questionnaire was created capturing the participants user experience of the tooltips (hereby UX questionnaire). In this article, we are only using the responses from the 15 participants mentioned above, as well as the responses Isaksen et al. used in their study.

4.6   Analysis

The recordings were structured and analyzed in a google sheet document (Fig. 4). The participants were differentiated by having separate sheets, listing all data elements from the program. The first two authors registered whether the participants entered correct information, and if they opened any tooltips. The sheets were set up to calculate successful tooltips, if both data entry was correct and the tooltip was opened.

	A	B	C	D	E	F	G	H	I	J	K	L	M
	Data element | Midwife nurse		Case 1			Case 2			Case 3			Case 4	
1													
2	O=opened, C=Correct, S=successful tooltip. =1 if true	O	C	S	O	C	S	O	C	S	O	C	S
3	Gravidity	1	1	1	1	1	1		1	0	1	1	1
4	Parity	1	1	1	1	1	1	1	1	1	1	1	1
5	Live born	1	1	1	1	1	1	1	1	1			0
6	Antepartum stillbirth	1		0	1		0	1	0	0		1	0
7	Intrapartum stillbirth	1	1	1	1	1	1	1		0	1		0
8	Stillbirth of unknown timing	1		0	1		0	1	1	1		0	0
9	Neonatal death		0	1	1	1	1	1		0	1		0
10	Abortion	1		0		0	1		0	1	1	1	1
11	SVD	1		0	1	1	1	1	1	1			0
12	Assisted vaginal delivery	1		0		0			0			0	0
13	C-section		1	0		0			0		1	0
14	Pre-eclampsia	1	0	0	1	0	0	1		0	1	0	0
15	Eclampsia	1	1	1		1	0	1		0			0
16	Hypertension		0	0	1	0	1	1	1	1	1	1	1

Fig. 4. Screenshot of the spreadsheet used to register opened tooltips and correct data entry

4.7   Motivation

In order to motivate the participants to take part of the experiment, they were told, at the end of the introduction, that if they did all their tasks, the tablet would be theirs to keep. This is probably part of the reason why everybody entered all cases, and gave feedback to the tasks. In addition, being aware of that their usage of the systems was being monitored, may also have resulted in a higher willingness to finish the tasks given. We did not start with introducing the reward, as we wanted to recruit somebody that were somewhat interested in the project.

5   Results

On average, there were 14 cases recorded per user, in addition we lost all recordings from one user and had one user where we only received eight recordings. This was probably due to connectivity issues, as we, during the post-interviews, found all 22 cases on their tablets.

After analyzing the information we received from the booklets and the interviews, we learned that the participants, on average, spent 20–25 min on each case, and it took them about 3 days to get comfortable with the system. However, many of the participants also stated that they wished they had more training with using the application, as for some of them, this was their first time using a touch screen.

Several informants requested more detailed cases, in order to diagnose the patients properly. They also stated that instead of camouflaging the information we should have written it straight forward, indicating that they were not fully aware of the goal of the experiments. This makes the results more trustworthy.

5.1   Tooltips

Below is a graphical presentation of the number of opened tooltips throughout the 22 cases. Normal Value represent the opened tooltips of normal values, while Explanation represent the opened tooltips of explanations. The x-axis shows the cases, while the y-axis represent the total number of opened tooltips for all participants. A trendline was added to better see the development from the first to the last case (Fig. 5).

The graph below shows that both normal values and explanation have a decrease in number of opened tooltips, normal values being slightly lower. This corresponds with what we learned from the post-interview, that the participants used the tooltips a lot in the beginning and less during the last cases. There is no significant difference between the two.

Through the post-interviews, we found that most of the participants confirmed that they used the tooltips less throughout the cases, because they had learned them by heart. This also corresponds with several of our results from the UX questionnaire, where the participants gave a 4.5 out of 5, on both "The need for opening the tooltips were less as the days went by" and "The tooltips helped me learn medical terms by heart". One of them even quoted the tooltip about eclampsia, proving that she really had learned the term. Another said that she "check with the information I got earlier",

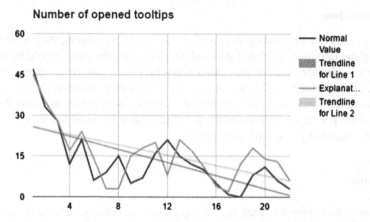

Fig. 5. Graph displaying opened tooltips throughout the cases

and further explained that she kept learning the terms when she opened the tooltips, and eventually she knew what to answer, without using them. One participant said she used the tooltips frequently in the first cases, but "Not frequently in the last cases because they helped us understand what it was.".

Another thing we noticed in the recordings, was that the tooltips were mostly used during the Previous Pregnancy stage, which may be because this is the first stage they enter information into. It may also be because pregnancies have different outcomes, and, therefore, it may be more difficult to differentiate between the different outcomes or delivery methods. Thus, it would require more of a need to consult with the tooltips. When we asked the participants during the interview what they found difficult in the system, the different stillbirths during previous pregnancies was mentioned several times. The difference between antepartum stillbirth, intrapartum stillbirth and stillbirth of unknown timing was confusing. Some also said that several of the terms used in the previous pregnancies stage, are terms that are more familiar to fully educated nurses and midwives, and might be difficult for people with less education to understand. Some also suggested that in order for non-medical personnel to understand what data to enter, signs and symptoms should be listed. This corresponds with the responses we received from the questionnaire regarding content types, that normal values is the most preferred content type.

The graph below show the percentage of successful tooltips from first to last case. The percentage was found by dividing number of successful tooltips with all opened tooltips. Its representation is mostly the same as the graph above, except from the y-axis, which represent the percentage of successful tooltips (Fig. 6).

The graph show that the percentage of successful tooltips increase towards the last cases. Also, as seen, the tooltips containing explanations has both a higher percentage of successful tooltips, and a steeper increase through the cases, than normal values.

During the post-interviews we found out that eleven of the 15 participants claimed that they open the tooltips first, and then enter the information. The last four entered

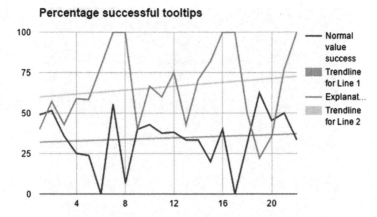

Fig. 6. Graph displaying percentage of successful tooltips throughout the cases

data first, and then used the tooltips to check the information they entered and to confirm their answer. We also found out that they had discussed with each other, and other colleagues, during the experiment, when solving the cases.

In addition to the interviews, we also used the booklet to find out what the participants thought. All of them wrote comments and thoughts for most of the cases, and also about the system and some of the tooltips they found useful. "I used the (i) to give me the meaning of the things or terms used" and similar comment are found in several of the booklets. A majority of the participants learned about gravidity and parity, and the different stillbirths. Especially did we notice that if the correct data entry was antepartum stillbirth, intrapartum stillbirth was quite often opened as well. "I learned the difference between antepartum and intrapartum stillbirth" one of the participants said. She often opened both tooltips to understand the difference between them. Also, we learned that ways of delivery contributed to learning. "The allow guided me on breech delivery" is a quote from one of the booklets, saying that the "allows", meaning the tooltips, taught her about breech delivery, something we also discussed during the interview.

Also, the tooltips for hypertension, pre-eclampsia and eclampsia were used more in the previous pregnancies stage. This was their first encounter with those tooltips during each case, and many of the participants found the terms confusing. We also found out that participants have different definitions of some terms, like for example pre-eclampsia. Some do not consider only protein in urine as a way of diagnosing pre-eclampsia, as it can indicate other diseases. Another interviewee said that "In our facility we don't have a lot of resources, so high BP means pre-eclampsia.", meaning they diagnose pre-eclampsia only based on high blood pressure. It is important to have formal definitions, however, it is absolutely vital to take into consideration the health facilities without the necessary resources for diagnosing certain conditions.

When analyzing the booklets and the post-interviews, several suggestion of improvement materialized. One participant suggested that we should add more vital signs to the data elements, another stated "Add more information to the i's. For example, can you have pre-eclampsia with only hypertension?". A third participant

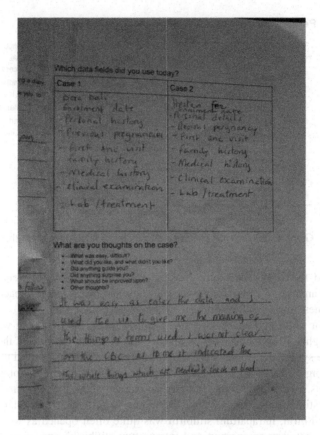

Fig. 7. An example from the tasks in the booklet

suggested that we should "for instance giving the normal ranges for BP". A fourth participant suggested signs and symptoms instead of formal definitions. She justified the statement by saying that non-medical personnel would not know what a condition is, based on the explanations. What is interesting is that all these participants had been using the testing program containing explanations as their content type for tooltips. These finding are also cohesive with the response from the UX questionnaire, where the following statements, "..should have provided more information.." and "..should have provided different information" received scores of 3.2 and 2.9 out of 5, indicating that they partly agree with the statements.

The chart below shows a scatter plot of the number of opened tooltips per user (x-axis) and % correct data (y-axis). Each dot represents a participant (Fig. 8).

There seems to be two users never or seldom opening tooltips who nevertheless enter data of with a high percentage of correctness (upper left). One of these was a nurse, who was sufficiently educated and outside the target group for the tooltips. Two other nurses participated.

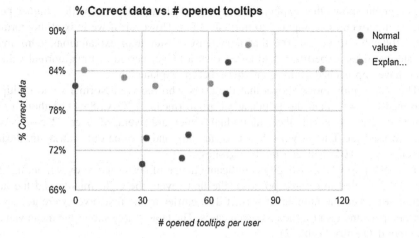

Fig. 8. A scatter plot of number of opened tooltips per user and % correct data

The other participants were scattered more linearly. A weak correlation between the number of opened tooltips and correct data entry was found (Pearson, r = 0.26). For successful tooltips correlated with correct data entry, r = 0.35, hence a moderate correlation.

5.2 Normal Values Versus Explanations

The graph below represents the correctness of data entry in all the cases (Fig. 9). The x-axis is the same as in the graph under "Tooltips", the cases, while y-axis is the correctness, measured in percent per case. Also here, a trendline was added in order to get a better view of the development from the first to the last case.

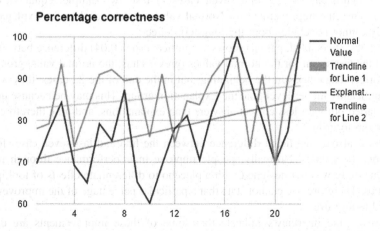

Fig. 9. A graph displaying the percentage of correctness (Color figure online)

The graph shows that explanations (red line) clearly start out with a higher percentage of correctness compared to normal values. However, if we look at the normal values (blue line), we can see that it increases faster than explanations. This may indicate that if the experiment had lasted over a longer period of time, normal values would have approached 100% correctness before explanations.

The scatter plot above shows that the users who received Normal value tooltips, performed less well than the Explanation group (means 77% vs 85%). Although the number of users is small, their individual scores are averaged over 22 cases. We therefore used the T-test (two-sided, two-sample), and it came out with a significant difference (p = 0.01) between the two groups.

To check possible statistically significant change of performance over time, the 22 cases were divided into three portions; the first seven, the eight middle and the last seven cases. Then the number of correct data entries in the first seven were averaged per participant and also for the last seven cases. The table below shows the mean values of correct data entry (Table 2).

Table 2. Results on correct data entry from logging use

	Average % correct first 7	Average % correct last 7
Normal values (n=7)	76	87
Explanations (n=6)	83	85
All participants	79	86

The difference in correctness between normal value tooltips (76%) and explanations (83%) is significant for the first seven cases (T-test, two-sample, equal variance) (yellow). Since the improvement for Normal values is stronger than for Explanations, the study cannot conclude about the long term effect.

The T-test (two sided, paired) shows a significant (p = 0.04) difference between the first and the last seven for the normal values (grey). Thus, the normal value group had fewer correct data entries in the beginning, but in the end of the 22 cases, they were at an insignificantly higher level than the Explanation group. This may be because normal values started out with less correct answers than explanations, and may therefore have "more room to grow".

There is also a significant difference between the first and last seven cases for the total group (p = 0.03). Normally, people improve their performance through repetitions. Our study was not designed with a placebo to differentiate effects of tooltips vs. no tooltips. Therefore, we cannot state that a particular percentage of the improvements followed tooltip use.

However, the interviews indicate that some of these improvements are due to tooltips, which is also cohesive with the UX questionnaire. "The tooltips helped answer correctly to the tasks given" received a total of 4.7 out of 5, meaning that they strongly agree with the statement. Also, there was a low correlation between opening of tooltips and correct responses (Pearson r = 0.26). The difference in performance between the Normal value and Explanation tooltips groups shows that the tooltips had effects. We therefore conclude that tooltips caused improvement in correct data entry.

Our usage of similar terms both in the cases and in tooltips containing explanations may have influenced the results of the experiment. This may be part of the reasons why the participants using the tooltips containing explanation had a higher correctness and higher percentage of successful tooltips, as they more easy could recognize the phrases used.

6 Conclusion and Further Research

The goal of this research was to find out whether tooltips helped users entering correct data and whether specific contents for tooltips were better than other. The study comprises an experiment with 30 users, where all their use of the software was logged and the participants were interviewed after completion. At the time of final paper submission, only 15 of the participants had completed the experiment, thus only the results for these 15 have been included in the paper. The results may therefore change after all participants have completed, and the final results will be presented during the conference.

Isaksen et al. [5] identified normal data values as the most preferred content type for tooltips for data fields. Formal explanations was the second most preferred type. Previous studies of tooltips [1, 7] have also come up with preferences and have not tested effects of long term use.

This study therefore compared the two types of tooltips during a two weeks experiment.

The explanations group had a higher percentage of successful tooltips, meaning instances of opening a tooltip and entering a correct value, possibly in the opposite sequence. The explanations group also had a steeper increase than normal values. We also found that, in terms of the correctness in data, explanations have a higher percentage. However, correctness for normal values increase faster, and after two weeks, the normal value group was slightly ahead of the explanations on correctness. When comparing the first seven cases with the last seven, we found that tooltips containing normal values has a significant increase in correctness. The difference in correctness between explanations and normal values for the last seven cases is insignificant, as is the increase in the explanations group.

Thus, we see no correlation between user preference and the usefulness of the different content types. In addition, the UX questionnaire revealed that the participants found the tooltips both helpful and understandable.

Both normal values and explanation has a decrease in number of opened tooltips from the first to the last case. The difference between them is not significant. This is also consistent with what we learned through our post-interviews, as participants told us that they did not need the tooltips at the end of the experiment, as the information was learned by heart. This is consistent in the increase in the percentage of successful tooltips from first to last case.

An unexpected finding was that users also opened tooltips after they had entered the data. During post-interviews, they said that this was in order to check that they had entered data correctly. This way of learning from tooltips has not been mentioned in previous user studies of tooltips [1, 7].

We also learned that they used tooltips more during the previous pregnancy stage, which was probably due to it being the first encounter with the terms, difficulties in differentiating the pregnancy outcomes, or because the terms are more used by nurses and midwives.

In order to increase the validity of the experiment, we could have included a control group of participants. Here, the aim would have been to compare the effects of a system with tooltips and a system without tooltips. This is similar to research on medication, where one group is given real medicine, while the other is given placebo medication. However, the comparison between the two groups would not have been symmetric, as one group would have been introduced to tooltips and the other group not. An alternative way could be create a testing program with some meaningless tooltips. This would have made the groups more symmetric, giving one group actual tooltips and the other group "placebo-tooltips".

Acknowledgment. This research has been supported by QU Horizon 2020 "mHealth4Afrika - Community-based ICT for Maternal Healthcare in Africa" (project 668015, topic ICT-39-2015), Norwegian Centre for International Cooperation in Education "Scholarly Health Informatics Learning" (UTF-2016-longterm/10032) and Norwegian Agency for Development Cooperation "Support to the Health Informations Systsem Project - HISP" (QZA-14/0337).

References

1. Dai, Y., Karalis, G., Kawas, S., Olsen, C.: Tipper: contextual tooltips that provide seniors with clear, reliable help for web tasks. In: CHI 2015 Extended Abstracts, pp. 1773–1778 (2015)
2. Duh, H.B.L., Tan, G.B.C., Chen, V.H.H.: Usability evaluation for mobile device: a comparison of laboratory and field tests. In: Proceedings of the 8th Conference on Human-Computer Interaction with Mobile Devices and Services, Helsinki, Finland, pp. 181–186 (2006)
3. Flaherty, K.: Diary Studies: Understanding Long-Term User Behaviour and Experiences. https://www.nngroup.com/articles/diary-studies/
4. Grossman, T., Fitzmaurice, G.: ToolClips: an investigation of contextual video assistance for functionality understanding. In: ACM Conference on Human Factors in Computing Systems 10, Atlanta, Georgia, USA, pp. 1515–1524. ACM (2010)
5. Isaksen, H., Iversen, M., Kaasbøll, J., Kanjo, C.: Design of tooltips for health data. Submitted for Publication
6. Michelsen, C.D., Dominick, W.D., Urban, J.E.: A methodology for the objective evaluation of the user/system interfaces of the MADAM system using software engineering principles. In: ACM Southeast Regional Conference, pp. 103–109 (1980)
7. Petrie, H., Fisher, W., Weimann, K., Weber, G.: Augmenting icons for deaf computer users. In: CHI 2004 Extended Abstracts on Human Factors in Computing Systems, Vienna, Austria, pp. 1131–1134 (2004)

The Application of Multi-view and Multi-task Learning for On-Board Interaction Design Based on Visual Selection

Bin Jiang[(✉)], JiangHui Ma[(✉)], and Di Zhou[(✉)]

School of Design Arts and Media,
Nanjing University of Science and Technology,
200, Xiaolingwei Street, Nanjing 210094, Jiangsu, China
jb508@163.com, 516082596@qq.com, zhoudi@njust.edu.cn

Abstract. The core of information visualization and visual selection is the mapping from abstract data to visual structure. The aim of information visualization doesn't lie in visualization itself, its ultimate aim is to collect information on the basis of visualization so as to offer support to decision making. Under the complex driving environment, Designers have to continue their research during the process of interface design. They can explore the implications and presentation methods of interface interaction inside the car in order to form an on-board interaction design system based on visual selection. This can also realize information sharing between cars and X (people, cars, roads and back-stage) and possess functions like strong sensation for complex environment, intelligent decision and mutual control. At the same time, on-board interaction equipment will have more diversified tasks. For example, the alternation of interaction and decision-making between multiple tasks like reality conformation, cluster display, gesture interaction, speech recognition, body sensation and eye tracking. At present, the new direction for interaction design is the analysis of multitask visual selection so as to realize secure, comfortable, energy-saving and efficient driving and finally the invention of a new generation of on-board interaction design system which can perform on human behalf. Through multi-view and multi-task learning, this paper gave an analysis of on-board interface design and concluded design scheme and suggestion with optimal user experience. By combing reasonable analysis of human intelligence and sensible interface design, this paper can provide new ways of thinking and methods for future on-board interface design.

Keywords: Information visualization · On-board interaction design · Interface design · User experience · Machine learning

1 Background

The core of information visualization is the mapping from abstract data to visual structure to strengthen interactive presentation of abstract data. As a result, visual design plays a very important part during the process. However, it is worth noticing that the aim of information visualization doesn't lie in visualization itself, it's only a

© Springer International Publishing AG 2017
A. Marcus and W. Wang (Eds.): DUXU 2017, Part III, LNCS 10290, pp. 79–93, 2017.
DOI: 10.1007/978-3-319-58640-3_7

means to an end. The ultimate aim is to collect information on the basis of visualization so as to offer support to decision making [1]. It doesn't mean the design of boring interface for the sake of functions or the gorgeous pictures for aesthetic forms. In order to convey information in a collect way, designers should combine both aesthetic forms and functions by analyzing huge amounts of complex information and achieve direct visual expression. Excellent works of information visualization is the product of imaginative design aesthetics and rigorous engineering science which present lengthy data in an extremely artistic way and thus achieving balance between aesthetic forms and functions.

Designers try to introduce information visualization to on-board interface design. One reason is that visual system is the most developed sensory system and one of the commonplace and important way for human to interact with electronic interface. Users can make decisions by understanding interface contents with visual information [2]. Another reason is that as information products, on-board equipment is in common use in human life. There are many differences between the designs of on-board interface and that of cell phones and computers. As users spend less time to stare at the screen, designers have to continue their research of interface design under complex driving environment.

For example, HUD head-up display (Fig. 1) is a kind of picture by projecting pictures from the window to extreme distances so that the driver can observe the dashboard while looking at the window.

Fig. 1. HUD head-up display

By conducting basic research on information visualization, building user task model and having eye-tracking test, designers explored the implications and presentation methods of on-board interface interaction so as to form a system based on information visualization.

2 Current Research and Development Trend

2.1 Current Situation of On-Board Interaction Design in the Automobile Industry

In china, with the rapid development of the automobile industry and the expansion and improvement of its variety, on-board equipment is very popular among the consumers. According to this trend, some famous car manufacturers implement on-board display as standard configuration for luxury cars like Audi A6L, Q5 from FAW-Volkswagen,

GL8 from SGM, E-level cars from Beijing Benz. The application of on-board equipment in China is still at the initial stage and has broad market prospects [3].

The popularity of smart phones and personal computers has promoted the prosperous development of the internet industry. However, there is also reform is in full spring for the cars at the other edge of the "mobile terminal". The integration of the information technology has brought new life to the automobile industry and intelligent on-board equipment has now become the top priority of many manufacturers and even internet companies. Participants from various fields are exploring how to create more intelligent on-board systems. Apple, Google and Microsoft are spending efforts into this aspect and came with the invention of Carplay and Android Auto from Apple and Google company respectively. Besides, traditional automobile industry are also conducting relevant research like Ford Sync from Ford, MyLink from Chevrolet, M.M.I from Audi, BlueLINK from Hyundai and so on.

In china, many internet companies and car manufacturers are beginning to conducting related research. Baidu has advantages in technology; its driverless cars have already been tested on the 5th Ring Road in Beijing. Open platforms of Tencent's car union include MyCar service, Car Union APP and Car Union ROM. Alibaba's strength lies in its AliCloud. New brand cars has integrated its YunOS for Car operating system with resources like bid data, Ali Communication, Autonavi, AliCloud Computing and XiamiMusic. Besides, Letv company put forward its own on-board system LeUI, mobile phone on-board connection system Ecolink and concept car FF zero1.

The research on interface design started much earlier at abroad and it tends to be more mature. But in China, the relevant research is still at the initial stage. Designers lack related design code when designing interactive interface so they rely much on experiential evaluations. However, just as the development of all things is depended on their internal contradiction, the development of HMI (human machine interface) reflects the relationship and contradiction between human and machine. If human machine relationship has promoted the evolution and advancement of vehicles, then the reform of means of labor and work prompted by vehicles will affect the development of human needs. The evolution of human machine relationship from "toughness" to "elasticity" reflected the transformation of car interface from scattered parts to the organic combination of the hard and soft, from simple operation space to pleasant mobile space (Fig. 2) [4].

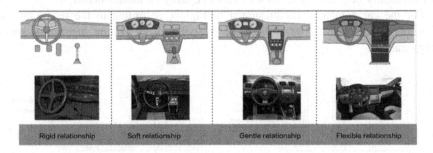

Fig. 2. Evolution of the relationship between human and machine

Human machine interaction based on cross-platform and multidisciplinary thinking is the new research direction for on-board interface design. Now much seemingly powerful on-board equipment is complex to operate and comprehend during actual use. Moreover, unreasonable software interface will make the driver feel the difficulty to operate when using it so that it will pose potential threats to driving safety.

2.2 Development Trend of On-Board Interface Design

The opening of the International Conference on Automobile User Interfaces and Interactive Vehicular Applications in 2009 had extremely important meanings. The conference divided the research category of HMI into four parts (Fig. 3). They included devices and interface, automation and instrumentation, evaluation and bench-marking and driver performances and behavior [5].

Devices & Interfaces	• Multi modal,speech,audio, gestural,natural input/output	• Text input and output while driving	• Sensors and context for interactive experiences in the car
	• In-car gaming,entertainment and social experiences	• Applications and user-interfaces for inter-vehicle communication	• Biometrics and physiological sensors as a user-interface component
Automation & Instrumentation	• Automated Driving and Interfaces for (semi-) autonomous driving	• Co-operative Driving/Connected Vehicles	• Information access (search, browsing,etc.)
	• Head-Up Displays (HUDs) and Augmented Reality (AR) concepts	• Assistive technology in the vehicular context	• Vehicle-based apps. web/cloud enabled connectivity
Ecaluation & Benchmarking	• Methods and tools for automotive user-interface research,including simulation	• Naturalistic/field studies of automotive user interfaces	• Modeling techniques for cognitive workload and visual demand estimation
	• Automotive user-interface frameworks and toolkits	• Automotive user-interface standards	
Driver Performance & Behavior	• Different user groups and user group characteristics	• Emotional state recognition while driving	• Detecting and estimating user intentions
	• Subliminal cues, warnings and feedback to augment driving behavior	• Detecting/measuring driver distraction	

Fig. 3. Research category of HMI (From auto-ui.org)

On the backdrop of the Internet comes the time for intelligent cars. Car manufacturers further extend their value chains to continuously innovate business structures and varieties. Future cars will combine the advanced on-board sensor and controller with modern communication, information technology to realize the information sharing between cars and X (people, cars, roads and backstage) and possess functions like strong sensation for complex environment, intelligent decision and mutual control. It will eventually be a new generation of cars operating on human behalf.

For the car company, (as illustrated in Fig. 4), according to the report on car consumer behavior in 2004, 80% of the interviewed are willing to pay for smart configurations.

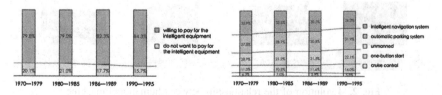

Fig. 4. Report on car consumer behavior

Viewing from the difference in their birth year, "post 85s" will be more willing to improve their budgets for smart configurations than people born before 1985. In terms of the performance and convenience, the interviewed said that they long most for "intelligent navigation system" and "automatic parking system" which are favored by 30% of consumers. Besides, consumers who hope for "driverless cars" also accounted for 20%.

The design of on-board interface has not only inherited parts concerning interactive design and information visualization but also has added its specific interactions. It includes not only information visualization design, interactive design, but also human machine engineering design, context awareness as well as task mode design. It can present text and static pictures like traditional interface as well as motion pictures and videos which provides designers with new design topics as well as a new design space. The development of on-board interface design is also becoming more mature. It can improve the utility of the interface which makes it more easy and efficient for operation and have instructive significance to the design and research of software interface.

3   Research Methods and Contents

Based on the theory of information visualization, research content is the study of on board interface design. By conducting research on users, designers try to study users' behavioral, physical and psychological features and analyze the methods and forms of visualized design inside the cars do as to build an on-board interface system based on information visualization (Fig. 5).

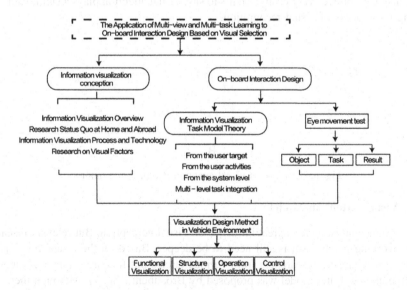

Fig. 5. Mold for on-board interface design

3.1   The Concept of Information Visualization

The concept of information visualization is developing rapidly. At first, information is only pieces of coarse raw data. The appearance of chart is the beginning of graph and its aim is to making abstract data easier to understand. With the advancement of technology and internet, different kinds of graphs began to appear which can help people to analyze and identify potential problems. Particularly, the rise of real-time and dynamic interactive visualization has greatly improved people's ability for analyzing and processing information.

Through interaction, people can screen and filter information independently and adapt appropriate ways to search for information in order to find the hidden rules for solving problems.

3.2   The Concept of Visual Attention

The fundamental function of attention is selection. The core of attention is selective analysis of information. By combing finite psychological resources, visual attention begins to identify important information in finite time. The processing method of visual sensation and visual perception are parallel and serial types respectively [6]. There is difference between them in terms of the amount of information they process. Visual sensation can possess much information than the latter one by make connections through visual attention mechanism. It can also stay at the front of the whole visual perception process and is a reliable guarantee for the identification process. (In Fig. 6), green right-angle from (A), big red circle from (B), two double sided arrow from (C) can catch our eyes very easily. That's to say, visual attention plays a significant role during the process of visual recognition.

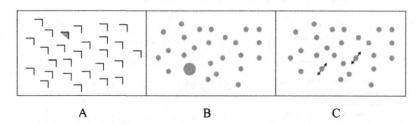

Fig. 6. Example of visual attention (Color figure online)

3.3   Visual Attention Model

Attention mechanism exerts great influence on visual perception. But relevant research on its working mechanism is still need to be deeper. Based on the research of visual attention mechanism, researchers from various circles put forward a range of theories and hypotheses. Filter model was proposed by Broadbent (Fig. 7). Although there are many stimulations to process passageways, information can only enter into advanced analytic processing channel through one single passageway which reflects the role of filter in attention selection.

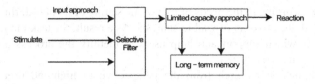

Fig. 7. Filter model

Professor Dewenci proposed the response selection model (Fig. 8). According to him, visual stimulation of information can step into advanced level by many passageways which can be perceived. While the attention mechanism acts as a feedback of stimulation rather than visual stimulation itself.

Fig. 8. The response selection model

The process of analyzing visual attention mechanism can presented as transforming complex visual stimulation into several simple visual recognition tasks. These simple processes mainly reflected in two ways: information recognition and information positioning.

In fact, the first step of the whole process of visual information positioning is to match subconscious memory to select the target that match the process. As we can see from (Fig. 9), the whole process is not the overall understanding of the object, but search according to basic information like directions and colors. By matching these characteristics with memory and getting feedback, these target information will be put into further analysis as key points and be used to position interest sectors in order to offer information support for separating pictures, identifying targets and analyzing situations in the following stage.

Fig. 9. The process of visual attention positioning

3.4 Forming On-Board Interface Task Models Based on Information Visualization

Information visualization is a serious of controllable processes that transforming raw data into visible forms and then into human perception. It is impossible to support the dynamic process of data analysis by a static picture. Designers have to conduct interactive analyses with graphic elements within the visible interface to achieve analysis target according to the needs of users. The setting of models during the process actually denoted objective set of visible analysis. As a result, the task model theory is a significant basis which support and help users to identify the process and guide the design of visual analysis system.

Firstly, conducting research from the perspective of high-end user targets and focusing on the users' intention. Secondly, starting from user activities and focusing on user behaviors. Thirdly, starting from the system itself and focusing on the system function structure. At last, integrating multitasks based on users' operation behaviors (Fig. 10). It is stated like this:

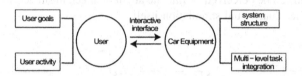

Fig. 10. Users' operation behaviors

To a certain extent, user target determines the whole framework of the on-board system. Its framework in turn also influences user target. At present, on-board system in the market mainly have four functions: electronic navigation, entertainment, shape control and mobile connection (Fig. 11).

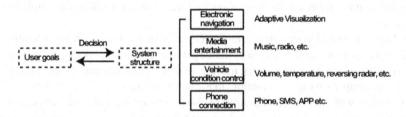

Fig. 11. Model framework

User activities include gesture interaction, speech recognition, body sensation and eye tracking. Among them, gesture interaction is the most universal and can easily achieve by technology. By applying interactive gestures like simple or double clicking, multi-touch, kneading and erasure to on-board system can better integrate it with the whole framework and connecting multi-tasks (Fig. 12).

Embedded interaction of products links classical interactive function with product function, which means that interaction can achieved by physical and digital ways. It can reach harmony between two sides and form the design trend for the integration between engineering design and interactive design.

Embedded and distributed ways of interaction and the continual appearance of new technology have greatly promoted the interactive design of the automobile like the design of Buick's concept car Riviera in 2013 (Fig. 13) and Benz's concept car FCV (Fig. 14) [7]. The combination of overall indoor design with human machine interface reflected the trend of the integration between engineering design and interactive design.

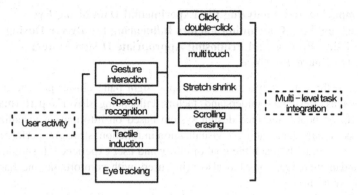

Fig. 12. Multi-task model

Fig. 13. Buick's concept car riviera   **Fig. 14.** Benz's concept car FCV

3.5 Eye Tracking Test Under Different Circumstances

Using the test result to describe and research user behaviors so as to make evaluations on the utility of the tested interface by referring to the variables achieved from the test. From the perspective of fixation time, fixation hot spot, sight path and task response, designers prepare the materials for the test and finally collect and analyze the experimental data (Fig. 15).

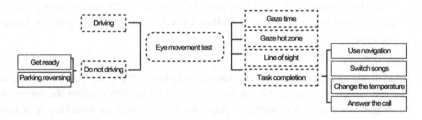

Fig. 15. Eye tracking test

3.6 Comparing and Analyzing the Experimental Data of the Eye Tracking Test, Concluding Factors Influencing the Driver During the Using Process and Proposing Appropriate Design System for On-Board Interface

According to the data analysis of the hot spot, sight path, cluster and the number of attention areas, designers understand factors influencing driver's performance and finally form on-board interface design system based on information visualization by linking task models. It can achieve visualization in function, structure, performance and controls and eventually reach the goal of utility and user experience. It should not only realize fundamental functions but also bring users with comfortable and harmonious operation experience.

With the further research of theory and the rise of precision device, the application of eye tracking technology in the field of interface design is becoming more mature day by day. It has the following three measurement indexes:

① Search process

- Scanning path. Scanning path is the spatial distribution of fixation points and saccades on the interface. The length of the path is the distance of two continual fixation points.
- Number of saccade. By observing the number of visual search behavior, the number of saccade can reveal the relevant organization degree of the screen.
- Frequency of saccade. Frequency of saccade refers to the spatial distance between fixation points.

② Manufacturing process

- Number of fixation points. The total number of fixation points concerns users' search efficiency. The unreasonable distribution of interface elements will cause the increase of the number of fixation points.
- Fixation rate of the interest sectors. Fixation rate of the interest sectors means the time ratio between the eye's fixations on the area.
- Average fixation time. Average fixation time reflects the difficulty of acquiring information. A long-time fixation means that it's rather difficult to acquire information from the interface. That's to say, there exists unreasonable factors on the design of interface zone.
- Number of fixation in the interest area. Number of fixation in the interest area is the total number of fixation in areas or particular elements preset by users. it can be used to check the visibility of interface elements and its surface meaning.

③ other indexes
Apart from measurement indexes mentioned above, there are also other indexes like retrospective saccade, hit rates and fixation times after finding the target. All these indexes can make usable evaluations of the software interface in a more profound way.

4 Data Analysis Based on Multi-task Multi-view Learning

Multi-task multi-view learning (MTMV) is a hot research topic of machining learning, which integrates muti-task learning (MTL) and multi-view learning (MVL) together [8]. As shown by (Fig. 16), many real-world problems contain more than one kind of information, known as multi-view data. Each view reflects one part of the problem's characteristics, and provides us one perspective to understand the problem. Compared with learning from the single view data, learning from multi-view can make better use of these different views and get improved results. Besides that, many real-world problems are similar or related to each other. For these problems, learning them jointly by using the multi-task learning strategies can usually improve the performance of each task compared to learning them separately. Therefore, as the combination of MTL and MVL, MTMV learning usually has a better performance.

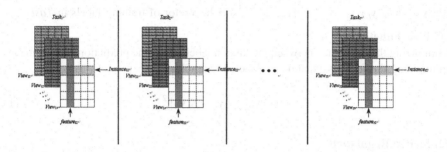

Fig. 16. Graphical representation of multi-view multi-task learning framework

The typical procedure for MTMV learning is to construct a model which reflects the relationships among different views and tasks first, then the objective function which represents this model should be converted to a convex one, and its parameters will be optimized by the alternative iteration method, which means optimizing these parameters alternately, every parameter is optimized while the others are fixed. After that, the prediction is possible to be done utilizing this trained model.

Generally speaking, the model of MTMV include 4 parts: the loss function measuring the misclassification, the sparse regulation, and 2 regularizations between task-task and view-view, respectively.

In order to fomulate the model of MTMV, we denote matrices with bold uppercase letters (e.g. $\mathbf{X}$), vectors with bold lowercase letters (e.g. $\mathbf{x}$), and scalars with italic letters (e.g. x), respectively. As illustrated by Fig. 1(a), suppose we have T related tasks ($Task_1, Task_2, \cdots, Task_T$) in totally. For each instance in $Task_t (t \in [1, T])$, it is described from V views ($View_{t1}, View_{t2}, \cdots, View_{tV}$). For the v-th view, we collect M_v features, let $M = \sum_{v=1}^{V} M_v$. And for $Task_t$, N_t is used to denote the number of instances it contains ($Instance_1, Instance_2, \cdots, Instance_{N_t}$). Specially, for $View_v$ in $Task_t$, the feature matrix is $\mathbf{X}_t^v \in \mathbb{R}^{N_t \times M_v}$, and $\mathbf{w}_t^v \in \mathbb{R}^{M_v}$ parameterize the linear mapping function.

For convenience, as shown by Fig. 2(a), we also denote $\mathbf{X}_t = (\mathbf{X}_t^1, \mathbf{X}_t^2, \cdots, \mathbf{X}_t^V) \in \mathbb{R}^{N_t \times M}$ and $\mathbf{w}_t = (\mathbf{w}_t^1, \mathbf{w}_t^2, \cdots, \mathbf{w}_t^V) \in \mathbb{R}^{M \times 1}$ as the concatenated feature matrix and parameters matrix for $Task_t$, respectively. Additionally, for the matrix $\mathbf{X}_t$, its i-th row and j-th column are denoted as $(\mathbf{x}_t)^i$ and $(\mathbf{x}_t)_j$ respectively. That is, from the sight of instance, $\mathbf{X}_t$ also can be understood as $\mathbf{X}_t = ((\mathbf{x}_t)^1, (\mathbf{x}_t)^2, \cdots, (\mathbf{x}_t)^{N_t})^T$, where $(\mathbf{x}_t)^i \in \mathbb{R}^{1 \times M}$ is the feature vector of $Instance_i$ in $Task_t$, as shown by each row in matrix $\mathbf{X}_t$. Conversely, $\mathbf{X}_t$ also can be understood from the sight of feature as $\mathbf{X}_t = ((\mathbf{x}_t)_1, (\mathbf{x}_t)_2, \cdots, (\mathbf{x}_t)_M)$, in which $(\mathbf{x}_t)_j \in \mathbb{R}^{N_t \times 1}$ is the j-th feature vector in $Task_t$, shown by the j-th column in matrix $\mathbf{X}_t$. In term of the parameters matrix, as shown in Fig. 2(b), for convenience, let $\mathbf{W} = [\mathbf{w}_1, \mathbf{w}_2, \cdots \mathbf{w}_T] \in \mathbb{R}^{M \times T}$. Each column in $\mathbf{W}$ is the coefficient vector for classifying the subjects of the specific task, $\mathbf{W} = ((\mathbf{w})_1, (\mathbf{w})_2, \cdots, (\mathbf{w})_T)$. Obviously, $(\mathbf{w})_t = \mathbf{w}_t$. In the same row, the coefficients record the contributions of the same feature toward different tasks, $\mathbf{W} = ((\mathbf{w})^1, (\mathbf{w})^2, \cdots, (\mathbf{w})^M)$. Let $\mathbf{y}_t = [y_{t,1}, y_{t,2}, \cdots y_{t,N_t}] \in \{1, -1\}^{N_t \times 1}$ be the vector of training labels in $Task_t$.

(1) Loss Function
Minimizing the difference between the known label $\mathbf{y}_t$ and the prediction results, means minimizing the misclassification on labeled examples.

$$L = \sum_{t=1}^{T} \|\mathbf{y}_t - \mathbf{X}_t \mathbf{w}_t\|_2^2 \tag{1}$$

(2) Sparse Regulation
The adoption of sparse regulation generally has two purposes: simplify the parameters matrix, and select common features across different tasks. Therefore, here we use $l_{2,1}$-norm to simulate this regulation:

$$R_{sparse} = \|\mathbf{W}\|_{2,1} \tag{2}$$

It has two advantages: Firstly, it ensures that a small number of features are jointly selected for all tasks. Secondly, the coefficients are encouraged to be similar across different tasks for joint feature selection at the same time.

(3) Task-Task Regularization
When modeling the task-task relationship, we mainly focus on the fact that, if the features of $Task_i$ and $Task_j$ are closely related, their corresponding coefficient vectors $\mathbf{w}_i$ and $\mathbf{w}_j$ should also be similar. In order to formulate this fact, we first measure the difference between $Task_i$ and $Task_j$ as follows:

$$g_{i,j} = exp(-2\|\bar{\mathbf{x}}_i - \bar{\mathbf{x}}_j\|_2^2 / \sigma^2) \tag{3}$$

Where $\bar{\mathbf{x}}_i = \frac{1}{N_i} \sum_{ins=1}^{N_i} (\mathbf{x}_i)^{ins}$ and $\bar{\mathbf{x}}_j = \frac{1}{N_j} \sum_{ins=1}^{N_j} (\mathbf{x}_j)^{ins}$ are the mean vector of $\mathbf{X}_i$ and $\mathbf{X}_j$, and $\sigma^2 = \sum_{i=1}^{T} \sum_{j=1}^{T} \|\bar{\mathbf{x}}_i - \bar{\mathbf{x}}_j\|_2^2 / T^2$. The larger the $g_{i,j}$ is, the more similar these two tasks are.

Therefore, by minimizing the product of $g_{i,j}$ and the difference between $\mathbf{w}_i$ and $\mathbf{w}_j$, we could encourage the convergence of $\mathbf{w}_i$ and $\mathbf{w}_j$ when $Task_i$ and $Task_j$ are closely related. Consequently, the relationship between tasks could be formulated as:

$$R_{task-task} = \sum_{i \neq j}^{T} g_{i,j} \left\| \mathbf{w}_i - \mathbf{w}_j \right\|_2^2 \tag{4}$$

(4) View-View Regularization

Although we observe an instance from V different views, it is reasonable to presume that the discriminant functions for different views tend to yield the identical label:

$$R_{view-view} = \sum_{t=1}^{T} \sum_{p,q=1}^{V} \left\| \mathbf{X}_t^p \mathbf{w}_t^p - \mathbf{X}_t^q \mathbf{w}_t^q \right\|_2^2 \tag{5}$$

Therefor, the final model of MTMV would be illustrated as Eq. (6):

$$\min F(\mathbf{W}) = \sum_{i=1}^{4} \mu_i \cdot f_i(\mathbf{W}) \tag{6}$$

Where μ_i, is a weight in the model, which should be specified based on the users' preference in a particular classification problem. $f_1(\mathbf{W})$, $f_2(\mathbf{W})$, $f_3(\mathbf{W})$, $f_4(\mathbf{W})$, respectively represent L, R_{sparse}, $R_{task-task}$, $R_{view-view}$.

Since there are a lot of variation in designing the interface of on-board display devices for cars, we apply MTMV learning strategy to optimize our design. Specifically, Eye Tracking System and Digitizing Collection, and others means are adopted in this paper to make a statistical analysis on the layout of control interface, optimum position of control button, and the setting of the interactive mode of each function by investigating six groups, including elder men (Age $> = 60$, Gender = Male), elder women (Age $> = 60$, Gender = Female), middle-aged men (Age, Gender = Male), middle-aged women (Age, Gender = Female), young men (Age, Gender = Male), and young women (Age, Gender = Female). That is, the author collects the optimal experience data of six different groups for each function of the on-board display devices to form a six-view information of on-board display devices. In addition, the author collects six-view information of the above groups aiming at five mainstream cars, including ordinary two-seater sports car, five-seater car, seven-seater commercial vehicle, sport-utility vehicle (SUV), and cargo truck. The author makes analysis on the six-view and five-task information and finally obtains corresponding design scheme and proposal for interface design of on-board display devices in various car models which can bring the optimal experience to users.

5   Conclusion: The Application of Visual Selection on On-Board Interaction Design

By referring to eye tracking experiment and multi-objective test, we can conclude that driver's interaction with and response to the outer environment comes from the input and identification of visual information. The process of noticing, responding and acting is a very complex one, among which visual selection is the most significant basis. Driver's initial process of visual selection is mainly caused by the environment. Here environment refers to exterior environment as well as the inside interface display (Fig. 17). The advanced stage of visual selection is determined by driver's ability, experience and the corresponding concept model. As a result, when conducting on-board interaction design, designers have to take urgent information as top priority and processing information according to their degree of emergency in order to keep drivers well informed of the danger. In that way drivers can step into the advanced stage of visual selection and behavioral stage more quickly.

Fig. 17. The inside interface display

Cognitive capture means the phenomenon of people's feeling of being disturbed by many stimulations. It is often in the way of visual stimulation, but other ones like hearing stimulation can also play a very important part. The influence of stimulation on drivers is usually determined by the brain load intensity brought by the information. Overloaded information will occupy many of driver's attention resources and dilute important information during the driving process. Although HUD can directly present information on the front windscreen and make it easier for drivers to receive relevant information, it will overlap with the external environment. For example, input ways using texts will weaken the existence of real roads, thus make them less noticeable to drivers. So when emphasizing important information, designers have to make the information easier to identify and also proving certain amount of time for presentation so that drivers can make prompt response. It is also necessary to set time for information presentation on on-board interface.

The research on product development suggested that product development process of hardware and software product have structural similarities which can correspond to their design rules, but they also have their own professional features. The design target of HMI has transcended interior and interactive design of cars. It's a significant factor generated from the intersection of these fields. We believe that there are overlaps with the design target of exterior trims and hardware HMI interface of cars. The manifestation is the display and controlling units in that they are not only design elements concerning interior appearance and details but also the main design target for hardware HMI interface. We also believe that software HMI interface needs to face complex interaction situation, driving tasks and interaction tasks. The understanding of interaction task will be one-sided if it is free from the boundary of driving task. The interaction methods and visual design of software designs depends on physical space provided by hardware HMI interface. Besides, the functional design of the display and controlling units of hardware interface can also reflect the configuration of software's system.

Despite its mature development, the start points of cars are safety and efficiency. Although the safety problem has already been solved technically, the task of interaction is becoming increasingly complex. How to elaborate designs to deal with complex problems when competing for driving resources? Under the backdrop of driverless cars, "safety" will rising from basic needs to user experience. Efficiency concerns not only the efficiency of machine operation but also machine's adaptability to human. From the perspective of human machine engineering, it reflected the concept of "machine to human". Offering solution which matches function can show the design's respect to human and thus evoke emotional felling. With the popularity of intelligent driving and driverless technology in future, the relationship between human and cars will be more diversified. Automobile HMI interface will bring users with experience beyond their expectation.

References

1. Consiglio, W., Driscoll, P., Witte, M.: Effect of cellular telephone conversations and other potential interference on reaction time in a braking response. Accid. Anal. Prev. **35**, 495–550 (2003)
2. Charissis, V., Papanastasiou, S., Vlachos, G.: Interface development for early notification warning system: full windshield head-up display case study. In: Jacko, J.A. (ed.) HCI 2009. LNCS, vol. 5613, pp. 683–692. Springer, Heidelberg (2009). doi:10.1007/978-3-642-02583-9_74
3. Sternberg, R.J., Sternberg, K.: Psychology Cognitive, 6th edn., no. 1 (2016). Translated by, Z. Shao. IBSN 978-7-5184-0650-0
4. Zeng, Q.: Integration of software and hardware interface for human computer interaction. HUNAN University (2016)
5. Zhang, Z.: Research on braking reaction time of driver in emergency state based on simulator. J. N. Chin. Inst. Sci. Technol. **03**, 27–30 (2009)
6. Charissis, V., Papanastasiou, S.: Human-machine collaboration through vehicle head up display interface. Cogn. Tech. Work **12**, 41–50 (2010)
7. Luo, S., Zhu, S., Sun, S.: Man-Machine Interface Design, pp. 1–2. Machinery Industry Press, Beijing (2004)
8. Wang, Q.: Ergonomics research and evaluation of software interface. J. Beijing Institute of Technology. **11**, 82–85 (2009)

Research on the Experience Design of Chinese Knowledge Sharing in the Information Age

Wenkui Jin[1(✉)], Renke He[1], and Xinxin Sun[2]

[1] School of Design, Hunan University, Yuelu Area, Changsha 410082, China
jinwenkui@foxmail.com, renke8@163.com
[2] School of Design Arts and Media, Nanjing University of Science
and Technology, Xuanwu Area, Nanjing 210094, China
sunxinxinde@126.com

Abstract. This paper is aimed to present the development process and status quo of knowledge sharing in the Internet age in China, and explore and analyze the factors which have an effect on knowledge sharing. By means of in-depth interview and questionnaire, purposes, behavior modes, and emotional experience of users on different knowledge sharing platforms were found. This paper also conducts an analysis for competitive products in view of five products of knowledge sharing in China, and explores the development process and the status quo of existing products of knowledge sharing in the Internet age in China. The experience design model of knowledge sharing is further created, and the selection of knowledge sharing platforms is discussed in this paper.

Keywords: Information age · Knowledge sharing · Experience design

1 Introduction

In the information age, knowledge extensively exists in every domain of the society, but individuals can only master a limited amount of data, information, and knowledge. In order to obtain and make use of knowledge while realize the value of knowledge, we need to consider knowledge sharing as the core task.

China has been a knowledge-learning advocator for long. Confucius says, "One should be fond of learning and not feel ashamed to ask and learn from his inferiors", which is a true saying respected by modern Chinese. Nowadays, the Internet channels of knowledge sharing include Baidu baike, Weibo, WeChat, Zhihu, and Fenda. In view of different website types, for example, Baidu zhidao is a platform operating in an instant question-and-answer form while Zhihu expects to help its users find better answers with correlated communities. For the operation aspect, besides the content itself, the great importance is increasingly given to copyright and benefit mechanisms. When it comes to interaction forms, based on the text, more forms such as pictures, voice, and videos have been developed. Under the background of sharing economy, it is significant to study design strategies and methods of knowledge sharing in order to deepen and develop the knowledge and customize the user experience for knowledge sharing platforms.

A. Marcus and W. Wang (Eds.): DUXU 2017, Part III, LNCS 10290, pp. 94–104, 2017.
DOI: 10.1007/978-3-319-58640-3_8

2 Background

2.1 Knowledge Sharing

Knowledge is now being seen as the most important strategic resource in organizations, and the management of this knowledge is considered critical to organizational success [1]. Knowledge sharing is an important part of knowledge management trilogy (knowledge creation, knowledge sharing, knowledge application) [2]. There is growing realization that knowledge sharing is critical to knowledge creation, organizational learning, and performance achievement [3]. As one knowledge-centered activity, knowledge sharing is the fundamental means [4]. Knowledge can be considered either tacit or explicit [5]. Information is "a flow of messages" whereas knowledge is based on information and justified by one's belief. All information is considered knowledge but knowledge is more than just information, i.e., knowledge includes information and know-how.

Studies suggesting that individuals are predisposed to certain work attitudes and behaviors [6]. There are many factors that affect knowledge sharing. The major factors that influence knowledge sharing between individuals in organizations: the nature of knowledge, motivation to share, opportunities to share, and the culture of the work environment [3]. We also found that social network and shared goals directly influenced the attitude and subjective norm about knowledge sharing and indirectly influenced the intention to share knowledge. Knowledge sharing is a communication and interaction process. Unlike products, it cannot be delivered freely. Upon sharing the knowledge of other people, reconstruction behavior is a must, and one is required to have a certain knowledge base to learn and share knowledge [7].

2.2 Internet-Involved Knowledge Sharing

The field of knowledge sharing has traditionally been dominated by information technology and technology-driven perspectives [8, 9].

In the second half of the 20th century, the emergence of the Internet had had a huge impact on human civilization, as significant as the discovery of a new continent. Gradually, a number of changes took place in the human society with regard to its organization and operation modes. In 1990, a research institute of the United Nations put forward the concept of knowledge economy, which clearly defined the nature of the new economy. In 1996, Organization for Economic Co-operation and Development named it as "knowledge-based economy", which is the first time to introduce the index system and measurement into the new economy. With the continuous development of the Internet and new media technologies, the network has become the most rapid and popular communication medium. Features of the Internet meet the demands of knowledge communication. Sharing knowledge on the Internet can not only effectively speed up the communication, but also enable the network users with the same interests to get together and form virtual communities on the website via knowledge sharing. As a result, various online communities of knowledge sharing sprang up. The gathered community members can both share knowledge and create new value with the shared knowledge. The mechanism of Internet-involved knowledge sharing is "acting not only as a medium for sharing technical knowledge, but as a place where one can seek advice, gather opinions, and satisfy one's curiosity about a countless number of things [10]." People share professional knowledge, various experiences, or daily recommendations on the websites. With the web 2.0 being popular and online Q-and-A communities emerging, the online information has been communicated bidirectionally other than been transferred in one way. Users are developed into the active creator of knowledge from the passive receiver of knowledge. Knowledge was no longer exclusively provided by professionals, but is now generated by the co-participation and creation of users. Network users are playing a role of creator, provider, and even communicator of knowledge rather than just receiver. Online communities used to be focused on the carried content on the websites, but now turn to users and pay more attention to social network relations derived from interpersonal connection, so that all sorts of virtual communities have been established.

Internet-involved knowledge sharing provides us with a network consisting of node paths, sharers, correlation mechanism, and value relations between them, which is of vital importance for knowledge sharing and communication behavior. Therefore, in order to do further research on knowledge sharing and communication behavior of knowledge sharing platforms, our concerns need to be centered on the purposes, behavior, and experience of participants, and also the content construction, copyright mechanism, interaction modes and other factors of products. The structural features of its networks can be better studied upon the exploration and analysis for the interaction relations based on the related theories in experience design.

3 Research Method

As knowledge sharing has increasingly become one of the important behaviors in people's daily life, the users' sharing behavior is driven by the corresponding value obtained from knowledge sharing. In order to know the status quo of knowledge sharing in China, the researchers conducted investigations for users and an analysis for competitive products, which is centered on people's motivations to use different platforms, as well as the differences of knowledge content and interactive design between each platform.

3.1 User Survey

By means of user survey combined with literature review and ethnographic research, the researchers studied and analyzed the factors which influence the occurrence of users' knowledge sharing. The user survey was conducted in four steps: user selection, user interview, questionnaire, and information arrangement. Based on the said steps, observation method was adopted so as to find users' behaviors varied according to knowledge sharing platforms during the using process.

Survey. A survey of 10 users through persona analyze by the in-depth interview and a five-person focus group. Our target users consist of students, housewives, and white collar workers. The in-depth interview lasted for about half an hour, in which these users were required to describe the complete process of using knowledge platforms, including the using condition, the platform selection based on different purposes, and the way to obtain/share knowledge. Then, they were provided with several prepared conditions and asked to illustrate how they would conduct knowledge sharing in these cases. For the focus group, the researchers displayed some typical problems and demands gathered from the in-depth interviews, and came up with some design proposals. Through these steps, the selections, requirements, behaviors, and psychological motivations of the users were known. Knowledge sharing involves a set of behaviors that aid the exchange of acquired knowledge.

Questionnaire. In order to obtain the opinions on knowledge sharing in a wider range, a questionnaire survey covered 100 people was conducted to verify the universality of the opinions acquired from the interview and the focus group.

3.2 Analysis for Competitive Products

Five knowledge sharing products in China are discussed in the paper to explore the development process and the status quo of the existing products of knowledge sharing in the Internet age in China. The advantages and disadvantages are discovered based on the results of the in-depth interview and questionnaires. What's more, the researchers also compare and analyze the existing platforms in China and present the development history and the status quo of knowledge sharing in China.

3.3 The Status Quo of Knowledge Sharing

This part mainly presents using motivations, behaviors, and feelings of users, seizes the most important tags of users, and classifies them according to categories based on the five most frequently used platforms including Baidu zhidao, Weibo, WeChat, Zhihu, and Fenda. In view of website types, for example, Baidu zhidao is a platform operated in the question-and-answer form while Zhihu expects to help its users find better answers with correlated communities. For the operation aspect, besides the content itself, the great influence are increasingly given to copyright and benefit mechanisms. For interaction forms, based on the text, more forms such as pictures, voice, and videos have been developed. We focused on both the user side and product side (Tables 1 and 2).

Baidu Zhidao. Baidu, with its popular slogan "Baidu it, and you'll know", dominates the search market with a considerable position in China. Baidu zhidao has been developed for such a long time with abundant accumulation, and a large amount of knowledge content generated by users has been collected, which is easy to be obtained via Baidu search engine. In most cases, if you search for questions on the Baidu, Baidu will give priority to the results searched in Baidu zhidao at the very top. For users, they use Baidu zhidao with a very clear purpose, which is knowing the answer in a simple and rapid way, and leave the page without more deep and systematic understanding of the related complex background knowledge about the questions. Therefore, their behaviors are conducted in a direct way that they firstly simplify the questions into

Table 1. The user side

Platform	Motivation	Behavior	Experience
Baidu zhidao	Specific questions and quick leaving with speedy answers	1. Search the similar questions 2. Obtain the related answers	Fast and convenient
Weibo	Obtaining more experience, related information without clear purposes, and highlighting the timeliness of information	1. Follow the verified celebrities; 2. Browse the information; 3. View the comments	Entertaining
WeChat	Obtaining the response of friends around	Send the moments wait for replies	Omnipotent moments and social relationship
Zhihu	Obtaining in-depth knowledge	1. Search the similar questions; 2. Obtain the answers from different perspectives	Professional and objective
Fenda	1. Obtaining knowledge of some specific persons; 2. Entertainment	1. Ask questions; 2. Answered by real persons	Strong interaction and real-person experience

Table 2. The product side

Platform	Position	Scenario	Similarity	Difference
Baidu zhidao	AQ-and-A interactive platform of knowledge sharing based on search	Questions are matched by search engine. Too detailed questions cannot be matched	Data-Information-Knowledge	From results searching to pages o related question Instant question-and-answer mode
Weibo	A platform of information sharing, communication, and obtainment based on user relationships	Real-time hot topics are displayed		Social contact; Publicity; An update in form of text within 140 Chinese characters (including punctuations) and real-time sharing Unidirectional and bidirectional following mechanisms Timeliness and randomness Convenient and speedy sharing of information
WcChat	Instant messaging service on intelligent terminal	Friends in the moments can answer the questions		Social contact; Privacy; Bidirectional adding mechanism; Design for mobile terminals; Official accounts + Moments; WeChat intelligent life; "Intelligent" living style; Connecting anything Question-and-answer mode; Copyright mechanism;
Zhihu	Authentic online community of questions and answers	Correlated communities are built to help users for better answers		Sharing professional knowledge experience, and opinions with each other; Answers are ranked according to the votes while invalid answers are hidden, by which to some extent great deal of useless information has been screened
Fenda	Pay answers in voice	Answer a question in one minute		Voice interaction; Profit mechanism: the question owner, the answerer, the eavesdropper; Cashable knowledge and skills; Various stars, and famous persons in different fields such as health care, financial management, and workplace; Create online celebrities of knowledge

several keywords and search the similar questions already being asked by others, rather than describe the complete questions. As a matter of fact, such answers they obtain also similar ones related to their personal questions. Although the questions are not asked by themselves, in most cases, the related answers are sufficient for solving their own questions, which provides a kind of convenient and fast user experience.

Weibo. The users of Weibo have no specific purposes for the knowledge content of knowledge sharing and pay attention to the topics and other users that they are interested in. The random knowledge content is sent by whom they follow. They themselves fail to have strong control force upon the obtained content, but through following the topics they are interested in after a longstanding screening, the obtained content is basically consistent with their loves and interests. Moreover, the content of Weibo was limited in 140 characters previously for a long time, and therefore the published content is also constrained, and usually about a single message. However, Weibo features comments. Users from various fields and with different knowledge backgrounds can give their comments in Weibo. The message can be highly expanded via these comments, and a knowledge system is established based on the comment content and message itself. Many people describe the phenomenon with humorous words that "information second, comments first." The users of Weibo obtain knowledge for entertainment in more cases, and highlight the timeliness of information.

WeChat. WeChat is a closed social platform, on which the WeChat friends are mostly intimate family members and close friends. When the users of WeChat are confronted with any problem, especially related to their life, they will send their problems in the Moments and wait for the answers. Thus, Moments is also called "omnipotent Moments". In most cases, users send their current problems are not actually for the knowledge to solve the problems, but for letting their friends know they are in troubles and need comfort, for strengthening their own sense of presence, or sometimes even for showing off by means of asking for help. For example, "I am going to attend a meet-and-greet of my idol and suddenly feeling nervous now. Could you please tell me what I can ask my idol, my omnipotent Moments?".

Zhihu. The users of Zhihu give more importance to the answers received on the platform and the knowledge sharers, who are basically well-educated with higher education backgrounds than those of many other platforms. The shared content is more objective and systematic while the knowledge sharers prefer to prove the objectivity of their opinion in virtue of literature and documents, and to share knowledge based on theories, practices, and experience with as less subjective assumptions and speculation as possible. In the information shared on Zhihu, the most valuable part is the experience sharing of their true life and the inspiration obtained from their own experience rather than the mere sharing of knowledge. On Zhihu, users are responsible for the information, comments, and discussion they post, and premise their behaviors on the belief that "my behaviors may affect the judgement of the newcomers".

Fenda. The users of Fenda pay more attention to the knowledge subjectivity, in other words, the source of knowledge. When they want to know the opinions of those hard-to-reach celebrities and popular figures on a certain question, they can ask on Fenda. When a question are submitted to a specific answerer, the answerer can answer the question in voice. The answerers of Fenda include various stars, and famous persons in different fields such as health care, financial management, and workplace, which is aimed to create online celebrities of knowledge.

4 Results and Discussions

4.1 Experience Design Model Building for Knowledge Sharing

As the exploration for knowledge sharing has reached the actual implementation from the theoretical study, how can knowledge sharing play a part in user experience has already become the research focus. By means of user survey and analysis for competitive products, the researchers matched and correlated users and products for comparison and analysis and found the regularity in the influence upon knowledge sharing experience. For the further research on the factors in knowledge sharing system, classification as well as extraction and induction, which influence the occurrence of knowledge sharing, this paper brings sharing contents, motivations, and behaviors into a unified system. The researchers built an experience design model of knowledge sharing, which includes three layers: content layer (data, information, and knowledge), motivation layer (personal, technical, incentive, and trust factors), and behavior layer (knowledge search and transfer) (Fig. 1). With an experience design model of knowledge sharing, the experience of users in the knowledge sharing process can be understood, and therefore people can know how to optimize the knowledge sharing platforms from the perspective of experience design.

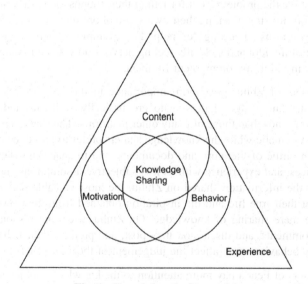

Fig. 1. Knowledge sharing model

Content Layer. Amidon once put forward a knowledge classification structure, called "information system" or "information pyramid" [11], in which the data, information, and knowledge are brought into a layered system with a pyramid shape (Fig. 2). We make analyses, give judgements, and take actions in our favor based on knowledge, which further constitutes human intelligence. On knowledge sharing platforms in the Internet, every concept in the knowledge classification structure has its own specific meaning. Data refers to a number, character string, image, or voice which has no specific background and meaning. Taking the topic "Today in the previous history" on Weibo as an example, for users, the dates without any specific background are simple and meaningless numbers. Data mining means find potential and useful information and knowledge in mass original data, such as concepts, rules, restrictions, modes, and constraints. Information refers to formatting, filtered, and integrated data used for displaying and explaining the results, which illustrates the relation between data. For example, "Today in the previous history" on Weibo can refer to the date of a certain historical event. Knowledge refers to meaningful information, manifested in the relations between data. For example, the users of Weibo can discuss a certain historical event itself under the topic "Today in the previous history", and further extend to the background, figures, process, significance, and evaluation of the event.

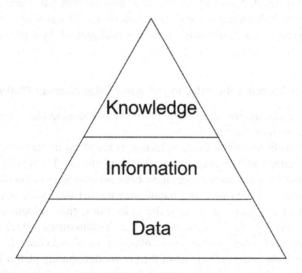

Fig. 2. Knowledge pyramid

Motivation Layer. From the user survey, it can be found that motivations of users on knowledge sharing platforms are varied. However, there are four widespread types of motivations including information search, social contact, value stimulation, and entertainment. Information search: The most essential driving force of knowledge sharing is the obtainment of knowledge and information, which is the common ground of the five said knowledge sharing platforms. Social contact: In the studied platforms, Weibo and WeChat are two knowledge sharing products featured with sociality based on social relations. Wherein Weibo shares knowledge based on weak relations, while WeChat based on strong relations. Value stimulation: Knowledge sharing needs the knowledge owner to share their knowledge, and therefore certain value is required by the group (knowledge owners) for stimulating the occurrence of knowledge sharing. Stimulating measures on the said platforms include virtual titles, actual money, and value exchange. For example, Fenda supports the question owner pays to the answerer and after that if other users want to know the answer, they can also pay for the answer. Entertainment: As the knowledge sharing purpose has been achieved, entertaining modes can better promote the occurrence of knowledge sharing and the sustainable development. For instance, Weibo allows its users to make comments with images, which is effective, convenient, and interesting.

Behavior Layer. Knowledge search and transfer are two important behaviors of users in knowledge sharing. The two behaviors can be found in the developing process of the content layer of "data – information – knowledge". Firstly, users find the data they are interested in, then form the key information, and finally correlate the information to be user knowledge. The knowledge search and transfer behaviors are varied according to platforms. For instance, Baidu zhidao makes users simplify the questions into several key words, search the existing questions related to their questions, and quickly leave the page without detailed reading. In the Moments of WeChat, users describe their questions in detail with natural language and wait for their friends' answers. On Zhihu, users read carefully, and profoundly know the background, system, and method of knowledge.

4.2   Factors Influencing the Selection of Knowledge Sharing Platforms

Upon knowledge sharing, users' selection of knowledge sharing platforms is influenced by factors from various aspects.

One important factors upon users' selection is based on the different purposes for obtaining knowledge and their acquaintance of the platforms. The relationship between platforms and users matters. Some users have been accustomed to a certain platform for the long-term use, and then their old habits may restrict their selections psychologically. For part of the users, especially the elder ones, they seldom change a new platform unless the current one cannot meet their requirements, which results in the lacking knowledge of other products, and influence users' selections in return.

On the other hand, users' selections of the knowledge sharing platforms is based on the result of self-evaluation. Another reason for selecting a certain media put forward by Wilbur Schramm is as follows: "Formula of selection = Expected return value/ Required efforts". The first level means before using a certain platform, the user wonders whether the medium can meet his requirements, that is, the expected return value. The second level means users tend to achieve the same or more satisfaction with less efforts. However, it is a process merely in mind for fast evaluation, which is evidently without any strict and rational calculation.

Users' selection may also be influenced by other users. A certain kind of environment created by other people will influence one's behavior. If one has been recommended by a user of a certain platform, and his friends around are the users of the platform, he is likely to use the platform once recommended by those friends.

These factors are varied according to users. However, it is necessary for knowledge sharing platforms to know about the factors, because users will make selections among the knowledge sharing platforms and transfer from one to another to ensure knowledge is available at need. Platforms are also required to expand their influence in order to make certain that users know where to find the knowledge they need.

5 Conclusion and Future Works

By means of content, motivations, and behaviors sharing, knowledge sharing explores and makes full use of the existing knowledge of human beings, plays a role as the lever, and promotes the creation and application of new knowledge. With the help of knowledge sharing, human beings establish shared libraries with abundant knowledge resources and come up with new technologies and methods so as to provide source power for social innovation. The cooperation and exchange as well as discussion upon knowledge between individuals can enlarge the value of knowledge in use and generate new knowledge. In this regard, knowledge sharing can be regarded as the core of innovation system. The researchers collect and present the practical methods and routes in knowledge sharing in the Internet age in China, analyze the factors influencing the occurrence of knowledge sharing, and build an experience design model, which will give guidance to the future design practice of knowledge sharing. For realizing the value of knowledge, knowledge sharing plays an essential role. However, in the actual application process, the false information, wrong "knowledge", privacy disclosure, and advertorials frequently occur on the knowledge sharing platforms, which brings negative social effects to knowledge sharing. Therefore, it is challenging in the future to ensure that users can obtain correct knowledge and improve users' ability to screen the knowledge.

References

1. Ipe, M.: Knowledge sharing in organizations: a conceptual framework. Hum. Resour. Dev. Rev. 2(4), 337–359 (2003)
2. Lu, L., Leung, K., Koch, P.T.: Managerial knowledge sharing: the role of individual, interpersonal, and organizational factors. Manag. Organ. Rev. 2(1), 15–41 (2006)
3. Bartol, K.M., Srivastava, A.: Encouraging knowledge sharing: the role of organizational reward systems. J. Leadersh. Organ. Stud. 9(1), 64–77 (2002)
4. Wang, S., Noe, R.A.: Knowledge sharing: a review and directions for future research. Hum. Resour. Manag. Rev. 20(2), 115–131 (2010)
5. Chow, W.S., Chan, L.S.: Social network, social trust and shared goals in organizational knowledge sharing. Inf. Manag. 45(7), 458–465 (2008)
6. Judge, T.A., Bono, J.E.: Relationship of core self-evaluations traits—self-esteem, generalized self-efficacy, locus of control, and emotional stability—with job satisfaction and job performance: a meta-analysis. J. Appl. Psychol. 86(1), 80–92 (2001)

7. Hendrikes, P.: Why share knowledge? The influence of ICT on motivation for knowledge sharing. Knowl. Process Manag. **6**(2), 91–100 (1999)
8. Davenport, T.H., De Long, D.W., Beers, M.C.: Successful knowledge management projects. Sloan Manag. Rev. **39**(2), 43–57 (1998)
9. Gourlay, S.: Knowledge management and HRD. Hum. Resour. Dev. Int. **4**(1), 27–46 (2001)
10. Adamic, L.A., et al.: Knowledge sharing and yahoo answers: everyone knows something. In: Proceedings of the 17th International Conference on World Wide Web. ACM (2008)
11. Amidon, D.M.: Innovation Strategy for the Knowledge Economy: The Ken Awakening. Routledge, Abingdon (1997)

The Effect of Video Loading Symbol on Waiting Time Perception

Woojoo Kim and Shuping Xiong[(⊠)]

Human Factors and Ergonomics Laboratory, Department of Industrial
and Systems Engineering, Korea Advanced Institute of Science and Technology
(KAIST), 291 Daehak-ro, Yuseong-gu, Daejeon, South Korea
{xml1324, shupingx}@kaist.ac.kr

Abstract. This study aimed to investigate the effect of different loading symbols and durations on waiting time perception of online video viewers. 60 young adults participated in this study and gave subjective ratings on waiting time perception through a 7-point Likert scale for 48 loading symbols (3 durations × 4 progress functions × 2 shapes × 2 embellishments). Results showed that duration and the progress function significantly influence the viewers' waiting time perception, while shape and embellishment do not. Loading symbols with the repetitive and linear progress functions are perceived longer than those of the power and inverse power progress functions. To indicate loading progress and to use manipulated progress functions are recommended, and design factors such as shape and embellishment are considered to be less effective. The findings of this study may serve as a useful input for loading symbol designers in creating better loading symbols.

Keywords: Video loading · Time perception · Symbol design · Progress indicators · Human-computer interface

1 Introduction

In these days, people watches a large amount of video media through video sharing websites and SNS services through personal mobile devices. Around 1/3 of China and 1/4 of U.S. internet users watch online videos every day [4]. The average time for US adults to watch digital videos was 21 min in 2011, and raised up to 76 min in 2015 [8].

Delay exists in every computer system, and many studies have shown that system delays can significantly affect user experience and performance [5, 22]. Users dislike delays [18] and web users start to lose interest in the current task at only 2 s of waiting [15]. In the same context, delayed video starts and stream interruptions have created a poor quality of experience for the viewer. Around 1/4 and 1/3 of viewers selected initial buffering and re-buffering respectively as the most frustrating aspect of internet video viewing [11]. Internet video viewers start to leave a website if the loading duration exceeds 2 s, and around half of them leave if the loading duration reaches 10 s [12].

The suffering from loading could be relieved by reducing the actual waiting time, but the actual waiting time cannot be shortened in many cases due to technical conflicts. An alternative approach to make users feel waiting time passes quickly can

© Springer International Publishing AG 2017
A. Marcus and W. Wang (Eds.): DUXU 2017, Part III, LNCS 10290, pp. 105–114, 2017.
DOI: 10.1007/978-3-319-58640-3_9

be attempted [17]. It was claimed that user experience is highly influenced by sub-jectively perceived time more than objective delay time [9, 23], because subjectively perceived time represents overall experience and extended waiting can arouse negative emotions [6].

Video loading symbols have been provided to notify the loading status and to relieve the boredom of viewers while waiting, but design guidelines for loading symbols were very limited. Therefore, arbitrarily designed loading symbols with repetitive progress have been popularly used among top video providers. However, many previous studies have argued the importance to provide feedback of loading progress to users [3, 15]. In addition, design factors of a loading symbol (such as its shape) may also influence the viewers' waiting time perception. In case of the web page usage, user experience and impression are highly influenced by the appearance [13], and users will leave if they feel frustrated with the design [16].

Some previous studies have found the effect of different loading progress behaviors on the progress bars in general human-computer interfaces. Myers reported that users had a strong preference for progress indicators in the graphical user interface during long tasks [14]. Harrison et al. also found that the loading with power progress function was perceived significantly shorter than the one with linear progress function [10]. However, very few studies have been conducted on the effects of different design factors (shape, progress function and embellishment) of a loading symbol on online video viewers' waiting time perception. The influential design factors, once identified, can be further considered in designing better loading symbols so that the waiting stress of online video viewers can be minimized.

The goal of this study is to examine the effect of different loading symbols on online video viewers' perception of waiting time. The effect of different loading durations on waiting time perception is also investigated in this study.

2 Methodology

2.1 Human Participants and Experimental Design

Sixty Koreans (26 males, 34 females) in the age range of 19-26 with normal or normal-to-corrected vision who are familiar with daily online video watching partici-pated in the experiment. Forty-eight loading symbols (Fig. 1), one for each combination of levels of four factors were used as stimuli in a 3 (durations) × 4 (progress func-tions) × 2 (shapes) × 2 (embellishments) repeated measures design. The sequence of loading symbols was randomized across all participants.

For duration, 5, 10 and 20 s were chosen based on the fact that 5, 10 and 20 s of startup delay of the online video lead to around 20%, 50% and 70% of abandonment rate, respectively [12]. For progress function, three non-repetitive progress functions varying in rates of the progress (Fig. 1) [10] and one repetitive function were used. Repetitive function progresses at 0.5 cycle/second repetitively, and linear function progresses linearly without any changes in speed. Power function progresses slowly at first and then rapidly accelerates, and inverse power function progresses fast at first and then rapidly decelerates. For shape, circle and bar were chosen as the two most

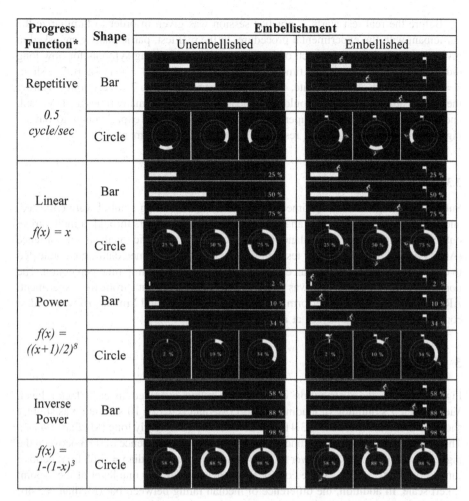

Progress Function*	Shape	Embellishment	
		Unembellished	Embellished
Repetitive 0.5 cycle/sec	Bar		
	Circle		
Linear f(x) = x	Bar		
	Circle		
Power f(x) = ((x+1)/2)^8	Bar		
	Circle		
Inverse Power f(x) = 1-(1-x)^3	Bar		
	Circle		

Fig. 1. Experimental stimuli of different loading symbols (Loading duration is not shown here due to the same symbol design) * *x: actual progress, f(x): displayed progress*

common shapes of the loading symbols used in online video platforms. For embellishment, a static small bicycle & flag figure was used. In order to minimize the influence of potential confounding variables, the length/width of the progress bar and size of figure/font were kept consistent for all loading symbols. All symbols were custom-made using Adobe Photoshop, After Effects and other computer programs.

2.2 Experiment Setting and Procedure

Loading videos were presented by a 24-inch monitor at 12 fps. Participants could freely decide the preferred sitting posture and the viewing distance to give close-to-real-life situations for more valid results.

Before the real test starts, a practice session was given in order to familiarize the participant with the experimental procedure. In the real test, participants were asked to give a subjective rating for each of forty-eight different loading symbols for how long did they feel about the waiting time in a 7-point Likert scale (1 = very short, 2 = short, 3 = slightly short, 4 = moderate, 5 = slightly long, 6 = long, 7 = very long). During the test sessions, participants could watch loading symbols as many times as they want, and their behavior was not supervised or controlled by the experimenter to have a higher ecological validity than research in controlled environments [7].

2.3   Data Analysis

Subjective ratings of waiting time perception for each loading symbol were collected, and arranged for the statistical analysis. After removing outliers through a multivariate outlier detection using Mahalanobis distance, nonparametric analysis of variance (ANOVA) and post-hoc Tukey test from aligned rank transformed data were conducted to check the statistical significance of each factor effect on waiting time perception. The nonparametric statistical test was used due to the ordinal data from the experiment. ARTool [25] was used to perform aligned rank transform, and Minitab 16 was used to conduct all statistical analyses at a significance level of 0.05.

3   Results

Figure 2 shows the distribution of subjective rating averaged in each factor level. Viewers felt 5 s duration of loading as short (Median = 2.12), 10 s duration as slightly short $\sim$ moderate (Median = 3.41) and 20 s duration as slightly long (Median = 4.81). The median rating of progress function factor showed the difference of 0.83 between the highest (Median = 3.04 for power function) and the lowest (Median = 3.88 for repetitive function) ratings, which can be considered somewhat close to one level of the 7-point Likert scale. In addition, the difference of median rating between bar (Median = 3.46) and circle (Median = 3.52) was very small (0.06), indicating negligible practical significance on the subjective rating. There was almost no difference on median ratings between unembellished (Median = 3.54) and embellished (Median = 3.56) symbols.

Further nonparametric statistical tests (Table 1) showed that rating on waiting time perception significantly differed among different durations (p < .001), progress functions (p < .001) and shapes (p < .001). However, no significant difference in waiting time perception was found from different embellishments (p = .233). The Tukey post-hoc grouping analysis showed that loadings with 5 s duration were perceived as the shortest (group A), followed by those with 10 s duration (group B), and those with 20 s duration were perceived as the longest (group C). Loading symbols with power and inverse power progress functions were classified in a group (group C) which was perceived significantly shorter than the ones with linear progress (group B) and repetitive (group A) functions. The difference of median ratings between bar and circle was statistically significant in spite of its negligible practical significance. In addition,

Rating by Duration, Progress Function, Shape, and Embellishment

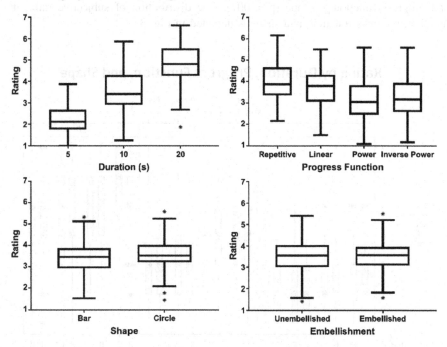

Fig. 2. Boxplot of average subjective rating for waiting time perception by each of duration, progress function, shape, and embellishment

Table 1. ANOVA results of effects of loading symbol factors on the rating for waiting time perception from aligned rank transformed data

Source	DF	F	P
Duration (D)	2	1825.84	**0.000**
Progress function (P)	3	117.32	**0.000**
Shape (S)	1	13.34	**0.000**
Embellishment (E)	1	1.42	0.233
D × P	6	3.15	**0.004**
D × S	2	2.00	0.135
D × E	2	0.51	0.602
P × S	3	4.55	**0.003**
P × E	3	2.12	0.095
S × E	1	1.22	0.269
D × P × S	6	0.82	0.556
D × P × E	6	0.70	0.647
D × S × E	2	0.11	0.898
P × S × E	3	0.56	0.643
D × P × S × E	6	0.72	0.636

significant interaction effects were found for duration × progress function (p = .004) and progress function × shape (p = .003). The distribution of subjective rating by duration, progress function, and shape is depicted in Fig. 3.

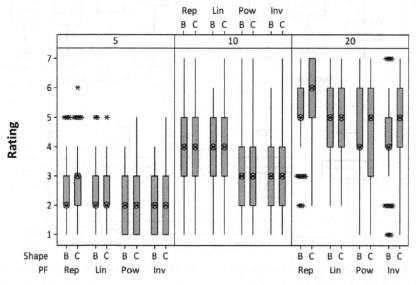

Fig. 3. Boxplot of duration, progress function, and shape on the subjective rating for waiting time perception. (Embellishment factor is not shown here due to the statistical insignificance.) *Note.* PF: Progress Function, B: Bar, C: Circle, Rep: Repetitive, Lin: Linear, Pow: Power, Inv: Inverse Power

4   Discussion

4.1   Main Effects

Non-repetitive loading symbols were perceived shorter than repetitive symbols, which is a consistent result with previous studies [3, 14, 15] that the user satisfies with the feedback on delay. Furthermore, loading symbols with power and inverse power progress functions were perceived significantly shorter than others. This result is partially consistent with the previous study [10] that found the power progress function was felt significantly faster than the inverse power and linear progress functions. The difference in their experimental settings (bar shape with 5.5 s duration only), evaluation methods (comparison between each pair of two progress functions) and tested populations might cause this inconsistency.

There could be two possible explanations for the reason why manipulated progress functions were perceived shorter. While static standard functions are relatively easy to conjecture when the loading will be ended, dynamic manipulated functions show continuous changes and make viewers difficult to know the expected end time of loading and to put more attention on subsequent changes in the loading speed. When a stimulus that requires more attentional resources is presented, the individual tends to perceive time intervals shorter [19, 26, 27]. Meanwhile, viewers are likely to satisfy more with manipulated progress, as it gives a rapid sense of conclusion through illusions caused by the adjusted progress. Users' perceptions about elapsed waiting time is strongly associated with overall satisfaction of the service [2, 21]. For these reasons, it is recommended to apply manipulated progress as power or inverse power functions rather than common repetitive or linear functions.

Even though the bar shaped symbol showed statistical significance to be perceived shorter than the circle shaped symbol, the practical significance was marginal considering a minor median difference of 0.06. On the other hand, the embellishment factor did not show significant difference in this study, which was contrary to our initial expectation and findings from the previous studies. When an interesting stimulus or a stimulus that requires more attentional resources is presented during the interval to be estimated, the individual tends to underestimate the temporal intervals [1, 19, 24]. A possible explanation for this surprising result is that the inserted bicycle figure used in this study might not be attractive enough for participants or they could get bored by watching the same static image for many times continuously. Overall, it can be concluded that shape and embellishment are less critical to be considered in design by taking practical significance into account.

4.2 Interaction Effects

A significant interaction was found between duration and progress function (p = .004). According to the distribution of rating, linear progress function seemed to be perceived shorter than repetitive progress especially at 20 s duration. A significant interaction between shape and progress function (p = .004) was also found, indicating tendency that the loading with a circle shaped symbol tends to be perceived a bit longer than the one with a bar shaped symbol especially at repetitive and progress functions. This leads to a surprising fact that the circle shaped symbol with a repetitive progress function, which is most commonly used in online video websites, showed worse performance than other loading symbols (Fig. 3).

4.3 Design Implications

It is better for loading symbol designers to provide feedback of loading progress to viewers, and apply manipulated progress of power or inverse power functions to effectively control viewers' perception for relief of stress from waiting. Harrison et al. investigated the effect of nine different progress functions of the progress bar with 5.5-second duration on user preferences [10], and found that the progress bar with the power progress function was significantly preferred than most of others. The effect of manipulated progress functions was validated at the broader use context including longer durations of 10 and 20 s, repetitive progress function, circular progress bar and embellishment. Design factors such as shape and embellishment can be considered to have less impact on designing a shortly perceived loading symbol. Even though this study was focused on loading symbols of the online videos, the findings of this study could be extended to other human-computer interfaces such as web page and mobile App loadings.

4.4 Limitations

Several limitations are inherent in this study. First, the main video content, which usually appears at the end of the loading, was not included in the stimuli. Second, a dynamic figure that can easily attract interest of viewers can be used as the embellishment. Third, some important factors that can influence the time perception such as user expectations [6] and predictivity [20] were not considered in this study.

5 Conclusion

This study shows that the duration and progress function of a loading symbol significantly affect viewer's perception of waiting time. Especially, loading of power and inverse power progress functions were felt significantly shorter than the repetitive and linear progress functions. It is suggested to provide feedback on progress and utilize adjusted progress functions to incite optimistic expectation of viewers. Design factors such as symbol shape and embellishment are less important for designing a better loading symbol. It should be noted that the circle shaped symbol with a repetitive progress function, which is most commonly used in online video websites, showed significantly worse performance than other loading symbols. The findings of this study may serve as a useful input for video service providers and loading symbol designers in creating shortly perceived loading symbols.

References

1. Angrilli, A., Cherubini, P., Pavese, A., Manfredini, S.: The influence of affective factors on time perception. Percept. Psychophys. **59**(6), 972–982 (1997)
2. Bleustein, C., Rothschild, D.B., Valen, A., Valatis, E., Schweitzer, L., Jones, R.: Wait times, patient satisfaction scores, and the perception of care. Am. J. Manag. Care **20**(5), 393–400 (2014)
3. Branaghan, R.J., Sanchez, C.A.: Feedback preferences and impressions of waiting. Hum. Factors: J. Hum. Factors Ergon. Soc. **51**(4), 528–538 (2009)
4. Brandt, M.: 1 in 4 U.S. internet users watches online videos daily. Statista, 28 August 2014. http://www.statista.com/chart/2627/internet-users-watching-online-video-every-day/
5. Ceaparu, I., Lazar, J., Bessiere, K., Robinson, J., Shneiderman, B.: Determining causes and severity of end-user frustration. Int. J. Hum.-Comput. Interact. **17**(3), 333–356 (2004)

6. Dabrowski, J., Munson, E.V.: 40 years of searching for the best computer system response time. Interact. Comput. **23**(5), 555–564 (2011)
7. De Pessemier, T., De Moor, K., Joseph, W., De Marez, L., Martens, L.: Quantifying subjective quality evaluations for mobile video watching in a semi-living lab context. IEEE Trans. Broadcast. **58**(4), 580–589 (2012)
8. eMarketer. US adults spend 5.5 hours with video content each day, 16 April 2015. https://www.emarketer.com/Article/US-Adults-Spend-55-Hours-with-Video-Content-Each-Day/1012362#sthash.4RDw7Swq.dpuf
9. Fredrickson, B.L., Kahneman, D.: Duration neglect in retrospective evaluations of affective episodes. J. Pers. Soc. Psychol. **65**, 45–55 (1993)
10. Harrison, C., Amento, B., Kuznetsov, S., Bell, R.: Rethinking the progress bar. In: Proceedings of the 20th Annual ACM Symposium on User Interface Software and Technology, pp. 115–118. ACM (2007)
11. Kishore, A.: Why quality of experience is the most critical metric for internet video profitability. Guardian (2013)
12. Krishnan, S.S., Sitaraman, R.K.: Video stream quality impacts viewer behavior: inferring causality using quasi-experimental designs. IEEE/ACM Trans. Netw. **21**(6), 2001–2014 (2013)
13. Lin, Y.C., Yeh, C.H., Wei, C.C.: How will the use of graphics affect visual aesthetics? A user-centered approach for web page design. Int. J. Hum. Comput. Stud. **71**(3), 217–227 (2013)
14. Myers, B.A.: The importance of percent-done progress indicators for computer-human interfaces. In: Proceedings of the 1985 SIGCHI Conference on Human Factors in Computing Systems, San Francisco, California, CHI 1985, pp. 11–17. ACM Press, New York (1985)
15. Nah, F.F.H.: A study on tolerable waiting time: how long are web users willing to wait? Behav. Inf. Technol. **23**(3), 153–163 (2004)
16. Parush, A., Shwarts, Y., Shtub, A., Chandra, M.J.: The impact of visual layout factors on performance in Web pages: a cross-language study. Hum. Factors: J. Hum. Factors Ergon. Soc. **47**(1), 141–157 (2005)
17. Pruyn, A., Smidts, A.: Effects of waiting on the satisfaction with the service: beyond objective time measures. Int. J. Res. Mark. **15**(4), 321–334 (1998)
18. Szameitat, A.J., Rummel, J., Szameitat, D.P., Sterr, A.: Behavioral and emotional consequences of brief delays in human–computer interaction. Int. J. Hum. Comput. Stud. **67**(7), 561–570 (2009)
19. Thomas, E.A., Weaver, W.B.: Cognitive processing and time perception. Percept. Psychophys. **17**(4), 363–367 (1975)
20. Thomaschke, R., Haering, C.: Predictivity of system delays shortens human response time. Int. J. Hum. Comput. Stud. **72**(3), 358–365 (2014)
21. Thompson, D.A., Yarnold, P.R., Williams, D.R., Adams, S.L.: Effects of actual waiting time, perceived waiting time, information delivery, and expressive quality on patient satisfaction in the emergency department. Ann. Emerg. Med. **28**(6), 657–665 (1996)
22. Thum, M., Boucsein, W., Kuhmann, W., Ray, W.J.: Standardized task strain and system response times in human-computer interaction. Ergonomics **38**(7), 1342–1351 (1995)
23. Tognazzini, B.: Principles, techniques, and ethics of stage magic and their application to human interface design. In: Proceedings of the INTERACT 1993 and CHI 1993 Conference on Human Factors in Computing Systems, pp. 355–362. ACM (1993)
24. Treisman, M.: Temporal discrimination and the indifference interval: implications for a model of the" internal clock". Psychol. Monogr.: Gen. Appl. **77**(13), 1 (1963)

25. Wobbrock, J.O., Findlater, L., Gergle, D., Higgins, J.J.: The aligned rank transform for nonparametric factorial analyses using only anova procedures. In: Proceedings of the SIGCHI Conference on Human Factors in Computing Systems, pp. 143–146. ACM (2011)
26. Zakay, D.: Attention allocation policy influences prospective timing. Psychon. Bull. Rev. 5 (1), 114–118 (1998)
27. Zakay, D., Tsal, Y.: Awareness of attention allocation and time estimation accuracy. Bull. Psychon. Soc. 27(3), 209–210 (1989)

Research on Image Emotional Semantic Retrieval Mechanism Based on Cognitive Quantification Model

Tian Liang, Liqun Zhang$^{(\boxtimes)}$, and Min Xie

Institute of Design Management, Shanghai Jiao Tong University,
Shanghai, China
zhanglliqun@gmail.com

Abstract. In the wake of the development of first-person engagement and crowdsourcing content creation, images are given abundant subjective dimensions of information, especially emotional ones. This research tried to purpose an approach for the image emotional semantic retrieval based on cognitive quantification model by using tags. In this research "Daqi", a typical Chinese emotional experience, is taken as an example to construct an emotional quantification model of it through semantic association analysis and statistical data analysis. The results of verification experiments indicated that it is practical and effective to rank images and recommend tags in image emotional retrieval system based on cognitive model. It is foreseeable that the theory of this research can be applied to other social digital resources, like music or video.

Keywords: Image emotional semantic retrieval · Cognitive quantification · Image annotation

1 Introduction

With the rapid development of Web2.0, first-person engagement and crowdsourcing content creation have boomed as new paradigms of interactions. Digital media resources, especially images, are given abundant subjective and expressive dimensions of cognitive contents, which advocates researches for retrieval of the emotional information. Human perception and understanding of image emotional information are operations mainly on the semantic level. However, "Semantic gap" between low-level image features and high-level emotional semantic can be hardly to bridge completely.

This research aims to purpose an approach for the image retrieval of emotional content based on tags. Tags are image description added by users directly, so image emotional semantic retrieval can be implemented based on text retrieval technology without the extraction of image information. To increase the number of tags, the channels of tag generation are expanded by including the relevant user interactive behaviors.

In this research, a cognitive quantification model of their emotional qualities or of their reception by users is constructed to organize and manipulate social image resources. Meanwhile, the model is applied to emotional semantic tag recommendation,

© Springer International Publishing AG 2017
A. Marcus and W. Wang (Eds.): DUXU 2017, Part III, LNCS 10290, pp. 115–128, 2017.
DOI: 10.1007/978-3-319-58640-3_10

which is beneficial to improve the efficiency of image annotation and the validity of image recommendation.

This research creatively proposes a mechanism for the emotional semantic retrieval of images. The mechanism has the following advantages,

- Retaining the user's subjective view of images maximally by using user-generated tags, which ensures the credibility of retrieval and is more lightweight.
- Binding the behaviors and views of users in image retrieval based on behavior psychology, which expands tag sources and provides more data for the modeling.
- Mining the potential emotional semantic of pictures based on the cognitive quantification model, which improve the effectiveness of image emotional semantic retrieval. Meanwhile diverse associated tags can be recommended according to the relevant weight in the model, which further improves the emotional image annotation.

The rest of the paper is organized as follows. An overview of the tag-based image emotional semantic image retrieval mechanism is presented in Sect. 2. Section 3 discussed the details of methods used in the mechanism. To verify the rationality of the proposed mechanism, experiments with small sample size have been done. The process and analyses are presented in Sect. 4. Section 5 is the summary and prospect.

2   Concepts and Methods

2.1   Concepts

Image Tag. Tags are the keywords added by users to describe the image contents. In particular, tags are not only the labels, but also can be the keywords in the titles, comments and so on. As tags are image descriptor, it is easy to recommend images directly based on text retrieval technology and there is no need to extract and analyze information of images.

An image can be added multiple tags, and a tag is also used to describe multiple images. The user is the creator of annotation behaviors, creating an association between images and tags.

At present, annotation behaviors are as follows,

- Adding the title or labels when uploading images;
- Adding the labels or grouping when collecting images;
- Making comments on images.

The tags generated by the above behaviors are "explicit tags". In fact, the above annotation behaviors are non-essential and costly behaviors for users, who is lacking of motivation. A large portion of the users only view images without leaving a tag.

However, studies have shown that the behaviors of users to retrieve images can reflect how much users agree with the retrieval results, revealing the relevance between the retrieval keywords and images. Using the data of users' browsing behaviors, "implicit tags" can be made. The details are discussed in Sect. 2.2.

Emotional Quantification Model. Image semantics has several levels. Emotional semantics lies on the highest level of abstract semantics, which can be defined as the semantics described intensity and type of feelings, moods, affections or sensibility evoked in humans by viewing images. It is usually represented in adjective form, romantic, brilliant etc.

Constructing an image emotional computational model usually involves three parts,

- extracting image perceptual features that can stimulate users' emotions;
- establishing the emotional recognition mechanism to bridge the semantic gap between low-level visual features and high-level emotional semantics;
- constructing the model to represent image emotional semantics that meet the needs of users' query.

Visual identity and machine learning are main methods in the first and the second parts. They are aimed to build an association between images and their emotional semantics that can be retrieved easily, which can be implemented just by "tags".

Based on tags, this paper is focused on the construction of the model to quantify image emotions which users search for.

In general emotional semantic models, the specific emotion is split and associated with the six basic dimensions of the emotion, anger, disgust, fear, joy, sadness, and surprise. The models relying on these six basic dimensions are not enough in emotional fine grain to represent complex emotional semantics or to distinguish between the various emotions clearly.

Learning from this idea, in this paper the emotional semantics are represented by more flexible and more targeted "emotional dimensions" which contain a variety of "emotional elements" associated with a certain relationship. The emotional semantic quantification model is expressed by "emotional dimensions", and the emotional dimension is extracted from "emotional elements".

2.2   Methods

Users' Retrieval Behavior. As mentioned in the previous section, it is non-essential and costly for users to add image tags and most users only browse images without leaving a tag. Studies have shown that users' behaviors to retrieve images can reflect the degree of users' recognition on the search results, in the image retrieval system, that is, the relevance of the search keywords and images.

Using the data of users' retrieval behaviors, it can be predicted whether the images are associated with the search keyword, and if so, the "search keyword" can be added to the images as an "implicit tag".

In users' retrieving images, the operations of generating "implicit tags" are as follows.

- click to view the image after retrieving;
- download/save the image after retrieving;
- snapshot the image after retrieving.

Among them, we remain neutral on the operation of clicking to view, because it is impossible to exclude behaviors that users click images to view due to curiosity and so on rather than recognition.

Combining the behaviors generating "explicit tags" mentioned in the previous section, the relationship between tags generated by users' behaviors ("explicit tags" and "implicit tags") and images is divided into three level, related_1, neutral_0.5 non-relevant_0, as follows (Fig. 1).

BEHAVIOR	TAG	RELEVANCE
add titles when uploading images	keywords in titles	1
add labels when uploading images	label	1
add labels when collecting images	label	1
add to groups when collecting images	group name	1
make comments on images	keywords in comments	1
download/save images after retrieval	search keywords	1
snapshot images after retrieval	search keywords	1
click images to view after retrieval	search keywords	0.5
other non-relevance behaviors	none	0

Fig. 1. Relevance of behavior and tag

A user may have more than one annotation for an image, but the above behaviors are not cumulative in relevance degree up to 1, that is, as long as there is a strong annotation behavior (relevance_1), the tag is added to the image by the user.

Tag Clustering Analysis. Clustering is a common data analysis tool and a basic algorithm for data mining. The essence of clustering analysis is to divide data into several clusters according to the relevance. Therefore, it has high similarity within clusters and big difference between clusters.

Tag clustering can be used to find semantic-related labels in social annotation systems, Begdman et al. The principle tag can be mostly represented by identifying the subject of the cluster. If the clusters constitute the special emotion, the principle tags of them is "emotional elements".

The semantic relevance of two tags can be obtained by relying on the semantic knowledge databases, such as Wordnet (for English) and CSC (for Chinese), to build a semantic correlation matrix (Fig. 2).

Tag \ Tag	t_1	t_2	t_3	...	t_n
t_1	1	0.2	0.4	...	0.3
t_2	0.2	1	0.5	...	0.8
t_3	0.4	0.5	1	...	0.7
...	...	...	...	1	...
t_n	0.3	0.8	0.7	...	1

Fig. 2. Semantic correlation matrix of tags

Based on the semantic relevance coefficient in the matrix to build N-dimensional space, the Euclidean distance formula (1) can be used to calculate the spatial distance of two tags. The closer, the more similar tags can be considered.

$$Euclid(1,2) = \sqrt{(x_1 - x_2)^2 + (y_1 - y_2)^2 + (z_1 - z_2)^2} \tag{1}$$

The shortest two clusters are merged into a large cluster until all small clusters are merged into a large cluster. The whole process can be shown in a form of a tree structure. Any number of semantic groups can be got through hierarchical clustering analysis (Fig. 3).

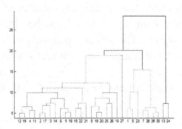

Fig. 3. Hierarchical clustering

Factor Analysis of Emotional Cognition. The main purpose of factor analysis is to reduce dimension by transferring lots of indicators into several comprehensive indicators under little information lost.

As tags increases, redundancy and uniqueness should be considered when performing image matching in the emotional space. Using factor analysis, an orthogonal emotional space can be constructed not only to retain the majority of original indicators meaning, but also to ensure the simplification of the model.

At the same time, the weight of each emotion dimension is allocated according to the contribution rate of each factor, rather than the artificial judgment, which makes the model more objective and reasonable.

Creating a tag-image matrix $S = \{s_{im}\}$ based on website image-tag database() (Fig. 4).

Tag / Image	T_1	T_2	T_3	...	T_m
I_1	s_{11}	s_{12}	s_{13}	...	s_{1m}
I_2	s_{21}	s_{22}	s_{23}	...	s_{2m}
I_3	s_{31}	s_{32}	s_{33}	...	s_{3m}
...	...	...	...	...	...
I_i	s_{i1}	s_{i2}	s_{i3}	...	s_{im}

Fig. 4. A tag-image matrix

s_{im} is the score of image I_i on tag T_m, determined by the number of T_m on I_i. Since the number of tags on different images are in a different order of magnitude, it needs to be standardized. For an image I_a and the number of tags $N = \{n_1, n_2, ..., n_m\}$, its score s_{ai}

$$s_{ai} = n_i / \max(n_i), \quad i = 1, 2, \ldots, m$$

After factor analysis, factors $F = \{F1, F2, \ldots, Fn\}$, that is the "emotional dimensions", and their variance contribution rate $A = \{a1, a2, \ldots, an\}$ can be got. The emotion Y can be represented by emotional cognitive factors F, as (2).

$$Y = a_1 F_1 + a_2 F_2 + \ldots + a_n F_n \qquad (2)$$

In addition, we obtain a factor load coefficients matrix of tags T and factors F. The rotation factor load coefficient matrix $B = \{b_{mn}\}$ can be obtained by using Varimax to rotate the initial factor load matrix. The rotation method can keep the factors orthogonal to each other, but the variance difference of each factor is maximized, so it is convenient to explain the factor.

Quantization models of each emotional dimension can be obtained.

$$F_i = b_{i1} T_{p1} + b_{i2} T_{p2} + \ldots + b_{im} T_{pm} \quad (i = 1, 2, \ldots, n) \qquad (3)$$

(3) into (2), we can get an emotional cognitive quantification model of Y

$$Y = c_1 T_{p1} + c_2 T_{p2} + \ldots + c_m T_{pm} \qquad (4)$$

$$C = AB \qquad (5)$$

3 Image Emotional Semantic Retrieval System

In the image emotional semantic retrieval systems, it is an important part to find most appropriate images for given tags and find the most appropriate tags for given images. That is, need to find the most appropriate match with each other tag-image pairs.

The system has three main functional modules,

First, recommend the relevant images according to users' search terms.

Second, recommend the relevant tags for the images that users agree with.

The third, based on users' feedback on the recommended results, expand the tag-image database.

Given an input tag T_a, the recommended image set $I_R = \{I_{r1}, I_{r2}, \ldots, I_{ri}\}$, and the recommended tag set for image $T_r = \{T_{r1}, T_{r2}, \ldots, T_{ri}\}$, the flow of the system is divided into the following steps (Fig. 5).

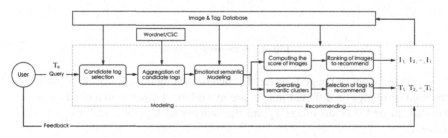

Fig. 5. Image emotional semantic retrieval system

3.1   Emotional Semantic Modeling

Candidate Tag Selection. Given an initial tag T_a, the tag set $T = \{T_1, T_2, ..., T_i\}$ where all tags associated with it are included is collected based on the coherence principle. The more images any two tags are annotated on by users at the same time, the more there are cognitive links with them. In order to avoid the tag noise, it is needed to set a threshold, usually an empirical value. There are experimental evidences found that the value set 10 can make the best performance.

Through synonyms to merger these coherence tags, get the candidate tag set $T_c = \{T_{c1}, T_{c2}, ..., T_{ci}\}$

Aggregation of Candidate Tags. Using the external semantic knowledge database Wordnet (for English) or CSC (for Chinese), establish a semantic association matrix according to the semantics relevance of T_c, shown as below. The correlation value is 0–1, the higher the value is, the higher the relevance is.

Then, cluster the candidate tags by the clustering algorithm to generate several original semantic clusters. A representative label is selected as a representative label to represent each cluster of the class, which forms emotional elements set $T_p = \{T_{p1}, T_{p2}, ..., T_{pm}\}$.

Emotional Semantic Modeling. Based on the website image-tag database, making factor analysis on T_p, to get the emotional dimension set $F = \{F_1, F_2, ..., F_n\}$ and its variance contribution rate $A = \{a_1, a_2, ..., a_n\}$, and then T_a emotional cognitive model can be expressed as follow.

$$Y = a_1F_1 + a_2F_2 + ... + a_nF_n \tag{6}$$

According to the rotation factor load factor matrix $B = \{b_{mn}\}$, each factor F quantization model can be expressed as follow.

$$F_i = b_{i1}T_{p1} + b_{i2}T_{p2} + ... + b_{im}T_{pm} \ (i = 1, 2, ..., n) \tag{7}$$

Combining the above two expressions to obtain the emotional semantic model of T_a with tag elements T_p,

$$Y = c_1T_{p1} + c_2T_{p2} + ... + c_mT_{pm} \tag{8}$$

3.2   Images Ranking and Tags Selection

Ranking of Images to Recommend. The value of each image on T_p is s_{mi}. The emotional value of each image on tag T_a can be calculated by using the formula (8). Recommended image are sorted by the emotional value from high to low.

Selection of Tags to Recommend. Each image has the highest score tag T_{p1} that is included in the emotional dimension F, where there are other tags T_p $\{T_{p2}, T_{p3}, \ldots, T_{pi}\}$. Tags are recommended according to the weight in the formula (7).

Feedback Collection. According to the user's browsing behavior, collect user's various types of annotation activities, which can generate explicit tags or implicit tags to enrich and expand the image-tag library data.

4 Simulation Experiment

4.1 Experiment Setting

"Daqi" was set as the special emotional term, and 25 testers (12 males and 13 females) were invited to participate in the experiment. 150 images from appliances, furniture, transportation, construction, utensils, jewelry and other fields were selected as exciter. Testers were asked to grade the correlation between images and some terms related to "Daqi", non-relevance 0, neutral 0.5, relevance 1. Using the experimental data to get the "Daqi" emotional semantic quantification model, some validation tests were made.

4.2 Experiment Process

Construct Emotional Quantification Model. Through the literature, online comments, and website etc., more than 140 adjectives appearing at the same time as "Daqi" were collected. Then, merge these terms into 45 terms through synonyms. Researchers, according to their own professional experience and cognition. A semantic correlation matrix (Fig. 6) of these 45 emotional terms were built on researchers' professional experience.

	concise	grand	elegant	solemn	funky	large size	delicate	strong	purely	symmetry	unite	smooth	generous	full	conception	strong	rounded	rough	delicate	peaceful	free and easy	structured	hale	simple and elegance	muddy	rigorous	vivid	uninhibited	tall	heavy
concise	1	0.3	0.4	0.2	0.7	0.6	0.2	0.2	0.8	0.5	0.5	0.6	0.7	0.4	0.3	0.2	0.6	0.3	0.7	0.8	0.7	0.7	0.5	0.9	0.3	0.4	0.4	0.4	0.5	0.3
grand	0.3	1	0.5	0.7	0.4	0.9	0.4	0.5	0.4	0.6	0.6	0.5	0.6	0.6	0.5	0.7	0.5	0.8	0.3	0.4	0.5	0.5	0.6	0.3	0.8	0.5	0.3	0.7	0.9	0.8
elegant	0.4	0.5	1	0.7	0.5	0.4	0.7	0.3	0.7	0.5	0.6	0.7	0.8	0.7	0.7	0.3	0.7	0.1	0.6	0.6	0.4	0.5	0.3	0.7	0.4	0.6	0.6	0.3	0.3	0.3
solemn	0.2	0.7	0.7	1	0.4	0.5	0.6	0.4	0.5	0.7	0.7	0.6	0.7	0.6	0.8	0.6	0.6	0.4	0.3	0.6	0.4	0.5	0.5	0.5	0.7	0.6	0.5	0.6	0.6	0.7
funky	0.7	0.4	0.5	0.4	1	0.5	0.3	0.4	0.8	0.5	0.6	0.6	0.6	0.5	0.4	0.2	0.5	0.7	0.6	0.8	0.8	0.5	0.5	0.8	0.4	0.4	0.5	0.4	0.3	0.5
large size	0.6	0.9	0.4	0.5	0.5	1	0.4	0.5	0.5	0.6	0.6	0.6	0.5	0.5	0.6	0.6	0.5	0.7	0.4	0.5	0.7	0.5	0.6	0.4	0.8	0.5	0.5	0.7	0.9	0.7
delicate	0.2	0.4	0.7	0.6	0.3	0.4	1	0.2	0.4	0.5	0.6	0.5	0.6	0.7	0.5	0.3	0.6	0.1	0.7	0.5	0.4	0.6	0.2	0.4	0.3	0.7	0.7	0.4	0.4	0.4
strong	0.2	0.5	0.3	0.4	0.4	0.5	0.2	1	0.4	0.4	0.5	0.5	0.5	0.6	0.4	0.7	0.4	0.8	0.2	0.3	0.5	0.4	0.8	0.3	0.8	0.6	0.5	0.7	0.7	0.6
purely	0.8	0.4	0.7	0.5	0.8	0.5	0.4	0.4	1	0.6	0.6	0.7	0.6	0.6	0.6	0.4	0.6	0.4	0.7	0.8	0.5	0.5	0.4	0.8	0.4	0.5	0.6	0.4	0.3	0.3
symmetry	0.5	0.6	0.5	0.7	0.5	0.6	0.5	0.4	0.6	1	0.8	0.7	0.5	0.6	0.5	0.4	0.6	0.3	0.5	0.6	0.5	0.7	0.6	0.7	0.5	0.7	0.5	0.5	0.5	0.6
unite	0.5	0.6	0.6	0.7	0.6	0.6	0.6	0.5	0.6	0.8	1	0.7	0.5	0.6	0.5	0.5	0.6	0.4	0.5	0.7	0.5	0.7	0.5	0.5	0.5	0.8	0.5	0.5	0.5	0.5
smooth	0.6	0.5	0.7	0.6	0.6	0.6	0.5	0.5	0.7	0.7	0.7	1	0.6	0.7	0.6	0.4	0.7	0.4	0.5	0.6	0.7	0.6	0.4	0.5	0.5	0.6	0.6	0.6	0.5	0.4
generous	0.7	0.6	0.8	0.7	0.6	0.5	0.6	0.5	0.6	0.5	0.5	0.6	1	0.6	0.6	0.4	0.5	0.4	0.4	0.6	0.7	0.5	0.5	0.6	0.6	0.6	0.6	0.5	0.5	0.4
full	0.4	0.6	0.7	0.6	0.5	0.5	0.7	0.6	0.6	0.6	0.6	0.7	0.6	1	0.6	0.3	0.8	0.4	0.4	0.5	0.5	0.6	0.4	0.5	0.6	0.6	0.7	0.5	0.5	0.5
conception	0.3	0.5	0.7	0.8	0.4	0.6	0.5	0.4	0.6	0.5	0.5	0.6	0.6	0.6	1	0.4	0.5	0.5	0.4	0.7	0.6	0.6	0.4	0.6	0.5	0.5	0.6	0.5	0.5	0.5
strong	0.2	0.7	0.3	0.6	0.2	0.6	0.3	0.7	0.4	0.4	0.5	0.4	0.4	0.3	0.4	1	0.2	0.6	0.2	0.2	0.4	0.6	0.7	0.3	0.7	0.6	0.4	0.6	0.7	0.6
rounded	0.6	0.5	0.7	0.6	0.5	0.5	0.6	0.4	0.6	0.6	0.6	0.7	0.5	0.8	0.5	0.2	1	0.4	0.5	0.6	0.6	0.5	0.2	0.5	0.6	0.5	0.6	0.4	0.5	0.4
rough	0.3	0.8	0.1	0.4	0.7	0.7	0.1	0.8	0.4	0.3	0.4	0.4	0.4	0.4	0.5	0.6	0.4	1	0.1	0.2	0.6	0.5	0.7	0.4	0.7	0.4	0.4	0.8	0.6	0.6
delicate	0.7	0.3	0.6	0.3	0.6	0.4	0.7	0.2	0.7	0.5	0.5	0.5	0.4	0.4	0.4	0.2	0.5	0.1	1	0.7	0.4	0.5	0.3	0.7	0.4	0.5	0.6	0.4	0.4	0.3
peaceful	0.8	0.4	0.6	0.6	0.8	0.5	0.5	0.3	0.8	0.6	0.7	0.6	0.6	0.5	0.7	0.2	0.6	0.2	0.7	1	0.6	0.5	0.4	0.7	0.5	0.6	0.4	0.4	0.5	0.5
free and easy	0.7	0.5	0.4	0.4	0.8	0.7	0.4	0.5	0.5	0.5	0.5	0.7	0.7	0.5	0.6	0.4	0.6	0.6	0.4	0.6	1	0.5	0.6	0.4	0.6	0.3	0.6	0.8	0.5	0.4
structured	0.7	0.5	0.5	0.5	0.5	0.5	0.6	0.4	0.5	0.7	0.7	0.6	0.5	0.6	0.6	0.6	0.5	0.5	0.5	0.5	0.5	1	0.5	0.5	0.6	0.7	0.6	0.5	0.5	0.5
hale	0.5	0.6	0.3	0.5	0.5	0.6	0.2	0.8	0.4	0.6	0.5	0.4	0.5	0.4	0.4	0.7	0.2	0.7	0.3	0.4	0.6	0.5	1	0.3	0.7	0.6	0.5	0.7	0.6	0.6
simple and elegant	0.9	0.3	0.7	0.5	0.8	0.4	0.4	0.3	0.8	0.7	0.5	0.5	0.6	0.5	0.6	0.3	0.5	0.4	0.7	0.7	0.4	0.5	0.3	1	0.4	0.5	0.6	0.4	0.5	0.3
since muddy	0.3	0.8	0.4	0.7	0.4	0.8	0.3	0.8	0.4	0.5	0.5	0.5	0.6	0.6	0.5	0.7	0.6	0.7	0.4	0.5	0.6	0.6	0.7	0.4	1	0.5	0.6	0.8	0.7	0.7
rigorous	0.4	0.5	0.6	0.6	0.4	0.5	0.7	0.6	0.5	0.7	0.8	0.6	0.6	0.6	0.5	0.6	0.5	0.4	0.5	0.6	0.3	0.7	0.6	0.5	0.5	1	0.6	0.5	0.5	0.6
vivid	0.4	0.3	0.6	0.5	0.5	0.5	0.7	0.5	0.6	0.5	0.5	0.6	0.6	0.7	0.6	0.4	0.6	0.4	0.6	0.4	0.6	0.6	0.5	0.6	0.6	0.6	1	0.6	0.4	0.3
uninhibited	0.4	0.7	0.3	0.6	0.4	0.7	0.4	0.7	0.4	0.5	0.5	0.6	0.5	0.5	0.5	0.6	0.4	0.8	0.4	0.4	0.8	0.5	0.7	0.4	0.8	0.5	0.6	1	0.6	0.4
tall	0.5	0.9	0.3	0.6	0.3	0.9	0.4	0.7	0.3	0.5	0.5	0.5	0.5	0.5	0.5	0.7	0.5	0.6	0.4	0.5	0.5	0.5	0.6	0.5	0.7	0.5	0.4	0.6	1	0.5
heavy	0.3	0.8	0.3	0.7	0.5	0.7	0.4	0.6	0.3	0.6	0.5	0.4	0.4	0.5	0.5	0.6	0.4	0.6	0.3	0.5	0.4	0.5	0.6	0.3	0.7	0.6	0.3	0.4	0.5	1

Fig. 6. A semantic correlation matrix

Through the clustering analysis, ward method, 16 related emotional terms, emotional elements, on behalf of each cluster respectively were obtained. They were Quality, Generous, Uniform, Smooth, Solemnly, Full, Rounded, Elegant, Simple, Artless, Pretty, Delicate, Angular, Hard, Huge, Uninhibited.

25 testers were asked to score the degree of correlation between 150 stimuli images and the 16 emotional terms, respectively. The result of factor analysis (Fig. 7) on the experimental data is as follow. KMO is 0.789 and the data is suitable for factor analysis.

Communalities

	Initial	Extraction
Quality	1.000	.872
Generous	1.000	.834
Uniform	1.000	.767
Smooth	1.000	.771
Solemnly	1.000	.894
Fulled	1.000	.789
Rounded	1.000	.910
Elegant	1.000	.774
Simple	1.000	.813
Artless	1.000	.895
Pretty	1.000	.768
Delicate	1.000	.867
Angular	1.000	.876
Hard	1.000	.767
Huge	1.000	.822
Uninhibited	1.000	.697

Extraction Method: Principal Component Analysis.

Total Variance Explained

Component	Initial Eigenvalues			Extraction Sums of Squared Loadings			Rotation Sums of Squared Loadings		
	Total	% of Variance	Cumulative %	Total	% of Variance	Cumulative %	Total	% of Variance	Cumulative %
1	5.538	34.614	34.614	5.538	34.614	34.614	4.362	27.262	27.262
2	4.131	25.816	60.429	4.131	25.816	60.429	2.694	16.840	44.102
3	1.923	12.018	72.447	1.923	12.018	72.447	2.458	15.361	59.464
4	.989	6.179	78.627	.989	6.179	78.627	2.399	14.994	74.457
5	.735	4.596	83.223	.735	4.596	83.223	1.402	8.766	83.223
6	.511	3.197	86.420						
7	.423	2.642	89.061						
8	.338	2.115	91.176						
9	.318	1.990	93.166						
10	.245	1.531	94.696						
11	.232	1.450	96.146						
12	.163	1.019	97.165						
13	.145	.909	98.074						
14	.124	.775	98.849						
15	.095	.594	99.443						
16	.089	.557	100.000						

Extraction Method: Principal Component Analysis.

Fig. 7. Communalities and total variance explained

To ensure a reasonable explanation, we choose the factor combination of which contribute is up to 83.223%. There are five factors in it. And the degree of extraction of each emotional term can reach more than 75%. Get the expression (9) of the five factors i, as follows (Fig. 8).

$$Y = 0.42F_1 + 0.31F_2 + 0.14F_3 + 0.07F_4 + 0.06F_5 \tag{9}$$

Component Matrix^a

	Component				
	1	2	3	4	5
Quality	.907	-.041	.037	.208	-.053
Generous	.852	.048	.279	.159	-.060
Smooth	.812	.276	.029	-.160	-.088
Uniform	.780	.172	.272	-.080	.219
Fulled	.729	.057	-.309	-.323	.232
Elegant	.709	.489	.084	.117	-.112
Delicate	.654	-.261	-.198	.503	-.280
Solemnly	.632	-.305	-.267	.235	.525
Hard	.255	-.730	.387	.108	-.084
Angular	-.200	-.730	.484	.256	.055
Pretty	-.202	.728	.284	.318	.122
Huge	.485	-.686	.133	-.262	.174
Rounded	.518	.684	-.349	-.146	-.173
Simple	.179	.629	.604	-.073	-.126
Uninhibited	.380	-.595	.383	-.429	-.262
Artless	-.187	.578	.664	-.055	.288

Extraction Method: Principal Component Analysis.
a. 5 components extracted.

Fig. 8. Component matrix

According to the composition of the score coefficient matrix, "Daqi" emotional cognition model can be got, as follows.

$$Y = 0.1T_1 + 0.12T_2 + 0.12T_3 + 0.17T_4 - 0.04T_5 + 0.11T_6 + 0.17T_7 + 0.15T_8$$
$$+ 0.13T_9 + 0.03T_{10} + 0.01T_{11} + 0.03T_{12} - 0.13T_{13} - 0.04T_{14} + 0.01T_{15} \quad (10)$$
$$+ 0.08T_{16}$$

Extract Emotional Dimensions. According to the rotation component matrix, five emotional dimensions can be made sure, and each emotional dimension inside the emotional composition is as follows (Fig. 9).

F_1 (Quality, Generous, Delicate, Elegant, Smooth, Uniform)
F_2 (Angular, Rounded, Hard, Full)
F_3 (Artless, Simple)
F_4 (Uninhibited, Huge, Pretty)
F_5 (Solemnly).

Rotated Component Matrix[a]

	Component 1	2	3	4	5
Quality	.873	.068	-.101	.179	.250
Generous	.860	.011	.142	.219	.164
Delicate	.767	-.143	-.506	-.024	.039
Elegant	.755	.376	.235	-.077	.033
Smooth	.689	.445	.131	.248	.138
Uniform	.646	.176	.334	.254	.377
Angular	-.089	-.891	-.048	.268	.012
Rounded	.452	.821	.054	-.165	-.033
Hard	.256	-.639	-.160	.514	.056
Fulled	.388	.524	-.121	.307	.505
Artless	-.069	-.031	.924	-.187	-.024
Simple	.334	.167	.772	-.034	-.276
Uninhibited	.204	-.221	-.044	.894	-.080
Huge	.200	-.249	-.199	.715	.411
Pretty	.067	.071	.598	-.618	-.137
Solemnly	.422	-.069	-.304	.033	.786

Extraction Method: Principal Component Analysis.
Rotation Method: Varimax with Kaiser Normalization.
a. Rotation converged in 13 iterations.

Fig. 9. Rotated component matrix

And the correlation matrix between the various emotional components is as follows (Fig. 10).

Correlation Matrix[a]

		Quality	Generous	Uniform	Smooth	Solemnly	Fulled	Rounded	Elegant	Simple	Artless	Pretty	Delicate	Angular	Hard	Huge	Uninhibited
Correlation	Quality	1.000	.815	.654	.669	.582	.554	.388	.654	.158	-.201	-.163	.656	-.094	.283	.415	.291
	Generous	.815	1.000	.652	.701	.456	.471	.384	.612	.322	.011	.005	.524	-.025	.289	.366	.343
	Uniform	.654	.652	1.000	.701	.377	.523	.367	.611	.336	.168	.030	.353	-.163	.141	.350	.231
	Smooth	.669	.701	.701	1.000	.342	.548	.641	.606	.288	-.006	.033	.377	-.353	-.013	.225	.237
	Solemnly	.582	.456	.377	.342	1.000	.549	.123	.235	-.256	-.318	-.317	.502	.032	.306	.464	.118
	Fulled	.554	.471	.523	.548	.549	1.000	.512	.439	.044	-.248	-.222	.325	-.372	.038	.314	.215
	Rounded	.388	.384	.367	.641	.123	.512	1.000	.643	.346	.043	.227	.194	-.790	-.476	-.256	-.229
	Elegant	.654	.612	.611	.606	.235	.439	.643	1.000	.471	.192	.203	.400	-.436	-.144	-.033	-.016
	Simple	.158	.322	.336	.288	-.256	.044	.346	.471	1.000	.668	.465	-.166	-.228	-.125	-.323	-.046
	Artless	-.201	.011	.168	-.006	-.318	-.248	.043	.192	.668	1.000	.609	-.453	-.082	-.266	-.317	-.190
	Pretty	-.163	.005	.030	.033	-.317	-.222	.227	.203	.465	.609	1.000	-.248	-.266	-.454	-.582	-.482
	Delicate	.656	.524	.353	.377	.502	.325	.194	.400	-.166	-.453	-.248	1.000	.069	.310	.319	.220
	Angular	-.094	-.025	-.163	-.353	.032	-.372	-.790	-.436	-.228	-.082	-.266	.069	1.000	.622	.411	.400
	Hard	.283	.289	.141	-.013	.306	.038	-.476	-.144	-.125	-.266	-.454	.310	.622	1.000	.509	.630
	Huge	.415	.366	.350	.225	.464	.314	-.256	.033	-.323	-.317	-.582	.319	.411	.509	1.000	.707
	Uninhibited	.291	.343	.231	.237	.118	.215	-.229	-.016	-.046	-.190	-.482	.220	.400	.630	.707	1.000
Sig. (1-tailed)	Quality		.000	.000	.000	.000	.000	.000	.000	.048	.017	.043	.000	.164	.001	.000	.001
	Generous	.000		.000	.000	.000	.000	.000	.000	.000	.453	.481	.000	.398	.001	.000	.000
	Uniform	.000	.000		.000	.000	.000	.000	.000	.000	.039	.378	.000	.144	.069	.000	.007
	Smooth	.000	.000	.000		.000	.000	.000	.000	.001	.476	.367	.000	.000	.447	.009	.006
	Solemnly	.000	.000	.000	.000		.000	.099	.007	.003	.000	.000	.000	.371	.001	.000	.108
	Fulled	.000	.000	.000	.000	.000		.000	.000	.322	.004	.010	.000	.000	.346	.000	.012
	Rounded	.000	.000	.000	.000	.099	.000		.000	.000	.327	.008	.021	.000	.000	.003	.008
	Elegant	.000	.000	.000	.000	.007	.000	.000		.000	.022	.016	.000	.000	.066	.366	.435
	Simple	.048	.000	.000	.001	.003	.322	.000	.000		.000	.000	.041	.008	.095	.000	.315
	Artless	.017	.453	.039	.476	.000	.004	.327	.022	.000		.000	.000	.195	.002	.000	.023
	Pretty	.043	.481	.378	.367	.000	.010	.008	.016	.000	.000		.004	.002	.000	.000	.000
	Delicate	.000	.000	.000	.000	.000	.000	.021	.000	.041	.000	.004		.235	.000	.000	.010
	Angular	.164	.398	.044	.000	.371	.000	.000	.000	.008	.195	.002	.235		.000	.000	.000
	Hard	.001	.001	.069	.447	.001	.346	.000	.066	.095	.002	.000	.000	.000		.000	.000
	Huge	.000	.000	.000	.009	.000	.000	.003	.366	.000	.000	.000	.000	.000	.000		.000
	Uninhibited	.001	.000	.007	.006	.108	.012	.008	.435	.315	.023	.000	.010	.000	.000	.000	

a. Determinant = 1.053E-006

Fig. 10. Correlation matrix

4.3   Experimental Verification

Verification of Model Calculated Value. To ensure similar cognition comparisons, "appliances" are served as test. 10 appliance images (Fig. 11) were shown to be scored on the relevance with "Daqi" and we collected the scores data from 100 volunteers (48 male and 52 female). Take the average to rank the image and compare with the theoretical values of model (10) (Fig. 12).

(1)   (2)   (3)   (4)   (5)

(6)   (7)   (8)   (9)   (10)

Fig. 11. Appliance image

No.	TEST	CAMPUT
10	0.87	0.94
6	0.80	0.81
7	0.80	0.70
3	0.73	0.76
4	0.73	0.72
9	0.73	0.72
1	0.67	0.65
2	0.60	0.59
5	0.60	0.65
8	0.53	0.62

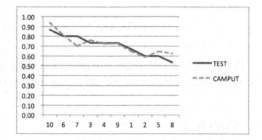

Fig. 12. Compare compute and test value

There are two ambiguities in the forecasting trend (No. 7 and No. 2), and the coincidence degree is as high as 80%. The model established can basically predict the emotional sensitivity of images.

Verification of Tag Recommended. Based on the emotional dimensions and the relevance between the terms, recommend the relevant label, some tags were selected to recommended, the maximum number 7, and asked 25 testers (12 male and 13 female) to choose the related ones from the recommended ones and calculated the use rate, the proportion of selected and provided tags.

Taking image No. 10 as an example, the highest-scored tags are Generous, Simple, and Rounded, in F1, F2 and F3 dimension, respectively. Combining the relevance matrix, as follows,

- Generous → F1 → Quality0.815, Smooth0.701, Uniform0.652, Elegant0.612, Delicate0.524
- Rounded → F2 → Full0.512
- Simple → F3 → Artless0.668

The recommended tags are as follow,
Generous, Rounded, Simple, Quality, Smooth, Artless, Uniform.
In this way, the recommended tags for the above 10 images and the average usage rate are as follows (Fig. 13).

NO	Tag max	Tag recommend	Use rate
1	Generous Simple Pretty	Generous Simple Pretty Quality Smooth Artless Uniform	0.94
2	Generous Hard	Generous Hard Quality Smooth Artless Uniform Angular	0.81
3	Quality	Generous Smooth Delicate Uniform Elegant	0.96
4	Smooth Delicate Hard	Smooth Delicate Hard Generous Uniform Quality	0.85
5	Simple Hard	Simple Hard Artless Angular	0.75
6	Quality Generous Simple	Quality Generous Simple Smooth Artless Uniform Elegant	0.97
7	Quality Simple Hard	Quality Simple Hard Generous Artless Uniform Angular	0.94
8	Uniform Hard	Uniform Hard Smooth Quality Generous Angular	0.90
9	Generous Simple	Generous Simple Quality Smooth Artless Uniform	0.88
10	Generous Rounded Simple	Generous Rounded Simple Quality Smooth Artless Uniform	0.96

Fig. 13. Average usage rate of 10 images

The average the adoption rate of the recommended tags is 89.6%. It is reasonable to recommend tags based on the emotional dimensions and emotional terms' relevance.

5 Conclusion

This paper initially envisages an image emotional semantic retrieval mechanism based on cognitive quantification model. Its core idea is to use semantic cognitive relevance of tags to divide some specific emotion into other relevant emotional dimensions and construct the emotional semantic cognition model.

At the same time, based on behavior psychology, tag generation channels are expanded by adding the users' retrieval behaviors which means "recognition", which provides more data for the modeling and make the model more representative.

As images need a lot of exposure to accumulate data to get a more accurate model, the idea of emotional semantic modeling is limited for cold-start images.

It is foreseeable that the theory of this research can be applied to other social digital resources, like music or video.

References

1. Ames, M., Naaman, M.: Why we tag: motivations for annotation in mobile and online media. In: Proceedings of the SIGCHI Conference on Human Factors in Computing Systems. ACM (2007)
2. Budanitsky, A., Hirst, G.: Evaluating wordnet-based measures of lexical semantic relatedness. Comput. Linguist. **32**(1), 13–47 (2006)
3. Cambria, E., Hussain, A., Havasi, C., Eckl, C.: Sentic computing: exploitation of common sense for the development of emotion-sensitive systems. In: Esposito, A., Campbell, N., Vogel, C., Hussain, A., Nijholt, A. (eds.) Development of Multimodal Interfaces: Active Listening and Synchrony. LNCS, vol. 5967, pp. 148–156. Springer, Heidelberg (2010). doi:10.1007/978-3-642-12397-9_12
4. Fukumoto, T.: An analysis of image retrieval behavior for metadata type image database. Inf. Process. Manag. **42**(3), 723–728 (2006)
5. Hanbury, A.: A survey of methods for image annotation. J. Visual Lang. Comput. **19**(5), 617–627 (2008)
6. Li, X., et al.: Low-rank image tag completion with dual reconstruction structure preserved. Neurocomputing **173**, 425–433 (2016)
7. Liu, N., et al.: Multimodal recognition of visual concepts using histograms of textual concepts and selective weighted late fusion scheme. Comput. Vis. Image Underst. **117**(5), 493–512 (2013)
8. Liu, Y., et al.: A survey of content-based image retrieval with high-level semantics. Pattern Recogn. **40**(1), 262–282 (2007)
9. Lu, Y., et al.: A unified framework for semantics and feature based relevance feedback in image retrieval systems. In: Proceedings of the Eighth ACM International Conference on Multimedia. ACM (2000)
10. Matusiak, K.K.: Information seeking behavior in digital image collections: a cognitive approach. J. Acad. Librariansh. **32**(5), 479–488 (2006)
11. Müller, H., et al.: Learning from user behavior in image retrieval: application of market basket analysis. Int. J. Comput. Vis. **56**(1–2), 65–77 (2004)
12. Sánchez-Rada, J.F., Iglesias, C.A.: Onyx: a linked data approach to emotion representation. Inf. Process. Manag. **52**(1), 99–114 (2016)
13. Scherer, K.R.: What are emotions? And how can they be measured? Soc. Sci. Inf. **44**(4), 695–729 (2005)
14. Schmidt, S., Stock, W.G.: Collective indexing of emotions in images. A study in emotional information retrieval. J. Am. Soc. Inf. Sci. Technol. **60**(5), 863–876 (2009)
15. Schröder, M., Pirker, H., Lamolle, M., Burkhardt, F., Peter, C., Zovato, E.: Representing emotions and related states in technological systems. In: Cowie, R., Pelachaud, C., Petta, P. (eds.) Emotion-Oriented Systems, Cognitive Technologies, pp. 369–387. Springer, Heidelberg (2011)
16. Sun, A., et al.: Tag-based social image retrieval: an empirical evaluation. J. Am. Soc. Inf. Sci. Technol. **62**(12), 2364–2381 (2011)
17. Wang, W., He, Q.: A survey on emotional semantic image retrieval. In: 15th IEEE International Conference on Image Processing, ICIP 2008. IEEE (2008)
18. Wei-ning, W., et al.: Image retrieval by emotional semantics: a study of emotional space and feature extraction. In: IEEE International Conference on Systems, Man and Cybernetics, SMC 2006. IEEE (2006)
19. Wu, L., et al.: Tag completion for image retrieval. IEEE Trans. Pattern Anal. Mach. Intell. **35**(3), 716–727 (2013)

20. Zha, Z.-J., et al.: Interactive social group recommendation for Flickr photos. Neurocomputing **105**, 30–37 (2013)
21. Zhang, H., Augilius, E., Honkela, T., Laaksonen, J., Gamper, H., Alene, H.: Analyzing emotional semantics of abstract art using low-level image features. In: Gama, J., Bradley, E., Hollmén, J. (eds.) IDA 2011. LNCS, vol. 7014, pp. 413–423. Springer, Heidelberg (2011). doi:10.1007/978-3-642-24800-9_38
22. Zimmermann, P., et al.: Affective computing – a rationale for measuring mood with mouse and keyboard. Int. J. Occup. Saf. Ergon. **9**(4), 539–551 (2003)

A Recommender System for Political Information Filtering

Kevin Lim[1], Chunghwan Kim[1], Gangsan Kim[1],
and Hyebong Choi[2(✉)]

[1] School of Computer Science and Electronic Engineering,
Handong Global University, Pohang, South Korea
klim6263@gmail.com, obparkl@naver.com,
21000048@handong.edu
[2] School of Creative Convergence Education,
Handong Global University, Pohang, South Korea
hbchoi@handong.edu

Abstract. Recommender system has been widely used and showcased its successful stories in e-business area for the last decade. It assists in making profits within a lot of companies by recommending their products that the customers would be interested in. Compared to many successful stories in e-business and industries, however, a recommender system has not been fully exploited in non-profit activities where people need information that is unbiased, accurate, up-to-date and mostly relevant to their interest, especially in politics. Even though choosing a right candidate with appropriate and accurate information is required to voters, it is not easy for them to keep up with the political issues due to the massive amounts of online media and its speed. To address these issues, we suggest a politician recommender system by using two widely used filtering: collaborative filtering and content-based filtering.

In order to build the recommendation system, we first collect public profile of current congress members in Korea and people's preference ratings to these politicians. These data are preprocessed and used in filtering methods to recommend politicians that a user would be favorable for. We compare the experimental results, and combine the two filtering whether the hybrid approach shows better performance than two individual methods. We anticipate this saves people's time and effort to obtain information to support their decision and makes people actively participate in political issues.

Keywords: Recommendation system · Data mining · Content-based filtering · Collaborative filtering

1 Introduction

Making a prudent and careful decision in political activities such as election would be substantially important to the people and the society for democratic countries to be ones of the people, for the people, and by the people. Compared to the tangible benefit, it takes substantial time and effort as well for them to obtain unbiased, up-to-date and accurate information to support their decision. It is due to the massive volume, speed,

A. Marcus and W. Wang (Eds.): DUXU 2017, Part III, LNCS 10290, pp. 129–145, 2017.
DOI: 10.1007/978-3-319-58640-3_11

variety of information that on/off-line mass media produce in every single minute. It may lead people to find easier way to make their decision with partial impression and gossip rather than focusing on intrinsic values before making decision that might change their life seriously.

To help this issue, it would be a sagacious choice to use a recommender system that filters the "Big Data" to find them out essential, unbiased, and accurate information. In this paper, we suggest an elaborate recommender system that reveals political information unbiased and closely-related to users in accordance with personal interest and inclination has been proposed. Recommender system is a system that recommends information in which a certain user has his or her own interests in the presence of too much information. In this study, it is expected that people are able to save their time and effort to obtain information to support their decision and to actively participate in political issues via the system that combines both collaborative filtering and content-based filtering algorithm.

Collaborative Filtering uses other people's evaluations to filter information. The basic idea is that people are interested in an item which other like-minded users. In contrast, the Content-based Filtering method provides recommendations by matching customer's profiles with content features. Content-based Filtering shows recommendations in the order of results measured by the similarity between users' area of interest and contents of items. Users indicate their opinions of how they think of the behavior of politicians via ratings. Hence, for this study, a survey made by 202 users' ratings about 300 politicians is used as the collected data, and the collaborative filtering correlates these numerical preferences with those of the other users to determine how to make future predictions. Also, collaborative filtering shares the ratings with others so that they can use them in making their own predictions. With this data, collaborative filtering applied by Cosine similarity is used, and to determine optimized the number of politicians recommended, the K-Nearest Neighbor algorithm has been applied. Cosine similarity is a measure to calculate the similarity among users with cosine values between two vectors of the groups, and it is applied only to the group for those who have sufficient number of record for politician preference. KNN algorithm gives K number of other highly similar neighbors, combining with users' profiles such as political orientation so that it can provide more accurate recommendation [1]. However, in the case that there is not sufficient number of users' preference data, we call it "Cold Start Problem." It degrades the recommendation quality. To mitigate the problem, content-based filtering is exploited, and it requires Jaccard similarity method due to the group for those who lack of preference records. It represents similarity among sets of binary data in terms of groups.

With comprehensive experiments in the study, two existing filtering methods with the one proposed above are compared. Since collaborative filtering with rating-based data via abundant data and content-based filtering with users' property-based data to overcome data scarcity, also called cold start problem, have been tested, Hybrid Filtering method that is mixture of collaborative and content-based filtering is suitable to politician recommender system.

2 Preliminaries

2.1 Dataset Description

User's Preference Data for Current Congress Members in Korea
We collect users' preference data of 300 politicians via surveys proceeded in mainly two terms, which were November 2016 and January 2017. Every user can do survey only once, and in every survey, there are totally 300 politicians who belong to different parties in South Korea. Users rate politicians on the scale of 1(very dissatisfaction) to 5 (very satisfaction), and they just rate politicians whom they know well due to more accuracy in a recommender system. In November 2016, which is the first term, we conducted online surveys of the preference about 300 congress members with 40 users in all age group. We gave a survey to every user so that he or she rated politicians whom they know well among 300 politicians. After that, we combined all surveys from 40 users, and Table 1 illustrates a part of the rating table combined with all surveys about 300 politicians as items by 40 users.

Table 1. Sample of a rating table with 40 users for 300 politicians

User	Item				
	Politician A	Politician B	Politician C	Politician D	Politician E
User 1	NA	NA	NA	NA	NA
User 2	NA	4	NA	NA	3
User 3	NA	3	3	NA	2
User 4	NA	3	3	NA	NA
User 5	NA	NA	NA	NA	NA
User 6	NA	3	NA	NA	NA
User 7	NA	NA	NA	NA	NA
User 8	NA	NA	NA	NA	NA
User 9	NA	1	3	NA	3
User 10	NA	3	NA	NA	NA

According to Table 1, NA represents a case when a user, who does not know a politician, ignores rating the politician. After the first data collection from 40 users, we decided to use 114 politicians for the second term of surveys because 114 politicians are only congress members who are rated by two or more users, and we need only this type of group to improve accuracy during evaluation of the recommender system. Through online surveys during the second term conducted in January 2017, we collected the data from 163 users of all age group on the preference of these 114 politicians. After the surveys, Table 2 is made by 195 users for 114 politicians. The reason for totally 195 users instead of 163 users is that we combined surveys of 40 users during the first term with surveys of 163 users during the second term, and we removed 8 users who did not rate at all and who rated only one politician during the surveys. This first data cleaning makes the recommender system more efficient in accurate recommendations with less error in evaluations.

Table 2. Rating table with 195 users

	Politician A	Politician B	Politician C	Politician D
User 183	0	2	0	0
User 184	0	2	0	0
User 185	0	1	0	0
User 186	2	4	5	3
User 187	0	1	0	0
User 188	0	1	0	0
User 189	0	4	0	0
User 190	3	2	0	4
User 191	5	4	0	3
User 192	0	2	0	0
User 193	0	1	0	2
User 194	0	3	2	3
User 195	0	2	5	5

Public Profile of Current Congress Members in Korea

In order to build a content-based recommendation system, we need items' attributes, so we collect the public profile of current congress members in Korea by using web-scraping from the website that monitors legislative activities. We obtain the item (politician) attributes matrix as described in Table 3. We decide to recommend a politician based on politician's attributes with five categories: Political Career, Standing Committee, Political Orientation, Specialization, and Military Service. In fact, there are sixteen standing committee in National Assembly of Korea, but we classify them into eight areas by considering their relevance as described in Table 4.

Party 1 is a ruling party and conservative. Party 2 is the first opposition party with the most seats and progressive. Party 3 is a moderate political party holding a casting vote. Political career is a standard that indicates whether a politician is a first-time member of National Assembly. In South Korea, every Korean man has to fulfill his

Table 3. Description of attributes matrix of congress members

Name	Party	Political career	Standing committee	Political orientation	Specialization	Military service
Politician A	Party 1	Two or more	Jurisdiction, culture and science	Conservative	Lawyer	Finished
Politician B	Party 3	Two or more	State affairs	Moderate	Police	Excepted
Politician C	Party 2	New	Welfare, jurisdiction, state affairs, society and economy	Progressive	Lawyer	Excluded (female)
Politician D	Party 3	New	Culture and science, state affairs	Moderate	Lawyer	Finished
Politician E	Party 3	New	Welfare, state affairs	Moderate	Politics	Finished
Politician F	Party 3	Two or more	Welfare, society and economy	Conservative	Public officer	Finished

Table 4. Description of standing committees in South Korea and their decision-making coverage.

Standing committee	Decision-making coverage	Classified
National defense	National defense	National security
Intelligence	National information	
Strategy and finance	Financial and economic policies	Society and economy
Trade, industry and energy	Trade, industry and energy	
Agriculture, food, rural affairs, oceans and fisheries	Agriculture, food, rural affairs, oceans and fisheries	
House steering	Matters concerning the operation of the national assembly	State affairs
Land, infrastructure and transport	Land, infrastructure and transport	
Security and public administration	Internal administration and election	
National policy	Political affairs	
Foreign affairs and unification	Foreign affairs and unification	Foreign and unification
Legislation and judiciary	Review and supervise matters concerning judicial institutions	Jurisdiction
Science, ICT, future planning, broadcasting and communications	Science, technology and broadcasting communication	Culture and science
Education, culture, sports and tourism	Education, culture, sports and tourism	
Environment and labor	Environment and labor	Environment and labor
Gender equality and family	Gender equality and family	Welfare
Health and welfare	Health and welfare	

duty of military service. However, some people do not have the duty of it for some reasons such as illness or difficulty in living. On the other hand, women are excluded from military service obligations.

2.2   Recommender System and Application

A recommender system is a system that guesses and recommends particular items that a user would prefer via information filtering among massive amount of information. The definition of filtering, one of the IT terms, is a technique to pick appropriate items out of various contents. There are mainly two algorithms used in a recommender system, which are an algorithm called collaborative filtering and an algorithm called content-based filtering.

The collaborative filtering filters information by using recommendations of other people. It is based on the idea that people who agreed with their evaluation of certain items in the past are likely to agree again in the future. In this type of recommendation, filtering items from a large set of alternatives is done collaboratively between users' preferences. The collaborative filtering only considers user preferences and does not take account of the features or contents of the items being recommended [2]. The collaborative filtering leads to an advantage in which this approach requires a large set of user preferences for more accurate results [2]. When more abundant data in terms of users and items has been collected, this filtering exploits better showcases of recommendation. In collaborative filtering, there are two variants of algorithms to approach, which are user-based collaborative algorithm and item-based collaborative algorithm.

User-based collaborative algorithm, also called memory-based algorithm, uses the whole user database to create recommendations by analyzing rating data from many individuals [1]. This algorithm gives a target user recommendation, which is also preferred by similar users. There is an assumption that similar users do rate similarly. However, the user-based collaborative filtering has some limitations. One is that it is difficult to measure the similarities between users because the size of data for making the recommender system keeps changing, so it is hard to find the optimal similarities. The other is the scalability issue. As the number of users and items increases, the computation time of the algorithm grows exponentially, thus it makes the system slower [3].

Item-based collaborative algorithm, also called model-based algorithm, produces recommendations based on the relationship between items inferred from the rating matrix [1]. In this algorithm, there is an assumption, which represents that users prefer items similar to other items they like. As item-based collaborative algorithm calculates similar items, it is proposed to overcome the scalability, which is a limitation of user-based algorithm. However, an issue is the ratings, which include some discrete values, and these ratings cannot provide much information about relationship between users and items [3].

In terms of collaborative filtering, if the size of information increases, accuracy of the recommender system is also improved. However, there is still an issue when using collaborative filtering only. The issue is called cold start problem, and it occurs in a case of the sparsity of information available in the recommendation algorithm. Even though the collaborative filtering has the cold start problem, the content-based filtering has a solution of this issue because it does not rely on users' preferences data for items.

Content-based filtering is a filtering method that recommends items based on similarity between user's profile and the contents of the items, so it basically recommends items that are similar to those that the user has bought or liked in the past. We can define the process of content-based filtering in three steps. First, it analyzes and categorizes items' attributes. Second, it retrieves user's profile based on user's interests or purchases of items. Third, it calculates the similarity between items and the user's profile in order to recommend the items to the user [2]. For example, in a movie recommendation system, the database contains the attributes of each movie such as genre, director, stars, and studio. If a user watched a movie 'Avatar' and rated high scores, the system would build this user's profile considering the attributes of the movie 'Avatar'. Then, the system recommends movies that have similar attributes to the user's profile.

Content-based filtering does not have cold start problem, since it does not require other customers' data to recommend items to users. This method can begin the recommendation as long as there is enough information about the items and the users in the database. On the other hand, this method has some disadvantages: limited content analysis and over-specialization. Limited content analysis refers to the situation where the recommendation's performance is not precise and poor due to a lack of attributes representing the items. Over-specialization, also known as serendipity problem, means that content-based filtering only recommends items within its expected range, so there would be no surprise recommendation that is not similar to the user's profile [4].

To build recommendations using both collaborative and content-based filtering algorithm, two similarity methods within neighboring range has to be calculated. First, collaborative algorithm requires calculation of similarity in order to predict the missing ratings based on neighborhood of either similar users or items. The range of neighborhood is measured via similarity between users or items, and there are two ways of measuring the similarity, which are Pearson correlation coefficient and the Cosine similarity. Pearson correlation coefficient is [2] a popular correlation coefficient calculated between two variables as the covariance of the two variables or users divided by the product of their standard deviations, and this is given by ρ (rho):

$$\rho_{X,Y} = \frac{cov(X, Y)}{\sigma_X \sigma_Y}$$

Cosine similarity is [2] a measure of similarity between two vectors or users of an inner product space that measures the cosine of the angle between them, and the equation is given by

$$similarity = \cos(\theta) = \frac{A \cdot B}{\|A\|\|B\|}$$

X, Y in Pearson correlation coefficient and A, B in cosine similarity denote the row vectors between two users. The range of both similarity methods is from −1 to 1. The value of negative one represents lowest similarity while the value of positive one is representing highest similarity. Higher similarity indicates closer relationship between two users. Second, for content-based filtering algorithm, Jaccard's coefficient is applied. Jaccard's coefficient is a measurement of similarity between binary sets of variables, and it is defined as the intersection of two data sets divided by their union. It becomes higher when the two data sets have more attributes in common.

$$Jaccard\ Coefficient(A, B) = \frac{|A \cap B|}{|A \cup B|}$$

Jaccard distance is a measurement of how dissimilar the two sets are, and the formula is [5]

$$Jaccard\ Distance(A, B) = 1 - Jaccard\ Coefficient(A, B) = \frac{|A \cup B| - |A \cap B|}{|A \cup B|}$$

2.3   Evaluation Metrics

Classification Accuracy Metrics

A confusion matrix [6] is a matrix which contains information about actual and predicted classifications, as described in Table 5.

Table 5. Confusion matrix with actual and predicted classifications

		Predicted	
		Negative	Positive
Actual	Negative	True negative	False positive
	Positive	False negative	True positive

Several standard terms have been defined as follows:

- The **accuracy (AC)** is the proportion of the total number of correct predictions. It is determined using the equation:

$$AC = \frac{TP + TN}{TP + TN + FP + FN}$$

- The **recall** is the proportion of positive cases that were correctly identified, as calculated using the equation:

$$Recall = \frac{TP}{TP + FN}$$

- The **precision** is the proportion of the predicted positive cases that were correct, as calculated using the equation:

$$Precision = \frac{TP}{TP + FP}$$

- The **F-measure** is the harmonic mean of precision and recall, as calculated using the equation:

$$F\text{-measure} = \frac{2\,Precision\,Recall}{Precision + Recall} = \frac{2}{1/Precision + 1/Recall}$$

ROC graphs are the way besides confusion matrices to examine the performance of classifiers. A ROC graph is a plot with the false positive rate on the X axis and the true positive rate on the Y axis [6]. The area under the curve means accuracy (Fig. 1).

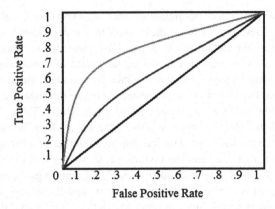

True Positive Rate

False Positive Rate

Fig. 1. ROC curve grap

Predictive Accuracy Metrics

Let y_i denote the ith observation and $\hat{y}_i$ denote a forecast of y_i. The forecast error is simply $e_i = y_i - \hat{y}_i$, and accuracy is measured based on e_i. The two most commonly used measures are based on the squared errors or absolute errors [7]:

$$\text{Root mean squared error: RMSE} = \sqrt{mean(e_i^2)},$$
$$\text{Mean absolute error: MAE} = mean(|e_i|).$$

The **root mean squared error (RMSE)** is the square root of the mean squared error. This is the statistic whose value is minimized during the parameter estimation process, and it is the statistic that settles the width of the confidence intervals for predictions.

The **mean absolute error (MAE)** is also measured in the same units as the data, but slightly smaller than, the root mean squared error. It is less sensitive to the occasional very large error because it does not square the errors in the calculation.

3 Methodology

3.1 Preprocessing

For both collaborative and content-based filtering, Table 2, which is a rating table with 195 users for 114 items or politicians, is mainly applied. However, if we just use the same rating table for both filtering algorithms, then optimized recommendations cannot be showcased because they basically use different similarity methods. According to the definition of filtering algorithms, collaborative filtering derives optimized recommendation mostly when enough items exist. On the other hand, content-based filtering is required when a scarcity of items occurs. To reduce this cold start problem, we specify a threshold of the amounts of items defining a word 'enough' so that we combine content-based filtering with collaborative filtering. However, data with few items rated by users degrades the system effect. To prevent this degradation, we assume that users who rated less than 10 items or politicians distract our experiment, and we thus make a new rating table by removing lists of these users in our experiment.

We convert the rating table into both real rating matrix and binary rating matrix. The real rating matrix is used in calculating similarity of collaborative filtering. In content-based filtering, we use Jaccard distance to calculate the similarity between items and users, and two binary datasets are needed to use this measure. The first binary dataset is acquired by transforming the item description matrix, Table 3, into the binary form as described in Table 6. This is a part of the binary form because there are 26 attributes in the item matrix. Each item has different number of attributes because they can belong to more than one standing committee, so we divided the each attribute by the square root of the total number of attributes of that item to give equal weights. The second binary dataset is a user profile binary matrix, and it is retrieved by combining the user's rating matrix and Table 6 in order to calculate the Jaccard distance between the items and the users. The user profile binary matrix is demonstrated in Table 7.

Table 6. Binary form of attributes matrix of congress members

Name	Society and economy	Culture and science	Welfare	State affairs	Jurisdiction	Progressive	Conservative	Moderate
Politician A	0	1	0	0	1	0	1	0
Politician B	0	0	0	1	0	0	0	1
Politician C	1	0	1	1	1	1	0	0

Table 7. Binary matrix for user-item (politician)

Item	User							
	User 1	User 2	User 3	User 4	User 5	User 6	User 7	User 8
Politician A	0	0	-1	-1	0	0	0	0
Politician B	0	0	0	-1	0	-1	0	0
Politician C	0	0	1	1	0	-1	0	0
Politician D	0	-1	-1	-1	0	-1	-1	-1
Politician E	0	0	1	1	0	-1	1	0

We normalize the user's rating matrix because different users have different criteria in rating items, and retrieve the user's profile for 26 attributes based on their preferences for politicians. In this method, we assume that a user is interested in attributes that belong to a politician whom he or she prefers. With this assumption, we obtain the user's profile from the user's preference data for the politicians and their attributes.

For collaborative filtering, it produces the recommendations based on the relationship between items or users inferred from the rating matrix. To reduce user-bias or item-bias problem, we first normalize the user-item rating matrix before computing similarity. We use a package *recommenderlab* in R language, which includes normalization in center basis.

With user-item real rating matrix, we make a tuple form reshaping the original data by *melt* function in R language in order to improve accuracy in evaluation. While the real rating matrix is composed of rows with users who rated items, the tuple consists of three columns, which are User, Politician, and Rating. If we use the user-item matrix, we use each row as a vector form when analyzing data in programming. However, if we use user-item-rating tuple as an object, we can easily proceed the experiment. Table 8 illustrates the tuple form with three columns of different contents in R language.

Table 8. Tuple of user-item-rating

User	Politician	Rating
2	Politician A	1
2	Politician B	4
2	Politician C	3
2	Politician D	2
2	Politician E	1
2	Politician F	5

3.2   Recommendation Model

A basic idea is that we build two types of recommender systems, which include collaborative filtering via *recommenderlab* and content-based filtering in R language. Before using the rating table for either real rating matrix or binary matrix, the table should be normalized to improve recommendations, and *recommenderlab* provides automatic calculation of normalization based on center in UBCF and IBCF methods. In contrast, since there is not any recommendation package in content-based filtering, we normalized each object directly. Depending on threshold of information, it is determined that which algorithm is applied to the boundary of the data. To set up the certain amount of 'enough' information, we find a boundary between two filtering algorithms to elicit optimized outcome.

Baseline Model
Using a *POPULAR* method in *recommenderlab*, we design a baseline model that recommends the most popular politicians that showed up in the user-rating matrix most frequently. Having a solid baseline based on the popularity makes it possible to identify why content-based and collaborative filtering are better than the baseline. Therefore, the baseline model is a tool of getting the optimized performance via both content-based filtering and collaborative filtering.

Defining the Training and Test Sets
We separate the entire data formed by tuples into two sets: training and test sets. The two sets are as follows:

Training set: This set includes users for the model to learn
Test set: This set includes users whom we recommend politicians.

To evaluate the model, we randomly split the data into training set and test set with fixed ratio of 8:2. The training set is used to train the model in collaborative filtering. To make better performance in collaborative filtering model, optimal training set is required, and we found out that randomly sampling 80% of the entire data is the best condition to make a training set due to sparsity of the information. The test set is to evaluate the performance of both collaborative and content-based filtering.

Application of Collaborative Filtering and Content-Based Filtering

In collaborative filtering, there are two ways to calculate similarity, which are cosine similarity and Pearson correlation coefficient. Comparing two methods, we observed which similarity method is the best fit for pursuing the most optimal recommender system. Figure 2 shows the comparison between Cosine similarity and Pearson correlation coefficient.

In Fig. 2, IBCF stands for item-based collaborative filtering, and UBCF stands for user-based collaborative filtering. According to the Fig. 2, regardless of which type of collaborative filtering is applied, a filtering used with cosine similarity shows better performance than a filtering used with Pearson correlation coefficient. Therefore, finding the optimal neighborhood is integrated by cosine similarity in Collaborative filtering. In content-based filtering, however, Jaccard distance similarity is calculated to measure the distance between two binary sets.

After making a decision of which similarity method is applied to, we do data cleaning work to find the threshold of 'enough' information because we can make a

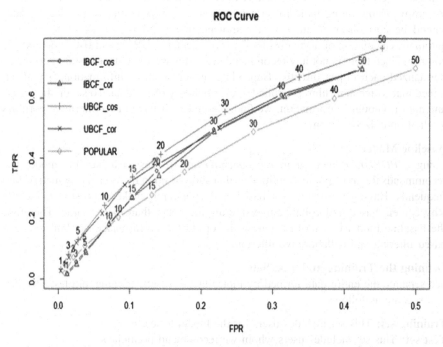

Fig. 2. IBCF and UBCF graph with cosine similarity and Pearson correlation coefficient

choice of which model has to be applied for outstanding recommendations at the boundary. Data cleaning work is done by a number of experiments of evaluation. To set up the boundary between collaborative filtering and content-based filtering, *F-measure* is applied after Top-N closest neighbors or politicians are recommended to a user. N is the number of items recommended to the user. Also, we check how precisely and correctly each model recommends items compared to baseline model.

Within the area of collaborative filtering, in order to compare the performance of user-based filtering to that of item-based filtering, we use *RMSE* and *MAE* figure in evaluation. *RMSE* and *MAE* show the efficiency of each algorithm by demonstrating a fact that lower value refers to less error detected, and the fact represents the better performance in the system. In our experiment, we prove that which model within collaborative filtering area shows the best function via *RMSE* and *MAE*.

4 Result and Discussion

Evaluation Measure
We proved that content-based filtering is essential for a group that consists of users who did not rate enough items, and collaborative filtering is necessary for a group that consists of users who rated enough items. After we removed a group of users who rated less than 10 politicians for more accuracy in preprocessing, we defined how 'enough' information or data is reliable. Table 9 shows the performance evaluation to compare each model to the baseline model, which is written POPULAR in the table. N represents the number of politicians recommended to users. CBF stands for content-based filtering.

According to the Table 9, the *F-measure* is measured via a group of users who rated 10 to 40 politicians. In this experiment, user-based collaborative filtering and content-based filtering outperformed the popularity-based model because all *F-measures* are higher than those of the baseline. Another observation is that *F-measures* with content-based filtering provide the better performance than those with collaborative filtering.

Table 9. F-measure average with comparison both UBCF and CBF to POPULAR

N	UBCF	POPULAR	CBF
10	0.243012	0.214243	0.332091
11	0.248496	0.211481	0.316799
12	0.239636	0.209155	0.302887
13	0.240742	0.204241	0.348843
14	0.239034	0.213361	0.356697
15	0.235963	0.205829	0.354188
16	0.232032	0.204934	0.356026
17	0.226061	0.204575	0.350058
18	0.219688	0.1984	0.32345
19	0.215003	0.193966	0.318362
20	0.209113	0.194544	0.314459

For the most optimized scale of N, which is the number of recommended politicians, we used Table 8. According to the Table 8, positive values represent that users relatively prefer politicians, but negative values represent that users do not prefer politicians. We observed that the average number of positive values where every user relatively prefers is about 10 politicians, and we concluded that the best scale of N is between 10 and 20. Figure 3 illustrates the superior performance of content-based filtering compared to other two models when recommending between 10 and 20 politicians with users who rated between 10 and 40 politicians.

However, for data cleaning based on the users who rated more than 40 politicians, collaborative filtering showed outstanding performance than the content based filtering in terms of recommendations among users who rated more than 40 politicians, Fig. 3 describes a graph for Table 10.

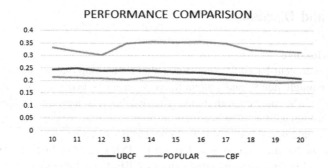

Fig. 3. Graph for comparison of the performance between two filtering model

Table 10. F-measures of 3 recommendation models

N	UBCF	POPULAR	CBF
25	0.546558	0.474066	0.370602
30	0.575327	0.511171	0.40977
35	0.598693	0.535087	0.432486
40	0.618448	0.561064	0.446404
45	0.631795	0.584981	0.457378

Since we have known that the average number of politicians who are rated positively by the users is about 37, we decided to make the scale of N from 25 to 45 as the number of recommended politicians.

According to Fig. 4, with higher performance of UBCF compared to CBF, we recognized that using UBCF is more efficient than using CBF within the threshold of more than 40 politicians rated by users. Also, we concluded that the threshold between collaborative and content-based filtering is about 40 politicians or items.

After a result that collaborative filtering makes higher performance than content-based filtering in data cleaning based on users who rated more than 40 politicians, we observed that which filtering algorithm in collaborative filtering exploits

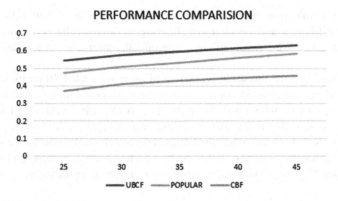

Fig. 4. Graph of performance comparison with more than 40 politicians

better outcomes. We proved that user-based filtering showcases less error than item-based filtering, which indicates that UBCF derives better function than IBCF. According to Table 11, after calculating the error via RMSE and MAE, we proved that user-based algorithm shows the better performance with less error value than item-based algorithm (Fig. 5).

Table 11. Accuracy between UBCF and IBCF

	RMSE	MAE
IBCF	1.052119	0.741415
UBCF	0.957778	0.679757
POPULAR	1.031537	0.779242

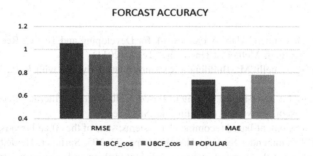

Fig. 5. Graph of RMSE and MAE for collaborative filtering methods

Result and Discussion

According to the experiments, we observed that there was not enough preference data to build a user's profile in terms of content-based filtering for users who rated less than 10 politicians. Also, in collaborative filtering, we removed the group of the users in order to prevent the degradation of the performance due to the scarcity of data.

After the elimination of the group, we realized that it is better to use both content-based filtering and collaborative filtering to improve the performance of the recommendations. We measured the appropriate threshold proceeded via the experiments.

We observed that the threshold is a group of users who rated 40 politicians. Based on the boundary, we applied content-based filtering algorithm into making recommendations for users who rated the politicians below the threshold. The optimal number of recommended politicians in content-based filtering was 10 to 20 politicians. On the other hand, for users who rated politicians above the threshold, we concluded that using collaborative filtering shows the best performance of recommendations with 25 to 45 politicians as the optimal number of recommended politicians.

5 Conclusion and Future Work

Through these experiments, we have confirmed that recommendations of items reflecting the users' profile and their preferences have improved the performance of the recommendation system. At the same time, however, there are some challenges to implementing a more accurate recommendation system. First, we expect that the system will produce a higher performance if the user's actual preference data for item attributes is reflected when building the user's profile in content-based filtering. Also, the data with about 200 users is insufficient for the recommendation system to achieve satisfactory performance. If a preference data with more users is collected, then it will also contribute to more accurate recommendations.

Our research can be used as a tool that can lead to a sagacious political decision-making and active political participation in democratic society for the future.

References

1. Hahsler, M.: recommenderlab: A Framework for Developing and Testing Recommendation Algorithms. Southern Methodist University, Texas (2011)
2. Gorakala, S.K., Usuelli, M.: Building a Recommendation System with R. Packt Publishing, Birmingham (2015)
3. Yao, G., Cai, L.: User-Based and Item-Based Collaborative Filtering Recommendation Algorithms Design. University of California, San Diego
4. Lops, P., et al.: Content-based recommender systems: state of the art and trends. In: Ricci, F., et al. (eds.) Recommender Systems Handbook, pp. 73–105. Springer, Heidelberg (2011)
5. Niwattanakul, S., et al.: Using of Jaccard coefficient for keywords similarity. Paper presented at International MultiConference of Engineers and Computer Scientists, Hong Kong, 13–15 March 2013
6. Hamilton, H.J.: Knowledge Discovery in Databases. University of Regina School of Computer Science (2012). http://www2.cs.uregina.ca/~dbd/cs831/index.html. Accessed 10 Feb 2017
7. Hyndman, R.J., Athanasopoulos, G.: Forecasting: principles and practice. OTexts (2013). https://www.otexts.org/fpp/2/5. Accessed 10 Feb 2017

8. Barragáns-Martínez, A.B., et al.: A hybrid content-based and item-based collaborative filtering approach to recommend TV programs enhanced with singular value decomposition. Inf. Sci. **180**(22), 4290–4311 (2010)
9. Kim, C.I., et al.: On the development of a course recommender system: a hybrid filtering approach. Entrue J. Inf. Technol. **14**(2), 71–82 (2015)
10. Shani, G., et al.: Evaluating Recommendation Systems. Microsoft Research (2009)
11. Wang, R.: Building a Movie Recommendation Engine with R (2015). https://muffynomster. wordpress.com/2015/06/07/building-a-movie-recommendation-engine-with-r/. Accessed 10 Feb 2017
12. Suh, B.W.: Development of Content Recommendation System Algorithm. Broadcasting Trend & Insight, vol. 5 (2016)
13. Information of 300 Politicians. http://watch.peoplepower21.org/. Accessed 10 Feb 2017

Look at My Face: A New Home Screen User Interface

Young Hoon Oh and Da Young Ju$^{(\boxtimes)}$

School of Integrated Technology, Yonsei Institute of Convergence Technology,
Yonsei University, Incheon, Republic of Korea
{50hoon, dyju}@yonsei.ac.kr

Abstract. Smartphone Technology grew up with mobile application. Mobile applications help users to conveniently access useful services. To instantly access desired information, bunch of apps are placed on the home screen which results in the visually complex user interface. In this paper, due to the lack of literature on wallpaper, we investigated which types of wallpaper people choose on their devices. We examined more than 200 participants for specific reasons of setting wallpaper and asked whether people concern the wallpaper occlusion. Based on the survey result, we present the prototype of home screen user interface which automatically organize objects on the screen. Additionally, we conducted focus group interview to get deeper insights on wallpaper and our prototype. Implicit meanings of setting wallpaper were covered. Finally, we discuss several implications of the prototype and limitation of the study.

Keywords: Wallpaper · Icon · User interface · Home screen

1 Introduction

User interface (UI) of the desktop environment is designed with the assumption that users stay in a limited space when using their device, while mobile device users are generally in motion and access their devices at various places. Due to the mobility and portability of mobile devices, they have a touchscreen as an alternative to the traditional PC interface such as mouse, keyboard, or pen. Therefore, the HCI community has conducted research on the method of improving the usability of touchscreen UI [1].

Existing mobile devices provide thousands of useful services through Google Play and Apple's App Store. More than 1.2 million apps are available on these platforms [2], and on average 26 apps are used on smartphone [3]. Downloaded apps are arranged in the form of an icon, widget, or browser shortcut on the grid-structured home screen. Despite these PC-like layout leveraging the familiarity and usability of the UI, little is understood so far about the home screen UI and how users arrange these objects.

Home screen UI is related to both usability and aesthetics because touching icons is the primary method of using smartphone. Home screen consists of the following elements. (i) Wallpaper on the background layer gives a first impression and creates the atmosphere of the visual interface. Therefore, most systems allow users to change the wallpaper to their favorite image. (ii) Icons and folders represent their functions, and users communicate with their device through an icon-arrayed interface. (iii) "Widgets

© Springer International Publishing AG 2017
A. Marcus and W. Wang (Eds.): DUXU 2017, Part III, LNCS 10290, pp. 146–163, 2017.
DOI: 10.1007/978-3-319-58640-3_12

provide small self-contained UIs for self-updating data" [4]. This reduces the amount of unnecessary steps needed to check information. (iv) Shortcuts enable users to launch specific webpages restrictively. All these elements contribute to the usability and constitute what is called a launcher.

Since smartphone launchers are highly customizable, users personalize the arrangement of these objects as well as the wallpaper [5, 6]. Personalization may result in a scene in which icons are spoiling the image as a whole. Although there are common intuitions and beliefs that people care about the aesthetics [7] of interfaces, there is little published research on the mismatch between the wallpaper and the objects on the home/lock screen interface. So far, we have not been able to support the personalization process and improve the usability of the interface. Important questions remain unanswered, such as whether people are concerned with the harmony of the wallpaper and icon arrangement. What is the actual purpose of setting wallpaper? It is unknown whether manually arranging icons influences usability. This paper contributes to the understanding of people's practices when customizing UI elements. We quantitatively investigate the users' concepts when setting wallpaper. For the design of a high-usability UI, we discuss the implications of our statistical results. We present our prototype of home screen UI, which harmoniously arranges objects according to the wallpaper image. Additionally, focus group interview (FGI) was followed to deepen our findings from the survey.

2 Related Work

2.1 Usability and Aesthetics

Usability has long been researched and it is generally defined as "the extent to which a product can be used by specified users to achieve specified goals with effectiveness, efficiency and satisfaction" [8]. Various factors can influence on usability; reducing errors with a careful graphic UI [9], context [10] or allowing configurable systems [11] may improve usability. Lee et al. [12] and Longoria [13] emphasized that learnability is essential for the mobile application. "Increasing importance is now given to the interface look and feel" [14]. Tractinsky et al. [15] showed a novel view on usability that the perceived aesthetics of the system is closely correlated with the perceived usability. Various reviews supported that context [14], combinations of color [16], or font [17] influence the user preference of a system. Mobile device is no exception. Specifically regarding the design of mobile apps, Clark [18] noted that an app icon should be aesthetic and identifiable because it is the only way to launch the app. Aesthetic factors may contribute to the overall success of a product or systems [19].

2.2 Icon Arrangement and Wallpaper

Research on users' practices for organizing icons, menus, or information was initiated from desktop domain. Barreau and Nardi [20] found that users preferred location-based searching to text-based searching on PC because people put icons at special places as a reminder. Ravasio et al. [21] investigated the practices of classifying documents from desktop users and identified that they organize documents by their types. In contrast to the continued research on PCs, it seems that HCI community has little focused on icon arrangement and wallpaper in the mobile domain. Recently Chen [22] conducted research about user preference on application (app) icon design and its influence on recognition, though the author only dealt with stylization of icon. To the best of our knowledge, research on users' practices for organizing app icons is limited to Böhmer and Bauer They presented the objective of a context-aware recommendation system [23, 24] based on the user's icon arrangement. Their pioneering work extended to the large-scale study on mobile app usage—which apps people use and how much time people spend on using apps [25]. Finally, the authors researched how people organize apps and found that people apply several concepts to arranging icons: usage frequency, relatedness, usability, aesthetics, and external concepts [4]. Although Böhmer and Bauer [24] implemented context-adaptive UI, there was little research on wallpaper and its integration with objects on the home screen. Therefore, from the next session, we will look back on the UI of commercial products and propose the new concept of interface based on the findings from literature and commercial products.

2.3   Current Home Screen User Interface

There are many commercial launchers available on popular mobile devices (e.g. TouchWiz by Samsung Electronics) and on app markets such as custom launchers, themes, and other decoration tools to help users customize UI elements (e.g., Go Launcher EX, Nova Launcher on Google Play). Personalizing an interface simply is required, while little scientific insight has been generated on the user practices of setting wallpapers or icon arrangement. Review of the usability or aesthetics of diverse manufacturer-customized interfaces has not been attempted either. Therefore, by analyzing representative smartphones' home screen UIs (Android OS on Fig. 1 and iOS on Fig. 2), we found that they have two shortcomings that may worsen the visual experience from the home screen:

Fig. 1. Examples of *Visual Incongruity* on smartphone

1. When setting wallpapers, current smartphones do not provide real-time screen previews (Fig. 2). Users must check the phone screen every time to see whether the objects and photo are harmonized.
2. We need to redesign existing home screen UIs which have no organic interaction between the objects and wallpaper (e.g., icon arrangement does not affect wallpaper settings and vice versa). The lack of an integrated UI results in an inharmonic appearance, which means that the wallpaper is entirely covered with objects. In this paper, we define this as "*Visual Incongruity.*" Figure 1 is the representative case of *Visual Incongruity* because users are not able to view the desired image, which not only damages the aesthetics of the device, but also causes users to modify the UI settings.

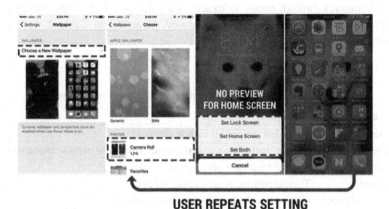

USER REPEATS SETTING

Fig. 2. Wallpaper setting in iOS

3 Survey of Wallpaper

Little is known about the wallpaper adoption and user behavior on wallpaper. No detailed prototype or solution has been presented yet. This led us to conduct a survey on wallpaper because we cannot develop solution without user practices of mobile UIs. We believed that the subsequent quantitative approach might provide us with design guideline of the new way to unravel the problems. For instance, if users prefer selfie as wallpaper, UI elements should not occlude faces. Thus our goal is to investigate wallpaper adoption quantitatively and to find whether or not users are concerned with *Visual Incongruity.*

3.1 Survey Design

The survey was conducted through online (197 participants) and offline (15 participants) with an identical design. Both were carried out from January 30 2015 to February 5 2015 and November 26 to 27. About 10% of participants were offered a gift compensation of about $4 but six participants who refused to fill in phone number were not rewarded. Except for the demographic investigation, four questions were asked. Descriptions of each part are:

Part 1. Demographics: We describe the survey participants.
Part 2. Distribution of home screens wallpaper and reasons. Among dozens of photos, we summarized them as the eight categories after several pilot studies. Pilot studies were conducted to verify the survey design, and we noticed that participants were confused to check the type of image. For instance, they had trouble deciding whether their wallpaper (e.g. 'default') was 'pattern' or 'retouched'. Therefore, we had to exactly define the category as shown on Table 1. We noticed users to mark 'photoswithface' if there were a face on their wallpaper. Considering non-tech savvy users, reference images were given right after investigating demographic information. We sent questionnaires through online to exactly show images. For offline survey participants, the images were black-and-white printed. Reasons on Table 2 were revised several times in the same way.

Table 1. Wallpaper categories (multiple responses not allowed)

Category	Description
Default	Preloaded images on mobile devices
Photoswithface	Portrait, including faces of people, animal, or cartoon characters
Landscape	Typical landscape photos w/o people
Pattern	Typical pattern images (logo, dot, etc.)
Livewallpaper	GIF image, Android live motion wallpaper, etc.
Retouched	Illustrated/retouched images with photo-editing tools
Inanimate	Inanimate objects like electronics, kitchen supplies, or goods
etc.	Does not fit into the above categories

Table 2. Reasons of choosing wallpaper (multiple responses allowed)

Reason	Description
Home_push	Order or request from others
Home_otherseye	Considering one's eyes
Home_unaware	Unaware of how to change wallpaper
Home_incongruity	Because I don't want the wallpaper to be covered when I change it to the other one
Home_tiresome	Because I am unwilling to change wallpaper
Home_time	Because it takes too much time to change wallpaper
Home_default	Because I hate preloaded images
Home_like	Because I prefer the image
Home_good	Because I think the photo is objectively good
Home_fit	Because it suits my phone
Home_etc	Does not fit into the above reasons

We asked why people chose the image among 11 reasons (Table 2). Multiple factors can influence on personal UI settings. Since smartphones are personal devices, individual trait is important. Given that smartphones are thought of as an item that the user always has on them, close friends may want users to change wallpaper to something specific (Home_push, Home_otherseye). Other people might not see the necessity to change their wallpaper (Home_tiresome). Old users may experience difficulties in customizing home screen (Home_unaware). Among these answers, all participants were allowed to choose up to three reasons.

Part 3. *Visual Incongruity* and user response: We were mainly interested in whether users dislike the appearance of wallpapers totally covered with icons. We asked how people responded to *Visual Incongruity* if objects (icons, widgets, etc.) cover the entire image on the home or lock screens. Table 3 lists the reactions when people were faced with *Visual Incongruity*. Listed items were designed with calculating number of cases (possible user actions*objects on the home screen). Multiple choices were allowed with no limitation.

Table 3. User response on *Visual Incongruity* (multiple responses allowed)

User response	Description
MoveIconWidget	I moved icon or widget
DeleteIconWidget	I deleted icon or widget
AlterWidgetSize	I altered the size of widget
PhotoEdit	I edited (e.g. cropped) wallpaper
ChangeWallpaper	I changed the wallpaper
DoNothing	I did nothing when faced with *Visual Incongruity*
etc.	None of the above

3.2 Survey Result

Part 1: Demographics. A total of 212 South Koreans responded to the survey, but six participants (aged above 40 years old) were deleted due to the little size of sample. One offline surveyee who did not fill in his/her name was excluded from the survey analysis. As a result, 205 participants (15 from offline) were considered to be an effective population. The mean age of participants was 22.84 (SD = 4.235, Range: 13–38), and college students, their friends, and those in neighborhoods near campuses were our targets. 101 participants were male and 104 participants were female, allowing a fairly balanced sex distribution among participants. For mobile phone operating systems, there were 124 Android OS users (60.49%), 79 iOS users (38.54%), and two Blackberry OS 10 users (0.98%). The portion of iOS users is bigger than twice the average of iPhone users [26].

Part 2: Distribution of Home Screen Wallpaper Adoption and Reason Why People Choose. As shown in Fig. 3a, the majority of the respondents was using portrait for their wallpaper. Teenagers especially preferred portrait image. To identify their own characteristic we grouped other three groups and compared them with

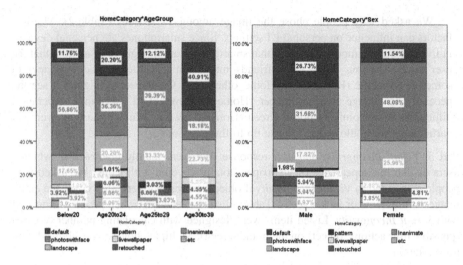

Fig. 3. Home screen wallpaper distribution by age group (Left, 3a), Home screen wallpaper distribution by sex (Right, 3b)

teenagers. The cross tabulation analysis supported that teenager's use of application of portrait is not identical with other groups (p-value = 0.005). Figure 3a shows that 'default' is unusually big from people in their 30s. From the aforementioned methodology, we found that people in their 30s significantly prefer 'default' more than the other three groups (p-value = 0.017).

We could find a distinct wallpaper preference between men and women from Fig. 3b. Cross tabulation analysis showed that overall wallpaper adoption was not identical (p-value = 0.029). When compared by gender, the preference of default image and portrait was significantly high in male (p-value = 0.007) and female (p-value = 0.022), respectively.

We then asked why they chose their images. Allowing multiple responses, 327 responses were collected. The hypothesis test showed that set of reasons are independent from age groups (p-value = 0.005, more than 20% of cells were counted less than 5). This means that distribution of reasons varies by age group. For instance, the distribution pattern of the 'Age30to39' showed a slight difference from that of other groups. As shown on Fig. 4, 'Home_like' (user preference) of people in their 30s is smaller than other groups. Cross tabulation analysis resulted in that user preference of people in their 30s were significantly lower than other three groups (p-value = 0.001). Secondly, 'Home_tiresome' of the group accounts for more than 30% which is larger than any other groups. Before analyzing the statistical result, we guessed old users might feel difficult to customize smartphone. However, of all the survey participants, there was no one who unaware of setting wallpapers. According to cross tabulation analysis, people in their 30s, compared to other three groups, have little interest in wallpaper settings (Home_tiresome, p-value = 0.023).

Part 3: Visual Incongruity and User Response. In Part 3, we asked whether people felt reluctant to *Visual Incongruity*. For this binary question, more than 77% of users

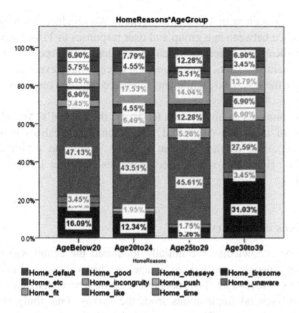

Fig. 4. Home screen wallpaper selection reason distribution by age group (Within AgeGroup, multiple choices allowed)

said the untidy icon arrangement is an eyesore. This trend was identical regardless of age group (data not shown) and OS (data not shown).

In sequence, we asked how people dealt with *Visual Incongruity*. Figure 5a shows that most people have moved icons or widgets except for people in their 30s. At least

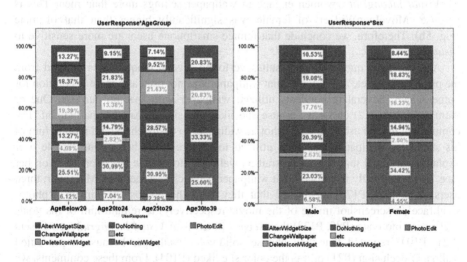

Fig. 5. User response by age group (Left, 5a, Denominator: sum of multiple choices for each age group, multiple responses allowed), User response by sex (Right, 5b, Denominator: sum of multiple choices for each gender, multiple responses allowed)

60% of each group dealt with *Visual Incongruity*. We conducted a hypothesis test to check independence between age group and user responses to *Visual Incongruity*. As a result, null hypothesis was rejected which means that user responses are independent by age group (p-value = 0.006, more than 20% of cells have expected cell counts less than 5). However there was no significant difference between respective variables and age groups.

From Fig. 5b, one sees an obvious sex tendency: the women's 'MoveIconWidget' is larger than that of men. We conducted cross tabulation analysis between sex and 'MoveIconWidget', and resulted in that there is significant difference by gender (p-value = 0.024). However, overall user responses were not independent from sex (p-value = 0.262).

3.3   Implications of the Survey

To the best of our knowledge, we initially identified the actual wallpaper that was adopted and why people selected an image as the wallpaper. Little background information led us to investigate how people use home screen elements. As a result, we empirically found several implications from the survey. One thing is that teenager significantly preferred portrait. The reason was simple; they like the image (Fig. 4). In contrast to people in their 30s, user preference of teenager is significantly bigger than other three groups (p-value = 0.047).

Another thing is that people in their 30s have less interest in home screen UI. They significantly preferred default image (Fig. 3a) and they answered they are unwilling to change wallpaper (Fig. 4). When we asked their response on *Visual Incongruity*, 'DoNothing' was the top response (Fig. 5a). We also identified the gender tendency through this research; Women significantly prefer portrait (Fig. 3b). When it comes to the *Visual Incongruity*, women engage in wallpaper settings more than men. This is because 'MoveIconWidget' of female was significantly bigger than that of male (Fig. 5b). Therefore, we conclude that female smartphone users are more sensitive to *Visual Incongruity*.

Analyzing the questionnaire results, we found several unique cases omitted from the prior section ('etc'). We found that wallpaper was not used as a mere decoration for home screen. Several respondents utilized wallpaper with specific purpose. One of them said she (P12) chose it because she liked the singer. Another participant (P9) commented that he used the screenshot as wallpaper to easily check and remind him of his schedule. Wallpaper was even utilized to change one's habit. One female user explained in detail that she set portrait as wallpaper to change her expression on her face. She specifically mentioned that wallpaper is the closest medium. Moreover, three users (P20, P85, P173) mentioned that they used the photos ('inanimate', 'photo-swithface', a screenshot image of the movie respectively) to remind him of his goals (P20) or to motivate (P85, P173) themselves. In terms of *Visual Incongruity*, two users (P21, P104) reported that they choose solid-color wallpaper because it prevented wallpaper occlusion (P21) or it is the color she liked (P104). From these comments, we were convinced that wallpaper can be utilized for various functions. For instance, some college students may conveniently check the new time table at a new school term because they are not accustomed to the new schedule or location of the classroom.

Although this study provides insight into wallpaper distribution, it is limited in that there is no analysis on the varying display size and resulting wallpaper settings. Since we did not want to overstrain our participants, screenshot image was not collected. Presented questions were limited to the smartphone platform as well. To the best of our knowledge, we looked into the wallpaper adoption for the first time with this survey research. Considering the saturation of smartphone markets and the importance of product differentiation, this survey is valuable for user experience designers and manufacturers.

4 Proposal of a New Home Screen UI

From our survey research and the existing literature, we took note of two tendencies. First, people choose portrait as wallpaper, and they set it because they prefer the image. Secondly, most users are concerned with *Visual Incongruity* and actually take action to cope with the problem. However, current UIs do not cope with *Visual Incongruity*, human prefer aesthetically pleasing system though [15]. In this regard, we propose a concept of new home screen UI. Our goal is to lessen the repetitive icon arrangement and reflect user behavior in the interface.

4.1 Rapid Prototyping with Framer.js

We developed several prototypes of new home screen UI with Framer.js which is an interactive prototyping tool. They were operated with mobile apps – Frameless, Frames (iOS, Apple iPhone 6s) and Framer (Android OS, Samsung Galaxy S6 Edge) - and were coded to display authentic home screen as native launcher. They do not work as native UI but provide real-feeling mobile interactions; Icons, widgets, or shortcut on the home screen are only allowed to act, animate, or display as programmed. Proto-typing process will be described from the following section.

4.2 Designing New Home Screen User Interface

Figure 6 shows the method and concept of proposing interface. It shows how messy home screen can be organized with moving or deleting icons. We describe several design implications of proposed interface from the following.

The first thing we had to choose was the wallpaper, which occupies the biggest part of the screen. Referring to the dominant preference on portrait, we focused on the portrait image to target mainstream users. Some images were downloaded from Google image search (Labeled for noncommercial reuse with modification). Since animals and cartoon characters have their own faces, they were collected as well (Classification issue mentioned before). We cropped and resized the images to fit on our mockup UI.

Second, we had to make decisions about the types and numbers of icons. For example, which types of apps would be placed on the dock? We tried to reduce

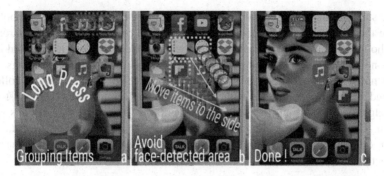

Fig. 6. Method of arranging icons on the proposing UI, (a) long press gesture triggers home screen items to be grouped, (b) items are moved to the side, (c) apps are rearranged

Fig. 7. Home screen prototype for Android OS, (a) long press gesture triggers the home screen setting menu, (b) menu is popped up with 'Relocation' button, (c) icons are rearranged

unfamiliarity from the prototype through adopting popular apps [25, 27]. As a result, Android and iOS prototype is presented in Figs. 6 and 7 respectively.

Next, we discussed how the object would be arranged. Following three factors constitute the pseudo-algorithm: Usage frequency, relatedness, and reachability.

Among three factors above, usage frequency is the top priority. There are two principles regarding usage frequency: (1) frequently launched items should be less moved than others at all time. (2) Icon arrangement is executed depending on the wallpaper occlusion. This means that if the face is occluded by icons, the proposing algorithm will move apps to create folder(s). If not, icon arrangement will be minimized because people organize items by location [20] and seldom change home screen panel [28].

Before apps are organized, relatedness of the apps is examined. The prototype clusters apps by category [4] because logical grouping helps users to get used to new home screen [28]. For instance, Angry Bird, Facebook, and Instagram can be grouped to a folder named 'Entertainment' (Fig. 6).

Last one is reachability, which is closely related with navigation time. If the desired apps are far from finger, users feel uncomfortable about using smartphone. Therefore, the prototype moves apps and (new) folders to the right side of the home screen because most users are right-handed. It makes much easier for the thumb to touch icon (e.g. Flipboard on Fig. 6). Detail configuration for left-handed users might be added in the future work.

In short, we propose the prototype of wallpaper UI with pseudo-algorithm. It works as following order: Checking usage frequency, relatedness, and reachability.

The interaction method is also important. Even if we develop sophisticated interface, users may not find how to launch the proposed function. Several prototypes using pinch to zoom, long press, or touch and drag were developed but we chose long press considering its compatibility on device. In this regard, we have applied long press to Android phone. Generally, long press on the home screen triggers the pop up menu which provides several options for home screen settings. Therefore, 'Relocation' button is integrated with existing context menu (Fig. 7). It is able to reduce the complexity of home screen interface. Without installing new apps, this gesture leads users to easily manage home screen elements.

5   Focus Group Interview

To get deeper insights into participant's rationale for home screen elements, qualitative approach was required. The FGI was held with 6 people (3 males, 3 females; aged 21–35, average age = 26.7, 58 min) on January, 2016. Two of them were Android OS users and four were iOS users. All of them were recruited near our institute. Participants were asked to share how they manage home screen elements – wallpaper, icon, folders and so on. Therefore, we focused on individual traits of managing home screen from the interview. The interview was semi-structured; before we start interview, we prepared the topics, keyword of questions, and our prototype. The proposed UI was displayed on iPhone using 'Frames' app which support wireless testing. None of the survey result was shared to avoid bias. Conversations were recorded with the consent of the participants and transcribed after the interview.

5.1   Wallpaper and Visually Incongruity

First keyword was wallpaper. All participants showed their phone to each other and freely discussed the wallpaper. They had all different purposes for wallpapers. P3 and P6 said there is no reason at the first time but they retracted that comment. P3 explained that he had set his nephew's photo before but he never use it ('photoswithface') anymore because he cannot see anything. As a result, he gave up using portrait and put all the things he uses on the home screen. P6 explained that he usually selects preloaded image because he could not find better one (Note: He uses 'livewallpaper' which is preloaded on iPhone 6s). P2 and P5 had strict criteria for setting home screen

UI. P2 specifically mentioned three requirements: (1) The color of wallpaper should match that of the phone case, (2) The icons should not be covering her favorite cartoon characters, and (3) no more than two rows of icons/folders should be on the screen. Her requirements are so strict that she seldom changes wallpaper. Along with P2, P5 set home screen UI in detail. He set wallpapers of his favorite celebrities to be shifted every hour. In the case of P4, her current wallpaper is landscape but sometimes she captures short to-do list on the Notes app and set it as wallpaper. From these cases, we found that wallpaper is not just a decoration. Setting wallpaper is simple but it implies complex user requirements.

We proposed the second keyword, *Visual Incongruity*. Among six participants, four mentioned that wallpaper occlusion is an eyesore. P4 recognized the inconvenience of *Visual Incongruity* because she had to write to-do list on the bottom of the screen. Then her memos are not fully occluded by icons. She pointed out that the real cause is lack of widget support (iOS). Furthermore, P2 and P5 were very sensitive to *Visual Incongruity*. P2 said she "never stops finding desired image until it is not occluded by icons." P5 fully understood P2 because he edits all images by hand to see his favorite celebrities. On the other hand, some users have less interest in the issue. P1 and P6 said they think it is not an important issue. From their wallpaper adoption (P1: 'pattern', P6: 'livewallpaper'), we guess that the type of image may indicate the user response to *Visual Incongruity*. This is because if we use pattern images (or live wallpaper) there is no way to avoid wallpaper occlusion. It always happens.

5.2 Icon Arrangement

Participants applied two or more concepts to arrange objects. They grouped items by relevance but frequently used items were put on the home screen panel. Except P4, they all placed 'Kakaotalk' on the home screen which is the most popular apps in Korea because they want to launch it quickly. Another example is P5. He integrated usage frequency, usability, aesthetics, and relatedness [4] into his phone. As shown on Fig. 8, he put Instagram and Facebook on the home screen because he used the two items more often than other social network services. Among participants, only P6 were unwilling to group items. He said he had grouped apps by color of the icon before, but now he left them as it is because it takes too much time to group his all apps (More than 125 apps installed).

Some participants depend on the dock but reasons were all different. P2 wanted visually simple interface that all apps were grouped to folders. P4 was similar with P2 but she put emphasize more on the short navigation time that not all apps were grouped to folders (See Fig. 8). In the case of P5, he put five apps on the dock. One is chrome which is his second most-used apps. He placed it on the dock because he can easily access information. But other apps – dialer, contacts, messages, app drawer – were left unchanged because it has been there from the first time.

Fig. 8. Screenshot images of FGI participants (P1, P2, P3, P4, P5 and P6 from the left)

5.3 Prototype UI

After prior discussion, we briefed them about the concept of our prototype. We specifically mentioned that it has only one function: icon rearrangement. Using the prototype, we attempted to draw implicit behaviors from participants. As our prototype has limited functions, we assumed that people would freely give out their opinions on it. We think their ideas would be helpful to develop improved prototype.

All participants were satisfied with the main idea: Icons do not occlude faces. However, most people wanted to customize or upgrade the grouping function. P2 wanted to arrange items by row because she think the rearranged state is not organized (See Fig. 6). In contrast, P5 hated the relatedness grouping. This is because he has not modified icon arrangement for 6 years. Every time he buys new smartphone, he put all items to be arranged as same as the old one. He just wanted to move icons ignoring grid layout. In the case of P1, she was positive about the relatedness-based grouping but she preferred manual control. She emphasized that she wants to arrange icons by herself because it helps her to memorize where they are [20].

P3 also prefers the presented concept of grouping items because he created several folders by relevance. Testing prototype UI, P4 disliked automatic grouping but she suggested a unique way to use her phone. She said, "How about using long press in the opposite way. If I long press the home screen, the folder is ungrouped for a while." She utilized the proposed method in an opposite way to reduce navigation time. Her idea could be helpful for users who have a lot of folders on the home screen.

5.4 Implications of the Focus Group Interview

FGI is able to provide design guideline of UI as well as complement the qualitative side of the survey research. We found that type of the image is not just limited to statistics. It is internally linked with user behavior, and people set wallpaper with various purposes. For instance, P6 said that when he uses default image, it reminds him of using the latest smartphone. This means that he feels satisfied with using smartphone. If we have not looked into FGI thoroughly, such psychological aspect would have gone overlooked.

We guessed participants may give their feedback on our prototype. Our prediction was right on the money; Interviewees were able to talk their needs which were not mentioned before we show the prototype. Most of them were positive on the concept of wallpaper occlusion. However, they said that the proposed grouping method is not enough. People usually create folders by relevance, but not all items were moved to folders (P5). Location of folder varies by user as well. In short, participants wanted to customize grouping mechanism to fit their needs. All these comments will help us to develop our prototype to improve user experience.

6 Discussion

6.1 Limitations of the Study

Due to the lack of literature review on smartphone's wallpaper, we had to conduct research empirically. We collected data on wallpaper category, reasons of setting wallpaper, and *Visual Incongruity*. We initially found implications from the survey but reliability of multiple response questions might be discussed. As we provided more than six options for each question, number of response was absolutely low. For instance, no one answered 'Home_unaware' from Fig. 4. It also has own meaning but this may influence on the reliability of the hypothesis test.

In this paper, we proposed the concept of home screen prototype but it has several limitations. First of all, the proposed method is limited to the portrait. Next, we applied three key concepts but it has limitation in that objects were moved as we coded. We also did not cope with cases when new apps are installed or deleted. Automatic icon arrangement will be further developed not to confuse users [29]. Moreover, the proposed UI was designed for mainstream users because most of them preferred portrait (Fig. 3a). Thus, based on the findings from the survey, it needs to reflect the characteristics of the old users in the future work.

6.2 Potential of the Proposed UI

Through our survey research and FGI, we found two potentials from the prototype. One thing is people really concern the wallpaper. This trend is assumed to be similar with other device platforms because a smartphone's UI structure resembles that of a desktop environment (e.g. Fig. 9). A PC has program shortcuts or widgets on the wallpaper as well. This means that the wallpaper is set on various other devices, such as a smart watch, laptop, tablet, or smart TV. We may identify whether the size of the display influences the wallpaper adoption and the existence of *Visual Incongruity*. An optimal UI for each device platform might be developed in the future.

Another thing is that our prototype may nudge people to communicate with others. Especially, it could be helpful for couples in a long-distance relationship or elderly people. Feedbacks from survey participants (P20, P85, P173) support this as well.

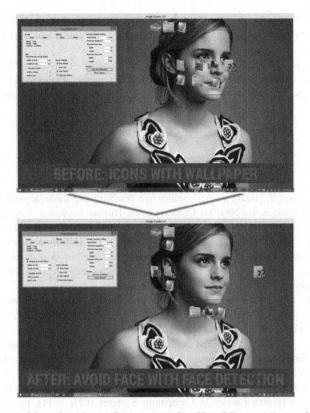

Fig. 9. Prototype of face detection software to resolve *Visual Incongruity* on desktop domain. Software developed using Haar Cascades and breadth first search algorithm.

7   Conclusion

Previous research investigated natural concepts how people arrange icons [4] but there is no prior research on wallpaper and its integration on the home screen UI. This led us to conduct empirical research with survey method. We investigated wallpaper adoption, reasons of setting wallpaper, and user response on *Visual Incongruity*. Several implications were found: (i) the majority of smartphone users set portrait as wallpaper. Teenagers and female significantly preferred portrait. (ii) Users were concerned about *Visually Incongruity*, and (iii) they took measures to avoid wallpaper occlusion (e.g. Move icons or widgets). Some unique cases showed the future potential of wallpaper which can be utilized for specific purpose. Based on the survey result and literature, we designed the prototype UI to reduce manual icon arrangement. We described the implications of our design in detail. We also conducted FGI to complement survey research. With six participants, we found that category of wallpaper is internally linked with user behavior. Moreover, we showed our prototype to interviewees and used it to get deeper insights on the given issue. As we have found from the survey, wallpaper can be utilized to provide specific function (e.g. to-do list, scheduler). Finally, we discussed the limitations of our research and its future potential. Deepening our findings from survey and FGI, we would like to improve our prototype in the future work.

Acknowledgments. This research was supported by the MSIP (Ministry of Science, ICT and Future Planning), Korea, under the "ICT Consilience Creative Program" (IITP-2017-2017-0-01015) supervised by the IITP (Institute for Information & communications Technology Promotion).

References

1. Roth, V., Turner, T.: Bezel swipe: conflict-free scrolling and multiple selection on mobile touch screen devices. In: SIGCHI Conference on Human Factors in Computing Systems, pp. 1523–1526. ACM Press, New York (2009). doi:10.1145/1518701.1518933
2. iTunes App Store Now Has 1.2 Million Apps, Has Seen 75 Billion Downloads To Data. http://techcrunch.com/2014/06/02/itunes-app-has-seen-75-billion-downloads-to-date/
3. Smartphones: So Many Apps, So Much Time. http://www.nielsen.com/us/en/insights/news/2014/smartphones-so-many-apps–so-much-time.html
4. Böhmer, M., Krüger, A.: A study on icon arrangement by smartphone users. In: SIGCHI Conference on Human Factors in Computing Systems (CHI 2013), pp. 2137–2146. ACM Press, New York (2013). doi:10.1145/2470654.2481294
5. Häkkilä, J., Chatfield, C.: Personal customisation of mobile phones: a case study. In: 4th Nordic Conference on Human Computer Interaction (NordiCHI 2006), pp. 409–412. ACM Press, New York (2006). doi:10.1145/1182475.1182524
6. Marathe, S., Sundar, S.S.: What drives customization?: control or identity? In: SIGCHI Conference on Human Factors in Computing Systems (CHI 2011), pp. 781–790. ACM Press, New York (2011). doi:10.1145/1978942.1979056
7. Bloch, P.H.: Seeking the ideal form: product design and consumer response. J. Mark. **59**, 16–29 (1995). doi:10.2307/1252116
8. Bevan, N.: International standards for HCI and usability. J. Hum.-Comput. Stud. **55**, 533–552 (2012). doi:10.1006/ijhc.2001.0483
9. Inostroza, R., Rusu, C., Roncagliolo, S., Jimenez, C., Rusu, V.: Usability heuristics for touchscreen-based mobile devices. In: 9th International Conference on Information Technology – New Generations, pp. 662–667. IEEE Computer Society, Washington, DC (2012). doi:10.1109/ITNG.2012.134
10. MacDonald, C.M., Atwood, M.E.: What does it mean for a system to be useful?: an exploratory study of usefulness. In: 2014 Conference on Designing Interactive Systems, pp. 885–894. ACM Press, New York (2014). doi:10.1145/2598510.2598600
11. Joyce, G., Lilley, M., Barker, T., Jefferies, A.: Smartphone application usability evaluation: the applicability of traditional heuristics. In: Marcus, A. (ed.) DUXU 2015. LNCS, vol. 9187, pp. 541–550. Springer, Heidelberg (2015). doi:10.1007/978-3-319-20898-5_52
12. Lee, V., Schneider, H., Schell, R.: Mobile Applications: Architecture, Design, and Development. Prentice Hall PTR, Upper Saddle River (2004)
13. Longoria, R.: Designing Software for the Mobile Context: A Practitioner's Guide. Springer Science & Business Media, Heidelberg (2004)
14. Angeli, A.D., Sutcliffe, A., Hartmann, J.: Interaction, usability and aesthetics: what influences users' preferences? In: 6th Conference on Designing Interactive Systems (DIS 2006), pp. 271–280. ACM Press, New York (2006). doi:10.1145/1142405.1142446

15. Tractinsky, N., Katz, A.S., Ikar, D.: What is beautiful is usable. J. Interact. Comput. **13**, 127–145 (2000). doi:10.1016/S0953-5438(00)00031-X
16. Ling, J., Schaik, P.V.: The effect of text and background colour on visual search of web pages. Displays **23**, 223–230 (2002). doi:10.1016/S0141-9382(02)00041-0
17. Bernard, M.L., Chaparro, B.S., Mills, M.M., Halcomb, C.G.: Comparing the effects of text size and format on the readability of computer-displayed Times New Roman and Arial text. J. Hum.-Comput. Stud. **59**, 823–835 (2003). doi:10.1016/S0171-5819(03)00121-6
18. Clark, J.: Tapworthy: Designing Great iPhone Apps. O'Reilly Media Inc., Newton (2010)
19. Norman, D.A.: Emotional Design: Why We Love (or Hate) Everyday Things. Basic Books, New York (2004)
20. Barreau, D., Nardi, B.A.: Finding and reminding: file organization from the desktop. ACM SIGCHI Bull. **27**, 39–43 (1995). doi:10.1145/221296.221307
21. Ravasio, P., Schär, S.G., Krueger, H.: In pursuit of desktop evolution: user problems and practices with modern desktop systems. J. ACM TOCHI **11**, 156–180 (2004). doi:10.1145/1005361.1005363
22. Chen, C.C.: User recognition and preference of app icon stylization design on the smartphone. In: Stephanidis, C. (ed.) HCI 2015. LNCS, vol. 529, pp. 9–15. Springer, Heidelberg (2015). doi:10.1007/978-3-319-21383-5
23. Böhmer, M., Bauer, G.: Improving the recommendation of mobile services by interpreting the user's icon arrangement. In: 11th International Conference on Human-Computer Interaction with Mobile Devices and Services, pp. 1–2. ACM Press, New York (2009). doi:10.1145/1613858.1613964
24. Böhmer, M., Bauer, G.: Exploiting the icon arrangement on mobile devices as information source for context-awareness. In: 12th International Human computer interaction with mobile devices and services, pp. 195–198. ACM Press, New York (2010). doi:10.1145/1851600.1851633
25. Böhmer, M., Hecht, B., Schöning, J., Krüger, A., Bauer, G.: Falling asleep with Angry Birds, Facebook and Kindle: a large scale study on mobile application usage. In: 13th International Conference on Human Computer Interaction with Mobile Devices and Services, pp. 47–56. ACM Press, New York (2011). doi:10.1145/2037373.2037383
26. Android and iOS Squeeze the Competition, Swelling to 96.3% of the Smartphone Operating System Market for Both 4Q14 and CY14. http://www.idc.com/getdoc.jsp?containerId=prUS25450615
27. Rahmati, A., Tossell, C., Shepard, C., Kortum, P., Zhong, L.: Exploring iPhone usage: the influence of socioeconomic differences on smartphone adoption, usage and usability. In: 14th International Conference on Human-Computer Interaction with Mobile Devices and Services, pp. 11–20. ACM Press, New York (2012). doi:10.1145/2371574.2371577
28. Hang, A., Luca, A.D., Hartmann, J., Hussmann, H.: Oh app, where art thou? On app launching habits of smartphone users. In: 15th International Conference on Human-Computer Interaction with Mobile Devices and Services, pp. 392–395. ACM Press, New York (2013). doi:10.1145/2493190.2493219
29. Ziefle, M., Bay, S.: Mental models of a cellular phone menu. Comparing older and younger novice users. In: Brewster, S., Dunlop, M. (eds.) HCI 2004. LNCS, vol. 3160, pp. 25–37. Springer, Heidelberg (2004). doi:10.1007/978-3-540-28637-0_3

Understanding the User

Extending the Concept of User Satisfaction in E-Learning Systems from ISO/IEC 25010

Andrés F. Aguirre[1]($\boxtimes$), Ángela Villareal-Freire[1], Rosa Gil[2],
and César A. Collazos[1]

[1] IDIS Research Group, University of Cauca, Popayán, Colombia
{afaguirre,avillarreal,ccollazo}@unicauca.edu.co
[2] Research Group on Human Computer Interaction and Data Integration,
University of Lleida, Lleida, Spain
rgil@diei.udl.cat

Abstract. Current trends in the development of educational applications bring new challenges that require both a rapprochement and an understanding of the elements implicit in the interaction of this type of system and the individuals who use them. One of the most relevant aspects in this interaction is user satisfaction; as a result, it is necessary to establish a broader and more precise definition of user satisfaction in the e-learning context, at the same time giving thought to the different constructs that characterize the software systems dedicated to learning. This article presents a proposal that extends the concept of satisfaction of use in e-learning environments through the ISO/IEC 25010 standard.

Keywords: User satisfaction · E-learning · User experience · Instructional design · ISO/IEC 25010

1 Introduction

Evaluating user satisfaction in applications dedicated to learning is a complex activity. This situation is due in large part to the increase in trends in learning styles, the diversity of students, technological advances, etc. [1]. These characteristics become important challenges for the definition of methods that allow the evaluation of designs of e-learning systems in a more precise and objective way with respect to the traditional methods.

The main task for a user when faced with an e-learning system is to learn. This is a rather abstract process. As such, professionals in the assessment of User Experience (UX) should significantly increase their efforts when dealing with such environments. Authors such as Squires point out the need to incorporate ease of use into learning in computer tools, and also point out the lack of reciprocity between the areas of Human Computer Interaction (HCI) and educational computing [2]. An educational application can be useful, but not in the pedagogical sense and vice versa [3–5].

© Springer International Publishing AG 2017
A. Marcus and W. Wang (Eds.): DUXU 2017, Part III, LNCS 10290, pp. 167–179, 2017.
DOI: 10.1007/978-3-319-58640-3_13

In this sense, it is necessary to make use of a model that is consistent with the new challenges implied in UX evaluation, in particular evaluation of user satisfaction in e-learning environments. For this purpose it has been found that ISO/IEC 25010 provides a definition that contemplates different nuances of general user experience that can be fully adapted to the human-computer system, including computer systems in use and software products in use [6]. Within this standard, satisfaction is divided into four sub-characteristics intended to identify user needs when using a system in a specific use context [6]: utility, confidence, pleasure and comfort. Although a product is satisfactory in one given use context, it may not be in another with different users, tasks or environments [7]. Therefore, it is considered important to focus more on the set of factors that determine the nature of an e-learning system, since these are the main components for adapting the satisfaction sub-characteristics established in ISO/IEC 25010 within the e-learning context. The adaptation of these sub-features will allow the defining of the parameters necessary to evaluating user satisfaction in e-learning environments.

2   User Satisfaction

2.1   Satisfaction in UX

Due to the current boom in technology use in society, it is logical that the satisfaction of the end user becomes the primary conditioner for the success or failure of any interactive system. In the event that the user does not achieve their objectives or the software does not meet their needs, they will simply abandon it in search of an alternative, from the competition [8]. User satisfaction is a complex concept, difficult to delimit, but of paramount importance since it will model the UX, making possible or preventing the achievement of its objectives [9]. In this context, several efforts have been made by the HCI community to establish the factors influencing satisfaction, to be able to manage them well in designing interfaces [10]. One of the widespread concepts that aid this aim is usability, which also seeks to provide elements for measuring the degree of satisfaction as well as the efficiency and effectiveness with which specific users can achieve specific objectives, in specific contexts of use [11,12]. Some authors extend this concept and establish two dimensions of usability: objective or inherent usability and subjective or apparent usability ([9,13,14] cited in [8]). The first refers to the functional or dynamic part of the interface and focuses on how to make the product easy to understand and learn (efficiency and effectiveness) [8,15]. Subjective usability, on the other hand, is more related to the visual impression of the interface, which the user perceives by means of design, aesthetics and interaction with the interface (user satisfaction) [8,14,15].

However, recent research has indicated that the usability of a product may not be the only, or even the main, determining factor in user satisfaction [16,17], due to the fact that in recent years there has been evolution in interactions between user and different interactive systems, in which this has gone from being a purely functional interaction, determined by the efficiency and effectiveness of the use of the product, toward being a sensory vision projected through pleasure, the subjective nature of the experience, the perception of a product and the emotional responses [16–18]. Thus, user satisfaction cannot be analyzed as an attribute of usability; instead, usability must be understood as a factor in the consolidation of elements that tend to satisfy user satisfaction [8]. UX then becomes a holistic view of interaction with a product [18], as it comprises the full set of effects brought about by the use of a product, including aesthetic experience, sense experience, emotional experience, and other aspects that involve user satisfaction [17].

2.2   Satisfaction in UX with E-Learning

Evolution in the concept of user satisfaction and in the understanding toward UX, also extends to teaching and learning systems. However, while virtual education is becoming one of the most representative approaches in the Internet [19], most studies conducted on evaluations of e-learning systems have provided minimal participation in UX aspects [20], reflected in educational applications having higher dropout rates compared to traditional courses led by an instructor. Many reasons may explain these high dropout rates, such as the relevance of the content, the level of comfort with the technology, the availability of technical support, etc., but one important factor is the lack of cognitive and emotional characteristics such as guidelines in the development of learning spaces with valid designs [1,21]. Consequently, evaluation studies of UX in e-learning are scarce [21].

Within such a scope, UX comprises an essential element in the ability of the student to acquire knowledge and competences in a satisfactory way. The evaluation of UX also therefore becomes a means of support so that learning and teaching processes are productive, since its objective is to design systems that are intuitive from which users can interact easily with e-learning systems and focus on acquiring the knowledge and skills provided in their training [22]. The less effort devoted to understanding and learning the functionality of the system, the more the student can devote to learning [23]. It should also be noted that one of the relevant aspects considered in UX - and in the particular case of e-learning have a substantial role - are emotions [24]. Several studies point out that emotions have a decisive influence on the motivation, attention span and performance of the student [25–27]. Therefore, in evaluating user satisfaction of e-learning systems, it is important to treat the affective qualities involved as an inherent component of UX, since these compromise the functional and non-functional attributes of a system, functional ones being understood as those related to usability, utility and accessibility, while in the case of the non-functional ones, these refer to aesthetic, symbolic, and motivational qualities, among others [25].

3   Traditional Approaches for the Assessment of User Satisfaction

User satisfaction assessment methods in e-learning are complex both in practice and in research [28] and are usually focused from a pragmatic perspective, in which assessment of the efficiency and effectiveness of an interactive system take precedence; or instead, they are oriented toward assessing the quality of the teaching, in the same way as happens in a traditional classroom [28,29]. This constant fluctuation between preferences in the way in which user satisfaction is assessed in e-learning causes fundamental aspects to be neglected that are part of the interaction with these systems and that require to be assessed. Following from this then is a compilation of the literature from two approaches:

3.1 Evaluation of User Satisfaction in Interactive Systems

User satisfaction can be considered as the main parameter in the use of inter-active systems [30]. From this point of view, several studies implement different types of work related to usability and user satisfaction [30]. However, many of these do not provide details on the questionnaires used for assessing satisfaction [9], several even rethinking the constructs and measures of user satisfaction, omitting validated and readily available questionnaires [9,30]. Among some of the questionnaires widely used in industry and academic environments are found the following described in Table 1.

Although these measures are widely used, their diagnostic value is diminished on comparison with more specialized measurement instruments, i.e. those based on particular aspects of a given context [43]. Although many authors support this premise, very little has been done to examine critically and in-depth the implications and specificities of assessing UX in e-learning (particularly user satisfaction) [44,45]. For this reason, there is a constant need in UX professionals to base their research on virtual educational contexts, on instructional models, and on learning styles, among other aspects that determine the quality of learning in e-learning systems. These fundamentals are one of the main reasons why it is necessary either to define new UX evaluation techniques in e-learning [44] or to complement existing ones. In addition to the elements of context, emotions are another critical conditioner in interaction with e-learning systems, given their value in cognitive processes. It is therefore crucial to consider the emotional states of users within the assessment parameters [44].

3.2 Evaluation of User Satisfaction in E-Learning

In the literature, a great number of studies measure various user satisfaction factors in e-learning systems. They usually focus on the quality of teaching and learning. However, these measures are not appropriate for an e-learning context, since the role of an "e-learner" is different from that of a traditional learner [28]. This special group of users (e-learners) has a unique view regarding satisfaction [29]. Table 2 shows some important research that has focused its efforts toward the definition of factors that affect user satisfaction in e-learning systems.

Table 1. Instruments for evaluating user satisfaction in interactive systems

Instrument	Description
QUIS	*Questionnaire for User Interaction Satisfaction* is a tool developed by researchers at the University of Maryland Human-Computer Interaction Lab. Designed to assess the subjective satisfaction of users on specific aspects of the human-computer interface [31]. The current version, QUIS 7.0, available in print and web in multiple languages [32], assesses the user's overall satisfaction in 6 hierarchically organized facets in each of the nine interface-specific factors defined in this tool: *screen factors, terminology and system feedback, learning factors, system capabilities, technical manuals, online tutorials, multimedia, teleconferencing and software installation* [32,33]. Each facet, in turn, consists of a pair of semantic differentials arranged on a 10-point scale [31,34]. The questionnaire is designed to be adjusted according to the analysis needs of each interface, in which only sections of interest can be considered
SUMI	*Software Usability Measuring Inventory* is a method of evaluating the quality of software that allows measuring satisfaction and assessing user perception [35]. SUMI is a commercially-available questionnaire for assessing usability of software developed, validated and standardized on international databases [35,36]. This method is referred to in standards ISO 9126 [37] and ISO 9241 as a recognized tool for evaluating user satisfaction via five dimensions of usability: *efficiency, affection, utility, control, and learning* [36]. This tool is also available in several languages [35,36]
WAMMI	*Website Analysis and Measurement Inventory* is an online service that emerged from SUMI. Both were developed at the *Human Factors Research Group* (HFRG) at University College, Cork. Unlike SUMI, which is designed for the evaluation of desktop software applications, WAMMI focuses on evaluation of websites [34,38]. This instrument consists of 20 questions that use 5-point Likert scales as answers [34,39] and makes it possible to create a questionnaire and link it to WAMMI classification scales [34]. The result of a WAMMI analysis is a measure of "global satisfaction" [49] that is divided into 5 dimensions [34,39] - attractiveness, control, efficiency, utility and learning - as well as providing an overall usability score
MUMMS	*Measuring Usability of Multi-Media System* was developed by the same group that designed SUMI and WAMMI. MUMMS consists of a questionnaire that enables assessment of quality of use for multimedia software products [40]. Measurement aspects are the same as those SUMI takes account of and it incorporates a new one related to the user's emotional perception toward the use of the system. This tries to capture information about the fascination the multimedia application exerts on users [40]
SUS	*System Usability Scale* is an interesting variation of the traditional questionnaires. It presents a combination of statements written positively and negatively, so that the user really pays attention to each of their answers [41,42]. SUS consists of a 10-item questionnaire, each with a Likert scale of 5 (or 7) points, which provides an overview of satisfaction with the software [41]

Table 2. Proposals for assessing user satisfaction in e-learning systems

Author	Description
Sinclaire [46]	Bases its study in the framework of quality of the *Online Learning Consortium* (formally Sloan Consortium) that identifies determinants in the overall satisfaction of the students with the online learning, related to: *interaction and communication, course design, learning, and individual self-efficacy factors of students and the ability to control the pace of individual learning*
Liaw [47]	The results of their research showed that *perceived self-efficacy* is a key factor influencing student satisfaction in e-learning. *Perceived utility* and *perceived satisfaction* contribute to the intention of students to use e-learning systems. Furthermore, the effectiveness of the e-learning system can be influenced by multimedia teaching, interactive learning activities, and the quality of the system
Wang [28]	Based on evaluation scales, efficacy of teaching, and user satisfaction, Wang conducted an exploratory study aimed at students of an e-course. The results of his work showed a total of 17 items applicable to the measurement of student satisfaction. These can be classified in the following dimensions: *content, personalization, learning community, and student interface*
Arbaugh [48]	In his study, this author considers as attributes that influence user satisfaction *perceived utility and ease of use, flexibility of the e-learning system, interaction with class participants, use of the platform by the student, and gender*
Thurmond et al. [49]	Refers to such aspects as computer literacy, courses taken, initial knowledge of e-learning technology, age, receipt of comments in time and form, availability of different assessment methods, scheduled discussions, teamwork, and relationship with instructors
Wont et al. [50]	In order to assess usability of e-learning systems, the authors take account of the following factors: *feedback from the e-learning system, coherence, error prevention, performance/efficiency, user like/dislike, error recovery, cognitive load, internationalization, privacy, and online help*
Ardito et al. [45]	In this paper, a methodology is set out for the evaluation of educational applications, in which *effectiveness and efficiency* are proposed as evaluation principles and considered from four dimensions: *presentation, hypermedia, proactivity of the application, and user activity*
Piccoli et al. [51]	These authors emphasize the importance of factors such as *motivation, comfort toward technology, attitudes to technology, epistemic beliefs, teaching styles, self-efficacy, availability, control, among others*; they affect directly and decisively a student's satisfaction with virtual education systems

4 Assessment of User Satisfaction in E-Learning Systems from ISO/IEC 25010

In response to the different problems and gaps that exist in the evaluation of user satisfaction in e-learning systems, the need arises to define the attributes that ought to be considered for evaluation. This approach is described below:

4.1 Attributes for Assessing User Satisfaction in E-Learning

To define the assessment attributes, a contextualization of each of the sub-characteristics of user satisfaction defined in ISO/IEC 25010 is carried out. For this purpose, the following treatment has been carried out on each sub-characteristic of satisfaction:

Utility. This corresponds to the degree to which a user is satisfied with the perceived achievement of *pragmatic goals*, including the results and the consequences of the use [6].

According to this concept, it is necessary to establish what will be considered as *pragmatic goals*. Hassenzahl [18], states that a product is perceived as pragmatic if it provides an efficient and effective means for achieving the objectives. In this sense, a student could have a large number of objectives when interacting with an e-learning system. However, in general terms the main objective of the student is to learn [52]. Consequently, it is considered that the pragmatic objectives will be directed to favor the learning process in such a way that this is achieved in a simple, fast way, using the least possible amount of resources.

To find a match for the above, studies are referred to from which the pragmatic goals of the student can be obtained and the usefulness thus determined of interacting with an online learning environment. An example of work suited to this purpose is the TAM Model [53], which emphasizes perceived utility, a concept that has been adapted by different authors and brought to the context of online learning environments [54–57]. Pragmatic objectives can be abstracted from these studies, such as performing learning tasks easily and quickly, facilitating the learning of course content, and improving learning performance, among others no less important.

Trust. Trust is understood as the degree to which a user has confidence that a product or system will behave as intended. Nevertheless, given that confidence is part of user satisfaction, which compromises a more generalized concept that is subject to the specific context of use [6], there is a clear need to consider elements from this context (in this case e-learning) that define a construct that supports confidence.

Consequently, the components that would become part of this purpose are obtained from instructional design, particularly the work of Keller [58], who has made several contributions to the subject and is considered one of the most representative authors in this area [59]. Keller proposes a model of four categories that make up the motivation of a student. These correspond to Attention, Relevance, Confidence and Satisfaction (ARCS) [58]. In this model, confidence is defined as strategies that help develop positive expectations for the achievement of student goals in e-learning, in such a way that the apprentices experience their successes as relating to their efforts and not to external factors such as luck or the difficulty of the task [58].

Moreover, from the perspective of interaction between a user and a software system, trust is positively affected by ease of navigation within the environment [60,61] and good use of visual design elements [4]. The model of confidence treated in [62] states that when an interface is consistent in terms of visual appearance, elements of interaction (buttons, menus, etc.), navigation, and terminology, this increases user confidence. Likewise, it has been identified that aspects such as lack of control by the user [62] and curt, non-constructive error messages ([63] cited in [62]) have a negative impact on user confidence.

Pleasure. The degree in which a user gets pleasure from fulfilling their personal needs [6]. Such needs may include needs to acquire new knowledge and skills, communicate personal identity and provoke pleasant memories [6].

Hassenzahl, one of the most influential researchers in the area of UX, compiles a list of the 8 psychological needs of humans, based on the needs proposed by Sheldon *et al.* [64]. In addition there are widely recognized studies, arising from outwith the psychology that support them: [65–68]. These needs involve the dimension of pleasure as the confirmation of the possibilities of a desirable event [64].

According to Hassenzahl's studies, stimulation, identification and evocation are considered important needs in the context of interactive technologies, and in turn correspond to the hedonic attributes that underlie pleasure [18]: *influence - popularity, pleasure - stimulation,* and *sense - self-realization.*

Comfort. This is related to the degree to which the user is satisfied with the physical comfort [6]. Jordan [69] and Tiger [67] establish that physical comfort is determined by the pleasures derived directly from such the senses, such as touch, taste and smell. This sub-characteristic of satisfaction will not actually be taken into account because of its apparent weak connection with conventional interaction styles in e-learning and its inability to emerge as a clear need for the present study.

Based on the above, the suggested approach allows a combination of interface design, the motivation construct in learning, and user experience. Thus, by including these structures within the UX evaluation process of e-learning systems, a more objective and accurate approach is obtained of both the pragmatic and hedonic objectives implicit in student satisfaction.

5   Conclusions

The absence of robust and reliable mechanisms for translating user needs into design features is a factor that considerably limits the assessment process of a system, resulting in a high degree of uncertainty in the results of the evaluator. Generally, this is due to the fact that the process is based on the experience of the evaluator and on his abstraction capacity, since it is based on the intuition and subjective criteria of the evaluator.

The way in which the different characteristics and sub-characteristics set out in ISO/IEC 25010 are defined (in particular satisfaction and its corresponding sub-characteristics) highlights the versatility of the standard to adapt it to a given context. This quality also facilitates the understanding of the elements of the context required to define the assessment parameters.

The need to redefine processes related to the assessment of user satisfaction in interactive systems, in particular e-learning systems, is evident, since traditional user studies focus on objective parameters, associated with measurable and verifiable aspects in an interactive product, neglecting hedonic components that are part of user satisfaction and are directly related to the degree of involvement and motivation that a person shows when using an e-learning system.

The majority of research related to the evaluation of user satisfaction in e-learning are oriented to considering satisfaction in a subjective way. In the present study we propose the integration of different structures that complement each other, in order to deal with the particularities implicit in the design of e-learning systems: learner-centered design, instructional design, and UX. This aspect allows a holistic view regarding the components that are part of the evaluation of user satisfaction in e-learning systems.

Current practice in the evaluation of UX suggests that the choice of UX measurement instruments is difficult and that the conclusions of some usability studies are weakened by the elements that they evaluate and by the way in which they use UX evaluation measures to provide support to the quality in use of software products. Suggestions on how to respond to identified challenges can provide tools that facilitate UX evaluation from an emotional perspective, and in turn establish more valid and complete UX measures regarding the perception of a student when faced with using an e-learning environments.

References

1. Zaharias, P., Poulymenakou, A.: Implementing learner-centred design: the interplay between usability and instructional design practices. Interact. Technol. Smart Educ. **3**(2), 87–100 (2006)
2. Squires, D.: Usability and educational software design: special issue of interacting with computers. Interact. Comput. **11**(5), 463–466 (1999)
3. Quinn, C.: Pragmatic evaluation: lessons from usability. In: 13th Annual Conference of the Australasian Society for Computers in Learning in Tertiary Education (1996)

4. Albion, P.R.: Heuristic evaluation of educational multimedia: from theory to practice. In: Proceedings of ASCILITE 1999: 16th Annual Conference of the Australasian Society for Computers in Learning in Tertiary Education: Responding to Diversity, pp. 9–15 (1999)
5. Squires, D., Preece, J.: Predicting quality in educational software: evaluating for learning, usability and the synergy between them. Interact. Comput. **11**(5), 467–483 (1999)
6. ISO/IEC 25010 - Systems and software engineering - systems and software quality requirements and evaluation (SQuaRE) - system and software quality models (2011)
7. Bevan, N.: Los nuevos modelos de ISO para la calidad y la calidad en uso del software. In: Calidad del producto y proceso software, Editorial Ra-Ma, pp. 55–75 (2010)
8. Hassan Montero, Y.: Factores del diseño web orientado a la satisfacción y no-frustración de uso. Rev. española Doc. científica **29**(2), 239–257 (2006)
9. Hornbæk, K.: Current practice in measuring usability: challenges to usability studies and research. Int. J. Hum. Comput. Stud. **64**(2), 79–102 (2006)
10. Rogers, Y., Sharp, H., Preece, J.: Interaction Design: Beyond Human-Computer Interaction, 3rd edn. Wiley, Hoboken (2011)
11. ISO 9241: Software Ergonomics Requirements for Office Work with Visual Display Terminal (VDT), Geneva, Switzerland (1998)
12. Hassan Montero, Y., Fernández, F.J.M., Iazza, G.: Diseño Web Centrado en el Usuario: Usabilidad y Arquitectura de la Información, Hipertext. net, no. 2 (2004)
13. Kurosu, M., Kashimura, K.: Determinants of the apparent usability [user interfaces]. In: IEEE International Conference on Systems, Man and Cybernetics, Intelligent Systems for the 21st Century, vol. 2, pp. 1509–1514 (1995)
14. Fu, L., Salvendy, G.: The contribution of apparent and inherent usability to a users satisfaction in a searching and browsing task on the web. Ergonomics **45**(6), 415–424 (2002)
15. Madan, A., Dubey, S.K.: Usability evaluation methods: a literature review. Int. J. Eng. Sci. Technol. **4**(2), 590–599 (2012)
16. De Angeli, A., Sutcliffe, A., Hartmann, J.: Interaction, usability and aesthetics: what influences users' preferences? In: Proceedings of 6th Conference on Designing Interactive systems, pp. 271–280 (2006)
17. Sonderegger, A., Sauer, J.: The influence of design aesthetics in usability testing: effects on user performance and perceived usability. Appl. Ergon. **41**(3), 403–410 (2010)
18. Hassenzahl, M.: The thing and I: understanding the relationship between user and product. In: Blythe, M., Overbeeke, K., Monk, A., Wright, P. (eds.) Funology, vol. 3, pp. 31–42. Springer, Dordrecht (2005)
19. Harun, M.H.: Integrating e-learning into the workplace. Internet High. Educ. **4**(3), 301–310 (2001)
20. Chuah, K.-M., Chen, C.-J., Teh, C.-S.: Designing a desktop virtual reality- based learning environment with emotional consideration. Res. Pract. Technol. Enhanc. Learn. **6**(1), 25–42 (2011)
21. Zaharias, P., Belk, M., Germanakos, P., Samaras, G.: User experience in educational virtual worlds. In: CHI 2011 (2011)
22. Ferreira Szpiniak, A., Sanz, C.V.: Un modelo de evaluacioón de entornos virtuales de enseñanza y aprendizaje basado en la usabilidad. In: IV Congreso de Tecnología en Educación y Educación en Tecnología, pp. 382–392 (2012)

23. Jonassen, D.H., Howland, J., Moore, J., Marra, R.M.: Learning to solve problems with technology: a constructivist perspective (2002)
24. Rager, K.B.: I feel, therefore, I learn: the role of emotion in SelfDirected learning. New Horiz. Adult Educ. Hum. Resour. Dev. **23**(2), 22–33 (2009)
25. Redzuan, F., Lokman, A.M., Othman, Z.A.: Kansei design model for engagement in online learning: a proposed model. Inform. Eng. Inf. Sci. **251**, 64–78 (2011)
26. MacFadden, R.J.: Souls on ice: incorporating emotion in web-based education. J. Technol. Hum. Serv. **23**(12), 79–98 (2005)
27. Wang, C., Ke, S., Chuang, H., Tseng, H., Chen, G.: E-learning system design with humor and empathy interaction by virtual human to improve students learning. In: Proceedings of 18th International Conference on Computers in Education, pp. 615–622. Asia-Pacific Society for Computers in Education, Putrajaya (2010)
28. Wang, Y.-S.: Assessment of learner satisfaction with asynchronous electronic learning systems. Inf. Manag. **41**(1), 75–86 (2003)
29. Shee, D.Y., Wang, Y.-S.: Multi-criteria evaluation of the web-based e-learning system: a methodology based on learner satisfaction and its applications. Comput. Educ. **50**(3), 894–905 (2008)
30. McNamara, N., Kirakowski, J.: Measuring user-satisfaction with electronic consumer products: the consumer products questionnaire. Int. J. Hum. Comput. Stud. **69**(6), 375–386 (2011)
31. Chin, J.P., Diehl, V.A., Norman, K.L.: Development of an instrument measuring user satisfaction of the human-computer interface. In: CHI 1988, Proceedings of SIGCHI Conference on Human Factors in Computing Systems, pp. 213–218 (1988)
32. Chin, J.P., Diehl, V.A., Norman, K.L.: Questionnaire for User Interaction Satisfaction (QUIS). Human-Computer Interaction Lab, University of Maryland at College Park (1988). http://www.lap.umd.edu/QUIS/index.html. Accessed 19 Jan 2015
33. Johnson, T.R., Zhang, J., Tang, Z., Johnson, C., Turley, J.P.: Assessing informatics students satisfaction with a web-based courseware system. Int. J. Med. Inform. **73**(2), 181–187 (2004)
34. Tullis, T., Albert, W.: Measuring the User Experience: Collecting, Analyzing, and Presenting Usability Metrics, 1st edn. Morgan Kaufmann, Burlington (2008)
35. Kirakowski, J., Corbett, M.: SUMI: the software usability measurement inventory. Br. J. Educ. Technol. **24**(3), 10–12 (1993)
36. Software Usability Measurement Inventory (SUMI). Human Factors Research Group, University College Cork (1993). http://sumi.uxp.ie. Accessed 22 Jan 2015
37. Obeso, M.E.A.: Metodología de Medición y Evaluación de la Usabilidad en Sitios Web Educativos. Universidad de Oviedo (2005)
38. Kirakowski, J., Claridge, N., Whitehand, R.: Human centered measures of success in web site design. In: Proceedings of 4th Conference on Human Factors and the Web (1998)
39. Lindgaard, G., Dudek, C.: What is this evasive beast we call user satisfaction? Interact. Comput. **15**(3), 429–452 (2003)
40. Measuring the Usability of Multi-Media System (MUMMS). Human Factors Research Group, University College Cork (1996). http://www.ucc.ie/hfrg/questionnaires/mumms/info.html. Accessed 21 Jan 2015
41. Brooke, J.: SUS - a quick and dirty usability scale. In: Jordan, P.W., Thomas, B., Weerdmeester, B.A., McClleland, I.L. (eds.) Usability Evaluation in Industry, pp. 189–194. Taylor & Francis, London (1996)
42. Hartson, R., Pyla, P.: The UX Book: Process and Guidelines for Ensuring a Quality User Experience. Morgan Kaufmann, Burlington (2012)

43. Sward, D., Macarthur, G.: Making user experience a business strategy. In: Proceedings of Workshop on Towards a UX Manifesto, pp. 35–40 (2007)
44. Zaharias, P.: A usability evaluation method for e-learning: focus on motivation to learn. In: CHI 2006 Extended Abstracts on Human Factors in Computing Systems, pp. 1571–1576 (2006)
45. Ardito, C., Costabile, M.F., Marsico, M.D., Lanzilotti, R., Levialdi, S., Roselli, T., Rossano, V.: An approach to usability evaluation of e-learning applications. Univers. Access Inf. Soc. **4**(3), 270–283 (2005)
46. Sinclaire, J.K.: Student satisfaction with online learning: lessons from organizational behavior. Res. High. Educ. J. **11**, 1–20 (2011)
47. Liaw, S.-S.: Investigating students perceived satisfaction, behavioral intention, and effectiveness of e-learning: a case study of the Blackboard system. Comput. Educ. **51**(2), 864–873 (2008)
48. Arbaugh, J.B.: Virtual classroom characteristics and student satisfaction with internet-based MBA courses. J. Manag. Educ. **24**(1), 32–54 (2000)
49. Thurmond, V.A., Wambach, K., Connirs, H.R., Frey, B.B.: Evaluation of student satisfaction: determining the impact of a web-based environment by controlling for student characteristics. Am. J. Distance Educ. **16**(3), 169–190 (2002)
50. Wong, S.K.B., Nguyen, T.T., Chang, E., Jayaratna, N.: Usability metrics for e-learning. In: On the Move to Meaningful Internet Systems 2003: OTM 2003 Workshops, pp. 235–252 (2003)
51. Piccoli, G., Ahmad, R., Ives, B.: Web-based virtual learning environments: a research framework and a preliminary assessment of effectiveness in basic IT skills training. MIS Q. **25**(4), 401–426 (2001)
52. Zaharias, P., Poylymenakou, A.: Developing a usability evaluation method for e-learning applications: beyond functional usability. Int. J. Hum. Comput. Interact. **25**(1), 75–98 (2009)
53. Davis, F.D.: Perceived usefulness, perceived ease of use, and user acceptance of information technology. MIS Q. **13**(3), 319–340 (1989)
54. Sun, P.-C., Tsai, R.J., Finger, G., Chen, Y.-Y., Yeh, D.: What drives a successful e-learning? An empirical investigation of the critical factors influencing learner satisfaction. Comput. Educ. **50**(4), 1183–1202 (2008)
55. Pituch, K.A., Lee, Y.: The influence of system characteristics on e-learning use. Comput. Educ. **47**(2), 222–244 (2006)
56. Saadé, R., Bahli, B.: The impact of cognitive absorption on perceived usefulness and perceived ease of use in on-line learning: an extension of the technology acceptance model. Inf. Manag. **42**(2), 317–327 (2005)
57. Ngai, E.W.T., Poon, J.K.L., Chan, Y.H.C.: Empirical examination of the adoption of WebCT using TAM. Comput. Educ. **48**(2), 250–267 (2007)
58. Keller, J.M.: First principles of motivation to learn and e-learning. Distance Educ. **29**(2), 175–185 (2008)
59. Ouimette, J., Surry, D.W., Grubb, A., Hall, D.A.: Essential books in the field of instructional design and technology. Australas. J. Educ. Technol. **25**(5), 731–747 (2009)
60. Xu, J., Le, K., Deitermann, A., Montague, E.: How different types of users develop trust in technology: a qualitative analysis of the antecedents of active and passive user trust in a shared technology. Appl. Ergon. **45**(6), 1495–1503 (2014)
61. Urban, G.L., Amyx, C., Lorenzon, A.: Online trust: state of the art, new frontiers, and research potential. J. Interact. Mark. **23**(2), 179–190 (2009)
62. Corritore, C.L., Kracher, B., Wiedenbeck, S.: On-line trust: concepts, evolving themes, a model. Int. J. Hum. Comput. Stud. **58**(6), 737–758 (2003)

63. Nilsen, J., Molich, R., Snyder, C., Farrell, S.: E-Commerce User Experience: Trust. Nielsen Norman Group, Fremont, CA (2000). http://www.nngroup.com/reports/ecommerce-user-experience/
64. Hassenzahl, M., Diefenbach, S., Göritz, A.: Needs, affect, and interactive products Facets of user experience. Interact. Comput. **22**(5), 353–362 (2010)
65. Maslow, A.H., Frager, R., Fadiman, J.: Motivation and Personality, vol. 2. Harper & Row, New York (1970)
66. Jordan, P.: Designing Pleasurable Products: An Introduction to the New Human Factors. CRC Press, Boca Raton (2000)
67. Tiger, L.: The Pursuit of Pleasure. Transaction Publishers, New Brunswick (2000)
68. Gaver, B., Martin, H.: Alternatives: exploring information appliances through conceptual design proposals. In: Proceedings of SIGCHI Conference on Human Factors in Computing Systems, vol. 2, no. 1, pp. 209–216 (2000)
69. Jordan, P.W.: Pleasure with products: human factors for body, mind and soul. In: Green, W., Jordan, P.W. (eds.) Human Factors in Product Design: Current Practice and Future Trends, pp. 206–217. CRC Press, Boca Raton (1999)

The International Effect of the Convention on Rights of Persons with Disabilities on Access in Society and Information

Leo Baldiga[1](✉), Jacob Gattuso[2], Sophia Baker[3], Holly Gruber[4], and Phillip J. Deaton[5]

[1] Department of Journalism, College of Communication Arts and Sciences, James Madison College, Michigan State University, East Lansing, MI, USA
baldigal@msu.edu
[2] Lyman Briggs College, Michigan State University, East Lansing, MI, USA
gattusoj@msu.edu
[3] College of Engineering, Michigan State University, East Lansing, MI, USA
bakersop@msu.edu
[4] Department of Human Development and Family Studies,
Department of Psychology, Michigan State University, East Lansing, MI, USA
gruberho@msu.edu
[5] Information Technology – Digital Content and Accessibility,
Michigan State University, East Lansing, MI, USA
deatonph@msu.edu

Abstract. Accessibility standards across the world have changed drastically since the 1970s, with many social reforms, building access requirements, and information technology being modernized to accommodate the needs of the differently abled. This paper seeks to analyze how the United Nations (UN) Convention on Rights of Persons with Disabilities (CRPD) has affected the social atmosphere of various states around the world that have implemented the CRPD to various degrees. This social atmosphere consists of three core components: socio-political perceptions, laws, and information access standards within each sovereign state. Each are aspects that directly affect the quality of life afforded to persons with disabilities that are citizens of these states.

Keywords: Convention on the rights of persons with disabilities · Disabilities · Accessibility · International law · Human rights · Infrastructure · Health care · Education · Transportation · Government · Web

1 Introduction

The rights of persons with disabilities (PWD) are supported by various institutions through society and government, and there are many different factors that influence the standard of protection provided by various nations across the globe. Different states have varying aspects of their laws and societal standards that provide more rights to PWD in comparison to other states; in addition, the implementation of these laws and

© Springer International Publishing AG 2017
A. Marcus and W. Wang (Eds.): DUXU 2017, Part III, LNCS 10290, pp. 180–198, 2017.
DOI: 10.1007/978-3-319-58640-3_14

the overall quality of life afforded to PWD varies from state to state. The United Nations (UN) Convention on Rights of Persons with Disabilities (CRPD), sometimes known as the UNCRPD was passed by the UN in 2007 to attempt to combat disparities in disability rights legislation [1]. This document acts to guarantee certain fundamental rights for PWD and ensures that the discrimination of PWD does not occur.

The CRPD aims to create the most accessible and inclusive environment for PWD. In Article 9, the CRPD requires that states who have ratified the document are obligated to eliminate any obstacle that can be identified as a barrier to PWD, both in physical and digital environments [1]. The CRPD plays a vital role in ensuring the social atmosphere PWD exist in is fair and accessible, and its effects reach down to most aspects of daily life for PWD. This includes general infrastructure and physical barriers that they may encounter, access to medical facilities and treatment, and the provision of accessible education. Each of these are an integral contributor to the quality of life of any given person, and the innate importance of their equitable provision is not exclusive to PWD.

The way these core aspects of human rights are provisioned has changed drastically since the advent of the digital age. The accessibility of most websites and applications on a technological device is often a second thought to most developers. To assist PWD in acquiring consistent standards of digital accessibility, the CRPD commits signees to promoting internet and information access in Article 9 of the document [1]. This article seeks to analyze the effects of the CRPD has had on each of the states selected based on aforementioned criteria, as well as the degree of ratification and implementation of the convention that the state has achieved. The expected conclusions of analyzing the effects in this way are that states that have ratified the CRPD will have more accessible environments than those who have only signed it or not signed it at all.

2 Methodology and Contextual Findings

The way in which global society views the way each state functions can be found by analyzing the nation's history of human rights and political movements. The style of governance it currently employs to manage its population and territory, whether its citizens have a high (or equitable) standard of living, and what the government provides for its citizens in terms of social programs and rights protections are also indicative of global perception. It is through these general criteria that each of these nations was chosen in order to present the most diverse range of findings, providing a snapshot into the lives of PWD under various conditions.

Each nation investigated in this paper is analyzed in terms of the quality of protections, services, and actualized quality of life its government provides to PWD through laws and societal norms. These may include the general rhetoric and language used when the topic of disability comes up in legal documents, the actualized access to medical facilities and social services that PWD have, the ease of movement they have in their environment, and other factors of access. Ultimately, this paper will primarily consider the digital interactions within these sectors. This paper will also hope to make connections between status of CRPD implementation and other laws and regulations that each state has.

By putting each state's socio-political atmosphere in context of the CRPD, a baseline measure for disability rights and accessibility can be determined, which we can measure against the digital accessibility of each state's website. There are multiple stages to the CRPD for states that choose to incorporate it into their legislation. The four stages of adoption are as follows: not signed, signed, ratified, and ratified with the optional protocol. The general assumption is that the quality of life afforded to PWD will increase as stages of signing and ratifying the CRPD increases. Seven states were selected based on various different statuses of ratification.

In order to qualify as a state with exceptional access standards, a state must incorporate inclusivity and access into the core of its legislative philosophy. By putting accessibility and civil rights first, a state in which every person, regardless of ability, race, or economic class is included in the system of government and culture is created. Laws that ensure building access, access to education that addresses the needs of persons with learning disabilities, and an inclusive political system are key in creating an atmosphere in which PWD are fully citizens of the state, with the same inalienable rights as persons without disabilities. The first section will detail aspects related to PWD and accessibility and the next section will connect that to the digital accessibility review that was done for this paper.

2.1 Canada

Canada has passed some of the most impressive legislature surrounding the fundamental rights of all citizens, central to which is The Canadian Charter of Rights and Freedoms. The charter guarantees fundamental freedoms, as well as a plethora of other rights that are incorporated into the lives of Canadian citizens [2]. The fundamental freedoms form the basis of the rights ensured to Canadian citizens in the rest of the charter. The freedoms are [2]: "Freedom of conscience and religion; Freedom of thought, belief, opinion and expression, including forms of the press and other media communication; Freedom of peaceful assembly; Freedom of association".

Nevertheless, these basic freedoms preempt further provisions of the Charter, following up the fundamental freedoms with sections that encompass democratic rights, mobility (residency) rights, and legal rights [2]. Each of these sections contain policies that ensure a more inclusive and equal environment for PWD. One of the most important sections within the charter to PWD is the Equality Rights sections. The Equality Rights section contains one of the most important clauses for protecting disability rights [2]: "Every individual is equal before and under the law and has the right to the equal protection and equal benefit of the law without discrimination and, in particular, discrimination based on race, national or ethnic origin, colour, religion, sex, age or mental or physical disability". This clause is vital as it ensures that PWD cannot be discriminated against due to a mental or physical disability, signifying that PWD have equal opportunity to exercise their rights as outlined in the Charter as much as any other citizen [2].

It should also be noted that the Charter contains sections outlining both enforcement as well as how the Charter is to be applied within society [2]. In general, the Charter protects a very wide variety of freedoms and rights, even though it lacks a lot of specificity.

The state also has the Canadian Human Rights Act. Perhaps the single most important clause for PWD within the Human Rights Act is [3]: "For all purposes of this Act, the prohibited grounds of discrimination are race, national or ethnic origin, colour, religion, age, sex, sexual orientation, marital status, family status, disability and conviction for an offence for which a pardon has been granted or in respect of which a record suspension has been ordered".

Once again, PWD have their rights specifically protected in an official piece of legislation. Canada excels at explicitly articulating the rights of many groups of people and minorities. Canada also does well in the aspect that they have the resources available to both apply and enforce their legislation so that the idealized equal environment becomes a reality. The Canadian Human Rights Act also has an entire Discriminatory Practices section where it is made illegal to discriminate against anyone on the aforementioned list in any of the following situations. The Discriminatory Practices section outlines further anti-discrimination in the following aspects [3]: "Denial of good[s], service, facility or accommodation; Denial of commercial premises or residential accommodation; Employment; Employment applications, advertisements; Employee organizations; Accessibility standards".

The "Accessibility standards" is of utmost importance, allowing legislation to be prescribed to PWD without infringement of other groups' rights. It also allows officials to recognize that certain accommodations must be recognized and implemented so that the environment that Canada is trying to create is as equal as possible.

Many policy groups in Canada actively pass legislation that is practicable and pragmatic. These policy groups seek to expand the existing environment to make it more inclusive to all people, including those with disabilities. One example is the Accessible Transportation group. The Accessible Transportation Group seeks to "provide accessibility to the national transportation network without undue obstacles" [4]. This group seeks to improve the quality of life afforded to those with disabilities, and expand upon and ensure those rights that are promised by both the Human Rights Act and the Canadian Charter of Rights and Freedoms.

Aside from the Canadian Charter of Rights and Freedoms, The Human Rights Act, and policy groups, there are many pieces of significant legislature surrounding the lives of PWD. One such piece of legislation is, The purpose of the Employment Equity Act is defined as: "To achieve equality in the workplace so that no person shall be denied employment opportunities or benefits for reasons unrelated to ability and, in the fulfillment of that goal, to correct the conditions of disadvantage in employment experienced by women, aboriginal peoples, persons with disabilities and members of visible minorities by giving effect to the principle that employment equity means more than treating persons in the same way but also requires special measures and the accommodation of differences" [5]. The Employment Equity act can be seen as an extension of the Human Rights Act, as outlined in the Discriminatory Practices Section that discrimination in employment is unacceptable.

Canada has made plenty of legal provisions for PWD. An anti-discrimination policy, that include both physical and mental disability, is found in Section 15 of the Charter. The Human Rights Act protects Canadians from discrimination while being employed or receiving services from "the federal government; First Nations governments; and private companies that are regulated by the federal government" [6].

The Canadian government has also created an Intercity Bus Code of Practice; this "voluntary commitment" is made and upheld by bus operators of intercity bus routes and scheduled services to "serve people with disabilities in a safe and dignified manner," [4]. This includes personal care attendants, wheelchair service, mobility assistance, carriage of aids and service animals, and many more; however, most of these services require an advance notice to the station or transportation service [4].

Health services in Canada and the implementation of laws is different in every province. For example, Ontario's health care plan includes assistance to PWD so that they can live where they choose, whether that be at home or in a facility. The government also provides services that help individuals research and implement options for assistance and accommodations [7].

While all of Canada's provinces have inclusive education policies, the implementation and specific laws supporting education differ from province to province, as does the definition of disability. One aspect that sets Canada apart from other states is that they attempt to set PWDs up for success not just with in school but after as well; plans to help PWD's transition from grade school to higher education or the job market are developed at different ages for disabled students per province. Canada may need to make several improvements to their laws surrounding education for PWD. For example, the laws can be out-of-date with current standards for education; student assessments are too generalized and do not take into account individuals with disabilities. Teachers and education staff sometimes do not have an appropriate amount of individuals who are sufficiently trained to meet the needs of students with disabilities. Disability education in Canada follows one of three paths: separate classrooms for PWD (veering towards the idea of Special Education), classes containing both PWD and non-disabled students (inclusive classrooms), or a mixture where PWD spend time in a "normal" classroom and a segregated one [8]. The inclusive track with PWD fully integrated in "normal" classrooms has been shown to have a positive impact on children; however, a large portion of PWD have been put into the segregated track. However, according to the Eaton v Brant County Board of Education case, the Canadian supreme court ruled that a school board has the right to place a student into a special education class [9].

Overall, Canada has excellent documentation of fundamental rights and freedoms guaranteed to its citizens, especially to PWD. Canada has also ratified the CRPD, which only further intensifies what is outlined in the Charter and Human Rights Act [10]. On top of highly inclusive policy, Canada also has the resources to make much of the legislation implementable. On top of pre-existing laws that protect the rights of Canadian PWD, the additional rights protections promised by the CRPD make Canada an example state when it comes to creating an equal, accessible, and non-discriminatory environment for PWD.

2.2   United States

The United States' society is advancing at a rapid rate, creating a more accessible, and equal environment for PWD, despite not having ratified the CRPD.

The United States has several pieces of legislature including the Rehabilitation Act of 1973, which defines what should and should not be done in certain societal aspects of the lives of PWD. Some of the more important sections in the act are [11]: Section 501; Section 503; Section 504; Section 508. Most of these sections require affirmative action on the part of the federal government, and all of them affect PWD, whether they ensure anti-discrimination policies, employment equity, or creating a digitally accessible atmosphere. Sections 501 and 503 both protect PWD from discrimination in the workplace, and Section 504 goes on to explain that "reasonable accommodation[s] for employees with disabilities" should be made in the workplace [11]. Section 508 finishes by stating that any electronic information developed be made accessible to PWD in a multitude of formats [11]. This signifies that the United States has not only ensured access to the physical world, but is also capable of recognizing the ever-expanding digital atmosphere.

Later, the United States passed Americans with Disabilities Act of 1990 (ADA), which implemented many changes to access in the states. It required publicly funded building built after the act was passed to be accessible to PWD, and that most public transportation systems be made accessible to PWD. Title I outlines that there cannot be discrimination of PWD in the workplace because of their disability [12]. This, coupled with Sections 501, 503, and 504 of the Rehabilitation act of 1973, make powerful workplace equity. The purpose of the ADA is that [13]: "the needs of people with disabilities [be accommodated], prohibiting discrimination in employment, public services, public accommodations, and telecommunications."

The telecommunications aspect of the ADA outlines the potential for legislature that can/will be passed later in time. It also states that, "Telephone companies must provide systems for people who use telecommunication devices for the deaf (TDD) or similar devices. They cannot charge extra for these types of service." [12]. This is important to note because without that part of the ADA, the smartphone community could be different for those who are deaf or hard of hearing.

The US has a strong background and way of interacting with PWD, and has strict guidelines as to how PWD should be treated and accepted in everyday life. According to United States Census Bureau, approximately 19 percent, or 56.7 million people, of the US population lives with a disability [14]. Because of the number of disabled citizens living in the US, the state has many laws and regulations that aim to give equality to everyone.

Infrastructure in the US is controlled by the ADA, which ensures that buildings and sites must meet access requirements. The ADA applies to buildings, sites, recreation facilities, streets, sidewalks, and transportation, with several exceptions. They are not, however, in areas that either lack funding or were created before the ADA was passed. These areas created before the ADA do not have to adhere to the accessibility standards laid out in new legislation.

In the US, PWD have "a number of options for health coverage" [15]. Medicaid and Medicare are the two largest health plans for PWD. PWD can, "fill out a Marketplace application to find out if you qualify for savings on a private health plan or for coverage through Medicaid" if they do not already have health coverage [15]. Both of these programs help those with disabilities get the attention they need, if they cannot provide it for themselves.

The Individuals with Disabilities Education Act (IDEA) has been implemented into American society, which is instrumental in providing the right to accessible education for PWD [11]. The main focus of IDEA is outlined in six defining principles [16]: Principle I: Zero Reject; Principle II: Nondiscriminatory Identification and Evaluation; Principle III: Free, Appropriate Public Education; Principle IV: Least Restrictive Environment; Principle V: Due Process Safeguards; Principle VI: Parent and Student Participation and Shared Decision Making.

The Individuals with Disabilities Education Act (IDEA) is a law ensuring services to children with disabilities, and affects upwards of 6 million students. [17]. PWD are also protected under Section 504 of the Rehabilitation Act of 1973. "The Section 504 regulation requires a school district to provide a "free appropriate public education" (FAPE) to each qualified person with a disability who is in the school district's jurisdiction, regardless of the nature or severity of the person's disability" [18].

Citizens of the United States have many fundamental rights guaranteed by the Constitution, and while the Rehabilitation Act and the ADA is largely directed toward PWD, it only further aids those who may have been overlooked by the Constitution. One flaw of the laws concerning PWD in the United States is that the United States has signed, but not ratified the CRPD [10]. Ratifying the CRPD could have a significant impact on improving the rights of PWD, so it is still a question as to why the CRPD has not been ratified and implemented within contemporary American society. Two-thirds majority in congress is needed to pass the CRPD. The resources are present, but the United States has not ratified it, so the inclusivity of the social environment in the United States could be improved by this commitment.

2.3   South Africa

In the past 25 years, South Africa has emerged from being one of the most repressive states to being highly inclusive. In the transition from apartheid government to democracy, South Africa has revolutionized the way all citizens' rights are protected, including PWD. The transitional government ensured that there were many layers of protection for all marginalized groups. While apartheid had primarily affected the black Bantu people, exclusive minority rule also led to Afrikaner and British PWD having incomplete protections of their rights.

During apartheid, the South African government implemented the "medical model" of disability as its primary directive in distributing services to PWD [19]. This model, like other deficit models, treats disability as a condition which must be treated. Rather than adapting their environment to the needs of PWD, it focuses on a person's weaknesses, rather than their strengths, and attempts to "fix" the person's disability. In order to execute this framework, very basic government programs provided rehabilitation services such as prosthetics and physical therapy to PWD. The medical model of disability is often criticized for neglecting to take into account the role that having a barrier free environment and the same universal rights as other citizens can have in ensuring the dignity of PWD and as such, it is regarded by most disability experts to be outdated and restrictive. The oversights of the medical model were further exacerbated by racial and patriarchal division under apartheid, leading to black PWD having dramatically fewer rights than white PWD [20]. The services provided to white PWD were significantly superior to those accessible to black PWD, with the gap in service quality and availability exacerbated even further by The Black Homeland Citizenship Act of 1970. The act forcefully relocated blacks into designated "Bantustans", segregated ghetto townships stricken with poverty [21]. This left most blacks with no reliable access to healthcare and other social services. What services were available were extremely underfunded [20].

This all changed in the transitional stages of South Africa's government. The new constitution that was introduced is widely regarded as one of the most libertarian and inclusive constitutional documents in the world today. In chapter 2 Section 9, the "equality clause" guarantees fundamental human rights to all citizens, stating that "The state may not unfairly discriminate directly or indirectly against anyone on one or more grounds, including race, gender, sex, pregnancy, marital status, ethnic or social origin, colour, sexual orientation, age, disability, religion, conscience, belief, culture, language and birth.", which is extremely robust language protecting all civil, social and political rights of the citizens [19]. This clause is further clarified by The Promotion of Equality and Prevention of Unfair Discrimination Act (PEPUDA) which defines discrimination as "any act or omission, including a policy, law, rule, practice, condition or situation which directly or indirectly (a) poses burdens, obligations or disadvantage on; or (b) withholds benefits, opportunities or advantages from any person on one or more of the prohibited grounds" [22]. PEPUDA also has a clause specifically dedicated to protecting against discrimination of PWD, requiring the removal of barriers to access and preventing the deprivation of facilities that are necessary for their functioning in society. The constitution also establishes a Pan South African Language Board in chapter 1, Section 6, which is required to "promote, and create conditions for, the development and use thereof" many languages, including sign language [19].

Throughout the transition, many legislative documents and organizations within the government were created which completely revamped the way in which disability was discussed and how disability services were disseminated to the people. Within the presidency, the Office on the Status of Disabled Persons (OSDP) was established, as well as within the offices of the premiers of the 9 provinces [23]. The OSDP started its work with the White Paper on an Integrated National Disability Strategy (INDS), enacted on December 3rd 1997 [23]. The main goal of the INDS was to introduce the "Social Model" of disability as the primary directive of disability rhetoric in South Africa. The INDS was drafted in response to The Disability Rights Charter of South Africa, a document produced by the collectivized PWD of South Africa to assert their rights in the transition [23]. INDS addressed how the current legislation did not protect the rights of PWD and exacerbated the conditions of unemployment, poverty, and societal exclusion that many were subjected to at the time. It also specifically addresses the struggles of blacks with disabilities by acknowledging that they had been systematically disadvantaged by the apartheid system. Through this, they had been more likely to be subjected to severe conditions of poverty, malnourishment, illiteracy, homelessness and racially and politically motivated violence as a result of systematically enforced inequality [23]. Having acknowledged this, INDS sought to rectify this institutionalized exclusion by adopting the social model of disability and beginning to work on creating a barrier free environment [23].

INDS was highly effective in what it sought to do. In changing disability rhetoric and creating a framework for barrier free access in all fields, the rights of PWD were revolutionized nearly overnight. While it was extremely progressive at the time it was introduced, it was updated and replaced by the White Paper on the Rights of Persons With Disabilities (WPRPD) on December 9th, 2015. The updates were introduced chiefly to comply with the requirements of the CRPD, which South Africa had signed and ratified without hesitation in 2007 [19]. While the WPRPD did not explicitly introduce any changes in policy, simply reiterating that the primary responsibility in ensuring equality for PWD lies with the federal government of South Africa with the vision of creating a "free and just society, inclusive of all as equal citizens". In order to do this, the WPRPD established nine strategic pillars to "task duty-bearers with the responsibility of eradicating the persistent systemic discrimination and exclusion experienced by persons with disabilities" [19]. By laying out a specific plan as to what needed to be accomplished and how it would do so, the OSDP provided a framework for progress in ensuring equality through this document [19].

The most recent development in South African disability legislature is the unveiling of the National Development Plan 2030 (NDP). This document outlines the government's aims to eliminate poverty and reduce inequality by 2030, doing so by "by drawing on the energies of its people, growing an inclusive economy, building capabilities, enhancing the capacity of the state, and promoting leadership and partnerships throughout society" [24] While its overall goals are not central to the discussion on disability rights, it makes specific mention of disability and poverty as codependents in a vicious circle and outlines ways in which the cycle may be broken through social assistance programs, programs designed to reduce unemployment among the disabled, and ensuring access to quality education for disabled children [24].

With the ratification of the CRPD and the adoption of these post-apartheid regulations, things have changed greatly for South Africa as a whole, and especially so on the front of medical service availability and affordability. In the INDS, methods for improving health care for PWD are discussed with the policy object being to make accessible health care tangible for those with disabilities. Beginning with the "development of a comprehensive universal health care system, at primary, secondary and tertiary level, that is sensitive to the general and specific health care needs of people with disabilities", the OSDP instituted a form of socialized medicine that works toward making quality care more accessible for all South Africans [20, 25]. Provided Furthermore, by following the guiding principles of the constitution and the CRPD the updated White Paper seeks to ensure that an "integrated and holistic basket of accessible and affordable healthcare services at a district and community level" is provided to PWD [19]. By these provisions, programs have been developed to ensure transportation and medical insurance is to those in need that cannot afford it.

In addition to revolutionizing medical care, South Africa has taken inclusion in the schooling systems seriously, as inequality in public schooling was a key part in the development and enforcement of the apartheid state. To ensure inclusion, many reforms to integrate schools have been instituted, although progress in this regard has been slow. This is partly due to the fact that many Afrikaner and British citizens send their children to private schools, making racially integrated public education a difficult thing to achieve [26]. While the White Paper has attempted to ensure equity for learners with disabilities in its schools by provisioning for programs to meet the needs of intellectually disabled students and training in South African Sign Language, it has fallen short in implementation due to lack of resources in schools and insufficient teacher training in Universal Design for Learning [19, 27]. It's likely that increasing the training around Universal Design for Learning would have an impact on the digital accessibility of educational resources as well.

South Africa has a plan set in place to help the infrastructure in the state reach the standards laid out in the CRPD, but the infrastructure currently is not accessible to those standards. The National Infrastructure Plan, adopted in 2012 as part of the NDP, seeks to improve all of the state's public infrastructure to ensure ease of movement and access to basic services such as clean water and electric power to all of its citizens [19]. The plan will take place over the next few years, however, due to lack of funding, the plan is off to a slow start. South Africa's failure to fund this plan is a result of prioritizing assets that require renovation more urgently [19]. In addition, South Africa also has specified architectural design standards for ensuring public facilities are accessible as evaluated in terms of "safe, comfortable and convenient use of the site, building or facility by persons with disabilities" [28].

2.4 India

India is the world's fastest growing nation in terms of population and economy, on track to exceed China as the world's most populous state by 2022 [29]. With poverty rates reaching nearly 30% [29], it is clear that the state has difficulty ensuring equality and adequate standards of living. This is important because poverty disproportionately affects PWD due to inequity in education access and employment.

While India's constitution does not explicitly protect citizens from discrimination on a basis of disability, there is other legislation that presumably extends the discriminatory protections outlined in article 15 to PWD [30]. However, it does "make effective provision for securing the right to work, to education and to public assistance in cases of ... disablement", delegating this responsibility to the states [30]. While these clauses are not especially robust when compared to many modern constitutions, they do fulfill a basic understanding of human rights and the need to protect those who are systematically disadvantaged.

The Rehabilitation Council of India was established in 1992 for "regulating the training of rehabilitation professionals and the maintenance of a Central Rehabilitation Register", providing regulation in the rehabilitation and therapy industry for PWD [31]. It established minimum education requirements for professionals, and defined disability in a legal sense for the first time. However, the legislative act that provided for the council's inception uses terminology and rhetoric that is now considered offensive, using "handicapped" as opposed to the now preferred "disabled" and even using "mental retardation" to refer to intellectual disability [32]. The act was amended in 2000 to extend the responsibilities of the council to promote research in the field of rehabilitation [32]. Despite its limitations, the enactment of this legislation was a step in the right direction for India's disability policy.

Disability legislation in India was revolutionized in 1995 by the Persons With Disabilities (Equal Opportunities, Protection of Rights and Full Participation) Act. As suggested by the title, it encourages the treatment of disability as a human rights issue, protecting the rights of PWD more fully [30]. Disability was redefined to include low vision, leprosy, and mental illness. Inclusive language is used more consistently throughout the document, although the use of "mental retardation" is maintained [33]. The issues of accessibility in education and employment are addressed and significant measures were taken to ensure that the needs of PWD were met in public schooling [33]. Additionally, 3% of jobs in public service were reserved for PWD (a form of affirmative action) [32]. Perhaps most importantly, Chapter VIII is dedicated entirely to non-discrimination. It requires a barrier free environment and prescribes the implementation of curb cuts, auditory signals at crosswalks, engraving on crosswalks and rail platforms, and accessible public transport, among other things, to accomplish this. It also forbids demotion or lack of promotion in the workplace based on disability, an important provision for ensuring employment rights [33].

Having signed and ratified the CRPD in 2007, India's legislative body passed the Rights of Persons with Disabilities Bill in 2014 bringing its laws up to compliance with the convention, simultaneously repealing and replacing the 1995 PWD act with more thoroughly inclusive legislation [34]. Article 3 states that the government will "ensure that the persons with disabilities enjoy the right to equality, life with dignity and respect for his or her integrity equally with others.", blanketing inclusivity into the core of the document's philosophy [34].

Despite of these legal measures and the work of a multitude of disability rights organizations dating back 50 years, rights for PWD have only progressed marginally, due to the negative cultural attitude towards PWD in India [35]. This stigma is widely shared by the people of India and is rooted in the Caste System, a system of social stratification based on cultural and religious beliefs in Karma and reincarnation that results in the exclusion of an entire class of people as "untouchable" [36]. While it is now outlawed, the Caste system still has a heavy influence in Indian Society, resulting in disability being seen as a result of bad karma. Counseling and education are being used to overcome this stigma, but progress is slow as these beliefs are deeply entrenched in society [36].

Another challenge in improving the conditions PWD are subjected to is the intense poverty that nearly 30% of India's citizens face [29]. The condition of extreme poverty tends to result in poor health and further deterioration of any pre-existing conditions or disabilities. This is not only due to harsh, unsanitary living conditions, but also to inaccessible health care, whether the inaccessibility results from an inability to travel to health care facilities, or the cost of service itself. This is especially prevalent, as people in poverty are considered to be a lower class, like PWD, providing aid faces a cultural block resulting in PWD living in slums being stigmatized two-times over [35].

While India has ratified the CRPD, the effects of it are slow to come into effect [36], especially in areas with higher poverty rates. The Indian Government will provide finances to states wanting to upgrade their accommodations and public facilities, but it is typically only new buildings that are accessible [36]. As one person put it, "Take a short wander around virtually anywhere in the state's capital and you are faced with stairs or steep, uneven pavements with stalls intruding on their spaces, running alongside unruly traffic" [35]. In economically prosperous areas the infrastructure is often very accessible, but as the relative wealth of an area decreases, so does the prevalence of accessible infrastructure.

The stigma surrounding disability has led to a lack of adequate discussion and knowledge on the subject. This disparity in information makes it difficult to both teach about disabilities and provide accessible education. Free education for disabled minors and equal access to education of any level is ensured in The Persons with Disabilities Act of 1995 [34]. Despite this, education for children with disabilities is not in the school curriculum. However, the Indian government is working on a separate curriculum that will provide schools with teachers trained specifically to teach students with special or additional needs, as well as a system that will monitor student progress [35].

Even though over a decade has elapsed since The Persons with Disabilities Act was passed, approximately 90% of India's disabled children still do not attend school. Only 9% have obtained an education higher than secondary while most do not move past primary school [34]. The inaccessible infrastructure of the school facilities themselves discourage students with disabilities from participating. Desks and chairs for physically disabled students are only reported to be provided in 15% of universities, and few universities provide assistive software, Braille books, or sign language interpreters for visually and hearing impaired students, significantly affecting the level of digital accessibility in higher education [34]. Mental and learning disabilities often remain undiagnosed due to stigma, with some teachers refusing to work with children with disabilities because they believe that they are incapable of learning [35].

2.5 Russia

The Russian Federation that emerged from the collapse of the Soviet Union in 1991 is a dramatically more inclusive and open state than existed previously. As the Russian superpower's government was restructured from a communist authoritarian state to recognizing open democracy as a valid means of governing, the former environment of secrecy and denial of basic human rights was dissolved, at least on paper.

The Soviet government's stance on disability was to deny of that disability was ever present. This led to the rights of PWD ultimately being refused. A "two-pronged policy of care and control" for managing disabled Russians was applied very unevenly in the USSR, leading to some PWD lacking any care, and some being institutionalized permanently without any retribution [37]. These and other policies prevented adequate educational and employment opportunities for PWD, keeping them politically weak.

Despite the "openness" of Mikhail Gorbachev's democratization of Russia, human rights violations against PWD continued to be purveyed by the state into the 2000s. Parents were pressured by doctors to relinquish guardianship of their disabled children so that they may be institutionalized and hidden from the world, given a second-class education, and live an unfulfilling life [38].

Issues with guardianship and power of attorney came to a head in the 2005 landmark European Court of Human Rights case Shtukaturov v. Russia. In this case, an individual with a mental disorder pressed charges against the state for violating his rights as outlined in Articles 6 and 8 of the Convention for the Protection of Human Rights and Fundamental Freedoms. His mother had institutionalized him in a psychiatric hospital against his will [39, 40]. The case resulted in Russia introducing legislation in 2011 to allow people denied of their legal personhood to initiate proceedings to regain it [40].

Russia ratified the CRPD in May of 2012, and the changes necessary to comply with the convention were implemented in October of that year. As a result of this, the number of disabled people in Russia grew from 4.7 million to 13.2 million people in 2013 [41]. By updating the definition of "disability" to the standards as defined in the CRPD, the ratification was the primary instrument of a 6% increase in relative weight of PWD in Russia's population [41]. By providing an avenue of recognition for their disabled status, the CRPD has allowed these people to more fully exercise their rights and receive benefits, thereby increasing their quality of life.

Despite carrying such population, PWD often find the infrastructure of the world around them to be inaccessible. In cities, "narrow doorways, no elevators, and steep wheelchair ramps that lack accessible handrails" exist [42]. Accessible busses and trains exist, but they are few, infrequent, and little information is provided about them making using one next to impossible. Trains are only accessible through narrow turnstiles that do not allow PWD to pass through to purchase tickets and board. Signs around public transport are not accessible to individuals with visual impairments. Discrimination by transportation service workers is prohibited by law but there is lax enforcement. Refusal to lower wheel chair lifts on buses and denial of entry onto flights based solely on disability has been known to occur [42].

One thing preventing children with disabilities are the infrastructure barriers; accessible transportation is very limited, and a lack of ramps make it difficult for children to enter buildings. Accommodations such as assistive technology and books for students with visual impairments are scarce. While schools specifically for PWD do exist, they are often located far from homes, offer limited academic programs, and lead to segregation between PWD and their peers [43]. While Russian law guarantees a right to education and include a ban on discrimination based on disability, Human Rights Watch discovered that children with disabilities were being denied admission by administrators on the grounds that, "they are unable to learn, are unsafe around other children, or engage in disruptive behavior" [43].

The main barrier for PWD when accessing health care is discrimination from health care services employees. People with auditory impairments have "difficulty communicat[ing] with healthcare professionals and getting emergency services" [42]. Sometimes medical professionals will refuse to talk to or accommodate PWD. In some more extreme cases, PWD are discouraged by health care workers from their right to a family; for example, abortions are encouraged for disabled parents. In one instance, a health care worker tried to separate a visually impaired woman from her infant daughter [42]. PWD also face a lack of adequate accommodations and care for their specific disability [42].

2.6   South Sudan

Having faced the horrors of the continent's longest running civil war, and persisting racially motivated violence, poverty, displacement and other conditions of social inequality continue to plague more than half of South Sudan's population [44]. These conditions affect PWD disproportionately due to lack of access to social services such as transportation, education programs, and medical care (there are an average of two doctors per 100,000 population) [44]. However, there are many government and nonprofit groups that are dedicated to making progress and improving the quality of life available to PWD.

The Transitional Constitution of the Republic of South Sudan, established as an update to the interim constitutional document drafted in 2005, specifically mentions disability and the rights of PWD in three contexts: guarantee of the right to education in Article 29 of the Bill of Rights, the dissemination of rehabilitation and benefits to disabled war veterans in Schedule A: National Powers, and the guarantee of equitable access to civil services in Part 9, Article 139 [45]. However, it does not provide an official definition of discrimination or assert that the government will protect PWD from discriminatory practices in access to public facilities and businesses.

Despite the setbacks that come along with enduring violence, the Government of South Sudan has been steadily making a concerted effort to generate progress. The goal is to develop a strong democratic nation that realizes freedom, equality, justice, peace and prosperity for all through a National Development Plan issued by the state at its inception in 2011 [46]. The plan outlines the government's goals of developing the kind of strong institutions required to have a transparent and accountable administration that can protect its people and provide social services to those who need them [46]. It also establishes the Ministry of Gender, Child, Social Welfare, Humanitarian Affairs and Disaster Management, which is to become the primary organization responsible for producing legislation and managing programs that ensure the welfare of those whose ability defend themselves is compromised [46].

In 2013, the Ministry of Gender, Child, Social Welfare, Humanitarian Affairs and Disaster Management produced the South Sudan National Disability and Inclusion Policy, a progressive document which claims to "address and respond to multiple vulnerabilities faced by PWD and promote and protect their rights and dignity in an inclusive manner" [47]. In order to accomplish this goal in such a politically turbulent environment, the policy lays out objectives to ensure access, encourage participation in society, and promote respect and the protection of the rights of PWD [47]. The policy also identifies barriers and goals for improving access to education for the disabled, acknowledging the difficulties that come with lack of infrastructure, widespread poverty and negative cultural perceptions of PWD. While South Sudan has not signed the CRPD, this policy makes specific mention of its influence and implements many of its principles to be more inclusive [47]. Perhaps most importantly, it seeks to mainstream disability and adopt a human rights based approach to the subject, ensuring nondiscrimination [47].

Infrastructure for providing accessibility in South Sudan lacks in all areas, from the architecture itself, to the roads, to the lack of access to clean water in rural areas. Public buildings often do not have ramps or lifts, and any lifts that do exist lack audio or

Braille instructions, making them inaccessible to those with visual impairments [47, 48]. Information on public transportation is inaccessible for both print and digital forms. However, the largest barrier for PWD in physical access is the inability to reach facilities; roads are the largest obstacle. They are both poorly maintained and the travel distance from rural areas is often too great for PWD to embark on safely.

According to article 31 of the Transitional Constitution, PWD's are entitled to health services, both traditional and specific to their condition [47]. However, many are deterred from receiving health care by the problems in infrastructure listed above. The lack of ambulances deters access to hospitals. For those able to reach facilities, inadequate drug supplies reduce treatment options. In addition to the lack of trained medical professionals, knowledge and information on disabilities is sorely lacking in the health care systems of South Sudan, leaving few with the skills to treat people, including PWD. This in turn leads to many health care workers holding negative attitudes towards PWD, resulting in substandard or no treatment. As for mental health, the lack of information often prevents treatment and access to medication [47].

While the Transitional Constitution grants a right to education to all South Sudanese citizens, "regardless of disability or gender" [47], due to a multitude of reasons many PWD have yet to obtain this right. Discrimination is still prevalent in South Sudan in the forms of violence, both physical and verbal in nature. This impedes education access for many South Sudanese PWD on the basis of discrimination and negative perceptions of disability, long distances that must be traveled on deteriorating roads to reach schools; lack of assistive devices and specialized schools and teachers; and inaccessible infrastructure within schools such as ramps and toilets [47]. In 2014, Inclusive Education Policy was instituted by the South Sudanese government to promote education for all citizens by providing accommodations and inclusion for students with both physical and mental disabilities [48]. Despite this initiative, South Sudan is far from providing accessible education to all.

3 Digital Accessibility Findings

A website maintained by each state's government was analyzed using manual accessibility evaluation by one inspector, in order to maintain consistency of results. The website selected was the titular site for these various states, which usually details government information and services, an essential feature for PWD to access. From this website, only one page was tested: the homepage for each. We used The Web Content Accessibility Guidelines 2.0 (WCAG 2.0), published by the World Wide Web Consortium (W3C) to conduct our research [49]. A non-normative document created by the W3C was used to interpret WCAG, the Understanding WCAG 2.0 document [50], and the strictest interpretation of the standard was used in this case. As soon as an error was found for each criterion, this was marked, so multiple errors per page were not gathered. There are several weaknesses to this approach.

Firstly, the full site was not analyzed. Secondly, all errors on each page were not gathered, as mentioned above, when an error was found per criterion, it was marked in the data as having error. Thirdly, severity of each violation was not gathered, so some of the impact on PWD may not be fully represented by this study. To minimize the interpretative nature of functional requirements (WCAG 2.0 is less a checklist and more a set of functional requirements), several success criterion were limited. For 1.3.1, heading hierarchy only was assessed. Several criteria were skipped, including all AAA criteria, and 1.4.3, 2.4.4, 2.4.5, 2.4.6, 3.2.3, 3.3.4, 4.1.1, and 4.1.2. So, in total 30 success criteria were evaluated. The website identified for South Sudan website was unable to be evaluated as it went down midway through the study (Table 1).

Table 1. Study results from digital accessibility evaluation.

Country	Passes	Fails	N/A	CRPD status
Canada https://www.canada.ca/en.html	23	-	7	Ratified
United States https://www.usa.gov/	19	3	8	Signed
South Africa http://www.gov.za/	16	9	5	Ratified with optional protocol
India https://india.gov.in/	19	3	8	Ratified
Russia http://government.ru/en/	19	4	7	Ratified without optional protocol
South Sudan http://www.goss.org/	-	-	-	None

4   Conclusion

While this paper details many effects of the CRPD, it is by no means a complete analysis, and instead hopes to contextualize how the CRPD interacts with legislation and regulations within other states and how that impacts digital accessibility. It is important to acknowledge that ratification status of The CRPD is not the only means to indicate a dedication to ensuring the rights of PWD. Although it seems to have a positive impact on digital and physical access, other laws and regulations outside of the protocols of the CRPD have similar effects. Furthermore, the effects of changing socio-political attitudes and the legislative trends that follow them are not to be overlooked in this regard. The CRPD also has an impact on the atmosphere of digital accessibility. It is seen in that the ratification status of the CRPD has a positive effect on the extent to which something is made accessible digitally, as it can be seen that the CRPD aims to make all aspects of life for PWDs more accessible. It would be logical to assume that if the ratification status increases, then digital accessibility would correspondingly improve.

This raises many other questions: Do international standards for digital information and electronic information technology appear in conversation by UN groups and other international bodies often enough? What makes some states have more/better digital governance than others? Are higher access standards a signature of more digitally mature states, and what means do they use to provide information to the public? It should also be brought into question why certain states have not implemented the

CRPD to a further extent even though they have the resources to do so. The prime example being the US. Furthermore, does change in government administration bring changes to the socio-political atmosphere that affect the daily lives of PWD? If so, then the CRPD implementation would surely have a positive effect during transitional periods of government, acting as a sort of baseline for the rights of PWD.

While many of the states analyzed have ratified the CRPD, the actualized impact of the convention is lacking in developing nations, where it often needed most. While these states have an intent to fulfill its accords, they often lack the funding and logistics to make progress in ensuring the rights of PWD in overall environmental accessibility and protection from discrimination. In more developed states however, the convention appears to have resulted in immediate and effective positive change, creating more accessible and inclusive environments for PWD. Even developed states that have not ratified the CRPD, such as the United States, have superior actualized disability rights than developing nations, making the maturity of the state, rather than ratification status, the core variable in the insurance of disability rights. This signifies that the overall effect of the CRPD is determined by a combination of factors that include available resources and logistics, ratification status, political and social attitudes, and pre-existing legislature.

References

1. United Nations General Assembly: Convention on the Rights of Persons with Disabilities. New York (2006). http://www.un.org/disabilities/documents/convention/convoptprot-e.pdf
2. Canadian Charter of Rights and Freedoms, Ottawa (1982). http://laws-lois.justice.gc.ca/eng/const/page-15.html
3. Canadian Human Rights Act, Ottawa (1985). http://laws-lois.justice.gc.ca/eng/acts/h-6/page-1.html#h-2
4. Accessible Transportation (2016). http://www.tc.gc.ca/eng/policy/acc-accf-menu.htm
5. Employment Equity Act (1995). http://laws-lois.justice.gc.ca/eng/acts/E-5.401/page-1.html
6. Rights of people with disabilities (2016). http://www.canada.pch.gc.ca/eng/1448633334025
7. Community Care Access Centres, Ontario (2015). http://www.health.gov.on.ca/en/public/contact/ccac/
8. Towle, H.: Disability and Inclusions in Canadian Education: Policy, Procedure, and Practice (2015). http://www.communitylivingkingston.org/Portals/11/Disability_and_Inclusion_in_Education.pdf
9. Pastora, J.S.: How the UN Convention on the Rights of Persons with Disabilities (CRPD) Might Be Used in Canadian Litigation. http://www.ccdonline.ca/en/socialpolicy/poverty-citizenship/legal-protections/crpd-in-canadian-litigation
10. CRPD List of Countries: Convention, Optional Protocol Signatures, Ratifications (2016). https://www.disabled-world.com/disability/discrimination/crpd-milestone.php
11. U.S. Department of Justice: A Guide to Disability Rights Laws (2009). https://www.ada.gov/cguide.htm#anchor65610
12. Rehabilitation Institute of Chicago: Americans with Disabilities Act (ADA): Summary of Key Points (2016). https://lifecenter.ric.org/index.php?tray=content&cid=16
13. Equal Opportunity Employment Commission: The Americans with Disabilities Act of 1990 (n.d.). https://www.eeoc.gov/eeoc/history/35th/1990s/ada.html

14. U.S. Census Bureau: Nearly 1 in 5 People have a Disability in the U.S., Census Bureau Reports (2012). https://www.census.gov/newsroom/releases/archives/miscellaneous/cb12-134.html
15. Coverage Options for Persons with Disabilities (n.d.). https://www.healthcare.gov/people-with-disabilities/coverage-options/
16. Heward, W.L.: Six Major Principles of IDEA (2013). https://www.education.com/reference/article/six-major-principles-idea/
17. U.S. Department of Education: Building The Legacy: IDEA 2004 (2017). http://idea.ed.gov/
18. U.S. Department of Education: Free Appropriate Public Education for Students With Disabilities: Requirements Under Section 504 of The Rehabilitation Act of 1973 (2010). https://www2.ed.gov/about/offices/list/ocr/docs/edlite-FAPE504.html
19. White Paper on the Rights of Persons with Disabilities (2015). http://www.gov.za/sites/www.gov.za/files/39792_gon230.pdf
20. Integrated National Disability Strategy (1997). http://www.independentliving.org/docs3/sa1997wp.pdf
21. Nigel Worden: The Making of Modern South Africa: Conquest, Apartheid, Democracy, 5th edn. (2012). http://site.ebrary.com.proxy1.cl.msu.edu/lib/michstate/reader.action?ppg=1&docID=10518634&tm=1488418309454
22. Promotion of Equality and Prevention of Unfair Discrimination Act, 2002 (2002). http://www.justice.gov.za/legislation/acts/2000-004.pdf
23. Disability Rights Charter of South Africa (n.d.). http://www.vut.ac.za/drop/disability/DISABILITY_RIGHTS_CHARTER.pdf
24. National Planning Commission: National Development Plan 2030. http://www.gov.za/sites/www.gov.za/files/Executive%20Summary-NDP%202030%20-%20Our%20future%20-%20make%20it%20work.pdf
25. United Nations General Assembly: Universal Declaration of Human Rights (1948). http://www.un.org/en/universal-declaration-human-rights/
26. Selod, H., Zenou, Y.: Private versus public schools in post-Apartheid South African cities: theory and policy implications. J. Dev. Econ. 71(2), 351–394 (2003)
27. Dalton, E.M., Mckenzie, J.A., Kahonde, C.: The implementation of inclusive education in South Africa: reflections arising from a workshop for teachers and therapists to introduce universal design for learning: original research. Afr. J. Disabil. 1(1), 1–7 (2012)
28. SABS Standards Division: The Application of the National Building Regulations South African National Standard (2011). https://law.resource.org/pub/za/ibr/za.sans.10400.s.2011.html
29. Central Intelligence Agency: The World Factbook, India: Census Data (2016). https://www.cia.gov/library/publications/the-world-factbook/geos/print_in.html
30. Government of India Ministry of Law and Justice: The Constitution of India (2015). http://lawmin.nic.in/olwing/coi/coi-english/coi-4March2016.pdf
31. Government of India Ministry of Law and Justice: Rehabilitation Council Act of India (1992). http://niepmd.tn.nic.in/documents/RCI%20Act.pdf
32. Government of India Ministry of Law and Justice: The Persons with Disabilities (Equal Opportunities, Protection of Rights and Full Participation) Act (1995). http://newsonair.nic.in/PWD_Act.pdf
33. Government of India Ministry of Law and Justice: The Rights of Persons with Disabilities Act (2016). http://www.prsindia.org/uploads/media/Person%20with%20Disabilities/Rights%20of%20Persons%20with%20Disabilities%20Act,%202016.pdf
34. Hiranandani, V.: Disability, economic globalization and privatization: a case study of India. Disabil. Stud. Q. 30(3) (2010). http://dsq-sds.org/article/view/1272/1302

35. Sarkar, M.: Disability in India: The Struggles of Infrastructure, Prejudice and Karma. CNN (2013). http://www.cnn.com/2013/12/27/world/asia/india-disability-challenges/
36. Abidi, J., Sharma, D.: Disability as Human Rights Issue: India's "Invisible Minority" in the Policy Realm. Yojana, April 2013 issue (2013). http://www.insightsonindia.com/wp-content/uploads/2013/09/disability-as-human-right-policy-yojana-april-2013.pdf
37. Phillips, S.D.: "There are no invalids in the USSR!": a missing soviet chapter in the new disability history. Disabil. Stud. Q. **29**(3) (2009)
38. Bonneville, K.: Civil Society and Human Rights. Topical Research Digest: Human Rights in Russia and the Former Soviet Republics, pp. 4–8 (2007). http://www.du.edu/korbel/hrhw/researchdigest/russia/russia.pdf
39. Council of Europe: Convention for the Protection of Human Rights and Fundamental Freedoms as Amended by Protocols No. 11 and No. 14 (1950). https://rm.coe.int/CoERM PublicCommonSearchServices/DisplayDCTMContent?documentId=0900001680063765
40. European Court of Human Rights: Case of Shtukaturov v. Russia (2008). http://www.mdac.org/en/content/shtukaturov-v-russia-judgment
41. The Committee on the Rights of Persons With Disabilities: Consideration of Reports Submitted by States' Parties in Accordance with Article 35 of the Convention: Russian Federation (2015). http://tbinternet.ohchr.org/_layouts/treatybodyexternal/Download.aspx? symbolno=CRPD%2fC%2fRUS%2f1&Lang=en
42. Mazzarino, A.: Barriers Everywhere: Lack of Accessibility for People with Disabilities in Russia. Human Rights Watch (2013). https://www.hrw.org/report/2013/09/11/barriers-everywhere/lack-accessibility-people-disabilities-russia
43. Human Rights Watch: Russia: Children With Disabilities Face Discrimination (2015). https://www.hrw.org/news/2015/09/01/russia-children-disabilities-face-discrimination
44. Central Intelligence Agency: World Factbook South Sudan. Census data (2016). https://www.cia.gov/library/publications/the-world-factbook/geos/print_od.html
45. Southern Sudan Legislative Assembly: South Sudan's Constitution of 2011 (2011). https://www.constituteproject.org/constitution/South_Sudan_2011.pdf
46. Government of Southern Sudan: South Sudan Development Plan 2011–2013 (2011). http://www.grss-mof.org/wp-content/uploads/2013/08/RSS_SSDP.pdf
47. Government of Southern Sudan Ministry of Gender, Child, Social Welfare, Humanitarian Affairs and Disaster Management: South Sudan National Disability and Inclusion Policy (2013). http://mgcswss.org/wp-content/uploads/South-Sudan-National-Disability-and-Inclusion-Policy.pdf
48. Republic of South Sudan Ministry of Education, Science and Technology: The National Inclusive Education Policy (2014). https://www.humanitarianresponse.info/system/files/documents/files/Draft%20Policy%20Position%20Paper_TC220514.pdf
49. Caldwell, B., Cooper, M., Reid, L.G., Vanderheiden, G.: Web content accessibility guidelines (WCAG) 2.0. WWW Consortium (W3C) (2008). https://www.w3.org/TR/WCAG20/
50. Caldwell, B., Chisholm, W., Slatin, J., Vanderheiden, G.: Understanding WCAG 2.0 (2007). https://www.w3.org/TR/UNDERSTANDING-WCAG20/

Coffee Cup Reading as an Inspiration for Looking into Augmented Mugs in Social Interaction

Ahmet Börütecene[1](✉), İdil Bostan[1], Gülben Şanlı[1], Çağlar Genç[1],
Tilbe Göksun[2], and Oğuzhan Özcan[1]

[1] Koç University - Arçelik Research Center for Creative Industries (KUAR),
Istanbul, Turkey
{aborutecene13,idbostan,gsanli15,
cgenc14,oozcan}@ku.edu.tr
[2] Department of Psychology, Koç University, Istanbul, Turkey
tgoksun@ku.edu.tr

Abstract. Augmented mugs are mostly used as non-interactive displays showing images, or providing information about the liquid content. However, there has not been sufficient research on what kind of affordances mugs could offer as tangible interfaces and how people might use them in face-to-face social settings. To fill this gap, we examined Turkish coffee fortune-telling, a socio-cultural practice based on deliberate physical interaction with coffee cup for reading and creating stories out of coffee ground shapes. First, we organized coffee cup reading sessions with 18 fortune-tellers whose analysis yielded 11 characteristics reflecting user behavior with cups. A follow-up cross-cultural study served as a first step for understanding the potential generalizability of these findings. Our main contribution consists of the characteristics we derived and the related potential interaction techniques we discuss for augmented mugs with an inner display. We also contextualize our findings by two scenarios in which the mug is used as a tangible interface in social interaction settings.

Keywords: Handheld devices · Cylindrical displays · Drinkware · Co-located interaction · Fortune-telling · Quantified self · Lifelogging

1 Introduction

Mugs may be one of the most pervasive objects that accompany us in daily life. Their natural presence in various activities such as business meetings, friendly conversations, morning commutes and small-talks in hallways mark them as a potential actor in social encounters. From this point of view, we consider that mugs are social objects worth investigating for HCI to explore the interaction opportunities that computerized everyday objects could present for enriching existing social interactions [6]. Although there are some efforts in augmenting mugs, the focus is mostly on designing smart drinkwares that provide information about the liquid content and drinking-related activities [24, 25], or on considering them as non-interactive flat displays for triggering social interaction [12, 23]. However, there has not been sufficient research on what kind

© Springer International Publishing AG 2017
A. Marcus and W. Wang (Eds.): DUXU 2017, Part III, LNCS 10290, pp. 199–218, 2017.
DOI: 10.1007/978-3-319-58640-3_15

of affordances mugs could offer as tangible interfaces and how people might use them in face-to-face social settings.

As an attempt to shed light on these gaps, we turned to Turkish coffee fortune-telling ritual, a socio-cultural practice based on "reading" coffee ground shapes inside the cup and narrating this visual content to the other; thus, creating from an ordinary mug a display and interface for social interaction (Fig. 1). Our choice was motivated by the approach in HCI that considers investigating cultural phenomena and practices as fruitful resources to exploit existing mental models of individuals and explore new metaphors for tangible interaction [11, 20]. As this fortune-telling practice is based on deliberate physical interaction with a coffee cup (revolving, tilting, touching, pointing etc.) in a natural setting it allowed us to gather empirical data on actions performed with/on cups. Second, as the practice requires the person to examine the visual content inside a cup, that is the coffee ground shapes, it helped us explore potential interaction techniques for handheld cylindrical objects with an inner display.

Fig. 1. Coffee ground shapes inside a cup (h: 5.5 cm, r: 5.5 cm) that people "read" to tell fortune.

Therefore, we first conducted coffee cup reading sessions with 18 fortune-tellers and analyzed their nonverbal behavior with the cup. The analysis yielded 11 characteristics that reflected how people used such a form factor with a visual content during social interaction. Following the analysis, we wanted to see whether these behaviors have the potential to be considered as valid and generalizable across cultures. Thus, we conducted a second study with 34 people (18 native Turkish and 16 native English speakers) that was designed on purpose to imitate the structure of coffee fortune-telling by concealing any direct cultural reference to it. Our aim was to observe whether people across cultures would still reflect the 11 characteristics in a setting where they were not exposed to the cultural dimension of the traditional practice. As a result, we observed a similarity between the groups in relation to the characteristics. Although this experiment alone would not be sufficient to prove that our findings are valid for all, it helped us to have an idea on the potential generalizability of the characteristics.

In this paper, we first provide a background on Turkish coffee fortune-telling and present the previous research on augmented mugs. We then report both of our studies in detail explaining the 11 characteristics we found, discussing the related interaction techniques we derived from each, and giving an account of the cross-cultural experiment. We conclude by contextualizing our findings by two potential scenarios in which an augmented mug is used as a tangible interface in a social interaction setting.

2   Background and Related Work

2.1   Overview of the Turkish Coffee Fortune-Telling

Turkish coffee drinking and fortune-telling sessions create an enjoyable, warm and sometimes humorous social environment. In other words, Turkish coffee fortune-telling transforms coffee from a simple drink into an object that mediates a friendly exchange of thoughts and emotions. As Turkish coffee is made by using a very fine powder, it leaves a considerable residue at the bottom of the cup. This coffee ground is believed to bear traces regarding the future of the drinker. Essentially, Turkish coffee fortune-telling ritual is based on "reading" this ground and telling what the person will face or what events will happen, how and when (Fig. 2). The fortune-teller uses the cup and saucer as a source of information to construct the fortune-telling discourse. Although, fortune-telling is generally associated with foreseeing the events to come, the practice is not limited to that. During the ritual fortune-tellers also refer to the past and present life of the person by discussing the state of various aspects such as emotions, friends, relationships, education, family etc. The perspective that fortune-tellers present is considered as a guidance which makes people reflect on their situation, behavior and actions. In other words, this phenomenon creates an opportunity for self-reflection and helps decision-making. Studies indicate that the fortune-telling is perceived as a method to seek social support and advice in different societies [1, 13, 14]. This supportive dimension of fortune-telling has also been examined from an interaction design point of view in terms of advice mediating handheld devices [4].

Fig. 2. Coffee cup turned upside down after drinking (1, 2, 3), reading the cup and saucer (4, 5)

2.2   Augmented Mugs

Studies that consider coffee mug as an interactive object and examine it thoroughly are rare. The most notable one is The Media Cup developed by Gellersen et al. which is an augmented ceramic coffee mug prototype with diverse sensors placed on the bottom [3]. Through these sensors the mug could perceive the temperature of the liquid it contained, sense its motion and send these data to other devices in the environment. The researchers' main interest here was to create a network of computerized devices that would communicate to each other. Therefore, they did not address comprehensively the social dimension that coffee culture presents. Although they tried to detect different positions and user gestures related to the use of the mug (stationary, moving, drinking out of it and fiddling with it), they did not examine or discuss the role of these in augmenting face-to-face social interactions.

Coffee mugs conceived as interactive objects to be used in social interaction are also rare. There are two related projects in this respect. One of them is the Paulig Muki, a coffee mug that allows people to share images with each other both remotely and in a co-located setting [23]. When people pour fresh coffee in their mug they see an image sent by a friend in the flat e-ink display on the outer surface of the mug. This project demonstrates that coffee mugs can introduce alternative ways of communication between people. Although it is a product that triggers social interaction and can be used in face-to-face settings, it does not sense how people handle the mug and benefit from the potential interaction techniques these gestures (drinking, holding, shaking the cup etc.) could offer to augment the cup and social interaction.

The other salient work is Mugshots, a coffee mug prototype with a small flat LCD display attached on the outer surface [12]. They were inspired from the theory of Goffman who suggested that social interactions are performative. By using the theater metaphor he explained that people perform differently in front stage and back stage, which correspond to public and private spaces. The aim of the researchers was to introduce the mug into the workplace to facilitate this switching between private and public performance. For instance, the user can see the picture on the flat display related to an incoming call from a relative in the personal office. When the user goes out on the corridor and meets with colleagues the picture on the display changes to an image predefined by the user for interactions in public. Although their study was exploring how coffee could be a social object and trigger conversations in face-to-face communication, they did not address how users handled the mug as an object and what kind of manipulative gestures they could perform with the mug during the conversation.

On the other hand, mug represents an unconventional form factor compared to flat surfaces as it has a cylindrical structure composed of curved surfaces. It is made of two circular adjacent areas: the inner and the outer surface. This way, it offers a potential space for cylindrical displays with both sides whose exploration could lead to novel interfaces and design challenges, however, we did not come across a study on how users could interact with these unconventional screens. The most relevant example of a seamlessly embedded curved screen is a mug designed by Intel that has LED lights integrated into the outer surface and displays basic images such as smileys, numbers or letters [22]. Although this mug makes it possible to use the outer surface of a cup for displaying information, it is not touch sensitive and it does not consider the inner surface as a space for interaction.

In summary, the literature review presented above indicates two research gaps: there is (a) no empirical data on how people tend to physically interact with mugs in a social setting and (b) lack of interaction techniques for handheld cylindrical objects that have a display on the inner surface. Our research aimed at addressing these gaps by conducting the studies reported in the following sections.

3   Study 1: Observing Fortune-Telling Rituals

3.1   Participants

Fortune-Tellers. We recruited 18 undergraduate students who were knowledgeable in fortune-telling and have been practicing it in a social context. There were 15 females and 3 males (M_{age} = 22.4, SD = 2.1).

Listeners. Two female university students, one 22 and the other 23 years old, were recruited to participate in the fortune-telling sessions. These participants were selected among female individuals who were undergraduate/graduate students and passionate about fortune-telling. Only one listener participated in each session. The purpose for recruiting two listeners was to schedule more sessions in a shorter time.

3.2 Procedure

The fortune-telling sessions were held at coffeehouses, or at cafes within the university campus. We chose coffeehouses as experiment space as they are popular places for fortune-telling activities. In order to obtain a consistency between each session we always conducted the study indoors and were attentive to maintain the same setting in each place: we selected calm environments, arranged participants to sit always at the table facing each other and placed the camera at the same angle and position. Each fortune-telling session was composed of a fortune-teller, a listener and the researcher. The fortune-teller and the listener were sitting at the table facing each other. The fortune-teller was telling the listener her fortune by reading the cup and saucer she used to drink the coffee on location. There was no limit to the duration of the session and the average duration of each session was around 10–15 min. Before each session the fortune-tellers were asked to complete an informed consent form and a questionnaire with demographic questions. The fortune-tellers were not given any instructions regarding gesture or object use. We used a cover research subject in the form to avoid participant bias and told the participants that our project aims to examine "Fortune-telling scenes in Cinema" and therefore compare real-life fortune-telling sessions with those depicted in films. We also planned a debriefing to send after the study.

The sessions started with the fortune-teller reading the cup of the listener. When the fortune-teller has finished with the cup s/he continued by reading the saucer. When the reading of the saucer was completed, the session ended. The sessions were video recorded with a smartphone camera by the researcher sitting at a distance from the table. A small tripod was also used in order to have a stable image, consistency in camera position and angle, and give freedom to the researcher to observe and take notes during the sessions. In some small locations we employed wide-angle lens to be able to maintain the same view. The camera was positioned to frame the hands, arms and faces of both participants to record the body movements.

3.3 Coding

After data was collected, all speech in the video recordings was transcribed into written format by native Turkish speakers. 2 researchers coded six participants (30% of the data), discussed conflicts and then the rest of the coding was completed based on agreed terms. We assumed both qualitative and quantitative approach in our coding. After watching all the videos we identified two main categories of bodily engagement with the cup during interaction: manipulative gestures and positioning of the cup. For the first category, we coded how fortune-tellers handled the coffee cup and what kind of actions they performed on and with it. For the second, we coded how the participants approached the cup and where they most engaged with it in the space around them. Regarding these categories, we aimed to capture the following instances during the coding: manipulative gestures performed on and with the cup; touch and mid-air gestures involving both surfaces of the cup; areas used for positioning the cup and frequency of contact with it; position of the cup according to body and the table.

Regarding the positioning areas the participants used, 4 different approaches emerged from the video recordings. We noticed that at some points during the sessions they were holding and manipulating the cup (1) *on table*; (2) at *lower torso*; (3) at *upper torso*; or (4) leaving it on the table and using only free-hand gestures. *On table* refers to manipulating the cup on the table surface. *Lower torso* refers to the area between the table surface and the chest while *upper torso* indicates the area from the chest to the eye-level. *No contact* refers to leaving the cup on the table, fully inter-rupting contact with it and starting to perform free-hand gestures. In determining these areas and calculating the spatial relationship between body, table and cup we consulted two sources [18, 19]. Beyond these points above we were attentive to search for interesting patterns or singular gestures that we could not predict prior to this study that could be a source of inspiration for the field. We thought that coding and analyzing these non-verbal behaviors could yield insights on how people bodily engage with coffee cups during social interaction and, this way, could inform us in designing interaction techniques for augmented mugs (Fig. 3).

Fig. 3. Still image from the first study. The listener on the left, the fortune-teller on the right.

3.4 Results and Discussion

In the light of the coding described above, we obtained characteristics that could be a reference for user interactions with Handheld Cylindrical Object (HCO). We grouped our findings into the 3 following categories: *Common Manipulative Gestures, Object-handling Styles* and *Idiosyncratic Behaviors*. For each characteristic we first describe the underlying user behavior, then propose and discuss the potential interaction tech-niques for augmented mugs with inner display. We included *Idiosyncratic Behaviors* as we wanted to gather all kinds of user engagement with the cup and indicate as many interaction techniques as possible for designers to consider for such a form factor.

Common Manipulative Gestures. Below we placed a table that shows the manipulative gestures performed by the fortune-tellers.

Table 1. Common manipulative gestures performed on/with the cup in the first study conducted with 18 participants.

Gestures on/with the cup	Count
1. Revolving and tilting	88
2. Revolving	88
3. Tilting	49
4. Touching	38
5. Pointing	33

Revolving and Tilting. These gestures were the most common manipulative gestures performed by the participants (Table 1). We intend by revolving, the hand gesture that turns the cup around itself. By tilting we intend the hand movements that change the inclination of the cup forward and backward in vertical axis. Revolving and tilting gesture performed together indicates that these two movements occur at the same time. The participants used this gesture as they were trying to see and browse through the visual content on the inner surface. Except for one participant, the most used gestures were revolving, tilting, or revolving and tilting together in every participant (Fig. 4).

Fig. 4. Revolving and tilting gestures were used to examine the visual content inside the cup

While revolving alone was used to browse contents inside the cup, tilting seemed also to provide different viewing angles of the inner surface. Beyond these, people also made slight gestures that moved the cup around such as downwards, upwards, towards self and away from self. Therefore, a Handheld Cylindrical Object (HCO) should be able to respond to these changes in angle and rotation. Let us think of a curved screen embedded into the inner surface of a mug. In terms of interaction, revolving the mug clockwise and counterclockwise can be used for basic navigation on this inner display (i.e., going to the next page). The speed of revolving gesture might be used to jump from one visual element to the other on the screen such as navigating among thumbnail photos. In this regard, tilting the HCO might correspond to vertical scrolling action. Furthermore, revolving and tilting gestures might also be used to create gradual changes in media elements on the inner display such as adjusting the visual content (i.e., changing the brightness/contrast of an image). Designers can exploit these gestures not only for manipulating the media inside the mug but also to control the surrounding devices such as TV screens [7].

Tilting the Cup to Share the Visual Content with the Listener. Almost half of the participants tilted the cup towards the listener and pointed to the exact spot where they recognized a visual element and made sure the listener was able to see it (Fig. 5). Such instances of sharing the information were observed in 8 out of 18 participants (Table 1).

Fig. 5. The cup was tilted towards the listener to share the visual content

Therefore, HCO should provide the possibility for data sharing with the conversation partner. This gesture demonstrates that the inner surface of the cup is considered as a space not only for examining content but for sharing as well. In terms of interaction, the mug can be interpreted as an interface that allows the user to switch between private and public content. It is up to the user to expose what s/he sees inside the mug. In this respect, it also shows that a coffee mug does not only remain a personal artifact but might become a shared one during social interaction. For instance, while the mug is tilted towards the conversation partner to show an image, the user can manipulate the image by moving a finger on the outer surface of the mug. Designers can explore the potential of content sharing on devices with such a form factor by employing in-air or touch gestures in the interaction process.

Touching. Touching the outer surface of the cup was also a common gesture (Table 1). There were cases where this action was a singular and slight touch, as if poking or rubbing the cup. In other cases, participants continuously played with the outer surface or engaged in various actions (Fig. 6a). For example, we observed that one participant tapped on the outer surface while she was trying to remember what she was going to say. She made the same action 3 times during her session. In this case, she uses the outer surface of the cup to communicate her frustration to the conversation partner.

We also observed contact with the inner surface of the cup. One participant believed she saw an image which signaled undesirable events so she touched the inner surface to

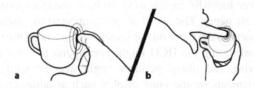

Fig. 6. Gentle and light touches were applied on the outer and inner surface of the cup

manipulate and erase the contents, therefore preventing those negative outcomes (Fig. 6b). This is intriguing in the sense that the participant got into contact with the inner surface with the intention of altering the information. It is also notable that an action which might not be socially acceptable, such as touching inside the mug, could be perceived as normal in the context created by an augmented mug. Therefore, the both surface of an HCO should be able to detect and respond to these types of contacts. In terms of interaction, touch gestures on the inner and outer surface of the mug can be used to select and manipulate content elements. Touching certain points on the mug can trigger actions such as sending messages, activating a process, responding to an incoming call etc. The fact that the user can see the inner and outer surface at the same time can create an interconnected touch space on the mug by providing a handheld double-sided display. For instance, while the user moves a finger along the outer surface, a visual element in the corresponding path on the inner surface can be triggered by this touch and start moving. Designer can benefit from this simultaneous touch interaction on both surfaces to explore novel interaction techniques for augmented mugs.

Pointing. Pointing was another common gesture among the participants. We found that 14 of them indicated the inner or outer surface of the cup during at least one instance of the conversation (Fig. 7).

Fig. 7. Pointing gestures indicated inner and outer surface of the cup

In pointing, participants indicated either a specific visual element inside the cup, or they pointed at the general direction of the cup to refer to a concept they were talking about, as if the referent was actually in the cup. For instance, a participant said "… but this is a man…" without actually showing the part that contains this specific image but instead indicating the cup in general. In this case, pointing is done mainly for the participants themselves as an expressive gesture and there is not an intention of sig-nifying the pinpoint location of visual element. However, their gesture helps to high-light the referent in the discourse. In terms of interaction, this demonstrates that people do not only tend to use touch gestures but also hover above and around the mug. This behavior opens up many possibilities for designers. Therefore, HCO should be able to detect this kind of in-air movement of a single finger. Around-device interactions have been discussed in HCI in terms of extending the interaction space around mobile devices to include also mid-air gestures as an input method [15]. While these studies focus on smartphones with flat screens, devices with unconventional handheld dis-plays, such as spherical ones, and cylindrical ones that have both inner and outer display, have not yet been explored. As we observed in our study, participants perceived the whole cup as the space where the elements of their narrative live and indicated these during the talk. These expressive gestures can be used to pull visuals from inside and send them to the outer display. They can also trigger various forms of media (i.e., visual, auditory, haptic) on the surrounding devices, or even smart clothes.

Object-Handling Styles. Below we show how the participants engaged with the cup in terms of contact and space.

Table 2. Indicates how frequently the cup was handled by the participants and in which positioning areas.

Cup	On table	Lower torso	Upper torso	No contact
Count	52	283	58	4
Percent	13,1%	71,3%	14,6%	1,0%

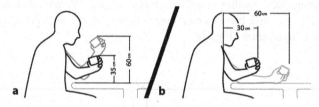

Fig. 8. (a) Approx. distance of the cup from the table surface; (b) approx. distance of the cup from the body;

Position of the Cup According to the Table Surface. The cup is mostly held in the space between the table surface and 35 cm above it. The highest point the cup was held was the eye level, which is 60 cm above the table surface (Fig. 8a). Table 2 lists the positioning areas in which the gestures were performed. Therefore, HCO should be able to recognize the gestures performed in this height range.

Position of the Cup According to the Body. The cup is mostly held approximately 30 cm in front of the body. While showing the contents to the listener, the participants extended their arms at most to approximately 60 cm (Fig. 8b). Therefore, HCO should be able to recognize the gestures performed in this range. The distances given in this characteristic, and the previous one, could also guide us in determining the visual content properties on the inner and outer surface of the mug in terms of visibility and readability (i.e., text size, image resolution etc.).

Contact with the Cup. In 86% of all gestures performed, the cup was held in hand (Table 2) (Fig. 9). Remaining 14% gestures were performed on table, although at least one hand was still holding the cup. Therefore, HCO should be designed in a way that its default status will be handheld. However, the interaction while the mug is left or handled on the table should not be ignored.

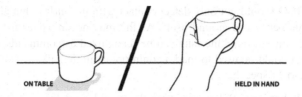

Fig. 9. Most of the gestures were performed while the cup was held in hand

Holding the Cup in a Straight Axis. Our observations revealed that the cup was mostly held in a straight axis, where the bottom was parallel to the table surface, although backwards and forwards tilting were also common (Fig. 10). Therefore, HCO should be able to recognize its different inclination states. The changes in inclination might seem problematic for designers in creating stable content on a mug. However, it might also be an opportunity in designing for fluid content [21] that user can control by revolving and tilting the mug (such as controlling a drop on the inner surface).

Fig. 10. Backwards indicates tilting the cup away from self. Forwards indicates tilting the cup towards self.

Interrupting Contact with the Cup. We noticed that participants performed most of the manipulative gestures while examining the visual contents. They carefully surveyed the cup, making many revolving and tilting actions, and once they began to speak, they left the cup on the table (Fig. 11b). Most slight touch gestures occurred during speech to indicate the contents, while angle or position changing motion gestures were mainly performed during silent examination periods. While the participants were holding the cup in air with both hands during this examination, one of them let go of the cup before they started speaking. In this case, one hand was holding the cup and the other was performing communicative gestures, which are used to express thoughts and intentions such as pointing at an object or hand movements describing a concept or thing [17] (Fig. 11a). In either way, contact with the cup was highest during examination and lowest during the conversation which is a commentary of the visual input.

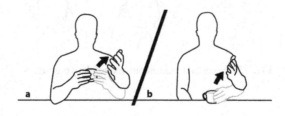

Fig. 11. The cup was used to regulate the talk.

Therefore, HCO should not only detect contact with the surface but also expressive hand movements performed around itself. As the mug accompanies the person while speaking, the gestures around the mug can be recognized as commands. For example, adjusting contact could be used to mark certain points in the talk, as leaving one hand indicates the start of speech.

Idiosyncratic Behaviors. Below we share the singular qualities of the participants' actions during fortune-telling.

Moving the Body Around the Cup Left on the Table. 2 participants left the cup on the table and had no contact with it. However, they moved their bodies around it to be able to see the inner contents instead of moving the cup itself (Fig. 12). They leaned forward or changed sitting position to get better visual frames. There were only 4 instances where the cup was left on the table without any contact however there was a gesture aiming at it. Therefore, HCO should be able to detect body movements around itself. The inclination of the body, head gestures and eye movements can provide information to the mug in terms of facial expression and gaze. The content inside the mug can change according to the proximity of the user's body.

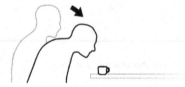

Fig. 12. Body moving around the cup

Using Long and Continuous Manipulative Gestures. We noticed that few participants continuously played with the cup in their hands and these manipulative gestures lasted much longer than other gestures (Fig. 13). Therefore, HCO should be able to detect a succession of movements as one action alone. Although a rare behavior, designers can explore the potential effect of long duration movements and continuous contact with the object for navigation purposes (e.g., browsing visual content slowly and in detail, zooming in a piece of data etc.).

Fig. 13. Long and continuous manipulative gestures

4 Study 2: Cross-Cultural Behavior Experiment

Our second study consists of a cross-cultural experiment to see whether the characteristics found in the first study tend to be culture-specific or generalizable.

4.1 Experimental Design

By conducting this study, we wanted to observe if people would still reflect the 11 characteristics found in the previous study when they were not exposed to the cultural dimension of Turkish coffee fortune-telling ritual. The traditional practice is based on two main components: examining the coffee ground on the inner surface of the cup and constructing a narrative on someone's life based on this content. In designing the experiment we imitated this underlying structure, but did not mention the cultural name and roles associated with it, that is, fortune-telling and fortune-tellers. Instead, we defined this narrative structure as a personal storytelling experience. Thus, we entitled the experiment as "Storytelling in Interpersonal Communication" and described it as a study on the role of storytelling between students in the campus. Complementary to this experimental setup, we included a non-Turkish population by recruiting native English speakers alongside native Turkish ones as narrators. These participants were asked to compose and tell a story, by looking at the symbols placed inside a mug, in which the protagonist was the listener.

In addition to the modifications above, we also changed the material components of the traditional practice. As the coffee cup is associated with fortune-telling practice in Turkey, we preferred to use a coffee mug, which is bigger in dimension, yet still manageable by single-hand, and usually not used for drinking Turkish coffee. It also presents a larger surface area that can be used for displaying visual content. To create the visual content on the inner surface, we used icons as symbols instead of abstract visuals resembling coffee ground, as otherwise this could have been perceived as a reference to the fortune-telling practice. First, we created a set of 16 icons from the website Flaticon[1]. In doing this, we looked for providing visual consistency within the set to avoid creating bias so we randomly selected the icons among black/white ones only, and those with similar visual qualities (Fig. 14). Then, we arranged these icons in two basic layouts, ordered and unordered, inside two identical mugs. The first layout was composed of grouped icons in columns, distributed in an ordered manner that

Fig. 14. The set of 16 icons we placed inside each mug

---

[1] www.flaticon.com.

contained four icons. The second layout was composed of ungrouped icons distributed irregularly around the inner surface of the mug. The motivation behind using these two basic layouts was to gather data on the possible effects of content arrangement on the narrators. Therefore, we printed two copies of the icons as 12 × 12 mm stickers and we placed each set on the inner surface of the mugs (Fig. 15).

Grouped Icons   Ungrouped Icons

Fig. 15. Mugs (h: 8.5 cm, r: 7.5 cm) with two different layouts (grouped and ungrouped icons)

Although we asked the participants just to look at the content inside the mug, we also placed some icons, selected and printed in the same manner, on the outer surface to break the potential association of the experiment setting with fortune-telling practice. In addition, we preferred calling the icons as symbols in order not to make the participants perceive the mug as a digital device.

4.2   Participants

Narrators. In total we had 34 participants as narrators. For the group of native Turkish speakers we recruited 18 people (M_{age} = 20.45, SD = 2.54) among the students at our university. For the group of native English speakers we recruited 16 people (M_{age} = 22.2, SD = 3.69) among the exchange students in the campus. The participants were awarded course credits and bookshop vouchers for their participation.

Listeners. Two female university students, one 20 and the other 21 years old, were recruited to participate in the sessions. Both were native Turkish speakers and had a good command of English. Only one listener participated in each session. They were awarded money for their participation.

4.3   Procedure

The experiment was held at the coffeehouse in the university campus to maintain the same environment as in the first study. The narrator, the listener and two researchers were present in the sessions. The narrator and the listener were sitting in front of each other at the table. One researcher recorded the sessions and the other gave the instructions to the participants. The sessions were videotaped with a digital camera. We used a tripod to have a stable image and consistent frame throughout the sessions. The camera was positioned to frame the hands, arms and faces of both participants to record the body movements, as in the previous study.

The sessions were held in two sections as there were two different mugs. Before each session the participants were asked to complete an informed consent form. In the first section we explained the procedure and asked them to compose a story to tell to the listener by examining the symbols on the inner surface of the mug given to them. We reminded the narrators to examine only the symbols placed inside the mugs and tell a story in which the listener would be the protagonist, as in fortune-telling sessions. We also told them that they were free to select, compose and interpret the symbols in any way they would like to. The listener was expected to follow the stories by providing basic verbal and nonverbal cues (e.g., saying yes-no, nodding) and ask questions whenever she was curious to know more about the details. Each story was expected to last for approximately 5 min. When the narrator was finished with the first mug, the second section started with the other mug following the same procedure in which we asked them to compose a different story. In order to prevent the primacy effect we changed the mug order in each experiment session. For example, if a session started with the mug of grouped icons, the following session with the next participant started with the mug of ungrouped icons. At the end of the sessions the narrators completed a survey with demographic information and questions related to the storytelling experience with the mug.

4.4   Results and Discussion

We coded the video recordings of the sessions according to the categories we used in our first study. We excluded one participant as he did not follow the procedure and created stories by using the icons on the outer surface of the mugs. Our analysis showed that the participants from both groups demonstrated considerably similar behavior in terms of the manipulative gestures with and on the mug (Table 2). Although the dimensions of the objects used in both studies were different, people tended to interact with the cup and the mug in similar ways. As in the first study, the most common manipulative gestures used by the participants were revolving and tilting and only revolving, which were mostly used to browse the icons inside the mug. Also tilting was a common gesture as a way to examine the inner surface. Touching and pointing, although performed less, were used to contact the mug with fingers and indicate the content (Table 3).

The motivation for conducting a cross-cultural study was not that of comparing different cultural groups but rather designing a setting that allowed us to observe if people across cultures would demonstrate similar behaviors in interacting with coffee mugs. The main finding of this follow-up experiment is that people, regardless of their cultural experience, tended to perform the same actions with and on a coffee mug in a social context. Their behavior reflected 10 characteristics out of 11, which indicates that the characteristics might not be culture-specific. However, further studies are required to evaluate this. We noticed that one characteristic, tilting, was not used in this

Table 3. Common manipulative gestures performed on/with the cup in the second study conducted with 33 participants.

Gestures on/with the cup	18 native Turkish speakers (count/percent)		15 native English speakers (count/percent)	
1. Revolving and tilting	146	34,76%	98	31,01%
2. Revolving	177	42,14%	159	50,31%
3. Tilting	47	11,19%	35	11,08%
4. Touching	23	5,48%	11	3,49%
5. Pointing	3	0,71%	3	0,95%

study for sharing the visual content with the listener, as it was the case with the coffee cup in the fortune-telling sessions. The ambiguous nature of the shapes created by coffee ground might have caused the fortune-tellers to share what they saw in the cup with the listener in the process of assigning a meaning to them. Instead, the icons in the mug were reflecting concrete images such as airplane, heart and thunder, and ready to be used as components for the stories without much need for interpretation. It seems that ambiguity created a collaborative space for making meaning together from the vague components of the visual content [9].

Regarding the role of the layout of the symbols, the survey at the end of the experiment showed that the grid-like, ordered layout on the inner cylindrical surface made it easier to compose stories as it provided a guide for navigating the visual content, and thus selecting and narrating the story components. Designers can explore this generative and supportive potential of a grid-based navigation in handheld cylindrical objects for storytelling purposes.

5   Potential Scenarios

The discussions around the results of our studies did not only demonstrate that the fortune-telling practice provided a natural and rich resource for identifying user behavior characteristics with coffee cups but also suggested two scenarios for the following contexts in which augmented mugs can be employed: (a) exploring lifelogs and (b) advising encounters.

5.1   Exploring Lifelogs

Elisa owns an augmented coffee mug that is connected to the apps and devices she uses for lifelogging and it receives the data they collect. This augmented mug presents Elisa's personal data by an interface on the inner display that covers the whole cylindrical surface inside. The outer surface of the mug is touch sensitive and used for interacting with the inner display. Elisa meets her date Erik today. She is so excited and thinks that she can bring her mug as an ice-breaker. After they have finished with their coffee, Elisa hands over her mug to Erik and asks him to tell what he sees through her personal data in the mug. Erik tries to understand what this data, represented by an abstract visualization for privacy and playfulness that are also present in coffee fortune-telling, could correspond to and how it could be part of a narration. Accompanied by Elisa he browses through the data and composes stories by combining different pieces to extend the conversation (Fig. 16).

Fig. 16. Generating new or unexpected connections through continuous and exploratory navigation offered by the mug.

This scenario illustrates how the coffee mug, a familiar component of social interactions, can be used as a tangible interface for sharing and examining personal data, and transforming it into narratives [5, 10]. In line with previous research, we argue that a way to understand the personal data and discover new connections might be changing our tendency from goal-directed information seeking towards an exploratory and serendipitous one [8]. In this regard, the coffee mug, a handheld cylindrical object, appears as a meaningful interface to extend and re-purpose the lifelog material for generating new connections and perspectives as its circular form factor embodies a continuous, random and exploratory navigation of the content.

5.2 Advising Encounters

Peter owns an augmented coffee mug that listens to the conversations around itself and provide information on the inner display regarding the content. The texts and visuals shown inside are visible only to Peter as the form factor of the mug prevents the other person to see the inner surface. One of his students, Mark, comes to see him to talk about his class project. During the talk he mentions a television show that the professor never heard of. As Peter do not want to interrupt his student's discourse, and appear ignorant, he triggers a search on the internet by touching the mug (Fig. 17a). While Mark is explaining his project, Peter is getting information on the show by looking at the results on the display (Fig. 17b). If Peter wants he can share the content with Mark on the outer display of the mug (Fig. 17c). As the search is saved, Peter can read more about the subject on computer after the meeting.

This scenario illustrates how an augmented coffee mug might be helpful for advisors' need for instant information during a meeting without revealing themselves as its form factor provides a private display space [16]. Sometimes advisors might not want to expose their search activity as they would not like to break the natural flow of

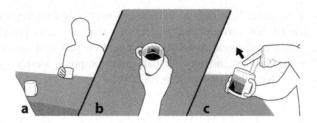

Fig. 17. The mug provides textual and visual information instantly

the communication as well as it might compromise their knowledgeable image in front of the others [2]. We believe that an augmented mug might be perceived less intrusive than other digital devices in an interpersonal communication as the mug is associated with social contexts like coffee talks. This natural presence makes it a suitable object to be employed as a tangible interface for social interaction.

6 Conclusion

In this paper, we presented our empirical investigation of Turkish coffee fortune-telling ritual, a traditional practice, as an inspiration for exploring the potential of augmented mugs in social settings. Our aim was to examine how people engage physically with coffee cups during social interaction and how these behaviors can inform the design of augmented mugs. In this regard, we conducted two studies. First one was an observational study with 18 fortune-tellers. Our analysis yielded 11 characteristics regarding the use of coffee cups that we grouped in three categories: 4 *Common Manipulative Gestures*, 5 *Object-positioning Styles* and 2 *Idiosyncratic Behaviors*. In this regard, the analysis showed that during the examination of the content inside the cup, people hold it with single hand and mostly at chest level; they use mostly revolving and tilting gestures; touching the outer surface and pointing at the cup are also common. In addition, we noticed that people move their body around the cup as well as perform long and continuous gestures with it. Furthermore, we found that the cup is used for social interaction purposes, such as leaving it on table as a sign for the start of a speech. This shows that coffee mugs are also used in guiding one's talk and as a support for marking certain points in communication. These characteristics demonstrated how people tend to physically interact with coffee cups and constituted an empirical ground that enabled us to discuss potential interaction techniques for augmented mugs with inner display.

Then, we wanted to observe if people would still reflect these 11 characteristics when they were not exposed to the cultural dimension of Turkish coffee fortune-telling ritual. Thus, we designed a follow-up cross-cultural study with 34 participants, native Turkish and English speakers, in which we imitated the structure of fortune-telling without including any direct reference to it. Our analysis showed that the participants reflected 10 characteristics out of 11, which indicates the possibility that almost all the findings from the first study might be generalizable; that is potentially not culture-specific. Regarding the composition of visual content, we found that people consider grid-based layout helpful as navigation structure for storytelling on the inner surface of the mug. This grid-based structure can be exploited in designing novel tangible interfaces for storytelling purposes with cylindrical form factor. Furthermore, as these results were obtained in a setting independent of the fortune-telling context, these characteristics can be exploited as part of a tangible interface for interpersonal communication in various contexts.

The outcomes of both studies helped us propose scenarios that describe an augmented mug as a tangible interface for two potential contexts: exploration of lifelogging data and need for instant information in advising encounters. We believe that our characteristics and scenario enable an informed discussion of potential contexts and novel interaction techniques for augmented mugs, and for handheld cylindrical objects in general. They also provide a base for making prototypes and conducting user studies for further exploration of interaction possibilities with such form factor in social settings.

References

1. Ægisdóttir, S., Gerstein, L.H.: Icelandic and American students' expectations about counseling. J. Couns. Dev. **78**(1), 44–53 (2000)
2. Anderson, F., et al.: Supporting subtlety with deceptive devices and illusory interactions. In: Proceedings of 33rd Annual ACM Conference on Human Factors in Computing Systems, pp. 1489–1498. ACM, New York (2015)
3. Beigl, M., et al.: Mediacups: experience with design and use of computer-augmented everyday artefacts. Comput. Netw. **35**(4), 401–409 (2001)
4. Börütecene, A., et al.: Informing design decisions for advice mediating handheld devices by studying coffee cup reading. In: Proceedings of 9th Nordic Conference on Human-Computer Interaction, pp. 7:1–7:10. ACM, New York (2016)
5. Byrne, D., et al.: Life editing: third-party perspectives on lifelog content. In: Proceedings of the SIGCHI Conference on Human Factors in Computing Systems, pp. 1501–1510. ACM, New York (2011)
6. Charlesworth, T., et al.: TellTale: adding a polygraph to everyday life. In: Proceedings of 33rd Annual ACM Conference Extended Abstracts on Human Factors in Computing Systems, pp. 1693–1698. ACM, New York (2015)
7. Corsten, C., et al.: Fillables: everyday vessels as tangible controllers with adjustable haptics. In: CHI 2013, Extended Abstracts on Human Factors in Computing Systems, pp. 2129–2138. ACM, New York (2013)
8. Dörk, M., et al.: The information flaneur: a fresh look at information seeking. In: Proceedings of SIGCHI Conference on Human Factors in Computing Systems, pp. 1215–1224. ACM, New York (2011)
9. Gaver, W.W., et al.: Ambiguity as a resource for design. In: Proceedings of SIGCHI Conference on Human Factors in Computing Systems, pp. 233–240. ACM, New York (2003)
10. Hilviu, D., Rapp, A.: Narrating the quantified self. In: Adjunct Proceedings of 2015 ACM International Joint Conference on Pervasive and Ubiquitous Computing and Proceedings of the 2015 ACM International Symposium on Wearable Computers, pp. 1051–1056. ACM, New York (2015)

11. Horn, M.S.: The role of cultural forms in tangible interaction design. In: Proceedings of 7th International Conference on Tangible, Embedded and Embodied Interaction, pp. 117–124. ACM, New York (2013)

12. Kao, H.-L.C., Schmandt, C.: MugShots: a mug display for front and back stage social interaction in the workplace. In: Proceedings of 9th International Conference on Tangible, Embedded, and Embodied Interaction, pp. 57–60. ACM, New York (2015)

13. Kawano, S., et al. (eds.): Capturing Contemporary Japan: Differentiation and Uncertainty. University of Hawaii Press, Honolulu (2014)

14. Kissman, K.: The role of fortune telling as a supportive function among Icelandic women. Int. Soc. Work. **33**(2), 137–144 (1990)

15. Kratz, S., Rohs, M.: HoverFlow: expanding the design space of around-device interaction. In: Proceedings of 11th International Conference on Human-Computer Interaction with Mobile Devices and Services, pp. 4:1–4:8. ACM, New York (2009)

16. Li, N., Dillenbourg, P.: Designing conversation-context recommendation display to support opportunistic search in meetings. In: Proceedings of 11th International Conference on Mobile and Ubiquitous Multimedia, pp. 12:1–12:4. ACM, New York (2012)

17. McNeill, D.: Hand and Mind: What Gestures Reveal About Thought. University of Chicago Press, Chicago (1992)

18. Neufert, E., et al.: Architects' Data. Wiley, Oxford (2002)

19. Openshaw, S., Taylor, E.: Ergonomics and Design: A Reference Guide. Diane Publishing, Collingdale (2006)

20. Svanaes, D., Verplank, W.: In search of metaphors for tangible user interfaces. In: Proceedings of DARE 2000 on Designing Augmented Reality Environments, pp. 121–129. ACM, New York (2000)

21. Wakita, A., Nakano, A.: Blob manipulation. In: Proceedings of 6th International Conference on Tangible, Embedded and Embodied Interaction, pp. 299–302. ACM, New York (2012)

22. Intel shows off a light-up smart mug, because why not? http://www.engadget.com/2014/01/07/intel-smart-mug-concept/

23. Paulig Muki. http://www.pauligmuki.com/index.php?lang=en

24. Vessyl. https://www.myvessyl.com/

25. Yecup: Your Perfect Wireless Smart Mug. http://yecup.org/

A LifeLike Experience to Train User Requirements Elicitation Skills

Silvia De Ascaniis[1(✉)], Lorenzo Cantoni[1], Erkki Sutinen[2], and Robert Talling[2]

[1] USI – Università della Svizzera italiana, Lugano, Switzerland
{silvia.de.ascaniis,lorenzo.cantoni}@usi.ch
[2] University of Turku, Turku, Finland
{erkki.sutinen,robert.talling}@utu.fi

Abstract. User Requirements Elicitation (URE) is a critical stage in the development of software systems. It is aimed at defining the information needs the system has to fulfill and the services it is expected to provide. The term "elicitation" points out the delicate role of the analyst, who has to take an active listening attitude in the dialogue with system stakeholders and intended users, being able to seek, uncover and elaborate requirements. The success of the process largely depends on the analyst's communication skills and expertise, since URE is communicative, interdisciplinary and practical in nature. Despite a variety of techniques and approaches to URE are proposed, there is not at the moment a systematic training method. In the paper, a behavioral simulator reproducing a lifelike URE conversation is presented, which was developed exactly to train URE skills. The didactical idea backing the simulator is an interaction between user and game, based on a narrative and relational model developed by one of the leading companies in the field. The effectiveness of the simulator was verified through an experiment, whose design, implementation and results are described. The experiment intended to verify the internal validity, that is if users playing systematically with the simulator improved their performance with the simulator itself, as well as the external validity, that is if users also enhanced their URE skills. Results showed users' improvements in both aspects.

Keywords: User requirements elicitation · Requirements engineering · Online applications · Behavioral simulator · Soft skills training

1 Introduction

The first step when designing an online application is to define the information needs it intends to fulfill and the services it is expected to provide. Contents and functionalities have to be implemented according to the typology of users the online application is mainly intended to reach. In order to use and enjoy it, in fact, users require the application to be able to satisfy their requests. The website of an enterprise devoted to baby care, for instance, will probably be visited mostly by parents of young children, parents-to-be, and people somehow related to the previous two groups; therefore, to meet the expectations of such users, the website must provide contents related to

© Springer International Publishing AG 2017
A. Marcus and W. Wang (Eds.): DUXU 2017, Part III, LNCS 10290, pp. 219–237, 2017.
DOI: 10.1007/978-3-319-58640-3_16

infants' needs like products available, location of stores, information about different stages of children's growth, and functionalities like buying online or having the complete view of expensive products (e.g. car seats). The process of defining users' requirements for online applications and, in general, for any type of software system, is called User Requirements Elicitation (URE). URE is one stage in the requirements engineering process, which comprises other activities such as requirements prioritization and operationalization, and it is, according to many, the most critical stage for the success of the project (Hofmann and Lehner 2001; Hickey and Davis 2002). The term "elicitation" points out the delicate role of the analyst, who has to take an active listening attitude in the dialogue with system stakeholders and with intended users, being able to seek, uncover and elaborate requirements. Literature about requirements engineering, however, does not provide a uniform presentation of the steps involved, not even a shared definition of this activity itself. It is commonly recognized, though, that URE is about learning and understanding the intentions of clients in developing the system as well as the needs of the users, with an important role being played by invention and creativity (Robertson and Robertson 1999; Maiden et al. 2004). The success of the process largely depends on the analyst's communication skills and expertise, since URE is (a) communicative, (b) interdisciplinary, and (c) practical in nature, as explained below.

(a) It can be seen as a dialogue among three actors: the client, whose intentions and expectations about the software have to be precisely clarified and made explicit; the intended users, whose characteristics have to be pointed out in order to understand their requirements; the analyst, who needs to collect the more elements as possible to realize the client's desires and fulfill users' needs.

(b) URE is performed in a variety of settings, from the development of websites and mobile applications to the design of complex pieces of software, from the implementation of enterprise systems to the development of market product lines. Different techniques are employed and approaches adopted, depending on the specific context of the project; such techniques and approaches have been borrowed and adapted from different disciplines, such as the social sciences (e.g. communication sciences, marketing), organizational theory, knowledge engineering, group dynamics. Only a few of them, though, have been developed specifically for URE (Zowghi and Coulin 2005).

(c) URE is an early but critical stage in the development of software systems, since in many cases, apart from a set of shared fundamental goals, functions, and constraints for the system or an explanation of the problems to be solved, contents and functionalities have still to be discussed, clarified, even identified. Stakeholders, then, might have different positions, or might be blind towards real users' needs or technical abilities. Moreover, most of the times stakeholders and analysts come from widely different professional areas, and do not share enough common understanding of concepts and terms; it is also often the case that the analyst has not enough familiarity with the problem, or that stakeholders do not realize what is actually feasible or realistic. All these drawbacks only emerge during the practice, that is in the actual system engineering, and require practical solutions.

As a communicative activity, URE is influenced by the multifaceted, unexpected, unforeseeable variables occurring in human interactions, and it is, thus, subject to a large degree of error. The establishment of a collaborative and positive attitude among the participants is essential to reduce incorrect, incomplete, inconsistent collection of information, and to overtake misunderstandings and misalignments between the parties involved. Despite the many techniques and approaches developed to perform URE, as well as classifications to organize such plethora of techniques and help analysts to select the most suitable one for their case, the training of novices still largely relies on practice (learning by doing) and experts' emulation (learning by observing). The need to work towards reducing the gap between experts and novices has been widely denounced, but "requirements elicitation still remains more of an art than a science" (Zowghi and Coulin 2005).

In this paper, an experiment is reported, which was designed to validate the effectiveness in training URE skills of a behavioral simulator, exactly developed for this task. The simulator derived from a joined idea between an academic stakeholder, who teaches and makes research in the area of online communication, and an industrial stakeholder, who is one of the leading international companies in the design, construction and validation of behavioral simulators to train soft skills in different working settings.

In what follows, we first set the state of the art of current techniques and approaches to URE, then we present the framework to understand and analyze online communication that led the design of the simulator. The experiment will be later described, results discussed, and future developments proposed.

2 Techniques, Methodologies and Models of URE

A wide variety of techniques, approaches and tools have been used for requirements elicitation. Zowghi and Coulin (2005) selected a core group of eight of them, which they claimed are representative of those that are both state of the art and state of practice. These eight 'families' of techniques are the following ones: interviews, in which stakeholders are interviewed by an analyst in a structured, unstructured or semi-structured manner and are best applied when there is a limited understanding of the domain from the part of the analyst; domain analysis, where related documentation and applications/competitor systems are examined; group work, implying a direct commitment of the stakeholders and cooperation among them; ethnography, which is particularly effective to investigate intended uses of the system and the addressed public; prototyping, implying building prototypes of the system to support the stakeholders and analysts to collaborate on possible solutions, which may be expensive but is extremely useful when entirely new applications have to be developed; goal based approaches, in which high-level goals of the system are decomposed and elaborated into sub-goals; scenarios, that are narratives describing expected interactions between users and the system; viewpoints, where the domain is modeled from different perspectives (such as from its operation, its interface, its competitors, its users) in order to have a complete description of the system.

The most commonly referenced empirical studies, when researching the effectiveness of elicitation techniques, are case studies (Takamoto and Carroll 2004; van Velsen et al. 2009; Martin et al. 2012) and experiments (Pitts and Browne 2004; Agarwal and Tanniru 1990). Several attempts have been made to aggregate the empirical research regarding URE to compare the effectiveness of elicitation techniques (Zhang 2007; Dieste and Juristo 2011; Davis et al. 2006).

Interviewing has emerged as the most used URE technique (Hadar et al. 2014; Davey and Cope 2008). Compared to other methods, interviewing is an interactive and engaging activity and enables the analysts to easily change the questioning strategy based on the received responses (Davis et al. 2006; Zowghi and Coulin 2005). Disadvantages of interviews are that they can be very resource demanding and require a longtime to collect answers from all the relevant stakeholders. Additionally, interviews are usually not exhaustive and do not explore all possible scenarios.

Usually, more than one technique or approach is adopted, because of the multifaceted and iterative nature of the URE process. Methodologies are reported in the literature, which propose combinations of approaches and techniques to achieve the best possible results in specific situations and environments (Checkland and Scholes 1990; Goguen and Linde 1993). When choosing a methodology, it needs to be tested in the context of use, because it can either enhance or constrain communication (Coughlan and Macredie 2014).

Process models have been proposed over the years to describe the different stages of the URE and, thus, to guide the selection of the techniques to be used (Sommerville and Sawyer 1997; Hickey and Davis 2002). Also frameworks for systemizing requirement elicitation methods have been developed (Carrizo et al. 2014). However, these models and frameworks only sketch generic roadmaps of the process; their inability "to provide definitive guidelines is a result of the wide range of tasks that may be performed during requirement elicitation, and the sequence of those activities being dependent on specific project circumstances" (Zowghi and Coulin 2005: 23).

A growing trend in software development is agile development, which poses new challenges on traditional requirement elicitation processes (Paetsch et al. 2003; Balasubramaniam et al. 2010). In agile development, an iterative URE process is used, where requirements emerge and are validated during software development. The focus is on continuous user interaction and user-centered design. A major advantage of iterative URE is the ability to adapt faster to changing requirements, but a major concern is that non-functional requirements (qualitative requirements) easily get neglected in the process (Ramesh et al. 2010).

Tools have been developed to aid URE process. A tool that provides the analyst with cognitive support is, for instance, Requirement Apprentice, which gives automated assistance for requirements acquisition (Reubenstein and Waters 1991). Other tools have been created for easier collaboration, like EasyWinWin, a collaborative user requirement negotiation software tool (Gruenbacher 2000). Some other tools aim at engaging stakeholders in the elicitation processes, as iThink, which has applied gamification to the URE process (Fernandes et al. 2012): it rewards the user with points for suggesting and analyzing user requirements.

Unfortunately, the adoption of new techniques and tools is limited, due to the lack of scientific evidence that they could provide cognitive support and domain knowledge to the analyst (Zowghi and Coulin 2005).

When committed to develop online communication projects, our research team also employs a mix of techniques to perform URE, including interviews, meetings and focus groups with stakeholders, as well as user scenarios. An original methodology developed by USI's team exactly for URE, is called User Requirements with Lego (URL) (Cantoni et al. 2009a, b). URL is based on Lego® Serious Play®, "an experiential process designed to enhance innovation and business performance" (Lego n.d.), by 'giving your brain a hand'; in fact, the core idea is doing while thinking, in order to stimulate and enhance creativity. URL is a sort of extension of Lego Serious Play, designed to support the definition of Information Architecture and content strategies in online communication. In particular, URL helps in finding tacit, difficult to grasp communicative requirements that usually do not emerge with other techniques. For this reason, URL has to be intended as an additional methodology, used besides formal and structured strategies (such as interviews and focus groups) to uncover and define user requirements.

The development of the URL methodology as well as the construction of the behavioral simulator presented in this paper, were led by the Online Communication Model (OCM), a model which ideally represents all the components of online communication artifacts – hereafter referred to with the generic term 'online applications' – like websites or mobile applications, and constitutes the framework of our understanding of URE. Differently from other models used to map URE, which are mostly based on processes and domain knowledge, OCM looks at computer-based systems from the point of view of communication, adopting a holistic approach.

In the dialogue between analysts and system stakeholders, then, a number of communication misunderstandings and misalignments may occur, which make it harder to design an online application that is able to satisfy the expectations of stakeholders and the needs of intended users. For this reason, after describing the OCM, some of the most common misunderstandings will be discussed, which were considered in the development of the simulator as well as in measuring the performances of students who took part in the experiment.

3   A Framework to Understand and Analyse Online Communication

3.1   Online Communication Model (OCM)

OCM (Cantoni and Tardini 2006, 2010; Tardini and Cantoni 2015) was developed to ideally consider all the elements and actors involved in a communicative activity taking place online. It goes beyond a naive dichotomy that sees online applications either as mere technological artefacts, to be handled by engineers or, on the opposite side, as advertising tools, to be managed by visual communication experts. The one or the other interpretation, in fact, are only partially true, and both suggest that online applications are static objects. OCM considers them as dynamic entities with a proper life and typical activities, like a shop or a press agency, and groups their constitutive elements in four dimensions or pillars (Fig. 1):

1. *contents and services/functionalities*: the more or less structured ensemble of information pieces and services provided in the application, such as information provision, news reporting, buying, chatting, product or service reviewing;
2. *accessibility tools*: the collection of technical instruments, which make the contents and services accessible, like hardware, software, and interface;
3. *people who manage*, who are the group of people who design, implement, maintain and promote the application;
4. *users/clients*, who are the group of people who access and use the application

The first two dimensions are related to 'things', while the other two ones are related to 'people'. There is, then, a fifth dimension that completes the framework:

5. *ecological context* or *relevant info-market*, which gives to every element of the application its precise meaning, value and place within the broader context of the web.

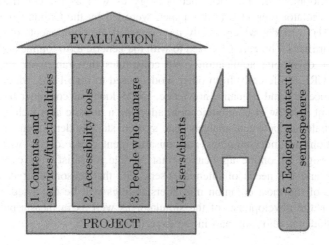

Fig. 1. Online communication model (adapted from Cantoni and Tardini 2006).

3.2 Communication Mistakes

As a result of a broad research they conducted with different teams of web design and development, Cantoni and Piccini (2004; see also Cantoni and Tardini 2006) defined the most common misunderstandings or mistakes between analysts and stakeholders of an online application referring them to three main scopes: (a) the *speakers* that are those who take part in the design dialogue; (b) the *relationship between the online application and the "world"* it is referred to; (c) the *time* spent to design and develop the application. Within each scope typical communication mistakes might occur, in particular:

1. concerning the speakers, it might happen:

   - a *mistake of person* that is when analysts and developers undertake the process of URE, design and development of the system with a person, who does not adequately represent the client, in the sense that has not a decision-making role or an adequate knowledge of the company's characteristics or needs;
   - that *each other's role and expertise are not valued*, because there are reciprocal prejudices, stereotypes or impatience;
   - that one *"can't see the forest for her trees"*, because the client and/or the analyst only focuses on one aspect of the system, which is not the most relevant, neglecting its final goal and the whole picture;
   - *to believe that the other speaker thinks and works as one does*, uses the same language, has the same knowledge of a field, follows the same procedures;
   - *to believe that one has to think as the other speaker does*, which can be the case both for the analyst, when s/he pushes the client to change some aspect of the company because s/he has a technical solution for it, as well as for the client, when s/he starts suggesting technical or implementation solutions s/he is not really expert about;
   - that one or the other of the speakers keeps *silence*, because s/he believes s/he has to think as the interlocutor but realizes s/he is not able to do so, and thus prefers to avoid the risk of failing or giving a bad impression;
   - that one of the speakers, usually the analyst, has a sense of *shyness*, due to the common belief that "the client is always right", and does not engage him/herself in an active dialogue with the client but passively obeys to his/her requests;

2. concerning the relationship between the "world" and the online application, three types of communicative mistakes can be distinguished:

   - *simulation* that is when the description made by the client of the "world" s/he wants to represent with the online application – which might be a company represented by a website, a service implemented on an online platform or a smartphone application – does not correspond to the reality, trying to make such reality more attractive than it is;
   - *dissimulation*, which is the opposite of simulation, and occurs when the client tries to hide aspects of the "world" that are considered weak or negative;
   - *utopia of the twofold* that is when the speakers – usually the client – believe that the online application will be a digital counterpart of the "world" it should represent, exactly reproducing its complexity;

3. concerning for the time factor, two are the most common types of communicative mistakes:

   - *haste* to have the online artifact ready, neglecting the time needed for its design, prototyping, implementation and testing, maybe just considering the ease of its technical production;
   - *hesitation*, mostly from the part of the client, who underestimates the time needed to realize the online application and continues to ask for changes and improvements.

4 Behavioural Simulators to Train Soft Skills

4.1 The Concept

Simulators are well known in education. Usually they are employed to train hard skills, which are specific teachable abilities that can be defined and measured, like typing, accounting, using a software. Simulators are also very popular to train procedural knowledge that is how to do things, like driving a car, flying a plane, operating a patient (see, for instance, the wide literature on surgical simulators or machine drive simulators). On the contrary, simulators for training soft skills are less known. Soft skills are personality-driven abilities, related to the emotive and communicative sphere, like patience, interpersonal relation, teamwork, communicative attitude. They can make a difference in the way a person performs in certain activities and at work, but are difficult to be defined, taught and, thus, measured.

The simulator validated in our experiment was designed to train URE skills, which comprise a number of soft skills, many of them related to people's communicative attitude, like negotiation style, self-control, empathy, complaints management. It was realized thanks to a joined idea of eLearning Lab, the laboratory of Università della Svizzera italiana in charge of improving the quality of teaching through the use of ICTs, and LifeLike Interaction, an international enterprise that designs and realizes behavioral simulators to improve job outcomes that rely in the interaction among people (LifeLike n.d.a). LifeLike simulators are based on the idea that "our brain does not accumulate data, rather, it memorizes experiences in the form of stories" (LifeLike n.d.b); different types of behavioral simulators have been developed by LifeLike for specific tasks, like to enhance customers' needs understanding, team management, communication effectiveness, sales closing, managing critical relationships, gathering information. In the next section, the simulator developed to train URE skills is presented.

4.2 How It Works

The didactical idea behind the simulator is an interaction between user and game, based on a narrative and relational model developed by LifeLike (the LifeLike Interaction®). The user plays an interactive game-interview, in which s/he plays the role of an online communication consultant, who meets a client willing to create a website for her enterprise. The game experience is highly realistic and based on emotion. In order for the dialogue to be as much realistic as possible, the situation has to be credible and the characters must have a professional as well as a psychological and private profile. The client, in our case, is Mrs. Manuela Cristicchi, the manager of a family-driven hotel on the Adriatic coast (Italy), who wants a website for her hotel, because she knows that her competitors also have a website and understands the potentiality of ICT as new promotion channels. The character of Manuela is played by a professional actor and the video sequences are built with advanced cinematographic techniques. All LifeLike simulators are built following the same technique. Actors are required a fine performance, since reading the script is not enough: they have to interpret a number of different moods and attitudes, which are communicated mostly non-verbally, with kinesics, facial expression, tone of voice (see Figs. 1 and 2). Real-time is mandatory, given that time has a real impact on the evolution of the interview and the reaction of the client; in fact, there is no pause button. Starting from a 'dream dialogue', that is the perfect dialogue between an analyst and a client, every dialogical turn was modified so to include a potential problem or an error in the URE process. The interview the user plays is the result of a unique combination of modified dialogical turns, according to his/her choices during the meeting with the client. About 16 million combinations are possible. The dream dialogue was elaborated by eLab, who has expertise in the field of online communication, URE and usability in particular; the dream dialogue was then modified by LifeLike according to its script rules.

(a)   **(b)**

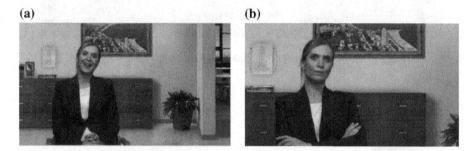

Fig. 2. (a) Mrs. Cristicchi in a welcoming attitude (b) Mrs. Cristicchi in an annoyed attitude

The game is articulated in the following steps:

1. the user logs into the system and is introduced into the simulator with a short video; s/he also receives a short description of Manuela Cristicchi's professional and personal profile;
2. the user plays the game: at each dialogical turn, s/he has to choose among three to five alternative statements, which might be either questions for or answers to Mrs. Cristicchi (see Fig. 3);
3. at the end of the game, the user gets: a score in percentage representing his/her performance in the URE dialogue according to the four stages of the game (opening, requirements analysis, solution proposal, closing) (see Fig. 4), an analytical feed-back on different stages of his/her dialogue with the possibility to check the game sequence (Fig. 5), a comment by Manuela, in the form of a telephone call she makes to her son and during which she reports her impression of the meeting and her decision;
4. the user is invited to play again to improve his/her performance.

The feed-back is based on the following indicators, weighted by the system to give the overall game score (see Fig. 5):

- negotiation style: refers to the user's spontaneous approach to the task. It can be assertive, aggressive or appeasing;

Fig. 3. Alternative choices in a dialogical turn of the LifeLike game.

(a)   (b)

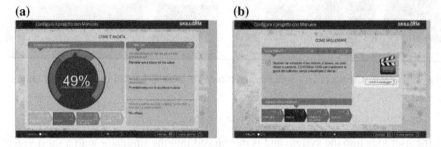

Fig. 4. (a) Overall game performance weighted according to the 4 stages of the dialogue (b) Analytical feed-back on each stage of the dialogue

- process of communication: indicates the extent to which the user was able to follow the ideal dialogical path, managing difficulties and unexpected situations;
- quality of relation: refers to the atmosphere created by the user during the dialogue, that is the extent to which s/he was able to put the client in a comfortable state;
- focus on the other part: is about the ability of the user at taking the right decision and accomplish the task without wasting time and disappointing the interlocutor;
- self-control: refers to the perceived consistency of the user's behavior;
- finalization: refers to the ability of "closing" the negotiation/dialogue.

At the end of the game, before the simulator gives its feedback, the user is asked to evaluate him/herself, through a set of questions related to the above indicators, to which s/he has to assign a score in percentage. Figure 5 reports the comparison between the scores assigned by the user to him/herself and the scores assigned by the system.

Like a muscle, soft skills need continuous and systematic training. As one single training session is not enough to strengthen a muscle, in the same way, one single game is not enough to enhance the desired skills. LifeLike Interaction fine-tuned a training protocol for behavioural simulators to be effective, which requires the trainees to play a certain number of games over one year, and their performances being monitored thanks to periodical check-ups.

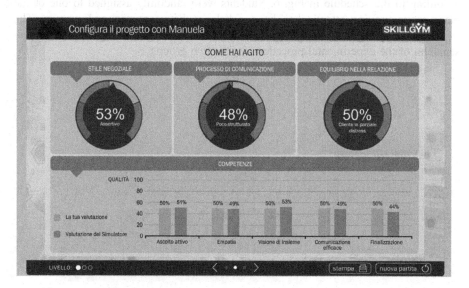

Fig. 5. Game performance according to the system indicators and comparison between the user's self-evaluation and the system evaluation

5   Validation of the LifeLike Simulator to Train URE Skills

5.1   Research Questions

The experiment was driven by two research questions:

(a) Do users playing systematically with the LifeLike simulator improve their performance with the simulator?
(b) Do users playing systematically with the LifeLike simulator enhance their user requirements elicitation skills?

Question (a) refers to the ability of players to reach better results practicing with the simulator, that is if they are able to understand the underlying rationale of the simulator and learn from it to improve their scores. If a selected group of trainees does not improve its performance with a tool/game by systematically training with it, this means either that trainees have some kind of learning difficulty – due, for instance, to a wrong estimate of the knowledge level required – or that the tool/game presents design failures – like unclear rules or inconsistent rationale.

Question (b), on the other side, represents the core of the experiment, as well as the success or failure of the simulator to accomplish the task it was developed for.

The experiment was conducted at USI with a class of 69 students, attending the second year of a Bachelor program in Communication Sciences, in the second semester of the academic year (17th February 2014–30th May 2014). The class was divided into two groups, the experimental and the control group, which trained with the simulator according to the schedule in Fig. 6. Students were randomly assigned to one or the other group, paying attention to have a balance between men and women. The experimental protocol followed five main steps described below. Figure 7 is a representation of the experimental procedure for the two groups.

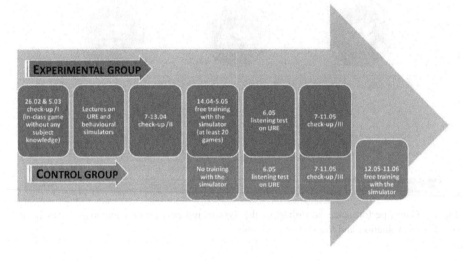

Fig. 6. Experimental protocol

5.2   Experimental Protocol

1. 1st check-up: both groups played 4 games over a 2 h class, after an overview of the experiment and a brief introduction to the simulator. Students were assumed to have the same level of specific knowledge (i.e. related to URE and online communication) and to have no experience with the practice of URE. Goal of the first check-up was to measure the individual as well as the group starting performance.

2. 2nd check-up: both groups played 4 games over one week (the game location being not relevant), after attending classes on URE and receiving details about the design, features and use of the simulator. Students were taught about different techniques and approaches to URE, case studies were discussed, and the OCM was presented as theoretical framework that drove the design of the simulator and constituted the point of reference for the URE practice. Goal of the second check-up was to measure the individual as well as the group improvement in playing with the simulator, after receiving field-specific and tool-related knowledge.

After the second check-up, students were split in groups. The experimental group was required to freely train with the simulator over 4 weeks (from 14th April to 5th May), playing a minimum of 20 games. After that period, accounts of students belonging to the experimental group were blocked.

3. 1st Listening test: after the training period, on May 6th both groups underwent a 'listening test' that is a test specifically designed to measure if students' URE skills benefited from the training. The name recalls the core of the elicitation activity, which implies the analyst to actively listen to his/her client, in order to uncover and clarify the requirements of the online application at stake. The test consisted in a video showing a lifelike dialogue between an analyst and a client willing to re-design the website for her luxury cruises enterprise (see Fig. 7a). Students had to carefully look – and listen! – at the video and annotate on a pre-set scheme three categories of elements:

   (a) what they learnt from the dialogue in terms of the 5 elements of the Online Communication Model (e.g. contents and functionalities of the website, people internal or external to the enterprise devoted to manage produce and manage it); this part was awarded 3 out of 10 points;

   (b) what else they need to know to successfully complete the URE, but that did not emerge from the dialogue, again in terms of the 5 elements of the OCM; this part was awarded 3 out of 10 points;

   (c) communication mistakes between the client and the analyst, listed according to the types described in Sect. 3.2 that are: problems regarding the speakers, problems regarding the world and its representation, and the time factor (Cantoni and Piccini, 2004); this part was awarded 4 out of 10 points.

4. 3rd check-up: the day after the listening test (May 7th), a final check-up was made, in order to test if the experimental group improved its scores thanks to the systematic training with the simulator. From May 8th until the exam, held on June 11th, the control group was given the possibility to freely train with the simulator, in order for those students to reach the same level of preparation for the exam as the students of the other group. Playing with the simulator did not directly grant students a higher score in the exam, but was supposed (as the experiment in fact later showed) to support their preparation to that part of the exam devoted to URE.

5. 2nd listening test: one part of the exam, held on 11th June 2014, was constituted by a second listening test, aimed at testing if students improved in understanding URE, thanks to the knowledge acquired during the course and to the activities proposed. An ad-hoc lifelike video (see Fig. 7b) was shot for the second listening test, showing a URE conversation between an analyst and the communication manager of a cultural association devoted to restoration of pieces of art in Venice (Italy), who wished to develop a website to let interested people know about the association activities and do fund-raising.

It has to be noted that students had access to the feedback part of the game only during the systematic training, while the check-up games did not give them any feed-back. This was to avoid that the control group could learn from its mistakes by listening to the feedback.

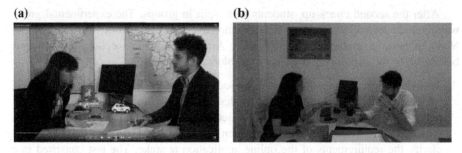

Fig. 7. (a) A frame of the first listening test (b) A frame of the second listening test

6 Results

6.1 Training with the LifeLike Simulator and Improvement in Game Performance

Charts 1 and 2 represent the values of mean and median of the control group (c.g.) respectively the experimental group (e.g.) across the three check-ups. The fact that the evolution of the median values followed the evolution of the mean values in every check-up shows that the two groups were normally distributed.

At the first check-up (c.g. $N° = 30$; e.g. $N° = 34$), the two groups performed almost the same (median = 51.3% and mean = 50.5% for the c.g.; median = 51.4% and mean = 50.6% for the e.g.), meaning that they had the same starting level of confidence with the use of the simulator.

After in-class lectures on URE and a familiarization with behavioral simulators, both groups improved a bit their performance: at the second check-up the mean value of the control group ($N° = 28$) reached 51.6% and that of the experimental group ($N° = 31$) reached 51.0%. The median values of both groups, however, slightly decreased. This result suggests that knowledge of the domain and of the type of tool alone do not influence game performance.

At the third check-up – that is at the end of the systematic training of the experimental group with the simulator over three weeks – a clear difference between the two groups was observed: experimental group ($N° = 25$) dramatically improved its performance, with a mean value that reached 58.6% and a median value that reached 57.5% (i.e. gaining 7.0% if compared to the first check-up). The control group ($N° = 22$ students) that did not play, on the opposite, had only a slight increase in the values: the mean value moved to 53.0% and the median value moved to 51.6% (i.e. gaining 0.3% if compared to the first check-up).

In order to verify if the difference in the groups' performance was statistically significant, a T-test between independent samples was performed for each check-up. The result of a T-test at 95% confidence level showed that the difference of the mean values was not significant on either of the three check-ups ($p = 0.768$ at the 1st check-up; $p = 0.498$ at the 2nd check-up; $p = 0.118$ at the 3rd check-up). It is, thus, not possible to state that a systematic training with the simulator allows to improve own

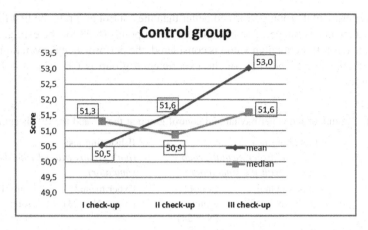

Chart 1. Mean and median values of control group across the three check-ups

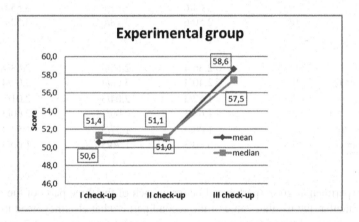

Chart 2. Mean and median values of experimental group across the three check-ups

performance with the simulator itself, even if this is what actually happened in the considered sample.

For the 3rd check-up, a T-test between independent samples was done also for specific indicators used by the simulator to calculate the performance. The difference between mean values resulted to be statistically significant for the following indicators: negotiation style ($p = 0.07$), self-control ($p = 0.048$), and finalization ($p = 0.049$).

6.2   Training with the LifeLike Simulator and Improvement in URE

Table 1 reports both the overall results (mean and median) of the two groups' performances in the first and the second listening test, and the values they obtained in each of the three parts of the listening tests.

The experimental group performed better than the control group in the first listening test, with a mean advantage of nearly one out of ten points (5.98 for the exp. g. against 5.04 for the c.g.). If the median value is considered, the performance is even higher: the value separating the higher half of the experimental group is 6.6 against 4.9 of the control group.

Table 1. Results of the experimental and control group at the 1st and the 2nd listening test

	I listening test (only the experimental group trained with the simulator)		II listening test (both groups trained with the simulator)	
	Experimental group (N = 23)	Control group (N = 24)	Experimental group (N = 23)	Control group (N = 24)
Mean	5.98/10	5.04/10	6.43/10	6.44/10
Median	6.60/10	4.90/10	6.23/10	6.47/10
Mean part (a) + (b)	3.11/6	2.64/6	3.61/6	3.55/6
Median part (a) + (b)	3.40/6	2.50/6	3.78/6	3.52/6
Mean part (c)	2.86/4	2.36/4	2.82/4	2.88/4
Median part (c)	3.10/4	2.40/4	3.00/4	3.00/4
Mean part (a)	1.67/3	1.57/3	2.04/3	2.01/3
Median part (a)	1.80/3	1.60/3	2.00/3	2.00/3
Mean part (b)	1.44/3	1.08/3	1.57/3	1.54/3
Median part (b)	1.70/3	0.80/3	1.70/3	1.60/3

The experimental group performed better in each of the three parts of the listening test, in particular, the median value of the second part ("what else they need to know") showed a relevant difference of nearly one point out of four (exp. g. 1.7 against c.g. 0.8). This result might mean that training with the simulator, users became more sensitive to the need of collecting all the relevant information to develop a successful application and, conversely, more alert in detecting the missing information.

Results of the second listening test showed a slight improvement for the experimental group – both overall and in the single parts of the test – but a dramatic improvement of the control group performances. It has to be remembered that after the first listening test the experimental group was denied access to the simulator. Instead, the control group systematically trained with the simulator: its mean and median scores raised of about 1.50 points out of ten. The median reached 6.47 against the previous value of 4.90, and the mean reached 6.44 against 5.04. If the single parts are taken into account, users' performances improved especially in the first two parts of the listening test ("what they learnt" and "what else they need to know"), more than in the third part ("communication mistakes"), confirming the above observation.

T-test for independent samples were performed also for the two listening tests, in order to verify if the difference in the mean values between the two groups was statistically significant. The T-test for the first listening test showed a significant difference between the two groups (p = 0.025) that is that a systematic training with the LifeLike simulator can improve URE skills. The T-test for the second listening test, instead, did not show a significant difference (p = 0.67).

7 Conclusion

Behavioral simulators are a new type of systems developed to train soft skills, which are personality-driven abilities related to the emotive and communicative sphere. In the paper, the design process, the development and the first results of an experiment aimed at validating a behavioral simulator to train user requirements elicitation skills were presented. The experiment involved students of a second-year Bachelor attending a course on Online Communication. Both their performance in playing with the simulator and their ability in the practice of URE were measured in order to verify the effectiveness of the simulator. Results showed that after a period of systematic training, the median values of the experimental group increased more than those of the control group that did not train with the simulator, even though such observation is not statistically significant, thus cannot be generalized. Results of the listening tests, which were designed to test students' URE skills out of the simulator environment, also showed an improvement in the performance of the experimental group, which was, instead, statistically significant; it is, thus possible to state that a systematic training with LifeLike simulator promoted an improvement in URE skills. In particular, users performed better in the parts of the test related to the requirements identification (i.e. what they learnt from the client's words), and to the unsatisfied requirements need (i.e. what else they need to know that did not come out from the dialogue with the client).

Some factors that probably influenced the experiment, and that are worth to be considered more carefully in a second experimental round, are the following ones: the size of the sample, the drop-out given to the type of users (i.e. students), the timeframe of the training that is usually much longer in non-experimental contexts (LifeLike suggests to play 20 games along 4 weeks). Further analysis, then, should be performed to test the correlation between performance and users' gender.

While, on the one hand, the promising results of the study open new educational opportunities to train designers in URE, on the other hand they raise several opportunities to enhance the technical design of the novel URE training platform. The student's performance can be observed not only by recording his/her choices on the screen, but by analyzing face muscles, by eye tracking, or by learning about his/her movements, breathing, skin, or voice. All the data collected can be mined for tracing the student's patterns and compared to those within a larger student community. The more a given student's behavior is observed and analyzed and opened transparently to the student, the more s/he can learn from his/her learning process and improve performance.

By having the student to talk to the simulator, it is possible to automatically transcribe the communication and analyze the student's oral communication, by using natural language processing, including sentiment analysis. These technologies would probably help the student to identify and self-analyze communication mistakes and thus improve the current system, which did not yet help students in this particular area.

References

Agarwal, R., Tanniru, M.R.: Knowledge acquisition using structured interviewing: an empirical investigation. J. Manag. Inf. Syst. **7**(1), 123–140 (1990)

Balasubramaniam, R., Cao, L., Baskerville, R.: Agile requirements engineering practices and challenges: an empirical study. Inf. Syst. J. **20**(5), 449–480 (2010)

Cantoni, L., Piccini, C.: Il sito del vicino è sempre più verde. La comunicazione fra committenti e progettisti di siti internet. Franco Angeli, Milano (2004)

Cantoni, L., Tardini, S.: Internet. Routledge, London, New York (2006)

Cantoni, L., Botturi, L., Faré, M., Bolchini, D.: Playful holistic support to HCI requirements using LEGO bricks. In: Kurosu, M. (ed.) HCD 2009. LNCS, vol. 5619, pp. 844–853. Springer, Heidelberg (2009a). doi:10.1007/978-3-642-02806-9_97

Cantoni, L., Marchiori, E., Faré, M., Botturi, L., Bolchini, D.: A systematic methodology to use LEGO bricks in web communication design. In: Proceedings of the 27th ACM International Conference on Design of Communication, Bloomington, Indiana, USA, 05–07 October 2009, pp. 187–192. ACM, New York (2009b)

Cantoni, L., Tardini, S.: The Internet and the Web. In: Albertazzi, D., Cobley, P. (eds.) The Media. An Introduction, 3rd edn, pp. 220–232. Longman, New York (2010)

Carrizo, D., Dieste, O., Juristo, N.: Systematizing requirements elicitation technique selection. Inf. Softw. Technol. **56**(6), 644–669 (2014)

Checkland, P., Scholes, J.: Soft Systems Methodology in Action. Wiley, New York (1990)

Coughlan, J., Macredie, R.D.: Effective communication in requirements elicitation: a comparison of methodologies. Requir. Eng. **7**(2), 47–60 (2014)

Davey, B., Cope, C.: Requirements elicitation – what's missing? Issues Inf. Sci. Inf. Technol. **5**(1), 53–57 (2008)

Davis, A., et al.: Effectiveness of requirements elicitation techniques: empirical results derived from a systematic review. In: Proceedings of the IEEE International Conference on Requirements Engineering, pp. 176–185 (2006)

Dieste, O., Juristo, N.: Systematic review and aggregation of empirical studies on elicitation techniques. IEEE Trans. Softw. Eng. **37**(2), 283–304 (2011)

Fernandes, J., et al.: iThink: a game-based approach towards improving collaboration and participation in requirement elicitation. Procedia Comput. Sci. **15**, 66–77 (2012)

Goguen, J.A., Linde, C.: Techniques for requirements elicitation. In: 1993 Proceedings of IEEE International Symposium on Requirements Engineering, pp. 152–164. IEEE, January 1993

Gruenbacher, P.: Collaborative requirements negotiation with EasyWinWin. In: Proceedings - International Workshop on Database and Expert Systems Applications, DEXA 2000, pp. 954–958 (2000)

Hadar, I., Soffer, P., Kenzi, K.: The role of domain knowledge in requirements elicitation via interviews: an exploratory study. Requir. Eng. **19**(2), 143–159 (2014)

Hickey, A.M., Davis, A.M.: The role of requirements elicitation techniques in achieving software quality. In: Proceedings of the 8th International Workshop of Requirements Engineering: Foundation for Software Quality, Essen, Germany, 9–10 September 2002

Hofmann, H.F., Lehner, F.: Requirements engineering as a success factor in software projects. IEEE Softw. **18**(4), 58–66 (2001)

Lego: Lego Serious Play (n.d.). http://www.seriousplay.com. Accessed 7 Feb 2017

LifeLike: Behavioral simulation (n.d.a). http://www.lifelikeinteraction.com/en/index.html. Accessed 7 Feb 2017

LifeLike: Simulators behavior (n.d.b). http://www.lifelikeinteraction.com/en/concept.html

Maiden, N., Gizikis, A., Robertson, S.: Provoking creativity: imagine what your requirements could be like. IEEE Softw. **21**(5), 68–75 (2004)

Martin, J.L., et al.: A user-centred approach to requirements elicitation in medical device development: a case study from an industry perspective. Appl. Ergon. **43**(1), 184–190 (2012)

Paetsch, F., Eberlein, A., Maurer, F.: Requirements engineering and agile software development. In: Proceedings of the Twelfth IEEE International Workshops on Enabling Technologies: Infrastructure for Collaborative Enterprises, WET ICE 2003, pp. 308–313 (2003)

Pitts, M.G., Browne, G.J.: Stopping behavior of systems analysts during information requirements elicitation. J. Manag. Inf. Syst. **21**(1), 203–226 (2004)

Reubenstein, H.B., Waters, R.C.: The requirements apprentice: automated assistance for requirements acquisition. IEEE Trans. Softw. Eng. **17**(3), 226–240 (1991)

Robertson, S., Robertson, J.: Mastering the Requirements Process. Addison Wesley, Great Britain (1999)

Sommerville, I., Sawyer, P.: Requirements Engineering: A Good Practice Guide. Wiley, Great Britain (1997)

Takamoto, Y., Carroll, J.M.: Designing a mobile phone of the future: requirements elicitation using photo essays and scenarios. In: 18th International Conference on Advanced Information Networking and Applications, AINA 2004, vol. 2, pp. 475–480 (2004)

Tardini, S., Cantoni, L.: Hypermedia, internet and the web. In: Cantoni, L., Danowski, J.A. (eds.) Communication and Technology, pp. 119–140. De Gruyter Mouton, Berlin (2015)

van Velsen, L., van der Geest, T., ter Hedde, M., Derks, W.: Requirements engineering for e-Government services: a citizen-centric approach and case study. Gov. Inf. Q. **26**(3), 477–486 (2009)

Zhang, Z.: Effective Requirements Development-A Comparison of Requirements Elicitation Techniques, p. 9. Tampere, Finland (2007). INSPIRE

Zowghi, D., Coulin, C.: Requirements elicitation: a survey of techniques, approaches, and tools. In: Aurum, A., Wohlin, C. (eds.) Engineering and Managing Software Requirements, pp. 19–46. Springer, Heidelberg (2005)

Comfortable Subjective Duration and User Experience of Face Recognition

Tingting Gan[✉] and Chengqiang Yi

Baidu, Beijing, People's Republic of China
{gantingting,yichengqiang}@baidu.com

Abstract. Face recognition, as an important biometric technique for personal identification, has been widely used in many departments as government, public security, banking, securities, taxation and army. However, most previous research paid more attention on technology in accuracy and speed and ignored user experience, which was our focus. We evaluated user experience of our and competing products, furthermore, quantitatively analyzed comfortable subjective duration of three stages called face detection, blink detection and picture-taking, adopting tolerance experiment and usability test. The result revealed that comfortable subjective duration of three stages were 1–2.5 s, 0.8–1.8 s, 0–0.7 s. Combined with the result of usability test, we optimized UE/UI design to enhance the user experience.

Keywords: Face recognition · Comfortable subjective duration · User experience

1 Introduction

Face recognition was the process of determining the size, location, position and orientation of human face from the input image, the research of which can be traced back to the 1960s. And it has become increasingly mature after decades of tortuous development [1, 2]. Face recognition was an important biometric technique for personal identification, has been widely used in many departments as government, public security, banking, securities, taxation and army. Most previous research focused more on technology in accuracy and speed [3–6], such as Galton proposed the use of the key points and their distances of the human face to represent the feature vector of the human face.

However, many researchers revealed that objective stimuli and subjective experience tended to be always inconsistent [7, 8]. Less studies assessed the user subjective evaluation in the process of face recognition in order to achieve not only the goal of a fast and accurate identification but only a good user experience. On the basis of this problem, our research paid more attention on the following questions:

1. What was the objective performance of our and competing product in terms of pass rate and recognition length after contrasting test?
2. What was the user's subjective evaluation of our and competing product? And was the subjective evaluation consistent with objective performance? If there is inconsistency, what was it and we needed to find out the reason in order to optimize UE/UI design.

© Springer International Publishing AG 2017
A. Marcus and W. Wang (Eds.): DUXU 2017, Part III, LNCS 10290, pp. 238–248, 2017.
DOI: 10.1007/978-3-319-58640-3_17

3. In the face recognition, what was the most appropriate subjective duration from the user perspective?

The current purpose might provide a direction of the further optimization direction on the users' subjective experience of face recognition through a comparison test and a rigorous experiment.

2 Research Method

2.1 Procedure

The whole study was divided into two parts. The first part was similar to usability test to obtain the objective performance of our and competing product. The second part was related to tolerance experiment, which was widely used in psychological experiment and aimed to obtain the intolerable length of time [9, 10].

Specifically, in the usability test we required our participants to conduct face recognition in our and competing products in sequential order. To balance order effect, half of the participants did our product first and another half did competing product first. Researchers recorded the pass rate and recognition length. And we also collected feedback of participants on the subjective experience during use.

In the tolerance experiment, participants were required to give an assessment on a five point Likert scale, namely 1-very unacceptable, 2-a little unacceptable, 3-moderate, 4-a little acceptable, 5-very acceptable, to a given duration of face recognition and then we calculated the duration interval of extremely well (4 points or more), moderately well (3–4 points), just passable (2–3 points) and completely intolerable (2 points or less). In order to facilitate targeted optimization, we divided the whole face recognition into three stages. The first stage was face detection, from the action of clicking the start button to the appearance on the page saying "face detected". The second stage was blink detection, from the appearance saying "please blink" to the appearance saying "blink detected". The third stage was taking a photo, from the appearance saying "please be ready to take photos" to the appearance saying "successfully completed" (see Fig. 1).

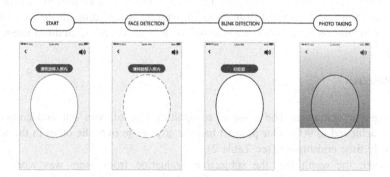

Fig. 1. The three stages of face recognition

We invited programmers to develop different demos in terms of duration for three stages respectively. As the first stage for example, it had 24 demos from 0.5 s to 15 s. The participant was given a demo at a time, the duration of which was programmed in advance, unrelated with actual behavior of the participant without his knowing. And he was required to evaluate his subjective acceptability for this given demo in a Likert scale. Every participant should evaluate all demos in an ascending or descending order. Similarly, half of them followed the former and the other half adhered to the latter to avoid sequential effect.

2.2   Material

Due to no need of develop demos for the first usability test, we adopted online version of our and competitive product to obtain comparable result in a real-world environment. However, the second part of tolerance experiment adopted demos which were scheduled time in advance. Before this, it was unknown what the appropriate quantity of demos and duration gap between the two adjacent demos were, which was determined in a pre-experiment. It was found out that 80% of participants cannot be tolerated if the duration exceeded 11 s, 9 s and 5 s for the three stages, namely face detection, blink detection and picture taken. As a precautionary measure, the duration for the three stages increased to 15 s, 11 s, 7 s. Duration gap between the two adjacent demos must fit in with the principle of neither so long to miss key turning point nor so short to unable to perceive discrepancy. Combining the previous studies which found out difference threshold distributed from 0.65 s to 1 s, we choose 0.5 s for the duration gap between the two adjacent demos.

Finally, the number of demos for first stage, face detection, from 0.5 s to 15 s, was 24. The number of demos for second stage, blink detection, from 0.5 s to 11 s, was 22. The number of demos for third stage, picture taken, from 0.5 s to 7 s, was 14. All demos in the same stage were equal excepted for duration (see Table 1).

2.3   Participants

We invited 10 participants for the pre-experiments and 28 for the formal experiment and usability test, whose occupations involved student, self-employed person and employee. Their age distributed from 18 to 25, with the mean value of 21. To avoid an impact of mobile phone models, we selected 16 IOS users and 12 android users.

2.4   Results

Objective Performance. The accurate recognition rate of both our and competing products achieved to 90%. Our product had the advantage over the other in the whole objectively time consuming (see Table 2).

However, the result that the subjective evaluation from users was worse than competing product was entirely unexpected. Further analysis revealed the most two

Table 1. All demos for three stages.

First stage (24 demos)	Second stage (22 demos)	Third stage 14 demos)
0.5 s	0.5 s	0.5 s
1.0 s	1.0 s	1.0 s
1.5 s	1.5 s	1.5 s
2.0 s	2.0 s	2.0 s
2.5 s	2.5 s	2.5 s
3.0 s	3.0 s	3.0 s
3.5 s	3.5 s	3.5 s
4.0 s	4.0 s	4.0 s
4.5 s	4.5 s	4.5 s
5.0 s	5.0 s	5.0 s
5.5 s	5.5 s	5.5 s
6.0 s	6.0 s	6.0 s
6.5 s	6.5 s	6.5 s
7.0 s	7.0 s	7.0 s
7.5 s	7.5 s	
8.0 s	8.0 s	
8.5 s	8.5 s	
9.0 s	9.0 s	
9.5 s	9.5 s	
10.0 s	10.0 s	
10.5 s	10.5 s	
11.0 s	11.0 s	
13.0 s		
15.0 s		

Table 2. The whole objective time consuming of our and competing products

Unit: s	iOS	Android
Our product	9.57	9.75
Competing product	10.82	12.05

important reasons were unsatisfactory interactive details and subjective perceived duration.

The former consisted of the following four details (see Table 3).

① The prompt frame of face detection included too many outlines of face and shoulder for user to manipulate in the given frame.
② Lack of clear and vivid hint, users cannot go forward according to our design.
③ When confronted the failure of face detection, users were at a loss what to do due to the inappropriate time and content of the prompt.
④ Our product was in short of interest, exquisite feeling and specialty.

Table 3. Unsatisfactory interactive details of our product

	Our weaknesses	Competing strength
Frame for prompt	1. The prompt frame of face detection included too many outlines of face and shoulder for user to manipulate in the given frame 2. The frame was so small that users needed to adjust mobile phone in a far position which was inappropriate for self-portrait	1. The prompt frame included only face 2. The frame was big enough for self-portrait
Prompts	1. The visual focus was in the prompt for frame, but word hit for prompt was on the top of frame. So it was difficult for users to observe. 2. Lack of Voice prompt 3. Visual cues were not obvious.	1. Obvious voice and visual prompt
Prompt of failure	1. When countering the failure of detection, users received the prompt too late 2. The contents was in common use without basing on the situation	1. The prompt appeared timely 2. The contents of the prompt was to a point 3. When monitoring a poor-light environment, the screen of competing product can be adjusted automatically
Visual effect		1. Users perceived less time with more dynamic effects 2. Full of exquisite feeling and specialty

The latter illustrated the inconsistence between subjective comfortable duration and objective duration. So what was the most subjective comfortable time of face cognition?

2.5   The Standard of Comfortable Duration

Every participant evaluated all demos of different duration and so we can calculate the mean value of all participants at every duration. Furthermore, the percentage of the participants who felt extremely well, moderately well, just passable at every duration can be calculated respectively.

In consideration of the two results, we can come to an agreement of a standard duration.

The result revealed that users felt extremely well from 1 s to 2.5 s (see Fig. 2), in the interval of which 70% of participants perceived comfortable in the face detection stage (see Fig. 3).

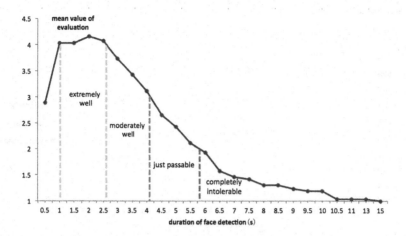

Fig. 2. The interval of users felt extremely well in the face detection stage 1-very unacceptable, 2-a little unacceptable, 3-moderate, 4-a little acceptable, 5-very acceptable

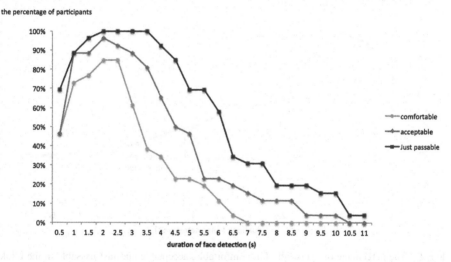

Fig. 3. The percentage of users who felt comfortable, acceptable and just passable in the face detection stage

Similarly, users felt extremely well from 0.8 s to 1 s (see Fig. 4), in the interval of which 80% of participants perceived comfortable in the blink detection stage (see Fig. 5).

And in the picture-taking stage the result was within 0.7 s (see Fig. 6). and 80% (see Fig. 7).

the percentage of participants

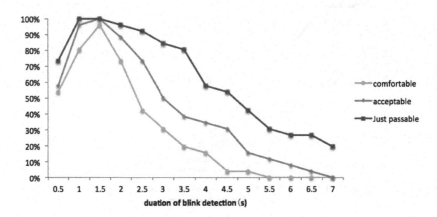

Fig. 4. The interval of users felt extremely well in the blink detection stage

mean value of evaluation

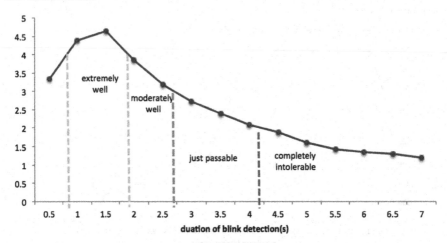

Fig. 5. The percentage of users who felt comfortable, acceptable and just passable in the blink detection stage

3 Discussion

In the interaction design of user interface, designers needed to guide users to go forward in line with your expectation to achieve product goal through the way of making the focal key points stand out. However, there existed some problems in the initial design.

We expected that users interacted in the sequence of hits-frame-other, however, people focused all their attention on the frame (see Fig. 8).

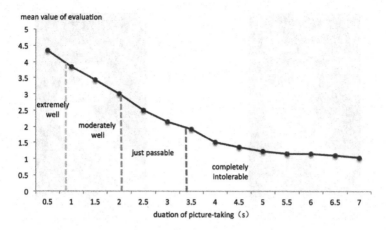

Fig. 6. The interval of users felt extremely well in the picture-taking stage

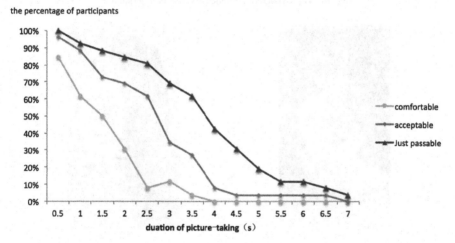

Fig. 7. The percentage of users who felt comfortable, acceptable and just passable in the picture-taking stage

So how to make the focal key points stand out was an important question. As our usual practice went, contents, color, size and distance might be in use (see Fig. 9). However, face recognition, as a novel Interactive mode, was difficult for users to understand. So we adopted more visual motion and sound in a subsequent improvement (see Fig. 10).

And we found out that in the face and blink stage, the subjective experience of users and the objective duration were inconsistent. Our data (see Fig. 10) revealed that current status of our product cannot meet users' demand in terms of degree of comfort. So we adjusted the time length of visual dynamic effect to increase the duration of detection by 1 s to push forward more participants' subjective experience into the comfortable interval (see Figs. 11 and 12).

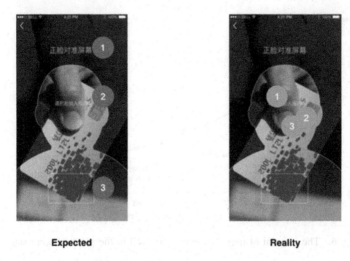

Expected   Reality

Fig. 8. The expected sequence vs. the real sequence

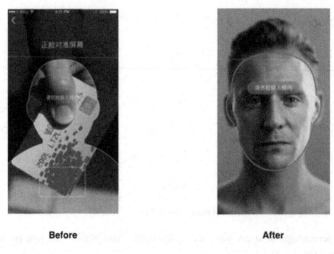

Before   After

Fig. 9. The product of before vs. after (Color figure online)

In the third stage, the longer the duration was, the better users perceived. So the performance of the recognition should be promoted in respect of technology.

As a whole, the present study tried to build a standard duration of face recognition in terms of users' subjective experience instead of objective technology, using usability test and tolerance experiment. We hope our result can give a reference to future optimization of related product.

However, we conducted the experiment in a normal environment, without considering circumstance differences, such as did the credit and financing circumstance do some different effect on the perceived duration? So we will conceive a more well-designed experiment to explore the subjective duration in more situations and more group division.

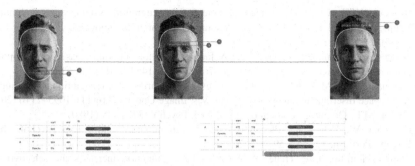

Fig. 10. Visual motion and sound in the face recognition

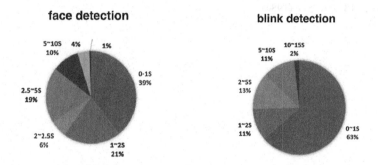

Fig. 11. In the face detection and blink detection before optimization

Fig. 12. Adjusting the time length of visual dynamic effect to increase the duration of detection by 1 s

References

1. Chellappa, R., Wilson, C.L., Sirohey, S.: Human and machine recognition of faces, a survey. Proc. IEEE **83**(5), 705–740 (1995)
2. Zhou, J., Lu, C.-Y., Zhang, C.-S., et al.: A survey of automatic face recognition. Acta Electronica Sinica **28**(4), 102–106 (2000)
3. Galton, F.: Numeralised profiles for classification and recognition. Nature **83**(2109), 127–130 (1910)

4. Bledsoe, W.W., Chan, H.: A man-machine facial recognition system: some preliminary results. Technical report, PRI 19A, Panoramic Research Incorporated, Palo Alto, USA (1965)
5. Wang, Z.H., Yuan, H., Jiang, W.T.: A face recognition algorithm based on composite gradient vector. Acta Automatica Sinica 37(12), 1445–1454 (2011). (in Chinese)
6. Sharma, A., Haj, M.A., Choi, J., et al.: Robust pose invariant face recognition using coupled latent space discriminant analysis. Comput. Vis. Image Underst. 116(11), 1095–1110 (2012)
7. Posner, M.I.: Orienting of attention. Q. J. Exp. Psychol. 32, 2–25 (1980)
8. Eriksen, C.W., Yeh, Y.Y.: Allocation of attention in the visual field. J. Exp. Psychol.: Hum. Percept. Perform. 11, 583–597 (1985)
9. Martinez-Trujillo, J.C., Treue, S.: Feature—based attention increases the selectivity of population responses in primate visual cortex. Curr. Biol. 14, 744–751 (2004)
10. Duncan, J.: Selective attention and the organization of visual information. J. Exp. Psychol.: Gener. 113, 501–517 (1984)

Taiwanese People's Wayfinding Personas and Tool Preferences

Chih-Wei Joy Lo[1], Chia-Ning Liao[2]([⊠]), I-Ping Chen[3],
and Tsuei-Ju Hsieh[4]

[1] Mass Communication Department,
Hsuan-Chuang University, Hsinchu, Taiwan
joylo810@yahoo.com
[2] Department of Educational Psychology and Counseling,
National Taiwan Normal University, Taipei, Taiwan
artning0905@gmail.com
[3] Institute of Applied Arts, National Chiao-Tung University, Hsinchu, Taiwan
iping@faculty.nctu.edu.tw
[4] Department of Information Communication,
Chinese Culture University, Taipei, Taiwan
tracy.tjhsieh@gmail.com

Abstract. Improving wayfinding system design is a challenge facing hospitals today, and as such this study seeks to improve the design of wayfinding systems by understanding patient routing patterns, wayfinding strategies, and wayfinder tool preference. The methodology of this study has three stages: The first is to administer the Wayfinding Strategies and Related Capabilities Survey [1] to a Taiwanese sample, and then to conduct a factor analysis to isolate important factors. Test subjects included 178 Taiwanese from different professional and education backgrounds. The second stage is based on the ratings of five wayfinding tools used by subjects (Google Maps, map signage, Hand-drawn maps, bystander assistance, and directional signage). A correlation analysis of the helpfulness of the tools and the factors isolated in stage 1 is conducted to separate the subjects into different wayfinding personas. The third stage is conducting interviews of exemplars of the personas found in the second stage. A factor analysis is conducted on the results of the survey, and important survey items are identified. Subjects are divided into one of the following 8 wayfinding personas based on their Wayfinding Ability and Wayfinding Strategy (survey or map strategy): Improvisational, Helpless, Capable, Brute Force, Orienteer, Road-Blind, Map Consultant, and Map-Blind. We advise that prospective designers of smart devices should, in addition to the current functions of Google Maps, consider the habit of hospital users to seek help, as well as the needs of the visually impaired.

Keywords: Wayfinding design · Wayfinding persona · Wayfinding strategy · Wayfinding tools · Wayfinding ability

© Springer International Publishing AG 2017
A. Marcus and W. Wang (Eds.): DUXU 2017, Part III, LNCS 10290, pp. 249–264, 2017.
DOI: 10.1007/978-3-319-58640-3_18

1 Introduction

Along with the great changes this generation has seen in the environment, many foreign medical centers are beginning to consider the importance and factors of innovation, and have thus begun rethinking their approach to improving user experience in a healthcare environment. When it comes to enhancing quality of care, now more than ever it is "out with the old and in with the new" when it comes to the development of medical processes, spaces, or products. Designers should, with a similar mindset, develop more innovative and practical designs for the medical field, such as management and inspection tools for assisting with medical decision-making, biometrics, home patient monitoring, healing environment design, etc. [2]. Wayfinding design is no exception. Recent advancements in science and technology have provided designers with many more choices of intelligent wayfinding tools. Future wayfinding designs will no longer be limited to additional floor plans in buildings, directional labeling, simple signage, and other such traditional wayfinding marking systems, but will also include technology such as smart wristbands, interactive signage, and iBeacon implementation [3].

Current interior space wayfinding equipment typically emphasizes information kiosks [4], indoor maps, and building markings. In recent years due to the popularity of the smart phone the availability of Google Maps has become more and more ubiquitous, and with modern people relying on it more and more, "smart" wayfinding design is an inevitable trend. However, while concerns about the development of hardware are well-founded, it is also important to match such hardware with user-centered software design. This requires the analysis and evaluation of the wayfinding behaviors, strategies, and tools utilized by users within indoor spaces. Doing so can only further enhance the user experience of the hospital.

2 Objective

This study's purposes are twofold: (1) To explore the wayfinding behaviors and wayfinding strategies of hospital visitors to classify Taiwanese hospital users into various wayfinding personas, and (2) to conduct interviews for each of the different wayfinding personas to help understand the wayfinding tool evaluation, expectations, and needs of each persona. We hope to care for the needs of a variety of hospital users in regards to wayfinding, and make recommendations for "smart" hospitals' future development of wayfinding tools.

3 Literature Review

In order to achieve the above objectives, we will first review the literature, including relevant articles for (1) understanding user wayfinding behaviors and how people choose wayfinding environmental information, (2) understanding user wayfinding strategies, (3) analyze the factors that influence user wayfinding, and (4) look for wayfinding strategy and capability literature to use as a reference for designing a questionnaire that can be added to the wayfinding survey tools currently used in modern indoor wayfinding design.

3.1 Wayfinding Behaviors

Wayfinding behaviors refers to all of the behaviors and cognitive responses of people in the context of purposeful travel [5]. When wayfinders are not familiar with the space they are in, and when they have done no preparatory work in advance (such as querying landmarks or obtaining a map), if there is time- or task-related pressure that causes anxiety, and the wayfinder will be forced to obtain useful information from the environment to and subsequently develop a wayfinding strategy.

Environmental Information Relating to Wayfinding. Experts have divided wayfinding data into three types: building information, circumstantial information, and language messages. Building information refers to elevators, stairs, partitions, walkways, and other building structures. Circumstantial information is attached to the structure of the building, such as signs, landmarks, and drawings. Language information includes spoken messages communicated by management services or by others [6, 7].

Wayfinding Options. After obtaining wayfinding information, people face a choice. Typically speaking, under normal wayfinding circumstances, the choice includes the following four subtasks [8]:

* Positioning: Use surrounding objects and try to determine the location of oneself in relation to the desired destination.
* Select one's path in accordance with the general direction of the desired destination.
* Monitor the route and direction to ensure that the current path is the correct one.
* Confirm and identify the desired location.

Confirming the position of oneself is the starting point of spatial cognition. When people determine their location, they need both building and environmental characteristics [9]. Maps are an ideal source of information about one's current location, and Devlin and Bernstein [9] discovered that, while on a school campus choosing environmental information, wayfinders will choose a map (69.8%), followed by directional signage second (53.3%), and then following a crowd (32.6%) or asking for directions (27.9%) [10]. Landmarks are another important source of information students rely on to confirm their location [11].

Wayfinding Strategies. When people encounter wayfinding problems, in order to solve the problem they will use collected routing information. How this information is applied is known as "wayfinding strategies," and varies from person to person and according to local conditions [12, 13].

Wayfinding strategies include survey strategies and route strategies. In a series of studies related to wayfinding strategies, Lawton [14] found differences in the use of wayfinding strategies between men and women. Women used route strategies more frequently, while men tended to use survey strategies. Routing strategies rely on using a series of directional markers to help determine the correct direction of travel, such as using landmarks or distinctive buildings to identify the correct path. Survey strategies are also called orientation strategies, and utilize an entire cognitive map to organize information on places and the links between them [14].

Survey strategies and route strategies are independent but not mutually exclusive, and wayfinders typically use both but with a tendency towards one or the other, rather than use one strategy exclusively. For example, Kato and Takeuchi [15] found that individuals who perform particularly well during wayfinding use both strategy types at the same time.

3.2 Individual Wayfinding Factors

Chen [16] found that factors affecting wayfinding effectiveness can be divided into individual factors, environmental factors, and social factors. Environmental factors include architectural design and environmental information, and social factors include group behaviors and education.

Among the above factors associated with indoor wayfinding, this study is primarily concerned with individual factors. Gärling et al. [17] and Kitchin [18] pointed out that an individual's ability to wayfind is affected by many factors, including their awareness of orientation, familiarity with their environment, wayfinding strategy preferences, gender differences, and others. Additionally, another individual factor influencing wayfinding ability is one's ability to read maps, which is related to reading speed, image memory, and cognition. Reading speed is, in turn, related to age, intelligence, and education. Image memory and cognition also affects how well one can apply wayfinding data [19].

By understanding individual factors of Taiwanese people's wayfinding as well as their preferred wayfinding strategies and tools, they can be sorted into categories of wayfinding personas. We expect an in-depth analysis of the differences in wayfinding strategies and mediums among these personas will allow us to put forward a more comprehensive and complete vision for future smart wayfinding systems.

3.3 Questionnaire Design

Chang and Ma [1] established a wayfinding behavior rating scale, developed measurement indicators of wayfinding ability, and, in different wayfinding situations, surveyed college students to collect wayfinding data and analyze it with Item Response Theory (IRT) and the Rasch model in a quantitative study of the difficulties and mental states encountered by wayfinders. The present study used the psychometric wayfinder questionnaire developed by Chang and Ma as its blueprint in measuring the wayfinding ability of (including awareness of orientation and route memory), participants' spatial anxiety while wayfinding, and wayfinding strategy preferences, in an attempt to, in accordance with the resulting individual wayfinding personas, facilitate the design of appropriate wayfinding markings, systems, and equipment to assist every type of hospital visitor.

4   Method

This study is divided into three stages:

1. In accordance with wayfinding psychometrics, we designed the Wayfinding Strategies and Related Capabilities Survey. We attempt to, through a factor analysis of the resultant data, induce the important factors of Taiwanese wayfinders.

2. In accordance with those important factors, subjects were classified into several different wayfinding personas.
3. Interview an exemplar of each wayfinding persona to understand the differences and similarities between indoor and outdoor wayfinding, typical assessments of existing wayfinding tools, and recommendations for future wayfinding tools.

4.1 The First Stage: The Wayfinding Strategies and Related Capabilities Survey

The Wayfinding Strategies and Related Capabilities Survey is composed of three parts: (1) First, subjects are asked for standard descriptive statistics such as age, gender, and education; (2) the second part uses the five-point Likert items from the questionnaire for the wayfinding ability of college students designed by Chang and Ma [1] to assess subjects' ability to deal with wayfinding problems (6 awareness of orientation items and 10 route memory items), the degree of anxiety in dealing with wayfinding problems (7 items), and wayfinding strategy (8 survey strategy items and 5 map strategy items). Because we are only concerned with indoor wayfinding strategies, items relating to the outdoors were revised[1] or deleted[2]. (3) In the third part, subjects were assessed with four-point Likert scale focused primarily on the degree each different type of wayfinding tool assisted with wayfinding behaviors.

Subjects included 178 people ranging between the ages of 18 to 80 years from either Taipei or HsinChu, Taiwan, separated into four generational categories: 18–30 (N = 91), 30–50 (N = 46), 50–60 (N = 26), and 60 and up (N = 8). In the sample, 71 were male, 106 female, and 1 undesignated. Education was divided into three categories: middle-school graduates (N = 3), 10th grade through some college experience (N = 82), bachelor degrees (N = 84), and other (N = 9).

The first part of the study was primarily focused on gathering the data necessary for stage 2 from the 178 subjects, including data on 36 items covering 36 variables. However, we believe that when it comes to dividing subjects into wayfinding personas, 36 is too many, and thus whenever possible attempted to reduce the number of items (please see Sect. 5.1 for the process and results).

---

[1] Items that were revised include: In item I-5, "While traveling, I kept track of the relationship between where I was and the center of town," "the center of town" was changed to "my destination"; in item I-6, "I make a mental note of the distance I had traveled on different road." "On the different road" was changed to "in the different corridor"; in item I-7, "While traveling, I visualized a map or layout of the area in my mind as I drove," "as I drove" was changed to "as I went"; in item II-2, "I made mental note of landmarks, such as buildings or natural features, that I passed along the way." was changed to "I will remember any special landscapes or wall patterns (or works of art) I see along the way".

[2] Items deleted include the following four: "I kept track of where I was in relation to the sun (or moon) in the sky as I went"; "I find it difficult to find where I parked my car in a large parking lot"; "When finding my way to an appointment in an unfamiliar area of a city or town, I find it difficult to locate the correct roads"; "When I take the bus, train, or mass rapid transit system, I will often take the wrong car and end up going in the opposite direction".

From the above factor analysis we found that there are in total four important factors that can be used to categorize Taiwanese wayfinding personas. We named these four factors Wayfinding Ability, Wayfinding Anxiety, Survey Strategy, and Map Strategy.

4.2 The Second Stage

In order to categorize wayfinding personas, this study used a Pearson correlation analysis to compare the relationships between the four major factors (Wayfinding Ability, Wayfinding Anxiety, Survey Strategy, and Map strategy) and subject wayfinding tool preference (for the process and results please see Sect. 5.2). From the four factors, three were significantly correlated with wayfinding tools subjects found useful, and all subjects were subsequently categorized into eight different wayfinding personas according to these three (for the process and results, please see Sect. 5.4). Additionally, the Pearson analysis was used to compare the correlations between various wayfinding tools in the hopes of discovering synergistic effects, if any (for the process and results, please see Sect. 5.3).

4.3 Stage 3

For each of the wayfinding personas, we tried to find one subject that could act as an exemplar and participate in a semi-structured interview. Within the study's time limit, we were only able to find and conduct individual interviews for six different exemplars.

Those interviewed mainly ranged between 30–55 years of age, with 5 men and 1 woman, all of which had bachelor degrees. The goals of the interview were threefold: (1) to understand the differences among subjects in outdoor and indoor wayfinding, as well as their wayfinding tool preferences; (2) to understand the assessments and recommendations from each type of wayfinder for each specific type of wayfinding tool (Google Maps, map signage, Hand-drawn maps, bystander assistance, and directional signage); and (3) to collect recommendations for future wayfinding tools from each wayfinding persona. The process and results are listed in Sect. 5.4.

5   Results and Discussion

5.1   Questionnaire Analysis Results

As for the second set of data gathered by the questionnaire, that is, the subjects' wayfinding ability and strategy self-assessment, we conducted a five-stage factor analysis, where we conducted five separate factor analyses, each time reducing the number of variables. Of the first four factor analyses, the worst results from KMO tests were KMO values that were more than 0.888, and Batlett's spherical test values always surpassed the .01 significance threshold, meaning that the data were suitable for a factor analysis. Factor extraction was performed by principal component, and factors were extracted one at a time. Because statistical analyses are not the focus of this study, only the final factor analysis will be reported (see Table 1).

Table 1. Final factor analysis results

	Factor 1	Factor 2	Factor 3	Factor 4	Communality
Eigenvalues	7.272	3.074	1.474	1.063	.764
% Variance explained	38.274	16.178	7.755	5.597	.719
Cumulative % variance explained	38.274	54.452	62.207	67.805	.769

Examining the resultant data using the KMO and Batlett's tests reveals that the KMO value of the final factor analysis is .902, the Batlett Spherical test value is 1860.319, and the degree of freedom is 171, which achieves a .01 level of significance, and means the data is suitable for factor analysis. To obtain results, factors were extracted by principal component analysis, along with the Varimax method (see Table 5): Only four factors were extracted with eigenvalues greater than 1. After the elemental matrix was rotated, it was confirmed that there are no items with a maximum factor load of less than 0.6, and therefore we maintained a total of 19 variables.

From the above factor analysis, we reduced the original 36 items on wayfinding personas to a mere 19, and we found that there are four important factors that can be used to classify Taiwanese wayfinder personas. We named these four factors, in accordance with their inherent qualities, as Wayfinding Ability, Wayfinding Anxiety, Survey Strategy, and Map Strategy: Wayfinding Ability is the ability of the subject to deal with wayfinding problems, including their awareness of orientation and route memory; Wayfinding Anxiety is the degree of spatial anxiety the subjects feel when confronted with any sort of wayfinding task (5 items); a Survey Strategy is any strategy where someone seeks to understand the distance and direction of the overall path, as well as each individual path, during wayfinding (4 items); Map Strategies include those where subjects use a map to gain information on where they are and where to go (2 items).

5.2 Factors Correlating to Wayfinding Personas

We used a Pearson's correlational analysis to understand any relevance and degree of benefit between the four individual factors and the five wayfinding tools presented in the third part of the questionnaire (Google Maps, map signage, Hand-drawn maps, bystander assistance, and directional signage; see Table 2). It was found that there was no significant correlation between Wayfinding Anxiety and the four important wayfinding factors, that is, whether a subject feels anxiety during wayfinding has no significant correlation with what tool they prefer. The other three categories (Wayfinding Ability, Survey Strategy, and Map Strategy) were more-or-less relevant to the tools subjects considered useful (See Table 2). Therefore, we used Wayfinding Ability, Survey Strategy, and Map Strategy to classify Taiwanese people's wayfinding personas.

Wayfinding Ability (Potential to Become Lost). Items associated with Wayfinding Ability are all inversely scored, that is, they let subjects assess how likely they are to get lost, including their awareness of orientation and route memory. On these items a

Table 2. Wayfinding factors and their correlations with wayfinding tools

		VI-2. Google map	VI-3. Map signage	VI-4. Hand-drawn maps	VI-5. Bystander assistance	VI-6. Directional signage
Wayfinding ability	Pearson correlation	−.125	−.182*	−.143	.071	−.173*
	Significance (two-tailed)	.100	.016	.060	.353	.023
Wayfinding anxiety	Pearson correlation	−.022	−.140	−.100	−.062	−.072
	Significance (two-tailed)	.778	.065	.188	.415	.345
Survey strategy	Pearson correlation	.324**	.141	.185*	.032	.120
	Significance (two-tailed)	.000	.063	.014	.679	.115
Map strategy	Pearson correlation	.040	.305**	.210**	.110	.171*
	Significance (two-tailed)	.596	.000	.005	.150	.025

high score indicates that subjects have a poor awareness of orientation or bad route memory, and thus easily feel confused during wayfinding. Low scores indicate that the subject has a strong awareness of orientation and a superior route memory, and is less likely to get lost. The Pearson correlation coefficients showed that the wayfinding tools most associated with Wayfinding Ability were map signage ($r = -.183*$, $p = .016$) and directional signage ($r = -.173*$, $p = .023$). This shows that for those with high Wayfinding Ability, their preferred tool is map signage followed by directional signage. Please see Table 3 for the related items.

Table 3. Wayfinding ability related questionnaire items and results

Factors related to awareness of orientation	
1	I can't make out which direction my hotel room faces
Factors related to route memory	
1	I have a lot of difficulties reaching the unknown place even after looking at a map
2	I have poor memory for landmarks
3	I become totally confused as to the correct sequence of the return way as a consequence of a number of left-right turns in the route
4	I often can't find the way even if given detailed verbal information on the route
5	I often (or easily) forget which direction I have turned
6	I cannot remember landmarks found in the area where I have often been
7	I can't verify landmarks in the turn of the route

Survey Strategy. For Survey Strategy, high-scoring subjects are those who make good use of survey strategies, tend to understand their entire journey before venturing forth, and will prepare mental maps of their destination and how to get there. The Pearson correlation coefficient showed that the wayfinding tools correlated with Survey Strategy include Google Maps (r = .324**, p < .001) and handheld maps (r = .185*, p = 0.14). People who tend to use a survey strategy are more likely to select Google Maps as their wayfinding tool of choice, followed by using Hand-drawn maps. Please see Table 4 for the related items.

Table 4. Survey strategy related questionnaire items and results

1	Before starting, I asked for directions telling how far to go
2	I make a mental note of the distance I had traveled in different corridors
3	I visualized a map or layout of the area in my mind as I walked
4	Before starting, I asked for directions telling me whether to go east, west, north or south at particular streets or landmarks

Map Strategy. Subjects with a high score in Map Strategy use maps well, and tend to find a map before departure for wayfinding reference. The Pearson correlation coefficient showed that the wayfinding tools associated with a subject's Map Strategy include map signage (r = .305**, p < 0.001), Hand-drawn maps (r = .210**, p = 0.005), and directional signage (r = .171*, p = 0.025). The more people are inclined towards using route strategies, the more they tend to find traditional wayfinder tools, such as maps and labels, useful. Please see Table 5 for the related items.

Table 5. Questionnaire items correlated to map strategy

1	Before starting, I asked for a hand-drawn map of the area
2	I referred to a published map

70% of subjects felt that Google Maps was helpful while wayfinding. 41% felt that map signage was helpful. 38.8% of subjects thought Hand-drawn maps were helpful. 55.6% found bystander assistance helpful. 54.5% felt that directional signage was helpful (Table 6).

Table 6. Helpfulness of wayfinding tools

	Wayfinding tool	Helpful	Unhelpful
1	Google map	70%	30%
2	Map signage	41%	59%
3	Hand-drawn maps	38.8%	61.2%
4	Bystander assistance	55.6%	44.4%
5	Directional signage	54.5%	45.5%

5.3   Correlations Between Wayfinding Tools

The results of the correlational analysis show that, besides the relationship between Google Maps and bystander assistance, all the other tools showed significant relationships. Of these, only map signage and Hand-drawn maps achieved a strong correlation ($r = .785^{**}$, $p < .001$), whereas bystander assistance and directional signage ($r = .506^{**}$, $p < .001$); and bystander assistance and map signage ($r = .462^{**}$, $p < .001$) achieved moderate strength correlations. Bystander assistance and Hand-drawn maps ($r = .253^{**}$, $p = .001$); Google Maps and Hand-drawn maps ($r = .159^*$, $p = .034$); and Google Maps and directional signage ($r = .199^*$, $p = .008$) only demonstrated weak correlational relationships. Please see Table 7 for details.

Table 7. Correlations between wayfinding tools

		Google maps	Map signage	Hand-drawn maps	Bystander assistance	Directional signage
Google maps	Pearson correlation	1	.253**	.159*	.076	.199**
	Significance (2-tailed)		.001	.034	.313	.008
Map signage	Pearson correlation	.253**	1	.785**	.425**	.462**
	Significance (2-tailed)	.001		.000	.000	.000
Hand-drawn maps	Pearson correlation	.159*	.785**	1	.464**	.496**
	Significance (2-tailed)	.034	.000		.000	.000
Bystander assistance	Pearson correlation	.076	.425**	.464**	1	.506**
	Significance (2-tailed)	.313	.000	.000		.000
Directional signage	Pearson correlation	.199**	.462**	.496**	.506**	1
	Significance (2-tailed)	.008	.000	.000	.000	

These results mainly reflect three phenomena: (1) Subjects that use Google Maps and subjects that believe in the usefulness of bystander assistance are unrelated. (2) Subjects that rely heavily on maps of any kind can be considered one social group, and this group, based on previous data demonstrating that these subjects also tend to have high Survey Strategy scores, can be shown to be able to convert abstract map data to real-world wayfinding information. (3) Subjects will interact with a multitude of wayfinding tools. For example, while subjects are asking bystanders for directions, they will simultaneously check maps and directional signage.

5.4   Wayfinding Personas

Because the above Pearson correlational analysis demonstrates that subjects do not feel there is any relationship between whether or not subjects found any particular way finding tool to be useful and wayfinding anxiety, we excluded wayfinding anxiety variables and only used Wayfinding Ability, Survey Strategy, and Map Strategy to categorize the subjects into the following eight types of wayfinding personas (see Table 8): Improvisational, Helpless, Capable, Brute Force, Overall Wayfinding Strategist, Road-Blind, Map Consultant, and Map-Blind.

Of these eight personas, subjects categorized into Improvisational, Capable, Overall Wayfinding Strategist, and Map Consultant all include subjects with Wayfinding Ability scores of less than zero, meaning they don't get lost easily; whereas Helpless, Brute Force, Road-Blind, and Map-Blind all include subjects with Wayfinding Scores above zero, meaning they get lost easily.

Wayfinding strategies can be divided into two types: survey strategies and route strategies. Of subjects that did not make use of any strategy, those with positive Wayfinding Ability scores were categorized into Improvisational, whereas those with negative Wayfinding Ability scores were categorized as Helpless. Of subjects that made use of route strategies, those with positive Wayfinding Ability scores were categorized into Map Consultant, whereas those with negative Wayfinding Ability scores were categorized into Map-Blind. Of subjects that made use of survey strategies, those with positive Wayfinding Ability scores were categorized into Overall Wayfinding Strategist, whereas those with negative Wayfinding Ability scores were categorized into Road-Blind. Of subjects that used both types of strategies, those with positive Wayfinding Ability scores were categorized into Capable, whereas those with negative Wayfinding Ability scores were categorized into Brute Force (see Table 8).

Table 8. The eight wayfinding personas

Wayfinding persona	Improvisational	Helpless	Capable	Brute force	Orienteer	Road-blind	Map consultant	Map-blind
Wayfinding strategy	None		Both survey and map strategies		Survey strategy		Map strategist	
Wayfinding ability	High	Low	High	Low	High	Low	High	Low
N	27	20	26	24	29	14	20	18
Percentage of total sample	15.2%	11.2%	14.6%	13.5%	16.3%	7.9%	11.2%	10.1%

5.5 Wayfinder Persona Interview Results

If hospitals of the future wish to develop smart wayfinding devices, we need to first understand what tools people use during wayfinding. Therefore, the last stage of this study was interviewing eight exemplars of each of the wayfinding personas to understand their views on wayfinding tool usage and their expectations for the future implementation of indoor smart wayfinding tools within hospitals. Because of time restraints, we were only able to interview six of eight exemplars. All of the exemplars were between 30 and 50 years of age, and had attained a university degree. Five were men, and one was a women. They each belonged to one of the following six wayfinding personas: Improvisational, Overall Wayfinding Strategist, Capable, Help-less, Map-Blind, and Road-Blind. The outline of the interviews are detailed below:

1. Wayfinding persona self-assessment: The wayfinding tools utilized at each stage of wayfinding and the wayfinding process for each wayfinding persona in a hospital setting.
2. Wayfinding tool evaluation: Individual evaluations by the exemplars for each type of wayfinding tool (Google Maps, map signage, Hand-drawn maps, bystander assistance, and directional signage).
3. Imagined future wayfinding tools: Suggestions by the exemplars for the creation of future wayfinding tools.

Wayfinding Personal Self-assessment and Wayfinding Tool Evaluation. The results of the interviews showed that the wayfinding tool preferences of the exemplars can be roughly divided into two parts: before wayfinding and during wayfinding.

Before Wayfinding. The large majority of the exemplars would, before departing, look up data relevant to their journey. Before Google Maps was released, these data were divided into "directions from friends or relatives" (as described by the Helpless exemplar) and "finding a map" (by the Orienteer exemplar). However, in the current Internet age, every single exemplar admitted to first checking Google Maps before departing. The only differences existed in whether or not they printed out a copy of the map, or wrote down detailed notes.

During Wayfinding

• Google Maps

1. The large majority of respondents agreed that accessing Google Maps on their handheld device was helpful, and that smart wayfinding devices will continue to trend into the future. If future hospital wayfinding design includes an indoor map application like Google Maps, so long as the data is accurate, download is convenient, and the user interface is clear, wayfinders will definitely download and use it.
2. The most helpful part of Google Maps was its ability to key in the desired destination directly, thus allowing the user to display a representation of where the destination was in relation to where the user was located.
3. Subjects with low Survey Strategy scores preferred to follow the route pre-planned by Google, while subjects with high Survey Strategy scores had no need to rely on such assistance, and just maintained a mental map that would allow them to walk in the correct direction, according to their own preferences.
4. Subjects with high Map Strategy scores liked to reference the map and possible route functions, whereas subjects with low Map Strategy scores relied on the textual instructions and street view features of their device. Subjects with low Map Strategy scores reported that they could not translate the two-dimensional map into the three-dimensional world, and thus could not rely upon the Google Maps overview or visualized route-planning functions. Instead, they use Street View to try and find landmarks to verify that their route was correct.

5. When it comes to subjects whose Wayfinding Ability is high, maps, Google Maps, and directional signage were all highly effective wayfinding tools. However, when it came to the three personas with low Wayfinding Ability, because their route memory and awareness of orientation are poor, they rely more upon step-by-step textual instructions, and need a reference to guide them through turns. The Map-Blind and Road-Blind exemplars hoped that future smart wayfinding design will have sounds or vibrations that report their future steps in advance and notifies them whenever they take a wrong turn, as well as clearly marked elevators and important intersections.

- Asking for directions

  1. The interviews revealed that, although most of the exemplars used some form of navigational device indoors, that within a hospital they habitually seek out information-services personnel. Because, typically speaking, finding one's way indoors is a simple matter, they often only had to ask for directions once or twice before finding their destination. It is so convenient that, currently, spending the extra effort to download a new APP would be uneconomical.
  2. Four of the six exemplars would, in a hospital, seek out information-services personnel or bystanders for directions. Only the Capable and Overall Wayfinding Strategist exemplars preferred not to do so. Both of these personas have excellent wayfinding abilities, the ability to understand maps, trust in their passing investigations, and trust in the planning and designs behind official information, and thus would only ask for directions when they are in a rush.
  3. Effective ways to guide: When bystanders were offering directions, the exemplars hoped that the bystander could inform them of the floor, distance, direction of their destination, as well as relevant landmarks and signboards that would be nearby.
  4. The exemplars pointed out that if all of the information presented by the bystander would lead them past three or more turns, they would have trouble remembering the directions. If bystanders sent them on a route with more than three turns, the exemplars hoped that these bystanders would be able to provide them Hand-drawn maps or written notes for reference, otherwise they'd end up having to ask someone else for directions later on. We refer to this phenomenon as the "three-turn rule."

- Hand-drawn maps

  1. Exemplars noted that if the directions for their route surpassed three turns, hand-held maps would be useful.

Suggestions for Future Wayfinding Devices

- Device aspects

  1. Of the six exemplars, five felt that in the future, should an indoor navigation device be released, that they would try using it. The only exception was the older woman exemplar of the Helpless persona, who said she would not use it.

2. As for opinions on wristbands or health-insurance cards with built-in chips, in addition to the potential added costs to the hospital, the extra work of renting or fixing the equipment may affect the willingness of wayfinders to utilize such tools.

3. Camera equipment in hospitals could be enhanced with facial recognition software that could pick up on an individual's face. This method does not require many external costs to the hospital, as they already have camera systems in place. However, this would raise privacy issues such that if facial recognition software was to be used, hospitals would need privacy protection mechanisms in place.

- Aspects of service design

1. Functions that allow for one to ask for directions: Five of the exemplars would, more than half the time, seek out service personnel whenever asking for directions. The results of our study show that subjects who use Google Maps do not ask for directions, and that those who ask for directions don't use Google Maps. Among the six exemplars, the exemplar for Capable did not like to ask for directions because the information they gather from their own planning efforts tends to be more reliable. In summary, when developing future smart wayfinding equipment, besides the functions already available on Google Maps, the ability to ask for directions or other humanized systems could be integrated into any new smart navigation equipment. This would help hospital wayfinders in the habit of asking for directions get official information.

2. Notification sounds and vibrations. Future smart wayfinding devices should, in advance, provide notification sounds or vibrations to report which direction wayfinders' should go and notify them whenever they take a wrong turn. These functions would also help the visually impaired.

3. Functions beyond wayfinding: Suggestions for the elderly included adding features for homecare, appointment reminders, and registration inquiry into the wayfinding device. The exemplar for Map Consultant also suggested that future devices could include a group positioning function, to allow for friends and family to find each other within the hospital.

6   Conclusion

6.1   Wayfinding Personas

We found that there are, in total, four major factors that can be used to categorize Taiwanese wayfinding personas: Wayfinding Ability, Wayfinding Anxiety, Survey Strategy, and Map Strategy. Of these, only three were correlated to wayfinding tool preference: Wayfinding Ability, Survey Strategy, and Map Strategy. From these three factors, we separated all of the surveyed subjects into one of the following eight personas: Improvisational, Helpless, Capable, Brute Force, Overall Wayfinding Strategist, Road-Blind, Map Consultant, and Map-Blind.

6.2 Wayfinding Tool Preferences

According to the questionnaire results, we found the following results surrounding wayfinding tool preferences: (1) 70% of Taiwanese believe that smart navigational devices are useful when wayfinding. 55.6% of Taiwanese felt that bystander assistance and directional signage were useful. (2) Subjects that used Google Maps do not think that bystander assistance is helpful, and vice versa. (3) Wayfinders who used map signage and Hand-drawn maps were strongly related, such that they can be combined into a single group. (4) Subjects will use a variety of tools when wayfinding, such as both asking for bystander assistance and looking at directional signage and maps.

6.3 Wayfinder Recommendations

Finally, the six exemplar interviews provided the following recommendations for future smart devices:

1. Google Maps already includes functions for inputting one's destination, routing, maps, and providing directions, such that the Capable, Overall Wayfinding Strategist, and Improvisational exemplars were all satisfied. However, for those exemplars with weaker wayfinding abilities, other functions may be necessary. For instance, an ability to ask for directions, or notification sounds beyond those associated with maps.
2. Consider the user persona before deciding on whether or not to give a wide range of map information. Survey strategists, before departure, tend to try and understand their journey as a whole, as well as the relative distances between each section of their travels. Users who make use of route strategies will, before departure, find a map to collect any relevant information. Thus, smart wayfinding tools should first identify what the user's style is, and then, if they are a survey strategist, give them more general information, and if they are a map strategist, provide a map.
3. For wayfinders who are not good at using either survey strategies or map strategies, they typically need detailed textual instructions for their route. Because of the "three-turn rule" we discovered, we recommend that for this type of user, wayfinding instructions should be given in stages, with three turns per stage.
4. Health care management and tracing functions could be integrated into future wayfinding tools for hospitals.

References

1. Ma, S., Chang, S.: Exploring the way-finding ability of college students and its affecting factors (Master's thesis) (2009). https://ir.nctu.edu.tw/handle/11536/42817. (in Chinese)
2. Lo, C.W.: Smart wayfinding for the future hospital. In: Yin, H.W. (eds.) SMART Hospital Design, pp. 334–345. Yonglin Foundation X-Lab, Taipei (2015). (in Chinese)
3. Lo, C.W., Yien, H.W., Chen, I.P.: How universal are the universal symbols? An estimation of cross-cultural adoption of universal health care symbol. HERD J. 9(3), 116–134 (2016)

4. Raven, A., Laberge, J., Ganton, J., Johnson, M.: Wayfinding in a hospital: electronic kiosks point the way. Exp. Mag. **14**(3) (2014). http://uxpamagazine.org/wayfinding-in-a-hospital/?lang=zh
5. Huang, J., Tzeng, S.: A study of wayfinding behavior in out-patient area-two single floor type for example. J. Des. **13**(4), 43–62 (2008). (in Chinese)
6. Hart, R.A., Moore, G.T.: The Development of Spatial Cognition: A Review, pp. 246–288. Aldine Transaction, New Brunswick (1973)
7. Siegel, A.W., White, S.H.: The development of spatial representations of large-scale environments. Adv. Child Dev. Behav. **10**, 9–55 (1975)
8. Canter, D.V.: Way-finding and signposting: penance or prosthesis? In: Canter, D.V. (ed.) Psychology in Action, pp. 139–158. Dartmouth Publishing Company, Hantshire (1996). http://eprints.hud.ac.uk/9227/
9. Devlin, A.S., Bernstein, J.: Interactive way-finding: map style and effectiveness. J. Env. Psychol. **17**(2), 99–110 (1997)
10. Weisman, J.: Evaluating architectural legibility way-finding in the built environment. Env. Behav. **13**(2), 189–204 (1981)
11. Murakoshi, S., Kawai, M.: Use of knowledge and heuristics for wayfinding in an artificial environment. Env. Behav. **32**(6), 756–774 (2000)
12. Magliano, J.P., Cohen, R., Allen, G.L., Rodrigue, J.R.: The impact of a wayfinder's goal on learning a new environment: different types of spatial knowledge as goals. J. Env. Psychol. **15**(1), 65–75 (1995)
13. Hunt, M.E.: Environmental learning without being there. Env. Behav. **16**(3), 307–334 (1984)
14. Lawton, C.A.: Gender differences in way-finding strategies: relationship to spatial ability and spatial anxiety. Sex Roles **30**(11–12), 765–779 (1994)
15. Kato, Y., Takeuchi, Y.: Individual differences in wayfinding strategies. J. Env. Psychol. **23**(2), 171–188 (2003)
16. Chen, G.: Wayfinding and Signage in Libraries. Flysheet Information Services Co., Ltd., Taipei (2007). (in Chinese)
17. Gärling, T., Böök, A., Lindberg, E.: Spatial orientation and wayfinding in the designed environment: a conceptual analysis and some suggestions for post occupancy evaluation. J. Archit. Plan. Res. **3**(1), 55–64 (1986)
18. Kitchin, R.M.: Cognitive maps: what are they and why study them? J. Env. Psychol. **14**(1), 1–19 (1994)
19. Thorndyke, P.W., Stasz, C.: Individual differences in procedures for knowledge acquisition from maps. Cogn. Psychol. **12**(1), 137–175 (1980)

The Role of Narrative Transportation Experience in Design Communication

Qiong Peng[1,2(✉)] and Jean-Bernard Martens[2]

[1] College of Culture and Art, Chengdu University of Information Technology,
Chengdu, China
q.peng@tue.nl
[2] Department of Industrial Design, Eindhoven University of Technology,
Eindhoven, The Netherlands

Abstract. User experience design requires communication to share design information and to integrate specialised knowledge to optimise design performance. Personal experience during communication process will influence individual participation, the output of communication and design performance. Defined by absorption into stories, narrative transportation will lead changes in beliefs and attitudes, which is potentially beneficial to design communication. This paper explores the role of narrative transportation in the communication of user experience design through literature review and experiments. The role of narrative transportation is positive proved by the increased effectiveness of design communication. It also provides a support of the importance to use storytelling in user experience design and implies the necessity of tools supporting storytelling.

Keywords: Narrative transportation · User experience · Design communication · Storytelling

1 Introduction

As Hassenzahl proposed that user experience is dynamic, context-dependent, subjective [1], the individual experience during communication will influence their participation and the performance of communication. User experience design usually requires designers and other stakeholders with various backgrounds to communicate together to share information, discuss design ideas and concepts and make decisions, especially in a large and complex project. Communication is the transmission of information [2]. It is a dynamic process in which people, both information senders and receivers [3], consciously and unconsciously interact with and affects by others through different channels [4]. During communication, information is transmitted, but it is not necessarily received or understood [2]. Although most of the design communication is positive, it frequently happens that there are arguments or disagreements from other stakeholders because of limited knowledge in related fields and lack of full understanding and empathy. It results in refusal of giving opportunities to the new ideas and frustrations for designers as well. Narrative, known as stories or testimonials, are a basic model of human interaction [5]. Narrative transportation, defined as absorption into a story [6] and proposed as a

© Springer International Publishing AG 2017
A. Marcus and W. Wang (Eds.): DUXU 2017, Part III, LNCS 10290, pp. 265–274, 2017.
DOI: 10.1007/978-3-319-58640-3_19

powerful persuasive means [7], can lead to emotional and cognitive changes. It has been mostly applied in psychological assessment but less practiced in design research. How to promote design communication is such an important problem as it requires hold an open mind, which means people should accordingly adjust individual attitudes and beliefs. It is easy in principle but hard in practice. This research proposed a discussion of the role of narrative transportation experience in design communication. In this research, theories of narrative transportation are introduced, experiments for evaluation of both narrative transportation and effectiveness of communication are conducted. It indicates that narrative transported people participate actively in communication, and efficiency of communication increased by less time on communication meetings, practical decision-making and reduced negative cognitive response by self-reported transportation. Since narrative transportation via stories does indicate not only mental imagery, but also physical medium as stories in the transportation, storytelling is theoretically supported in user experience design.

2 Related Theories Review

2.1 Narrative Transportation Theory

Narratives have been assumed and proved to be effective for persuasion in fields like psychology and marketing. Stories are one of the narratives, with a plot consisting of beginning, middle and end, and provides people with a simple way to share information and communication. Narrative transportation is proposed as absorption into a story and an integrated melding of attention, imagery, and feeling by Green and Brock [6]. It can provide people with a vivid experience through narrative transportation via stories. Transported people, who are absorbed into or get lost in a story [6, 15] can image the story, share the emotions presented in the story and easily focus on the story, thus become prone to be engaged in the activities.

Since transportation is a convergent process during which mental activities such as emotion, attention and imagery focus on events occurring in the narrative [6], the Transportation-Imagery Model (TIM) proposed by Green and Brock [6, 9] indicated that the transported people are subjectively distance from reality [10], provoked with strong emotions and motivation, and exhibit greater change in attitude and belief in response to stories [9]. It can foster emotional and empathetic connections with story. Then beliefs and attitudes can be affected by vivid imagery which makes narratives seem like a real experience.

Narrative Transportability Scale including 11 universal items and a varying number of items addressing the experience of the character in a specific story, was developed to measure differences in individual state of being transported into the narrative world [7]. The Transportation Scale-Short Form (TS-SF) was proposed for practice by Appel et al. [10] because the former one turns out to be too long.

Narratives are a promising method to create a shared understanding within design group/team, and the process of narrative transportation can help people to image what will be like of a design idea and make a reference to it. Then it is highly possible to promote communication during design process.

2.2 Communication in User Experience Design

Communication is a system of transmitting information and interaction of personal beliefs. Communication is necessary because there are possible differences in cognition of information senders and receivers. Information can be transmitted through verbal forms, written words and visual images. Mind reading [11] which is necessary in communication to acquire information and knowledge about other people's beliefs and desires, is easy to achieve through transportation. Communication theory [12] has been studied in various disciplines for different purpose. In design, communication has been got more attention since design has changed from individual activities to collaboration, especially for a complex and large design project. Brilliant ideas, feedback, and suggestions need to be explained in a way that others can read, hear, understand and respond to. As Fig. 1 shows that in the communication of user experience design, it is a dynamic system including people, content, channels or mediums, cognitive process, mental mind etc. People can get to know unknown or new things and ideas during communication. Designers are likely to convey information about details such as functionality, form, shape, colour, technology, value, user needs and creativity etc. to other stakeholders. Meanwhile, others give feedback, advice, and arguments about all the aspects for design. Consultation, negotiation, evaluation, confirmation and decision-making are usually achieved during design communication. The effectiveness of design communication directly affects final decision-making and outputs of user experience design. Previous studies mostly focused on the results and patterns of design communication. Effectiveness of design communication has also been stressed. However, it is common to be addressed from the perspectives of communication methods, tools supporting, and from an organisational view, rarely be concerned of personal experience during communication.

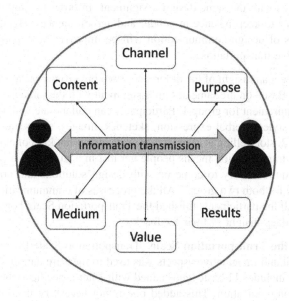

Fig. 1. Design communication

In design communication, empathy is another important aspect which can influence effectiveness. Empathy means seeing with the eyes of another [13]. It can promote communication by understanding or feeling what another person is experiencing. Empathy can be enhanced through narrative transportation because people experience emotional changes in transportation and easily to imagine and understand what the main character experience in the story. In design, empathy is possible promoted by narrative transportation via visual stories, because to visual something is to construct a visual image that resembles the visual experience you would undergo [13].

3   Studies

3.1   Study 1

Introduction. To determine whether people are transported into a narrative and the role of narrative transportation to design communication, an experiment of the evaluation was conducted. The context is designed as a workshop for the early design of user experience with people involved having a communication meeting. A design assignment is given with a written description. It simply describes the problem encountered by a master student, who is from east Asia and just begins his life in Netherlands. Due to the special rainy weather in Netherlands, he/she always has the problem for navigation when he is riding a bike outside. 20 university students from Industrial Design, Psychology, Computer Science as participants took the experiment. They were half-half divided into two groups with 3 small teams respectively. In each small group, 3–4 participants are mixed with different backgrounds. At least one design student is required in a team. All the groups have communication meetings separately in different places with the same design assignment. In order to simplify the research procedure, we try to keep balance in gender and age differences. Hypothesis 1 is that the effectiveness of design communication will be improved with participants' experience of narrative transportation.

Procedure. To get an insight of the differences, two big groups are required differently for comparison. Based on the same design assignment with the same introduction, there is no special requirement for group 1. Participants can collaborate with the design work in their normal styles. Verbal expression, sketches, images, slides are allowed to use freely. In group 2, storytelling is asked to use, no matter what kind of expression for the story. Narrative transportation means people get lost in a story, and it mostly a mental activity. It is required to try to come up with design solutions and no specified procedure to follow for both two groups. All the processes of communication are observed and recorded. All the participants finished the Transportation Scale Form and joined an interview for a deep insight of their feedback.

Adaptation of the Transportation Scale. Transportation Scale [8] referring to cognitive, emotional and imaginative aspects was used to measure narrative transportation (see Table 1). It includes 11 basic items added with 1 item specific to the character used in the design communication. This added one is not necessary if no character or no

Table 1. Transportation scale for measurement

General items	
1	While I was reading/seeing the narrative, I could easily picture the events in it taking place
2	While I was reading/seeing the narrative, activity going on in the room around me was on my mind
3	I could picture myself in the scene of the events described in the narrative
4	I was mentally involved in the narrative while reading it
5	After finishing the narrative, I found it easy to put it out of my mind
6	I wanted to learn how the narrative ended
7	The narrative affected me emotionally
8	I found myself thinking of ways the narrative could have turned out differently
9	I found my mind wandering while reading the narrative
10	The events in the narrative are relevant to my everyday life
11	The events in the narrative have changed my life
Item specific to the character in the story (if necessary)	
12	While reading/seeing the narrative I had a vivid image of XXX (the character's name)

story in their communication. The measurement is evaluated by a 7-point Likert scale ranging from 1 (not at all) to 7 (very much).

Analysis and Results. During the communication meetings, participants were organised to discuss the design assignment, express their ideas in various ways. In group 1, all the 3 teams communicated in conventional ways, such as verbal talking and discussion, visual sketches, mind-map drawing. 1 team also used persona and storyboard which are often used in user experience design. In group 2, storytelling is the requirement for communication. Storytelling here is different to simple storyboard with persona and scenario. It consists of a beginning, middle and end, and the plot development as well as a climax. Giving to limitations of visualization, it can be used in verbal language, written words and visual storyboard or images. For narrative transportation measurement, the means of each participant for the 11 items in the scale are analysed (see Fig. 2). 30% of the means is higher than the scale average state of point 4 in group 1, which indicates that the narrative transportation was not experienced a lot in this group. But small percentage does not mean that the other 70% participants did not experience transportation at all. Compared with the former one, 80% means are higher than the average 4 in group 2. We cannot conclude that how much narrative transportation was experienced by participants in group 2 only from the average numbers. However, the different data shows that it is possible to say it is easy to narrative transported because more people get narrative transportation with the help of storytelling. By SPSS analysis, gender and age have no significant influence to individual narrative transportation. For item 3 referring to cognition and 7 referring to emotion, there are significant differences (item 3: $p = 0.037 < \rho$, item 7: $p = 0.029 < \rho$). This means that participants in group 2 experienced changes in cognition and emotion significantly. It can also support the hypothesis that stories can promote narrative transportation by emotional changes.

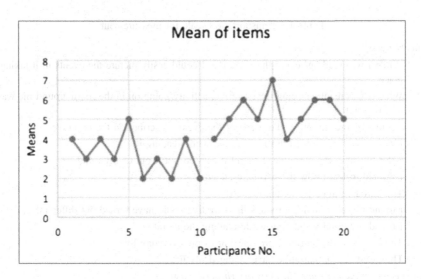

Fig. 2. Means of narrative transportation

As to the evaluation of the effectiveness of communication, data was collected from the following aspects: time for communication meeting, how many design solutions are proposed, whether to make a design decision. Meanwhile, a questionnaire based on literature of assessment of communication [4, 14], was developed to get the feedback of personal opinions. Questions cover the holistic evaluation of the communication and personal feelings in engagement and understanding. The results show that, on the whole, more design solutions were proposed in group 2 with less time spent (see Fig. 3). The workshop was designed to finish within 2 h. The time for communication is little differently in minutes. All the teams in group 2 got their final decision-making, and only one team in group 1 did not make decision. Analysis of the questionnaire indicates that there is no significant difference of personal engagement in the communication ($p = 0.867 > \rho$). However, the difference of personal understanding with

group	team	time spent on communication (hours)	number of design solutions	decision-making (Yes/No)
1	1	2.0	3	Yes
	2	1.67	2	Yes
	3	2.0	2	No
2	4	2.0	4	Yes
	5	1.67	3	Yes
	6	1.83	5	Yes

Fig. 3. Data for communication in each team

others is quite significant (p = 0.316 < ρ) and the same in holistic satisfaction of the whole communication (p = 0.348 < ρ). To some extent, this proves that the effectiveness of communication has been increased.

The data from recorded videos and interviews are translated literally and analysed. It is obvious that in group 2, nearly 80% of the participants reported that they changed their attitudes after constructing stories and they are prone to understand other team members' opinions and to engage themselves in the stories. It is consistent with the result of narrative transportation measurement by the scale, which means they had experienced narrative transportation. There are more interactions among the team members in group 2 by more talking, more eye contacts. A higher percentage of satisfaction of the communication is calculated in group 2 compared with group 1.

3.2 Study 2

Because narrative transportation has a direct relation with stories by its definition, stories are constructed and expressed mentally. Then transported people are influenced by the characters in stories to change their beliefs and attitudes. Studies for narrative transportation mostly try to explain it terms of internal cognition. How about the external medium for stories? The stories can be shown in written words and visual storyboard. In design, we proposed hypothesis 2: Visual storytelling can be used as stimuli to enhance the generation of narrative transportation. In this study, 10 students (6 male and 4 female) participated in two groups with 5 ones randomly distributed in each group. Given to visualization which may need some sketch skills, only industrial design students were recruited in this study. The same design topic used in study 1 was used as well. The difference is that written stories are required for communication in

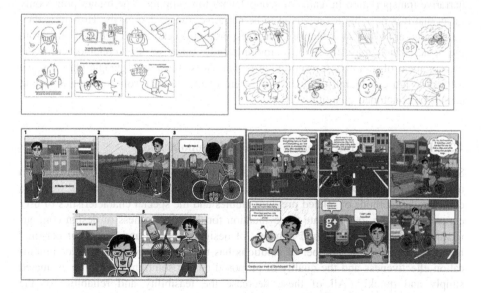

Fig. 4. Visual storytelling by group 2

group 1, and visual stories in group 2. The Narrative Transportation Scale with a 7-point Likert scale is employed to measure individual transportation immediately after the end of the communication.

The results indicated there is no significant difference in the means of the 12 items ($p = 0.842 > \rho$) in Narrative Transportation Scale. However, all of the participants in group 2 using visual stories get higher points in all the 12 items, and they proposed more design solutions (shown in Fig. 4) both in hand sketches and image storyboard than group 1 within the same time. They also explained that it is easily to engage in the communication and experience empathy through constructing and expressing of the visual stories.

4   Discussion

For narrative transportation, more studies have been made in different fields but less practiced in design research. This paper proposes a research of its role in design communication with the aim to find alternative ways to promote design communication and design performance. However, there is still some space for further discussion.

4.1   Measurement of Narrative Transportation

In this research, Narrative Transportation Scale is used to measure individual narrative transportation according to recommendations from previous studies. However, narrative transportation is a process rather than a statement, we can limitedly get to know there are individual differences in the transportation with the different number assessing experience of each item in the scale. In study 1, we cannot conclude that there is no narrative transportation in teams of group 1 with lower points. The higher points only mean that it is possible for a person to be narrative transported easily. How long they transported and to what extent of their transportation to cannot be deduced only from the scale, which may affect the communication. What we can conclude from the measurement of narrative transportation is that easily transported people play positive role in design communication. But the extent of the positive role to communication cannot be concluded quantitatively.

4.2   Evaluation of Effectiveness of Design Communication

Since limited research of communication theories applied in design, there are no universal standards for evaluation of design communication. In this research, we try to combine the methods of related previous studies and the special characteristics of user experience design to formulate the evaluation for the effectiveness of design communication by recording time and numbers of design solutions and survey of personal feelings. However, the number of solutions has no direct correlation with communication effectiveness and the quality of proposed design solutions cannot be evaluated simply and quickly. All of these decrease the feasibility and reliability of the evaluation. It is possible to conclude that the effectiveness of communication is influenced by easily transported people and the influence is positive.

4.3 Limitations in Both Two Studies

There are limitations in both two studies. There are no significant differences in some items in Narration Transportation Scale. This can be attributed to the limited number of participants, especially in study 2. The analysis of information from video records and interviews is plain to a certain degree and not enough to provide support for the hypothesises. Narrative transportation is a process which involves complicated mental activities. It is not enough to decide people experience transportation by their self-report neither by their body languages and behaviours.

4.4 Visual Storytelling

It is shown in study 2 that visual storytelling contributes to experience narrative transportation. Narrative transportation is essentially associated with story. Visual storytelling can promote construction of stories in mental processing, then promote narrative transportation. An interesting finding is that participants in study 2 visualize stories by hand-sketches and with the help of tools. Since not everyone involved in user experience design are skilled in sketch, it is necessary and valuable to explore tools supporting visual storytelling which can make storytelling fast and easily.

5 Conclusion

Transportation is a process into a narrative which involves cognitive and emotional investment. In this research, individual narrative transportation in design communication is studied to support the hypothesis that effectiveness of design communication can be improved through narrative transportation. The role of narrative transportation is positive and beneficial. Meanwhile, the visual storytelling in design communication shows its special benefits. It provides an alternative method to promote design communication by experiencing narrative transportation. It also gives us a research direction of tools supporting visual storytelling to promote narrative transportation.

Acknowledgement. The research reported in this paper was supported by the 2016 project (16ZB0217) and 2014 project (GY-14YB-13). Thanks to all who were involved in.

References

1. Hassenzahl, M.: Experience Design. Technology for all the Right Reasons. Morgan & Claypool, San Rafael (2010)
2. Littlejohn, S.W., Foss, K.A.: Theories of Human Communication, 9th edn. Thomson Wadsworth, Belmont (2008)

3. Shedlosky, R.: The experience of psychological transportation: the role of cognitive energy exertion and focus during exposure to narratives. The Ohio State University (2010)
4. Chiu, M.-L.: An organizational view of design communication in design collaboration. Des. Stud. **23**(2), 187–210 (2002)
5. Williams, J.H., Green, M.C., Kohler, C., Allison, J.J., Houston, T.K.: Stories to communicate risks about tobacco: development of a brief scale to measure transportation into a video story - the ACCE project. Health Educ. J. **70**(2), 184–191 (2010)
6. Green, M.C., Brock, T.C.: The role of transportation in the persuasiveness of public narrative. J. Pers. Soc. Psychol. **79**(5), 701–721 (2000)
7. de Graaf, A., Hoeken, H., Sanders, J., Beentjes, H.: The role of dimensions of narrative engagement in narrative persuasion. Communications **34**(4), 385–405 (2009)
8. Mazzocco, P.J., Green, M.C., Sasota, J.A., Joens, N.W.: This story is not for everyone: transportability and narrative persuassion. Soc. Psychol. Pers. Sci. **1**, 361–368 (2010)
9. Green, M.C., Brock, T.C.: In the mind's eye: transportation-imagery model of narrative persuasion. In: Brock, T.C., Strangem, J.J., Green, M.C. (eds.) Narrative Impact: Social and Cognitive Foundations, pp. 315–341. Lawrence Erlbaum Associates Publishers, Mahwah (2002)
10. Appel, M., Gnambs, T., Richter, T., Green, M.C.: The Transportation Scale-Short Form (TS-SF). Media Psychol. **18**, 243–266 (2015)
11. Frith, C., Frith, U.: Theory of mind. Curr. Biol. **15**(17), R644–R645 (2005)
12. Craig, R.T.: Communication theory as a field. Commun. Theory **9**(2), P119–P161 (1999)
13. Davis, M.H.: Empathy: A Social Psychological Approach. Westview Press, Boulder (1996)
14. Sonnenwald, D.H.: Communication roles that support collaboration during the design process. Des. Stud. **17**, 277–301 (1996)
15. Nell, V.: Lost in a Book: The Psychology of Reading for Pleasure. Yale University Press, New Haven (1988)

A Requirements Engineering Process for User Centered IT Services – Gathering Service Requirements for the University of the Future

Dominik Rudolph$^{(\boxtimes)}$, Anne Thoring, Christian Remfert,
and Raimund Vogl

University of Münster, Münster, Germany
{d.rudolph, a.thoring,
c.remfert, r.vogl}@uni-muenster.de

Abstract. The process of digitalization challenges universities worldwide, in particular the universities' IT. Using ITIL and the ITSM-focused application of software requirements engineering as a basis, qualitative interviews with students were conducted to gather information on service requirements. Three service categories clearly dominate the students' wishes for IT support: study organization, online literature and software provision. As regards the study organization, a centralized platform granting access to all relevant information and services (e.g. schedule, exam administration, certificates, study progress, contact information) is particularly important. From the students' point of view, IT should enable them to focus on the content of their studies, provide support for organizational problems, and grant easy access to resources, such as literature and software, while at the same time require little effort.

Keywords: Digitalization · ITIL · ITSM · Service engineering · Qualitative study · Higher education

1 Introduction

The digitalization does not stop at higher education and is challenging universities to develop appropriate strategies in order to shape this trend. Particularly in teaching, a great potential is suspected, and that is why the subject increasingly receives attention [1–4]. In this context, it is often referred to as a revolution [e.g. 5–7] or a shift [8]. The discussion is partly fueled by companies who, not least in their own interest, see a multitude of possibilities [e.g. 9]. The question of costs is often focused, since a cost-cutting effect is ascribed to the digitalization in higher education [e.g. 10].

However, the aspect of use is often missed out in the discussion. An insight into the needs of students and their view on digitalization is required in particular. With the students' help the university IT can provide relevant services in order to support the academic studies in an ideal way.

To address the changes that the digital transformation with the ever more pervasive use of information technology creates for the support for teaching and learning in higher education (e.g. time-shifted learning via podcasts, digital materials and

© Springer International Publishing AG 2017
A. Marcus and W. Wang (Eds.): DUXU 2017, Part III, LNCS 10290, pp. 275–293, 2017.
DOI: 10.1007/978-3-319-58640-3_20

annotation or real-time interaction in class), a comparison of specific characteristics of software and IT services has been done to find out where they differ and if IT services might eventually be suitable for being used with software requirements engineering (SRE) [11–13] processes. In a further step, a literature review has been conducted to identify possible SRE processes with their methods and a checklist has been developed to check which methods might address IT services and their specific characteristics at best. Based on this, we designed workshops to test a prototypical process for SRE use in the field of ITSM. Also, we wanted to identify and develop requirements for specific new services in the area of IT-supported learning. We thus conducted workshops with different student groups, each comprised of 5–6 people. These groups were asked to conduct the full process of requirements engineering under supervision of a researcher, who was introducing the methods and acted as a moderator, but was not taking an active part in the discussion and the development of the requirements.

1.1 The IT Infrastructure Library (ITIL)

This study was conducted as part of a joint research project of the IT center (ZIV, Zentrum für Informationsverarbeitung) and the Institute for Information Systems of the University of Münster. The project was set up to establish a service catalog for the ZIV's IT operations. The idea for such a catalog is rooted in the so-called IT Infrastructure Library (ITIL) [14, 15], a de facto standard for managing IT operations. ITIL has been developed since the beginning of the 1990s and its underlying concepts have been discussed in academia under the paradigm of IT service management (ITSM) since the turn of the millennium. According to ITIL and ITSM [16], the IT and the business functions of an organization act like provider and customer – a situation which is called "market-orientation". As on regular markets, the provider offers services that the customer can order. The customer, on the other hand, has a demand for services that the provider tries to address. To stay competitive, it is necessary for the provider to always look for new service ideas that might be relevant for the customer.

The IT service itself is the core concept of service orientation as described by ITIL and ITSM. Such an IT service supports the customer's business processes by processing a business process object, thereby generating value for the latter. It is provided continuously, automatically and care-free by an IT-based infrastructure, and, furthermore, customizable to meet the customer's specific requirements. Consequently, the customer does not have to know details on how the service is provided or which technical components are used. The support of the business processes and the generated value are in focus [17]. This is in contrast to the traditional approach of IT functions, which were only providing technical assets without questioning for which purpose those assets were used.

Over time, the IT-based infrastructure of the University of Münster has grown a lot. While catering only for a small number of researchers with information technology needs in the beginning, the ZIV nowadays operates an IT infrastructure that supports about 45,000 students and nearly 8,000 employees. But not only the number of users has grown, the spectrum of supported technologies has expanded as well. While only a few mainframe systems were operated in the 1960s, today complex networks, server systems, application systems and a broad range of end-user devices are maintained. To keep control over this infrastructure, it seems to be helpful to standardize processes and assets. Here, IT services are helpful as they are standardized by definition. This standardization is reflected in the processes that are used to provide a service which in turn leads to a standardization of the result.

Although the idea of a service catalog seems appealing and clear at first sight, it is also challenging: Most practitioners struggle with understanding IT services and therefore find it hard to define them. Furthermore, selecting the ideal range of IT services to be offered is challenging as well. Against this background, the ZIV decided to bring in the Institute for Information Systems to support the introduction of a service catalog. While discussing which services should be included in the ZIV's service portfolio, the management board mentioned that nowadays students and employees do not solely use ZIV services for their studies and work, but also services from commercial providers. Especially apps which support the administration of university life (e.g. exam registration, requesting of grade reports) are used a lot by students. While those apps are convenient for the student, they bear a risk for the university, as system interfaces are used without consultation or knowledge on how to interact with them. What is more, reverse engineering revealed how to access these interfaces, causing not only technical issues on the server side, but also privacy issues as all data is routed via server systems of the commercial providers. Both issues are highly relevant for the university. The use of such apps reflects that the ZIV's services currently do not suit the students' needs well enough. Although the ZIV does not have to prevail on a free market, its services need to be competitive too. Therefore, it does not suffice to improve the existing IT services, but it is necessary to produce and bring forward ideas for new IT services as well.

1.2   Challenges of Service Development

The identification of new IT services is a challenging task and relevant literature based on ITIL is quite limited. The few existing contributions suggest different approaches. Zarnekow et al. [18] for example, propose to analyze the business process and derive potential services from them. Other approaches suggest to start with the technical infrastructure (e.g. Braun und Winter [19] or Brocke et al. [20]). They propose to bundle components of the technical infrastructure, so that they support a business process or task. While these approaches might be feasible in organizations with defined business processes, they do not work in a university setting. Here, the typical business tasks, that is teaching and research, are very creative and, thus, hard to standardize in terms of business processes. The same applies to the learning activities of students. Furthermore, it is neither efficient nor good practice to define IT services for the support of students and employees based on speculations.

ITIL proposes to simply ask the customers for new services, assuming that they are able to express their requirements and can also assign them to one of four categories: service demands, solutions, values and specifications. This assumption is astonishing, bearing in mind that according to ITIL it is already hard to understand what an IT service is and thus questionable if customers are really able to reflect their needs in this way.

A first test was conducted by Teubner and Remfert [21], who asked the users of a German university for their service requirements. For the participants, it was indeed difficult to explicitly formulate their requirements: No one was able to specify service demands, only a few mentioned values, and the majority listed solutions or specifications. Although these are just the results of one study, they indicate that it is not enough to simply ask for services – as proposed by ITIL. As a consequence and for a better understanding, the authors extended their interviews asked participants to also explain their daily work routine and corresponding needs.

1.3 Digitalization in Higher Education

Although there are some studies focusing the digitalization in the field of higher education, they are either very specific and their results can only be generalized to a very limited extent, or they are designed as a quantitative study and therefore allow only a very general view of the subject. A good overview of the status of digitalization is provided by the annual ECAR studies by EDUCAUSE, which focus on both the students (50,000 participants) [22] and the lecturers (13,000 participants) [23] in the USA. Despite the lecturers' high willingness to use innovative tools in teaching and the ever-increasing technical equipment available to students, the results show that digitalization is only at an early stage of development. Other studies focus individual subtopics of digitalization, such as the use of mobile devices and online services in university libraries, the use of apps by medical students [24], or the use of online literature and online references for studying [25]. There is still a lack of qualitative studies which provide insights into the digitalization of university life and the wishes of the students, in order to harness their findings for university IT. This is the starting point for this study.

1.4 Limitations of the Study

The present study is deliberately designed as a qualitative pilot study in order to gain first insights into the topic of digitalization from a student's perspective. Due to the method, these insights are subjective assessments of the participating students, which are not representative. Moreover, results have to be evaluated in relation to the circumstances at the University of Münster and are therefore not necessarily transferable to other universities, especially those outside of Germany. We believe, however, that they can give good insights into the study situation and the mindset of the current generation of students.

2 Research Methodology

In the absence of recent studies on the digitalization at universities from the students' point of view, the following study is designed as a pilot study.

2.1 Research Questions

First of all, it is necessary to clarify how digitized the academic studies already are from the students' point of view. Differences between the disciplines are to be expected. *Research Question 1 (RQ1): How digitized are academic studies at present?*

To identify improvement opportunities, it is necessary to find out which university IT services are relevant to the students and how their user experience proves to be. *Research Question 2 (RQ2): How do users evaluate their experience with university IT services?*

In this context, it is also interesting to know which applications are used for study purposes that are not offered by the university, but by commercial providers. *Research Question 3 (RQ3): Which commercial services are used for study purpose and why?*

Aside from concrete improvement opportunities, the study also aims to determine which new services the students want the university to provide. *Research Questions 4 & 5 (RQ4, RQ5): What services should the university provide? Which is particularly important?*

We suspect that the prioritization of the services will be different between students from technical disciplines and those from rather non-technical courses. *Research Question 6 (RQ6): Do priorities differ between students from technical and non-technical subjects?*

2.2 Setting

Students from various departments of Münster University were recruited by means of flyers, the ZIV's website and Twitter profile, and the university's Facebook group. Vouchers with a value of €25 were used as incentives. The focus groups took place in a neutral meeting room on two dates within a week in January 2017. The conversations were recorded and subsequently transcribed by assistants.

2.3 Population

The recruitment was supposed to deliver a diverse picture of the students' situations and wishes. For this reason, it was initially planned to form specific focus groups for first-term students, more experienced students and foreign students. However, targeted recruiting was dismissed, since first-term and foreign students proved to be very difficult to contact because they are (still) comparatively loosely connected with the university and not (yet) organized as a group. The attempt to recruit first-term students through a special flyer handed out at the university's freshmen fair was unsuccessful. It was therefore decided not to differentiate based on the study phase and nationality.

Instead, two homogeneous groups were formed in consideration of the students' subjects of study, differentiating between technical and non-technical backgrounds. It was assumed that students from technical disciplines will have different requirements and wishes regarding IT support and will communicate them differently as well due to their wider knowledge in this field. This approach allows to compare both groups and, simultaneously, avoids that participants with little technical knowledge are intimidated and, thus, passive. The group size should not extend 6 persons, in order to ensure a dynamic conversation, enough speaking time per person and an efficient management of the discussion.

2.4 Data Analysis Strategy

The transcribed interviews comprise a total of 56 pages (30,300 words). The data were cleansed, structured and subsequently assigned to the research questions. Significant statements were extracted and clustered into subject areas. The participants' prioritizations of services were also grouped into thematic areas [26].

3 Method

Since no relevant studies are available for the research questions, this survey is designed as a qualitative pilot study. In the run-up, participants were given very limited and general information on the subject of the study to avoid framing. A two-method design was applied. In the first hour of the focus group interview, the participants were given short assignments, which they had to solve with Lego Serious Play (e.g. modeling typical study situations such as group work with its specific problems and possible solutions). This part should introduce the participants to the topic and loosen up the atmosphere. The actual survey consisted of a 1.5-h guided interview.

3.1 Interview Instrument

In the run-up to the study, according to the recommendations in the literature [27, 28], an interview guideline was developed to structure the discussion in view of answering the research questions. A guideline from a previous study, which was designed to uncover students' requirements concerning a web portal, was used as a starting point. As the method had proved successful, only content adjustments had to be made.

The guideline divided the focus group interview into three sections: In the first part, after a short round of introductions, the participants were asked to describe their own experiences with the use of IT during their studies. The aim was to determine which parts of the academic studies are already digitized and which are still processed offline. In this context, used services – offered by the university or by external providers such as WhatsApp or Facebook – and usage problems were of particular interest. The usage situation was also discussed. Finally, the participants were asked to make suggestions on how the university could simplify their studies by means of IT.

In the second part, the participants were asked to write down the most important IT services and functions that the university should offer. These were subsequently presented and classified by the participants.

In the third part, the collected services had to be prioritized. For this purpose, each participant could assign a total of ten points to the mentioned services, with the possibility to assign all points to one service. Subsequently, the participants were asked to disclose their respective decisions and give reasons. A ranking list was formed from the prioritizations.

3.2 Participants

Eleven students from various disciplines were selected to participate in the two focus groups. Both groups were formed as homogeneous as possible with regard to the students' subject of study (technical vs. non-technical) in order to check for differences between these groups. The first group was made up of students from IT-related courses such as information systems, computer sciences and mathematics, while the second group consisted of students from non-technical courses such as psychology, history, politics or chemistry. However, most participants in the second group also considered their technical affinity as above-average. The participants were between 20 and 35 years old and studying between the 1st and 11th semesters. Two out of eleven participants were female. The targeted equal distribution of both genders could not be achieved due to the self-recruitment procedure. The participants did not know each other. Five participants had previously studied at foreign universities and were able to contribute these experiences to the discussion. One participant was already working and studying part-time.

4 Findings

In the following, the results of the focus group interviews will be presented with regard to the research questions.

4.1 Status Quo of Digitalization

The participants perceive the degree of digitalization of their studies very differently. As expected, there are major differences between the fields of study. When it comes to **lecture materials**, about half of the participants still work the traditional way using paper copies. These are usually provided by the lecturer in form of a printed reader.

RQ1-A: "Sure, the university provides digital slides and digital materials, sometimes a script or something similar. This was always very handy, but in general I print digital materials to work on them – non-digital so to say."

RQ1-B: "As regards scripts, in the first session they always say: 'Yes, go to the copyshop in the Frauenstraße. Ask for my name to get a printed material collection.' Then you get a three-thousand-page doorstopper."

Many participants, however, do not want to change this situation, as they prefer reading printed instead of digital copies. On the one hand, they expect a higher learning effect by working on paper.

RQ1-C: "I always attach a lot of importance to working on paper, taking notes on paper, writing abstracts on paper. Because, in my opinion, you just learn more comfortably - at least I do. Once you've written and summarized everything by hand, you know it."

On the other hand, annotating and taking notes with digital tools is still perceived as complicated or not suitable for all situations.

RQ1-D: "Okay, so I tried it, but in chemistry you have to draw so many formulas. You could write those with OneNote as well by now, but the software just reacts so badly that you can't keep up."

If, on the other hand, the documents are already provided digitally by the lecturer, they are usually processed digitally as well.

RQ1-E: "I hate working on paper, so I do not print any lecture notes and I never have money on my copy card. No, it would be too much effort to manage all the lectures. I read lecture notes on the computer where I have the PDFs and when I make notes during the lecture I add them directly afterwards. I hardly ever use paper."

One participant even takes the trouble to digitize all handwritten notes and handouts himself.

RQ1-F: "I scan the notes afterwards. I don't keep anything on paper. My handwritten notes lie on the shelf for the current term and if the writing pad is used up, it is disposed of."

With regard to teaching, participants also report that the Moodle-based e-learning platform Learnweb is used widely for the provision of materials and has a very good reputation.

RQ1-G: "I have the impression that there is actually good response, even among professors. There is always an entry for lectures, and slides and materials are available."

RQ1-H: "The professors upload everything, and they do it relatively promptly ... and there actually is nothing else I might want."

Sometimes, however, lecturers do not use the Learnweb due to a lack of technical competence.

RQ1-I: "All of our lecturers in both subjects fail at this. In Chemistry, lectures are not offered in Learnweb as a matter of principle and seminars rarely – and that's about it."

Apart from lectures materials, there are other aspects of studying that are not yet digitized entirely: The **registration for courses and examinations** usually takes place online, but individual participants from the humanities report that in their discipline registration lists on paper are still used sporadically. As regards attendance and performance records, paperwork is still dominant.

RQ1-J: "For practical courses, which we had to complete in addition to our actual studies, we had to get a copy from the professor and bring it to the Examination Office basically every time. Nothing is digitized yet."

When it comes to **literature research**, some departments (e.g. theology) still make use of card indices instead of computer workstations. From the students' point of view, especially the online provision of literature (i.e. essays and books, in particular) is still in its infancy. The participants strongly agree that all literature should be available online to avoid that students have to compete for scarce book resources or cannot access required literature in time for seminar papers. One participant who had previously studied in the Netherlands would even pay significant tuition fees for online access.

RQ1-K: "In the Netherlands you are paying about € 1,018 of tuition fees each year and the whole library is available online which makes literature research just super easy."

With respect to the issue of digitalization in general, students see the problem that they are faced with ever-increasing demands, not least regarding **technical resources**. But not every student has the necessary hardware.

RQ1-L: "If you'd say, okay, we do everything computer-assisted, then you would have to presuppose that every student has access, that is a computer, the whole hardware and other things. I'm not sure if this is de facto possible, because that would make it a basic requirement and I don't think that all students could fulfill it."

If the university wanted to increase the degree of digitalization, it would have to solve this problem first.

RQ1-M: "The process of digitalization is in a transitional phase, where no more than 50% are fulfilled. The reason is that students have to provide the resources themselves – they are not provided by the university."

In summary, it can be stated that the degree of digitalization is very heterogeneous: While the registration for examinations is largely digitized, the administration of the examination results is largely paper-based. Digital badges are not yet used. Notes and scripts are only partially digital, but the majority of the students do not regard this as a disadvantage. According to the participants, the university could increase the degree of digitalization in some cases by providing the necessary hardware and training for the lecturers.

In general, the students have a rather conservative understanding of digitalization which, essentially, includes the online provision of material as well as online registration possibilities. New forms of learning such as MOOCS, interactive classroom systems or even virtual reality are irrelevant, and mobility is not a big issue either. Students still predominantly study at home using a PC or a book. According to the students, this will hardly change in the coming years. Lectures where attendance is expected are also considered appropriate and future-oriented. Infrastructural aspects (e.g. audio-visual equipment in the auditorium, WLAN) were of very little importance in the interviews.

4.2   User Experiences with University IT Services

Discussing relevant systems of the university IT, participants primarily mention the Learnweb, the exam registration system QISPOS, the cloud storage service sciebo and the library online public access catalog OPAC. In addition, most participants use standard software which is available via terminal servers, the Office 365 software package which is available at a special price to university members, and, to a somewhat lesser extent, the e-mail service. With the exception of the printing service Print&Pay, the students to not bring into focus other university IT services (e.g. websites, communication infrastructure, media technology).

While the Learnweb receives an entirely positive evaluation, the **exam administration system** has the greatest potential for improvement from the students' point of view. Almost all participants have heard of or made negative experiences because the system apparently is complicated and generates misunderstandings. They have, for example, not received important examination results and thus had some serious disadvantages in their course of studies.

RQ2-A: "There were problems with my fellow students. They had, for example, registered online and learned after the registration deadline that the system had kicked them out. They were allowed to register again two terms, that is one year, later and some were not allowed to do the exam before."

RQ2-B: "Someone I know had also met the registration deadline and believed until the end that his registration was successful, but the system had thrown him out after the deadline had passed, without him noticing."

RQ2-C: "For me, QISPOS is confusing, too. You have to click through tree structures until you find your course or module. I think that this is no longer up-to-date and causes problems for the examination office that could be avoided if something better was chosen."

Especially in the case of combined degree programs which do not meet the standard, the system seems to reach its limits.

RQ2-D: "Trying to combine two subjects of study using this system feels like hell."

Foreign students in particular, seem to have difficulties with the low degree of standardization regarding exam administration procedures which differ greatly depending on the department, course combination, the responsible examination office and its respective system.

RQ2-E: "It would be nice if everything was standardized, so that you know at the moment you enter the university how this process works. Otherwise if you're new, especially for me for instance, I am not, I wasn't used to the German system."

Other universities have a different approach where students are registered for exams automatically with an opt-out option:

RQ2-F: "For these automatic administration at my home university for my bachelors, we just got registered immediately the moment we sign in for the course, and we could de-register during that semester, so that's way simpler. We just get automatically registered and then, if you don't want to take your exam, you can just de-register."

Learnweb and QISPOS are university systems that students do not use in private contexts and, thus, there are little opportunities to draw comparisons. This, however, is different for the university **cloud service** sciebo and the **e-mail service** perMail which participants can compare to privately used commercial services such as Dropbox and Google. In comparison, students criticize that university services are more complicated to use (sciebo) and have a rather old-fashioned interface (perMail).

RQ2-G: "perMail looks as if someone assembled it using Microsoft Frontpage and did not improve it during the last one hundred thousand years. I cannot even look at it, because it really hurts my eyes. The buttons are labeled with Times New Roman, that's just ... no."

From the students' point of view, commercial services benefit from their high integration with other services and their optimization due to a higher competition.

RQ2-H: "We've talked about user friendliness. Google Drive and Dropbox have proved their worth. They must prevail in the free market and – without addressing reproaches to the university – I would say therefore they are just better. [Using Google

Drive,] I can just invite others by e-mail and it is connected with all my Google services and that is just easier."

Students perceive these services as better developed and more intuitive in general.

RQ2-I: "If you look at Dropbox or Google Drive: Just give me your e-mail address and it's ready. But with sciebo you have to enter the exact university e-mail address. You cannot say, ok, I just enter 25 e-mail addresses. Instead, you must enter each one individually. Drag and Drop, as I know it from Google Drive, OneDrive and other services, does not work either."

Often networking effects are relevant as well - for example, when sharing data with sciebo.

RQ2-J: "If one person does not use it, it doesn't work for the others either."

RQ2-K: "The situation is already exhausting enough: Someone doesn't use WhatsApp, so you have to switch to a Signal, Telegram or Facebook group. You end up with seven messengers and do not need another one from your university."

The **search engines** of the university and the university library, too, are compared to Google's search engine and do poorly from the students' point of view.

RQ2-L: "The search engines are really super slow and thus totally unattractive. Perhaps you miss out on results because the search engine is just so bad."

RQ2-M: "With the OPAC, you can't say: Search only items that are available online. That doesn't work. You have to enter everything super exactly which is really... I don't know. With Google, you only enter roughly what you are looking for and it will work in some way. The same with Google Scholar. But using the OPAC, you have to enter the exact title or you will get 100 books with "the" in the title."

RQ2-N: "The university's internal search doesn't find anything, so I mostly use Google to search something on the university website. The internal search does not find its own contents."

In general, the participants are skeptical about university systems and see no need to replace commercial systems with university solutions.

RQ2-O: "You already know Dropbox. You have it and can also assume that everyone else has that. Thus, it is always a question of convenience if I continue using it. It would be the same with WhatsApp. Even if the university would offer the perfect WhatsApp or Facebook alternative, the acceptance would still be less. Not because of technical features, but simply because of the 'First come first serve'-principle."

RQ2-P: "It is challenging if the university offers something in this area. I think you cannot dictate which services students should use."

Participants who have studied abroad prefer the commercial solutions implemented there, with Google or Microsoft providing the basic services such as cloud, mail and Office software.

RQ2-Q: "[At my university in the Netherlands] everything is based on Office 365. The university e-mail address, too. All services are based on this. That works quite well actually. Yes, everything is included: Office is included, Cloud is included – virtually everything in one service."

RQ2-R: "[At my university in Australia] everything was based on a Google e-mail address. You got a new account, but you could also link it with an existing account. That was well done, because you already knew the services from your private account."

From the students' point of view, German universities face the disadvantage that they have to implement legal regulations on **data protection** more strictly than private companies.

RQ2-S: "I believe that the big companies simply do not care about legal matters. In Germany, things have to be a certain way, and the university has to stick to it."

The issue of data security is assessed ambivalently by the participants: While they indicate that data security is important to them, they prefer to use commercial rather than university services because the latter are too complicated. Some students believe that security cannot be guaranteed anyway.

RQ2-T: "When it comes to data security, solutions, no matter how you design them, always remain a bad compromise because no one can guarantee absolute security. This is the problem."

RQ2-U: "There is no place, where the data are absolutely secure, unless they are offline. That's a fact."

Apart from university systems, participants often use software which is provided by the university (e.g. Office 365, SPSS) and wish for further free or discounted software, especially from Adobe. It is criticized that there is no central download platform, making it hard to find the available software.

Overall, the user experience of university IT systems is rather poor. Due to commercial models, the students have very high requirements and believe that the university cannot compete, in particular with regard to the ease of use and the interface design. University applications have a bad image and some are not even given a try if there are commercial alternatives. Regarding data protection, there are concerns about commercial providers, but they do not have an effect in practice because user friendliness and the exchange with other users are of significantly higher importance.

4.3 Usage of Commercial Services for Studying

As regards commercial services used by students during their studies, the same providers, which are favored for private use, dominate. These are Facebook, WhatsApp and Skype for the coordination of groups (group function). In some cases, these services are also used to digitize non-digital processes. The participants report, for example, that exam results lists, which the university only releases in form of a bulletin in the faculty building, are photographed by a student and sent to all course participants or published on Facebook.

In addition, the participants use tools that are included in Google and Microsoft 365 suites (in particular, Office and e-mail services) as well as Dropbox for storage purposes. For the students, using these services has a great advantage, because they have already used them before and will still use them after their studies. Thus, they do not have to learn and configure a new system.

4.4 Service Requirements of Students

The new services and service improvements identified by the students can be divided into six categories: study organization and management, literature provision, software provision, learning and communication, minor improvements of existing services, and others. Overall, 19 services were proposed. Most fell into the category of study organization, followed by minor improvements of existing services such as a more stable WLAN or more favorable prices for printing.

4.5 Service Prioritization of Students

By prioritizing the services, individual opinions were filtered out and a clear trend could be identified (see Table 1). The three most important services were a centralized platform where all services are integrated (23 of 110 points, quoted by 7 of 11 participants), the online provision of literature (15 points/7 quotations) and a standardized exam administration system (12 points/5 quotations). The centralized service platform stands out as a clear favorite – especially, since a dedicated university app with quite similar functionalities received another 8 points. All other services received less than

Table 1. Prioritization of services

	G1	G2	Total
Study organization	33	19	**52**
Centralized service platform	15	8	**23**
Standardized course and exam registration process	10	2	**12**
University app	0	8	**8**
Improved schedule planner	5	0	**5**
Improved administration portal	3	0	**3**
Course evaluation system	0	1	**1**
Library	9	8	**17**
Online literature	9	6	**15**
Standardized system for literature research	0	2	**2**
Software and hardware	5	9	**14**
Software platform	5	1	**6**
Free software	0	6	**6**
Soft-/hardware partnerships	0	2	**2**
Learning and advice	0	7	**7**
Interactive online learning	0	4	**4**
Messenger	0	3	**3**
Other	13	7	**20**
Minor service improvements (virtual machines, cloud, printing, WLAN)	8	7	**15**
Media equipment training for lecturers	4	0	**4**
ZIV service notifications	1	0	**1**
Total	60	50	**110**

10 points and a maximum of two quotations. Seven out of 19 services received points from only one person, usually the proposer.

4.6 Differences Between Fields of Study

Comparing the service prioritizations of the Group 1 (technical background) with those of Group 2 (non-technical background), some minor differences are evident. The issue of study organization is most important in both groups, but in group 1 it is considerably more prominent. Only Group 2, on the other hand, addresses the aspect of mobility (app) with regard to a centralized service platform. The provision of application software is more dominant in group 2 as well. In the case of library services, however, both groups arrive at the same rating.

5   Discussion

5.1   RQ1: How Digitized are Academic Studies at Present?

The results show that, from the students' point of view, the degree of digitalization has not exceeded a medium level yet. It is striking that the students – in contrast to the stereotype of the digital native and in line with the findings of Bennett et al. and others [29–33] – do not have high expectations of the technical support at their university. In fact, they understand digitalization primarily as the digital provision of lecture notes and online interaction possibilities with the university (i.e. registration for exams, communication with lecturers and fellow students). Nonetheless, the participants would welcome a significantly stronger degree of digitalization, but they predominantly demand minor improvements of individual systems and no fundamental reform of the academic studies (e.g. in form of online lectures).

5.2   RQ2: How Do Users Evaluate Their Experience with University IT Services?

Students are particularly critical of those university services where they also use commercial alternatives from providers like Google, Dropbox or Microsoft. The latter are generally considered superior, as they must prove themselves in a competitive environment. Compared to commercial services, university services do significantly worse in terms of ease of use and look & feel. The basic advantage of the university services – the higher data protection – is noticed by the students, but it has virtually no effect on their usage behavior.

The participants consider the lack of integration, a feature that they value with services of commercial providers, as a major disadvantage of university systems. At the university, students often need a separate ID for each system, and media disruptions also hinder their use. As a matter of principle, university systems have an image problem and some are not even given a try if commercial alternatives exist.

5.3 RQ3: Which Commercial Services are Used for Study Purpose and Why?

As described above, numerous commercial services are used both privately and for study purposes. They are mainly used to perform communication tasks, such as the exchange of information in group works or with lecturers. For this purpose, the real-time communication services of WhatsApp and Facebook are typical tools. The university's e-mail service, on the other hand, is avoided. The service is perceived as old-fashioned and complicated, but the main reason is the medium e-mail in itself, which it is deemed to be too formal, too slow, too complicated and too little group-based. WhatsApp & Co., on the other hand, offer easy-to-use functions for file sharing, video telephony, chat and status information. If e-mails services are used, it is those of commercial providers like Google or Microsoft which offer an integrated user experience. Overall, a convenient and seamless integration of all services (storage, collaborative work, e-mail, chat, Office applications) plays an important role in the preference for commercial providers, while most university services are not interfaced with each other or with privately used commercial services.

Another advantage of commercial services, such as Dropbox, is the fact that they are used by nearly everyone, so collaboration with others is very easy.

5.4 RQ4: What Services Should the University Provide?

As noted above, the students' pictures of a digitized university are less visionary, but rather pragmatic. Although most of the participants had an above-average technical background knowledge according to their self-assessment, there are hardly any suggestions that go beyond the improvement of existing services. However, the big issue outshining everything else is an integration and standardization of these services.

5.5 RQ5: Which Service is Particularly Important?

From the participants' point of view, it is not a new service, but the integration and standardization of existing services that has top priority. In concrete terms, the students expect a portal in form of a website or an app, which requires only one login and merges the most important status messages, information and a transcript of records. The displayed information should be highly personalized and match their specific subject of study and their study objective (examination regulations, schedule, information about lecture rooms). Ideally, this application would be complemented by intelligent features, which – similar to GoogleNow – take over a counseling function. These features should, for example, display suitable course modules based on examination regulations and previously completed courses, calculate the overall average score or show the next appointment including relevant location plans.

5.6   RQ6: Do Priorities Differ Between Students from Technical and Non-technical Subjects?

Due to the small number of participants and the different group sizes, variances in the response behavior of the two groups have only very limited explanatory power. The only significant differences were observable with regard to software provision, possibly because the technophile group is already better equipped with software. The otherwise rather small differences suggest that the services identified are considered to be important across the disciplines.

6   Implications for Research and Practice

Although this pilot study can only give limited insights due to the small, non-representative sample and the specific situation at the University of Münster, it provides a lot of valuable information, especially for those responsible for university IT. From a practitioner's point of view, the good news is that students have a much more grounded and pragmatic view on the development in the next few years than company representatives suggest at symposia. The students do not want a digital revolution in teaching but essentially minor improvements of the core services of university IT.

However, a major problem of university IT could arise from the fact that users are affected by commercial services of large providers such as Google, Microsoft, Facebook and Dropbox. They expect the same integration of services they are accustomed to as well as an intuitive and simple way of use. However, university systems are usually developed over many years due to historic reasons and are operated decentrally. Thus, numerous unconnected systems co-exist (e.g. university library, data center platforms, university administration platforms, exam registration systems of various departments, various e-learning systems), making it necessary for students to use several IDs and understand different system logics. Furthermore, universities rarely invest in the design of their services. Instead they focus security aspects, which are usually associated with a lower usage comfort. Students, however, value security aspects rhetorically at most. Therefore, the universities have to find a tradeoff between necessary security and desired user friendliness. Students support cooperation between higher education institutions and commercial providers instead of university in-house developments, because they put it past commercial providers only to have the resources for competitive products. As the interviews indicate, most of the university services are no longer in the comfortable situation that they have to be used due to lack of competition, no matter how bad the user experience is.

Great potential inheres in the creation of a centralized access to existing services. But unlike most university apps which merely summarize general information with a cafeteria meal plan and a map, the students wish for a personalized solution that simplifies their study organization.

Depending on their field of study, the participants have made very different experiences with the degree of digitalization, implying that digitalization does not happen automatically, but is strongly dependent on individual actors who are able to promote or slow down the issue. In order to avoid a two-tier society, universities should develop a digitization strategy at an early stage, in which they define the objectives and the implementation procedures. The results suggest that further research should examine in more detail the question which services the university itself should offer and which it should outsources (either completely or in form of a cooperation) to private providers. A larger sample and quantitative methods are needed, in order to test the validity of the results and support them in a representative way, as well as to transfer them to other universities and, if appropriate, other countries. The requirements of university employees would also be a fruitful research objective, which could be analyzed using the methods developed here.

7 Conclusion

To date, digitalization at universities has been an extensively discussed but widely diffuse topic. Most studies focus on single aspects such as mobile apps or e-learning tools, or look into technical issues. Based on the ITIL framework and the basics of service engineering, this study attempts to identify essential IT services which universities should provide from the students' point of view. In addition, it delivers a genuine insight into the current state of digitalization from a user's perspective.

As previous studies have demonstrated, the idea of the modern student as a permanently online, technically well-informed and equipped digital native is a myth. Though the technical background knowledge is extensive, some of the participants do not have the necessary hardware and, moreover, the majority does not strive for a considerably intensified digitalization of the academic studies. New learning formats such as lecture recordings or interactive elements are generally welcomed as additional possibilities, but they are not claimed for insistently.

The degree of digitization within the university differs significantly depending on the particular faculty culture. Reasons include the students' lack of technical equipment as well as the lecturers' lack of knowledge.

For studying, commercial and university services are used in parallel as a matter of course. Commercial services from the private sphere are used in the university sphere as well, provided they seem suitable. University systems are considered old-fashioned, complicated, and less intuitive. In particular, the lack of integration of different services (and the accompanying need for different IDs for each system) is a major disadvantage. Thus, the majority of the participants argues for a cooperation between the university and commercial providers such as Google or Microsoft, although there generally are diffuse concerns about data protection. However, these are ignored because students believe their own data is either undeserving of protection or not protected anywhere anyway, not even at the university.

Three service categories clearly dominate the students' wishes for IT support: study organization, online literature and software provision. As regards the study organization, a centralized platform granting access to all relevant information and services (e.g. schedule, exam administration, certificates, study progress, contact information) is particularly important. From the students' point of view, IT should enable them to focus on the content of their studies, provide support for organizational problems, and grant easy access to resources, such as literature and software, while at the same time require little effort. In consequence, higher education institutions face significantly higher requirements for the design of their systems, because students measure their value compared to experiences with privately used IT services. However, it is difficult to reconcile the integrated user experience and intuitive handling with the security requirements for university IT systems which are particularly high in Germany. Nevertheless, universities are well advised to develop and implement digitalization strategies in order to actively shape this change.

References

1. Hanna, N.: Mastering Digital Transformation. Towards a Smarter Society, Economy, City and Nation. Emerald Publishing, Bingley (2016)
2. Hochschulforum Digitalisierung: Diskussionspapier: 20 Thesen zur Digitalisierung der Hochschulbildung, Berlin (2015)
3. Brown-Martin, G., Tavakolian, N.: Learning {Re}imagined. How the Connected Society is Transforming Learning. Bloomsbury Academic, London (2014). An imprint of Bloomsbury Publishing Plc
4. Craig, R.: The technology of higher education. TechCrunch (2016)
5. Shark, A.R. (ed.): The Digital Revolution in Higher Education. How and Why the Internet of Everything is Changing Everything. Public Technology Institute, Alexandria (2015)
6. Bischof, L., Stuckrad, T.V.: Die digitale (R)evolution? Chancen und Risiken der Digitalisierung akademischer Lehre. CHE, Gütersloh (2013)
7. Bischof, L., Friedrich, J.-D., Müller, U., Müller-Eiselt, R., Stuckrad, T.V.: Die schlafende Revolution - Zehn Thesen zur Digitalisierung der Hochschullehre. Centrum für Hochschulentwicklung gGmbH, Gütersloh
8. Biddix, J.P., Chung, C.J., Park, H.W.: The hybrid shift. Evidencing a student-driven restructuring of the college classroom. Comput. Educ. **80**, 162–175 (2015)
9. Cisco: Digitising Higher Education. To enhance experiences and improve outcomes (o.J.)
10. Bowen, W.G.: Higher Education in the Digital Age. Princeton University Press, Princeton (2013)
11. van Lamsweerde, A.: Requirements Engineering: From System Goals to UML Models to Software. Wiley, Chichester (2009)
12. Thayer, R., Dorfman, M.: Software Requirements Engineering. IEEE Computer Society Press, Los Alamitos (2000)
13. Pohl, K.: Requirements Engineering: Fundamentals, Principles, and Techniques. Springer Publishing Company, Incorporated, Berlin (2010)
14. Brenner, M.: Werkzeugunterstützung für ITIL-orientiertes Dienstmanagement. Ein modellbasierter Ansatz, Norderstedt (2007)
15. van Bon, J., van der Veen, A., Pieper, M.: Foundations in IT Service Management Basierend auf ITIL. Van Haren Publishing, Zaltbommel (2008)
16. Barafort, B., Betry, V., Cortina, S., Picard, M., Renault, A., St-Jean, M., Valdés, O.: ITSM Process Assessment Supporting ITIL (TIPA). Van Haren, Zaltbommel (2009)
17. Teubner, A., Remfert, C.: Towards a theoretical backing for IT services. In: Proceedings of 19th International Conference on Human-Computer Interaction, Vancouver, Canada (2017, forthcoming)

18. Zarnekow, R., Hochstein, A., Brenner, W.: Service-Orientiertes IT-Management: Best Practices und Praxisbeispiele. Springer, Berlin (2005)
19. Braun, C., Winter, R.: Integration of IT service management into enterprise architecture. ACM (2007)
20. Brocke, H., Uebernickel, F., Brenner, W.: A methodical procedure for designing consumer oriented on-demand IT service propositions. Inf. Syst. e-Bus. Manag. **9**, 283–302 (2011)
21. Teubner, A., Remfert, C.: ITOMEx – Eine Fallstudie zum IT Service Management. In: Working Papers of the Institute for Information Systems (2016)
22. Dahlstrom, E.: ECAR study of undergraduate students and information technology, 2015 (2015)
23. Brooks, C.: ECAR study of faculty and information technology. Research report, Loisville, CO (2015)
24. Briz-Ponce, L., Juanes-Méndez, J.A.: Mobile devices and apps, characteristics and current potential on learning. JITR **8**, 26–37 (2015)
25. Connaway, L.S., Lanclos, D., Hood, E.M.: I Find Google a Lot Easier than Going to the Library Website. Imagine Ways to Innovate and Inspire Students to Use the Academic Library. Indianapolis (2013)
26. Ruddat, M.: Auswertung von Fokusgruppen mittels Zusammenfassung zentraler Diskussionsaspekte. In: Schulz, M., Mack, B., Renn, O. (eds.) Fokusgruppen in der empirischen Sozialwissenschaft, pp. 195–206. Springer, Berlin (2012)
27. Prickarz, H., Urbahn, J.: Qualitative Datenerhebung mit Online-Fokusgruppen. Plan. Anal. **28**, 63–70 (2002)
28. Schulz, M., Mack, B., Renn, O.: Fokusgruppen in der empirischen Sozialwissenschaft: Von der Konzeption bis zur Auswertung. Springer, Berlin (2012)
29. Margaryan, A., Littlejohn, A., Vojt, G.: Are digital natives a myth or reality? University students' use of digital technologies. Comput. Educ. **56**, 429–440 (2011)
30. Lei, J.: Digital natives as preservice teachers. J. Comput. Teach. Educ. **25**, 87–97 (2009)
31. Kolikant, Y.B.-D.: Digital natives, better learners? Students' beliefs about how the Internet influenced their ability to learn. Comput. Hum. Behav. **26**, 1384–1391 (2010)
32. Jones, C., Ramanau, R., Cross, S., Healing, G.: Net generation or digital natives. Is there a distinct new generation entering university? Comput. Educ. **54**, 722–732 (2010)
33. Bennett, S., Maton, K.: Beyond the 'digital natives' debate. Towards a more nuanced understanding of students' technology experiences. J. Comput. Assist. Learn. **26**, 321–331 (2010)

Understanding Voting Barriers to Access for Americans with Low Literacy Skills

Kathryn Summers[1]([✉]), Jonathan Langford[2], Caitlin Rinn[1],
Joel Stevenson[1], Emily Rhodes[1], Jaime Lee[1], and Rachel Sherard[1]

[1] University of Baltimore, Baltimore, USA
ksummers@ubalt.edu
[2] Interactive Educational Systems Design, River Falls, USA
jlang2@pressenter.com

Abstract. For our democracy to be truly representative, all adults who wish to vote need to be able to vote successfully and independently. But 42% of adult Americans read at Basic or Below Basic levels, according to the National Adult Literacy Survey, and PEW research shows that citizens with lower literacy levels vote at much lower rates than citizens with higher literacy levels. Similarly, adults with disabilities vote at much lower rates than adults without disabilities. Prior research has identified some of the barriers that affect voting access for adults with disabilities; this in-depth ethnographic study explores the barriers that affect voting access for adults with lower literacy skills. Understanding these barriers sheds light on the human implications of current voting system controversies.

While this research focuses on activities related to voting, the barriers, behaviors, and coping strategies observed also have implications for the design of other public services. The research joins a growing body of data-driven insight into how to design information and services for this 42% of American adults. It also provides insights that are useful for other populations who don't read well, such as English Language Learners, and for older adults who sometimes experience reduced functional literacy.

Keywords: Voting · Low literacy · Civic literacy · Disabilities · Ethnography

1 Introduction

Literacy—defined as "using printed and written information to function in society, to achieve one's goals, and to develop one's knowledge and potential"—represents an important qualification for successful interaction with many elements of modern life. Yet according to the 2003 National Assessment of Adult Literacy, 43% of adults in the United States experience low literacy, defined here as scoring at the levels of Below Basic or Basic in prose literacy [15]. This presents substantial problems for civic participation in many areas, including voting.

Research has long established that low literacy has a negative impact on voting activity [13–15]. These findings represent a call to action for identifying and addressing elements of voting participation that are especially challenging for adults with low

© Springer International Publishing AG 2017
A. Marcus and W. Wang (Eds.): DUXU 2017, Part III, LNCS 10290, pp. 294–312, 2017.
DOI: 10.1007/978-3-319-58640-3_21

literacy. This call to action is made more urgent by the overrepresentation of older Americans, individuals from racial/ethnic minorities, and Americans of lower socioeconomic levels among the ranks of those with low literacy [15].

In order to understand and effectively address barriers to voting participation, it is important first to understand the voting experience of individuals with low literacy. This study explores factors such as family experience and attitudes toward voting, voting activities—including registering to vote, travel to the polling place, and polling place experiences—and preferences related to voting options such as machine versus paper voting, early voting, and absentee voting.

A fundamental goal of such understanding is to identify both barriers to voting—elements that get in the way of voting for low-literacy individual—and facilitators, defined as anything that promotes a positive experience during the voting process. The current research is designed to help provide this information through in-depth interviews conducted with low-literacy voters, using an approach adapted from similar research into the voting experiences of people with disabilities [25].

2 Methods

This ethnographic study uses qualitative analysis of 54 in-depth interviews in order to understand the voting experience of adults with low literacy skills. The goal was to engage participants in discussion and storytelling about their experiences with voting—what they believe, what they do, and why—in order to better understand the complex nature of their experience.

30 participants were accompanied to a polling place on an election day or an early voting day, then interviewed about their experience and their voting history immediately after voting. These interviews, conducted in or just outside a polling place, right after a voting experience, helped participants provide the most reliable accounts of their experience possible without direct observation (researchers did not, of course, observe participants while voting). Of the 30 interviews conducted at polling places, 16 observations/interviews were conducted during early voting of November 2014, 5 observations/interviews took place on election day, November 4, 2014, and an additional 9 observations/interviews were conducted on election day, November 8, 2016. 8 of the participants were voting for the first time when interviewed.

To allow a broader sample, an additional 24 participants were interviewed about their voting experiences and voting history in the University of Baltimore's User Research Lab. These additional interviews were not accompanied by an immediate voting experience. However, researchers encouraged participants to tell the stories of actual voting experiences as much as possible. Of these 24 interviews, 10 were conducted during August 2014, 4 during December 2014, and 10 during April and May 2015.

The semi-structured interviews examined the following issues:

- Sense of civic responsibility and importance of voting, with questions about family voting patterns and history, personal voting history, and the meanings and significance of voting.

- Past and current voting experiences, with questions about preparation for voting (learning about candidates and issues, getting registered, finding the polling place), questions about the experience of voting (getting to the polling place, interacting with poll workers, interacting with ballots).
- Feelings about voting, as indicated by the adjectives chosen, spontaneous statements about emotional state or emotional impact, and presented affect during the interview.

2.1 Participants

Participants were recruited for the study from a database of participants maintained by the University of Baltimore, through street recruiting, and using snowball sampling, a non-probability sampling technique used in sociology and statistics research in order to research a population which may be difficult for researchers to access.[1]

All 54 participants were African Americans living in or close by Baltimore, Maryland. Not every participant chose to share their age, educational level, or employment status, but those who did ranged in age from 18 to 71, with an average age of 45 years. In order to participate in the survey, the participants were required to qualify as low literate, i.e., reading at the eighth grade level or below as measured by the Rapid Estimate of Adult Literacy in Medicine (REALM) [7].[2] Participants' REALM scores ranged from 15 to 60, with an average score of 51 (Table 1).

2.2 Analysis

Audio recordings of the interviews were transcribed and converted to a spreadsheet format for qualitative analysis. The primary researcher conducted open coding to identify patterns and themes related to the research questions. Axial coding was then conducted to identify relationships among the open codes, and a set of standardized thematic categories was developed for systematic analysis [4, 9, 26].

---

[1] Snowball sampling is the most commonly used sampling technique for studying hard-to-recruit populations. Its potential disadvantages are minimized by using a diverse seed (a diverse group of initial contacts, found in a variety of ways), which was done, and multiple recruitment waves (asking at least three rounds of participants to recommend additional participants), which was done [11].

[2] The REALM is one of several possible instruments for estimating adult literacy levels. It is comprised of a list of 66 words that a participant reads aloud as a facilitator keeps score of words pronounced correctly; the score is the number of correct words a participant pronounces. Although originally designed to measure health literacy, REALM has several advantages for field work—primarily in that it takes 2–5 min, requires minimal training to administer, and does not feel like a literacy test to participants. The REALM has been shown to reliably distinguish between adults at lower literacy levels [1], although it does not distinguish between adults at a 9th grade reading level or above. The REALM is also highly correlated with the Wide Range Achievement Test-Revised $(r = 0.88)$, the revised Slosson Oral Reading Tests $(r = 0.96)$, the revised Peabody Individual Achievement Test $(r = 0.97$, and the TOFHLA $(r = 0.84)$ [6, 17]. The REALM also has a high test-retest reliability $(r = 0.97)$ [7].

Table 1. Demographic characteristics of study participants.

Gender		
Male	33	61.1%
Female	21	38.9%
Reading level (REALM)		
3rd grade or less (0–18)	1	1.9%
4–6th grade (19–44)	9	16.7%
7–8th grade (45–60)	44	81.5%
Age (52 of 54 reported)		
18–40 years	21	40.4%
41–60 years	26	50.0%
61 or more years	5	9.6%
Education (51 of 54 reported)		
9th grade or below	3	5.9%
10–12th grade	29 (may include some grads)	56.9%
HS graduate or GED	5	9.8%
Some college	10	19.6%
A.A. or A.S.	3	5.9%
Bachelor's degree	1	2.0%
Employment (32 out of 54 reported)		
Working full-time or part-time	12	37.5%
Not working or on disability	20	62.5%

Each transcript was then reviewed for matches to the thematic categories by the primary researcher and one of the other researchers. Differences in coding decisions between the two researchers were discussed and settled by consensus agreement.

3   Findings

In our analysis of the interview transcripts, we focused on participants' feelings about voting, their voting history—including the role of voting in their family history—and in the aspects of their voting experiences that seemed to pose challenges or to make the process of voting easier.

3.1   Personal Voting History

Voting history of the participants varied widely. All but two had voted at least once. Some were voting for the first time on the day they were interviewed. They ranged from dedicated voters who had voted in nearly every election for decades, to occasional voters who had voted between 3–5 times over an extended period, to rare voters who had voted just once or twice over an extended period, to new voters who were voting for the first or second time. Some voters only vote in presidential elections, others focus on local elections (for mayor, city council, etc.), and some vote in both federal and local elections. Voters who participate in local elections express a strong sense of the mayor and of their city councilman, and a conviction that these officials have power over their day-to-day welfare.

Some voters talked about voting shortly after they turned 18, alluding to a sense of growing up and entering the adult world.

P7.   The first time I voted? Oh my God. I think I was about 18 or 19; I don't know. When I first got that voters card. I was excited. Just go vote; didn't even know who I was voting for.

P3.   I felt like somebody because I voted.

P51.   Yeah… yes, because I was excited. 'Cause I was old enough to vote.

Note, however, that after participant 51's initial election, he didn't vote again until he was a grandfather. This suggests a need to follow up on initial enthusiasm in order to help build a regular habit of voting.

3.2 Family History of Voting

Some participants reported a strong family history of voting. They had memories of accompanying their parents to polling places before they could vote, of parents or siblings helping them get registered, of the pride of going with family members to vote for the first time after turning 18. 61% of the participants said their parents vote, or voted when they were alive. 48% told stories of family members actively encouraging voting, compared to 26% who said their families did not emphasize voting or place much value on it.

P26.   School told us too but it was more so by your parents taking you…. I grew up with my mother so I got the experience of going to vote and see how it was for them.

P37.   Yeah; my parents, I've never known them not to vote…. Election time would come, they would stand right at our door… to hand out ballots…. My mother would always tell us to offer them something warm to drink or if it was summertime, offer them something to drink.

Sometimes this family history led to regular voting by the participant; other times it did not. A much smaller number of participants talked about successfully passing this emphasis along to their children. Others described their failure to do so:

P34.   Only my son, he can vote now but he ain't voted…. He feels like you vote and they still don't get the right person…. He feels it's all fixed.

P34.   [My son don't vote] but that's because he a boy…. One of my brothers they won't vote. Me and my sisters, we be there, we be pumped up, have our shirts on, ya know. We want to win. Have our little shirts on…. [My son's] silly. He 20 but he's like 15 for real.

Others had memories of some family members voting, or some relatives who advocated voting, but voting was not necessarily emphasized.

3.3 Feelings About Voting

Participants' feelings about voting ranged from a deeply felt personal commitment, to lukewarm commitment, to paying lip service to the importance of voting (often coupled with a poor actual voting history), to explicit questioning of the efficacy and utility of voting. Reasons for voting were similarly varied—some participants cited a need to protect their benefits. Others expressed a personal sense of obligation to particular city officials. A few cited the problems facing the world, with the hope that voting could make a difference.

Reasons for Voting

By far the most frequently expressed, and foundational, motivation to vote was a belief that election outcomes influence governmental decisions—whether at local or national levels.

P20.   My one vote or not vote might be the reason why somebody didn't get in. So I really try to pay attention to who I am picking as well so I don't pick the wrong person.... Because we gotta choose the people that speak for us. We can't do it ourselves.

The next most common motivation for voting expressed by participants was their own social and economic welfare. These participants explained that voting would help to protect their benefits, or the benefits of others, or community institutions such as schools and libraries:

P4.   Because I want to select candidates who have my interest in mind.

P17.   I grew up in a poor family and voting is important so they won't try to cut out their benefits, you know, like social service or SSI or Social Security.

P21.   Some of the presidents be making good decisions for the community and some doesn't like health benefits. I just voted for this year because of health benefits. For health and jobs. I think there be more jobs in the community.

Some voters expressed a desire to protect their children:

P51.   I'm out here voting [because].... I got a better chance with [candidate A].... I been in this neighborhood about 14 years, living next to white people. And [candidate B] get in that chair, lord knows the white people I'm living next door to, their true colors might come out... It makes a difference. I got grandkids, I got a son.

P38.   Who runs the city that you live in... it's important because it depend on [i.e., determines]... what's gon' happen within the next generation... far as health, everything.

A few voters expressed a sense of pride or obligation to past champions who had to fight for the right to vote.

P1.   I want to know who's running the country.... I want to have a say in it.... This is what my forefathers fought for.

P52.   Our ancestors and stuff foughted for us to have this opportunity... and to not use it is like a kick in their ass.

Reasons Not to Vote

The most frequently cited motivation not to vote was a belief that politicians are dishonest or that the system is rigged, so that voting doesn't make a difference.

P6.   I believe they going to put who they want in there so to me it's a waste of time.

P3.   Some people say they into looking out for schools, trying to make schools better, but once they get into it, get their votes in, they don't actually do it. So that's the reason why I don't vote.

P19.   My family just don't vote. I don't know why. Their attitude is no matter who you put in the seats, they're going to do what they want to do anyway. They tell you one thing, when they get in office they totally do the opposite.

P32.   All of them is the same thing anyway. Always give you promises and never really stick to them at all.

Concerns of this type were expressed by 17% of the participants who discussed their feelings about voting. This included several participants who expressed elsewhere in their interviews a belief that their votes could make a difference—in some cases suggesting conflicting feelings about engagement and marginalization among these voters, in others reflecting changing views over time.

This feeling was also cited by participants who had voted once, upon turning 18, but who had not voted again (One of our participants had voted at 18, but then had not voted again until choosing to participate in the study, at age 51.). This suggests a window of opportunity for generating enthusiasm and educating new voters. For example, schools and other organizations could provide opportunities for high school seniors and others of the same age to contact locally elected leaders, could conduct voter registration, and could walk new voters through how to educate themselves about election issues and go about voting.

Quality of Voting Experience

Although all of the participants who voted during the study had a positive experience, a few participants had memories of very negative experiences with voting:

P21.   It was like dreadful because I didn't know nothing about it. They explained but I still didn't understand but I got the hang of it. That's why I really don't vote because there's a lot that you got to do.

P22.   The last time I voted it was crazy…. You had to sometimes you had to do your own voting, like write down the vote or something like that. You had sometimes machines… that would break down. Like you stick your vote in and it would just break down or you had to re-do it or the machine wasn't working. So it was really difficult for voters to vote or to stand in line or to wait or to do anything.

Not everyone who worried about voting had actually had a negative experience. Some participants worried prospectively that casting their votes would be difficult or require a lot of effort, or that they would not be successful. Others were afraid of not knowing what to do or of looking "ignorant."

P45.   I was nervous before I went in there because I thought I wasn't going to get no help…. People think you slow because you need a help. I got to stop thinking like that. If I need help I just say excuse me, I need a little help. You may think I'm ignorant or whatever.... There used to be a time I wouldn't even ask. I'd sit there and pretend that I know and knowing that I don't know.

Several of these apprehensive voters chose to vote as part of the study. Afterwards, they expressed pleasure and relief at how positive their voting experience had been, describing the process as easy.

P12.   It was easy for me and I liked it. So I'll probably come and vote again.... Can't wait to do it again.

P35.   I look forward to doing it again next year.... I was all proud; I said can I have one of your stickers—because I want to show that I been voting today. I'm going to rub it in too. I wish I could bring some more people with me, come out here and vote.... Like I say for me for the first time, I'm thinking it going to be a bunch of people; it was going to be all these machines and I'll be confused which one to push and wouldn't be able to understand or couldn't read, you know, to that nature. It was nothing of the sorts. It was nothing of the sorts.

P39.   It was a simple process. And me personally, I thought it was going to be much harder and that was another reason why I hadn't voted in the past.... I thought it would be harder than actually what I thought it would be.... [I expected it to be] complicated. A lot of reading. It wasn't. It wasn't.

P57.   Oh wow, I really did it! And it was not complicated whatsoever!... I feel really nice. And look how many daggone stickers I got!

This positive reaction suggests another window of opportunity to increase voter participation, if ways to allay this preliminary anxiety could be found.

3.4   Issues of Civic Literacy

Before voting, would-be voters must navigate some fairly complex processes, such as getting registered, finding their polling place, and forming opinions that can guide their votes. Their success in navigating these processes is often hampered by a lack of civic literacy, which often accompanies low literacy in general [21, 22, 24].

Learning About Issues and Candidates
Knowing where to find information about issues and candidates and then interpreting that information to make voting decisions is a challenge related to both civil literacy and literacy in general [13, 22].

Most participants (78%) relied on television for information about issues and candidates. The next most frequently mentioned sources of information and guidance were the internet (30%) and other people—family, neighbors, or casual conversations during daily activities (35%). Billboards, newspapers, and fliers (from campaigners or in the mail) were also mentioned. Some participants (9%) reported that they formed opinions in part by meeting with candidates or volunteers going door-to-door or walking around the neighborhood.

Many participants claimed to feel "prepared" before going to vote, but the details of their experience contradicted this statement. Many mentioned seeing items on the ballot that they were not prepared for. Very few mentioned the sample ballot as a source of information, even though one is sent in the mail to voters in Maryland.

P20.   So I don't mind just going for just the President. You get up there and vote, and you think you're going to be there for two minutes to vote, and two minutes turn to ten, who the hell are all these other people? I never heard of them one time, you know what I mean?... You don't know how many people you going to look at. A lot of us just younger come in and it's that.

One person wished he could learn about the ballot online before going to vote:

P4.   I think there should be somehow even prior to the voting, election, there should be some site where people can go to and they can see what is up for what will be in the ballot. I don't know if there's such a thing. Like if they're going to be voting for bonds or whatever.

Participants who did use the internet often used it as a follow-up source of information —they would see a billboard or a commercial, and then look up that person online. Only a few participants felt confident that they could do "deep" research online, such as researching candidate backgrounds or prior history. Several participants considered themselves to be still learning about the internet—newly available to them through a smartphone—although some of the younger participants relied heavily and with confidence on Google.

P10.   Normally I learn through TV, 'ya know; commercials. Things of that nature. As far as doing deep research, no; I've never been the type that did that.... [Online I look] just like who's the councilman of my district; stuff like that. Or who's about to run for council.

P46.   I'm learning it from this [Android phone].... I'm learning. I'm not going to tell you I'm a whiz with it. There's a lot of things on here—a lot of apps I haven't even got into yet. So it's like I'm an infant when it comes to technology.

P33.   No; just looking for information about candidates for voting. That's how I look up. I Google.... I bring in—I write off everything from my computer, put it in my pocket, bring it with me.

How to Handle Lack of Preparation

A few participants (7%) indicated that they did no preparation for voting. Some thought no preparation was needed. Others asked for help from a poll worker—and were sometimes disappointed to find out that the poll workers could not help them vote.

P6.   Like if you didn't know more they came and explained to you who the person was, what they did; stuff like that.

P36.   She was trying to help me with that but it wasn't really much she could tell me because I got to do it on my own. But once I started voting, and I read everything carefully, I felt good.

A handful of participants ended up relying on the campaign literature provided outside the polling place.

P27.   I know what I hear. I watch the news and everything. I read the stuff that they give us [outside the polling place].... It's helpful. They give the pamphlets for you to read through it and see what works for you; who you're against and who you're for.

P35.   When I came in they gave us some brochures on certain candidates so I just took some of those and read them.

Perhaps inevitably, participants regularly encountered questions on the ballot that they did not expect or were not prepared for. For some of these, such as ballot measures, they would routinely do their best to decipher the language of the measure and make a decision on the spot.[3]

P34.   When I get there and I read it, I just decide then right when I'm there.

P58.   I gave it a quick thought, and made the best selection I could.

Two participants indicated that they could also use personal experience to make decisions about judges:

P33.   This time I was much more prepared because I had my own computer. I already knew what I had to do. Looked everything up ahead of time. So it was much easier when I saw the names pop up and everything. Oh yeah—and I was fortunately to be in front of some people like the judges. I been in front of them so I know which one was good and which one I wouldn't want to be in front of again.

Registration

Registration was a hurdle for many voters and would-be voters. Among participants who talked about how they had registered to vote, many did so as part of another institutional transaction (e.g., social services, MVA, jail, or the draft). Others had registered at the instigation of their parents or other family members, or as part of a registration drive in a mall or in their neighborhood. In short, participants who had succeeded in registering to vote typically received external support in figuring out the required procedures.

In general, most participants didn't understand how registration worked. They were unaware that there is a deadline for registering before an election, so they sometimes registered past the deadline without realizing it (they sometimes received a provisional ballot, but were unaware that their vote might not count). Most participants did not know how to update their registration, or even that they needed to update it. Some of our participants simply went back to their old precincts to vote; others attempted to use a polling place closer to their current address, but were given provisional ballots or were re-directed to their prior precinct.

P20.   Because you only can go to vote in areas that you're really close to. I was down the street trying to go to another place.... You don't think it should matter because voting is voting and everything is confidential.... If I didn't have a

---

[3] This finding suggests the value of including a plain summary such as is provided on ballots in California to assist voters with low literacy in interpreting the intent of ballot measures.

vehicle it'd be kind of hard because there's no bus line that goes to the elementary school [his prior precinct]. Hear what I'm saying? That's what I mean by shouldn't matter what area you live in because you might have to go somewhere that's off the bus line.

About 26% of respondents who discussed voter registration could not remember where or when they had registered. Seven participants (13%) had tried to vote at some point and been unable to do so because they were not registered, or had been asked to use a provisional ballot. Of the 30 interviews that occurred just after the participant had voted, five participants (17%) thought they were properly registered but had to use a provisional ballot.[4] None of these participants realized that they had used a provisional ballot or realized that the problems with their registration might lead to their vote not being counted.

Participants who register without the kind of help provided in an institutional setting may think they have registered correctly when in fact they have not. Some of our participants talked about filling out registration paperwork at home or at a mall, but not receiving a registration card even though many weeks had passed. When they went to vote, sometimes they filled out a provisional ballot, but this solution is less than ideal as these votes will not be counted unless the problem with their registration is resolved. In a few cases, voters without valid registration were turned away completely by poll workers.

P32.   I went to vote one year and my name wasn't on the paper. So I had to fill out this form. But they let me vote. I had to do something. Fill out some papers where I put the address put back in the county.

P36.   It was cool but they didn't really explain. They just gave me the paper to fill out. I just filled it out. They said they was going to mail me.

P8.   Right now; I don't really know. I was under the impression that I was able to vote but every time I try, they tell me no I can't vote… Yes, I filled it out but no go…. I assume they wouldn't have because I never heard anything from them. That's why I'm saying that.

P28.   I had to start all over again then wait for them to send me another voter's card. I couldn't even vote this year.

One participant whose registration had not been successful (although she did not realize that) talked about the "difficulty" of the form, even though the questions were "ordinary" and not "hard":

P40.   [My sister] brought me a form home and we filled the form out to get our voters card which we haven't got it back yet…. The voting application [questions were] just ordinary—where you live at, date of birth, mother's maiden name; stuff of that nature. She helped me do all that; fill most of that out…. Well, it was kind of difficult for me because it was the first time I ever did it. It was kind of difficult. But hard; no. I wouldn't say it was hard to do but it was difficult.

---

[4] Researchers determined this because they saw the participants get directed to the provisional ballot table, or inferred that they had voted using a provisional ballot because they had used "paper" rather than the electronic voting machines that were standard in 2014.

In several of these comments, the voter's frustration leaks through: they don't understand what went wrong and wish it was easier to "just vote." Sometimes the barriers to voting posed by the registration process felt like deliberate obstruction:

P47.   I think maybe the voter registration [is] crap. I ... [It] shouldn't be so complicated sometime if you don't have your voter registration card or if you change address or whatever.... [I]f you a citizen of the United States and can prove that you are, it should never be an issue about having to re-register and that day you should already be... inside somebody's computer saying yeah; this guy's a registered voter. Should have no problem wherever you moving around the country. Should be able to vote. Wherever you want.... I ain't going to say [they] trying to take away people's voting rights, but make it harder for people to vote so they can get in or whatever to what they doing legally to try to get people not to vote. It puzzles me because it's not a complicated thing. It shouldn't be.

Finding the Polling Place

Another difficulty faced by participants was figuring out where to vote. The most common sources of information were following the address on their voting card or asking neighbors or family members. Some participants remembered their polling place from prior elections. Others saw the signs and activity surrounding a polling place near their home and followed the lines.

The complexities of the registration process also affected the task of finding the right polling place. Many participants did not know how to update their registration, and sometimes didn't know they could, so about 12% of participants simply went to the polling place for a prior address in order to vote. A somewhat smaller group (8%) went to the wrong polling place and were re-directed to the polling place associated with their registration status, but another 10% were simply handed provisional ballots. Only two participants (4%) looked up their polling place online.

P20.   You only can go to vote in areas that you're really close to. I was down the street trying to go to another place. It was not far off but as far as your locations in your area, they want you to stay into the area. You don't think it should matter because voting is voting and everything is confidential.... If I didn't have a vehicle it'd be kind of hard because there's no bus line that goes to the elementary school. Hear what I'm saying? That's what I mean by shouldn't matter what area you live in because you might have to go somewhere that's off the bus line.

The role of poll workers was crucial in helping the sizeable contingent of voters who were in the wrong precinct or who had not successfully registered. Poll workers who just handed voters a provisional ballot without explaining what it was, or (worse) just turned voters away as unregistered, lost an important opportunity to act as facilitators.

Lack of Knowledge about Election Logistics

A sizeable number of participants showed limited knowledge about election logistics. Many of the participants had never heard of early voting. Many seemed unaware that elections include both presidential and mid-term elections, and unaware of the difference between municipal elections and federal elections. Participants tended to identify their voting history by what candidates or what offices they had voted for:

P6.   The Democrat. And I do the government one. That's it.

P57.   [I vote in] General, and (pause) just general election.... Yeah, when it was like [pause] that [pause] Catherine Pugh [mayor of Baltimore] thing.

Of the 43 participants who discussed or were asked about absentee voting, 65% revealed in their responses that they hadn't heard of it or were uncertain about what it meant. Of those who did know about absentee voting, several had concerns about it—including worries that the ballot could get lost in the mail, that they might forget to mail it in time, or that absentee ballots might be counted differently from votes cast in person.

P34.   You never know about the mail. You know, like if it's getting there or they receive now like the door like that. Other people touches it and stuff.... I'd just rather use a computer to cast my own ballot because too many hands touch the mailed in one. I just think it's better this way, doing it through the computer. Because you get to do it yourself and you know at the end it's already cast.

4   Implications for Improved Voting Practices

4.1   Barriers

The convergence of many of the challenges described in the Findings above can add up to significant difficulty in voting successfully. Potential voters may not know when and where they should go to vote, what will be on the ballot, or how to register, or what the registration deadlines are. Because participants are unfamiliar with election policies and practices, they are more likely than other voters to vote out of precinct, or to not be properly registered. They are less likely to know about early voting options or the possibility of absentee voting. Their anxiety about complex reading-based activities can lead to anxiety or a lack of confidence about their ability to vote successfully [15]. Their primary source of information, television and news, may not provide sufficient depth or breadth of information about election practices. Compared to more literate potential voters, adult Americans with low literacy are less likely to have at-home internet access, and often have limited internet experience, making them both less likely and less able to find information or solve problems online—although it is true that smartphone usage among this demographic is growing, making it possible that their propensity to find voting information online will increase [18–20].

These barriers provide opportunities for election experts and officials to find ways to improve the voting experience of Americans with low literacy skills.

4.2 Facilitators

The study also provided insight into a number of facilitators that help individuals with low literacy achieve success in voting. These included support in helping voters get registered successfully, the potentially positive influence of poll workers, the advantages provided by early voting, the convenience of having polling places within walking distance, and the simplified interaction and reduced cognitive load that can be provided by electronic ballot marking machines [27].

Assisted Registration
As reported above, many respondents reported institutional support as part of successful voting registration. This speaks to the value of building voting registration into governmental processes such as social service visits or interactions at departments of motor vehicles, as well as well-organized registration drives sponsored by public or private organizations.

Convenient Polling Place Locations
Of the participants who talked about how they got to the polling place, 54% reported that they walked; 37% drove or got a ride from someone with a car; and 17% had to take public transportation (generally because they lived outside the city or were traveling to the polling place for a prior address). This speaks to the importance of convenient location as a facilitator for low-literacy voters who may find it more difficult to get to polling places that are inconvenient or further away.

Helpful Poll Workers
Poll workers clearly played a major role in making the experience of voting a positive one, and in helping voters feel successful. 75% of participants reported that poll workers were helpful.

P16. At first it was kind of difficult until there was one helpful person that came over. She went through everything with us.

P40. It was pretty good. I really learned something today…. I never voted before, and I thought it would be hard. But it's not hard, especially when you got someone standing there and helping you and directing you through the steps.

In contrast, only 15% of participants reported negative experiences with poll workers:

P20. I might look at a lady facial features and see something like that. Why are you irritated? This is your job! You're here to help. What is wrong?

P21. Some people be mean and nasty…. Like they rude. Like if I have a problem, if they take it out of my hand, like snatch it and stuff like that. Like take it next, next. Don't say welcome, thanks for coming, don't say nothing just next, next.

Unfortunately, these negative experiences with poll workers—even though they were relatively rare—tended to magnify the discomfort voters were already anticipating.

Early Voting
Some participants who were concerned about voting were asked to try early voting. Those who described their reactions were universally pleased.

P36.   Even though it's early voting, I did expect a lot more people. People go to vote, there be a lot of people. So I just expected more people. But it wasn't. It was calm. It was cool.

P26.   I guess like this early voting thing would make it a 10 for me. If I can do all my votes like this early? I'll be very happy because that means it's more comfortable for me, I don't have a line, I don't have the next person saying well, how long is she going to be going to that ballot or for the next person to feel uncomfortable about how long I'm going to be at that poll. So, yeah.

Voting Machines

The state of Maryland moved from direct recording electronic (DRE) voting machines to paper ballots in 2016. Thus, most of the participants used voting machines unless they had to fill out a provisional ballot or were among the nine voters who were interviewed in November 2016. Some participants remembered paper ballots from before the switch to voting machines, and a handful remembered the old lever machines used before 2004.

57% of the participants had the opportunity to compare experiences with touch-screen voting and paper ballots. Of those, 81% preferred touchscreen voting, and 10% preferred paper. Participants liked the touchscreen because it made voting faster, because it was simpler (voting one race at a time), because the text size could be enlarged, and because it felt to some participants as if the machine required less writing. Some participants felt safer with the touchscreen machines because they felt more able to fix mistakes; voters who used paper generally assumed they would be unable to correct an error.

P1.   You can have the text normal, large or extra large because there is buttons on it where you're able to read it. Like I said it's clear and if you make a mistake, you can go back and push the button—the same button that you pushed—to erase your mistake. The thing I like about it is at the end, if there is any mistakes, that you actually can go back into the voting and change them.

P26.   You don't have to write anything. You just touch it.... I think it's better for a lot of people because you might have some people that really don't know how to write or really don't know really what to do so the touch screen is a lot better—not only for us but for older people.

Some participants thought the touchscreen voting machine provided more information or help than a paper ballot.

P34.   They helpful like when it tell you to choose like more than one. They tell you how many you can choose if you want to pick more than one. And they tell you to hit next if you ready to move on. There wasn't nothing not helpful to me.

P39.   Because everything is explanatory on the computer as you just read and make a choice.

A few participants felt more trust that machines would be impartial and less vulnerable to error than paper ballots, which they incorrectly assumed would involve human handling.

P24.   Just press one button. Press it boom, for that person. Instead you got to scan, or fight it down, put it in a box, people got to count the vote. Negative. I think that be shaky a little bit. My vote might throw away or something like that. It's just crazy.

P50.   [Dismayed in 2016 to be using paper ballots again] This old way of reading things, that's so obsolete. You know it should be computerized now.... [instead of] you know, you having people sitting there, counting...

One participant was afraid that having the paper ballot exist permanently might make his votes less confidential:

P56.   I didn't particularly care for the paper ballot, and I asked a question was it shredded after, you know, it went through the machine, and he [the poll worker] said yes, but I didn't hear a shredder machine.... I would have felt more comfortable with it being shredded.

Many of the participants thought they would need help with the electronic voting machines, but most needed only minimal help.

P12.   Because I didn't know what to do at first. But once she showed me, I was on—I did it on my own.

P15.   The assistance I needed—I think it was how you started. How you needed to start it. That's all.

Some of the older participants spoke positively about the technology, but their unfamiliarity with it and their uncertainty about it lingers in their descriptions, while a handful expressed outright discomfort and preferred paper.

P45.   I'm not good with computers. I can learn. I like it though. I just have to get used to the technology. But I like it though. It was quicker.

P53.   I guess cause I'm so old school with the reading, I like to read.... [On paper] the ink is nice and bold where I can understand it, but it seems like the computer screen it could be big, but it still seem like I just don't get it,... I think it's a timing issue.... You know, where in reading I could take my time and read the line.... I don't like the touch screens.

One major concern in voting is whether or not voters can successfully make changes to correct an error or reflect a change of heart. A surprising number of participants did not realize it was possible to correct a mistake on their ballot, but of the 35 participants who discussed making changes, 88% of those who used touchscreen voting machines were able to figure out how to make a change, while of those who used paper, 71% assumed they could not make changes.

P51.   No. 'Cause it was in pen... If somebody behind me had said "Oh, I might have made a mistake" I'd say, well, if you did, I think your mistake about to go through!

4.3   Suggestions for Improvement from Participants

At the end of the interviews, participants were asked if there was anything election officials could do to help them have a better voting experience. Some participants did not have suggestions for improvement, but many did.

Several participants requested features or services that are already widely available. One participant (see above) asked for a website that would allow potential voters to see what would be on the ballot before the election, and would provide summary information about candidates. Another asked if the words could be enlarged on electronic voting machines. A participant asked for confirmation that absentee votes were actually received and counted (most states already provide a way to confirm that absentee ballots have been received). One participant asked if there was a way she could just sit comfortably at home, figure out her choices, and mark her ballot without coming to the polling place. The reactions of these participants suggest the potential value of already existing strategies for improving the voting experience, but also speak to the need to communicate and publicize available options more clearly for low-literacy populations.

Other services or features requested by participants have been offered in some jurisdictions, although not in Maryland. An older woman with poor health doesn't always know in advance how she will feel physically, so she wanted free transportation to the polling place, because "sometime I might be feeling good and.... I want to vote but can't get there." Free or discounted rides on election day are available in some cities, but this is by no means universal.

Some suggestions from participants would require legal action and perhaps even experimental research into appropriate implementation, such as including photographs next to candidate names to help voters whose "reading is not up to par" and to help voters remember "who was who." Election experts have not reached consensus on how photographs could be included on ballots without introducing bias [12, 28].

Other changes would require both legal action and technological advances. One participant asked if the voting machine could talk to voters—but this participant wanted more than just an audio ballot. He wanted to be able to ask questions, and to have the machine be prepared with mini-summaries of who the candidates are and what they stand for. Another participant had a similar desire, wanting to be able to speak her choices in an entirely verbal interaction. Several participants asked why you have to vote in one particular polling place if you are a citizen and can prove your identity— raising the controversial political and technological issue of how voter identities can be confirmed.

And, of course, some participants echoed the plea increasingly heard from many younger voters of "why can't I just vote on my phone?"

5   Limitations of This Study

This study was conducted in a single large urban center. It is likely that voting challenges and circumstances related to low literacy would be different in rural areas, or for other ethnic groups, or in areas of the country with substantial cultural differences. To help address these issues, at least one follow-up study is planned for the next election cycle in rural areas of West Virginia.

Due to legal requirements that prevent researchers from accompanying voters as they vote, there was no possibility to include direct observation as part of this research effort. Instead, the study relied on self-reporting via in-depth interviews. Because of this, the findings are less reliable, for several reasons. Due to the stigma associated with inability to read well, participants may have overstated their success and underreported problems related to literacy issues, as has been shown to be the case with medical treatment [3, 8, 16]. Additionally, as shown in several instances in this study, low-literacy individuals do not always recognize their own difficulties [2, 10].

Potential strategies to alleviate difficulties in voting suggested by these findings or directly by study participants will need to be tested for efficacy. In some cases, such as use of voting machines with touchscreens, findings from this study already confirm that these strategies have value for some voters. However, many of these suggested strategies will need additional investigation to maximize their effectiveness and to identify and minimize any new problems they may create.

References

1. Alqudah, M., Johnson, M., Cowin, L., George, A.: Measuring health literacy in emergency departments. J. Nurs. Educ. Prac. **4**, 1–10 (2014)
2. Alton, N.A., Romm, C., Summers, K., Straub, K.: Using eye-tracking and form completion data to optimize form instructions. IEEE Xplore (2015). doi:10.1109/IPCC.2014.7020389
3. Baker, D.W., et al.: The health care experience of patients with low literacy. Arch. Fam. Med. **5**, 329–334 (1996)
4. Charmaz, K.: Constructing Grounded Theory: A Practical Guide Through Qualitative Analysis. Sage, London (2006)
5. Davis, T.C., Crouch, M.A., Long, S.W., Jackson, R.H., Bates, P., George, R.B., Bairnsfather, L.E.: Rapid assessment of literacy levels of adult primary care patients. Fam. Med. **23**, 433–435 (1991)
6. Davis, T.C., Kennen, E.M., Gazmararian, J.A., Williams, M.V.: Literacy testing in health care research. In: Schwartzberg, J.G., VanGeest, J.B., Wang, C.C. (eds.) Understanding Health Literacy: Implications for Medicine and Public Health, pp. 157–179. American Medical Association, Chicago (2005)
7. Davis, T.C., Long, S.W., Jackson, R.H., Mayeaux, E.J., George, R.B., Murphy, P.W., Crouch, M.A.: Rapid estimate of adult literacy in medicine: a shortened screening instrument. Fam. Med. **25**, 391–395 (1993)
8. Easton, P., Entwistle, V.A., Williams, B.: How the stigma of low literacy can impair patient-professional spoken interactions and affect health: insights from a qualitative investigation. BMC Health Serv. Res. **13**, 319 (2013). doi:10.1186/1472-6963-13-319
9. Glaser, B.G., Strauss, A.L.: The Discovery of Grounded Theory: Strategies for Qualitative Design. Transaction, Rutgers (1967)
10. Graham, S., Brookey, J.: Do patients understand? Perm. J. **12**, 67–69 (2008)
11. Heckathorn, D.D.: Snowballs versus respondent-driven sampling. Soc. Meth. **41**, 355–366 (2011). doi:10.1111/j.1467-9531.2011.01244.x

12. Johns, R., Shephard, M.: Facing the voters: the potential impact of ballot paper photographs in British elections. Pol. Stud. **59**, 636–658 (2011). doi:10.1111/j.1467-9248.2010.00874.x

13. Kaplan, D., Venezky, R.L.: Literacy and voting behavior: a bivariate probit model with sample selection. Soc. Sci. Res. **23**, 350–367 (1994). doi:10.1006/ssre.1994.1014

14. Kirsch, I.S.: Adult literacy in America: a first look at the results of the National Adult Literacy Survey. U.S. Government Printing Office, Washington, DC 20402 (1993)

15. Kutner, M., Greenberg, E., Jin, Y., Boyle, B., Hsu, Y., Dunleavy, E.: Literacy in everyday life: results from the 2003 National Assessment of Adult Literacy. NCES 2007-490. National Center for Education Statistics, Washington, DC (2007)

16. Pankh, N.S., Parker, R.M., Nurss, J.R., Baker, D.W., Williams, M.V.: Shame and health literacy: the unspoken connection. Patient Educ. Couns. **27**, 33–39 (1996)

17. Parker, R.M., Baker, D.W., Williams, M.V., Nurss, J.R.: The test of functional health literacy in adults: a new instrument for measuring patients' literacy skills. J. Gen. Intern. Med. **10**, 537–541 (1995)

18. Pew Research Center. Mobile fact sheet, 12 January 2017. http://www.pewinternet.org/fact-sheet/mobile

19. Pew Research Center. Smartphone dependency by education, 11 January 2017. http://www.pewinternet.org/chart/smartphone-dependency-by-education

20. Pew Research Center. Smartphone dependency by income, 11 January 2017. http://www.pewinternet.org/chart/smartphone-dependency-by-income/

21. Quesenbery, W.: Map of the voter experience: entering the polling place: marking, pre-marking, casting. Presentation at the Meeting of the User Experience Group VSAP [Voting Systems Assessment Project], 8–9 April 2014

22. Quesenbery, W., Chisnell, D., Davies, D., Schwieger, J., Newby, E., Goddard, R.: How voters get information: final report: recommendations for voter guides in California. Center for Civic Design. http://civicdesign.org/wp-content/uploads/2014/05/FOCE-how-voters-get-information-final-14-1015.pdf

23. Rachal, J.R.: We'll never turn back: adult education and the struggle for citizenship in Mississippi's freedom summer. Amer. Educ. Res. Q. **35**, 167–198 (1998)

24. Redish, J., Chisnell, D.E., Newby, E., Laskowski, S.J., Lowry, S.Z.: Report of findings: use of language in ballot instructions. NISTIR 7556. National Institute of Standards and Technology (NIST) (2009)

25. Sanford, J.A., et al.: Understanding voting experiences of people with disabilities. In: Working Paper #5, The Information Technology and Innovation Foundation, Washington, DC (2013)

26. Strauss, A.L., Corbin, J.: Basics of Qualitative Research: Techniques and Procedures for Developing Grounded Theory, 2nd edn. Sage, Thousand Oaks (1998)

27. Summers, K., Langford, J.: The impact of literacy on usable and accessible electronic voting. In: Antona, M., Stephanidis, C. (eds.) UAHCI 2015. LNCS, vol. 9178, pp. 248–257. Springer, Cham (2015). doi:10.1007/978-3-319-20687-5_24

28. Voting operations. ACE Newsletter (n.d.). https://aceproject.org/ace-en/topics/vo/voc/voc02/voc02a

Bifurcating the User

Nicholas True[1,2]([✉]), Shad Gross[1], Chelsea Linder[1],
Amber McAlpine[1], and Sri Putrevu[1]

[1] Angie's List, 1030 E. Washington St., Indianapolis, IN 46202, USA
nic.true@angieslist.com
[2] Department of Informatics, Umeå University, MIT-huset Campustorget 5,
Umeå Universitet, 901 87 Umeå, Sweden

Abstract. Within the design of technology, the notion of the user, and user-centered design, has become a guiding principal for creating successful products. However, the concept of "user" is a non-trivial notion. HCI has historically viewed "the user" as an abstract concept, that is to say, it has been a reductive definition. As the field has become increasingly transdisciplinary the definition of "the user" has evolved overtime to reflect more breadth and depth. However, this is not always the case within industry practice. In this paper we present a situation and case study where, in industry, the reductive notion of the user posed distinct impediments to progress, how we were able to identify those and blend academic thinking into an industry approach to more success than either alone.

Keywords: Service Design · Sharing Economy · HCI · Design

1 Introduction

Within the practice of design, the concept of user-centered design [10, 17] has had considerable traction and success as a philosophy and method for how designers should approach solving problems. Within this approach, considerations of the user – a person who a designer considers or involves in the making of an interface, system or service – are quite important and fundamentally guide design decisions. Due to this, knowing the user, or the different tiers of users [3] that a system is designed for is an important part of creating useful and usable designs.

While considerations of the user and user involvement are powerful tools for design, this way of thinking may not be sufficient to cover the changes resulting from shifts in the ways that technology, products, and services have changed. For example, the move from individual, owned products to a "Sharing Economy" [14] introduces systems and interfaces intended to bring together people with different motivations and goals around a shared artifact and Service Design [22] where numerous different people are brought together, often through different interfaces, around a service. In both of these contexts, the idea of a singular user or a tiered set of users may be blurred as the very aspect that makes these approaches valuable is the coordination of multiple sets of perspectives and goals.

© Springer International Publishing AG 2017
A. Marcus and W. Wang (Eds.): DUXU 2017, Part III, LNCS 10290, pp. 313–329, 2017.
DOI: 10.1007/978-3-319-58640-3_22

In this paper we detail and reflect on a case study of a business model that does not readily fit into classifications of primary, secondary and tertiary users. Specifically, we describe the challenges that arise from having two primary user groups with different scales, concerns, and goals. These differences may put users at odds with each-other. While this case does not aim to give singular, prescriptive solutions to the situation of multiple primary users, it does explain what seems to be a trend in design (through businesses such as AirBnB and Uber), highlight some of the unique challenges that come with such a situation and, as these situations become more common, directions for find context-specific resolutions. We then apply these newer concepts of the user to the context of our own ethnographically-inspired investigation at Angie's List—a company focused on facilitating and assisting transactions and providing a marketplace for those transactions. Finally, we reflect upon these different situations in juxtaposition – highlighting the particular challenges and difficulties that arise from designing for multiple primary users.

2   Previous Work

The idea of multiple primary users is rooted in three main areas of thinking. First is User-Centered Design (UCD), from which the idea of "users" and the division of users into different classes emerges. The second is the Sharing Economy, in which the idea of a single, primary user is challenged by the notion of the "Sharing Economy". Finally, the third concept is Service Design, in which there are further differences between the people who are users of any given interface, all with differing roles and perspectives on how the service will unfold.

2.1   User-Centered Design

While it is not exclusive to the design of interfaces and technology, much of the relationship between HCI and design practice is rooted in the concept of UCD. The concept originated in the work of Norman and Draper [18] and subsequently developed further in The Psychology of Everyday Things [17]. This approach became of significant importance leading to the establishment of an international standard through ISO 13407 [8] (which would later be replaced by ISO 9241-210 [10]). While UCD has had a couple of different names and specific standards attached to it, it is evident that the concept is wide-spread and accepted as an approach to design.

In Abras et al.'s Encyclopedia of Human Computer Interaction, UCD is defined as "a broad term to describe design processes in which end-users influence how a design takes shape…. There is a spectrum of ways in which users are involved in UCD but the important concept is that users are involved one way or another." [1]. The core element of the process, then, is the involvement of the user. From this perspective, understanding users psychologically [e.g. 17], cognitively [e.g. 19], and even phenomenologically [e.g. 4] is important because it will aid in making design decisions that are better and, ultimately, interfaces that are better in usability or "the extent to which a system, product or service can be used by specified users to achieve specified goals with effectiveness, efficiency and satisfaction in a specified context of use" [9]. The idea of "specified users" is important here – as the different means of understanding users also can result in divisions across different groups of people. This is echoed in the sentiments of social informatics with regards to the effects of technology – "ICT (Information Communication Technologies) uses shape thought and action in ways that benefit some groups more than others and these differential effects often have moral and ethical consequences" [21]. Thus, reaching the goals of UCD begins with understanding who the user is.

Understanding the user may not be straight forward. As a means of accounting for this, Eason [3] divides the singular concept of "user" into three distinct groups: Primary users who frequently directly interact with the system through input and output; Secondary users who occasionally interact with the system or must work directly with the output of the system; and Tertiary users who do not directly interact with the system but are in some way affected by it. Although not to the same degree, this notion of different ranks of users has also been raised in less formal contexts as a means of describing interactions with technology in the context of hospitals: describing the doctors and nurses as the primary users and their patients as secondary users [23]. In both cases, the idea of a single user gets changed to include considerations of other users who are effected by the system.

The concept of the user, and a weighted hierarchy of users, create an extremely useful model for pursuing the goals of UCD. However, there have been changes to the ways that users are understood that also seem to prompt some reconsideration. Specifically, the rise of the "Sharing Economy" and Service Design will be presented as two such concepts, which we will examine here through the examples of two contemporary, successful examples – AirBnB and Uber.

2.2 Sharing Economy

In one sense, the two examples presented here are part of what has been described as the "Sharing Economy." This has been defined as "collaborative consumption made by the activities of sharing, exchanging, and rental of resources without owning the goods." [14]. Alternately, the Sharing Economy has also been defined as "The peer-to-peer-based activity of obtaining, giving, or sharing the access to goods and services, coordinated through community-based online services." [7]. Combining these definitions, we arrive at our working understanding of the Sharing Economy – it involves collaborative consumption of durable goods or services and frequently some sort of digital networking to make connections. While the idea of sharing is not something new, its ubiquity across large populations, the goods in question, and the electronic means of making connections all present new opportunities and challenges to this system of sharing.

Two of the most successful examples of the Sharing Economy in action are AirBnB and Uber. AirBnB (www.airbnb.com) is a platform where people who wish to visit a place (guests) can connect with people who have a place to stay (hosts). The shared element in this system is the living space, with the hosts generally owning or at least leasing the space and sharing that space with guests based on a pre-determined agreement. Uber (www.uber.com) applies similar thinking to automobiles. Like a taxi, the driver picks someone up who has requested a ride and takes them to their destination. In this example the shared item is the automobile, like the living space in AirBnB, with the driver frequently owning or leasing the vehicle and sharing the ride with the person who has placed the request.

Both examples not only fit the definition of "Sharing Economy" – they are peer-based networks based off the sharing of durable goods and, indeed, are raised as examples of the concept both in a more beneficial light [e.g. 7, 13, 20] and a negative one [e.g. 15, 16]. Regardless of larger social benefits of such a mindset, it has proven to be a viable business model at the least.

Framed by the Sharing Economy, the matches between users for both AirBnB and Uber make sense. The person who hires an Uber driver does not need their own car, they just need an easier, less expensive, and often better maintained means of transportation than alternatives such as taxis, while the person who owns the car is given an additional means to earn income. Similar things can be said of AirBnB, where the value of having lodging that is cheaper and more culturally embedded than a hotel drives one side and the monetization of property drives the other. The important factor, then, becomes creating an interface that connects these two groups.

Considering the different needs of the different user groups means creating different interfaces for them. For example, the levels of access, intentions and needs for information would be quite different for an Uber driver versus a passenger. The passenger needs to have expectations set for the trip, including a tracker for when the car will arrive, what kind of car it will be, and who will be driving it—all of which are provided by the passenger interface. Alternately, the driver needs to know how to get where the passenger is going, should no specific course be offered. These are low level concerns, but when creating features of an application they become the core needs of the users that are being fulfilled.

For AirBnB, the host may be lining up several different guests at once, while the guests are most likely planning a one-time visit, hosts may be coordinating the plans of multiple guests. In both this and the case of Uber, there is a difference in terms of goals and what is needed from an interface to fulfill those goals. Hence, it seems reasonable to declare both user groups for the service, even if there still may be some way to shoehorn these different users into primary, secondary, and tertiary status.

The companies AirBnB and Uber provide these different groups of users with different senses of how the interaction should take place, with different applications and features to reach their individual goals. While this relationship is not intrinsic to the Sharing Economy, it does seem like it is a part of current, successful implementations. The implication is that in such a context, the designation of one of the types of user as primary, secondary or tertiary, at the level of the business, seems murky.

2.3 Service Design

Another rising concept that equally challenges the idea of a singular, or neatly ranked set, of users is Service Design. "Service Design is an emerging field focused on the creation of well thought through experiences using a combination of intangible and tangible mediums" [22]. Like other user experience approaches, the focus on Service Design is the creation of an experience for one or more people. However, unlike the notion of the Sharing Economy presented above, there is not necessarily a specific physical object that the experience is connected to. A somewhat older, more business/operations –centered definition focuses on the "service concept," breaking this down into operation, experience, outcome, and value of the service [2, 6, 11]. From this perspective, the core components of a service are how the service is executed, the over-all feeling of the service for the user, the result for that user, and the value of those results.

The examples of AirBnB and Uber equally fit within these definitions. There are also divisions that emerge. There are some issues that apply broadly to both the host and the guest such as the concerns of the "nebulous regulations surrounding Airbnb" [16] that could result in concerns for safety of goods or person. The goal of the experience, overall, is to replace those concerns with a more positive experience. However, others are more pointed at one end of the moral hazard problem of damage to the renter in AirBnB transactions [24]. Similarly, one could imagine a similar situation when hiring an Uber driver – the lack of knowledge about the driver presenting the chance that the passenger could have a bad experience during the ride, due to bad driving or unsafe vehicles, or worse. This is not to say that being a guest at an AirBnB house or a driver for Uber is without its own risks and concerns, more that these concerns differ in terms of objects and nature. Returning to the core components of a service concept, there is a broad similarity between the hosts and guests but they also provide different operations for the service—e.g. hosts set up the space, guests find it, different experiences—e.g. having someone stay in their house, visiting a different culture, outcomes—e.g. making money and staying somewhere, and value—e.g. mitigation of moral hazard, staying somewhere cheaper than a hotel.

One telling aspect of the ways that these services create two groups of primary users is in how AirBnB models their experience. Storyboards and journey maps are common tools of Service Design [22]. A unique aspect of AirBnB's approach is that the story is told from different perspectives [12], namely the host and the guest, and that these stories create two distinct yet intertwined journeys. These two different journeys highlight the idea that there are two different users, both of which who have some claim to primacy within the service, but have considerably different operation, experience, outcome, and value of the service.

From the examples of AirBnB and Uber, framed through the lenses of the Sharing Economy and Service Design, the concept of a single, primary user begins to break down. In both situations, there is not just one user, but rather the interrelation of different users, each with their own set of concerns. To further explore this, we now turn to research done in a context that presents a similar situation, with regards to the consideration of multiple primary users.

3 Historical Context of Angie's List

The business context for this work is Angie's List – a company focused on facilitating and assisting transactions and providing a marketplace for those transactions between providers of home services (Service Providers) and those that consume home services

(Home Owners). Angie's list was founded in 1995 in Indianapolis, Indiana by Angie Hicks and Bill Oesterle as a continuation of their Columbus Neighbors venture which, itself, was a continuation of the Indianapolis Unified Neighbors venture. Across these initial ventures, the core component was bringing together people's information and resources as a neighborhood community. One such resource that became extremely useful was reviews of Service Providers, which helped the members of the community to make decisions regarding who to hire when they needed work done on their homes. This concept was moved from Indianapolis to Columbus and then back to Indianapolis, focusing on the specific concerns and pools of Service Providers in these areas.

In 1999 Angie's List began the transition from analog to digital when the website was launched. This extended the reach of the original business model, meaning that it no longer had to be limited to the specific area where the business was located. This broadening of reach came with a narrowing of focus, moving from a more general fostering of community action to the useful and popular reviews – written descriptions of working with Service Providers within a specific area. What grew from this was a subscription-based crowd-sourced repository of reviews for Indianapolis service providers. As part of the focus on reviewing Service Providers, users could submit reviews of the people that they had worked with, and those reviews were accompanied by a "grade" of A, B, C, D or F (like the American school system) with an A representing exceptional work and F representing work that had failed in some way.

In the 7 years that followed the initial introduction to digital services and the web, Angie's List continued to extend the breadth of areas covered – going from the Midwestern United States to encompassing the entire country. This had the benefit of expanding the business and the reach of the services, but also presented new challenges for the subscription-based model. Specifically, the focus on a few small communities had become more about the evaluation of service providers. As of 2016, the member base had extended to 5 million registered users with 10 million reviews from all over the United States (https://www.angieslist.com/news-releases/angie-s-list-membership-tops-five-million.htm). There still was a community element to the services but, as the reach of Angie's Lists' services extended, the focus of the community became increasingly about the evaluation of Service Providers and less about other aspects of the community.

This shift of focus from communities to the Service Providers who work in them also brought about a reconsideration of the company's business model. In response to this, the company moved away from the subscription model and began to focus more on the connections between Service Providers and Home Owners - facilitating connections, offering guarantees to work, and facilitate positive experiences between Service Providers and Home Owners. Whereas initially the focus of the company, and subsequently the concept of primary user, was attached to Home Owners, now Service Providers had become invested in the service to a degree like those described in the AirBnB and Uber examples. While it wasn't obvious at the time, at this point those focused on User Experience at Angie's List were dealing with two primary users. How we became aware of this situation was through the process of an ethnographically-inspired investigation with the goal of understanding our users.

4 Researching the Users

This study was conducted with Angie's List members, both Homeowners and Service Providers, in Indianapolis, Indiana and surrounding areas during August and September of 2016. The goal of our research was to understand the experience of getting work done around the home. One of the main tools that we aimed to employ to this end were the kinds of alignment documents commonly employed by companies to help gain alignment on customer experiences. Within this approach, however, the first of the divisions between our users became apparent. Due to the prior focus on Home Owners and their experience of having work done on their homes, one of the key alignment documents – a customer journey map – had already been constructed. This meant that even though our research would be simultaneously looking at both the Service Provider and Home Owner experiences, the specifics of how the research would unfold would need to be adapted to bring the level of understanding regarding the Service Provider experience up to the pre-existing level of the Home Owner experience.

To account for the differing level of pre-existing understanding, two main groups were formed within the team. Two researchers were dedicated to engaging in Home Owner research and two researchers were dedicated to Service Provider research. In addition to these teams, there were two researchers who would float between the teams. One of these researchers split his time between visits to homes and visits to businesses; the other researcher focused more on synthesis, bringing together pre-existing data from surveys together with the new data and more generally aiding in the synthesis process. One consequence of this division was that, despite the floating team members, the planning, execution, and sharing of research were handled separately by each team, independent of the other. In sum, this meant that even though the research was done under the heading of one project, the felt experience of the researchers was closer to two projects running in parallel.

For the Home Owner side of the project, participants were collected by means of a screener survey. This survey contained questions about demographic information (e.g. gender, age group, family status, etc.) as well as some more specific questions about home status (e.g. home ownership status, value of home). In addition to the questions, the survey outlined how participants would be reimbursed for their time participating in the study. From this information, we selected participants that were homeowners in the greater Indianapolis area (where the research team was based). This selection process was based off the goals of our study – with homeowners having greater ability and, subsequently, experience getting work done around their homes - and pragmatic considerations of project budget, timeline, desired number of participants, research team size and risk of fatigue with travel. Additionally, we targeted the age group 21–34 a little more than other age groups due to an under-representation of this age group within our pre-existing surveys. Beyond these aspects, we attempted to get a variety of participants based on gender, marital status, and family status. Specifics of our participants can be found in Table 1.

In terms of data collection, two approaches were used – on site home visits and probes. The first, which had ten participants, was based off contextual inquiry – taking

Table 1. Home Owner Participants

Participant	Gender	Age	Marital status	Family status	Visit/Probe
P1	M	21–34	Married	No children	V+P
P2	F	65+	Separated	No children	V+P
P3	M	21–34	Married	Children	V
P4	M	55–64	Married	No children	V
P5	M	55–64	Separated	No Children	V+P
P6	F	21–34	Partnered	Children	V+P
P7	F	45–54	Separated	No children	V+P
P8	M	65+	Married	Children	V
P9	F	35–44	Married	Children	V
P10	M	35–44	Married	Children	V
P11	F	55–64	Single	No children	P
P12	F	21–34	Married	Children	P
P13	F	35–44	Married	Children	P
P14	F	35–44	Married	Children	P

the form of a home tour to highlight various work done, semi-structured interviews, and a canvas activity over the course of three to four hours. We had initially wanted to time our research activities to coincide with actual work getting done on the home. This, however, proved to be prohibitively difficult, due to a combination of the infrequency of work done on the home both in terms of number of projects and time of day that work is done. So while we could not conduct research in the middle of work being done with all participants, we did have participants who were at various stages in projects.

The probes were helpful in this regard, allowing us to extend our data collection to a longer timeline.

For the home tour, participants were prompted to give us a guided tour of as much of their home as they felt comfortable sharing, speaking aloud about the different aspects that they thought were important and highlighting areas that they had work done. Following this, the semi-structured interviews involved researchers following-up on topics and concepts that came up during the home tour as well as inquire further into pre-defined areas of research (e.g. what makes you decide to have someone do work on your home as opposed to doing it yourself, how do you feel about the current state of your home?). Finally, the stimulus activity involved having participants look at sheets of stickers with either words or images on them related to experiences. Participants were directed to pick out the words and images that they associate with success and arrange them into groups on a large sheet of paper. As with the tour, participants were encouraged to talk through their process. The goal of this was to define what values were most important to our participants, flesh them out, and obtain more details around who they are as people and what core values drive their decisions.

The second approach that we used for data collection was a probe kit. The probe kit was loosely designed off cultural probes [5] and contained a set of prompts, activities, and artifacts for participants to encourage consideration and reporting of their feelings during work on their homes. Most of these items were arranged into envelopes to be opened daily throughout the time that participants had the probe. For example, on the first day of the probe participants opened an envelope to find two cards. One card read:

DAY ONE Record your thoughts about the work being done to your home. The prompt is a suggestion, but feel free to tell us anything else we need to know from today.

Prompt: When you are starting a project, how do you decide to DIY or hire a professional? If you choose to hire a professional how do you go about this process?

The second card had a few more pointed prompts created to both inspire as well as amuse, with prompts ranging from What if you had unlimited money? How would you change your home? to What if the roof of your house suffered meteor damage? What steps would you take to initiate the repair process? In addition to the daily cards, the probe kits contained a frame for participants to draw in, a suggestion box, and (for half of the probes) a digital camera. We dropped the probes off at nine houses, five of which were also part of the home visits (see Table 1 for the breakdown). Participants had the probes for five days, after which we would come and pick them up. Of the 9 probes we sent out, we only got 7 back, with two participants ceasing contact with the research team.

Like the Home Owner side, Service Provider participants were gathered by means of a screener. While this screener did ask demographic questions that were like the Home Owner side, there were also several questions oriented more towards the nature of providing services. Specifically, participants were selected to give a variety of different company sizes - based off the number of employees and general job duration – based off the type of job done in the industry. See Table 2 for a breakdown of these aspects of our Service Provider participants.

Table 2. Service Provider Participants

Participant	No. Employees	Location	Industry
SP1	1	All onsite	Painting
SP2	4	Onsite + Office	Garage work
SP3	3	Onsite + Office	Electrician
SP4	5	All Office	Auto repair
SP5	10+	Onsite + Office	Roofing

One major difference between the approach taken with the Service Providers and the Home Owners was the duration and location of the visits. While the Home Owners had one centralized location to visit, Service Providers frequently have an office that they work out of as well as the onsite visits that comprise their services to homeowners. Two of our participants did not map directly to this; one participant worked out of his truck and the mechanics had a garage that customers would bring their cars to, meaning that they did not do onsite visits. The remaining three spent their time divided across working in an office and visiting homes. With this in mind, we wanted to get experience with both the office and onsite aspects of the job, and oriented our visits accordingly. Visits lasted for a full day (approx. 8 h) and were scheduled around when participants would be doing onsite work. Overall the goal of this was to get exposure to the whole of the service provider experience.

The data collection approach was like the approach on the Home Owner side, involving a combination of participant observation, semi-structured interview, and stimulus activity. The only difference in approach was that more questions were prepared in advance, as opposed to organically emerging from the participant observation. This was due to the need to bootstrap our knowledge of Service Providers and to gain their perspective on the issues that had emerged from previous research on Home Owners. For example, from the Home Owner side, a major pain point is Service Providers who do not return calls requesting service. As such, we wanted to ensure that we probed service providers regarding why this happens, what other issues exist, and ultimately where meaningful interventions can be made.

In addition to the in-situ visits we also sent out two surveys, one for Home Owners (n = 1335) and one for Service Providers (n = 1589). These included several questions based on the findings of the qualitative research to give some quantitative support as well as more open-ended questions to supplement the data already collected.

Even just in describing the approach to research, schisms between our two sets of users emerge. On one hand, Home Owners represent users with a centralized location, infrequent work, and with a strong emotional connection to their site. Alternately, Service Providers had multiple locations that they work at, engage in several jobs in a single day, and have a different kind of emotional relationship with their business. These different elements of scale and connectivity would continue to play out across the narratives that we collected.

5   Research Findings

We present our findings as a series of concerns for both Home Owners and Service Providers. Through this, we hope to highlight some of the differences that these two user groups have and the challenges that these present to designing for both of them.

5.1   Home Owner Concerns

Through the semi-structured interviews we learned much about people, their homes, and their home projects. Home Owners have many concerns when planning and commissioning services for their homes. These concerns are broad in nature, some of the most often mentioned concerns include security, communication/scheduling, and price/speed.

Security. For this study security is defined as the feeling of safety when allowing a previously unknown person into someone's home. Home, as we mentioned, is an emotional space, and allowing an unknown person into the home can be a difficult experience. For example, one participant (P2) said "…I don't like to leave people alone in the house" about completing home projects. Another participant (P8) mentioned "Once I've selected a contractor, by doing due diligence up front, I trust them." [In reference to having work done in a home with children.] Security as a feeling by Home

Owners often ladders up to a general feeling of trust in the Service Provider. In the case of security, trust has more of an emotional connotation with many participants pointing to the importance of feeling comfortable with the provider and establishing trust. For Home Owners, allowing someone into their home is a very different experience than for Service Providers, who often enter homes to complete projects. Through our research we found that online reviews, especially those on Angie's List, are a way for people to begin to build trust with the Service Providers they hire.

Communication. Another top concern among Home Owners was communication. Again, due to the strong emotional attachment to the home as being the most expensive thing most people own communication emerged as a concern when working on projects. Firstly, communication was indicated as a metric of success for a home project. "The responsiveness and communication you have with a service provider are the key to getting the job done and being satisfied with how is (sic) turned out. ...if they don't communicate well to their client, it may not be a good experience" (Survey Response). This sentiment was echoed many times over, so regardless of the overall quality of the job, without adequate communication the experience suffers. Other comments simply and directly stated how important communication was: "Contact with us is very important" (P11). In other cases, communication was referenced contextually: "Dealing directly with the service provider has been working well..." and "We were attached at the hip" (P2). While these comments may not overtly mention communication, efficient and reliable communication were key to positive outcomes. The research points to communication as being of such high importance because people want to know what is happening to their home due to the high emotional and financial investment the home represents. While the work being done may be routine for Service Providers, it is more unusual for Home Owners. Relevant, timely, and open communication, have been found, are reliable indicators of the overall experiential quality of home projects. This is due, in part, to the correlation of communication and trust between parties.

Scheduling/Speed/Price. While there were, many concerns uncovered during our research we have chosen to focus on the most often stated. While not mentioned as frequently as security and communication scheduling, speed, and price were oft echoed concerns. Scheduling was mentioned in the context of wanting to know when things were going to be started and completed. Specifically, pain points tended to revolve around delayed start dates and unforeseen issues necessitating extended time-tables. One tale of a particularly large project mentioned the frustrations scheduling can cause: "Sometimes we've had to work around the weather and be flexible with that even so far as waiting from fall to the following spring once and vice versa. And just waiting for supplies to come in and then planning around the workers' schedules on my own. We always make it work. Always" (P2). This project even involved a work stoppage over winter where the participant and their family had to live with work-in-progress for an entire winter. Overall, most Home Owners, drawing from the emotional attachment to their home, want their projects to be scheduled and completed quickly so they can get back to enjoying their home.

As a tie-in to scheduling is speed, that is, the quickness with which a project can be completed. Once a project begins, the focus moves to, "how effective they are at beginning on time and finishing on time" (P5). Overwhelmingly, participants commented on how important a project being finished on time, or before, was to the overall experience. Specifically, this can be tied to the disruptive nature of home projects. Having a Service Provider in their homes is disruptive to the Home Owner. Service Providers recognize this as mentioned in our interviews. "...being in someone's home. Their life is still happening, even though this may be just a "job" to you and your staff" (P11). This epitomizes why speed is important to the success of a home project, the faster it is done the faster the Home Owner can return to their normal routine.

Another repeating theme was price. Many of our participants were very concerned with being "charged a fair price". The interesting thing that emerged in this area was that fair price was not always, or even often, associated with the cheapest price. The most common sentiment expressed was some variation of "I want quality work at a fair price." However, it should be noted that many participants cited "fair price" rather than "best price" which is typified by the following statement: "...a fair price - which is not necessarily the cheapest price" (Survey Response). We presupposed going into the study that price would be the biggest concern, and were intrigued when it rated somewhere near the middle. This is interesting because it ladders to trust. People are willing to pay a fair price in exchange for aspects they deem important to the experience, price is not always the largest determining factor. These factors and concerns, and how they are handled, similarly coalesce into trust. In conclusion, when it comes to Home Owner concerns they all hinge on allowing unknown Service Providers into their homes to do projects and managing the life disruption around those projects.

5.2   Major Concerns-Service Provider

During the semi-structured interviews with Service Providers we learned that their concerns have very little overlap with those of Home Owners. For the most part the concerns of the Service Providers, much like the concerns of the Home Owners, are self-oriented. For Service Providers there were many concerns we noted, however the most common were finding quality clients and doing "good" work.

Quality Clients. The concern we noted with most frequency was that of finding quality clients. Through further interaction we developed the operational definition of "quality clients" to mean: clients that are interested and motivated to purchase a service at a fair price and intend to purchase a service in the very near future. This definition is to disambiguate those prospective clients that intend to purchase a service but in the not-so-near future or those who are simply exploring options or those who purchase solely based on the lowest cost option. Many participants commented on providing estimates as a way to determine the seriousness of a client. This fits with the trend of service providers in some areas, most notably plumbing, charging a service call fee to travel to a home. These fees are generally used to discourage less serious clients from requesting a quote/estimate they don't intend to act on soon. Succinctly stated in the following "If customers pay for a quote they are more serious customers..." (SP3) In addition Service Providers may employ tactics to try to screen clients for seriousness. One example we uncovered during our research is that when advertising with coupons a Service Provider would "always do a 2 week lead time on coupons because it will help weed out customers that aren't really interested." (SP3) A common pain point mentioned by Service Providers is clients who schedule a service but cancel on short notice, this necessitates the evaluation of client seriousness as a way to avoid lost work.

Following seriousness of clients we enter into a desire from Service Providers to find clients that appropriately match their offerings. Service Providers resoundingly have a sense of pride in the professionalism and quality of their work, another are they use to identify quality clients is when they feel the prospective client has hired them due to their reputation for high quality work. This leads to the evaluation of clients based on appropriateness to Service Provider offerings. For example one participant said that after "3–4 years" of running the business they began to be "more selective" of the clients they worked with, looking for people who wanted higher quality work, were willing to pay for that work, and acknowledged the providers expertise. (SP3) These observations, while different from Home Owner concerns, still relate to trust, although this time it is trust in the fact that the prospective client will follow through with the purchase of the service and trust they are purchasing the proper service.

Doing "Good" Work. Continuing on the theme of quality referenced above Service Providers often mentioned "doing good work". We initially took the comment at face value, meaning, Service Providers have a deep sense of professional pride and value performing their trade and achieving excellent high quality outcomes. However, through the research process we discovered that good was used to mean both good as in quality, and good as in virtuous. Service Providers often mentioned performing charitable acts for members of their community that were in need. Doing "good work" in both senses of the term was a source of satisfaction for Service Providers.

Professionalism was a term repeated throughout our studies, this tended to relate to a sense of pride in the practice of a trade, or craftsmanship. The first aspect of doing "good work" we observed is that of producing high quality outputs and deriving satisfaction as a result. The satisfaction experienced by a Service Provider of creating a high quality output can be attributed to two different sources: 1. the pride intrinsic to creating a quality outcome, and 2. the pride of seeing how the work positively impacted the client. For example one Service Provider commented on their attitude toward goodwill "We probably do one pro-bono job every day - single mom, elderly - trying to help by giving back to the community." (SP4).

Another avenue of "doing good work" as a concern of Service Providers is applying their chosen trade in such a way as to produce excellent outputs through craft. One Service Provider spoke to the importance of quality through the framing of interest. They spoke about how applying their trade and seeing how the results impacted the client was extremely satisfying, enough so that they would continue to accept residential jobs even though commercial work pays more. "I like the satisfaction of someone coming out and saying 'wow' at the work you did." (SP1) The same Service Provider also said that at this point in their career they had little interest in working on jobs where quality was not the number one priority: "I'd rather do good work or no work at this point in my life" – (SP1) Our observation here is that there are aspects other than price which impact decision making, that is not to say price is not a factor it is just not always necessarily the primary factor.

6 Discussion and Conclusion

When considering the goals of Service Providers and Home Owners, the level at which they are examined is important. At one level, the goals are quite similar, with the Service Provider wanting to do good work and the Home Owner wanting to have good work done. From this perspective, the job of anyone who is facilitating this experience is only to help encourage good work. However, within this area challenges arise in the operations of good work, the scale at which good work takes place, and the ways that such good work fits into larger plan and goal structures for the Home Owner and the Service Provider. Here we will reflect on these challenges of mechanics, scale, and goal structures.

Challenges of operations were the most frequently reported points where the perspectives of our two Primary Users divided. These are the tasks that either a Home Owner or Service Provider needs to accomplish for work to be done. This makes sense as they are often the most visible and immediately impactful aspects of the interaction.

Along with being more noticeable, challenges of operations make up the components of products or features for multiple users under one business. Just as Uber has one application for drivers and another for passengers, the differences in these applications must, to be successful, relate to the differences between how users fulfill their role in the service. They must also not contradict each other. An application that only tells passengers where drivers are without telling drivers how to get to them would be comparable to a service that solves a problem for a home service provider by exacerbating a problem for homeowners or vice versa. Our approach to this challenge is to weigh different products and features across both sets of users – considering not only the benefits of one opportunity in terms of how it effects the user group who will be directly using the service, but also how it will affect the other user group. This is not an easy task, but the benefit of the approach is that it can give a clear means of evaluating features and keeping them to a manageable set.

Challenges of scale are a step up from the more operational issues that can differentiate two different groups of Primary Users. These are the aggregate of operational challenges, showing how they combine to create larger functional blocks that align at key points but can also diverge at others.

These would be the kinds of perspectives that come from frequency or involvement in a specific service. One example would be AirBnB's situation where a host may have any number of different guests from several different places in a relatively short amount of time. The trip for the guest, alternately, may be a once-per year venture or a once in a lifetime situation. In the case of Home Owners and Service Providers, a similar difference in scale occurs – with some home renovations only happening annually or once in the lifetime of a home from the perspective of the Home Owner, but being daily affairs for the Service Provider. In both example cases, it is the scale of the work that becomes important in terms of the expectations that are set regarding its execution and the overall experience of the interaction.

When facilitating interactions between groups with different operations and scales of functioning in that interaction, even the process of modeling that interaction can become difficult. Finding a common unit, then, becomes one way to move forward. In our case this meant focusing on intersections between the user groups, and the specific concerns raised within those intersections. The activity of creating alignment documents (Customer Journey Maps, Experience Models, etc) was helpful in this regard, but with a somewhat different approach that that which is normally taken. Rather than representing the journey of one user and aligning it with the touchpoints, products, and features of the business, the journey is represented through a map showing the alignment of the two users and how they do or do not match up throughout the process. This helped us to see not only where some of the mechanics of both sides broke down, but also in the process of creating stages for each side how difference of scale created points for meaningful intervention.

While operations are at the level of individual operations in the interaction and challenges of scale operate at the level of how mechanics are aggregated into larger frames of reference, it is within the challenges of definition, or meaning, that some of the most subtle and impactful challenges seem to arise. These challenges are not always forthcoming, and as such require rich understanding of the two Primary Users as well as the ability to meaningfully discuss their interrelations.

Just as the elegance of AirBnB's system could be described in terms of economic theory that may be felt, but not easily articulated, by the users of that service, these are the ways that mechanics and scale are given meaning in the minds of different Primary Users. In the context of Home Owners and Service Providers, these challenges amount to the ways that trust can be developed in their interaction. This occurs in a context where, for homeowners, good work is positive interactions with work at a place that is important to the user's identity. For Service Providers, the context is one of numerous different sites and continuous reproduction of work across numerous different sites, each having their own sets of Home Owners, as a means of doing enough work to maintain a business. These perspectives are not uniform across Service Providers, but do illustrate how different operations aggregate into different scales which, in turn, aggregate into different meanings. Given that these operations are different across user groups, so too are the meanings.

Compared to the challenges of mechanics, the challenges of definition are much harder to identify and to mitigate in the context of design. Such ideas are often summative of the other challenges, but tacit in nature. The challenge here is not only surfacing these concerns, but doing so well for each individual group. The ethnographically-inspired approach that we took on this project was particularly useful in this regard. By having two different sets of users our individual participation observations built two different empathetic relationships. While this presented its own challenges for the discussion and synthesis of data, it allowed us to materialize those conversations and, within the team, work collaboratively towards resolution.

The issues of mechanics, scale, and definition do not present an insurmountable task for the facilitation of good experiences in the interactions between Service Providers and Home Owners. Indeed, these are simply the areas for opportunity to bring together these different primary users in ways like how Air Bnb brings together hosts and guests and Uber brings together drivers and passengers. For us this is a continual process, but as an overall guiding principal it is important to remember the common core elements in these groups. Specifically, that they must interact with each other and take away from those interactions a feeling that the process has been devoid of static, and full of substance. Thus, rather than a primary user or even two primary users, the focus becomes on the connections, intersections, and overlaps between these people. Thinking about the individual issues that arise in each primary users' respective journey then becomes a process of framing those issues considering the connections, and developing features and products that resolve those issues through the lens of those connections. To use a networking metaphor, the focus should not be the nodes (users) but rather the edges (connections).

The strategies that are presented here are not hard-and-fast answers to this situation. We have had success in applying them, but they may not work in every context. We present them more as considerations as the singular idea of the user becomes something that design may not be able to sustain going forward. Through the examination of Air BnB and uber, along with our own work and reflections on an ethnographically-inspired investigation into Home Owners' and Service Providers' respective journeys, our aim is merely to begin discussions about what it means to have multiple primary users and how these challenges can be addressed going forward.

References

1. Abras, C., Maloney-Krichmar, D., Preece, J.: User-centered design. In: Bainbridge, W. (ed.) Encyclopedia of Human-Computer Interaction, vol. 37, no. 4, pp. 445–456. Sage Publications, Thousand Oaks (2004)
2. Clark, G., Johnston, R., Shulver, M.: Exploiting the service concept for service design and development. In: Fitzsimmons, J., Fitzsimmons, M. (eds.) New Service Design, pp. 71–91. Sage, Thousand Oaks (2000)
3. Eason, K.: Information Technology and Organizational Change. Taylor & Francis, London (2005)
4. Frauenberger, C., Good, J., Keay-Bright, W.: Phenomenology, a framework for participatory design. In: Proceedings of the 11th Biennial Participatory Design Conference, pp. 187–190. ACM (2010)
5. Gaver, B., Dunne, T., Pacenti, E.: Design: cultural probes. Interactions 6(1), 21–29 (1999)
6. Goldstein, S.M., Johnston, R., Duffy, J., Rao, J.: The service concept: the missing link in service design research? J. Oper. Manag. 20(2), 121–134 (2002)
7. Hamari, J., Sjöklint, M., Ukkonen, A.: The sharing economy: why people participate in collaborative consumption. J. Assoc. Inf. Sci. Technol. (2015)
8. ISO 13407. Human-centred design processes for interactive systems (1999)
9. ISO/DIS 9241-11.2. Ergonomics of human-system interaction – part 11: usability: definitions and concepts (2016)
10. ISO 9241-210. Ergonomics of human-system interaction – part 210: human-centred design for interactive systems (2010)
11. Johnston, R., Clark, G.: Service Operations Management. Prentice-Hall, Harlow (2001)
12. Kessler, S.: How Snow White Helped Airbnb's Mobile Mission. Fast Company (2012). https://www.fastcompany.com/3002813/how-snow-white-helped-airbnbs-mobile-mission. Accessed 08 Feb 2017
13. Lampinen, A., McGregor, M., Brown, B.: The Role of Money and Reputation in the Sharing Economy. https://scholar.google.com/citations?user=NmdJtOAAAAAJ&hl=en

14. Lessig, L.: Remix: Making Art and Commerce Thrive in the Hybrid Economy. Penguin, New York (2008)
15. Malhotra, A., Van Alstyne, M.: The dark side of the sharing economy… and how to lighten it. Commun. ACM **57**(11), 24–27 (2014)
16. McNamara, B.: Airbnb: a not-so-safe resting place. J. Telecomm. High Tech. L. **13**, 149 (2015)
17. Norman, D.A.: The Psychology of Everyday Things. Basic Books, New York (1988)
18. Norman, D.A., Draper, S.W.: User-Centered System Design: New Perspectives on Human-Computer Interaction. Erlbaum, Hillsdale (1986)
19. Oviatt, S.: Human-centered design meets cognitive load theory: designing interfaces that help people think. In: Proceedings of the 14th ACM International Conference on Multimedia, pp. 871–880. ACM, October 2006
20. Puschmann, T., Alt, R.: Sharing economy. Bus. Inf. Syst. Eng. **58**(1), 93–99 (2016)
21. Sawyer, S., Eschenfelder, K.R.: Social informatics: perspectives, examples, and trends. Ann. Rev. Inf. Sci. Technol. **36**(1), 427–465 (2002)
22. Stickdorn, M., Schneider, J., Andrews, K., Lawrence, A.: This is Service Design Thinking: Basics, Tools, Cases. Wiley, Hoboken (2011)
23. Tenhue, N.: User Experience: Primary and Secondary Users in Healthcare. Medium (2016). https://medium.theuxblog.com/user-experience-primary-and-secondary-users-in-healthcare-8dd4c5c61490#.us8nl6s7y. Accessed 09 Feb 2017
24. Weber, T.A.: Intermediation in a sharing economy: insurance, moral hazard, and rent extraction. J. Manag. Inf. Syst. **31**(3), 35–71 (2014)

The Challenges Found in the Access to Digital Information by People with Visual Impairment

Karolina Vieira da Silva Bastos$^{(\boxtimes)}$ and Ivette Kafure Muñoz

Universidade de Brasília, Brasília, Brazil
karollinna@gmail.com, ivettekead@gmail.com

Abstract. This study presents a study project which objective is to identify the challenges of access to information faced by people with visual impairment when interacting with digital information environments. The research circumstances are presented from the visual impairment perspective, studies of users oriented to the visually impaired, Assistive Technology for people with visual impairment and digital accessibility. Considering the scope and the objective of the research, a descriptive study is being developed using the mixed method as methodological approach, which will have the qualitative method as the main guide of the project, and a secondary database, in which the quantitative method will be incorporated within the qualitative method in order to play a supporting role in the procedures. As a research method, the survey will be adopted using the interview technique, using the semistructured script as an instrument to collect data about the target audience and their preferences, thoughts and behaviors. Pre-tests were performed to improve the instrument for collecting data and adding value to the intended objectives. After a preliminary analysis it was verified that the introduction of digital resources brought benefits to the life of the visually impaired people. However, difficulties were also identified. It is hoped that this research highlights the importance of knowing the particularities and needs of visually impaired users so that the development of interfaces and digital resources become increasingly accessible and inclusive.

Keywords: Assistive Technology · Digital accessibility · Factors in interaction with information · Need for information · Users study · Visual impairment

1 Introduction

In recent years, improvements in the production, processing and dissemination of information and knowledge have led to clear social changes, which were generated mainly by the development and dissemination of Information and Communication Technologies (ICTs) and the World Wide Web. Those improvements characterize the Information Society [3, 6], which is described as an environment of informational abundance and ICTs arise as tools to deal with the problem of the intensifying of production and organization of information, enhancing the access and connecting the people to the products of the mind [10], so that information in digital format has been one of the main forms of disseminate and promote access to information, by the ease of access and publication, low cost and, mainly, by the high celerity which this

© Springer International Publishing AG 2017
A. Marcus and W. Wang (Eds.): DUXU 2017, Part III, LNCS 10290, pp. 330–346, 2017.
DOI: 10.1007/978-3-319-58640-3_23

information reaches the users [13]. This allows social authors to acquire autonomy and independence in educational, professional, domestic, leisure and entertainment activities [48].

However, in spite of the many advantages that such computational technologies make emerge, it is observed that they can cause digital exclusion if users who have any limitations when interacting with digital environments are deprived of access to information due to difficulties of access, of browsing, or for not understanding the information provided [42, 43]. The action of providing services and information through technological resources alone does not guarantee the functionality of access to information, especially if there are access barriers that jeopardize their effective use. This reality instigates debates and researches on the accessibility of digital content, which is indispensable for providing access to information for citizens [42, 43].

Specifically in the case of users with visual impairment, the accessibility of digital content is paramount, since a considerable part of the information available in these contents is predominantly visual. To access them, visually impaired users need to use some Assistive Technology [39]. In the case of people with total loss of vision the screen reader can be used, which, through a voice synthesizer, digitally vocalizes all the textual information contained in a digital document [39]. Thus, these users are unable to view links and select them with the mouse. They navigate the pages using pre-defined key combinations and simultaneously listen to their content [42]. Therefore, images, graphs and maps should be described in text in order to provide the visually impaired with as much information as possible contained in the document [39]. The tables must also be carefully structured, so that their data is properly understood when read cell by cell or in linearized mode (line by line) [39]. In relation to the difficulties faced by people with low vision, they are generally smaller compared to those faced by people with total loss of vision, but also deserve due attention [39]. Text with appropriate font sizes to each particular need must be provided, as well as the contrast of both images and text colors and background are important to facilitate their understanding [39].

Thus, it is important to ensure that digital content be designed in accordance with the accessibility guidelines, and it is fundamental to ensure that the visually impaired user is able to interact with the websites [42]. In addition to the adoption of accessibility guidelines, which guarantee Assistive Technology access to the website, it is important to know the needs, skills and behavior of visually impaired users of different types, so that content can be organized to facilitate the access to it [42]. In face of that context, ascertaining the importance of knowing the particularities of the visually impaired user and understanding their specificities for the construction of websites best suited to this profile of users, this research project intends to answer the following question: What are the challenges of access to information faced by people with visual impairment in the interaction with digital information environments?

In order to answer the research question, it is defined as the research goal: to identify the challenges of access to information faced by people with visual impairment in the interaction with digital information environments. The specific goals, necessary to achieve the main goal, are: (1) To identify the demographic profile of the visually impaired person according to sex, age, educational level, geographical location of residence, social level, level of visual impairment and level of digital inclusion;

(2) Check the information needs that the visually impaired person seeks to satisfy when accessing digital environments; (3) Identify the digital resources and locations that the person with visual impairment uses to obtain access to digital information; And (4) Identify the advantages and difficulties encountered by the visually impaired person when accessing information through digital resources.

2 Visual Impairment

Vision is one of the main senses in the capture of stimuli, spatial projections, mediating the subject's relationship in their social environment [37]. Through the vision, one has the possibility of communicating with another, identifying objects, distinguishing colors, shapes and sizes, knowing places, distances, namely, allowing the subject to fully enjoy the world [37]. A person, having an irreversible condition of loss or reduction of visual response in both eyes on a permanent basis, even after medical treatment, surgeries or the use of lenses, is characterized by having visual impairment, which can be classified in the condition of blindness or low vision [30, 42]. Under these two designations are a vast number of visual disturbances in people with varying degrees of vision, including residual, and there are also several terms and definitions such as medical and pedagogical [42].

In a medical definition a person is considered blind when their visual acuity is equal to or less than 20/400 (.05 in decimal scale), i.e., if they can see at 20 feet (6 m) what a person with normal vision range can see at 400 feet (120 m) [53], or if the widest diameter of his field of vision implies an arc not greater than 20°, although his visual acuity in that narrow field may be greater than 20/400 [14]. In this context, a person with low vision is characterized as having visual acuity in values between 20/60 (.3 in decimal scale) and 20/400 (.05 in decimal scale) [53].

In an educational approach, the functional vision of the visually impaired person is the guideline of the adequate conceptualization for this purpose, so that the vision assessment will consider visual acuity, visual field and efficient use of vision potential [44]. Thus, from 1970 on, the diagnosis of the visually impaired person began to evaluate the forms of perception of the subject in addition to considering the clinical patterns: if he understands the world through touch, smell, synesthesia, among other senses [36]. Thus, visual efficiency is achieved through the quality and use of visual potential according to the conditions of stimulation and activation of visual functions, which means that the individual's emotional factors, environmental conditions and life contingencies directly interfere with the potential use of vision [44].

From this, under the sociocultural perspective of Vygotsky and taking his work as support, the person with visual impairment is not only that person who has an absence of visual perception, but also one who uses the other senses to learn the world and gives emphasis on the integrity of the individual and the unique adequacy of his personality in relation to the different experiences lived and the multiple influences received [40]. This means that the development of the person with visual impairment will occur considering the peculiar characteristics of the individual, linked to the biological aspect and also the secondary peculiarities, originating from the social aspect [40].

Similarly, from the point of view of González Rey, founder of the theory of subjectivity with historical and cultural basis, the person with visual impairment is a concrete individual whose disability will participate in the constitution of his subjectivity in a particular way due to the characteristics of the socio-relational systems in which he participates and the subjective senses that it produces in him [40]. In this way, it is observed that both Vygotsky and González Rey demarcate the dynamic constitution of the individual and his personality in the articulation between the individual and the social [40].

Thus, the absence of vision is a complex and diverse phenomenon. The causes of disability, timing and form of visual loss, whether it is progressive or sudden, the psychological, familial, and social context will influence how the person with visual impairment will learn and how they will cope with their blindness status [36].

Against this background, it is important to study the visually impaired user and understand the biological characteristics, individual experiences and socio-cultural heritage before offering any type of information in any type of resource or support.

3 Visually Impaired Users Study

Access to information is a fundamental element in favor of the development of the human being, especially in the case of visually impaired people, who face difficulties in accessing and acquiring information [33], primarily when it comes to access to digital environments that are mostly developed without considering their particularities [42].

Accessing the information becomes crucial factor for their socialization and educational training, particularly when it comes to information in the digital environment, which has brought to this community a range of information and, as a consequence, more autonomy [33].

The Information Science, which aims to study the general properties of information (its nature, genesis and effects), and to analyze its construction, communication and use processes, has sought to study the relations between the man and the information [32]. That man, in Information Science has been studied as information user, which is the objective and main focus of studies and professional practice in the area [15].

The main questions that cover the relationship between users and information can be mainly of three types: information need, information use and behavior in the search and use of information [15]. The field of study within the Information Science that investigates this diversity of relationships is called informational behavior, which includes, among other aspects, the so-called user study [15].

The user study can be termed as surveys that are done to find out what people need in terms of information or whether these people are satisfied and being attended properly by their information providers. These studies also include the investigation of how and for what purpose the information is used, and what factors affect such use, as well as the ways that those needs are expressed and known within a thematic area or by those using the products and services of an information unit or information system [18, 24, 25].

In terms of historical evolution, the origin of the study of users dates back to the 1930s, in the city of Chicago, when the first studies were done about users' reading habits and the socializing potential of public libraries. Over time, other issues became the focus of these studies, leading them to go through different steps ranging from the goal of creating new services based on user profiles and enhancing existing libraries to understanding the needs of information of the user from their cognitive, social, cultural, organizational and affective contexts [17, 24, 25].

User studies are guided by two approaches: traditional and alternative. The traditional approach, consolidated in studies prior to the 1980s, directs the focus to the product, the service or the information system, based on quantitative data, which are evaluated practically disregarding the one to whom they are intended, whether the user is individual or collective [17]. In other words, in this type of approach studies are oriented to the use of information and emphasize how organizations treat information [17]. By contrast, the alternative approach arises in the early 1980s, which focus changes from the system to the user. That is, it is characterized by user-centered studies of information, its individual characteristics and perspectives, focusing on the human factor [17].

From the late 1990s, new studies began to try to reconcile the traditional and alternative approaches, seeking to overcome the tendencies that sometimes saw the user as void, totally determined by their belonging to a socio-demographic profile (as in the traditional approach), sometimes saw users as being isolated, endowed with unique criteria (totally individual) to judge information, feeling and defining in their mind something like "information need" (as in the alternative approach). Such studies are characteristic of the so-called social approach presented by Capurro [11]. Within social approach, the social-epistemological paradigm, developed by Hjørland and Albrechtsen, argues for a socio-cognitive approach to Information Science, i.e., relates the cognitive paradigm within a social context [11]. The socio-cognitive view tends to give epistemological treatment to the subjects of psychology (that means to see the knowledge of the individual in a historical, cultural and social perspective) [29]. It even discerns in Information Technology a contribution to the social paradigm in Information Science, because it has managed to change the perspective of individual information services and to have founded a new perspective, much more general and flexible [29].

In this context, the socio-cognitive view is shown as an appropriate scientific approach for interaction studies between the visually impaired person and the digital information environments, since, besides the application of accessibility guidelines, the cognitive aspects of visually impaired users, especially those with total loss of vision, are a fundamental component to be considered to guarantee the accessibility of digital contents [42]. Thus, it is desirable to know the cognitive aspects regarding the historical and sociocultural context of these users, as well as their other diverse dimensions (individual, social, motivational, emotional) [42].

With this in mind, it can be seen that the user study can contribute to the development of more accessible websites, since direct contact with the users is necessary to know their needs and behaviors [32]. And it is also observed that understanding disabled users and their behaviors is not always a trivial process, since their physical and/or cognitive abilities differ from the abilities of non-disabled users [42].

4   Assistive Technology for the Visually Impaired

Assistive technology has several concepts, both internationally and nationally. The "Assistive Technology" term was created in 1988 as an important legal element within the US law known as Public Law 100-407 and it was renewed in 1998 as Assistive Technology Act 1998 (PL 105-394, S.2432). It establishes, with other laws, the American with Disabilities Act (ADA), which regulates the rights of citizens with disabilities in the United States, and provides the legal basis for public funds to purchase the resources they need. In Europe, a consortium was created in 1999 among countries to deal with Assistive Technology throughout that entire continent called Empowering Users Through Assistive Technology (EUSTAT) [21].

According to EUSTAT, "support technology", the name given to Assistive Technology, encompasses all products and services capable of compensating for functional limitations, facilitating an independent way of life and helping the elderly and disabled people to realize their full potential [21]. This Consortium produced four important documents, the result of studies developed with the help of partner institutions and published by the European Commission [20]:

- Assistive Technology Education for End-Users - Guidelines for Trainers.
- Go for it! A User Manual on Assistive Technology.
- Critical factors involved in end-users' education in relation to Assistive Technology.
- Programs in Assistive Technology education for End-Users in Europe.

Within the European Commission, between 2004 and 2006 the EASTIN Consortium, which is a European information network on support products for people with disabilities, was set up to create an international information network on All European countries by providing a full range of query tools in the field of Assistive Technology in all official languages of the European Union in a facilitated and accessible manner [19].

In Brazil, the Technical Assistance Committee (CAT), which later changed its name to the Brazilian Assistive Technology Committee [52], at its plenary meeting on December 14, 2007, approved the following concept for Assistive Technology: an area of knowledge with an interdisciplinary feature that encompasses products, resources, methodologies, strategies, practices and services that aim to promote the functionality related to the activity and participation of persons with disabilities, disabilities or reduced mobility, aiming at their autonomy, independence, quality of life and social inclusion [8]. That is, Assistive Technology refers to the research, manufacture, use of equipment, resources or strategies used to enhance the functional abilities of people with disabilities. The Assistive Technology application covers all orders of human performance, from the basic tasks of self-care to the performance of professional activities [9].

Therefore, because Assistive Technology is an area of knowledge that encompasses a range of resources and services, it is important to separate it into categories to promote the organization of its area of expertise and to study, research, develop, promotion of public policies, organization of services, database cataloging and formation to identify the most appropriate resources to meet a functional end-user need

[45]. Thus, according to the proposal of classification based on the guidelines of the American with Disabilities Act (ADA) Assistive Technology resources are divided into 11 categories: aids for daily living; CAA (CSA) - augmentative (supplementary) and alternative communication; computer accessibility features; environmental control systems; architectural designs for accessibility; orthoses and prostheses; postural adequacy; mobility aids; aids for the blind or people with low vision; aid for the deaf or hearing impaired; and adaptations in vehicles [45]. This article, as it focuses on the category of aid for blind or partially sighted people, will then present the various programs/devices available to the visually impaired [49, 50]:

Interfaces for people with low vision:

- Hardware: Electronic magnifying glass for TV or manual electronic loupe.
- Software: LentePro, Magic and operational system accessibility resources (MS Windows).

Interfaces for blind users:

- Hardware: Braille printers, tactile relief table, Thermoform, spoken Braille, Braille Terminal (Braille line) and Braille lite.
- Software: Dosvox, screen readers (Virtual Vision, Jaws, NVDA and Orca), OpenBook, Braille Fácil, Monet, Letra System (Electronic Read), Lynx and Voice Mail.

With technological convergence and the growing demand to be constantly connected, regardless of location, portable communication solutions such as notebooks, tablets and cell phones became popular [23]. Among them, cellular phones acquire a central role [23]. In this sense, it is also necessary to present the main Assistive Technology interfaces used for the interaction of the visually impaired person with mobile devices.

Screen readers for mobile devices with a touch screen have a movement/gesture reading, that is, it has to enable visually impaired people to scroll through the options by touching the screen to hear a description of the item their finger, being able to pass commands to your device by touching, dragging or sliding [22].

To date, there are two major players in the mobile landscape: Apple and Google, who run the mobile device industry [28].

The iOS operating system running inside iPhone, iPad and iPod touch devices, manufactured by Apple, has integrated a screen reader called Voice Over, which has accessibility features that were not available in other devices [23], as well as other user-assisted features with visual impairment.

For smartphone users using Google's Android operating system, there is the TalkBack screen reader, an app that comes pre-installed on most Android devices [26]. There are other applications developed for Android that are meant to be accessible that are available for download on Google Play, some of which are free and other are paid.

It should be noted that the indication of the most appropriate technology for each case depends on the individual characteristics of each subject and the learning phase of the use of Assistive Technology [22]. Also, family and external influences are considered as potentially important contributors to skills acquisition in Assistive Technology and access [35].

From the foregoing, it has been found that accessibility devices are essential for the visually impaired, as it allows access to digital information, assuring them independence and autonomy, generating motivation and producing opportunities for inclusion in the digital environment and in the communities contained therein [47].

However, for such artifacts to work properly, it is necessary to standardize and harmonize between websites and browsers. This standardization is proposed through guidelines and guidelines for accessibility and laws that determine accessibility to the digital environment [42].

5   Digital Accessibility

Digital accessibility means enabling all people to access, maintain, and interact with the computer and its resources [51]. This means that systems that allow the access to information and services in digital environments should be flexible enough to meet the users' needs, whether these users are disabled or not, also benefiting seniors, users of alternative browsers, of Assistive Technology and mobile access [4].

Within the digital accessibility, it is possible to highlight accessibility on the Internet as one of the most studied and disseminated themes currently [31]. This is mainly because, in recent times, the greatest obstacle faced by people with disabilities is the access to information, and therefore to important information-related aspects such as education, work and leisure [51]. In this sense, the current concern of accessibility advocates is to ensure that these principles are also observed in the digital space, which is a space of information and communication [51]. Thus, the Internet has been widely used to exemplify this concept, since it contains basic aspects of both technologies [51]. Thus, accessibility in this medium refers itself to sites that are available and accessible on the web, at any time, place, environment, access device and by any type of user [31].

In this sense, to ensure web growth, reaching its maximum potential so that sites are accessible to everyone regardless of equipment, browsers or special needs, the World Wide Web Consortium (W3C), an international committee made up of large Internet companies which acts as an Internet policy manager, has made remarkable international effort, pro-accessibility in digital space [51]. Thus, in order to define recommendations for the construction of web pages and other documents available in digital space, the committee created the Web Accessibility Initiative (WAI), which its main responsibility is to elaborate and maintain a set of recommendations that guarantee the construction of sites with accessible content for all people when properly followed, regardless of the hardware, software, network infrastructure used, or their language, culture, geographical location or physical and mental capacity [58].

As a result of this work, in May 1999 the WAI published the Web Content Accessibility Guidelines (WCAG 1.0) [54]. The guidelines are intended for all web content and authoring tools developers [54]. The main objective of those guidelines is to promote accessibility [54]. In December 2008, the guidelines were updated, giving rise to WCAG 2.0, which is, until now, the main worldwide reference in terms of web content accessibility [56].

After mentioning the importance of developing a site following the accessibility guidelines, it is essential to know if the site code meets these guidelines [31]. The code can be verified through the code validators of the W3C consortium.

Next, the accessibility assessment of the site must be carried out through automatic and human mechanisms.

The automatic validation is performed through a validator, online software that detects and analyzes the HTML of a web page and compares it with established guidelines according to each priority level [48]. In case errors are found when evaluating a page, the validator will gather the descriptions and location of each error, as well as suggestions for improvement. If the validator does not find any errors, it will provide a seal that certifies to the page the status of consonant with the accessibility guidelines [48]. Overall, according to the World Wide Web Consortium there are 87 automatic validation tools in the Internet [57].

Human validation is another step of assessing the accessibility of a site [54]. It is imperative because, although automatic validation is fast and convenient, it is generally not possible to identify all accessibility problems of a site mechanically [54]. Thus, human validation will help ensure language clarity and ease of navigation [54].

Even with all these initiatives, it is noted that the opportunities for access to informational digital environments in the context of the visually impaired still differ from the opportunities of those who see, since currently most sites and software still have accessibility barriers which make it difficult or impossible to use the Web for many people with disabilities [55]. In this way, it is verified that there are still some paths to be covered in order to achieve full access to information in the digital environment.

6 Methodology

Regarding the purpose of the research, this study is characterized as descriptive in nature, since this study intends to describe and comprehend from an in-depth perspective the relevant characteristics of the phenomenon of interaction between the visually impaired person and the digital information environments [38, 46].

As a methodological approach, the mixed method will be used, which tends to collect and analyze data both qualitatively and quantitatively, with the aim of providing a better understanding of the research problem [16]. Thus, the concurrent embedded strategy will be used as a research strategy, which aims to use a single phase of data collection to collect both qualitative and quantitative data [16]. Thus, following the concurrent embedded approach, the research will have the qualitative method as the main guide of the project and a secondary database that will play a supporting role in the procedures [16]. Therefore, receiving less priority, the quantitative method will be incorporated within the qualitative method [16]. Therefore, the combination of the data of the two methods will enrich the description of the research participants [16].

The survey will be adopted as a research method, since descriptive statements will be made about the group of people with visual impairment to discover the distribution of certain traits and attributes that determine their characteristics [2]. The interview will be used as a technique of this method in order to collect data about people and their preferences, their thoughts and their behaviors in a systematic way [5]. The interview will be semistructured, since a script will be elaborated with main questions, complemented by questions that may arise during the moment of the interview, because in this research the importance of the collected information results from associations made by the interviewee [34].

As research instruments will be used: pen, paper and audio recorder, as researchers conducting interviews should use as a research tool to record the information: handwritten notes on forms; audio recordings and video recordings [16], whereas, even if the interview is recorded, it is appropriate for the researchers to make notes, since the electronic equipment is subject to failure [16].

7   Pre-tests: Collection and Analysis

In order to improve the data collection techniques to be used in the research and to verify if the specific objectives can be achieved and consequently reach the general objective of the research through the variables to be studied, two pre-tests were carried out in the months of September and October of 2016. The data collected in pre-test 1 consisted of interviews with two people with visual impairment, one with low vision and the other blind, at Instituto Benjamin Constant (Rio de Janeiro), applying the semi-structured script prepared for the research. The data were analyzed in two sets: demographic data and data access in the digital environment. Pre-test 2, held in the discipline "Special Topics in Communication and Mediation of Information: Human Factors in Information Interaction (FHI)" of the Graduate Program in Information Science of the Universidade de Brasília (PPFCINF) is presented after the data set regarding access to information in the digital environment, because it fits in and complements one of the items addressed in this block.

7.1   Pre-test 1

From September 26 to 30, 2016, the researcher participated in the Course on Computer Science in the area of Visual Disability, carried out by the Instituto Benjamin Constant in Rio de Janeiro. The course provided learning about notions of visual impairment and computer programs available in the area of visual impairment. The course was accompanied by theoretical classes and practical activities that allowed her to obtain the experience of how a person with visual impairment uses the digital resources to access the information. The teacher who taught the classes has low severe vision and one of the class members has total loss of vision. These factors contributed to a proper environment to the pre-test. Therefore, the teacher and the blind class member were invited to be interviewed for this purpose.

The semi-structured script used in the interview is an adaptation of the present script in Silva's work [47], whose approach to research follows the same theme. In this roadmap for better data collection and analysis, the variables studied are separated into two sets: demographic data and data access in the digital environment.

The responses were recorded in audio, with permission of the participants, for later transcription and analysis of the data.

The data collected revealed that, when surveying the demographic profile of interviewees, it is possible to know the audience studied and understand the context they are inserted. This factor is fundamental for the development of the research because, under a socio-cognitive view of the study of users to evaluate the information needs of people with visual impairment interacting with digital information environments, it is necessary to first understand who these users are, as well as their actions, which are inseparable from their historical and sociocultural context, to later raise other aspects and carry out analyzes [1, 52].

By analyzing the data on access to information in the digital environment, the information needs of the interviewees were raised and it was observed that they are diversified, varying according to their personal objectives, contextual situation, social, economic and cultural factors. In addition, it was found that the information needs of the visually impaired person did not differ from the other users [33]. What distinguishes them are the information and technology used to gain access to information, which should not impose or have an exclusionary barrier [33].

In doing so, it was verified that there are several technological resources used by people with visual impairment to access information in the digital environment, such as: the interviewee with low vision uses the accessibility features of Windows, iPhone accessibility features, the NVDA screen reader, the DOSVOX operating system and the Magic screen magnifier; the blind interview used the accessibility features of iPhone, DOSVOX, Jaws screen reader and the standalone text reader, a special scanner available at work.

Also, it was verified that technological resources promote facilitations in people's lives, bringing autonomy, quality of life and inclusion in social life [55], since, after insertion of the digital resources in the life of the interviewee, it was possible she gets more information, in a faster way, and it's easier to store all the information she wanted. The participant emphasized the aspect of these resources to increase independence in activities carried out in everyday life and also to be instruments of sociability, and also emphasized the fact that nowadays those who do not have or do not know how to use digital technologies become digitally excluded and, consequently, socially.

However, it was also possible to perceive that, although there are several paths that promote access to information, there are also many difficulties placed on the path of the visually impaired person, such as: lack of accessibility to the computer - software/hardware compatibility with screen readers programs; Browser accessibility - exchange of versions that are not accessible and do not have originally the resources that are needed; and accessibility in the development of web pages - if laws and guidelines of recommendations to make the content of websites accessible are not followed a series of difficulties can be generated, such as images, graphics and maps without textual description.

Another difficulty expressed is the factor of documents having graphics, mathematical formulas and chemical compounds with a specific symbology that is very difficult for the screen reader to authenticate the information expressed in the content to the visually impaired person. In this perspective, Reis et al. [41] tested in their research the reading of the NVDA screen reader and DOSVOX operating system for notations commonly used in chemical equations and representations of the periodic table, such as: X^2, X2 and X2, and they report that in these expressions the digit two represents different characters, which can be readily ratified when making use of the vision, because the first digit two is overwritten, the second in natural size and the third subscript [41]. This is a playful resource commonly employed to specify the dissimilarity of meanings in chemistry teaching [41]. However, such significance will not be perceived by people with visual impairment who are accessing such characters through screen readers, since the sound will be exactly the same for all three expressions [41]. The authors also tested the notations H^1 and H1, in which the first, with superscript, represents the atomic number of the chemical element and the second notation, with subscription, the number of atoms; however the screen reader does not provide such information [41]. In this sense, the inability to transmit singular aspects of content in audio prevents these tools from conferring trustworthiness to the basic principles of Chemistry [41].

Also there are difficulties related to personal and social aspects, which prevents the visually impaired person from reaching the desired information and, therefore, important aspects related to information, such as education, work and leisure.

Still, the CAPTCHA in image with or without corresponding audio version was also cited by the interviewees as a hindrance to information access in web pages. CAPTCHA is a security program used to protect sites against bots, which is a software designed to simulate human actions repeatedly in the standard way, in the same way as a robot would do [12]. Thus, sites use CAPTCHA that generate classification test that humans can pass, but current computer programs cannot [12]. In other words, the CAPTCHA certifies and identifies the access by humans and eliminates the action of the bots [12]. A common type of CAPTCHA test is a randomly generated sequence of letters and/or numbers that appears in the form of an image and a text box [27]. To pass the test and prove your human identity, users have simply to type in the text box the characters that they see in the image [27]. For security guidelines, to implement the CAPTCHA image at sites, the sequence of letters and/or numbers should be randomly distorted before being presented to the user; and it means they should be unreadable by computers [12]. Thus, the CAPTCHA, because of it is designed to prevent automated software from performing actions that degrade the quality of service of a system, is naturally designed to be difficult to read and understand. It means it is inaccessible by its nature; it is not read, nor interpreted by screen readers, effectively rendering the service unusable by some people [7]. For this reason, when implementing a CAPTCHA image in a site an existing alternative resource it is necessary to provide a corresponding audio code, i.e., a set of letters and/or numbers that are reproduced by a distorted synthetic speech [12].

7.2 Pre-test 2

On October 5, 2016, during the "Special Topics in Communication and Mediation of Information: Human Factors in Information Interaction (FHI)" class of the Graduate Program in Information Science of the Universidade de Brasília (PPFCINF), a research exercise was carried out under the supervision of Professor Ivette Kafure and with the consent of the students. The intention of the exercise was to put the 12 students of the class, all of them visually not-impaired, in the position of visually impaired users.

In order to carry out the exercise, the participants were asked to close and keep their eyes closed. The intention was to test the CAPTCHA in audio, which has the distorted synthetic speech, to verify how the information transmitted to them only by the sound medium would be understood. For this purpose the researcher accessed two government sites that offer services and information essential to citizens' lives and that use the CAPTCHA image technology with an audio correspondent in their forms and asked participants to listen to the code, write down and then report what they heard.

The first site accessed was the individual taxpayer income tax refund query page hosted in the Receita Federal website. To perform the query on the page the person is asked to fill in the fields related to the Individual Taxpayer Registration (CPF) number, the birthdate, the tax year and the CAPTCHA with alphanumeric text image options and its correspondent audio version.

The second site accessed was the social security ticket value calculation page hosted on the Dataprev website. To perform the query on the page a person is asked to choose the calculation category, fill in the taxpayer registration data and the CAPTCHA with alphanumeric text image options and alternative sound code. By choosing the sound code, the CAPTCHA image is suppressed and an audio file is offered to be downloaded and listened using audio programs that the user must have already installed on his computer. This file has a different code then the one that was previously displayed in the image.

A difficulty regarding the understanding of the spoken code in the corresponding audio of the CAPTCHA was verified in the execution of the pre-test, since in both pages accessed the audio of the CAPTCHA could not be understood by any of the 12 members of the class.

The CAPTCHA image contained in the individual taxpayer income tax refund query page hosted on the Receita Federal website displayed the code "us93ez" in both the image and the corresponding audio. Participants understood sound reproduction in different ways. Five participants comprised only letters, four of which comprised the same code "ksjjoy". It should be noted, therefore, that the code understood has no similarity or correspondence with the code presented in the page consulted. Others still comprised smaller sets, with three, four or five digits, none of them corresponding to the code intended by the site mechanism.

In the second site accessed, social security ticket value calculation page hosted on the Dataprev website, a similar situation happened to that of the previous website. The participants understood the sound code in different ways. In this case, there was still one more obstacle: the sound code does not match the same as the CAPTCHA image code. If the person with visual impairment wishes to request help from a sighting person to check the audio with the image, this would not be feasible because of that difference. The user must repeatedly hear the audio code and insert their impression in the designated field until they have understood the correct code. In this aspect, it is verified that although the Receita Federal and the Dataprev websites, both Federal Government institutions, offer the alternative in audio for the CAPTCHA in image, this alternative does not completely solve the problem of accessibility.

8 Preliminary Research Considerations and Contributions

It is verified through the pre-tests that the obtained results were satisfactory to validate the research techniques and instruments; and to verify that through the variables to be studied the specific goals can be reached and, consequently, the general goal of the research can be reached, too.

Also, it is verified that the information accessibility is necessary for the people with visual impairment to reach the desired information, and for this reason this work is proposed. Thus, at the end of the research, when the challenges of access to information faced by people with visual impairment in the interaction with digital information environments will be identified, it is possible to know these users and their demands, in order to understand if the information they seek are accessible, to highlight through their experiences, needs and perceptions what can still be improved regarding accessibility in the digital environment. This knowledge would contribute to draw the attention and improve the perspective of technology developers working together with producers and managers of information, seeking to better understand the needs and expectations of users before offering them technologies and services.

References

1. Araujo, C.A.A.: Paradigma social nos estudos deusuários da informação: abordagem interacionista. Inf. Soc.: Est. **22**(1), 145–159 (2012)
2. Babbie, E.: Métodos de pesquisas de survey. UFMG, Belo Horizonte (2003)
3. Barbosa, J.S.: O setor de acessibilidade das fábricas de cultura das regiões Norte e Sul da cidade de São Paulo. In: 8th Seminário Nacional de Bibliotecas Braille: Cultura, Educação e Inclusão. Febab, São Paulo, 28–30 April 2014
4. Behar, P.A., et al.: A importância da acessibilidade digital na construção de objetos de aprendizagem. R. Nova Tecn. Educ. **6**(2), 1–10 (2008)
5. Bhattacherjee, A.: Social science research: principles, methods, and practices. USF Tampa Bay Open Access Textbooks Collection. Book 3 (2012)
6. Borges, C.V.S., et al.: Proposta de acesso inclusivo dos portadores de deficiência visual na Biblioteca Universitária José de Alencar da Faculdade de Letras da UFRJ. In: 8th Seminário Nacional de Bibliotecas Braille: Cultura, Educação e Inclusão. Febab, São Paulo, 28–30 April 2014
7. Brasil. Ministério do Planejamento, Orçamento e Gestão. Secretaria de Logística e Tecnologia da Informação. Departamento de Governo Eletrônico, eMAG: Modelo de Acessibilidade em Governo Eletrônico (2014). http://emag.governoeletronico.gov.br. Accessed 26 May 2016
8. Brasil. Presidência da República. Secretaria Especial dos Direitos Humanos. Coordenadoria Nacional para Integração da Pessoa Portadora de Deficiência, Ata da VII Reunião do Comitê de Ajudas Técnicas - CAT CORDE/SEDH/PR realizadas nos dias 13 e 14 de dezembro de 2007 (2007). http://www.infoesp.net/CAT_Reuniao_VII.pdf. Accessed 27 Feb 2017
9. Brasil. Presidência da República. Secretaria Especial dos Direitos Humanos. Subsecretaria Nacional de Promoção dos Direitos da Pessoa com Deficiência. Comitê de Ajudas Técnicas, Tecnologia Assistiva. CORDE, Brasília (2009)

10. Campello, B.: O movimento da competência informacional: uma perspectiva para o letramento informacional. Ci. Inf. **32**(3), 28–37 (2003). doi:10.1590/S0100-196520 03000300004
11. Capurro, R.: Epistemología y Ciencia de la Información. Enlace **4**(1), 11–29 (2007)
12. Carnegie Mellon University. CAPTCHA: Telling Humans and Computers Apart Automatically (2010). http://www.captcha.net/. Accessed 13 Oct 2016
13. Caselli, B.C.A.: Acesso à informação digital por portadores de necessidades especiais visuais: estudo de caso do Telecentro Acessível de Taguatinga. Dissertation, Universidade de Brasília (2007)
14. Conde, A.J.M.: Definindo a cegueira e a visão subnormal (2012). http://www.ibc.gov.br/? itemid=94. Accessed 11 Oct 2016
15. Costa, S.M.S.: Informação, usuários de informação, necessidade de informação; suportes de informação e meios de acesso à informação. UnB/CID, Brasília (2003)
16. Creswell, J.W.: Projeto de pesquisa: métodos qualitativo, quantitativo e misto, 3rd edn. Artmed, Porto Alegre (2010)
17. Cunha, M.B., Amaral, A.S., Dantas, E.B.: Manual de estudo de usuários da informação. Atlas, São Paulo (2015)
18. Cunha, M.B., Cavalcanti, C.R.O.: Dicionário de biblioteconomia e arquivologia. Briquet de Lemos, Brasília (2008)
19. EASTIN. O que é EASTIN (2005). http://www.eastin.eu/pt-pt/whatiseastin/index. Accessed 27 Feb 2017
20. Empowering Users Through Assistive Technology. Documentos Públicos disponíveis para o projeto (1999). http://www.siva.it/research/eustat/download_por.html. Accessed 27 Feb 2017
21. Empowering Users Through Assistive Technology. O que é o EUSTAT (2000). http://www.siva.it/research/eustat/leaflet_por.html. Accessed 27 Feb 2017
22. Façanha, A.R.: Uma proposta para acessibilidade visual e táctil em dispositivos touchscreen. Dissertation, Universidade Federal do Ceará (2012)
23. Façanha, A.R., Viana, W., Pequeno, M.C., et al.: Estudo de interfaces acessíveis para usuários com deficiência visual em dispositivos móveis touchscreen. Nuevas Ideas en Informática Educativa **7**, 144–149 (2011)
24. Figueiredo, N.M.: Avaliação de coleções e estudo de usuários. Associação dos Bibliotecários do Distrito Federal, Brasília (1979)
25. Figueiredo, N.M.: Estudos de uso e usuários da informação. IBICT, Brasília (1994)
26. Google Play. Google TalkBack (2016). https://play.google.com/store/apps/details?id=com.google.android.marvin.talkback. Accessed 25 Oct 2016
27. Google. G Suite. O que é CAPTCHA? Ajuda do Administrador do G Suite (2016). https://support.google.com/a/answer/1217728?hl=pt-BR. Accessed 17 Nov 2016
28. Goos, B.M.: Informação móvel para todos: acessibilidade em aplicativos jornalísticos para dispositivos móveis. Dissertation, Pontifícia Universidade Católica do Rio Grande do Sul (2015)
29. Hjørland, B.: Epistemology and the socio-cognitive perspective in information science. J. Assoc. Inf. Sci. Technol. **53**(4), 257–270 (2002)
30. Instituto Benjamin Constant. Os conceitos de deficiência: as diversas definições (2005). http://www.ibc.gov.br/?catid=83&itemid=396 Accessed 11 Oct 2016
31. Kade, A., et al.: Acessibilidade virtual. In: Sonza, A.P., et al. (eds.) Acessibilidade e tecnologia assistiva: pensando a inclusão sociodigital de PNEs, pp. 313–364. Instituto Federal do Rio Grande do Sul Campus Bento Gonçalves, Bento Gonçalves (2013)
32. Le Coadic, Y.-F.: A ciência da informação, 2nd edn. Briquet de Lemos, Brasília (2004)

33. Malheiros, T.M.C.: Necessidade de informação do usuário com deficiência visual: um estudo de caso da biblioteca digital e sonora da Universidade de Brasília. Dissertation, Universidade de Brasília (2013)
34. Manzini, E.J.: A entrevista na pesquisa social. Didática **26/27**, 149–158 (1991)
35. Wong, M.E., Cohen, L.: School, family and other influences on assistive technology use: access and challenges for students with visual impairment in Singapore. Br. J. Vis. Impairment **29**(2), 130–144 (2011). doi:10.1177/0264619611402759
36. Nunes, S., Lomônaco, J.F.: O aluno cego: preconceitos e potencialidades. Psicol. Esc. Educ. **14**(1), 55–64 (2010). doi:10.1590/S1413-85572010000100006
37. Oliveira, M.G., Pagliuca, L.M.F.: Análise comparativa da acessibilidade para cegos: contextos culturais. Benjamin Constant **57**(1), 92–103 (2014)
38. Pinsonneault, A., Kraemer, K.: Survey research methodology in management information systems: an assessment. J. Manag. Inf. Syst. **10**(2), 75–105 (1993)
39. Ponte, M., Salvatori, T., Sonza, A.P., et al.: Material digital acessível para deficientes visuais: ampliando o acesso à informação. Benjamin Constant **18**(53), 16–29 (2012)
40. Raposo, P.N., Martínez, A.M.: A aprendizagem dos alunos com deficiência visual: reflexões a partir de uma pesquisa no ensino superior. In: Martínez, A.M., Tacca, M.C. (eds.) Possibilidades de aprendizagem: ações pedagógicas para alunos com dificuldade e deficiência, pp. 237–272. Alínea, Campinas (2011)
41. Reis, L.S.A., Araujo, A.C.B., Ribeiro, K.P.: O desenvolvimento WEB no processo de ensino e aprendizado de química para deficientes visuais. In: 6th Simpósio Hipertexto e Tecnologias na Educação, 2nd Colóquio Internacional de Educação com Tecnologias. UFPE, Recife, 7–8 December 2015
42. Rocha, J.A.P.: (In)acessibilidade na web para pessoa com deficiência visual: um estudo de usuários à luz da cognição situada. Dissertation, Universidade Federal de Minas Gerais, Belo Horizonte (2013)
43. Rocha, J.A.P., Duarte, A.B.S.: (In)acessibilidade na web para pessoa com deficiência visual: um estudo de usuários à luz da cognição situada. In: 14th Encontro Nacional de Pesquisa em Ciência da Informação, Universidade Federal de Santa Catarina, Florianópolis, 29 October–1 November 2013
44. Sá, E.D., Campos, I.M., Silva, M.B.C.: Inclusão escolar de alunos cegos e com baixa visão. In: Sá, E.D., Campos, I.M., Silva, M.B.C. (eds.) Formação continuada a distância de professores para o atendimento educacional especializado: deficiência visual, pp. 13–38. SEEP/SEED/MEC, Brasília (2007)
45. Sartoretto, M.L., Bersch, R.: O que é Tecnologia Assistiva. In: Assistiva Tecnologia e Educação (2016). http://www.assistiva.com.br/tassistiva.html#topo. Accessed 27 Feb 2017
46. Sekaran, U.: Research Methods for Business: A Skill-Building Approach, 4th edn. Wiley, New York (2003)
47. Silva, K.V.: A inclusão digital e as dificuldades do acesso à informação para pessoas com deficiência visual. Monograph, Universidade de Brasília (2010)
48. Sonza, A.P.: Ambientes virtuais acessíveis sob a perspectiva de usuários com limitação visual. Thesis, Universidade Federal do Rio Grande do Sul (2008)
49. Sonza, A.P., et al.: Tecnologia assistiva e software educativo. In: Sonza, A.P., et al. (eds.) Acessibilidade e tecnologia assistiva: pensando a inclusão sociodigital de PNEs, pp. 199–312. Instituto Federal do Rio Grande do Sul Campus Bento Gonçalves, Bento Gonçalves (2013)
50. Sonza, A.P., Salton, B.P., Carniel, E.: Tecnologia Assistiva como agenda de inclusão de pessoas com deficiência visual. Benjamin Constant **22**, 21–39 (2016)
51. Torres, E.F., Mazzoni, A.A., Alves, J.B.M., et al.: A acessibilidade à informação no espaço digital. Ci. Inf. **31**(3), 83–89 (2002). doi:10.1590/S0100-19652002000300009

52. Vitorini, E.F. Uso da linguagem documentária na busca da informação em bibliotecas universitárias: a perspectiva dos deficientes visuais. Dissertation, Universidade Estadual Paulista (2015)
53. World Health Organization. International Statistical Classification of Diseases and Related Health Problems (2016). http://apps.who.int/classifications/icd10/browse/2016/en#/H54. Accessed 11 Oct 2016
54. World Wide Web Consortium. Web Content Accessibility Guidelines 1.0 (1999). https://www.w3.org/TR/WCAG10/. Accessed 22 Oct 2016
55. World Wide Web Consortium. Introduction to web accessibility (2005). https://www.w3.org/WAI/intro/accessibility.php. Accessed 23 Oct 2016
56. World Wide Web Consortium. Web Content Accessibility Guidelines (WCAG) 2.0 (2008). https://www.w3.org/TR/WCAG20/. Accessed 22 Oct 2016
57. World Wide Web Consortium. Web accessibility evaluation tools list (2016). https://www.w3.org/WAI/ER/tools/. Accessed 23 Oct 2016
58. World Wide Web Consortium. Web Accessibility Initiative (WAI) (2016). https://www.w3.org/WAI/. Accessed 22 Oct 2016

How the Inhabited Space Helps Consumers Customize Good Products

Liang Zhou and Kanliang Wang(✉)

School of Business, Renmin University of China, Beijing, China
xinquan2008@163.com, klwang@ruc.edu.cn

Abstract. Consumers could derive benefit from the preference fit through the online customization. However, consumers' preferences are often ill defined and sometimes unstable. Many methods are discussed to solve this problem in online customization. In this research, the authors propose a new method to examine whether the inhabited space would have different influences on consumers' perception of preference fit in an online customization context. Also, the mediating role of psychological distance between the consumers and the products is examined. Using subjects from a Chinese university, they report a study involving real customization tasks on a well-known Chinese customization website. The study arrives at the conclusion that the configurator with a higher inhabited space will help the consumers to customize more preferred products, which would be partial mediated by the psychological distance between the consumers and the customized products. The results would offer insightful guidelines to customization websites.

Keywords: Customization · Inhabited space · Preference · Psychological distance

1 Introduction

According to Forbes, many consumers nowadays customize products on mass customization websites in order to get their most preferred goods. Online customization is becoming increasingly more popular among consumers, firms, governments and researchers [1, 2]. One of the crux problems in online customization is the configurator which is a toolkit for the consumers to customize the products. Research has also confirmed that configurator used in the mass customization websites could help consumers construct their preferences, which in turn creates values for customers and thus enhances their willingness to pay as well [3]. And the configurator is also regarded as an interaction toolkit and value co-creation between the consumers and the company [4]. According to Prof. Piller's study, the cost of the configurator is very high (often more than 100 thousand dollars) [3]. And only when the consumers are satisfied with the configurator in online customization, they may be able to finish the customization, and purchase the products, return to the website and even recommend it to others [5]. Riemer [6] finds that users' satisfaction toward the configurator may directly influence their satisfaction to the final products. Therefore, How to design the configurator is a key problem in the online customization.

© Springer International Publishing AG 2017
A. Marcus and W. Wang (Eds.): DUXU 2017, Part III, LNCS 10290, pp. 347–356, 2017.
DOI: 10.1007/978-3-319-58640-3_24

Therefore, there are many studies about online configurator. Prior studies on customization configurator most focus on the functional requirements and structural features of a product family as well as information presentation format of the toolkit [1, 7, 8]. Some other studies focus on design principles of the configurator and some features such as starting solution, which could be buried in the configurator to influence consumers' perception and behavior [9–12]. All these studies regard the configurator as an Online Customization Toolkit which provides functions for the consumers to customize their products.

However, the configurator is also a central interaction interface between the customer and the mass customization company as well as the product itself [5]. The mass customization company provides product modules and presents relevant information in this configurator and in turn the consumer elicits their needs for this product to the company during the customization process. And the configurator also provides customers with a chance of trial and error so that they can try all options available in this configurator. Actually, the atmospherics of a retailing store, which is defined as "conscious designing of the space/web environments to create positive effects in users in order to increase favorable consumer responses", has significant impact on consumers' purchasing behavior both online and offline [13–16]. Only a slight change in a picture used in the website design can change consumers' purchase intention [17].

Prior research suggests that the interaction in virtual world can be enhanced through inhabited space, which refers to the degree of being situated in a context and in a meaningful place [18], because this inhabited space provides relevant atmosphere with context, meaning, and history. Applied to the online customization environment, inhabited space can be defined as the context where the product will be used. For example, a configurator for a swimsuit with a background of beach can give the feeling that the users are trying these swimsuits on the beach. Hence, this beach background provides inhabited space by showing a meaningful place.

In this paper, we investigate how the inhabited space of the configurator affects consumers' perception and attitude during the online customization process. We suggest that a configurator with a higher degree of inhabited space will lead to a higher perception of preference fit for the consumers. According to prior studies, consumer's preference is constructed during the decision process rather than buried in the memory [19, 20]. Actually, many researchers consider that consumers have ill defined and unstable preferences, which is a big challenge in the online customization [21]. And some following studies suggest that providing specific context cues such as starting solutions and peer suggestions can help consumer form initial design and get high preference fit [12, 22]. Accordingly, the inhabited space which refers to the context where the product will be used is also a context factor for the consumers. And compared with the context without inhabited space, the configurator with an inhabited space can help the consumer construct his/her preference more easily and also get a high perception of preference fit. Moreover, one problem in online customization is the separation of the design environment and the using context. The consumers design the products in the online configurator but will use these products in a specific context. For example, the consumer will design a flower vase which is intended to be put in a bedroom with a modern decoration. Therefore, in order to get a higher preference fit in the online customization, the product information as well as the using context information should be presented to the consumers at the same time. The inhabited space may solve this problem.

Besides, according to the endowment effect, the fact that the consumer feels like the originator of the object may generate values to the product so as that the consumers may be willing to accept a low-quality outcome. This effect is called as 'I designed it myself' effect [23]. In another word, the psychological distance between the consumer and the customized product may influence the consumer's evaluation about the product. At the same time, the inhabited space can decrease the psychological distance among the users in an virtual environment [24]. So, we also want to know whether the inhabited space in the customization configurator can decrease the psychological distance between the users and the customized products. If this effect existed, then the inhabited space may enhance the endowment effect in the online customization so that the consumer may get more from the feeling of 'I designed it myself'.

While most studies about the online customization configurator focus on the customizable product itself, we highlight the space design in this customization context. Actually, this paper is the initial step to explore the environment design in the online configurator, which contributes to the design science of online customization. And this paper also discusses the psychological distance between the consumer and the customized product. The empirical results may help to understand how the inhabited space helps to customize a good product.

Moreover, our research also has practical implications for practitioners. Our research results provide the insights about how to design an interactive configurator in online customization.

2 Theoretical Background

2.1 Inhabited Space

Hornecker and Buur [18] suggested that the inhabited space can enhance the quality of interaction in virtual world. They define that the inhabited space is the context where interaction takes place, which refers to the degree of being situated in a meaningful place. So a high degree of inhabited space is like real space where action takes place through the relevant atmosphere such as sound and visual stimuli. For example, some museum exhibits ancient products with computer-based pictures, videos, as well as recordings; so that the visitors can feel that they are really in the ancient time with this product on the side. Hornecker and Buur [18] also designed an sensoric garden in a public place. They installed a keyboard and audio tools on a path. Visitors walking on this path are just like walk on a real keyboard and can hear the sound the time they step on a key. And in nowadays, we can also see piano steps in some cities.

Besides in physical world, the inhabited space has also been deployed in virtual environment. When we upload our video to YouTube, we can set our background. For example, we can set our video background as a theatre when we upload our own music performance so that the users can perceive that we are performing in a theatre rather than at home.

An empirical study also suggested that inhabited space could enhance the co-experience in the social-media enhanced real-time streaming video [24]. In their study, the authors developed a social median enhance real-time video playing room which enables all participants watching a real-time football game together. In the high inhabited space version, the video is situated in the middle of a virtual football field with the stands around. On the contrast, in the low inhabited space version, the participants only can see the video without any background. The experiment results support the idea that higher inhabited space can decrease the psychological distance between the users in the playing room, which in turn leads to a higher perception of co-experience.

In this paper, we apply the inhabited space concept into our specific customization context. We define the inhabited space in online customization as the context where the customizable product will be used. For example, if the consumer wants to customize a suit to join a college party, the high inhabited space is the background of a party room, while the low inhabited space is a background of an office. So, the party room is a meaningful place with a relevant atmosphere for this consumer.

2.2 Preference

Initially, the researchers considered that the consumers' preferences are well-defined and stable all the time, which is regarded as the premise of customization that the consumers know their preferences well and can freely express the preferences to the companies through the configurator. However, as the following studies suggested, the researchers reach an consensus that the consumers often do not have well-defined preferences [25], and usually construct them during the decision making process [19, 26].

Furthermore, there is another dimension of preference, the preference insight, which represents the degree to which consumers know their preferences, including the stability and clarity of those preferences [21]. Therefore, Simons [21] divided consumers into four groups according to these two dimension of preferences. Consumers in the first group have well-defined preferences and good preference insights, which enables them to judge correctly whether a customized offer fits their preferences. In the second group the consumers have well-defined preferences but poor preference insight. In this condition, the consumers' preferences are stable and clear, but they do not know this, which may lead to customize an unfit product. The third group of consumers has ill-defined preferences but good preference insights. This means that actually the consumers do not have stable and clear preferences, and they also know this situation. So they may accept others' opinion or companies' recommendation easily. Consumers in the fourth group have ill-defined preferences and poor preference insights. These consumers' preferences are unstable and not clear, but they always think that the final customized products fit their preferences. For example, he/she does not distinguish the taste of Coca-Cola and Pepsi-Cola, but he/she believes that Coca-Cola is superior.

Though prior empirical studies suggested that online customization can enhance consumers' preference fit through the online configurator [27], the consumers' ill-defined preferences and poor insight into preferences are key challenges for the companies, and many designing strategies are employed to solve this problem. For example, a starting solution is a common design to facilitate the customization process [12], and side-by-side comparison is another method to help consumers to generate initial designs [28].

2.3 Psychological Distance

As construal level theory suggests, psychological distance between two objects can influence the level of mental construal. Specifically, people will construe a distant object at a high level which is more abstract and construe a close object at a low level which means more concrete [29].

Generally speaking, there are three kinds of psychological distance: spatial distance, temporal distance and social distance [29]. All these distance have similar meaning in construal level theory. For example, people always use the spatial distance to represent the social distance and temporal distance (for a review see Trop and Liberman's work [29]). It always takes more time for a person to get to a distant place than a close place, which means that the spatial distance represents the temporal distance. And a person always takes a seat far away from another person to indicate the social distance and sits close to a person to show the more intimate relationship. However, though they are related with each other, they have different effect in some respects.

The psychological distance also has effects on consumers' preferences. Trope and Liberman [30] found that when people make decision about a distant object, they will focus on the central features of this product, while pay more attention to the peripheral attributes in the close distance context. Some other studies also suggested that people would give more weight to the most important attribute when they make a distant decision, and would consider all features as the equally important when they evaluate a close object [31, 32]. Furthermore, consuming a product in a distant future leads people to pay more attention to the nonalignable attributes of this product [33]. The authors show two brands of potato chips with the same attractiveness which is tested by a pretest to the participants. One brand is better on its alignable attributes, while the other is designed to be better on its nonalignable attributes. And all the participants are randomly assigned to two conditions: one is to get this brand rightly after this experiment and the other is to get this product after this semester. The results of this study show that when people choosing a product in a distant future, the nonalignable attributes play a greater role than the alignable attributes. That's because that with the increasing of psychological distance, people would like to represent the product in a high level, more abstract attributes, which meets the requirement of nonalignable attribute comparing.

3 Hypothesis Development

As noted earlier, consumers often have unstable preferences. Specifically, in different context, consumers' preferences may change a lot. For example, in the office, a lady may prefer a modern style cup, while she may keep a cup of cartoon style in her bedroom. So, when consumers use the configurator to customize a unique product, they may need to specify the environment where the product will be used. Without this, the consumers' preference may be not clear, which lead to a hard decision making during the customization process. Inhabited space enables the consumers to directly know whether the customized product fits the environment so that they can modify their choices in time if necessary. This helps the consumers to customize a higher preference fit product.

Besides, customization configurator provides a try-and-error process for the consumers to create their own products [34]. And the inhabited space makes the consumers can try in a real like environment so that they can design a closer fit between their preferences and the products. In line with prior studies, a higher preference fit between the measured preference and the customized product can generate values to the outcome of customization. So we propose the first hypothesis as follows:

H1: higher inhabited space will lead to closer fit between the measured preference and the customized product attributes, which leads to a higher WTP.

Human beings recognize objects in a holistic way instead of a separated view. So only providing the product itself may cut off the link between the product and the context, leading to a harder choice. Instead, inhabited space makes the design environment more familiar to the consumers. In line with construal level theory, when consumers feel more familiar, then the psychological distance between them decreased.

Furth more, inhabited space makes the design environment more real to the consumers. Then the relevant context can reduce the consumers perceiving of the psychological distance through two factors. One is the real context of the product makes the consumers feels that he is right now using this product, which reduce the spatial distance between the product and the user. The second is the temporal distance. The inhabited space makes the consumers to feel trying the product right now which is very close temporal distance.

According to 'I designed it myself' effect, the more feeling of as the originator of the product, the more benefit is derived from the customization. Therefore, the higher inhabited space leading to a shorter psychological distance between the consumers and the products will also lead to a higher WTP for the product.

H2: higher inhabited space will lead to shorter psychological distance between the consumers and the products, which also lead to a higher WTP for the product.

We also argue that the close distance between the product and the consumer will lead to a high preference fit. Consumers in a close distance situation will focus more on the details and concrete attributes. As we discussed above, in a close distance situation, consumers give almost average weight to each attribute, which means they need to seriously consider all attributes. So he will try more options during the customization process, which means a higher possibility to create a product that fits the preference.

H3: the effect between the inhabited space and consumers' preference fit is partial mediated by the psychological distance between the products and the consumers.

4 Research Method

4.1 Experiment Design

A lab experiment is conducted to test this hypothesis. We recruit 60 university students who are randomly assigned to 2 groups. A flower vase customization configurator is developed as the experiment stimuli. The participants are told that they need to customize a little flower vase which will be placed on their bedroom desk. They can customize the frame, color, and pictures on the vase. The high inhabited space group is a configurator with a bedroom picture as the background, where the customizable vase is on the lab desk, and the low inhabited space group is only a vase configurator with no background. All the options for each attribute of the vase are generated from a real website. The bedroom background with a simple decoration is chosen among 10 pictures from a 10 persons' pretest. And in line with prior study, we limit the number of options for each attribute to prevent information overload [8].

4.2 Participants and Procedures

All of the participants are indicated that they need to customize a flower vase which will be put on their bedroom's desk through this website. When the participants arrived at the laboratory, they are randomly assigned to the two groups. We will record all of the customization process for further analysis. When finish the customization, they are asked to answer some questions. Each participant will be paid by 20 RMB and a chance to win the vase customized by himself/herself, which is worth about 200 RMB.

4.3 Measurement of Variables

We modify the items used in Lim's work to measure the inhabited space [24]. We adopt the method to measure the preference fit from prior studies [27, 35]. And the psychological distance measure is from Lim's work [24]. We also measure the willingness to pay (WTP) for the customized products by using an open ended question.

4.4 Data Analysis and the Result

The hypotheses are supported by this experiment results.

5 Conclusion

5.1 Theoretical Contribution

This paper contributes to the configurator design in online customization. This is an initial step to explore the space effect in the customization context. As prior researches most focused on the customizable product itself, the result of this paper may remind us paying attention to the customization environment. As the atmospherics of a mall or a supermarket are well discussed in the prior studies, the online atmospherics also influences the consumers' behavior [13, 36]. And we consider this is more important in the online customization context than in the normal electronic purchasing context because this online configurator is not only a place for consumers to buy a product but also a place for them to interact with the companies and the products. The inhabited space provides context cues for the consumer to the trial-and-error process. The mediating effect also contributes to the construal level theory.

5.2   Practical Implication

This paper has significant implications for the online customization companies. As the inhabited space can increase the consumers' perception of preference fit, the customization companies can provide many backgrounds for their configurator so that the users can set the backgrounds according to their own purchasing goals. Moreover, the websites can provide the function that the consumers can upload their own pictures to the configurator as the background. And the companies should also collect the data about how and where the consumers use their products so that they can provide the appropriate inhabited space for consumers. And as the result that closer distance may lead to a higher preference fit suggests, the online customization websites may provides some functions to decrease the psychological distance between the products and the consumers. For example, they can give a quicker delivery so that the consumers can get the product in a near future.

5.3   Limitation and Future Research

Though the empirical results support the hypotheses, there are still some limitations. First, all the measurement in this paper is self reported. Actually, in virtual world some objective data should be collected to test these hypotheses. Second, only one product category is discussed in this paper. In the future research, we should extend the product categories so that the results get a higher generalizability.

This paper shows that the inhabited space can influence the consumers preference fit in the online customization context. In the future, we can explore more atmospherics factors, such as the music, and the interaction effect between these different atmospheric factors.

Acknowledgment. This research was supported by the National Natural Science Foundation of China with grant # 71331007.

References

1. Fogliatto, F.S., da Silveira, G.J.C., Borenstein, D.: The mass customization decade: an updated review of the literature. Int. J. Prod. Econ. **138**(1), 14–25 (2012)
2. Goduscheit, R.C., Jørgensen, J.H.: User toolkits for innovation – a literature review. Int. J. Technol. Manag. **61**(3), 274–292 (2013)

3. Piller, F.T.: Mass customization: reflections on the state of the concept. Int. J. Flex. Manuf. Syst. **16**(4), 313–334 (2004)
4. Friesen, G.B.: Co-creation: when 1 and 1 make 11. Consult. Manag. **12**(1), 28–31 (2001)
5. Franke, N., Piller, F.T.: Key research issues in user interaction with user toolkits in a mass customisation system. Int. J. Technol. Manag. **26**(5), 578–599 (2003)
6. Riemer, K., Totz, C.: The many faces of personalization - an integrative economic overview of mass customization and personalization. Braz. Oral Res. (2001)
7. Ong, S.K., Lin, Q., Nee, A.Y.C.: Web-based configuration design system for product customization. Int. J. Prod. Res. **44**(2), 351–383 (2006)
8. Kamis, A., Koufaris, M., Stern, T.: Using an attribute-based decision support system for user-customized products online: an experimental investigation. MIS Q. **32**(1), 159–177 (2008)
9. Levav, J., et al.: Order in product customization decisions: evidence from field experiments. J. Polit. Econ. **118**(2), 274–299 (2010)
10. Coker, B., Nagpal, A.: Building-up versus paring-down: consumer responses to recommendations when customizing. J. Retail. **89**(2), 190–206 (2013)
11. Jin, L., He, Y., Song, H.: Service customization: to upgrade or to downgrade? An investigation of how option framing affects tourists' choice of package-tour services. Tour. Manag. **33**(2), 266–275 (2012)
12. Hildebrand, C., Häubl, G., Herrmann, A.: Product customization via starting solutions. J. Mark. Res. **51**(6), 707–725 (2014)
13. Turley, L.W., Milliman, R.E.: Atmospheric effects on shopping behavior: a review of the experimental evidence. J. Bus. Res. **49**(2), 193–211 (2000)
14. Gao, L., Bai, X.: Online consumer behaviour and its relationship to website atmospheric induced flow: insights into online travel agencies in China. J. Retail. Consum. Serv. **21**(4), 653–665 (2014)
15. Sun, H.-M., et al.: The effect of user's perceived presence and promotion focus on usability for interacting in virtual environments. Appl. Ergon. **50**, 126–132 (2015)
16. Dailey, L.: Navigational web atmospherics: explaining the influence of restrictive navigation cues. J. Bus. Res. **57**(7), 795–803 (2004)
17. Cyr, D., et al.: Exploring human images in website design: a multi-method approach. MIS Q. **33**(3), 539 (2009)
18. Hornecker, E., Buur, J.: Getting a Grip on Tangible Interaction: A Framework on Physical Space and Social Interaction (2006)
19. Bettman, J.R., Luce, M.F., Payne, J.W.: Constructive consumer choice processes. J. Consum. Res. **25**(3), 187–217 (1998)
20. Dhar, R., Gorlin, M.: A dual-system framework to understand preference construction processes in choice. J. Consum. Psychol. **23**(4), 528–542 (2013)
21. Simonson, I.: Determinants of customers' responses to customized offers: conceptual framework and research propositions. J. Mark. **69**(1), 32–45 (2005)
22. Franke, N., Keinz, P., Schreier, M.: Complementing mass customization toolkits with user communities: how peer input improves customer self-design*. J. Prod. Innov. Manag. **25**(6), 546–559 (2008)
23. Franke, N., Schreier, M., Kaiser, U.: The "I designed it myself" effect in mass customization. Manag. Sci. **56**(1), 125–140 (2010)
24. Lim, S., et al.: Getting closer and experiencing together: antecedents and consequences of psychological distance in social media-enhanced real-time streaming video. Comput. Hum. Behav. **28**(4), 14 (2012)
25. Payne, J.W., Bettman, J.R., Johnson, E.J.: Adaptive strategy selection in decision-making. J. Exp. Psychol. Learn. Mem. Cogn. **14**(3), 534–552 (1988)

26. Payne, J.W., Bettman, J.R., Johnson, E.J.: The Adaptive Decision Maker. Cambridge University Press, New York (1993)
27. Franke, N., Schreier, M.: Product uniqueness as a driver of customer utility in mass customization. Mark. Lett. **19**(2), 93–107 (2008)
28. Randall, T.: Principles for user design of customized products. Calif. Manag. Rev. **47**(4), 68 (2005)
29. Trope, Y., Liberman, N.: Construal-level theory of psychological distance. Psychol. Rev. **117**(2), 440–463 (2010)
30. Trope, Y., Liberman, N.: Temporal construal and time-dependent changes in preference. J. Pers. Soc. Psychol. **79**(6), 876–889 (2000)
31. Kray, L.J.: Contingent weighting in self–other decision making. Organ. Behav. Hum. Decis. Process. **83**(1), 82–106 (2000)
32. Kray, L., Gonzalez, R.: Differential weighting in choice versus advice: I'll do this, you do that. J. Behav. Decis. Mak. **12**(3), 207–218 (1999)
33. Malkoc, S.A., Zauberman, G., Ulu, C.: Consuming now or later? The interactive effect of timing and attribute alignability. Psychol. Sci. **16**(5), 411–417 (2005)
34. Huffman, C., Kahn, B.E.: Variety for sale: mass customization or mass confusion? J. Retail. **74**(4), 491–513 (1998)
35. Randall, T., Terwiesch, C., Ulrich, K.T.: User design of customized products. Mark. Sci. **26**(2), 268–280 (2007)
36. Koo, D.-M., Ju, S.-H.: The interactional effects of atmospherics and perceptual curiosity on emotions and online shopping intention. Comput. Hum. Behav. **26**(3), 377–388 (2010)

DUXU for Children and Young Users

Teenagers' Destination Website Navigation. A Comparison Among Eye-Tracking, Web Analytics, and Self-declared Investigation

Edoardo Cantoni, Elena Marchiori$^{(\boxtimes)}$, and Lorenzo Cantoni

Faculty of Communication Sciences,
Università della Svizzera italiana, Lugano, Switzerland
{edoardo.cantoni, elena.marchiori,
lorenzo.cantoni}@usi.ch
http://www.webatelier.net

Abstract. The aim of this study is to verify if teenagers' actual navigation through webpages match with their self-declared preferences (in terms of tourist attractions), and if these preferences are in line with the official DMO data about most viewed pages. Particularly, self-declared attractions are confronted with the contents visualized during navigation, thus making possible to understand to what extent the exposure to certain themes influence preferences towards certain attractions. Results from this comparison suggest that contents that teenagers pay attention to during navigation are not always what they declare to prefer as tourist attraction.

In a second stage, a comparison with the official DMO data showing the most viewed pages is carried out in order to verify if there are any commonalities in terms of preferred attractions. Results show commonalities in terms of preferences: outdoor/sports and events/concerts are the preferred themes across all sources. But results also show discrepancies. In fact, at the same time, according to each type of approach used, the ranking of preferred themes changes. Therefore, results suggests that a multi-source approach helps to eliminate possible biases that may occur if only one approach is adopted.

Keywords: Website navigation · Eye-tracking · Online behaviour · Teenagers · Web-analytics · DMO

1 Introduction

Eye-tracking, intended as the technique that allows understanding where a person is looking (Nielsen and Pernice 2010) is becoming a relevant source of information not only for usability studies, but also for investigating online consumer behaviour (Gidlöf et al. 2013; Venkatraman et al. 2014). Understanding the online consumer behaviour of its own costumers is also crucial for a Destination Management Organization (DMO), in particular for understanding preferences of prospective tourists who might use online sources (e.g. official website) to get information and inspiration on their next travel. DMOs generally study log files, and online behaviour happened on their own website (s) thought web analytics data (Yang et al. 2014), and several managerial decisions

© Springer International Publishing AG 2017
A. Marcus and W. Wang (Eds.): DUXU 2017, Part III, LNCS 10290, pp. 359–370, 2017.
DOI: 10.1007/978-3-319-58640-3_25

might be based on such source of data; for example: from a decision to improve a specific section of the website as a result that majority of people visited it, till a consideration to repute a specific tourism attraction as more relevant as majority of people mainly viewed a page dedicated to it. Nevertheless, offline market research and other source of information are generally used to integrate such decisions, however relying only on web analytics data might limit the interpretation of the online behaviour. Moreover, relying only on traditional method such as a user test based on pre-post questionnaire with self-reported perceptions on a website content/structure, might limit the interpretation of the data and might contain biases (Marchiori and Cantoni 2015).

Therefore, this study proposes a new approach to triangulate three sources of information: eye-tracking, web analytics, and self-declared investigation, with the objective to better understand the relevance of using a multi-source approach on online consumer behavior investigation. The official website of a Swiss destination at the border with Italy is used as case study, and a specific segment is analyzed. The segment under investigation is a group of teenagers living in an Italian city at the border with Switzerland. This specific segment allowed to identify if there is (or not) particular tourism attractions which attract them the most, and which type of elements of the pages generally capture their attention.

Understanding teenagers' online preferences (Gidlöf et al. 2012; Loranger and Nielsen 2013; Kaplan 2013) is still a sensitive segment for the difficulties to have access to teenagers (e.g. need of a consent form signed by their parents or legal representatives), and for their velocity to adapt to new trends and preferences. However, a DMO might find relevant to understand if this specific segment presents specific preferences, and in turn, might decide to create a dedicated section, and/or web navigation apt for them, and/or provide/improve specific services offline. Therefore, this study wants to contribute to the body of knowledge on the use of a multi-source approach to investigate tourism-related online consumer behavior, and at the same time, providing new evidences on teenagers' online consumer behavior when it comes to navigate an official DMO website.

As an introduction to this work, the concept of eye tracking, its application to the tourism industry, and the online behaviour the teenager segment are introduced. The research design and discussion of the results are then presented. Contributions of this study and future research are finally discuss in the conclusions.

2   Literature Review

2.1   Eye-Tracking Technique and Tourism

With the term "eye-tracking" is intended a technique that allows understanding where a person is looking, more precisely to measure the movements of the eyes with respect to the head (Nielsen and Pernice 2010). The concept of eye tracking evolved over time, from the first techniques based on direct observations on eye movements till the most recent ones based on modern eye-trackers hardware and software. Nowadays, thanks to technological advances, the eye tracking technique has been applied in various fields, and particularly has been proved to be a very effective tool specifically in psychology and marketing to gain a deeper understanding of users' behaviour (Gidlöf et al. 2013; Venkatraman et al. 2014). In recent years, eye-tracking has been also applied to investigate the online consumer behaviour in the tourism and hospitality domain. For example, the eye-tracking technique has been used in the hospitality sector to investigate the online decision-making process of potential clients (Noone and Robson 2014). Another study focused the attention on people's perception of tourism-related images according to ethnicity (Wang and Sparks 2014). Eye-tracking research has been carried out in the field of social media and tourism as well. Taking as a reference point previous studies applying an eye-tracking approach to social media (Wan Adnan et al. 2013), this branch of research has attempted to analyse what are the digital aspects that attract users the most while are navigating on tourism-related social media pages (Marchiori and Cantoni 2015). Moreover, other studies used the eye-tracking technique to analyse advertising effectiveness on tourism-related blogs, social networks and reviews portals (Méndez 2015).

2.2 Teenagers' Online Behaviour

One of the main studies carried out on the teenager segment has been developed by Gidlöf et al. (2012), analysing the exposure of Swedish teenagers to online advertising. Particularly, the study found out that out of all the potential online advertisings to which teenagers were exposed, only the 10 percent of it was actually seen, revealing great resistance to this type of advertising. The research also found that teenagers' visual attention is significantly influenced by the size and position of the online advertisement, whether the gender of the users appeared to have not influence. A study by Khan and Locatis (1998) about information retrieval on the Internet, found that when it comes to prioritize tasks, experienced high school students are more efficient than novices, even though their success rate in search process is less higher. In line with these results, Lazonder et al. (2000) observed that experienced high school students can locate websites (in terms of online navigation) better than inexperienced ones, but at the same time, results show that experienced students are not better at browsing in websites to find information. A more recent article by Kaplan (2013) analysing online purchasing behaviour of teenagers, pointed out that this particular segment has short attentions spans towards online advertisement. However, an effective way to gain their attention is to adopt a concise and transparent messaging style. Loranger and Nielsen (2013) analysed the online behaviour of teenagers and their performance in achieving tasks. Their study underlined that despite feeling confident while navigating online, teenagers have a lower success rate (71%) in accomplishing tasks compared to adults (83%). That is, teenagers tend to leave a task uncompleted quite fast if they are not able to find what was desired, showing a lower level of patience and cautious compared to adults. Moreover, the study discovered that teenagers have the highest success rate in e-commerce websites, while have more difficulties on dealing with government and non-profit ones. The study also proved that teens don't like to read a lot on webpages, and prefer contents that are presented visually, entertaining, and quick to be loaded online.

3 Methodology

For the present study, an ad-hoc eye-tracking experiment was design and performed. The case study selected for the experiment was the official website of Regional Destination Management Organization located in the South of Switzerland. The group of teenagers' object of the experiment were instead from a border city located in the North of Italy. A total of 23 participants aged between 17–19 years recruited on a voluntary basis took part to the test. Participants have been recruited from a high school of an Italian city located in the North of Italy, a neighbouring region of the Swiss destination under study. A consent form signed by the parents of the students have been required in order to involve them in the test.

3.1 Setting of the Experiment

The setting of the test was structured as follows: each participant was invited to sit in front of a PC, equipped with the Tobii X2-60 hardware mounted below the PC screen. Once the eye calibration process was completed, the test started. The test was based on a user free navigation of the official destination website of Canton Ticino, the Italian-speaking region in Southern Switzerland on the border with Italy (www.ticino.ch). The navigation time for each participant was fixed to five minutes, after which the test automatically ended. Each participant was also asked to complete a pre-post questionnaire, aimed to investigate teenagers' self-reported preferences on the aspects viewed during their website navigation. This study reports the results for a specific question that asked which attractions of the destination impressed them the most. The self-reported top attractions were then classified according to themes in order to obtain a map of what contents appeal participants the most. This classification was then compared with the themes that were visualized the most during the free navigation, which were instead resulted from the heat maps analysis emerged from the eye-tracking.

3.2 Eye-Tracking Data Analysis

The free navigation analysis was performed using Tobii Studio 3.4.5 software. Results from free navigation were studied analysing heat maps generated by the software, that is, coloured maps showing where participants fixated over each page. A single page might contains several areas coloured by the heat maps corresponding to different top fixation areas within that page as in Fig. 1. A total of 126 pages were viewed by the 23 participants (16 pages viewed in average per participant). Out of those 126 pages, 82 have been analysed. The pages not considered for the analysis were the ones that reported a loading error caused by a technical problem with the Tobii eye-tracker.

Specifically, the heat map analysis followed a four-step process:

(1) *Selection of the pages to analysis from the official DMO website*: (web) pages considered for the analysis were selected according to the number of participants visiting each page. For example, the heat map related to the homepage has been

Fig. 1. Example of a page with heat-areas

ranked first, being visited by all the 23 participants, while the heat map for the page "Explore" has been visited by 10 participants, and ranked second, and so on. In order to be considered for the analysis, at least 2 people had to have seen a single page.

(2) *Identification of the heat-areas within each web page*: heat maps for each page were analysed identifying heat areas where fixations were concentrated the most, namely those areas where the colours resulted more intense towards yellow/red.

(3) *Content analysis of the topics corresponding to the heat-areas*: the specific topics over which colours were more intense were then content analysed by one coder and classified into themes. The analysis of the most viewed topics considered the number of participants who visualized each page (data provided by the Tobii software). For example, for a page visualized by 10 participants, there might be two heat-areas to be coded in order to define the topic of the elements viewed. If the element of the first heat-area (e.g. a picture) was about the topic "lake of Lugano", it was considered visualized 10 times. Then, if in the same page the second heat-area (e.g. a text) was again about the topic "lake of Lugano", this specific topic gained 10 more visualizations, bringing the total count to 20 views, meaning that the person was expose twice to that specific topic.

(4) *Ranking of most visualized themes:* the ranking of all the macro themes emerged by summing all the visualizations per specific topic. Macro-themes emerged after a saturation process, listing all the single topics and then assigning them to themes.

3.3 Comparison Among the Data Gathered from the Self-reported, Eye-Tracking, and Web Analytics Investigation

Results coming from the eye-tracking analysis (namely heat maps investigation) are confronted with the self-reported description of the top attractions mentioned by the participants, allowing to verify any relation between what has been seen and what has been declared. Most visualized themes in free navigation and most cited self-declared attractions are then confronted with the official web analytics data provided by the DMO. In order to match with the segment investigated, the web analysis data have been filtered selecting the age (e.g. 18–24), and the same geographical area of the respondents. Then, the ranking of the most visualized pages according to the analytics is confronted with the most visualized themes and most cited attractions.

4   Results

4.1   Top Tourism Attractions Emerged from the Three Different Dataset

Self-declared top attractions: Among the 23 participants, 15 declared to have visited the destination to which they were exposed to. In the post-questionnaire, where participants were asked to declare their preferred attractions after the free navigation on the official DMO website, the most cited ones were falling in 14 macro-themes (see Fig. 2), namely: Sports/Outdoor Activities, Lugano and the Lake (8 attractions each), Events/ Concerts, Beaches/pools (6 attractions each), Nature, Shopping, Lake Maggiore (4 attractions each), Nightlife, Attractions (3 attractions each), Locarno, Culture/ Museums, Accommodation, Gastronomy (1 attraction each).

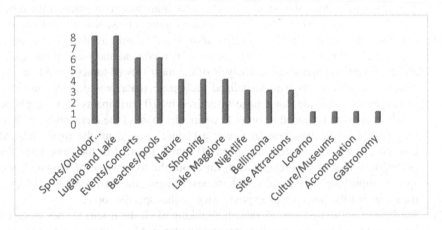

Fig. 2. Themes of most cited attractions

Most viewed contents (eye-tracking data analysis): The most visualized contents gathered from the heat-maps analysis resulted in the following 19 macro-themes (see Fig. 3), individuated thanks to heat-areas: Nature (100 visualizations), Sports/Outdoor Activities (47 vis.), Lugano and the Lake (39 vis.), Shopping (29 vis.), Site Attractions (28 vis.), Beaches/pools (27 vis.), Seasons (22 vis.), Nightlife (21 vis.), Culture/

Museums (vis.), Events/Concerts (18 vis.), Other (18 vis.), Gastronomy (15 vis.), Lake Maggiore (10 vis.), Locarno (10 vis.), Transports (9 vis.), Ascona (7 vis.), Accommodation (4 vis.), Mendrisiotto (3 vis.), Bellinzona (1 vis.).

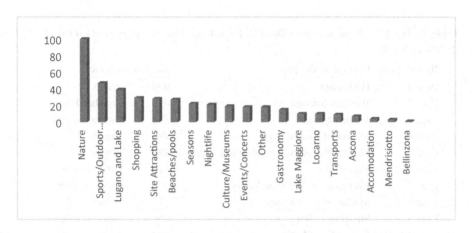

Fig. 3. Ranking of the most viewed contents

As part of the research, the same heat-areas were analyzed in terms of type of graphic elements. For the analysis, six types of graphic elements were considered: Picture, Picture with text, Text, Central text (that is, a main text –a title for example– presented at the centre of a page), Google maps tool, Google street view tool. The most viewed graphic elements resulted to be in order: Picture with text (no. 258), Text (86), Central text (66), Picture (54), Google maps tool (12), Google street view tool (5) (see Fig. 4).

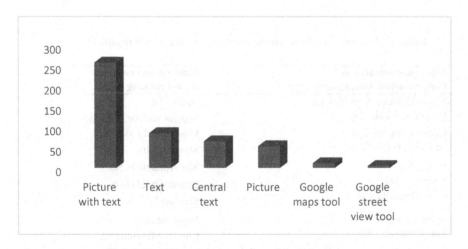

Fig. 4. Ranking of the most viewed graphic elements

Most Viewed Pages (DMO data): According to the Web Analytics data provided by the DMO under study, filtered about online sessions of users aged 18–24 coming from the same province of the Italian respondents area, the first 10 pages which received more sessions are showed in the following table (Table 1):

Table 1. Top 10 web pages of the official DMO website (filtered for the 18–24 segment, and a specific province)

ID web page	Content of the page	Sessions	Themes
Page 1	Homepage	906	Varies
Page 2	Weather forecast	891	Weather Forecast
Page 3	Tibetan bridge	532	Outdoor/sports
Page 4	Market of Como, Italy	496	Events
Page 5	Market of Como, Italy (German version)	399	Events
Page 6	Excursions	343	Outdoor/sports
Page 7	Excursion in Verzasca Valley	302	Outdoor/sports
Page 8	Market of Como, Italy	174	Events
Page 9	Sledging at Nara	159	Outdoor/sports
Page 10	Fair of San Martino	159	Events

4.2 A Comparison Between the Results Gathered from the Eye-Tracking Data vs Self-reported Attractions

From the eye-tracking analysis emerged that participants viewed mainly contents related to the theme "Nature" during their navigation (100 visualizations), while (see Table 2), after the free navigation participants reported mostly attractions related to the theme "Sports/Outdoor Activities", and specifically "Lugano and the Lake" (8 cited attractions each, occupying the first place in the ranking of the most cited attractions).

Table 2. A comparison between the eye-tracking data vs self-reported attractions

Most cited attractions (Self-reported Attractions)	Most viewed contents (Eye-Tracking data)
Sports/Outdoor Activities 1st	Nature 1st
Lugano and Lake 1st	Sports/Outdoor Activities 2nd
Events/Concerts 2nd	Lugano and Lake 3d
Beaches/pools 2nd	Shopping 4th
Nature 3rd	Site Attractions 5th
Shopping 3rd	Beaches/pools 6th
Lake Maggiore 3rd	Seasons 7th
Nightlife 4th	Nightlife 8th
Site Attractions 4th	Culture/Museums 9th
Locarno 5th	Events/Concerts 10th

The second most cited attraction was related to "Events/Concerts" and "Beaches and Pools" (6 attractions each). During navigation instead, contents related to this two themes were not ranked in a very high position in terms of visualized contents (respectively 27 and 18 contents, occupying 6th and 10th place in the ranking of most visualized contents).

At the third place in the ranking of the most cited attractions there are the ones related to the themes "Nature", "Shopping" and "Lake Maggiore" (4 attractions each). As mentioned before, during navigation contents related to "Nature" were the most visualized (100 visualizations) while "Shopping" occupies a quite high position (29 visualizations, occupying 4th place), and "Lake Maggiore" a quite low one (only 10 contents visualized, occupying 13th place). In the fourth position among the most cited attractions there are the ones related to the themes "Nightlife" and "Site Attractions". During navigation, contents related to "Nightlife" were visualized 21 times (occupying 8th position) while contents related to "Site Attractions" were visualized 28 times (occupying 5th position). All the other cited attractions were cited only once, all occupying the fifth position.

This result suggests that what participants looked at during navigation does not reflect exactly what they cited as preferred attraction. For example, even if participants viewed mainly contents related to nature, they cited more attractions related to sport/ outdoor and to the destination Lugano. However, even if not in the first position, among the most viewed themes we find as well sport/outdoor (2nd place) and Lugano and the Lake (3rd place), meaning that in both rankings these themes are significant. Attractions related to events and concerts are also cited often, but find little correspondence with the number of visualizations (only 18), meaning that despite the little number of visualized contents, teenagers were impressed by this type of attractions. This is the same case for the beaches and pools, which in the ranking of the most cited attractions are second, but recorded a relatively low number of visualizations. Therefore, it is possible to argue that, as confirmed also by previous studies the eye-tracking technique represents a valid aid in identifying the most relevant contents within a page, but this does not automatically means that what they look more is what they like the most.

Moreover, it is possible to sum up what appeared to be the most successful type of page layout for teenagers navigating a tourism related website. If we consider that the most viewed graphic elements are pictures with text, and the most viewed contents are related to "Nature", we can state that this combination could be the one that appeals the most teenagers. Even though, it should be more precise to include the most cited attractions: "Sports/outdoor" and "Lugano and the Lake". Including these data, the best possible layout should include pictures with text related to the themes "Nature", "Sports/Outdoor" and "Lugano and the Lake".

4.3 A Comparison Among Eye-Tracking, Web Analytics, and Self-declared Investigation

The following paragraph reports the results from a comparison among eye-tracking, web analytics, and self-declared investigation.

Table 3 reports the themes emerged from the top 10 web pages of the official DMO website (filtered for the 18–24 segment, and a specific province), and the top themes emerged from the eye-tracking and self-declared investigation.

Table 3. Summary table of most relevant themes across the three dataset

Most relevant themes for the teen segment	Self-reported (cited attractions)	Eye-tracking (viewed contents)	Web analytics (online sessions)
Sports/Outdoor activities	8	47	1336
Events/Concerts	6	18	1228

From the official DMO web statistics, the homepage is the page that receives the majority of sessions being the most popular page of the website. This is in line also with the results coming from the free navigation, where all participants visualized the homepage as all of them were forced to start from that page.

The second most viewed page according to the web analytics data, was the thematic page "weather forecasts". This theme doesn't appear in the ranking of most cited attractions and most visualized themes, and this probably due to the fact that weather conditions are normally checked only in the very short time before the visit to the destination, and don't represent attractions themselves.

Interestingly, the web analytics fata for the segment teen for a specific province of Italy, revealed that the third position is occupied by the "Tibetan Bridge" page (related to the theme of Outdoor/Sports). The sixth and seventh most popular pages are also related to the theme of Outdoor/Sports, namely the pages "Excursions" and "Excursion in Verzasca Valley". Therefore, the sessions counted for the Outdoor/Sports theme are 1336. As reported in Table 3, the presence of these pages among the most popular ones is in line with what participants declared to appreciate as a favourite attraction, and as well as with what people looked at during navigation.

In fourth, fifth and eighth position in the ranking of the most popular pages we find pages related to the "market of Como", which can be attributed to the theme "Events". The ninth position is also occupied by a page related to the same theme, namely the page "Fair of San Martino". Sessions for this theme reach a total of 1228. The theme "Events" is very popular in the self-declared attractions, although less in the ranking of most visualized themes during navigation.

Overall, it is possible to argue that there is a correspondence between some specific themes that people see during navigation, themes that people declare to be attracted by after navigation and themes belonging to the pages that received more sessions. Relating these results with the specific segment under study, it is possible to state that (Italian cross-border) teenagers visiting the destination website are attracted the most by sports/outdoor activities and events, which are the common top themes emerging from the three different sources.

5 Conclusions

The study compared the results from three different research approaches, namely: eye-tracking, web analytics, and self-declared investigation in order to gain an understanding of teenagers' preferences in terms of tourist attractions for a specific destination. The study identified two main types of preferred attractions themes: Sports/Outdoor Activities and Events/Concerts. These themes revealed to be the only ones appearing in the results of all the three approaches, while other themes were less or more relevant according to each research approach adopted. In fact, the study revealed certain correspondences in terms of preferred themes, but some results may seem contradictory. For example, even if participants mostly looked at themes related to the theme "nature", the majority of self-declared attractions belong to the theme "sports/outdoor", indicating that what users look at does not always reflect their preferences. This shows the importance of adopting a multi-source approach: if only one approach is used, possible biases may occur in identifying teenagers' online preferences. The research is not free from biases though. A major bias comes from the DMO data about online sessions. These data comes from teenagers of a specific city in Italy. Moreover, teenagers from other regions may have different preferences. Future research might consider to specify the nature of the online user, being it a local or a tourist. Furthermore, future research should also consider to enlarge the sample to other regions, and confront the results with other segment in order to better understand specific web navigation path.

References

Gidlöf, K., Holmberg, N., Sandberg, H.: The use of eye-tracking and retrospective interviews to study teenagers' exposure to online advertising. Vis. Commun. **11**(3), 329–345 (2012)

Gidlöf, K., Wallin, A., Dewhurst, R., Holmqvist, K.: Using eye tracking to trace a cognitive process: gaze behaviour during decision making in a natural environment. J. Eye Mov. Res. **6**(1), 3–14 (2013)

Kaplan, M.: Teenage Online Shopping Trends. http://www.practicalecommerce.com/articles/4073-Teenage-Online-Shopping-Trends. Accessed 20 June 2013

Khan, K., Locatis, C.: Searching through cyberspace: the effects of link display and link density on information retrieval from hypertext on the World Wide Web. J. Am. Soc. Inf. Sci. **49**(2), 176–182 (1998)

Lazonder, A.W., Biemans, H.J., Wopereis, I.G.: Differences between novice and experienced users in searching information on the World Wide Web. J. Am. Soc. Inf. Sci. 576–581 (2000)

Loranger, H., Nielsen, J.: Teenage Usability: Designing Teen-Targeted Websites. https://www.nngroup.com/articles/usability-of-websites-for-teenagers/. Accessed 4 Feb 2013

Marchiori, E., Cantoni, L.: Studying online contents navigation: a comparison between eye-tracking technique and self-reported investigation. In: Tussyadiah, I., Inversini, A. (eds.) Information and Communication Technologies in Tourism 2015, pp. 349–359. Springer, Cham (2015). doi:10.1007/978-3-319-14343-9_26

Méndez, J.H.: Travel 2.0 tools: User behavior analysis and modelling. Special emphasis on advertising effectiveness through the eye-tracking methodology. University of Granada (2015)

Nielsen, J., Pernice, K.: Eyetracking web usability. Pearson Education, Upper Saddle River (2010)

Noone, B., Robson, S.K.: Using Eye Tracking to Obtain a Deeper Understanding of What Drives Online Hotel Choice. Cornell University (2014)

Venkatraman, V., Payne, J., Huettel, S.A.: An overall probability of winning heuristic for complex risky decisions: Choice and eye fixation evidence. Organ. Behav. Hum. Decis. Process. **125**(2), 73–87 (2014)

Wan Adnan, W.A., Hassan, W.N.H., Abdullah, N., Taslim, J.: Eye tracking analysis of user behavior in online social networks. In: Ozok, A.A., Zaphiris, P. (eds.) OCSC 2013. LNCS, vol. 8029, pp. 113–119. Springer, Heidelberg (2013). doi:10.1007/978-3-642-39371-6_13

Wang, Y., Sparks, B.: An eye-tracking study of tourism photo stimuli: image characteristics and ethnicity. J. Travel Res. **55**(5), 588–602 (2014)

Yang, Y., Pan, B., Song, H.: Predicting hotel demand using destination marketing organization's web traffic data. J. Travel Res. **53**(4), 433–447 (2014)

Using Storytelling to Support the Education of Deaf Children: A Systematic Literature Review

Leandro Flórez Aristizábal[1,2(✉)], Sandra Cano[3], and César Collazos[1]

[1] IDIS Group, University of Cauca, Popayán, Colombia
lxexpxe@gmail.com, ccollazo@unicauca.edu.co
[2] GRINTIC Group, Institución Universitaria Antonio José Camacho,
Cali, Colombia
learistizabal@admon.uniajc.edu.co
[3] LIDIS Group, University of San Buenaventura, Cali, Colombia
sandra.cano@gmail.com

Abstract. Education of deaf children has always been a challenge due to communication problems, that's why different teaching and learning strategies must be taken into account in order to address language issues and make use of the visual input to overcome the loss of the auditory one. Storytelling is one of such strategies that's been proven to be effective in teaching and learning processes of hearing children. Therefore, a systematic literature review was conducted to identify how this technique has been used in the education of deaf children and how could interactive storytelling engage children with learning processes in different areas of knowledge. A total of 623 studies were found in different databases but just 24 of them were selected for this review.

Keywords: Storytelling · Deaf · Children · Sign language · Education · Learning · Systematic review

1 Introduction

Deaf children learn at different paces compared to their hearing peers [1] and this has aroused interest among researchers and teachers who are constantly looking for new and different ways to improve education processes of these children. As technology advances and teaching strategies changes, new tools can be implemented to support the education of people with disabilities. In this study, we want to know how a teaching strategy like storytelling has helped deaf children in their education and how the inclusion of ICT could improve these teaching and learning processes through interactive storytelling.

This paper is structured as follows. In Sect. 2 we give an overview about storytelling and how Human-Computer Interaction (HCI) is involved in interactive storytelling. In Sect. 3, the methodology to conduct the systematic review is presented. Section 4 shows the results obtained after data extraction and analysis. Finally, Sect. 5 concludes this study.

© Springer International Publishing AG 2017
A. Marcus and W. Wang (Eds.): DUXU 2017, Part III, LNCS 10290, pp. 371–382, 2017.
DOI: 10.1007/978-3-319-58640-3_26

2 Background

In this section, we present a short overview of storytelling, and how it can be enriched by means of technology and HCI. Moreover, education of deaf children is also introduced in this section.

2.1 Storytelling + HCI

Storytelling is known as a social and cultural activity of creating or sharing stories and it has lately being a topic of interest in fields like HCI and Artificial Intelligence (AI) [2, 3] Storytelling is pervasive in different aspects of children's life such as the development of skills in communication or to enforce the relationships with peers and adults [4]. In the field of education, storytelling has demonstrated to be a great resource to work in different areas like natural sciences [5], foreign language teaching [6], sign language [7, 8], programming [9] and literacy [10–14].

According to the National Storytelling Network (NSN) high-quality storytelling must be interactive [15] and nowadays technology provides new opportunities for children not just to have fun but also to learn. Interactive storytelling is an interdisciplinary field in which the humanities meet artificial intelligence [16] where stories are told by combining personal narratives with technology and this is essential in order to engage the new generation of digital natives [17]. Therefore, Human-Computer Interaction (HCI) plays a key role in the design and development of interactive environments for children, especially for those with disabilities who present specific problems and incorporate unusual forms of interaction [18].

2.2 Education of Deaf Children

The Salamanca statement [19] is a document that is informed by the principle of inclusion and proposes that education systems should be designed in order to consider the wide diversity of children and their unique characteristics, interest, abilities and learning needs [20]. Unfortunately, deaf children are facing difficulties in different areas of knowledge mainly due to the late acquisition of a first language which should be a sign language (SL). Some SL are legally recognized in national laws or constitutions, or are mentioned in the laws of different countries [21]. Children must be exposed to an accessible language during the first five years of age [22] and for deaf children it should be the SL used or accepted in their countries but unfortunately for some of them this language is not acquired properly at home due to 90% of them are born to non-deaf parents [22, 23] who do not use this language.

It is then clear that in order to acquire any kind of knowledge, it's necessary to have a proper communication channel and that's why a bilingual education should be adopted [24] where SL is seen as primary language in order to start developing skills in a second language (written language) and other areas like math. One of the main reasons deaf children don't finish higher education is poor literacy skills according to [25]. Literacy problems may affect the development of other skills and learning of other areas such as math and science [26] and this leaves deaf people in a disadvantage compared to their hearing peers.

Taking into account that sign language is the primary communication channel of deaf children, different educational strategies must be implemented in order guarantee the fundamental right to education for these children as stated in [19].

3   Research Method

This study was carried out by following Kitchenham and Charters [27] guidelines to perform a systematic literature review in software engineering. These guidelines define the procedures to be followed in order to identify and summarize existing data about a particular subject. In subsequent sections, the steps followed to perform the review are presented.

3.1   Research Questions

The main objective of this study is to answer the following research questions.

RQ1: How is storytelling being used to support education of deaf children?
RQ2: How could interactive storytelling support education of deaf children?

3.2   Data Sources and Search Strategies

We searched for papers that are written in English and Spanish. The search was made in electronic databases with very specific keywords and filtering criteria. The following electronic databases were used.

English search:

- IEEE Xplore (http://ieeexplore.ieee.org)
- ACM Digital library (http://dl.acm.org)
- SCOPUS (https://www.scopus.com/home.uri)
- Springer (http://link.springer.com)
- ProQuest (http://search.proquest.com)

Spanish search:

- ProQuest (http://search.proquest.com)
- Dialnet (https://dialnet.unirioja.es)
- Redalyc (http://www.redalyc.org)

The keywords to address the search in order to find relevant studies in English and answer the research question were: *Storytelling, deaf, children, learning or education, sign language*. The same words were used in Spanish: *Cuentos, niños, sordos, aprendizaje o educación, lengua de señas o lenguaje de señas*.

From this group of keywords, it is mandatory that the words *storytelling (cuentos)*, *deaf (sordos)* and at least one of the other ones are included in all the results, that is how we came up with the following strings in each of the databases:

IEEE Xplore. It has an advanced search that allows to find articles where the keywords are found just in the title and abstract. After applying a full string with all the words, we obtained more than 80000 articles irrelevant for the search, that is why we decided to perform individual searches were the words *storytelling* and *deaf* were combined with each one of the others, getting as a result that only three words (storytelling, deaf and children) were necessary to get the only relevant paper this database offers to help answer the research questions.

("Document Title":storytelling AND "Document Title":deaf AND "Document Title":children OR "Abstract":storytelling AND "Abstract":deaf AND "Abstract":children)

ACM Digital Library. It also has an advanced search where keywords can be found only in the title and abstract. The structure of the string is the same used in IEEE Xplore but with all the keywords included.

acmdlTitle:(+"storytelling" +deaf +(learning children education "sign language")) OR recordAbstract:(+"storytelling" +deaf +(learning children education "sign language"))

SCOPUS. It lets perform a search where the words can be found not just in the title and abstract but also in the keywords of the document. In this database all the words were included.

(TITLE-ABS-KEY (storytelling AND deaf) AND TITLE-ABS-KEY (learn* OR child* OR education* OR "sign language"))

Springer. It does not allow to find the keywords just in the title and abstract, instead, it performs the search finding the words in the whole document. Since Springer could offer relevant results in chapters of books, these ones were also included in the search.

storytelling AND deaf AND (learning OR children OR education OR "sign OR language")

ProQuest (English and Spanish). ProQuest was used to find papers in English and Spanish. The same structure of the string used in the previous databases was used for both searches.

(storytelling deaf) AND (children OR "sign language" OR education OR learning)

(cuentos sordos) AND (niños OR "lenguaje de señas" OR "lengua de señas" OR educación OR aprendizaje)

Dialnet. It does not have an advanced search where operators like AND/OR can be used. This is why the search had to be done using the 2 most important keywords in order to find enough results to be filtered by us.

cuentos sordos

Redalyc. It has a poor engine to perform searches, even though it is one of the most relevant databases for literature in Spanish, so we decided to perform the search using Google where we can filter a search by site and filetype. All the words could be used here.

cuentos sordos niños OR "lengua de señas" OR "lenguaje de señas" OR educación OR
aprendizaje site:redalyc.org filetype:pdf

3.3 Management of Studies and Inclusion/Exclusion Criteria

The exclusion criteria (EC) are all the reasons why some studies found are not included into the systematic review.

- EC 1: Document not available to download
- EC 2: Document not in English or Spanish
- EC 3: Document not related to storytelling and deaf people

On the other hand, the inclusion criteria (IC) show the factors to consider a paper as relevant to answer the research questions. In our case, there is only one reason to include a paper in the systematic review.

- IC: Document related to the use of storytelling with deaf people.

3.4 Data Extraction

We developed a template to register all the results given by each database. On this template, we were able to record relevant information of every paper such as: (a) Name of database, (b) String used, (c) Inclusion or exclusion criteria, (d) ID of paper, (e) Authors, (f) Paper Title, (g) Keywords, (h) DOI, (i) Year of publication, (j) Name of conference or journal where the study was published, (k) Type of publication. The search of this systematic review was performed in September 2016. We obtained 623 studies from all databases. Once the inclusion and exclusion criteria was applied, only 24 studies were selected for the review process. Table 1 shows detailed data about the number papers found on each database and relevant studies selected from them.

Table 1. Summary of search results

Database name	Search results	Duplicated papers	Relevant papers
IEEE Xplore	1	–	1
ACM	3	–	3
SCOPUS	14	5	6
Springer	269	9	1
ProQuest (English)	233	26	9
ProQuest (Spanish)	11	–	0
Dialnet	18	–	1
Redalyc	74	–	3
Total	**623**	**40**	**24**

4 Data Analysis and Results

In order to determine how storytelling is being used to support the education of deaf children, the selected papers were classified into different categories:

Skill. Research that clearly shows the support to a specific skill to be developed.
ICT. Research that makes use of any kind of technology to support learning.
Development. Research that proposes the development of a tool, app or platform to support learning.
Strategies/Activities. Research focused on presenting strategies or activities developed to support learning with or without ICT.

Figure 1 shows the number of papers that fitted in each category.

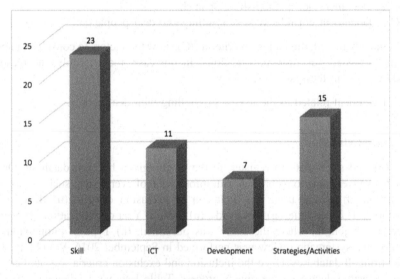

Fig. 1. Classification of articles

96% of the papers aimed to develop or strengthen a particular skill [S1–S20, S22–S24], 46% showed the use of ICT as a resource [S1–S5, S11, S18, S19, S21, S23, S24], 29% had an app, tool or platform as a result to support teaching/learning [S1–S5, S18, S21] and 62,5% presented activities or strategies as part of the educational process [S5, S6, S8–S17, S20, S22, S23]. Some papers matched more than 1 category.

The category *skill* was divided into 3 subcategories identified in the papers in order to know what are the target areas of knowledge.

Figure 2 shows that 65% of the researches aim to support literacy in deaf children skill [S1–S3, S5–S8, S10, S11, S14, S15, S17, S18, S22, S24], 26% sign language [S4, S5, S8, S11, S14, S19] and 43% narrative [S4, S9, S10, S12–S14, S16, S17, S20, S23].

From the strategies/activities category, we identified that 33% of the papers involved a collaborative work of children with peers [S5, S6, S8, S10, S15] (Fig. 3).

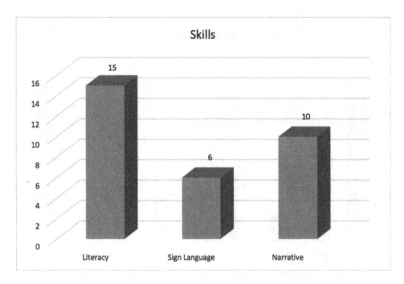

Fig. 2. Skills aimed to be developed or strengthened

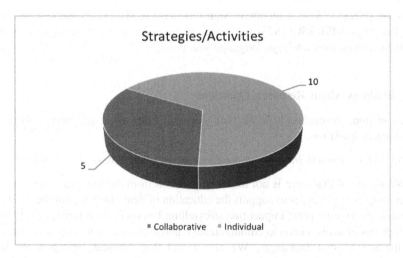

Fig. 3. Papers with collaborative or individual strategies/activities

Finally, we wanted to know which sign languages were used by users in the different researches in order to identify if these were used as primary communication channel (Fig. 4).

From all the papers, 33% of them did not mention the use of any sign language [S3, S6, S7, S10, S13, S18, S20, S21], while 29% made use of American Sign Language (ASL) [S1, S8, S9, S11, S14, S19, S22], 12,5% made use of Brazilian Sign Language (BSL) [S5, S8, S24] and 8% used Chilean Sign Language (ChSL) [S15, S16]. Arabian Sign Language (ArSL) [S2], Spanish Sign Language (SSL) [S4], Hong Kong Sign

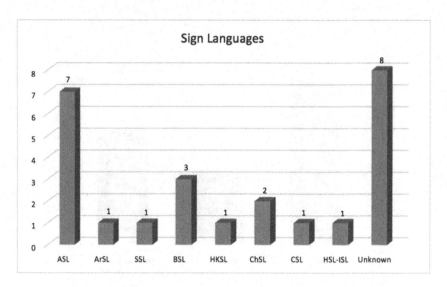

Fig. 4. Sign languages used as primary communication channel in researches

Language (HKSL) [S12], Colombian Sign Language (CSL) [S17], Hebrew and Israeli Sign Language (HSL-ISL) [S23] were each mentioned in one different paper. In some researches, more than one sign language was used.

4.1 Findings About Research Questions

In this section, we discuss how the data extracted from reviewed papers address our two research questions.

RQ1. *How is storytelling being used to support education of deaf children?*

We identified that there is not much information from the last five years about the use of storytelling in order to support the education of deaf children, but the 24 studies reviewed showed the great impact that storytelling has on deaf children, mainly in the development of skills related to communication and language such as literacy, narrative and the use of sign languages. We also found that different strategies are being implemented in the classroom in order to address this issues related to communication and that almost half of the studies showed the implementation of technology not just to be used in the classroom, but also at home. Finally, some studies show the use of collaborative strategies with great results.

RQ2. *How could interactive storytelling support education of deaf children?*

The studies reviewed showed that the inclusion of ICT engages children and allow them to take the education process outside the classroom. Through interactive story-telling, children will not be restricted to a fixed story, instead, they will be direct authors of it and this could improve not just skills like sign language, literacy and narrative but also imagination. Unfortunately, there is even less efforts made in order to use interactive storytelling, since just a small part of the reviewed papers show the inclusion of interactive stories, but this is also an opportunity to propose a methodology that could motivate researchers to start working towards the inclusion of deaf children in society through education.

5 Conclusions and Future Work

We have conducted a systematic review where 24 out of 623 papers were selected to answer the research questions. After data extraction and analysis, we can determine that skills related to language and communication are the most common among researches that involve the use of storytelling as an educational resource for deaf children. Storytelling has been used for a long time with this community but according to the last five years there is not much research around the use of this strategy to educate deaf people and we think there should be made more efforts taking into account that new technologies such as smartphones and tablets open a new set of opportunities to impact positively in the lives of these children through a well-known strategy such as storytelling.

Nowadays, deaf children are also considered digital natives and this could make interactive storytelling an even more effective strategy for them, but unfortunately, we noticed that there is not an established methodology to make use of interactive storytelling through the use of ICT.

According to the results of this study, for future work we identified a great opportunity to propose a methodology to design interactive storytelling where researchers can integrate technology and education in order to remove barriers in the way of deaf children by letting them tell their own stories. The findings of this systematic review will be enhanced by including studies where interactive storytelling supports education in general without restricting the search to just deaf children.

Appendix: Papers Included in the Review

S1. M. Malzkuhn and M. Herzig, "Bilingual Storybook App Designed for Deaf Children Based on Research Principles," in Interaction Design and Children, 2013, pp. 499–502.

S2. A. Alsumait, M. Faisal, and S. Banian, "Improving Literacy for Deaf Arab Children Using Interactive Storytelling," in iiWAS '15 Proceedings of the 17th International Conference on Information Integration and Web-based Applications & Services, 2015, p. 5.

S3. K. Hart and R. Ahmed, "Using Demibooks Composer to Create Remedial Learning Apps for the Profoundly Deaf," in Proceedings of the 13th International Conference on Interaction Design and Children, 2013, pp. 573–576.

S4. S. Peix Cruz, "Carambuco : cuentos y actividades en lengua de signos," Boletín de la asociación andaluza de bibliotecarios, no. 107, pp. 50–59, 2014.

S5. C. Guimarães, D.R. Antunes, L.S. García, A.L. Pires Guedes, and S. Fernandes, "Conceptual meta-environment for deaf children literacy challenge: How to design effective artifacts for bilingualism construction," Proceedings - International Conference on Research Challenges in Information Science, p. 12, 2012.

S6. H.P. Karasu, "Group Activities for Literacy Preparation during the Pre-School Period of Hearing-Impaired Children," Education and Science, vol. 39, no. 173, pp. 297–312, 2014.

S7. L.K. Entwisle, K. Brouwer, E. Hanson, and J. Messersmith, "A Systematic Review of Emergent Literacy Interventions for Preschool- Age Children With Cochlear Implants," Contemporary Issues in Communication Science and Disorders, vol. 43, pp. 64–76, 2016.

S8. D. Chen Pichler, J.A. Hochgesang, D. Lillo-Martin, R. Müller de Quadros, and W. Reynolds, "Best Practices for Building a Bimodal/Bilingual Child Language Corpus," Sign Language Studies, no. January, pp. 361–388, 2016.

S9. J.S. Beal-Alvarez and J.W. Trussell, "Depicting Verbs and Constructed Action: Necessary Narrative Components in Deaf Adults' Storybook Renditions," Sign Language Studies, pp. 5–29, 2015.

S10. L. a Pakulski and J.N. Kaderavek, "Reading intervention to improve narrative production, narrative comprehension, and motivation and interest of children with hearing loss," The Volta Review, vol. 112, no. 2, pp. 87–112, 2012.

S11. D. Golos and A. Moses, "Supplementing an Educational Video Series with Video-Related Classroom Activities and Materials," Sign Language Studies, no. January, pp. 103–125, 2016.

S12. F. Sze, G. Tang, T. Lau, E. Lam, and C. Yiu, "The development of discourse referencing in Cantoneseof deaf/hard-of-hearing children.," Journal of child language, vol. 42, pp. 351–393, 2015.

S13. A.N. Asad, L. Hand, L. Fairgray, and S.C. Purdy, "The use of dynamic assessment to evaluate narrative language learning in children with hearing loss: Three case studies," Child Language Teaching and Therapy, vol. 29, no. 3, pp. 319–342, 2013.

S14. K. Snoddon, "Ways of taking from books in ASL book sharing," Sign Language Studies, vol. 14, no. 3, pp. 338–359, 2014.

S15. M.R. Lissi, K. Svartholm, and M. González, "El Enfoque Bilingüe en la Educación de Sordos : sus implicancias para la enseñanza y aprendizaje de la lengua escrita," Estudios Pedagógicos, vol. 38, no. 2, pp. 299–320, 2012.

S16. X. Acuña Robertson, D. Adamo Quintela, I. Cabrera Ramírez, and M.R. Lissi, "Estudio descriptivo del desarrollo de la competencia narrativa en lengua de señas chilena," Onomázein, vol. 26, pp. 193–219, 2012.

S17. L.S. Prieto Soriano, "La Pedagogía por Proyectos de Aula: una alternativa para enseñar castellano escrito a niños y niñas de primer ciclo," Educação & Realidade, vol. 41, no. 3, pp. 789–806, 2016.

S18. P. Bottoni, D. Capuano, M. de Marsico, and A. Labella, "DELE framework: An innovative sight on didactics for deaf people," Journal of E-Learning and Knowledge Society, vol. 8, no. 3, pp. 165–174, 2012.

S19. J.S. Beal-Alvarez and S.G. Huston, "Emerging Evidence for Instructional Practice: Repeated Viewings of Sign Language Models," Communication Disorders Quarterly, vol. 35, no. 2, pp. 93–102, 2013.

S20. T. Boons, L. De Raeve, M. Langereis, L. Peeraer, J. Wouters, and A. van Wieringen, "Narrative spoken language skills in severely hearing impaired school-aged children with cochlear implants," Research in Developmental Disabilities, vol. 34, no. 11, pp. 3833–3846, 2013.

S21. P. Bottoni, F. Borgia, D. Buccarella, D. Capuano, M. De Marsico, and A. Labella, "Stories and signs in an e-learning environment for deaf people," Universal Access in the Information Society, vol. 12, no. 4, pp. 369–386, 2013.

S22. B.K. Strassman and K.O'Dell, "Using open captions to revise writing in digital stories composed by D/deaf and hard of hearing students," American Annals of the Deaf, vol. 157, no. 4, pp. 340–357, 2012.

S23. S. Eden, "Virtual intervention to improve storytelling ability among deaf and hard-of-hearing children," European Journal of Special Needs Education, vol. 29, no. 3, pp. 370–386, 2014.

S24. R.I. Busarello, V.R. Ulbricht, P. Bieging, and V. Villarouco, "Deaf students and comic hypermedia: Proposal of accessible learning object," Lecture Notes in Computer Science (including subseries Lecture Notes in Artificial Intelligence and Lecture Notes in Bioinformatics), vol. 8011 LNCS, no. PART 3, pp. 133–142, 2013.

References

1. Bueno, F.J., Alonso, M.G., del Castillo, J.R.F.: Assisting lecturers to adapt e-learning content for deaf students. ACM SIGCSE Bull. **39**, 335 (2007)

2. Riggs, S.: "Kanju": integrating HCI to tell better stories in immersive environments. In: Proceeding SIGGRAPH International Conference on Computer Graphics and Interactive Techniques, Anaheim (2016)

3. Riedl, M.O.: Computational narrative intelligence: a human-centered goal for artificial intelligence. In: CHI 2016 Workshop on Human-Centered Machine Learning, 5 p. (2016)

4. Garzotto, F., Paolini, P., Sabiescu, A.: Interactive storytelling for children. In: Proceedings of the 9th International Conference on Interaction Design and Children IDC 2010, vol. 2, p. 356 (2010)

5. Pérez, D., Pérez, A.I., Sánchez, R.: El cuento como recurso didáctico. 3Ciencias 1–29 (2013)

6. Reyes, A., Pich, E., García, M.D.: Digital storytelling as a pedagogical tool within a didactic sequence in foreign language teaching. Digit. Educ. Rev. 1–18 (2012)

7. Peix Cruz, S.: Carambuco: cuentos y actividades en lengua de signos. Bol. Asoc. Andaluza Bibliotecarios 50–59 (2014)

8. Beal-Alvarez, J.S., Huston, S.G.: Emerging evidence for instructional practice: repeated viewings of sign language models. Commun. Disord. Q. **35**, 93–102 (2013)

9. Burke, Q., Kafai, Y.B.: Programming & storytelling: opportunities for learning about coding & composition. In: Proceedings of the 9th International Conference on Interaction Design and Children - IDC 2010, p. 348 (2010)

10. Moreno de León, T.A., Rangel, L., De León, E.: Promoviendo el desarrollo de la competencia lectora a través de cuentos con imágenes sin palabras en preescolar. Revista Internacional de Educación Preescolar e Infantil **2**(1), 49–64 (2016)
11. Malzkuhn, M., Herzig, M.: Bilingual storybook app designed for deaf children based on research principles. In: Interaction Design and Children, pp. 499–502 (2013)
12. Alsumait, A., Faisal, M., Banian, S.: Improving literacy for deaf arab children using interactive storytelling. In: iiWAS 2015 Proceedings of the 17th International Conference on Information Integration and Web-based Applications & Services, Bruselas, p. 5 (2015)
13. Lissi, M.R., Svartholm, K., González, M.: El Enfoque Bilingüe en la Educación de Sordos: sus implicancias para la enseñanza y aprendizaje de la lengua escrita. Estudios Pedagógicos **38**, 299–320 (2012)
14. Prieto Soriano, L.S.: La Pedagogía por Proyectos de Aula: una alternativa para enseñar castellano escrito a niños y niñas de primer ciclo. Educação Realidade **41**, 789–806 (2016)
15. National Storytelling Network: What is Storytelling? http://www.storynet.org/resources/whatisstorytelling.html
16. Koenitz, H.: Interactive storytelling paradigms and representations: a humanities-based perspective. In: Nakatsu, R., Rauterberg, M., Ciancarini, P. (eds.) Handbook of Digital Games and Entertainment Technologies, pp. 361–375. Springer, Singapore (2017). doi:10.1007/978-981-4560-50-4_58
17. Alsumait, A., Al-Musawi, Z.S.: Creative and innovative e-learning using interactive storytelling. Int. J. Pervasive Comput. Commun. **9**, 209–226 (2013)
18. Bottoni, P., Borgia, F., Buccarella, D., Capuano, D., De Marsico, M., Labella, A.: Stories and signs in an e-learning environment for deaf people. Univ. Access Inf. Soc. **12**, 369–386 (2013)
19. Nations, U.: The Salamanca Statement and Framework for Action on Special Needs Education. Salamanca (1994)
20. Domínguez, A.: Educación para la inclusión de alumnos sordos. Revista Latinoamericana de Educación Inclusiva **3**, 45–61 (2008)
21. World Federation of the Deaf: Sign Language. https://wfdeaf.org/human-rights/crpd/sign-language
22. Mellon, N.K., Niparko, J.K., Rathmann, C., Mathur, G., Humphries, T., Napoli, D.J., Handley, T., Scambler, S., Lantos, J.D.: Should all deaf children learn sign language? Pediatrics **136**, 170–176 (2015)
23. Guimarães, C., Pereira, M.H.R., Fernandes, S.: A framework to inform design of learning objects for teaching written Portuguese (2nd Language) to deaf children via sign language (1st Language). In: Proceedings of the Annual Hawaii International Conference on System Sciences, pp. 2–10 (2015)
24. World Federation of the Deaf: Bilingualism as a basic human right for deaf children in education. https://wfdeaf.org/news/bilingualism-as-a-basic-human-right-for-deaf-children-in-education
25. Bueno, F.J., Alonso, M.G., del Castillo, J.R.F.: Assisting lecturers to adapt e-learning content for deaf students. In: ITiCSE 2007 Proceedings of the 12th Annual SIGCSE Conference on Innovation and Technology in Computer Science Education, Dundee, pp. 335–335 (2007)
26. Michaud, L., McCoy, K.: An intelligent tutoring system for deaf learners of written English. In: Proceedings of the Fourth International ACM Conference on Assistive Technologies, Arlington, pp. 92–100 (2000)
27. Kitchenham, B., Charters, S.: Guidelines for performing systematic literature reviews in software engineering. EBSE Technical report Software Engineering Group, School of Computer Science and Mathematics Keele University (2007)

Research on Online Education Products Designed for Chinese Young Women's Interest Development

Xuan Li[(⊠)], Jingya Zhang, Qijun Chen, Nan Wang, and Yi Yang

Baidu, Beijing, People's Republic of China
{lixuan03,zhangjingya02,chenqijun,
wangnan01,yangyi01}@baidu.com

Abstract. Among Chinese netizens, young women account for a relatively high percentage and become active users. As living standard improves, their focus have changed from the basic needs of life to the improvement of the quality of life and happiness, especially spending a lot of time on interest developing. Some Internet giants and many online educational institutions have paid attention to it, and released a number of online education products for young women to develop interests. In this research, we defined "Young women" in China and "Interest Developing" according to available data. We performed a detailed analysis in the group of "young women", including their demographic characteristics, living styles, needs on interest developing, and specific learning processes. Then we took Baidu's product for young women as an example, in comparison with other products on the Chinese market, to explore the design concepts, design style and operational activities of online interest-developing products. Finally, we summarized the strengths and weakness of existing products, and see what this industry is really achieving or how it's trending. This research hopes to help design interest-developing products for Chinese young women, and even.

Keywords: Online education · Interest development · Chinese young women · Product design · Baidu Nuomi

1 Introduction

In China's Internet report, among Chinese netizens, young women account for a relatively high percentage and become active users (The age structure of internet users in China as shown in graph 1). More than 73% of the female have an undergraduate degree, with good educational background [1]. Young women are 18–35 years old women with characteristics of intellectual, spiritual independent and freedom. The women's lifetime is as follows: childhood, primary and middle school period, College student, taking up an occupation, being a wife and being a mother, children independence and the retirement life in the later years. While young women may be at the stage of college student, employment, or being a wife (Blackbody as shown in graph 2). They have a deep love for life and family, so in addition to work and study, approximately 80% young women spend a lot of time on doing things they love and

© Springer International Publishing AG 2017
A. Marcus and W. Wang (Eds.): DUXU 2017, Part III, LNCS 10290, pp. 383–392, 2017.
DOI: 10.1007/978-3-319-58640-3_27

experiencing life [2]. Many young women choose to develop interest based on their hobbies. Interest refers to the individual's tendency of the attitude, emotions and idea to a particular thing, activity. Interest developing is the process of forming interest. Any interest developing experiences emotional satisfaction in obtaining knowledge of it and participating in related activities. Interest development is crucial to improving of the quality of life, experiencing the beauty of life and living a more colorful life. But time become a sore point for young women to develop interest because of works and study taking up too much time (Figs. 1 and 2).

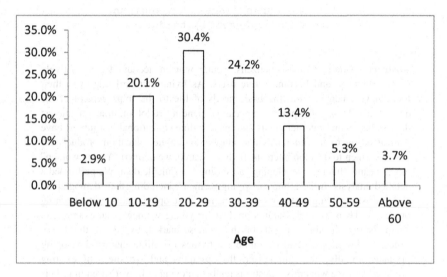

Fig. 1. The age structure of internet users in China

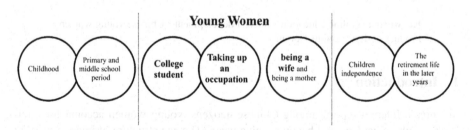

Fig. 2. Graph 2 the women's lifetime

Fortunately, this is a society with internet, human can get what they want on the Internet at any time any place because of development of online education. In China, according to the way of the resources operation of platforms, online education's product forms mainly include B2B2C platform, B2C service, assessment tools and online Internet schools [3]. Apart from the pure online form, the combination of online and offline gradually become a new trend, such as O2O pattern, and Nuomi education of Baidu is a notable example. It is undeniable that K-12 students' course learning content and vocational training of adult in online education are enormous. But some Internet giants and many online educational institutions have paid attention to young women and their need, and released a number of online education products for young women to develop interests.

2   Young Women's Interest Developing

2.1   The Characteristics of Young Women's Interest Developing

Women in different stages have different roles, and interest points and the process of interest developing change correspondingly. For young women, first of all, they can do whatever they want to do and learn anything. Before, because of the restriction of money and decision-making ability, parents often make a decision for them, which is possibly inconsistent with their interest points. Secondly, the realistic utility of young women's interest development is weak, and what they want is to experience a variety of activities to make their life more exciting. Thirdly, young women also want to make friends by developing interest and get a better interpersonal relationship. It is a wonderful life that your friends have common interests with you. Fourthly, many young women still hope to develop interest to their own strong point and highlight, and eventually it is beneficial to their work and other areas of life. Last but not least, because the computer and network are essential for young women and their time is relatively not so easy, many young women will choose online or the combination of on-line and off-line to learn.

2.2   The Interest of Young Women

Based on our previous research as well as the existing data, we divide species of interest into seven: literature and art, entertainment, life skills, life emotion, health, maternal-baby and parent-offspring, financial investment (as shown in Table 1). Literature and art has been popular with all ages, especially the instruments. Recently years, Chinese Classics, based on various schools of thought in the Pre-Qin and the essence of culture of Chinese different historical periods, is certainly growing in popularity. The main group of the entertainment activities is young people. Life skills make life more refinement, enrichment and simpleness, which attract the attention of adults. Life emotion, maternal-baby and parent-offspring are the focus of people who have a family or lover. Human wouldn't lose concern on health at any time and fitness is a new trend in the 21th century. The types of sports are various and 55.4% of women choose running [4]. From 2012, with the gradual implementation of a series of national financial policies, it opens up a broader development space for the investment banking market. Financial investment is sought after by young and middle-aged people.

For the above-mentioned information, it is not difficult to find that young women have wide-ranged interests and their interest are mainly distributed in literature and art,

Table 1. The classification of interest

Literature and art	Entertainment	Life skills	Life emotion	Health	Maternal-baby and parent-offspring	Financial investment
China studies	Travel	Gastronomy	Love and marriage	Fitness	Pregnancy	Finance
Literature	Constellation	Roasting	Parent-child communication	Health care	Early education	Fund
Painting	Tarot	Mixed drink/coffee	Family relationships	Ball games	Child care	Stock
Photography	Magic cube	Fashion beauty		Yoga	Parent education	Futures
Calligraphy	Animation	Home decoration		Martial arts	Developmental psychology	Insurance
Chess	Online game	Handwork DIY				Heavy metal
Music	Automobile	Pet				
Dance		Green plants				
Robot/ programming		Life tips				
		Social etiquette				

entertainment, health and life skills. Some new words to describe young women, such as "artistic female youth", "secondary yuan girl", "life Daren" and so on, also reflect it.

2.3   The Process of Young Women's Interest Developing

Taking into account our previous studies and other related materials, the process of young women's interest development is as follows: finding potential interest, experiencing an interest activity and enhancing individuals' capability. (as shown in graph 3). Next, we take the guitar as an example to specify the process. Firstly, young women can find potential interest in some circumstances, for example, when they look a movie that leading man like play guitar; Wechat subscription or Big V Weibo push an article that depicts guitar as very interesting; some people in online interest community make friends because of liking guitar; or their friend become to learn guitar. These can attract their attention on guitar and want to further know it. Based on the knowledge of guitar, young women hope to find some way to experience it. At the very beginning, they will find some experience courses on a number of platforms, such as Nuomi education. After experience guitar, they will confirm if they really like it and are ready to spend more time and money on it. Further systematic study is important to enhance individuals' capability of play guitar. In the last two stages, people need to make a purchasing decision. Before making decision, young women will go through the two stages of preliminary screening and quality identification. On the stage of preliminary screening, based on the feature of interest itself and their time and other information, young women choose study way (online, offline or the combination of online and offline) and screen several alternative learning institute. When identifying quality, they appraise learning organization on account of course duration, instructor, score and related factors about institution. Of course, many young women may just arrive at second path, and they just want to experience an interest activity and touch more thing. Experiencing an interest activity itself is an exciting thing for young women (Fig. 3).

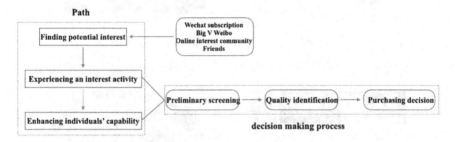

Fig. 3. The process of young women's interest developing

2.4   Product Analysis- Baidu Nuomi as Example

As mentioned before, some Internet giants and many online educational institutions have paid attention to the trend of interest development. We take Baidu Nuomi for case study to see how to design products for these young women.

Baidu Nuomi is an online platform providing offline local life service, including food, movies, entertainment, beauty and so on. What users do on Nuomi, especially on the mobile side (APP for IOS & Android), is about more relaxing life issues. Further more, the main and active users of Nuomi are young women aged 18 to 35, who are spending a lot of time on interest development. Considering these features, the new "Learning Channel" of Baidu Nuomi APP (hereinafter referred to as Nuomi Learning) is improving its product to meet the users' needs.

2.5   Product Concept

From the very beginning, what to show on the home page is based on what users want to see. When a young woman opens Nuomi Learning, she is probably trying to find some interesting courses, but doesn't know which fits herself. Therefore, the target of home page is to help users to find out their existing or potential interests.

To show the interesting factors of a course on home page is not so easy. Some other products concerning interest development are also making efforts to it. For example, Dazhongdianping shows interest developing courses by thematic activities [5]. Mianbaolieren highlights the joy of course by entertaining decoration [6].

Dazhongdianping   Mianbaolieren

Above may be some of good patterns to arouse users' interests. For Nuomi Learning, we believe that there could be something more to do. First, we confirmed by research as discussed before that users would like to seek out their interest on home page. So we plan to show contents of good quality instead of group-buying courses. It is to say, we are not going to be an online shop that pushes customers to decide what to buy and buy it immediately. Instead, we are going to act as a guide that gives our users some tips and recommendations for a particular area of interest development. Next, we need to consider how to be a good guide. As young women wandering around home page of Nuomi Learning, they are probably green hands and need someone experienced to show them around. Thus, a talent or expert, or what we call "Da Ren", in some area by your side may be a good idea. This Da Ren tells you more information about what the area is, what you could get from it, who may be suitable for it, or how you get started. For example, there may be some articles discussing the effect of doing yoga, or strategy of learning to play an instrument. Further more, a better guide could be talking to you as a human being. AI (Artificial Intelligence) may be a solution to it. We are trying to put methods of AI into practice on Nuomi learning.

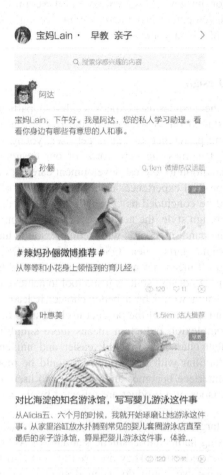

(Part of) New Conceptual Design of Nuomi Learning

As we can see on the new conceptual design of Nuomi Learning home page, there is no longer showing course name and price simply. Instead, there are articles of experiences or recommendations. In fact, here we find the 3 most important factors affecting users when seeking their new interest. That is, a particular sort of interest development, the quality of it and the distance between the user and the location where she can take courses. To recommend a particular sort of interest development that the user may be interested in, we push the articles to her based on what she had chosen. Then we try to show the quality of the relevant courses not only by comments to a particular course, but also by articles of experiences or recommendations at a higher level. Users care about the distance a lot, because they are not just wandering around an online platform like Nuomi Learning. They want to find something to learn offline in an actual place and take courses to improve themselves actually. Within 3 km may be a suitable distance. So the "Da Ren" showing on one users' home page must be nearby her, not far more than 3 km. Also, in the upper right corner of the article we push to her, there shows the exact distance.

All in all, it is a try for our new conceptual design of Nuomi Learning home page. We try to make interest development easier and more interesting from the beginning, to meet the growing needs of China young women.

2.6 User Experience Design

After information design, here comes user experience design, particularly at the level of surface. Before getting started on visual design, the overall design style should be defined. It depends on the preference of our target user, young women. Obviously, "young" and "feminine" becomes the key words of our design style. Besides, the young women who pay attention to interest development care a lot their living quality, so as the high quality of product experience. Therefore, the DNA of visual design style of Nuomi Learning could be concluded as "young", "feminine" and "high-quality".

Defining the overall design style, the new design plan of Nuomi Learning changes in two aspects. On the one hand, it accords with "complexion reduction", a new trend in mobile design. This trend starts when iOS6 upgraded to iOS7, replacing skeuomorphism with flat design. It means no need any more to imitate the real items when designing mobile products. As design style is just a tool to achieve the ultimate goal of being easy to use, flat design would be a better choice. It leads users to pay more attention to the content and function of the product itself, instead of how exquisite it is from the appearance. Complexion reduction means more simplified interface color, larger and more prominent characters in bold, easier and universal icon. As users getting more and more familiar with the product, it could be modified gradually to simplification. Then the interface becomes anonymous, and users focus on functional experience. The characteristics of a product are reflected by the content itself, not the interfacial design.

Young women, the target users of Nuomi Learning, are active users of most mobile APPs. So their using habits and aesthetic standard of APPs are finally shaped by the trend of complexion reduction. They are used to, and also love, the clean and simple design. That is what we could do when designing for the new edition of Nuomi Learning. For example, in the previous edition, we used card type design. The problem is that the whole page is divided into different parts and looks a bit complex. This kind of design is not easy for user to find the information he wants. So we broke through the cards and made the structure simple. Also, we leave more blank, keeping elements away from others. It means putting the key point on the Golden Section and leaving blank on other sections, so that users will not be distracted from the main information.

On the other hand, we try to design delicate edition for privileged (VIP) business users, despite the new trend of Flat Design. The merchants that provide offline interest development courses hope to attract more customers from online users, and Material Design meets the users' needs of quality. For example, pink is the dominant hue of Nuomi as women prefer feminine and warm color. But in this privileged edition, we use black as the interface color. Black tells the feeling of the high quality of a product. Also, users love gold when talking in high level. So we highlight the important information in the effect of gold plating. In this way, the interface looks more valuable.

As we found out that young women cares a lot the high quality of product experience especially when concerning interest development, this privileged edition is totally custom-built for them.

(Part of) Privileged Edition of Nuomi Learning

3 Summary and Prospect

To conclude, first of all, young women's interest developing is to experience life, grow up and make friends, and their choices depend on themselves and choosing online or the combination of on-line and off-line to learn. Second, they have wide-ranged interests and their interest are mainly distributed in literature and art, entertainment, health and life skills. Third, the process of young women's interest development is as follows: finding potential interest, experiencing an interest activity and enhancing individuals' capability. Before making decision, young women will go through the two stages of preliminary screening and quality identification. Last but not least, we take Baidu Nuomi for case study to see how to design products for these young women from product concept and user experience design.

Based on the important role of women in the economic growth, a new word is created as "she economy". In the contribution of mobile terminal to Internet traffic, female users become huge groups and they get wide attention from Internet giants and many online institutions. There are more and more products designed only for meeting women's need in many fields in China, such as meiyou, meilishuo, weimi and so on. Some suggestions were given to design products only for young women in this article, for example the DNA of visual design style of Nuomi Learning could be concluded as "young", "feminine" and "high-quality",and the recommendations of "Da Ren" to help young women find what they want. We hope that the paper can help design interest-developing products and other products for Chinese young women, and even all other potential groups of users in some way. Of course, we also have many deficiencies and will learn more knowledge for improving our products.

References

1. The statistical analysis report of development condition of China Internet network. http://www.cnnic.net.cn/hlwfzyj/hlwxzbg/hlwtjbg/201608/P020160803367337470363.pdf
2. QQ big data: the report of Chinese interest. http://www.techweb.com.cn/news/2016-09-09/2390397.shtml
3. Chinese Internet learning white paper. http://www.360doc.com/content/16/0321/17/1609415_544089792.shtml
4. Chinese women's digital fashion users white paper – lifestyle. http://www.199it.com/archives/435982.html
5. Interface of Dazhongdianping Learning. http://www.dianping.com/events/m/index.htm
6. Interface of Mianbaolieren. https://itunes.apple.com/cn/app/mian-bao-lu-xing-you-ji-gong/id521964741?mt=8

Technology as an Extension of the Self: Socialising Through Technology for Young People with Autism

Lye Ee Ng[(✉)]

Victoria University, Melbourne, Australia
lye.ng2@live.vu.edu.au

Abstract. Technology has a profound impact on the well-being of young people with autism. Through technology, they are able to socialise, learn and gain sensory relief, creating positive communication experiences and self-conceptions. Using qualitative participatory methods, this research illustrates how The Lab, a technology club for young people with autism, enables individuals on the spectrum to socialise beyond the perceived limitations of their disability through the use of technology. The findings of this research suggest that technology can provide young people with the avenue to learn, practice and define their own sociality, defying the medicalised notion of autism.

Keywords: Autism · Technology · Video ethnography · Online participatory ethnography · Socialisation

1 Introduction

"all technologies are extensions of our physical and nervous systems... Any extension, whether of skin, hand, or foot, affects the whole psychic and social complex." – McLuhan (1964), p. 4 & 90

The well-being of individuals with autism has been closely linked to technology. From a medical perspective where disablement for individuals with autism is in part characterised by the inability to communicate and socialise, the use of technology is linked to the notion of the cyborg (APA 2013; Campbell 2009). Drawing from Haraway's (1999, p. 272) 'cyborg manifesto' where she critiques that humans have become cyborgs, a "hybrid of machine and organism" that condenses the "image of both imagination and material reality", disability scholars such as Campbell (2001, 2009) and Garland-Thompson (2015) argue that the use of technology by disabled persons is a way of internalising ableism to create the "perfect body". In Foucault's term, 'technologies of self':

"Permit individuals to effect by their own means, or with the help of others, a certain number of operations on their own bodies and souls, thoughts, conduct, and way of being, so as to transform themselves in order to attain a certain state of happiness, purity, wisdom, perfection, or immortality." (Foucault et al. 1988, p. 166).

© Springer International Publishing AG 2017
A. Marcus and W. Wang (Eds.): DUXU 2017, Part III, LNCS 10290, pp. 393–402, 2017.
DOI: 10.1007/978-3-319-58640-3_28

A physically disabled person may, for example, require prosthetics to help them gain the ability to walk or perform specific labour – attaining a "state of happiness" in accordance to the rules laid out by our ableist society. In the case of autism, assistive-technologies such as visual learning tools aim at helping individuals with autism learn communicative, speech and social skills. In other words, the use of technology from this perspective hopes to compensate for autistic behaviours. The medical model views impairments and unusual behaviours such as those exhibited by individuals on the autism spectrum as deficits (Baron-Cohen 2002) – assuming the existence of the "perfect body" and viewing technology as a viable means for achieving this state of being. The role of technology then is to be applied and used in a directive way, similar to how perceived within education (i.e. as a tool for learning - see Sect. 4.1).

On the contrary, from a social constructionist perspective, disability is seen as a social construct where ideologies, governance and policies contribute to the disablement of people rather than their impairments. The use of assistive-technology has sometimes been regarded as a fallacious argument for improving the lives of these individuals. Instead, it strengthens the ableist rhetoric, "a set of assumptions (conscious or unconscious) and practices (e.g. use of technology) that promote the differential or unequal treatment of people because of actual or presumed disabilities" (Campbell 2009, p. 4). Nonetheless, disability scholars admit that access to technologies for people with disabilities is still important as it has the potential to incorporate inclusion and "create wide new vistas for civic engagement, education, employment, and social interaction" (Jaeger 2012, p. 33). Within the social constructionist perspective, people with impairments or unusual behaviours are disabled by the ableist culture produced and reinforced by the medical paradigm. Technology in this instance is adapted and used as a form of resistance or communication rather than compensation.

While these two perspectives seem to present polarising arguments, they demonstrate the importance of technology to people with disabilities. They reveal that impairments affect the lives of people in both tangible and intangible ways because it creates inconvenience perpetuated by discrimination. While sociality, referring to "the social processes through which [individuals] develop an awareness of social norms and values and achieve a distinct sense of self", is a constructed view, the discrimination and stigma faced by young people with autism is real and affects their state of well-being (Giddens and Sutton 2014, p. 69).

Therefore, there is a need to address both the immediate and practical means of relieving individuals with disability from discrimination while at the same time, enabling them to progressively change the disability rhetoric through the use of technology to improve their well-being now and in the future.

In this paper, I will be using the case study of The Lab, a technology club for young people with autism, to illustrate how the use of technology can enable them to socialise beyond the perceived limitations of their disability.

2   The Lab and the Research Project

The Lab is a network of technology clubs for young people between ages ten and 16 who are on the autism spectrum. It is a not-for-profit organisation which currently runs 12 sites around Australia.

Each site runs weekly two-hour sessions facilitated by two or three young and tech-savvy mentors who may be graphic designers, game developers, etc. During the sessions, participants of The Lab are encouraged to bring in their personal laptops and learn computing skills from the mentors. In the event where participants are unable to bring in their laptops, computers are made available on-site. The Lab emphasises on self-motivated, interest-based learning where the young person is responsible for his/her education. Hence, participants of The Lab are free to engage in any technology-based activities such as coding, gaming and robotics. Some young people, for example, may prefer watching YouTube videos or playing games for the week and resume learning computing skills another time. Unlike a classroom, learning and teaching (by the mentors) are casual and unstructured.

As the mentors have different skills and the physical spaces of The Labs vary from one site to another, over time, each Lab has been observed to develop its own culture. Having visited a few Labs myself and interacted with the young people, I found that while the activities differed from each lab, they showed consistent positive interactions between peers and mentors.

An evaluation of The Lab by Donahoo and Steele (2013) suggests that, contrary to prevailing knowledge, young people with autism are able to socialise within this shared environment. The evaluation found that The Lab has provided an avenue for these young people to relax and make friends, some for the first time, which has had a direct impact on their emotional and mental health. Parents have reported the reduction of anxiety and anti-depressive medication for their children since attending The Lab. In some instances, the child has reportedly reduced the infliction of self-harm or self-blame since then as well.

Two mitigating factors were attributed to the success of The Lab. Firstly, the utility of a combination of unstructured physical and online spaces gave Lab members mobility and the freedom to interact, learn and play at their own pace. Secondly, the unrestricted use of a variety of technologies brought in by mentors, parents or participants enabled young people at The Lab to explore their interests and learn through sharing with peers and mentors.

Informed by these observations, the broader aim of this research is to understand how physical, online and psychosocial spaces, theorised as *differentiated spaces*, enable young people with autism to socialise and develop interpersonal and technology-assisted relationships (Ng et al. 2015). Within which, it looks at how young people perceive themselves and their autism, learn skills to communicate and socialise through experiences at The Lab and online, as well as develop positive self-conceptions, self-esteem and identity. I will specifically be focusing on how technology and the online space enable young people with autism to communicate and define their own sociality within this paper.

3 Methodology

In this research, three qualitative methods were used to understand how young people with autism socialise within The Lab. They were namely participant observation, video ethnography and online participatory ethnography. These methods were largely used in an adaptive and participatory manner where participants were encouraged to give input and feedback throughout the data collection phase.

According to MacLeod et al. (2014), participatory methods "sought to overcome barriers to [research] participation" for autistic people who are often deemed as "problematic" to communicate with. This was in line with an evaluation of The Lab where Donahoo and Steele (2013) found that traditional forms of qualitative research imposed stress on participants. Therefore, the choice of qualitative methods were used to mitigate this stress by building relationships with participants and placing them as equally important in their input as the researcher within the project (Mertens 2015, pp. 25–27).

3.1 Video Ethnography and Participant Observation

Video ethnography is the video recording of a stream of activities engaged by subjects in their natural setting, in order to experience, interpret, and represent culture and society (Pink 2007, p. 22). Apart from aiding the researcher in recording data, the process of video ethnography enables participants to present a specific and detailed narrative of their disability (Pink 2012; Harris 2016). While the presence of the video camera involuntarily affects the way participants react, it gives them the opportunity to present their best qualities for the recorded material (Pink 2012). Together with participant observation, it enabled me to holistically understand participants and their activities at The Lab, learning the nuances within their speech and body language.

A total of 31 members of The Lab participated in this part of the research which took place over three Australian school terms (or approximately 36 weeks). They were asked to continue with their routine activities at The Lab while I observed, interacted and videoed them. All observations and interactions were noted in a diary after each session. Together with the video transcriptions, they were analysed through critical discourse analysis. This segment was particularly interesting as the young people often negotiated with me on when and how they wanted to be videoed. They asked questions such as "Will this be published on YouTube?" or "Can you film me from a distance instead?" which brings up interesting discussions about online personas and image, and technology as a form of surveillance. Some of these discussions will be highlighted in the next section.

3.2 Online Participatory Ethnography

Online or "virtual ethnography" is an adaptive form of ethnography using digital tools within an online community (Steinmetz 2012). "Participatory" refers to two different aspects of participation in this case. Firstly, it was conducted in a consultative process through feedback sessions – even the theme of project was negotiated as a group. Secondly, instead of studying an established online environment which is often the case in virtual ethnography (Steinmetz 2012), participants were requested to build this online environment. This was in-line with The Lab's ethos of self-motivated and interest-based participation and was welcomed by the participants.

16 members of The Lab participated in this phase of the research which took place over one Australian school term (or approximately 12 weeks). Participants were asked to create an online world within Minecraft, a 3D sandbox simulation game, in teams of two to four under an agreed upon theme (e.g. Build a useful application/graphic for the specific Lab – Some participants went on to create a banner for the official Facebook page). I was given access to their worlds to observe and participate in their projects. Each fortnight, I would go around the teams to discuss their progress, some of the problems they may have encountered and understand their process of communication. The overall results suggest that members of the team had to maintain communication with each other online - beyond just the game space or the physical space of The Lab – to spark continual interest. Many teams ended their projects prematurely as they felt that there was a lack of communication and enthusiasm between team members. Generally, team members who were able to text each other over mobile phones (i.e. Older participants), or used the same online messenger programmes such as Skype were able to complete their projects – bringing into question as to how accessibility to specific technologies may affect the way young people with autism learn to communicate and socialise.

4   Findings and Discussion

The overall findings reveal that communication and socialisation through online and mobile technologies are equally important and impactful on young people with autism in comparison to physical communication which is often prioritised in understanding sociality (Giddens and Sutton 2014). Walking into The Lab, you often see young people talking to each other while texting on their phones and messaging on Discord or Skype. They travel between and within multiple spaces at the same time, learning to socialise as they communicate on different platforms. In many cases, the ways they communicate in online and offline spaces are more similar than different within the context of The Lab. Socialisation is no longer one-dimensional within the relativity of time and space but rather, it occurs simultaneously within multiple spaces and "screens" across different time zones (Merriman 2012). Therefore, there is a need to redefine sociality with the inclusion of technology. Technology has changed our attitudes, behaviours and patterns of communication, both positively and negatively, and it should be regarded beyond simply tools that are used to improve performance, enhance learning, etc. – the implication here being that they are separate rather than integral aspects to our lives. As suggested in the beginning of this paper, technology has become an extension of the self. This is supported by the findings of this research presented below.

4.1   Learning Through Simulation

Young people with autism have been observed to emulate behaviours and speech from what they learnt online.

Learning by simulation or simulated-learning is not a new concept. It has been used in education, particularly in higher education, to "replace and amplify real experiences with guided ones, often "immersive" in nature, that evoke or replicate substantial aspects of the real world in a fully interactive fashion" (Lateef 2010, p. 248). Lateef (2010) argues that it is a "technique" as opposed to a form of "technology" – although he acknowledges the role of technology in enhancing this technique. This is similarly implied by Clayton and Gizelis (2005) and Zigmont et al. (2011) where simulation, a form of role-playing that can occur within physical or online settings, is used as a method of teaching. It assumes that learning through simulation is directive rather than organic. Similar to the medical model of personhood, technology is seen as a specific tool built for an explicit purpose: teaching. However, the results of my research at The Lab reveal that young people with autism learn social and communication skills through simulating gameplay. This is often constituted under the behavioural effects and impacts of gameplay; a common rhetoric, for example, is that playing violent games lead to aggressive and addictive behaviours (Griffiths 1999; Anderson 2004). While these behavioural changes may be seen as consequences of playing games, they are nonetheless a form of learning – albeit not with the common, positive connotations of learning.

During one of the sessions, I sat with a 10-year-old child playing Emily is Away, a narratively-based chat game where you either pick preprogrammed lines or type in personal responses to engage in a conversation with the computer-generated character, Emily (Fig. 1).

This child developed a romantic relationship with Emily within the game through choosing lines that he did not seem to fully understand. At some point, he turned around and asked me if these were speech you would normally use to pursue a girl.

In other instances, young people at The Lab often speak in a similar fashion to the way they communicate online. Aside from shorthand such as "LOL", "BTW" or "BRB", they also learn to negotiate through trading online. On Minecraft servers, for

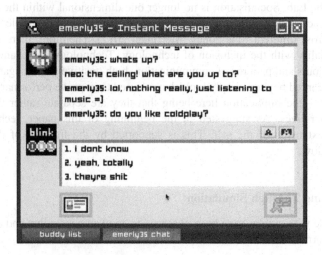

Fig. 1. An ongoing game of "Emily is Away"

example, young people at The Lab learn simple sentences and phrases through reading ongoing chats online (e.g. "You sell armor?", "How much?", "You trade weapons?"). This is sometimes reflected in their conversations at The Lab where they speak in a relatively condensed and abrupt manner.

These examples illustrate the impressions online conversations and communication may have on young people, especially those on the spectrum who may be unable to discern between what is acceptable speech on a day-to-day basis. Some young children with autism have been reported to have negative or very little interactions with their peers face-to-face (Donahoo and Steele 2013). Thus, they may begin to speak or behave through simulating their positive experiences online, injecting shorthand into their speech or engaging in conversational styles similar to that of their online communication. This will be further explored in my next point.

4.2 Network Sociality and Beyond

Inspired by Manual Castell's work on network society, Wittel (2001) conceptualised the term 'network sociality' – a form of socialisation enabled by technology that is largely interest-based and requires lower commitment in comparison to traditional notions of socialisation and communication. It enables people to socialise within extensive networks focused on individual connections rather than membership-based, exclusive communities. Wittel's 'network sociality' suggests that we communicate at high levels of intensity on a need basis, similar to that of a social contract between two or more people. He argues that this is because of the way we connect with each other online which is largely through networks rather than communities.

This is evident not just within the online space but also the physical space of The Lab. While some young people develop friendships that extend beyond The Lab, most interact solely within the sessions based on the activities they are engaged in.

A group of young people, for example, have been working on their Minecraft world for over a year now. While they continue doing so in their own time, my conversations with them indicate that do not communicate with each other much except through in-game messaging when necessary. However, when they are at The Lab, they converse intensely, discussing issues from their personal lives to their individual progress on the world with much enthusiasm, comparable to the likes of what we traditionally understand as "best friends". Within The Lab sessions, they have also drawn up plans, lists and sketches for what needs to be built in their Minecraft world. However, in-game building is often worked on individually and anyone who is trusted by the players are free to join.

This form of physical and online interactions mirror Wittel's concept of network sociality. Any form of communications is done in short-bursts (i.e. at The Lab sessions) and with great intensity. They communicate base on common interests or on a need-basis, concerning him- or herself to individual activity or person rather than a group or community. However, beyond the weekly meetings, members keep to themselves and have low commitment to each other.

This re-enactment of Wittel's 'network sociality' within both physical and online spaces urges us to rethink the definition of socialisation once again.

4.3   The Physicality of Technology

Unlike other spaces, the online/digital space is mediated and requires a physical medium. Therefore, in understanding sociality through technology, the physicality of medium must be considered.

Disability geographers Davidson and Parr (2010, p. 72) argue that the online space is enabling because individuals with autism are able to interact without the nuances of physical communication such as body language, eye contact and emotional cues. Similarly, within the physical space of The Lab, young people with autism have used their screens as a way to avoid these nuances of physical communication. For instance, two young people may be sitting beside each other but interacting silently through online means. In other instances, the young people may be chatting without ever looking directly at their peers. Instead, their eyes are concentrated on the screens in front of them. One young person often talks to someone in between talking to his console or laptop – he would comment on his game (e.g. Come on! You can win this Pikachu) and interject with a reply to someone else's comments or conversations then return to talking to himself/the console or laptop.

The physicality of technology creates a form of distraction for these young people who gain sensory relief (i.e. keeping eye contact to the minimal) while simultaneously engaged in conversations. It enables them to express themselves within a physical setting without having to comply with the general rules of physical communication. This form of communication is not limited to young people with autism and demands a redefinition of the social norms guiding communication. When some parents enter the room, they demand their child to look at them or the mentors while talking to them. In their perspective (and many others within mainstream society), making eye contact while speaking to someone is polite. However, for individuals on the spectrum, the presence of the technological medium enables them to overcome some of the physical discomfort from sensory overload and effectively converse or communicate to others in their means. Therefore, we need to expand and rethink what we understand to be socially acceptable, or "polite", forms of communication so as to create a more inclusive society.

On another front, the physicality of technology may also impede communication. While I was videoing the sessions, some participants were visibly nervous or unusually quiet and composed. Others asked questions about what I was using the footage for and if I could delete certain sections of it. The video camera hence became an imposition on their freedom; it became a surveillance tool. According to Davidson and Parr (2010) as well, the physicality of technology and the online space may also restrict people with autism from wanting to learn and communicate with others who are not on the spectrum as they may retreat into their comfort zones, creating exclusive groups and communities rather than trying to be included by others who are different from themselves. The intricacies and complexity of technology call for more considerations to be taken into account when analysing their use as a medium for communication.

5   Conclusion

In McLuhan's (1964) most influential works, he discusses technology as an extension of the self and the human body. Although McLuhan wrote his research 30 years before the World Wide Web (WWW) was created, he prophesied the potential of web technology as an "extension of consciousness" that would include "television as its content, not as its environment", where information retrieval and communication would be enhanced and "speedily tailored" (cited in Guertin 2012, p. 39). He implores us to understand technology beyond simply a tool, but an amplification of ourselves that have broader social consequences. McLuhan's theories were exemplified at The Lab where technology has become an integral part to its members' ability to communicate and socialise – beyond the perceived limitations of their disability imposed by the medical view of their differences.

In my research, technology has demonstrated itself to be an extension of these autistic youth's individual psyche and mode of communication and expression. Through technology, they are able to learn and emulate patterns of interaction and create different styles of communication that are both comfortable for themselves and their peers around them. In the process of which, they illustrate how Wittel's concept of 'network sociality' can transcend between physical and online spaces, calling upon us to rethink and reconceptualise notions of sociality with the inclusion of technology as an integral part of communication and life.

Ringland et al. (2016, p. 1259) similarly found through their analysis of an online gaming platform and forum dedicated to young people with autism that "members of the [community] search for, practice, and define sociality". This view is confirmed by my research at The Lab.

Acknowledgements. This research is sponsored by Victoria University (Melbourne, Australia) and the Young and Well Cooperative Research Centre. An ethics application was submitted to and approved by Victoria University in early 2016 (ID: 0000024193). I would like to thank Associate Professor Timothy Corcoran and Dr Stefan Schutt for their supervision and advise to this research project.

References

Anderson, C.A.: An update on the effects of playing violent video games. J. Adolesc. **21**(1), 113–122 (2004)

APA: Diagnostic and Statistical Manual of Mental Disorders, 5th edn. American Psychiatric Association, Arlington (2013)

Baron-Cohen, S.: Is Asperger syndrome necessarily viewed as a disability? Focus Autism Other Dev. Disabil. **17**(3), 186 (2002)

Campbell, F.A.: Inciting legal fictions: 'disability's' date with ontology and the ableist body of law. Griffith Law Rev. **10**(1), 77 (2001)

Campbell, F.K.: Contours of Ableism: The Production of Disability and Abledness. Palgrave Macmillan, Basingstoke (2009)

Clayton, G., Gizelis, T.I.: Learning through simulation or simulated learning? An investigation into the effectiveness of simulations as a teaching tool in higher education. In: Proceedings from British International Studies Association Conference (2005)

Davidson, J., Parr, H.: Enabling cultures of disorder online. In: Chouinard, V., Hall, E., Wilton, R. (eds.) Towards Enabling Geographies: "Disabled" Bodies and Minds in Society and Space [e-book], pp. 63–83. Ashgate, Burlington (2010)

Donahoo, D., Steele, E.: Evaluation of The Lab: A Technology Club for Young People with Asperger's Syndrome. Young and Well Cooperative Research Centre, Melbourne (2013)

Foucault, M., Martin, L.H., Gutman, H., Hutton, P.H.: Technologies of the Self: A Seminar with Michel Foucault. University of Massachusetts Press, Amherst (1988)

Garland-Thomson, R.: A Habitable World: Harriet McBryde Johnson's "Case for My Life". Hypatia **30**, 300–306 (2015)

Giddens, A., Sutton, P.W.: Sociology. Polity, Cambridge (2014)

Griffiths, M.: Violent video games and aggression: a review of the literature. Aggression Violent Behav. **4**(2), 203–212 (1999)

Guertin, C.: Digital Prohibition: Piracy and Authorship in New Media Art. Bloomsbury Publishing USA, New York (2012)

Haraway, D.: A cyborg manifesto. In: During, S. (ed.) The Cultural Studies Reader, pp. 271–291. Routledge, New York (1999)

Harris, A.: Video as Method: Understanding Qualitative Research. Oxford University Press, Melbourne (2016)

Jaeger, P.T.: Disability and the Internet: Confronting a Digital Divide. Lynne Rienner Publisher, Boulder (2012)

Lateef, F.: Simulation-based learning: just like the real thing. J. Emerg. Trauma Shock **3**(4), 348–352 (2010)

MacLeod, A.G., Lewis, A., Robertson, C.: 'Charlie: please respond!' Using a participatory methodology with individuals on the autism spectrum. Int. J. Res. Method Educ. **37**(4), 407–420 (2014)

McLuhan, M.: Understanding Media: The Extensions of Man. ARK Paperbacks, London (1964)

Mertens, D.M.: Research and Evaluation in Education and Psychology: Integrating Diversity with Quantitative, Qualitative, and Mixed Methods. SAGE Publications, California (2015)

Merriman, P.: Mobility, Space and Culture. Taylor and Francis, Hoboken (2012)

Ng, L.E., Schutt, St, Corcoran, T.: Technology use and teenagers diagnosed with high-functioning autism: in and across differentiated spaces. In: Corcoran, T., White, J., Whitburn, B. (eds.) Disability Studies: Educating for Inclusion. Sense, Rotterdam (2015)

Pink, S.: Doing Visual Ethnography. SAGE Publications, Melbourne (2007)

Pink, S.: Advances in Visual Ethnography. SAGE Publications, Melbourne (2012)

Ringland, K.E., Wolf, C.T., Faucett, H., Dombrowski, L., Hayes, G.R.: "Will I always be not social?": re-conceptualizing sociality in the context of a Minecraft community for autism. In: Proceedings of the 2016 CHI Conference on Human Factors in Computing Systems (2016)

Steinmetz, K.: Message received: virtual ethnography in online message boards. Int. J. Qual. Methods **11**(1), 26–39 (2012)

Wittel, A.: Toward a network sociality. Theor. Culture Soc. **18**(6), 51 (2001)

Zigmont, J.J., Kappus, L.J., Sudikoff, S.N.: Theoretical foundations of learning through simulation. Semin. Perinatol. **35**(2), 47–51 (2011)

Service Design for Improving Adolescents' Cyber Language Habit

Jae Sun Yi$^{(\boxtimes)}$, Chanmi Jeon$^{(\boxtimes)}$, and Yeji Yu$^{(\boxtimes)}$

School of Contents Convergence Design, Handong Global University,
Pohang, Republic of Korea
creativel@handong.edu, {cksalsp,isu5519}@naver.com

Abstract. This study aims to improve excessive usage of slang and indiscriminate language habit of Korean adolescents, and the consequent social problem called 'Cyber Bullying'. A desk research is conducted to examine adolescents' language habit and the reality of cyber bullying, and the problems of current systems is analyzed to propose a new service design that can compensate the defects. Not only that, through analysis on the traits of teenagers that use lots of swear words and psychological characteristics of adolescents, a smartphone keypad and application are developed that help adolescents to check their language habit and improve it by themselves in everyday life since adolescents tend to feel resistance about coercive external interference. Teenagers can correct their language habit as soon as they type swear words by immediate feedbacks and given substitutable words, and also can recognize their habitual usage of swear words by the accumulated data of usage. The significance of this study is improving teenagers' language habit by using refined expressions instead of violent slangs, and to prevent secondary problems which can result from negative language habit.

Keywords: Design for social impact · Adolescents language habit · Mobile application and keypad · Slang tracking and recognition system

1 Introduction

Recently, the indiscriminate and violent language habit of adolescents in Republic of Korea has been a serious problem. More than two thirds of teenagers are using swear words habitually and unconsciously, and the awareness of the problem is considerably low. Using slangs in adolescence and having bad language habit can lead to brain damage so that the brain cannot grow and develop normally, and consequently the vocabulary, cognitive ability, and emotion control ability will decline. Moreover, it leaves psychological damage and aftereffect to the person who listen to swear words, which can result in depression, and the consequent problems such as difficulty in interpersonal relationship and social life. The reason why the usage of slang of Korean adolescents is a serious problem is that it not only occurs in oral conversation in daily life but also in online chats, so it causes secondary problems such as cyber verbal violence. Hence, this study defined adolescents' violent language habit as an issue, and designed a service which helps adolescents who want to improve their language habit to do so on their own. When it comes to the oral language habit, it is hard to implement

© Springer International Publishing AG 2017
A. Marcus and W. Wang (Eds.): DUXU 2017, Part III, LNCS 10290, pp. 403–414, 2017.
DOI: 10.1007/978-3-319-58640-3_29

the technology that catches slang among every word said and gives immediate feedback. Besides, since the online verbal violence called 'Cyber Bullying' that is happening among teenagers is an arising social problem, a service platform is needed to make it easy to improve cyber language habit. The goal of this study is to make teenagers recognize the unconscious usage of swear words, not just once but continuously through a slang tracking system, so that it is helpful to improve their language habit. Ultimately, it aims to reduce the potential number of the victims and attackers of cyber bullying and to prevent subsequence crimes and various social problems caused by adolescents' verbal abuses.

2　The Problem of Korean Adolescents' Usage of Swear Words

2.1　Korean Home Education

Traditionally, Korea is influenced by Confucianism which considers community as being more important than individual and emphasize manners, and old generation parents are known for strict discipline on their children's language and behavior. However, double-income family increased [1] as a result of modern society, so children and parents have less time to spend together. At the same time, the rising education fever in Korean which is the highest among the world [2] and the social atmosphere that places importance on school scores and competition, the significance of home education has been relatively weakened. Accordingly the interest of parents in children's language habit waned, and the number of teenagers who use swear words unconsciously and indiscriminately are increasing for there is no specific restriction at home. The language habit of children has been changed for the worse because of the society atmosphere which considers usage of slang as the subculture of adolescents [3]. In addition, they are constantly exposed to violent contents from movies or TV shows, and learning swear words from the media and become accustomed [4].

2.2　Current Status of Korean Adolescents' Usage of Swear Words

In an observational study conducted by Korean Educational Broadcasting System [5], it has been observed that nearly every sentence in the conversation of adolescents included swear words, and it seems to be impossible to continue the conversation without using swear words because of replacing considerable number of words with slang words. It is more serious since these problems are not limited to the delinquent teenagers called troublemakers. Teenagers, regardless of gender, grade, and age, are found to be using a lot of slangs, which suggests that there is a problem with the language habits of all Korean adolescents. According to a survey conducted by a daily newspaper [6], elementary, middle, and high school teachers answered that the biggest reason why students use slang is "habitually" which was 39%, and "afraid of being alienated from friends" which rated 22.1%. It showed that teenagers have a significant meaning in their peer groups, and they tend to use swear words more than their intention in order to communicate with their peers using their common language.

2.3   Effect of Using Swear Words on Adolescents

2.3.1   Physical Damage

According to a paper published in the Journal of Mental Health [7], people who suffered from verbal abuse of people and colleagues in childhood including adolescent, had smaller corpus callosum than that of normal people because of excessive production of stress hormone called 'cortisol'. The corpus callosum is a bridge between the left and the right side of the brain, and once it is damaged, the exchange of information between the left and right side of the brain is not smooth that it results in degradation of linguistic ability and social skill.

In addition, the frontal lobe of the brain, which is responsible for rational thinking, grows greatest in teenage years, and it is hard to be developed appropriately when exposed to verbal abuse at this time. As a result, it is more likely that the instinctive and emotional limbic system will supervise the person, resulting in an impulsive and violent act [8].

Swear words have negative effect on not only those who listen to it, also those who use it. In an observational study conducted by Korean Educational Broadcasting System in cooperation with a psychological research team from Seoul National University [5], the group using a lot of slang showed a higher score in the sector of unplanned impulse which means being unable to make a plan and practice it (Fig. 1). It shows that the use of slang leads teenagers to haphazard and impulsive tendencies. In the same study, the group with high frequency of using swear words showed activated parasympathetic nervous system when hearing violent cursing, which indicates that the more frequently they use slang, the more and often they use slang as they get used to slang.

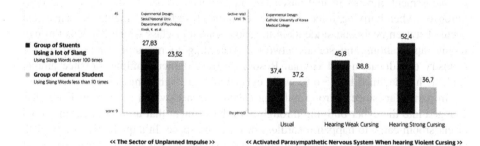

Fig. 1. The sector of unplanned impulse and activated parasympathetic nervous system when hearing violent cursing (Source: *EBS*, 2012)

2.3.2   Psychological Problems

Slang causes not only physical damage, but also contributes to the psychological problems of teenagers. When a teenager suffers from verbal abuse, he or she is likely to develop a negative self-image. Accordingly the self-esteem declines, and a person with low self-esteem can hardly have a healthy ego since it it difficult to correct a self-image. Low self-esteem often accompanies depression, and depression causes a feeling of helplessness and loss of will to live, resulting in suicide in serious cases. In fact, a teenager who suffered from cyber language abuse in Korea in 2012 showed how constant verbal violence wreak great damage on adolescents by committing suicide [9]. In a qualitative research conducted in 2014 [10], one of the common answers of students suffering from verbal abuse was 'There is a great deal of aftereffects due to verbal abuse.' The most common forms of verbal abuse found among teenagers are negative expression about appearance, or verbal abuse such as 'Go kill yourself.' [10] These are demeaning comments made to blindly harass and hurt someone, and these are not made because the victim has done something wrong or 'deserves' it. Especially, verbal abuse occurs in mobile SNS where many young people say swear words or curses on a particular person continuously. Thus, it is not easy for the victim to deal with it, and the damage gets bigger because of repeated verbal abuse. In the end, the scars left by these verbal abuse and memory remain unsolved, deteriorating the quality of life and leaving psychological aftermath.

3 Cyber Bullying Issues in Korea

3.1 Appearance of Cyber Bullying

Recently, with the spread of smartphones, physical school violence committed offline has changed into a new type of online violence called 'Cyber Bullying'. A common definition of cyber bullying is that the individual or a group with malice bully someone intentionally or repeatedly via e-mail, web site, social networks, chatting, and so on [11]. Mostly, cyber bullying among teenagers is based on the SNS(Social Network Service), though there are types of media outlets, such as photos and videos, most of the harassment appears in text-based language violence [10]. In this study, the definition of cyber bullying refers to direct or indirect verbal and mental violence that occurs between peers and students in the same school or class which happens through mobile applications and social networks. According to research conducted by the Ministry of Education and Human Resources Development, offline violence among students has declined by 13.6%, while cyber bullying is growing steadily over time.

In particular, since a group bullying called 'outcast' which appears in Korea has changed into the cyber bullying through SNS, harassment that used to occur in school or classroom came to happen regardless of time and space. In a qualitative study [10], teenagers suffering from cyber bullying said that because it is not physical type of violence, it leaves no sign of violence on the victims, that it is hard for their parents or people around them to recognize that someone is experiencing it. In addition, it is almost impossible to find out specific attacker and punish them when reported, for it is done in groups.

3.2 Current Status of Cyber Bullying Occurrence and Problems
with Current System

Currently, 34% of Korean teenagers are experiencing cyber bullying, which means that a third of teenagers are victims or attackers of cyber bullying [10]. Whereas school violence off-line is decreasing over time (Fig. 2), cyber bullying is steadily increasing

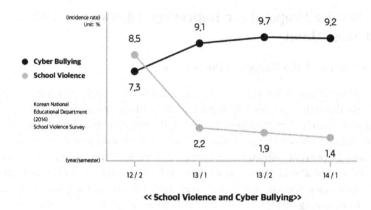

<< School Violence and Cyber Bullying>>

Fig. 2. School violence and cyber bullying (Source: Korean National Educational Department, 2014)

since its first sighting, and it is expected to grow further. Especially, one of the characteristics of cyber bullying in Korea is that the victims and attackers are acquaintances, and more than half of them belong to the same school [10]. Therefore, a solution from school or government is urgent, but schools fail to offer other solutions except for media education and campaigns. Through the interview [10], it is found that the content of media education and campaigns is all about encouraging teens to be aware of the harmfulness of cyber bullying, so most of students responded that they did not agree with the content. Other opinions were like these; 'Because education is not frequent, it is likely to forget about it instantly.', 'I don't know how to deal with it specifically when I get a cyber bullying even after the education.' Most of the responses were negative, so it seems that education and campaigns are not practical to solve the problems of cyber bullying [10]. Also, the problem is not improved unless the victims ask help for their parents or teachers when cyber bullying happens, and it is common that even if the adults help, the problem is repeated again, such as bully students revenge the victims with cyber verbal abuse after being punished [10]. Most of the measures were aimed at mending and managing the bullying after it happens rather than the precautionary level, and the victims need to cope actively to deal with the problem.

Results of analyzing the situation and how to deal with the cyber verbal abuse, the reason why the methods currently being implemented are not working properly are as follows. (1) The education and campaigns are not ongoing and ran on event variables, and (2) they are simply conveying messages suggesting that cyber bullying is bad, not suggesting a specific action. (3) Most of the measures to deal with the cyber bullying are compulsory such as including the third party, and (4) there is a limit to the fact that the victims' reports are needed to deal with the aftermath of cyber bullying and that they cannot reduce the number of potential victims and attackers.

4   The Service Proposal for Improving Adolescents' Cyber Language Habit

4.1   The Goal and the Target of the Service

The top priority of this study is to enable adolescents to manage their habitual usage of swear words through a service platform that they often encounter in daily life, help them improve their cyber language habits easily without outside intervention. Ultimately, it aims to reduce the potential number of the victims and attackers of cyber bullying and to prevent subsequence crimes and various social problems caused by adolescents' verbal abuses. Since more than 60% of teenagers said it was their "4–6th grade of elementary school year" when they first started learning swear words [12], teenagers from the age of 11 to 18 were chosen as targets. In particular, in order to improve language habit, the user's willingness to reduce the use of habitual and repetitive slang is crucial, and also this service regards it meaningful to help adolescents do it voluntarily, thus teenagers who have the intent to improve language habits is the target of this service.

4.2   Analysis on Current Usage of Swear Words and the Users

In the study of Korean national language centers [13], adolescents aged 13 to 18 were asked how many times they use slang a day, and the highest response was '1 to 2 times' with 38.9%, and the next was '3 to 9 times' with 30.4%. Seven out of ten students believe that their use of slang is less than 10 times a day. However, in an observational study of Korean Educational Broadcasting System [5], teenagers used 400 swear words for 8 h on average. This shows that teenagers actually use a lot more slangs than they think, and do not fully recognize their use of it.

Despite the fact that teenagers are not aware of their use of swear words accurately, they clearly know that they use slang. According to a research by the KEDI [12], one of the four students was interested in improving language habits and having a critical mind with their language habits. Nevertheless, by a research of the Korean Federation of Teachers' Associations(2011) [14], half of teenagers who use slang are habitually used to use it, and it seems to be difficult to break the habit since it is already routinized as a result of continuous usage of swear words. In case of students whose brains are damaged from habitual use of slang, the vocabulary is limited and it is not easy to think of the appropriate language expression in a moment because they had replaced a lot of words with slang. In an observational study conducted by Korean Educational Broadcasting System in cooperation with a psychological research team from Seoul National University [8], it is found that teenagers who use more swear words had lower vocabulary level compared to another group as shown in (Fig. 3). Even in the experiment of filling in the blank with correct proverb and writing the antonym, the group who use more slang showed relatively poor results than the group that use less slang, which indicates that using slang words lowers the language ability.

Autonomy is an important characteristic of adolescent psychology, and a study on self identity in adolescence suggests subjecthood (.791), initiative (.768), and goal

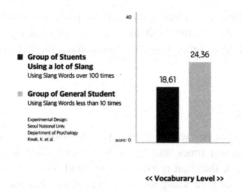

Fig. 3. Vocabulary level (Source: *EBS*, 2012)

orientation (.722) as important features [15]. This means that it will be effective to respect the autonomy of teenagers to help resolve the problem without resorting to compulsory methods or external intervention.

Based on the preceding issues, the user's needs to be considered in the service is as follows; (1) let the teenagers recognize their current status since they are not aware of the fact they use slang more than they think, and (2) manage their language habit through constant feedbacks for it is hard to break the bad habit because of chronic and indiscriminate usage of slang. (3) Suggest replaceable words for teenagers having limited vocabulary and expressiveness, and (4) all the procedure and experience of the service should guarantee the autonomy of the users. Also (5) encourage the users and give them feeling of fulfillment so that they can be interested and receive positive stimulus.

4.3   Choosing Service Platform

The most important criteria of platform for this service is if the platform is able to provide an environment, in which adolescent can improve the langue habits themselves. Due to the nature of cyber bullying, there exist multiple attackers, and that attackers are also potential victims at the same time, so it is difficult to differentiate between victims and attackers of cyber language violence. For that reason, it is not easy to deal with the problem when the third party such as teachers, school, or police are involved, and there is no significant effect of compulsory treatment due to the psychological repulsion of adolescents. Therefore, the focus of this service is on helping teenagers reduce the usage of slang and change their behaviors at their own wills. As a result, we concluded that the most effective platform that teenagers meet in everyday life and have no resistance is the smartphone keypad, which they directly enter slang with. It is also because more than 40% of teenagers spend more than three hours a day using smartphones, mostly using the SNS (76%) with smartphones [16]. Moreover, it makes the reason of choosing the platform clear that it is possible to respond to the user as soon as they type slang with the keypad, so that the typed slang can be purified or blocked before it is sent. Thus, the main platform is a smartphone keypad of android operation system, which is relatively easy to develop and customize. With the keypad, there is an application that counts the frequency of usage of slang and shows change of the frequency according to time, in order to keep track the improvement of language habit consistently.

4.4   Service Features

- *Cumulative data of swear words usage.* The users can compare the frequency of today to that of recent times and check how much slang is used, and using the monthly data record, they can recognize what kind of slang is the most frequently used and the level of their slang usage compared to other users.
- *Instant warning.* When entering slang into a keypad, it tells them they used it right away by sending immediate vibrant or sound alarm with an instant message. Also, it is not just noticing the fact that they entered slang, but also delivering a message encouraging to consider the other people who will receive the message.
- *Suggesting replaceable words.* The user can turn on/off the function which automatically replace a slang into better expression as soon as it is typed. It gives a solution by suggesting replaceable words rather than forcing to stop using the slang.
- *Award and penalty, concept of report card.* A system that awards an prize when the user achieves certain number of daily goals and gives penalty on excessive usage of certain slang word gives young adults a motivation to improve their language habits. In addition, the concept of a school report card is applied in order to make the teenagers feel fulfilled when they receive good grade through improving the language habit, as they care a lot about getting high grades in school.

4.5   Information Architecture

(1) The main screen of the application contains informations that should be most accessible, such as today's grade and the frequency of using swear words, which changes in real time. The users are able to check daily frequency and do self check simply on the main screen. (2) The accumulative data of slang usage on daily, weekly, and monthly basis is shown with line graph so that it is easy to compare the frequency for a particular period of time at a glance. (3) In award and penalty menu, there are award cards, which is given when the users achieve their goal for a certain number of time, and penalty cards that show what slang is most frequently used and the replaceable expression. The user can see and check the list and content of award and penalty cards by simply swiping and tapping the screen. (4) The report card is a cumulative and arranged data of slang usage received at the end of each month, and it consists of frequency of the languages used in that month, the ranking of the most used slangs, and overall grade of user's language habit. The grade system is similar to that of Korean high school which classify every user of the service into 9 different grades. (5) The frequency is automatically detected and counted by slang database when a slang word is typed, and there appears an immediate notification to alert the user. Also,

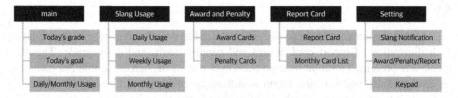

main	Slang Usage	Award and Penalty	Report Card	Setting
Today's grade	Daily Usage	Award Cards	Report Card	Slang Notification
Today's goal	Weekly Usage	Penalty Cards	Monthly Card List	Award/Penalty/Report
Daily/Monthly Usage	Monthly Usage			Keypad

Fig. 4. Information architecture

the slang can be changed automatically into better expression or replaceable words are suggested with the keypad (Fig. 4).

5 The Process of Producing Final Output of the Service

5.1 Branding

The name 'Anslang' is a compound word of Anti and slang, which has a meaning of being against to use slang, and at the same time, in Korean it means 'I'm not going to use it!' that shows strong will of the user. The logo design reflects the contents of the service, which is school uniforms, signs of teenager students, and a firm commitment to improving language habits by the pose of the arms. 'A' in the middle stands for 'Anslang' and also the highest grade of report card that is the design concept of this service. The main colors applied to design the logo and application are purple and mint, and pastel soft colors make it easy to see the application screen. Moreover, we tried to give a neutral mood so that it is suitable for every teenagers regardless of gender, and added cute line illustration considering the preference of young adolescents. The fonts used throughout the logo and application design are vivid and cute, and harmonized with the whole concept (Fig. 5).

Fig. 5. (1) Logo (2) application icon

5.2   GUI Design

The overall design concept is to provide a desirable design environment for teenagers with illustration of report card, award and penalty cards, and daily grade. The main menu was presented with an icon on the lower part of the screen so that the menu can be easily found, and selected menu is differentiated by the difference in opacity. In addition, it is possible to visually identify the key content and other contents by using the coloring point to highlight the focal point while general color scheme is unified. Looking at the details of major screens, (1) today's grade, which is the most important visual information, is placed in the middle the main screen and it takes the largest part of design in order to capture the attention of user. Today's goal and the frequency of using swear words are presented with a text information as well as a graph to help the user's understanding. (2) In the accumulative data page, it is easy to switch the category by tapping the subordinate category button that places in the upper part of the screen. The amount of slang usage is shown in line graph to make it easy to compare the data of each day visually, and the user can check the graph by swiping the screen, and the frequency of today, this week, and this month is emphasized using point colors. (3) The recent report card, of last month, is on the report card menu, and when tapping

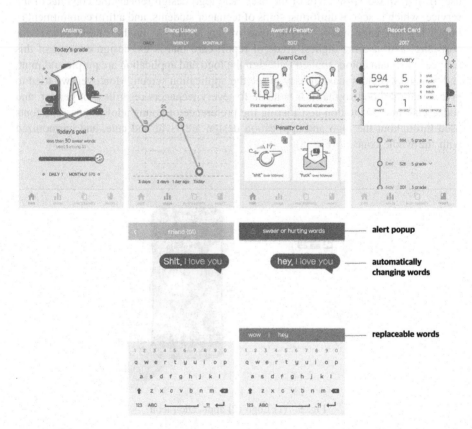

Fig. 6. Graphical user interface design: (1) main page (2) accumulative data page (3) award/penalty page (4) recent report page (5–6) keypad

the time line of monthly report card list that is below, the monthly report will be displayed on the top of the screen. (4) The keypad has the same form of existing one, and there is a space that shows replaceable words when entering slang. Also, the notification of using slang appears on top of the screen so it does not bother the user (Fig. 6).

6 Conclusion and Proposal of Further Study

The use of slang in Korean teenagers is not just a matter of language habits, but a serious problem that can greatly affect the brains and emotions of teenagers, and even created a social phenomenon called cyber bullying. The study expects that using purified and refined language instead of offensive and violent language will have a positive impact on youth's emotions and language development, and suggests concrete measures that reduce the use of swear words by presenting instant feedback and the alternate words. Continuous cumulative data enables to self-check the usage, thereby improving the long-term language habits. It aims to help the users reduce their usage of coarse language habits in everyday life with an android smartphone keypad and application that is accessible for the teenagers, and ultimately, reduce the potential number of the victims and attackers of cyber bullying.

In future follow-up studies, it is necessary to modify and supplement the application through usability test, and after that, verify that if there is real improvement of language habit using the service, and whether the change of cyber language habit is applied to oral dialogue as well. Additionally, the results of this study are solely driven by Android operating systems on smartphones, so it needs to be expanded by developing a new application for the iOS, in order to provide the service in all smartphones.

References

1. Lee, J.: South Korean family after patriarchy: from normality to flexibility. In: The Korean Cultural Studies, S.283–S.310. Korea Cultural Research Institute Ewha Womans University, Seoul, Korea (2015)
2. Coughlan, S.: Asia tops biggest global school rankings. BBC (2015). http://www.bbc.com/news/business-32608772
3. Khil, E.B.: Study on adolescents' use of slang and jargon – adolescents' verbal deviance, is it a culture of passage rites? Korean J. Youth Stud. 21(2), 469–489 (2014)
4. Lee, J.-K., Woo, H.-J.: A study on intention to calling bad language of adolescents: exposure to curse on TV, perceived seriousness of curses on TV, stress, and variables of theory of planned behaviors. Korean J. Journalism Commun. Stud., S.356–S.380 (2011). Korean Society for Journalism & Communication Studies, Korea
5. Korean Educational Broadcasting System. Do we use slang language? Doucumentary Prime. EBS (2012)
6. Yoo, S.-J.: Korean Language Disease. Chosun (2013)
7. Martin, H.T., et al.: Hurtful words: association of exposure to peer verbal abuse with elevated psychiatric symptom scores and corpus callosum abnormalities. U.S.: Am. J. Psychiatry 167, 1464–1471 (2010)

8. Lee, J., Byun, J.: When teenagers listen to severe slang, their brains get hurt for lifetime. dongA Science (2012)
9. Baek, S.: A silent harassment, cyber bullying. Asia Today (2016)
10. Lee, C., Shin, N., Ha, E.: A study on the situation of youth cyberbullying and measures to prevent it. Natl. Youth Policy Inst. Stud. **1**, 1–268 (2014)
11. Li, Q., Cross, D., Smith, P.K.: Predicting student behaviors: cyberbullies, cybervictims, and bystanders. In: Li, Q., Cross, D., Smith, P.K. (eds.) Cyberbullying in the Global Playground: Research from International Perspectives. Blackwell Publishing, Hoboken (2012)
12. Yang, M., Kang, H., Cho, S.: Usage of Slang in School Life and Purification Counterplan. Korean Educational Development Institute (KEDI), Seoul (2010)
13. Korean National Language Centers. How Often Adolescents Use Slang per a Day (2011)
14. Korean Federation of Teachers' Associations. Students' Language Usage Studies (2011)
15. Kim, W., Park, Y.-H., Kim, J.: A structural model of the relationships among basic psychological needs, ego identity, and career identity of middle school students in South Korea. Educ. Psychol. Stud. **28**(2), 333–352 (2014). Korean Educational Psychology Association
16. Park, H.-J.: A Study on the Perception of SNS Peer Culture and Potential of Cyber-Bullying in Adolescents. Chonbuk National University, Chonbuk (2016)

Let's Play (While Far Away)! Using Technology to Mediate Remote Playdates for Children with Autism

Annuska Zolyomi[(✉)], Ankitha Bharadwaj, and Jaime Snyder

University of Washington, Seattle, WA, USA
{annuska, jasl208}@uw.edu, ankitha.bharadwaj@gmail.com

Abstract. Play is an essential social, emotional, and intellectual developmental activity for children, including those with autism. Parents, educators, and therapists of autistic children strive to create opportunities for children to engage in mutual play with peers. Among other benefits, play enables children to develop the ability to see the world through someone else's eyes, a process described by the "Theory of Mind" (ToM), a concept formulated by developmental psychologists. This awareness of another's perspective has been identified as particularly challenging for people with autism. To examine the potential for technology to support play and ToM skills, we interviewed parents of children with autism about their current play practices. We found that parents struggle to implement in-person playdates due to the challenges of finding appropriate nearby peers and busy schedules filled with medical and therapy appointments. To explore alternatives to in-person playdates, we conducted an exploratory study in which pairs of autistic and neurotypical children interacted via two remote technologies: Microsoft Skype and Microsoft IllumiShare, a shared surface system. Our interaction analysis revealed that, through embodied interaction with real and virtual objects, the children engaged in mutual and parallel play. However, at times, the constraints of the technology impeded joint attention and perspective-taking. We contribute empirical findings based on interaction analysis of neurodiverse playmates playing remotely with tangible objects in a shared surface environment. We recommend design considerations for remote technologies to support mutual play and ToM skills.

Keywords: Remote technologies · Embodied interaction · Theory of mind · Play · Autism

1 Overview

Play is an essential social, emotional, and intellectual developmental activity for children [3, 19], including those with Autism Spectrum Disorder (ASD).[1] While parents, educators, and therapists of autistic children strive to create play opportunities, play is not a simple prospect for autistic children [10]. During play, we draw upon our social, verbal, and non-verbal communication skills. These are the very abilities

---

[1] We use identity-first ("autistic children") and person-first language ("children with autism") interchangeably to reflect the range of preferences within the neurodiversity community [15].

© Springer International Publishing AG 2017
A. Marcus and W. Wang (Eds.): DUXU 2017, Part III, LNCS 10290, pp. 415–432, 2017.
DOI: 10.1007/978-3-319-58640-3_30

impacted by autism [1]. Play enables children to develop the ability to see the world through someone else's eyes, a process described by the "Theory of Mind," (ToM) a developmental psychology theory developed by Alan Leslie [11, 16]. Simon Baron-Cohen's research in the autism field has shown that this awareness of another's perspective can be a challenge for people with autism [2, 13]. Children with autism are also likely to be highly sensitive to sensory inputs [1]; therefore, they can experience discomfort with dynamic environmental changes often associated with play including loud noises and bright lights. Even simply the unstructured nature of playtime can be challenging to many autistic children who can have difficulty managing transitions and typically prefer structure. Given the juxtaposition of the importance of play with its challenges, our research investigated the current play practices of autistic children and the opportunities for technology to facilitate play.

Remote technology has become increasingly pervasive and affordable, enabling people to communicate while not physically co-located. For example, FaceTime from Apple and Skype from Microsoft are pre-installed on many mobile and desktop devices. These video-based technologies enable a user to view and hear a remote partner. The IllumiShare, a prototype system created by Microsoft Research, provides the additional ability for partners to share any arbitrary surface. The IllumiShare device is a lamp with a web camera and a projector embedded next to the light bulb [14]. In this system, each user has in front of them a desktop including physical objects, overlaid with a projection of their partner's desktop and objects. Figure 1 illustrates paired IllumiShare desktops. The girl is placing her hand on her desktop, which is projected to her partner. He is tracing her hand with his pen. The illuminated rectangle on the table establishes a space for *joint interaction* [5].

Fig. 1. In the left-hand image, the girl places her hand on her IllumiShare desktop and sees a projection of her partner tracing her hand. She can also see his face and hear him via Skype. In the right-hand image, the boy traces the projection of his partner's hand.

In exploring the use of IllumiShare and Skype during remote playdates, we drew upon the concept of *embodied interaction* [7], which addresses the ways in which interactions with and through technology are fundamentally social and embodied. Embodied approaches to design strive to make a system's mediating interfaces recede in order to make user experiences directly tangible. Previous research exploring how neurotypical (NT) children play using IllumiShare and Skype [14] demonstrated that, when using IllumiShare, physical toys and their digital representations blend together into *tangible objects* to be used in play. By interacting with these digitally enabled tangible objects, the children engaged in technology-mediated social interactions. We build upon this research to study the remote play of neurodiverse (ND) pairs (comprised of neurotypical (NT) and neuro-atypical). From this perspective, we investigated our research questions:

R1: What are current playdate practices for families with children with autism?
R2: How can remote technologies be used to create authentic play experiences for children with autism?
R3: How do children with autism interact with remote technologies during play?

To address our research questions, we interviewed parents of autistic children and found that, while they value play as important to their child's development, they struggle to implement face-to-face playdates due to the challenges of finding appropriate nearby peers and busy schedules filled with medical appointments. We then conducted an exploratory user study with pairs of children, each consisting of a child with autism and a NT playmate. The children interacted via Microsoft Skype and IllumiShare while in different lab rooms. Our interaction analysis revealed that, through embodied interaction with real and virtual objects, the children created meaning in the form of mutual and parallel play, supporting important ToM skills. The children successfully negotiated variations of remote technology features. However, at times, the constraints of the technology impeded joint attention and perspective-taking. We contribute empirical findings based on parent interviews and interaction analysis of neurodiverse playmates playing remotely with tangible objects in an shared surface environment. We recommend design considerations for remote technologies to better support mutual play and ToM skills.

2 Related Work

In this section, we establish a connection between ToM and the cognitive and social skills involved in play. We highlight research on play among neurodiverse peers and recent research on technology-mediated play of children with autism.

2.1 Theory of Mind Skills and Play for Autistic Children

While no one theory holistically describes autism, we draw upon the ToM to better understand stages of cognitive development that are related to play. ToM, coined by Premack and Woodruff [18] and extended upon by Alan Leslie [16], is "the ability to infer other people's mental states (their thoughts, beliefs, desires, intentions, etc.), and the ability to use this information to interpret what they say, make sense of their behavior and predict what they will do next" [13]. Through conceptual perspective-taking tests designed to detect a child's awareness that their belief about an experimental situation is different than others, Baron-Cohen et al. found that "autistic children as a group fail to employ a theory of mind" [2, p. 43]. Due to this ToM gap demonstrated by research and seen in practice, researchers, parents, educators, and therapists aim to build ToM skills of autistic children. They do so by targeting key skills of engaging in pretend play, developing emotional literacy, and understanding information states (perspective taking and joint attention) [13, p. 2]. These skills are used during play. By conducting our research within the context of play, we used the real-world scenario of play to investigate ways children demonstrate ToM skills.

When children play, they are actively engaged in experiences that are pleasurable, intrinsically motivated, and flexible [26]. A key motivator for paired play is enjoying the camaraderie of playmates. Wolfberg et al. [25] found that integrated play groups are an effective forum for both neurodiverse and neurotypical children to develop relationships. Inclusive play provides autistic children the opportunity to develop social communication and reciprocity, while neurotypical children gain knowledge and skills to be flexible and responsive. Based on the benefits of integrated play groups, our study examines the verbal and non-verbal communication and reciprocal exchanges that arise during the free play of autistic children with their neurotypical play mates. We draw from Wolfberg's model of inclusive play to analyze our user study.

2.2   Technology-Mediated Play for Neurodiverse Children

Research on the play practices of autistic children focuses on the role of digital games in building social relationships and cognitive skills. Boyd et al. examined the usage of iPad games, finding that games support building friendships through features that enable children to fluidly join an activity and to coordinate their actions [4]. In research on how inclusive pairs used an iPad picture-taking application, Sobel et al. investigated the role of technology in enforcing cooperation and prompting for interactions [22]. On both dimensions, they had mixed results that depended on the naturally-occurring dynamics of the children. This points to the need for flexible game environments that can be adjusted based on the children's goals and dynamic. Both Boyd et al. and Sobel et al. discussed that the children bonded over being able to comment and share their gaming experience.

Specifically exploring embodied interactions, Farr et al. researched social interactions of autistic children playing with tangible objects on an Augmented Knight's Castle play set [9]. The researchers conducted interaction analysis and coded for play modes (e.g., disengaged; co-operative-social play) plus object-related actions (solitary versus parallel sensori-motor play). They found that the children who were allowed to extend the functionality of the objects (by activating pre-recorded audio) were motivated by the immediate feedback of the object and sought the attention of others to share the effects. Our research also employs interaction analysis and uses a similar play code scheme. However, our research is distinct in that we studied remote play in which the role of technology was to convey verbal and non-verbal interactions. In our case, the use of objects was intrinsic in the children's embodied interactions.

A popular platform for remote play is the Minecraft online gaming environment. Some Minecraft servers, such as AutCraft, are dedicated to players with autism and related neurodiverse conditions. Research on these dedicated servers has found that the players engage in social learning, problem solving, and community building through their use of the game's communication affordances (chat windows, avatars, and play activity) [20, 27]. Our research builds upon this examination of remote play by exploring the set of communication affordances supported in remote technology (audio, video, and a shared surface).

Overall, this body of knowledge informs our research with its emphasis on inclusive play experiences and exploring the role of technology to support play rather than constrict it. We use the methods of interaction analysis and video coding to identify evidence of ToM skills.

3   Method

We conducted semi-structured interviews with four mothers of children with Autism Spectrum Disorder (ASD) to gain an understanding of current playdate practices. They were recruited via a local autism therapy clinic and a local company's email list of self-selected employees with an interest in autism. In each hour-long interview, we inquired about their child's autism diagnosis and characteristics, current school and therapy strategies, current play goals, logistics, positive experiences, and challenges, and the use (if any) of technology for remote communication with friends and family. The children were all male, aged 3.5–11. Their parents identified them as having autism (with one child also having low cognition and a visual impairment). Two of the children attended mainstream class in public school. One child attended a class comprised of 50% ASD and 50% NT children. Another child attended special education class in public school and spent 1.5 h per day in a general education class. To analyze the interview results, two researchers used the affinity diagramming technique to generate themes.

Next, we conducted an exploratory user study with four pairs of children, each consisting of an autistic child and a neurotypical playmate. We recruited the children from the parents who participated in our interviews and from a local autism community group. All of the autistic children (4 male, ages 9–13) were confirmed as being on the autism spectrum by their parents and were verbal. None of the playmates (3 male, 1 female, ages 8–13) were identified by the parents as being on the autism spectrum. In this report, we changed the children's initials and indicated which child had autism by appending their initial with an apostrophe. The University of Washington Human Subjects ethics board approved this research.

During each session, the pair of children first interacted face-to-face to help researchers establish a baseline for their interactions. The children were instructed to spend 5 min playing together with any of the toys available on a nearby table (cards, cars, mermaid doll, and a Question and Answer style book). The NT child was then escorted to another lab. Each lab had similar toys and was equipped with a Microsoft Surface tablet running Skype, plus an IllumiShare device. As shown in Table 1, the pairs cycled through three conditions in random order: (1) Skype audio and video, (2) IllumiShare plus Skype audio and video, and (3) IllumiShare plus Skype audio only. Each pair experienced the "IllumiShare plus Skype audio and video" twice since the IllumiShare was novel technology that none of the children had previously experienced. (The children had previous experience with remote video applications.) They

Table 1. The pairs cycled through 3 conditions. "IllumiShare + Skype" was done twice. Audio and video were on for the "Skype" condition. Only audio was on for the "Skype-Audio only" condition.

Pair	Intro	1st	2nd	3rd	4th
1 (A' and D)	Face-to-face	IllumiShare + Skype	Skype	IllumiShare + Skype	IllumiShare + Skype-Audio only
2 (F' and G)	Face-to-face	Skype	IllumiShare + Skype	IllumiShare + Skype-Audio only	IllumiShare + Skype
3 (H' and K)	Face-to-face	IllumiShare + Skype	IllumiShare + Skype-Audio only	IllumiShare + Skype	Skype
4 (N' and P)	Face-to-face	IllumiShare + Skype-Audio only	IllumiShare + Skype	Skype	IllumiShare + Skype

played in each condition for no more than 10 min, with a researcher entering the room to adjust the equipment for each condition. The sessions ended by debriefing each child separately, during which they were asked their favorite play activity and if anything was bothersome about the play session.

Our analysis of video recordings followed Goodwin's protocols of interaction analysis, a method often used in the systematic investigation of mundane activities ranging from families at the dinner table [8] to interactions of adults with communication disorders [23]. By conducting a detailed interaction analysis, Goodwin describes an "embodied participation framework" comprised of body positioning, artifacts, gestures, gazes, and linguistic markers. Order matters when it comes to interpreting gestures, language, and structure in the environment, making it important to develop a coding technique that accounts not just for isolated instances but sequences of actions. In our analysis, we closely examined specific interactions, prioritizing depth and richness of data over quantity of participants. We followed Erickson's [8] inductive procedure in which researchers iteratively view the video corpus to identify major events, transitions, and themes. The first analytic pass occurred during the sessions as two researchers coded for the Play Categories listed in the first column of Table 2: disengagement, parallel play, mutual play, and negotiation. After all the sessions were completed, we discussed the major events and themes we had coded while observing the sessions and then wrote memos defining, clarifying, and refining observations. The refined Social Play codes and definitions are the result of these analytic activities and are based directly on Wolfberg et al.'s [25] research on integrated play groups. With both empirical and theoretical support for this inductive schema, one of the researchers coded the video corpus to these more refined Social Play Codes. For Isolate and Onlooker-orientation codes, we observed instances where both children showed this behavior. Therefore, we appended ASD and NT as appropriate. Finally, we transcribed key excerpts for salient talk, singing and paralinguistic elements.

Table 2. Codes and definitions for our interaction analysis.

Initial play categories	Refined social play codes	Refined social play definitions
Disengagement	Isolate – ASD Isolate – NT	Child acts unaware of peer. Wanders, occupies self.
Parallel play	Onlooker-orientation – ASD Onlooker-orientation – NT	Child looks at peer or at their play materials. Does not enter into play.
	Parallel-proximity	Child plays independently beside peer.
Mutual play	Common focus	Child interacts with peer with shared attention on the play. Indicated by joint action, mutual imitation, sharing emotional expression, sharing materials, taking turns, giving and receiving assistance.
	Common goal	Child and peer cooperate in play by planning and executing a shared agenda. Indicated by defining rules and roles, negotiating, compromising, coordinating and supplementing.

4   Results

4.1   Families Face Challenging Play Logistics

During our interviews with parents, we found that families struggled to incorporate playdates into busy schedules of school, doctor's appointments, and regular and intense therapy in the following areas: physical, occupational, speech, social skills, Applied Behavior Analysis, and Relationship Development Intervention. The parents value the benefits of playdates (i.e., learning typical social skills; negotiating), noting that mutual play with appropriate-level peers is critical for their children. The parents described difficulties finding playmates with complementary schedules, play skills, and interests. All of the families had previously used Skype or FaceTime on their desktop computers or mobile devices. Two families regularly used FaceTime with family members, for example a traveling parent or grandparents who live far away. Based on these experiences, parents expressed a primary concern that conversations using these tools can easily became stifled unless the other party was entertaining and engaging.

Additionally, parents expressed worries about the social dynamics presented by their children's play environments. To these parents of ASD children, positive social engagement in face-to-face play means that their child is very animated, participating in the activity, and laughing at appropriate times. Importantly, parents did not consider eye contact to be a critical component of play. Instead, they valued parallel play, such as sitting side-by-side while playing video games independently. For example, P4's mother speculated that not being forced to make eye contact with his friend allowed her son to feel more comfortable. Other parents noted similar difficulties their children experienced during face-to-face play due to tendencies of being rigid and having difficulty conforming to play activities. Some parents noted that their children sometimes have problems taking turns and sharing toys. The parents said that due to these challenges, play can quickly turn to arguments and disruptive behavior (e.g., throwing things). Difficult social interactions, changes in routines, and being in unfamiliar environments can wear out the children, increasing the likelihood that children will need to perform self-soothing behaviors such as hand flapping, putting their head down, hitting their face with a stuffed animal, and, with a parent's guidance, taking deep breaths.

4.2 Mutual Play Through Embodied Interaction

Taken together, *common focus* on each other and materials, along with setting and executing *common goals*, result in mutual play [25]. In our study, the children's mutual play began during the face-to-face baseline session in which they discussed what they thought they were going to do, and played with the toys or spun in the chairs. In some pairs, one child was more vocal than the other; in other pairs, both children were equally vocal. When the children were placed in separate rooms, researchers assessed typical markers of conversational alignment [12] such as tone of voice, body language, and amount of dialog. Based on these markers, the children exhibited play dynamics that were consistent with their face-to-face behaviors. Throughout the sessions, the children jointly established their common focus and goals through technology-mediated verbal exchanges and non-verbal communication using their body and objects. For example, their mutual play was based on negotiating how to co-create using physical and virtual artifacts (e.g., taking turns tracing each other's autographs), cooperating to use material only accessible to one child (e.g., a book; digital media from tablet), and planning how to use jointly-accessible artifacts used in combination to create a shared surface game space (e.g., card game).

Common Focus. We observed instances of all aspects of common focus, as defined in our codebook: joint action, mutual imitation, sharing emotional expression, sharing materials, taking turns, giving and receiving assistance, and directives. Upon starting their remote play, all pairs began establishing a baseline of what their partner could see and hear. The children jointly made sense of their environment through this inquisitive form of play. As illustrated in Excerpt 1, we can look at interactions between A' and his younger sister, C, who their mom described as often taking a "nurturing, mothering" role with A'.

Excerpt 1, First Interaction[a]	
1D:	A', are you drawing on a separate piece of paper?
2A':	I'm drawing autographs." ((holding pen))
3D:	Wait, where are you...where are you drawing it on? Are you drawing on the paper that's taped? ((*feels the edges of her paper*))
4A':	(.5 s) N::no.
5D:	Okay
6A':	(1 s) Hey, let's thumbs up! ((*reaching right hand out toward Skype, into IllumiShare desktop, with his thumb up*)) (Fig. 2)
7D:	Thumbs up! ((*forms thumbs up with her hands, extending toward Skype and over IllumiShare*)) (Fig. 3)

Fig. 2. In the left-hand image, A' says, "Hey, let's thumbs up!" and extends his right hand. In the right-hand image, his thumbs up is projected to D via Skype and IllumiShare.

Fig. 3. D returns A's thumbs up

[a]We used the Modified Jefferson transcription convention [24]. Turns at talk are numbered for identified speakers. Continuous speech at turn boundaries is shown with = equal signs, while onset of [overlapping talk is shown with left brackets. EMPHATIC talk is shown in caps, and elong:::ated enunciation is shown with repeated colons. ((*Activity descriptions*)) appear within double parentheses and in italics, and > comparatively quick speech < appears in angle brackets. We extended the convention in two ways: (1) The child with autism is indicated with an apostrophe, and (2) {{*Technology descriptions*}} appear within double curly parentheses and in italics.

Joint Attention. Attending to a person or object is a behavior that tends to be difficult for children with autism. This was evidenced when the pair directed their actions toward a common object or activity. The children demonstrated that they were attending to the same object or activity through verbal communication, gestures, moving objects, or drawing pen marks. When a child looked toward the Skype video, we made general observations that they were looking for the presence of their peer or for visual communication. When a child was looking at another object, such as a book, instead of at the IllumiShare desktop, we observed that they were at least partially engaged by the object. In the case of Pair 3, H' and K, their sociotechnical interactions were enriched by their personal tablets, which they brought to the study. According to H''s mother, they primarily played video games when together. During the face-to-face portion of the session, K was preoccupied with his tablet, watching YouTube videos of Minecraft gameplay. H' started playing with cars. When Illumishare + Skype was introduced, the two expressed excitement with comments like "wow" and "this is so cool." H' spent the majority of the time drawing a cat character, even using his iPad to look up the character as a reference. In one interaction, K gave explicit directions to H' asking for visual access to his marks (Excerpt 2). This type of interaction through drawing has been established as an important form of communicative practice [21].

Excerpt 2, Placing Marks	
1H':	Draw in the middle of the paper so I can see what you're drawing.
2K:	(1 s) I can totally see your drawing too.

In another example, F' and G spent almost the entire session playing cards, actively engaged with playing and, as conditions changed, expressing delight and talking about what to adjust in their game. In their first condition (Skype), F' directed play, asking if G could see his cards and telling G to hold up his cards. Sometimes, a physical action was adequate to convey meaning, with no words necessary, as shown by G holding up his card in Excerpt 3.

Excerpt 3, Verbal and Visual Checks	
1F':	((holds up cards to the camera)) "Show your cards to the other person."
2G:	((holds up his cards))
3F':	Currently you have 14 chips, is that correct?
4G:	Yeah.

During mutual play, they placed joint attention on the artifacts and, when they oriented themselves toward the camera, toward each other.

Taking Turns. Turn taking is another behavior that tends to pose challenges for children with autism. People can asynchronously and explicitly take turns (such as making a move during chess) or they can take turns more informally (such as dressing a doll together). In our study, we observed both styles of turn-taking. As an example of asynchronous turn-taking, A' and D began their session with A' writing Disney princess autographs, while D followed along, tracing what A' drew. The IllumiShare + Skype-Audio condition enabled their mutual play of writing and tracing. They negotiated their Disney signature tracing activity with the use of words, drawing, and observing. (Excerpt 4). When the IllumiShare was turned off and they just had Skype, they continued drawing autographs in a more parallel play fashion. They then switched to a "Would you rather?" verbal exchange for a few minutes.

Excerpt 4, Explicit Directions	
1A':	How do you like that? ((After drawing the signatures across the page.))
2D:	Keep it right there, I'm gonna trace.
3A':	((watches, waits for her to trace))
4D:	Who's next?

For Pair 4, N' and P, a major play activity was choreographing the signing of a song about the U.S. states. In the IllumiShare condition, N' spontaneously began writing down the state names, and P, recognizing the order of the states as a song they learned in school, began singing them as N' wrote. N' and P switched roles as writer and singer. When the condition changed to Skype, N' did not realize that the Illumi-Share was now off. He put his finger on one of the lyrics and asked P to sing, but P said he could not see where N' was pointing. As shown in Fig. 4, N' then decided to hold up the paper to the Skype camera so P could see where he was pointing. It took N' a while to find a successful way to show P where to start singing. This example demonstrates a technological barrier to the children fluidly taking turns in this condition.

Fig. 4. N' struggles to simultaneously point to the correct word while showing it to P.

Common Goal. During mutual play, children establish common goals about their activities and roles. Mutual goal setting involves negotiation and compromise, requiring a child to express his views and consider the views of others. We observed negotiation as play began, at points within play when roles or activities were clarified or changed, and as technology conditions changed. The sociotechnical nature of the study required the children to negotiate how to share materials (e.g., playing with cards shared between their physical and virtual space) and the IllumiShare desktop. When the latter occurred, the children needed to accommodate the changed video and audio modes of communication. They re-established how the play activity would proceed and negotiated how they would share materials. The majority of children expressed delight when Skype video was back on and they could see each other. For instance, K commented "I can see your face!", and both waved at each other. When Skype video was turned off, the children often adapted by being more vocal. P3 (H') and his friend (K) had to verbally check in with each other to see if the other was active and paying attention during their play.

When F' and his friend G were in the Skype-only condition, they struggled to play a card game without visual access to the desktop. F' tried so show G his cards on the table by physically re-orienting the tablet running Skype, but the tablet fell on the table. When the IllumiShare came on, they quickly adjusted their actions to leverage visual access, which eliminated the need to hold up their cards to Skype, thus freeing up their hands (Excerpt 5). The pair used explicit statements questioning to establish their mental model of their own perspective and their peer's visual perspective, which is a key step in building ToM.

Excerpt 5, Checking In	
1F':	I have a question, can you see these cards on the ground? o::oh::h!
2G':	I can see the cards.
3F':	Oh, you can actually see them! That is so awesome! Can you see me?

In Excerpt 6, F' and G figured out how to strategize their play when they lost video and could only rely on IllumiShare + Skype - Audio. (Note that F' also broke the fourth-wall of research, instructing the researchers to "turn the video back on" and contemplating the researchers' intentions.) They used a verbal exchange, informed by knowledge of what the other child could see, to re-affirm their common goal.

Excerpt 6, Figuring Things Out	
{{Skype is turned off.}}	
1F':	Hello?
2G':	Huh? Our video is turned off?
3F':	We need to think of a new way to play…that's what they wanted us to do….Turn the video back on! Just kidding! <Spoken into the room> I'm thinking…Oh wait, you can still see the table! So we can still play the same game, but with showing them on the table.

4.3 Nature of Parallel Play and Disengagement

We observed multiple instances of parallel play in the form of onlooker-orientation and parallel-proximity play. We based our coding on evidence of independence such as: (1) attention on different types of objects, (2) absence of dialog or gestures about play goals and activities, and (3) uncoordinated drawing on separate places in the IllumiShare. For example, A' and D exhibited parallel play when they drew independently without speaking or coordinating their drawings. As illustrated in Excerpt 7, at one point, A' wanted D to comment on his drawings, but D did not respond. Upon further prompting, D gave a minimal, onlooker-type response, even though she actually could not see his drawing. This example demonstrates the difficulty in sustaining mutual play, especially when the technology was not flexible enough to show A' what D was actually engaged in.

Excerpt 7, Missed Connection	
1A':	(8 s) ((A' drawing map of animal park, within IllumiShare frame. D is reading book, out of IllumiShare frame.)) ((A' folds up his paper with map. Paper ruffling.))
2A':	Hey, D. ((looking at Skype))
3D:	(1 s) Haha! ((A' glances down and back at Skype))
4D:	(.5 s) What?
5A':	= H::here's a map of Sudden Defiance Animal Map ((unfolding map to reveal it. Holds it vertically to Skype. D only can see A''s hand and the top edges of A''s paper. D moving her paper off IllumiShare frame with one hand, keeping her place in book with other hand.))
6D:	Oh, that's cool. ((Puts down pen, glances at Skype, looks down at book. A' looking at Skype, which shows user icons.))
7A':	What's your favorite so far? ((Leaning his map back so he can see it, which is still out of the IllumiShare frame))
8D:	I like the…um::m…((glances at IllumiShare frame, which does not show the map, then back at book)) … the ocelots. (Figure 5)
9A':	Usually at my zoo, they'll be two ocelots. ((holding up two fingers))
10D:	Yeah. ((eyes remain down at book))

Fig. 5. A' is writing "ocelot" and talking to D, who is engrossed in her book.

Disengaged. On rare occasions, the children shifted from parallel play to disengagement. One striking example is Pair 4, H' and K. In their face-to-face condition, H' and K sat far away from each other, with H' wandering around the room and K playing on his tablet with his headphones in. This dynamic was occasionally replicated when they were in separate lab rooms. K was intent on streaming music and video from his tablet. The audio streamed automatically to H' via Skype audio. H' focused mainly on drawing his cat characters. At one point, K wanted to show H' a video so he put his tablet down on the IllumiShare desktop. Unfortunately, H' said he could not see it, which was due to the screen glare caused by the IllumiShare lamp, so he resumed drawing. This demonstrates that even when the children attempted to establish a common focus, the technology barrier and a lack of a common goal prevented mutual play.

5 Discussion

To summarize the nature of the children's remote play, they used fluid, intrinsically motivated embodied interactions while engaging in both mutual and parallel play. Their remote play dynamics were congruent with their baseline face-to-face play dynamics. The children exhibited the ability to focus jointly on a common goal. They exhibited ToM skills such as taking turns and predicting actions when they sang, traced autographs, and played cards. The mutual and parallel play categories that established by previous work on face-to-face play extended effectively to remote play. However, the remote-nature of their play had its challenges, which we surfaced through inter-action analysis. The children needed to adapt their play to account for the changing capabilities and constraints of the remote technology. The new audio and visual capabilities were not always readily apparent to the children. In these cases, their interactions became strained when a child continued playing as if the original com-munication channel (e.g., Skype video) was still available. The children also had difficulty pulling their peer back into previously established goals if their peer had independently shifted to a new activity. Despite being disappointing to the child when this happened, disagreements over play activities is a natural aspect of free-play. Therefore, we conclude that the children exhibited authentic play while not co-located.

There were some unique qualities of being remote that facilitated play and strengthened their ToM skills. Once in different rooms, the children were motivated to establish a connection with their peer. They articulated their sense of self by explaining their sensory capabilities (what they could hear, see, and do) and compared that to their peer's experience. The children made discoveries about how they could share materials and adjust rules of games to play collaboratively. The children engaged in all types of play (mutual and parallel), regardless of the specific remote technology. We found it counter-intuitive that the condition with the *richest* modes of interaction, Illumi-Share + Skype, was *not* immune to the *least* desirable mode of interaction, isolated play. And the condition with the *least-rich* communication channel, Skype, was suf-ficient for *mutual* play. This achievement means that children, with today's publically available technology, can host authentic playdates.

Another implication of effective technology-mediated play is that the children's interaction styles were successful over communication channels that are more restricted than face-to-face communication. In our case, and in other research such as Minecraft servers geared toward autism communities [20, 27], there is synergy between autistic children's communication preferences and technology-mediated communication. A remote technology channel distills social interactions down to dialog (aloud or in chat), body language (projected or embodied in an avatar), and manipulation of objects (physical and digital). Aspects of social interactions that can be difficult for people with autism are limited (e.g., eye contact) or eliminated altogether (e.g., physical touch).

Technology-mediated communication also facilitates asynchronous communication, which can be a preference for people with autism [17], thus loosening the expectations of managing synchronous, unpredictable in-person communication. Interestingly, adding the IllumiShare desktop, which enriches the communication channel, also benefitted the children. They could more easily engage in familiar, table-based activities and did not have to engage in extra work to share the materials and their actions. This points to an element of authentic embodied interaction—the value of easily communicating and sharing embodied actions without requiring an extra step to explicitly share the interaction with each other.

Although our research yielded rich qualitative data, we had a limited number of interview and study participants. By conducting the study in a lab, the children were asked to play in an unknown environment with unknown researchers, which can be disorienting for children with autism. Future studies could be conducted in a setting familiar to the child, such as home or school, and perhaps over a longer period of time to evaluate the effect of novel technology. Future research could also explicitly explore symbolic play with objects, which is a component of Wolfberg's play model and could lead to deeper insights on the role of tangible objects [25].

6 Design Considerations

Based on our exploratory research and given the limitations of our study, we offer the following design considerations for remote technology toward enhancing mutual play and ToM skills. We target our design direction toward (1) reinforcing embodied interactions to scaffold mutual play and (2) using technology to strengthen shared experiences.

6.1 Reinforcing Embodied Interactions to Facilitate Mutual Play

Our first design direction aims to help children successfully establish mutual goals and focus, which requires navigating shifts in play. The remote technology environment should amplify the children's embodied interactions to emphasize directions toward mutual play. Shifts between mutual and parallel play tended to occur when a child became interested in another activity. These transitions between activities were often accompanied by (1) new objects being used, or (2) verbal and non-verbal communication from a child without reciprocal communication from his peer. Interestingly, the child who left the original activity for a new one was often the neurotypical child, perhaps because the autistic child was often still immersed in the original activity. This points to a common trait among people with autism—the ability to deeply pursue interests [1] and engage in activities that are personally motivating [6]. Regardless of who tried to initiate mutual play with a new activity, unsuccessful attempts to engage over time resulted in both children becoming absorbed in their own activities.

At these vulnerable points, it would be helpful for a child to gain the attention of their peer in a more purposeful and concrete manner. This could be accomplished by making the system aware of the children's gestural attempts to engage each other.

When the pair's non-verbal, verbal, and object movements indicate there is a vulnerable point of play, the system could initiate visual cues (e.g., changing the color hue of the IllumiShare light) or audio cue (a beep) to draw the pair's joint attention. An alternative approach could be to provide controls (e.g., a button on the IllumiShare surface), "smart" tangible object (one with knowledge of its location, user, and state of play), or a gesture vocabulary to the children, so they can activate sounds and visual cues in the shared environment.

To further promote joint attention when the pair is veering off to different activities within the IllumiShare space, there could be features that nudge the pair toward a common area of the IllumiShare desktop. For instance, if one child is focusing on one corner (e.g., drawing animals) and their peer is focusing on another corner (e.g., writing), the IllumiShare could display visual cues to bring their attention together, perhaps using a trail of lights. As with any auto-detection software, care would need to be taken to correctly distinguish between desired (mutual) and less desired (parallel-proximity) activities.

6.2   Strengthening Relationships Through Shared Experiences

Our second design direction is toward strengthening the bond between the children. As discussed in the Related Work section, children valued being able to comment on their coordinated experiences and share them with others. In our study, the children verbally and physically checked in with each other (e.g., giving each other thumbs up), and often discussed what they were able to see, hear, and do. By taking a step back and discussing their experience, they were establishing a common understanding and frame of reference. The technology could do more to create a sense of joint experience with mechanisms for capturing the experience. The children could take screen captures of each other on Skype and their IllumiShare desktops. When they experience something funny or confusing, they could request that the system retroactively capture the last two minutes of the experience, for example. They could then review their experience from their vantage point or from their peer's. Along with being a compelling way for a child to be immersed in the sensory experience of their peer, this flipped vantage point could help the pair resolve confusion about their play strategies. Ultimately, the children may choose to share their vignettes with other peers and trusted adults, deepening each other's understanding of the play experiences of the children.

7   Conclusion

Motivated by the barriers faced by children with autism to participate in inclusive play, we examined the opportunity of conducting playdates over remote technologies. Through video conferencing and a shared surface, the children in our study carried out embodied interactions, thus leveraging their non-verbal communication skills to convey their intentions to, and interact with, their peer. This naturalistic style of play contributed to authentic, socially appropriate play experiences that our parent interviewees desire for their children. Although it is not possible to observe mental states, we observed behaviors that point to mental states that support a child's ToM. We found that there is not a direct correlation between the type of play (mutual versus parallel) and the specific remote technology. The design of remote technology can amplify children's embodied interaction, and therefore, scaffold mutual play. Remote play technology can facilitate reflecting and sharing play vignettes, toward the goal of strengthening social bonds. Although remote technologies provide a less-rich communication environment than face-to-face interactions, the communication and dynamics of remote technologies are adequate for inclusive play, and in some ways may be more ideal for children on the autism spectrum.

Acknowledgements. Thank you to Microsoft Research, especially Sasa Junuzovic, for guidance on this research and access to the IllumiShare. Thank you to Julie Kientz for direction on our project, Kiley Sobel for piloting our codebook, and Katie Headrick Taylor for inspiration on interaction analysis.

References

1. American Psychiatric Association. Diagnostic and Statistical Manual of Mental Disorders (5th ed.) (2013)
2. Baron-Cohen, S., Leslie, A.M., Frith, U.: Does the autistic child have a "theory of mind"? Cognition **21**(1), 37–46 (1985)
3. Boutot, E.A., Guenther, T., Crozier, S.: Let's play: teaching play skills to young children with autism. Educ. Training Dev. Disabil. **40**, 285–292 (2005)
4. Boyd, L.E., Ringland, K.E., Haimson, O.L., Fernandez, H., Bistarkey, M., Hayes, G.R.: Evaluating a collaborative iPad game's impact on social relationships for children with autism spectrum disorder. ACM Trans. Accessible Comput. **7**(1), 1–18 (2015). https://doi.org/10.1145/2751564
5. Clark, H.H.: Using Language. Cambridge University Press, New York (1996)
6. Dawson, M., Mottron, L., Gernsbacher, M.A.: Learning in autism. In: Learning and memory: A Comprehensive Reference: Cognitive Psychology, 759–772. Elsevier, New York (2008). http://www.epubbud.com/read.php?g=ET5HW22S&p=1. Accessed 18 Dec 2016
7. Dourish, P.: Where the Action Is. MIT Press, Cambridge (2001). http://cognet.mit.edu. offcampus.lib.washington.edu/book/where-action. Accessed 17 Dec 2016
8. Erickson, F.: Talk and social theory: ecologies of speaking and listening in everyday Life. Polity (2004). http://www.polity.co.uk/book.asp?ref=9780745624709. Accessed 1 Apr 2016
9. Farr, W., Yuill, N., Hinske, S.: An augmented toy and social interaction in children with autism. Int. J. Arts Technol. **5**(2–4), 104–125 (2012)
10. Freeman, S., Kasari, C.: Parent–child interactions in autism: characteristics of play. Autism **17**(2), 147–161 (2013)
11. Alvin I. Goldman. 2012. Theory of Mind. The Oxford Handbook of Philosophy of Cognitive Science, pp. 402–424
12. Gumperz, J.J.: Discourse Strategies. Cambridge University Press, Cambridge, UK (1982)
13. Howlin, P., Baron-Cohen, S., Hadwin, J.: Teaching Children with Autism to Mind-Read: A Practical Guide for Teachers and Parents by Patricia Howlin. Wiley, Chicago (1999)
14. Junuzovic, S., Inkpen, K., Blank, T., Gupta, A.: IllumiShare: sharing any surface. In: Proceedings of the SIGCHI Conference on Human Factors in Computing Systems, pp. 1919–1928 (2012). http://dl.acm.org/citation.cfm?id=2208333. Accessed 10 June 2016

15. Kenny, L., Hattersley, C., Molins, B., Buckley, C., Povey, C., Pellicano, E.: Which terms should be used to describe autism? Perspectives from the UK autism community. Autism (2015). http://dx.doi.org/10.1177/1362361315588200

16. Leslie, A.M.: Pretending and believing: issues in the theory of ToMM. Cognition **50**(1–3), 211–238 (1994)

17. Morris, M.R., Begel, A., Wiedermann, B.: Understanding the challenges faced by neurodiverse software engineering employees: towards a more inclusive and productive technical workforce. In: Proceedings of the ACM SIGACCESS Conference on Computers & Accessibility (ASSETS 2015), pp. 173–184 (2015). http://dl.acm.org/citation.cfm?id=2809841. Accessed 9 Apr 2016

18. Premack, D., Woodruff, G.: Does the chimpanzee have a theory of mind? Behav. Brain Sci. **1**(4), 515–526 (1978). https://doi.org/10.1017/S0140525X00076512

19. Quill, K.A.: Teaching Children with Autism: Strategies to Enhance Communication and Socialization. Cengage Learning, Boston (1995)

20. Ringland, K.E., Wolf, C.T., Faucett, H., Dombrowski, L., Hayes, G.R.: "Will i always not be social?": re-conceptualizing sociality in the context of a minecraft community for autism. In: Proceedings of the 2016 CHI Conference on Human Factors in Computing Systems (2016)

21. Snyder, J.: Visual representation of information as communicative practice: journal of the American society for information science and technology. J. Assoc. Inf. Sci. Technol. **65** (11), 2233–2247 (2014). https://doi.org/10.1002/asi.23103

22. Sobel, K., Rector, K., Evans, S., Kientz, J.A.: Incloodle: evaluating an interactive application for young children with mixed abilities, pp. 165–176 (2016). https://doi.org/10.1145/2858036.2858114

23. Streeck, J.: Gesture as communication I: its coordination with gaze and speech. Commun. Monogr. **60**(4), 275–299 (1993)

24. Taylor, K.H., Hall, R.: Counter-mapping the neighborhood on bicycles: mobilizing youth to reimagine the city. Technol. Knowl. Learn. **18**(1–2), 65–93 (2013). https://doi.org/10.1007/s10758-013-9201-5

25. Wolfberg, P., DeWitt, M., Young, G.S., Nguyen, T.: Integrated play groups: promoting symbolic play and social engagement with typical peers in children with ASD across settings. J. Autism Dev. Disord. **45**(3), 830–845 (2015). https://doi.org/10.1007/s10803-014-2245-0

26. Wolfberg, P.J.: Play and Imagination in Children with Autism, 2nd edn. Teachers College Press, New York (2009)

27. Zolyomi, A., Schmalz, M.: Mining for Social Skills: Minecraft in Home and Therapy for Neurodiverse Youth. In: Proceedings of the 50th Hawaii International Conference on System Sciences (2017). http://scholarspace.manoa.hawaii.edu/handle/10125/41569. Accessed 6 Jan 2017

DUXU for Art, Culture, Tourism and Environment

Perception of Source Credibility Within Touristic Virtual Communities: A Cross-Generational Examination

Aleksander Groth(✉), Giulietta Constantini, and Stephan Schlögl

Interaction Lab, Department Management, Communication and IT,
Management Center Innsbruck, Innsbruck, Austria
{aleksander.groth, stephan.schloegl}@mci.edu,
giulietta.constantini@outlook.com

Abstract. Online reviews are an important factor in the pre-purchase phase of tourist products, but lack social cues to enable an evaluation of the source's trustworthiness, leading to uncertainty towards the source itself. Drawing upon generational theory, generations differ in their attitudes towards the credibility of online information and their touristic purchase behaviors. A differentiation between actively and passively sought cues regarding source (e.g. profile pictures) and message characteristics (e.g. trustworthiness) is made, in order to better understand the attitudes towards online reviews. An eye tracking study with ten participants of Generation Y and seven of Generation Baby Boomer was conducted on the travel site Tripadvisor.com. Results show that Generation Y and Generation Baby Boomer differ significantly in their attitude towards user generated content. Generation Baby Boomer relies less frequently on reviews than Generation Y, reads reviews less frequently and seeks for elements indicating the level of source credibility. For both generations, message characteristics including factors such as the quality of the language, the length of a message and the congruence with personal interests represent the most important cues in the evaluation of source credibility. Generation BB does not pay attention to source characteristics at all but derives some of them, such as travel interests or the experience of a reviewer, from message characteristics.

Keywords: Source credibility · Electronic word-of-mouth · Eye tracking

1 Introduction

The rise of online booking and reservation systems has led to changes in the strategic and operational processes in travel agencies and destination management organizations, offering new opportunities for tourists in their purchase decision making processes and in the possibility to browse past experiences and reviews of touristic products [1]. Electronic word-of-mouth (eWOM) functionalities, like online reviews, have been integrated in and transformed social media sites into active virtual online communities or touristic online review sites, such as e.g. TripAdvisor [2]. Travelers are given the opportunity to exchange and consume touristic experiences online through text, videos and photographs [3].

© Springer International Publishing AG 2017
A. Marcus and W. Wang (Eds.): DUXU 2017, Part III, LNCS 10290, pp. 435–452, 2017.
DOI: 10.1007/978-3-319-58640-3_31

Due to the intangible character of experience goods, an evaluation of such products in the pre-purchase phase proves to be difficult. Hence, purchase decisions evolve around interpersonal influences, which are generated through online reviews and shared on virtual online communities [4]. In order to mitigate the prevailing feeling of uncertainty, consumers seek for online information about a product and for shared experiences by former customers, which leads to indirect purchasing experiences [5].

Since eWOM does not provide any nonverbal or contextual cues, consumers are confronted with the obstacle to base their evaluation about the credibility and integrity of a source on the information provided by the website. While a connection and significant tie-strength between information sender and receiver is remarkable in traditional word of mouth, no social connection can be recognized in eWOM. Even more, a main characteristic of eWOM is its indirect - and mostly public – communication, wherein no emotional connection between sender and receiver can be recognized [6]. This weak tie strength between information sender and receiver leads to a difficult assessment of a source's credibility. Therefore, cues for source credibility are sought to reduce feelings of uncertainty. Individuals browse and look for information displayed on the website, that provides them with cues about the reliability of a source. Such cues help in the assessment of the credibility of a reviewer and play an essential role in consumers' decision making processes [7].

This study investigates relevant information cues in online reviews of touristic products and how such cues are evaluated regarding the credibility of an information source in touristic virtual communities, based on the example of TripAdvisor. It is analyzed, whether user-generated content is relevant at all for these two generations, when booking a vacation online. In a further step, the study aims at investigating how source credibility is perceived differently by Generation Y and Generation Baby Boomer and through which factors such a difference is manifested. Since generations are said to have diverse attitudes towards online media and purchase behaviors, the question arises, whether this theory can also be applied to the topic of source credibility. Thus, the following research question is derived: *What are the differences in perceived cues for source credibility between Generation Y and Generation Baby Boomers in touristic community websites?*

2   Source Credibility Theory

Hovland refers to credibility as the degree of perceived believability of a set of information or a source [8]. Fogg and Tseng [9] describe credibility as "*a perceived quality (…), it does not reside within an object, a person or a piece of information.*" Hence, people who are described as credible are considered believable and information that is described as credible is regarded as believable information. Further, a distinction between source credibility and message credibility can be made.

There are various models explaining source credibility and its elements, with many based on the original model introduced by Hovland. This model consists of two factors, namely *perceived expertise* and *perceived trustworthiness*. The rating of these parameters lies in the subjective perception of the receiver. Source credibility is proven to have a positive effect on overall message credibility. Due to the intangible character and the associated economic and psychological risks within touristic decision making, as well as the absence of physical cues within eWOM, source credibility plays an especially important role in the travel and tourism industry [10]. Perceived source credibility has a significant impact on the attitude, opinion formation as well as the future behavior of the message receiver [8].

Ayeh et al. extended the model of source credibility by including a consumers' attitude towards a product, brand or company through three factors: Trustworthiness, Expertise, and Homophily [2].

Trustworthiness is defined as *"the degree of confidence in the communicator's intent to communicate the assertions he/she considers most valid."* [8] Mayer and Davis similarly describe trustworthiness as *"the willingness of a party to be vulnerable to the actions of another party based on the expectation that the other party will perform a particular action important to the trustor, irrespective of the ability to monitor or control that other party"* [11]. Ohanian agrees with this definition, stating that trustworthiness describes the consumer's confidence in the reviewer providing honest and objective information. Trustworthy reviewers do not have any intention to mislead the customer and are willing to tell the truth based on their experiences. Thus, perceived trustworthiness can lead to a change in someone's attitude and has the potential to influence purchase intentions. It is assumed that perceived trustworthiness positively effects the attitude towards using eWOM as a source for travel planning [12].

Expertise is said to influence the credibility of a source immensely [8] and is defined as the extent *"to which user generated content contributors are perceived to be a source of valid assertions"* (p. 23). It is the degree to which someone considers the information provider to possess enough knowledge and skills in order to make qualified statements about a topic [12]. In the context of touristic eWOM, expertise is regarded as a component of the *"multi-dimensional construct of prior knowledge that includes the elements familiarity and past experience."* [13] Someone who is considered an expert in a special field of interest is likely to produce more product- and purchase related messages than a non-expert. That is, an expert's opinion is taken into consideration more often than the opinion of non-experts. Due to their knowledge and degree of experience, experts are perceived as more influential and possess a higher degree of persuasion power than non-experts [14].

Homophily is an element which has derived from McGuire's "Source-Attractiveness Model" and is defined as the similarity between the sender and the receiver of a message regarding specific attributes [15]. The fundamental principle of social homophily can be found in Laumann's theory and represents the so-called "like-me principle" which states that individuals tend to establish relationships with people that are similar to them in their interests and attitudes and belong to an equal social status [16]. While in former times, homophily was rather regarded as a characteristic based on similar demographics, it is nowadays seen as a construct of shared mindsets and interests [17]. Individuals tend to interact with people that are like them. Hence, when reading reviews, consumers tend to seek for characteristics, mindsets and values of a reviewer fitting their own values. If similar values as well as similar preferences are recognizable, an increased extent of perceived homophily can be recognized [15].

Consumers tend to rather rely on eWOM created by people that have similar interests and mindsets. The perceived trustworthiness and expertise of an information source are determined by the congruence between the sender's and the receiver's mindsets [2]. Still, in online communication social homophily does not necessarily need to have an impact on credibility or attitude formation. A reason can be the lack of personal knowledge, which may be substituted by specific cues in online communication [14].

3 Source Characteristics as Cues for Source Credibility

As information providers are typically unknown within eWOM, individuals can only make assumptions about their intentions. Thus, they are searching for cues in order to assess the credibility of an information source, which subsequently determines the credibility of the review and the overall attitude. Source characteristics are often used to make judgements about the credibility of a source. Many consumer review sites allow a reviewer to display personal information. Such cues of information are an aid for readers in the formation of impressions and judgments [7]. The disclosure of identity information of a reviewer has an impact on the overall credibility of a message and its' source. It reduces uncertainty, which frequently evolves from the lack of social cues in online communication [18]. Moreover, the presence of social information leads to an increased perception of interpersonal warmth and affection [19].

A distinction between self-generated and system-generated cues can be made. Self-generated cues refer to information provided by the information sender, whereas system-generated cues include elements such as the reputation among other users [7].

3.1 Self-Generated Cues

Self-disclosure explains the phenomenon of individuals enclosing inner private and intimate information to a broader public within virtual communities. In a broader sense, it explains the phenomenon of conveying messages that are related to themselves and include thoughts, feelings and experiences. This also refers to individuals creating a so-called online identity – a special kind of social identity within virtual communities or web spaces [7]. Self-disclosure leads to an enhancement of interpersonal relationships; intimate relationships are built. A communication partner who encloses personal details is perceived as more credible. Credibility increases as the information enables the receiver to conform to the previous expectations about the sender [20]. Nevertheless, reviews including personal information are perceived as less credible than reviews providing no personal information at all [21].

Profile Picture. Within Uncertainty Reduction Theory, individuals avoid the feeling of uncertainty in interpersonal relationships. In order to reduce this feeling online, profile pictures are disclosed. This can reduce the feeling of uncertainty and transforms the impersonal relationship into a personal conversation [22]. The theory of Perceived Social Presence is regarded as an antecedent for this phenomenon, stating that sources including a profile picture are to be perceived of higher social presence than those without. Social presence is defined as the extent to which a medium gives users the impression that their communication partner is psychologically present [23]. Moreover, physical attractiveness has an impact on the perception of source credibility. Physical attractive communication partners are perceived as more credible, as they are subjectively perceived as individuals possessing more expertise over a certain topic [24].

Gender. Women and men do not only differ in their attitude towards the credibility of a review, although each sex tends to rate articles by the opposite gender as more credible than articles written by the same sex [25]. However, other sources state that reviews not containing any information about the source's gender are perceived as more helpful than those giving information about the gender of the information provider [21]. Still, gender does not play such an important role as previously predicted and no significant influence is remarkable [26].

Location. When a review is related to a specific location, information delivered from sources living at or close to this location is considered more credible. It is assumed that the source has good knowledge of the esoteric aspects of the location. According to a study analyzing travel blogs and touristic virtual communities, individuals living close to a particular place, so called residents, have more influential power over this place than former tourists living further away [27]. Also, reviews by people living close to a specific hotel are perceived as being more credible [21].

Age. Consumers perceive a source being approximately of the same age as more credible. People have the feeling that they are confronted with the same wishes and problems and have similar mindsets [28]. A reviewer's age significantly impacts the perception of eWOM and is thus regarded as a central predictor of source credibility [26].

3.2   System-Generated Cues

Such cues include reputation as the endorsement of a reviewer by others. Reputation is regarded as the extent to which information receivers judge an information source to be honest and to have a concern about others. Reputation, a factor that heavily impacts the feeling of perceived credibility towards a particular person, is built through the collective view of others [29]. Reputation cues are aggregated opinions by others about a comment or a reviewer and serve as collective endorsements. Individuals are more likely to have a credible attitude towards a person if a comment is rated as helpful by a large number of peers and this information is displayed on the information source's profile or next to the comment [30]. Such popularity has a positive impact on the perceived level of source credibility [31]. This phenomenon is also referred to as the "Bandwagon effect". A reviewer who is endorsed by a large amount of people is rather trusted as a lot of other consumers trust him. The so-called bandwagon heuristic explains that opinions of the majority are taken for granted [32].

3.3 Additional Cues

Within virtual communities, especially TripAdvisor, additional cues will be considered as well. Travel frequency plays an important role and is another predictor for the level of perceived source credibility [26]. It is assumed that this cue influences source credibility, since it determines whether a source is experienced and therefor influences the level of perceived expertise. In addition, travel interest is understood to have a major impact on perceived source credibility [7]. It is assumed that travel interests influence the perceived feeling of homophily of an information receiver towards the source.

A list and summary of all operationalized factors regarding source credibility can be found in Table 1.

Table 1. Operationalization of constructs.

Construct	Definition/background	Operationalization
Trustworthiness	*"The degree of confidence in the communicator's intent to communicate the assertions he/she considers most valid"* [8]	Trustworthiness strongly influences overall perceived source credibility through: Profile picture, location, age, gender, travel interests, member since, number of visited places, helpful ratings on website [2]
Homophily/ trustworthiness	Homophily significantly impacts perceived trustworthiness of a source [2]	When I have the feeling that a reviewer is similar to me due the above stated characteristics, my feelings towards perceived trustworthiness is increased
Expertise	*"The extend "to which user-generated content contributors are perceived to be a source of valid assertions"* [8]	Expertise strongly influences perceived source credibility through: Profile picture, location, age, gender, travel interests, member since, number of visited places, helpful ratings on website. [2]
Homophily/expertise	Homophily significantly impacts perceived expertise of a source. [2]	When I have the feeling that a reviewer is similar to me due the above stated characteristics, my feeling s/he possesses expertise in the field is increased
Profile picture	Physical attractiveness is said to have an important impact on the perception of eWOM. [24]	Did you look at the physical attractiveness of the source? What did the profile picture tell you?

(continued)

Table 1. (*continued*)

Construct	Definition/background	Operationalization
Location	When a topic of discussion is related to a specific place, input which is delivered from sources living at or close to the destination is considered more credible [27]	Is (and why) the location of a reviewer important to you? Does it matter whether s/he lives at the place of interest or not?
Age	Consumers are likely to have a high feeling of perceived credibility when the information source is approximately of the same age [26]	Is (and why) the age of a reviewer important to you? Do you consider sources of similar / different ages as important?
Gender	Women and men do not only differ in their attitude towards credibility of a review, but each sex also tends to rate the opposite genders' articles as more credible than same genders' articles [25]	Is (and why) the gender of a reviewer important to you? Do you perceive a male or a female source as more credible?
Travel interests	Travel interests have an important impact on perceived source credibility. It is assumed these have an effect on the perceived feeling of homophily of an information receiver towards the message source [7]	Which role do travel interests play for you? Are you looking for travel interests similar to your own?
Member since		Do you consider the duration of the reviewers' membership?
Number of visited cities	Travel frequency plays an important role and can predict perceived source credibility [26]	Is (and why) the frequency of previous travel activities important to you?
Endorsement	Individuals are more likely to have a credible attitude towards a person if a comment is related as helpful by a large number of peers and this number is displayed on the information source's profile or next comment [30]	Is (and why) the helpfulness rating important to you? Do you consider sources more credible when they are endorsed by other people?

3.4 Message Credibility

Message credibility, in contrast, consists of the factors *Content,* manifested in the clarity and valence of the message, and *Consensus,* whether someone agrees because the own values fit the ones of the sender of a message. The latter consists of receiver judgment and review consistency [33].

Although a distinction between source and message credibility is made, these two kinds of credibility are interlinked. Credible sources are expected to provide credible information and credible messages are likely to be written by credible sources. When consumers are confronted with purchase decisions, purchase related messages – such as eWOM in the form of online reviews – are sought. Moreover, evidence which helps in the evaluation of an information source's credibility, is looked for. Positive characteristics of an information source can lead to an increase in the perceived credibility of the content delivered in a message, which again leads to an increased likelihood of the information receiver to accept the message. Most sources tackling the issue of source credibility prove, that a source, which possesses a high degree of perceived credibility, is more persuasive than a source being perceived as non-credible. A review provided by a source which possesses a high degree of credibility leads to more favorable behavioral intentions, whereas a source perceived as non-credible, leads to the opposite behavior [8].

4   Generational Attitudes Towards EWOM

The term generation describes a set of people born within the same time span. Each generation spans approximately twenty years and slowly transforms into the next generation. During their life span, each generation experiences similar events and is exposed to similar external influences in the form of historical or social events. Thus, members of a generation develop similar shared values that evolve through these experiences. All members of a generation are understood to possess similar personality traits, also referred to as "peer personality" [34].

4.1   Generational Approach Towards Online Media

Different generations employ different ways to handle, use and evaluate eWOM. There are some remarkable differences between different generations in their attitude towards online media and eWOM. While older generations are less likely to use eWOM in a purchase decision making process, younger generations tend to use travel reviews more frequently, especially in the middle of the planning process to limit alternatives to choose from, and consequently select the best available product [26].

Within this study, a focus will be put on Generation Y and Generation BB. It will be examined how these two generations differ in their behavior regarding the evaluation of source credibility in touristic eWOM. Although studies have made clear that different generations view online information differently, only little research has been conducted regarding the difference between the two generations in perceived cues for source credibility.

4.2   Generation Y

Regarding the aspect of trust in online media and eWOM, members of Generation Y are more likely to exhibit trust than former generations [35]. However, Generation Y is considered a generation that is the most careful of all generations in online social networks. They are more likely, than any other generation, to consider perceived risks before engaging in online activities [36]. From this perspective, it can be understood that Generation Y is the more careful generation that might check for source credibility cues more thoroughly. Professional advice does not play a significant role for Generation Y; it is considered the least important factor [37].

Regarding their holiday behavior, Generation Y takes shorter vacations but therefore tends to go on holiday more frequently. Travel reviews are mainly used in the planning process to narrow down alternatives and to create a set of options to choose from. Moreover, reviews are mainly used in order to reduce uncertainty [26].

4.3 Generation Baby Boomers (BB)

Generation BB has grown up with mass marketing and has seen the rise of the internet, networks and television. This generation is characterized by their revolutionary outlook as they have experienced constant social change. They are frequent travelers who prefer new and distant countries. BB tend to travel a lot and have ambitious plans for the future. Moreover, internationalization of trade, food and culture has played an important role and determined their lives [38]. Also regarded as the Generation 50 plus, the grey generation or the third generation, they can be defined as a generation that is mobile, interested in and rapidly adapting to changes and new trends [39]. Although people expect this generation to be put off from new technologies, sources state that they are experienced in using such technologies and are quick adapters, as they have been confronted with technological and other social changes throughout their whole life [40]. Members of the BB generation are longing for more input in the buying process and seek for control within it. Unlike Generation Y, they are mainly searching for products that offer good value. They look at actual features and characteristics of a product whereas image-related messages are not taken into consideration [41].

The BB generation utilizes the Internet more and more often in purchase decision processes; especially in the process of vacation planning [42]. Although the number of those consumers seeking online information in the pre-purchase phase has been increasing over the last years, only few BB purchase online [43]. One reason, why many senior citizens are put off from using the Internet for shopping purchases, is a lack of confidence in online media [44]. However, although senior citizens rarely do shop online, they often use the Internet as a medium to get informed about products and to search for information needs [45]. Still, there is a remarkable difference compared to Generation Y regarding the relevance of eWOM in travel related topics, as older consumers are less likely to read other travelers' reviews [26]. Members of the BB generation are, when utilizing reviews, less likely to evaluate the credibility of an online source and tend to accept information without checking for cues indicating the reliability of the source. They focus on the actual message and search for cues identifying message credibility, whereas cues indicating the credibility of the source itself are not taken into consideration [46].

5 Methodology

The main goal of this study is the examination of the role of source credibility in eWOM in the touristic context, focusing on how Generation Y and Generation BB differ in their perceived cues for source credibility. In this context, the role of source as well as message characteristics, such as content with regard to the perception of source credibility, will be examined. Since attentional behavior is compared with self-reported behavior, a distinction between actively and passively sought cues is made (cf. Table 2).

Table 2. Framework for eye tracking analysis

Actively sought	Actively sought within AOI	The characteristic is sought within the eye tracking experiment and per the post-test questionnaire also a characteristic which has been paid attention to
	Actively sought somewhere else	The characteristic is not sought within the AOI but per the post-test questionnaire it is a characteristic which is regarded. It can be derived that it is fixed to another item or characteristic
Passively sought		The cue is sought within the experiment but per the post-test questionnaire it represents a cue which has not been paid any attention to

Relevant characteristics were marked as areas of interest (AOI). AOIs represent zones on a website that are significantly meaningful. The following AOIs were created: *Profile picture*, *Location*, *Member since*, *Endorsement* and *Message characteristics* (the actual message and the subject headline). For these AOIs, the following measures were calculated: *Time to first fixation*, *fixation count* and *visit duration*.

5.1 Experiment

The experiment was conducted utilizing a Tobii T60 Eyetracker using the travel website TripAdvisor.com. The procedure followed a standardized process including the following steps [47].

- **Pre-test questionnaire.** The questionnaire included questions about the participants' online shopping behavior and their vacation behavior.
- **Task scenario.** Participants were asked to act like in a real-life situation and in case they were currently planning a seven-day trip to their preferred destination on TripAdvisor. Therefore, all had to think about their travel destination, travel party composition and travel dates before they started the experiment and write this down.
- **Post-test questionnaire.** This includes questions about topics that cannot be directly observed. These are rather related to feelings and opinions. On a four-point Likert scale (1 – not applicable to 4 – applicable), participants were asked if they have looked at reviews provided by former customers and which cues they had sought in order to evaluate the source credibility. The first part covered attitudes

towards source and message characteristics during the experiment, the second part asked about general attitudes towards these. The third part aiming at attitudes regarding Ayeh's model of source credibility, followed by questions regarding factors influencing personal vacation decisions and perception towards source credibility. The last part asked for demographic data.

- **De-Briefing interview.** In order to develop a better understanding of what the participants have done and experienced during the experiment.

5.2 Participants

In total, twenty people were tested within the experiments, ten from Generation Y (17–38 years old) and seven[1] from Generation BB (50–72 years old) using a randomized sample. Generation Y consisted of eight females and two male participants with 60% spending more than five hours online per day; nine travel several times a year, with none booking offline and all being familiar with TripAdvisor. Recommendations by friends (3.2), virtual communities (3.1) and destination websites (3.0) were the most frequently consulted sources for Generation Y in the process of vacation planning, via travel agencies the least (1.3). Generation BB consisted of four females and three male participants with 71% spending 1–2 h online per day; four travel several times a year, booking their holidays online (7), direct (4) and via a travel agency (2). Destination websites (3.3) and virtual communities (2.3) and recommendations by friends (2.1) were the most frequently consulted information sources for travel planning, travel agencies (1.9) and social media (1.4) the least.

6 Results

Regarding the aspect of source credibility, it can be recognized that for both generations, source characteristics play a less important role than message characteristics. Regarding the metrics gained from the AOIs, it could be derived that the review itself was the element which was most often fixated, first fixated and represented the highest visit duration. Combining these observations with the results from the post-test questionnaire and the de-briefing interviews stating that message characteristics are the most frequently mentioned characteristic regarding source credibility, it can be derived that message characteristics represent for both generations more valuable and reliable cues in the evaluation of source credibility than source characteristics (cf. Figure 1). While it is remarkable that source characteristics are sought by some members of Generation Y, they are not at all referred to by Generation BB. This goes along with Liao und Fu's statement reporting that BB mainly focus on the actual message and search for cues

---

[1] The original sample constituted of ten participants. Two participants had to be omitted due to reporting over-confident IT-skills and already asked a lot of computer-usage related questions in the pre-test questionnaire stage. One participant was over-strained in the trip planning stage and chose "any" hotel, in order to finish the task "somehow".

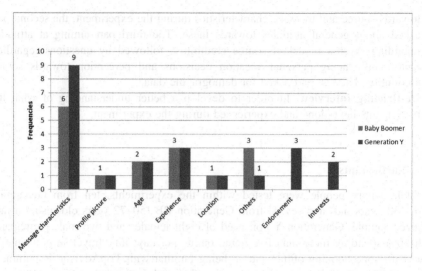

Fig. 1. Source credibility cues by generation

identifying message credibility whereas cues giving information on how credible the source could be are almost not sought at all [46].

6.1 The Role of Message Characteristics

Message characteristics play the most important role, also in the evaluation of source credibility. This goes along with Moran and Muzellec [33] stating that message and source credibility are interlinked. When it comes to message characteristics, the following characteristics are paid attention to by both generations:

- Grammar and spelling
- Length of a message
- Congruence with personal interests

Moreover, and in contrast to Generation Y, Generation BB mentions to pay attention to the level of the objectiveness of a message. A message has to be coherent, conclusive and justified so that a source can be regarded as credible. Moreover, statements praising everything as extremely good are not regarded as being credible and have a negative influence on the perceived level of source credibility.

6.2 The Role of Source Characteristics

Figure 2 sums up the insights gained from the eye tracking data and post-test questionnaires regarding the role of source characteristics.

Regarding the role of source characteristics, a differentiation between those source characteristics sought within the relevant areas (factor *Endorsement* until *Member*

	Generation Y							Generation BB			
	Time to first fixation	Visit Duration	Fixation Count	Actively within AOI	Actively regarded but sw. else	Influence on elements of SC	Passively regarded	Actively within AOI	Actively regarded but sw. else	Influence on elements of SC	Passively regarded
Endorsement	74,22 sec	0,37 sec	11,14 sec	44% (4 out of 9)	11% (1 out of 9)	TW 3 out of 4 EP 3 out of 4	34% (3 out of 9)	0%	0%		0%
Profile Picture	88,86 sec	0,24 sec	6 sec	22% (2 out of 9)	0% (0 out of 9)	TW 2 out of 4 EP 2 out of 4	44% (4 out of 9)	0%	0%		0%
Location	124,06 sec	0,34 sec	2,25 sec	20% (2 out of 10)	20% (2 out of 10)	TW Median=1 EP Median=1	20% (2 out of 10)	0%	25% (1 out of 4)	TW 0 EP 2 out of 4	0%
Member since	248,35 sec	0,33 sec	1,67 sec	11% (1 out of 9)	22% (2 out of 9)	TW Median=2 EP Median=3	22% (2 out of 9)	0%	0%		0%
Travel Interests				40% (by 4 out of 10)		TW Median =3 EP Median=3			17% (by 1 out of 6)	TW Median 4 EP Median 4	
Age				30% (by 3 out of 10)		TW Median = 2 EP Median = 3			29% (by 2 out of 7)	TW Median = 2 EP Median = 2	
Gender				Not regarded at all		No influence			Not regarded at all	No influence	
Number of visited cities				10% (by 1 out of 10)		TW Median = 3 EP Median = 3			14% (by 1 out of 7)	TW Median = 4 EP Median = 4	

Fig. 2. Summary of source characteristics (TW - Trustworthiness, EP - Expertise)

Since) and the source characteristics not regarded within those areas but regarded somewhere else, such as the message itself, is made (*Travel interests* until *Gender*).

Although less frequently referred to than message characteristics, source characteristics tend to play a more important role for Generation Y than for Generation BB. Similarly to what has been discovered within the eye tracking analysis, the factor *Endorsement* represents a cue which is most frequently sought and fixated. Moreover, an impact on source credibility, with both a remarkable effect on the perceived trustworthiness and expertise can be recognized. This goes along with findings from the post-test questionnaire and the eye tracking analysis. Moreover, the factor *Duration of Membership* – although representing the highest time to first fixation and lowest fixation count – plays an important role influencing the perception of source credibility, since it affects the level of perceived expertise to a large extent. The factors *Endorsement* and a reviewer's *Profile picture* are factors that are frequently sought passively; these two were sought within the eye tracking experiment but not stated as being regarded within the post-test questionnaire. Following Just and Carpenter's [48] eye-mind hypothesis, it can be derived that they could have a subconscious influence on the level of perceived source credibility.

The source characteristics *travel interests*, *number of visited cities*, *age* and *gender* were not clearly discernable in the eye tracking experiment. Since these characteristics were not sought within the relevant areas of interest, it is derived that they are fixed to message characteristics, such as the content itself, and not as a singular characteristic. Interesting factors are *travel interests* and the *age* of a reviewer. Although only regarded by one participant, the number of visited cities is another factor that plays an important role in the perception of source credibility.

Generation BB, in contrast does not regard source characteristics at all. No participant regarded any source characteristics within the relevant areas but rather derived some of them from the message itself. *Travel interests* as well as the *number of visited cities* play an important role for Generation BB. Also, according to the findings of the de-briefing interview, the experience of a reviewer is rated as important.

6.3 The Impact of Homophily on the Perception of Source Credibility

The factors *trustworthiness* and *expertise*, which represent the antecedents of *source credibility*, are determined by *homophily*, according to what Ayeh et al. [2] state within their model of source credibility. Within our study, the influence on the factors *trustworthiness* and *expertise* was examined, by taking generational differences into account. Whereas Generation Y defines homophily as the similarity in *travel interests*, Generation BB manifests homophily in the similarity of *age* and *gut feeling*; also the *level of education* was mentioned to be a factor indicating the degree of homophily.

According to Generation Y, homophily has an important impact on the perceived level of trustworthiness, the perceived level of expertise and the perception of overall credibility. In contrast, Generation BB regards the influence on the perceived level of trustworthiness as most important, whereas the impact on expertise and overall credibility is regarded as minor.

7 Summary

The following contributions to literature were made. It is notable that Generation Y and Generation BB differ in their attitude towards eWOM – Generation BB relies less on reviews than Generation Y. Moreover, we can confirm that Generation BB tends to be less concerned about source credibility and source characteristics.

For Generation Y, message characteristics represent the most important cue regarding to source credibility. Parts of the relevant message characteristics are the length of a message, the style of writing and the congruence with personal interests and purposes. Although source characteristics are regarded as less important, these are sought cues which influence the perceived level of source credibility. *Endorsement* is a factor that is most frequently sought and has a high impact on the perceived level of source credibility, by influencing both – the level of perceived trustworthiness and the level of perceived expertise. Although not as frequently sought, *duration of membership* is another important indicator influencing the level of perceived expertise. Furthermore, *travel interests* and *age* of a reviewer influence the level of perceived source credibility. However, they are not sought within the areas providing actual source characteristics but are expected to be derived from the message itself, which again proves the influence of message characteristics and the review itself. Moreover, it is remarkable that some characteristics, such as the reviewers' profile picture, are frequently passively sought which could result, following the eye-mind hypothesis, in a subconscious influence on the perceived level of source credibility.

Similar to Generation Y, Generation BB regards message characteristics as most important factor in the evaluation of source credibility. They also pay attention to the length of the message, the writing quality as well as the congruence with personal interests and purposes. Moreover, the degree of objectiveness within statements plays an important role in the evaluation of source credibility. Source characteristics on the other hand do not play any important role. They are rarely sought and when sought are not derived from the areas providing this information, but are derived from the message itself. Among those characteristics, *travel interests* as well as the *number of previously visited cities* of a reviewer are important factors influencing the level of perceived source credibility.

Moreover, the degree of homophily between a reviewer and a review reader is said to influence source credibility. Both generations agree that homophily influences the level of perceived trustworthiness towards an information source; however, its impact on perceived expertise and overall credibility seems controversial, with Generation Y reporting these factors as being more influential regarding to source credibility than Generation BB.

8 Limitations and Further Research

This experiment comes with several limitations. In particular, the small number of participants limits its explanatory power. Generation BB had to exclude three participants due to several reasons. Within the brief window of testing, we were unable to recruit new participants on such a short notice. Still, timing and testing this generation needs double the preparation and testing time than actually planned and needs to be prepared with extensive care. The test scenarios opted for an unstructured exploration by the user on TripAdvisor, which led to completely different search paths through the website, and consequently made comparing and harmonizing all relevant areas of interest challenging.

Further research should put emphasis on the message characteristics and investigate the elements of message credibility in further detail. Ayeh et al.'s model of source credibility was not applied to the factor message characteristics, which represents another field for further investigation. Additionally, further studies could examine the influence of online search behavior of Generation BB and focus further on the perception of source credibility. Moreover, other generations such as Generation X, may be taken into account.

References

1. Buhalis, D., Law, R.: Progress in information technology and tourism management: 20 years on and 10 years after the Internet—The state of eTourism research. Tour. Manag. (2008). doi:10.1016/j.tourman.2008.01.005

2. Ayeh, J.K., Au, N., Law, R.: "Do we believe in TripAdvisor?" examining credibility perceptions and online travelers' attitude toward using user-generated content. J. Travel Res. (2013). doi:10.1177/0047287512475217

3. Xiang, Z., Gretzel, U.: Role of social media in online travel information search. Tour. Manag. (2010). doi:10.1016/j.tourman.2009.02.016

4. Litvin, S.W., Goldsmith, R.E., Pan, B.: Electronic word-of-mouth in hospitality and tourism management. Tour. Manag. (2008). doi:10.1016/j.tourman.2007.05.011

5. Ye, Q., Law, R., Gu, B., Chen, W.: The influence of user-generated content on traveler behavior: an empirical investigation on the effects of e-word-of-mouth to hotel online bookings. Comput. Hum. Behav. (2011). doi:10.1016/j.chb.2010.04.014

6. Hennig-Thurau, T., Gwinner, K.P., Walsh, G., Gremler, D.D.: Electronic word-of-mouth via consumer-opinion platforms: What motivates consumers to articulate themselves on the Internet? J. Interact. Market. (2004). doi:10.1002/dir.10073

7. Park, H.L., Xiang, Z., Josiam, B., Kim, H.M.: Personal profile information as cues of credibility in online travel reviews. In: Cantoni, L., Xiang, Z. (eds.) Information and Communication Technologies in Tourism 2013, pp. 230–241. Springer, Berlin Heidelberg, Berlin, Heidelberg (2013)

8. Hovland, C.I., Janis, I.L., Kelley, H.H.: Communication and Persuasion. Psychological Studies of Opinion Change. Greenwood Press, Westport (1982). ©1953

9. Fogg, B.J., Tseng, H.: The elements of computer credibility. In: Williams, M.G., Altom, M. W. (eds.) The SIGCHI conference, Pittsburgh, Pennsylvania, United States, pp. 80–87. doi:10.1145/302979.303001

10. Loda, M.D., Teichmann, K., Zins, A.H.: Destination websites' persuasiveness. Int. J. Culture Tourism Hosp. Res. (2009). doi:10.1108/17506180910940351

11. Mayer, R.C., Davis, J.H.: The effect of the performance appraisal system on trust for management: a field quasi-experiment. J. Appl. Psychol. (1999). doi:10.1037/0021-9010.84. 1.123

12. Ohanian, R.: Impact of celebrity spokespersons' perceived image on consumers' intention to purchase. J. Advertising Res. **31**, 46–54 (1991)

13. Kerstetter, D., Cho, M.-H.: Prior knowledge, credibility and information search. Ann. Tourism Res. (2004). doi:10.1016/j.annals.2004.04.002

14. Lis, B.: In eWOM we trust. Bus. Inf. Syst. Eng. (2013). doi:10.1007/s12599-013-0261-9

15. McGuire, W.J.: Attitudes and attitude change. In: Lindzey, G., Aronson, E. (eds.) Handbook of Social Psychology. Special fields and applications, 2nd edn., pp. 233–346. Random House, New York (1985)

16. Laumann, E.O.: Prestige and Association in an Urban Community: An Analysis of an Urban Stratification System. Bobbs-Merrill, Indianapolis (1966)

17. Brown, J., Broderick, A.J., Lee, N.: Word of mouth communication within online communities: conceptualizing the online social network. J. Interact. Mark. (2007). doi:10. 1002/dir.20082

18. Sussman, S.W., Siegal, W.S.: Informational influence in organizations: an integrated approach to knowledge adoption. Inf. Syst. Res. (2003). doi:10.1287/isre.14.1.47.14767

19. Tidwell, L.C., Walther, J.B.: Computer-mediated communication effects on disclosure, impressions, and interpersonal evaluations: getting to know one another a bit at a time. Hum. Commun. Res. (2002). doi:10.1111/j.1468-2958.2002.tb00811.x

20. Derlega, V.J.: Self-disclosure. Sage series on close relationships. Sage Publications, Newbury Park (1993)

21. Lee, H., Law, R., Murphy, J.: Helpful reviewers in TripAdvisor, an online travel community. J. Travel Tourism Market. (2011). doi:10.1080/10548408.2011.611739

22. Berger, C.R., Calabrese, R.J.: Some explorations in initial interaction and beyond: toward a developmental theory of interpersonal communication. Hum. Commun. Res. (1975). doi:10. 1111/j.1468-2958.1975.tb00258.x
23. Gefen, D., Karahanna, E., Straub, D.W.: Trust and tam in online shopping: an integrated model. Manag. Inf. Syst. Q. **27**, 51–90 (2003)
24. Patzer, G.L.: Source credibility as a function of communicator physical attractiveness. J. Bus. Res. (1983). doi:10.1016/0148-2963(83)90030-9
25. Flanagin, A.J., Metzger, M.J.: The perceived credibility of personal Web page information as influenced by the sex of the source. Comput. Hum. Behav. (2003). doi:10.1016/S0747-5632(03)00021-9
26. Gretzel, U., Yoo, K.H.: Use and impact of online travel reviews. In: O'Connor, P., Höpken, W., Gretzel, U. (eds.) Information and Communication Technologies in Tourism 2008, pp. 35–46. Springer Vienna, Vienna (2008)
27. Arsal, I., Baldwin, E.D., Backman, S.J.: Member reputation and its influence on travel decisions: an case study of an online travel community. J. IT Tourism **11**, 235–246 (2009)
28. Münz, K., Sergiunaite, V.: Electronic word of mouth (eWom): The relationship between anonymous and semi-anonymous eWom and consumer attitudes (2015)
29. Zacharia, G., Maes, P.: Trust management through reputation mechanisms. Appl. Artif. Intell. (2000). doi:10.1080/08839510050144868
30. Metzger, M.J., Flanagin, A.J., Medders, R.B.: Social and heuristic approaches to credibility evaluation online. J. Commun. (2010). doi:10.1111/j.1460-2466.2010.01488.x
31. Huang, L.-S.: Trust in product review blogs: the influence of self-disclosure and popularity. Behav. Inf. Technol. (2013). doi:10.1080/0144929X.2014.978378
32. Moe, W.W., Schweidel, D.A.: Online product opinions: incidence, evaluation, and evolution. Market. Sci. (2012). doi:10.1287/mksc.1110.0662
33. Moran, G., Muzellec, L.: eWOM credibility on social networking sites: a framework. J. Market. Commun. (2014). doi:10.1080/13527266.2014.969756
34. Strauss, W., Howe, N.: The Fourth Turning. An American prophecy, 1st edn. Broadway Books, New York (1998). ©1997
35. Strutton, D., Taylor, D.G., Thompson, K.: Investigating generational differences in e-WOM behaviours: for advertising purposes, does X = Y? Int. J. Adv. (2011). doi:10.2501/IJA-30-4-559-586
36. Lu, J., Yao, J.E., Yu, C.-S.: Personal innovativeness, social influences and adoption of wireless Internet services via mobile technology. J. Strateg. Inf. Syst. (2005). doi:10.1016/j. jsis.2005.07.003
37. Li, X., Li, X., Hudson, S.: The application of generational theory to tourism consumer behavior: an American perspective. Tour. Manag. (2013). doi:10.1016/j.tourman.2013.01. 015
38. Parment, A.: Generation Y vs. baby boomers: shopping behavior, buyer involvement and implications for retailing. J. Retail. Consum. Serv. (2013). doi:10.1016/j.jretconser.2012.12. 001
39. Haynes, L.: Baby boomers. Brand Strategy **179**, 31 (2004)
40. Brown, P.: Are the forties the new thirties? Brand Strategy **153**, 26 (2001)
41. Wolf, M., Carpenter, S., Qenani-Petrela, E.: A comparison of X, Y, and baby boomer generation wine consumers in California. J. Food Distrib. Res. **36**(1), 186–191 (2005)
42. Beldona, S., Nusair, K., Demicco, F.: Online travel purchase behavior of generational cohorts: a longitudinal study. J. Hospitality Market. Man. (2009). doi:10.1080/ 19368620902799627
43. Wood, S.L.: Future fantasies: a social change perspective of retailing in the 21st century. J. Retail. (2002). doi:10.1016/S0022-4359(01)00069-0

44. Eastman, J.K., Iyer, R.: The elderly's uses and attitudes towards the Internet. J. Consum. Market. (2004). doi:10.1108/07363760410534759

45. Leppel, K., McCloskey, D.W.: A cross-generational examination of electronic commerce adoption. J. Consum. Market. (2011). doi:10.1108/07363761111143150

46. Liao, Q.V., Fu, W.-T.: Age differences in credibility judgments of online health information. ACM Trans. Comput.-Hum. Interact. (2014). doi:10.1145/2534410

47. Rubin, J., Chisnell, D.: Handbook of usability testing. How to plan, design, and conduct effective tests, 2nd edn. Wiley Pub., Indianapolis, IN (2008)

48. Just, M.A., Carpenter, P.A.: A theory of reading: From eye fixations to comprehension. Psychol. Rev. (1980). doi:10.1037/0033-295X.87.4.329

Gender Differences in Tourism Website Usability: An Empirical Study

Zhao Huang[1,2(✉)] and Liu Yuan[1]

[1] Key Laborartory of Modern Teaching Technology, Ministry of Education,
Xi'an 710062, People's Republic of China
{zhaohuang,yuanliu}@snnu.edu.cn
[2] School of Computer Science, ShaanXi Normal University, Xi'an 710062,
People's Republic of China

Abstract. The emergence of the Internet and web technologies has made unprecedented effect on the tourism industry. To keep the competitive advantages in the tourism industry, most travel agencies have built their own websites for promotion, marketing, and online transactions. Nowadays, thousands of electronic tourism websites become accessible, providing a variety of online information and services online. Usability has been recognized as a vital factor in the success of tourism websites because usability has been shown to change users' attitudes, achieve users' satisfaction. However, there are limited studies exploring gender differences in usability of tourism websites. It can be arguable that gender differences significantly influence usability design of tourism websites. Thus, this study aims to assess the usability of current tourism websites from a gender difference perspective. The results show significant differences of usability perception between genders. More specifically, the common usability that males require most includes visibility of system status, user control and freedom and efficiency of use. The usability that females require most covers aesthetic design, help and documentation and security and privacy. These findings can provide deep insights into gender differences in usability to support tourism website design.

Keywords: Gender differences · Usability assessment · Tourism websites

1 Introduction

The emergence of the Internet and World Wide Web (WWW) has made unprecedented effect on the tourism industry [1]. To keep the competitive advantages in the tourism industry, most travel agencies have established their own websites for promotion, marketing, and online transactions [2]. Tourism websites can be seen as an interface of electronic tourism where users have their initial interaction with the tourism industry [5]. Today, thousands of electronic tourism websites are accessible, making a variety of online information and services widely available online [1]. Among them, usability is one of the most important factors in the success of tourism websites because it usually affects usage and acceptance, and increases users' interaction with those websites [2]. Past research has revealed the importance of gender to information system usability

A. Marcus and W. Wang (Eds.): DUXU 2017, Part III, LNCS 10290, pp. 453–461, 2017.
DOI: 10.1007/978-3-319-58640-3_32

(e.g. [3, 4, 19]). However, there are limited studies exploring gender differences in usability of tourism websites. We argue that such lack of studies may hinder the development of more personalized and user-centered tourism websites. Therefore, this study aims to explore gender differences in usability design, focusing on the four specific tourism websites. By doing so, it can provide insights into gender differences in usability to support tourism website design.

Accordingly, the paper is presented as follows: Sect. 2 presents related studies from literature to demonstrate the importance of gender differences to usability in tourism websites. In Sect. 3, an empirical study is designed to explore gender differences in tourism website usability. This allows the detection of gender difference results related to usability of the target tourism websites which are discussed in Sect. 4. Finally, conclusions are drawn and possibilities for future study are recommended in Sect. 5.

2 Study Background

Studies of gender differences in various computer-related systems and online commercial applications are indicated in the literature, such as car navigation systems [4], blog interface [6], mobile commerce [8] and hypermedia learning systems [9]. These studies show that males and females have diverse perceptions, expectations, preferences and performance with computer-related information systems. For example, perceived ease of use is more salient to females [3]. Female have higher expectation of accessible information quality than males [3]. Females prefer blogs whose layouts feature more images than text, while males prefer blogs with a greater proportion of text than images [6]. Moreover, females are more likely than males to seek out discounts and hunt for bargains [4].

Many research (e.g. clinical and experimental research) study the gender from biological differences in the brain scheme, showing lateralization of two hemispheres in human brain [10]. Others focus gender differences on information processing [11], information quality [12], IT adoption [13], online shopping [6], social networking site use [14], online auctions [15] and mediated communication [16]. Within the tourism websites context, the magnitude and presence of gender differences is also highlighted in the recent literature. For example, females have more favorable perceptions of tourism website functionalities and content than males have [7].

3 Methodology

Having indicated the importance of gender differences to computer-related information systems, this paper reports on an empirical study to explore gender differences in tourism website usability. To conduct the study, three research instruments are used, namely a set of tourism website samples, the task sheet and the questionnaire. Four tourism websites: Airbnb, Ctrip, Travelzoo and Yelp are selected for study since these websites are popular, highly used, and of high quality. The task sheet details a set of tasks for users to perform. These tasks are representative activities that users would be expected to perform on tourism websites. The questionnaire is based on Nielsen's usability heuristics to capture users' perception towards usability of tourism websites. The questionnaire design has three steps. Step one: the existing heuristics are extended by adding three new guidelines: Interoperability; Interactivity, and Security and Privacy to meet tourism website specific needs (see Table 1). Step two: a set of evaluation criteria is developed for each heuristic. Step three: the questions are developed from these associated criteria. Study participants are initially allowed to have free interaction with tourism websites. Therefore, a general perception of tourism websites can be developed. Subsequently, a task-based interaction assigns users to complete a series of tasks. Finally, the users are asked to fill out the questionnaire to express their perceptions for the usability of tourism websites.

Table 1. Usability heuristics

No.	Usability heuristic	Interpretation
H1	Visibility of system status	To keep users informed about their progress
H2	Match between system and the real world	To use the user' language, follow real-world conventions, make information appear in a natural and logical order
H3	User control and freedom	To make undo, redo functions available during interaction
H4	Consistency and standards	To keep the same design features, follow platform conventions
H5	Error prevention	To support users overcome errors, prevent same problem occurrence
H6	Recognition rather than recall	To make information easily remembered
H7	Flexibility, efficiency of use	To consider usage for both novice and experienced users
H8	Aesthetic design	To make minimalist design
H9	Help user recover errors	To precisely indicate the problem, constructively suggest a solution
H10	Help and documentation	To provide help to support user's task completion.
H11	Interoperability	To ensure exchanged information, services work together via different systems
H12	Interactivity	To provide rich interactive and social experience
H13	Security and privacy	To protect users' information and secure personal services

To analyze users' perception of usability of the target tourism websites from the gender perspective, the data collected from the questionnaire was coded using IBM SPSS for windows (version 23.0). The significance value (P) was predefined as less than 0.05. The independent variables were the four tourism websites and the gender, while the dependent variables were the participants' perception.

4   Results and Discussion

4.1   Descriptive Profile

Figure 1 shows the participants' gender information among the four target tourism websites. Note that the distribution of participants' characteristics is equally allocated across the four tourism websites.

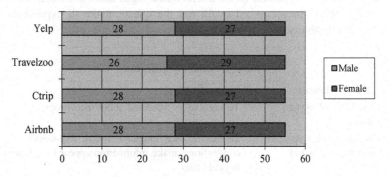

Fig. 1. Participants gender distribution

Additionally, the analysis of the usability heuristics reliability was conducted by calculating Cronbach's alpha. An alpha value between 0.7 and 0.95 shows high reliability [20]. In this study, the alpha values of each usability heuristic were higher than 0.7, showing good reliability (see Table 2).

Table 2. Reliability of usability heuristic

	Airbnb	Ctrip	Travelzoo	Yelp
Usability heuristic (number of items)	Cronbach'Alpha			
H1.Visibility of site status (4)	0.737	0.710	0.758	0.803
H2.Match site and real world (3)	0.740	0.715	0.754	0.771
H3.User control and freedom (3)	0.779	0.703	0.748	0.758
H4. Consistency (3)	0.704	0.721	0.711	0.739
H5. Error prevention (3)	0.738	0.707	0.794	0.743
H6. Recognition (4)	0.701	0.711	0.763	0.701
H7. Efficiency of use (3)	0.784	0.715	0.762	0.730
H8. Aesthetic design (3)	0.704	0.707	0.775	0.753
H9.Help user recover errors (2)	0.737	0.746	0.721	0.786
H10.Help and documentation (2)	0.781	0.745	0.752	0.790
H11. Interoperability (2)	0.746	0.779	0.706	0.786
H12. Interactivity (4)	0.767	0.704	0.755	0.788
H13.Security and privacy (4)	0.788	0.797	0.765	0.721

4.2 Overall Assessment

Overall, the results show that females have the higher scores of the overall usability assessment than males have (see Fig. 2). As a high score indicates a bad overall assessment of usability, it indicates that females have the worse overall assessment of usability. Accordingly, these may imply that females have a higher level of usability requirements than males.

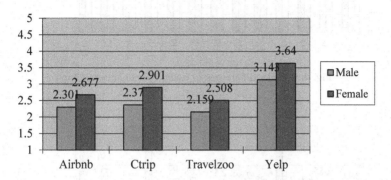

Fig. 2. Participants gender distribution

4.3 Gender Differences to Usability Heuristics

Given the gender difference in the overall usability perception, this section describes the detailed level of gender difference in usability heuristics. Figures 3, 4, 5, 6 shows the significant differences of usability heuristics perception between genders among the four tourism websites.

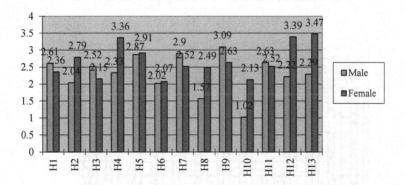

Fig. 3. Gender differences to usability heuristics in Airbnb

Among the four tourism websites, the common usability heuristics that males require most are Visibility of system status (H1), User control and freedom (H3) and Efficiency of use (H7). Visibility of system status is used to keep users visually informed about their progress. It seems that males consider and largely rely on subset

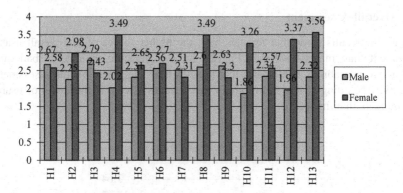

Fig. 4. Gender differences to usability heuristics in Ctrip

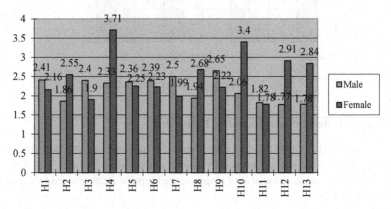

Fig. 5. Gender differences to usability heuristics in Travelzoo

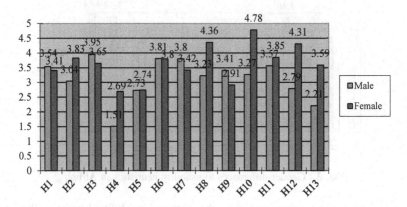

Fig. 6. Gender differences to usability heuristics in Yelp

of highly available visual cues when they interact with tourism websites [18]. User control and freedom is about users having good control and a high degree of freedom. The results imply that males are more likely require control, mastery and self-efficacy to pursue self-centered goals [6]. They normally advantage for spatial navigation through a website and have higher self-reports on sense of direction or spatial confidence [4]. Regarding efficiency of use, it appears that males place a greater emphasis on perceived ease of use and they tend to perceive the link between ease of use and their attributes more strongly than females counterparts [13].

Moreover, the common usability heuristics that females require most are Aesthetic design (H8), Help and documentation (H10) and Security and privacy (H13). Aesthetic design refers to the set of visual design elements of tourism website. It can be seen as apparent usability, which is perceived more quickly than other attributes of usability [17]. Our findings suggest that females are more process-oriented which means females are not limited by the nature of the target technologies (e.g. usefulness of help function, personal information protection), but more open to various possible design aspects (e.g. aesthetic, ease of use and enjoyment). Regarding help and documentation, it implies that females may place greater emphasis on internal and external supporting factors, while males may rely on facilitating conditions. Similarly, females are more concerns and apprehensive about the risk threats associated with online services. As explained by Lin and Chien [4], females are found to have higher computer anxiety than males. Thus, they always ask for a higher level of online service protection.

Furthermore, the significant differences of usability heuristics perception between genders have been identified on each tourism websites. More specifically, on Airbnb, usability heuristics that have the higher scores by males are Visibility of system status (H1); User control and freedom (H3); Efficiency of use (H7); Help user recover errors (H9) and Interoperability (H11), while usability heuristics that have the higher scores by females are Match site and real world (H2); Consistency and standards (H4); Error prevention (H5); Recognition (H6); Aesthetic design (H8); Help and documentation (H10); Interactivity (H12); Security and privacy (H13). Regarding Ctrip, usability heuristics that have the higher scores by males are Visibility of system status (H1); User control and freedom (H3); Efficiency of use (H7); Help user recover errors (H9); while usability heuristics that have the higher scores by females are Match site and real world (H2); Consistency and standards (H4); Error prevention (H5); Recognition (H6); Aesthetic design (H8); Help and documentation (H10); Interoperability (H11); Interactivity (H12) and Security and privacy (H13). As for Travelzoo, usability heuristics that have the higher scores by males include Visibility of system status (H1); User control and freedom (H3); Error prevention (H5); Recognition (H6); Efficiency of use (H7) and Help user recover errors (H9), while usability heuristics that have the higher scores by females are Match site and real world (H2); Consistency and standards (H4); Aesthetic design (H8); Help and documentation (H10); Interoperability (H11), Interactivity (H12) and Security and privacy (H13). For Yelp, usability heuristics that have the higher scores by males are Visibility of system status (H1); User control and freedom (H3); Efficiency of use (H7) and Help user recover errors (H9), while usability heuristics that have the higher scores by females are Match site and real world (H2); Consistency and standards (H4); Aesthetic design (H8); Help and documentation (H10); Interoperability (H11); Interactivity (H12) and Security and privacy (H13).

These findings show that in each target tourism website, females have more usability heuristic requirements, covering a wider range of tourism websites design than males.

5 Conclusion

The development of tourism websites has been rapid. Users can use tourism websites to receive updated travel-relative information and services, share personal experiences and form communities of exchange. Usability should be importantly considered and addressed into tourism website design on the basis of gender differences. This study's results identify a number of significant differences of user perception of usability features between females and males in the tourism websites. More specifically, the results show that females have a wider range of usability requirements than males. This implies that females are more process-oriented, which means females are not limited by the specific nature of usability (e.g. usefulness), but more open to various possible applications throughout the whole process of tourism website usage (e.g. ease of use and enjoyment). However, males are more motivated by productivity-related or task-oriented factors. Furthermore, our results find the significant differences of user perception of the specific usability features between males and females within each target tourism websites. For example, on Airbnb, females are more concerned and apprehensive about the security and privacy than males on tourism websites. On Ctrip, female subjects' fixation spread over a larger area, and they search for more details compared with the male subject. On travelzoo, females focus on particular navigation features, while males approach navigation from a global perspective. As for Yelp, females focus more on establishing and maintaining relationships with people and social contexts than males do.These may provide a better understanding of whether travel agencies should develop their websites that meet users' requirements and preferences based on gender.

This study has limitations. For example, this study considered a small (four) sample of tourism websites, which might provide limited empirical insight. Additionally, it would be interesting to conduct a study that explores users' performance with tourism websites. The results may provide deep insights into users' behaviors, which may better inform tourism website design.

Acknowledgments. This study was supported by a research grant funded by the "Open Research Project of Key Laboratory of Modern Teaching Technology, Ministry of Education" (SYSK201502), "the Scientific Research Foundation for the Returned Overseas Chinese Scholars, State Education Ministry", and "the Fundamental Research Funds for the Central Universities" (GK201503066).

References

1. Wang, L., Lawa, R., Guilleta, B.D., Hung, K., Fongb, D.K.C.: Impact of hotel website quality on online booking intentions: eTrustas a mediator. Int. J. Hospitality Manag. **47**, 108–115 (2015)

2. Vladimirov, Z.: Customer satisfaction with the Bulgarian tour operators and tour agencies' websites. Tourism Manag. Perspect. **4**, 176–184 (2012)

3. Nasan, B.: Exploring gender differences in online shopping attitude. Comput. Hum. Behav. **26**, 597–601 (2010)

4. Lin, P., Chen, S.: The effects of gender differences on the usability of automotive on-board navigation systems-a comparison of 2D and 3D display. Transp. Res. Part F **19**, 40–51 (2013)

5. Chung, N., Lee, H., Lee, S.J., Koo, C.: The influence of tourism website on tourists' behavior to determine destination selection: a case study of creative economy in Korea. Technol. Forecast. Soc. Change **96**, 130–143 (2015)

6. Hsu, C.: Comparison of gender differences in young people's blog interface preferences and designs. Displays **33**, 119–128 (2012)

7. Ladhari, R., Leclerc, A.: Building loyalty with online financial services customers: is there a gender difference? J. Retail. Consum. Serv. **20**, 560–569 (2013)

8. Okazaki, S., Mendez, F.: Exploring convenience in mobile commerce: moderating effects of gender. Comput. Hum. Behav. **29**, 1234–1242 (2013)

9. Pérez, S.J.G., Pérez, B.L., Fernández, D.M., Gayo, J.E.L.: Interoperability between platforms without a defined referential model: a semi-automatic learning system for structural pairing. Comput. Hum. Behav. **51**, 1351–1358 (2015)

10. Kim, D.Y., Lehto, X.Y., Morrison, A.M.: Gender differences in online travel information search: implications for marketing communications on the internet. Tourism Manag. **28**, 423–433 (2007)

11. Lenney, E., Gold, J., Browning, C.: Sex differences in self-confidence: the influence of comparison to others' ability level. Sex Roles **9**, 925–942 (1983)

12. Liu, Y., Li, Y., Zhang, H., Huang, W.: Gender differences in information quality of virtual communities: a study from an expectation-perception perspective. Pers. Individ. Differ. **104**, 224–229 (2017)

13. Faqih, K.M.S., Jaradat, M.R.M.: Assessing the moderating effect of gender differences and individualism-collectivism at individual-level on the adoption of mobile commerce technology: TAM3 perspective. J. Retail. Consum. Serv. **22**, 37–52 (2015)

14. Dhir, A., Torsheim, T.: Age and gender differences in photo tagging gratifications. Comput. Hum. Behav. **63**, 630–638 (2016)

15. Hou, J., Elliott, K.: Gender differences in online auctions. Electron. Commer. Res. Appl. **17**, 123–133 (2016)

16. Kimbrough, A.M., Guadagno, R.E., Muscanell, N.L., Dill, J.: Gender differences in mediated communication: women connect more than do men. Comput. Hum. Behav. **29**, 896–900 (2013)

17. Tractinsky, N.: Aesthetics and apparent usability: empirically assessing cultural and methodological issues. In: Proceedings of ACM Conference on Human Factors in Computing Systems. ACM Press, New York, 115–122 (1997)

18. Yang, J.C., Chen, S.Y.: Effects of gender differences and spatial abilities within a digital pentominoes game. Comput. Educ. **55**(3), 1220–1233 (2010)

19. Liang, L., Zhou, D., Yuan, C., Shao, A., Bian, Y.: Gender differences in the relationship between internet addiction and depression: a cross-lagged study in Chinese adolescents. Comput. Hum. Behav. **63**, 463–470 (2016)

20. Sun, J., Hsu, Y.: An experimental study of learner perceptions of the interactivity of web-based instruction. Interact. Comput. **24**, 35–48 (2012)

Energy UX: Leveraging Multiple Methods to See the Big Picture

Beth Karlin[1(✉)], Sena Koleva[1], Jason Kaufman[1],
Angela Sanguinetti[2], Rebecca Ford[3], and Colin Chan[4]

[1] See Change Institute, Los Angeles, USA
bkarlin@seechangeinstitute.com
[2] UC Davis, Davis, USA
[3] University of Oxford, Oxford, UK
[4] Yardi Energy, Vancouver, Canada

Abstract. Engaging the public to decrease their carbon footprint via energy feedback has become a significant topic of both study and practice and understanding how to best leverage technology for this purpose is an ideal question for the field of HCI to address. One common example is Home Energy Reports (HERs) and Business energy reports (BERs), which are paper or electronic reports that display a consumer's energy use alongside various benchmarks and "tips" to help (and persuade) them to save energy. While HERs and BERs show great promise, average savings hover around 1–3% with the potential savings in the average home and/or business closer to 15–20%, leaving potential room for improvement. This paper presents a mixed-methods research framework that is being used to improve BER user experience and energy savings. It blends inductive research methods from the fields of design and HCI with deductive methods drawn from psychology and behavioral economics to develop and test hypotheses and translate findings into real-world application. After introducing the framework, a case study is presented in which these steps are followed over two years of research with one BER product across multiple utility pilots. Implications for both energy feedback specifically as well as suggestions on how this framework can be applied across the broader field of usability are discussed.

Keywords: Energy · Feedback · Usability · Psychology · Multi-disciplinary

1 Introduction

One potent route to changing the way that people use energy, particularly motivating them to conserve, is providing feedback on their energy use [1]. The efficacy of feedback operates under the assumption that most people are uninformed about the relationship between their behaviors and their energy use and, in a larger sense, their impact on the environment; feedback is an attempt to "bridge this 'environmental literacy gap'" [2]. Energy feedback shows promise for supporting energy reduction (or energy shifting), though the results on the extent of its impact are mixed. While much research has investigated effectiveness of feedback (vs. a control group), the design of feedback interventions that may increase energy savings has received less attention.

© Springer International Publishing AG 2017
A. Marcus and W. Wang (Eds.): DUXU 2017, Part III, LNCS 10290, pp. 462–472, 2017.
DOI: 10.1007/978-3-319-58640-3_33

Energy feedback falls squarely in the world of HCI research, as it involves the presentation of energy use data (often collected from the smart meter) back to consumers [2]; these communications necessarily must consider the interface with its human consumers. To be effective energy feedback must not only reach and engage consumers, but should also effectively lead them to change their behavior in some way. Persuasive HCI in this domain should thus consider both design elements and the impact of these elements on customer behavior [2]. Different empirical methods reveal different insights into these processes; thus, understanding how to use them together and individually is key to maximize learning.

This paper presents a multi-method framework for effectively designing HCI to engage consumers in energy saving behavior. To illustrate this framework, we detail a case study of approximately two years of collaborative research with Yardi Energy. Yardi offers a diverse range of products in the area of asset management, energy cost analysis, and energy efficiency software for real estate companies and energy utilities. One of these products is their Business Energy Report (BER) program. BERs are paper or electronic reports that communicate computer-generated energy use data to commercial utility customers and encourage them to use less energy, either through capital investments in efficiency upgrades or through behavior change. BERs include features such as benchmarking (e.g., comparisons between customers' energy use and their peers) and energy-saving "tips," (e.g., information on efficient lighting). Our central question throughout this research was: "How can the design elements of BERs be leveraged to most effectively support energy reduction goals?"

2   Background

Feedback, the process of providing information about the result of an action that can be used to reinforce and/or modify future behavior, is considered an important dimension of behavior change [3] and has been used in fields ranging from education [4] to health behavior [5]. Eco-feedback, specifically, refers to feedback that is provided about behavior with the goal of reducing environmental impact [2].

Eco-feedback has received much attention in the energy space over the past decade due to changes in the electricity grid that enable real-time data collection and the processing of large data sets [6], and the proliferation of new feedback products on the market [7]. A recent meta-analysis of energy feedback studies [1] identified several variables that moderate its effectiveness, including frequency, medium, comparison message, duration, and combination with other interventions (e.g. goal, incentive). However, these variables have not been experimentally manipulated in most of these studies, with a focus on testing feedback vs. a no-feedback control group. Further, design variables have not been tested consistently for their role in feedback effectiveness.

A review of past empirical research on eco-feedback identified two primary fields that have conducted studies in this area: psychology and HCI [2]. The authors found that the HCI literature was primarily focused on the visual design of eco-feedback using qualitative methods whereas psychology literature was primarily focused on the effectiveness of eco-feedback interventions using experimental methods; there was little overlap between the two field in terms of references and citations. They concluded that "perhaps a future goal for HCI should be to initiate collaborations with environmental psychologists" [2].

3   Research

The current research presents a framework that integrates methods from the HCI and psychology fields; it progresses from observational methods with a "user-centered" focus to the development and testing of hypotheses, and finally to the optimization of eco-feedback design and the testing of the generated materials in the field. It has three phases: (1) Observe, (2) Test, and (3) Apply (see Fig. 1 below). The first phase, "Observe," involves customer research and literature review; the objective is to assess the opinions and thoughts of potential users in an inductive fashion and review and integrate relevant literature from across disciplines. This phase serves to generate hypotheses and inform methods to test them in the subsequent "Test" phase. This phase includes user testing and A/B testing to measure both stated and revealed preferences of design features with users. In the final "Apply" phase, insights from testing are used to optimize the design and launch it with actual users in an applied setting.

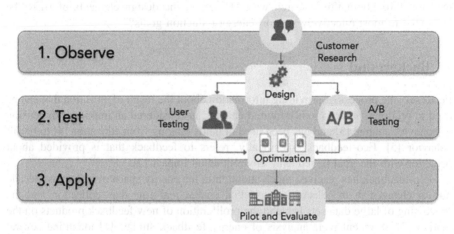

Fig. 1. Research framework

This framework is both multi-disciplinary and iterative. While the benefits of individual elements are recognized by researchers and practitioners alike, they are often used in isolation rather than as part of a holistic, programmatic approach. Thus, the framework's unique strength lies in how various methods can work together and inform one another. To that end, the process does not stop at the "Apply" phase; one can also evaluate the effectiveness of the final product "in the real world" and use these results in restarting the process. For example, the findings might show that certain materials were more successful for one group of recipients than another, at which point one can go back to the literature ("Observe") for clues on relevant group differences and/or redesign and test new materials with these insights in mind ("Test").

While a variety of research methods can be employed through each phase, certain methods are particularly well-suited to achieve the most common goals of each one. Table 1 summarizes each method, its benefits, and in which phase of the process it can be used. Below this table, we describe each phase in more detail and in the next section present a case study, with resulting findings, from each method.

Table 1. Multidisciplinary methods for studying human-computer interaction

Method	Description/benefits	Observe	Test	Apply
Literature review	Understand research and theory across disciplines	x		
Ethnography	Assess attitudes, feelings, actions, and barriers of potential users	x	x	
Content analysis	Reduce textual data to a set of codes with specific definitions	x	x	
Focus groups	Ask a fixed set of questions to several participants in a group setting	x	x	x
Interviews	Ask a fixed set of questions to one participant in a one-on-one setting	x	x	x
Surveys	Collect both quantitative and qualitative self-reported data at scale	x	x	x
Eye tracking	Understand how users interact visually with a designed image		x	
User testing	Systematically walk a user through interactions with a product		x	
Experimental design	Understand differences in response between multiple versions		x	x

3.1 Observe Phase

The goal of this phase is to remove or reduce preconceptions regarding what may be effective and simply observe, both the users that we plan to target, as well as existing relevant research and theory across disciplines. This step is similar to the first step in the design thinking process – Empathize – which suggests that one should not approach a problem with a potential solution in mind, but instead by "immersing yourself in [the] experiences [...] of the user for whom you are designing" [8]. While there are multiple methods that can be used in this phase (e.g., surveys, focus groups, ethnography), we discuss the way we used literature review and interviews in our case study.

Literature Reviews. Perhaps the broadest method for establishing a general understanding of a topic or theme is to examine past theory and research on the subject. For example, in brainstorming new ways of framing BER content, we conducted a literature review on lesser-utilized types of persuasion, such as Omega strategies. Prior work in eco-feedback has largely been rooted in Alpha strategies, which focus on increasing motivation to move towards a goal (e.g. by increasing the trustworthiness of the message source). In contrast, Omega strategies promote change by reducing the motivation to move away from the goal (e.g. addressing barriers). Reviewing the literature thus provided us an expanded pool of strategies for testing and improving BER content that we would have missed without taking this step.

Another topic in our literature review that led to testable hypotheses was the use of images in sustainability communication. We located studies that showed that visual content aids in information recall [9], that people prefer vertical bar charts for historical benchmarking of energy usage and horizontal bars for social benchmarking [10], and that images of people dominate visual representations of climate change and so could fit more closely with customers' existing mental representations on the topic [11]. Based on this "observation" of the literature, we hypothesized, and subsequently found, that the images in BERs attract readers' attention and that images of people in BER tips could increase their appeal.

Interviews. Interviews can be used to assess user beliefs, needs, behaviors, or barriers to action. They can be conducted in-person or remotely (e.g., by phone) and can be free form (following a natural conversation with very little pre-determined content), structured (following a script of set questions), or semi-structured (set questions with allowances for deviation or deeper probing). Interviews can provide an in-depth understanding of the characteristics and mental processes of individual participants. In 2016, Yardi's data science team identified a set of small-medium business (SMB) customers who were using heating, ventilation, and air conditioning (HVAC) while their businesses were closed. Before jumping into designing an intervention, we wanted to get a better sense of these businesses' perceptions of their heating and cooling use. We conducted phone interviews with a random selection of these pre-identified customers. Rather than asking them why they used their HVAC during closed business hours (which might prematurely steer the conversation or make them defensive) the interview protocol instead assessed their awareness, attitudes, and actions surrounding their HVAC use through general questions (e.g., "How is your air conditioning system at your place of business controlled?").

This design was critical as it allowed us to discover that, despite the fact that Yardi had specifically identified these businesses as using HVAC systems during closed hours, 100% of the interviewees claimed that they turned their cooling either down or completely off during those times. This finding revealed a vast disconnect between how SMB owners think they are using energy and how they are actually using energy. Participants agreed that HVAC use during closed hours is useless and expressed interest in HVAC efficiency to cut business costs. Thus, while we started this research to understand why SMB owners were using their HVAC systems during closed hours, we came to a very different conclusion: that many SMB owners are running their HVAC systems during closed hours unknowingly. This fundamentally altered our approach; for example, instead of suggesting to SMB owners that they should not use their HVAC systems during closed hours, we needed to first help them realize that they were unknowingly doing so.

3.2   Test Phase

While the methods of the "Observe" phase can provide an unbiased understanding and help to develop hypotheses about how to design interventions, the methods of the "Test" phase can test these hypotheses using actual prototypes and controlled experiments. Through iteration, these hypotheses can be refined and used to design and optimize operational prototypes. The two "Test" phase methods we discuss in our case study are usability testing with eye tracking and experimental design (aka A/B testing).

Usability Testing with Eye Tracking. Eye-tracking uses specialized computer hardware to track the eye movements of a user as (s)he looks at material on a screen or page. Eye-tracking is best used when it is thought that someone's gaze direction and eye movements reveal something that is otherwise outside conscious awareness, and thus cannot be assessed via self-report. While other forms of testing measure what a person says would catch their attention, eye-tracking shows where people are looking. Heat maps are one type of output generated by this method and show where and how long someone looks at different parts of the material on a screen.

The efficacy and utility of eye-tracking can be increased by combining it with other methods of usability testing, such as a think-aloud procedure in which participants speak their thoughts and feelings aloud as they view and interact with the material. Depending on the software used, think-aloud audio and eye-tracking heat maps can be synchronized. What participants self-report with the think-aloud, when triangulated with where their eyes are fixating, can provide valuable insight above and beyond what each of these methods can offer alone.

Based on our review of the literature on sustainability communication, we predicted that images would disproportionately attract users' attention, and particularly images of people engaging in efficiency behaviors. To test this, we conducted an eye-tracking study with four SMB owners while they examined a sample BER. As the heat maps below show, we found evidence to support our hypothesis: customers' gazes were indeed more drawn to big numbers, infographics, and pictures relative to the text on the report pages (Fig. 2). This suggested that one route to increasing the appeal and effectiveness of the BER would be to optimize these visual elements.

Experimental Design (A/B Testing). While qualitative research can be a great way to generate hypotheses (e.g., the idea that people struggle to remember shutting off large devices when leaving on vacation), it is not as effective for testing hypotheses, especially ones involving complex relationships (e.g., the idea that one message frame will more effectively change a certain behavior among younger, but not older, customers). A/B testing using online samples allows such questions to be answered quickly, cheaply, and at scale. Within an experiment, participants are randomly assigned to view and respond to one of several versions of a design or product. While another option is to show participants all the options at once and ask them to pick their favorite, this measures individuals' stated preferences. Studies show that stated preferences may or may not match actual preferences in an applied setting [12]. By randomly assigning participants to view just one version, an experimental design allows assessment of customers' actual, or revealed preferences. If additional questions are added, it is also

Original   Heat Map

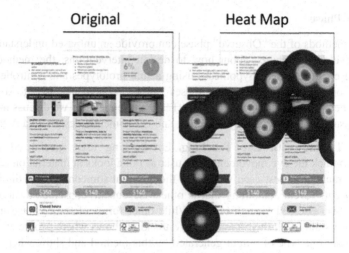

Fig. 2. Eye-tracking heatmaps on BER "tips".

possible to look for moderating relationships among variables (e.g., do property renters and owners respond differently to an image?).

Over the course of this research, we conducted a series of experimental tests using Amazon's Mechanical Turk (mTurk), which is an online marketplace in which people participate in short online surveys in exchange for small monetary compensation [13]. In an average study, our sample included ∼15% business owners, with a mean age of ∼35 years and a 50/50 gender split between male and female. Participants were randomly assigned to one of several versions of a BER image (minimum 50 participants per condition) and asked about their behavioral intention (i.e., self-reported likelihood of engaging in a proposed action) based on the materials they were shown. We also assessed the usability of the material using a scale measuring trust, satisfaction, engagement, and ease of use [14].

In a series of experimental studies based on the literature and our usability findings, we examined the hypothesis that images of people in BER tips would increase behavioral intention to engage in them. The first of these tests compared a single tip with an image of a person with a tip with an image with an inanimate object, and found that people in tip images had a highly significant effect on increasing behavioral intention, supporting our hypothesis. Our next test compared two groups of three tips: one with three images without people, and one in which one of three images had a person in it. In this second study, we found that tips without images of people might actually wash out the effect we had previously observed from a tip with an image of a person, since in this test there was no significant difference in behavioral intention. Our third test re-tested this phenomenon across a spectrum of three tip groups: one in which none of the images had people in them, one in which one of the three images had people, one in which two of the three images had people, and one in which all three images had people. The group with no images of people was rated significantly less useful than tip groups with images of people as a whole; however, this test also showed that groups with a mix of images with and without people outperformed the group where all three images had people. Collectively, the findings of these three tests do not necessarily reveal that images of people are always the best, but they do suggest that images of people influence the effectiveness of the BER.

Beyond these findings on images, we have tested hypotheses regarding bench-marking language, tip length, rebate banners, and framing business identities, to name a few. Some findings include the fact that greater discrepancies in benchmarking are more engaging and more likely to lead to a change in behavior and that including banners with dollar savings amounts increase the usability and trust of a BER.

3.3 Apply Phase

The third and final step of our research process takes place once materials have been developed and optimized for use with real customers. While the goals of the Observe and Test phases are to, respectively, generate and optimize content with in relation to a particular variable (e.g., images in a report), this final step allows us to combine results from multiple tests of different design elements and measure how this overall design affects actual user behavior. Two methods in this phase we will discuss from our case study are field experiments and field surveys.

Field Experiments. The basics of experimental testing in the field are similar to those in an online setting, as described in the Test phase; respondents are randomly exposed to one of a number of conditions or versions of a treatment (or a non-treatment control group) with comparisons between outcomes measured. While pre-testing only allows for a comparison of reported attitudes or preferences (e.g., behavioral intention), field testing allows for a comparison of responses in an applied setting. While they are not as fast or inexpensive as online pre-testing, field experiments provide greater external validity that the product will work in practice. In one experiment, we randomly assigned BER recipients to receive one of two differently framed BER Welcome Letters and measured the percentage that returned a tear-off survey at the bottom of the letter. Half of the participants received a letter with a "corporate" tone and the other half received a letter with a "personal" tone (Fig. 3).

Fig. 3. Welcome letter AB test.

Businesses who received the "corporate" version of the letter returned 7.2% of the tear-off surveys, compared to 6.4% who received the "personal" version; this difference was statistically significant. While this finding was surprising (e.g., we had hypothesized the personal tone would outperform the corporate one), we identified a possible confounding variable in the first paragraph ("Your business has been selected" in the corporate vs. "I'm writing to invite you" in the personal). We reasoned that feeling "selected" might have signaled more personalization than being simply "invited" which resulted in the higher response rate. We later compared these two sentences in an online test and confirmed this hypothesis.

Field Surveys. Field surveys can capture insights from actual users of a design or product in an applied setting (vs. user testing, which is typically conducted with potential users who are recruited to participate). They can include a combination of quantitative data (e.g., "On a scale of 1–5, how satisfied are you with the Business Energy Reports mailed to your organization") and qualitative data (e.g., "What, if any, behaviors have you engaged in as a result of receiving these reports?"). Tear-off surveys are one approach for programs like Business Energy Reports, in which the survey is attached to the report and customers are invited to complete, detach, and return the tear-off section by mail. Often, the survey also includes a web address where the survey can be submitted online instead of by mail.

Multiple field surveys from large-scale utility pilots were deployed during our two years of research with Yardi Energy. Synthesizing findings from 6 tear-off surveys across different utilities revealed both high satisfaction with and self-reported behavior change resulting from the reports. Sixty percent of respondents across surveys rated their satisfaction as either "4" or "5" on a scale of 1 to 5 where 5 indicated the highest level of satisfaction (mean = 3.7/5, st. dev. = 1.3). We also gained a much clearer sense of the actions that were being taken by report recipients. The most popular behavior was enacting a recommended tip (ranging from 18–40%), visiting an online portal (11–24%), and researching available rebates (8–22% of respondents).

4 Discussion

In order to effectively utilize the smart grid and its potential for engaging consumers to save energy, interested governments and energy utilities must identify and deploy the most effective strategies to process and present energy data to customers in a way that is clear, engaging, motivational, and trustworthy. Looking across theory and methods from the disciplines of HCI and psychology enables the benefits of both to be leveraged and synthesized to improve programs and products. In this paper, we have described a case study that walked through a multi-method framework and deployed dozens of individual research "studies" to examine and refine Business Energy Reports (BERs).

This process allows for a clear path from understanding customers to testing hypotheses and deploying in the field. Exploring theory and customer perceptions through literature review and interviews can help generate hypotheses rooted in observation. Eye-tracking and experimental pre-testing can then be used to test hypotheses and iteratively optimize design before field implementation. Once in the field, A/B testing and tear-off surveys can be used to measure and validate insights. Collectively, these methods can work together to streamline and improve the ways humans interact with computer-generated data, and, in this case, to most effectively use that data to design energy feedback aimed at motivating behavior change.

There are several key takeaways that highlight the benefit of triangulating findings across the methods embedded in this framework. Our unbiased observation of customers and the literature allow us to generate hypotheses that relate these observations to the specific elements of BERs. After targeting businesses whose smart meter data revealed that they were most likely using their HVAC systems during closed business hours, we found that these customers were unaware (or unwilling to admit) that they were in fact using their HVAC systems then. We were only able to discover this because we kept our initial research observational by simply asking how respondents used their HVAC systems in general. This disconnect between what people do and what they think they do clearly has implications for how we might design an intervention, such that customers are first carefully convinced that they do engage in this behavior.

Likewise, literature review suggested that images and benchmarks are important and that loss frames are the best way to present motivational messaging [15]. Relating these observations to actual BER elements allowed us to develop specific hypotheses about the best way to present them (e.g., images of people and loss framing will increase the behavioral intention of BER recipients). Methods used in the Testing phase led to findings that at times agreed with the existing literature and at other times deviated from it. For example, consistent with the literature, we found that it is as important to consider BER imagery as BER text and that the language and construction of the benchmarks impacts readers differently (e.g., business owners prefer social benchmarks to goal-based benchmarks, and larger discrepancies in benchmarking more effectively engage customers). In contrast, we also found that gain frames sometimes outperformed loss frames (contrary to many assumptions in behavioral science). These insights allowed us to revise and optimize BER content. Lastly, field testing in the Apply phase allowed us to measure the impact of these reports in their entirety (as opposed to refining just their individual components) on actual customers, as they engage with them.

While we reviewed this process and these methods in a very specific context – Business Energy Reports designed to inspire greater energy efficient behaviors – the framework and methods we have discussed can certainly be adapted and applied in a number of situations in which humans are interacting with computer-generated data.

References

1. Karlin, B., Ford, R., Zinger, J.: The effects of feedback on energy conservation: a meta-analysis. Psychol. Bull. **141**(6), 1205–1227 (2015)
2. Froehlich, J., Findlater, L., Landay, J.: The design of eco-feedback technology. In: Proceedings of the 28th International Conference on Human Factors in Computing Systems - CHI 2010 (2010)

3. Bandura, A.: Principles of Behavior Modification. Hold, Rinehart & Winston, New York (1969)
4. Bridgeman, B.: Effects of test score feedback on immediately subsequent test performance. J. Educ. Psychol. **66**(1), 62–66 (1974)
5. Becoña, E., Vázquez, F.L.: Effectiveness of personalized written feedback through a mail intervention for smoking cessation: a randomized-controlled trial in Spanish smokers. J. Consult. Clin. Psychol. **69**(1), 33–40 (2001)
6. Chopra, A.: Modeling a green energy challenge after a blue button. White House Office of Science and Technology Policy (2011). http://www.whitehouse.gov/blog/2011/09/15/modeling-green-energy-challenge-after-blue-button
7. Karlin, B., Ford, R., Squiers, C.: Energy feedback technology: A review and taxonomy of products and platforms. Energy Effi. **7**(3), 377–399 (2014)
8. A Design Thinking Process. ME 113. N.p. (2012). Web, 01 Mar 2017
9. Smith, N., Joffe, H.: How the public engages with global warming: a social representations approach. Publ. Underst. Sci. **22**(1), 16–32 (2012)
10. Fischer, C.: Feedback on household electricity consumption: a tool for saving energy? Energy Effi. **1**(1), 79–104 (2008)
11. O'Neill, S.J., Boykoff, M., Niemeyer, S., Day, S.A.: On the use of imagery for climate change engagement. Glob. Environ. Change **23**(2), 413–421 (2013)
12. Nolan, J.M., Schultz, P.W., Cialdini, R.B., Goldstein, N.J., Griskevicius, V.: Normative social influence is underdetected. Pers. Soc. Psychol. Bull. **34**(7), 913–923 (2008). doi:10.1177/0146167208316691
13. Karlin, B., Ford, R.: The usability perception scale (UPscale): a measure for evaluating feedback displays. In: Marcus, A. (ed.) Proceedings of the 2013 Human Computer Interaction (HCII) Conference. Springer, Heidelberg (2013)
14. Kahneman, D., Tversky, A.: Prospect theory: an analysis of decision under risk. Econometrica **47**(2), 263 (1979)

Optimizing User Interface Design and Interaction Paths for a Destination Management Information System

Dimitri Keil[1,2], Wolfram Höpken[1($\boxtimes$)], Matthias Fuchs[2], and Maria Lexhagen[2]

[1] University of Applied Sciences Ravensburg-Weingarten,
Weingarten, Germany
wolfram.hoepken@hs-weingarten.de
[2] European Tourism Research Institute (ETOUR), Mid-Sweden University,
Östersund, Sweden

Abstract. Destination Management Organizations (DMO) being the central units in destination management within European destinations face increasing pressure due to effects of globalization. At the same time, effects of digitalization combined with methods summarized by the umbrella term of Business Intelligence create opportunities to tackle these challenges. Höpken et al. (2011) described how destinations can evolve to so-called *knowledge destinations*. With the help of a Destination Management Information System (DMIS) managers of DMOs as well as its various stakeholders are provided with holistic decision support when working on strategic development of the destination. The objective of this study is to conceptualize a novel DMIS user interface and evaluate its usability. The study (1) defines different analysis perspectives and corresponding performance indicators enabling a powerful decision support for destination managers and tourism stakeholders, (2) defines interaction paths along different abstraction levels to support drill-down analyses, and (3) evaluates the usability and understandability of the DMIS interface in the south-western Swedish destination Halland.

Keywords: Destination Management Organization (DMO) · Destination Management Information System (DMIS) · Management Cockpit (MC) · User interface (UI) design · Usability · Business intelligence

1 Introduction

Since 2000, tourism has seen a steady increase in revenues worldwide with an industry volume of $ 1,309 billion for 2014. Since 2010, the number of tourist arrivals rose steadily. In 2015, global tourist arrivals grew four percent compared to the previous year (UNWTO 2016:16). At the same time, the surrounding conditions of international as well as national economic competition have changed dramatically. Bieger and Scherer (2003:10–11) refer progress in information and communication technology (ICT), transport technology and deregulation of markets as drivers for these changes. Thus, these developments lead to increased market transparency while, at the same

© Springer International Publishing AG 2017
A. Marcus and W. Wang (Eds.): DUXU 2017, Part III, LNCS 10290, pp. 473–487, 2017.
DOI: 10.1007/978-3-319-58640-3_34

time, reduce the cost of travelling, which gives both consumers and private companies access to new markets.

The described opening of global tourism markets leads to increased competitive pressure in many countries of the world. Companies must respond to these changes with innovative power and flexibility and, thus, need the ability to develop new competences (Fischer 2009:1). Information and knowledge, which foster the early recognition of development trends and customer needs, help companies to succeed. Changed market conditions affect competition in the broad tourism industry. Next to individual tourism service providers in the field of accommodation or transportation, this especially applies to geographical target areas as competitive units, in tourism also referred to as destinations. Consequently, in the context of global competition, tourism destinations must cope with saturated markets and increasingly demanding customers, while product life cycles are shrinking at the same time (Fischer 2009:3). In addition, the public character of the so-called Destination Management Organizations (DMO) strengthens the interests of its numerous stakeholders. Next to local politicians and the various service providers, important stakeholder groups consist of the local population, the DMO's employees and investors as well as the visitors of the destination (Fischer 2009:66–68; Bieger and Beritelli 2013:91).

The described market changes combined with the claim towards professional management making informed and transparent decisions place new challenges on electronic management support. At the same time, more and more data is available as a consequence of ongoing digitalization processes. However, especially at the destination level, these data about customers, products and competitors often remain unused (Pyo 2005; Fuchs et al. 2014; Höpken et al. 2015). The use of Business Intelligence (BI) and its capabilities to convert data into information for decision-support helps to overcome changes in economic conditions and, thus, to ensure increased competitiveness. According to Bieger and Beritelli (2013:107), an ideal indicator system for measuring competitiveness must, next to other things, be simple, transparent and comprehensible to the practitioner but also based on theoretical models or theories in order to have explanatory power and, thus, be suitable as a strategic basis for decision-making. The research challenge now is to structure relevant information in a meaningful way and to present it in the best possible way to meet these managerial requirements.

The objective of this study, therefore, is to conceptualize a novel destination management information system (DMIS) user interface and evaluate its usability. Specifically, the study will (1) define different analysis perspectives and corresponding performance indicators enabling a powerful decision support for destination managers and tourism stakeholders, (2) define interaction paths along different abstraction levels to support drill-down analyses, and (3) evaluate the usability and understandability of the DMIS interface with input from major stakeholders from the south-western Swedish destination Halland. In more detail, the following research questions will be answered: *What basic structure should a DMIS have or how should content be subdivided within a DMIS?* Management information is to be divided logically, considering the specificities of tourism, thus, provide the greatest possible overview of the overall situation within a destination. *How should key figures be displayed within a DMIS?* Concretely, this question is about delimiting the flood of information within the

DMIS. In addition to the selection of suitable diagram types, the various levels of indicator visualization are discussed. Overall, this is intended to improve the understanding of economic contexts in destination management, since key performance indicators (KPIs) often have a causal link.

The paper is structured as follows. The first chapter introduced challenges, opportunities and resulting research questions for this work. The second chapter provides basic definitions and summarizes all related studies and concepts that inspired the creation of the concept, which is then presented in the third chapter. Chapter four covers the methodology regarding the concept's evaluation before concluding this paper and providing a suggestion for future work based on the presented findings.

2 Background

2.1 Success Factors of Tourism Destinations

A tourist destination is defined as a geographic area selected by a particular guest or guest segment. A destination should, by definition, include all the necessary accommodation, catering and entertainment facilities for a particular stay. Thereby, a destination is seen as the major competitive unit in tourism and should, therefore, be managed as a strategic business unit (Bieger and Beritelli 2013:54).

Tourists perceive and assess the overall performance of the destination as one single product. Thus, destinations are increasingly competing with other destinations sharing a similar range of tourism products and services, which require their continuous optimization, reconfiguration and promotion (Dettmer 2005:19; Bieger and Beritelli 2013:56). Furthermore, this work focuses on destinations that correspond to the so-called *community-model* (Flagestad and Hope 2001:452), implying a large amount of small-sized tourism suppliers and a dominant role of the DMO.

Usually, a DMO covers all functions of strategic management within a destination. This includes safeguarding the normative framework and ensuring the long-term cohesion of stakeholders. In addition, safeguarding the strategic competitiveness of the destination is another important task. Finally, the DMO also secures the operational tasks within the destination (Bieger and Beritelli 2013:102).

Destinations are often described as systems in which the various actors are related. In the center, there are the different individual service providers, coordinated by the DMO. At the same time, the system is embedded in different environmental spheres, which provide the natural, social, political and economic framework conditions for the provision of services. The demand side, which is strongly interrelated to the economic environment and, thus, the economic success of the destination, is another external factor of influence (Bieger and Beritelli 2013:62).

In summary, destination management deals with the constant monitoring and analysis of the environment, in particular tourist demand but also available resources and competition. The results are then incorporated into the strategy planning of the destination (Bieger 1997:129).

In a recent study, Bornhorst et al. (2010) identified determinants for the success of DMOs and destinations. They elaborated a model that explains the relationship between the success of DMOs and destinations based on selected indicators. Accordingly, it is factors related to organizational efficiency that contribute to the success of a DMO. Supplier relations, effective management and strategic planning are examples of success factors of a DMO. The success of a destination, on the other hand, is measured by factors, such as product and service offerings and the quality of visitors' experience. Finally, community relations management, marketing and economic key figures contribute to the success of both DMOs and destinations (Bornhorst et al. 2010:587–588).

The findings of the mentioned study have been confirmed by Volgger and Pechlaner (2014). The authors investigated the role of network capability when measuring success of DMOs and destinations and found that network effects are increasing with the rise of power and acceptance of the respective DMO (Bornhorst et al. 2010:517–518; Volgger and Pechlaner 2014:72).

2.2 Business Intelligence in Tourism

Airline companies were pioneers within the tourism domain when it comes to analyzing customer transaction data as input to process and product optimization. The most prominent application areas of business intelligence (BI) in the airline industry comprise demand forecasting (Subramanian et al. 1999) and the prediction of customers' cancellation behavior and no-shows (Garrow and Koppelman 2004). A prominent example in the area of revenue and yield management in the airline industry is the DINAMO system introduced by American Airlines in 1988 (Smith et al. 1992). DINAMO builds on American Airline's GDS SABRE as the data source, providing comprehensive information on all transactions related to the areas reservation/booking, cancellation (no-show) and offerings/resource management.

Early applications of BI can also be found in the area of tourism destinations and the hospitality industry. A common example is the Austrian tourism marketing information system TourMIS (Wöber 1998), offering market research information and decision support for tourism destinations and stakeholders. TourMIS supports analyses of tourism performance indicators like arrivals, overnights or visits aggregated on the level of tourism destinations, regions, countries, or customer characteristics like sending country.

The Tyrolean (Austria) benchmarking tool Destinometer™ analyses representative survey data on customers' satisfaction with the destination offer (e.g. accommodation, gastronomy, animation, wellness, sport, shopping, etc.) as well as supply-side destination data (e.g. overnight stays, price levels for the various accommodation categories) and destination resource data (e.g. bed base, marketing costs, cost for energy, water and recycling and aggregated wages for tourism personnel) (Fuchs 2004b; Fuchs and Höpken 2005; Weiermair and Fuchs 2007).

MANOVA WEBMARK (Kepplinger 2006), a management information system for Austrian tourism stakeholders, supports tourism destinations, accommodation providers, attraction providers and ski lift operators in their operative and strategic decision making process. Tourism indicators like arrivals, overnights, visits, and passengers/transportations as well as guest feedback and satisfaction are collected and support the analysis of guest satisfaction (based on guests' demographic characteristics, travel motives and consumption behavior), performance indicators and trends, benchmarking as well as strategic analyses like SWOT analyses or importance/performance analyses (IPA), respectively.

DestiMetrics (www.destimetrics.com) supports performance analyses and decision making for tourism destinations and accommodation providers in the United States and Canada and offers performance indicators like occupancy rates, daily average room rates, or revenue per available rooms (RevPAR). The system interlinks them with contextual factors influencing tourism demand (e.g. holiday information) and offers benchmarking functionalities for tourism suppliers within as well as between tourism destinations.

T-stats (www.t-stats.co.uk), another management information system (MIS) for tourism destinations, supports descriptive analyses and benchmarking functionality in the areas of accommodation (i.e. indicators like occupancy rates, average room rates, RevPAR, etc.), attractions (i.e. indicators like the number of visitors, expenditures per visit, etc.), general tourism statistics (e.g. arrivals, expenditures, car parking, visitors of information centers, visits to events and festivals, weather data, exchange rates, etc.), customer feedback and satisfaction (based on customizable surveys) and website statistics (i.e. web navigation behavior).

Thus, almost all BI components are gradually being used in destination management. However, Höpken et al. (2015) criticize the fact that these solutions typically are isolated solutions, thus, only covering small areas of relevant business processes within tourism. The authors, therefore, describe a holistic system architecture that precisely meets this challenge, namely the generation of knowledge across all relevant business processes of a destination (Höpken et al. 2015; Fuchs et al. 2014).

2.3 Dashboard Design

A further challenging aspect is the design and implementation of a management cockpit which is highly accepted by its users. While Few (2006) provides instructions on how to design meaningful BI dashboards, Georges (2000) focuses on a holistic organizational level when designing the concept of the Management Cockpit (MC). Its goal is to increase the productivity and effectiveness of a team of executives in any type of organizations. This is achieved by the creation of a common communication framework within a special meeting room (Daum 2006:313). The central structural element is a Wall Display System, consisting of a blue, black, red and white wall, respectively. They cover different tasks within the decision-making process and, thus, provide answers to the following questions (Daum 2006 p. 314):

- Where do we stand in relation to our overall goals? (Black Wall with the main indicators - the Black Wall integrates the Balanced Scorecard if it is used)
- What about our resources? What can we do? (Blue Wall with detailed indicators and information on resources and internal processes)
- What are the (external) obstacles and critical success factors that need to be overcome? Where do we have to act? (Red Wall with detailed indicators and information on customers, markets and competitors)
- What are the critical decisions that need to be taken now? (White Wall with information on previously agreed, ongoing measures, strategic projects, etc.)

The White Wall is usually represented by a separate whiteboard or presentation screen, which is used for monitoring previously taken decisions. The remaining walls are divided into six screens (i.e. Logical Views) which deal with information on the six most important questions per wall. Each of these six screens, in turn, contains exactly six individual pieces of information, which, in their combination, are supposed to provide answers to the respective question. Georges (Georges 2000; Georges 2000:133) justifies the restriction to six information blocks with the limitation of a human's short-term memory, i.e. the capacity to process information.

Additionally, the MC also defines different levels of visualization (Daum 2006:315):

1. Level 1 shows the overall status for the whole *Logical View* and for each of the corresponding six indicators, using a common traffic lights color scheme.
2. Level 2 uses specific diagram types to support managers to capture the overall status at a glance (e.g. a tachometer).
3. Level 3 shows further details within the relevant *Logical View* by utilizing commonly used chart types, such as line or bar charts, respectively.
4. Level 4 provides an additional level of detail and e.g. allows a drill down to the level of single transactions, spreadsheets, and reports used for aggregations.

Similar to Few's (2006) instructions on dashboard design, the SUCCESS rules by Gerths and Hichert (2013:17–37) define how business information can be presented in a standardized and clearly structured way (Schneider 2016:33). It also serves as the theoretical foundation for the non-profit association IBCS (International Business Communication Standards, www.ibcs-a.org), which is committed to the dissemination of standards for shaping successful business communication (Schneider 2016:33). More precisely, SUCCESS consists of seven rule areas that can be used to assess the quality of business charts and are referred to as SAY, UNIFY, CONDENSE, CHECK, ENABLE, SIMPLIFY and STRUCTURE (Gerths and Hichert 2013:17–37).

3 Conceptualization of DMIS User Interface

The concept presented in this section provides a suggestion for the general structure of the user interface for a DMIS as a special form of information system, described in the concept defining the *knowledge destination* (Höpken et al. 2011).

In the Management Cockpit (Georges 2000), indicators are divided into three walls with each having a different focus to answer relevant managerial questions. This holistic approach allows cross-industry usage of the concept.

According to Bieger (1997:129), constant monitoring and analysis of the environment, in particular the demand side, but also available resources and competitors, are the most important tasks in destination management. Combined with the findings on success factors in tourism and inspired by the MC, the proposed concept divides information into three perspectives, namely *Resources*, *Performance* and *Demand*.

With reference to the related model by Bornhorst et al. (2010), the depicted process and input variables within that model essentially correspond to the *Resources* available to the DMO and the destination for the optimization of the overall destination product. These findings strongly correlate with the definition of the *Blue Wall* within the MC.

Furthermore, the measurement of success is represented by means of *Performance* variables. These could be economic key indicators, such as the return on investment (ROI) or tourist arrival data. But also qualitative indicators, such as the assessed visitor experience, could be used to measure success. These figures should, however, always be analyzed in relation to direct competitors to better evaluate success or failure. The success measurement, thus, ranks among the main tasks in destination management, which, in turn, has parallels to the *Black Wall* within the MC.

The strong influence of the *Demand* side on the success of a destination can be explained by the fact that a destination is mainly defined and interpreted by the final customer (i.e. tourist). Thus, the range of products and visitor services is constantly

Table 1. Identified perspectives including exemplary list of indicators

Resources	Performance	Demand
Community/supplier relations • Articles in newspapers & magazines • Fairs, festivals and other events • Community/supplier polls	*Economic indicators* • Tourist arrivals, overnights • Bed occupancy rate • Season length • Revenues o Products o Services • Market share • Guest engagement areas	*Psycho-graphic segmentation* • Pull/push motives *Socio-demographic segmentation* • Country of residence • Age (range) • Marital status • Household income
Growth statistics • Population • Capacity metrics • Number companies • Employment rates in touristic sector • Salary development • Tax income • GDP	*Satisfaction rates* • Guests o e.g. towards products and services • Residents o e.g. regarding tourism development • Employees o e.g. regarding salary development • Members o e.g. regarding market development	*Social media statistics* • Likes, tweets, mentions, reviews, rankings • Sentiment analysis *Web usage statistics* • Website visitor tracking • Search statistics *Location tracking* • Guest movement • Consumption • Weather
Corporate social responsibility (CSR) • Protective areas • Recreational areas • power/heat consumption • Energy mix • Waste accumulation • Share of regional products • Public project presentations • Urban/rural development	*Competitor/* • Market share • Main competitors	*Corporate social Responsibility (CSR)* • Guest awareness measurement • Used transportation types *Currency rates* • Most important sending countries *Risk analysis* • Technology shifts • (natural) disasters • Terrorism

adapted to the needs of the clientele. Destination guests also show specific travel motivations that are either intrinsic or influenced by the destination itself. In this context, researchers refer to so-called push and pull factors of travel motivation (Klenosky 2002). Economic revenues in tourism are only sustainable if demand meets suitable elements out of the overall destination product. However, customers can also be influenced by unforeseen factors, such as political decisions, price fluctuations or even the weather (Bornhorst et al. 2010:587). Thus, the demand-side comprises the critical success factors for the goal achievement, namely the success of the destination. Here we have the connection to the *Red Wall* within the MC.

Table 1 summarizes the three interface perspectives with related exemplary indicators. The latter are deduced from a literature review paired with several expert interviews (Bornhorst et al. 2010; Bieger and Beritelli 2013; Fuchs and Weiermair 2004; Weiermair 1993).

Figure 1 on the following page displays the prototypical implementation of the Resources view in the form of a dashboard within a prototypically implemented BI portal. The first highlighted area (1) in the figure shows the navigation elements used to access the three predefined views. The second highlighted area (2) frames the collapsed sub-categories (Logical Views within the MC) of this perspective. In this example, these are National Economy, Organization, Products & Services and Infrastructure. Finally, the third highlighted area (3) shows various indicators assigned to the sub-categories National Economy and Organization.

On each of the above described perspectives or dashboards, DMIS users will be able to create an unlimited number of sub-categories and within these an unlimited amount of information boxes, which summarize customized analysis results configured by users. Furthermore, the presented concept uses three visualization levels.

Fig. 1. Resources dashboard

On the first level, information boxes display a description (e.g. 'Are we satisfying our guests?' or just 'guest satisfaction') paired with details on associated indicator(s). The optional status for each information box is visualized using a traffic lights color scheme. The green status corresponds to the desired target value of a selected indicator. In the example in Fig. 2, the target value would be $\geq 10\%$.

Level I: Overview   Level II: Details

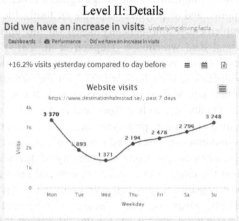

Level III: Report

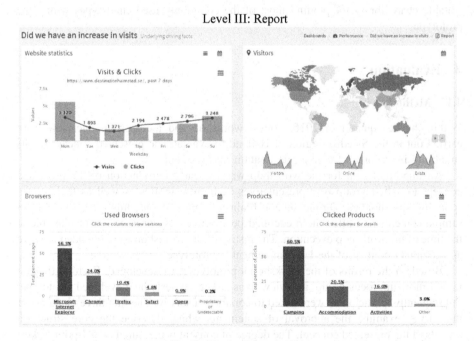

Fig. 2. Navigation overview

The second level shows the corresponding underlying data of a selected information box using appropriate chart types following the SUCCESS rules (Gerths and Hichert 2013:17–37). Additional grouping elements, such as grouping visits on a website by operating system and changes on the time interval of chart data from a daily to a weekly or monthly level, are also available.

The third level serves as the report layer for each information box. Based on the selected indicator, various aggregation functions and available grouping elements are applied and displayed in separate customizable charts. These additional charts could be implemented automatically based on the information within a holistic, multidimensional data warehouse (Höpken et al. 2013). This level also includes model-based results such as visitor segments based on similarities in their click behavior. The chart widgets can then be rearranged on the screen to finally be printed and shared with colleagues or used in business presentations.

Finally, the technologies and frameworks used for the implementation of the presented interface prototype are briefly summarized. *AdminLTE* (almsaeedstudio. com/themes/AdminLTE/documentation), based on the popular framework *Bootstrap* (getbootstrap.com) provides the layout framework of the prototype. *Bootstrap* takes over the entire user interface design and ensures that the prototype is presented in the best possible way on all commonly used devices. For the manipulation of different HTML elements, pure *Javascript* (JS) and special JS frameworks like *jQuery* (jquery.com) were used. Finally, *highcharts* (www.highcharts.com) was selected as a suitable chart library for plotting most of the commonly used chart types within the prototype.

4 Evaluation

4.1 Method

Within the last quarter of 2016, both a workshop and focus-group interview were carried out in the Swedish region of Halland to evaluate the presented concept for its suitability in the area of tourism destination management.

An important goal for the workshop was the early introduction of the presented concept to a first group of representatives both from DMOs as well as their corresponding stakeholders. During several brainstorming sessions, this group did collect sample contents and filled the predefined perspectives. No prototype was available at the time of the workshop execution. The results of the workshop were intended to serve as exemplary content of the later implemented prototype.

Based on the results of the workshop a prototype was developed. Each participant in a follow-up focus-group interview was asked to test the developed prototype. Subsequently, participants were asked to complete a survey. The first three elements of the survey examine the approval of statements which describe the core structural aspects of the presented concept. The degree of consent is measured on a 4-point Likert scale (strongly agree, rather disagree, strongly disagree), to force respondents to give a clear opinion (Likert 1932). In addition, respondents can add additional comments in a text field provided for each topic area.

Following the questions on the concept, participants should provide the likelihood towards a given set of statements in the areas of perceived usefulness and ease of use. These statements are based on the Technology Acceptance Model (TAM) as described by Davis (1989) and often used in conjunction with system installations and the measurement of user acceptance. Respondents can specify their consent using a 7-point Likert scale (extremely likely, quite likely, slightly likely, not likely, unlikely, slightly unlikely).

4.2   Results

A total of nine participants took part in the workshop. Next to the organizer representing the entire Swedish region of Halland, DMO representatives from three additional sub-destinations were present. Moreover, stakeholders representing hotels, hostels and camping sites mainly covered the accommodation sector. Two other participants finally represented a winter sports center. The results of the brainstorming sessions were used to fill the three predefined dashboards of the later implemented interface prototype with corresponding exemplary content.

A first focus-group interview was conducted with a total of five participants, four of which also answered the corresponding survey. Moreover, all participants work for DMOs, mostly in the field of destination development.

The results show a strong agreement among three of the four survey participants regarding the grouping of analysis results into the three predefined dashboards. The other respondent would also rather agree to the corresponding statement. Similar results can be observed regarding the levels of visualization. Here, however, the relationship between stronger and weaker consent is balanced. One participant also expressed the desire for further levels within the comments section. Finally, the result regarding the overall understanding of the developed concept is equal with the first statement, where three out of four respondents strongly agree and one respondent still rather agrees with the statement (see Fig. 3 for reference).

	strongly agree	rather agree	rather disagree	strongly disagree
1. The grouping of analysis results into the three predefined dashboards (i.e. Resources, Performance and Demand) appears to be logical	3	1	0	0
2. The levels of visualization effectively reduce information overloads (i.e. level I: target control -> level II: target value details -> level III: related data)	2	2	0	0
3. Overall, I understand and like the way information is structured within the DMIS.	3	1	0	0

Your comments regarding structure of and navigation within the system:
I want more levels.

Fig. 3. Survey results: concept details

Regarding perceived usefulness of the system, three out of four respondents considered it to be extremely likely that the system would make it easier to do their jobs. The other respondent also votes for a weak but still positive likelihood. Furthermore, two of the respondents consider it highly likely that tasks could be accomplished faster by using the system, and another two are very positive regarding the overall usefulness of the system. The other two respondents for each of the above statements would agree, too. Finally, two respondents believe that using the system would improve their job performance, productivity and effectiveness, respectively. The other respondents also rather or slightly agree with these statements (see Fig. 4 for reference).

	extremely likely	quite likely	slightly likely	neither likely nor unlikely	slightly unlikely	quite unlikely	extremely unlikely
8. Using the system in my job would enable me to accomplish tasks more quickly	2	2	0	0	0	0	0
9. Using the system would improve my job performance	2	1	1	0	0	0	0
10. Using the system in my job would increase my productivty	2	1	1	0	0	0	0
11. Using the system would enhance my effectiveness on the job	2	1	1	0	0	0	0
12. Using the system would make it easier to do my job	3	0	1	0	0	0	0
13. I would find the system useful in my job	2	2	0	0	0	0	0

Fig. 4. Survey results: perceived usefulness

Concerning ease of use, one respondent considers the system to be extremely user-friendly. Two other respondents think this is quite likely and a last one would also slightly agree. Moreover, two respondents would consider the system to be extremely flexible to interact with and two others think that it would be easy for them to become skillful at using it. The other respondents share these assessments by evenly assuming a slight or stronger likelihood towards the according statements. Another three of the respondents indicate that operating the system would be easy. The other respondent could not take a decision towards this specific statement. Finally, three respondents are quite convinced that interaction with the system would be clear and understandable with another three respondents believing the system will do exactly what they expect. Each of the other respondents assume a slightly likelihood towards the corresponding statements (see Fig. 5 for reference).

	extremely likely	quite likely	slightly likely	neither likely nor unlikely	slightly unlikely	quite unlikely	extremely unlikely
14. Learning to operate the system would be easy for me	0	3	0	1	0	0	0
15. I would find it easy to get the system to do what I want it to do	0	3	1	0	0	0	0
16. My interaction with the system would be clear and understandable	0	3	1	0	0	0	0
17. I would find the system to be flexible to interact with	2	1	1	0	0	0	0
18. It would be easy for me to become skillful at using the system	2	1	1	0	0	0	0
19. I would find the system easy to use	1	2	1	0	0	0	0

Fig. 5. Survey results: perceived ease of use

5 Conclusion and Future Work

Destination Management Organizations (DMOs) as central units for the management of European destinations face great challenges by the progressive effects of globalization. The use of Business Intelligence (BI) and its ability to transform data into information and knowledge input for decision-support helps to tackle these challenges while ensuring competitiveness (Fuchs et al. 2014; Höpken et al. 2015). In this context, the present work deals with the optimal structuring and presentation of these data based on selected design concepts, such as the Management Cockpit (MC) or SUCCESS rules for data visualization (Georges 2000; Gerths and Hichert 2013:17–37). The defined concept was first discussed and pre-evaluated within a workshop with destination stakeholders. The next step was to implement a first prototype, which then was used as input for a focus-group interview accompanied by a survey. The main findings were that the overall concept is well-understood and accepted by its selected users. All members of the focus group also think that a functional system based on the proposed concept would be useful in their daily business. Ease of use was also positively evaluated, although there is still room for improvement. Yet, the main goal was to get a first impression by practitioners regarding the developed concept. On the basis of these findings, a next logical step would be the successive development of the existing prototype into a functional prototype. This way, the whole concept could be tested under real conditions and over a longer period of time. Similarly, on the basis of a larger user group, a quantitative evaluation could follow in order to verify the concept's particular suitability to display BI-based knowledge in the domain of tourism destination management.

References

Bieger, T.: Management von Destinationen und Tourismusorganisationen. Oldenbourg, Munich (1997)

Bieger, T., Beritelli, P.: Management von Destinationen. Oldenbourg, Munich (2013)

Bieger, T., Scherer, R.: Clustering und integratives Standortmanagement - von einem theoretischen Konzept zur konkreten Handlungsstrategie. Clustering - Das Zauberwort der Wirtschaftsförderung, pp. 9–26. Haupt, Bern (2003)

Bornhorst, T., Ritchie, J.B., Sheehan, L.: Determinants of tourism success for DMOs & destinations: an empirical examination of stakeholders' perspectives. Tour. Manag. **31**(5), 572–589 (2010)

Daum, J.H.: Management Cockpit War Room. Controlling, Heft **6**, 311–318 (2006)

Davis, F.D.: Perceived usefulness, perceived ease of use, and user acceptance of information technology. MIS Q. **13**(3), 319–340 (1989)

Dettmer, H., Eisenstein, B., Axel, G., Hausmann, T., Claude, K., Werner, O., et al.: Managementformen im Tourismus. Oldenbourg, Munich (2005)

Few, S.: Information Dashboard Design: The Effective Visual Communication of Data. O'Reilly Media Inc, Sebastopol (2006)

Fischer, E.: Das kompetenzorientierte Management der touristischen Destination - Identifikation und Entwicklung kooperativer Kernkompetenzen. Gabler, Wiesbaden (2009)

Flagestad, A., Hope, C.A.: Strategic success in winter sports destinations. Tourism Manag. **22**, 445–461 (2001)

Fuchs, M.: Strategy development in tourism destinations: a data envelopment analysis approach. Poznań Univ. Econ. Rev. **4**(1), 52–73 (2004)

Fuchs, M., Höpken, W.: Towards @Destination: a data envelopment analysis based decision support framework. Information and Communication Technologies in Tourism, pp. 57–66. Springer, New York (2005)

Fuchs, M., Höpken, W., Lexhagen, M.: Big data analytics for knowledge generation in tourism destinations - a case from Sweden. J. Destination Mark. Manag. **3**(4), 198–209 (2014)

Fuchs, M., Weiermair, K.: Destination benchmarking: an indicator-system's potential for exploring guest satisfaction. J. Travel Res. **42**(3), 212–225 (2004)

Garrow, L., Koppelman, F.: Predicting air travelers' no-show and standby behavior using passenger and directional itinerary information. J. Air Transp. Manag. **10**(6), 401–411 (2004)

Georges, P.M.: How management cockpits facilitate managerial work. In: Küting, K., Weber, C.-P. (Hrsg.) Wertorientierte Konzernführung. Kapitalmarktorientierte Rechnungslegung und integrierte Unternehmenssteuerung, Stuttgart, pp. S.431–S.466 (2000)

Georges, P.M.: The management cockpit - the human interface for management software: reviewing 50 user sites over 10 years of experience. Wirtschaftsinformatik **42**(2), 131–136 (2000)

Gerths, H., Hichert, R.: Geschäftsdiagramme mit Excel nach den SUCCESS-Regeln gestalten: Tipps und Tricks für Excel 2003 und 2007/2010. Haufe, Freiburg Munich (2013)

Höpken, W., Fuchs, M., Höll, G., Keil, D., Lexhagen, M.: Multi-dimensional data modelling for a tourism destination data warehouse. Inf. Commun. Technol. Tourism **2013**, 157–169 (2013)

Höpken, W., Fuchs, M., Keil, D., Lexhagen, M.: Business intelligence for cross-process knowledge extraction at tourism destinations. Inf. Technol. Tourism **15**(2), 101–130 (2015)

Höpken, W., Fuchs, M., Keil, D., Lexhagen, M.: The knowledge destination - a customer information-based destination management information system. Inf. Commun. Technol. Tourism **2011**, 417–429 (2011)

Kepplinger, D.: Tourismus WEBMART - Interaktive Datenerfassung und Ergebnisdarstellung durch Online-Datenbanken. Innovationen in der Tourismusforschung: Methoden und Anwendungen, pp. 63–76. Lit Verlag, Vienna (2006)

Klenosky, D.B.: The "Pull" of tourism destinations: a means-end investigation. J. Travel Res. **40**(4), 385–395 (2002)

Likert, R.: A technique for the measurement of attitudes. Arch. Psychol. **22**(140), 5–55 (1932)

Pyo, S.: Knowledge map for tourist destinations. Tourism Manag. **26**(4), 583–594 (2005)

Schneider, C.: Management Reporting: Stand und Herausforderungen. Managementberichte gekonnt visualisieren: Standards und Design-Grundsätze für ein aussagekräftiges Reporting, pp. 23–40. Freiburg Munich, Haufe (2016)

Smith, B.C., Leimkuhler, J.F., Darrow, R.M.: Yield management at American Airlines. Interfaces **22**(1), 8–31 (1992)

Subramanian, J., Stidham, S., Lautenbacher, C.: Airline yield management with overbooking, cancellations, and no-shows. Transp. Sci. **33**(2), 147–167 (1999)

Volgger, M., Pechlaner, H.: Requirements for destination management organizations in destination governance: understanding DMO success. Tourism Manag. **41**, 64–75 (2014)

Weiermair, K.: Some reflections on measures of competitiveness for wintersport resorts in overseas markets. Tourist Rev. **48**(4), 35–41 (1993)

Weiermair, K., Fuchs, M.: Productivity differentials across tourist destinations - a theoretical/empirical analysis. Productivity in Tourism - Fundamentals and Concepts for Achieving Growth and Competitiveness, pp. 41–54. Erich Schmidt, Berlin (2007)

World Tourism Organization: UNWTO Annual Report 2015. UNWTO, Madrid (2016)

Wöber, K.: Global statistical sources- TourMIS: an adaptive distributed marketing information system for strategic decision support in national, regional or city tourist offices. Pac. Tourism Rev. **2**(3), 273–286 (1998)

Modeling a Systematic-Innovation Approach for Green Product Design

Yao-Tsung Ko[1(✉)], Meng-Cong Zheng[2], and Chi-Hung Lo[1]

[1] Department of Industrial Design, Tunghai University, Taichung, Taiwan
{mike.ko,chlo}@thu.edu.tw
[2] Department of Industrial Design, National Taipei University of Technology,
Taipei, Taiwan
zmcdesign@gmail.com

Abstract. Technology developing always impacts environment. Designers must consider the balance between technical innovation and environmental protection when creating an innovative product. This paper presents a systematic-innovation design method for green product based on the QFD approach and TRIZ tools. Conceptual design is considered to be one of the pivotal components in New Product Development (NPD) process which has a significant impact on downstream NPD activities. Despite the recognized importance of conceptual design, there is a lack of a systematic and effective innovation creating process for green product. To address this gap, a useful and powerful design method of systematic innovation is created for green product, depending on the capability of QFD detailed problem analysis and the prowess of TRIZ innovative idea generation. The proposed design method was developed with QFD-I and an eco-contradiction matrix identifying the contradiction between customer needs and eco-efficiency elements for deriving TRIZ invention principles. The related specific solutions are conducted from these invention principles. The eco-innovative product could be created depended on these specific solutions. A case study of the innovative garden eco-light design was demonstrated for the applicability of this method and the results validated the feasibility and effectiveness.

Keywords: Systematic-innovation · Green product · QFD · TRIZ · Eco-contradiction matrix

1 Introduction

Without creativity in design there is no potential for innovation. Technological advance often conflicts with environment. It usually emphasizes the advantage and novelty of an innovation product but ignores its environmental impact (Hsu 1999). Corporate has the responsibility to make its activities be more environmentally friendly. Environmentally conscious design (eco-design) is particularly important in manufacturing industry. To implement eco-design concept, it is critical to take environmental aspects into account in the early phases of design, such as the planning and the conceptual design phases. Many eco-design methods (Fiksel 1996; Behrendt et al. 1997; Chen and Yen 1999) have been developed to assist the design engineers for reducing the environmental

© Springer International Publishing AG 2017
A. Marcus and W. Wang (Eds.): DUXU 2017, Part III, LNCS 10290, pp. 488–500, 2017.
DOI: 10.1007/978-3-319-58640-3_35

impact of the product throughout its life cycle. Nevertheless, those methods are focused on the redesign or optimization of existing products. Design engineers always attempt to reduce the harmful impact from products or processes; however, it is not easily achieved. It seems to be an irreconcilable problem for design engineers. Therefore, it is necessary to develop a product eco-innovation design process. The purpose of this study is to develop a more innovative product eco-design methodology based on QFD approach and TRIZ tools. The rest of this paper is organized as follows: In Sect. 2, the related works of eco-design method is presented. In Sect. 3, the proposed methodology is described in detail. In Sect. 4, a case study is illustrated to verify the feasibility and effectiveness of the proposed method, and finally, in Sect. 5, the paper is concluded.

2 Related Works

Many design methods and tools have been developed to support systematic-innovation. Cascini et al. (2011) aimed to bridge systematic invention practice with product life cycle management systems by integrating TRIZ principles within a computer aided design system. Concerning eco-invention, Fresner et al. (2010) applied TRIZ in cleaner production to have a more rational use of materials and energy to reduce waste and emissions in industrial activities. Sakao (2007) proposed another extension, coupling TRIZ and quality function deployment by integrating life cycle analysis. In another research Grote et al. (2007) presented, a methodology based on TRIZ, design for X tools and life cycle analysis to develop an eco-inventive methodology. Low et al. (2000) used TRIZ evolution patterns to explain the relationship between product function and service. Chen (2002) developed an eco innovative design method by incorporating green evolution rules and ideality laws to create products and processes that are innovative, useful, and environmentally friendly. Justel et al. (2005) utilized TRIZ evolution patterns to get the evolution of joint parameter for disassembly. Although life cycle assessment (LCA) (Wenzel et al. 1997) is an essential evaluation method for systematic-innovation based on the life cycle approach, in LCA the environmental burden is not evaluated until the detail design phase. Also, there are few quantitative methods for improving a product using LCA data. With regard to QFD (Akao 1990) analysis approach, QFD determines product design specifications (how) based on customer needs (what) and competitive analysis (why), which represents a customer-driven and market-oriented process for decision-making. It is quite natural to use QFD in decision making for such purposes as determining customer needs (Stratton 1989) and development priorities (Crowe and Cheng 1996; Han et al. 1998; Jugulum and Sefik 1998). Karsak et al. (2002) presented a QFD systematic decision procedure in product planning, which has been traditionally based on expert opinions and consider the interdependence between the customer needs and product technical requirements, and the inner dependence within themselves, along with resource limitations, and design metrics such as extendibility and manufacturability. Tsai et al. (2003) used fuzzy QFD approach with an optimistic index in the priority ranking procedures. This fuzzy index can correct bias problems in a consistentway for prioritizing strategic functions. A priority change display in the priority ranking according to different scenarios can provide "what-if" analysis in a decision-making environment. However, QFD is easy to use for clarifying key components from both the quality and environmental aspects in the initial design phases (Masui et al. 2000), but it does not support the generation of solution ideas. At the product level, it is important to detect local conflicts in products and to resolve those conflicts. TRIZ which is useful for resolving conflicts of parameters in the product is an inventive problem-solving method. Because of the capability of solving conflict problems, the ideas of implementing TRIZ for eco-innovative design have been proposed (Chen and Liu 2003; Jones et al. 2001). There is still a disadvantage of finding hardly the contradiction parameters for invention principles.

Although some above researches have successfully integrated QFD and TRIZ for NPD, these approaches and models are still very difficult to use in practice. Most of them just provide a procedure or guidelines instead of an operational model. However, this paper provides a more enhanced and robust method. The proposed systematic-innovation approach utilises TRIZ more effectively for green product. This will bring more efficiency and feasibility to the problem-solving processes. Meanwhile, this paper also proposes a operational model of eco-contradiction matrix to help designers generate more conveniently and effectively creative outcomes in NPD.

3 Methodology

The proposed method is a systematic-innovation design method based on the eco-efficiency elements, QFD-I and TRIZ tools.

3.1 Eco-Innovation Design Process

From the ecological and environmental perspective, the development of technology is important for a national economic growth but it also impacts the ecological environment. Air pollution, energy and material consumption, noise, and toxic waste water constantly influence the ecosystem directly or indirectly. They have made the greenhouse effect stronger, unknown diseases spread, and many species vanish. Therefore, the World Business Council of Sustainable Development (WBCSD) has identified seven major eco-efficiency elements for companies which develop eco-friendly products or processes in order to reduce environmental impacts (Desimone and Popoff 1997).

A. Reduce the material intensity of its goods and services (material reduction).
B. Reduce the energy intensity of its goods and services (energy reduction).
C. Reduce the dispersion of any toxic materials (toxicity reduction).
D. Enhance the recyclability of its materials (material retrieval).
E. Maximize the sustainable use of renewable resources (resource sustainable).
F. Extend the durability of its products (product durability).
G. Increase the service intensity of its goods and services (product service).

As each element improves or more elements improve simultaneously, it produces high eco-efficiency products or services.

The proposed eco-design method was established based on the above seven eco-efficiency elements. This eco-design method integrated QFD-I and TRIZ concept to create innovative product. An new eco-contradiction matrix was proposed to find the conflict features. It can help a design engineer find the eco-conflict features easier than the traditional TRIZ contradiction matrix. The important point in the utilization of the eco-contradiction matrix is the identification of pairs of contradictory characteristics and their conversion into the standard terms in TRIZ. For this reason, a method to identify contradictory parameters using the QFD-I matrix and to find links to the eco-contradiction matrix has been proposed. In eco-design, in addition to quality characteristics and environmental characteristics must also be considered at the same time. Therefore, the QFD-I approach and eco-efficiency elements were utilized to identify conflict features for use in eco-contradiction matrix in this paper.

The procedure of the proposed eco-design method is shown as Fig. 1. First, define the seven eco-efficiency elements clearly for product design. Second, find the customer requirements and quality characterictics based on QFD-I approach. Then calculate the importance of the quality characterictics and set top priority of the quality characterictics for use in next phase. Third, put the quality characterictics and eco-efficiency elemnets into the eco-contradiction matrix and converse they to the standard technical features used in TRIZ. Review the matrix and find the conflict points. The proposed invention principles of TRIZ were derived based the contradiction parameters. A design engineer can generate a novel solution idea for eco-innovative product based on the derived invention principles.

3.2 QFD-I Approach

QFD was first introduced by Akao (1990) at Kobe Shipyard of the Mitsubishi Heavy Industries Ltd. in 1972. QFD develops a series of matrices to associate customer requirement items with technical attribute items, thereby identifying the design specifications from the customer requirements. The QFD is an implement to translate customer needs into product technical requirements of new products and services that have been developed from Japan in the late 1960s to early 1970s (Chan and Wu 2002). The main concept of traditional QFD considered four relationship matrices that included product planning, parts planning, process planning, and production planning matrices, respectively (Karsak et al. 2002; Akao 1997). Each translation used a matrix, also called house of quality (HOQ), as shown in Fig. 2. In the first place, the product planning matrix is established. The customer needs translated to the second QFD as inputs for the development of product design requirements. Secondly, in the part planning matrix, important design requirements are linked to part component characteristics deployment. Furthermore, the part component characteristics are similarly linked to manufacturing operations. In the production planning matrix, the process parameters and control limits are determined in the same way. This study is to consider the construction of product planning matrix (the first of the four matrices) because most innovative ideas will be created at the QFD-I phase. That is, the quality characteristics of the new product are defined by the QFD model.

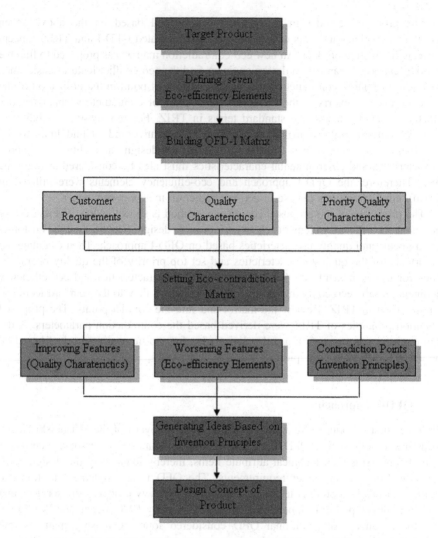

Fig. 1. The workflow of eco-innovation design process.

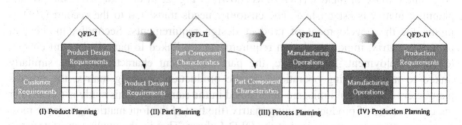

Fig. 2. The process of QFDs.

QFD-I Matrix			Quality Characteristics (j)						
	Item	Impartance pi	QC$_1$	QC$_2$	QC$_3$	QC$_4$	QC$_5$	...	QC$_m$
	CR$_1$	$p1$	a_{11}	a_{12}	a_{13}	...	...	...	a_{1m}
	CR$_2$	$p2$	a_{21}	a_{22}	a_{23}	...	...	...	a_{2m}
	CR$_3$	$p3$	a_{31}	a_{32}	a_{33}	...	...	...	a_{3m}
	CR$_4$	$p4$	...	...	...	...	...	...	...
	CR$_5$	$p5$	...	...	...	...	...	...	...
	CR$_6$	$p6$	...	...	...	...	...	...	...
	...	...	...	...	...	...	...	...	...
	CR$_n$	pn	a_{n1}	a_{n2}	a_{n3}	...	...	...	a_{nm}
Sum=$\Sigma pi*QCj$									
Relative Importance $p*j$									

(Customer Requirements (i) — left vertical label)

Note:
1. Relationship: strong concern=5; concern=3; weak concern=1
2. Importance Ratio: 1~5

Fig. 3. QFD-I matrix

QFD is a very useful tool to realize the real customer requirements and the quality characteristics of a product. The QFD-I process was adopted to extracte the quality characteristics based on the voices of customers (VoC) (Sanchez et al. 1993) in this paper, and an eco-contradiction matrix is then created by combining eco-efficiency elements, quality characteristics and TRIZ tools. In Fig. 3, the relative importance values $p*j$ are computed by Eq. (1).

$$p_j^* = \frac{\sum_{i=1}^{n} p_i a_{ij}}{\sum_{i=1}^{n} \sum_{j=1}^{m} p_i a_{ij}}$$

The customer requirements i (CR1,...CRn), their importance pi, the quality characteristics j (QC1,...QCm), and the relationship a_{ij} between i and j are described in the QFD-I matrix (Fig. 3). A designer can utilize QFD-I matrix to get the quality characteristics and its relative importance for further conflict analysis in eco-contradiction matrix.

3.3   Eco-Contradiction Matrix

TRIZ proposed by Altshuller (1984) is based on scientific observations and on extensive analysis of invariant design strategies applied across technical domains. The most powerful tool of TRIZ is the contradiction matrix including 39 engineering parameters and 40 invention principles (Altshuller 1996). The proposed eco-contradiction matrix was built for creating eco-innovative products based on the traditional contradiction matrix of TRIZ.

Note that the use of eco-contradiction matrix is not the same as the contradiction matrix of TRIZ. Figure 3 is for setting main conflicts in the target product and to identify them with the eco-contradiction matrix of TRIZ. In order to make it easy to set confliction points, the top priority quality characteristics that have the higher values of $p*j$ are selected from QFD-I and the eco-efficiency elements are also considered in Fig. 4. The selected quality characteristics would be regarded as the improving features and the eco-efficiency elements would be regarded as the worsening features in the proposed eco-contradiction matrix. The steps of eco-contradiction matrix is shown as follows:

Eco-Contradiction Matrix				Worsening Parameter Eco-efficiency Elements (i)						
				A	B	C	D	E	F	G
		Item	TRIZ No.	EE-EP1	EE-EP2	EE-EP3	EE-EP4	EE-EP5	EE-EP6	EE-EP7
Improving Parameter	Quality characteristics (j)	QC1	QC-EP1				X			
		QC2	QC-EP2	X					X	
		QC3	QC-EP3					X		
		QC4	QC-EP4		X					
		QC5	QC-EP5							X
		...	...							
		QCn	QC-EPn			X		X		

Note:
A: reduce the material intensity of its goods and services (material reduction)
B: reduce the energy intensity of its goods and services (energy reduction)
C: reduce the dispersion of any toxic materials (toxicity reduction)
D: enhance the recyclability of its materials (material retrieval)
E: maximize the sustainable use of renewable resources (resource sustainable)
F: increase the service intensity of its goods and services (product durability)
G: extend the durability of its products (product service)

X: Contradiction

Fig. 4. Eco-contradiction matrix

STEP 1: Put the quality characteristics into the improving column and the eco-efficiency elements into the worsening row.
STEP 2: Replace quality characteristics and eco-efficiency elements with standard features in TRIZ intuitively.
STEP 3: Sets contradiction marks (X) between the technical terms in TRIZ.
STEP 4: Derive invention principles based on the TRIZ contradiction matrix.
STEP 5: Develop eco-innovative product concept based on the invention principles

The use of the eco-contradiction matrix facilitates the generation of a novel solution idea at the product level.

4 A Case Study

Company A, which is an international original brand manufacturing electronics company in Taiwan would like to coorperate with us to develop a all new garden eco-light with green energy. The proposed systematic-innovation design method was employed to create a innovative outdoor eco-light for Company A.

4.1 Customer Requirements

The target product is a outdoor garden eco-light. The cuctomer requirements were carried out after discussing with the marketing members of Company A. The product features were listed as follows:

Easy to use; (2) Good shape; (3) Eco-material; (4) Good brightness; (5) Easy to setup; (6) Environment friendly; (7) Multi-functional; (8) Long life cycle; (9) Easy to maintain; (10) Green power

4.2 QFD-I Matrix of Garden Eco-Light

According to the cuctomer requirements, the related quality characteristics were defined in this design project. The importance ratio of the cuctomer requirements and the scores of the quality characteristics cooresponding to each cuctomer requirement were identified based on the judging rules of QFD-I mentioned previously in sub-Sect. 3.2. Finally, The QFD-I matrix of this garden eco-light was established as following Fig. 5.

4.3 Eco-Contradiction Matrix of Garden Eco-Light

In order to make it easy to set conflict points, the top five quality characteristics that have the higher values of the relative importance $p*j$ were selected from QFD-I. The five selected quality characteristics were considered as the improving parameters and the seven eco-efficiency elements were considered as the worsening parameters. These two different categories of parameters were put into the eco-contradiction matrix together to discuss the conflict for innovations in Fig. 5.

Meanwhile, the selected quality characteristics and eco-efficiency elements were transferred to the corresponding TRIZ engineering parameters shown as TRIZ No. on row and column in Fig. 6. For example, "Energy consumption" can be transferred to "loss of energy (TRIZ No.22)"; "Illumination intensity" can be transferred to "Illumination intensity (TRIZ No.18)". All of the quality characteristics and eco-efficiency elements were transferred to the standard features in TRIZ with the same manner. Finally, three contradictions were identified after reviewed the eco-contradiction matrix.

QFD-I Matrix			Quality Characteristics (j)							
Customer Requirements (i)	Item	Importance pi	Energy consumption [kWh/year]	Setup time [hr]	illumination intensity [lux]	Added function [quantity]	Maintenance time [hr]	BOM cost [USD]	Useful Lifetime [year]	Recyclability ratio [%]
	1. Easy to operate	3				3				
	2. Good form	4	1					1		
	3. Eco-material	4								5
	4. Good brightness	4	3		5			1	3	
	5. Easy to setup	3		3			1			
	6. Environment friendly	3				5				
	7. Multi-functional	2	1							
	8. Long life cycle	4			3				5	3
	9. Easy to maintain	3				3	5			
	10. Green power	5	5		3			3	5	1
Sum=Σpi *QCj			37	15	47	33	18	23	57	37
Relative Importance p*j			13.9%	5.6%	17.6%	12.4%	6.7%	8.6%	21.3%	13.9%

Note:
1. Relationship: strong concern=5; concern=3; weak concern=1
2. Importance Ratio: 1~5

Fig. 5. The QFD-I matrix of the garden light

They were $X1$, $X2$ and $X3$, respectively. $X1$ means if we want to enhance the brightness of light, it will impact the goal of energy reduction and product service ($X2$); $X3$ means if we want to add more functions on product, it will impact the goal of material retrieval.

4.4 Invention Principles

In order to get innovative idea triggers, the invention principles were derived based on the above-mentioned contradiction parameters. The specific solutions were proposed from the generic solutions with some creativity and imaginations. The design thinking process is shown in Table 1.

Finally, the solution ideas for the garden eco-light design is listed as follows:

(1) Use solar power for green energy.
(2) Use LED light for reducing power consumption.
(3) Install a light sensor for the automatic turning on/off function.
(4) Separation concept for multi-functional uses between garden light and portable light.

Eco-Contradiction Matrix				Worsening Parameter						
				Eco-efficiency Elements (i)						
				A. Material reduction	B. Energy reduction	C. toxicity reduction	D. Material retrieval	E. Resource sustainable	F. Product durability	G. Product service
		Item	TRIZ No.	23	20	31	32	34	27	33
Improving Parameter	Quality characteristics (j)	Energy consumption [kWh/year]	22							
		Illumination intensity [lux]	18		X₁					X₂
		Added function [quantity]	33				X₃			
		Useful lifetime [year]	23							
		Recyclability ratio [%]	31							

Note: Mark X*n* indicates that there is a contradiction between improving and worsening parameters.

Fig. 6. The Eco-contradiction matrix of the garden light

Table 1. Specific solutions for the garden light.

Contradiction	Invention principle	Generic solution	Specific solution
X_1 = [18, 20]	(32, 35, 1, 15)	35: Parameter changes 32: Color changes	1. Solar power 2. Colorful LED
X_2 = [18, 33]	(28, 26, 19)	19: Periodic action	1. Light sensor
X_3 = [33, 32]	(2, 5, 12)	2: Taking out/separation	1. Double uses

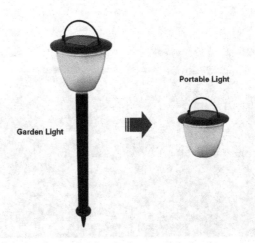

Portable Light

Garden Light

Fig. 7. Multi-functional uses for the garden eco-light by the separation concept.

4.5 Design Concept of the Innovative Garden Eco-Light

Considering the factors of enviromment friendly and convenient use, the design concept of solar power and multi-functions are utilized to create the garden eco-light (Fig. 7.). In order to create a variant atmospheres the LED light is adopted. Finally, the garden eco-light was created based on the above analysis results. The detail design of the eco-light is illustrated as following Fig. 8.

Fig. 8. The concept design of garden eco-light.

Fig. 9. Scenarios of variant LED lights.

We hope that the innovative garden eco-light has not only single color function, but also has variant colors for creating fancy environment (Fig. 9.).

5 Conclusions

Creativity is the most important part of the concept design process in new product development (NPD). There is no potential for innovation without creativity in design. Future products must have not only novelty but also the environment-friendly features. Therefore, design engineers will meet more and more challenges while developing eco-innovative products. Contradiction will be the largest block on the road for new generation of solution ideas. The systematic-innovation design process integrating quality characteristics of QFD-I and WBCSD eco-efficiency elements into the proposed eco-contradiction matrix is established for solving the eco-innovative product design. The solution ideas of eco-innovation design will be effective approaches towards sustainable development. The proposed eco-design method based on the above-mentioned ideas indeed can assist designers to create eco-innovative product. A case study example demonstrated the applicability and feasibility of the proposed eco-design method. Moreover, the new eco-contradiction matrix could help designers find quickly the conflict points between different parameters for invention principles. We believe that although innovation may be accidental, systematic innovation is destined. The proposed process of eco-design method provides a possible way for destined innovations.

References

Akao, Y.: Quality Function Deployment. Productivity Press (1990)

Akao, Y.: QFD: past, present, and future. In: Proceedings of the International Symposium on QFD 1997, Linko ping (1997)

Altshuller, G.S.: Creativity as an Exact Science: the Theory of the Solution of Inventive Problems. Gordon and Breach, Amsterdam (1984)

Altshuller, G.S.: And Suddenly the Invento, 2nd edn. MA Technical Innovation Center, Worcester (1996)

Behrendt, S., Jasch, C., Peneda, M.C., Van Weenen, H.: Life Cycle Design, a Manual for Small and Medium Sized Enterprises. Springer, Berlin (1997)

Chan, L.K., Wu, M.L.: Quality function deployment: a literature review. Eur. J. Oper. Res. **143**, 463–497 (2002)

Cascini, G., Rissone, P., Rotini, F., Russo, D.: Systematic design through the integration of TRIZ and optimization tools. Procedia Eng. **9**, 674–679 (2011)

Chen, J.L., Yen, M.: Development product design methodology by using life cycle assessment for design for environment tasks. In: Proceedings of International Conference on Cleaner Production and Sustainable Development 1999, 13–17 December, Taipei, Taiwan, pp. 361–370 (1999)

Chen, J.L.: Green evolution rules and ideality laws for green innovative design of products. In Fourth International Symposium on Going Green-Care Innovation (2002)

Chen, J.L., Liu, C.C.: An eco-innovative design approach incorporating the TRIZ method without contradiction analysis. J. Sustain. Prod. Des. 1(4), 262–272 (2003)

Crowe, T.J., Cheng, C.C.: Using quality function deployment in manufacturing strategic planning. Int. J. Oper. Prod. Manag. 16(4), 35–48 (1996)

Desimone, L.D., Popoff, F.: Eco-efficiency: the business link to sustainable development. Massachusetts Institute of Technology, Cambridge (1997)

Fiksel, J.: Design for Environment. McGraw-Hill, New York (1996)

Fresner, J., Jantschgi, J., Birkel, S., Barnthaler, J., Krenn, C.: The theory of inventive problem solving (TRIZ) as option generation tool within cleaner production projects. J. Cleaner Prod. 18(2), 128–136 (2010)

Grote, C.A., Jones, R.M., Blount, G.N., Goodyer, J., Shayler, M.: An approach to the EuP directive and the application of the economic eco-design for complex products. Int. J. Prod. Res. 45, 4099–4117 (2007)

Han, C.H., Kim, J.K., Choi, S.H., Kim, S.H.: Determination of information system development priority using quality function deployment. Comput. Ind. Eng. 35(1–2), 241–244 (1998)

Hsu, M.Y.: Promoting innovation for environment by green patent system. In: Proceedings of International Conference on Cleaner Production and Sustainable Development 1999, 13–17 December, Taipei, Taiwan, pp. 485–494 (1999)

Jones, E., Harrison, D., Stanton, N.A.: The application of TRIZ tools in an eco-innovation process. In: Proceedings of World Conference on TRIZ Future 2001, 7–9 November, Bath, UK, pp. 57–78 (2001)

Justel, D., Vidal, R., Chiner, M.: TRIZ applied to innovate in design for disassembly. In: 1st IFIP TC-5 Working Conference on CAI, IFIP-TC5 ULM, Germany (2005)

Jugulum, R., Sefik, M.: Building a robust manufacturing strategy. Comput. Ind. Eng. 35(1–2), 225–228 (1998)

Karsak, E.E., Sozer, S., Alptekin, S.E.: Product planning in quality function deployment using combined analytic network process and goal programming approach. Comput. Ind. Eng. 44, 171–190 (2002)

Low, M.K., Lamvik, T., Walsh, K., Myklebust, O.: Product to service ecoinnovation: the TRIZ model of creativity explored. In: International Symposium on Electronics and the Environment, pp. 209–214. IEEE, San Francisco (2000)

Masui, K., Sako, T., Aizawa, S., Inaba, A.: Design for environment in early stage of product development using quality function deployment. In: Reichl, H., Griese, H.-J. (eds.) Proceedings of the Joint International Congress and Exhibition—Electronics Goes Green, vol. 1. VDE Verlag, Berlin (2000)

Sakao, T.: A QFD-centred design methodology for environmentally conscious product design. Int. J. Prod. Res. 45(18–19), 4143–4162 (2007)

Sanchez, M., Ramberg, J.S., Fiero, J., Pignatiello, J.J.: Quality by design. In: Kusiak, A. (ed.) Concurrent Engineering : Automation, Tools, and Techniques. Wiley, New York (1993)

Stratton, B.: The refined focus of automotive quality. Qual. Prog. 22(10), 47–50 (1989)

Tsai, C.Y., Lo, C.C., Chang, A.C.: Using fuzzy QFD to enhance manufacturing strategic planning. J. Chin. Inst. Ind. Eng. 18(3), 33–41 (2003)

Wenzel, H., Hauschild, M., Alting, L.: Environmental Assessment of Products. Chapman & Hall, London (1997)

Cultural Calibration: Technology Design for Tourism Websites

Emanuele Mele[1(⊠)] and Erkki Sutinen[2]

[1] The Faculty of Communication Sciences,
USI - Università della Svizzera italiana, Lugano, Switzerland
emanuele.mele@usi.ch
[2] Department of Information Technology, University of Turku, Turku, Finland
erkki.sutinen@utu.fi

Abstract. With favourable socio-economic and political conditions, tourism has registered an impressive growth both at the international and domestic level. According to the figures released by UNWTO (2016), the total number of international tourist arrivals worldwide was 1.186 billion in 2015, forecasting to reach 1.8 billion in 2030 with a growth of 3.3% a year. Supporting this phenomenon, Information and Communication Technologies (ICTs), particularly the Internet, play a major role at every stage of the tourism experience. As a consequence, Destination Marketing/Management Organizations (DMOs) should leverage on good-quality websites to answer visitors' needs and prevail over competitors. Especially for National Tourism Organizations (NTOs), given their role in promoting the destination abroad, the elaboration of online marketing strategies should also take into account culture-bound preferences and needs of reference publics. Within this context, the concept of cultural calibration refers to any technology that transforms contents and tools that people use to communicate with each other in an effort to match with their culture-dependent expressions. Despite the recognized effects of culture on online behavior and willingness to travel, content managers often have to rely on common sense when designing country-specific website editions. In addition to that, differently from eLearning, ecommerce, and online marketing areas, little research has been done regarding software design for adaptation activities in the eTourism context. Consequently, the objective of this paper is to provide a design concept for a software for cultural calibration of destination websites. Its relevance for researchers and practitioners is also presented, together with the evaluation of its functionalities and possible applications.

Keywords: Cultural calibration · eTourism · Website design

1 Introduction

Cultural calibration describes any technology that transforms contents and tools that people use to communicate with each other, in an effort to answer their culture-dependent preferences. Addressing the latter, Barber and Badre (1998) refer to it as "cultural markers", which characterize the choice of layout and multimedia contents for any website from a specific cultural group. Coining the term "culturability", the

© Springer International Publishing AG 2017
A. Marcus and W. Wang (Eds.): DUXU 2017, Part III, LNCS 10290, pp. 501–513, 2017.
DOI: 10.1007/978-3-319-58640-3_36

researchers propose that the usability of a website is strongly affected by cultural variables, especially in the travel context. Indeed, on the one side, prospects seek novelty and inspiration on the web to escape from their usual environment. On the other side, the Information Retrieval (IR) process for the planning phase can become frustrating if website design is perceived as unfamiliar or unusual by online visitors (Barber and Badre 1998). Appearing as an inner contradiction, the issue of finding a balance between novelty and familiarity is probably one of the most challenging aspects for online tourism promotion (Mele and Cantoni 2017). This applies especially for NTOs, whose promotional activities are mostly aimed at attracting international markets (Pike 2008). Addressing these issues, Cantoni and Tardini (2006) underline the importance of adapting elements like units of measure, symbols, and calendars to the culture of the reference audience to enhance communication between hosts and visitors. The authors add that historical, religious, and culinary notions also require adaptation according to the cultural background of the reference audience (Cantoni and Tardini 2006). On the same topic, after showing the presence of cultural-bound preferences on destination websites, research by Tigre Moura et al. (2014) highlights the negative effects of making a tourism website appear completely familiar to specific international users. Such adaptation process is known as "localization" and it comprises a set of activities to tailor a website according to the culture of the reference audience (Mele et al. 2016). Also suggesting coexistence of cultural familiarity and novelty in destination websites, a study by Toyama and Yamada (2012) shows the possibility of decreasing risks of disappointments by adapting communication in key areas of the website (Toyama and Yamada 2012). Not at all distant from the concept of localization, cultural calibration aims at facilitating information retrieval on destination websites, while keeping culture-bound preferences on a quantitative and comparable (yet different) relation. Given the peculiarities of the tourism domain, the following paper aims at (i) providing a design concept for a software for cultural calibration of destination websites; (ii) clarifying its relation and differences with existing concepts and tools; (iii) and illustrating its relevance for researchers as well as practitioners. To achieve such goals, the concepts of culture, localization, (semi-)automatic adaptation, and contextualization are described first. These are followed by the construct of cultural calibration and its design challenges. Afterwards, the outline on possible designs and implementations is presented, along with a discussion on how cultural calibration enhances technologies for eTourism. Discussion, concluding remarks, and limitations are presented at the end.

2 Literature Review

The construct of culture presents an extensive amount of definitions, which highlight the complexity of all its dimensions (Wallerstein 1990). For the purpose of this study, culture will be described as a set of values, behaviors, and customs that are transmitted and learned across generations within a specific societal context (Hofstede et al. 2010). Among the most known researchers and anthropologists examining it, Geert Hofstede's studies are probably the most used and (also) criticized ones (Jones 2007). According to the author, this complex concept can be defined as the mental programming of human beings, which conditions their reactions when facing specific situations and guides their preferences in life. Providing more details, the anthropologist compares culture to an onion and its layer structure (Hofstede et al. 2010, p. 8). For the scope of this paper, an example related to website design will be associated with each element. The first and outer level is composed by symbols, which carry a specific meaning for a group of people and may change over time. For example, the icon of a flag may not be a synonym of "switch language" for all international users accessing a website. The second layer contains the present and past heroes belonging to a specific society. In the context of destination websites, for instance, the granularity of their description (including the amount of words) may increase for those publics that have a relatively distant culture from the object of communication. The third layer contains all rituals performed within a specific society (Hofstede et al. 2010). Within the tourism context, educating prospects about the value of local heritage for the local population is regarded by researchers as an important step toward promotion of responsible and sustainable behaviors at the destination (Ndivo and Cantoni 2016). The fourth and inner layer describes the values that (consciously or unconsciously) influence behaviors and choices of individuals from a certain society. In addition to that, Hofstede adds that such inner layer is the less subject to changes over time (compared to the others), which only happen gradually across cultures allowing researchers to instantiate comparisons among them (Hofstede et al. 2010). According to a study developed by Alexander et al. (2016), such cultural values influence experts' decisions regarding design attributes. After analyzing a sample of 460 "government" and "news and media" websites in English, Chinese, and Arabic, findings show significant differences on elements like layout, visual representations, and textual contents. Concluding their study, the authors highlight the importance for both Human Computer Interaction (HCI) researchers and practitioners to adapt websites to culture-bound preferences of the reference audience. At this regard, the researchers add that a culturally suitable user interface design has the power to enhance user experience on the website, relating directly to their values and attributes (Alexander et al. 2016). Addressing this aspect, Barber and Badre (1998) coin the term "culturability". According to the authors, the usability of any piece of software not only does depend on elements like user's goal and context, but also on culture-bound components. The latter are defined as "cultural markers" and they represent a set of predominant elements that characterize design and multimedia content of any website from a specific cultural group. Consequently, their absence can negatively affect user ability to retrieve information while browsing it (Barber and Badre 1998). The importance of considering cultures for website design is also highlighted by Marcus (2001), who invites professionals to abandon culturally biased paradigms, regarding concepts like usability and aesthetics. Also other research supports the idea that online communication is constellated by cultural preferences, although the Internet does not know geographical distances or borders. Especially in the ecommerce sector, where suppliers are often in contact with international customers, researchers highlight the importance of investigating the impact of culture values on e-commerce platforms acceptance, for constructs including trust and ease of use (Kim et al. 2016). Addressing these issues, a study by Bartikowski and Singh (2014) does an empirical analysis of ecommerce websites contents designed for the French market. Among the findings, cultural markers appear to be one of the most important trust drivers. These take the form of celebrities, monuments, pictures, and symbols that match with the culture of the reference audience (Bartikowski and Singh 2014). In addition to this area, the importance of culture and cultural dimensions have also been reported by researchers in other domains, including eGovernment (Zhao et al. 2014), eLearning (Tarhini et al. 2016), and tourism (Tigre Moura et al. 2014). To support the measurement of cultural expressions on the web, studies in the tourism area, like those developed by Mele et al. (2016) and Tigre Moura et al. (2014), are based on the model elaborated by Singh et al. (2003) for business websites. Being defined as the best coding scheme to examine in a quantitative way the presence of culture-bound elements on the web (Vyncke and Brengman 2010), the authors provide a framework based on Hofstede's (2010) and Hall's (1976) theories. In addition to this model, it is important to mention that there are others available to researchers and practitioners in the field of HCI and cross-cultural communication. For instance, a study by Rao (2011) employs the GLOBE (Global Leadership & Organization Behavior Effectiveness) model to examine the role of cultural dimensions for eLearning activities in India. The analysis and measurement of cultural values serves, first, to understand their transposition into multimedia contents and design (for example, Tigre Moura et al. 2014). Second, researchers suggest practitioners to adapt their online communication strategies according to culture-bound preferences and needs of the reference audience (for example, Calabrese et al. 2014). At this regard, localization describes the adaptation of design and multimedia contents, including also units of measure, calendars, and currencies to the culture-bound preferences of the addressed audience (Cantoni and Tardini 2006). Research in the area of business and ecommerce underlines that the process of localization can be applied to lower perceived risks related to purchasing products on websites or using online services (Bartikowski and Singh 2014). Such dynamic increases its relevance especially in the tourism domain, where prospects engage in extensive information search before taking their final decision on intangible dominant products or services (Sirakaya and Woodside 2005). Consequently, it comes as no surprise that companies in this sector can benefit from such activities. Indeed, by making parts of online communication culturally familiar to the receiver, there is the possibility to increase understanding lower the risk of disappointment (Toyama and Yamada 2012). Nevertheless, researchers warn against the limits of localization, by suggesting that given the novelty-seeking purpose of leisure tourism and the hedonic purposes of prospects, this process may be actually counteractive (Tigre Moura et al. 2014). Adding a new perspective to this interesting finding, research by Mele and Cantoni (2017) suggests that localization activities should improve mutual understanding in the tourism area, without hindering its attractiveness and novelty. The authors explain that, on the one side, content editors and web designers should provide online visitors with activities, attractions, and experiences that reflect the uniqueness of the destination. On the other side, they should integrate localization processes to ease information retrieval and promote responsible behaviors at the destination. The latter applies especially in the context of cultural tourism, where visitors have the possibility to learn online about the value attributed to (tangible or intangible) heritage by the local population (Mele and Cantoni 2017). Following this line of thought, familiarity and novelty must be addressed as co-existing and synergic concepts, instead of contrasting ones (Toyama and Yamada 2012). For the scope of this research, it is important to underline that localization is not the only available option to build appropriate online communication strategies in the tourism domain. For example, content adaptation or (semi-)automatic personalization on-the-fly is an area of great interest for computer science researchers (Ferretti et al. 2016). This includes the analysis of three main components of web adaptation process: content, navigation, and presentation (De Virgilio et al. 2006). Addressing this topic, a study developed by Kardaras et al. (2013) examines the importance of customized content presentation and media adaptation in the tourism area by employing fuzzy logic techniques. The latter allows to automatically translate user perceptions of service quality into characteristics of an adaptive website. After testing a static and (in a second moment) a customized hotel website on study participants, results reveal that most valuable contents and features should prevail over the less important ones, which can be suppressed or even omitted by website managers (Kardaras et al. 2013). In addition to localization and (semi-)automatic personalization, contextualization comprises a set of online communication design techniques that take as a starting principle user context rather than recorded preferences on specific content (Majid et al. 2013). A study developed by Majid et al. (2013) explores this area by elaborating a context-aware personalized travel recommendation system. While details of the study will not be presented here, for the scope of this overview it is important to mention that one of the main advantages of this strategy consists of increased precision of prediction. Briefly explained, authors show that by considering the context of user queries and the most popular context for visiting specific locations, the system can increase the fraction of correct predictions in the total number of personalized recommendations made (Majid et al. 2013). All of the above mentioned strategies aim at increasing the relevance and meaningfulness of displayed website features, in an effort to make them satisfactory for an increasingly contended audience. To increase their efficiency, within the area of computer science, a study developed by Mushtaha and De Troyer (2016) presents the design and functioning of a software for supporting website content localization, following the framework presented in a previous research by the same authors (Mushtaha and De Troyer 2014). Leveraging on the concept of cultural markers, such tool provides researchers and practitioners with guidelines to localize websites at different depths, according to the needs of the commissioners. While the technical details of the LWDA (Localized Website Design Advisor) will not be explained in this section, it is certainly important to mention the reason of its development. Indeed, the authors underline that due to the scattered presence of sources regarding this process, website designers tend to proceed following common sense or benchmark. However, different contexts of use of the same strategy may cause diverging results. Consequently, the WLDA is meant to provide consistent point-to-point guidelines according to a specific case (Mushtaha and De Troyer 2016). Given the peculiarity of the tourism domain, which requires content analysis approaches that differ from those generally used for business websites (Tigre Moura et al. 2014; Cappelli 2008), there is the need to develop a comprehensive tool for guiding the evaluation and elaboration of culturally suitable destination websites.

3   Cultural Calibration: Concept as a Design Challenge

A key challenge of interaction design, when understood from a broad perspective of designing technologies that enhance interaction between people, is to find a mechanism for cultural calibration. This concept refers to any technology that adjusts the contents and tools that people use to communicate with each other, in an effort to answer their culture-dependent preferences. From a theoretical viewpoint, it has connections with semi-automatic content adaptation, contextualization, and localization activities (see Table 1). However, it also does present distinguishing characteristics. Proceeding from left to right, similarly to semi-automatic adaptation, the design concept of cultural calibration highlights the possibility of providing suggestions on multimedia content entries and layout characteristics, assisting online managers for the elaboration of country-specific website editions. As for localization activities, one of the most important variables taken into account in the design concept is culture-bound preferences of the reference audience. However, differently from this concept, cultural calibration considers all cultural markers on the same continuum, registering them as quantifiable and comparable (yet different) elements. Hence, the focus is on creating calibrated equivalences among cultures, rather than highlighting specificities. To delimit the scope of the concept, it is key to clarify the aspect of culture taken into consideration.

Table 1. Cultural calibration and related concepts

For the purpose of this study, in addition to Hofstede's et al. (2010) definition mentioned in the previous section, culture will be treated as a form of communication, as for Hall and Hall's (1990) theories, composed by specific preferences and markers. Other anthropological and sociological aspects of the construct go beyond the scope of this research. Following this logic, the concept of cultural calibration aims at expanding the knowledge horizons of prospective tourists, by adjusting information on culture-sensitive topics to make them more understandable. In this sense, it tackles the problem of several personalization systems based on static user profiles, which prevent visitors from exploring a wider information spectrum (Shukla et al. 2013). In relation with the concept of contextualization, another design challenge is to include the possibility of presenting contents on destination websites according to the actual location of online visitors. Indeed, a focus on visitor context, rather than visitor preferences, may enhance the usefulness of the website throughout the tourist journey, from the planning phase to the conclusion of the experience itself. Providing an overview on the most important design challenges, a software for cultural calibration can be composed by the following elements. The first and inner layer presents a database gathering country-specific preferences in local destination websites for (i) design, (ii) visuals, and (iii) textual contents – including word-clouds. The interpretations regarding differences among countries will be done by applying major cross-cultural models (Minkov 2011, p. 45). Differently from this one, the second layer can offer specific suggestions regarding the elaboration of a country-specific website, from the choice of layout to the granularity of textual content. For the elaboration of the design concept and its implementation, explained in the next section, the present paper follows the overall structure of the Information Systems (IS) research framework developed by Hevner et al. (2004) (see Table 2). Briefly explained, Hevner et al. (2004) state that researchers have to explore the relevant environment to discover the phenomenon of interest. People, organizations, and technologies represent the main stakeholders for the definition of business needs. After detecting one, design science aims at building theories and artifacts, using the raw materials provided by the knowledge base to satisfy the identified need (Hevner et al. 2004). Connecting it to the present paper, on the one side, the relation between the design concept and the environment provides relevance to the IS research and the possibility to test it against the real environment. On the other side, the knowledge base provides rigorousness to the proposed design concept for cultural calibration.

Table 2. information system research framework (Hevner et al. 2004)

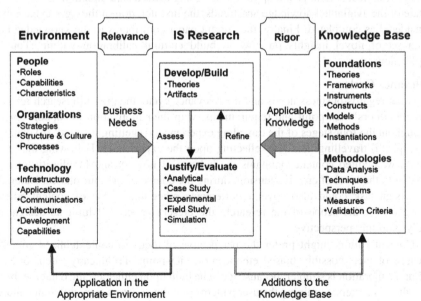

Throughout (and not only after) the co-design process with a group of stakeholders, the design concept will be iteratively concretized, piloted with a set of subsequent versions, and formatively evaluated. The latter can be done, for instance, via 30-minute open-ended interviews with researchers in the eTourism domain, who have had collaborations with the industry. In this way, interviewees not only will be able to provide precious insights regarding the knowledge base, but add their viewpoints on the evolving environment. Further improvements to the design concept are presented in the section dedicated to discussion and concluding remarks.

4 Design and Implementation

This section shows how content editors' expectations, as described in Sect. 2, can be transformed into a functional application that implements the ideas of cultural calibration. To reach this goal, the present research employs the Design Science (DS) approach, presented in the previous section, as a guide for the design process. DS is particularly useful for tackling complex and even wicked problems of which the integration of cultural calibration in eTourism is a good example, as shown in the plethora of different and even contradictory perspectives of the literature review.

Rigor Cycle

DS forms a foundation for a constructive research-based activity that consists of three interdependent cycles: relevance cycle, design cycle, and rigor cycle (Hevner et al. 2004). In the literature review, there is an overview of the contemporary state of research regarding the aforementioned design problem from the viewpoints of the role of culture in eTourism applications. In addition to that, there is also the presentation of a set of technical solutions and opportunities going toward said direction. Hence, being aware of the available knowledge and trends, the first iteration of the rigor cycle can be considered as completed. Finally, the current paper contributes to the knowledge base by a set of novel insights on how to build cultural calibration within eTourism applications.

Relevance Cycle

For what regards business needs and the relevance cycle, the present research refers to content editors' viewpoint and requirements, with their motivation to support tourists throughout the four stages of the travelling experience: (i) getting inspired, (ii) planning the trip, (iii) travelling, and (iv) reflecting upon the experiences. Following the literature, a well-edited content maintains the balance of novelty and familiarity, or even raises it to the level of creative tension, during the course of the four phases. Naturally, the design task could also cover requirements other than those of content editors. However, for the scope of the research, the present paper will limit its design and analysis to this perspective.

Content editors might prefer the perspective of focus to contextualized contents, because of their possibly biased ethnocentric viewpoint. Technically, focus-oriented cultural calibration is simpler, because it can be built upon either a static database, based on cultural markers, or mining the user patterns of online visitors from different cultures. Focus-oriented cultural calibration resembles social navigation in ecommerce or eLearning applications, whose aim is to optimize users' track to goals, determined by services providers, in our case content editors. However, contextualizing the contents is a customer-oriented approach and requires a more open attitude from content editors. While they can employ metadata to attract visitors from a given culture to specific contents, in principle all the edited content is freely accessible and semi-automatically adapted or adaptable to any visitor, independently of their background. In this case, technically more demanding than that of focus-oriented cultural calibration, visitors can explore contents that are retrieved semi-automatically from, for instance, visitors' travel diary. Compared to focus-oriented cultural calibration, contextualized content uses calibration that honors the individual preferences of the visitor. To summarize, while focus-oriented cultural calibration is technically close to the static localization approach, contextual content calls for semi-automatic adaptation where content is not given but retrieved on-demand. Contextualization, as a dynamic approach, serves a visitor on-the-move, for both focus orientation and contextual content.

The rigor loop highlighted the nested layers of culture as values, rituals, heroes, and symbols (Hofstede et al. 2010). From the representation of data perspective, the level of abstraction increases by each layer from the innermost (values) to the outmost one. While values may be explicitly stated by a commonly agreed document of a given culture, each member of a culture might have their own concrete navigation map based on their value system. Values generate sets of rituals and behaviors, together with a range of variations. Heroes and their behaviors represent the grand narratives of a culture, as represented, for example, in sacred texts. Finally, easy-to-identify-and-represent symbols seal heroes' grand narratives. Thus, when a version of a cultural calibration technology is taken to a real-life test in a given environment, to finish an iteration of the relevance loop, it should be tested against all layers, as follows:

- The extent to which cultural calibration facilitates a constructive *value* dialogue that promotes mutual understanding between tourists and the culture they are experiencing;
- The extent to which cultural calibration allows the tourist to identify, accept, and interpret *rituals* and, more broadly, culture-dependent *behaviors*;
- The extent to which cultural calibration translates between the grand *narratives* of tourists' own and visited culture; and helps identify traces of those within what they observe;
- The extent to which cultural calibration recognizes and maps *symbols* of the visited environment onto the tourists' own system of symbols.

While testing cultural calibration technology against the layers, it must be reminded that a functional solution promotes creative tension rather than boring balance between tourists and hosting culture.

Design Cycle

The implementation of cultural calibration is performed in the design loop, by applying agile methods for fast prototyping. Table 3 shows the technologies that can be used to build cultural calibration for different layers of culture. For a value dialogue, focus oriented cultural calibration warns of differing values between tourists' culture and visited one. Contextualized contents needs to calibrate visitors' own values onto the

Table 3. Technologies for building cultural calibration for different cultural layers

	Focus orientation	Contextual contents
Values	Early warning systems	Ethically contextualized stories
Behaviors	Guidance to culturally acceptable activities	Match making
Narratives	Adaptive summarizing grand narratives	Embedding visitors in non-familiar grand narratives
Symbols	Symbol screening	Symbol mining

ethical spectrum of the visited culture by making use of stories characterized by ethically sensitive contents. Such activity requires advanced human language technologies. For what regards interpreting behaviors, focus orientation guides tourists to experience activities allowed by their culture. For contextualized contents, various match making technologies can help tourists explore and find attractive activities. As of (grand) narratives, cultural calibration can either – leading tourists to determined goals – summarize narratives or – for more explorative tourists – embed them with a foreign narrative. Addressing the symbolic layer, superficial cultural calibration helps screen symbols in an alien milieu, whereas contextual calibration maps between new and known symbols.

Besides standard database solutions, various adaptation and data mining techniques can be used for the implementation of focus-oriented cultural calibration. Whereas, contextualized contents require text mining and digital story telling tools for cultural calibration. Finally, each iteration in the design loop requires a light (but systematic) and well planned evaluation. Such activity can be performed by organizing a focus group that represents content editors and addressed tourists from diverse cultural settings.

5   Discussion and Concluding Remarks

Far from being a mere tool for content editing, a cultural calibration software for the tourism domain presents implications for both researchers and practitioners. From a theoretical viewpoint, calling for a variety of approaches, the design concept presented in this paper goes well beyond the traditional solutions of semi-automatic adaptation, localization, and contextualization that are commonly used to tailor online communication in the tourism realm. In this sense, the concept of cultural calibration aims at sustaining a tension between novelty and familiarity in the DMO's website throughout the tourism experience. Rather than being interpreted in a negative sense, such state is meant to promote creativity while experiencing the destination/s. More specifically, instead of confirming stereotypes and pre-conceived ideas regarding the hosting culture, a software for cultural calibration aims at enriching the quality of the experience by tailoring website multimedia and textual contents to pursue the following objectives: (i) promoting value dialogues in terms of mutual understanding; (ii) enhancing identification and interpretation of rituals of the hosting culture; (iii) increasing the understanding of local narratives; (iv) and providing support for the recognition and interpretation of symbols at the destination/s. Taking the third (iii) point as an example, a country-specific edition of a NTO's website may provide information regarding a local celebrity or hero by leveraging on certain common historic threads that already exist between the reference audience and the hosting country. In this way, also aiming at stimulating the curiosity of online visitors before visiting the destination. From a managerial viewpoint, a software for cultural calibration can work as a plug-in to be installed into an existing computer program for content editing, thus providing clear guidelines to website managers regarding culturally calibrated multimedia and textual contents to improve the communication toward a specific audience throughout the tourism experience.

The authors of this research have devised a concept of cultural calibration to be utilized within eTourism application development and a scheme to design implementations of cultural calibration. The study shows that the design concept of a platform that allows content editors of tourism website to create culturally calibrated contents requires a tight co-design effort from a diverse team of experts and stakeholders. Cultural calibration can be understood also from the viewpoint of a *tourist as a content provider*, located in the intersection of their own culture (possibly physically remote) and the culturally novel environment they are visiting at the time of the authoring. Such aspect is becoming increasingly relevant at the time of tourist bloggers. Moreover, sharing economy aspects are winning ground also in tourism. Traditional expert culture is transforming towards a culture of collaboration, where it is extremely challenging to differentiate between an expert, or a content editor, and a layman, or an information consumer. In this case, sharing economy would require cultural calibration between those that co-author or co-experience a given tourism site.

References

Alexander, R., Thompson, N., Murray, D.: Towards cultural translation of websites: a large-scale study of Australian, Chinese, and Saudi Arabian preferences. Behav. Inf. Technol. 1–13 (2016). doi:10.1080/0144929X.2016.1234646

Barber, W., Badre, A.: Culturability: the merging of culture and usability. In: Conference on Human Factors and the Web. AT&T Labs, New Jersey (1998). http://zing.ncsl.nist.gov/hfweb/att4/proceedings/barber/. Accessed 19 Sept 2016

Bartikowski, B., Singh, N.: Doing e-business in France: drivers of online trust in business-to-consumer websites. Glob. Bus. Organ. Excell. 33(4), 28–36 (2014)

Calabrese, A., Capece, G., Di Pillo, F., Martino, F.: Cultural adaptation of web design services as critical success factor for business excellence: a cross-cultural study of Portuguese, Brazilian, and Macanese web sites. Cross Cult. Manag. 21(2), 172–190 (2014)

Cantoni, L., Tardini, S.: Internet. Routledge, New York (2006)

Cappelli, G.: The translation of tourism-related websites and localization: problems and perspectives. In: Voices on Translation, RILA Rassegna Italiana di Linguistica Applicata, pp. 97–115 (2008)

De Virgilio, R., Torlone, R., Houben, G.J.: A rule-based approach to content delivery adaptation in web information systems. In: 7th International Conference on Mobile Data Management (MDM 2006), p. 21. IEEE (2006)

Ferretti, S., Mirri, S., Prandi, C., Salomoni, P.: Automatic web content personalization through reinforcement learning. J. Syst. Softw. **121**, 157–169 (2016)

Hall, E.T.: Beyond Culture. Anchor Books, New York (1976)

Hall, E.T., Hall, R.M.: Understanding cultural differences. Intercultural Press, Yarmouth (1990)

Hevner, R.A., March, T.S., Park, J., Ram, S.: Design science in information systems research. MIS Q. **28**(1), 75–105 (2004)

Hofstede, G., Hofstede, G.J., Minkov, M.: Cultures and Organizations: Software of the Mind, 3rd edn. McGraw-Hill, New York (2010)

Jones, M.L.: Hofstede - Culturally questionable? In: Oxford Business & Economics Conference (OBEC), pp. 1–9. Oxford (2007)

Kardaras, D.K., Karakostas, B., Mamakou, X.J.: Content presentation personalisation and media adaptation in tourism web sites using Fuzzy Delphi Method and Fuzzy Cognitive Maps. Expert Syst. Appl. **40**(6), 2331–2342 (2013)

Kim, E., Urunov, R., Kim, H.: The effects of national culture values on consumer acceptance of e-commerce: online shoppers in Russia. In: 4th International Conference on Information Technology and Quantitative Management, pp. 966–970. Elsevier, Asan (2016)

Majid, A., Chen, L., Chen, G., Mirza, T.H., Hussain, I., Woodward, J.: A context-aware personalized travel recommendation system based on geotagged social media data mining. Int. J. Geogr. Inf. Sci. **27**(4), 662–684 (2013)

Marcus, A.: Cross-cultural user-interface design. In: Human-Computer Interface International Conference, pp. 502–505. Lawrence Erlbaum Associates, New Orleans (2001)

Mele, E., Cantoni, L.: Localization of national tourism organizations websites: the case of ETC members. In: Schegg, R., Stangl, B. (eds.) Information and Communication Technologies in Tourism 2017, pp. 59–71. Springer, Cham (2017). doi:10.1007/978-3-319-51168-9_5

Mele, E., De Ascaniis, S., Cantoni, L.: Localization of three European national tourism offices' websites. an exploratory analysis. In: Inversini, A., Schegg, R. (eds.) Information and Communication Technologies in Tourism 2016, pp. 259–307. Springer, Cham (2016). doi:10. 1007/978-3-319-28231-2_22

Minkov, M.: Cultural Differences in a Globalized World. Emerald Group Publishing Limited, Bingley (2011)

Mushtaha, A., Troyer, O.: the cultural conceptual model for simplifying the design of localized websites. In: Marcus, A. (ed.) DUXU 2014. LNCS, vol. 8518, pp. 158–169. Springer, Cham (2014). doi:10.1007/978-3-319-07626-3_15

Mushtaha, A., Troyer, O.: Localized website design advisor: a web-based tool providing guidelines for cross-cultural websites. In: Marcus, A. (ed.) DUXU 2016. LNCS, vol. 9747, pp. 396–406. Springer, Cham (2016). doi:10.1007/978-3-319-40355-7_38

Ndivo, M.R., Cantoni, L.: The efficacy of heritage interpretation at the Lalibela Rock-Hewn Churches in Ethiopia: exploring the need for integrating ICT-mediation. Int. J. Relig. Tour. Pilgrim. **4**(3), 17–28 (2016)

Pike, S.: Destination Marketing. An Integrated Marketing Communication Approach. Elsevier, Oxford (2008)

Rao, P.: E-learning in India: the role of national culture and strategic implications. Multicultur. Educ. Technol. J. **5**(2), 129–150 (2011)

Schmiedel, T., Muller, O., Debortoli, S., vom Brocke, J.: Identifying and quantifying cultural factors that matter to the IT workforce: an approach based on automated content analysis. In: Twenty-Fourth European Conference on Information Systems (ECIS). AIS Electronic Library, Istanbul (2016). http://aisel.aisnet.org/cgi/viewcontent.cgi?article=1182&context=ecis2016_rp

Shukla, R., Silakari, S., Chande, K.P.: Web personalization systems and web usage mining: a review. Int. J. Comput. Appl. **72**(21), 6–13 (2013)

Singh, N., Zhao, H., Hu, X.: Cultural adaptation on the web: a study of American companies' domestic and Chinese websites. J. Glob. Inf. Manag. (JGIM) **11**(3), 203–220 (2003)

Sirakaya, E., Woodside, A.: Building and testing theories of decision making by travellers. Tour. Manag. **26**, 815–832 (2005)

Tarhini, A., Hone, K., Liu, X., Tarhini, T.: Examining the moderating effect of individual-level cultural values on users' acceptance of E-learning in developing countries: a structural equation modeling of an extended technology acceptance model. Interact. Learn. Environ. 1–23 (2016). doi:10.1080/10494820.2015.1122635

Tigre Moura, F., Gnoth, J., Deans, K.R.: Localizing cultural values on tourism destination websites: the effects on users' willingness to travel and destination image. J. Travel Res. 1–15 (2014)

Toyama, M., Yamada, Y.: The relationships among tourist novelty, familiarity, satisfaction, and destination loyalty: beyond the novelty-familiarity continuum. Int. J. Mark. Stud. **4**(6), 10–18 (2012)

UNWTO: UNWTO World Tourism Barometer and Statistical Annex, March 2016. From UNWTO eLibrary: http://www.e-unwto.org/doi/pdf/10.18111/wtobarometereng.2016. 14.2.1. Accessed 2 May 2016

Vyncke, F., Brengman, M.: Are culturally congruent websites more effective? An overview of a decade of empirical evidence. J. Electron. Commer. Res. **11**(1), 14–29 (2010)

Wallerstein, I.: Culture as the ideological battleground of the modern world-system. Theory, Cult. Soc. 31–55 (1990)

Zhao, F., Shen, N.K., Collier, A.: Effects of national culture on e-government diffusion - a global study of 55 countries. Inf. Manag. **51**, 1005–1016 (2014)

"deBallution" - A Prototype of Interactive Artwork Based on Cultural Heritage

Je-ho Oh[1], So-young Kim[2], Yun Tae Nam[3], and Chung-kon Shi[1(✉)]

[1] GSCT, KAIST, Daejeon, Republic of Korea
{aomewho, chungkon}@kaist.ac.kr
[2] CDE, UNIST, Ulsan, Republic of Korea
ahyne@naver.com
[3] sensiLab, Monash University, Clayton, Australia
yun.nam@monash.edu

Abstract. Based on cultural heritage plays about throwing action, we made a public interactive artwork by throwing pseudo-balls, "deBallution." Audience members participated in interactive artwork not only for pleasure but also as part of their cultural heritage, maintaining and also disrupting social orders and structures. First of all, this research extracted the audience's basic activities from cultural archetypes. Then, it applied audience activities to a basic model of public interactive artwork for playing on a media façade to participating in collective performance for disruptive social structures. The interactive artwork concept is to catch audience members' throwing movements on a virtual screen and drawing various generated kaleidoscope images to predict points from the audience throwing on the screen. We made prototype "deBallution" and then exhibited it and evaluated user tests. Through evaluation results for the prototype, we revised "deBallution" artwork contents for developing artistic values and produced overall interactive artwork.

Keywords: Interactive artwork · Cultural heritage · deBallution

1 Introduction

1.1 Background and Motivation

The audience member has often been just a spectator in public art, not a participant or creator [1–3]. Digital technologies allow audience members to help build a city's scenery by their own action [4, 5]. It is possible to change the city's landscape using audience members' activities, mediated by digital technologies through interaction. This public experience put audience members in cooperation and competition to change a city's landscape. Digital art is avant-garde, because it makes use of digital media, which prompt interactive, participatory art, which—for its part—prompts participatory democratic society [6].

Values of public artwork make public participation an "unforgettable experience," not just a private experience of artwork. These experiences could lead to direct audience action mediated by digital technologies. In the viewpoint of the audience

© Springer International Publishing AG 2017
A. Marcus and W. Wang (Eds.): DUXU 2017, Part III, LNCS 10290, pp. 514–528, 2017.
DOI: 10.1007/978-3-319-58640-3_37

participation, Claire Bishop proposed "participatory aesthetics." These aesthetics were different from Bourriaud's "Relationship Aesthetics" [7, 8]. According to Bishop, "The artist's practice, and his behavior as producer, determines the relationship that will be struck up with his work. In other words, what he produces, first and foremost, is relations between people and the world, by way of aesthetic objects." The work of art has a social and historical context, but its role is not to engage directly with society; art is disengaged, and it has its own space. Bishop asserted that the Relationship Aesthetics concept is the ideal form of audience collaboration and cooperation. Through the public interactive artwork for media façade by audience interaction, audience members actively participate in and change contents producing a landscape of the city.

The main motivation of this paper is to produce a digital interactive artwork, building on a cultural archetype. Cultural heritage directly supports public interactive artworks in audience action and in the embodiment of contents. This audience action not only involves body movements from passive observers and performers for choosing the scene; it also involves generating energy for changing social views of politics. This aesthetic values public artwork based on cultural heritage. Through the archetypes, it was possible to extract original emotion and activity from the human universal model and derive artwork's contents—narrative, visualization, sonification, and embodiment of artwork's objective [9, 10]. Audience members participated in the public artwork and saw their shadows changing due to other audience's action on video. Cultural heritage have seen use in digital games, especially narrative ones, to extract a main character's action for their features and graphic images. Cultural heritage can also support artwork to enhance the aesthetics' values through the audience's universal activity patterns. This is because audience members have situations with mythical or traditional experiences and return to the origin model of humanity through the culture heritage.

1.2 Related Work

Public digital artwork has been produced in various ways. These public digital artworks gave new artistic values for collaborated or competed experience to participating audience. Lozano-Hemmer Rafael has made a public interactive artwork installation based on digital technologies, "The city as interface." Lozano-Hemmer showed that an alternative interface design is possible which stimulates brief encounters as part of everyday urban life [11]. Emily et al. proposed "The VideoMob," an interactive video platform and artwork that enables strangers visiting different installation locations to interact across time and space through a computer interface that detects their presence, video-records their actions while automatically removing the video background through computer vision, and co-situates visitors as part of the same digital environment [12]. Beyer et al. proposed "The Puppeteer Display," a wide interactive banner display installed at a city sidewalk, and two long-term field studies investigated the opportunities of public displays to actively shape the audience [13]. However these artworks or research works have not used audience archetypes to make new artwork contents. Audience members just had an experience of real life, with much the same patterns. Audience members did not know various meanings of their own actions and so duplicated their usual actions. This was because this artwork and research did not consider human psychology and cognition—in view of objective and result from their own actions. These audience actions effected on temporarily and not expanded public experience for making new society—new rules, communities, and role of humans. Applied archetypes will create new, expanded experiences, making various layers generate audience action—beyond space and time, age and gender.

2 Artwork Overall Design

2.1 Artwork Concept

The basic artwork concept is to make new artwork form audience members' whole-body action. The audience action will influence social values, mediated by public media.

The meanings of the title "deBallution" are as follows.

First, it means a digital revolution by throwing balls, a symbolic revolution mediated by digital artwork, a change from tradition to digital technologies. Second, it means devolution by throwing balls. Devolution is the transfer of some authority or power from a central organization or government to smaller organizations or government departments. The audience here performs symbolic devolution. Audience members threw the pseudo-balls for media façade and caused symbolic digital revolution, devolution [14].

This paper chose the throwing action to make audience resistance and destruction activities for competition and antagonism, generating a new world—not passive media or society. Why did we focus on the throwing action in the artwork? The throwing action is related to disruptive aesthetics. Concerning disruptive aesthetics, our motive was "overthrowing a society." In summation, the term "overthrowing" means "beyond throwing," which regards the accomplishment of objective through the throwing activities [15]. Overhand throwing is a basic throwing action used in war, hunting, and sports. It is a direct, fast, and accurate throw by moving the hand over the shoulder. This throw is a symbol for a strong motivation to hit a target and change a target condition.

This artwork referred three throwing games that are part of different cultural heritages.

(1) Greek "Hyakintos" Myth

Throwing discus myth content is about the origin of the flower "Hyakintos" from a relationship between a god and ordinary people in terms of friendship, love, and jealousy. However, this myth told a story about the origin of throwing action sports, which in Greece involved the discus. Unlike other sports games, throwing discus is not war game. It is a pure competition game for records [16] (Fig. 1).

Fig. 1. Greek Hyakintos Myth [16]

① Main objective – Throwing a discus for a long distance single-handedly.
② Activities – Throwing discus with three-quarters movement, according to the rules.
③ Values – A thrown discus will come back just like a boomerang, as will friendship and create entertainment in a group.

(2) Stone War from Korean Traditional Play

A war of throwing stones is a traditional Korean game [17]. Two communities separated and began throwing stones each other. This game came from real war but had been developed as a traditional folk game in the festival. The game enhanced a group relationship through competition in each community (Fig. 2).

① Main objective – Competing and winning by throwing stones for communities.
② Activities – Throwing real stones and avoiding or defending against stones from opponents
③ Values – Establishing cooperation within the community and competition with opponent communities. The ultimate value was to strengthen both for future real battles.

(3) Battle of the Oranges from Ivrea in Italy

The Battle of the Oranges is a festival at Ivrea in Italy. It involves some thousands of towns people, divided into nine combat on-the-ground teams, who throw oranges at tens of card-based teams—with considerable violence—during the last three carnival

518   J. Oh et al.

Fig. 2. War of throwing stones in Korea [17]

days [18]. People wearing a red hat will not be considered part of the revolutionaries, and therefore will not have oranges thrown at them. These traditional games were based on participators throwing. The participators enjoyed the game like they were playing at war and felt the pleasure of rebellion and victory (Fig. 3).

Fig. 3. Battle of the oranges in Ivrea [18]

① Main objective – Throwing real oranges to opponents and win the official guards as traditional carnival.
② Activities – Throwing real oranges and avoid flying oranges
③ Values – Revolution for ordinary people in carnival game and visualization pleasure by crushed oranges.

These archetypes have features for throwing action by individual or group and are beyond making festival play, making a new world.

2.2 Scenario Design

We created "deBallution's" scenario design based on the previous artwork concept and applied by narrative forms [19].

(1) Audience members watched video contents about city's landscape on a media façade or a large display.
(2) Audience members threw pseudo-balls onto the media façade or the large display.
(3) Video contents in the media façade or the large display broke or generated pseudo-balls.
(4) Audience members disrupted the video content when they filled the media façade or the large display with broken or generative images.
(5) The new content that played in the media façade or the large display symbolized a new world.

2.3 Graphic Design

The main concept of graphic design is to visualize audience throwing action to generate new images on the throwing point. The contents express visually that participants desire to overthrow reality by throwing. The first screen images are realistic and fanciless, reflecting everyday life. After participants throw, a festival starts on the screen, but the screen begins to be damaged. At any point where a participant throws, a kaleidoscope image expands just like images of crushed oranges. The throwing action has usually happened at festival in the past. The throwing action in this project means that participants gather and they set off firecrackers by making a festival. The kaleidoscope images are like firecrackers and reminiscent of festivals. The many points of the action signify the many participants. Ernest Edmund used kaleidoscope images in basic interactive research to generate various pattern images from audience action [20, 21]. These repeated throwing actions of participants creates recurring but diverse patterns of firecrackers. These lead participants into a rhythmic fireworks festival. The various images of firecrackers depend on the motion of the participants. This is intended to emphasize the diversity of individuals. After festival ends soon, strange images like errors appear on the screen. These little errors lead to big changes and damages. Finally, participants overthrow the screen image. The glitch effect is used for the damage effect, as it is similar to the principle of a glitch. Unintended simple errors by participant generate the new screen. This gives a positive meaning to errors, failure, and the participants' ultimate conquest of the screen (Fig. 4).

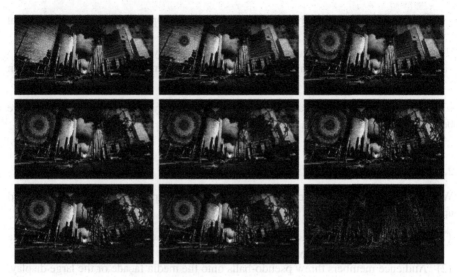

Fig. 4. Examples of graphic design [14]

2.4   Applied by Aesthetics for Artwork

Audience members could put their emotions in the artwork and change their emotions through participation in the artwork. This artwork is based on technical implementation and graphic design. However, these technical factors of the interactive installation would not lead to interactive artwork without aesthetic values. This project did not serve designs or technical devices, but two aesthetic values—pleasure framework and disruptive aesthetics.

(1) **Pleasure Framework**

The concept of pleasure framework proposes thirteen pleasures—creation, exploration, discovery, difficulty, competition, danger, captivation, sensation, sympathy, simulation, fantasy, camaraderie, and subversion by participation in an interactive artwork. These are only possible categories that a participant might feel pleasure in during an interactive art experience [22]. Audience members could experience the following emotions, typically by participating in "deBallution" through a pleasure framework.

① Creation – Audience members felt they were part of the creation when they drew a new painting by making a circle, making a new world through their own actions.

② Discovery – Audience members discovered new unfamiliar scenery of the city. Particular actions may provoke different images and transformed contents.

③ Difficulty – Audience members had difficulty making circles on the screen precisely where they wanted to draw them. This difficulty gamified the experience, focusing them on achieving a goal.

④ Competition – Audience members participated in "deBallution," in collaboration. They tried to achieve a defined goal together. Completing the goal could involve working with or against another human participant when making a new world.

⑤ Subversion – Audience members could destroy the background image on the screen and create the new world through their own action.

(2) Disruptive Aesthetics

Artworks each have their own artistic values. Disruptive aesthetics placed artistic value on social meanings [23]. Especially, they lead audience members to break down traditional social values. The audience overthrows the social order and proposes a new world (Fig. 5).

① Audience – Audience threw pseudo-balls.

② Interactive installation – The installation represented a screen video and covered circle images, influenced by audience action.

③ Artwork contents – The previous background video broke down after the audience filled it with generative circle images; a new, futuristic video ensued.

④ Breaking a rule/community/role – Audience members disrupted the city landscape in the screen by their own activities. Such disruptive aesthetics in "deBallution" broke down the rule of maintaining community and created a new world.

These aesthetics will influence the artwork, creating a new artistic value and experience independent of design values or technical implementation issues.

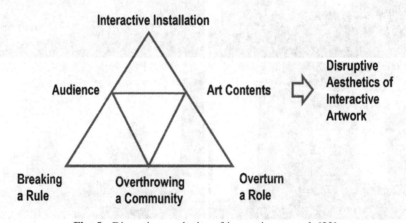

Fig. 5. Disruptive aesthetics of interactive artwork [23]

3   Prototype and Evaluation

3.1   Prototype Implementation

The prototype focused on audience throwing action and reflecting on the screen circle images.

These audience activities could be possible to two or three participants. Those images filled the screen and disrupted background images. This distorted content is a new world the audience itself created by changing city scenery.

The prototype made by openFrameworks, used C++ programming connected by Kinect. This is because, in the prototype test, video about scenery of the city played on a small screen instead of a media façade and focused on audience activities not on video contents. Audience members made throwing gestures in front of the screen, which generated circle images at the positions of the audience's throwing by calculating virtual location through Kinect, connected by openFrameworks programming. Audience members continued throwing and circle images at the position of the previous images and new images expanded on the screen progressively until the screen filled with images covering up the scenery of the city. At that time, the screen was full of various circle images. The origin video was a reversal of the screen and the audience's throwing play was completed.

Video cuts from prototype exhibition are as follows (Fig. 6).

Fig. 6. Still frames of prototype "deBallution"

3.2   Evaluation Factors

After the prototype exhibition, we evaluated the user test and group interview.

Ten participants (5 males, 5 females) performed in the prototype test. Their ages ranged from 22 to 38 years old ($\bar{x} = 28.2$); eight were right-handed, and 2 were left-handed.

Participants could throw pseudo balls as much as they wanted without a restriction on time or throwing numbers. After a survey, we interviewed the participants. In the participant interviews, we focused on two questions involving social group play experimentation and development ideation for increasing the artwork value.

3.3   Results and Discussion

(1) Main objective

The highest factor concerning the main objective of the participants was making circles in the content (Fig. 7).

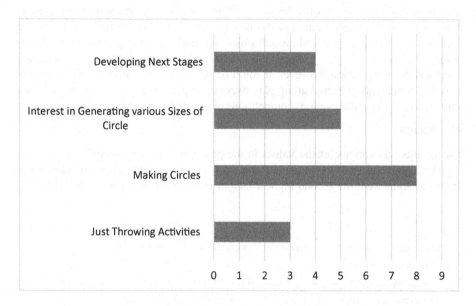

Fig. 7. Result of main objective

This means that participants wanted to know the results of their own activities, and just the throwing action would be possible to influence content. Participants were interested in the throwing action for making circles and developing next stages. The participants' objectives influenced content development because they wanted to change the media through interaction. This objective is different in regards to observation or appreciation from Bishop's viewpoint of participatory aesthetics. However, participants had different objectives and desires. In the developing artwork, we focused on participant activities of adjusting different images by throwing actions, reflecting their own desire and creating antagonism and competition between the participant groups.

(2) **Activities**

The average number of throwing actions was 37. Continued throwing activities by the audience meant that the participants were immersed in the "deBallution", because the test did not ask how many throwing activities were performed.

Participants performed voluntary throwing actions in the prototype test. This was because participants wanted to watch the "deBallution" content of their own actions and were interested in participation by making circles. Then, participants acted on the artwork with various throwing actions and poses, just like game play. For example, participants jumped for power-up throwing, shot-put throwing, and throwing with both hands. The original throw for this artwork was the overhand throw, which means "overthrowing the rule, community, and role," by participants; however, participants made various throwing actions: side-arm, underhand, three-quarters, twisted throwing, and jump throwing. Trials of a throwing action with a whole body movement especially influenced audience emotion through participation. This result means that the audience wanted to act on various self-objectives and were not controlled by installation limitations. This is because the "deBallution" installation fit the audience overhand throwing action; however, it could be perceived with other throwing actions as well. Participants preferred group play over single play. This means that participants wanted to play in collaboration, competition, or conflict for self-motivation.

(3) **Values**

Participants had various artistic values in the prototype of "deBallution."

The highest factor of the pleasure framework was the creation pleasure. Subversion and simulation were the second highest factors in this framework (Figs. 8 and 9).

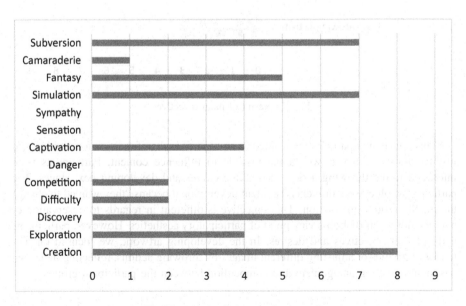

Fig. 8. Result of pleasure framework

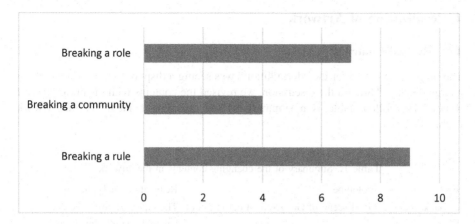

Fig. 9. Result of disruptive aesthetics

The highest factor of disruptive aesthetics was the overthrowing rules. The highest factor of content developing the artwork was the circle image changing to other images.

Narrative development, background image modifying, and competition among participants were the highest factors in the developing elements. In the interview, participants proposed various background images and videos. The participants also wanted to perform by stage level, developing like storytelling or gamification. In general, participants' interests and immersion were increased by group performance. This is because competition influenced participants' throwing objectives and enhanced their throwing action skills. In short, participants wanted to experience dramatic visualization by their own activities and changing of artwork values. These elements were our intended objective.

We found the pleasure framework and disruptive aesthetics in the artwork. The interactive artwork outcome generated intended or unintended audience participation [24]. Participants were absorbed with the "deBallution" merely by the throwing activities. Participants drew their own images of their own throwing actions. They wanted to draw circle images where they drew—just like the abstract drawings of Kandinsky or Jackson Pollock. Participants wanted to draw the same size and location image as the previous throwing points due to their reflection desire. This means that they wanted to draw an in-depth layered visualization of the circle image and background. Participants had a duplication desire for their own creatures and developed the next stages. These participant-desired actions will adjust the realization of public interactive artwork "deBallution." They will generate more active unintended actions and create a new image relation between the background image and the participants generating images. These artwork values were values of participatory artwork by Claire Bishop, influencing a new world by direct participant activities [7]. These results mean that the throwing action autonomously influenced various participant activities. Using these activities, it was possible to make developing contents and artistic values. In the prototype test, audience members threw imaginary objects and generated extended circle images. Those images filled the screen and disrupted background images. This distorted content is a new world the audience itself created by changing city scenery.

4 Realization of Artwork

4.1 Revised Contents

The original objective for the "deBallution" was seeing a display for a media façade or a large display. Through the discussion, we revised the contents with the prototype test results. The follow table is a summary of the changing contents in the artwork (Table 1).

Table 1. Summary of the changing contents in the artwork

Factors	Prototype	Realization "deBallution"
1. Background image	Fixed scene of GangNam street in Seoul	The Opera House in Sydney – Changing color and image
2. Audience throwing action	Audience throwing generated various circles in the screen in terms of location and speed	Audience throwing generated various kaleidoscope points on the screen in terms of location and speed
3. Visualization for throwing action	Just visualized circle, but size varied	Circle changed to kaleidoscope images, and the kaleidoscope images expanded
4. Climax scene	N/A	Background image changed to various color tones and blurred outlines
5. Ending scene	N/A	Background image changed to cultural heritage image

For increased audience participation, we applied these audience action patterns in the prototype to generate random kaleidoscope images.

4.2 Realization "deBallution"

The system was designed to recognize the users' throwing actions and patterns. The 6 main parameters included the elbow's x, y, and z positions and the hand's x, y, and z positions. These were observed and analyzed to make a decision as to whether or not throwing actions happened. The patterns of the audience's throwing experiences were used to describe interactivity in levels (low, medium, high). The "high" level of interactivity concerns a meaningful interaction between the system and the participants. The audiences become active authors or creators. The diversity of interactivity levels comes in different shapes, sizes, and colors of 3D generative kaleidoscopes. For instance, high-level interactions make bigger sizes, dynamic shape changes in animation, and vibrant shades of red. Based on color theory, this is associated with different meanings: energy, strength, power, and celebration. "Medium" levels of interaction are possible to make a middle range of sizes, animation, and comfort shades of green that create feelings of relaxation, balance, and soothing emotions. "Low"

Fig. 10. Exhibition of "deBallution" (Color figure online)

levels of interaction create small sizes, changes, and sophisticated shades of blue that are associated with emotions of calmness, spirituality, and futurism [14] (Fig. 10).

4.3 Conclusion

In this paper, we proposed the basic prototype of interactive artwork "deBallution" based on cultural heritages. Audience members threw pseudo balls on a screen and could make a new world by their own activities in the interactive artwork based on cultural heritage.

References

1. Hu, J., Funk, M., Zhang, Y., Wang, F.: Designing interactive public art installations: new material therefore new challenges. In: Pisan, Y., Sgouros, N.M., Marsh, T. (eds.) ICEC 2014. LNCS, vol. 8770, pp. 199–206. Springer, Heidelberg (2014). doi:10.1007/978-3-662-45212-7_25
2. Narumi, T., Yabe, H., Yoshida, S., Tanikawa, T., Hirose, M.: Encouraging people to interact with interactive systems in public spaces by managing lines of participants. In: Yamamoto, S. (ed.) HIMI 2016. LNCS, vol. 9735, pp. 290–299. Springer, Cham (2016). doi:10.1007/978-3-319-40397-7_28
3. Zhang, Y., Frens, J., Funk, M., Hu, J., Rauterberg, M.: Scripting interactive art installations in public spaces. In: Kurosu, M. (ed.) HCI 2014. LNCS, vol. 8510, pp. 157–166. Springer, Cham (2014). doi:10.1007/978-3-319-07233-3_15
4. Bullot, N.J.: The functions of environmental art. Leonardo (2014)
5. Liang, F., et al.: Information-based development trend of building skin design. Leonardo **47** (2), 173–175 (2014)

6. Best-Dunkley, A., Puustinen, M.: RE/F/r. ACE: a participatory media artwork. Digit. Creativity **23**(2), 136–143 (2012)
7. Bishop, C.: Antagonism and Relational Aesthetics. MIT Press, Cambridge (2006)
8. Bishop, C.: Contingent Factors: A Response to Claire Bishop's Antagonism and Relational Aesthetics'-Response, vol. 115, p. 107, October 2006
9. She, J., et al.: Drag a star: the social media in outer space. In: Proceedings of the 23rd Annual ACM Conference on Multimedia Conference. ACM (2015)
10. Kriss, R.-B.: Shadowed by images: Rafael Lozano-Hemmer and the art of surveillance. Representations **111**(1), 121–143 (2010)
11. de Waal, B.G.M.: The city as interface. Digital Media and the Urban Public Sphere (2012)
12. Emily, G., et al.: The VideoMob interactive art installation connecting strangers through inclusive digital crowds. ACM Trans. Interactive Intell. Syst. **5**(2), 7 (2015)
13. Beyer, G., et al.: The puppeteer display: attracting and actively shaping the audience with an interactive public banner display. In: Proceedings of the 2014 Conference on Designing Interactive Systems. ACM (2014)
14. Oh, J.-H., Kim, S.-Y., Nam, Y.T., Shi, C.-K.: deBallution –interactive artwork by throwing pseudo balls based on cultural heritages. In: Proceedings of the 2016 IEEE International Symposium on Mixed and Augmented Reality Conference (2016)
15. http://www.etymonline.com/index.php?term=overthrow&allowed_in_frame=0
16. Bulfinch, T.: Bulfinch's Greek and Roman Mythology: The Age of Fable. Courier Corporation, North Chelmsford (2012)
17. http://terms.naver.com/entry.nhn?docId=1010795&cid=50221&categoryId=50230
18. http://www.storicocarnevaleivrea.it/la-manifestazione/glossario/glossario-b/battaglia-delle-arance/
19. Oh, J.-H., et al.: A study of interactive art in the narrative form of "magic monkey". In: Proceedings of the Eighth International Conference on Computer Graphics, Imaging and Visualization, pp 39–46. IEEE (2011)
20. Costello, B., et al.: Understanding the experience of interactive art: Iamascope in Beta_space. In: Proceedings of the Second Australasian Conference on Interactive Entertainment. Creativity & Cognition Studios Press (2005)
21. Muller, L., Edmonds, E.: Living laboratories: making and curating interactive art. In: SIGGRAPH 2006 Electronic Art and Animation Catalog, pp. 160–163 (2006)
22. Costello, B., Edmonds, E.: A study in play, pleasure and interaction design. In: Proceedings of the 2007 Conference on Designing Pleasurable Products and Interfaces, pp. 76–91. ACM (2007)
23. Oh, J.-H., Shi, C.-K.: Disruptive aesthetics for interactive artwork. In: Proceedings of the International Symposium on Electronic Art (2015)
24. Ernest, E.: The art of interaction. Digit. Creativity **21**(4), 257–264 (2010)

Research on the Design of Nanjing Museum Cultural and Creative Product from the Perspective of Experience

Xinxin Sun[1(✉)], Wenkui Jin[2], and Chao Li[1]

[1] School of Design Arts and Media, Nanjing University of Science and Technology, Xuanwu Area, Nanjing 210094, China
sunxinxinde@126.com, 260082785@qq.com
[2] School of Design, Hunan University, Yuelu Area, Changsha 410082, China
jinwenkui@foxmail.com

Abstract. This paper aspires to shed light on creative cultural product design by referring to document research and conducting on-the-site investigation. During the process, we also had profound discussion, conducted survey on user groups through questionnaire and explored user need. Cultural elements consist of aesthetic consciousness, code of conduct and moral value while design properties consist of physical, logical and emotional aspects. They are closely related with each other and make up a traditional design model for cultural experience so as to support creative cultural product design. By referring to Nanjing Museum and studying its cultural elements, we came up with a design strategy which can be applied to design practice.

Keywords: Cultural product design · Experience design · Cultural and creative industry · Nanjing Museum

1 Introduction

With the increasing popularity of creative experience parks and tourism industry, the experience economy has embraced a development upsurge in the cultural experience industry. As an important carrier of cultural diffusion, creative cultural product design has become a critical trend in the global market. Product functions can be divided into two categories: utilitarian and useless ones. One product can possess these two functions at the same time. In recent years, creative cultural products like adhesive tape which inscribe the copy of Emperor Kangxi's works from Taiwan have catching the trend. It has also triggered our thinking about "consumer culture" [1]. At present, designers have already focused on the integration and application of traditional culture with product design while problems like lack of innovation and poor presentation of product culture still remain [2]. They can be illustrated as follows: (1) the lack of meaning in local modern design. There is a lack of individual culture in current design. Many designers like to blindly imitate western design models by making use of western ideas to design products which are unique in oriental culture. They lack the ability to think problems from a Chinese perspective which render it difficult to showcase Chinese civilization among the world culture. (2) The transplantation of traditional cultural elements. Now

A. Marcus and W. Wang (Eds.): DUXU 2017, Part III, LNCS 10290, pp. 529–539, 2017.
DOI: 10.1007/978-3-319-58640-3_38

many Chinese designers have already realized the importance of inheriting traditional culture with the result that lots of designs have taken advantage of traditional Chinese culture. But many so-called local designs are still at the stage of simple transplanting of product appearance like patterns and forms. Designers ignored the spiritual strength and experience that exerting intangible impact on users. When seeking inspiration from traditional culture, designers are easy to be tempted by splendid cultural representations and ignore the role played by intangible culture so that they fail to integrate material culture with intangible culture during the design process. The so-called local design is just a piece of "gorgeous coat" in the disguise of tradition and lacks emotions. So it is impossible to making traditional culture located deep in all forms of cultural life. (3) the bottleneck problem of experience need, establishment and extension. Under the back-drop of experience economy, the idea of design diversity is on the rise. Toffler, the author of The Third Trend, once predicted that "all industries in the future can only depend on providing user experience to achieve success." At the same time, the dean of institute of futurology in Copenhagen (one of the largest and most authoritative research institutions in the world) put forward a bold prediction that "future products must offer spiritual comfort for users". As a result, with people's increasingly higher expectations and requirements for products, designers not only have to design products that meet customers' basic demand but also satisfy their emotional and experience need. In 2005, ICSID gave a new definition for industrial design: design is a strategic way or process for solving problems. It can be applied to products, systems, services and experience in order to realize innovation, achieve success and improve the quality of life. This defi-nition has brought new thinking and opportunity for product design and innovation activity under the information society. So current product design has gone through the evolutionary process of "function—form—emotion—experience." Because of poor quality, similar function and lack of cultural connotation, designers have to optimize product designs from the perspective of experience.

Based on the Above-Mentioned Problems, this Paper will Conduct the Following Research: The first one is to study and explore the cultural features and elements of collections in Nanjing Museum. The second is to study the experience design models if creative products. The last is to study and practice design strategy used by creative cultural products. Based on the application of traditional culture in creative cultural design and user experience theory, this topic shed light on the reflection relationship between experimental, cultural and design dimensions so as to form design strategy of creative cultural products in Nanjing Museum based on experience. It will contribute to a better interaction between traditional culture and modern products, creating products more of the characteristics of Nanjing Museum. The idea of linking culture with product design from the view of experience can bring users with a better cultural experience.

2   Background

The essence of a museum is not lingering on the past or the existence, but exploring, discovering and creating the unknown and future. It's a materialized "past" which inspires and gives birth to new life. Museum should not only be a place for reserving and researching cultural objects but also a place to fully utilize resources, creating profound spiritual wealth and bringing a unknown world. It's a non-profit organization which means that it's not profit-oriented. Although the creative culture industry doesn't encompass in museums' principles, it's an important means for museums to realize their goals. On the basis of non-profit organizations, museums can improve their educational and recreational functions by promoting creative cultural products that are beneficial to cultural diffusion, artistic innovation and knowledge popularization. While meeting people's spiritual need for culture, the invention of creative cultural products and the development of this industry can also help museums to expand their influence on society.

Located at the south of Purple Mountain and the north of Zhongshan Gate and with a territory of over 70,000 square meters, Nanjing Museum now have more than 420,000 pieces of collections which can dating back to the Paleolithic period (Fig. 1). They came from Jiangsu province as well as the whole country. These collections include excavations, loyal treasures and social donations. As a result, Nanjing Museum is acknowledged by the public as a magnificent art treasure of the Chinese nation.

Fig. 1. Nanjing Museum and its cultural relics

Nanjing Museum is a pioneer of the cultural industry among all Chinese museums by setting up a museum shop in 1979. Until now, the shop mainly sells academic books, replicas of historical relics, aesthetic presents, handicrafts, souvenirs, famous paintings, four treasures of the study, Chinese jades, Nanjing brocade as well as office supplies. All these products give a full play of the cultural characteristics of Nanjing Museum.

3 Research Method

By targeting potential users of creative cultural products in Nanjing Museum and analyzing experience design theory, the research formed design models of traditional culture in modern products so every level can reflect with each other and establish experience design models of traditional culture that can finally support creative cultural design.

The research has three steps. Firstly, we conducted survey on former users by using questionnaires so as to select all the collected information and set up powerful user information. Secondly, we formed creative cultural product design from the perspective of experience. At last, we also organized and extracted the cultural elements and information of Nanjing Museum.

3.1 User Positioning and Analyze of Creative Cultural Produces in Nanjing Museum

Visitors are important targets of museum's service. Museum's basic principle is to understand, to get familiar with, to organize, to provide service and meet visitors' needs. As a result, how to provide service for visitors is an issue that can't be denied in the development of creative cultural products. It is very significant to conduct research on users before developing these products. By conducting relevant research, we got to know the following four points: Firstly, the age, education background and occupation of museum visitors. Secondly, the time they sent in culture shops and traces. Thirdly, visitors' purchasing motive. Lastly, visitors' preference and aesthetic needs in different age groups. By conducting these research and understanding user needs for creative cultural products, we can design products in a more reasonable way.

The main processes include information collection, information analysis, distribution of preliminary research, questionnaire analysis, questionnaire correction, open publication and data analysis. By using a large number of questionnaires, we can get more precise data. The research contents are like these: museum visitors' basic information (age, race and education background), the frequency for visiting museums, purchasing purpose and usage, purchasing tendency and affordable product price [3]. We also had a clear understanding of customer expectation for creative cultural products during the process. They mainly include cultural essence, beautiful appearance, utility, convenience, reasonable price, unique feature and excellent experience.

Scientific analysis of research is the basis for development and positioning. At the same time, it's also an important process for cultural products in the museum to evolving from concept design to real market.

3.2 User Need for Creative Cultural Products in Museums

The Combination of Utility with Aesthetics. "Aesthetics" is a pretty important principle to attract consumers to appreciate and purchase creative cultural products in museums. It's also a basic rule for the development of this kind of products. However, apart from aesthetics, products should also possess utilitarian function. Under the premise of commemorative meaning and aesthetic function, many museum visitors require that creative cultural products should also be convenient for use.

The Combination of Culture with Experience. The focus of creative cultural products in museums is innovation. It is deeply rooted in culture with the feature that it has added value for cultural and creative experience. So if designers want to resonate with users, they have to come up with excellent cultural ideas and create product experience. By "reinventing" the visual image, designers can integrate the depth of art with the breadth of experience to satisfy users [4]. This way can also create touching stories, cultural connotation and aesthetic atmosphere. As a result, all the designed products have their unique history, operation philosophy and creative value. At the same time, these products are embedded with cultural connotation which can separate them from others as well as extend their life cycles. The life cycles of creative cultural products in museums depend on innovation strategy, among which design can exert great influence on product's life cycles.

The Combination of Theme with Series. The design of serial products abides by the aesthetic principle of "variety in unity". Now with the increasing trend for market competition, more and more visitors are paying attention to creative cultural products which can further contribute to the promotion of these brands in museums. Meanwhile due to the family feature of serial products, if customers develop trust on one of the serial products, they will naturally trust other products of the same series as well. Serial products stress the overall presentation of appearance and have their unique cultural features. It lies in the fact that the increase in product numbers can catch people's eye and avoid situations like disconnection between product designs and incongruity of styles. Moreover, if creative cultural products want to leave customers with happy memory, they should be confined in certain themes. A good theme is also the essence of this kind of products. It can establish a bond between products and customers. Creative cultural products with a certain theme have two advantages. One is that they can easily can visitors' eye so as to better promote the cultural elements. The other is that they can contribute to the exploration of product depth, the expansion of breadth and the improvement of product structure.

3.3 Establishing Experience Design Model

Based on experience, Donald Norman put forward classification of emotional design which included instinctive, behavior and reflective aspects. In order to research the application of traditional culture in modern product design, designers have to analyze the connotation and extension of traditional culture of the research object, then explore, collect and select cultural elements and symbols of value of regional characteristics. Moreover, this step can also contribute to the discovery of visual symbols which are deeply rooted in culture and are powerful enough to stimulate target groups' perception and imagination. Here, the traditional culture can be divided into aesthetic consciousness, code of conduct and moral value.

The following is the design model based on the application of traditional culture in modern product design. Experience level consists of instinctive, behavior and reflective aspects. Cultural elements consists of aesthetic consciousness, code of conduct and moral value. Design properties consist of physical, logical and emotional aspects. Every level can reflect with each other to form experience design models based on traditional culture and support creative cultural design (Fig. 2).

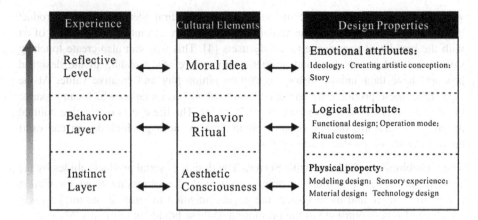

Fig. 2. Design model for creative cultural products

4 Product Design Strategy and Practice

Nanjing is an ancient city with a long history and a treasure house for national cultural resources. Nanjing Museum has over 400,000 works of art like stone objects, jade, pottery, bronze wares, china, paintings, calligraphy as well as sculptures which can dating far back to the Paleolithic Age. Among them, 1062 pieces of collection were granted as first class treasure in China. "Stringed jade ornaments" from the Paleolithic Age, "gold and silver pot" from the Warring States Period, "gold beast" from the Western Han Dynasty, "jade seal of prince Guangling" from the Eastern Han Dynasty, "bronze beast statue" from the Western Jin Dynasty, "painting of seven sages of forest" from China's southern Dynasties and "vase with plum blossom inscription" from the Ming Dynasty are all national cultural relics. With a wide variety of collections, Nanjing Museum has the unique advantage for developing cultural industry by extracting significant elements like form, function, structure and cultural connotation from key cultural relics. At the same time, it is also famous for culture from Kingdom of Wu, culture from regions south of Yangtze River and culture from the Republic of China. Particularly, culture from the Republic of China has integrated with Nanjing's regional characteristics which can be further explored.

Based on user need, experience design has the purpose of providing user experience. That's to say, it's a kind of customer-oriented design. Experience design of creative cultural products stresses user's experience during different development stages [5]. Most importantly, this kind of design is reflected on products themselves so as to satisfy customers and reveal the hidden cultural connotation. Through design practice, we will put design model into actual use and create relevant products.

4.1 Product Design of Creative Cultural Products that Extend Visual Elements Originated from Nanjing Museum

The instinctive level of creative cultural products focuses on the display of cultural features. By representational transformation, we can display elements such as forms and patterns of traditional culture to modern products. This can in turn design products that can extend visual elements originated from Nanjing Museum. Excellent visual experience can transform into excellent products. The application of elements is a very straight and clear way as typical symbols can bring typical differentiation degrees. Typical symbol can also express concepts, further connotation and ideas. It a very effective way to implant element symbols to relevant product carriers (Fig. 3).

Fig. 3. The exhibition hall of the Republic of China in Nanjing Museum

The exhibition hall of the Republic of China in Nanjing Museum showcased the splendor of Nanjing (capital of the Republic of China). The dressing culture of that period is a very typical representative of traditional culture. Cheongsam is one of the most typical dressings in this period. It became extremely popular in 1930s and 1940s. This period also marked the height of women dressing in China. Cheongsam has the following characteristics: buttons down on the right, straight collar, single piece of cloth, plane cutting and so on. It is also a king of dressing full of Chinese cultural elements. By extracting this element and applying it to mugs can help people to remember the past and to reflect on the present. Inside of the mug are the lines of Cheongsam with unique patterns so as to extend cultural symbols (Fig. 4).

4.2 Creative Cultural Product Design Based on Code of Conduct

Experience design of the behavior level originates from people's way of life, operation process and behavior. It can be manifested in the utility, completeness and convenience of products. The process of using a product is also the process for interpretation. It actually mean the interpretation of products' forms, symbolic features and connotation which can prompt the transformation of product utility to cultural diffusion.

Green-glazed bottle with eight diagrams, a cultural relic in Nanjing Museum, was made in the period of Qianlong Dynasty. It shaped like a jade rice dumpling with eight

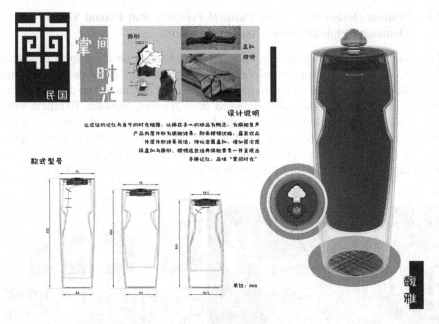

Fig. 4. Mug design by Nanjing Museum

diagrams on the surface which represented the profound Chinese culture like Yin and Yang in Taoism. This object also has a coded lock the eight diagrams on the surface of the bottle were designed as the key. The flat base was the unlock button. When using this product, unlocking it is not only a simple action but also the discovery of its cultural connotation. This kind of design can help visitors to better understand culture and enable interactive experience between visitors and objects (Fig. 5).

4.3   Creative Cultural Design Embedded with Emotional Experience in Nanjing Museum

Emotional reflective level is also called mental or psychological level. It's a measurement of reflection and product value after seeing the product and making use of it which can correspond to product's ideological level. In term of creative cultural products, the reflective level includes product history, emotion, cultural features and connotation. This kind of products can express their cultural contents by telling stories and using metaphor.

The key for the theoretical innovation of souvenirs lies in the application of artistic connotation and life concept to products. We can start from the interaction between users and products to pay attention to product experience and user feeling, reserving untouchable experience with perceivable ways.

Seeking inspiration from female pottery figures from the Tang dynasty, this sauce bottle made full use of features of dressing, hairstyle and accessories used by pottery figures which gave full play of the female gentle disposition in the Tang dynasty. The

Fig. 5. Coded lock based on eight diagrams

free combination of the cap and bottle also adds interest to the cooking process. Due to the integration of bottle and cap, it can produce a very interesting effect when using it. These sauce bottles just like several ancient females standing in an array (Fig. 6).

女性在多数情况下是厨房的绝对主角，本产品是以唐代女性陶俑为灵感，设计的一款面向女性的厨房调味瓶。产品提取人物服饰、发型、帽饰等元素特点，体现女性""温婉""的特征，可以自由组合的瓶身与瓶盖设计为料理或饮食的过程增添了一丝情趣。除了自己使用之外，亦可作为趣味礼品赠予佳人。

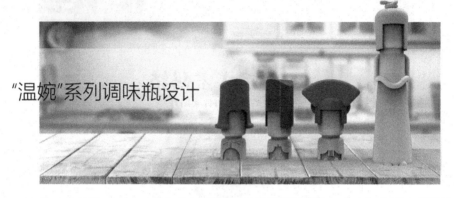

"温婉"系列调味瓶设计

Fig. 6. The Design of sauce bottles

5   Conclusion and Future Works

Based on the creative cultural product design in Chinese museums, this paper gave an analysis to how to optimize product design from the perspective of experience under the backdrop of the reform drive in China. In order to have a better understanding of museum visitors, we conducted survey on target groups based on important factors like their needs, interests, motivation and faithfulness [6]. According to the theory of experience design, we established a design model by applying traditional culture to modern product design. It goes like this: Experience level consists of instinctive, behavior and reflective aspects. Cultural elements consists of aesthetic consciousness, code of conduct and moral value. Design properties consist of physical, logical and emotional aspects. Every level can reflect with each other to form experience design models based on traditional culture and support creative cultural design.

There are so many colorful and diversified advanced productivity force and cultural relics left by the ancient people. They all displayed the wisdom and strength of designers and researchers. Experience products focus more on connecting personal feeling with materials and the short-term or repeated interaction between two parties. This kind of interaction can bring users with totally different feelings, satisfy their needs and create beautiful memory.

Acknowledgement. The authors are grateful for the financial support provided by "Research on the development mode of the integration of production, design and communication of cultural industry under the visual threshold of experience" (No. 16YB19).

References

1. Meixian, H.: The concept and practice of the cultural creative industries development in museums in Taiwan. Southeast Culture **05**, 109–118 (2011)
2. Yinyin, Z., Xiping, S., Jingyan, Q.: Service oriented sustainable experience design of museum. Packag. Eng. **22**(36), 1–4 (2008)
3. Stickdorn, M., Schneider, J.: This is Service Design Thinking: Basics, Tools, Cases. Wiley, Hoboken (2012)
4. Min, W.: Interactive programs design of museum temporary exhibitions. Southeast Culture **01**, 117–120 (2015)
5. Solomon, S., Weisbuch, G., de Arcangelis, L., Jan, N., Stauffer, D.: Social percolation models. Phys. A **277**, 239–247 (2000)
6. Guidi, G., Trocchianesi, R., Pils, G., et al.: A virtual museum for design: new forms of interactive fruition. In: International Conference on Virtual Systems and Multimedia, pp. 242–249. IEEE (2010)

An Exploratory Case Study into Curatorial Intervention Within the Context of HCI

Deborah Turnbull Tillman[1,2(✉)], Jorge Forseck[2], and Mari Velonaki[2]

[1] New Media Curation, University of New South Wales, Sydney, Australia
deborah@newmediacuration.com
[2] Creative Robotics Lab, UNSW – Art & Design,
University of New South Wales, Sydney, Australia
j.forseckrauhhain@student.unsw.edu.au, m.velonaki@unsw.edu.au
http://www.crl.niea.unsw.edu.au/

Abstract. This paper presents the results of the first of two experimental interventions in human computer interaction within the context of curating and evaluating digital interactive art. This study is situated within a larger inquiry of detecting and understanding human activity (namely engagement, experience and discursive language) regarding human-computer interaction at the cross-disciplinary research facility, the Creative Robotics Lab at the University of NSW. The methodology and engagement frameworks sit within a practice-based research approach to creative practice. Here art and technology lead the inquiry, highlighting the importance of HCI methods such as evaluation, reflection and iterative approaches to the refinement of one's own appreciative system. The research process is then situated within the scope of HCI interactive scenarios and the experimental user interface.

Keywords: Disruption · Disruptive technologies · Prototyping · Authenticity · Curating · Action research · Criteria · Audience experience · Interactivity · Evaluation · Reflection · Appreciative systems

1 Introduction

This paper aims to contribute to new ways of exploring human-computer interaction by positioning an HCI Case Study within an artistic environment, thus transforming the engagement experience, and generating new knowledge that can be applied across disciplines. By using an art exhibition as a platform for the Case Study instead of confining it solely within a laboratory or gallery environment, certain constraints are lifted and data more specific to the research can be collected that aims to reveal new behavioural patterns. There are some tendencies that can be clearly identified and improved upon, and others that fall into a more exploratory vein. The scope ranges from working with emerging art practitioners, their early work, and experimental spaces; to established practitioners in later states of their work, in more finished spaces. This exploration

© Springer International Publishing AG 2017
A. Marcus and W. Wang (Eds.): DUXU 2017, Part III, LNCS 10290, pp. 540–555, 2017.
DOI: 10.1007/978-3-319-58640-3_39

sets the groundwork for a second Case Study as indicated in the methodology section (Fig. 1). In revealing the demands of art designed, prototyped and evaluated within an HCI context, the authors have been able to test an articulated methodology for experimental making and exhibiting, which resulted in engaging an audience and evaluating their experience at the prototype phase of the work of emerging practitioners. In collecting, collating and analysing the data, and then presenting it here, the authors are aiming to contribute to new techniques in evaluating interactive systems through staging experimental curatorial interventions away from the laboratory in socially engaged spaces.

The curatorial intervention discussed in this paper is *Denouement*, the first of two experimental interventions into curating and evaluating digital interactive art. This study is situated within a larger inquiry of detecting and understanding human activity regarding human-computer interaction. The methodology and engagement frameworks sit within a practice-based research approach to creative practice. Here, art and technology lead the inquiry, highlighting the importance of HCI methods such as evaluation, reflection and iterative approaches to both artistic practice and the refinement of the curatorial appreciative system. The research process is then situated within the scope of HCI interactive scenarios and the experimental user interface. These experimental interventions contribute to a PhD inquiry identifying emergent techniques for evaluating participation in interactive art and which variables might contribute to the audiences experience of it.

2   Process

The process to be employed for the case studies will be practice-based, drawing upon the action research approach made famous by Lucy Suchman in the 1980s and relating to the way that humans and machines communicate with each other [9]. Relevant interdisciplinary models for engagement include E.T. Stringer's approach into educational action research using terminology like LOOK → THINK → ACT. His work in 2003 is based in social reform and draws on Kurt Lewin's Spiral of Steps model from 1947. Here Stringer attempts to depict comparative research on the conditions and effects of various forms of social action (such as art), and research leading to social action (art research) [8]. Social scientist Richard Johnson revised Lewin's Spiral model in 2008, allowing for responsive engagement and utilizing words such as UNFREEZING → CHANGING → REFREEZING [7]. As recently as 2006–2010, artists and social scientists have responded to a call for more distinct language frameworks describing how audiences experience interactive art specifically within the context of HCI. As detailed by Edmonds in [3], Brigid Costello developed what she calls a 'pleasure framework' for play. This taxonomy articulates 13 different descriptions of pleasure that people experience when engaging with gamified or interactive art forms. Dialogue around descriptions of exploration, competition, captivation, sympathy, camaraderie, and subversion emerged, to name a few. In active research, Zafer Bilda has developed a model of engagement, specifying interaction modes and phases that a user might move through when experiencing interactive art. Modes are described with words like unintended, deliberate, intended/in control, intended/uncertain, and unexpected; where phases are described in stages of learning, adaptation, deeper understanding and anticipation. In developing interactive systems for expert users rather than general audiences, Andrew Johnston has identified language around digital music, namely engagement that is instrumental (the musician plays the system), ornamental (the system adds something to the original sound), and conversational (where the expert and the system respond to each other) [3].

Around the same time, a specifically curatorial take on these approaches is outlined in Lizzie Muller's close reading and application of Donald Schön's reflection-in-action approach to curating [5]. She developed Beta_space, a public lab for testing interactive art systems and processes at the Powerhouse Museum, Sydney, between 2004–2011, in fact, much of the foundation work in the above frameworks were also tested in Beta_space. In learning to curate under Muller at the Beta_space public laboratory, Turnbull Tillman is a product of Muller's experimental approach to curating interactive art which utilises HCI methods in design and implementation via her documented process of designing → experimenting → reflecting → prototyping → iterating → publishing [5]. The experimental curatorial frameworks established by Muller and experimented with in Beta_space are what the researchers are working from, extending on and experimenting with here.

In measuring the experience of interactive art across disciplines and groups, conceptual development takes place with the curator offering a brief and the practitioners responding to it. This is not to say the curator is the catalyst of an artist's creative idea or a technologist's animation of that idea, but they are definitely becoming a participant in new media and interactive practice. In meeting with, evaluating, iterating and exhibiting prototypes with an emerging or established practitioner, this will feed the reflective curatorial process, as will the evaluation of audience experience. Each of the below steps in the curatorial, exhibition and evaluation process represents the creative and professional progression of Turnbull Tillman's practice-based research, incorporating the design functions of art experience through human computer interaction [1].

Where detailed accounts of the theoretical and philosophical frameworks for this study can be found in earlier publications by these authors [10], this paper will present the pragmatic results of the examination of responsive systems, where media artists, curators and audience members engage critical and creative spaces via speculative design, experience and evaluation, as with [6]. Reflection on the part of researchers is presented here, in analysis of the data collected. The exhibition for examination was produced by PhD researcher Turnbull Tillman through research initiative New Media Curation (NMC)[1]. Finally, in working through the reflection-in-action practice based research methodology (Fig. 1), this study is an opportunity for Turnbull Tillman to reflect on the way her appreciative system has developed over 8 years of independant curation, taking

---

[1] www.newmediacuration.com.

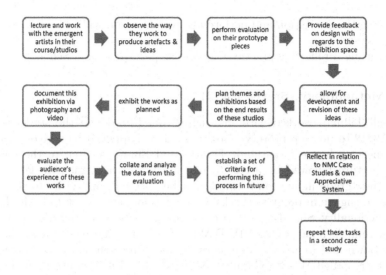

Fig. 1. New Media Curation research methodology/process. (2015)

note of any behaviors or critical language that may have emerged around the audience's experience of interactive art, as her practice developed[2], The methodology for presentation is well situated in the Creative Robotics Lab[3], where the author's studies are based on responsive systems and human interaction.

3   Results from Intervention #1: *Denouement*

3.1   Intervention #1 Exploratory: *Denouement*

SOMA3412 and Musify+Gamify (26 May–6 June 2015) www.musifygamify.info
   Denouement is a curated set of gamified film clips created by emergent practitioners, namely the students of undergraduate media arts course SOMA3412[4]. This curatorial intervention was staged from February–May 2015 and its design occurred in 4 stages:

1. Working with the students in SOMA3412 in Semester 1 of the 2015 school year to bring viable ideation to a set of working prototypes suitable for exhibition;
2. Securing partners, exhibition space, and ethics approval to promote and support a study that disrupts the audience's experience of interactive art in a public space;

---

[2] This methodology has since been modified as a reflexive practitioner model for Curators-as-Producers in Fig. 12.3 of [11], p. 191.

[3] www.crl.niea.unsw.edu.au.

[4] SOMA 3412 was a media arts course offered at the UNSW School of Art and Design titled Critiques of Narrative in Moving Image and was taught by Tom Ellard.

3. Staging the exhibition and performing evaluation on willing audience participants; and
4. Producing a reflective practice exercise, as per Muller and Schön.

3.2   Methodology (Stages 1 & 2)

Turnbull Tillman worked with Instructor Tom Ellard and the students from SOMA3412 to develop prototype artworks. This happened by way of a preliminary meeting between Turnbull Tillman and Ellard, a pitch to the students during lecture followed by a call to participate as an extracurricular activity (as in their grade in the course would not be affected), and visits to the media studios to engage in progress checks on the developing artwork in both ideation and functionality. She also worked on securing a site and exhibition to experiment within. As a part of the VIVID Music Festival, fellow media arts colleagues Oliver Bown and Lian Loke were curating an exhibition at the Seymour Centre Theatre called Musify+Gamify[5]. NMC was hired to produce the exhibition component of the project, and after surveying the site, Turnbull Tillman became aware of an outdoor screen and courtyard that might be used for displaying the prototype interactive works for the curatorial intervention. With all of the other interactive artworks and the performances situated inside, curators Bown and Loke agreed that the courtyard needed an attractor [3] and were amenable to the proposed intervention.

3.3   The Artworks and Designed Engagement Experience (Stage 3)

Where 10–12 students showed interest in exhibiting prototype works, only two prototype works from the SOMA3412 class were selected to exhibit in this experimental setting: *Puppet Boyfriend*, by Lauren Wenham, and; *Apollo Vs/...*, by Seunghyun Kim. This was largely because these were the only two students who followed through on their interest to exhibit and test their prototypes, which were both robust enough for exhibition with the public, and sophisticated enough in both ideation and functionality that they could engage that public. Wenham's work consisted of a series of sonified and animated photographs that the audience engaged with through a track-ball mouse. By moving the track-ball and clicking the mouse buttons, a simple switch patch created in IsadoraV2 gave the audience control over Lauren's *Puppet Boyfriend* for as long as they chose to choreograph his movement (Fig. 2).

Kim's work was slightly more complex. It was a game comprised of tiny moving squares meant to represent cells. Here the audience member (the offense) engaged with the work to battle a disease (the defence). Designed in Adobe Flash, it had an engagement timeline of no longer than 5 min. The input mechanism for *Apollo Vs/...* required a keyboard with a trackpad for both movement through the gamespace and the generation of cells on either side of the battle (Fig. 3).

---

[5] www.musifygamify.info.

Fig. 2. Lauren Wenham, *Puppet Boyfriend*, with IsadoraV2 patch visible. (2015)

Fig. 3. Installation shot of *Denouement*, consisting of Seunghyun Kim's *Apollo Vs/...* (2015) and Lauren Wenham's *Puppet Boyfriend* (2015). Plinth and engagement mechanisms also shown.

The overall engagement was speculatively designed by Turnbull Tillman as a single disruptive experience prior to entering the main exhibition space. The screens displaying the works served as the attractors, where the plinths displaying input mechanisms (trackpad/keyboard and track-ball mouse) served as sustaining mechanisms [3]. As such, the questions on the survey for audience evaluation queried the two artworks as one experience (Fig. 4). The evaluation methodology of surveys over semi-structured interviews or video-cued recall were selected because of the location, the time the audience might be able to commit

Fig. 4. Engagement (foreground) and Evaluation (background) in situ.

before viewing a ticketed concert, and the data set suggested for the study which was minimum 100 people.

Immediately after the participants interacted with the artworks, they were asked to complete a simple survey designed specifically for this experiment. The survey consisted of a set of 16 questions divided into three groups: Demographic, General, and Experiential (Appendix). The data was then captured, categorised and analysed to pinpoint any emergent trends. In the next section, interdisciplinary collaborators Forseck and Turnbull Tillman present the findings most relevant to their investigation into curating digital interactive art, beginning with the audience's experience of and engagement with it.

3.4   Data

Demographic: During the six days of data collection 96 subjects were surveyed with their age ranging from 18 to 65 with an average of 30.62 and a standard deviation of 10.85, the age distribution is shown on Table 1.

Table 1. Age distribution.

Age range	Age
15–24	32
25–34	37
35–44	15
45–54	5
55–64	5
65+	1

The first 2 indicators on the survey began with a general audience demographic querying gender (Table 2) and profession. We also tallied how many people appeared in each category. The male/female ratio is 1.07:1, slightly higher on the male side, with only a very small number of people not wanting to reveal their gender. Regarding profession, a high number of participants were textbook professionals expected to attend an interactive exhibition; they are either students at the nearby university, working in relevant academic fields, the arts, computer & IT, or engineering. A few financiers and retirees attended, and the 'other' category was made up of independent subject types, such as travellers, baristas, or massage therapists, for example.

Table 2. People in attendance per day, by gender.

Date	Male	Female	Und.	Total
26/05	12	8	0	20
28/05	10	8	0	18
29/05	11	9	1	21
30/05	9	9	0	18
03/05	3	2	0	5
04/05	4	8	0	12
TOTAL	0	2	0	2

General (Questions 1–3): Questions 1–3 were included for the venue's marketing team, to monitor what affectively attracts people to the site. The results showed that the festival branding and word of mouth (or friends) were the main reasons people had heard about the program and attended, but also that the majority of people who did so had been to the site previous.

Experimental (Questions 4–13): The remaining questions centred around what we, the researchers, wanted the subjects to explore regarding their experience by recording what they remembered about it immediately afterwards (Fig. 4). They were asked general questions, mostly to be able to determine in a "yes/no" way, if the prototype works created by emergent practitioners were effectively recognised as artworks (quantifying) and, if they were enjoyable, why (qualifying). In several of the questions we offered a "why" qualifier to a "yes/no" response; prompting the subject to think about why they answered yes or no. Sometimes very detailed responses were obtained, but if the question was too direct or a bit confronting, we tended not to receive an answer at all, as is indicated by the no comment section in Q4a being the largest percentage (Table 3). As the results show the audience members where experiencing a humanities definition of authenticity in relation to the artworks; one that recognized the experience as related to art and as enjoyable enough to maintain engagement [4,12,13].

Table 3. Reasons for lack of awareness ranked by percentage.

Given reasons	Percent
No comment	33%
Didn't know what it was	15%
Thought it was a game	15%
Advertising	7%
Usually something else in the space	7%
Personal limited idea of art	7%
It is interactive	4%
Looks like a model	4%
Part of Vivid	4%
People sitting and writing	4%

3.5 Results

This Case Study was designed to record and analyse, in an exploratory way, how and why people engage with interactive art. This was done through applying a curatorial practice-based research approach to working with emerging practitioners and partnering with a public festival where participating artists and curators were interested in learning more about the medium they are working in. The survey used to evaluate the audience's experience engaging with the work asked a series of open or closed questions. As the results will inform the next Case Study, this section contains a brief report of the data generated by these responses.

For the next experiment, which will be designed for a more specific interactive experience, we would suggest to ask less open questions, resulting in clearer data. As in Q4a, this question was so open that 1/3 of the participants didn't know how to articulate the qualifying aspect of it (Table 3). In the instances of the "no comment" answers, if we wanted to know why, we would have to contact the subjects and perform a follow up interview. Alternately, in the next experiment, participants won't be permitted to leave the experiment until all questions are answered. As this first experiment was an exploratory study, we left issues like this open to the subject.

We see an example of this in Q5 we see where a "yes/no" question was asked and received a largely positive response with 5.4:1. When again followed with a qualifying question, the largest percentage of subjects didn't know or couldn't verbalize how they knew the work was interactive, and didn't understand until they were told by researchers.

The proposed explanation for this results according to the authors is that there is a difference in the two fields we are approaching the data from. From a design/engineering point of view quantitative data is more useful than the qualitative, subjective data collected from question 5a. This is, again, largely because the question is too open, and more than half of the participants that were unable to identify the intervention as *interactive* couldn't articulate an answer

Table 4. Responses of subjects who couldn't identify the Intervention as interactive.

Given reasons	Percent
No comment	53%
Not until I was told	33%
Is not on my eye level	7%
Thought it was other type of setup	7%

(Table 4). However, a possible method to fix this situations is for the researchers to follow up and interview those that responded with the no clarification and ask them to explain or to explore the grey areas of their experience.

The trend changed for Q6 and 6a. Where more people answered no to the closed question, people were a little more specific in the open question. Still, the largest number of answers in percentages were "not applicable", and "no comment" was tied with understanding the work was interactive within a timeframe of under 10 s and between 1–2 min (Fig. 5). Though Q8 was an open question, we received a variety of answers, the largest of which was NOT a "no" or "I don't know" response. This leads us to conclude that not only are the works recognisable and effective, but that they are so in relation to art or design related subject matter, largely gaming (Table 5).

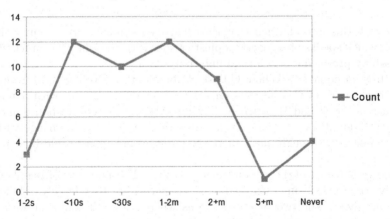

6a. How long do you think it took you to realise this?

Fig. 5. Survey question 6a

Q9 is more about specifically engaging with digital interactive art with a sample rate of 1:1.77 that leans towards a lack of engagement. But considering those who responded 'yes', we can see again that the works were largely recognised as digital art and/or media by 59.4% (Games, art, dance, media, movies, music, emotions, and people; as shown in Table 5). Those that associated the

Table 5. What do the artworks made the subjects think of.

Response	Percent
Games	35.42%
Biology	10.42%
Art	7.29%
Computer science	5.21%
Dance	3.13%
Media	3.13%
Movies	3.13%
Music	3.13%
Emotions	2.08%
People	2.08%
Chaos	1.04%
Future	1.04%
Life	1.04%
Marketing	1.04%
Science	1.04%
Doesn't know	1.04%
Other (<1%)	11.46%
No comment	6.25%

works with this also clarified that they had seen similar work at university or school, which speaks of a generic sophistication, with the emergent practitioners successfully producing at a formal university level.

Q10 is an equaliser. Where Q9 asked about interactive art, Q10 wanted to know how many of the subjects engaged with art in general, with a positive response of 2.8:1; and then where (Table 6). Here the "no" response and "no comment" qualifiers are about even. After that most subjects engage with art at Art Galleries, through music or through digital media, as would be expected from this audience.

The responses to Q11 are quite encouraging. The majority of people could conceive the works being exhibited in other spaces, but they largely didn't comment on where. The two biggest sections where they did comment were at a gallery, or in any public space. Some of the strongest answers in this section are in a "Private/Dark Room", as a "3-D facade projection", "shopping malls", "train stations", and even as an "e-birthday card".

In Q12 and Q13 we did ask some more of the pointed questions that are hard to posit. We asked if they would revisit this kind of work and if so, why? 91% of the subjects said YES, 36% of them said because they had fun, 21% because it was interesting, and curiosity and uniqueness tied at 9%.

Table 6. Response to where do the subjects with art.

Response	Percent
Art galleries	26%
Music	13%
Digital media	7%
Anywhere	6%
Museums	5%
Online	4%
Theatre	4%
School	3%
VIVID	2%
Dance	1%
Outdoor exhibitions	1%
No comment	27%

We felt positive about these responses, even about the more specific Q13, on how the experience might be improved. The largest number of subjects wanted improvements relating to the design. As a prototype and experimental exercise for the makers and the producer, this makes sense. After this, 13% wanted a better interface, 11% a better sound/audio integration, and 8% wanted clearer exhibition design.

3.6 Detailed Analysis

Interactivity and Engagement: Overall, this first experiment is considered successful as an intervention within a larger exhibition environment, largely because people recognized it as art that was interactive, and because they were willing to both acknowledge and participate in realizing this art form. As shown in the data, people came along to the larger event, noticed our intervention, they used it and had fun, and they were interested and engaged with both the systems and research.

Further analysis of the data as collated shows that people were confident of the interactivity present in both pieces and engaged with them quickly on a 5.4:1 ratio. Furthermore, this happened even when it was not completely clear to people how the interface worked since far less (2:1) of the surveyed people claimed to have understood it.

Other indications of success include that the works were recognisable in their prototype form as interactive artworks and professionals in similar and related fields recognised this, though they wanted more from the experience once they hit the limitations of the systems. Table 7 below shows the percentages to which they were aware of the works and how they understood that the works were meant to be interactive, ranging from didactics to visual cues to actually being

Table 7. Reasons given for awareness of an interactive piece.

Given reasons	Percent
It says "Click me"	34.57%
Controllers (Keyboard/Mouse/Headset)	25.93%
Other people interacting	8.64%
The Setup/display	8.64%
I was told	3.70%
No comment	18.52%

told as much by the researchers. From this data we are comfortable concluding that with 91% of the audience willing to return, and with 2/3 of this total qualified with a positive response, our audience experienced the works in an authentic manner.

Repetition and Improvement: Another important factor in the audience's response noticed by the researchers is their willingness to engage with interactive art, more than 90% (Table 8). The reasons provided for this willingness are varied, with 'Fun' and 'Interesting' being the most common, at more than 55% combined (Table 9). Because of these results, we (the art and technology collaborators who delivered the experiment and analysed the data), see value in the qualitative/quantitative analysis, and can better advise each other on how to formulate more focused questions in the next survey relating to more established practitioners and more finished works.

Table 8. Percent of people that would engage with this kind of work in the future.

Future engagement	Percent
Yes	90.63%
No	6.25%
Unsure	3.13%

Table 9. Percent of people that would engage with this kind of work in the future.

Given reasons	Percent
Fun	36%
Interesting	21%
Curiosity	9%
Different/uncommon	9%
Enjoy new things	6%
Enjoyable/entertaining	6%
Other	12%

Design for the next experiment in this curatorial study relies on what the audience felt could be improved in the design of this intervention. Table 10 shows the percentages of what the audience felt could be improved in the overall design and the engagement factors.

Table 10. Suggestions given of improvement of the interactive piece.

Given suggestions	Percent
Design	44.79%
Interface	12.50%
Audio/sound	11.46%
Exhibition design	8.33%
No comment	14.59%
N/A	8.33%

4   Discussion

In conclusion, the researchers are satisfied with the intervention inasmuch as it is meant to be exploratory, to gather general information about how audiences experience interactive art within the scope of HCI user scenarios and an experimental user interface. In this early stage, the results remain general, with not all the data being usable without further investigation. Important findings that the authors did take away from this intervention, and which will be incorporated into the design of the second Case Study are:

1. When there are multiple artworks with different engagement mechanisms, they should be treated as independent interactions within the survey. Though, they were both there as a single disruption and in essence, they have the same fundamental principles, they operate in a different way, and therefore, the experience was then different for the participant. This is articulated in the want by the participants to have a cleaner, better design, largely in regard to the interface (Table 10).
2. We found that some of the questions asked were too open even for an exploratory study, which resulted in confusing the participants and making it difficult for them to articulate the hows and the whys of their engagement. This then rendered the analysis of certain data too broad to accurately identify any possible pattern. Where this doesn't necessarily mean that the questions were badly designed for the experiment, there is an opportunity in the second intervention to have the questions more closely focused on the exhibition space (and place) as part of the experience (Table 10).
3. Both the curatorial methodology and process call for a reflective practice Case Study (stage 4 of *Denouement*'s design). At the time of this initial exploratory Case Study, Turnbull Tillman was scheduled to produce *ISEA 2015: Disruption* in Vancouver, British Columbia. In learning from the disruptive nature

of *Denouement*, Turnbull Tillman was able to iterate her methodology, again in a public art setting, and this time analysing her own process and honing her appreciative system, rather than the audiences experience of the work. Her journey and findings are detailed in a co-authored book chapter *Disruption and Reflection: A Curatorial Case Study* in [11]. The new Case Study will again be focused in the audience's experience.

5   Conclusion

This paper reports the results of the first experimental intervention made by the collaborators to identify emergent techniques for curating, evaluating and speaking about interactive art across disciplines. In addition, this paper aims to contribute to new ways of exploring human-computer interaction by positioning the Case Study in an artistic environment, thus transforming the engagement experience and incorporating new terminology. There are some tendencies that can be clearly identified and improved upon, and others that fall into a more exploratory vein. This exploration sets the groundwork for a second intervention as per Turnbull Tillman's iterative methodology. We can now incorporate more details based on what we have discovered here. In collecting, collating and analysing the data, and then presenting it here, we are hoping to contribute to new techniques in evaluating interactive systems through staging experimental interventions away from the laboratory and into social spaces.

Appendix

5.1   Questionnaire from Intervention #1: *Denouement*

Demographic Questions

- Age:
- Gender:
- Profession:

General Questions

1. Why are you visiting the Seymour Centre?
2. Have you been here before?
3. How did you hear about the current program?

Experience Questions

4. Before we approached you, where you aware that this screen displaying art? Yes/No Why?
5. Where you aware that it was interactive and/or of the interface? Yes/No How?

6. Did you understand how the interface worked? How long do you think it took you to realise this? Yes/No/Comments:
7. Did you notice anything in particular about the works you have engaged with?
8. What do the artworks present make you thing of?
9. Do you engage with *this* kind of art often? Yes/No When?
10. Do you engage with *any* kind of art often? Yes/No What?
11. Could you imagine this work in any other kind of space? Yes/No/Comments:
12. After experiencing this kind of work, would you engage with this kind of work again? Yes/No/Comments:
13. How might this experience be improved?

References

1. Brown, C.M.: Human-Computer Interface Design Guidelines. Intellect Books, Bristol (1998)
2. Card, S.K., Moran, T.P., Newell, A.: The keystroke-level model for user performance time with interactive systems. In: Communications of the ACM, New York, USA, vol. 23, no. 7, pp. 396–410 (1980)
3. Edmonds, E.: The Art of interaction. In: Routledge, T.F. (ed.) Digital Creativity, vol. 21, no. 4 (2011)
4. Greer, J.: Digital companions: analyzing the emotive connection between players and the NPC companions in video game space. In: Webber, N., Riha, D. (eds.) Part 4, Article 1 in Exploring Video Games. E-book with Inter-Disciplinary Press (2013). ISBN 978-1-84888-240-9
5. Muller, L.: Learning from experience a reflective curatorial practice. In: Candy, L., Edmonds, E. (eds.) Interacting: Art, Research and the Creative Practitioner, pp. 94–106. Libri Publications, UK (2011)
6. Silvera-Tawil, D., Velonaki, M., Rye, D.: Human-robot interaction with humanoid diamandini using an open experimentation method. In: IEEE, pp. 425–430 (2015)
7. Smith, M.K.: Action research, the encyclopaedia of informal education (1996). www.infed.org/research/b-actres.htm. Accessed 2001 and 2007
8. Stringer, E.T.: Action Research in Education. Prentice Hall, Upper Saddle River (2003)
9. Suchman, L.: Plans and Situated Action: The Problem of Human-Machine Communication Communications of the ACM. Cambridge University Press, New York (1987)
10. Turnbull Tillman, D., Velonaki, M.: Curating: a disruptive technique for disruptive technologies. In: Proceedings of the 21st International Symposium on Electronic Art. Vancouver, Canada (2015). http://isea2015.org/proceeding/submissions/ISEA2015_submission_82.pdf
11. Turnbull Tillman, D., Velonaki, M.: Disruption and reflection: a curatorial case study. In: England, D., et al. (eds.) Curating the Digital: Space for Art and Interaction. Springer Series on Cultural Computing, pp. 181–201. Springer International, Switzerland (2015)
12. Turnbull Tillman, D., Velonaki, M., Gemeinboeck, P.: Authenticating experience: curating digital interactive art. In: TEI 2015, Stanford, CA, USA, pp. 429–432 (2015)
13. Turkle, S.: Authenticity in the age of digital companions. In: Interaction Studies, vol. 8(3), pp. 501–517. John Benjamins Publishing Company, Philadelphia (2007)

DUXU Practice and Case Studies

The Role of UX in Government System Expansion

Fuad Abujarad[1]([⊠]), Ian O'Bara[2], Sarah J. Swierenga[2],
and Eric D. Raile[3]

[1] Yale School of Medicine, New Haven, CT, USA
fuad.abujarad@yale.edu
[2] Usability/Accessibility Research and Consulting,
Michigan State University, East Lansing, MI, USA
{obaraian, sswieren}@msu.edu
[3] Montana State University, Bozeman, MT, USA
Eric.raile@montana.edu

Abstract. In order to design an expansion for an existing government system that satisfies the strategic requirements of having public value, legitimacy, and feasibility, the expanded system must create something real and substantial that the target population can make use of. Our User Experience (UX) framework helps to identify areas where public value, legitimacy, and feasibility are strong, and also need more attention. We show how we used a hybrid approach that combines usability evaluation, focus groups, and online surveys to identify the user and stakeholder experiences that drive design forward in a way that leads to the success and stability of the implemented expansion.

Keywords: Criminal background checks · User experience · Health information technology · Usability · Government

1 Introduction

With population growth in the U.S. slowing, the population is becoming older and more diverse. Those individuals 65 years and older will increase by 55% from 2015 to 2030 and will represent 20% of the population by 2050 [1]. Consequently, the number of Americans becoming dependent on long-term care is increasing [2–5]. The methods by which care is provided to this population have evolved over the last two decades, moving from institutionalized care to increased options for home and community based networks of care. With this shift there was significant increase in the demand for individuals who provide services for older adults outside long-term care facilities and the fastest growing occupations being personal care workers (PCWs). As the population needing long-term care at home increases, so does the need for special protective measures to ensure the safety of older adults who are at the highest risk for abuse, neglect, and exploitation [6, 7].

Systems for pre-employment background screening of workers therefore play an important role in maintaining a secure and stable healthcare system [8, 9], and in the past decade national legislation has reflected this need in the changing healthcare landscape

A. Marcus and W. Wang (Eds.): DUXU 2017, Part III, LNCS 10290, pp. 559–569, 2017.
DOI: 10.1007/978-3-319-58640-3_40

(Section 6201 of the U.S. Patient Protection and Affordable Care Act Pub. L. 111–148, 124 Stat. 119–124, Stat. 1025, enacted March 23, 2010). Most states currently require pre-employment background checks for workers with direct access to residents in nursing homes or other long-term care facilities or who provide services to those receiving federal funding in long-term care, however this does not include PCWs. With the previously mentioned shift to in home care and the increased demand for PCWs, system expansion is needed to keep up with the evolving state of long-term care.

One state where this expansion is of particular importance is Michigan, where 28.6% of households with a family member in long-term care reported that they experienced one or more forms of abuse including physical, caretaking, verbal, emotional, neglect, sexual, and material exploitation [6, 10, 11]. Michigan launched a statewide pre-employment background check system in 2006 to combat this issue, which covers licensed long-term care facilities. In this paper we discus expanding this system to cover PCWs that provide in home services.

2 Program Background

The Michigan Workforce Background Check (MWBC) system (Fig. 1) is in place to conduct the fingerprint-based background checks of qualifying individuals. The MWBC uses the job applicant's name to check available name-based registries. In

Fig. 1. MWBC registry checks screen from the system

addition, it uses digital fingerprints scanning to conduct checks of Michigan State Police (MSP) and Federal Bureau of Investigation (FBI) criminal history records. The name-based registries checks include the Health and Human Services Medicare/ Medicaid Exclusion List registry (OIG); the Michigan Offender Tracking Information System (OTIS); the Michigan Nurse Aide Registry (NAR); and the Michigan Public Sex Offender Registry (PSOR). After completing the comprehensive background checks, prospective employers receive either a "yes" or "no" determination about an applicant's qualification status following the MWBC evaluation. To maintain continuous monitoring, the system includes a State "rapback" function that provides notice to an employer immediately if a current employee is subsequently arrested, arraigned, or convicted.

Michigan also requires background checks through alternative mechanisms for entities associated with the Michigan Medicaid MI Choice Waiver program, alternatively known as "MI Choice." MI Choice allows for support and service alternatives to facility-based care for Medicaid beneficiaries (i.e., older adults and persons with disabilities) and has both personal care and community living components. Michigan requires criminal background checks through the MI Choice operating standards and through contractual provisions with waiver agents. "Waiver agents" have the authority to determine whether an individual qualifies to receive supports and services in her or his own home or in the setting of her or his choice (e.g., adult foster homes or homes for the aged). Based on the contract provisions, waiver agents and care provider agencies must conduct a name-based criminal history screening for all paid staff and volunteers who will enter the home of a MI Choice participant. At a minimum, waiver agents and care provider agencies must use the Internet Criminal History Access Tool (ICHAT) provided by the Michigan State Police in conducting such checks.

However, there is currently no uniform statewide standard for conducting background checks on direct care workers in general across programs. PCWs in Michigan are subject to a variety of background check procedures, since formal background check standards for this workforce have not been developed. The MI Choice program contractually requires name-based criminal history checks (i.e., ICHAT) for PCWs paid with program funds, but similar requirements are not in place for PCWs hired through other mechanisms. Given the shift to in-home and community based services and the increased role of PCWs in long-term care it is necessary to include more rigorous screening of PCWs in the MWBC system.

While an expansion to the MWBC that would cover PCWs can be shown to fill a gap in the current system, government system expansion does not come easy and requires a great amount of buy in and support, not only from those who will be maintaining and funding the system, but from those who will be using it and those who are the target of its use as well. One way to take the experiences of all those affected into account is through the use of User Experience (UX) methodologies. Using the proposed expansion of the MWBC system as an example, this article hopes to create a UX based model for system expansion that others can follow.

3   User Experience Approach to Expansion

When developing a government system, the developers need to show that the system has the following three elements: public value, legitimacy, and feasibility. Policymaking and the creation of government systems requires an alignment of these three elements in what Moore called the strategic triangle (value, legitimacy, and feasibility), in order to provide a meaningful and lasting outcome [12]. The same can be said of government system expansion. In order to create public value the system must create something real and substantial that the target population can make use of; legitimacy can be achieved if the system has political and public support, and feasibility requires the technical and human resources, as well as the commitment to apply those resources to the system.

Specifically, the expansion of a government system like the MWBC system can only be shown to be effective if it has the resources and the organizational will to do so. Moreover, the stakeholders need to buy in to the idea of the system and feel it will provide them with perceived benefits. One way to design a system expansion with these elements for success in mind is to take UX into account. The Nielsen Norman group defines UX as encompassing "all aspects of the end-user's interaction with the company, its services, and its products" [13]. In a government system context, this means taking into account the feelings about the system of those affected by it and the experiences and interactions they have with that system. With the strategic success of government system expansion being dependent on stake holder perception and experience of the system therefore committing the required resources the researchers designing the Michigan Workforce Background Check Expansion (MWBCE) chose to adopt UX methodologies in order to create a system that could be seen to have public value, legitimacy, and feasibility. The research methods of usability testing, focus groups, and surveys were adopted to meet these goals.

4   Methods

As the proposed MWBCE was an expansion of the current MWBC system, we needed to evaluate the usability of current system before any additional functionality could be implemented. We conducted a usability evaluation of the MWBC system as a first step to ensure both the public value it provided users and stakeholders as well as the technological feasibility of expanding the system. This in turn leads to the increased legitimacy of the proposed MWBCE. Moreover, it is not just enough to show that the system can be expanded, the proposed changes need the support of those who will be using it, as well as those who it will effect, showing it has the public value to give it the buy in for legitimacy and insure it has the resources it needs for feasibility. To test this a stakeholder analysis consisting of focus groups and a survey was conducted. In this section, we discuss the usability evaluation and the focus groups outcomes in detail.

4.1   Usability Evaluation of the MWBC System

A usability evaluation was performed to identify any user interface design issues with a redesigned version of the MWBC system, which was upgraded to meet HTML5 coding standards [14]. The goal was to test the technological feasibility as well as the public value from the experience and interaction of the user. The six participants worked in long-term care in various capacities and all had conducted background checks as part of their job responsibilities. The hour-long sessions consisted of representative end users completing several tasks that included: creating new applications, determining employment eligibility for applications with and without hits, and managing the account.

Usability was measured based on the three components of efficiency, effectiveness, and satisfaction [15]. Effectiveness was measured as the percentage of tasks completed successfully. Efficiency was measured as the average time to perform a task and assessed based on issues observed during performance of the tasks. Satisfaction was measured by user satisfaction ratings (i.e., from post-task and post-study questionnaires that included the System Usability Scale (SUS)) written feedback on the questionnaires, and verbal comments from each session. While effectiveness and efficiency measures were quantitative, satisfaction was measured qualitatively.

The findings of the study indicated that users who perform background checks as part of their job responsibilities were mostly successful in completing the tasks and indicated that they had a favorable impression of the redesigned MWBC system [14], which was also in line with previous evaluations of earlier versions of the system [16–18]. In general, tasks that involved performing registry checks, locating existing records in the MWBC system, and updating hiring decisions for employees or applicants that no longer worked at the facility were relatively straightforward. However, tasks that involved making the correct eligibility determination when there was a non-disqualifying hit in a name-based registry, e.g., a misdemeanor offense that was not disqualifying to work in long-term care according to the State statute, were more challenging for some of the users [14].

After attempting all of the task scenarios, participants were asked to use the System Usability Scale (SUS) to rate their experience with the MWBC system. The SUS, created by John Brooke, is an industry standard used as a quick and reliable tool for measuring usability that can be used for small sample sizes [19, 20]. The SUS score for the MWBC system was 94.6, which is considered a very high score [14]. Overall, participants viewed the redesigned provider user interface to be is usable, accepted, and efficient. The results from the usability evaluation are mapped to the public value and feasibility of creation government system expansion and provide theoretical foundation for a meaningful and lasting outcome.

4.2 Stakeholder Focus Groups Analysis Strategy and Methods

A "stakeholder analysis" involves a researcher assessing the attitudes of various stakeholder groups about a particular program or prospective change. The broad goal of this research study was identification of the normative (i.e., how things "should be") and structural obstacles to expanding fingerprint-based background checks to PCWs. The researchers gathered stakeholder attitudes and beliefs because program success ultimately would depend on views about the need for, viability of, and effectiveness of expanded background checks. The researchers deliberately gathered both positive and negative views, as well as feedback about the balance between the two. In order to gather a cross-section of views effectively and comprehensively, the researchers employed a mixed-methods approach with both focus groups and a survey.

4.3   Stakeholder Analysis Participant Profile

Although stakeholder analysis can take various forms, the researchers focused on analyzing the attitudes and interests of a broad cross-section of important stakeholder groups. The initial step was identification of the key stakeholder groups to be included in discussions of a potential change process. This first step resulted in the categorization of stakeholder groups as shown in Table 1 below.

Table 1. Stakeholder groups

(1) Participants (older adults and persons with disabilities) receiving supports and services and their relatives and advocates
(2) PCWs and job applicants
(3) Waiver agents and fiscal intermediaries
(4) Care provider agencies
(5) Employees of nongovernmental organizations (NGOs) whose work intersects with background checks and/or the healthcare workforce
(6) Government employees whose work intersects with background checks and/or the healthcare workforce

For purposes of the research study, Group 1 (participants receiving supports and services and their relatives and advocates) focused on individuals qualifying for in-home assistance under MI Choice. As for the other groups, Group 2 (PCWs and job applicants) included individuals hired through MI Choice, including some who had undergone fingerprint-based background checks in the pilot program. Group 3 included employees of a number of waiver agents that make waiver determinations for the State. Group 3 also included employees of fiscal intermediaries, which are entities that help individuals with money and financial matters and/or help organizations with tasks such as payroll and conducting background checks. Fiscal intermediaries may also conduct background checks on individuals hired in self-determination situations. Group 4 included owners and employees of care provider agencies working in the pilot program's geographic coverage area. Such agencies were either firms or non-profit organizations that hire PCWs to provide supports and services for individuals. A range of NGO employees (Group 5) were part of the study, including some working from the perspective of participants receiving supports and services and some working from the perspective of PCWs. Finally, Group 6 included government employees at both the county and State levels.

4.4 Stakeholder Analysis Procedure

The researchers planned and convened five focus group sessions to gather information and feedback from the stakeholder categories listed previously (excluding the government employee category). Per methodological standards, the target size for each focus group was approximately 6–10 participants. The focus group sessions lasted between 75–90 min each. In terms of additional resources, Michigan State University provided two note takers (both familiar with user experience evaluation methodologies) and two digital audio recorders for the focus group sessions and arranged for transcription of the raw data. The notes supplemented the digital audio recordings and provided additional data for the transcriptionist. The researchers debriefed with the note takers after each session. The exact number of participants for each focus group was: twelve in Group 1, thirteen in Group 2, six in Group 3, seven in Group 4, and six in Group 5. Differences between the two slates of questions reflected differences in the nature and interests of stakeholder groups, for example questions about organizational processes would not be appropriate for the group of participants receiving supports and services.

Groups 5 and 6 were the subject of a web-based survey the researchers distributed to employees of both governmental and nongovernmental organizations with responsibilities related to PCWs and/or background checks. The survey used both closed and open-ended questions that were informed by the results of the previous focus group sessions. The researchers initially recruited 30 governmental and nongovernmental employees via email. Individual responses were delinked from the identifying information. The researchers had followed up with prospective respondents on multiple occasions. The response rate for the survey was 60% (i.e., 18 out of 30).

4.5 Stakeholder Analysis Results

General Concerns Related to Personal Care Workforce. Multiple stakeholder groups made it clear that background checks were part of a web of general issues related to the personal care workforce. In terms of labor economics, focus group and survey participants mentioned low average pay, high turnover, and the transience of the PCW workforce as concerns. Focus group and survey participants also expressed concern over the increasing need for PCWs as the general population ages; demographics will continue to drive greater demand. Also prominently mentioned were concerns over the lack of standardized training, licensing, and certification requirements for PCWs.

PCWs expressed worries about their own safety and about the need for greater protection from family members of some participants receiving supports and services. The PCWs felt that some participants receiving supports and services also needed greater protection from their own family members. Further, PCWs worried that government funding programs do not currently cover sufficient hours of work, meaning that participants receiving supports and services are not receiving all the care they need. Personal care agencies, on the other hand, mentioned the logistical difficulties of supervising PCWs who are widely spread out as they work in homes. Personal care agencies also mentioned the economic pressures introduced by increasing minimum wages in Michigan.

Perceived Benefits of Expansion. A widespread opinion across groups was that fingerprint-based background checks are necessary. Half of the survey respondents cited the lack of fingerprint-based background checks as problematic. Focus group participants indicated that such checks were "desperately needed" and that the current lack of a requirement for fingerprint-based checks for PCWs was "amazing." Survey respondents similarly noted that background checks are required in related healthcare professions and that measures should be taken to limit the cases of fraud and abuse that harm the entire direct care industry. In the view of such persons, fingerprint-based background checks would legitimize the industry, improve its reputation, and professionalize PCWs. Widespread belief existed that fingerprint-based background checks improve the actual safety and security and feelings of security for participants receiving supports and services.

Another widespread belief was that background check requirement would dissuade problematic individuals from applying for jobs. Focus group participants thought that the cost of such background checks alone might deter some unfit applicants, if those costs were borne in part or whole by the workers. According to focus group and survey participants, deterrence would result in improved quality of the personal care workforce overall. Participants in multiple focus groups and some survey respondents thought that fingerprint-based background checks might serve as a source of pride and of feelings of professionalism for PCWs, as well. Background checks could function as a credential of prequalification for PCWs.

Focus group participants noted that a statewide fingerprint-based background check system might produce cost savings by weeding out unfit applicants or employees quickly, thereby enhancing the quality of the workforce and reducing turnover. Personal care agencies were also hopeful that better, standardized checking procedures might reduce the cost of liability insurance, given the potential for a better quality workforce.

Potential Concerns About Expansion. This section discusses the types of issues and concerns the State might try to address in implementing any new background check system, with an emphasis on fingerprint-based background checks. The costs of fingerprint-based background checks and the question of who pays for the checks for PCWs were clearly the biggest concerns across all focus groups. Among survey respondents, 78% were "very" or "somewhat" concerned about both increased costs and about who pays for them, though at least one survey respondent felt that organizations that really cared would have no problem covering the costs. Each stakeholder group had different ideas about who might be responsible for covering the cost, with such ideas including the State, personal care agencies, PCWs, participants receiving supports and services, and health insurance companies. PCWs and participants receiving supports and services all expressed a clear belief that their own group could not carry the costs. Various focus groups argued that costs ultimately would get passed on to PCWs or to participants receiving supports and services regardless of who paid initially. NGOs asserted that the State and the personal care agencies were the only feasible options, given that State law prohibits job applicants from paying the costs of fingerprinting.

Focus group participants also saw a system as insufficient if it did not capture relevant non-criminal offenses on the part of a job applicant or worker. Finally, focus group participants pointed out that abuse occurs sometimes even when fingerprint-based background checks are present; as one participant observed, you cannot "forward-check" a job applicant or worker. Survey respondents also noted that you are not likely to catch the "clever" unfit actors and that background checks do not assess personality.

The researchers did not see the anticipated level of privacy concerns related to the process of taking and storing fingerprints. The expression of such worries was minimal across focus groups and even in the PCW group, though the latter group was not necessarily representative of the whole PCW population. A number of focus group participants shared the view that privacy is nonexistent in our society now anyway. However, half of survey respondents indicated that they were "very" (17%) or "somewhat" (33%) concerned about worker privacy.

In replying to a question about benefits versus costs on the survey, 56% of respondents said the benefits outweighed the costs, 33% were unsure, and only 11% said the benefits did not outweigh the costs. Some survey respondents mentioned direct balancing tests. For example, the decision might come down to weighing the prevention of misconduct against access to service concerns.

5   Conclusion

Using a UX framework can help to identify areas where public value, legitimacy, and feasibility are strong and need more attention. This UX framework helps to identify user and stakeholder experiences and drive design forward in a way that will lead to the success and stability of the implemented expansion. Getting these experiences helps to triangulate where public and political will are strong or lacking, and helps to find the required resources for implementation. Starting with an evaluation of the current system provides the designers with insight into the technological feasibility moving forward, as well as feedback about the value of the current system to those who use it and all those it affects. Using usability evaluation, focus group, and survey UX methodologies we were able to identify where the proposed MWBC design expansion for PCWs was strong and also areas that need more attention moving forward.

The usability evaluation highlighted that users are willing to take the time to learn the current MWBC system because they recognize the benefits in terms of time conservation, consistency, and patient safety, demonstrating that the MWBC system has the public value and the backing to show the expansion has legitimacy. Users of the MWBC system also stated that it is user-friendly and works for a diverse group of end users, showing that the current system has the technological feasibility to serve as the basis for expansion.

The UX methodology of focus groups and survey provided a great deal of insight into unforeseen opinions and concerns with the MWBC expansion among stakeholders highlighting their usefulness in expansion design. While originally hypothesized to be a larger issue, privacy was shown to be of little concern to all stakeholder groups, whereas cost was the main concern. Stakeholders across groups had concerns about the increased funding needs and who would be responsible for covering the cost showing a feasibility challenge in terms of resources and ownership. Stakeholders did believe that the benefits of expansion outweighed the costs, though, as a widespread opinion throughout the groups was that fingerprint-based background checks are necessary; the MWBC expansion was shown to increase the public value of the current system and had the legitimacy in terms of public and political backing to be implemented. Moving forward, additional research and planning will have to be done in the area of cost. By continuing to highlight the user experience, we will focus on designing an expansion where the resources associated with cost and ownership will be mitigated as much as possible to increase feasibility.

Highlighting all of these experiences as part of a user centered design of system expansion shows that UX methodology can be used by other states and organizations to better test the public value, legitimacy, and feasibility of their proposed system expansions. By first testing the current system for public value and feasibility, and then getting feedback from those the proposed expansion effects on the legitimacy and feasibility of implementation, a more strategic, valuable, and successful system can be designed.

Acknowledgment. Funding for this research came from the Centers for Medicare & Medicaid Services of the U.S. Department of Health and Human Services under the Ninth Announcement CFDA #93.506, Funding Opportunity Number CMS-1A1-13-002.

References

1. US Census Bureau: The Older Population: 2010 Census Briefs (2011). http://www.census.gov/content/dam/Census/library/publications/2011/dec/c2010br-09.pdf
2. Friedland, R.B.: Caregivers and long-term care needs in the 21st century: Will public policy meet the challenge? (2004). http://caregiverslibrary.org/Portals/0/caregivers%20and%20LTC%20needs%20and%20Public%20Policy.pdf
3. Luz, C., Swanson, L., Ochylski, D., Turnham, H.: Michigan's 'Building Training … Building Quality' personal and home care aide state training program. Final report for the Michigan Office of Services to the Aging (2014). http://phinational.org/sites/phinational.org/files/research-report/michphcast-finalreport-20141219.pdf
4. National Center for Health Workforce Analyses: Nursing aides, home health aides, and related health care occupations – National and local workforce shortages and associated data needs (2004). http://bhpr.hrsa.gov/healthworkforce/reports/rnhomeaides.pdf
5. Paraprofessional Healthcare Institute: Facts 3: Who are direct-care workers? (2011). http://www.phinational.org/sites/phinational.org/files/clearinghouse/NCDCW%20Fact%20Sheet-1.pdf
6. Department of Health and Human Services, Office of Inspector General: Nursing Facilities' Employment of Individuals with Criminal Convictions. Report OEI-07-09-00110, March 2011
7. Cooper, C., Selwood, A., Livingston, G.: The prevalence of elder abuse and neglect: a systematic review. Age Ageing **37**, 151–160 (2008)

8. Post, L.A., Salmon, C.T., Prokhorov, A., Oehmke, J.F., Swierenga, S.J.: Aging and elder abuse: projections for michigan. In: Murdock, S.H., Swanson, D.A. (eds.) Applied Demography in the 21st Century, pp. 103–112. Springer Science and Business Media, Heidelberg (2008). ISBN 1402083289

9. Post, L.A., Swierenga, S.J., Oehmke, J., Salmon, C., Prokhorov, A., Meyer, E., Joshi, V.: The implications of an aging population structure. Int. J. Interdisc. Soc. Sci. **1**(2), 47–58 (2006)

10. Galantowicz, S., Crisp, S., Karp, N., Accius, J.: Safe at Home? Developing Effective Criminal Background Checks and Other Screening Policies for Home Care Workers. AARP Public Policy Institute, September 2010

11. Blumstein, A., Nakamura, K.: Redemption in the presence of widespread criminal background checks. Criminology **47**(2), 327–359 (2009)

12. Moore, M.H.: Creating Public Value: Strategic Management in Government. Harvard University Press, Cambridge (1995)

13. Norman, D., Nielson, J.: The Definition of User Experience (UX) (n.d.). https://www.nngroup.com/articles/definition-user-experience/

14. Abujarad, F., Swierenga, S.J., Dennis, T.A., Post, L.A.: The impact of usability on patient safety in long-term care. In: Nah, F.F.-H., Tan, C.-H. (eds.) HCI in Business, HCIB 2015, LNCS 9191, pp. 221–231. Springer International Publishing, Switzerland (2015)

15. International Organization for Standardization: Ergonomic Requirements for Office Work with Visual Display Terminals (VDTs) – Part 11: Guidance on Usability. (ISO Reference No. 9241-11:1998[E]) (1998)

16. Swierenga, S.J., Abujarad, F., Dennis, T.A., Post, L.A.: Real-world user-centered design: the Michigan Workforce Background Check system. In: Salvendy, G., Smith, M.J. (eds.) Human Interface, Part II, HCII 2011, LNCS 6772, pp. 325–334. Springer, Berlin (2011)

17. Abujarad, F., Swierenga, Sarah J., Dennis, Toni A., Post, Lori A.: Rap backs: continuous workforce monitoring to improve patient safety in long-term care. In: Marcus, A. (ed.) DUXU 2013. LNCS, vol. 8014, pp. 3–9. Springer, Heidelberg (2013). doi:10.1007/978-3-642-39238-2_1

18. Swierenga, S.J., Abujarad, F., Dennis, T.A, Post, L.A.: Improving patient safety through user-centered healthcare background check system design. In: Proceedings of the International Symposium of Human Factors and Ergonomics in Healthcare HFES 2013 (2013). Hum. Factors Ergon. Soc. **2**(21), 21–26 (2013)

19. U.S. Department of Health & Human Services: System Usability Scale (SUS). usability.gov (n.d.). http://www.usability.gov/how-to-and-tools/methods/system-usability-scale.html

20. Brooke, J.: SUS: a retrospective. J. Usability Stud. **8**(2), 29–40 (2013)

Pervasive Information Architecture and Media Ecosystem: A Brazilian Video on Demand User Experience

Luiz Agner[1(✉)], Barbara Jane Necyk[2], and Adriano Bernardo Renzi[3]

[1] Faculdades Integradas Helio Alonso/Facha, Rio de Janeiro, Brazil
luizagner@gmail.com
[2] Pontifícia Universidade Católica do Rio de Janeiro, Rio de Janeiro, Brazil
07barbara@gmail.com
[3] Serviço Nacional de Aprendizagem Comercial/Senac-Rio,
Rio de Janeiro, Brazil
adrianorenzi@gmail.com

Abstract. This paper evaluates user's consumption and interaction with video on demand focused on the Globo Play app provided by Brazil's largest TV network: TV Globo. Globo Play stands as an answer to the video on demand request addressed by Globo in a market scenario filled with world competitors like Netflix and Youtube. Cooperative evaluation and SUS results pointed out that there still is much to do in order to improve and to meet user's requirements in what concerns quality of interaction, according to pervasive information architecture guidelines. User sessions indicated non-attendance to some usability issues as well. We came to the conclusion that the new world of ubiquity and pervasiveness probably does not make the traditional aspects of usability and user's experience disappear.

Keywords: Brazil · Media ecology · Pervasive information architecture · TV · UX

1 Introduction

Brazil is a country with continental proportions and a huge population (206 million people). In 2015, 39.3 million households (57.8% of all) had internet access, of which 99.8% had broadband connection, according to the Brazilian Institute of Geography and Statistics [1]. Nearly 102 million people are internet users and 139 million people have a mobile device for personal use. 97.3% of private school students and 73.7% of public school students use internet. The digital TV signal reaches now 49.4% of urban households and 17.6% of rural households.

Brazil is the third country in the world to spend a large amount of time on mobile phones [2]. Brazilians spend about 3 h 40 min online on cell phones and watch 6 h of TV shows in a daily basis [3].

This paper studies the user consumption and interaction of video on demand, focused on Globo Play app, provided by Brazil's largest TV network, TV Globo. This research regards the user experience of young middle class undergraduate students of

© Springer International Publishing AG 2017
A. Marcus and W. Wang (Eds.): DUXU 2017, Part III, LNCS 10290, pp. 570–580, 2017.
DOI: 10.1007/978-3-319-58640-3_41

Rio de Janeiro, Brazil's second largest city. We conducted an evaluation of the user experience and information architecture.

TV Globo produces and exhibits a large number of shows, such as soup operas, sitcoms, drama series, special shows, news broadcasting and varieties. TV Globo's network spreads out through a vast ecosystem based on linear TV, smart TVs, notebooks, PCs, tablets and smartphones providing a cross-device user experience. The app provides real-time and non real-time on-demand video through the internet.

In order to collect qualitative insights about Globo Play app utilization a descriptive research based on cooperative evaluation sessions has been driven. Pervasive information architecture and media ecosystem theories were regarded as a fundament to understand the case study as well as usability heuristics.

2   Pervasive Information Architecture and New Media Ecosystem

Rosenfeld et al. [4] emphasize that information has been more abundant than ever due also to many available devices: smartphones, tablets, smart watches, etc. Many artifacts around us are connected to fulfill daily tasks and influence new ways to interact with information. A broader range of interconnectivity takes place, transforming the interaction of humans with isolated computers to a human-information interaction into a dynamic interaction ecology. As an example, Rosenfeld *et al.* [4] mention CNN's responsive adaptations for publishing news through different devices.

Arango [5] emphasizes that information architecture has to start from systemic thinking, since a diversity of products and services interact with each other through several channels. Nowadays, as physical and digital environments are integrated experience, information architecture needs a holistic approach.

It is worth mentioning the notion of ecosystem applied to media. The ecosystem idea was first proposed by Marshall McLuhan and Neil Postman in the American and Canadian academia. In 1968, the concept was formally exposed and defined in a lecture as a "study of media as environment". According to Postman [6],

"[…] human beings live in two different kinds of environments. One is the natural environment and consists of things like air, trees, rivers, and caterpillars. The other is the media environment, which consists of language, numbers, images, holograms, and all of the other symbols, techniques, and machinery that make us what we are" [6].

The idea of information architecture as ecosystem is observed in Resmini and Rosatti's [7] pervasive information architecture manifesto. The authors highlight that:

"When different media and different contexts are intertwined tightly, no artifact can stand as a single, isolated entity. Every artifact becomes an element in a larger ecosystem. All of these artifacts have multiple links or relationships with each other and have to be designed as part of one single seamless user experience process" [7].

Another important aspect in the manifesto regards the users' role transformation:

"Users are now contributing participants in these ecosystems and actively produce new content or remediate existing content by ways of linking, mash-ups, commentary, or critique. The traditional distinction between authors and readers, or producers and consumers, becomes thin to the point of being useless" [7].

The concept of pervasive information architecture came up as a result of media convergence process. Smartphones, computers, tablets, smart TVs, smart watches, braces, social networks, tend to converge as an integrated system. Each one of these channels helps constructing one whole narrative. There is a complex ecosystem loaded by the production of continuous content that represents the new dynamics of information flow. The thin line between editors and readers cease to exist as well as the boarders from one media to another. Hybrid languages bring everything together.

In a scenario marked by fast evolution of technology possibilities, consumers' behavior has been transformed. Users not only search, access and use information; since web 2.0, people also cite, create, reinterpret, edit, mix and recreate information through various interconnected channels. Consumers became *prosumers* and information tends to flow as a transmedia narrative.

The renewal of information architecture into new conceptual aspects perceived by Resmini and Rosatti is stressed by Morville [7], who pointed out its new role:

"(...) the design of ecosystems for way-finding and understanding promotes a holistic approach to information architecture and user experience that draws insights from multiple disciplines and historical contexts" [7].

Information architecture reframing led Resmini and Rosatti [7] to present five new principles of pervasive experience: (1) Place making – refers to the capacity to build a sense of self-localization. The principle suggests that architecture reduces the possibility of user disorientation. The heuristic interconnects conceptually with notions of space, place and context; (2) Consistency – refers to a model of pervasive information that attends goals, contexts and users, keeping the same logic in different medias, environments and necessities; (3) Resilience – refers to the capacity of the pervasive information model to adapt to specific users, their needs and search strategies; (4) Reduction – refers to the capacity of managing a huge quantity of information and organizing it for easy access which minimizes cognitive stress and frustration; (5) Correlation – refers to the relevant connections between pieces of information, services and products to help users reach objectives or stimulate latent needs.

3 Aspects of Brazilian TV System

TV broadcasting system was launched in Brazil in 1950, in São Paulo, and rapidly became reference for the population behavior, profoundly influencing the country's politics and cultural trends. TV Globo station was founded in 1965 and soon become one of the biggest references in Brazilian teledramaturgy [8]. In the 70s, the company stood out bringing one of the major commercial products of the Brazilian TV, the soup opera, and shortly after, in 1982, the company dazes competitors expanding to successful mini-series. In 1995, TV Globo retained Latin America's biggest TV production, as 90% of its TV shows' schedule were produced in-house. The Globo Group incorporates TV Globo, GloboSat (cable channel), Globo.com (internet portal), Editora Globo (publishing house), Som Livre (record music company) and Zap (real state portal), among other companies. Nowadays, TV Globo produces 3,000 h of entertainment as well as 3,000 h of sports related shows and news per year, with international award winning contents. It is a huge corporation with 119 affiliated broadcasters through open TV, covering 99.5% of Brazilian population. In 2016, the company reached 98.44% of the country's territory throughout 5,482 cities [8].

However, over the latest years, TV Globo has been suffering strong impact from other TV corporations, as well as digital competitors as Youtube, Netflix, Facebook and Twitter, leading its national influence to a gradual decline.

4 Case Study: The Globo Play App

In order to face adversities, TV Globo recently launched the digital app Globo Play, aimed to several integrated systems that became known as the Globo's version of Netflix. In four months, Globo Play app reached five million downloads on mobile devices. The app is available for iOS, Android, smart TV (LG, Sony and Samsung) and Chromecast. There are development projects for other TV manufacturers and Apple TV. Awarded in 2016 as the app of the year in media and entertainment categories, Globo Play app means to bring ubiquity to the Brazilian TV system.

Globo Play app enables users to watch the national newscast, *Jornal Nacional*, or any other show at any time, out of the official schedule. It also provides TV broadcast in real time to smartphones and other devices connected to the internet. Nonetheless, there are access restrictions to the most awarded and popular shows (soup operas, mini-series sitcoms) and only paying subscribers have access to it.

The app's information architecture categorizes its content in seven major topics: soup opera and mini-series, sitcoms, variety, reality shows, news, sports and specials. There are three different levels of users: (1) the anonymous user – watches the news broadcast, parts of sports, variety and reality shows; (2) the logged on user – watches the TV shows on real time; and (3) the paying subscriber – watches soup operas, mini-series, sitcoms and has access to all archive of older shows. Besides the direct use, there is a social network layer that enables likes, comments and sharing.

Fig. 1. Home of the app Globo Play for Ipad (photo: Luiz Agner).

The Globo Play app goal is to bring a multiple device experience to users, in a cross-channel interaction journey, as it can start with video consumption on tablets, followed later on with smart TV or on the website. The Globo.com portal is a technological partner, responsible for the system's infrastructure and front-end interaction. Apple TV, Android TV and videogames are part of future developments for the app (Fig. 1).

5 Research Method

In this research we applied cooperative evaluation method and System Usability Scale (SUS) to evaluate the Globo Play app user experience. As Monk et al. [9] explain:

> "Cooperative evaluation is a procedure for obtaining data about problems experienced when working with a prototype for a software product, so that changes can be made to improve it. What makes cooperative evaluation distinctive is the collaboration that occurs as users and designers evaluate the design together. [...] This makes the procedure seem very natural to the users and requires fewer resources than more formal testing methods" [9].

The goal of an interface is "to communicate with its users, however sometimes there is a problem of communication". According to Monk *et al.* [9], cooperative evaluation can be seen as a method that brings together evaluators and users "in a cooperative context where the user completes work and is encouraged to think aloud about problems experienced". Evaluators allow users to make mistakes and, from user's questions, are able to take the investigation deeper in order to get further information about the interface. When a user finishes the set of tasks, the evaluator interview him/her about the session to deepen the investigation and clarify any miscomprehended observations. This is called a debriefing interview.

Cooperative evaluation should be applied agilely, with low cost procedures and conducted as a natural process. The interaction sessions used in this research were recorded by Lookback tool, using a MacBook Air and a Mini Ipad.

The cited authors [9] expose that cooperative evaluation sessions provide two kinds of data about the user experience: unexpected behaviour and user comments. User comments are important subjective evaluations of the interface. They reflect the user's experience with the system and may be recorded in audio or video format during a debriefing interview. It is basically a qualitative research.

Most tasks we proposed to Globo Play app users involved finding video on demand using the app's categories, as well as interacting with the social layer. The following examples are tasks presented to users during the cooperative evaluation sessions (Table 1):

Table 1. Some of the tasks proposed to users during the cooperative evaluation of Globo Play app.

1- Using the app, access the "Small Business, Great Business" video and watch the story on the US market for smartphones
2- Share this story in your Facebook timeline
3- Indicate that you liked a video from the TV comedy show "Zorra"
4- Send your comment about the video "Malhação - Pro Dia Nascer Feliz"

In order to get a quantitative score, we applied the SUS scale as a post-test questionnaire before recording debriefing interviews. These responses helped guiding the interviews. According to Brooke [10], SUS questionnaire is a tool that aims to measure people's subjective perceptions of a system, during short period breaks within evaluation sessions.

SUS scores can vary from 0 to 100. The value 68 is considered the average score for a SUS questionnaire. Any scores above 68 would be considered above average and scores below 68 are to be considered below average. SUS has become an industry standard, with references in over thousands of articles and publications. One benefit of using SUS is that it can be used on small sample sizes with reliable results (see Sauro) [11].

The seven participants invited for the cooperative evaluation and the SUS were young students of Social Communication selected from a college in Rio de Janeiro city. They were between 18 and 35 years old, with moderated or moderately high experience with information technology and with experience in apps like email, entertainment (audio and video), news, social networks and instant messengers.

6 Observed Interactions

Table 2 shows, in a condensed form, commentaries from users regarding their experience using the Globo Play app (for Ipad) while trying to accomplish pre-determined tasks as well as their profile. The goal was to register problems that could be related to the fundamentals of pervasive information architecture and interaction experience associated to the SUS score. Considering the most relevant, this paper presents data from four sessions (Table 2), with two Globo Play paying subscribers and two non-subscribers.

Table 2. Highlighted comments on Globo Play app based on users speeches collected during cooperative evaluation sessions, associated to each individual profile and SUS score.

User	User profile	User comments	SUS score
3	15–19 years old, female. Undergraduate student Technology experience: moderate Daily internet access: more than 8 h Operational system experience: Android Globo Play app experience: some previous experience Linear TV: 4–6 times a week TV experience on mobile devices and PCs: moderate Preferences: series, soup operas and movies	Do not intend to use the app in future experiences because she got disappointed. She believes that Globo Play app could be much better. She believes that the app enables only a small part of TV Globo content. Her evaluation points out that the app is time consuming because it demands users to figure out where preferred content is located. The app lacks objectivity, as content identification is not obvious to her. There is a fake look of simplicity provided by colorful nice displays. She reported that quitting out would have happened if there had not been a continuous encouragement by the moderator. The app's functions are not integrated because they don't make sense for her. It has inconsistencies, irrelevant search results and lack of related content (as it would be expected in any website). She said that it is an awkward app. She got irritated with the waste of time. Although she considers herself a young and technological driven person, she found herself "beating her brain out". Her	30.0

(continued)

Table 2. (*continued*)

		self-confidence status got lower and she thinks that the app should be released "with a user manual"	
4	25–29 years old, female. Undergraduate student Technology experience: high-moderate Daily internet access: more than 8 h Operational system experience: Android, Windows and Apple iOS Globo Play app experience: high-moderate experience Linear TV: everyday TV experience on mobile devices: high-moderate TV experience on notebook and PCs: some experience Content preferences: soup operas, mini series and varieties Paying subscribed user	She is a paying subscribed user for about a month and used the app in her Android smartphone and smart TV. She watches Globo Play content after her daily classes' routine at night She considers the app "quite confusing" and should be "more organized". She thinks the content categories should be available at the side menu She wouldn't take it as an easy going app and states that her mother would get lost It presents an excess of fragmented featured shows that brings confusion and a lot of scroll downs is required The user complained "the comment button is decorative". The insert comment task was blocked by a security issue. The app demands a validation login code sent through SMS, which the user included twice with no success. "Anyone would quit… It takes so much to comment." She thinks that it is a non-friendly app because it doesn't provide search field throughout the pages Although she already knows how to use the app, she doesn't have confidence. For her, the best improvement should be a side menu with video categories	32.5
5	30–34 years old, female. Public relations bachelor Technology experience: moderate Daily internet access: more than 8 hours Operational system experience: Windows and Apple iOS Globo Play app experience: high-moderate experience Linear TV: 4–6 times a week TV experience on mobile devices, notebook and PCs: moderate Paying subscribed user	She is a regular Globo Play paying subscriber (US$3.00 per month). She uses the app on a daily basis in order to keep up with the soup operas at night and weekends, using a HDMI connection to a regular TV She said that there is a different experience in each device: tablet, notebook and smartphone. She adds that there is no consistence among these devices. The user pointed out divergences on the Globo Play ecosystem. The version for desktop (Globoplay.globo.com) was considered the best experience She criticized the fact that there is many featured content and said that it would be much easier if users could find all categories on the top of the display. This would avoid the over scrolling down to find content Her assumption is that the app would automatically recognize the user's preferences and load up the full content She points out that users like her mother would have a hard experience with Globo Play app. She did not like the experience with the app tablet version She had difficulties to find specific shows, as the interface interaction is very different from the other options. "It has too much content at the same time" For the app tablet version she would eliminate the featured shows and leave only the live stream as well as the main shows categories She didn't understand why she could not include a comment, since she is a paying subscriber. "Some kind of error did not let me comment, nor read other users comments". "I have never noticed the social layer" She insisted on fulfilling this task but verified that the add comment icon did not work, the sharing icon showed no problem, and the like icon asked for a subscriber login confirmation	57.5
6	20–24 years old, male. Undergraduate student Technology experience: moderate Daily internet access: 3–8 h Operational system experience: Windows, Android and Apple iOS	Considers that Globo Play app is not easy to use, compared to Netflix and Youtube. "When using Youtube, I easily search through keywords, while here I put every all information possible, but the results are not-related. It was hard to understand its logic. If I use Youtube to find a specific scene, probably I will find it faster than using Globo Play app."	42.5

(*continued*)

Table 2. (*continued*)

Globo Play app experience: some experience Linear TV: everyday TV experience on mobile devices: some TV experience on notebook and PCs: moderate	"The search presents three results for subscribers, despite the fact that I am not a subscriber…That's kind of stressful". "Most of the featured scenes are just for subscribers. This sucks." The user added that the keywords search doesn't present the results in the alphabetical order, nor in chronological order. "The first top result is not the most relevant and it brings too many exclusive results to subscribers – this is a dangerous strategy because it could lead to the belief that most part of the content is reserved for subscribers only". "This dynamics could drive users off" The user tried to include a comment with no success. He considered the app hard to learn. "If I had given this app to my mother, it would have taken her two days at least to completely interact with it" The app has too many steps before it is possible to reach the category menu, causing cognitive overload: "It is different from Netflix, that presents featured content options based on your previous preferences, instead of putting upfront what Globo thinks is the most important" "Youtube and Netflix have an interaction that I am already used to. With this app, I didn't have confidence to enter too much further and leave the chance to go backwards all over again. You get apprehensive" "On the release week, I downloaded the app to try it out, but right on the first experience, I though it complicated and deleted" The user suggests some improvements: the main category menu should go the top or side position. "Soup operas and mini-series have some free content, but scenes are too short". "There could be a map to help navigation" "How to become a subscriber? The app doesn't explain…". "I was upset because the app said: *This is an exclusive content for subscribers* ". "But there is no option to become a subscriber. It seems like the message is: If you are not a paid subscriber, get out of here!"

If we take into account the average of all SUS score generated through the cooperative evaluation it would point out the 59.64 score, which is considered to be a low score in the System Usability Scale. Furthermore, if we take the SUS average only regarding the paying users subcribers, we would get a 45 score, which is even lower than the first one. These are not a good results, considering that the average score with SUS studies is 68 [11]. Below this value it is advisable to promote new studies over the detected problems in order to ensure an optimised system usability.

7 Discussion and Conclusion

Globo Play app stands as an answer to video on demand requests addressed by Brazil's main TV network in a market scenario filled with competitors like Netflix and Youtube. It also represents an attempt to reverse the downward trend in linear TV audiences as well as in the decrease in publicity income, driven over the last years by social media and other internet services.

This has been Globo Play app's goal since it was launched by TV Globo station as a cross-platform software. Aimed at the young public in order to gain contemporary and future audiences, Globo Play app designs an ecosystem that offers a cross-channel experience.

Globo Play app faces the huge challenge to be competitive within well-established practices that take place with public use of other apps and social media like Facebook, Netflix and Youtube. Competition gets even more difficult taking into account that TV Globo is a traditional open TV station. Broadcasting business and content production are its main features.

The cooperative evaluation and SUS results pointed out that there still is much to do in order to improve and to meet the user requirements in what concerns the quality of interaction according to pervasive information architecture guidelines.

The cooperative evaluation sessions with young users indicated the non-attendance to some pervasive information architecture and usability heuristics as follows (see Table 3).

Table 3. List of problems based on users comments on Globo Play's cooperative evaluation associated with heuristic categories based on Resmini and Rosati [7], Nielsen [12], Norman and Nielsen [13], and Oliveira et al. [14].

Heuristics	Insights/Observations	References
Consistency; Standards	- Inconsistency in the search field application (search fields on all pages were required by users) - Absence of upper global navigation bar or side menu with IA categories. The web version has this function (as a side menu) but tablet and smartphone versions do not	Resmini and Rosati Nielsen
Match between system and the real world	- Taxonomy categories do not reflect the user's mental model. Users have difficulty in finding videos by browsing the categories proposed by the app	Nielsen
Reduction; Aesthetic and minimalist design	- Excessive featured video scenes in the homepage leads to extra scroll down procedures. The attempt to find anything is difficult and disturbing	Resmini and Rosati Nielsen
Resilience; Flexibility and efficiency of use	- Contents are not loaded according to the logged on user's profile. - Previous content experiences are not loaded in the navigation history. The absence of history also does not help in the cross-platform continuity throughout devices, as Netflix does	Resmini and Rosati Nielsen
False affordances	- The comment icon isn't actionable - Categories labels are taken for affordances - The label See More Scenes is taken for affordance	Norman and Nielsen
Resilience	- Comments are not allowed in some videos - Non-subscribers have more difficulty to post their comments	Resmini and Rosati
Interoperability	- SMS validation code is requested to approve comments insertion in the cross-platform experience. Interoperability among devices is reduced by the rigid security that breaks the flow of experience	Oliveira et al.
Correlation; Recognition, diagnosis, and recovery from errors	- The interdiction message Content Available to Paying Subscribers Only does not help the user on how to become a subscriber, breaking the flow of the experience	Resmini and Rosati; Nielsen

The Globo Play app performance for Ipads as part of a media ecosystem proved to be unsatisfactory taking into account that the usability and UX requirements in the new pervasive scenario increased. New information architecture guidelines are related to a network that had incorporated complexity based on ubiquity and heterogeneity.

People inhabit this media ecosystem where prosumers, a new kind of user, also wish to participate, to share, to comment and to produce content. The needs and goals of a prosumer call for a more rigorous set of requirements of experience to which all ecosystem components should fit in.

With various emerging device/interaction paradigms, platforms like Globo Play app are emerging from tools to ecosystems. This context brings new horizons for IA: according to Rosenfeld *et al.* "what is needed is a systematic, comprehensive, holistic approach to structuring information in a way that makes it easy to find and understand – regardless of the context, channel, or medium the user employs to access it" [4].

However, the cooperative evaluation sessions conduced in this research produced results that highlighted some experience aspects which are not reflected upon pervasive IA heuristics. Some traditional usability, IA and experience problems were not overcome yet and they need to be taken into account also in the pervasive information scenario. We are talking about problems such as a match between system and the real world, hidden affordances, usable categories, interoperability or recovery from errors.

Regarding ecosystems, as users mentioned in their interviews, insights force us to conclude that probably the new world of ubiquity and pervasiveness does not make some traditional aspects of experience disappear. On the contrary, these aspects are enhanced. Much of the experience can be impacted by generic problems, as Renzi [15] has already pointed out when proposing his heuristics for cross-channel scenarios.

Our observations also made us perceive that pervasive information architecture heuristics should probably be expanded to address, explain or reflect ancient problems of user experience which are still there. New research must be carried out in this direction.

Acknowledgements. The authors are grateful for the support of Faperj - Fundação Carlos Chagas Filho de Amparo à Pesquisa do Estado do Rio de Janeiro (APQ1/2014).

References

1. IBGE: Pesquisa Nacional por Amostra de Domicílios. Acesso à internet e à televisão e posse de telefone móvel celular para uso pessoal: 2015/IBGE, Coordenação de Trabalho e Rendimento. – Rio de Janeiro, 87 p. IBGE (2016)
2. Folha de S. Paulo: Brasil é terceiro país do mundo que fica mais tempo on-line no celular. http://www1.folha.uol.com.br/tec/2015/09/1679423-brasil-e-terceiro-pais-do-mundo-que-fica-mais-tempo-on-line-no-celular.shtml. Accessed 15 Dec 2016
3. Folha de S. Paulo: Em 2015, brasileiro passa 6 horas por dia na frente da televisão. http://f5.folha.uol.com.br/televisao/2015/12/1723883-brasileiro-passou-5-horas-por-dia-assistindo-tv-em-2015.shtml. Accessed 9 Dec 2016
4. Louis, R., Peter, M., Jorge, A.: Information Architecture for the World Wide Web for the Web and Beyond, 4a edn, p. 400. Sebastopol, O'Reilly (2015)

5. Arango, J.: For everybody. Accessed 29 Dec 2015. http://jarango.com
6. Postman, N.: The Humanism of Media Ecology. Keynote Address Delivered at the Inaugural Media Ecology Association Convention. Fordham University, New York. http://www.media-ecology.org/publications/MEA_proceedings/v1/humanism_of_media_ecology.html. Accessed 9 Dec 2016
7. Resmini, A., Rosati, L.: Pervasive Information Architecture: Designing Cross-Channel User Experiences. Elsevier, Burlington (2011)
8. Rede, G.: http://redeglobo.globo.com/Portal/institucional/foldereletronico/. Accessed 5 Dec 2016
9. Monk, A., Wright, P., Haber, J., Davenport, L.: Improving Your Human-Computer Interface; A Practical Technique. Prentice Hall, New York (1993)
10. Brooke, J.: SUS: a retrospective. JUS – J. Usability Stud. **8**(2), 29–40 (2013). http://uxpajournal.org/sus-a-retrospective/. Accessed 15 Dec 2016
11. Sauro, J.: Measuring Usability With The System Usability Scale (SUS). http://www.measuringu.com/sus.php. Accessed 5 Dec 2016
12. Nielsen, J.: 10 usability heuristics for user interface design (1995). http://nngroup.com/articles/ten-usability-heuristics. Accessed 9 Dec 2016
13. Norman, D., Nielsen, J.: Gestural interfaces: a step backward in usability. Interactions **17**(5), 46–49 (2010)
14. Oliveira, H.P.C., Vidotti, S., Bentes, V.: Arquitetura de informação pervasiva [recurso eletrônico], 1a edn. Cultura Acadêmica, São Paulo (2015)
15. Renzi, A.B.: Experiência do usuário: a jornada de designers nos processos de gestão de suas empresas de pequeno porte utilizando sistema fantasiado em ecossistema de interação cross-channel. Doctorate thesis, 239 p. Escola Superior de Desenho Industrial. Rio de Janeiro (2016)

Simplified Thermal Comfort Evaluation on Public Busses for Performance Optimization

Guilherme Valle Loures Brandão,
Wilian Daniel Henriques do Amaral,
Caio Augusto Rabite de Almeida,
and Jose Alberto Barroso Castañon$^{(\boxtimes)}$

Universidade Federal de Juiz de Fora, Juiz de Fora, Brazil
{guilherme.loures,wilian.amaral}@engenharia.ufjf.br,
caioaugusto.arq@gmail.com, jose.castanon@ufjf.edu.br

Abstract. This paper consists on a simplified methodology proposal for thermal comfort evaluation inside short-haul urban busses using dry and wet bulb temperature readings paired with the air relative humidity and then compare each situation to a predefined comfort zone based on common literature parameters. To demonstrate the method application, readings were made in the morning, noon and late afternoon over 65 working days during late winter through mid-spring seasons in the city of Juiz de Fora – Brazil.

Keywords: Thermal comfort · Urban bus · Hygrothermal comfort · Comfort evaluation

1 Introduction

Human behavior, perception and productivity are very affected by the environmental characteristics in which an individual is inserted. Some can be controlled and adjusted but others are inherent to the local. When a certain physical environment answer the user's functional (physical and cognitive) and spatial (psychologic) needs it most certainly will have a positive impact on task fulfillment.

On public transportation vehicles, such as urban busses the vehicle heating, ventilation and air conditioning (HVAC) systems are the most flexible tools to control users comfort level and so ensuring the best environment possible to both driver and passengers inside the vehicle. According to Riachi and Clodic [1] the higher we find the occupation rate to be, more efficient air control and exchange systems are required. Thermal comfort plays an important role as per the driver under optimal conditions won't be distracted and users would be more likely to choose the bus as their way of transportation.

Urban busses environment differs from those found inside buildings, which have fixed geographical orientation and low relative occupation rates, making thermal control through ventilation openings management more effective.

A. Marcus and W. Wang (Eds.): DUXU 2017, Part III, LNCS 10290, pp. 581–593, 2017.
DOI: 10.1007/978-3-319-58640-3_42

The project for thermal comfort in automotive vehicles is one of the most important features at the conception phase and must consider variants as air flux, humidity, human and environmental heat exchanges among others [2–5]. Without this system, thermal comfort is acquired by adjusting windows and hatches for optimal airflow and therefore heat exchanges. In Brazil, notoriously famed by its tropical climate, HVAC technologies aren't systematically applied to the urban bus fleet, reason why it's so important to verify the possibility of thermal comfort status acquisition through passive solutions on heat exchanges. The regulation "ABNT NBR15570:2011 – Transport— Technical specification for vehicles of urban characteristics for public transport of passengers manufacturing" [6] oversees the urban bus characteristics and specifies the number and area of windows and other ventilation devices, allowing projects with window openings in the top, bottom or both halves.

Thermal comfort sense evaluation, considering the human body and environment interactions is a serious topic to ensure the best comfort state for both passengers and driver inside the vehicle. Several studies focus on thermal well-being on humans and a considerable amount of information is available in the literature, with most studies considering stable and uniform thermal conditions amongst the various vehicle occupants [7, 8].

In a general manner, thermal comfort can be defined a condition when the body temperature doesn't change abruptly, skin moisture is low and the physical effort to temperature regulation is at its minimum [9]. As this concept changes, accordingly to the local climate and user adaptation to the bioclimatic features, as well as their psychological and physiological factors, it is possible to define through a bioclimatic diagram – in which relations between temperature and air relative humidity are related using a local climatologic series – the hygrothermal comfort values throughout the year.

To be possible to assume a certain individual to be in a thermal comfort situation, Frota and Schiffer [10] says that some premises must be evaluated such as the subject's thermic neutrality (which consists on dissipating all the body heat to the environment throughout conductive, radiative and evaporative heat exchanges), the sweating rate and skin temperature must be under acceptable limits according to the activity in play, considering the energy needed to perform the given task and the fact that the individual must be free from stress caused by temperature differences due distinct object's heat absorption rates or wind gusts. Lamberts [11], in the other hand, uses the information provided by the ISO 7730 [12] regulation to suggest that a person dressed with regular clothes (insulation = 0.6clo) is in a comfort situation between 23 °C and 27 °C.

To Lin et al. [13] studies on urban transportation vehicles can be classified on two types: the first approach consists on tests under controlled laboratory circumstances and does allow large scale production vehicles to be studied under a variety of scenarios such as the influence of infrared radiation on windows with and without tinted films. Many regulations rely on this approach, like the ISO 14505-2:2006 [14]. In the second approach, which consists on study the thermal comfort at the field, the premise that user's behavior cannot be reproduced on laboratory controlled environments and any attempt implies on uncertainties about real-life conditions which can affect the obtained results is made. Field experiments, on the other hand, could detect and analyze physiological, psychological and behavioral variables and, therefore, can determine how certain local groups relate with the thermal environment in ways that cannot be completely covered by mathematical models of thermal balance.

The authors also found differences in the preferred way to reach a comfort status between short-haul and long-haul bus lines users. Short-haul trips have an average duration of 30 min and average speed of 40KPH and passengers usually adjust airflow to obtain thermal comfort, as opposed of long-haul trips, which last an average of 60 min at an average speed of 100KPH, where the users prefer to adjust solar incidence by opening or closing the curtains.

Even though vehicular HVAC technology has been improving rather fast over the last few years, the studied short-haul bus scenario doesn't seem to follow the trend on most cities leaving both passenger and driver under poor environmental conditions.

2 Review of Current Standards

The assessment of thermal environment inside a vehicle cabin correlates several variables and can be carried out trough different approaches. In response to these different possible evaluation forms the standards present several methodologies and procedures to obtain the most reliable results when considering the environmental and physiological variables that can be applied in predictive mathematical models which can end up in objective results or personal and psychological results that addresses the individual's perception of the environment and can vary individually [15].

The Brazilian standards for thermal comfort assessment are predominantly focused to be applied on buildings [16–18]. The ABNT NBR-15570 [6], which brings the technical specifications to produce urban vehicles with characteristics suited for public passenger transport, briefly presents design requirements and partial evaluation – as in the case of motor insulation – to achieve thermal comfort without, however, presenting a methodology for evaluating the entire environment. In the case of vehicles equipped with HVAC systems, it is possible to apply NBR 16401-2 [17] as an alternative.

When talking about international standardization, there's a significant range of standards dealing with indoor thermal environment analysis. The most used are the ISO 14505 [14, 19, 20], which deals directly with the matter applied to vehicles and the ASHRAE 55 [21], although not referring to vehicle cabin application, defines the conditions for human thermal comfort using factors such as the air relative humidity, considered as an influential factor if less than 30% or greater than 70%, and effective temperature, if less than 20 °C and greater than 24 °C [22].

Medeiros [9] indicates ISO 14505: 2007 [14, 19, 20] – Ergonomics of the thermal environment - Evaluation of thermal environments in vehicles as the most relevant in the context of the evaluation of the thermal environment in vehicles, since it is the most used worldwide by vehicle producers in the development and conformity verification of their products, reason why we will emphasize their study. The ISO 14505 [14, 19, 20] is segmented into three parts: the first one introduces the principles and methods to determine the thermal stress, the second indicates how the equivalent temperature must be determined and the third part defines how to evaluate the thermal environment through analysis of individual's subjective response.

On its first part the ISO 14505-1:2007 [19] – Principles and methods for assessment of thermal stress, it is determined that the thermal environment inside vehicles is influenced by both the climatic conditions of the external environment and the capacity of the HVAC system to act in the internal environment reducing the unfavorable effects on the influence of the external environment. The standard directs the evaluation of the internal thermal environment according to the effects verified in the conditions of heat stress, cold stress or thermal discomfort. After determining the cause of the thermal problem verified by this previous assessment it is suggested the application of subsidiary standards focused on each condition as per specific characteristics of the situation found.

On its second part, the ISO 14505-2: 2006 [14] – Determination of equivalent temperature, guidelines are presented for the evaluation of the thermal conditions inside the vehicle cabins and could be applied in the assessment of other confined spaces with asymmetric climatic conditions, focusing on the evaluation of thermal conditions in situations which deviation from the thermal neutrality is relatively small. This part is based on the determination of the equivalent temperature to verify its applicability – since it is possible to determine the relation between temperature measured in real and ideal conditions (in which, theoretically, there would be neutrality among the body and the interior environment by the sensible heat exchange between them in the same proportion) through the determination of the equivalent temperature that receives different approaches according to the objective of the evaluation. Another valid method is the application of thermal sensors in either manikins that simulate individuals or on human beings using real life clothing, dividing the body into zones that allow correct measurements in both cases. The reliability of the method should be treated with caution when skin evaporation, body transpiration and other human factors are involved.

On its third part, the ISO 14505-3: 2007 [20] – Evaluation of thermal comfort using human subjects, guidelines are given and a standard method of testing for the human perception of thermal comfort in vehicles is presented. The proposed method for evaluation is not restricted to a single vehicle style and makes possible the verification through general principles that can be used to measure and determine the performance of the thermal environment under a given condition of interest, causing it to be applied in both development and verification of product reliability. For those modals without cabins in which the user is directly exposed to the external environment, the speed of movement and the meteorological conditions may interfere excessively in the evaluations. However, the principles of this standard remain applicable and its application is also possible to passengers and operators simultaneously as it does not interfere with the safe operation of the vehicle.

After presenting the standard, it is possible to realize that although the ISO 14505 [14, 19, 20] should be used in the design phase of the vehicles and in the validation of the results obtained by researches that verify the thermal characteristics of the thermal environment inside the vehicle its application is laborious and relies on specific materials, tools and certified technicians. Due these factors, it is proposed the preliminary verification of the thermal environment through this work proposed methodology, enlightening the initial problem understanding through simplified procedures therefore facilitating the decision-making process and reducing efforts to define the nature of the problem.

3   Methodology

Based on the analysis of ISO 14505 [14, 19, 20], ASHRAE 55 [3] and NBR 15570 [6] standards, the main variants to be applied in the method were defined by its ease of measurement with simple tools or could be measured using an instrument capable of multi-variable measurements or mathematic models. The variants were defined as per below: (Table 1).

Table 1. Chosen variants

	Variant	Definition	Unit
1	Dry Bulb Temperature (DBT)	It is the temperature of air measured by a thermometer freely exposed to the air but shielded from radiation and moisture, the true thermodynamic temperature [21]	°C
2	Wet Bulb Temperature (WBT)	It is the temperature in which a parcel of air would have if it were cooled to saturation (100% relative humidity) by the evaporation of water into it, with the latent heat being supplied by the parcel [21]	°C
3	Air Relative Humidity (RH)	It is the ratio of the partial pressure of water vapor to the equilibrium vapor pressure of water at a given temperature [21]	%
4	Internal surface temperature (IST)	It is the temperature of cabin internal surfaces measured by an infrared thermometer	°C
5	Effective Temperature Index (ET)	It is a relation between Dry Bulb Temperature and Air Relative Humidity which allows the thermal comfort evaluation by a graphic plot	°C

The measurement of Dry Bulb Temperature, Wet Bulb Temperature and Air Relative Humidity (variants 1–3) can be done by a digital thermo-hygrometer with relative ease. In general, it is recommended to switch on the instrument at least 2 h before taking the measures to ensure the time needed for sensors stabilization, although this period may vary for each instrument manufacturer, as the gap between single measurements. The Internal Surface Temperature (variant 4) can be measured by a simple infrared thermometer.

Based on the measurement procedures recommended by the standards, it was decided to carry out the measurements in one point at the center of the vehicle, at a 1.10 m height from the vehicle floor, which is common to sitting or standing passengers, instead of the three heights proposed by the standards. The decision to concentrate the measuring points at the central point is based on the fact that, due to the central doors in the vehicles to apply accessibility criteria, the three standardized measurement points have similar characteristics. In this proposal, vehicle engine is considered as thermally isolated, without contributions to interior cabin heating. To ensure a more reliable result, it is recommended that the measures are made under a real travel, by the period of 30 min, taken every 5 min. These measurements can be after normalized in a mean value that will be used on calculation.

586   G.V.L. Brandão et al.

The measurement of the internal surfaces temperatures taken by the infrared thermometer allows verifying if there are significant radiant temperature influences over the other parameters. If the surfaces temperatures are close to Dry Bulb Temperature values, it could be ignored and, if they're significantly different it is recommended to report this could be an interference factor on the results. This may be used as an additional data once the measurement of the real radiant temperature depends of a Black Body Thermometer, which makes no sense when talking of a simplified methodology.

After the proposed measurements were taken, it is suggested to use the Effective Temperature Index calculated and the Air Relative Humidity value to cross-check the data. The Effective Temperature Index (variant 5) can be calculated by Eq. (1), the Nieuwolt equation [21].

$$ET = DBT - [0.55 * (1 - 0.01RH) * (DBT - 14.5)] \tag{1}$$

In which:
ET   – Effective Temperature Index
DBT   – Dry Bulb Temperature
RH   – Air Relative Humidity

After calculating the Effective Temperature Index the results can be plotted on a graphic that correlates RH and ET. Although its subjective character and wide matter discussion, the proposed comfort zone will remain between Effective Temperature 20 °C to 24 °C and Air Relative Humidity 30% to 70%, once they could be considered as restrictive values. The comfort zone is illustrated on Fig. 1.

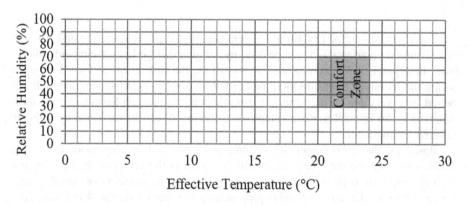

Fig. 1. ET – RH comfort zone

In purpose of simplifying the methodology, the influence of the activity was deliberately disregarded, considering the users in rest and thermal equilibrium with the environment and not considering the interference of the clothing in the thermoregulation of the organism.

4   Application

The method was tested by taking measurements inside a bus used to transport students inside the Federal University of Juiz de Fora (UFJF) campus. This vehicle shares the same model as the other city busses found in Juiz de Fora city – Brazil, as well as the same seat and window configuration plus have a fixed daily route and schedule. The bus, as all other Juiz de Fora city urban busses does not have a HVAC system, relying only on window management to achieve thermal comfort.

It is important to say that according to ABNT [16] Juiz de Fora city is included under the bioclimatic zone 3, which corresponds to a highland tropical climate, showing slight lower mean temperatures as found in a typical tropical climate region, this is due the altitude difference. Juiz de Fora also is known for high thermal amplitudes during the day. Although occurring throughout the whole year, precipitation is more intense during late winter and mid spring seasons.

Measurements were taken at 08h00m, 12h00m and 17h00m on every day for 65 working days in between September 1st and November 30th 2016. Each trip had an average time of 30 min and measurements were made every 5 min (Fig. 2).

Fig. 2. Bus route inside the campus (Color figure online)

During the trip, with the route illustrated in red on Fig. 2, variables 1 through 4 (described in Table 1) were simultaneously measured using an ICEL TD-990 infrared thermometer and an Instrutherm HTR-157 digital thermohygrometer. The infrared readings showed the bus internal surface temperatures quite near the dry bulb air temperatures, and therefore allowing the radiant temperature effects to be neglected without highlighting its possible influences within the thermal environment. After the measurements, the obtained values were normalized and organized in a graph which corresponds to the relations between DBT, WBT and RH, as shown below: (Fig. 3).

At 08h00m is possible to verify high RH rates while the temperatures remain relatively low. This situation is due the local climate factor added the fact it's the beginning of spring in the southern hemisphere and therefore the rain season, that falls mostly during the night keeping the RH high until the middle of the mornings (Fig. 4).

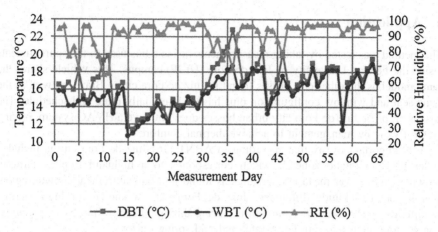

Fig. 3. 08h00m series measurement

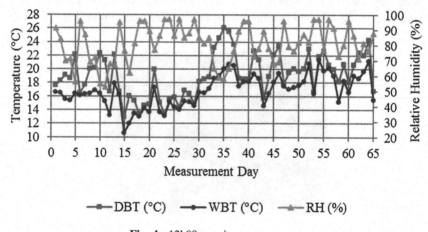

Fig. 4. 12h00m series measurement

By noon, the high temperature and RH rate variation became more evident, as well as the temperature increase with the summer approach. The verified situation is due the higher solar incidence which increase the temperatures, some sparse rain occurrence increasing RH rates on a few days, while on other days it is possible to perceive a drastic reduction when compared to the 08h00m readings. The increased distance between DBT and WBT readings is mainly due this reduction in RH (Fig. 5).

At 17h00m it's possible to verify an overall raise in temperatures and a further reduction on RH due to the increase in solar incidence and the higher temperatures. The variations between DBT and WBT are caused by the lower RH measured with a few peaks due sparse rains in the end of the afternoon.

With all the data acquired and in possession of the Nieuwolt equation previously described, the effective temperature index calculation was possible. These calculations were done to all three series of data as presented in the following images: (Figs. 6, 7 and 8).

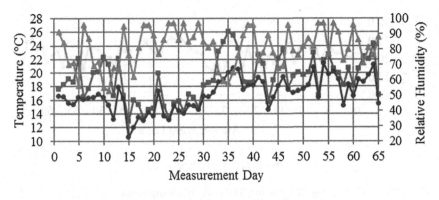

Fig. 5. 17h00m series measurement

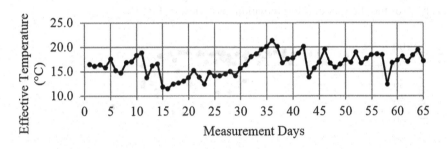

Fig. 6. 08h00m series effective temperatures

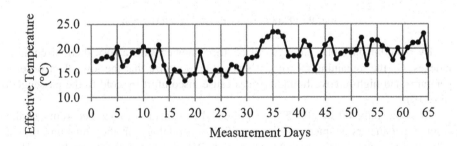

Fig. 7. 12h00m series effective temperatures

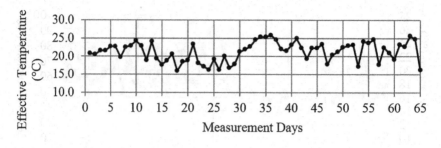

Fig. 8. 17h00m series effective temperatures

After comparing each effective temperature for a given day and time with its relative humidity rates, the graph presented on Fig. 1 could be populated for a better analysis of the thermal comfort situation, as follows: (Fig. 9).

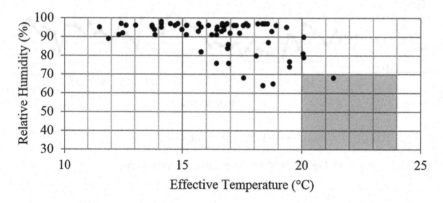

Fig. 9. 08h00m series thermal comfort graph

By 08h00m only one amongst all 65 trips showed satisfactory thermal comfort indexes. On the remaining 64 trips, it's possible to realize that the low effective temperatures and high relative humidity rates cause discomfort by cold to the passengers (Fig. 10).

At noon, only 09 of all 65 trips presented satisfactory values according to the comfort parameters adopted in this simplified methodology. In the remaining trips a cold discomfort can be perceived when high RH and low ET are combined. Heat discomfort is found when high RH and comfortable ET values occur, giving the passengers a fug sensation (Fig. 11).

The biggest comfortable situation found in this survey occurred in the end of the afternoon, when 28 out of 65 trips presented ET and RH readings amongst the adopted comfort parameters. In this scenario, cold discomfort is caused by low ET readings and high RH, while heat discomfort is caused by high RH readings at comfortable ET readings and high RH readings paired with high ET values.

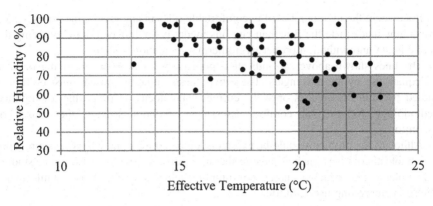

Fig. 10. 12h00m series thermal comfort graph

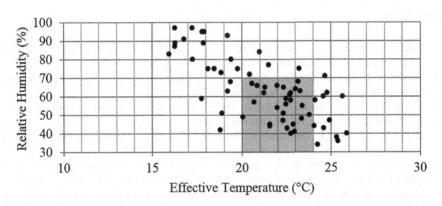

Fig. 11. 17h00m series thermal comfort graph

5   Conclusions

Analyzing the results presented in the previous section, a table containing the absolute number of comfortable and uncomfortable trips was formulated and presented as follows: (Table 2).

Table 2. Comfort rates by each measurement series

Time	Trips	Comfortable trips	Comfortable trips (%)	Uncomfortable trips	Uncomfortable trips (%)
08:00	65	1	1.5	64	98.5
12:00	65	9	13.8	56	86.2
17:00	65	28	43.1	37	56.9

It's evident the high number of uncomfortable rides in any given time series, which shows how inadequate the Brazilian city bus model is for Juiz de Fora City facing the local climate and without a proper hygrothermal regulation system.

The rates shown above can indicate a poor open window dimensioning or even inadequate use by the passengers. These hypothesis, although raised, must be further studied by future researches once the current paper focus on proposing a simplified methodology for thermal comfort assessment, without seeking the causes of discomfort.

Although the problems could be extinguished by adopting an HVAC system, more sustainable alternatives, such as passive shading and ventilation devices, can be studied and implemented reducing energy consumption and operator expenses while maintaining or improving user comfort.

References

1. Riachi, Y., Clodic, D.: A numerical model for simulating thermal comfort prediction in public transportation buses. Int. J. Environ. Prot. Policy 2(1), 1–8 (2014)
2. Fanger, P.O.: Thermal Comfort: Analysis and Applications in Environmental Engineering. McGraw-Hill Book Company, New York (1972)
3. ASHRAE.: Fundamentals Handbook. American Society of Heating, Ventilating and Air-Conditioning Engineers. Atlanta, USA (2001)
4. Danca, P., Vartiresa, A., Dogeanua, A.: An overview of current methods for thermal comfort assessment in vehicle cabin. Energy Procedia 85, 162–169 (2016)
5. Körbahti, B., Kucur, M., Kaykayoglu, C.R.: An innovative computational model of the thermal comfort conditions in city/inter-city buses. In: ECCOMAS 2000 - European Congress on Computational Methods in Applied Sciences and Engineering, pp. 11–14, Barcelona (2000)
6. Associação Brasileira de Normas Técnicas.: NBR 15570: Transporte - Especificações técnicas para fabricação de veículos de características urbanas para transporte coletivo de passageiros. ABNT, Rio de Janeiro (2011)
7. Ivanescu, M., Neacsu, C.A., Tabacu, I.: Studies of the thermal comfort inside of the passenger compartment using the numerical simulation. In: International Congress Motor Vehicles & Motors 2010, Kragujevac, pp. 7–9 (2010)
8. Pala, U., Oz, H.R.: An investigation of thermal comfort inside a bus during heating period within a climatic chamber. Appl. Ergon. 48, 164–176 (2015)
9. Medeiros, E.G.S.: Estudo Termoambiental em Viaturas Utilizadas nos Serviços de Radiopatrulhamento no Estado da Paraíba. Masters degree thesis, Universidade Federal da Paraíba (2014)
10. Frota, A.B., Schiffer, S.R.: Manual de Conforto Térmico: Arquitetura. Urbanismo. Studio Nobel, São Paulo (2001)
11. Lamberts, R.: Conforto e Stress Térmico. Technical report, Universidade Federal de Santa Catarina Civil Engineering Department (2014)
12. International Organization for Standardization.: ISO 7730: Moderate thermal environments - Determination of the PMV and PPD indices and specification of the conditions for thermal comfort. ISO, Geneva (2005)

13. Lin, T., Hwang, R., Huang, K., Sun, C., Huang, Y.: Passenger thermal perceptions, thermal comfort requirements and adaptations in short and long-haul vehicles. Int. J. Biometeorol. **54**, 221–230 (2010)
14. International Organization for Standardization.: ISO 14505-2: Ergonomics of the thermal environment – Evaluation of thermal environments in vehicles. Part 2: determination of equivalent temperature. ISO, Geneva (2006)
15. Ormuž, K., Muftić, O.: Main ambient factors influencing passenger vehicle comfort. In: Proceedings of 2nd International Ergonomics Conference, Zegreb, pp. 21–22 (2004)
16. e diretrizes construtivas para habitações unifamiliares de interesse social. ABNT, Rio de Janeiro (2005)
17. Associação Brasileira de Normas Técnicas.: NBR 16401: Instalações de ar-condicionado – sistemas centrais e unitários. ABNT, Rio de Janeiro (2008)
18. Associação Brasileira de Normas Técnicas.: NBR 15575: Edificações Habitacionais – Desempenho. ABNT, Rio de Janeiro (2013)
19. International Organization for Standardization.: ISO 14505-1: Ergonomics of the thermal environment – Evaluation of thermal environments in vehicles. Part 1: Principles and methods for assessment of thermal stress. ISO, Geneva (2007)
20. International Organization for Standardization.: ISO 14505-3: Ergonomics of the thermal environment – Evaluation of thermal environments in vehicles. Part 3: Evaluation of thermal comfort using human subjects. ISO, Geneva (2007)
21. ANSI/ASHRAE.: Standard 55: Thermal Environment Conditions for Human Occupancy (2013)
22. Zhou, Q.: Thermal comfort in vehicles. Technical report, Faculty of Engineering and Sustainable Development (2013)
23. Dunlop, S.: A Dictionary of Weather. Oxford University Press, Oxford (2008)

Shaping the Experience of a Cognitive Investment Adviser

Heloisa Candello[1(✉)], Claudio Pinhanez[1], David Millen[2],
and Bruna Daniele Andrade[1]

[1] IBM Research, São Paulo, Brazil
{heloisacandello, csantosp}@br.ibm.com,
bandrade2@gmail.com
[2] IBM Watson, Cambridge, MA, USA
david_r_millen@us.ibm.com

Abstract. In this paper we describe the design process of a multi-bot conversational system to assist people to make more informed decisions about finance. Several user activities were held to understand the experience of investment decisions, the opportunities to design financial cognitive advisers, and the user perceptions of such systems. Valuable information was gathered from four user studies which assisted the project team to decide what would be the best approach to help people to make more informed decisions about investments using technology. The user studies findings highlighted that financial decisions are made based on information people receive from friends, news, and social networks, which led us to explore intelligent systems that would gather such information and play the role of financial advisers in a multiparty conversational system. We discuss the main design implications of our studies in the context of a prototype called *CognIA* and conclude discussing several challenges of designing conversational systems.

Keywords: Conversational interfaces · Dialogue systems · Multiparty dialogue · User experience

1 Introduction

Our main research focus is the often-blurred connections between human and machines which result in better decision-making. Every day people make decisions based on information they receive from social networks, news, and friends. Nowadays intelligent machines are starting to take the space of advisers informing or (not) informing us to make better or worse decisions. Intelligent advisers are known by various names such as virtual personal assistants, intelligent assistants, or cognitive advisers. They are present in several areas, such as health, well-being, finance, commerce, and education to mention some. In certain contexts, such as finance, the challenge to design for those systems is even bigger since private information is shared by humans with machines and trust is essential in those contexts.

Many technological advances in the early 2010s in natural language processing (spearheaded by the *IBM Watson*'s victory in *Jeopardy*) spurred the availability in the early 2010s of text-based chatbots in websites and apps (notably in China [1]) and

A. Marcus and W. Wang (Eds.): DUXU 2017, Part III, LNCS 10290, pp. 594–613, 2017.
DOI: 10.1007/978-3-319-58640-3_43

spoken speech interfaces such as *Siri* and *Cortana*. However, the absolute majority of those chatbot deployments were in contexts of *dyadic dialog*, that is, a conversation between a single conversational agent with a single user.

Human-computer interaction, in practice, has also been mostly about dyadic interaction since the dawn of computer systems in 1950s. The two dominant interaction paradigms, *command-line* and *point-and-click*, are both not well suited for multi-user interaction (one application with more than one user engaged in the same activity) or multi-app interaction (one user interacting seamlessly with more than one application), and even more for generic multiparty applications (many users and many bots simultaneously). Notably exceptions are surface interaction and multi-user games but the mainstream of human interaction with computers remains one-to-one.

In this sense, conversational interfaces powered by chatbots are an important breakthrough from the past of computer interaction because they naturally enable multiparty applications. By exploiting the many social protocols human had developed for multi-person conversations since the advent of language, conversation-based interfaces may finally break from the dyadic paradigm in computer interaction.

In this paper, we consider a scenario of wealth management where advice is provided by multiple chatbots. We highlight our design process and several design activities undertaken with potential users with limited financial knowledge to understand their rational when making investment decisions. The information gathered from user studies assisted us to define and refine the concept and graphical user interface of a financial adviser. We then explore opportunities to use this knowledge in the context of a multiparty dialogue system called *CognIA* (Cognitive Investment Adviser) which is a chat system aiming to help users with low knowledge of finances to take more informed decisions about their investments.

2 The Design Process and the Role of User Studies

The specific methods and tools used in this research were detailed and organized according to the main stages of the *Design Research* methodology [2, 3]. An overview of the design process is depicted in Fig. 1. As we see, the beginning of the design process was guided by user experience studies supported by theories, competitors' analysis of financial advisers, and technology availability and its constraints. We explain in detail the different methodologies, processes, and findings in the remainder of the paper.

Notice that at the beginning of the process there were no pre-selected form for the finance advising system: the decision to use a conversational system was a result of the overall design process. Although many aspects and activities were performed, the key components of the design process were four user studies we conducted to explore the needs of our users and, later, the nuances of human-machine interaction which informed the design of our conversational system *CognIA*. The aim of the user studies was threefold: understanding the everyday practices which prevent people to make better investment decisions; exploring how a system could be to help people to make more conscious investment decisions; and designing the basic information for the future system to work (the language/knowledge corpus used in the conversational system).

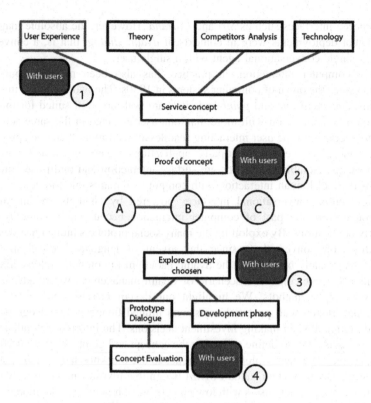

Fig. 1. Design process of CognIA

CognIA is targeted to investors who have limited knowledge of finance (and often not willingly to spend time learning it) but nevertheless would like to make good investments. We focused on people younger than 40 years old, well-educated, and with medium-high income. As reported by previous research [4] most Brazilians in this segment (about 70%) save money in basic, low-yield savings accounts, instead of investing in other financial products available.

Some of those products have returns much better than savings accounts, low risk, and reasonable liquidity, so many investors fail to make money simply due to lack of information. We recruited participants with those characteristics for our qualitative user studies, marked in Fig. 1 as "With users". The first user study aimed to understand financial practices, motivation stoppers to invest, and interaction channels to make investments (circle "1" in Fig. 1). The second user study focused on testing user preference concepts (circle "2" in Fig. 1). Users evaluated three service concepts envisioned by the project team. A concept based on an intelligent financial adviser was chosen by the design team based on the results of the second study. But further explorations were needed to design an intelligent financial adviser which led to the third user study (circle "3" in Fig. 1). Questions such as: How people would add data into the system? How people would interact with the system and receive feedback? Which kind of interaction modes are more suitable for our target audience?

Results of those preliminary activities guided the designers of the project team to design a graphical user interface for *CognIA*, envisioned as a multiparty dialogue system. An animated video demo which demonstrated how the application would work was created to guide our multi-disciplinary team to develop the UI. The video was a reference for discussions on interaction flow and visual design decisions in the team meetings. In parallel to system development, designers evaluated the first impressions of the system by potential users (circle "4" in Fig. 1). A video-card perception technique was employed to gather first impressions from users. This technique is a mix of using our video demo as scenario and the reaction card method.

In the next sessions, we explain with more details of our design research stages and how design activities were conducted and assisted us on project decisions and directions. But before going into the details of the design process, it is important to understand that our design challenges are bedded in the general context of how people make economical and finance decisions, an area often known by the term *Behavior Economics*.

3 Behavior Economics and Finance

For this project, we were informed by social science theories which could help us understand financial behavior and investment decision-making. In particular the work of [5] known as *Prospect Theory* was extremely helpful to us. Prospect Theory is based on four key elements: reference dependence, loss aversion, diminishing sensitivity, and probability weighting. Briefly, *reference dependence* is based on observations that people derive utility (value) from gains or losses relative to a specific reference point. Thus, individuals assess the outcome of a financial decision relative to a current value (e.g., current value of an investment). *Loss aversion* describes the asymmetry in sensitivity which people experience between loses and gains. Individuals are significantly more sensitive to a loss of a specific amount than to a gain of the same amount. *Diminishing sensitivity* and *probability weighting* describe how people behave unreasonably at the extremes of the value distribution.

There have been several attempts to exploit some of these principles in financial systems and interfaces. For example, [6] attempted, with mixed results, to overcome loss aversion by presenting more explicitly and detailed risk assessments and expected returns for financial investment decisions. [7] explored the influence of both few financial thought leaders and aggregated crowd choices on the investment decisions of older adults. They found that individuals who took aggregated crowd choices into account were able to make less risky investment decisions. [8] created an investment interface that highlighted potential losses (and gains) and motivated changes to investment allocations to minimize future losses. They effectively demonstrated that by appealing to loss aversion tendencies they could motivate investment changes.

For our purposes, we considered how to reasonably *frame* the investment decision and outcome so the user would have a frame of reference for the expected (or actual) gain or loss. We also considered design alternatives for presenting investment losses and gains to remedy the decision bias associated with loss aversion.

4 First User Study: Understanding Financial Decisions

Having explored the general decision framework of behavior economics, we start the description of our design process by describing the first user study which aimed to understand people's perceptions and their attitudes towards investment decisions and how they manifest themselves in practice. Additionally, the outcomes of this study oriented team discussions by considering real issues and situations reported by participants. The study consisted of a set of semi-structured interviews which were carried out to understand everyday practices, motivation stoppers, and interaction channels to make investments.

Participants. Twelve participants aged from 29 to 43 years old were interviewed. All the participants were Brazilians. Five were men and seven were women, and four participants had children. All the participants had a university degree and premium bank accounts in Brazil (clients with medium, high income).

Method. Twelve semi-structured interviews were conducted in May of 2015 taking approximately 20–30 min each. Participants were initially recruited by a snowball sample. A consent form was filled out by participants before the study started. The semi-structured interviews covered open-ended questions about the participants' past investments decisions, factors they consider when making investment choices, and sources they consult before investing. The interview also included a practical question about investments: *"If you had R$ 20.000,00 to invest, which type of investment you would do and why?"* All the sessions were audio-recorded and researchers took notes during the interviews.

Data Analysis. An exploratory and qualitative approach was undertaken to conduct the data analysis. The data was analyzed having three research questions as guidance: (1) What are the most common investments of participants? (2) What are their challenges when deciding where to invest? (3) Which kind of people and/or information sources they consult to know more about investments? The data was coded after semi-structured interviews and audio transcriptions. Categories emerged from the data and relationships emerged between the categories. This process was facilitated using *NVivo* software.

Findings. The most common investment types of our participants are savings accounts and fixed income investments (for example, treasury bonds known as *CDB* and *DI*). Ten participants considered themselves "conservative" investors, and not having enough knowledge of investing. Two participants, the ones who considered themselves as "moderate" investors, have used professional financial advisers in the past and had already taken elementary financial education. Two participants had lost money in the stock market previously and admitted they did not have enough knowledge and confidence to do this kind of investment. Most of our participants seem to overweight risk over returns. The ones who invested in fixed income investments followed advice from their bank managers or family and friends. Some of the challenges our participants faced when deciding to invest are described below with quotes from our participants:

Lack of Knowledge – Financial education is not a priority for our participants. Also, families do not pass information of how to invest to other family members, since money a private issue of which people do not talk about frequently. Bank managers are the main source of information but they are regarded by our participants as vendors. Participants sometimes rely on their advices in case of fixed income investment, or leave their money in less profitable and popular investments such as savings accounts. Bank managers also use terms and jargons which some of our participants are not familiar with ("risk protection", "liabilities", "liquidity"). In our participants' opinions, bank managers usually have a restrict portfolio of investments to offer and there is no *"transparency in relation to taxes and return" (P4)*. They also mention that good bank managers do not show only the good investment options but also talk about the ones which are less profitable.

Lack of Time and Interest – Our participants do not feel attracted by financial information, most of them find boring to look for information in this area or to read it. Moreover, most of them think investing will be time consuming – *"I have friends who are slaves of their investments" (P6)*. Occasionally, participants prefer to follow an advice of which they are not aware of all the constraints due lack of time to monitor investments, interest, and/or motivation. Financial information sounds complicated and difficult to them *"It is very difficult to know how do I make money investing." (P3)*.

Emergency Funds and Liquidity – All the participants mentioned the necessity to have an emergency fund in case they need of cash. Single participants usually save money for travelling and leisure. Married participants with children usually save money for a future home purchase, eventualities, and family holidays.

Communication Channels – Bank managers usually contact our participants by phone, often in commercial hours. This is considered disrupting and annoying by our participants since talking about an investment portfolio is a private matter not to be discussed at work and also because they are not available to talk at the moment of the call. They prefer to receive e-mails than calls from the banks.

The most common information source participants consult before making an investment are family and friends with experience in investing. Trust was a big issue for our participants, and the lack of trust on bank managers sometimes results on choosing not so profitable investment choices. Four participants also rely on news and financial websites to validate options suggested by bank managers or family and friends. Even though, those four participants focus their reading on investments they were not confident to better compare with the other investments.

5 Designing the Service Concept

Having determined the key financial needs, issues, and worries of people in the target segment and understood deeper the rich mental and behavior processes involved in financial decision making, we proceed with a design phase whose aim was to determine the best approaches to serve the needs of this population. It is important to notice that we are not simply interested in designing a computer system which could support investors. Our approach was to look to the problem holistically and target the designing of a *service* to be provided by a financial institutional or similar, including how it would be created and maintained, its business model, the flow of information, and its support systems.

In other words, it was a problem of *service design*, albeit with a strong IT component. After looking into different methodologies used in service design as described [9–12], we decided to use the notion of *service concept* as the central structuring element of this design phase. Edvardsson describes the service concept as *"a detailed description of the customer needs to be satisfied, how they are to be satisfied, what is to be done for the customer, and how this is to be achieved."* [13].

Based on this framework we researched and explored different innovative ideas and models which were being proposed in the finance landscape around 2015, as well as performed some ideation sessions, aiming to collect different service concepts (existing, planned, or futuristic) which could be a solution to our design goal. The result was a list of 10 service concepts which included services based on cognitive advising systems, social wisdom platforms, finance learning systems, etc. As a way to visualize and better compare the service concepts, we mapped them according to the source of the financial knowledge employed by the system, which could be the user, experts, wisdom-of-the-crowd, or from a machine. Figure 2 shows this mapping and the relative position of the 10 service concepts.

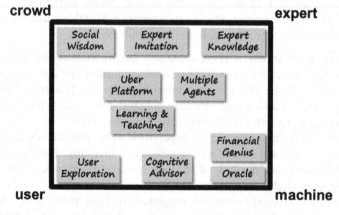

Fig. 2. The 10 service concepts mapped according to the source of finance knowledge used by the system.

To compare and select the most promising candidates for the next phase of the design process, we analyzed each service concept according to four dimensions: quality of *user experience*, matching to economic and finance *user behavior models*, level of maturity of the *supporting technology* required, and the number of players in the *competitive landscape*. This analysis was performed by four different individuals in the group who were experts in the corresponding area.

User Exploration

	Good	Bad	Ugly
User Experience	allows trial & error allows learning integration of information	interactive financial simulator can overwhelm people too much work for users	requires financial literacy personalization to literacy level lack of expert to trust
User Behavior Models		hard to overcome cognitive bias	
Technology	Watson Explorer APIs journalistic data published	financial data search engine financial reasoning models temporal reasoning	
Competitive Landscape	not really something as nicely aggregated out there	lots of similar stuff which people do not use	

Fig. 3. Table showing the result of the *Good/Bad/Ugly analysis* for the service concept *User Exploration*.

To collect the analysis in a comparable format, we employed a technique we call the *Good/Bad/Ugly* analysis[1]. For each service concept and dimension we listed its positive aspects (*The Good*), negative aspects (*The Bad*), and possible road blocks (*The Ugly*). Figure 3 shows the resulting table for a service concept where the user can explore freely financial terms, concepts, and products. Using the Good/Bad/Ugly tables created for each service concept, the four experts discussed and compared the different concepts and selected three of them as the most promising:

- **User Exploration:** a finance information aggregation system where all kinds of financial information (markets, social media, simulators) could be searched and explored freely by the user.
- **Expert Knowledge:** a human advisers-based system where the user could watch videos and read opinions from experts and celebrity investors, combined with some level of automatic personality and profile matching.
- **Cognitive Adviser:** an intelligent system able to match investment needs to products with support for user exploration through question-and-answer and provision of evidences and opinions to support financial decisions.

Having found three service concepts with enough potential and feasibility, it became clear that to go further in the design process we would need to have user feedback not on the service concepts but on actual realizations of them.

6 Second User Study: Exploring Service Concept Mockups

We then quickly proceeded to develop basic *mockups* of the service concepts, wireframe prototypes with sample interactions for each of the three service concepts selected in the previous design phase. Figure 4 shows sample screens from each of them.

---

[1] Inspired by 1966 Sergio Leone's classic western *The Good, The Bad, and The Ugly*.

Fig. 4. Sample screens of the mockups built for the three service concepts: user exploration (left), expert knowledge (middle), and cognitive adviser (right).

To perform a user evaluation of the three mockups, a qualitative, inductive and interpretative approach was taken in which we employed the foundational theoretical ideas about how people make investment decisions and access financial information sources emerged from preliminary user studies and the previous design research activities. In other words, as well as delivering requirements for such a system, these activities generated issues about the different design parameters – interaction mode and flow, layout, navigation system, activity type, information design and many more – for which recommendations were generated. The main goal of the second design study was to gather user's impressions of three different mockups and to identify which aspects people expect from financial advisers supported by technology.

Participants. Fifteen participants aged from 26 to 40 years old participated in the study. All the participants were Brazilians. Seven were men and eight were women, and only one participant had children. All the participants have a university degree and premium bank accounts in Brazil (clients with medium, high-income). Participants were from diverse backgrounds and most of them had savings accounts. According to them savings accounts have a high liquidity and for this reason was the preferred investment choice. The majority preferred to use Internet and mobile banking and rarely would go to a bank branch. The ones who preferred to go to the branch bank would do so to withdraw money or to make financial transactions. Those considered going to the bank safer than doing online transactions.

Methods. In the lab sessions participants interacted with the three mockups guided by a scenario and answered questions with answers ranked by a *Likert scale*. The study took approximately 45 min for each participant. The moderator made clear that researchers were interested to know about the concepts and not keen on evaluating graphic design features. First, participants answered demographic questions and commented their previous investments experiences. Participants read aloud the scenario and then started the interaction with the mockups:

Scenario: *Consider you have an income of R$10.000,00 and you just received R $25.000,00 as bonus. You want to buy a new house (or car) to replace your older one in about 2 years. Your plan is not to use this money before 2 years. You need some help* *deciding which kind of investment is the best for you. Therefore, you are testing some investment apps.*

Each interactive mockup illustrated one service concept and it was used as a *prop* to foster discussions with participants. In the first mockup users explored a tag cloud containing investment names with links to financial websites. In the second, an intelligent assistant based on the user's profile provided best investment choices with levels of confidence. The third was an interactive knowledge map which users could explore by interacting with topics and listening to audio samples from a celebrity human financial adviser. Participants were exposed to the three mockups counterbalanced. Participants were asked to think aloud and report their choice of investment after experiencing each mockup. For each mockup interaction, participants were asked to describe how they thought that mockup works and their expectation for the service offered by it. Additionally, they answered a Likert 5-point scale regarding 7 statements. They also were encouraged to give their rational choices while filling out the Likert scale. At the end of the study, participants were encouraged to compare the concepts and report their preferences.

Data Analysis. A qualitative approach was undertaken to conduct the data analysis. The data was analyzed with the aim to elucidate user preferences of design concepts and key facts that might affect financial decisions. The Likert scale was analyzed and served as a source to understand participants rational and concept choices. The data was coded after the user sessions and audio transcriptions. Categories emerged from the data and relationships emerged between the categories. This process was facilitated using *NVivo* software.

Findings. The main categories affecting financial decisions were: family opinions, lack of trust in bank managers and government, debts, and having or not children. Three of our participants were planning to have children, therefore their opinions tended to be more conservative. Other factors also affected how people share their service concept preferences: lack of experience with investments, previous experiences with investments, knowing the source of information, and expectation to validate information offered by our service concepts. Regarding each mockup, the following summarizes the findings:

User Exploration – Participants with more motivation and experience with previous investments preferred this option. Others with low knowledge of investments evaluated this option overwhelming, due to information overload, and likely time consumed. Participants also found this option an incentive to learn about investments while accessing the financial webpages links. This option also inspired credibility because of the variety of information sources.

Expert Knowledge – People not keen on investments do not like to spend time reading and investigating about investments. In our participant words *"It's straightforward, does not make me go around and search like the other one (UE)"*. Also, most of the participants considered this option narrow and biased in one expert opinion. All the participants said that they would validate investment options suggested in this concept with friends and family. The ones who know the expert valued this option with higher degree. It was also evident the importance of having up-to-date information in this option more than on the others.

Cognitive Adviser – Participants with no previous experience with investments, except savings accounts, preferred this option. It was considered more straightforward than other options. They appreciated building their profile in collaboration with the system by choosing pictures which would match their profiles. For some participants, it is not transparent knowing the reasons why they are categorized by the banks as conservative, moderate, or aggressive investors. Although, this option was the preferred of our target audience, it was also considered less trustful than other options because it lacked data source transparency.

In our participant's views, all the service concepts should have detailed information of output values, including tax deductions. They also wanted more types of investments to help comparison. Moreover, information sources should be up-to-date and this should be more explicit in the service concept interfaces (e.g., showing the update date). Information curation and ownership was also highlighted as paramount to have knowledge of and as an issue to affect investment decisions. Overall, people with low financial knowledge preferred the intelligent assistant concept while people with some financial knowledge preferred exploring web sources. Most of our participants found narrow and not appealing the expert knowledge option, they argued the need for more than one adviser perspective. Most of participants preferred not having this kind of service being directly offered by banks due to information bias. Based on the results of this user study the project team decided that the most promising direction was the Cognitive Adviser, augmented by some ideas from the other service concepts which have received high praise from the participants of the study.

7   *CognIA*: A Cognitive Investment Adviser

Having converged the design process towards a conversational advising system, we start exploring the advantages and challenges of the approach. A key concern of the design team was how to build a system which inspired trust from its users. We had identified in the user studies the propensity of participants to see the advice of their bank managers and financial advisers as biased by a selling proposition. Concerned that the same problem would affect the perception of the advice provided by a machine, and inspired by some appearing automatic debating systems, we decided to take an approach where the user would converse not with a single chatbot but with multiple advisers, each advocating for a particular financial product, in a dialogue moderated by a trusted, non-partisan financial adviser.

Following this concept, we developed *CognIA* which is a multi-bot conversational system which helps people to make better investment decisions. In the current version three bots participate in the same dialogue with the user. *Cognia* is also the name of the agent which moderates the conversation; *SavingsGuru* is an agent which answers questions about savings accounts; and *CDBGuru* is an agent which answers questions related to CDB investments (a kind of treasury bond). A multi-bot platform, called

Sabia, is used to define the entities, relationships, and behaviors needed for the creation of coordinated chatbots which react or pro-actively act using natural dialogue.

The interaction starts with the *Cognia* agent which asks basic questions about the user needs. Then the *Cognia* agent can invite one or more chatbots in the chat into the conversation considering appropriate investments for the user. *Cognia* is able to redirect the topics based on the user's utterances and to enforce that the chatbots only send allowed messages. The *CognIA* visual/interaction design process has been informed by the design activities described in the last section. The questions embodied in the system and their intents were gathered from the results of the *Wizard of Oz* study described in the next section. The answers were composed based on financial websites and financial experts' posts. Then a concept video was produced to guide the design and deployment of *CognIA*.

8   Third User Study: Discovering Conversation Patterns

This experiment was designed to examine user dialogues mediated by a cognitive investment advisor using the *Wizard of Oz* technique [14, 15]. Participants believed they were interacting with a functional system. Fifteen user sessions were conducted in October 2015. Participants were invited to test a "the first version" of an intelligent financial adviser dialogue that could answer questions related to two kinds of investments: Savings accounts and a fixed-income investment called CDB (Bank Deposit Certificate). Participants followed a Wizard of OZ protocol. The user tests were remote and took approximately 30–40 min. The main data gathered were notes, audio and video recordings (screen captures). Participants were young adults (26 to 43 years old), highly educated and high-income bracket. All the participants described themselves as not interested or not keen on finances, particularly investments. All the participants answered positively to the consent form document, allowing us to use the data gathered.

Procedure. Participants were recruited by a snowball sampling [16] and invited to be part of the remote study. The sessions started with demographic questions and questions of their financial investment experiences. Following that, they shared their screen with the researcher and started interacting with the chat mock up, the supposed Intelligent Financial adviser. A human operator, that was not the same as the researcher facilitating the user session, answered their questions using a protocol. The human operator used a small table of content to answer the questions. The table was composed of 36 small paragraphs extracted from popular financial websites. The content relied on investment definitions, pros (return) and cons (risk) of two types of investments. Every table cell had a label (e.g. interest, safety, minimum value) to help the operator find the questions quickly during the sessions. The human operator could use sample answers in case she did not have an answer (1.I don't know; 2. Ask again please; 3. I don't have enough information). In the end of the session, the facilitator asked the participants to give their impressions about the system and disclosure the identity of the intelligent system.

Data Gathering and Analysis. Lightweight and heavyweight analyses were the approaches to analyze the data [17]. The lightweight analysis consisted in an affinity cluster extracted from notes and offered guidelines for the main categories to look for in the audio transcriptions. In the heavyweight analysis, the Nivivo software was used to analyze the data. Notes, Chat transcriptions and videos were analyzed. Categories from the affinity cluster phase were used as a base to analyze Chat transcriptions and video transcriptions. Videos were mainly a source for understanding why people wrote some questions for the Financial advisor. For example, sometimes people repeated a question, or rephrase a question before write the question and not always they typed what they wanted to know. Some reactions and contextual information were only possible to gather from watching some sessions again.

Findings. The main results were a categorization of questions, a set of questions of each investment (Savings and CDBs) and 18 design recommendations. Overall, 125 questions were gathered: 86 questions about CDB investments and 39 questions about Savings. The main categories of information for both investments were: definitions; advantages and disadvantages to invest; simulation of values and profitability; liquidity, fees; and risk (Table 1). Questions were asked in an informal language, although participants usually reframed their question thinking aloud before writing. Some participants were not sure if the system would understand them, for example: punctuation marks. Others expected the system would know Acronyms and main jargon from investments. In occasions, they received a negative answer from the system they were usually upset but forgiving. They also repeated variations of the same question when they did not get a satisfactory answer from the system (human operator). Additionally, results provided insights and recommendations for designing our prototypes of chat-based cognitive investment advisors. It also provided the first corpus for *CognIA*.

Table 1. Examples of categories and questions extracted from the study

Categories	Sample question	
Definition	What are the types of CDB?	Quais são as modalidades de investimento CDB?
Advantages and disadvantages	What are the advantages to invest on CDB?	Quais são os pontos contra para investir em cdb?

9 Visual Design and Graphical User Interface

The graphical interface design paradigm was created based on the familiarity of our participants with conversational apps such as *WhatsApp* and *Skype* and behavioral theories. The visual identity was designed to reach the audience of our project. A mood board, a semantic panel with graphical elements (colors, typefaces, shapes) with perceptual aspects gathered from the user studies, were created to guide the visual design. Graphical elements were added to the chat interface to create the sense of multiparty dialogue, such as: icons of the agents, location of icons on the screen, distinct colors for each agent. Visual comparison and calculation features were considered essential features by design activities participants and were added to the system. Several interaction modes were included into GUI inspired by behavioral theories.

Mood boards are collections of images to represent concepts, sensations in response to a product or service. It is an instrument for designers to communicate with each other and with the clients and the project team [18, 19]. Designers working as part of the project team chose five words to serve as the base for the visual language of *CognIA*: finance; trust; motivation; technology and intelligence. Those words were inspired by user study findings. Those words referred to characteristics people value when making decisions about investments and characteristics the project team wanted to transmit with *CognIA*. Based on those words, designers searched for images using search websites (*Google images, Instagram, Pinterest*). The images were selected and grouped by the chosen words, Afterwards, common colors to compose the color scheme of *CognIA* were extracted from each group of images (see Fig. 5).

Fig. 5. Mood board – pictures related with concept areas (Color figure online)

Based on the observation of shapes and colors found in the mood board, designers created a *semantic panel* with three principal columns: *concept, perceptual aspects* and *results* (see Fig. 6). The concept column included rows for finance, intelligence, motivation, trust, and technology (Fig. 6 shows only the *finance* row). The *perceptual*

Concept	Perceptual Aspects		Results		
			Typography	Shape	Color
Finance Choose the best investment option.	Economy Control Investment Rate	Rational Graphics Measurement	Helvetica Neue Regular Sans Serif	Arrow Lines Right angles Scale	▨ Yellow ◧ Blue ■ Dark Blue ■ Dark Green

Fig. 6. Part of semantic panel shows the *Finance* row (Color figure online)

aspects column contains terms which describe the characteristics which can be observed in the mood board, economy, investment, rational, graphics, etc. The *results* column was divided into three visual elements subgroups: typography, shape, and color. The *typography* column contains choices of the best typefaces for the project.

The *shape* column shows choices of shapes which fit to the concept. The *color* column shows colors options related to the concept which fit the guidelines of the sponsoring organization. The semantic panel was used as a resource for designers to create the visual identity and graphical user interface of *CognIA*.

Designers then explored several versions for the graphical user interface applying colors, shapes, and typefaces available in the semantic panel described above (see Fig. 6). One version was chosen in a shade of green, since this version was visually distinct from current financial apps in the marketplace (Fig. 7).

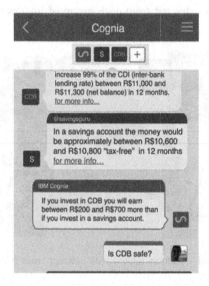

Fig. 7. Cognia's conversational user interface (Color figure online)

A user scenario was developed to illustrate the interaction flow of the system. This scenario was used to create the basic interaction flow of the systems and the expected behaviors of each chatbot. Since the project team is multidisciplinary, composed of computer scientists, designers and engineers we used a video demo as tool to guide the team through the development process of *CognIA*. The team would have an example of how the envisioned concept should work and based on it the functions illustrated in the video were developed. The video case scenario was inspired by previous design activities to understand investment decisions with real users. It was made by the designer members of the team. The video length was about three minutes and showed how the multiparty cognitive dialogue helped a user to make an investment decision.

The first part of the video consisted in a short introduction with an initial phrase *"Cognia has detected that you have considerable money in your bank account"* to introduce the case scenario. Next, a user receives a push notification from the system with a message *"Your account in Banco Blue has R$ 16.000 that is not receiving any interest. Would you like to invest some of this money?"* This message acts like a trigger for opening the application. After that, *Cognia*, the moderator agent, displays three options with different values to be invested. The user selects one of those options and *Cognia* replies: *"There may be a penalty for early withdrawal for your investment. How long do you plan to leave the money in this investment?"* and shows three options of investment horizon. The user chooses one and *Cognia* invites two more expert agents to participate in the dialogue, one is *SavingsGuru* and the other is *CDBGuru*. *CDBGuru* provides a simulation of the value selected by the user and after *SavingsGuru* does the same. The user asks a question a clarifying question, *"What is CDB?"* and *CDBGuru* answers it. *Cognia* then compares the answers from the product gurus showing the user which investment is more profitable. *CDBGuru* and *SavingsGuru* show then some web articles with links which can be useful for the user. An interactive visualization comparing values is also shown for the user in the video. *Cognia* then asks for a decision and the user chooses the CDB option. *Cognia* redirect the user to a fictitious *Bank Blue* page where he can complete the transaction.

10 Fourth User Study: Evaluating the *CognIA* Prototype

As part of the design and development process we performed an evaluation study to understand the desirability and issues of the prototype of our multi-bot chat advising system, *CognIA*.

Participants. Ten Brazilian participants were recruited by a snow-ball sample. The background of our participants was varied (Linguistic, Design, Computer science, Anthropology, Computer science, Tourism, and Engineering). All the participants worked in the same technology company. Five participants were female and five were male, with an average age of 35 years. All of them had previous experiences with savings account and four of them with other types of investments (including CDB). It was the first-time participants have contact with a multiparty dialogue system. All the participants we recruited were familiar with chatrooms.

Method. In the first part of the study, participants were asked to watch a video demo and make any comments they judged necessary (see Figs. 8, 9, and 10). The instructor asked them first to select 10 adjectives of 118 *product reaction cards adjectives* [20] written in individual paper cards and to think aloud while making their choices [21, 22]. Afterwards, participants were asked to choose 5 adjectives among the 10 adjectives previously chosen and to give reasons for the choice to the instructor. Participants were also requested to add any words they did not find in the stack of 118 cards and to explain why. Following the reaction cards activity, participants were asked to watch again a specific fraction of the video in which *CognIA* invites other agents to participate in the conversation. Then, the instructor questioned the participant: *"Who are the participants of this conversation? What is your impression of this concept?"* Participants then shared their thoughts of multiparty dialogues with the instructor.

Fig. 8. Participant watches the video.   **Fig. 9.** Participant choosing cards.   **Fig. 10.** Cards used in the study.

At the end of the session participants answered a semi-structured interview with demographic questions and their previous experience with investments. A consent form was filled out by participants before the study. The experiment was conducted in a lab and in some cases remotely via video conference. For the remote participants, the paper cards were substituted by a table with the adjectives. Remote participants were asked to highlight 10 words in red and the 5 words in bold. The length of the session was on average 15–25 min. All the sessions were audio- and video-recorded. The observation data was analyzed with the support of the notes which researchers took during the sessions. The use of a notepad was vital to gather information in case any problems might happen with the video recording. Participants were rewarded with a small gift.

Data Analysis. The data was analyzed using descriptive statistical methods and qualitative methods. Basic statistical analysis was carried out to analyze the data from the questionnaires: demographic data, semantic scales, and design preferences. Tables and cross tabulation were applied to compare the results among participants and the use of the system. The restricted number of participants in the study was not enough to ensure the validity of the statistical analysis. Research questions were kept in mind while the data was classified and codified. Relevant issues were classified into sets of codes. The principal set of issues emerged from the data were: reactions of multi-agent concept and reactions to interface and information design (positive and negative adjectives). The transcriptions of the videos, observation analysis and coding were assisted by a qualitative software.

Findings. Participants chose 35 words from 118 reaction cards. Thirty-two words selected were positive and three negative (Fig. 11). The positive words more frequently chosen by participants were: *Easy to use, Sophisticated, Friendly, Straightforward, Helpful,* and *Connected.* The three negative words chosen by participants were: *Scary, Insecure,* and *Intimidating.*

The interface was considered familiar and easy to use, and participants identified similar tools they already use similar to *CognIA* concept. The dialogue styles were recognized as useful since participants perceive this mode as allowing them to type and ask what they desire. Overall, participants found useful the separation of investments in agents. Some of them considered this approach useful for information design since

Fig. 11. Tag cloud results

each agent has a different color which helps in organizing and distinguishing information in the chatroom screen. Others did not notice the agents' separation. *"Funny, I found interesting this approach, but for me I was talking to CognIA all the time. It was what I felt. Even though we had characters (CDB and Savings) for me the interface is the app, the system."* Some participants emphasized the importance of the quality of the information and not the way it was delivered (single bots or multi-bots).

Additionally, participants highlighted that having different agents for different investments helped them to compare investments and decide which investment would be more suitable for them. A better job could have been done to distinguish the differences between agents in the system. Even though they liked the separation it was not possible to be sure they understood the system was multi-agent. It was also clear the option of having multi-agents in the system did not affect negatively the participants' perceptions. For more details of this study please see [23].

11   Conclusion and Further Research

We described in this paper a design process of a financial adviser system which led to the development of a prototype of a multi-bot conversational system. The design process went through multiple steps and used four different user studies to guide key design choices and to validate the multi-bot approach. Multiple design and user study methodologies were combined to address the complexity of the challenge and needs of the multi-disciplinary design team. The resulting prototype of the CognIA system was highly evaluated by potential users. At the moment of the writing of this paper the prototype is being refined and improved to be deployed in a financial information website in Brazil.

In today's point-and-click interfaces, it is very hard to two or more people to explore together the options in an investment website and even harder in a smartphone app. In most cases, mouse control is appropriated by one of the users, creating a natural dominance which is not inductive to collective decision-making. This can be addressed in our proposed system, a multiparty chat where investment chatbots and humans can talk to each other in the same dialogue. In the next version of the system, it will be possible to bring to the conversation their spouses, family, or other people they trust such as a human investment adviser. Similarly, multiparty chats naturally allow competitive behavior and its effective management. In the investment scenario, the users could bring banks with competitive products to a single conversation, allowing easier comparison and even auction-like competition between the bots.

Challenges to design multi-bot systems are to understand and implement humans' protocols, managing and monitoring turn-taking in a dialogue [24], track of threads and topic changes, and to design to support multiple roles (for example bank managers, family) [25]. Those are key technical challenges to be overcome to effectively deploy multiparty conversational systems.

References

1. Olson, P.: Get Ready for the Chat Bot Revolution: They're Simple, Cheap and About to be Everywhere. Forbes (2016). http://www.forbes.com/sites/parmyolson/2016/02/23/chat-bots-facebook-telegram-wechat/. Accessed 19 Aug 2016
2. Nieveen, N., Mckenney, S., Van Den Akker, J.: Educational design research: the value of variety. In: Van Den Akker, J., et al. (eds.) Educational Design Research: The Design, Development and Evaluation of Programs, Processes and Products. Paperback, New York (2006)
3. Zimmerman, J., Forlizzi, J., Evenson, S.: Research through design as a method for interaction design research in HCI. ACM (2007)
4. SPC (2015). https://www.spcbrasil.org.br/imprensa/pesquisas
5. Kahneman, D., Tversky, A.: Prospect theory: an analysis of decision under risk. Econometrica: J. Econom. Soc. 263–291 (1979)
6. Zhang, Y., Bellamy, R.K.E., Kellogg, W.A.: Designing information for remediating cognitive biases in decision-making. In: Proceedings of the 33rd Annual ACM Conference on Human Factors in Computing Systems. ACM (2015)
7. Zhao, J.C.: To risk or not to risk? Improving financial risk taking of older adults by online social information. In: Proceedings of the 18th ACM Conference on Computer Supported Cooperative Work & Social Computing. ACM (2015)
8. Gunaratne, J., Nov, O.: Informing and improving retirement saving performance using behavioral economics theory-driven user interfaces. In: Proceedings of the 33rd Annual ACM Conference on Human Factors in Computing Systems. ACM (2015)
9. Chase, R.B.: It's time to get to first principles in service design. Manag. Serv. Qual. 14(2/3), 126 (2004)
10. Holmlid, S.: Service design methods and UCD practice. In Proceedings of the INTERACT 2005 Workshop on User Involvement in e-Government Development Projects, Rome, Italy (2005)
11. Mager, B., Gais, M.: Service Design. Fink, Paderborn (2009)
12. Curedale, R.: Service Design: 250 Essential Methods. DCC Press, Topanga (2013)
13. Goldstein, S.M., Johnston, R., Duffy, J., Rao, J.: The service concept: the missing link in service design research? J. Oper. Manag. 20(2), 121–134 (2002). doi:10.1016/S0272-6963(01)00090-0

14. Steinfeld, A., Odest, C.J., Scassellati, B.: The Oz of wizard: simulating the human for interaction research. In Proceedings of the 4th ACM/IEEE International Conference on Human Robot Interaction, HRI 2009, pp. 101–108. ACM, New York (2009). doi:10.1145/1514095.1514115

15. Grill, T., Tscheligi, M.: The ConWIZ protocol: a generic protocol for wizard of Oz simulations. In: Moreno-Díaz, R., Pichler, F., Quesada-Arencibia, A. (eds.) EUROCAST 2013. LNCS, vol. 8112, pp. 434–441. Springer, Heidelberg (2013). doi:10.1007/978-3-642-53862-9_55

16. Bryman, A.: Social Research Methods. Oxford University Press, Great Britain (2008)

17. Goodman, E., Kuniavsky, M., Moed, M.: Observing the User Experience: A Practitioner's Guide to User Research. Elsevier, Amsterdam (2012)

18. Chang, H.M., Díaz, M., Català, A., Chen, W., Rauterberg, M.: Mood boards as a universal tool for investigating emotional experience. In: Marcus, A. (ed.) DUXU 2014. LNCS, vol. 8520, pp. 220–231. Springer, Cham (2014). doi:10.1007/978-3-319-07638-6_22

19. Mcdonagh, D., Storer, I.: Mood boards as a design catalyst and resource: researching an under-researched area. Des. J. 7(3), 16–31 (2004)

20. Benedek, J., Miner, T.: Measuring desirability: New methods for evaluating desirability in a usability lab setting. Proc. Usability Professionals Assoc. 2003, 8–12 (2003)

21. Love, S.: Understanding Mobile Human-Computer Interaction. Elsevier, Oxford (2005)

22. Preece, J., Rogers, Y., Sharp, H.: Interaction Design: Beyond Human-Computer Interaction. Wiley, New York (2007)

23. Candello, H., Andrade, B.D.: Evaluating multi-agent conversational interfaces in the early stages of the design process. Revista de Design, Tecnologia e Sociedade 3(1), 1–15 (2016)

24. Traum, D.: Issues in multiparty dialogues. In: Dignum, F. (ed.) ACL 2003. LNCS, vol. 2922, pp. 201–211. Springer, Heidelberg (2004). doi:10.1007/978-3-540-24608-4_12

25. Dignum, F.P.M., Vreeswijk, G.A.W.: Towards a testbed for multi-party dialogues. In: Dignum, F. (ed.) ACL 2003. LNCS, vol. 2922, pp. 212–230. Springer, Heidelberg (2004). doi:10.1007/978-3-540-24608-4_13

User Experience Evaluation for User Interface Redesign: A Case Study on a Bike Sharing Application

Jonas Forte$^{(\boxtimes)}$ and Ticianne Darin

Virtual University Institute, Federal University of Ceará, Fortaleza, Brazil
jonasforte@alu.ufc.br, ticianne@virtual.ufc.br

Abstract. Mobile application redesign requires the accurate use of design methods and guidelines, as well as detailed evaluation. In the context of alternative and environmentally friendly transportation supported by mobile applications, the redesign process can help enhancing the user experience resulting in a greater adherence of the citizen. To illustrate this scenario and inspire designers to further consider the user experience aspects, we present a case study of the redesign of *Bicicletar*, a Brazilian bike-sharing application. Our main goal is to analyze how the User Experience (UX) with this outdoor mobility application may affect the design choices in the User Interface. Overall, our iterative redesign process comprised: (1) UX evaluation of the application in the real usage context; (2) re-design of the application through a high-fidelity prototype; and (3) prototype validation. The results showed that the user experience problems regarding the identification and interaction with the main features of *Bicicletar* affected the perceived usability of the application. On the other hand, the redesigned prototype improvements on the user interface positively affected not only the user experience but also how the users trust the application. The present research is a starting point for the implementation of improvements in *Bicicletar* and in over 10 variations of this application in other Brazilian states, benefiting the local community, and serving as a reference for the redesign of other mobile applications.

Keywords: Evaluation · User experience · User interface · Redesign process · Design recommendations · High-fidelity prototype · Outdoor mobility

1 Introduction

In recent years, there has been a growing concern in providing broad and democratic access to urban space. Through monitoring and analyzing citizen data, governments and companies have been planning on how to improve cities inhabitants' life quality [1], as well the cities mobility design [2]. Consequently, multiple initiatives and technological aids aiming to support urban mobility frequently encourage the use of public transportation and environmentally sustainable vehicles. The users of such applications must be provided with a pleasurable experience and have their needs met when interacting with the application [3] as they commute, even when using a small screen or experiencing a limited internet connection. They need to feel encouraged to handle the

© Springer International Publishing AG 2017
A. Marcus and W. Wang (Eds.): DUXU 2017, Part III, LNCS 10290, pp. 614–631, 2017.
DOI: 10.1007/978-3-319-58640-3_44

applications while using private or public transportation in multiple contexts. Therefore, mobile applications to support outdoor mobility must not only work properly but also provide a positive User Experience (UX) and have a good User Interface (UI) design [4], which can be seen as the most important element of a computer-based system [5]. Such applications must be easy to use, flexible, have a simple and intuitive interface, maintain data integrity and provide an easy user adaptation, according to the usage context [6]. However, during the design process of a user interface, designers and practitioners frequently do not address the most common usability and experience issues, resulting in user's frustration [5]. Redesigning the UI according to the users' expectations and experience tends to positively affect the application usability [7]. Several approaches have been carried on to evaluate the usability of such applications and to assure they meet the user needs, focusing on user's attention in the context of use [8], or in techniques performed by specialists [9]. Numerous studies focus on conceptualization, development and evaluation [4, 10, 11] of user interfaces in this context, however, the evaluation usually takes place in a laboratory, often ignoring the diverse aspects of the outdoor context of use that may affect the user experience.

In order to provide the users of such mobile applications with a positive experience and help them to engage into a pleasurable experience with the city outdoor mobility, we present a case study of the UI redesign of a bicycling mobility application based on the UX evaluation involving users in their real context of use. Our analysis is mainly based on observing the user behavior while interacting with the UI, which indicates the actual feedback of the users, and allows comparison of their experiences [4]. We address different techniques used for user interface evaluation based on a combination of methods in real context [11], whose outcome served as feedback to the redesign process, effectively covering user's requirements. The redesign process was based on user-centered design [10] and prototype evaluation [12].

Our target application is the bike-sharing mobile application *Bicicletar*, which allows citizens to borrow public shared bicycles, in various Brazilian's metropolises. The main contribution of this work is the analysis of how the aspects of UX with outdoor mobility applications may affect the design choices for the user interface. As a result, we propose the redesign of *Bicicletar*'s interface and discuss a set of design recommendations for outdoor mobility applications designers.

2 Methodology

2.1 Study Object

For this study, we chose an application called *Bicicletar*[1], which allows access to a public bike sharing system in Fortaleza, a Brazilian city with over 2 million inhabitants and with 216 km of cycling infrastructure. This application features include: registration, acquisition of usage credentials, a function to borrow bikes from a station, and the ability to locate stations on the map. We used the Android version of the app because it is the most common operating system in Brazil for mobile devices, with

---

[1] Version 1.5 updated July 22, 2015.

92.4% of its market share [13]. In addition, in 2012, the bicycle was pointed as one of the most used vehicles for commuting in Brazil [14], which shows the relevance of this mean of transportation in the routine of the Brazilian people. In this research, we carried out a regional-focused evaluation in order to value local initiatives to support mobility. Furthermore, the results obtained will be forwarded to the responsible companies for implementation, so that the evaluation and redesign proposal can generate real improvements and benefits for the community.

2.2   Materials

The interface portion evaluated (Fig. 1) corresponds to the main functions of the application, which comprises six interfaces:

Fig. 1. Evaluated sections of *Bicicletar* application.

1. acquisition of passes through the application;
2. location and details of stations;
3. information on the number of parking spaces and availability of bicycles;
4. choice and release of bicycles;
5. mailbox and
6. registration.

Four smartphone models were used during user testing and inspections and are listed in Table 1. To create both high-fidelity prototypes the POP 2.0 tool was used on Primary Redesign (web version[2]) and Final Redesign (mobile app[3]). A digital camera was used to record the interactions during all user tests, in addition, OBS Studio[4] was used to capture the computer screen and webcam images while *AZ Screen Recorder*[5] app was used to capture the smartphones' screen.

Table 1. Details of the devices used

Model	Operational system	Display
Positivo Selfie S455[a]	Android 5.0.2	4.5 inches 854 × 480 pixels
Motorola Moto G 1st generation	Android 5.1	4.5 inches 720 × 1280 pixels
Xiaomi Redmi 2 HM 2LTE-BR	Android 4.4.4	4.7 inches 720 × 1280 pixels
LG G4[b]	Android 6.0	5.5 inches 2560 × 1440 pixels

[a]Used only in inspections
[b]Used only in user tests with Final Redesign

2.3 Stages of Research and Application of Methods

For the research planning, we followed the DECIDE [15] framework. The general objectives defined were: (i) analyze how the UX with outdoor mobility applications affect the design choices for the UI; (ii) propose the redesign of *Bicicletar's* interface; and (iii) discuss the set of design recommendations for outdoor mobility application designers. Figure 2 summarizes the methods used and the results generated in each

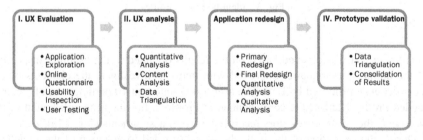

Fig. 2. Overview of the stages in this survey

---

stage of the research. Four stages were defined to conduct the research, based on the objectives: (I) UX evaluation, (II) UX analysis, (III) application redesign and (IV) prototype validation, each one of those containing a step to consolidate the results based on the adequate qualitative or quantitative analysis of each set of data.

UX Evaluation. To get familiarized with apps that aim to facilitate urban mobility, we made a comparative analysis based on user data using 6 of the main apps that serve Brazilian metropolises. The following apps were used: *Bike BH, Bike Brasilia, Bicicletar, Bike PoA, Pedala SP* and *Bicidade*. The evaluators registered their perceptions on the apps conforming to Norman's model [16] of interaction and the fundamentals of Information Architecture [17]. Still, in the same stage, we applied an online questionnaire to gather some data about the usage of *Bicicletar*. The evaluation of the application occurred in two complementary phases. We performed usability inspections of *Bicicletar* application in a laboratory context and user tests were carried out in the real context of use. It is important to emphasize that the usability evaluation was performed because it can contribute to the quality of the user experience indirectly, making the user feel easier and probably fulfilled [3]. The application' inspection was based on the usability checklist proposed by [18].

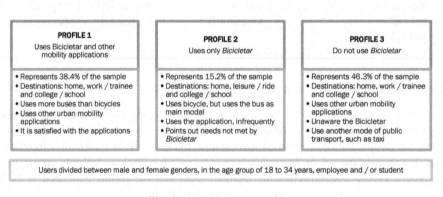

Fig. 3. Identified user profiles

The user test was planned based on the results obtained in the usability inspection and the online questionnaire, improved with items to investigate the elements of the user experience proposed by [19]. The user test counted on 10 participants, of which 5 attended Profile 1 and 5 that corresponded to Profile 2. For the accomplishment of the procedures, the trio of evaluators received different assignments (Fig. 11a).

During the execution of the tests, the users were led to a station of the *Bicicletar* system and the evaluators used contextual observation and Think Aloud [20] technique. The tests included performing specific tasks for the application such as getting a bike using the application and consulting a specific station and informing the number of bike spots available. The post-test questionnaire was based on Computer System Usability Questionnaire (CSUQ) [21] and Questionnaire for User Interface Satisfaction (QUIS) [22]. Finally, users responded to the Self-Assessment Manikin (SAM) [23, 24].

UX Analysis. A Content Analysis technique [25] was used to interpret the results of the user tests. A quantitative analysis of the data generated by the questionnaires was also included. To prepare the data, audios and videos from pre and post-test interviews were organized to get an overview of application usage. In addition, the videos recorded during the tests were transcribed. Then content units were organized and specific codes were assigned to each unit. Finally, the units were categorized and analyzed.

Application Redesign. In order to propose the redesign of *Bicicletar* interface, the UCD processes [10] were used. To produce the redesign of *Bicicletar* application the UI development [10] process was divided into two phases, conceptualization and prototyping. Two proposals of redesign were created for this work, a primary redesign and a final redesign. In both proposals, a UX evaluation was made. However, the evaluation of the primary redesign occurred in a laboratory (Fig. 11b) with 5 users [26], and the evaluation of the final redesign happened in real context of use (Figs. 11c, d) with 10 users.

Prototype Validation. At the end of each stage, the collected data were interpreted, organized and cross-referenced to obtain answers to questions about how UI changes affected UX. The data collected in the questionnaires pre and post-test was quantitatively analyzed for the creation of comparative graphs, interview information and usage observations were analyzed qualitatively to be compared with the questionnaire data.

2.4   Ethical Issues

Four aspects are relevant to IHC research involving people: the need for informed consent of subjects, the preservation of their anonymity, the protection of vulnerable groups and the guarantee of the well-being of individuals [27]. Thus, participants in both methods voluntarily agreed to participate. Vulnerable groups such as minors and disabled people did not participate.

2.5   Limitations and Threats to Validity

The redesigns proposals of the interface were created based on User Centered Design processes [10] and tested with 15 users through a high-fidelity prototype, because many authors [28–32] have argued that the prototypes are primarily used for the communication, exploration, refinement, and evaluation of design ideas. During the tests with *Bicicletar* the performance was evaluated, but due to the use of prototypes to present the new UIs, this aspect was not considered on evaluation of redesign proposals.

As described, a Content Analysis was done, but due to the large volume of data generated - combined with the limited experience of the evaluators – the Unitarization and Categorization processes were difficult, which impacted on the execution time of the later stages, causing delays in the research schedule. For that reason, to consolidate the results of the redesign of the application only qualitative and quantitative analysis were done.

3 Results

3.1 Overview of Top Bicycling Mobility Applications in Brazil

In the first stage of the research, which sought to identify and compare the main services and applications focused on bicycling mobility, we obtained an overview, although superficial, of the applications of this type available to Brazilians. Some similarities were found between the applications, including the functions offered, such as the number of vacant spots and bicycles available and the display of stations per map, we also found similar problems, such as delays in the update of information and bad overall performance. In the opinion of users, bad experiences are common because of these problems, and their comments often associate those bad experiences with difficulties during use.

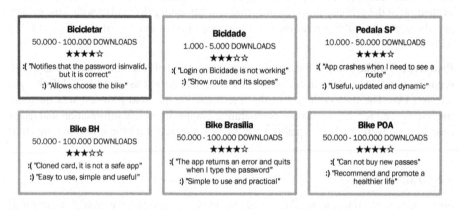

Fig. 4. Overall experience identified in the comparison of similar applications at Google Play

Figure 4 shows the comparison of the overall experience identified in the 6 applications. The results showed that the main problems in all applications are related to feedback, affordances, labeling, navigation, and organization, explaining several of the complaints from users on Google Play. Among those apps, *Pedala SP* was the most problematic. The review given by users on Google Play confirms the analysis's findings.

3.2 Online Questionnaire

Through the data collected in the online questionnaire, we created user profiles, (Fig. 3), that identified problems that affect the user experience and outlined an overview of users' perceptions of *Bicicletar*.

3.3 Usability Inspection of *Bicicletar*

With the inspections, we obtained two sets of results: the checklist results with the usability rate of each application specifying which heuristics were affected positively and negatively and a set of problems encountered while operating the interfaces.

To calculate the usability rate, the "yes" and "no" answers were counted and the non-applicable items were ignored. The percentage of positive responses constitutes this indicator. The resulting usability rate for *Bicicletar* was 57%, based on items with positive evaluation. Figure 5A represents the distribution of responses to the checklist, considering the 90 items that did not apply to *Bicicletar*. Figure 5B represents the distribution of 140 valid responses for analysis (i.e., disregarding non-applicable items).

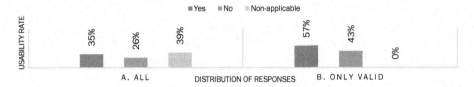

Fig. 5. Distribution of responses to the checklist

The portion of the interface most affected was the stations section, with 19 of the 56 problems discovered. Many problems that affect the interface, in general, have also been detected, such as the location of the exit button and the misuse of colors, this group being the second largest concentration with 13 problems. Considering that a problem may affect more than one heuristic, the most affected ones were: (H8) aesthetic and minimalist design, (H7) flexibility and efficiency of use, (H3) user control and freedom and (H1) visibility of system status. Figure 6 exemplifies some of the violations identified.

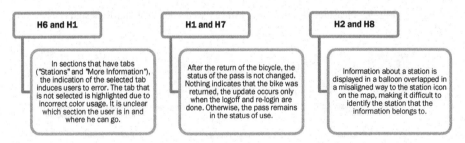

Fig. 6. Examples of problems identified in the *Bicicletar* inspection on laboratory

3.4   User Tests

This section presents the results of user tests with 25 people (10 of current *Bicicletar* application, 5 of Primary Redesign and 10 of Final Redesign), and the comparative graphs of users' opinions collected by SAM (Figs. 7, 8 and 9) and post test questionnaires (Fig. 10).

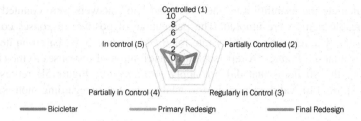

Fig. 7. Dominance: *Bicicletar* vs. Primary Redesign vs. Final Redesign

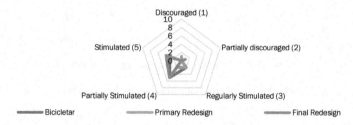

Fig. 8. Arousal: *Bicicletar* vs. Primary Redesign vs. Final Redesign

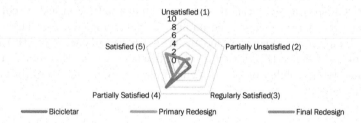

Fig. 9. Pleasure: *Bicicletar* vs. Primary Redesign vs. Final Redesign

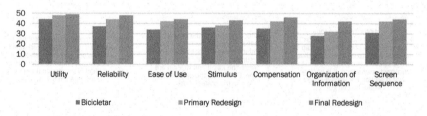

Fig. 10. Overview of users' opinions on general aspects

Fig. 11. User tests in real and laboratory context of use

***Bicicletar* in Real Context of Use.** The sample of users of *Bicicletar* (Profiles 1 and 2) had 10 participants combined. 70% of the members of this group alleged they knew how to use all the functions of the app, 80% reported having their needs met by the application and 80% felt partially satisfied with it. The feeling of control divides the opinion of the participants: 40% of users rated it as partially low and the other users are divided between regular, partially high and high. A pattern was noticed in the users of the application: they feel satisfied even if they do not feel in control (Figs. 7 and 9). In the data from the analysis of the post-test questionnaire 40% of users stated that the application is partially confusing. Regarding the sequence of screens, 40% rated *Bicicletar* as partially clear, 10% as confusing and 10% as partially confusing. The information presented by *Bicicletar* on stations and use only has validity for the users if they are correct in terms of use. It was observed in the reports that the imprecision of this information frustrates the users and creates a feeling of insecurity. In addition, the break in the flow of navigation makes the interaction dull and confusing. Problems of communication and usability indicated that the conceptual model of the application does not correspond to the mental model of the users. Some users do not notice the

Fig. 12. Primary redesign's screens

presence of features in the application, such as (1) the time of use of shared bikes, (2) indication of the return of the bike at the station and (3) the use status of the pass. In all three cases, this happens because the information is barely visible and the changes that indicate the status update are not perceived.

Primary Redesign in Laboratory Context. During the analysis of the data set of user tests with *Bicicletar* app, suggestions for improvement were identified by evaluators and users, which were met in the primary redesign proposal (Fig. 12). This evaluation was conducted in the laboratory and through a computer-based [11] high-fidelity prototype was evaluated by the users. In it, 60% of users had a partial high feeling of control, 80% presented partial satisfaction with the application and 40% affirmed to feel partially exciting during the tests. 60% of the users pointed having a high feeling of control, and their sense of satisfaction was equally divided between partial and fully satisfied.

Final Redesign in Real Context of Use. In general, the UI changes in the final redesign (Fig. 13) highlighted a very positive UX in this evaluation stage, for 80% of users the application became partially easy to use and presented a partial clear screen sequence as well as partially organized.

4   Discussion

4.1   User Experience: *Bicicletar* vs. Primary Redesign vs. Final Redesign

To evaluate the adequacy of the functionalities and the interaction problems, 6 objectives were defined. Each of these objectives is discussed below based on the results obtained with the triangulation of data collected throughout the research.

Do the emotional aspects inherent in the use point to a positive and enjoyable experience?

On Bicicletar. Partially. In general, users were satisfied with the application. However, feelings of frustration, confusion, fatigue and insecurity permeate the use of the application. Errors and difficulties in interaction made users feel incapable, ashamed or technically unprepared. Frustration is not just application-driven, as users take the blame for the flaws and are disappointed in themselves.

On Primary Redesign. Partially. The level of user satisfaction remained constant, this first version of redesign obtained a positive evaluation in the aspect of the dominance of the SAM questionnaire. It was evident the need to change in the conceptual model of purchase of a new pass in the application, because in the Primary Redesign only aesthetic aspects (UI) were changed, the conceptual model and sequence of screens of the bicycle application were preserved.

On Final Redesign. Yes. All users were satisfied, an explicit fact of 100% of positive ratings on the pleasure, arousal and dominance items of the SAM questionnaire. During the interactions, 15 reactions or indications of positive feeling were scored, as were the expressions or attitudes that demonstrate satisfaction of expectation.

Fig. 13. Final Redesign' screens

Are the users able to properly detect the main features of the application?

On Bicicletar. No. The lack of clarity in information architecture complicates user perception. Users had some difficulty in locating certain stations, but those difficulties were overcome with a closer examination of the interface.

On Primary Redesign. Partially. There were problems in detecting the cycling display feature in the map, 40% of users believe that bike lane view functionality does not exist on the map section, while it does. In the primary redesign, this functionality was not easily identified and raised questions during interactions.

On Final Redesign. Yes. In the quantitative analysis of the observations of use were counted 107 occurrences of executing an activity purposely, without making a mistake.

Users reacted positively while executing the main features of the application. It was noticed that the perception of the users was benefited by the changes of the interface.

Are the users able to perform the main functions of the application?

On Bicicletar. Yes. After exploring interface elements and functions. Users reported problems with: application crashes, updating real-time information, interacting with the map and organizing the list of stations. It was also noticed that the start of the borrowing process of the bicycles does not match their expectations. In addition, the lack of information or their conflict about sections and their apparent disabled status confuse users and limit their possibilities of interaction.

On Primary Redesign. Yes. The effort required to understand the new elements of the redesign proposal was not painful. The problems of low usability were corrected, however, due to the limitations of the prototype, the performance could not be evaluated.

On Final Redesign. Yes. Users have demonstrated high ability to perform the main functions, indicated by the 107 occurrences of running an activity purposely without making a mistake. Aspects evaluated in the SAM and post test questionnaires as control feeling, satisfaction, ease of use, compensation and organization of information had 100% of Positive ratings. There were 18 occurrences of comparison with previous experience, which indicates that users were familiar with the elements of the interface and that there is a good relationship between the conceptual model and the mental model.

Do the users properly understand the interface elements and the application concept?

On Bicicletar. Partially. In general, users understand the elements of the interface and understand the concept of the application as a whole, however, the concept of passes is not well understood, which makes it difficult to perform the function of borrowing a bicycle, one of the main functions. The lack of integration between *Bilhete Único/* Student Identity and the application contributes to the existence of this gap. In the post test, 40% of users said the application is partially confusing.

On Primary Redesign. Partially. The elements of the interface were understood by most users, as perceived in the post test questionnaire, in which 80% of users claim that the application is partially stimulant and to 60% of users organized. To allow clear communication, a brief description of the operation and rules of use were added to the interface element representing the Pass.

On Final Redesign. Yes. In the selection section of the bike, details about the available accessories were added through visual elements in the interface, and these were also perceived during the interactions. The application presented 100% of positive ratings in the post test questionnaire, in which users claim to feel compensated. Organization of information and ease of use also presented 100% of positive ratings.

Do the users' needs match the features available in the application?

On Bicicletar. No. Users have some needs that are not met by the application, the main ones are updating the information, needs relating to helping section, status of bicycles and stations, notifications, display of bike paths on the map and search for stations by address. In SAM, 80% of users say they are partially satisfied with the application, and this is the one with the highest positive ratings. Of the users who feel partially satisfied, 50% rated the application as partially rewarding.

On Primary Redesign. Yes. User needs are met, features reported as missing were made available, such as the help section, search option in the stations section, and the display of cycle paths. In the post test questionnaire, 80% presented partial satisfaction with the application. The compensation sentiment received 100% of positive ratings. 80% of users claim that the application is fully rewarding and 20% that the application is totally rewarding.

On Final Redesign. Yes. As in Primary Redesign, the final version redesign met the users' needs, as they stated partial or total satisfaction. For 40% of users the application is partially rewarding and 60% that the application is fully rewarding.

Can social and environmental aspects influence the experience of using the application?

On Bicicletar. Yes. The use of mobile devices to borrow bicycles must happen at stations, a public environment, which gives users a sense of insecurity and sets up a usage situation that requires speed and convenience to perform operations. The application is expected to be easy to use, simplify access to important information, provide quick responses and clear feedback, and instantly update the necessary data.

On Primary Redesign. Yes. The use of a larger screen of laptop during the tests and the absence of adverse conditions such as constant noise, distractions and a sense of insecurity allowed users to better understand the interface elements. Due to the good environmental conditions, such as the pleasant temperature and the use of chairs in the laboratory tests, the users felt more stimulated to express opinions and suggestions of improvement.

On Final Redesign. Yes. In addition to the social aspects, it has been noticed that ambient lighting conditions (e.g. sunlight) can also affect the visibility of the interface elements, especially in devices that have screen protectors, because depending on the material (e.g. glass). This accessory may negatively influence the user experience. However, the use of high contrast colors reduced the negative impact of both factors.

4.2   User Interface Components Used on Redesigns Proposals

The use of the green color and bicycle icon was preserved in redesign proposals to keep the user interface associated with other components of Bicicletar, like stations and bicycles, that also have the same characteristics. Colors, typography and elements (Fig. 14) used on redesigns proposals are based on Google's Material Design guidelines for Android applications to ensure the consistency and patterns with the Operating

Fig. 14. Examples of components and patterns of material design used on redesign proposals (Color figure online)

System, like floating action button to main functions, subheaders to group similar information on lists; fixed tabs to enable content organization at a high level, such as switching between views, toolbar, above app content highlighting important features and section name and the side navigation to allocate application's sections, enabling quick navigation between unrelated views and reducing visibility of infrequent destinations.

4.3   Design Recommendations for Outdoor Mobility Applications Designers

Users need to have information reliable and constantly updated, presented in a concise and organized way, since the context of use and the nature of the application requires speed and practicality. The sequence of screens should be logical and simple, the use of wayfinding on the top of the screen is recommended. Interrupting the flow of navigation by changing unnecessary screens and organizing information in many sublayers makes it difficult to use, making it an arduous process that requires concentration, which is not recommended for outdoor mobility applications. This type of application should not present a conceptual model that differs from the mental model of users, so that users do not feel incapable or confused. This problem can be avoided by developing a clear organizational structure. Uniformity in User Interface is a good way to ensure that your design communicates effectively without confusing or overwhelming the users. The confirmation or error messages should be short and easy to interpret, keeping in mind that there is difficulty in capturing user perception due to the context of use, as external environments, moving, divided attention, and how users use the application, as brief consultations and rapid implementation of actions. The main functions of the application should be easily found and in some cases, allow more than one way of execution. Using contrast as a tool to draw the user's attention is a good way to help the user understand the relationships between functions and elements. The frequency of use of the application should be considered in the design process, because if users do not perform long and continuous use experiences, the learning curve is compromised. The frequency of use is related to ease of understanding, learning and use.

5   Conclusion

The *Bicicletar* app benefitted the people who depend on the public transportation system of *Fortaleza*. Due to the quality and variety of the experiential aspects explained by this research, result of the association of different methods, we noted that users recognize the usefulness and relevance of the provided information, and for this reason, they act with a certain tolerance towards the problems that negatively affect their experience with the application. The identified problems are the same as other applications from several states in Brazil, as initially identified in comparative research step, which makes this research more relevant. Changes in the UI positively affected the UX. Improvements in the sequence of screens, organization of information and visual elements have generated an increase in users' feelings of pleasure, dominance and security. The Public Transportation System in large metropolises is complex and linked to problems that affect the user's commute. Designers of outdoor mobility applications need to consider situations of stress, discomfort and insecurity that are part of the users' routine. The design process of these applications should be based on the understanding of mental model and context of use, meeting user's needs, with an UI that provide easy of use and a pleasurable experience. Due to the good receptivity of UI redesign, our next steps will be to implement and test with more users.

References

1. Batty, M., Axhausen, K.W., Giannotti, F., Pozdnoukhov, A., Bazzani, A., Wachowicz, M., Ouzounis, G., Portugali, Y.: Smart cities of the future. Eur. Phys. J. Spec. Top. **214**(1), 481–518 (2012)
2. Jensen, O.B., Lanng, D.B., Wind, S.: Mobilities design – towards a research agenda for applied mobilities research. Appl. Mobil. **1**(1), 26–42 (2016). doi:10.1080/23800127.2016.1147782
3. Hassenzahl, M.: User experience (UX): towards an experiential perspective on product quality. In: 20th International Conference of the Association Francophone d'Interaction Homme-Machine, pp. 11–15 (2008). http://doi.acm.org/10.1145/1512714.1512717

4. Mohamed, A., Ozkul, T.: User-interface usability evaluation. Int. J. Comput. Sci. Secur. (IJCSS) **10**(2), 88–94 (2016)
5. Sridevi, S.: User interface design. Int. J. Comput. Sci. Inf. Technol. Res., vol. **2**(2), pp. 415–426 (2014). www.researchpublish.com. ISSN 2348-120X
6. Weiss, S.: Handheld Usability. Wiley, West Sussex (2002)
7. Park, H., Song, H.D.: Make e-learning effortless! Impact of a redesigned user interface on usability through the application of an affordance design approach. Educ. Technol. Soc. **18** (3), 185–196 (2015)
8. Kjeldskov, J., Graham, C., Pedell, S., Vetere, F., Howard, S., Balbo, S., Davies, J.: Evaluating the usability of a mobile guide: the influence of location, participants and resources. Behav. Inf. Technol. **24**(1), 51–65 (2005)
9. Nielsen, J.: Heuristic evaluation. In: Nielsen, J., Mack, R.L. (eds.) Usability Inspection Methods, pp. 25–62. Wiley, New York (1994)
10. Kikuchi, H., Kimura, S., Ohkubo, S., Inamura, H., Takeshita, A.: User interface development from conceptualization to prototype evaluation through UCD processes. NTT DOCOMO Tech. J. **12**(3), 33–41 (2010)
11. Carneiro, N., Pinheiro, M., Mesquita, V., Coelho, B., Forte, J., Darin, T.: Transporte e Tecnologia: Avaliação da Experiência de Uso de Aplicativos de Apoio à Mobilidade Urbana. In: TISE - XXI Congreso Internacional de Informática Educativa, 2016, Santiago, vol. 12, pp. 253–264. Nuevas Ideas en Informática Educativa, Santiago (2016)
12. Lim, Y., Pangam, A., Periyasami, S., Aneja, S.: Comparative analysis of high- and low-fidelity proto-types for more valid usability evaluations of mobile devices. In: Mørch, A., Morgan, K., Bratteteig, T., Ghosh, G., Svanaes, D. (eds.) Proceedings of the 4th Nordic Conference on Human-computer Interaction: Changing Roles (NordiCHI 2006). ACM, New York, pp. 291–300 (2006). http://dx.doi.org/10.1145/1182475.1182506
13. Kantar Worldpanel ComTech. Smartphone OS sales market share (2016). http://www.kantarworldpanel.com/global/smartphone-os-market-share. Accessed 28 July 2016
14. das Cidades, M.: Caderno de Referência Para a Elaboração de Plano de Mobilidade Urbana (PlanMob) (2010)
15. Preece, J., Rogers, Y., Sharp, H.: Design de Interação: além da interação humano-computador. Bookman (2013)
16. Norman, D.A.: Cognitive engineering. In: Norman, D.A., Draper, S.W. (eds.) User Centered System Design: New Perspectives on Human-Computer Interaction, Hillsdale, USA, pp. 32–65 (1986)
17. Rosenfeld, L., Morville, P.: Information Architecture for the World Wide Web, 3rd edn. O'Reilly, Sebastopol (2006)
18. Yáñez Gómez, R., Cascado Caballero, D., Sevillano, J.L.: Heuristic evaluation on mobile interfaces: a new checklist. Sci. World J. **2014**, 1–19 (2014)
19. Garrett, J.J.: The Elements of User Experience: User-Centered Design for the Web and Beyond, 2nd edn. New Riders, San Francisco (2010)
20. Nielsen, J., Clemmensen, T., Yssing, C.: Getting access to what goes on in people's heads?: reflections on the think-aloud technique. In: Proceedings of the Second Nordic Conference on Human-Computer Interaction (NordiCHI 2002), pp. 101–110. ACM, New York (2002). http://dx.doi.org/10.1145/572020.572033
21. Lewis, J.R.: Psychometric evaluation of the computer system usablity questionnaire: the CSUQ. Int. J. Hum.-Comput. Interac. **7**(1), 57–78 (1992)
22. Chin, J.P., Diehl, V.A., Norman, K.L.: Development of an instrument measuring user satisfaction of the human-computer interface. In: O'Hare, J.J. (ed.) Proceedings of the SIGCHI Conference on Human Factors in Computing Systems (CHI 1988), pp. 213–218. ACM, New York (1988). http://dx.doi.org/10.1145/57167.57203

23. Bradley, M.M., Lang, P.J.: Measuring emotion: the self-assessment manikin and the semantic differential. J. Behav. Ther. Exp. Psychiatry **25**, 49–59 (1994)
24. Lang, P.J. Bradley, M.M., Cuthbert, B.N.: International affective picture system (IAPS): instruction manual and affective ratings. Technical report A-4, The Center for Research in Psychophysiology, University of Florida (1999)
25. Moraes, R.: Análise de conteúdo. Rev. Educação **22**(37), 7–32 (1999)
26. Nielsen, J., Landauer, T.K.: A mathematical model of the finding of usability problems. In: Proceedings of ACM INTERCHI 1993, pp. 206–213 (1993)
27. Leitão, C., e Daniela Romão, D.: Pesquisas em IHC: um debate interdisciplinar sobre a ética. In: Atas do Workshop sobre Interdisciplinaridade em IHC, CLIHC, pp. 6–7 (2003)
28. Preece, J., Rogers, Y., Sharp, H.: Interaction Design: Beyond Human-Computer Interaction, 3rd edn. Wiley, New York (2011)
29. Buchenau, M., Suri, J.F.: Experience prototyping. In: Boyarski, D., Kellogg, W.A. (eds.) Proceedings of the 3rd Conference on Designing Interactive Systems: Processes, Practices, Methods, and Techniques (DIS 2000), pp. 424–433. ACM, New York (2000). http://dx.doi.org/10.1145/347642.347802
30. Gutierrez, O.: Prototyping techniques for different problem contexts. In: Bice, K., Lewis, C. (eds.) Proceedings of the SIGCHI Conference on Human Factors in Computing Systems (CHI 1989), pp. 259–264. ACM, New York (1989). http://dx.doi.org/10.1145/67449.67499
31. Schneider, K.: Prototypes as assets, not toys. why and how to extract knowledge from prototypes. In: 18th International Conference on Software Engineering (ICSE-18), Berlin, Germany, pp. 522–531 (1996)
32. Thompson, M. Wishbow, N.: Prototyping: tools and techniques: improving software and documentation quality through rapid prototyping. In: Proceedings of SIGDOC 1992, pp. 191–199. ACM Press (1992)

Teleconsultation Process for Physicians Working with ASD Patients: Insights from a Usability Evaluation

Jennifer Ismirle[1(✉)], Hannah Klautke[1], Sarah J. Swierenga[1], and Lauren O'Connell[2]

[1] Usability/Accessibility Research and Consulting, Michigan State University, East Lansing, MI, USA
{ismirlej,klautkeh,sswieren}@msu.edu
[2] Department of Pediatrics and Human Development, College of Human Medicine, Michigan State University, East Lansing, MI, USA
LOconnel@hurleymc.com

Abstract. We describe a usability evaluation of a teleconsultation model for primary care physicians (PCPs) with patients with autism spectrum disorders and a developmental-behavioral pediatrician (DBP) with relevant expertise. Six PCPs participated in a total of 12 consultations with a DBP. Detailed observations and user ratings and comments were collected. Standard usability metrics were used, and the communication quality and interactions of the two participating parties (PCP and DBP) were examined. High post-task and post-study ratings (including System Usability Scale, Communication Quality, and attitudes toward teleconsultation process scores), as well as the positive comments from participants, indicated that the teleconsultations were successful, and demonstrated the effectiveness of this type of communication, particularly for validating PCPs' ideas and strengthening their confidence in talking with families, providing new ideas and redirected their thinking, and connecting PCPs with location-sensitive resources. PCPs found value in the opportunity to connect with an ASD specialist in a timely and efficient manner. Most indicated that the video element of the consultation enhanced clarity and understanding, attention, engagement, and collegiality, while acknowledging drawbacks such as reduced ability to multitask compared to consultations by phone. Recommendations for enhancements of the teleconsultation process focus on supporting PCPs in getting started with Zoom; providing ground rules and establishing procedures; creating information sharing/summary templates for the teleconsultation process; and fostering communication quality in a mediated environment.

Keywords: Telehealth · Autism spectrum disorders · Usability · Teleconsultation · Communication quality

© Springer International Publishing AG 2017
A. Marcus and W. Wang (Eds.): DUXU 2017, Part III, LNCS 10290, pp. 632–644, 2017.
DOI: 10.1007/978-3-319-58640-3_45

1   Introduction

Telehealth initiatives have often focused on connecting patients with medical providers in order to improve access to specialized knowledge and to provide medical services to remote users [1–3]. A smaller portion have been geared at connecting physicians with other physicians or particular medical specialists (e.g., [4]). This current study focuses on such physician-physician consultation, specifically in the area of developmental-behavioral pediatrics.

Developmental-behavioral pediatricians (DBP) are pediatricians with subspecialty training and experience that allows them to consider, in their assessments and treatments, the medical and psychosocial aspects of children's and adolescents' developmental and behavioral problems, such as autism spectrum disorders (e.g., autism disorder, Asperger's syndrome, Rett syndrome), attention and behavioral disorders (e.g., ADHD, depression, anxiety disorder) and learning disorders. DBPs work closely with family members and advocate for their patients by working with schools, preschools, and other agents, such as social workers or relevant agencies involved with developmental care and education [5]. This pediatric subspecialty is marked by substantial personnel shortages [6], turning primary care physicians (PCPs) into key players in the management of autism spectrum disorders. For primary care physicians caring for patients with Autism Spectrum Disorders (ASD), there is a critical need for just-in-time guidance by DBP specialists, suggesting telehealth approaches as one possible solution to alleviate access issues.

Our user experience evaluation team (Michigan State University (MSU) Usability/Accessibility Research and Consulting) consulted on a research project with the Department of Pediatrics and Human Development (in the College of Human Medicine at MSU) to conduct a usability evaluation that assessed the potential of a teleconsultation process to improve communication between PCPs and a DBP with expertise in ASDs. The research focused on understanding the extent to which autism-related information needs of PCPs can be met by consulting an autism specialist or DBP at a distance, and given the complexity of cases involving ASD patients, allow for high quality communication between primary care providers and the specialist and provide relevant and actionable support to the PCP.

While the details of virtual provider-specialist consultations can vary based on local contexts, for the purposes of this research, teleconsultations consisted of pre-arranged, approximately 15-minute long interactions via HIPAA-compliant Zoom teleconferencing software and were offered to PCP participants wishing to consult a DBP with expertise in the diagnosis and management/treatment of ASD. Our pilot study to determine the usability of teleconsultations is one element of a multifaceted initiative to enhance support services for Michigan children with ASD and their families.

2   Methods

Our usability study concentrated on obtaining performance, observational, and subjective satisfaction data from representative users performing typical tasks using the teleconsultation process. In addition to this investigation of user-system interaction, user-user interaction (i.e., interaction between a PCP and a DBP) was analyzed. While effectiveness, efficiency, and satisfaction remain relevant parameters, this combination introduces other elements of interest, such as communication quality and interactivity between users.

We examined the extent to which actual PCPs consulting with the DBP reported feeling that their concerns and questions were being heard, understood, and adequately responded to by the remotely located specialist to allow for the provision of quality care to the patient. Given the pilot function of the current version of the process, this study also aimed to understand PCPs' perceived value of the teleconsultation process and their needs, preferences, perceived obstacles, and concerns. Finally, the study aimed to capture observations regarding the communicative aspects of teleconferencing in order to make recommendations for enhancements of this process.

2.1   Participants

Six practicing primary care physicians (PCPs) were recruited via an email requesting their participation in a 1-hour session including a "mock teleconsultation and an exit interview" geared at "testing the feasibility of mobile consultations." Participants did not receive any incentive or compensation for their participation. All six participants were pediatricians practicing in either East Lansing, Lansing, Flint, or Grand Rapids. Participants ranged in age from 38 to 62 and had between 9 to 33 years of practice. They reported seeing autistic children in their practice between "less than once per week" (but no less than once per month) to "2–5 times per week." All of them used electronic health records (Centricity, EPIC, CPS 11, New Gen, or eMDs) and reported using a desktop computer and the Internet daily. In contrast, exposure to videoconferencing technology varied widely between "2–5 times per week" and "less than once per month." With one exception, participants approached the teleconsultation session with interest in teleconferencing-based access to a developmental behavioral pediatrician, and had positive expectations regarding effects of such access on their knowledge and ability to provide quality care.

A developmental-behavioral pediatrician served as the consultant for the sessions. This DBP, who practices medicine in Flint, Michigan and specializes in the diagnosis and management of autism, had prior experience with an electronic health record, used a laptop and the Internet daily, and had significant experience with videoconferencing technology.

2.2   Procedure and Metrics

We conducted 60-minute sessions with six users (primary care physicians) and a DBP to determine the effectiveness of the teleconsultation process. PCPs were recruited from the surrounding areas of southern Michigan by the MSU Department of Pediatrics and Human Development. For two of the primary care physicians, the timing of the scheduled consultations enabled a member of the department to be present to assist with setting up Zoom teleconferencing software in person. The remaining PCPs were instructed on how to set up Zoom through emailed instructions.

After the PCP, DBP, and the session moderator met virtually in the designated 3-party Zoom session, the moderator greeted the participant, made introductions, and read a description of the study. For each teleconsultation task, participants were asked to first describe a case scenario, which had been provided to them at random and in advance of the session. The case scenarios consisted of a set of case notes describing a young patient with ASD-relevant symptoms and his or her medical, social, family, and medication history, results of previous assessments, and a list of possible questions. These cases were developed by a pediatrician with expertise in autism spectrum disorders in conjunction with Usability/Accessibility Research and Consulting.

After providing the overview of a case, PCPs were asked to pose specific questions from their scenario to the DBP to guide her input in the case (and the DBP did not have exposure to the cases or questions in advance). PCPs were encouraged to flesh out details as needed, especially if the specialist were to ask follow-up or clarification questions that were not answered within the stimulus materials but that they would likely be able to answer if the child in question were an actual patient of theirs.

The DBP responded with thoughts on additional evaluations or, if sufficient diagnostic clarity had been established previously, prioritized suggestions of treatment options. If sufficient diagnostic clarity had not yet been established previously, she occasionally provided hypothetical treatment options contingent on the outcomes of the additional evaluations, as well as other relevant advice on navigating insurance constraints and identifying and connecting with locally available resources.

To increase the naturalness of the consultation, the moderator turned off their video component (and still observed and listened to the consultation) while the PCP consulted with the DBP, and re-enabled their video portion only after the conclusion of each 10–15 min long consultation in order to administer the post-task satisfaction survey while the specialist temporarily left the meeting to fill out her own post-task satisfaction form. For this survey, the PCPs and the DBP were asked to rate the effectiveness of the consultation and to identify the main questions(s) that had been asked during the consultation to allow for comparison across the two parties.

After the two rounds of case consultation and post-task questionnaires, a post-study questionnaire (consisting of 25 items) was administered to participants to assess the effectiveness of the teleconsultation process, physicians' satisfaction with the technical aspects of the process, the perceived quality of the communication that occurred, and professional usefulness of the process. The DBP completed only the communication quality portion of this questionnaire to examine the user-user interaction, and she provided qualitative feedback on the overall process.

The System Usability Scale (SUS) was used for the first portion of the post-study questionnaire with PCPs rating their level of agreement to ten statements (e.g., I thought the teleconsultation process was easy to use) to assess the usability of the overall process. The SUS, created by John Brooke, is a quick and reliable tool for measuring usability that can be used for small sample sizes [7]. Participant responses are calculated and averaged to find the overall SUS score (which ranges between 0–100).

To assess the perceived quality of the video-based interaction within the teleconsultation, participants were asked to complete a portion of the Communication Quality Questionnaire [8] as part of the post-study questionnaire. This measures the degree to which interactions are smooth, efficient, yet personal and overall satisfying to the two parties involved and has been used in both face-to-face and computer-mediated contexts (e.g., [9]). This portion of the questionnaire consisted of ten five-point semantic differential items, such as "Please rate the quality of the communication that occurred in the teleconsultation process on the following dimensions: In-depth (5)–Superficial (1)."

Finally, PCPs were asked to rate their level of agreement to statements aimed at gathering their attitudes towards the teleconsultation process (e.g., I felt comfortable using the teleconsultation process), and open-ended questions were asked verbally to gain feedback on how the teleconsultation process could be enhanced (e.g., Would you like the option to send notes, video, etc. before and/or during the teleconsultation?).

3 Results

At the conclusion of each of the two consultation tasks, the PCPs and the DBP were asked to rate their level of agreement to the following statement on a scale of 1–5 (Strongly Disagree to Strongly Agree): "The consultation provided answers to the question asked and would assist me (the PCP) in providing care to the patient." Generally, the DBP tended to rate the consultations more critically (averaging 3.7) than the participating PCPs (averaging 4.8). In addition, the PCPs and the DBP were asked separately what the main question(s) was that was posed to the specialist, and comparison showed that each user understood the focus of each consultation in these sessions (which is an important factor for this process).

The average scores from the post-study questionnaire are included in Table 1. The average SUS score for the teleconsultation process was 77.5 for the PCPs, which is in the acceptable range (above 70 is considered acceptable). Two participants had lower scores that fall in the marginally acceptable range (between 50–70), and these participants in particular had major difficulties when attempting to set up Zoom and when entering the teleconsultation meeting, which likely contributed to the lower ratings they gave for the SUS and the statements related to their attitudes toward the consultation process; in contrast, they gave high post-task ratings and high ratings for the Communication Quality Scale.

Table 1. Quantitative post-study results: System Usability Scale (SUS), Communication Quality (CQ), and attitudes toward the teleconsultation process

	SUS Score for PCPs	Perceived CQ by the PCPs	Perceived CQ by the DBP	I felt comfortable using the teleconsultation process (PCPs)	I would use this teleconsultation process if it were offered (PCPs)
AVG*	77.5	4.7	4.2	4	3.8

*Note: Average overall SUS scores can range between 0–100; CQ and attitude ratings are on a scale of 1–5 (Strongly Disagree to Strongly Agree)

The average Communication Quality score for the teleconsultation process was 4.7 for the PCPs, and 4.2 for the DBP. In the scale's original validation work [8], respondents rated their average satisfaction with routine interactions with others as about 7 on the 9 point scales (9 being high, 1 being low), which is equivalent to a score of 4 on the 5-point scale used in this study. As such, especially the PCPs' scores are on the high end. Furthermore, one particular item that tended to lower the score was the "Formal (1)–Informal (5)" item. Given the professional context of these interactions, some formality is not necessarily as indicative of lack of immediacy/warmth as it is in the context of everyday interactions on which the scale is designed. Therefore, the positive ratings can be seen as conservative estimates of the PCPs' perceived communication quality. On the other hand, a concern about social desirability and politeness in responding may operate more strongly on the PCPs' side than on the side of the DBP as participant-researcher, which may explain the DBP's slightly less positive ratings.

In addition to the Communication Quality questionnaire, observations regarding the communication and interactivity of participants and the overall process setup were examined to determine considerations for a successful teleconsultation process, which are overviewed in the next section. These observations (based on previous work such as [3, 10]) included both nonverbal and verbal communicative behaviors (including facial expression, eye contact, gestures, and interactivity in terms of conversational back-and-forth, clarification questions from both parties, mirroring, and expressions of mutual understanding/engagement/rapport); the situational contexts in which doctors used the technology (including work interruptions, phone calls, settings); and the performance of the specific teleconferencing software used, different ways in which the relevant hardware (monitor, keyboard, webcam, mic, speakers) was set up across users, and challenges related to its use. We found a variety of communicative and interaction behaviors, some of which is more conducive to the consultation's quality. For example, a pattern of presenting the case description, asking a question, listening to the advice, asking another question(s) and listening, and finally thanking the DBP could be noted in participants that tended to be less expressive during the consultation (i.e., using less back channeling such as nodding). With other participants, we observed repeated turn-taking between both parties that became more conversational with back channeling throughout (e.g., nodding, smiling, saying "okay," "makes sense," etc.) to indicate understanding. Several participants also mentioned that this type of session was not necessarily typical because they would likely be multi-tasking during a consultation and would not be entirely focused on the conversation. We also noted variation in terms of participants' positioning in relation to their camera and screen, with some appearing back-lit with hard to discern facial expressions.

Process enhancements are discussed in the next section, but overall the teleconsultations were perceived as valuable by the PCPs because of the following:

- validating the PCPs' ideas for patient plans and strengthening their confidence in talking with families;
- providing new ideas and redirecting their thinking;
- connecting PCPs with additional resources while considering their location;
- and providing a high level of specificity and sequential ordering of advice.

4 Tips for Enhancing Teleconsultation Process

Based on the overall results and feedback, recommendations for enhancements of the teleconsultation process include the following areas:

- Support PCPs in setup of video conferencing tool and include the option to use a telephone for flexibility and simplicity
- Establish a procedure for sharing patient information and dealing with interruptions during a teleconsultation
- Foster communication quality and interaction in a mediated environment
- Provide a summary of the teleconsultation through use of a template
- Consider additional implementation factors including HIPAA compliance, billing and costs, scheduling logistics, and the participation of third parties

Flowcharts to illustrate examples of the setup process before a teleconsultation (Fig. 1) and the teleconsultation process using a video conferencing tool (Fig. 2) are also included.

4.1 Support PCPs in Setup of Video Conferencing Tool and Include the Option to Use a Telephone for Flexibility and Simplicity

Three of the four participants who did not have in-person technical support for downloading and using the Zoom software for the first time encountered difficulties, and one of the two participants who did receive support stated a lack of confidence in his ability to tackle unfamiliar computer-related tasks. Therefore, successful adoption of offered teleconsultations is likely to hinge on easing these initial technical challenges for users, although participants also thought the process would become much easier after they became familiar.

Possibly more effective than very specific set up instructions for Zoom would be efforts to provide a contact person who can walk interested PCPs through the process and test the teleconferencing tool with them for the first or second time. Similarly, participating institutions could eliminate the downloading and installation part of the process by having IT support preinstall the program on PCPs' preferred computers for this purpose.

To maximize the potential of video conferencing, PCPs need digestible information or just-in-time support for checking and meeting computer requirements including the webcam and microphone, connection, as well as Zoom-specific functionality such as screen sharing or the chat function for the sharing of links. Additionally, it seems ideal to pick a platform like Zoom and not change to a different tool, to the extent possible, so that users do not have to go through the initial learning curve repeatedly.

The option to consult via telephone in addition to the option to use videoconferencing is also needed to meet the needs of the users by allowing for flexibility and simplicity (e.g., not requiring Zoom meetings only). Although most of the PCPs and the DBP felt that using videoconferencing for consultations was ideal, most also mentioned that this medium of communication may not always be feasible or practical when they have limited time available to schedule and prepare for a consultation and likely will be multitasking. After having some difficulty with the Zoom setup or mentioning a lack of computer usage, the option to use telephone in some instances was preferred. For example, an initial video consultation could help establish the relationship and rapport between the PCP and DBP, and then the option to schedule telephone consultations could be available as needed.

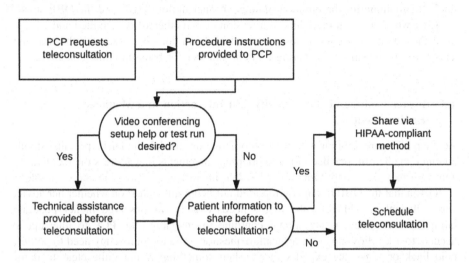

Fig. 1. Example of setup process before first teleconsultation using video conferencing tool

4.2 Establish a Procedure for Sharing Patient Information and Dealing with Interruptions During a Teleconsultation

A procedure needs to be established to allow PCPs to share patient information with the DBP before, during, and after consultations (e.g., if a follow-up is scheduled). For example, PCPs mentioned the desire for this option and a variety of methods for sharing information, including: using fax or email to send patient information and reports from other providers (e.g., from psychologist, etc.), providing access to a patient's entire chart, holding up textual/visual information to the camera while videoconferencing, and sharing video of the patient (e.g., live or pre-recorded). However, determinations are needed to ensure any methods used are HIPAA-compliant, as well as what types of information will be useful for the DBP to help avoid overwhelming amounts of content being shared.

A template and/or checklist is needed which indicates the key types of information that are useful for the DBP to have before or during a consultation (e.g., any previous evaluations/screenings/referrals and the results, past medications used, developmental milestones and behaviors, etc.). Instructions could indicate to the PCP that they should be prepared to present these types of patient information and also what they feel is important, or to send the template to the DBP before with the requested content (e.g., provide a means for the PCP to organize the patient history and their thoughts). In addition, a procedure is then needed to establish how the patient information will be shared with the DBP to ensure privacy, and (if possible) how additional types of content can be shared, such as videos.

A few important ground rules should be established in advance, such as how to deal with common interruptions during a teleconsultation, especially if potentially private information may be mentioned during an incoming phone call or when a medical staff member stops by in-person. Users should therefore be instructed on how to briefly mute one's microphone for the duration of such an interruption. PCPs and the DBP should consider whether or not recording of a session or parts thereof is permitted and what to do if the Zoom connection is lost or technical disruptions interfere with the timeline. This could be as simple as sharing a phone number for back-up communication.

4.3   Foster Communication Quality and Interaction in a Mediated Environment

As the party more familiar with the teleconferencing model, the DBP specialist should continue the helpful practice of using orienting statements that address the fact that the approach may be initially unfamiliar but that interactivity is possible and desirable.

Given that the DBP frequently reported not being quite clear on whether her advice was sufficient or addressed the PCP's needs exactly (as observed in her post-task ratings and comments), she should continue to encourage the PCP to interrupt as needed, to ask follow-up and clarification questions, and to not feel any need to politely hold back or "save the expert's face" when something is not quite clear to them. Continuing the conversational tone of the meeting and monitoring non-verbal expressions can provide clues on the level of understanding reached as well, although consulting DBPs will have to be aware that some participants are unlikely to be quite as expressive and less prone to back channeling as others in this regard. And even though the video component likely reduces multitasking, in the hectic reality of the medical field some of this may still occur along with more substantial interruptions by third parties.

Other orienting statements could include whether or not notes or a session report will be provided, whether or not parties are expected to take notes (and hence will look occupied either with their screen or a notepad at times), and whether multiple monitors are being used (which would explain why the other party appears to not be looking at the participant).

To improve the richness of the mediated communication, participants can avoid back lighting which makes facial expressions hard to see and position their webcam near the top of their screen to improve eye contact and turn-taking regulation. They can position themselves close enough to the computer to ensure sufficient audio quality but not so close that their gestures and body language are cut out from view. Additionally, if audio quality was insufficient in a test run, they can use an external microphone/headphones to minimize the detrimental effects that having to strain to hear or repeatedly talking over each other can have on the flow of the communication and the establishing of rapport.

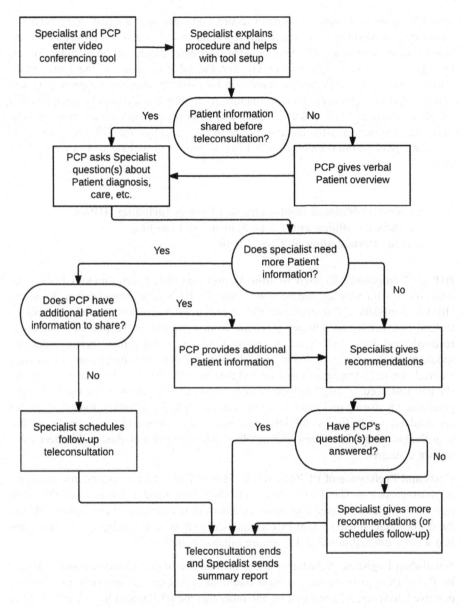

Fig. 2. Example of teleconsultation process (Note: Telephone would be used instead if there was an insufficient connection for video conferencing.)

4.4 Provide a Summary of the Teleconsultation Through Use of a Template

A summary report or overview of the consultation would be very useful for PCPs to ensure they have a record of the advice and plan provided by the specialist. This report would likely become part of a patient's record, and therefore a template for this type of summary is needed to ensure consistent reporting and to establish a procedure for the type of information that should be included (and what should not be included for this record). A template would also ensure that the DBP is aware of the types of the information they are expected to summarize for the PCP, allowing for productive and efficient note-taking during the consultation. A "toolkit" should also be compiled that includes information on possible resources, evaluation tools, information packets, diagnostic requirements for insurance, and so on, providing the DBP with an easily accessible pool of information to pull from as needed to include with a report for a PCP.

4.5   Consider Additional Implementation Factors Including HIPAA Compliance, Billing and Costs, Scheduling Logistics, and the Participation of Third Parties

HIPAA Compliance Related to Information Sharing. Determinations need to be made on how information can be shared with the DBP for teleconsultations to ensure HIPAA compliance. For example, the overall teleconsultation procedure needs to include instructions on whether a release from a patient or the patient's parents is required (and for which types of information), or whether these teleconsultations should avoid the sharing of identifying information and be considered part of necessary medical care (e.g., similar to a referral and thereby not require a release from a patient). Privacy and security requirements also need to be considered when establishing a procedure for sharing patient information with the DBP. Additionally, the locations that are available for PCPs and the DBP to communicate should be considered, and if a consultation occurs in a (semi-)public place, whether and how this could affect compliance concerns.

Costs and Preference of PCPs to Bill for Their Time. Billing procedures should be considered, such as: Can PCPs bill for consultation time and if yes, how so? Or would consultations be considered a professional courtesy in their current conception? Would the documentation that several PCPs requested contribute to turning the consultations into a more official/formal and therefore billable event?

Scheduling Logistics. Scheduling issues include two of the main concerns mentioned by PCPs: How to find time for these additional consultations and how to minimize possible interferences? For example, the times that the DBP would be available need to be determined (e.g. certain days per month, during what times, after hours or day time only). Billable consultations may alleviate the concern about finding time in the day, and scheduled times rather than random call backs would address concerns about interruptions. Times determined in advance may or may not allow the PCP to schedule certain patients strategically around that time as well. Having a strategy for handling various levels of consultation requests may be beneficial, and considerations should be made regarding possible support for follow-up communication (e.g., consider how consultation can be arranged on PCP side). Existing consulting models (e.g. psychiatry) may provide insights. If additional DBPs are added to the pool of consulting experts, scheduling should take into account the PCPs' preference for continuity by providing access to the same expert across teleconsultations.

Including Third Parties. Suggestions by the DBP to connect the PCP with a familiar social worker who would assist in navigating local resources for the patient were repeatedly greeted with strong interest. This could take the shape of three-way video conferencing meetings unless the DBP and the social worker are collocated during some of the set-aside consultation times. Similarly, it may or may not be possible to involve the patient and/or his or her parents directly in interactions with the DBP, as suggested by another PCP. Therefore, additional scheduling/logistical strategies related to such third-party involvement should be considered.

5 Conclusion

Overall, the teleconsultation process was well received by both the PCPs and DBP in this study. The high post-task and post-study ratings (including System Usability Scale, Communication Quality, and attitudes toward the teleconsultation process scores), as well as the positive feedback from participants, indicated the effectiveness of the teleconsultations and satisfaction with this process. In this pilot study, efficiency was also observed through consultations being completed within the expected time range of 15 min or less. Based on qualitative feedback from the participants, the teleconsultations:

- validated the PCPs' ideas for patient plans and strengthened their confidence in talking with families;
- provided new ideas and redirected their thinking;
- connected PCPs with additional resources while considering their location;
- and provided a high level of specificity and sequential ordering of advice.

PCPs especially expressed their interest in the opportunity to connect with an ASD specialist in a timely and efficient manner, and most felt that the video element of the consultation was ideal, and that the teleconsultations enhanced clarity and understanding, attention, engagement, and collegiality.

Enhancement considerations offered above can be used to determine clear procedures and implementation factors and to foster communication quality and interaction for teleconsultations. More broadly, these insights can be used for mediating communication and improving the process of video conferencing between professionals.

Acknowledgements. This research was conducted for the Department of Pediatrics and Human Development, College of Human Medicine, Michigan State University and through their grant from the Michigan Department of Health and Human Services (MDHHS), "Autism Spectrum Disorders: How Michigan State University Can Make a Difference", PIs: Gage, Douglas; English, Boyce; Plavnick, Joshua; Marisa Fisher, 10/1/2014–8/31/2016. Michigan Department of Health and Human Services (formerly Michigan Department of Community Health), MDCH 20152523 Gage.

References

1. Hernandez, M., Hojman, N., Sadorra, C., Dharmar, M., Nesbitt, T.S., Litman, R., Marcin, J.P.: Pediatric critical care telemedicine program: a single institution review. Telemed. e-Health **22** (1), 51–55 (2016)
2. Mehrotra, A., Jena, A.B., Busch, A.B., Souza, J., Uscher-Pines, L., Landon, B.E.: Utilization of telemedicine among rural Medicare beneficiaries. J. Am. Med. Assoc. **315**(18), 2015–2016 (2016)
3. Sabesan, S., Allen, D., Caldwell, P., Loh, P.K., Mozer, R., Komesaroff, P.A., Talman, P., Williams, M., Shaheen, N., Grabinski, O.: Practical aspects of telehealth: doctor–patient relationship and communication. Intern. Med. J. **44**(1), 101–103 (2014)
4. Beste, L.A., Mattox, E.A., Pichler, R., Young, B.A., Au, D.H., Kirsh, S.F., Chang, M.F.: Primary care team members report greater individual benefits from long- versus short-term specialty telemedicine mentorship. Telemed. e-Health **22**(8), 699–706 (2016)
5. American Academy of Pediatrics: What is a developmental-behavioral pediatrician? (2007). http://depts.washington.edu/dbpeds/Orientation/WhatisDevBehPeds.pdf
6. Soares, N.S., Langkamp, D.L.: Telehealth in developmental-behavioral pediatrics. J. Dev. Behav. Pediatr. **33**(8), 656–665 (2012)
7. Brooke, J.: SUS: a retrospective. J. Usability Stud. **8**(2), 29–40 (2013)
8. Duck, S., Rutt, D.J., Hurst, M.H., Strejc, H.: Some evident truths about conversations in everyday relationships: all communications are not created equal. Hum. Commun. Res. **18**, 228–267 (1991)
9. Umphrey, L.R., Wickersham, J.A., Sherblom, J.C.: Student perceptions of the instructor's relational characteristics, the classroom communication experience, and the interaction involvement in face-to-face versus video conference instruction. Commun. Res. Rep. **25**(2), 102–114 (2008)
10. Watts, L., Monk, A.: Telemedical consultation: task characteristics. In: Proceedings of the SIGCHI Conference on Human Factors in Computing Systems, pp. 534–535. ACM, New York, March 1997

Visual Standards for Southern California Tsunami Evacuation Information: Applications of Information Design in Disaster Risk Management

Claudine Jaenichen[✉] and Steve Schandler

Chapman University, Orange, CA, USA
jaenichenstudio@yahoo.com

Abstract. Community participation and reaction during evacuation is rarely an individual and isolated process and the outcomes are systemic. Ineffective evacuation information can easily attribute to delayed evacuation response. Delays increase demands on already extended emergency personal, increase the likelihood of traffic congestion, and can cause harm to self and property. From an information design perspective, addressing issues in cognitive recall and emergency psychology, this project examines evacuation messaging including written, audio, and visual presentation of information, and demonstrates application of design principles and the role of visual communication for Southern California tsunami evacuation outreach. The niche of this project is the inclusion of cognitive recall of visual presentations of information based on quantitative data of a 4-year cognitive recall study that included over 300 participants as the driving influence in how the messaging was developed, distributed to the community, and formal design decisions were made. The outcome of this work feeds into a current project, Visual Standards for Tsunami Evacuation Information, an open-source tool for communities to create and self-sustain tsunami evacuation information specific to location. The project will act as a hub that provides a "starter kit" for community decision-makers and emergency management that are hoping to create cohesive and branded tsunami evacuation information in place for their city and counties.

Keywords: Design patterns · Design philosophy · Design thinking · Design/evaluation for cross-cultural users · Education/training · Information design · Design for disaster planning · Emergency management · Mapping · Wayfinding · Wayshowing · Cognition · Public education

1 Introduction and Background

Emergency management departments in the United States distribute informational and instructional messaging to its residents and communities before an evacuation is required in hopes to make the population "information aware" and therefore more prepared [1]. Emergency management is a public authoritative agency interconnected

© Springer International Publishing AG 2017
A. Marcus and W. Wang (Eds.): DUXU 2017, Part III, LNCS 10290, pp. 645–663, 2017.
DOI: 10.1007/978-3-319-58640-3_46

with agencies responsible for the safety, response, recovery, and preparedness protecting "communities by coordinating and integrating all activities necessary to build, sustain, and improve the capability to mitigate against, prepare for, respond to, and recover from threatened or actual natural disasters, acts of terrorism, or other man-made disasters." [1]. Local departments are funded and regulated at the county, state and federal level.

Claudine Jaenichen is a graphic designer who is also certified emergency medical technician and member of Santa Barbara Sherriff Search and Rescue. In 2005, she decided to investigate the role of design in emergency evacuation procedures.

The specific focus of evacuation information centers in its systemic and capacious variables. Evacuations require different cognitive processing of information due to the unpredictable onset of stress and sudden sense for protection of self, family and property. In a national collection of over 20 official outreach material on evacuation preparedness used for hurricane, flood, and tsunami, the implementation of a map as the main visual infrastructure to communicate messaging was used. The majority of the maps were repurposed roadmaps or inundation maps originally intended for internal emergency planning. The maps were inconsistent in the use of visual variables, amount of graphic density, symbology, semiotics, and severe qualities in legibility and usability.

There are currently no guidelines, regulations, or methodology that include stakeholders in the process of developing and evaluating these maps and their messages. Nor is there data to support that materials are being understood, are memorable, or useful. A problem in conveying evacuation information using a "map" as the main visual infrastructure is assuming the skill set necessary in map reading. An individual will need the following skillset in basic map reading and comprehension; (1) how to use a legend or key; (2) how to determine orientation of the map to physical space; (3) understand meanings of color, texture, and symbols; and (4) how to determine self location to destination in order to create a route. Maps can be confusing to read and dense with information. They can also be authoritative and can imply that the user must understand the map instead of the map being developed to understand the user's needs.

Ineffective evacuation information can easily attribute to delayed evacuation response and communities not evacuating at all. Evacuation behavior and decision-making is rarely an individual and isolated process and responses become systemic. Ineffectual behaviors increase demands on an already extended emergency personal, increase the likelihood of traffic congestion, and harm to self and property. Evacuation materials need to be developed with the inclusion of emergency cognition and disaster psychology. The ability to problem-solve, make rational decisions and recall information becomes vulnerable when confronted by urgent situations. Processing information during high levels of stress contribute to information overload, tunnel vision, temporary cognitive paralysis, and forms of denial. Tunnel vision is associated with extreme stress and exhaustion in which primitive tasks become central to cognitive processing and problem-solving capabilities are limited. Temporary cognitive paralysis, such as when people "freeze", is also associated with people experiencing dramatic shifts in cognitive demands as a result of an abrupt change in the environment. Even though panic is not a likely response in evacuation behavior these cognitive phenomena effects how a person receive and retains information. Variables that contribute to cognitive paralysis include limitation of reaction time, perception of danger to self, and previous training or experience. This is especially true if people do not receive instructions and evacuation information until the time of evacuation is required. Findings from the 2012 FEMA National Survey found that 92% of respondents received their information from the media with the top three sources from local television, national television, and radio. Emergency management departments in Southern California are consistent in relying on these sources, including the web, for evacuation information. Media sources are problematic for two main reasons; (1) they are audio reliant, which data from our study demonstrated was the lowest performing outcome in information recall; and (2) information is usually distributed or accessed at the time of impact providing new information on a population already in distress.

In other related work, airline safety cards share the same objective of informing emergency procedure using visual communication to air passengers. Jaenichen collected international safety cards to assess them in the same way she assessed evacuation maps. She found more unity and cohesion in messaging and use of visual variables across all local and international airlines. A major contributor is having a governing body that dictates and regulates how emergency and safety information is presented. The Federal Aviation Administration's Office of Airport Safety and Standards and National Transportation Safety Board requires that all airlines flying into the United States comply with their regulations. Airline safety cards demonstrated more consistency in their use of symbology, iconography, and text in a cross-cultural environment. Success can also be attributed to repetition when passengers fly regularly. Repetition allows for people to develop and improve a cognitive framework for emergency procedure helping to memorize a cadence and rhythm of information. Relating this work to evacuation material Jaenichen developed a syntax for visual communication that could be universally applied to tsunami evacuation preparedness outreach.

2 Methodology

2.1 Context

The U.S. Geological Survey (USGS) and the California Geological Survey (CGS) provide geologic and seismic expertise to local and government offices that include inundation maps for the purpose of emergency planning. These maps are for "local governmental agencies [to] use these new maximum tsunami inundation lines to assist in the development of their evacuation routes and emergency response plans". Yet, Jaenichen found a number of these maps were used in its original format, or slightly altered, for public outreach. The presentation of these maps have serious issues in readability, scale, labeling, and graphic density for a person who does not have, or should have, experience in topology or geographical map reading. When one of these maps from a public outreach brochure was tested in Santa Barbara, comprehension and cognitive recall failed by 100% early in the study and was excluded from further testing.

2.2 Cognitive Recall Study

To map or not to map—this was the first question to ask before a redesign would be explored. In 2011, Jaenichen approached Dr. Steve Schandler, director of Chapman University's Cognitive Psychophysiology Laboratories, to systematically evaluate evacuation material and improve the quality of content and recall of information by going into the community and testing materials. To date, they have data from over 300 participants in the control group at Chapman University and 100 participants recruited from the communities of coastal cities including Santa Barbara and San Clemente (the evacuation information was directly relevant to participants in these cities, resulting in a study group that was highly motivated to learn the information). Jaenichen and Schandler tested 3 different presentations of information; written, audio, and visual (e.g. map). All participants were evaluated for corrected vision and hearing, educational level, literacy level, and general health status.

Participants served individually in one study session, followed 24-h later with a phone call interview. One third of the subjects were given the visual redesign evacuation map; one third received a written description of the same movement routes; and one third was presented with a digital audio recording describing the same movement routes. They either had 4 or 2 min to review or listen to the material. Immediately following the presentation of the information, the subject completed a 15-question multiple-choice test regarding the information that was presented. Twenty-four hours later the subject was contacted via telephone and completed another test regarding the information presented in the first session. The review period was determined by the average time people spent looking at direct mail marketing because the scenario and distribution of the proposed campaign will mimic how people retain information without cognitive impairments.

Across all groups and both review periods, the visual (map) presentation of information produced better retention (less forgetting) of information from Day One to Day Two.

2-Minute Review Period: For all information types, Day One and Day Two recall were greater for the community sample suggesting higher motivation for persons most affected by the evacuation information. Compared to the other information forms, the greatest recall scores were associated with the written presentation of information. However, compared to the visual (map) presentation, proportionally less written information was recalled during Day Two. Auditory information presentation was associated with the greatest reduction in information retention from Day One to Day Two.

4-Minute Review Period: Increased information review time increased recall for each information type. This was exactly what was predicted. The recall superiority of the visual (map) presentation of information remained, indicating that its effectiveness is due more to the information type than due to the time allowed to evaluate the information. The increased processing produced more permanent storage of the information. Compared to written information, the auditory information presentation also benefitted more from the increase in review time.

In summary, the written presentation of evacuation information resulted in the greatest immediate recall for both groups. However, visual presentation produced the most stable recall across the 24-h retention period. This is particularly significant in trying to initiate a preparedness campaign prior to a disaster event so at the time an event occurs, experience with the information would have already made a cognitive imprint reducing the amount of learning new information under stress.

2.3   Design Principles and Wayshowing

During an evacuation, learning is already compromised by anxiety. Because evacuation information is given under levels of stress, recalling information reduces the ability to process and learn new information. Jaenichen and Schandler revised the map by simplifying it down to only relevant layers of information. They formulated length and levels of components (e.g. compositional space and hierarchy) and use of visual variables. This approach was particularly critical for the continuity and application of other tsunami evacuation campaigns to be used in other coastal cities. The redesign prioritized a distinct clarification between foreground and background information driven by "wayshowing" principles. This approach changed the main visual infrastructure from a geological, topology, or road map to assimilating the more commonly recognized diagrammatic public transportation map.

In 2005, Mollerup [2] coined the term "wayshowing", derivative of the term "wayfinding" originated by Lynch [4] from The Image of a City in 1960. Mollerup suggested that in order to assist in wayfinding, principles of wayshowing is needed. Maps are static forms of communication relying on the reader to decode the information, finding out where they are on the map, navigating the space, and determining which routes are relevant. By approaching the map from the perspective of the user, information takes an active role indicating directions for movement and instructions. Formal decisions of visual variables included conventions already used by public transportation in southern California, including what Jacques [5] defined as *visual verbs*—presentation of arrows—which made the maps less static and effectively communicated directions and instructions for movement.

Texture

Texture creates visual noise, a vibration or disruption, of the composition causing the eye to move towards that noise. When used sparingly, texture can help with calling attention to significant areas on the page. Texture was used to create noise indicating possible road closure due to inundation. The use of high-contrast "checker" texture was used to cause disruption in order to make potential closures on major routes and highways a priority top-level read (see Fig. 1). The Orange County Transportation

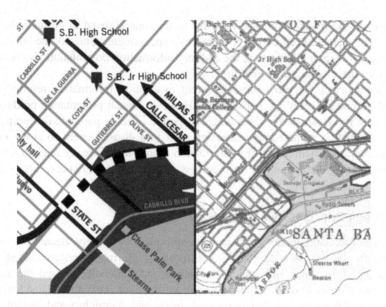

Fig. 1. The first map uses texture intentionally to bring attention to areas of importance. The second map shows when too much texture is used, there is no place for the eye to settle.

Authority currently uses this texture for possible route closures on bus maps syncing the conventional meaning of this pattern to the tsunami maps.

Another texture used in cities with military or natural preserved restricted areas was a crosshatched pattern. Crosshatches, made from patterns of "x", represent the idea of "fencing-off", restricted, or "do not enter (Fig. 2)."

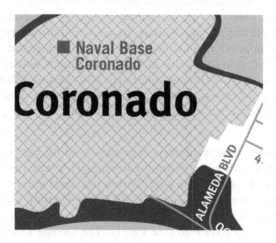

Fig. 2. Cities like Coronado, San Diego, have significant military bases not accessible to the public. A crosshatch texture is used to signify this restricted area.

Standardizing visual guidelines for tsunami information still allows for political, organizational, governmental, and individual flexibility for the need of each city. In Santa Barbara, emergency management designated an area that would be immediately impacted during a tsunami evacuation, not by the inundation zone itself, but the congestion that would follow an evacuation. Not every city has needed this visual variable, but when needed, diagonal lines is the standardized texture for this specific communicative message (Fig. 3).

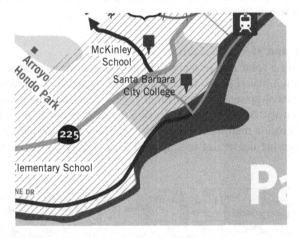

Fig. 3. Some cities designate a "high warning" area reflected here as diagonal lines.

Three more visual variables using texture indicate a form of a route; rail, path, and beach entry seen in Fig. 4 below.

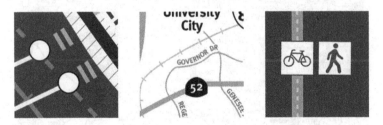

Fig. 4. From left to right: parallel strokes represent beach entry; thin line with hatch pattern represent a rail/train route; and shorter dash lines represent walking or biking paths.

There is a total of 6 visual levels using texture seen in Fig. 5 below.

Fig. 5. From left to right: restricted area, high warning area, route effected by flooding, train or rail route, walk/bike path, beach entry

Density: Color and Stroke Weights

When developing a color and stroke weight palette, we accounted our analysis of the original evacuation materials we reviewed and the inconsistent variations of density. Density is the visual presence of an overall page. Color and stroke weights are attributes to page density. A bad example of a very dense page reliant on color and strokes is the Texas evacuation map seen in Fig. 6 below. Many maps Jaenichen and Schandler reviewed had varying degrees of unsupported page density with no clear function.

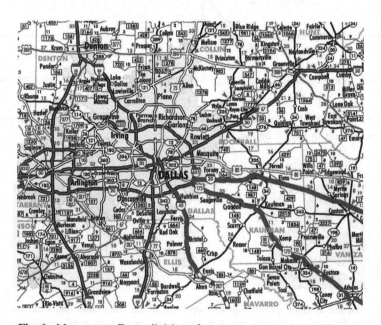

Fig. 6. Map source: Texas division of emergency management, Houston

Their approach to color was based on defined functions—they would not add color or change variance without this rule. We reviewed color semiotics and conventions established in the area. All evacuation routes are indicated as blue. The California Department of Transportation had already officially "branded" the color blue by implementing tsunami evacuation route and evacuation site identification signage throughout coastal cities (see Fig. 7). Although using blue for the tsunami evacuation routes could be confused with flood direction or movement of water rather than safety routes—because the symbolic meaning between signified, water, and signifier, blue, is iconic—they felt confident that the convention of evacuation route had already been well-too established with coastal communities to flip its meaning.

Fig. 7. State of California - Department of Transportation (2007)

They relied on the conventional meaning of red for the inundation area—associated with meanings such as emergency exit signs, fire (fire trucks, extinguishers, etc.), emergency room signage, emergency call and stop buttons, and the American Red Cross. In Fig. 8 below, "flooding" is indicated in red and the evacuation route in blue.

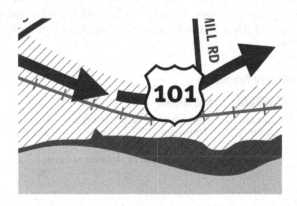

Fig. 8. The red represents the inundation area, whereas the blue is coded for the evacuation route based on the color code already established by the Department of Transportation's tsunami evacuation route signage. (Color figure online)

A third color, gold, was used for landmarks functioning as spatial orientation devices. The remaining neutral color palette, screens of black, functioned as background and foreground control, providing levels hierarchy and priority of information (Fig. 9).

Primary functions

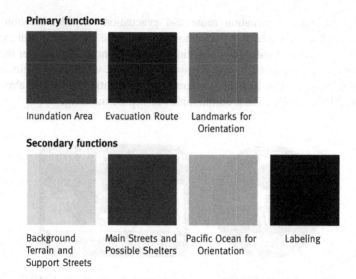

Inundation Area   Evacuation Route   Landmarks for
                                       Orientation

Secondary functions

Background   Main Streets and   Pacific Ocean for   Labeling
Terrain and   Possible Shelters   Orientation
Support Streets

Fig. 9. There is a total of 6 visual levels using color. (Color figure online)

Stroke weights play a role in density, not only in their own representation on the page with its mark and color, but also how they layer and interact with one another. Joseph Albers [6], author of *Interaction of Color* and *Color Theory*, explains that the negative "white space" in between elements is an actual graphic element. The unintentional negative space created by intentional visual variables influence design principles such as composition, tension, tangents, and overall legibility. Stroke weights and color were only added when its function were clearly defined (Fig. 10).

Primary functions

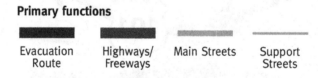

Evacuation   Highways/   Main Streets   Support
Route   Freeways   Streets

Fig. 10. There is a total of 4 stroke weights.

Typography

One of the most important revisions Jaenichen and Schandler negotiated was content. Major cuts were made in the amount of information in existing evacuation material. They identified relevant streets, landmarks, and routes, removing any other "visual noise" that was too specific for the public's use. A great deal clutter was removed as seen in Fig. 11 below.

A disciplined typographic approach was established into 5 levels of hierarchy. The following list of information was given a consistent type size, use of caps, and color in every map they have produced. The order is from the most prominent, foreground information, to lower level, background information:

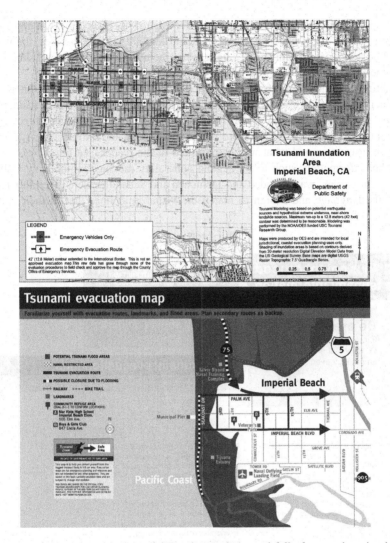

Fig. 11. The first map used by Imperial Beach was dense and full of competing visual noise. The second map demonstrates how our revisions improved legibility revealing and usable and relevant information intended for the public to use.

(1) Identification of the city represented.
(2) Identification of neighboring cities and major highways for spatial orientation.
(3) Names of landmarks, including train stations, hospitals, parks, tourist sites, and in some cases, well known residential areas known to the people who live in the city.
(4) Street names and highways of evacuation routes
(5) Other smaller, but relevant, street names needed in order to connect to the major evacuation routes

They used Meta, a humanist sans serif designed by Erik Spiekermann [7] and released in 1991, because of its cleanliness and legibility. In some cases, the typeface had to be legible at 7 points and Meta's subtle inclusion of serifs helped shape words the same way serif typefaces do.

Editing the amount of information was also a significant and successful negotiation in reducing text when applied to the content of brochures mailed out to residents and businesses in the inundation areas. They re-stylized the writing using direct conversational (e.g. using "you", "your", etc.) throughout the material to be more specific and direct in instruction and what was being asked of the reader (see Fig. 11).

Other information, such as the legend and safety message required by California Geological Survey, was included and Jaenichen and Schandler were given flexibility to revise the language and design to match the visual guidelines that fit their approach (Fig. 12).

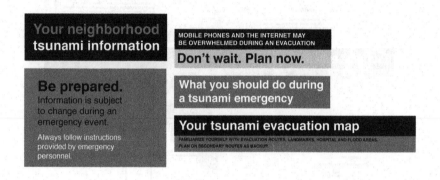

Fig. 12. Example of mastheads and copywriting using direct conversational style in brochure that was mailed to residents

Walking Sign Systems

Santa Barbara, Coronado, and Marina del Rey have major foot and bike traffic and are especially populated with tourists and people who do not know the city well. We explored a walking sign system that would address the populated tourist areas and help this demographic make decisions in an area that may be unfamiliar to them. For example, if someone was on the pier in Santa Barbara and an evacuation order was given, signage would indicate that walking 5 min to safety would be better than retrieving a car in a parking lot that is further away and in the direction of the potential inundation area.

We require that maps included in the walking sign system be aligned in a heads-up position and that the placement and unique orientation will correspond to the direction the user is facing (see Fig. 13). We conducted walk-throughs of pedestrian traffic areas

Fig. 13. Example of heads-up positioning for a walking sign system in Santa Barbara and Huntington Beach

and identified areas where signage would benefit decision-making in the event of an evacuation. Due to limited budgets, we were required to use kiosks or sign posts that were already in place.

Print vs. Web

Web is the most cost effective and efficient mode of information from the perspective of emergency management. Changes can be uploaded instantly with no limitations in the amount of content. There are major problems relying on virtual information whether distributed before a tsunami event or during. Research continues to support that sudden influx placed on telecommunications will most likely overwhelm infrastructure. Technology is an invaluable resource, but limita-tions must also be acknowledged. A report written by Townsend and Moss [8], Telecommunications Infrastructure in Disasters: Preparing Cities for Crisis Communication (2005), sheds light on the increasing concern of relying on technology for communication distribution:

> The breakdown of essential communications is one of the most widely shared characteristics of all disasters. Whether partial or complete, the failure of telecommunications infrastructure leads to preventable loss of life and damage to property, by causing delays and errors in emergency response and disaster relief efforts. Yet despite the increasing reliability and resiliency of modern telecommunications networks to physical damage, the risk associated with communications failures remains serious because of growing dependence upon these tools in emergency operations.

This investigation by Townsend and Moss revealed 3 causes of failure that is still relevant today; (1) physical destruction of network components; (2) disruption in supporting network infrastructure; and (3) network congestion. FEMA's tips for communicating during an emergency (2014) emphasizes the need to have charged devices with advanced knowledge of an event, but this excludes disasters that are unpredictable and devices need infrastructure to function.

Even though people are encouraged to learn about evacuation preparedness, they do not volunteer to do so prior to evacuation. A person must volunteer to access virtual community outreach. Jaenichen and Schandler surveyed L.A. and Orange County residents in 2009 and 86% of those surveyed did not know what to do in case of an evacuation and 80% would not how they would be notified. Emergency management spends a lot of energy on community outreach, including online and social media presence. Websites such as Ready.gov and TsunamiZone.org are valuable resources of information and Jaenichen would be interested to measure how many people from the public visit these sites and how they use the information. Until then, she has advocated for an "information confrontation" approach to distributing information, similar to direct-mail marketing campaigns. Aside from consumer-targeted marketing, these direct-mail pieces also come from city utility agencies. People spend an average of 2-min reviewing the relevance of direct-mail information before making the decision to either save or discard the material. This interaction places evacuation information in front of people so they take responsibility to confront the material. Reoccurring and repetitive cadence of mailings (at least annually) is also critical so information begins to build a cognitive framework. Fire drills and airline safety demonstrations are good examples of successful repetitive exercises. Below are examples of the final printed formats where all the visual and text variables are combined into its final intentional messaging.

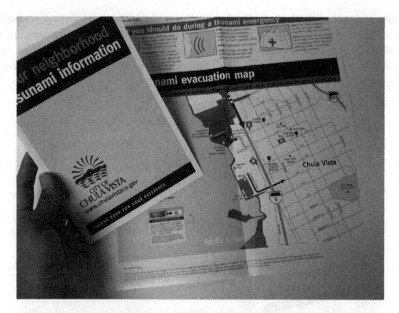

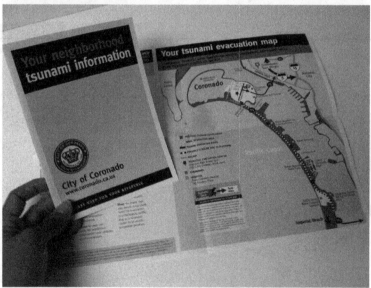

3   Implementation

Since 2011, this project has generated interest from the Emergency Management community, California Geological Survey, and invitations to present at the National Evacuation Conference, the California State Emergency Management Conference, and

California State Tsunami Steering Committee meetings. Jaenichen has also been invited to be a permanent member of the CA Tsunami Steering Committee, not only demonstrating the relevance of our work, but also the role of design in civic service and the significance of design principles in safety and health risk communication. Below are examples of completed redesigns for tsunami evacuation instructions.

To date, we have completed work for 23 coastal cities in Southern California for San Diego, Los Angles, and Orange Counties including, Santa Barbara, Huntington Beach, Carlsbad, City of San Diego, Coronado, Chula Vista, Del Mar, Encinitas,

Imperial Beach, National City, Oceanside, Solana Beach, Venice, Marina del Rey, Harbor City, Long Beach, Santa Monica, Malibu, El Segundo, Hermosa Beach, Palos Verdes Estates, Redondo Beach, Rancho Palos Verdes, and Manhattan Beach. Within the established design standards, flexibility is necessary to meet the individual needs and politics of counties and cities.

4 Future Work

Because of this work, Jaenichen has reached out to a global network of scientists, designers, and design thinkers creating Design Network for Emergency Management (DNEM). DNEM is an international think tank that consists of experts from five of the world's seven continents. The core group specialize in diverse fields such as design, research, science, emergency planning, and policy. By encouraging quality research, collaborations, and applications of design and design thinking in the specialized area of emergency planning, DNEM will build a stronger body of universal knowledge, credibility, and applications of design methodologies in disaster risk management. DNEM provides transdisciplinary expertise on the applications of design thinking and evidence-based design principles before, during and after emergencies.

The core group of DNEM will work on publishing usability guidelines, Visual Standards for Tsunami Evacuation Information (VSTEI). The purpose of VSTEI is to convey the importance of distributing precise emergency evacuation information, empower city infrastructure and management to feel comfortable implementing VSTEI, and encourage accurate cognitive recall of tsunami evacuation information for residents, tourists, students, commuters, and employees in tsunami risk cities. VSTEI will provide a tool to educate emergency management on the benefits of data-supported design principles when developing and visualizing content for the public. Emergency planners will be able to create and distribute tsunami evacuation and preparedness information that is coherent, cohesive, and memorable.

The Governor's Office of Emergency Services (CalOES), U.S. Department of Commerce National Oceanic and Atmospheric Administration (NOAA), and United States CA Geological Survey (CGS) has endorsed VSTEI. VSTEI will be a resource hub for emergency management as they develop tsunami evacuation information for their community and will provide guidelines and tools that are cohesive, visually "branded," and State-endorsed.

References

1. FEMA. Guide to Emergency Management and Related Terms, Definitions, Acronyms, Programs and Legislation (2008). https://training.fema.gov/hiedu/docs/terms%20and%20definitions/terms%20and%20definitions.pdf
2. www.fema.gov. 2012 FEMA National Survey Report (2013). https://www.fema.gov/media-library-data/662ad7b4a323dcf07b829ce0c5b77ad9/2012_FEMA_National_Survey_Report.pdf
3. Mollerup, P.: Wayshowing: A Guide to Environmental Signage. Lars Muller Publishers, Switzerland (2005)

4. Lynch, K.: The Image of the City. The M.I.T. Press, Massachusetts Institute of Technology, Cambridge, Massachusetts, London, England (1960)
5. Jacques, B.: Semiology of Graphics: Diagrams, Networks, Maps. The University of Wisconsin Press, Wisconsin (1993). Trans. William J. Berg
6. Albers, J.: Interaction of Color. Yale University Press, New Haven (2006)
7. Erik Spiekermann is an information architect, type designer (FF Meta, ITC Officina, FF Info, FF Unit, LoType, Berliner Grotesk), author of books and articles on type and typography, and founder of MetaDesign—Germany's largest design firm with offices in Berlin, London and San Francisco
8. Townsend, A.M., Moss, M.L.: Telecommunciation Infrastructure in Disasters: Preparing Cities for Crisis Communications (2005). www.nyu.edu/ccpr/pubs/NYU-DisasterCommunications 1-Final.pdf

SmartPA: An Electronic Solution for Secure Prior Authorization Processing

Ramandeep Kaur[1], Patricia Morreale[1(✉)], and Marvin Andujar[2]

[1] Department of Computer Science, Kean University, Union, NJ, USA
{kramande, pmorreal}@kean.edu
[2] Computer Science and Engineering Department,
University of Florida, Gainesville, FL, USA
manduja@ufl.edu

Abstract. Electronic Prior Authorization (Electronic PA) is a fast and efficient way of ensuring that prior authorization, needed for medical drug and treatment dispensing, is accurately and promptly completed, supporting quick delivery of medications to patients. Electronic PA (ePA) solutions are the next big revolution in healthcare industry after the introduction of electronic health records. ePA is a time saver for prescribers as well as a cost-saving solution to insurance companies and Medicare services. ePA is new to the industry and due to a knowledge gap among medical professionals and their IT solution providers, ePA applications lack sophisticated components to ease the workflow. Instead of being time-saving, broken ePA processes become time consuming. A research study identified common gaps around the PA process by interviewing and gathering feedback from key stakeholders in the process. The results of the study have demonstrated how a new electronic solution that was developed working with the stakeholders has helped close some of the identified gaps. The resulting solution, SmartPA, provides a secure, reliable interface in support of medical standards, as well as enhancing the PA workflow process.

Keywords: User centered design (UCD) · Electronic prior authorization (ePA) · Digital healthcare systems

1 Introduction

Scenarios where the transition to electronic health records from paper charting caused the documentation process to become more tedious have been documented [1, 2]. The target user community of medical professionals was not happy with the change to the new electronic health records (EHRs) or the lack of communication that the change was to occur. Along with designing novel technologies for the benefit of the users, developers must include user input and ideas from early on to avoid disappointments in the resulting system design. One of the overarching goals of human- computer interaction (HCI) research has been to increase the good experiences and possibly reduce or mitigate horrible first experiences with technology [1]. When migrating to a new technology, the transition should be smooth.

© Springer International Publishing AG 2017
A. Marcus and W. Wang (Eds.): DUXU 2017, Part III, LNCS 10290, pp. 664–676, 2017.
DOI: 10.1007/978-3-319-58640-3_47

A more efficient solution to prior authorization (PA), as it is currently in practice, is needed. PA is a vital procedure that involves prescribers (doctors, nurses, nurse practitioners, physician assistants), patients, pharmacists as well as insurance companies and companies that manage their benefits (PBM). Insurance companies maintain drugs in lists called formulary lists and non- formulary lists. Drugs listed under the formulary list category are dispensed using a process called Prior Authorization. These formulary drug lists have prescriptions that have been tested and researched to be safe and effective, as well as less costly to both the insurance carrier and the member. The insurance companies see formulary drug lists as a way to increase safety and effectiveness (although, it can be debatable if their formularies have the best prescriptions out there, it just depends on the specific case and insurance carrier) while also keeping costs down for both parties. Both brand name drugs and generic drugs can be found on formularies, however, generic drugs are almost always less costly and chemically equivalent to brand name drugs [19].

Several of the drugs that are restricted in nature due to clinical usage or even cost are controlled using the PA process. In a typical scenario, a patient goes to a doctor's office for treatment of a condition they are experiencing and the prescriber writes a prescription for the medication. The patient takes the prescription to a pharmacy for fulfillment. The pharmacist will run this script through the dispensing system. For the formulary drugs, if the patient is denied the medication, he/she is requested to contact their prescriber to the next action. A call is placed to the prescription benefit management (PBM) company that serves the insurance plan for further action. Once, the prescriber calls the PBM, he/she is taken through the PA process flow where they are asked detailed questions for the usage of the medication. The PBM will then make a decision of "Approval" or "Denial" for the requested medication. In case of an approval, the patient can return back to the pharmacy and receive their medication. In case of "Denial", further case reviews occur. Figure 1 details the Prior Authorization workflow process.

Non-formulary prescriptions aren't on the insurance policies list of preferred drugs. Knowing that, non-formularies are costlier as well as experimental in nature. The PA process to receive this medication is often very complicated due to the nature of their

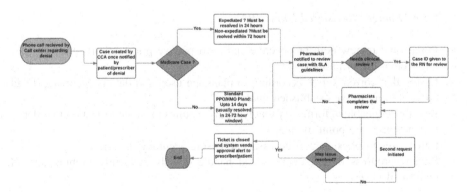

Fig. 1. Prior authorization workflow process.

administration. Most of the patients receiving these drugs will be in the hospital and closely monitored [20]. Non-formulary drug PA processes are excluded from this paper.

An ineffective PA process can have a significant impact on healthcare [3, 4]. The U.S. spends four times as much money on PA compared to Canada [5]. Most of the money goes to physician income due to the amount of time they spend in negotiation between pharmacies and PBMs to resolve a denial case [6]. Patient care could be improved if the PA process was less time-consuming for physicians [7, 8]. Therefore, an effective electronic solution is required to make this cumbersome process simple for the users who are prescribers, pharmacists, and PBM employees and for the overall benefit of the patients [9].

2 Methodology

It is essential for developers to engage stakeholder when attempting to rebuild old broken processes [10]. A key stakeholder is defined as an individual, a group, or an organization who may affect, be affected by, or perceive itself to be affected by a decision, activity, or outcome of a project, program, or portfolio [10]. The following are the identified key stakeholders and their defined roles in the process of electronic prior authorization [11, 12]:

- *Managed Care Pharmacists*

- Work with other health professionals to establish drug utilization guidelines and administrative policies for prior authorization criteria.
- Design communication protocols to be used in call centers to ensure that the correct information is collected as required for PA processes.
- Analyze prescription claim data to identify problematic prescription use patterns.
- Ensure safe drug distribution, encourage appropriate prescribing and proper use of medications by reviewing PA requests, determine if additional information is needed, work with other health care professionals to make a decision on the request and meet turn-around times.

- *Case Manager Registered Nurse (RN)*

- Initiate and review both prospective and retrospective prior authorization requests (electronic, fax or phone).
- Ensure that correct forms according to plans are used and data is accurately filled out according to the established guidelines.
- Be knowledgeable of formulary that typically requires prior authorization in order to take action at the point of care.
- Refer cases to physicians if necessary to ensure accuracy of forms.
- Review progress of PA requests and handle denials efficiently. Submit second requests if necessary.

- *Call Center Agent*

– Aid prescribers in the PA process, especially those who are still performing the process manually.
– Assist prescribers in obtaining correct PA forms and faxing them.
– Inform prescribers of requirements for letters documenting medical necessity.
– Handle the request by phone.
– Notify prescribers of the status of their PA request.

For this study, participants were recruited from different backgrounds to accurately present the user community. An initial survey was circulated among potential users who initially expressed interest in taking part in the study. The survey had an informed consent to ensure users did not feel compelled to participate and knew their right to withdraw at any time from the study. Figure 2 presents the questions included in the initial survey:

Three focus groups were conducted based on user's role, and include pharmacists (4), case management nurses (4), and call center agents (3):

Managed care pharmacists are the most vital part of the prior authorization process. They perform end-to-end business roles including receiving the claim information from the prescriber, reviewing the claim for drug interactions or misuse, drug distribution

1. What is current role at your place of employment ?
    a. Physician/Nurse Practitioner
    b. Registered Nurse
    c. Pharmacist
    d. Call Center Agent
    e. Other: _____
2. How long have you been employed at your current job ?
    a. Less than a year
    b. 1 - 5 years
    c. 5 - 10 years
    d. Other: _____
3. Is your primary job responsibility related to prior-authorization ?
    a. Yes
    b. No
    c. I'm not sure
4. How many hours do you spend working with prior authorization process in a week ?
    a. Less 3 hours
    b. 3 - 6 hours
    c. 6 - 10 hours
    d. More than 10 hours
5. Do you have an opinion you would like to share regarding making the current prior authorization process that you work with more efficient ?
    a. Yes
    b. No

Fig. 2. Initial survey questions.

and dispensing, ensuring patient safety as well as business and cost management [16]. These pharmacists are doctorate-prepared professionals with a minimum of five years' experience in the traditional pharmacy setting before being recruited onto managed care responsibility [11].

Case management nurses bring a different perspective to the business. Their role is to certify the medical necessity provided by the prescriber regarding the prescribed drug or procedure. They make their decision based on detailed medical information about the patient such as current diagnosis, lab results, scans, previous prescriptions, hospital visits, etc. They are highly trained and usually possess five years or more industry experience along with a graduate degree in case management nursing [12]. Their input is essential to patient safety and quality administration.

Call center agents (CCAs) are an important part of the prior authorization process and are usually the first point of contact for patients and prescribers. They should possess prioritization and organization skills. They can be hired for the position if they have a high school diploma and knowledge of primary medical terminology. All CCA's should have basic HIPPA training to protect confidential patient information.

3   Survey Results

All survey participants were informed that participation in the focus group was voluntary and they could withdraw their participation at any time per protocol of NIH PHRP [21]. Each focus group was carried out by one facilitator and lasted an average 30 min, during which the facilitator invited users to expand on their thought and suggestions [13]. An open dialogue format was used during the discussion [14, 15]. The top concerns brought up by the users based on their roles are presented here.

Managed care pharmacists had the most input with several key concerns associated with the system they are using currently:

- One of the pharmacists initiated the discussion by suggesting that he has witnessed multiple users accessing the same case ID for a patient at the same time resulting in simultaneous entries which can cause medical errors.
- Additionally, everyone had the same consensus about the process being extremely manual. For a given patient case ID, three to seven screens need to be accessed across several systems to gather pertinent information about a single patient. This can cause delay and excessive frustration.
- One user reported that existing systems are slow and based on some highly unstable old platforms. Any updates from the technology team causes system failures.
- Another user reported lack of Auto save function in case the application crashes, which is quite common.
- In general, users said there is no standard user interface across the different business areas. If a job change happens, users have to learn a new system every time.
- Finally, no update tags or user edit comment functionality is provided in the current system. If multiple users work on a single case ID, it is difficult to determine who made the last change.

Case management nurses also had their fair share of disappointment with the current systems due to the fact that they don't get a distinction in the application.

- The system lacks access control and according to the users, everyone has the same access control in the application causing information overload for nurses.
- These users have to go fishing for the data. There is no dedicated workflow for nurses to get assigned cases. They must receive case IDs from the call center or pharmacists to pick up their assignment.
- Once the case ID is manually entered, the users are bombarded with information and based solely on their experience, they review pertinent data.
- The system also lacks a patient 360-degree view that would provide assessment data, previous history, etc. for facilitating case reviews.
- Finally, no workflow setup is present to transfer the case back to the call center agent or pharmacists once reviewed by the nurse.

Call center agents were not as happy after they learned that developing a more efficient electronic PA might cut down on the total number of call centers. However, they were reassured that an efficient PA will affect them equally compared to other users and a comprehensive prior authorization process should have call centers to include physicians that are not using electronic health record or CoverMyMeds® system in their offices.

- Some CCA users reported there was no easy way to read drug usage information to assist the patient on the phone. From the focus group discussion, it was noted that if a patient call in, a CCA will answer any drug information related question.
- One of the user's internal company surveys revealed that approximately 25% of the faxes and phone calls are misdirected to the wrong department causing user frustration. The misdirection is possible due to an ineffective integrated voice recognition (IVR) component of the ePA.
- Users reported that case details are in different pages and tabs without a summary view to read out to the patient when they call in to ask about their case decision. The lack of a summary page of case details results in lengthy call times.
- Lastly, no easy workflow exists for transferring case requests to a pharmacist or RN, which seems to be a common failure point in all three user groups. It requires manual calls along with passing of an explicit and correct case id instead of direct workflow routing.

4 Design Concept

The web-based platform developed is designed to identify and introduce complete automation in the existing manual process. Future functionality will have the call center agent processing cases in 1/10th of the time as it takes in the manual spread sheet driven process. The time calculation is based on the reported time it takes to "create case" in manual environment versus expected automated process. The patient's medical record alone with the physician request for the formulary medication will be presented to the call center agent using highly efficient web services. These XML web services will fetch the data from the back end repositories and provide it to the call center agent for case processing. The web services will perform the role to streamline the data and present only relevant pieces of information in an efficient manner. This will avoid direct SQL calls to the backend data stores and will encapsulate business data safely and efficiently.

SmartPA, a JavaScript/CSS based web application, is a real-time, end-to-end electronic prior authorization solution that is scalable and integrated within the physician and pharmacy application workflow. A basic PA application helps in processing coverage reviews of any PBM eligibility and claims adjudication system. This system monitors the status and outcomes of coverage reviews made by PBM and manages coverage reviews of prescription rejections. The application also administers client specific coverage criteria with complete adherence to Medicare and HCR rules and other state specific regulations. Prior Auth application design follows a layered architecture (Fig. 3).

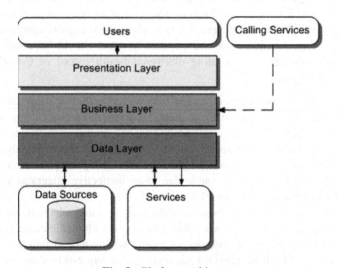

Fig. 3. Platform architecture

This particular PA application is designed to support four types of users.

1. Pharmacists
2. Case Management nurses
3. Customer care representatives
4. Physicians (using a separate end of the application)

Presentation layer components implement the functionality required to allow users to interact with the application. This layer contains UI components and UI validation components. User interface (UI) components provide the mechanism for users to interact with the application. They format data and render it for display, and acquire and validate data entered by users. PA application uses HTML components for UI.

UI validation component ensures data integrity in the system and protects the process by imposing data validation. PA application uses Java script based UI validation.

5 Usability Testing

5.1 Overall User Testing

User testing was conducted at an off-site facility to keep the bias to a minimal from the current system that users are exposed to already. There were total of eight attendees who participated in Test 1 after development cycle 1 and six in Test 2 after development cycle 2. Typically, a total of six to eight participants are involved in a usability test to ensure stable results [13]. Each individual session lasted approximately fifteen minutes. Test scenarios differed from test 1 versus test 2. In general, all participants found SmartPA to be clearer, more straightforward, and overall better system to use. During Test 1, 85% thought the SmartPA was easy to use, was a more stable environment and was easy to navigate. 15% of the participants thought that application can be improved significantly.

During Test 1 following were the identified minor problems:

– Lack of auto-save function in the application
– Manual ID entry is the only way to look up a patient or an existing case
– Clients cannot see a sequential break-down of the case components

During Test 2 following were the identified minor problems:

– Inability to save entered information in the forms during application crash was one of the initial problems recognized in the legacy system.
  - In first round of testing, users were not able to verify if that function exists in the application. During the application testing in developing environment, application was stopped during "debug" mode to test for data retention during application crash.
  - During round 2 testing, users were able to go back to the previous page and see the stored information in the previously filled forms, however, that does not guarantee application's ability to retain entered data in an event of a crash. To properly assess that, we will need to create a crash simulation in the user (deployment) environment.
– It was successfully assessed that manual user entry has dual advantage in the SmartPA application system.
  - It will be ensured that user ID's entered in the directory for each user will match their member ID's as well. Entering the user ID will add an additional security feature by making it hard for application users to browse non-essential health records.
  - Only essential, case-pertinent health records should be accessed by users as well as the application allows only one health record to be opened at a time. However, users are able to do "last name" look up for ease of case search.

- Multiple users are prohibited from accessing the same health record on multiple machines to keep data entry accurate and information up to date. This removes the need for data cleaning and comment association for each change.
- Lastly, clients are able to see sequential breakdown of the case summary including member information, physician contact information, details regarding the case as well as coverage review decision
  - This prevents the need to toggle between different applications as well as potentially reducing errors by displaying all patient information on one screen.
  - In client focus interviews, 100% of the participants preferred single screen display versus multiple page information gathering.

Users were also given a wireframe diagram of a superior electronic PA system to study and identify major differences between their legacy app and this wireframe simulation of a sophisticated ePA summary screen (Fig. 4)

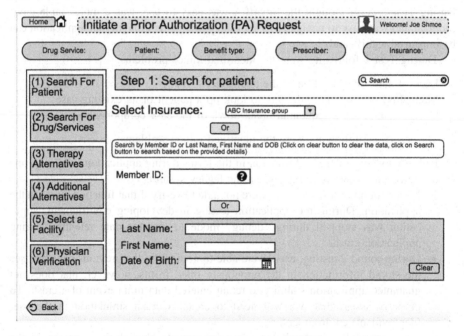

Fig. 4. SmartPA reference wireframe

Unfortunately, all focus groups returned with mission critical failures they have noticed in their legacy systems. Major key points included:

- application UI crash or hang-up in the middle of case creating queue which leads to patient frustration and increased call times
- One single sign-on for all roles and no work-queue segregation causing full exposure of patient data for all members
- Need to toggle among applications to retrieve information
- Significant amount of manual entry forms

The representatives of ePA teams suggested that it is all about keeping up with the latest technology. Migration to better systems will potentially help save money by reducing maintenance costs. Failing to keep up with IT trends makes any business lose their competitive edge. There are several competitor products that have been launched to support ePAs in various environments. As a business, being unable to keep up with the strong currents of technology will seriously affect company earnings and potential extinction [18].

5.2   Test Methodology

Task-Based Evaluation: After the application was completed in development cycle 2, the participants were invited to perform user acceptance testing (UAT) on the application to assess the usability of SmartPA. Participants were assigned two task sequences to complete major functions of the SmartPA: Case create and Case review. UAT was performed by employing a usability tool called "Task decomposition" during which user is given a task sequence to follow and their activity time is recorded [17]. These results are primarily based on test 2 of the application development due to completeness of the app and a better workflow achieved after the 2nd round of development. The participants were grouped together for the sake of simplicity and also due to the fact that the two major functionalities are synonymous on all of the user screens. Three categories of users were provided with three separate logins, one for each user category, which was a major improvement over the legacy systems. RNs, pharmacists and CCAs each had their own individual logins into SmartPA. The group had six members and two from each group representation.

All participants successfully completed Task sequence 1 ("Case Search"). Five of the six (84%) completed Task 5 within expected time which was 2 min and 46 s with a standard deviation of 51 s.

Approximately half (50%) of participants were able to complete Task 2 (Case create, Fig. 5) in expected time of 4 min and 15 s with a standard deviation of 54 s.

Since there was no effective measure of key logging or error capturing, if a participant had felt that they had reached a point of no return in the sequence, they were allowed to restart the task and measuring stop- watch allowed to be reset. The previous

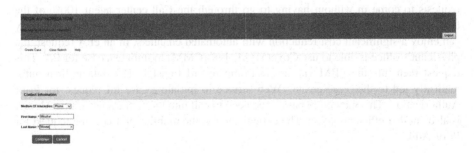

Fig. 5. "Create Case" screen in SmartPA

score was discarded. Records reflected in the log are only where the user successfully completed the sequence.

Task Rating: Task rating is an essential measure to be done when performing task decomposition. This establishes the efficacy of the new features in a product versus legacy features. [13, 17]. After the completion of each task, participants were asked to rate the ease or difficulty of performing these functions since these will be essential parts of their work routine. Following three factors were considered in ratings:

– As a user, it was easy to find my way to this information from the homepage.
– As a user, as I was searching for this information, I was able to keep track of where I was in the website.
– As a user, I was able to accurately predict which section of the website contained this information.

The 5-point rating scale ranged from 1 (Strongly disagree) to 5 (Strongly agree). Agree ratings are the agree and strongly agree ratings combined with a mean agreement rating of >4.0 considered as the user agrees that the information was easy to find, that they could keep track of their location and predict the section to find the information [17].

All participants agreed it was easy to create a case (mean agreement rating = 4.23) and 76% found it easy to perform coverage review for a case (mean agreement rating = 4.11).

6 Future Recommendations

With an application such as SmartPA, there are significant opportunities for future implementations. Many enhanced features can be added to the application such as RFID two factor authentication to pad security features, e-fax ability and fax queuing as well as e-letter generation during case rejections. Based on budget allocation and manpower, the application can integrate with several other electronic methods of data feeds such as CoverMyMeds®, leading EHRs and e-pharmacy systems. The call center agent will also benefit from the questions and answers in an electronic fashion. This will be much faster and more efficient than the current manual fax and phone call process. The data will be electronically sent over to the application and stored in the system of record database. Several channels such as ePA and Mobile will allow for requests to come in without having to go through the Call center agent 100% of the time. This is a highly efficient and organized way to handle PA requests and a company can enjoy a significant cost reduction with automated channels. In an ePA request, the physician's office is able to use CoverMyMeds® (CMM) to initiate a case for PA. This request then hits the PBM via an electronic record transfer. The data is then automatically fed to the 'case create" Web service to initiate a case for request for Prior Authorization. This method bypasses the need to call into the Call center. Using Mobile is also another efficient option. The patient can use the mobile app to open a request for Prior Auth.

The questions and answers are then sent and received electronically via mobile. The entire process is quick and cost efficient. Thereby, the combination of Call Center application streamlining along with reducing the load to the call center via self-service automated channels allows for a much leaner and efficient Prior Authorization process.

7   Conclusions

A majority of the participants found SmartPA to be well-organized, comprehensive, and uncluttered UI. This resulted in an effective, easy-to-use application overall. Some of the less technically experienced individuals had difficulty picking up the technology. SmartPA presents users with a centralized portal to find information, a positive factor enhanced by application stability while maintaining patient privacy. Implementing the recommendations from this research and continuing to work with users in practical settings will ensure the continued development of a user-centered application for ePA in the future.

References

1. Opoku-Boateng, G.A.: User frustration in HIT interfaces: exploring PAT HCI research for a better understanding of clinicians' experience. In: AMIA Annual Symposium Proceeding, pp. 1008–1017, November 2015
2. Magsamen-Conrad, K., Checton, M.: Technology and health care: efficient, frustration, and disconnect in the transition of electronic medical records. GSTF J Media Commun. 1(2), 23–27 (2014)
3. Quallich, S.: The price of prior authorization. Urol. Nurs. 35(2), 109–110 (2015)
4. CoverMyMeds: Electronic Prior Authorization (ePA). EPA National Adoption Scorecard. CoverMyMeds (2015)
5. Frost & Sullivan: The Impact of the Prior Authorization Process on Branded Medications, pp. 3–9 (2015)
6. Demystifying Electronic Prior Authorization (ePA), 23 January 2015. http://surescripts.com/docs/default-source/products-and-services/surescripts-white-paper—demystifying-electronic-prior-authorization_final.pdf
7. Allscripts Services for Hospitals and Health Systems. H&HS Services. Allscripts http://www.allscripts.com//market-solutions/hospitals-health-systems/services
8. PAHub™ Prior Authorization Software Features. (n.d.). http://www.agadia.com/solutions/utilization-management-solutions/electronic-prior-authorization/pahub-features/
9. The State of Drug Electronic Prior Authorization (ePA), 5 September 2013. http://www.pocp.com/PDF/State of ePA - 9-5-13 (Final).pdf
10. Hack, N.B.: How Deeply Engaging Stakeholders Changes Everything, 3 May 2011. http://www.forbes.com/sites/85broads/2011/05/03/how-deeply-engaging-stakeholders-changes-everything/#3860057e1808
11. Roles of Pharmacists, June 2013. http://www.amcp.org/RolesofPharmacists/
12. Marshall, C.C., Shipan, F.M.: Experiences Surveying the Crowd: Reflections on Methods, Participation, and Reliability. ACM, 2 May 2013. https://www.microsoft.com/en-us/research/wp-content/uploads/2013/05/websci13-methods-final.pdf

13. Shneiderman, B., Plaisant, C., Cohen, M., Jacobs, S., Elmqvist, N.: Designing the User Interface: Strategies for Effective Human-Computer Interaction, 6th edn. Pearson Higher Ed, New York (2017)
14. Greever, T.: Articulating Design Decisions. O'Reilly, Sebastopol (2015)
15. Yan, P., Guo, J.: The research of web usability design. In: IEEE Proceedings of the 2nd International Conference on Computer and Automation Engineering (ICCAE), pp. 480–83 (2010)
16. Prior Authorization, April 2012. http://www.amcp.org/prior_authorization/. Task analysis, (n.d.). http://www.usabilitynet.org/tools/taskanalysis.htm
17. Software Evaluation Survey Template | SurveyMonkey. (n.d.). https://www.surveymonkey.com/mp/software-evaluation-survey-template/
18. Lawson, R.: Reasons to move away from legacy systems, 10 August 2015. http://www.arrkgroup.com/thought-leadership/reasons-to-move-away-from-legacy-systems/
19. Formulary versus Non-Formulary Prescription Drugs, 22 August 2014. http://www.biabenefit.com/formulary-versus-non-formulary-prescription-drugs/
20. Holdford, D.A., Brown, T.R.: Introduction to hospital & health-system pharmacy practice (2010). http://www.ashp.org/doclibrary/bookstore/p2371/p2371samplechapter4.aspx
21. Resources | Research Involving Human Subjects https://humansubjects.nih.gov/resources

Research on the Cognitive Evaluation Method of Subway Signs Design in the Aging Society

Jian Liu[1], Jian Dai[1(✉)], Yanrui Qu[1], Zhenwei You[2],
Xiaochun Wang[2], and Junfeng Cui[3]

[1] College of Architecture and Urban Planning,
Beijing University of Technology,
No. 100, Pingleyuan, Chaoyang District, Beijing 100124, China
LJYM66@163.com, 1853119576@qq.com
[2] School of Digital Media and Design Arts,
Beijing University of Posts and Telecommunications, Beijing 100876, China
[3] Academy of Arts, Zhengzhou University, Zhengzhou 450001, China

Abstract. Currently, design and research targeting the elderly people are still in their fledgling days. Problems are resolved mainly through knowledge and experience of the designers. But when it comes to the technological and theoretical contradictions occurring in solving the complicated ones, ambiguity and instability between the problems and solutions arise. Besides, the solutions are mostly open-ended and unfinished. This paper, with the elderly as the test subjects and through questionnaires distributed after the subjects take the subway, conducts cognitive evaluation of the Beijing Subway Station signs based on Semantic Differential (SD) and establishes an evaluation method that is systemic and readily available. Such a method is conducive to delivering stable designs.

Keywords: Design methods · Aging · Subway sign system · Human factors · Cognition

1 Introduction

In the traditional design and research procedures, researchers tend to base clear and objective fundamental principles on previous questionnaires. Then, researchers and designers would combine their subjective opinions to explore problem space and establish problem framework. By so doing, they give rise to design concepts and use them as the primary directions for design. For instance, in a research on the railway station signs comprehensible to the elderly conducted in 2000, Japan Railways carried out a satisfaction survey on 260 senior citizens in terms of font size, spacing, color in the signs by filling in questionnaires and answering questions orally [1]. In the design and research of signs for the elderly, [2] conducted a satisfaction survey on signs among the elderly in the residential areas in Beijing through questionnaires [2]. In the research on the subway station signs and evaluation research from the perspective of the elderly, [3] and her colleagues did a survey on the elderly passengers at the Guangzhou Subway Station through questionnaires. Evaluation and analysis of

© Springer International Publishing AG 2017
A. Marcus and W. Wang (Eds.): DUXU 2017, Part III, LNCS 10290, pp. 677–689, 2017.
DOI: 10.1007/978-3-319-58640-3_48

univariate descriptive statistics were made to offer suggestions for the sign design at the Guangzhou Subway Station [3]. Data can be collected within certain domain in a short span by means of such traditional survey questionnaires, which provides support for design later by analyzing objective data. However, quantified analysis lacks essential support for inaccurate and non-value data. Therefore, while analyzing quantified data in previous literature, this paper adopts Semantic Differential (SD) to analyze the feelings of the elderly after viewing the signs, set the scale of "sign semantic", evaluate and analyze the descriptive parameters of all scales, describe the concept and construction of spatial targets with figures, and establish correlations between demands and sign design factors. This paper, with the elderly as the subjects, conducts SD-based cognitive evaluation of the Beijing subway signs by letting the elderly take the subway with questions provided and through distributing questionnaires, and constructs an "evaluation system" of the subway signs. Here is a list of some of our main proceedings series:

- First, it points out that the traditional questionnaires for subway signs tend to be temporary and unfinished; whereas semantic analysis in the past is mostly objective and denotative when it comes to the cognition of the elderly toward subway signs. As a result, in this chapter, a guiding experiment from cognitive logic to systematic logic is carried out. Semantic terms summarizing and describing the subway signs are collected, analyzed and later selected, screened and matched by combining the previous literature. Adjective terms in the SD scale evaluation axis are made and evaluation scale designed, thus constructing a scale that targets evaluation of the elderly toward subway signs.
- Next, native and non-native elderly people are invited to take the subway with questions provided. After that, based on the results of 60 SD evaluation data files, this paper uses factor analysis to extract the cultural, physiological and psychological factors. Combining that and the Functional Model Theory proposed by Kantowitz [7], this paper subdivides the cognitive process of the elderly toward subway signs into: cognitive system, processing, execution and maintenance system in the progressive order.
- At length, variance analysis is adopted to identify the distinction between the native elderly and the non-native ones in their evaluation of the cultural factor. The research shows that due to the asymmetry in the cultural background, needs for information of the non-native elderly and designer model of the Beijing subway signs, their evaluation is comparatively low. Against the vacuum in the research of subway signs for the elderly, this chapter establishes the problem framework through the results and analysis of this research.

2 Empirical Study Based on SD

From March 1 to October 10, 2016, during the period of the survey, 60 elderly people were invited to take the subway, participate in a test and evaluate the SD scale. Prior to that, preparations for the survey were done, including specifying research objects, collecting adjectives in the factor axis and determining the scale of evaluation to complete the SD scale. Procedures of the experiment include evaluation of the basic characteristics of analysis on the average, application of factor analysis in pursuit of internal relevance and pattern within the semantic and then classification. Procedures are as follows (Fig. 1):

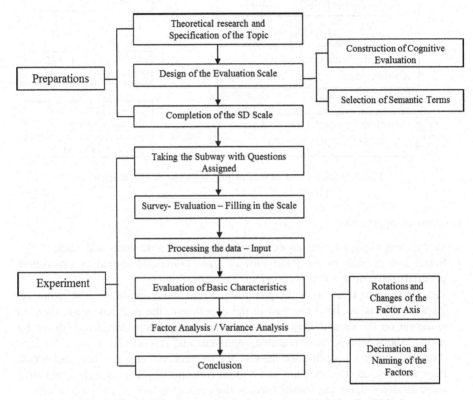

Fig. 1. Evaluation system of the subway signs (Made by the Writer)

Design of the evaluation scale based on SD means conducting semantic summarization and description toward the relevant factors of the subway signs in accordance with the characteristics and research targets of the signs. That is to say, via the guiding experiment procedures from cognitive logic to systematic logic, selecting the typical semantic space based on the semantic cognition of the elderly. First, in order to prevent subjective decisions made by the researchers in selecting semantic terms and use terms in line with the cognitive features, knowledge and experience of the elderly, this research deploys Evaluation Grid Method (EGM) [4]. It starts with the cognition and feelings of the elderly, and by way of comparing strong points and weaknesses of the design, identifies their initial comprehension of the signs. Then, it guides the elderly to divide their appeal into different layers, with comprehension emphasizing details at the bottom of the pyramid and that based on systematic feelings at the top [5]. Construction of user feelings is shown as below (Fig. 2).

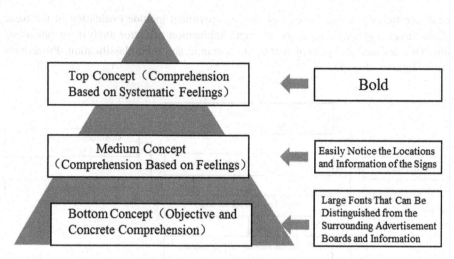

Fig. 2. Construction of user cognition (Made by the Writer)

Experiment Approaches:

- Researchers explain to the subjects about experiment procedures and rules;
- Select five pictures of the good subway signs home and abroad as experiment materials through research on previous literature.
- Ask the subjects to compare the pictures and rank them according to in sequence. As the subjects are fully engaged in the experiment, the researchers ask them to comment on the current Beijing subway signs and propose new requirements by listing "shortcomings" and "possible improvements" respectively.
- After the subjects have finished the test, the researchers interview them and divide their answers into top, medium and bottom concepts. Positive as well as negative ones are determined, thus being used as the evaluation indicators in the scale.

Through the guiding experiment from cognitive logic to systematic logic, the elderly users help or independently design the cognitive dimensions at different levels, including the bottom concept emphasizing details and the top concept based on systematic feelings. Six unified, clear, simple, straightforward and bold adjectives indicating directions are obtained, which can be used in making the adjective terms in SD scale evaluation axis. Yet previous research shows that seven adjectives are still subjective and broad for the summarization and analysis of signs. While they may be insufficient to construct the SD scale evaluation axis, generally 15–20 will do. In addition, seven semantic terms clearly cannot summarize all the characteristics of the signs and there might be some downsides (using pictures as the experiment materials may fail to present complete systematic space to the subjects). For example, whether the circulation plan is smooth or not and the continuity of how the signs are set cannot be evaluated. Besides, how the elderly living with cataract view the signs cannot be observed.

According to results of the questionnaires and features of the Beijing subway signs, 15 evaluation items are selected and are converted into adjective phrases comprehensible to the elderly based on their cognitive traits. Eight of them are about the features of signs: planned locations of the signs, specification of the destinations, specification of the main roads, comprehensible marks, readable combinations of colors, understandable formats, straightforward information and sufficient lighting; The remaining seven are about the feelings of the elderly: sense of security, direction, memory, pleasure to the eye, relaxation, dependency and subjective evaluation (Table 1).

This paper classifies the semantic terms into positive and negative categories and hence constituting adjective terms (Fig. 3). Evaluations are made based on the bi-polar principle in the hope of obtaining more objective data. The semantic evaluation factor axis is evaluated as per seven sections of an hierarchical structure, with the score ranging from -3 to $+3$. Take "lighting" as an example, the corresponding semantic terms are "dim" and "bright". Based on the lowest score of -3 and the highest $+3$, the elderly subjects evaluate in the light of their personal feelings.

Table 1. SD semantic terms.

	No.	Item	Adjective terms
Basic Features of the Signs	1	Planned Location of the Signs	Discontinuous – Continuous
	2	Specification of the Destinations	Ambiguous – Bold
	3	Specification of the Main Roads	Scattered – Unified
	4	Comprehensible Marks	Comprehensible – Incomprehensible
	5	Readable Combinations of Colors	Identifiable – Unidentifiable
	6	Understandable Formats	Appropriate Layout – Inappropriate Layout
	7	Straightforward Information	Simple – Complicated
	8	Sufficient Lighting	Dim – Bright
	9	Secure	Sense of Danger – Sense of Security
	10	Direction	Weak Sense of Direction – Strong Sense of Direction
Feelings of the Elderly Passengers	11	Memory	Forgettable – Memorable
	12	Straightforward	Abstract – Straightforward
	13	Pleasing to the Eye	Ugly – Beautiful
	14	Dependency	Will Use – Will Not Use
	15	Subjective Evaluation	Good – Bad

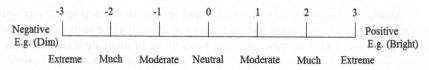

Fig. 3. Evaluation scale setting (Made by the Writer)

The evaluation scale is made through the aforementioned cognitive construction research, selection of semantic terms and evaluation criteria setting. The scale is primarily used to evaluate the feelings of the elderly after they have taken the subway with questions provided.

3 Survey and Research on Taking and Transferring Subway Trains by the Elderly

3.1 Survey Targets and Approaches

The subjects are required to take the subway with questions provided on the basis of the evaluation scale established according to the research above. The survey includes two parts: first, basic survey on the inside, entrance and exits of the Beijing subway stations; second, record and survey the behaviors of the elderly passengers while they take and transfer subway trains, and then analyze their needs for signs.

3.2 Selection of Subjects

- Selection of the subjects participating in the test: use MMSE (Mini Mental State Examination) scale to conduct the test, thus ensuring that the subjects comply with the experiment requirements.
- The famous American scholar Collier [6] points out that comparative analysis is a research method targeting at small samples or small cases. By focusing on the comparable samples and controlling the number of the variables, it increases the credibility of the experiment.
- Confirmation of the Tested Sample Quantities: in user experience design, researchers always call for user-oriented design. But in actual work, due to time and resource constraints, they cannot but make decisions on their own without data or with partial data. Owing to problems such as "how many sample will suffice to reveal the problem", "whether the result is reliable or not", etc., it is difficult to search for user demands. This test chooses 60 samples (aged 67 on average) by applying the problem-spotting probability model to evaluate the sample quantities. By combining the realities of the elderly Chinese and the research target, this paper determines on the basis of probability that the age 65 is the boundary. Although some research argues that individual cases vary a lot, seen from probability, when people turn 65, their cognitive abilities and physiological functions degenerate. The boundary conforms to the standards using Nominal Group Technique (NGT).

- Categorization of Samples: in this research, the elderly subjects are categorized into the native ones (30) and the non-native subgroup visiting Beijing (30). The native ones are also dubbed as the road-finding experts because they are familiar with the Beijing subways and the local culture. The non-natives visiting Beijing are those who take the subway for the first time and are not familiar with the Beijing Subways and the transfer lines. But the latter are required to be literate.

3.3 Cognitive Walkthrough

This paper adopts Cognitive Walkthrough while recording the behaviors and experience of the elderly who take the subway, as the results are unpredictable and the subjects might be missed out. During the test, the researchers treat themselves as XX and personally experience it without any hypothesis based on previous experience. Through months of actual survey, hundreds of data files are obtained.

3.4 Procedures of the Test

- For each train-taking and transferring task, it is designed as choosing a destination in the subway map that the subjects have never been to. The subjects will need to transfer during the course (Fig. 4);
- Each subject chooses a train-taking and transferring task randomly from the list. If they have been to the destination, then re-choose one;
- To ensure objectivity and authenticity, the subjects are only allowed to arrive at the destinations with the guidance of the Beijing subway signs. They should not ask others for help, nor should they resort to maps and smartphones.

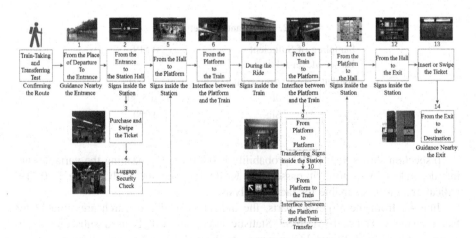

Fig. 4. Hierarchical task analyses of the signs during the test

- During the process, a researcher will record how each subject is doing with a smartphone to capture informal conversations. The subjects should describe their feelings toward the entire process to the researchers, which should be noted down. The researchers may ask appropriate questions, but should not help searching for information.
- During the process or after the test is done, the subjects fill in the "SD Survey on Subway Signs Form" with the assistance of the researchers.

4 Results of the SD Survey

Input and calculate the data files regarding the 60 subjects and questionnaires with EXCEL. The average evaluation value of the two groups of subjects toward the subway sign sematic terms can be obtained (calculate the average value of each semantic term sample and then delete the largest deviation in the sample). Then input the value into the SD evaluation curve scale.

4.1 Factor Analysis

This paper contains as many as 15 summarizing and descriptive semantic terms as regards relevant factors of the subway signs. Excessive descriptive variables might complicate the research and analysis later. In a bid to analyze the evaluation of the elderly passengers toward the Beijing subway signs, this paper extracts the major common factors among the intricate adjective variables through factor analysis, input the original indicator data after standardizing it, and conduct factor analysis. Before that, indicator inspection shall be conducted to make sure that it is suitable for the analysis. This paper deploys KMO and Bartlett's test for the inspection and the results are shown in Table 2 as follows:

Table 2. KMO and Bartlett's Test

Sampling of Sufficient Kaiser-Meyer-Olkin		0.519
Bartlett's Test	Approximate Chi-square	173.717
	df	105.000
	Sig.	0.000

Inspection shows that: KMO probability is $0.00 < 0.01$, meaning the variables are interdependent. Therefore, it passed the KMO test and the KMO value is 0.519, indicating that it is suitable for factor analysis.

Judging from the aforesaid parts, the indicators in this research are suitable for factor analysis. Hence IBM SPSS Statistic (Version 21.0) is used subsequently to conduct analysis and Principal Component Analysis (PCA) is applied. Ultimately, three factors are extracted through cumulative variance explained rate and Screen Plot analysis factors. The characteristic value of the three factors are respectively 3.320, 2.036 and 1.861, while the rotated variance explained rate are 22.135%, 13.571% and 12.406% respectively. Besides, it can be told from the Screen Plot that when four factors are extracted, the fourth one will become comparatively stable. While if three factors are extracted, they will be steep. Therefore, it is more appropriate to extract three and the final accumulative variance explained rate is 48.112%. Lastly, the research rotates the factors using Varimax Rotation and the factor loading matrix thereby obtained is as follows:

Finally, name the three factors as physiological, psychological and cultural factors. However, such naming is not specific enough. Therefore, it requires a comparatively stable theoretical framework to summarize the research and describe the cognitive process of the elderly toward the signs. By combining factors and the Functional Model Theory proposed by Kantowitz [7], the cognitive process of the elderly toward the signs can be divided into: cognitive system, processing, execution and maintenance system in a progressive manner. Among them, the information cognitive system indicates the source of information regarding the cognition of human senses toward the basic attributes of objective things. Combining Table 3, it can be told that: Factor 2 corresponds to four indicators, comprised of the complexity of color identification, whether the signs can be clearly seen, whether the setting of the sign locations is suitable for the heights of the elderly, characteristics of the five senses, and the influence of lighting. Based on whether the subway signs meet the needs of the elderly

Table 3. Rotated Component Matrix a

	Component		
	1	2	3
1 Insecure – Secure	**0.815**	0.188	0.075
2 Weak Sense of Direction – Strong Sense of Direction	**0.719**	−0.324	−0.324
3 Forgettable – Memorable	**0.673**	0.106	0.188
4 Complicated – Simple	**0.665**	−0.251	0.026
5 Abstract – Straightforward	**0.646**	0.07	0.459
6 Incomprehensible – Comprehensible	**0.638**	0.01	0.021
7 Unidentifiable – Identifiable	0.227	**0.82**	0.01
8 Ambiguous – Clear	−0.017	**0.819**	0.08
9 Inappropriate Layout – Appropriate Layout	−0.123	**0.69**	0.16
10 Dim – Bright	0.242	**0.545**	−0.303
11 Ugly – Beautiful	−0.058	0.419	**−0.718**
12 Discontinuous – Continuous	0.237	0.175	**0.548**
13 Feeling Bad – Feeling Good	−0.33	0.153	**0.449**
14 Scattered – Unified	0.038	−0.045	**0.44**
15 Will Not Use – Will Use	0.089	0.048	**0.35**

Extraction Method: Principal Components.
Rotation Method: Varimax Rotation, or Kaiser.

a. Convergence is realized after six iterations of rotation.

passengers in terms of their physiological features and with information received about the signs through the cognitive system, procedures including cognition, interpretation and evaluation are established, which lays a solid foundation of cognition for information processing in the next step. As a result, they are named as physiological factors.

Nonetheless, divide arises in the bridge connecting the information processing system, indicating mismatch between the physiological functions of the elderly and the current signs. Hence, we need to target those living with eye conditions such as cataract, maculopathy, narrowing horizon, etc., and establish a "coding system" of comprehensible signs by means of quantifying the brightness and color of the current sign environment, conducting Cognitive Walkthrough research by experimenting and wearing cataract patients experience glasses and designing as well as comparing literature and standard theoretical research. In doing so, a cognition interface can be provided to activate the information processing system, thus avoiding negative feelings triggered while the elderly passengers are viewing the signs and realizing they are "aging" because of the degenerating physiological functions [8].

The information processing system means conducting context construction, establishing code of conduct and arriving at certain conclusions or decisions with the obtained information. It is the premise for the executive system to act. Factor 3 corresponds to five indicators, i.e. pleasure to the eye, continuity of the signs, subjective opinions, unity and dependency. They represent the psychological recognition of the elderly toward subway signs, hence named as psychological factors. Nevertheless, psychological changes in the crystallized intelligence and fluid intelligence of the elderly lead to a divide in the bridge connecting the executive system. Consequently, the executive system fails to act. In view of that, we need to focus our efforts on the crystallized as well as fluid intelligence [9] of the elderly, and establish a decoding system that strengthens the input, storage, guidance and free-forward control of the psychological schema. That will facilitate effective performance by the executive system.

Via the cognition interface established based on the physiological cognitive system, conduct psychological processing of the information and carry out the act through the information executive system. Factor 1 corresponds to six indicators, including sense of security, sense of direction, memorability, loading capacity of the information, comprehensibility and Straightforwardness. But variance analysis below shows that there is distinct difference between the evaluation of the native group and non-native group in the statistics sense. Specifically, the native group give a higher score to common factor 1, while the non-native group lower. That is because the latter are unfamiliar with the transfer lines and locations of the Beijing subways, thus getting lost, confused, wandering during the process. It results in a divide in the bridge connecting the executive system and is named as the cultural factor. Given that, a knowledge framework that elevates "cross-cultural adaptability" to the subway signs should be established. Building on the aforementioned conclusions, this paper also gives play to the scientific factor establishment and maintenance system, making sure that the three factors function soundly. To make that happen, smart facilities shall be applied to put forth the idea of designing "exclusive" signs for the elderly. In this manner, straightforward sign information can be provided to the elderly, their energy can be saved while trying to find the roads, and their sense of fulfillment can be enhanced.

4.2   Variance Analysis

This part aims to study the abovementioned two types of samples with two-way variance analysis. Analysis will be made on whether they are significantly different in terms of the three factors and if there is obvious variation between the average of each factor. Conclusion will be drawn for further study and made into Fig. 5.

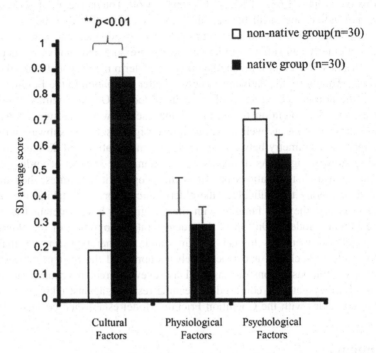

Fig. 5. Results of variance analysis

Figure 5 shows that there is no evident difference between the physiological and psychological factors. But the two groups give comparatively low score to the two factors, which speaks to the fact that the current sign design does not accord with the physiological and psychological features of the elderly. For instance, the sign information is discontinuous and signs as well as advertisement boards are mixed, compromising readability and causing visual interruptions. Moreover, the setting of color, height and lighting does not take into consideration the viewing distance of the elderly passengers [9]. As a consequence, it is difficult for the cognitive system to experience the basic attributes of the objective things relying on senses. Nor can it provide a fine cognition interface for the procession and execution of cognitive information later.

As a whole, noteworthy distinction is seen between the two groups in terms of the cultural factor, as $p < 0.01$. To make it more specific, the average score of the non-native group is −1.19 while the native 0.88. Furthermore, apparent distinction is seen among all the six indicators corresponding to factor 1. As for security, the native group score 2.20 on average while the non-native one −1.03, showing that the former give higher evaluation to security indicators. Similarly, variation is spotted in the following five indicators: discontinuous – continuous, forgettable – memorable, complicated – simple, abstract –straightforward, incomprehensible- comprehensible. Average score of the native group are respectively 0.47, 0.40, 0.80, 1.67, 0.53, while of the non-native group −1.63, −1.83, −1.67, 0.63, −1.60. The native group scores higher than the non-native one at all the six indicators, showing that they better recognize them. Study shows that due to the accumulation of experience and achievements in learning, the elderly can suffer from less cognitive pressure and can be less dependent on signs. Besides, it is helpful to lengthen their short-term memory and make them feel more secure. Therefore, the native group gives better evaluation to the Beijing subway signs than the non-natives in terms of the cultural factor. On the contrary, owing to a lack of user model cognition (cognition of the users toward the signs) toward the locations, subway stops as well as circulation design inside the subway stations in Beijing, there is asymmetry between the needs for information and designer model of the Beijing subway signs (As designers tend to name the stations according to local culture and construct the stations based on the geographical features, they may not understand or predict the difficulties the elderly encounter when taking the subway. One reason is that they are familiar with the design and have a detailed as well as complete Mental Model.). On top of that, degenerating cognition of the elderly passengers (such as memory, logical thinking and degenerating senses) make the non-native elderly unclearly and inaccurately comprehend the System Object Model and cannot continuously construct as well as renew correct psychological schema. Consequently, they get lost, confused or become resistant against taking the subway. The result coincides with the Cognition Friction Model established Norman [10].

5 Summary

In the past, designers opt to make judgment issues in designing based on their experience and inspiration, which can be unspecified and ambiguous. With the rapid development of the Internet technologies and the expansion of design objects, the dualism featuring traditional function and form as well as art and science gradually converts into problem-oriented research model, and resolution to problems in designing is acquired based on relevant knowledge. This paper, with the elderly as the subjects, conducts SD-based cognitive evaluation of the Beijing subway signs by letting the elderly take the subway with questions provided and through distributing questionnaires. Later, by analyzing the research results with the help of statistics, it specifies the problem framework and constructs an evaluation method that is systemic and readily available. That is helpful for the stable output of the design.

References

1. 財団法人共用品推進機構編: 高齢者にわかりやすい駅のサイン計画. 東京:都市文化社 (2000)
2. Qian, C.: Study on the design of sign system for aging population. Central Academy of Fine Arts (2009)
3. Beifen, Z.: Research and evaluation of subway station signage system based on aging perspective. South China University of Technology, Guangzhou (2012)
4. 福田忠彦研究室編: 人間工学ガイド感性を科学する方法, pp. 125–172. サイエンティスト, 東京 (2011)
5. 讃井純一郎: 商品企画のためのインタビュー調査: 従来型インタビュー調査と評価グリッド法の現状と課題. 品質 **33**(3), 13–20 (2003)
6. Collier, D., Mahon, J.: Conceptual 'Stretching' revisited: alternative views of categories in comparative analysis. Am. Polit. Sci. Rev. **87**(4), 845–855 (1993)
7. Kantowitz, B.H.: Selecting measure for human research. Hum. Factors **34**(4), 387–398 (1992)
8. Scialfa, C., Spadafora, P., Klein, M., Lesnik, A., Dial, L., Heinrich, A.: Iconic sign comprehension in older adults: the role of cognitive impairment and text enhancement. Can. J. Aging/La Revue du vieillissement **27**, 253–265 (2010)
9. Clay, O.J., Edwards, J.D., Ross, L.A., Okonkwo, O., Wadley, V.G., Roth, D.L., Ball, K.K.: Visual function and cognitive speed of processing mediate age-related decline in memory span and fluid intelligence. J. Aging Health **21**(4), 547–566 (2009)
10. Norman, D.: Cognitive engineering. In: Norman, D.A., Draper, S.W. (eds.) User Centered System Design. Lawrence Erlbaum, Hillsdale (1986). Copyright 1986

Developing an ATM Interface
Using User-Centered Design Techniques

Arturo Moquillaza[1(✉)], Edward Molina[2], Edilson Noguera[2],
Leidi Enríquez[2], Adrián Muñoz[2], Freddy Paz[1], and César Collazos[2]

[1] Pontificia Universidad Católica del Perú, Lima, Peru
{amoquillaza, fpaz}@pucp.pe
[2] Universidad del Cauca, Popayán, Colombia
{eamolina, eynoguera, leidi, jorgevelasco,
ccollazo}@unicauca.edu.co

Abstract. ATM interfaces nowadays present serious issues in usability and accessibility, frustrating users' interaction and leading them to make operational mistakes. For this reason, we present the development of graphical interfaces for ATMs of BBVA Continental Bank, which follows a process of user-centered design. The priority was to identify the real needs of users based on the context, and to understand how they interact with the interfaces. In order to validate our proposal, we established a model and a functional prototype. Later, we evaluated this new design with a usability test. Based on the defects that were found, we applied changes to improve the interfaces. Finally, after an in-depth analysis, we concluded that the designed interfaces were suitable for implementation in the ATMs of BBVA Continental Bank, due to the process followed and the acceptance by users.

Keywords: Human-computer interaction · Semiotic engineering · User-centered design · Usability · Automatic teller machine

1 Introduction

According to the study performed by Granollers et al. [1], Latin-American industry is worried about HCI, UX and usability. In this line, BBVA Continental Bank, which is one of the leading financial entities in Peru, is worried about user experience in all its channels. A few years ago, they changed their ATM application. They noted that the interfaces of their software systems needed improvements in in usability. However, there is not much information or methods in industry to develop usable interfaces for ATMs. There are several guidelines about how to design web interfaces, but little information about how to apply those principles to ATM or self-service interfaces.

According to the study performed by Cooharojananone et al. [2], there are two relevant aspects that should be considered when we design interfaces for ATMs: (1) the software application process sensitive information, and (2) the interface has limitations because of the number of buttons. The first aspect could influence the customer's behavior. The second feature gives the experience a strong limitation, which impact directly on the usability of the system.

© Springer International Publishing AG 2017
A. Marcus and W. Wang (Eds.): DUXU 2017, Part III, LNCS 10290, pp. 690–701, 2017.
DOI: 10.1007/978-3-319-58640-3_49

Regarding the methods and techniques that have emerged to develop usable ATM interfaces, the study performed by Rosenbaum [3] states that the conventional Nielsen's heuristics can be applied, especially (N3) User control and freedom, (N5) Error prevention, and (N1) Visibility of system status.

According to Van der Geest et al. [4], a good ATM service should achieve two goals:

- The feeling that there is a reliable, responsive, empathetic, and knowledgeable service employee available to help us
- The belief that an organization is committed to caring for about us, because our customer experience matters to them

In this context, BBVA Continental Bank contacted "Universidad del Cauca" in order to present its case and requested improvement of its interfaces. BBVA Continental Bank requested the design of a new usable interaction that would prevent user frustration. The design would need to permit the following functions: Payment to companies and Updating of personal data.

Then, the case was taken up by "Universidad del Cauca" in an HCI undergraduate course. The teacher proposed this case for developing along the whole course. The final product for students was to be a prototype validated by users.

For developing those proposals, we used the following techniques: activity theory, user profiles, and semiotic engineering, among others.

For validation of the prototype, we used user testing. Then, the design was validated with real users. This validation permitted getting feedback and new information, which was used to improve the prototype.

Finally, the prototype was delivered to BBVA Continental Bank, which valued positively the whole experience and the product received.

2 Background

2.1 Human-Computer Interaction (HCI)

According to the study performed by Peres et al. [5], HCI can be defined as a discipline with focus in the design, evaluation and implementation of interactive systems for human use, and what happens when a human and a computer system perform tasks together.

2.2 Usability

Usability is defined in ISO 9241 (2002) as *"The effectiveness, efficiency and satisfaction with which specified users achieve specified goals in particular environments."* According to this definition, and Peres et al. [5], there are three analyses we have to make in order to measure usability:

- The characteristics required of the product in a specific context of use;
- The process of interaction between user and product;
- The efficiency, effectiveness and the satisfaction resulting from use of this product.

2.3   User Profile

According to the study performed by Moreno [6], user profiles describe users of the computer system and provide details of their relevant characteristics. This way, requisites capture is centered on the most relevant for the user, and let a design with an adequate level of usability. User profiles are fundamental in user-centered design processes.

2.4   Semiotic Engineering

We can apply concepts of Semiotic Engineering in design and building of artifacts. The word Artifact (De Souza, 2005) describes something created by humans, and its meaning or value is intrinsically associated with the creator's intention, and the interpretation of the users about how, when or where it can be used [7].

This concept is centered in communication, but in a new type. Designer interaction is the emitter, and the designer communicates by symbols defined for the understanding of a determinate user, the receiver. Those symbols should be translated by computers, which are the mediator between emitter and receiver, carrying the message [7].

2.5   Activity Theory

According to the study performed by Carvalho et al. [8], Activity Theory is a line of investigation started by some Russian psychologists, among them Vygotsky and Leontiev. This theory studies the human practices and its development processes. The basic elements of analysis are the activities of people, which are volunteer interactions between a human and an element or object.

HCI take an activity as an action that a user wants to perform, and a computer as his tool or object, besides every button and every interface as another class of objects for the user to accomplish his task.

Activity Theory emphasizes the social dimension in which the activity is located in a determinate context. This social vision permits, from different perspectives, emphasis in every moment the elements which take place in the performance of every task [9].

2.6   Usability Test

Several usability methods were proposed in order to evaluate the level of usability of computer systems. According to the study perfomed by Holzinger [10], these methods are divided into two groups: usability inspection methods and usability testing methods. According to Paz et al. [11], the main difference between them is that in inspection methods; usability problems are detected by specialists using inspection techniques, and in testing methods, usability problems are found through the user's observations while they are using or making comments about the interface of a computer system.

3 Case Study: Design of the ATM Interfaces for BBVA Continental

3.1 Purpose of Study

The purpose of this study was to design usable interfaces for ATM of BBVA Continental; however, there were not typical functionalities such as Cash Withdrawal or Balance Inquiry. Then, this new interface should give support to the following requirements: payment to companies and updating of personal data.

The Bank provided all the related information in order to students could develop their proposals according to requirements and complementary information. Three objectives were established by the Bank, for any proposal:

- Proposing an interaction design of ATM interfaces that fulfills users' needs of usability.
- Applying an interaction design process for building good interactions with quality.
- Validating the interaction design by the executing of a usability test.

3.2 Methodology

Interface design was developed following a user-centered process. According to disciplines reviewed in the previous section, and developed in class to students, students adapted in a process made by the following steps:

1. Identify User Profiles

Students identify characteristics of possible representative user of system. The importance of this activity is letting the designer know for who he designs, what the user expects and in what way. Interface design proposed should be oriented to the user, organized and structured according to profiles defined in this step.

2. Analyze Existent ATM Interfaces

Students analyze current ATM interfaces of the Bank and ask questions about business rules and style guides predefined. The importance of this activity is proposing interfaces that respect guides and rules previously established, and discover what of these rules can be broken by new proposals.

3. Brainstorming

Students identify by Brainstorming relevant assets for interfaces, having aspects of usability, accessibility, culture and emotions, under semiotic engineering and activity theory.

4. Prototyping

In this step, students design prototypes according with requisites given and items identified in previous steps.

5. Running a Usability Test

In this step, students prepare a usability test to real users, which should be selected from user profiles defined in previous steps.

As prerequisite for the test, students designed a physical mockup similar to a real ATM in order to validate their proposals and to apply the Test. The principal activities of this step are: Planning, Execution and Analysis.

The result of this step permitted identifying and proposing improvement to proposal and getting feedback of real users about interfaces and other aspects related, normally ignored in design time.

6. Make Improvements Over Prototypes

In this step, students improve their own proposal. This activity is very important because is the materialization of the feedback of real users, obtained by a formal method (Usability Test). Prototypes with improvements can be shown to new users in less formal tests. At the end of this step, prototype is already validated with actual users, then, the proposal is ready for being delivered to the Bank.

3.3   Interface Design

User Profiles. All BBVA Continental customers were identified as users, and were separated into three user profiles. The principal difference was the level of expertise using ATMs.

All the users have the same objectives: Doing a payment to companies and Updating his personal information, both by the ATM.

Semiotic Engineering. The interaction design process should ensure the adequate expression about what we can communicate, so that users interpret them from their context, as if they were communicating directly with the designer.

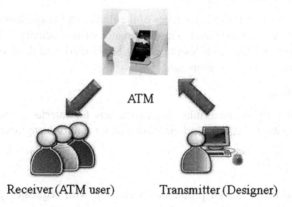

Fig. 1 Semiotic engineering in the interaction designer- ATM-user

Considering this principle, we generated scripts that define the steps that designers of interfaces expect that users understand when they use the interfaces in the ATMs.

The sequence defined in each phase then was translated into interfaces for the ATMs, which are interpreted and displayed by the user, according to the following scheme (Fig. 1):

Activity Theory. By this theory, we identified the tool, the rules and how is organized the division of work.

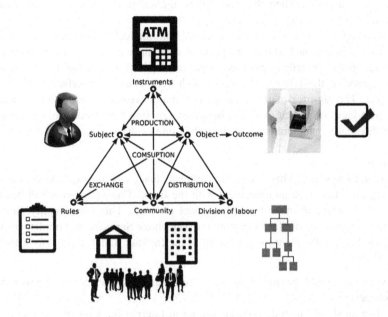

Fig. 2 Application of activity theory

According with Fig. 2 above, we made these interpretations:

- Community: The set of individuals who are clients of BBVA Continental, and can be established in one of the profiles described.
- Division of work: Every individual of community will have a role.
- Rules: Requisites defined by community in order to use the tool. In this case, rules can be: Being a BBVA Continental client, having a Card, etc.
- Tool: BBVA Continental ATMs.
- Goal: Directly the realization of a payment and Updating his personal information, both by the ATM.
- Result: Refers directly to success of every of two goals described before.

Other Relevant Aspects. Other relevant aspects about interfaces that were considered are elements of accessibility, culturalism and emotions.

- Accessibility: Prototype proposed can be used by tactile o physical (buttons). Every interaction with the screen generates a sound. Additionally, we considered type and size of letters. Those permit that users with certain disability can use the ATMs.
- Affordance visual: Keyboard icon permits that the user associates this image with the functionality, which is, deploy the tactile keyboard.
- Culturalism: According to García [12], images, symbols and objects used in interfaces do not carry the same meaning in different cultures. Therefore, for the interface success in an international market, the images must be selected and designed carefully. Then this concept is applied in the design of the interfaces requested.
- Emotions: Given the concept of emotional communication between the system and the user, it is approached from the point of view that a particular client can dispel his frustration due to failed operations with messages that help the individual to feel less guilty of the failure. The cases with very effective interfaces consider this subject. The absence of this concept is a major weakness in the interaction as it tends to focus on the rational user behavior, ignoring their emotional behavior [13]. For this reason, this point is considered as one of the key issues in this work.

Scenarios

Payment to Companies. This covers the payments that a customer can do to institutions and companies that have an agreement with the Bank. These payments will be able to do by ATM independently of ATM's model or mark. This functionality should be based in a screen flow similar to Payment of Telephone Services, and implementing the navigation like the Payment to companies of the Internet Banking (screens were given by the Bank).

- Navigation should be based in Services Payment (flow already known by the customer).
- Navigation should include sections shown in Internet Banking (because is the new functionality).
- It should as far as possible try to have similar flows in channels (in this case Internet Banking and ATM).

The design challenge is to make various proposals that seek to achieve the objectives, knowing the constraints of an interface like an ATM. In that sense, the proposals can zoom in or out of some goals, even stop fulfilling some of the requirements. It has this flexibility because the transaction is completely new in ATM. Finally, flows are constantly under review and refinement.

Updating of Personal Data. This covers the customer requirement of updating his personal data managed by Bank for communicating with him. Additionally, the authorization that enables to Bank to use this data for sending promotions, offers or other info that the Bank considers convenient. The channel in which customer can do this will be the ATM, independently of ATM's model or mark. The workflow of Updating of Personal Data was provided by BBVA to designers.

For both scenarios, we build Use Case Diagrams and Activity Diagrams in order to model the behavior and understand requisites.

4   Results of the User-Centered Design

As result of the process described, we proposed interfaces and sent to BBVA Continental Bank. Some of the screens proposed were the following (Figs. 3, 4 and 5):

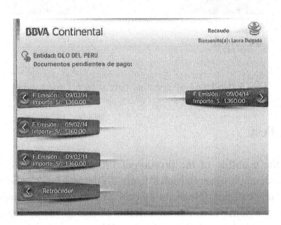

Fig. 3 Payment to companies screen 3 (prototype)

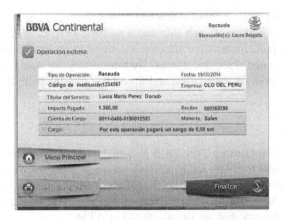

Fig. 4 Payment to companies screen 6 (prototype)

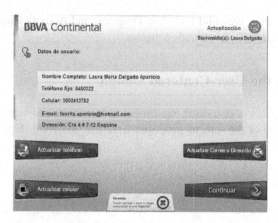

Fig. 5 Updating of personal data screen 1 (prototype)

5 Usability Test

In order to test the usability of the prototypes proposed, there was made a Usability Test, from the systematic observation of users doing real tasks. These tests permitted verifying the existence of possible usability problems in interfaces, and finding possible solutions for the problems detected. The test was run in three steps: Planning, Execution and Analysis.

5.1 Planning

As prerequisite, we made a physical mockup with measures closer to reality, which had a LCD monitor, 4 buttons in each side and a numeric keypad, as real ATM.

After that, 8 participants were selected according to profiles identified.

Also, we prepared three documents: Data necessary for doing tasks, Test cases, with variants in tasks for every user, and a Post-test questionnaire (Fig. 6).

5.2 Execution

Tests were made on October 27th, 2015 in Vereda Torres, Popayán.

After welcoming the users and explaining what was going to be done, each one was given a format with the necessary data to perform the tasks and another with the three tasks that had to be performed. Users lined up to perform the tests one after the other, simulating also the row that are usually found at ATMs.

When each user finished the test, they filled out the post-test questionnaire, where they presented their experience with the ATM. In addition, while each user was doing his tasks with the ATM, it was noted the possible defects of the interface, not only the visible defects, but also those expressed by the users' facial and body movements. Figure 7 shows to a user working with the physical mockup of an ATM.

Fig. 6 Physical mockup of an ATM with prototypes proposed running

Fig. 7 User doing tasks

5.3 Analysis

From the obtained results, we can affirm that:

- 87.5% of the users were able to update their data (telephone, cellphone, email, address) according to the assigned task. In addition, this same percentage of users (87.5%) stated that the interfaces for updating data are clear. In the other hand, at the time of seeking the action, 25% of users consider that they did not easily find the option (button) to update their data.
- 75% of the users were able to make their payments using the ATM in a traditional way (with physical buttons). This figure coincides with the percentage of users who consider that the interfaces to perform payments were clear (75%). Similarly, 75% of users say that they quickly found the option to do them. In the other hand, 62.5%

of users were able to make their payments using the touch interface and this same number considers that this option is easily found.

Then, from the feedback of users, we identified defects and grouped them into the categories presented below:

- Names of actions are not representative.
- Several actions on the same screen are ambiguous.
- Inaccurate language when giving orientation to the client.
- Important information should be highlighted.
- When requesting information, do so in the form of a question to the user.

These defects identified were corrected in a new version of the ATM interface prototype. Finally, prototypes improved were sent to BBVA Continental Bank.

6   Conclusions and Future Work

At the end of this process, we can conclude that prototypes delivered permit the user more freedom and use of the system with better satisfaction.

Also, we conclude that is necessary to follow an interaction design process, in order to ensure a design centered in the real needs of user. This will permit that they can do the tasks they need in an effective and pleasant way, reducing the mistake probability.

Given the results obtained from the usability test, we can affirm that the majority of the customers did the tasks without major difficulty. Then, interfaces delivered are adequate for implementing in BBVA Continental ATMs, because of the process followed and the users' acceptance.

According to the previous points, we affirm objectives given by the Bank were fulfilled.

Finally, we recommend to BBVA Continental Bank implement a systematic process of interaction design based on the techniques described in this work.

Acknowledgment. The authors thank to all the participants involved into the experience required to perform the presented study. The study was highly supported by BBVA Continental Bank, "Universidad del Cauca" and IDIS.

References

1. Granollers, T., Collazos, C., González, M.: The state of HCI in Ibero-American countries. J. Univ. Comput. Sci. **14**(16), 2599–2613 (2008)
2. Cooharojananone, N., Taohai, K., Phimoltares, S.: A new design of ATM interface for banking services in Thailand. In: Proceeding of the 10th Annual International Symposium on Applications and the Internet, July 2010, pp 312–315 (2010)
3. Rosenbaum, S.: Creating usable self-service interactions. In: 2010 IEEE International Professional Communication Conference (IPCC), pp. 344–349 (2010)

4. Van der Geest, T., Ramey, J., Rosenbaum, S., Van Velsen, L.: Introduction to the special section: designing a better user experience for self-service systems. IEEE Trans. Prof. Commun. **56**(2), 92–96 (2013)
5. Peres, R., Cardoso, E., Jeske, J., Da Cuhna, I.: Usability in ATMs. In: Proceedings of the 2011 IEEE Systems and Information Engineering Design Symposium, University of Virginia, Charlottesville, Virginia (2011)
6. Moreno, L.: Perfiles de usuario. In: AWA, Marco metodológico específico en el dominio de la accesibilidad para el desarrollo de aplicaciones web. Universidad Carlos III de Madrid (2010). http://labda.inf.uc3m.es/awa/es/node/66. Accessed 21 Nov 2016
7. Garrido J: Ingeniería Semiótica: Recuperando la Simpleza de la Comunicación. In: Faz: Revista de diseño de interacción (2014). http://www.revistafaz.org/n6/faz6_01_ingenieria_semiotica.pdf. Accessed 21 Nov 2016
8. Carvalho, M., Bellotti, F., Berta, R., et al.: An activity theory-based model for serious games analysis and conceptual design. Comput. Educ. **87**(C), 166–181 (2015)
9. Barros, B., Vélez, J., Verdejo, F.: Aplicaciones de la teoría de la actividad en el desarrollo de sistemas colaborativos de enseñanza y aprendizaje. Experiencias y resultados. Inteligencia Artif. Rev. Iberoamericana de Inteligencia Artif. **8**(24), 67–76 (2004)
10. Holzinger, A.: Usability engineering methods for software developers. Commun. ACM **48**(1), 71–74 (2005)
11. Paz, F., Villanueva, D., Rusu, C., et al.: Experimental evaluation of usability heuristics. In: Proceedings of the 2013 10th International Conference on Information Technology: New Generations, 2013, pp. 119–126 (2013)
12. García L: La cultura en el Diseño Centrado en el Usuario. In: Revista UX Nights (2015). http://revista.uxnights.com/la-cultura-en-el-diseno-centrado-en-el-usuario/. Accessed 21 Nov 2016
13. Hassan, Y., Martín, F.: Más allá de la Usabilidad: Interfaces 'afectivas'. In: No Solo Usabilidad (2003). http://www.nosolousabilidad.com/articulos/interfaces_afectivas.htm. Accessed 21 Nov 2016

Challenges to Patient Experience: Documenting Evidence-Based Practice in the Family Health Center

Dawn S. Opel$^{(\boxtimes)}$ and William Hart-Davidson

Michigan State University, East Lansing, USA
{opel.dawn, hartdav2}@msu.edu

Abstract. In the clinical setting, documenting evidence-based decision making is, increasingly, an important and time-consuming part of work. In the abstract, few health and medical professionals doubt the value of evidence-based medicine and practice. Evidence-based medicine and practice as a concept is well-researched, documented in health and medical literature, and has gained wide acceptance among researchers and practitioners alike. There are significant financial incentives for implementing evidence-based practice models. However, there are also challenges to implementation. During the clinical patient encounter, the need to attend to the knowledge work of documenting evidence-based decisions can distract if not disrupt work. There is understandably considerable resistance to new technology among providers in mission-driven clinics when the need to document evidence causes profound changes in work practice and, just as importantly, changes in the way they identify as being a healthcare provider.

In this article, we draw on a user experience research project of evidence-based practice in a mission-driven organization, a family medicine clinic. Our experience design research is a response to adaptive challenges in these healthcare providers' work lives. We document design challenges posed by technologies implemented to align work practice with evidence and to produce a record of evidence-based decisions, with particular emphasis on electronic medical records. We discuss three themes drawn from this research and the implications of these for UX researchers and practitioners.

Keywords: User experience · Electronic medical records · Relational coordination · Evidence-based practice

1 Introduction

Health services research is increasingly turning its attention to the study of patient experience in the primary care setting, and particularly, the effect of processes inherent in service delivery on the patient experience [1, 2]. While studies often gauge "patient satisfaction" with their health and medical treatment, it is often difficult for patients to see how internal clinical processes bear a relationship to their satisfaction with their care. Some may be visible, and some may not be. For example, if a patient is left in the waiting room for an hour, and they are told that their doctor is running an hour behind,

© Springer International Publishing AG 2017
A. Marcus and W. Wang (Eds.): DUXU 2017, Part III, LNCS 10290, pp. 702–712, 2017.
DOI: 10.1007/978-3-319-58640-3_50

they are not likely to know why, but their satisfaction is affected adversely by the experience of waiting. This highlights how far patient satisfaction surveys can potentially inform UX research, particularly as health services research to improve patient experience.

So to get at what is keeping that clinic schedule an hour behind, UX research is needed that evaluates evidence-based clinical practice, and what might be causing slowdowns in that practice. There are many ways to evaluate workflow processes in organizations. Relational coordination is one such framework that looks at how employees communicate and relate for the purpose of task integration. This framework focuses helping researchers identify specific communication and relationship ties needed to drive coordination and performance in an organization [3]. With this framework, researchers learn what communication takes place across what roles in an organization, and what relationships with what roles are valued most. This framework has been used in industries as far ranging as automotive, higher education, banking, and now health care [3].

Process improvement and patient experience is also affected by the role that the patient is allowed to play in management of care. The "Literate Care Model," introduced and promoted by the U.S. Office of Disease Preventions and Health Promotion, is a holistic approach to primary care and, especially, to helping patients manage risks associated with chronic illness [4]. Our project, then, begins with questioning not only how to improve patient experience in the primary clinic through improved processes, but how the primary care clinic can create workflow processes that support improved patient engagement as well as experience through the use of the Literate Care Model.

2 Background

This work took place as a part of an initiative called the Clinic Transformation Project, undertaken by a committee of administrators and providers from the College of Human Medicine and the Family Health Center at Michigan State University. The Family Health Center is a clinical practice on Michigan State University's campus that provides primary care services for adults and children in the mid-Michigan area. It is also a federally qualified health center (FQHC), which means that it provides medically necessary services regardless of ability to pay. The fourteen providers in the clinic (MDs, DOs, and PAs) all hold faculty positions at Michigan State, so they work approximately one to two days per week in the clinic. While on rotation in the clinic, they not only see patients, but also supervise medical students who also rotate through the clinic. Meanwhile, nurses and medical assistants (MAs) work full-time to staff the clinic on a day-to-day basis.

The purpose of the Clinic Transformation Project was to re-envision clinical service delivery processes for the improvement of patient experience in the Family Health Center. A provider on the project contacted the authors in the early stages of the project to conduct qualitative research that could inform a potential intervention to improve the delivery of care in the clinic.

2.1   Methodology and Study Design

The overall study design for this project contains three phases: a needs analysis, an intervention designed from that needs analysis, and an evaluation of the intervention. This paper focuses on the first phase, a needs analysis informed by Spinuzzi's *Topsight*, a set of observation-based research methods for identifying communication patterns that impact an organization's mission [5]. We used these methods specifically to study the clinic's practices by role with specific emphasis on locating discoordinations, contradictions, and breakdowns in day-to-day, mission-critical work routines. Discoordinations are not usually big problems when they occur, but are more often just small problems in routine practice. But patterns of them shift the focus of work to solving these rather than working on what workers understand to be their "real work." Contradictions are moments when an issue seems at odds with the mission or goals of the clinic. These can be felt as personal disruptions: "this isn't what I'm supposed to be spending my time doing," or as shared ones: "we are not getting the job done." Breakdowns are moments when patient expectations are not met. These may result from patterns of discoordination or moments of contradiction.

Our data collection included, after IRB approval, over twenty hours of observation and contextual inquiries in the clinic. These observations included a dimension of contextual inquiry, because we needed to ask questions from time to time to learn about our participant's use of technologies, such as electronic medical records. We created a schedule to conduct these observations and contextual inquiries by role, over five weeks, in order to shadow all roles in the clinic (providers, nurses, medical assistants, and billing and front desk staff) at least once. We also created a standard observation form that allowed us to record all routine communicative practices chronologically by phase (pre-delivery of care, during care, post-delivery of care) throughout our observation, as well as to include photographs of artifacts used for communication or documentation between and among roles in the clinic. (We did not observe inside the treatment rooms or collect any data with patient information.) After each observation, we entered our handwritten notes into a word processing program and added more detail to our field notes.

Data from these observations and contextual inquiries was coded through two separate first cycle coding methods: attributive and descriptive coding. Attributive coding was used to code all observational data by the communicative "attributes," that is, what kind of activity involving communication or documentation was taking place at a given time. Separately, we coded the data into descriptive codes, also known as topic coding [6], with codes that matched the "optimization" items to be addressed over the next year by IT professionals as the clinic transitions its electronic medical record system (see Sect. 2.2). These first cycle coding processes were then used for subsequent thematic analysis that appears in the discussion below.

Also as a part of the needs analysis design, we administered a survey to all providers, medical assistants, and nurses in the clinic. This survey asked people in each role to answer questions about their knowledge and appreciation of other roles in the clinic. These questions were based on the framework of relational coordination, which posits that workflow performance improvements are the result of the raising of human and social capital [7]. This survey data collection is still in progress.

2.2 A New Electronic Medical Record Rollout

The Clinic Transformation Project began months before the clinic was scheduled to transition its electronic medical record system (EMRs) to a new system, athenahealth. While it was not anticipated that we would study the EMR rollout, we happened to be conducting observations in the clinic when the initial "go live" took place. As a result, after the "go live," much of what we observed in terms of disrupted workflow practice was EMR transition-related, and we began to take notes on this. Our observations, then, include both pre and post "go live" data.

3 Discussion

We identified three themes that organize our findings from this first phase of needs analysis in the clinic. For each theme, we will explain the phenomena we have seen in the clinic as it relates, and then talk about both short term and longer term implications for each theme that may help us to think about ways to improve the patient experience in the clinical setting.

3.1 The Clinic Provides Care

It is essential to good patient experience to see the entirety of the patient experience, not just the face-to-face point of contact with the patient during the visit. However, inside the clinic, workflow processes are designed to keep a clinical worker's focus entirely on his or her role, and, for providers and MAs, this is also mostly focused on the patient encounter in the clinic. Even the scheduling of the calendar is organized around patient encounters. But what the patient sees is that the clinic delivers care throughout their lives, including coordination of prescriptions, outpatient services, questions and follow-ups to questions, and billing concerns. This is particularly the case for those with chronic conditions that require a greater amount of support from the clinic outside of the face-to-face visit. Figure 1 represents the disparity between the providers' and patients' point of view of the patient experience:

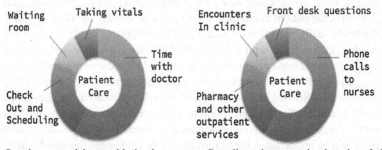

Fig. 1. Discrepancies in perceptions of patient experience: synchronous to coordinated views

Viewed from a communication design standpoint, it is easy to see why the clinic has difficulty valuing the patient experience beyond the encounter. The physical space is designed to facilitate the encounter, from waiting room to treatment room. Clinic staff refer to office space as "gopher holes," places where staff are sequestered for asynchronous work. Whiteboards set up in the treatment areas have the names of the providers on duty and the MAs who are assigned to facilitate their schedule of patient encounters. Meanwhile, the paperwork that facilitates asynchronous care coordination outside of the clinic—signatures for specialists, prescriptions, communications with instructions for patients—are housed in an alleyway shut off from the main treatment area, and clinical staff see that paperwork as what is done last, if all other tasks related to the patient encounter have been accomplished.

Electronic space reflects the physical space. The EMR system is workflow-oriented to reflect the calendar of those attending to the patient encounter. This means that for providers, asynchronous care is hidden from the interface, which focuses on the calendar of appointments for the day. In the clinic, MAs and nurses have responded to the interface design of the EMR by creating physical workarounds such as post-it notes. When a patient calls with a question that only a provider can answer, MAs and nurses stick a post-it on the desktop of the provider. When the provider has a spare minute (or more likely, when the provider returns to her desk to find the note, she borrows against the calendared time for a patient encounter), she responds, often leading to work interruption to physically track down the note-writer. These interruptions then create waiting room backlog for patients, as asynchronous care is pitted in a zero sum game with the appointment calendar.

Further, because nurses only conduct phone triage in the clinic, they are far removed from the synchronous encounter, and may never have met the patient face-to-face. This also affects patient experience, because nurses have not been able to establish the kind of relationships that providers and MAs have with patients, yet they may be the ones who have the most frequent communication with them. This is a missed opportunity to develop a richer patient relationship across roles, and causes patients to rely that more heavily on their provider and the in-patient encounter when there is a breakdown in care.

The implications for UX design are both related to the EMR and to clinical role coordination and training to support better synchronous and asynchronous patient care. The accepted practice of workflow-based EMR interface does not work when workflow is defined as only the patient encounter. There must be design for asynchronous tasks integrated into the daily workflow of healthcare providers.

This works hand in hand with the design of the daily schedule and the design of payment and reimbursement schemes. As long as time increments are assigned for bill-for-service schemes, there cannot be time built into the workday for providers to do asynchronous work. Service delivery reform efforts undertaken by the Center for Medicare and Medicaid Services are piloting Advanced Alternative Payment Models (APMs) for the purpose of incentivizing structural changes to workflow and payment [8]. UX designers will be important in the scaffolding of these changes through EMR design.

We see that transformation of the clinical experience is tied to greater attention to both what happens in the patient encounter, and what happens when the patient needs the clinic outside of that encounter. This involves a greater fluidity of all roles in both

Table 1. The clinical workflow is not set up for care coordination beyond the synchronous visit.

Contradiction	Providers consider it an afterthought to communicate with other roles for asynchronous care coordination
Discoordination	The identity of the provider centers around working shifts of synchronous encounters
Breakdown	Patients often cannot get help when they need it from home, as nurses are swamped with phone triage

synchronous and asynchronous care, which currently is not the structure of this clinic (see Table 1). This can begin with mindfulness on the part of providers and MAs about the growing importance of asynchronous care, but eventually, this must be built in structurally, with all roles, including nurses, working in both synchronous and asynchronous contexts, and a scheduling and EMR system that allows for asynchronous care as a built in part of the workday.

3.2 Primary Care Is a Collaborative Writing Task

In their well-known book *Laboratory Life,* Latour and Woolgar write about their observational study of the Jonas Salk Institute [9]. One of the interesting findings from that book is the way the laboratory acts, holistically, as a writing space: literally a place that produces research articles. This does not negate the idea that the Salk institute also produces other things: scientific knowledge, medical breakthroughs, or even new vaccines. However, a key part of the success of all of these other outcomes is related to the way the institute writes. It cannot succeed any other way.

The Family Health Center also writes. Good patient care depends on it, even if the ways it happens are so embedded in the daily routine so as to go unnoticed most of the time. The diagram (Fig. 2) illustrates how we understand it working.

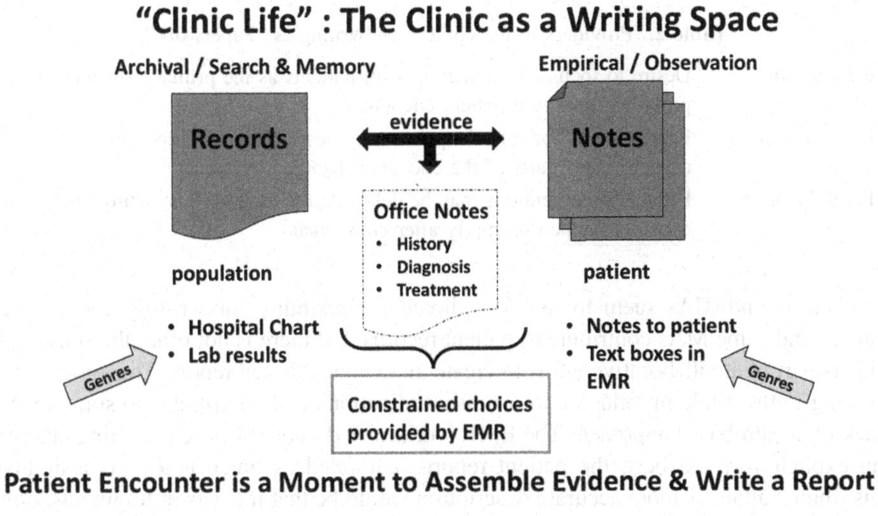

"Clinic Life" : The Clinic as a Writing Space

Patient Encounter is a Moment to Assemble Evidence & Write a Report

Fig. 2. "Clinic life:" the clinic as a writing space

The writing that the clinic needs to do has a very specific purpose: document evidence based decisions about patient care. The existence of this documentation is very important for making sure that patients' care plans will pay for their care, but it is also important for other things: continuity of care for chronic illness, executing an intervention that involves, say, medication or physical therapy, and of course helping patients and family members stay engaged in their care.

If we think about documenting evidence-based decisions as a primary rather than a secondary thing—which we can do if we talk about what is likely to really help patients—then the patient encounter and the clinicians themselves play interesting roles as evidence gatherers and writers. Two sources of evidence go into the report: one is archival, coming from patient records. The other is empirical, coming from observations that happen during an encounter and analysis, and interpretation of test results that happen before or after an encounter. All of these data need to come together in a coherent report about the patient's status in order for them to receive good care.

Implications for UX Design: Creating Effective Writing Spaces and Interfaces. Different roles in the clinic—providers, MAs, nurses, and even office staff—can play different roles in this writing process. But there is significant discoordination and contradiction—two problems revealed by the *Topsight* approach—involved, too. At least some of this is attributable to problems with writing support available in the clinic, both in the EMR and in various ad hoc technologies (e.g. their smartphones) that clinicians use to supplement their work as writers.

One problem we observed was that providers and especially physicians are very aware of the need to document evidence-based decisions. But their writing work is usually not the focus of their activity when they are in the clinic (see Table 2). It's more often thought of as secondary—as "paperwork"—rather than as a central component to ensuring the quality of the patient's care. But what happens with paperwork often has a lot to do with the patient's experience, and possibly with patient health outcomes, too.

Table 2. Providers in the clinic view writing as "Paperwork"

Contradiction	Desire to focus on interacting with patients as the primary element of providing care in a patient encounter
Discoordination	Patient needs for follow-up (consults, tests, Rxs) are important, but asynchronous parts of the encounter handled by nurses
Breakdown	Patients' interventions may be delayed or disrupted if asynchronous work does not happen promptly after clinic visit

Nurses and MAs seem to feel less direct responsibility for writing. To be sure, nurses and some MAs contribute to patient records, but there is not often the sense that this is part of a collaborative effort to create an evidence-based report. The systems for writing in the clinic introduce a lot of discoordinations that contributes to some of the lack of a team-based approach. The EMR workflows do not always cue writing tasks in an explicit way. At best, the patient report—compiled as office notes—is a highly-distributed affair. A more accurate description would be that it exists in fragments, only occasionally pulled together into one coherent report.

Despite these challenges, though, we did see providers and MAs working together in ways that did acknowledge the roles everyone on the team could play in building good office notes. In these teams, MAs did exercise their writing and research ability. They also felt more central to the process of delivering quality care in those cases. Providers were, in turn, able to focus more of their effort on the encounter and seeing patients.

Framed as a design challenge, the EMR interface should be designed to better accommodate team-based writing. Without a team-based approach, the work of writing piles up for providers who must stay late or otherwise squeeze in time to catch up after their workday.

3.3 Encounter Teams Provide the Best Patient Experience

Attention to both synchronous and asynchronous care are critical to the patient experience, and we have found through the needs analysis that it takes a highly coordinated team to deliver quality care that extends beyond the patient encounter. The Family Health Center has the appearance of teams through its schedule, but in actuality, this is just an assignment schedule by role, and those on shift at any given time have little to do with one another, except in pockets of cases where the provider and MAs are working in tandem. Our evidence indicates that these pockets occur where the practice style of the individual provider involves a team-based approach to the encounter.

Several factors contribute to the lack of team-based coordination in the clinic. One is just the manner in which providers are scheduled. With so little time in the clinic per week, it is hard to take the lead of a team. Further, there is very uneven training and professional development, particularly for MAs, such that what MAs do varies considerably from MA to MA. Third, the front desk, billing, and nurses work in isolation under the current model, which in turn puts asynchronous care in isolation, unless nurses request counsel or need a signature from a provider.

The Family Health Center does not currently have a structure where teams can thrive. Much of this is related to the scheduling of providers such that they are not in the clinic with enough routine to establish and lead for a consistent team mentality. Some providers have a routine down that encourages this, others have different management and work styles. As a result, MAs sometimes do not ask and are confused about their work, particularly if they have less experience or training (see Table 3). Meanwhile, nurses feel sequestered from decision-making about a patient's care, and as a result, their work feels more administrative than care-oriented, which further isolates

Table 3. Team cohesion is uneven in the clinic.

Contradiction	MAs and nurses are uncertain of what tasks to do when; often wait for instruction from physicians instead of acting
Discoordination	Some MAs feel that their work is more valuable because they are assigned higher-order research tasks. Nurses feel sequestered doing triage only
Breakdown	Slowdown in practice workflows; uneven quality of care based on which provider is on duty and which MAs are assigned

them. Nurses relish the opportunities to see patients face-to-face to do bloodwork, but these appointments are not integrated into the encounter schedule or the patient care strategy.

The new EMR rollout intensified the unevenness of teambuilding in the clinic, as technological know-how is now concentrated in a few members of the clinic staff, and others feel increasingly isolated. Asynchronous care continues to take more of a backseat as the difficulties with the new EMR exacerbate encounter workflow slowdown.

We see a few strategies to build well-coordinated encounter teams in the Family Health Center. Shorter-term strategies would be to vary the scheduling of providers and MAs across "sides" of the clinic (the physical shape of the clinic has two wings of treatment rooms, and providers and MAs have become routinely assigned to one side with particular providers or MAs scheduled together every time), in order to distribute the expertise and training across the entire clinic. This would also expose all MAs to the provider styles that currently embrace more of a team-based approach to the encounter schedule.

Longer-term strategies involve moving the Family Health Center to an agile team approach, an alternative project management framework where a small, cross-functional team responds to challenges through iterative and adaptable communication processes. This framework is increasingly being explored for adaptation from the software development to the healthcare setting, as healthcare increasingly must face uncertain environments and need to move from a fixed operations focus to an adaptation focus [10]. We could see this working in the clinic with groups across roles having a short early morning meeting to make game plans together for the encounters scheduled for the day. This would include the research and writing tasks for those encounters, and the plan for following up with care after the encounter is over. In this team approach, the provider may act as the quarterback to initiate the play, but the other roles work alongside to execute it. All are knowledgeable about the goals for the patient, and at all phases of care.

4 Implications

How might both UX practitioners and academic researchers get involved in the design for the themes we present to improve the patient experience in the clinical setting? Our analysis in this initial phase of work aligns well with Spinuzzi's discussion of "unintegrated scope" as a source of problems for workplaces and as challenges for user-centered researchers and designers [11]. Briefly, the problem with unintegrated scope is that observational studies like ours reveal challenges at the macro-level: goals, mission, and even professional identity. But solutions to address these challenges may miss the way these are tied to micro (operational level) discoordinations rooted in mundane tasks and perpetuated by meso (activity level) disruptions that become habituated. We hope our suggestions below start conversations that bridge these gaps such that UX professionals might usefully contribute to holistic solutions in clinical settings.

4.1   For UX Practitioners

In this project, we had the opportunity to view a new EMR rollout not as the EMR technical experts responsible for testing and evaluating the software setup in the clinic, but instead, as researchers viewing from a much more holistic perspective the experience of clinical staff when attempting to adapt to change, and in an already complex and uncertain environment. The main takeaway we offer for practitioners is, when setting up a new clinic on a new EMR system, to not jump immediately into the operational level of technology integration, but instead, to spend much more time first understanding the climate for that integration, and the barriers to integration and customization prior to the "go live."

For example, the EMR IT support team sent a 500-page procedures manual to the clinical staff prior to the transition, a move that upset the clinical users and further caused worry about the transition to the new EMR. The training that the clinical staff received was in modules that were unrelated to the real workflows of the clinical setting, and as a result, those uncomfortable with technology (many of whom are the same staff with little training that were discussed earlier), felt even more isolated and incapable of doing their jobs well. For this reason, these staff members feared the EMR rollout was designed to eliminate their positions, a belief which was unsubstantiated, but deeply felt nonetheless. UX practitioners should gain information about the context of use, learning about the themes such as we found in this needs assessment, and gaining trust from the users before moving to the operational phase of an EMR transition.

4.2   For Researchers

For researchers, we see two issues that might be pursued further to inform good patient experience design. The first is the role of professional identity and authority when re-distributing work to a collaborative, team-based environment to improve quality of care. As we have discussed, much of the problem that we see is the "let doctors be doctors" rationale for the design of an EMR, a rationale that identifies being a doctor with the synchronous patient encounter and its verbal communication in that encounter, is that it is positioned opposite communication that must take place to shape a more complete patient experience that incorporates writing for asynchronous care.

The second issue that we see of importance is the tension at a systemic level to keep clinical professionals focused on the big picture when they must also be documenting in a very granular manner. This big picture includes the continuum of care in and out of the clinic and communicating for that continuum across roles. It also includes the very real need for providers to be present during the clinical encounter. The need for virtual and physical spaces to accommodate increasingly flexible and distributed communication is the UX design challenge we must address in order to support clinicians and ultimately, to create meaningful patient experiences.

5 Conclusion

In this study, a needs analysis of a family medicine clinic for improved patient experience, we discovered that several design challenges exist in the structured workflow of clinical staff that thwart the ability of the clinic to provide quality care across the patient's experience in and out of the clinic. The most major impediment is the viewpoint of clinicians of patient experience as focusing primarily on the synchronous patient encounter. This is re-emphasized by the workflow design of the EMR system, increasing demands of providers to provide evidence-based documentation of decision-making without the time or the support to do that work, the relegation of certain roles to entirely asynchronous work, and the lack of cohesive encounter teams in the clinic. For UX designers and researchers, the challenges lie in finding design solutions that incorporate coordinated teams of researcher-writers—from every role in the clinic—to support evidence-based practice that strengthens patient engagement and experience.

References

1. Kringos, D.S., Boerma, W.G., Hutchinson, A., van der Zee, J., Groenewegen, P.P.: The breadth of primary care: a systematic literature review of its core dimensions. BMC Health Serv Res. **10**, 65–78 (2010). doi:10.1186/1472-6963-10-65
2. Eide, T.B., Straand, J., Melbye, H., Rortveit, G., Hetlevik, I., Rosvold, E.O.: Patient experiences and the association with organizational factors in general practice: results from the Norwegian part of the international, multi-centre, cross-sectional QUALICOPC study. BMC Health Serv Res. **16**, 428–437 (2016). doi:10.1186/s12913-016-1684-z
3. Hoffer Gittell, J.: Transforming Relationships for High Performance: The Power of Relational Coordination. Stanford University Press, Stanford (2016)
4. Office of Disease Prevention and Health Promotion. Health Literate Care Model. http://health.gov/communication/interactiveHLCM
5. Spinuzzi, C.: Topsight: A Guide to Studying, Diagnosing, and Fixing Information Flow in Organizations. Amazon Createspace, Austin (2013)
6. Saldaña, J.: The Coding Manual for Qualitative Researchers. Sage, Thousand Oaks (2009)
7. Relational Coordination Research Collaborative, Brandeis University. http://www.rcrc.brandeis.edu
8. Center for Medicare and Medicaid Services. CMS announces additional opportunities for clinicians under the Quality Payment Program (2016). http://www.cms.gov/Newsroom/MediaReleaseDatabase/Press-releases/2016-Press-releases-items/2016-12-15.html
9. Latour, B., Woolgar, S.: Laboratory Life: The Construction of Scientific Facts. Sage, Beverly Hills (1979)
10. Tolf, S., Nyström, M.E., Tishelman, C., Brommels, M., Hansson, J.: Agile, a guiding principle for health care improvement? Int. J. Health Care Qual. Assur. **28**(5), 468–493 (2015). doi:10.1108/IJHCQA-04-2014-0044
11. Spinuzzi, C.: Toward integrating our research scope: a sociocultural field methodology. J. Bus. Tech. Commun. **16**(1), 3–32 (2002). doi:10.1177/1050651902016001001

The Labor Judicial Expert from Sergipe State, Brazil and Propositions of Use of Tools Ergonomic in the Sustenance of Causal Connections in Disturbances Bone-Muscle

Marcos André Santos Guedes[1]([⊠]), Maria Goretti Fernandes[2],
and Marcelo Marcio Soares[3]

[1] Federal University of Sergipe, Av. Augusto Franco, Nº 3500 Cond. Morada
das Mangueiras, Casa 94, bairro Ponto Novo, Aracaju, SE 49047-670, Brazil
marcosguedes@hotmail.com
[2] Dept. de Fisioterapia, Federal University of Sergipe, Cidade Univ. Prof. José
Aloísio de Campos Av. Marechal Rondon, s/n, Jd. Rosa Elze São Cristóvão/SE,
Aracaju, SE 49100-000, Brazil
fisiol00@yahoo.com.br
[3] Centro de Artes e Comunicação–Dept. de Design, Federal University of
Pernambuco, Av. Prof. Moraes Rego, 1235-Cidade Universitária, Recife, PE
50670-901, Brazil
soaresmm@gmail.com

Abstract. The judgment in many of the labor lawsuits involving litigations provoked by musculoskeletal disorders is made through the production of expert evidence produced by judicial experts. Such evidence must naturally be clothed with the most compelling scientific methodologies. In this context, the objective of this study was to discuss the profile of the judicial expert in proceedings carried out in one of the sticks of work in Sergipe (Brazil) combined with the hypothesis of using ergonomic tools to enable the technical arguments of these expert professionals to be demonstrated, in order to demonstrate. That it is possible the use of ergonomic methodologies as a reinforcer of the conclusions of nexo-causal in lides caused by musculoskeletal constraints. In view of the analysis made in this study, it was concluded that it is entirely feasible to include in the labor judicial processes a multidisciplinary methodology of investigation of osteomuscular causal neurosis, shared with investigative tools of an ergonomic nature, and which predominates experts with training in the health area when in Specific processes of dealing with the causal nexus in musculoskeletal constraints.

Keywords: Labor judicial expert · Ergonomic tools · Nexo-causal osteomuscular

© Springer International Publishing AG 2017
A. Marcus and W. Wang (Eds.): DUXU 2017, Part III, LNCS 10290, pp. 713–723, 2017.
DOI: 10.1007/978-3-319-58640-3_51

1 Introduction

Resolving judicial labor litigation supported by expert judicial evidence has been an increasingly common practice in Brazilian labor court courts. In fact, the technical-scientific knowledge that supports an expert methodology adds strength in the expert conclusions reached making them often so solid and forceful that there is no glimpses of the succumbing party and thus facilitating the conclusions expressed by the learned judge in the process.

At this juncture, the professional training of the expert body, when faced with labor disputes involving musculoskeletal diseases, requires a degree of specialization of permanent mastery of the use of tools and methods of ergonomic investigation, as well as reinforce the effects of the conclusions evidenced in the expert reports. The labor conflicts with disruption in occupational diseases of the musculoskeletal segment contribute to the Brazilian justice system the hope in the recognition of a causal nexus favorable to the worker. In fact, it has been observed that in such disorders legal behavior has been used more and more of the production of expert evidence from expert experts in the subject and in this the technical-scientific knowledge has contributed a guiding medium in judicial judicial decisions. Therefore, the professional training of the expert body in specialized areas such as Human Engineering assumes real contribution value in the support of the nexus-causal or nexus-concausal of expert evidence produced.

The Brazilian legal system, through Article 145 of the Code of Civil Procedure (CPC), evidences the need for expert evidence in the face of the complexity of the case and when the proof of the fact depends on technical-scientific knowledge. The selection of experts is linked to the discretion of the judge by professionals of university level, duly registered in the competent class body that must prove their specialty in the matter on which they should comment. Nascimento (2010) demonstrated how relevant it is to meet all the requirements in the legislation especially regarding the quality of the expert, in the areas of engineering, medicine, among others, to perform a certain skill. The Brazilian judicial expert must possess sufficient technical and scientific knowledge to the point of being able to clarify the causal link in expertise involving diseases and work activity. In this sense, it is urgent to signal the difference that technical-scientific knowledge can provide in solving problems through the study of human movement (kinesiological) and physical interventions in the combined movement (Biomechanics), in addition to environmental ergonomic science.

The word expertise is deposited in the morphological study of the Portuguese language as belonging to the class of feminine words being attributed five specific meanings: (1) Quality of the expert, (2) skill, dexterity, (3) inspection or technical and specialized examination, (4) Set of experts (or one) who does this survey, (5) knowledge, science (Aurélio, 2013).

The judicial expert should therefore have technical and scientific knowledge capable of clarifying the causal link in skills involving work activity. Causal nexus is defined as the referential element between conduct and outcome (Cavaliere Filho 2012). It is through him that we can conclude who caused the damage. For this, it is necessary to study the human movement (kinesiological) and the physical interventions of the combined movement (biomechanics), besides the environmental ergonomics.

It has been demonstrated a great challenge, in countries with strong processes of industrialization, to identify the causal nexus of work-related pathologies (Carrara and Abreu 2012). It is also stated that these diseases have great legal implications in the life of patients, and their recognition is governed by norms and laws that must guarantee the health of the worker.

The identification of the pathological causal nexus presents enormous challenges, especially when dealing with musculoskeletal diseases, a multi-causal disease that requires a deep and extensive investigation of the worker and personal habits of the worker-claimant (Menegon et al. 2002).

The carrying out of judicial investigations to prove nexo-causal of musculoskeletal diseases assumes ample complexity, not for the difficulty of the matter by itself, but for the lack of specialized technical body to use of the investigative tools of the Human Engineering as another resource in support of the nexus -Bausal (Bernardes et al. 2010).

According to the Statistical Yearbook of Social Security - AEPS (2013), the year 2013 represented a new record among the largest participations in the concession of benefits already granted involving pathologies of the LER/DORT group: with 21.91% due to shoulder injuries (CID M75), dorsalgia (CID M54) with 6.36%, and 13.56% of the total involving pathologies such as synovitis and tenosynovitis (CID M65). This scenario induces the constant need for reflections either by the expressive number of cases in the granting of social security benefits or simply if the data could not be much greater if there were conjectures by ergonomic routes that could support the recognition of these diseases linked to work kinesiology.

According to de Azevedo (1999), when choosing an area as an auxiliary resource in causal nexus research, it is imperative to gather scientific and social relevance within a methodological framework defined by the researcher.

The Brazilian Law no. 11,430/06, regulated by Decree no. 6.042/07, imposes on companies the need to prove that an accident or sickness of their employee is not related to the nature of their function. The proposal to reverse the burden of proof almost always rests on the need to use scientific knowledge that can irrefutably remove or approximate liability through a causal link, especially with regard to the pathologies inherent to the LER/DORT group. It is therefore of practical importance in the application, development and improvement of current ergonomic methods so that they can issue expert reports of the best category and scientific basis, either at the request of the justice or the public authorities.

Judicial decisions take into account other factors of analysis and resolution of proceedings when faced with expert witness reports, that is, reports produced initially that lose their importance in clarifying the magistrate's doubts in such a way that the confirmation of the existence of a causal link must be Treated by multidisciplinary means of investigation (Guimarães, 2012).

For Martins J.R. et al. (2011) it is necessary to change the methods of analysis in the case of judicial expertise for a new look of the ergonomic sciences based on the analysis of the activity developed. Stella (2010) stated that although activities with risks raise in recognition of causal nexus with occupational diseases, yet judgments based on different criteria are not guarantees of success.

Tailoring competencies between judicial branches does not seem to be new. According to Marins (2004) the judiciary, since its inception, has relentlessly sought the evolution and adequacy of its services to the human needs of each era.

According to Yee (2009), it is considered as adaptive and/ or modern competence jurisdictions of justice advents such as the Brazilian Constitutional Amendment No. 45, dated 12/30/2004, where it was defined that the jurisdiction to prosecute and adjudicate actions of indemnity By accident of work would be transferred from the Common Justice to the Specialized Justice, that is to say, the Labor Justice. In this context specialized judgments require specialized fundamentals within the scenario investigated in a special way with the use of expert resources.

According to Vidal (1997), the applications that ergonomics can bring to society are innumerable in several planes, and for the organizational plan of the companies, a new area of action is created through the creation of an expert act involving the worker in his/ her working environment.

For Bernardes and Júnior (2011), the demand for professionals specialized in specialized areas of RSI/DORT cases is necessary. This behavior can be observed punctually through Technical Standard of the Unified Ministry of Labor and Social Security when the framework for assessing the disability of citizens and their consequent grant of financial benefit.

The judicial expert must possess technical and scientific knowledge capable of clarifying the causal link in expertise involving diseases and work activity. Identifying the causal nexus in different musculoskeletal conditions does not consist of a simple work, but represents a great challenge in the face of surreal importance for the maintenance of balances in a trial counter.

The investigative scope of this study sought to know the dominant professional profile of the Sergipe judicial experts working in one of the working branches of the Sergipe capital (Brazil), and whether this would be directly related to the hypothesis of absences in the use of elucidative ergonomic tools in nexus skills Causal osteomuscular.

2 Methodology

The research was classified as qualitative/ quantitative applied to the solution of the hypothesis of ergonomic tool use in ergonomic constraints attested by Judicial Skills. The research approach involved a survey in the electronic database of the 2nd Labor Court of the Regional Labor Court in Sergipe (Brazil) involving labor judicial processes in which the rights claim resulted in judicial expert actions of causal links involving musculoskeletal system pathologies.

The legal proceedings were analyzed according to the information contained in each one of them whose scope of interest involved the following parameters: Expert Medical Report, Technical Report produced by Technical Assistant, Manifestation on Expert Report, Expert Report on Lent, initial petition produced by the lawyer Of the claimant, Scheduling of expertise, Technical Report on Environmental Working Conditions-LTCAT, Judgment.

Once the documents belonging to all judicial processes of interest have been collected, that is to say, they deal with the health of the worker; A sample composed only of processes involving judicial expertise in musculoskeletal injuries were analyzed.

The decision for this scope of research, thus presented, was made as a consequence of the chosen Labor Court to cover complaints from workers in the capital and from the geographically surrounding municipalities, and thus, to gather an incidence of companies with a major economic activity suggestive of the existence of Osteomuscular occupational pathologies.

3   Results and Discussion

The population population surveyed reached 246 different expert reports, of which only 28 of these reports had dealings involving occupational pathologies such as: Osteomuscular, Noise-Induced Auditory Loss - PAIR, psychiatric diseases, work accident, other issues with health repercussions, Psychological illnesses, etc.). In a special way, only 11 investigative processes of osteomuscular tract pathologies were identified, and thus they were submitted to a thorough analysis in order to gather potential in the implantation of ergonomic tools as an auxiliary resource in the definition of causal nexus of occupational diseases of the musculoskeletal segment.

Among all the judicial experts appointed to act in the judicial processes of musculoskeletal diseases, it was observed, through Fig. 1, that half (50%) had academic training in the medical field, and the remaining final one with training in physiotherapy, thus totaling 5 experts Total.

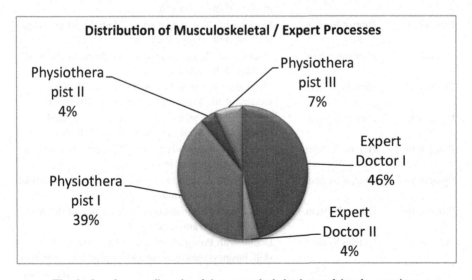

Fig. 1. Legal proceedings involving musculoskeletal complaints by appointee

It should be noted that the 28 lawsuits analyzed in detail in only 12 of them were conducted by an expert with medical education and postgraduate in ergonomics. From the Table 1 It is possible to know the academic formation among the expert professionals named in the judicial processes of investigations of the ergonomic constraints of osteomuscular character.

Table 1. Processes distribution when versus is wrapping LER/DORT without straight/indirect causal connection for the expert body employed methodology

Process	Expert evaluation with focus in	Professional formation of the expert body
Process 1	Human	Physiotherapist with Postgraduation in: Physical therapy of the Work and certified by ABERGO
Process 2	Human	Physiotherapist
Process 3	Human/System	Doctor with Postgraduation in: Medicine of the work, medical skill, ergonomic
Process 4	Human	Doctor with Postgraduation in: Medicine of the work, medical skill, ergonomic
Process 5	Human/System	Doctor with Postgraduation in: Medicine of the work, medical skill, ergonomic
Process 6	Human/System	Doctor with Postgraduation in: Medicine of the work, medical skill, ergonomic
Process 7	Human	Doctor with Postgraduation in: Medicine of the work, medical skill, ergonomic
Process 8	Human	Physiotherapist with Postgraduation in: Physical therapy of the Work and certified by ABERGO
Process 9	Human/System	Doctor with Postgraduation in: Medicine of the work, medical skill, ergonomic
Process 10	Human/System	Doctor with Postgraduation in: Medicine of the work, medical skill, ergonomic
Process 11	Human/system	Doctor with Postgraduation in: Medicine of the work, medical skill, ergonomic
Process 12	Human/System	Physiotherapist with Postgraduation in: Physical therapy of the Work and certified by ABERGO
Process 13	Human/System	Physiotherapist with Postgraduation in: Physical therapy of the Work and certified by ABERGO
Process 14	Human/System	Doctor with Postgraduation in: Medicine of the work, medical skill, ergonomic
Process 15	Human/System	Doctor with Postgraduation in: Medicine of the work, medical skill, ergonomic
Process 16	Human/System	Doctor with Postgraduation in: Medicine of the work, medical skill, ergonomic
Process 17	Human/System	Doctor with Postgraduation in: orthopedy, medical skill, business management and hospital administration

(*continued*)

Table 1. (*continued*)

Process	Expert evaluation with focus in	Professional formation of the expert body
Process 18	Human	Physiotherapist with Postgraduation in: Physical therapy of the Work and certified by ABERGO
Process 19	Human/System	Physiotherapist with Postgraduation in: Physical therapy of the Work and certified by ABERGO
Process 20	Human	Physiotherapist with Postgraduation in: Physical therapy of the Work and certified by ABERGO
Process 21	Human	Physiotherapist with Postgraduation in: Physical therapy of the Work and certified by ABERGO
Process 22	Human	Physiotherapist with Postgraduation in: Physical therapy of the Work and certified by ABERGO
Process 23	Human	Physiotherapist with Postgraduation in: Physical therapy of the Work and certified by ABERGO
Process 24	Human	Doctor with Postgraduation in: Medicine of the work, medical skill, ergonomic
Process 25, 26, 27, 28	Damaged due to: death of the claimant, decision still not hands, still not carried out Skill	

The existence of experts with a postgraduate degree in ergonomics alone does not represent a total guarantee regarding the inclusion of ergonomic tools in investigative nexus-causal methods. In only 54% (thirteen processes) of the processes there was an investigative focus through considerations of the system in which the complainant had been inserted and of analyzes of his/her clinical/mental history.

The non-predominance of evaluations with an ergonomic look can be explained by the possible technical ignorance regarding the propositions of ergonomic tool use in the auxiliary support of the osteomuscular causal links, although actions of the Federal Council of Brazilian Medicine are observed through technical guidance so that other scientific areas, Like ergonomics, can combine and produce scientific synergy in the establishment of the technical nexus by correlating the diagnosis of the disease with work.

The results of the Table 1 Also show that it is possible to apply knowledge of the Ergonomic Analysis of Work to the processes, after all it suggests to be a powerful ally of the Expert Expert Judicial in the understanding of kinesiogenesis and the evolution of the occupational pathologies with repercussions in the causal nexus.

According to Reis (2005) occupational diseases should be observed through the adoption of multicausal and multifactorial eyes, especially those that are portrayed of musculoskeletal disorders.

The Table 2 Makes the crossing of 11 specific processes of musculoskeletal pathological regions with the possibility of applying ergonomic tools observed in ISO 11228-3.

Table 2. Suggestion of ergonomic tools pointed out by ISO 11228-3, its characteristics, quali/quanti, applied to the LER/DORT processes where no causal link was recognized.

Process	Affected bodily region claimed in the proceeding	Ergonomic tools suggested by ISO 11228-3	Main features of ergonomic tool
Judicial process 1	Trunk	OWAS	(A)
		REBA	(B)
		PLIBEL	(C)
		QEC	(D)
Judicial process 2	Upper limbs	STRAIN INDEX	(E)
Judicial process 3	Trunk	OWAS	(A)
		REBA	(B)
		PLIBEL	(C).
		QEC	(D)
Judicial process 4	Trunk	OWAS	(A)
		REBA	(B).
		PLIBEL	(C)
		QEC	(D)
Judicial process 5	Trunk	RULA	(F)
		STRAIN INDEX	(E)
		OSHA CHECKLIST	(G)
		HAL/TLV ACGIH	(H)
		UPPER LIMB EXPERT TOOL	(I)
		OCRA INDEX	(J)
		OCRA CHECKLIST	(K)
Judicial process 6	Upper limbs	RULA	(F)
		OSHA CHECKLIST	(G)
		HAL/TLV ACGIH	(H)
		UPPER LIMB EXPERT TOOL	(I)
		OCRA INDEX	(J)
Judicial process 7	Trunk	OWAS	(A)
		REBA	(B)
		PLIBEL	(C)
		QEC	(D)
Judicial process 8	Mixed joints	STRAIN INDEX	(E)
Judicial process 9	Trunk	OWAS	(A)
		REBA	(B)
		PLIBEL	(C)
		QEC	(D)

(*continued*)

Table 2. (*continued*)

Process	Affected bodily region claimed in the proceeding	Ergonomic tools suggested by ISO 11228-3	Main features of ergonomic tool
Judicial process 10	Trunk	OWAS	(A)
		REBA	(B)
		PLIBEL	(C)
		QEC	(D)
Judicial process 11	Lower members	OWAS	(A)
		REBA	(B)
		PLIBEL	(C)
		QEC	(D)

SUBTITLE:

(A) OWAS: Analyzes postures of different body segments; Also considers their frequency during the transfer of work

(B) REBA: Similar to the RULA (checklist). Considers all body segments at the same time

(C) PLIBEL: Check List to identify different risk factors for different body segments; Considers postures, movements, equipment and other organizational aspects

(D) QEC: Quick method to estimate exposure level; Considers different postures, strength, load handled, duration of task with assignment of scores

(E) STRAIN INDEX: A careful method that considers the following risk factors: effort intensity, duration of effort per cycle, exertions per minute, hand/wrist posture, work speed and duration of the task per day

(F) RULA: Fast coded analysis of static and dynamic postures; It also considers frequencies of force and action: the result is an exposure score for which preventive measures should be taken

(G) OSHA CHECKLIST: Checklist proposed during development of the OSHA standard (revoked); Considers repetitiveness, inadequate postures, strength, some additional elements and some organizational aspects

(H) HAL/TLV ACGIH: Detailed method based mainly on the analysis of frequency of actions and peak of force; Other key factors are generally considered

(I) UPPER LIMB EXPERT TOOL: Workload scanning evaluation method; Considers repetitions, force majeure, inadequate postures, duration of the task and some additional factors

(J) OCRA INDEX: A careful method that considers the following risk factors: frequency of actions, repetitiveness, inadequate postures, strength, additional factors, lack of recovery periods, repetitive task duration

(K) OCRA CHECKLIST: Checklist proposed during development of the OSHA standard (revoked); Considers repetitiveness, inadequate postures, strength, some additional elements and some organizational aspects

4 Conclusion

The absence of direct/indirect causal nexus attested by the expert body to the 28 lawsuits shows that even the professional body possessing postgraduate in ergonomics, nevertheless it was not observed application of consecrated tools of the ergonomics that could strengthen the conclusive process with consequent less possibility Of future challenges.

In fact, the mere use of investigative methods based on clinical, kinesiological and biomechanical aspects, among other aspects, are not sufficient guarantees for a nexus-causal conclusion free of vices or inaccuracies involving musculoskeletal disorders. It is necessary to include in the methodological scope expert essential visits to the work environment of the worker with consequent use of ergonomic tools consecrated scientifically, such as those listed by ISO 11228-3.

The 2nd Labor Court of Sergipe (Brazil) has postponed the appointment of experts with specialized training restricted in ergonomics, waving so that the experts proceed in their conclusions without technical complements in terms of ergonomic tool that could distance or approximate the rationale for the existence of A causal link. The development of this work confirms the belief that it is possible to include in the labor judicial processes a methodology of investigation of musculoskeletal causal links shared with investigative tools of an ergonomic character, especially those indicated by ISO 11228-3, since they do not meet international scientific requirements Good analysis by body region.

A perfect fit between the subject of technical expertise and the special knowledge on the subject suggests that it is the best decision to make when the appointment of an expert.

References

Alberto, V.L.P.: Perícia Contábil. Ed. atlas (2012)
de Azevedo, I.B.: O prazer da produção científica. 7.ed. UNIMEP, Piracicaba (1999)
Bernardes, J.M., Moro, A.R.P., Merino, E.: Pericias judiciais em casos de LER/DORT: Modalidade prática da ergonomia? (2010)
Bernardes, J.M., Júnior, J.R.V.: A atuação do fisioterapeuta nas perícias judiciais de LER/DORT. Revista Fisioterapia Brasil 12(3), 232–236 (2011)
Cavaliere Filho, S.: Programa de Responsabilidade Civil, 10th edn. Atlas, São Paulo (2012)
Carrara, P.R., Abreu, M.J.: A utilização de ferramentas ergonômicas em perícias judiciais de DORT. http://www.sefit.com.br/sefit2012/wp-content/uploads/2012/01/A-Utiliza%C3%A7%C3%A3o-de-Ferramentas-Ergon%C3%B4micas-em-Per%C3%ADcias-Judiciais-de-DORT-Priscila-Romano-Carrara.pdf Accessed 02 May 2014
de Holanda Ferreira, A.B.: Dicionário Aurélio da Lingua Portuguesa. Brasil (2014)
de Macedo Guimarães, L.B.: Série monográfica ergonomia. Ergonomia de processo. FEENG, V 1, UFRGS, Porto Alegre (2004)
Marins, M.M.M.L.: Ergonomia e sua Implantação no Poder Judiciário. In: monografia de conclusão de curso em administração judiciária, Rio de Janeiro: FGV (2004). http://www.google.com.br/url?sa=t&rct=j&q=&esrc=s&source=web&cd=1&ved=0CC8QFjAA&url=http%3A%2F%2Fwww.tjrj.jus.br%2Fdocument_library%2Fget_file%3Fuuid%3D171d613b-9b2f-4d66-8bb3-0018af6f41d3%26groupId%3D10136&ei=5wdjU_szzpPIBNXggbgD&usg=AFQjCNES8-LC7dSc4BqlukcTe0Pv4J1J1g&sig2=r2XEELMUpq9KThfbMIuPDg&bvm=bv.65788261,d.aWw&cad=rja. Accessed 14 Feb 2014
Menegon, N.L., Camarotto, J.A., Bernardino, M.T.S.M.: OPAPEL DA ERGONOMIA NO RECONHECIMENTO DO NEXO CAUSAL. In: VII Congresso Latino-Americano de Ergonomia, Recife. Sessão Técnica, São Paulo (2002)

Nascimento, J.A.: Pericia Judicial Teoria e prática: Lições de um Magistrado. Aracaju: jus fórum (2010)
Vidal, M.C.: Introdução a Ergonomia. Apostila do curso de especialização em ergonomia do OPPE/UFRJ (1997)
Yee, Z.C.: Perícias de Engenharia de Segurança do Trabalho: Aspectos Processuais e casos práticos. Juruá, Curitiba (2009)

The Open University of the Unified Health System in Brazil (UNA-SUS/UFMA): Identification and Hierarchization of Problems in Distance Learning Courses

Carla Galvão Spinillo[1]([⊠]), Stephania Padovani[1],
Kelli C.A.S. Smythe[1], Juliana Bueno[1],
and Ana Emília Figueiredo de Oliveira[2]

[1] Department of Design, Federal University of Parana, Curitiba, Brazil
cgspin@gmail.com, kellicas@gmail.com,
oieusouaju@gmail.com, s_padovani2@yahoo.co.uk
[2] UNA-SUS/UFMA – Federal University of Maranhão, São Luis, Brazil
oliveira.anaemilia@gmail.com

Abstract. This article reports a study of heuristic evaluation and hierarchization of the problems found on four distance learning courses offered by the Open University of the Unified Health System in Brazil (UNA-SUS/UFMA). It is part of a broader research on information architecture, interaction design and information design on e-learning courses. The sample was assessed through 88 heuristics and recommendations, followed by the FIP (Frequency, Impact and Persistence) technique to establish the severity of the problems found. The results showed that the sample did not meet (a) the information design principles of consistency, proximity, and hierarchy; and (b) the interaction design criteria of adaptability, explicit control and consistency. The sample also presented weaknesses in the information architecture systems of navigation, labeling and search. The heuristic evaluation followed by the hierarchization of problems have proved to be advantageous at the beginning of the evaluative research project. Recommendations were proposed to improve the distance learning courses.

Keywords: Health education · Evaluation · Online courses · Information design

1 Introduction

The improvement of the quality of health services for people is a major challenge faced by countries worldwide. It is also one of the core Millennium Development Goals of the World Health Organization [1]. More than four million people on the planet are estimated to be affected by poor health services [1]. The health service crisis is the result of a lack of economic, social and educational policies on health quality for people in a number of countries. Improving the skills of the health workforce so as to meet the demands of the population is one of the key issues to promote health quality services.

© Springer International Publishing AG 2017
A. Marcus and W. Wang (Eds.): DUXU 2017, Part III, LNCS 10290, pp. 724–739, 2017.
DOI: 10.1007/978-3-319-58640-3_52

Thus, programs aiming at educating and training the health workforce will contribute to overcoming the health service crisis.

In line with this, the Brazilian Ministry of Health created in 2008 the Open University of the Unified Health System (UNA-SUS) to provide training to health professionals through distance learning courses. This virtual learning modality made the access to training courses possible for health professionals working in remote and rural areas of Brazil.

The distance learning courses offered by UNA-SUS are developed in partnership with a number of Brazilian universities, one of the most active partners being the UFMA - Federal University of Maranhão [2]. From 2014 to 2016 UNA-SUS/UFMA offered 55 distance learning courses to 179,301 health professionals, among them medical doctors, nurses and dentists. In order to improve the quality of their courses, a research on information design and interaction design was conducted. The aim of the research was to propose recommendations for the courses' developers in these fields, and it consisted of a heuristic evaluation study, followed by users` experience (UX) testing. This article reports the heuristic evaluation study. This study made the identification and hierarchization of problems in the distance learning courses possible, providing the basis for the UX study.

2 Setting the Ground

The literature on human interaction with digital systems/artifacts has produced a number of approaches, frameworks and tools to analyze, design and evaluate such systems/artifacts [3, 4]. In the scope of education, principles and recommendations have been proposed for designing/developing learning applications [5, 6] to avoid the declining of users' learning performances. Principles and recommendations are also intended to minimize learners' cognitive load and to promote motivation. In this sense, Sera and Wong [5], based on Hashim, Ahmad and Rohiza`s principles [6], claim that an application should:

- Be quickly learnable and user-friendly;
- Often minimize scrolling;
- Provide clear, simple and consistent navigation throughout its pages;
- Keep the positions of similar actions and elements the same (e.g., buttons, icons);
- Present flexibility of the display in the interface design;
- Provide users with the necessary information only;
- Favor the use of animation and of pictorial/graphic representations of information to textual information; and
- Allow user control over the application.

Researchers have also been interested in understanding users' experience with digital artifacts [4, 7]. In this regard, Garrett [4] has proposed a classification of the elements of users' experience into five planes:

1. Strategy plane: the identification of users' needs and the objectives of the system/artifact developed.

2. Scope plane: functional specifications of the system/courses, along with content requirements to be made available.
3. Structure plane: the information architecture (how the information nodes are interconnected) and the design of the interaction (conceptual model and predominant interaction style).
4. Skeleton plane: objects of the interface, the navigation system (how the user can move inside the system) and diagrams of the system screens.
5. Surface plane: the graphic and/or multimedia attributes that represent the information in the system to users.

According to Garrett [4], a design process which focuses on these planes seeks to ensure that aspects of the user's experience with digital artifacts are taken into account. For that, it is necessary to employ the User-Centered Design approach to digital artifacts. Such an approach entails: (a) considering what users want to do, rather than what technology can do; and (b) designing for diversity and to better connect people in an effectively way [8]. In this sense, evaluation therefore, becomes fundamental to guarantee a usable system. Engaging users in the design process and/or conducting user testing of digital artifacts/systems are at the core of the User-Centered Design approach.

However, the evaluation of digital artifacts/systems by experts prior conducting user testing can also be a valid way to identify artifacts/systems' drawbacks, making improvements in the testing material possible. Such evaluation prevents testing poor designed digital artifacts with users. It also allows foreseeing any problems/difficulties users may face when interacting with the artifact/system, which can be accounted for in the testing design. Thus, expert evaluation prior conducting user testing is beneficial to User-Centered Design research.

One of the most popular methods of expert assessment is the heuristic evaluation. Heuristic evaluation is the inspection of the usability of artifacts/systems by specialists, through a set of consolidated principles that lead to the discovery and resolution of problems [3, 9]. Heuristic evaluation may consider the artifact/system information architecture, interaction design and/or information design.

Information architecture refers to the specification of how users find information in the system, and it involves organization, navigation, labeling and search systems [10]. The navigation system specifies ways for the user to move through the informational space. The organization system determines how the organization and categorization of content are presented. The labeling system defines verbal (terminology) and visual (iconic) signs for each element of information and of navigation support to users. Finally, the search system determines the questions users can ask and the set of answers that will be obtained when making a query in the database [10, 11].

Interaction design concerns how actions are taken between users and the system, considering interdependent factors, such as the context of use, type of task and of users. Interaction design aims to reduce the negative aspects of the user experience and, at the same time, to improve the positive ones [12]. In this sense, ergonomic criteria may be employed to minimize ambiguities in the identification and classification of qualities and problems in interaction design evaluation of digital artifacts/systems [13]. The following criteria are considered of relevance for interaction design [14]:

- User Guidance criterion: it refers to the advising and instructing resources offered to users when interacting with a system, such as alarms and messages.
- Workload criterion: it considers elements of the interface that may reduce users' cognitive and perceptual load, and may rise dialogue efficiency.
- Explicit control criterion: it considers users' control over the system when it processes their actions, as well as the system processing of explicit users' actions.
- Adaptability criterion: it regards the system ability to react according to context and to user's needs and preferences.
- Error management criterion: it refers to resources for preventing or reducing the occurrence of errors, as well as for recovering from errors, such as incorrect data entry, or entries with inappropriate formats.
- Consistency criterion: it refers to ways to conform the elements/aspects of the interface design in similar contexts and to differ them when applied to different contexts, such as codes and formats.

Finally, information design considers the communication and optimization of information conveyed in print and/or digital artifacts/systems [15]. It embraces the analysis, planning, presentation and understanding of a message, taking into account its content and form [16]. The evaluation of artifacts/systems from an information design viewpoint should range from general to specific aspects of representing a content. Thus, the following aspects should be taken into account:

- The general presentation of the content, that is its broad graphic relations and structure within and between pages, and overall use of color;
- The presentation of the verbal mode regarding typographic aspects of the text (e.g., font size, column width, text alignment, use of whitespace);
- The presentation of the pictorial mode (static and/or dynamic images) regarding clarity in depiction, graphic emphasis and text-image relations; and,
- The presentation of the schematic mode regarding the clarity and emphasis of graphs, diagrams, tables and infographics.

To assess the information design aspects of content representation, principles and recommendations have been proposed, whether for the verbal, pictorial and schematic modes [17–21], or to the overall design of artifacts [22, 23]. These principles and recommendations aim at increasing quality of design projects, focusing on users in order to improve their interaction experience with artifacts/systems. Principles and recommendations are suitable for heuristic expert evaluation, and were, therefore, considered in the assessment of the UNA-SUS/UFMA courses in the scope of information design.

Lipton [22] and Pettersson [23] proposed information design principles concerning essential aspects of content communication that are relevant to digital artifacts/systems. They based their principles upon theories of perception and cognition allied to design good practices and research outcomes. Lipton [22] suggested the principles of *Consistency* in the way elements/relations are presented; *Proximity* between related elements; *Chunking* elements to provide groups of information at a time; *Alignment* of the elements of a page; *Hierarchy* of elements differing in importance; *Structure* of elements to organize the content; and *Clarity* in language.

Similarly, Pettersson [23] also suggested the principles of *Clarity, Structure* and *Consistency* (referred to as *Unity*) together with others, which he grouped into the categories: Functional, Aesthetics, Cognitive and Administrative. The Administrative category concerns financial, principled and legal aspects of the design process, which the author considered to be the principles of *Information Access, Information Cost, Information Ethics,* and *Securing quality.* The Cognitive principles regard the users' domain, aiming to facilitate their *Attention, Perception, Processing and Memory.* On the other hand, the Functional and Aesthetics principles regard the designers' domain and their decision making for message representation.

Since heuristic evaluations are conducted by experts, they are within the designers' domain. Therefore, the Functional and Aesthetics principles are pertinent to heuristic evaluation on information design. The Aesthetics principles proposed by Pettersson [23] are *Harmony* and *Proportion,* which regard the arrangement of elements in a visually balanced manner. For the Functional principles, Pettersson [23] proposed the principles of *Simplicity* (conciseness and accuracy to improve reading flow and image understanding); and *Emphasis* (highlighting elements to attract, direct and maintain users' attention), together with *Clarity, Structure* and *Unit* (consistency). It is worth mentioning that Pettersson [23] proposed *'Defining the problems'* as a functional principle which regard the identification of the aspects/issues to guide and/or constrain the design process.

3   The UNA-SUS/UFMA Distance Learning Courses

The UNA-SUS/UFMA courses are similar in the technical and design aspects. They present a common visual language for illustrations, screen layout, menus and typographic resources for the texts. The courses are in the Moodle platform, and can be accessed by the users enrolled on a course. Users are allowed to manage their profile and interact with other users on the same course. The courses are structured in modules and units, which provide users with learning objects, such as e-books, videos, games and animations, as well as learning activities and virtual discussion forums. With the exception of the Moodle platform's own profile settings, the other contents of the courses are accessed through external links.

UNA-SUS/UFMA offers postgraduate (specialization/diploma) courses, training courses and self-instructional courses. All courses are free of charge, and some are open to the public, as for instance, the community healthcare. A tutorial is available to get users acquainted with the course/system environment and the virtual rooms.

The development of distance learning courses at UNA-SUS/UFMA involves teams of experts from the fields of health (medical doctors, nurses), education (instructional designers, pedagogues), computer science (information technologist, programmers) and design (graphic designers, illustrators). The design of a course at UNA-SUS/UFMA is an iterative process. However, in general, the production of a course begins with the teams of health and education experts. These experts are responsible for developing the courses' contents, particularly the texts to be presented on the courses. Depending on the topic of the course, the content developers may vary (e.g., cardiologists, nurses). Once the content of a course has been decided, it goes to the computer science and design teams. The computer science team is in charge of the technical aspects of the course, such as programming requirements and database resources. The design team is responsible for the interface design of the course, choosing/creating its elements (e.g., icons, illustrations, type fonts).

Despite the professional efforts of the UNA-SUS/UFMA's teams to produce courses for effective learning, users/learners and information designers are not yet engaged in the development of the courses. Since user centered design approach and information design expertise are of relevance to produce useful artifacts/systems, neglecting them may compromise the effectiveness of the courses in communicating contents to users. The study reported herein is part of a research project that attempts to fulfil this gap.

4   The Study on Identification and Hierarchization of Problems in the UNA-SUS/UFMA Courses

A study on identification and hierarchization of problems in the UNA-SUS/UFMA courses was conducted to produce recommendations for improving their quality, allowing the design of appropriate material for testing in the UX study.

To define the scope of the study on identification and hierarchization of problems, the heuristic evaluation regarded the planes of Structure, Skeleton and Surface [4], of the UNA-SUS/UFMA courses. However, when and where necessary, the courses` developers were requested to provide information on the scope and strategy planes.

The heuristic evaluation was carried out by six researchers from the Federal University of Parana with expertise in information design and interaction design. The methodological procedures consisted of:

1. Overall examination of the system used for the courses to identify the main usability weaknesses of the system;
2. Delimitation of the course sample to be analyzed;
3. Selection of the heuristics and recommendations to assess the sample;
4. Evaluation of the sample through specific protocols; and
5. Hierarchization of the problems identified in the sample. The FIP (Frequency, Impact and Persistence) technique was employed to establish the severity of the problems.

4.1   The Sample and Selection of Heuristics

A sample of four distance learning courses was selected by the UNA-SUS/UFMA team for the evaluation. Each course offers an e-book as a supporting learning artifact, a virtual café, a notice board, and a forum of activities. Since the courses have a common visual language and system design, the four-course sample was then representative of the UNA-SUS/UFMA courses. The courses in the sample were the following:

1. Specialization Course: More Medical Doctors Program, Module 2, Health and Society, Unit 1, How to understand health?
2. Self-instructional course: PROVAB, Module 1, Sexual and Reproductive Health 1, Unit 1, Prenatal risk of habitual assistance in humanized childbirth.
3. Self-instructional Course: PROVAB, Module 3, Comprehensive Health Care for Children 1, Unit 3 Food and immunization.
4. Training Course: Portuguese Language, Module 1, Spelling and Accentuation, Unit 2, Use of the hyphen.

To select the heuristics/recommendations for the study, the following tasks were carried out by the researchers: change profile; access course units; visit each available link and, return to the home page. As a result, 88 heuristics/recommendations were selected to evaluate the sample, being:

- 26 for information architecture regarding navigation, labeling, orientation and information search [11];
- 27 for interaction design on user guidance, workload, explicit control, adaptability, error management and consistency [14]; and
- 35 for information design concerning functional and aesthetic principles of content representation [23][1]. These regard the overall representation of content, and the presentation of the verbal, pictorial and schematic modes. Thus, they covered typographic aspects of text layout, static and dynamic images, text-image relationship, and information visualization.

The heuristics were arranged in rows in a table (evaluative protocol), and the columns were intended for the researchers expert judgment. The researchers should consider the heuristic to have been *Complied* (C), *Not Complied* (N) or *Partially Complied* (P) in each course. Figure 1 shows a detail of the table used for heuristic evaluation in interaction design.

Fig. 1. Detail of the protocol of the heuristic evaluation for interaction design

---

[1] The functional principle *Defining the problems* [23] was not considered in the information design heuristic evaluation as it is related to the strategy and scope planes.

4.2 Levels of Evaluation and Hierarchization of Problems

The evaluation of the sample was conducted at a macro level and at a micro level. At the macro level, general aspects of the virtual leaning environment of the UNA-SUS/UFMA courses were analyzed. This allowed an overview of the courses' system and its structure, as well as the identification of problems and eventual disparities across the courses. At the micro level, a module and a unit of each course and the e-books of the sample were evaluated. This made it possible to identify specific weaknesses of the courses/e-books, particularly regarding information design aspects of content representation in the sample. The heuristics evaluation on information architecture and interaction design was carried out at the macro and micro levels, and the recommendations on information design at the micro level only.

After the heuristic evaluation, a syntheses of the problems identified at the macro and micro levels was generated to make the hierarchization of the problems possible. The FIP (Frequency, Impact, and Persistence) technique [3] was used for this purpose. Such technique aims at answering the following questions:

- How often does the problem occur?
- What is the impact of the problem?
- How persistent is the problem?

To apply the FIP technique, protocols were developed. In each one of the protocols the researchers evaluated the problems identified, assigning a consensus score ranging from 1 to 10 for each of the three aspects: frequency, impact and persistence. The scores were, then, placed in the following formula so as to calculate the severity of each problem:

$$\text{severity} = \frac{\text{score(frequency)} \times \text{score (impact)} \times \sqrt{\text{score (persistence)}}}{\sqrt{10}} \tag{1}$$

In the FIP formula, the scores were in a scale of 0 to 100. The problems ranging from 100 to 70 are highest in severity; those ranging from 69 to 30 were intermediate in severity; and those ranging from 29 to 0.1 were lowest in severity for the UNA-SUS/UFMA courses. The problems which scored 0.0 in severity were disregarded and did not require recommendations for improvements.

The results of the heuristic evaluation and problem hierarchization were analyzed qualitatively. The qualitative approach was considered appropriate, since the results were to produce recommendations for the UNA-SUS/UFMA courses, providing improved material for the UX study. Thus, the numbers herein are only intended to show the occurrence of the results in each item evaluated, with no statistical purpose.

5 Results and Discussion

5.1 Heuristic Evaluation

At the macro level, the heuristics on information architecture and interaction design satisfactorily fulfilled were: 11 in information architecture, with a higher incidence in

Navigation (N = 5) and; 13 in interaction design, with a higher incidence in Workload (N = 6). For example, the heuristics for actions/elements positioned in a logic manner on the screen, and adequate clusters of information presented per page to avoid overwhelming users with contents, were considered fulfilled in the four courses.

On the other hand, 11 heuristics on both information architecture and interaction design were not fulfilled. For instance, the heuristic for allowing different ways for searching was not fulfilled (N = 5), and neither were the 06 heuristics on consistency. Those partially fulfilled were 04 on information architecture (Navigation) and 03 on interaction design (User guidance, and Adaptability).

At the micro level, the heuristic evaluation on information architecture and inter-action design was carried out for each course of the sample. This generated a total of 104 occurrences on information architecture (26 heuristics × 4 courses) and 108 on interaction design (27 heuristics × 4 courses) across the courses. The highest figure of heuristics satisfactorily fulfilled was 23 occurrences in both Workload (interaction design) and Navigation (information architecture). Navigation also presented a high figure of heuristics not fulfilled (N = 19 occurrences). Moreover, the sample has not fulfilled all heuristics on information architecture for Search (N = 20 occurrences); and those on interaction design presented the highest figure on User guidance (N = 15 occurrences).

The heuristic evaluation on information design (micro/e-book level) generated a total of 140 occurrences (35 heuristics × 4 courses). The highest figure of heuristics satisfactorily fulfilled was in the verbal mode (N = 14 occurrences) followed by the pictorial mode (N = 12 occurrences). The verbal mode had also the highest figure of heuristics not fulfilled (N = 10 occurrences), followed by the schematic mode (N = 07 occurrences). The pictorial mode also presented the highest figure of heuristics partially fulfilled (N = 17 occurrences).

5.2   Hierarchization of Problems

The results of the heuristic evaluation were ordered according to their degree of severity (FIP technique). A total of 52 problems were identified (Table 1): 13 high severity problems (N = 100 to 70), 22 medium severity problems (N = 69 to 30), and 17 low severity problems (N = 29 to 0.1). The problems of high and medium severity (N = 35) were considered to negatively affect the distance learning courses produced by UNA-SUS/UFMA.

Table 1. Occurrence of the degree of severity of the hierarchical problems (FIP)

	Severity rank			Total occurrences
	High	Medium	Low	
Information architecture	6	8	2	16
Interaction design	3	8	5	16
Information design	4	6	10	20
Total occurrences	13	22	17	52

In information architecture the highest severity problems with a maximum FIP score (FIP = 100) were absence of navigation aid (e.g., site map); and of tools for searching didactic content. As for the interaction design, the most severe problems had to do with the lack of tools for customizing the course interface (FIP = 100), and for allowing users to resume reading the e-book (FIP = 90).

Finally, within the scope of information design, the problems of greater severity regard typographic aspects of text, text-image relation and pictorial representation of contents. Justified alignment of text, misuse of bold and italic, and poor hierarchy in headings (FIP = 80) were typographic deficiencies (Figs. 2 and 3) found throughout the courses and which may affect reading/legibility. Windows opening outside the page to display information (FIP = 80) were some of the weaknesses found in text-image relation (Fig. 4). These remove users/learners from the page context and may affect their attention to and understanding of information.

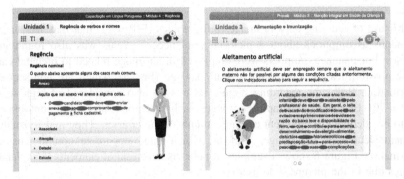

Fig. 2. Examples of inappropriate text alignment that resulted in 'holes' in the text lines indicated by the red dots in these screen shots (Copyright permission by UNA-SUS/UFMA). (Color figure online)

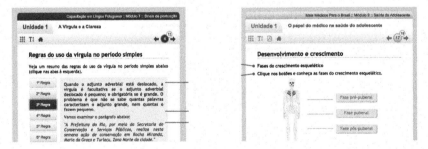

Fig. 3. Examples of misuse of bold and italic; and poor heading hierarchy which are indicated by the red lines in these screen shots (Copyright permission by UNA-SUS/UFMA). (Color figure online)

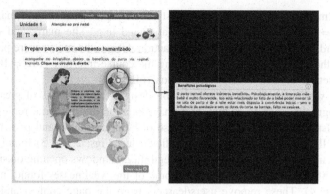

Fig. 4. Example of an unnecessary window to display the image caption. The red line/arrow shows the image caption in this screen shots (Copyright permission by UNA-SUS/UFMA). (Color figure online)

Misuse of ordering cues in images/infographics (FIP = 72) that may lead users to erroneous assumptions about a pictorial sequence of events was also found in the courses. For instance, numbers were employed in an image related to prenatal care to show possibilities for calculating gestational age (Fig. 5), which are non-sequential information. Problems regarding picture style were also considered of high severity (FIP = 70). Flat and oversimplified images, lacking color contrast and contours seem not to be adequate to represent certain contents of the courses. They make visualizing elements/details of the images difficult, which may jeopardize comprehension of information. Figure 6 shows examples of poor visualization of elements in explanatory images due to the picture style used.

Fig. 5. Misuse of numbers to show possibilities for calculating gestational age which is non-sequential information (Copyright permission by UNA-SUS/UFMA). (Color figure online)

Furthermore, the sample presented other weaknesses in the pictorial representation of information in the e-book pages. Different icons were used to convey the same

Fig. 6. Examples of problems in picture style that make visualization of elements in explanatory images difficult (Copyright permission by UNA-SUS/UFMA).

message, indicating inconsistency in the use of icons across courses. For instance, the concept of 'bibliographic references' is conveyed by two icons (a quotation mark and a magnifying lens), whereas the concepts of 'attention' and 'to learn more' (Fig. 7) are both represented by the same icon: an exclamation point (!). In addition, some images were not related to the content presented in the page, and had a decorative function only. Although such images are usually intended to promote a pleasant visual experience (Fig. 8), they may distract users and affect their learning focus if not carefully placed.

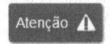

Fig. 7. The same icons to represent 'Attention' and 'To learn more'

Fig. 8. Cartoonlike characters used in e-book pages of the sample (Copyright permission by UNA-SUS/UFMA).

The sample also presented cartoonlike characters (Fig. 8), possibly intended to make the contents more enjoyable to users, giving 'lightness' and 'grace' to their representation. This, however, may constrain the acceptance of pictorial representation by users, who may consider cartoonlike characters to infantilize contents, lacking the seriousness expected in adult learning environments.

6 Conclusions

In general, the outcomes of the heuristic evaluation of the UNA-SUS/UFMA course sample and the hierarchization of problems showed design flaws in the planes of structure, skeleton and surface [4]. Weaknesses were found in information design, information architecture, and interaction design. The courses/e-books were not in accordance with the information design principles [22, 23] of *consistency* in the way elements are presented (icons), *proximity* between related elements (text-image relation), and *hierarchy* of elements differing in importance (headings). In the domain of information architecture, the sample presented weaknesses in the *navigation* (navigation aid to users), *labeling* (ambiguous icons), and *search* (lack of search tools to the didactic content) *systems* [11]. Finally, in the scope of interaction design, the courses have not fully met the ergonomic criteria [13, 14] of *adaptability* (limited customization), *explicit control* (not allow users to go back to a page for continuing the reading), and *consistency* (variation in the presentation of clickable areas). The courses' system also seems to fail when it comes to preventing/reducing and recovering from errors (*error management criterion*).

These deficiencies may compromise the communication and pedagogical effectiveness of the UNA-SUS/UFMA courses/e-books, thus, negatively affecting the user learning experience. Errors or confusion may occur during the interaction with the courses/e-books, and may result in difficulties in, or even lack of understanding of information. In order to improve UNA-SUS/UFMA courses and e-books, recommendations have been made on information architecture, interaction design and information design.

7 Recommendations and Final Considerations

Based on the outcomes of the study, 20 recommendations on information design, 16 on both interaction design and on information architecture were put forward to improve the UNA-SUS/UFMA courses. These recommendations have a flexible character so as to accommodate the variety of situations and contents to be represented. The recommendations should be followed by the courses' developers, who are capable of interpreting/adapting them to the particularities of each content representation, resulting in useful design solutions. The main recommendations regard the high severity problems (FIP score = 100 to 70), which are shown in Table 2.

The heuristic evaluation followed by the hierarchization of problems with FIP technique have strengthened the research design by supporting decision making for UX testing. They have proved to be advantageous at the beginning of the evaluative research process, preventing the testing of material with flaws on information design, information architecture and interaction design. As a result, the UX testing protocols

Table 2. Recommendations regarding the high severity problems found in the sample

Problem	Recommendation
Information architecture	
The system does not offer navigation aid to users	Provide navigation tools for node-to-node navigation (e.g., site map, index, shortcut window) in both the system environment and e-books
The system does not provide search tools to the didactic content	Provide search tools for content in the courses and the e-books to make it possible for users to do: (a) a basic search (user does not need to configure the search) and (b) an advanced search (users can set the search parameters)
The system does not allow navigation to previously visited pages (e.g. no return page)	Allow chronological and hierarchical navigation back to any accessed page
The system does not indicate what was viewed/accessed by the user	Use a graphic differentiation to sign content (images, texts), icons, bottoms, links already viewed/accessed by the user
The system does not indicate the clickable areas of a page to users	Visually indicate the clickable areas of a page. If possible, show distinct visual stages (a) before clicking, (b) mouse-over and (c) after clicking, to make clickable areas explicit to users
At the end of an e-book unit, the system does not provide information on the next unit to be learned	Provide a link to the next e-book unit at the end of every unit. For the last unit, make it clear to users that it is the final unity of the module/e-book
Interaction design	
The system does not allow interface customization (except for profile and privacy settings)	Allow customization of the user interface (e.g., highlight contents to be viewed later, make notes about the content of the pages)
The system does not allow users to mark a reading- stopping point in the e-book to allow them to resume the reading later on	Provide resources to allow users to come back to a particular page of the e-book, after a break in the reading
The presentation of clickable areas differs in the courses' pages	Standardize the presentation of the clickable areas according to their information content/function (e.g., icons, buttons)
Information design	
Typographic drawbacks in text alignment (justified), in the use of bold and italic for paragraphs, and in hierarchy of headings	Align texts left to avoid 'holes' between the words of a typeset line, use bold and italic to emphasize words only (not paragraphs), and differ the headings to indicate levels of importance (e.g., 1 and 1.2; font size variation)

(*continued*)

Table 2. (*continued*)

Problem	Recommendation
Unnecessary windows opening outside the e-book pages to display information	Do not overuse modal resources. Preferably, use tooltip or pop out boxes to show additional information on e-book pages
Misuse of sequential cues, and poor representation of proportion in images/infographics	Use ordering cures in sequential images only and represent proportion accurately in images/infographics
Flat and oversimplified images, lack of color contrast and contours to properly represent certain contents of the courses	Increase color contrast, add contour/outline and the necessary details to images to improve their clarity and to ease the identification/perception of relevant information by users

(e.g., usability tasks) were developed taking into consideration the problems identified in the study.

Moreover, this study ratified the importance of considering information design aspects in the production of UNA-SUS/UFMA distance learning courses, to improve their communication quality.

References

1. WHO – World Health Organization. http://www.who.int/en
2. UNA-SUS/UFMA. http://www.unasus.ufma.br
3. Nielsen, J.: Usability Engineering. Academic Press, Cambridge (2003)
4. Garrett, J.J.: The Elements of User Experience: User-Centered Design for the Web and Beyond, 2nd edn. New Riders Publishing, Thousand Oaks (2010). ISBN: 9780321683687
5. Seraf, M., Wong, C.Y.: A study of user interface design principles and requirements for developing a mobile learning prototype. In: International Conference on Computer and Information Science (ICCIS), pp 1014–1019 (2012)
6. Hashim, A.S., Ahmad, W.F.W, Rohiza, A.: A study of design principles and requirements for the m-learning application development. In: International Conference on User Science and Engineering (i-USEr), pp. 226–231 (2010)
7. Marcus, A. (ed.): Design, User Experience, and Usability: Novel User Experiences. Springer International Publishing, Heidelberg (2016)
8. Benyon, D.: Interação Humano-Computador, 2nd edn. Pearson Education, São Paulo (2011)
9. Preeece, J., Rogers, Y., Sharp, H.: Design de Interação: além da interação humano computador, 3rd edn. Bookman, Porto Alegre (2013)
10. Morville, P., Rosenfeld, L.: Information Architecture for the World Wide Web. O'Reilly, New York (2007)
11. Agner, L.: Ergodesign e arquitetura da informação: trabalhando com o usuário. Quartet Editora, Rio de Janeiro (2006)
12. Saffer, D.: Designing for Interaction: Creating Innovative Applications and Devices, 2nd edn. New Riders, San Francisco (2010). ISBN-10: 0-321-64339-9

13. Cybys, W.A., Betiol, A.H., Faust, R.: Ergonomia e Usabilidade Conhecimentos. Métodos e Aplicações, Novatec Editora São Paulo (2007)
14. Bastien, C., Scapin, D.: Ergonomic criteria for the evaluation of human-computer interfaces. Technical report no. 156. Rocquencourt, France: Institut National de Recherche en Informatique et en Automatique (1993)
15. SBDI- Sociedade Brasileira de Design da Informação. http://www.sbdi.org.br
16. Pettersson, R.: Information Design Basic ID-concepts. Institute of Infology, Tullinge (2013)
17. Bringhurst, R.: Elementos do estilo tipográfico. Cosac Naify, São Paulo (2005)
18. Lupton, E.: Pensar com tipos: guia para designers, escritores, editores e estudantes, 2nd edn. Cosac Naify, São Paulo (2013)
19. Hammerschmidt, C., Spinillo, C.: Articulação tipográfica em bulas digitais: estudo analítico a partir do Bulário Eletrônico da Anvisa. In: Proceedings of the 6th Information Design International Conference, pp. 1068–1083. Blucher, São Paulo (2014)
20. Spinillo, C.: Diseño de información de instruciones visuales, vol. 1, 1st edn. CEAD- Centro de Estudios Avanzados de Diseño, A.C, Puebla (2010). 59 p.
21. Engelhardt, Y.: The language of graphics. Sewn, Amsterdam (2002)
22. Lipton, R.: The Practical Guide to Information Design Hoboken. Wiley, Hoboken (2007)
23. Pettersson, R.: It Depends: ID – Principles and Guidelines Tullinge Institute for Infology (2007)

Case Study: Building UX Design into Citizen Science Applications

Brian Traynor[1(✉)], Tracy Lee[2], and Danah Duke[2]

[1] Mount Royal University, Calgary, Canada
btraynor@mtroyal.ca
[2] Miistakis Institute, Calgary, Canada
tracy@rockies.ca, danah@rocikes.ca

Abstract. Citizen science is the engagement of the public in science or monitoring to address real world problems. Citizen science programs have the ability to provide excellent data for researchers at large spatial and temporal scales. Advancements in technology has resulted in a proliferation of citizen science programs and many are dependent on website and smartphone applications to facilitate data collection, data usability and communication of results. Citizen science applications need to be developed so that they are easy to use and any interface issues identified and resolved before release. Usability reports during the development cycle provide evidenced-based prioritization recommendations. In this paper, two case studies are presented. The Call of the Wild application involved the testing of a high fidelity prototype to collect data on work flow and ease of use. The Wild Watch application provided data on task success and SUS scores that supported release readiness. Both projects continue to have improvements identified based on usability testing.

Keywords: Citizen science · Usability testing

1 Introduction

The Citizen Science Association[1] defines citizen science as "involvement of the public in scientific research – whether community-driven research or global investigations [1]." A powerful value proposition for citizen science is that programs are able to achieve multiple outcomes, including both science and public engagement goals [2]. From a science perspective citizen science can help generate datasets over large geographic and temporal scales; speed up field detection, and enable the classification of large datasets [2]. These benefits are exemplified through the discovery of significant scientific results associated with citizen science projects including documenting range shifts [3], assessing vulnerable species [4], effects on water resources, species management [5] and disaster and conflict resiliency [6]. From an education and engagement perspective citizen science has been shown to advance both individual and societal outcomes including environmental stewardship [7], community capacity [8], environmental justice [9], and co-production of knowledge and practice [8].

---

[1] http://staging.citizenscience.org/.

© Springer International Publishing AG 2017
A. Marcus and W. Wang (Eds.): DUXU 2017, Part III, LNCS 10290, pp. 740–752, 2017.
DOI: 10.1007/978-3-319-58640-3_53

The role of volunteers in citizen science projects can be diverse, from citizens contributing field observations, or sorting or classifying images from their home computers, or identifying and addressing a local issue of concern [1, 10–12]. In addition, citizen science projects can range in scale from a local conservation challenge (e.g., pollution in a local water body) to global in scope (e.g., tracking monarch butterflies across North America) [13, 14].

In the last two decades, citizen science approaches to gathering biodiversity and natural resource information have proliferated [15, 16]. Researchers have identified three factors leading to the recent proliferation of citizen science programs: (1) the evolution and accessibility of technical tools to improve communication, dissemination of information, and data collection; (2) appreciation by professional scientists and others that the public represents a valuable source of labor, skills, computation power, and funding; and (3) the increased value realized by improving the public's understanding of research and monitoring through engagement in the scientific process [17].

In this paper we explore the role of technology and more specifically the contribution of HCI expertise in enhancing program design in two citizen science programs.

2 Role of Technology in Citizen Science

Low cost user friendly technology has enabled global participation in citizen science programs which continue to expand in an effort to engage the public in biodiversity research [18]. In 2016, 90% of North Americans have access to the internet and 67% of Canadians and 72% of Americans own a smartphone [19]. In addition, it has been estimated that by 2020 80% of people globally will own smartphones [20]. Smartphone applications (mobile apps) developed for citizen science programs enable real time reporting of observations, with functionality such as recording sound, taking photos and video and pin point locational accuracy using global positioning systems [21, 22].

Supportive applications built for smartphones, computers and other emerging technology together have the ability to engage a large number of volunteers, improve data collection, control data quality and usability of the data [23], all important variables of citizen science programs. Engaging a large number of volunteers is exemplified by the success of projects on the Zooniverse on-line citizen science portal, where the Galaxy Zoo project enlisted volunteers who collectively classified 50 million galaxies within the first year of operation. Snap Shot Serengeti, another Zooniverse platform, saw 28,000 volunteers classify over 1.51 million remote camera photos [11, 12]. Technology has improved data collection experience for the user through the building of streamlined interface. *Fold it*, a collaborative citizen science gaming application is responsible for the identification of the structure of a protein integral to AIDS [24]. This virtual citizen science approach greatly increased the speed at which this scientific discovery was made, contributing significantly to the scientific process. Data quality can also be improved using smartphone applications. For example, some OPAL (Open Air Laboratories) projects include a requirement to upload photos to help with verification of observations [25]. OPAL includes volunteer engagement in environmental research in the United Kingdom. Lastly, data sharing and usability of data can be greatly improved, for example Project Budburst developed a smartphone app where participants monitor phenology (observing seasonal changes such as plants leafing, flowering and fruiting) and can upload photos with notes and information on the observations creating an on-line community [26]. All of these examples rely on technology and usability of the technology.

The use of HCI in citizen science has been limited due to inadequate interaction between citizen science practitioners and HCI specialists [27]. Preece identified HCI as having a key role to play in supporting citizen science but examples of collaboration are limited. Frameworks to support the design and implementation of citizen science do not include specific reference to usability testing for data collection, data usability and communication applications [16, 28].

The usability of a citizen science application relies on the development process. Developers and information design specialists should be engaged early in the process and feedback should be obtained from end-users. A recent review of nature based applications on Google Play found 6031 nature based applications of which 33 supported citizen science. A review of the applications concluded that no application captured the full potential of capabilities available and most failed to capture the public imagination [29]. This example highlights the need for HCI specialists to have an increased role in citizen science program development. Newman et al. highlight

"...volunteers require simple features that are within their cognitive access. They need to experience initial easy success. Once successful, they may explore complex questions in more depth and have patience for more complex user interface designs and features..." [30].

Examples exist of research exploring methodologies and tools to enhance participation in research and emphasize the importance of the development phase for smartphone apps [21]. Newman et al. provide a comprehensive discussion of their User-Centric Design (UCD) approach to the development of the geospatially enabled www.citsci.org website [30]. They detail the 'iterative investigation, design, requirements specification, development, implementation, testing, and maintenance' development cycle with particular emphasis on the task-based usability evaluation with 16 participants. A further 10 participants were engaged in post-production feedback. The authors reported that participants had difficulty with complex tasks, especially if they were unfamiliar with map features and navigation. Participants also pointed out the need for integrated tasks between citizen scientists and volunteer coordinators [30]. Ease of use and simplicity were also identified as important for adoption. This example highlights the importance of integrating HCI with citizen science to optimize the utility of smartphones and websites to advance citizen science initiatives.

2.1 Usability Evaluation and Reporting

There are multiple opportunities to solicit end-user feedback during the development life-cycle. Tullis and Albert [31] identify formative usability as evaluation activities that attempt to identify design issues and improvements before release and frequently make iterative changes with feedback from smaller numbers of participants. They identify summative usability as evaluation activities that allow the developers to assess performance or yield comparison to identified goals or expectations [31]. Figure 1 shows how these evaluation approaches can overlap during a development cycle. A selection of usability test methods (in green text) has been included in this diagram to highlight how different usability tests can be integrated into product development. For example, rapid paper prototyping might be carried out with a few participants to guide interface design, while performance testing is done with many participants to measure effectiveness, efficiency and satisfaction later in the development cycle. Development teams also recognize that they need to be strategic with their investment in usability testing as there are usually limited resources and tight schedules associated with any project. Guidance on the type of evaluation approaches can be found in many user experience textbooks and the ISO/IEC 25061 standard [32].

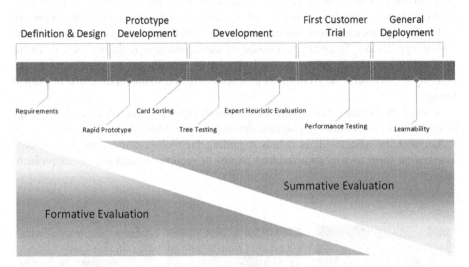

Fig. 1. Overlap of formative and summative evaluation during a product development life-cycle. (Color figure online)

An important consideration for any team should be the reporting of usability evaluation activities. Excellent guidance can be found in the ISO/IEC 25066 standard [33]. The reporting should be appropriate for the type of usability test activities and participant engagement, and should be communicated to stakeholders accordingly. Little has been published in the Citizen Science-HCI literature on the advantages of usability evaluation and reporting on the overall adoption of these applications by contributors and scientists. This paper highlights two case studies that integrated usability testing in unique citizen science programs focused on biodiversity conservation. In both cases the results from the usability testing led to significantly improved applications, ultimately improving the quality of data collected, actual use of data, and sharing of information.

3 Call of the Wetland Case Study (Formative Evaluation)

Call of the Wetland is an urban citizen science program to be launched in April 2017 that enables the public to survey wetlands and report their observations of amphibians, tadpoles or eggs, record amphibian calls and submit photos of amphibian species. The program was developed with two goals: (1) to document where different amphibian species are occurring in the City of Calgary, Alberta, Canada to support biodiversity planning, and (2) to engage the public in wetland conservation by visiting and studying amphibians in urban wetlands. Call of the Wetland has been developed by a team of specialists with a diversity of backgrounds including biologists, communication, information technology and HCI.

Program design elements were informed by a user needs assessment workshop with program collaborators, where program goals, objectives and measures of success were outlined. The user needs assessment laid the foundation for program development and outlined design elements and functionality of collection tools and program website and mobile application. The primary method of data collection is through a Call of the Wetland smartphone application. HCI specialists contributed to the design of the usability test protocol, the recruitment process and the presentation of results in a report format.

Call of the Wetland participants contribute by reporting their observations through an open source smartphone application developed specifically for the program (Fig. 2). Participants are able to fill in details regarding their observation through a wildlife observation form as well as uploading photos or recorded sound files of amphibians calling.

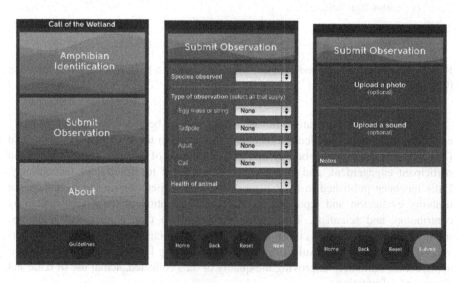

Fig. 2. Call of the wetland smartphone application pre-testing.

3.1 Usability Method

A high-fidelity prototype was developed as proof of concept and to fully scope out data collection and work flow. It was important to get early feedback on the prototype not only to identify design improvements, but also to gain some first-hand experience with potential end-users. Two test protocols were developed: (a) moderated think aloud prototype exploration, (b) unmoderated field evaluation. Program partners, interested participants and volunteers were recruited for these evaluation activities.

The moderated concurrent think aloud usability test included (1) participant consent and study purpose (script), (2) participant demographics/technology experience, (3) moderated tasks and difficulty assessment (identify amphibian, record a sound, submit a photo, ease of use scenarios) and (4) participant experience (frequency likelihood, assistance/learnability). Test participants were recruited from a diverse pool ranging from researchers, environmental specialist, and public volunteers.

The goal of these usability evaluations was to surface design issues and rapidly iterate improvements. Participant feedback and experience was also valuable as the initial test activities were carried out with a broad user base. A number of open-ended questions allowed for participants to express their experiences in their own words.

3.2 Results

Moderated Evaluation

Fourteen participants, including program partners and volunteers likely to participate in the program were included in the usability testing. Information was collected on participant occupation, age, comfort with technology, and amphibian knowledge. The majority of participants (78.6%) indicated that they were very comfortable using a tablet/smartphone prior to using the app. In addition, 57.1% of participants indicated that they were not familiar with amphibians and their habitats prior to the testing.

Participants were asked to identify the ease of use for a number of functions, using the amphibian wildlife identification guide, submitting an observation, uploading a photo and uploading a sound file. For example, half the participants reported having trouble navigating the steps between uploading the audio/image and submitting it (Fig. 3), indicating adjustments were needed.

The resulting data allowed the researchers to identify a number of key issues such as, improvement to the amphibian identification page, ambiguity in the application guidelines, challenge to upload a sound and/or photo process, verification of file uploads, and reporting of no sightings. The qualitative responses also provided excellent feedback on application ambiguity, learnability and overall design.

Unmoderated Field Evaluation

Four participants completed the unmoderated usability test protocol. This allowed respondents to provide input on using the application for opportunist observation and systematic assignments. The self-reported comments identified similar issues to the moderated session, but also included possible issues/enhancements such as adjustments

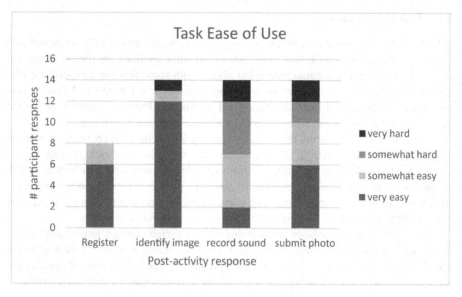

Fig. 3. Participant ease of use reported by task.

to the audio recording instructions, better understanding of how a participant corrects submitting errors, and ability to record the wetland survey number they have agreed to survey.

A summary consolidated report was prepared at the end of the testing phase. This report included recommendations on how to address identified issues. The report was shared with project partners and changes to the smartphone application were then prioritized.

3.3   Impact of Report

Following the usability testing, the smartphone application underwent major adjustments based on recommendations (significant overhaul of the amphibian identification guide, photo and sound upload process, registration process and ability to report no sightings). The changes significantly improved the data collection experience for users. The smartphone application will be released this spring. Further evaluations are planned to assess application performance.

4   Wild Watch Case Study (Summative Evaluation)

Wild Watch was created in partnership with Cenovus Energy and Shell Canada to increase employee awareness of wildlife stewardship and to generate a real-time spatial digital dataset of wildlife observations and human-wildlife interactions to inform industrial site wildlife management plans. Wild Watch participants (employees and contractors working at northern industrial sites) use a smartphone app and/or online mapping tool to enter their wildlife observations.

Historically, both industrial partners supported wildlife reporting programs where participants reported observations via hard copy forms. The programs were underutilized, and the data was ultimately deemed unusable as locational information was poorly reported. The growth and success of citizen science programs and role of technology provided an opportunity to improve multiple aspects of the program including data collection, data management and usability of the data.

Key features of the Wild Watch program include streamlined data collection; improved location accuracy of observations; reporting on human wildlife conflicts and other activities of interest (on infrastructure, on road, in garbage or wildlife vehicle collision); alerting environmental staff when a human wildlife conflict or endangered species are reported, providing access to real time data that can be searched by species, activity of by date; and automated upload into government wildlife reporting form. These features are all dependent on human interacting with the Wild Watch program via the project website (Fig. 4), online mapping tool and smartphone application.

HCI specialists played an important role in the development phase and undertook usability testing and recommendation on the smartphone application and online mapping tool (Fig. 4). The program has been running since 2013 and annual reviews identify adaptations to improve the user experience. The program continues to evolve as staff and participants interact with the site and find ways to improve the experience.

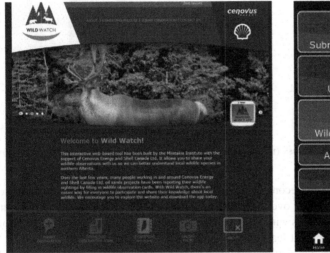

Fig. 4. Wild Watch web interface and smartphone application.

4.1 Usability Methods

A two-stage test protocol was developed: (1) moderated think aloud task performance evaluation of website and a self-rated experience using a SUS questionnaire, and (2) moderated think aloud task performance evaluation of application, self-rated experience using a SUS questionnaire, and a session debrief with participants.

For both the website and app, the participants were asked to undertake the following tasks: (1) register for an account (Website only), (2) add an observation (information provided), (3) upload a photo (photo provided), and (4) find information about moose. Test participants were recruited from Cenovus employees likely to be using this application.

4.2 Results

Figure 5 summarizes task (listed above from 1–4) success for six participants performing with both the web (W) and mobile application (A). While all participants completed the four tasks, minor problems were noted.

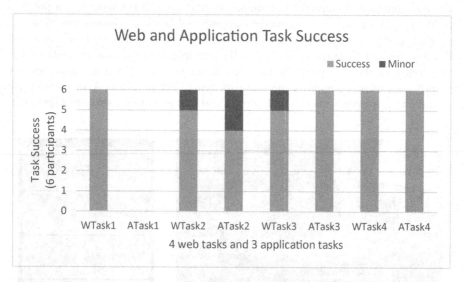

Fig. 5. Participant task success (minor indicates a task completion with some minor issue)

Only task success was recorded. Some learnability could result in the higher success rates for the application over the website. However, with three of the participants having some minor problems with task 2, (adding an observation via the mapping tool) this pointed the development team to particular areas for improvement.

Figure 6 offers insights to the participants' impression of their satisfaction with their experience. The advantage of using a standard instrument such as the SUS questionnaire is that it allows you to compare with other reported SUS scores. A SUS score in the 50–70 range as being marginal, SUS above 70 indicates acceptable level [31, 34]. The high average SUS score is an excellent indicator of the website and application perceived ease of use.

This combination of task success and SUS scores supports the development effort, allows for future comparison and is a good indicator of the likely acceptance of the

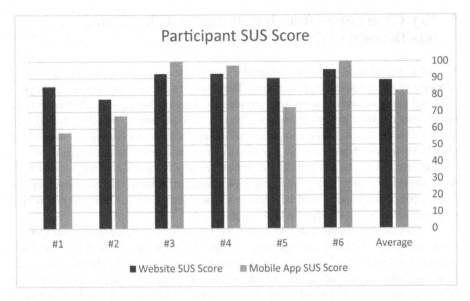

Fig. 6. Six participant SUS scores for Wild Watch web and smartphone application.

application. A comprehensive usability report was provided with an executive summary identifying positive findings, areas for improvement and associated recommendations. These were separated by website and application. The report also included a full description of the test method, moderator scripts, tasks and questionnaires used. Collected data was collated and presented in a way that other researchers might easily follow. This approach suggests that the test protocol was executed consistently and could easily be duplicated or reused.

4.3 Impact of Report

The report was shared with program partners, recommendations were discussed and where appropriate incorporated into the website mapping and smartphone applications prior to release of the program. Major adjustments focused on changes in language, placement of key features and changes to design of functionality components such as registration and locational pin for marking observations on the mapping tool. Wild Watch launched in 2013, and since this time annual program evaluations (interviews and surveys) have identified additional improvements to the usability of data (improved search functions and display of data on mapping tool), and development of environmental email alerts (i.e. species at risk reports). The Wild Watch program highlights the value of the HCI specialist role in enhancing design and functionality of the developed applications, ultimately improving program success.

5 Key Observations from Integrating Usability Testing into Development

The HCI specialist or user experience designer plays a crucial role in the successful adoption of citizen science applications. There are lots of usability test methods possible and the development team needs to identify what methods provide the maximum benefit that consider project resources. The test methods and resources allocated will depend to some extent of the complexity of the application and the legacy products in use. Development teams should pay particular attention to the recruitment of test participants. Formative test activities can provide early feedback on design issues with small numbers of participants. Where demonstrated performance targets are set, then a larger pool of participants will be necessary (for example, if you want to report significance levels when comparing two designs).

While usability testing can add to the work load of a development team (preparation, planning, execution and reporting), the advantages are many. A well-defined test protocol can be reviewed and consideration given to the demands on the test participant as well as the integrity of the data collected. In effect, the team can assess the ethical quality of the test protocol and ensure that appropriate professional standards are met. Efforts made to recruit end-users in testing allow the team to demonstrate readiness for product release. The resulting usability test report is an excellent vehicle for communicating to stakeholders. These reports provide guidance on the prioritization of ongoing development, and also engage the development team with end-users. Since recommendations are evidence-based, it is easier to reach consensus on development priorities. The captured data also provides baseline data against which these future changes can be measured.

These case studies did not have a usability research question to be examined. However, their goal was successful adoption with accurate, meaningful data collected in the field and then the analysis and use of the resulting data to help with environmental management decisions. The ubiquitous availability of mobile technology offers fantastic potential for data collection. However, ease of use will be essential to adoption of citizen science applications and usability testing is integral to a successful development process.

5.1 Areas for Future Research

Some potential areas of applied research include: planning and stakeholder engagement models, recruitment strategies and the influence of incentives, change management and consensus decision making during development, stakeholder communication through usability reports and long-term assessment of engagement through diary studies and usage reports.

Acknowledgements. Wild Watch is generously supported by Cenovus Energy and Shell Canada. Call of the Wetland is generously supported by Enbridge, TD Friends of the Environment and The Calgary Foundation.

The authors wish to thank information design and communications students from Mount Royal University whom assist with the usability testing, including Amy Lai, Alexis Handford, and Devon Henry. In addition we thank participants whom undertook usability testing for Call of the Wetland and Wild Watch programs.

References

1. Bonney, R., Phillips, T.B., Ballard, H.L., Enck, J.W.: Can citizen science enhance public understanding of science? Public Underst. Sci. **25**, 2–16 (2015). doi:10.1177/0963662515607406
2. Mckinley, D.C., Miller-Rushing, A.J., Ballard, H.L., et al.: Published by the Ecological Society of America ESA Management and Environmental Protection (2015)
3. Wilson, S.: Citizen science reveals an extensive shift in the winter distribution of migratory western grebes. PLoS ONE **8**, e65408 (2013). doi:10.1371/journal.pone.0065408
4. Westgate, M.J.: Citizen science program shows urban areas have lower occurrence of frog species, but not accelerated declines. PLoS ONE **10**, e0140973 (2015). doi:10.1371/journal.pone.0140973
5. Delaney, D., Corinne, D., Sperling, S., et al.: Marine invasive species: validation of citizen science and implications for national monitoring networks. Biol. Invasions **10**, 117–128 (2008)
6. Tidball, K.G., Krasny, M.E.: Civic ecology: a pathway for earth stewardship in cities. Front. Ecol. Environ. **10**, 267–273 (2012)
7. Evans, C., Abrams, E., Reitsma, R., et al.: The neighborhood nestwatch program: participant outcomes of a citizen-science ecological research project. Conserv. Biol. **19**, 589–594 (2005)
8. Ballard, H., Belsky, J.: Participatory action research and environmental learning: implications for resilient forests and communities. Environ. Educ. Res. **16**, 611–627 (2010)
9. Wing, S., Horton, R., Marshall, S., et al.: Air pollution and odor in communities near industrial swine operations. Environ. Health Perspect. **116**, 1362–1368 (2008)
10. Wiggins, A., Crowston, K.: From conservation to crowdsourcing: a typology of citizen science (2011). doi:10.1109/HICSS.2011.207
11. Cox, J., Oh, E.Y., Simmons, B., et al.: Defining and measuring success in online citizen science. Comput. Sci. Eng. **17**, 28–41 (2015). doi:10.1109/MCSE.2015.65
12. Swanson, A., Kosmala, M., Lintott, C., Packer, C.: A generalized approach for producing, quantifying, and validating citizen science data from wildlife images. Conserv. Biol. **30**, 520–531 (2016). doi:10.1111/cobi.12695
13. Haywood, B.K., Parrish, J.K., Dolliver, J.: Place-based and data-rich citizen science as a precursor for conservation action. Conserv. Biol. **30**, 476–486 (2016). doi:10.1111/cobi.12702
14. Ries, L., Oberhauser, K.: A citizen army for science: quantifying the contributions of citizen scientists to our understanding of monarch butterfly biology. Bioscience **65**, 419–430 (2015). doi:10.1093/biosci/biv011
15. Pocock, M.J., Chapman, D.S., Sheppard, L.J., Roy, H.E.: A strategic framework to support the implementation of citizen science for environmental monitoring. Final report to SEPA, p. 67 (2014)
16. Shirk, J.L., Ballard, H.L., Wilderman, C.C., et al.: Public participation in scientific research : a framework for deliberate design. Ecol. Soc. **17**(2), 20 (2012). Article 29, doi:10.5751/ES-04705-170229

17. Silvertown, J.: A new dawn for citizen science. Trends. Ecol. Evol. **24**, 467–471 (2009). doi:10.1016/j.tree.2009.03.017
18. Baker, B.: Frontiers of citizen science. Bioscience **66**, 921–927 (2016). doi:10.1093/biosci/biv011
19. Poushter, J.: Smartphone ownership and internet usage continues to climb in emerging economies. Pew. Res. Cent., 45 (2016). http://www.pewglobal.org/2016/02/22/smartphone-ownership-and-internet-usage-continues-to-climb-in-emerging-economies/
20. The Economist: The truly personal computer. Econ. (2015). http://www.economist.com/news/briefing/21645131-smartphone-defining-technology-age-truly-personal-computer
21. Teacher, A.G.F., Griffiths, D.J., Hodgson, D.J., Inger, R.: Smartphones in ecology and evolution: a guide for the app-rehensive. Ecol. Evol. **3**, 5268–5278 (2013). doi:10.1002/ece3.888
22. Dehnen-Schmutz, K., Foster, G.L., Owen, L., Persello, S.: Exploring the role of smartphone technology for citizen science in agriculture. Agron. Sustain. Dev. **36**, 25 (2016). doi:10.1007/s13593-016-0359-9
23. Newman, G., Wiggins, A., Crall, A., et al.: The future of citizen science: emerging technologies and shifting paradigms. Front. Ecol. Environ. **10**, 298–304 (2012). doi:10.1890/110294
24. Curtis, V.: Online citizen science projects: an exploration of motivation, contribution and participation. Ph.D. thesis. The Open University, Milton Keynes, UK (2015). http://oro.open.ac.uk/42239/
25. Davies, L., Fradera, R., Riesch, H., Fraser, P.L.: Surveying the citizen science landscape: an exploration of the design, delivery and impact of citizen science through the lens of the Open Air Laboratories (OPAL) programme. BMC Ecol. **16**, 1–13 (2016). doi:10.1186/s12898-016-0066-z
26. Graham, E.A., Henderson, S., Schloss, A.: Using mobile phones to engage citizen scientists in research. Eos (Washington DC) **92**, 313–315 (2011). doi:10.1029/2011EO380002
27. Preece, J.: Citizen science: new research challenges for human-computer interaction. Int. J. Hum. Comput. Interact. **32**, 585–612 (2016). doi:10.1080/10447318.2016.1194153
28. Chase, S.K., Levine, A.: A framework for evaluating and designing citizen science programs for natural resources monitoring. Conserv. Biol. **30**, 456–466 (2016). doi:10.1111/cobi.12697
29. Jepson, P., Ladle, R.J.: Nature apps: waiting for the revolution. Ambio **44**, 827–832 (2015). doi:10.1007/s13280-015-0712-2
30. Newman, G., Zimmerman, D., Crall, A., et al.: User-friendly web mapping: lessons from a citizen science website. Int. J. Geogr. Inf. Sci. **24**, 1851–1869 (2010). doi:10.1080/13658816.2010.490532
31. Tullis, T., Albert, B.: Measuring the User Experience: Collecting, Analyzing, and Presenting Usability Metrics. Morgan Kaufmann, Amsterdam (2013)
32. ISO/IEC: ISO/IEC 25062:2006 - Software engineering—Software product Quality Requirements and Evaluation (SQuaRE)—Common Industry Format (CIF) for usability test reports (2006)
33. ISO/IEC: 25066:2016 Systems and software engineering—Systems and software Quality Requirements and Evaluation (SQuaRE)—Common Industry Format (CIF) for usability—Evaluation report (2016)
34. Sauro, J.: A Practical Guide to the System Usability Scale. Measuring Usability LLC, Denver (2011)

Participatory Design in the Development of a Smart Pedestrian Mobility Device for Urban Spaces

Wiktoria Wilkowska[✉], Katrin Arning, and Martina Ziefle

Human-Computer Interaction Center,
RWTH Aachen University, Campus Boulevard 57, Aachen, Germany
{wilkowska,arning,ziefle}@comm.rwth-aachen.de

Abstract. Pedestrian mobility is an important component in urban mobility concepts. Walking is a highly flexible means to reach nearby places, to access public transport, or to bridge the "last mile" between the parking space and one's office or home. Smart pedestrian mobility devices (PMD) can support pedestrians' activities, either by offering ride-on functions or assistance in everyday activities (e.g., as a carrier for goods) and thereby enhance pedestrians' connectivity and flexibility. To ensure a high acceptance and adoption rate of PMD, a design approach is needed that explicitly focuses on users' interests and requirements. We present a multi-level and iterative participatory design approach for the development of smart mobility devices, that reaches from (a) requirement analysis and use case development, (b) communication design, (c) personalization/identity design, (d) exterior design evaluations, to (e) practical driving experience testing. The application and specific suitability of empirical qualitative and quantitative methods is demonstrated and results regarding (a) general acceptance, perceived benefits, barriers, usage conditions and purchase criteria, (b) visual and auditory signal sets for communication design, (c) usability and learnability evaluations after riding on a prototype are presented. The findings demonstrate a high willingness of users to participate in the design process, but also highly differentiated perceptions and requirements regarding a PMD. Even though still in the prototype stage, PMD yield a high potential to serve as a day-to-day mobility assistant (especially for older people) but also as a fun ride-on device (for younger and physically fit people).

Keywords: Smart mobility · Communication design · User factors · User-centered design · User experience · Technology acceptance

1 Introduction

The mobility of today changes. Considering growing urbanization, increasing environmental pollution, and varying job-related challenges, mobility requirements are changing and novel mobility concepts are needed to counteract the resulting challenges in modern societies [1, 2]. Although current public transport systems comprise extensive bus networks as well as urban and intercity railways that extend to most major destinations, an efficient access for pedestrians to these means of transport is

A. Marcus and W. Wang (Eds.): DUXU 2017, Part III, LNCS 10290, pp. 753–772, 2017.
DOI: 10.1007/978-3-319-58640-3_54

often limited [3]. Also, drivers who need cars for their job or carry out other accomplishments with the help of cars are often confronted – especially in urban spaces – with difficult parking situation and are urged to walk greater distances. In addition, the ratio of older persons in Western countries is growing steadily. In an aging society it is very important to develop devices which can support and assist the elderly in their daily life, since their mobility significantly degrades with age and differs from the mobility patterns of the younger members of the society [4, 5]. Understanding the dynamics of daily mobility patterns is therefore essential for the management and planning of urban facilities and services [6], as well as for the development of mobility innovations that meet the demands of today's users of urban spaces.

In view of these facts, a comprehensive approach is needed that offers pedestrians of different age and physical fitness integrated "door-to-door" mobility services that enhance their connectivity, provide flexibility and assistance in everyday activities, and potentially increase the transit ridership [3]. At the same time, the mobility of tomorrow must be more climate and resource-efficient, more effective, and safer [7]. Due to the current mobility trends, it is foreseeable that in the near future a high proportion of electric vehicles will dominate the urban transport which opens up great possibilities for new (smart) technological developments. And, considering the congested (inner-)cities, especially the pedestrian mobility devices are likely to play a considerable role.

In the last years, an increasing number of mobility devices for pedestrians has become visible on the streets. A prominent example is the Segway, regarded as the first electrically powered, self-balancing transportation device for persons [8], which was introduced in 2001. Since then a rising competition on the market could be observed (e.g., electric scooters, hover boards). However, none of the technical innovations in this area was equally successful, or dominated the market: either, they addressed too narrow target groups, or they were simply poorly conceived. To develop flawless, functioning and well accepted pedestrian mobility devices for use in urban spaces, sophisticated ideas are needed to open up larger market shares to remain competitive. The technology must be absolutely effective, assistive, environmentally sound, safe for urban traffic, and fun for diverse user groups. To achieve this, however, in addition to technical ingenuity, a sophisticated research methods are necessary, which successfully involve all stakeholders in the design process: designers, researchers, but especially the potential end-users.

This article describes the application of such a participatory design [9, 10] to the development of a smart pedestrian mobility device (PMD), which is meant to support the pedestrians in their everyday activities (e.g., go shopping), ease the way to school, work or the bus stop, and just to have fun, cruising in the urban environment. To ensure a high user acceptance and widespread adoption of such devices, a user-centered approach was pursued that focused on the user's particular interests and requirements. To achieve this, potential users were continuously integrated into all steps of the developmental and design processes (participatory design). "Typical" development and design processes of technical devices include the user at later stages, when the (merely) technical requirements are defined and a beta-version of the final product is produced. The users' role is usually limited to some "fine-tuning" aspects, when designing the exterior or the HMI (human-machine-interface) of the device. However, an early integration of the user into the design process has been proven as useful and effective for developing "acceptable" technical devices, systems and interfaces (e.g., [11–13]).

In the following, we present the single research steps of the development process, from the concept stage to the development of the first prototype and the first usability evaluation of a smart PMD for the use in an urban context. The participatory research design plays an important role in the empirical approach and explores the users' perceptions and needs in different aspects of use. The paper is structured as follows: Firstly, we present the conceptualization of the specific PMD that was to be developed (Sect. 2). In the next step, we describe the participatory design process for the user-centered (communication) design development of the device (Sect. 3) and outline research methods used in the participatory design approach (Sect. 4). Next, the main results are presented (Sect. 5) and discussed in Sect. 6. Finally, the limitations and future research duties are described in Sect. 7.

2   Specification of the Smart Pedestrian Mobility Device

The smart PMD, which served as the technical concept basis for the participatory design approach presented in this paper, is a multi-purpose mobility robot and assistant that unites many helpful functions in one compact, easy to use, and fun-to-drive electrically operated device. It has four multi-directional wheels – two each at the front and the back – for stable and easy riding and handling, making it usable for a large group of people (commuters, urban residents, tourists, elderly people, teens, etc.).

The innovative PMD has two main functions: One is the ride-on function for persons commuting through urban areas. The user rides on the device in a standing position and controls the ride through weight shifting (e.g., when the rider leans forward, the PMD moves forward and when the rider leans back, it moves back, or stops). A connection via an app on the smartphone shows all necessary data, like battery status, range, or the navigation area. Another designated function is the tethering function. The device is equipped with a semi-autonomous "follow-me" feature. Using the smartphone connection, the GPS position of the user is continuously detected and the mobility robot follows user's every step while carrying heavy items (e.g., purchases from the grocery store).

For the communication with the user, different channels are designated: One is a LED-stripe on the device which gives the user visual feedback about various functions (e.g., turn left/right) and driving events (e.g., slowing down). A second communication channel is possible through built-in speakers, enabling an acoustic feedback. A further communication opportunity is the app, where all the important data regarding the state of the device, technical data, navigation maps, etc. can be displayed in more detail.

The PMD is conceptualized as a convenient device designed to bridge the last mile(s) to the peoples' destinations, for fun rides and as an overall helpful assistant in the everyday life. In the following, the empirical approach to develop a first prototype of a PMD which is adapted to users' requirements and needs, easy to use, and perceived as useful is described.

3 Participatory Design Process for a User-Centered (Communication) Design Development

In this article we examine communicative, functional, and operative requirements of users to the electrically operated, semi-autonomous PMD concept specified above. The aim was to identify criteria that can be used as a basis for a user-centered development process. These criteria should be addressed to deploy the full potentials of such mobile robots for the future (urban) mobility.

In this section, we describe aspects in the process of designing a pedestrian mobility device, which were considered in the scientific approach. Figure 1 depictures this process in detail.

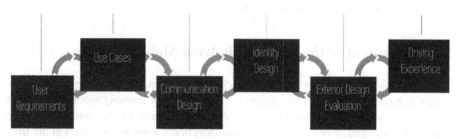

Fig. 1. Single steps of the research process in the design of the PMD

3.1 Determining User Requirements and Use Cases

Determining effective requirements for the PMD is pivotal to produce a device that meets the users' real needs. To do so, in the present research a multi-methods approach was applied to gather relevant information about the requirements among users. However, the requirements device needs to meet can vary greatly, depending on user characteristics (e.g., age, mobility patterns).

Thus, defining relevant target groups is the first important step to get insights into the particular needs and demands of the targeted users. To create a mobility robot for the broadest possible use and/or assistance, persons of different age and gender, students, young professionals as well as professionally established persons took part in the research process. The composition and assignment of the participants to the respectively applied research methods are described in detail below (see Sect. 4).

In the early stage of the scientific process, the participants were encouraged to express their general opinions about the smart pedestrian device which had been introduced in basic terms. They were asked to reflect on possible benefits and to ask themselves, whether they would use such technology in the future. In addition, as it is sometimes easier to identify associated barriers associated with a particular device, the respondents explicitly focused on possible obstacles with the PMD, discussing possible facts which would lead them to reject the device. In group discussions (Fig. 2), participants suggested solutions for the identified barriers or formulated conditions under which the use would be possible for them.

All ideas and opinions regarding perceived benefits and barriers as well as the mentioned demands and conditions were collected and evaluated later in the scientific process.

Fig. 2. Discussion about perceived benefits and barriers of the use of a PMD

3.2 Creating Communication Design

A PMD that is highly sensitive to the needs of its user, that is attentive to the permanently changing surroundings, and traffic safe, requires a sophisticated communication ability which provides the user with unambiguous and intuitive signals.

The process of the creation of such an explicit and clear language, which provides the user with precisely outlined, clear, and situationally presented hints (i.e., audible, visual, and/or haptic), is a very challenging task. There are some relevant points to be considered:

- It is important to develop communication patterns that allow for a flawless user interaction.
- The communication system should be perfectly adapted to the function/task, purpose or goal at which it is aimed.
- The communication design should consider the already existing, deeply anchored signals which are intuitively understood in a certain way (e.g., red light for warning).
- Different signaling modes must be correspondingly matched to one another and must be "dosed" accordingly for the user.
- The visual and acoustic signals need to be redundantly coded but they should not be too complex or overload the user.

In the present study, participants "developed" the communicative signs for different functions and given events (e.g., on/off, braking, turn signals) linked to the daily use of the PMD from scratch. They created the signals in two modes: visual, using a spectrum of 265 colors on an LED-stripe, and acoustic, using a keyboard or their own voice which was recorded (as exemplary shown in Fig. 3).

The procedure followed three successive steps: In the first step, groups of participants generated events in which communication between the user and the device is necessary/desirable. In the second step, they made their own signal suggestions for

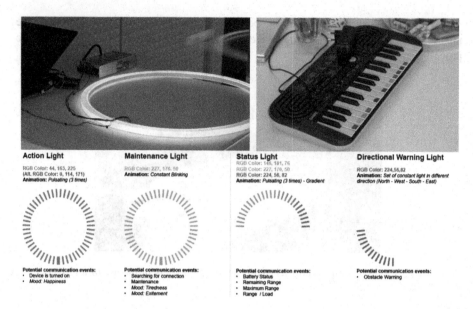

Fig. 3. Top: tools for creation of visual and acoustic signals; bottom: examples of visual signal presets for different driving events for the pedestrian mobility device (Color figure online)

specific functions and/or events, depending on their previous decision, whether an acoustic and/or visual signal was essential or not. In the third step, the group presented their signal proposals, giving the other participants of a focus group (see Sect. 4.1) a forum for discussion and evaluation of their results. All signals were then repeatedly evaluated during later stages of the research process.

3.3 Exploring Identity Design

According to the ever-increasing tendency of personalized technology (e.g., in the area of medical technology [14], mobile commerce [15, 16], or e-learning [17]), the next question which was relevant for the process of designing the smart PMD was the importance of identity characteristics and personalized character traits. The aim was to explore how potential users perceive and wish the device to be or to behave. The central question was if users wish the PMD to be equipped with a social identity, serving as an electronic "friend", who knows its user's personal needs, wishes and preferences to a given (day-)time or a specific situation. Participants also discussed about the importance of displaying basic emotions in the mobility device (e.g., joy/fun, distress, anger).

In a "do-it-yourself" workshop (Fig. 4) participants worked on the identity topic in three successive steps. In the first part, the brainstorming method was applied, where the persons tried to identify potentially relevant identity features. In the second step, they created paper prototypes of the device trying to highlight the characteristics that were especially important to them with regard to identity. In the third step, all paper prototypes were presented and discussed with the other participants.

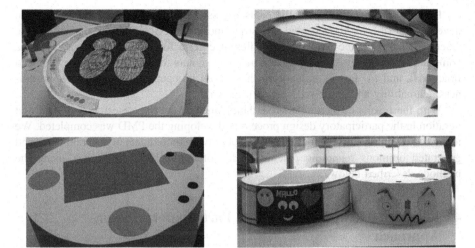

Fig. 4. Various concepts for personalized prototypes of the pedestrian mobility device

Finding of the personal identity preferences was important for the design process at least for two main reasons: Firstly, it affected the interaction with the user to a great extent, and secondly, it has played a decisive role in the development of the exterior design of the PMD.

3.4 Prototype Driving Experience and Usability Testing

Based on the information gained in the workshops, a first prototype of the pedestrian mobility device was assembled, which allowed for the actual interaction (i.e., driving experience) with users.

In a driving event, participants explored the driving features, trying to identify possible weaknesses. Initially, each person was exposed to a free driving and handling experience, for which there was no time limit. After gaining some driving routine, everyone had to run a route with obstacles as effectively and error-free as possible.

After the active driving experience, besides the evaluation of the mandatory usability criteria according to ISO 9241-11 [18], i.e., effectiveness, efficiency, satisfaction, participants had to assess their individual opinions regarding riding comfort, learnability, driving safety, and the perceived fun.

Finally, in short interviews participants expressed their opinions regarding driving properties and suggestions for improvements and optimization of the driving ability.

3.5 (Exterior) Design Evaluation

Eventually, the information gathered up to this point was evaluated and validated in a larger group of potential users.

In a quantitative survey, participants assessed different aspects relevant for the development of a highly-accepted pedestrian mobility device. They evaluated: (1) the exterior design, (2) the relevance of different criteria for buying the device, (3) the communication design (i.e., visual and acoustic signals for various driving events and functions), and (4) factors influencing the overall acceptance (e.g., perceived usefulness, learnability and perceived ease of use, fun).

With the results of the quantitative data gained in the five research steps, the first iteration in the participatory design process in developing the PMD was completed. We identified communicative, functional, and operative requirements of different users and generated opinions regarding potential fields of application (use cases), using the methods described below.

4   Research Methods Used in the Participatory Design Approach

In this section, the research methods used in the participatory design approach are described. We applied a mixed methods approach: qualitative (Sect. 4.1) and quantitative (Sect. 4.2) methods as well as hands-on experience. Such a "triangulation" (e.g., [19–21]) that means a combination of multiple research methods in the study of the same phenomenon, is very powerful for gaining insights and results, and for assisting in making inferences and in drawing conclusions [22]. Thereby, effectiveness of this triangulation is based on the premise that the weaknesses in each single method will be compensated by the counter-balancing strengths of another [23]. In this section, the particular methods used to gain relevant data and the associated samples of participants are described in more detail.

4.1   Qualitative Data Collection

To gain first insights into perceptions of an upcoming innovative technology, qualitative research methods represent an appropriate instrument. Qualitative methods focus on the content of relevant properties associated with the research question or study material [24] and are primarily used for exploratory purposes, allowing to gain an understanding of underlying reasons, opinions, and motivations. Their inductive feature allows that propositions may be developed not only from practice, or literature review, but also from ideas themselves [23].

In the process of designing the PMD, qualitative research methods were used both, individually and in groups. In the following, the methods used for the exploration of the respective main topics are briefly described.

Focus Groups. Based on the interaction between participants in discussions about a specific topic, the method of focus group discussions aims at collecting qualitative data. Qualitative data is a source of rich descriptions and explanations of processes in the specific context. A systematic group interview allows to increase the depth of the inquiry and to unveil aspects of a phenomenon. In addition, group interactions may accentuate members' similarities and differences, and give rich information about the range of perspectives, opinions, and experiences [25, 26].

In the present research, three focus groups were conducted to determine user requirements and demands in the following aspects of the use of a PMD:

- In the first focus group (N = 6; age range: 27–66 years; 4 women and 2 men) participants initially reflected on the question, which *requirements, benefits* and *barriers* the utilization of a PMD can bring along. In addition, they discussed about conceivable *use cases* (as described in detail below) and considered under which conditions they would use such a technology innovation. In the further course of the focus group, participants conceived their own communication design for the specific functions and the specific events related to the drivability of the PMD.
- The second focus group (N = 10; age range: 23–37 years; 4 women and 6 men) aimed at determining of the importance of the *device's identity* and answered the question in how far the mobility robot needs to be personalized to its user. The main part of the meeting was the creative workshop (as described below) and the final discussion on this topic.
- In the third focus group (N = 15; age range: 18–24 years) the main focus was the verification and validation of the communication design as well as evaluation of the exterior design. Presets of acoustic and visual signals for certain functions and events in the traffic were presented and discussed in the group. The most suitable signal, or variants with the most intuitive effects on participants, were included.

Use Cases. The method of use cases is an important technique for the collection and specification of functional requirements [27]. They are specifically suited to understand the device from the user's perspective and allow to find out in which situations the potential users are willing to use it.

In the present study, the method of the use cases was applied to define possible interactions between users and the device. As a part of the first focus group discussion, participants identified different use cases for the pedestrian robot: possible functions (e.g., ride function, "pack mule" function), different roles (e.g., personal assistant, dog sitter), and cases of application (e.g., as an entertainment/fun tool). The use cases gave impulses for later concepts of communication and exterior design.

Creativity Workshop. The creative workshop played a very special role in the process of the development of the PMD. Considering that some people are less talkative, timid, and/or quickly distracted through the opinions of other discussion partners, creating space for their creativity and free thinking can truly bear special fruit.

In the present research participants of the workshop were free to either work alone or together with others in small groups. The task was to create a paper prototype of a pedestrian robot with all possible characteristics, functions, and elements desired for such a device. There was no time limit and the participants were provided with a variety of handicraft materials. In fact, some of the persons chose to work alone. Apparently, they took the opportunity to work undistracted and in this way expressed their own ideas, presenting the creations without the support of others.

User Interviews. User interviews are a key activity for understanding different aspects, tasks, and motivations of the users for whom the device is designed. For the purposes of the presented study, short interviews were used as informal chats. As a part of the evaluation of the first prototype, participants were interviewed about the perceived pros and cons of the device. In addition, they were asked to make suggestions for improvement and they rated their physical and mental efforts when driving with the pedestrian robot.

4.2 Quantitative Research Methods

Quantitative research focuses on explanation of phenomena by collecting numerical data that is analyzed using mathematically based methods [28] and is a complemental addition to qualitative methods. An advantage of quantitative methods is that they provide precise, quantifiable, and reliable data that is usually generalizable to some larger population as long as the data is based on random samples of sufficient size. It allows researchers to test specific hypotheses that are constructed before the data is collected, and is useful for studying larger numbers of persons. The results are relatively independent from the researcher and can be evaluated by the quality criteria objectivity, reliability and validity (e.g., [23, 29, 30]).

In the present study, complementary to the above mentioned qualitative techniques, quantitative questionnaire as well as usability testing (hands-on experience) were applied to gain best possible knowledge for an optimal development of the pedestrian mobility device. In the following, the methods are described in more detail.

Questionnaire. In addition to the qualitative techniques, a quantitative questionnaire consistently examined diverse factors that are essential for the acceptance and successful adoption of the pedestrian mobility device. Apart from demographic data and their habits to use different mobility devices, participants answered questions regarding requirements and demands with respect to the PMD. In addition to user factors, they were queried about their opinions regarding the ownership modality, i.e. whether they could imagine buying, sharing or renting it. Also, purchase criteria for the PMD and a general attitude towards technical innovations (e.g., "It's fun to try out novel technical equipment.") were part of the questionnaire. Moreover, the traditional aspects of technology acceptance, like perceived usefulness, satisfaction, and fun had to be rated. The questions had to be answered on 6-point Likert scales ranging from 0 (= strongly disagree) to 5 (= strongly agree).

Hands-On Experience. The prototype of the pedestrian robot allowed first hands-on experiences with the device and brought significant insights regarding practical usage aspects. Following the first impressions after an introduction and driving instructions, participants had the opportunity to ride on the device. After a free driving and the first handling experience they had to complete a parkour ride. In a subsequent evaluation, the drivers were asked for usability ratings and shared their opinions, discussing the existing driving properties and their suggestions for improvement.

4.3   Participants in the Research Process

Empirical data was acquired from a wide range of potential users (N = 41). The recruitment aimed at reaching young, middle-aged, and older adults to account for different interests and opinions regarding the variable utilization opportunities of the PMD.

The age range of the participants was between 18 and 66 years (M = 29, SD = 11.7; 63% female) and comprised of people with various professional backgrounds (e.g., business economists, architects, psychologists, physicians) as well as students of different scientific fields (e.g., communication science, UI Design, computer science). Most participants were very open-minded with regard to technical innovations. The sample reached relatively high average values on the scale "technology fascination", i.e., with regard to possession of technology devices ("I love to own new technical devices."; M = 3.5, SD = 1.2 of 5 points), trying them out ("I like to watch new technical devices on the Internet or in shops."; M = 3.7, SD = 1.5), fun with technology ("It's fun to try out technical equipment."; M = 3.9; SD = 1.2), and facilitation of some areas in everyday life ("Technical equipment makes everyday life easier for me."; M = 3.9, SD = 0.7). These results indicate a quite tech-savvy sample.

In addition, most participants held a driving license (92%) and liked to drive a car (70%). Considering the required posture to ride on the PMD, participants also referred to their (more or less frequent) use of boards: 35% of the sample indicated to have used a skateboard and a longboard, 28% have done surfing, and almost every second person (48%) referred to have some experience in snowboarding. Thus, from the personal experience at least some of the participants could anticipate how the PMD is going to work when ready for the street.

Despite the fact that the PMD was still in the concept stage and not available as consumer product on the market, participants of the focus groups and workshops were asked about the conceivable and preferred usage modality: ownership, sharing, or renting. Interestingly, there was significantly less interest for buying the pedestrian device (27.5%) than for the idea to share (49%) or lend it (60%). Most of the sample (68%) perceived – at least in this time period – no need for a regular/daily use of the mobility robot. The idea to use it as a companion in leisure activities (33%) and/or as a domestic helper (45%) were rather more popular. About one third of the queried persons (31%) could imagine a use 'just for fun' of the PMD.

5   Results of the Participatory Design Approach

The results of the different stages of the participatory design process were elaborated from scratch according to the user-centered research and were analyzed, depending on the used methods as well as the nature of the collected data. Qualitative data were analyzed via content analysis. Quantitative outcomes were calculated by means of statistical methods.

Considering the early development phase of the PMD concept and the fact that most data originate from qualitative techniques, we confine the presented results to the main findings. These aspects are presented in a descriptive way by means of a central tendency of a variable and its dispersion [mean values (*M*) and the associated standard deviations (*SD*)]. Due to a relatively small sample size, the authors relinquish extensive inferential statistical analyses at this point. In the following, the main results are summarized by topic.

5.1   The User's Requirements and Acceptance of a PMD

General Opinions About the Smart Mobility Robot. Overall, the analysis of the empirical data showed a moderate positive attitude toward using the mobility device. As correlates to acceptance of the investigated device, participants responded to questions about their perceived usefulness (PU), perceived ease of use/learnability (PEU), practical use, supporting tool (to get things done faster), and fun. Figure 5 depicts the average values for the mentioned aspects.

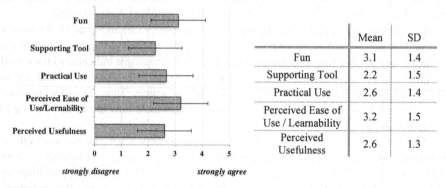

	Mean	SD
Fun	3.1	1.4
Supporting Tool	2.2	1.5
Practical Use	2.6	1.4
Perceived Ease of Use / Learnability	3.2	1.5
Perceived Usefulness	2.6	1.3

Fig. 5. Aspects of acceptance of pedestrian mobility device concept: bar charts (left) and measures of central tendency [mean and standard deviation (SD); right].

In general, the participants acknowledged the perceived usefulness and the practical use, but they appreciated the fun with the device more. Also, on average, respondents assessed learning to drive or navigate the device as easy. However, as can be seen from Fig. 5, the acceptance of the PMD concept was rather restrained due to the early stage of development: The mean values only just reached the middle of the scale (i.e., a neutral response).

Perceived Benefits. Despite the rather low acceptance of the innovative mobile technology, the participants, who were encouraged to express their opinions about the device in the concept stage in the focus group discussion, perceived a lot of possible advantages of the PMD. Some of these ideas are listed below:

- Convenient/natural posture: Driving the pedestrian robot demands a natural standing position and is controlled by natural (intuitive) movements.
- High efficiency: Driving with the device is faster than walking.

- Last mile device: Improvement of the "door-to-door" mobility and/or enhancement of connectivity between, for instance, work place and home.
- Easy-to-use tool to link home, work, and other activity targets.
- Potential enhancement of transit station access (e.g., for professional commuters, to get to the station more quickly).
- Mobility tool in professional context to cover long distances (e.g., on university campus, industrial halls, medical center, etc.).
- Service on demand (if someone needs help, e.g., with carrying of the groceries from the supermarket home).
- Guide for strangers: To find one's bearings in new/unknown places.
- Replacement for the car in the city.
- Reasonable costs of maintenance (electronically powered).
- Environmentally conscious mobility alternative.
- Fun tool: Simply good to stroll through the area.

In addition, there were many beneficial use cases the respondents could imagine with regard to the smart PMD:

- Autonomous delivery service (e.g., for medication needed in case of illness);
- Urban rental device (e.g., for the way home from the city);
- Tourist guide/City tours guide;
- Guide dog for the blind;
- "The mule/donkey"/Assistant on long walking distances (e.g., on airports, trade fairs, big manufacturing facilities);
- Assistance for motion-restricted persons;
- "Dog sitter" (i.e., autonomously walking the dog).

In view of the number of the presented beneficial ideas, it is quite conceivable that potential users can adopt a positive attitude toward the use of the PMD. On the other hand, there are also some negative aspects that could dampen the merits; these are described in the next paragraph.

Perceived Barriers. Besides the advantageous possibilities associated with the use of the mobility device, participants also considered possible disadvantages.

- Loading area too small for purchases: In reality most people make one large purchase a week; thereby the device would fail due to loading space restrictions.
- High accident risk, especially on crowded urban streets.
- Unstable driving experience (e.g. high speed in bends).
- Less physical activity in the daily life: For people who are less likely to take care of their physical fitness, this would mean even less exercise ("Why stand, if you can sit?").
- Uncomfortable, i.e., too big and too heavy to be carried (e.g., to continue the journey by train or bus).

Discussing the use cases in this context, brought a comment regarding a missing focus on specific target groups (e.g., it would be too dangerous for people who are restricted in their mobility). However, the respondents perceived substantially less barriers than benefits of the pedestrian mobility device, which is very promising result.

In addition, some perceived downsides were directly linked to additional conditions which could enhance the use of the PMD – provided a compliance with the conditions. These are presented hereafter.

Conditions of Use. Besides the clearly defined pros and cons of the use, in the group discussions participants revealed a conditional acceptance of the pedestrian mobility device. They identified the conditions listed below:

- Special parking stations/safe storage areas for the device (to avoid having to carry it with you when shopping or using public transportation services);
- Adequate battery service life (of a *rechargeable* battery);
- Anti-theft protection in general and for the loading;
- Protecting the loading from dropping down;
- Attractive and functional design.

Generally, the respondents tended to positively assess the pedestrian mobility device. Conditions, like the ones presented above helped to structure their opinions, bringing to light some interesting topics, issues, and practicable solutions at the same time. Careful consideration of these conditions and the associated demands of potential users may lead to greater acceptance and adoption among potential future users.

5.2   Purchase Criteria

Although the participants had a high general technical affinity (as described in Sect. 4.3), most respondents were not particularly willing to buy the device, reaching on average only $M = 1.6$ ($SD = 1.2$) out of 5 possible points (5 = high agreement). In the early development of the mobility robot, they would rather rent or share the device with others. However, it was an important concern to find out what is important to potential buyers.

From the beginning of the study respondents were asked to rate the relevance of different buying criteria on a 6-point Likert scale ranging from 0 (= not important at all) to 5 (= very important). The descriptive results are summarized in Fig. 6.

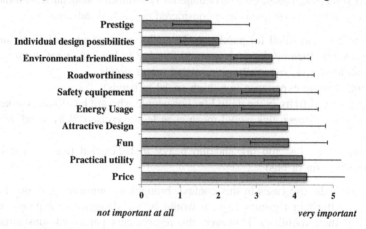

Fig. 6. Ratings of the relevance for different purchase criteria for PMD

The most important criteria for purchasing the PMD were price ($M = 4.3, SD = 0.8$) and its practical utility ($M = 4.2, SD = 1.2$), but fun ($M = 3.8, SD = 1.2$) and attractive design ($M = 3.8, SD = 1.1$) also played a considerable role. Prestige ($M = 1.8, SD = 1.3$) and the individual design possibilities ($M = 2, SD = 1.3$) were rather unimportant purchase criteria. Apart from these, the other mentioned criteria, like energy usage, safety and roadworthiness, as well as the environmental factors were rated as (quite) important, reaching mean values between $M = 3.4$ and $M = 3.6$ of 5 possible points.

Moreover, focus groups discussions revealed further highly relevant requirements: safety issues in the everyday road traffic, ergonomic factors (e.g., the weight of the device), the aspect of physical fitness since the device might replace walking as healthy lifestyle habit, as well as aspects of the interaction with the user (ease of the use). The latter requires a particularly careful and thorough processing. Hence, the following section elaborates in detail on the communication between the user and the PMD.

5.3   Expectations Regarding Communication Design

The development of the communication design of a smart pedestrian device that provides driving safety and is roadworthy ("ready for the streets"), is a complex process and calls for many iterative steps to get to an optimal final outcome. As described in more detail in Sect. 3.2, the process of PMD communication design development began with the (1) identification of relevant driving functions (e.g., turning right/left, to set the brake, reversing) and communication events (e.g., low battery charge level), over (2) group discussions on desired signal modalities and creation of signal presets, to (3) evaluations and ended with (4) determination of the particular visual and acoustic signals for specific functions and driving events. However, it should be stressed at this point that the authors do not claim finality or completeness of the presented results. Rather, the first general insights with regard to the preferred signal modalities, which were gained within the qualitative studies, are described in the following.

The main requirements for the visual signals were:

- "Not too colorful": Traditional color allocation according to deeply anchored schemata of known signals (red/yellow/green), eventually extended by some neutral colors (e.g., blue for the signal of stand-by status of the device).
- Demand for intuitive color scheme for the typical driving events (e.g., red = "stop", yellow = "steady", green = "go").
- Unambiguous signaling for the user and for the environment: The use of existing traffic light system leads to intelligible understanding and interpretation of visual signals.

- References for the visual signal characteristics:
  - Moderate pulse duration in order not to delay the traffic flow;
  - Customizable brightness, depending on light conditions outside;
  - Moderate and repeated rotation of the colors for a better perception of the signals in the footwell area.

W. Wilkowska et al.

The lessons learned for the design of audio signals were:

- Non-intrusive but clearly perceptible acoustic signaling.
- Clearly interpretable acoustic signals, especially as a warning signs (e.g., caution, an obstacle ahead!).
- Precise matching of the acoustic and the visual signals.
- Certain redundancy of the acoustic with visual signals, without stimulus overflow.

Concerning some general requirements with respect to the communication design, all discussion partners came to the congruent conclusion that, whenever possible, a reduction of signals should take place. Guided by the motto "Less is more", participants argued that too many signals could distract the user too much from driving, and rather stress out than provide fun or assistance.

On the other hand, it should also be possible that the communication design adapts to the needs of the particular user. For instance, someone who suffers from color blindness would benefit considerably from enhanced acoustic signals for the pedestrian device, especially since the spatial arrangement, as is known from the traffic lights, is missing here. Then again, someone with hearing difficulties, would profit significantly more from the visual signal stimuli. Thus, flexible design would certainly increase the usability.

6 Discussion

Since the concept of smart pedestrian mobility devices presents a valuable solution for short distances as well as a cost and energy effective opportunity for locomotion in urban spaces, it is relevant to spread the idea and utilization in growing urban areas. To enhance the adoption of this new kind of mobility and to reach a high sustainability in the development of smart pedestrian mobility devices, an inclusion of users' perceptions and demands, as well as a diligent implementation of insights derived from the participatory design process is highly recommended.

The aim of the presented study was to apply a participatory design approach and, thereby, identify criteria which can support the user-centered development process of such a mobility device, so that the best possible preconditions for the acceptance of the new technical device are created. Overall, the inclusion of future users in early stages of the technology development process was proven to be highly useful. Although still in the concept stage, participants were able to imagine using the PMD without being able to look at, or touch a prototype in the requirement and use case sessions. However, the resulting low willingness to buy the mobility robot indicated that the use cases and potential business models of the PMD are not sufficient, and need more refinement and elaboration. Different reasons are conceivable for explaining the low willingness to buy a PMD: First, in the early and explorative stage of the design process participants are forced to anticipate a technological concept, with which no familiarity is given and no real "hands-on" experience with a mature device is possible. Depending on the imagination, creativity, and innovativeness of the participant this might lead to a rejecting attitude and to an underestimation of acceptance. Another reason might be the nature or state of the device itself. Apparently, the technical device alone – at least in the early concept stage – is not enough to convince the (potential) user of its usefulness, and to evoke the desire to own a PMD. In this case, for successful mobility potentially more infrastructural background is required which is connected to the device. A potentially promising starting point is the integration of PMD in a multimodal public sharing system, which has a respective urban infrastructure available with renting stations combined with (e-)bikes and (e-)cars.

In line with ongoing research activities and recent innovations in autonomous driving, the PMD could also benefit from continued development of its autonomous functions, e.g., autonomous delivery of goods (e.g., bringing home your bags after shopping, delivering medicaments from the pharmacy) or as a city guide/physical navigation assistant. Here, it is important to consider that these different application contexts might activate qualitatively and quantitatively different acceptance-relevant benefits or barriers among users, which need to be captured by continuously involving the user in the design process. This refers for example to the safety aspect – for the mobility robot itself (protection against theft) as well as for its transport load (alarm signal when the goods are falling off or if goods are stolen from the PMD).

A further aspect which is related to the desire to 'have one', is the identity or personality of a PMD. Referring to "hedonic design approaches" [31], a device should elicit positive emotions and minimize negative emotions, in order to lead to a positive experience and high levels of customer loyalty. Hence, when designing a PMD it is important not only to give him "a life" (i.e., technical functionalities) but also "a soul" (i.e., communicative and emotional features), which make the PMD a valuable assistant and helper or even a friend. Designing a technical device which serves as a friend might provide a suitable solution for supporting "livable" life conditions for singles, elderly, and impaired people. Understanding the dynamics of the inhabitants' daily mobility patterns is essential for the planning and management of urban facilities and services [32]. Creating a well-functioning, accepted, environmentally friendly, and economically reasonable mobility device that serves the user as an assistant or even as a friend could lead to a significant change of the cityscape and perhaps to a better emotional state of urban residents.

The purpose of this article was to present how the participatory design, using qualitative and quantitative research methods can be useful to explore and improve our understanding of the users' needs with regard to technology innovation in the context of urban mobility. A key feature of multi-method research is its methodological pluralism or eclecticism, which, compared to mono-method research, frequently results in superior research [33].

In the described research project, there was enough time to carefully plan and conduct a suitable research approach. A successful use of different empirical methods, as it was described in detail above, led to multifaceted, informative, and for the various target groups specific results. However, we are aware of the fact that other (industry) projects are under higher time and cost pressure, which might limit the scope and/or variety of methods applicable in the design process. In case of time or cost restrictions, we recommend to involve the user at later stages in the design process, preferably in the second iteration level, i.e., to pre-develop design sets (e.g., visual and/or sound sets for communication design) as a starting point for the evaluation and fine-tuning by participants. Still, the researcher has to remain open if participants reject the designed pre-sets and has to allow the development of alternatives and own creative ideas.

7 Limitations and Future Research

Future research and developmental activities should ensure that the present needs of the users are accordingly considered without compromising the ability of future generations to meet their own requirements. This means a further integration of the potential users in the subsequent in-depth design processes.

Moreover, it is increasingly important for transport planners and public officials to decide how nonmotorized facilities should be managed. Decisions should be made about where and when specific modes and activities should be allowed, the rules everybody should follow, and how such rules should be promoted and enforced [34].

A further possible development of intelligent pedestrian mobility device could enhance the focus on the assistive function, like it is proposed for the i-Walker for elders [5]. This target population includes, but is not limited to, persons with low vision, visual field neglect, spasticity, tremors, and cognitive deficits. Technology which supports such users in their daily routine would strengthen their autonomy and (self-)confidence.

Finally, participatory research and design on PMD should be iteratively continued with technically advanced prototypes in more elaborated usage scenarios to capture more accurate and valid judgements, demands, and requirements by users.

Acknowledgments. Authors thank participants for their time and patience to volunteer in this study. Thanks to Kilian Vas, Daniel Hari, and Uwe Wagner. Thanks also to Barbara Zaunbrecher for valuable remarks on this work, and all research assistants for their support in the project. This work was funded by the Excellence initiative of German states and federal government (project Urban Future Outline).

References

1. Himmel, S., Zaunbrecher, B.S., Ziefle, M., Beutel, M.C.: Chances for urban electromobility – field-test of a prototype for multimodal mobility and the effects on travel behavior. In: Marcus, A. (ed.) DUXU 2016. LNCS, vol. 9747, pp. 472–484. Springer, Cham (2016). doi:10.1007/978-3-319-40355-7_45
2. Wilkowska, W., Farrokhikhiavi, R., Ziefle, M., Vallée, D.: Mobility requirements for the use of carpooling among different user groups. In: Advances in Human Factors, Software, and Systems Engineering, vol. 6, pp. 129–140. AHFE Conference (2014)
3. Shaheen, S.A., Finson, R.: Bridging the last mile: a study of the behavioral, institutional, and economic potential of the segway human transporter. Trans. Res. B. Paper 03 **4470**, 13 (2003)
4. Martins, M.M., Santos, C.P., Frizera-Neto, A., Ceres, R.: Assistive mobility devices focusing on smart walkers: classification and review. Robot. Auton. Syst. **60**(4), 548–562 (2012)

5. Annicchiarico, R., Barrué, C., Benedico, T., Campana, F., Cortés, U., Martínez-Velasco, A.: The i-Walker: an intelligent pedestrian mobility aid. ECAI **178**, 708–712 (2008)
6. Batty, M.: Cities and Complexity: Understanding Cities with Cellular Automata, Agent-Based Models, and Fractals. MIT Press, Cambridge (2005)
7. Litman, T., Burwell, D.: Issues in sustainable transportation. Int. J. Glob. Environ. Issues **6** (4), 331–347 (2006)
8. Sawatzky, B., Denison, I., Langrish, S., Richardson, S., Hiller, K., Slobogean, B.: The segway personal transporter as an alternative mobility device for people with disabilities: a pilot study. Arch. Phys. Med. Rehabil. **88**(11), 1423–1428 (2007)
9. Sanders, E.B.-N.: From user-centered to participatory design approaches. In: Design and the Social Sciences: Making Connections, pp. 1–8. CRC Press (2002)
10. Spinuzzi, C.: The methodology of participatory design. Tech. Commun. **52**(2), 163–174 (2005)
11. Kowalewski, S., Arning, K., Minwegen, A., Ziefle, M., Ascheid, G.: Extending the engineering trade-off analysis by integrating user preferences in conjoint analysis. Expert Syst. Appl. **40**(8), 2947–2955 (2013)
12. Wilkowska, W.: Acceptance of eHealth Technology in Home Environments: Advanced Studies on User Diversity in Ambient Assisted Living. Apprimus, Aachen (2015)
13. Ziefle, M., Schaar, A.K.: Technology acceptance by patients: empowerment and stigma. In: van Hoof, J., Demiris, G., Wouters, E. (eds.) Handbook of Smart Homes, Health Care and Well-being, pp. 1–10. Springer, Switzerland (2014). doi:10.1007/978-3-319-01904-8_34-1
14. Kerssens, C., Kumar, R., Adams, A.E., Knott, C.C., Matalenas, L., Sanford, J.A., Rogers, W.A.: Personalized technology to support older adults with and without cognitive impairment living at home. Am. J. Alzheimers Dis. **30**(1), 85–97 (2015)
15. Ho, S.Y., Kwok, S.H.: The attraction of personalized service for users in mobile commerce: an empirical study. ACM SIGecom Exchanges **3**(4), 10–18 (2002)
16. Li, Q., Wang, C., Geng, G.: Improving personalized services in mobile commerce by a novel multicriteria rating approach. In: Proceedings of the 17th International Conference on World Wide Web, pp. 1235–1236. ACM (2008)
17. Huang, Y.M., Liang, T.H., Su, Y.N., Chen, N.S.: Empowering personalized learning with an interactive e-book learning system for elementary school students. Educ. Tech. Res. Dev. **60** (4), 703–722 (2012)
18. International Organization for Standardization: ISO 9241-11: Ergonomic Requirements for Office Work with Visual Display Terminals (VDTs): Part 11: Guidance on Usability (1998)
19. Yin, K.: Case Study Research: Design and Methods. Sage Publications, Newbury Park (1994)
20. Jick, T.D.: Mixing qualitative and quantitative methods: triangulation in action. Adm. Sci. Q. **24**(4), 602–611 (1979)
21. Wilson, C.E.: Triangulation: the explicit use of multiple methods, measures, and approaches for determining core issues in product development. Interactions **13**(6), 46–ff (2006)
22. Fellows, R., Liu, A.: Research Methods for Construction. Blackwell Science Limited, Oxford (1997)
23. Amaratunga, D., Baldry, D., Sarshar, M., Newton, R.: Quantitative and qualitative research in the built environment: application of "mixed" research approach. Work Study **51**(1), 17–31 (2002)
24. Mitzner, T.L., Dijkstra, K.: E-health for older adults: assessing and evaluating user centered design with subjective methods. In: Ziefle, M., Röcker, C. (eds.) Human-Centered Design of E-Health Technologies: Concepts, Methods and Applications, pp. 1–21, Hershey, PA (2011)
25. Lambert, S.D., Loiselle, C.G.: Combining individual interviews and focus groups to enhance data richness. J. Adv. Nurs. **62**(2), 228–237 (2008)

26. Hennink, M.M.: Focus group discussions. Oxford University Press, Oxford (2013)
27. Kulak, D., Guiney, E.: Use cases: requirements in context. Addison-Wesley, Boston (2012)
28. Creswell, J.W.: Research Design: Qualitative & Quantitative Approaches. SAGE Publications, London (1994)
29. Sukamolson, S.: Fundamentals of Quantitative Research. Language Institute, Chulalongkorn University (2010)
30. Johnson, R.B., Onwuegbuzie, A.J.: Mixed methods research: a research paradigm whose time has come. Educ. Res. **33**(7), 14–26 (2004)
31. Chitturi, R.: Emotions by design: a consumer perspective. Int. J. Des. **3**(2), 7–17 (2009)
32. Liu, L., Biderman, A., Ratti, C.: Urban mobility landscape: real time monitoring of urban mobility patterns. In: Proceedings of the 11th International Conference on Computers in Urban Planning and Urban Management, pp. 1–16 (2009)
33. Rouzies, A.: Mixed methods: a relevant research design to investigate mergers and acquisitions. In: Advances in Mergers and Acquisitions, pp. 193–211. Emerald Group Publishing Limited (2013)
34. Litman, T., Blair, R.: Managing personal mobility devices (PMDs) on nonmotorized facilities. In: Annual General Meeting, Transportation Research Board, Washington DC (2004)

Service Design for Inter Floor Noise Problem: Using a Floor Noise Reduction Device Technology and Network System in Apartment Complex

Jae Sun Yi[1]([⊠]), Seona Kim[2]([⊠]), and Hahyeon Sung[1]([⊠])

[1] School of Contents Convergence Design,
Handong University, Pohang, Republic of Korea
creative1@handong.edu, tjdhaaa@gmail.com
[2] School of Communication Arts and Science,
Handong University, Pohang, Republic of Korea
kimsunaaa@naver.com

Abstract. Due to the rapid change in the residential style, about 70% of the population of South Korea reside in multi-unit dwelling today. As many people share the same building as a residential area, the neighboring interlayer noise problem becomes a serious social problem leading to murder, arson attack, etc. However, it is practically impossible to improve the buildings or introduce new building technologies to ones already built to prevent the inter floor noise. When noise occurs, there are no appropriate system or laws for people to impose special sanctions on the perpetrator. Most solutions are either too long in terms of process or indirect. It is necessary to have a process, which solves the problem directly and continuously. The survey results, that targeted people living in apartment houses, show that perpetrators are not aware of the actions that cause noises. Not only that, results show both victim and noise attacker's lack of awareness of precise standards of interested noise. Above all, anyone living in the apartment houses can be a victim or a perpetrator of inter floor noise problem. Therefore, this study proposes a service in which the perpetrators can monitor, manage and supervise interlayer noises that they create. This service will help perpetrators be more keen to their own noise, ultimately preventing problems caused by interlayer noises. Through the service, it is expected that the number of victims suffering from the noise will be decreased and ultimately, the inter-floor noise complaint rate, which is increasing every year, will be reduced so it prevents neighbor's conflicts and disputes.

Keywords: Service design · Inter floor noise · Floor noise reduction device technology · Behavior change · Home IoT

1 Introduction

Residential forms in Korea have been changed fast. Territory area of South Korea is the world's 109th largest which is one over a hundred seventy of world's largest country, Russia. However, population density in South Korea is world's 12th highest country

© Springer International Publishing AG 2017
A. Marcus and W. Wang (Eds.): DUXU 2017, Part III, LNCS 10290, pp. 773–783, 2017.
DOI: 10.1007/978-3-319-58640-3_55

which is higher than Canada, United States and Japan. As the tertiary industry developed, people needed to live in small area effectively. Thus, housing forms evolved from detached house into apartment house. Three of four South Korean today live in apartment houses include dwelling houses, tenement house, apartment buildings and condominium-style housing complex called 'villa'. The most common of all, is apartment houses, of which buildings are not interlayer noise proof, due to high demand of construction in a short period of time. Especially, the changes of structure type, which is for building as fast as possible, worsen the noise problem. As a result, inter-floor noise problem pose growing social issues. Recently, a middle-aged man in Korea attacked a couple living upstairs with a sickle over a noise complaint. Also, a man of 30s killed his neighbor in another case of fatal noise-related conflict in apartment complexes and a 49-year-old man set fire to the house above his in a multifamily dwelling after a long dispute over noise. It became not only a neighbor dispute but also a serious social problem, which leads to retaliatory crime, assault and even murder.

2 Current Inter-floor Noise Problem

2.1 An Architectural Perspective

One of the reasons why the floor noise problem occurs is due to a change in the architectural technology in South Korea. In response to rapidly changing industrial technology, the building design has been changed from a pillar-type to a wall-type in order to build a lot of apartments in a short period of time. As shown in the Fig. 1, the pillar-type (the ramen structure) is a structure in which large pillars support the ceiling and multiple beams are laid under the slab[1]. Especially, the noise transmitted from the

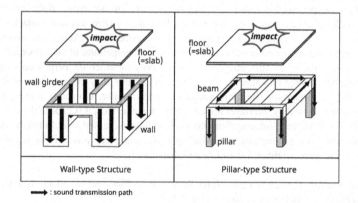

Fig. 1. Wall-type and pillar-type structure

---

[1] Structural Concrete Slabs are constructed to provide flat surfaces, usually horizontal, in building floors, roofs, bridges, and other types of structures. The slab is supported by walls, by reinforced concrete beams usually cast monolithically with the slab, by structural steel beams, by columns, or by the ground.

floor is dispersed by beams and pillars, which is advantageous for reducing the inter-floor noise. Until the 1980s, there were many cases where apartment complexes were constructed with this type of structure in South Korea. On the other hand, the wall-type is a structure that bearing walls support the ceiling without pillars, which means the impact is completely delivered to the floor. Also, the impact sound is transmitted to upper floor as well as to downstairs through the wall, which makes the buildings exposed to the noises [1]. In accordance with the research, which is conducted by the Ministry of Land, Infrastructure and Transport, the pillar-type structure has 1.2 times higher interlayer noise blocking effect than the wall-type structure. Nevertheless, the pillar structure heightens the house so number of floors should be limited, which means the number of houses are reduced. Adding to that, the construction process with pillar structure is slow and costly, leading construction companies to avoid building with such types [2]. As a matter of fact, 85% of the apartments built in South Korea between 2009 and 2011 were constructed with wall structures and only 2% were pillar structures. It is important to reduce the noise transmission by adopting a new structure which is helpful to prevent noise problem, despite the high costs. However, the construction industry emphasizes strengthening of the design rather than the structural change as it is more affordable and no feasibility in business [3]. Ministry of Land, Infrastructure and Transport had set the standard floor structure of Korea as 50 dB for heavy-weight floor impact noise and 58 dB for light-weight floor impact noise. If these standards are exceeded, it is not acceptable to build apartment houses. On contrast, Japanese construction standards are in much more detail by dividing it into five levels with a rating system [4]. Since Korea's heavy-weight floor impact sound standards are equivalent to Japan's 4th grade, and even light-weight floor impact sound standards are at the lowest level in Japan, apartment houses designed with Korean standards are difficult to be built in Japan [5]. Therefore, Korean construction standards are very vulnerable to noise.

2.2 Problems in Coping Situation When Noise Occurs

At present, when the actual floor-to-floor noise is generated, the victim can cope with the situation in four patterns, but the limitations are as follows (Fig. 2). The vertical axes of the table represent each step, and the horizontal axis represents the behaviors experienced in the step, thoughts in action, and pain points that occur.

2.2.1 Individual

Generally, when a noise occurs, the victim goes to the neighborhood where the noise is generated and complain. According to the survey, however, that conducted to about 361 people of various ages by Google online form from March 28 to April 10, 2016, 27% of the respondents answered 'yes' to the question 'Have you ever complained to your neighbors due to the noise between floors?', confirming that the number of people who actually protested is a minority. The highest response rate (42%) were those with passive responses of not notifying the noise in order to avoid worsening the relationship with neighbors. In fact, more than half (52%) of those affected by noise said they tolerate more than three days before complaining. Especially, when asked 'How to

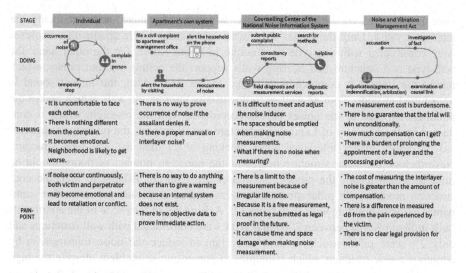

STAGE	Individual	Apartment's own system	Counselling Center of the National Noise Information System	Noise and Vibration Management Act
DOING	occurrence of noise — complain in person — temporary stop	file a civil complaint to apartment management office — alert the household on the phone — alert the household by visiting — reoccurrence of noise	submit public complaint — search for methods — consultancy reports — helpline — field diagnosis and measurement services — dignostic reports	accusation — investigation of fact — adjudication(agreement, indemnification, arbitration) — examination of causal link
THINKING	· It is uncomfortable to face each other. · There is nothing different from the complain. · It becomes emotional. Neighborhood is likely to get worse.	· There is no way to prove occurrence of noise if the assailant denies it. · Is there a proper manual on interlayer noise?	· It is difficult to meet and adjust the noise inducer. · The space should be emptied when making noise measurements. · What if there is no noise when measuring?	· The measurement cost is burdensome. · There is no guarantee that the trial will win unconditionally. · How much compensation can I get? · There is a burden of prolonging the appointment of a lawyer and the processing period.
PAIN-POINT	· If noise occur continuously, both victim and perpetrator may become emotional and lead to retaliation or conflict.	· There is no way to do anything other than to give a warning because an internal system does not exist. · There is no objective data to prove immediate action.	· There is a limit to the measurement because of irregular life noise. · Because it is a free measurement, it can not be submitted as legal proof in the future. · It can cause time and space damage when making noise measurement.	· The cost of measuring the interlayer noise is greater than the amount of compensation. · There is a difference in measured dB from the pain experienced by the victim. · There is no clear legal provision for noise.

Fig. 2. Customer journey map of coping situation when noise occurs

react if the noise keep loud even though you complained?', 50% of respondents answered that they would re-complain only by the administration office of apartment complex. Additionally, 45% of those who would not re-complain answered that they gave up to complain because they do not want to make any neighbor troubles. Thus, when the noise occurs, the victim feels uncomfortable to face with the perpetrator directly, and it can be confirmed that victims are fearful of emotional response that can lead to retaliation or conflict.

2.2.2 Apartment's Own System

The apartments in South Korea are ran based on management offices. For the convenience of apartment residents, the management office is involved in a variety of tasks including garbage collection, caring of flowerbeds around the apartment, complaints handling, etc., and has internally defined rules of life. When a complaint about neighbor noise comes in, the apartment manager can ask the households to be quiet, but there is no compelling reason to suppress the noisy residents. In Seoul, the capital city of the Republic of Korea, it is stipulated that it should refrain from making noise in the apartment [6]. Actually, it is difficult to verify the act immediately when the noise is generated by these activities. Most of all, in multi-unit dwelling like apartments, it is difficult to regulate noisy residents in some cases because they do not know exactly where the noise is occurring.

2.2.3 Counseling Center of the National Noise Information System

In 2012, the Government of the Republic of Korea established the Inter-floor Noise Neighborhood Center of the Ministry of the Environment in consideration of the ever-increasing inter-floor noise complaints and the seriousness that leads to social problems in neighboring conflicts. Interventions of the National Noise Information System was established in order to promptly and reasonably adjust the dispute caused by inter-floor noise. However, when examining the process of using the center, it only serves as a guide or a counselor to dispute procedures. Thus, the center is not an adequate solution to prevent noise or resolve disputes, it incites conflicts instead. In addition, there are many cases in which the victim gave up the dispute process because of fear for retaliation or worry about the neighbor relationship. It is because the victim is a subject who actively seeks the ways to resolve noise problem while the perpetrator does not participate at all. According to the number of dispute resolution cases and the customer satisfaction index of the Interventions of the National Noise Information System analyzed by the National Environment and Labor Committee[2], the number of consultations received at the Center is high. However, after a certain period of time following the consultation, the applicant's satisfaction decreased due to recurring noises as noise is a product of lifestyle [7]. Hence, the conflicts surrounding the floor-to-floor noise must be solved directly and through a continuous process rather than an indirectly method such as through counseling.

2.2.4 Noise and Vibration Management Act

If noise damage occurs, the majority of people want active intervention by a third party such as a security guard or a police officer, but there is no way to impose special sanctions on the perpetrators of noise in terms of laws of the Republic of Korea, except for asking to be quiet. In the case of the UK and Germany, detailed provisions for the Noise Control Law are clearly defined, and high fines are imposed to prevent conflicts in advance [8]. However, it is unreasonable to regulate interlayer noise with the current Korean law. The law on punishment for misdemeanor crimes is regulated[3], but the scope and strength of punishment is not clearly defined. Also, if the police cannot detect the noise when the case is dispatched, the punishment cannot be enforced. Therefore, in Republic of Korea, there is no effectiveness of law that prevents noise from neighbors, and if victim wants to impose punishment, it is impossible unless disputes occur.

3 Analysis of Noise Offenders and Victims

3.1 Cognitive Level

3.1.1 Recognition of Behavior

According to the survey mentioned before, over 60% of noise makers are not aware of that they made noise until they got complained. In addition, 57.1% of people who maintained their situation even though they received complaints from neighbors thought 'I did not make any noise problem.' Thus, the noise makers do not recognize

---

[2] The number of consultation applications (2012–August 31, 2014) is 78,255, with about 1,500 monthly average and about 71 daily average.

[3] Article 3 of the Penal Law for Misdemeanors, Law of the Republic of Korea.

① A person who falls under any of the following subparagraphs shall be punished by a fine, detention or fine of not more than 100,000 won.

-21. (Disturbance nearby) A person who made too loud, or sang loud sounds such as musical instruments, radio, television, loudspeaker.

that their behaviors could make loud sounds until somebody let them know. Moreover, people usually do not know that could be themselves who make noisy sound. Letting people to understand these things should be the first step. In the survey, 91.1% of noise offender said they tried to be quiet after they got complained but the 51.6% of victims said that nothing is changed even after they asked to. It is confirmed that there are a lot of differences between perpetrators and victims in cognitive level of behavior. Therefore, it needs to give recognition to perpetrators when they make loud noise.

3.1.2 Recognition of Noise

Today in South Korea, there is a floor noise standards enacted by the Ministry of Land, Infrastructure and Transport. It is 40 dB in the daylight and 35 dB in the night, and if it lasts for one minute, victims can receive the damages. However, people do not even understand the concept of decibels and it is hard to understand how loud the standards decibel is in the actual life. 72.7% of people who file a civil complaint to Counseling Center of the National Noise Information System complained about children's jumping noise but it is relative and subjective. Although it is necessary to make standards in specific decibel level, most of people do not know the government's standards and it is hard to adjust noise to a standard which is written in number. Therefore, both victims and perpetrators cannot recognize the specific standards.

3.2 Relationship Between Neighbors

Through the research, there are two leading points in relationship between neighbors. First of all, as a sociologist Katz said, people tend to be more awkward to the face-to-face situation in these digital media and new media era [9]. Adding to that, in recent research of Korea Social Integration Survey-field of social communication, 55.1% of responded people thought there are no communications between neighbors. People in Korea are getting uneasy to be closed to their neighborhood. Secondly, giving an advance notice could prevent the discord with neighbors. To deeply research about these, it is necessary to interview 3 cases who are in circumstances that are prone to make noise. (1) Family with 3 children, (2) One with instrument as a hobby, (3) Family with dogs. One interviewee answered that advanced request for the loud sound was acceptable, and it made people more generous to understand the situation even though there is a noise problem. Considering the social trends which people avoid the face-to-face situation, it is inappropriate to compel neighbors to communicate each other. It is important to have third party intervention rather than communication between neighbors.

4   Proposal of Service of Inter-floor Noise Recognition

4.1   Technology and Device Selection

4.1.1   Noise Reduction Device of LNSC

Recently, a noise reduction device that gives a warning when noise occurs has been invented in Korea. The company LNSC's interlayer noise reduction system is a system in which the vibration sensor collects the level of noise and transmits it to the management server. A warning sound is emitted by a device for noise above a certain level. In the management server, the inter-floor noise bill is made with the collected data and it is possible to transmit it to each household and transmit the warning through SMS. Particularly, the invented technique of the interlayer noise reduction induction device improves accuracy in analyzing the noise pattern by collecting noise intensity, cycle, epicenter, spatial distribution and history. However, the beeping sound is transmitted only by sound, so there is no great effect in paying attention and easy to be drowned in other sound. In addition, unnecessary data is collected because these beeps are continuously generated for noise that cannot be avoided like moving or construction. The LNSC noise reduction system operated the system to accumulate data on the management server and issue reports and bills. However, access to records is difficult because such data can only be viewed by administrators on a particular server. In addition, issuing and using such a bill will actually increase the work of the apartment management office, and it is troublesome to separately dissever the noise management tasks in addition to the apartment management work.

4.1.2 Wall-Pad in South Korea and Networking System

In South Korea, as the smart home market grows, the functions of the Wall-Pad[4] are gradually expanding. Especially, as the world has entered an era of Internet of Things (IoT), Smart home (or home IoT) is growing in the Korean market as personalization of IT is expanded to the private space such as home. The key services of Wall-Pad are in-house call control, door control, home security (CCTV, fire etc.), and home control (energy, lighting, etc.) [10]. In the early days, the function was limited to the connection with the outside of the house such as visitor identification, security guard, and call. However, as the home network market has grown, the Internet has recently been connected and it is possible to provide a service that is involved in the life of the user such as healthcare, remote monitoring [11]. The Wall-Pad is connected to the complex network and the household network, so it is not only capable of connecting to the management room and the household, but also to each household. Through this, it is possible for the management office to perform comprehensive management of the complex, to store various kinds of data, to provide information and services. On the individual side, home security and home control as well as digital content and communication services between residents can be provided. The Wall-Pad is a convenient device in apartment complexes. Modern Koreans who are sensitive to privacy and personal information can communicate within the apartment without providing unnecessary personal information such as phone number or name. From the standpoint of managing apartment buildings, even if there is no personal information of the residents, it can be used as a medium to facilitate the communication between the residents of the apartment and the management room.

---

[4] A wall pad is a touch screen type device that attaches to a wall. It is a system that provides the basic functions of a home network through an LCD of about 5 to 15 in., and is also referred to as a video phone or an interphone.

Thus, this service is to develop a device that can reduce the noise itself by complementing technology of LNSC and selecting the device as the Wall-Pad of Korea that can interoperate with the apartment and web in the apartment management server.

4.2 Service Contents

4.2.1 Service Goals

Based on the type of service previously selected, this service will provide audiovisual warning through the Wall-Pad to the abuser in case of inter-floor noise, and will seek to strengthen and prevent perception of floor noise by checking data. This service is intended to provide an environment in which the perpetrator can consider first by seeking consent in advance through the Wall-Pad. In addition, it aims to establish its own system to enable continuous management supervision on the inter-floor noise by data accumulation through the apartment management office.

4.2.2 Service Scenario

When the perpetrator is targeted, the situation can be divided into two cases regarding inter-floor noise. First, a warning is given to the perpetrator who may or may not know that they have made a noise, and second, the abuser informs in advance in case they are about to make a noise. Therefore, the service scenarios based on service content are as follows (Fig. 3).

First, when noises are generated, the inter-floor noise is detected by the noise sensor installed in each household, and when the noise exceeds the standard, the touch screen of Wall-Pad gives a visual and audible warning to the user to recognize the interlayer noise that is occurring. As a result, when the interlayer noise ceases, the situation is terminated. However, if the interlayer noise level is continuously exceeded, device repeatedly re-warns about the noise generated by the user through the touch screen interphone. At the same time, the data is accumulated in the management system and the administrator can confirm it, so that the manager can grasp the area where the interlayer noise is generated when the complaint is received. If civil complaints due to continuous inter-floor noise are received at the management office, the management room first grasps the floor noise source and gives a warning to the floor noise source through the ARS[5]. At this time, if the ARS is received from the household and the floor noise is reduced or decreased below the standard value, the situation will be terminated. However, if additional complaints are received, the apartment management room will visit the noisy residents and warn them. Also, if the ARS is not received in the generation where the floor noise occurs, the service will be terminated by visiting directly and giving a warning to the perpetrator. If the perpetrator announces possibility of future noise in advance of the situation, the user can select the type of situation through the notification menu in the touch screen Wall-Pad, and neighbors will be able to check that announcement via the Wall-Pad.

---

[5] Automatic Response Service. A system that stores various kinds of information in voice in a storage device and automatically delivers information desired by the user.

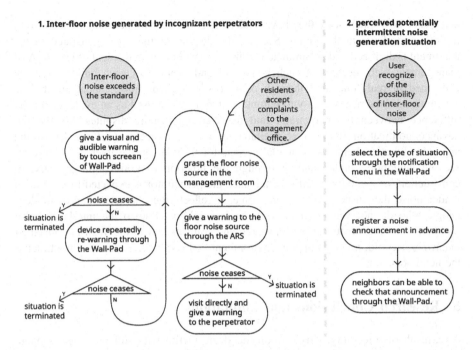

Fig. 3. Service scenario in two major situation

4.2.3 Service Functions

The functions of the service can largely be divided into cognitive function, data management and accumulation function, and notice in advance function (Fig. 4).

First, the cognitive function detects the noise with the device of the inter-layer noise reduction of the LNSC, and gives the audiovisual warning to the noise maker's Wall-Pad so that the user can recognize the noise generated by the user oneself. From the app's Information Architecture, a warning screen would pop-up with the buzzer sounds. If user press the button 'I'll be careful' on the screen, the perpetrator can confirm the data of the noise that perpetrator just made, so user can resolve the difference from the noise perception standard between perpetrator and the victim. In addition, by checking the real-time and monthly statistics of the App-IA, users can see

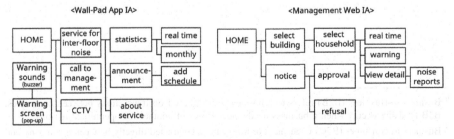

Fig. 4. Information architecture of wall-pad app and management web

at a glance how much noise they have made, and compare it to the standard and also to the other residents in the graph. Second, the decibel of the noise generated in the apartment is digitized and accumulated on the server of the management office. In IA of management web, decibel of each household and average of each building can be confirmed in real time, and through comparison, it helps noise management. The accumulated data makes it easy to output, so that it can be used as an evidence for the difference between the perpetrator and the victim in future disputes. Finally, the advance notification function is available in the announcement of the IA of the app. This function helps the potential perpetrator to work on the inter-floor noise by seeking neighbors' understanding through the function of notification on moving, construction, or a certain meeting in advance the perpetrator is expected to generate a louder noise than usual. At the same time, it reflects the characteristics of modern people who do not want to meet with their neighbors due to the interlayer noise problem, announcements can be registered and confirmed with the Wall-Pad installed in each household, thus creating an environment that can be considered without facing the neighbors.

5 Research Conclusions and Limitations

As a result of this study, it is recommended the victim who suffered noise damage should seek a more aggressive method in order to solve the noise conflict in Korea. In addition to this, this paper proposes a service that gives the perpetrator a task and alerts with the sound of the doorbell in conjunction with the pad for instant recognition of the sensory noise. Through this service, the perpetrator stops himself/herself by perceiving a situation that he/she is making a noise and induces a self-check through a noise report. The awareness of perceived noise and behavior makes it possible for the perpetrator to prepare for future cases, in which the noise is to occur, beforehand using the advance notification function. This service is important as it helps the perpetrator to actually recognize by providing an environment to be careful and caring first.

However, since the noise reduction induction technology used in this service should be buried on the floor and all households in one apartment building should be installed, the service proposal can be only in the form of B2B[6], not B2C[7]. In addition, feedback of the victim is necessary because the noise criterion is relative and subjective. Future research will try to find a way to set the noise criterion by allowing the victim's feedback through the Wall-Pad.

---

[6] Business-to-Business (B2B) refers to a business model based on transactions between companies. B2B typically occurs when a business needs the services of another for operational reasons.

[7] Business to consumer (B2C) is business or transactions conducted directly between a company and consumers who are the end-users of its products or services.

References

1. Park, Y., Kang, K.: A basic study on apartment floor noise management. Korea Environment Institute, pp. 44–45 (2013)
2. Jeon, B.: 'Perforated' interlayer noise, the alternative is a pillar type. Kyunghyang (2016). http://news.khan.co.kr/kh_news/khan_art_view.html?artid=201608201832011&code=940100
3. Jee, H.: Inter-floor noise building, the problem is 'structure'? Newdaily (2014). http://biz.newdaily.co.kr/news/article.html?no=10030515
4. Japan Standards Association: JIS A 1418: acoustics—measurement of floor impact sound insulation of buildings. In: Part 2: Method Using Standard Heavy Impact Source. Japan Standards Association, Tokyo (2000)
5. Lee, C.: Problems and future tasks of inter-floor noise in multi-unit dwelling. Natl. Assem. Res. Serv. **58**, 44 (2013)
6. Seoul Government: Standard Apartment Management Rules, article 58, clause 3 (2008)
7. Yoo, E.: Inter-floor noise dispute, limit by phone counseling only. GreenPostKorea (2016). http://www.greenpostkorea.co.kr/news/article.html?no=67658
8. Defra: The Clean Neighbourhoods and Environment Act 2005, pp. 82–85 (2005)
9. Katz, E., Blumler, J.G., Gurevitch, M.: The Public Opinion Quarterly: Uses and Gratifications Research. Oxford University Press on behalf of the American Association for Public Opinion Research, pp. 509–523 (1974)
10. Jeong, Y.: Design and Implementation MoIP Wall-Pad Platform for Home-Network, pp. 16–17. Chungju National University, Chungju (2011)
11. Shin, Y.: Research on a SmartHub Design for Improving the Usability of SmartHome, pp. 24–26. Hongik University, Seoul (2016)

Analysis of Users' Mental Model and Expectations from Usability and Information Design Point of View in e-Contracts: A Case of Hotel Reservation

Renata Zappelli Marzullo[1], André Ribeiro Oliveira[1],
and Adriano Bernardo Renzi[2(✉)]

[1] Escola Superior de Desenho Industrial, Rio de Janeiro, Brazil
rvzappelli@gmail.com, ribeiro74@gmail.com
[2] Serviço Nacional de Aprendizagem Comercial/Senac-Rio,
Rio de Janeiro, Brazil
adrianorenzi@gmail.com

Abstract. For a successful business negotiation it is essential that all parts involved understand their duties and rights clearly in order to close the deal with mutual trust. The contract is the legal tool that can assure this communication between two or more parties. With the gradual technological advancements and the expansion of services and commerce to the internet, the contract function gets subdued, instead of being use as a tool for legal communication. The fragility of electronic contracts, can be observed by the number of users that contract and pay for services or products without even reading the terms of use. This research debates the role of e-contracts and its relation to Information Design, data organization and usability. These integrated areas of study are the foundation to build an online questionnaire applied to interaction design experts in order to map the interaction flow from specialists' perspective. The presented results expose usability issues related to information absorption and impact further discussion on the use of graphics to help improve e-contracts.

Keywords: Information design · Usability · Human computer interaction · e-Contract

1 Introduction: Contracts and e-Contracts

The comprehension of contracts can be helpful in communication between companies and its clients. According to Passera et al. [1], contracts are frequently analyzed from a juridical logic point of view, in which portray documents to be interpreted by law principles. For this, contracts are mostly created with the objective to solve legal disputes, instead of promoting a relation between the parts involved, which should be a requirement for any business.

The jurist César Fiuza [2] describes a pedagogical function of contracts, responsible for stimulating social relations between the parts involved in a business: "approximate people, abate their differences. The contractual clauses give the involved parties a sense

© Springer International Publishing AG 2017
A. Marcus and W. Wang (Eds.): DUXU 2017, Part III, LNCS 10290, pp. 784–803, 2017.
DOI: 10.1007/978-3-319-58640-3_56

of respect to the other, as well as to oneself, since it is pledged one's word. By means of contracts, people acquire their rights, as a contract is a miniature of a legal order, in which each part involved has their rights and duties expressed in clauses".

When businesses are conducted through online channels, the contract function gets even more subdued in the process. In an article published by The Guardian in 2011 [3], a research by Skandia (a company specialized in investments) presents the fragility of electronic contracts, since the percentage of people that contract and pay for services or products without even reading the terms of use is high.

This research showed that only 7% of clients read the terms of use when purchasing an online product of service, while 21% acknowledged having suffered later for marking the contract agreement box without reading its content. For every ten interviewed users, at least one felt attached to a contract longer than estimated as a result for not reading the contract clauses. And one in every twenty people lost money for not being able to cancel or change hotel reservations. According to the Newspaper, 43% of people do not read the terms and conditions of contract for considering a boring activity or for not fully understanding the clauses. Stanford University verified that 97% of users click the agree box without even reading the terms and private policies related to the services purchased [4]. Based on these facts, Alves and Araújo [5] alert that "consumers' vulnerability became higher with e-commerce, as the interlocutor does not fully comprehend the characteristics of a company that offers products and services through internet".

However, in face of the facilities of the web and technologies advancements, it was expected a more agile communication between the parts involved. Information about products, or services, should be more accessible and detailed to users, since there is no physical limit to the amount of data regarding a product. Likewise, contract terms can be available on the internet without the necessity of physical storage, using papers. The possibilities of visual information and objective search engines in dynamic online systems can also bring easiness to users in relevant information identification and comprehension. In theory, as concluded by Schreiber [6], the consumer should have lesser obstacles in e-commerce than the traditional brick and mortar businesses.

It is important to emphasize the security issues related to online purchases, a big influence in users buying decision. The perception of consumers regarding a company's credibility on security, privacy of information and usability has direct impact on their trust in the company. For this reason, Kim et al. [7] suggest that the key to success on e-business is the construction of reliable trustworthy transactions processes, where e-sellers offer a trustful environment. Likewise, Renzi and Freitas' research [8] has presented the integrated mutual feeding of usability and reliability in the e-commerce of books: planned information to bring good usability in a website can help increase users' trust.

Passera et al. [9] propose the use of information design in contracts, given its potential to change definition, structure and management foundations of commercial relations. The researchers suggest the use of visual direction to facilitate the assimilation of juridical terms, as well as to take contracts beyond mere legal documents and make them efficient communication tools.

In this context, becomes evident the necessity to study the influence of information design, its foundations and methodologies, and usability on online contract processes and their connection to digital environments that users trust and comprehend.

The present research has the objective to introduce the topic of information design, usability principles and infographic information as a mean of interaction and communication between companies and consumers through digital contracts and present preliminary results of an online questionnaire applied to HCI specialists regarding the topic, using Booking.com (the hotel reservation site most used worldwide, according to a research from Skift [10]) as the object of study. The decision to analyze hotel reservation e-contract processes came from the verification of the high number of users worldwide that use primarily the internet to search and book hotels.

The questionnaire objectify confirm relevant variables of information design, identified in theories, that may influence the usability of e-contracts. It is expected to have a general understanding of users' mental model and their expectations regarding organization of information during their assimilation and decision processes when booking a hotel.

2 Information Design, HCI and Usability

Shedroff [11] presents the beginning of information design from graphic design and editorial fields of knowledge, with the objective of organizing and presenting data in order to transform them into information with meaning and value. The International Institute for Information Design (IIID) [12] describes information design as "the definition, plan and modeling of a message content and the context it is inserted with the intention of satisfying the information needs of the receptors". Bonsiepe [13] characterizes Information Design as when content are visualized by means of selection, order, hierarchy, connections and visual distinctions that result in an efficient action. The design can facilitate the reception and interpretation, allowing therefore, more efficient actions. Frascara [14] defines it as a contemporary society's necessity, as it enables a great volume of information to be clear, in a homogeneity access. Its objective is to assure the effectiveness of communication through the easiness of perception processes, reading, comprehension, memorization and use of the information. For the author, a good information design makes information accessible, appropriate, complete, concise, meaningful – to fulfill users objectives – opportune, comprehensible and appreciated for its usefulness. It invites to be used, reduces tiredness and errors in the process of assimilation, speeds the work and makes the information attractive and adequate to contexts is fit in.

The efficiency of assimilation of information is also highlighted by Jacobson [15], who points that Information Design is to improve society's capacity in acknowledging, processing and disseminating information in order to create understanding. It is verified that diverse definitions of Information Design focus mainly on users and the efficiency of their actions, similar concerns of study from Interaction Design.

Preece et al. [16] put Interaction Design's primarily objectives as the reduction of negative aspects of user experience, such as frustration, and highlight of positive aspects, building interactive products with easiness, efficiency and pleasant to use. It is important to integrate studies of Information Design with HCI investigation to understand users' mental model, expectations and the most relevant information for better decisions. Studies from Nielsen, Schneiderman, Mijksennar, Tufte etc. are relevant to a deeper understanding of this relation and base to build a questionnaire suitable for this research.

Three principles for managing written content for the web are exposed by Nielsen [17]: be objective; write content for easy reading; use hypertexts to segment long information throughout pages. The author emphasizes the importance of presenting most important content first, since users do not waste too much time when reading on the web. Users need to identify in a quick visual browse what is the major content of the page and how it can help them. Nielsen complement about legibility: high contrast, flat colors for background and typography big enough for users to read easily. Mijksenaar [18] goes further and points the best way to design information is "to give form to information; to emphasize or to minimize; to compare or to ordain; to group or to classify; to select or to omit; to choose between immediate or slow recognition; and present it in an interesting way".

The author defines two major categories: (1) differentiation, which points to type distinction, colors and shapes, and (2) hierarchy, which indicates relevance distinction with the use of size and intensity.

Tufte [19] proposes principles to help guide informational projects from a visual point of view: show the data; induce the viewer to think about the substance rather than about methodology, graphic design, the technology of graphic production, or something else; avoid distorting what the data have to say; present many numbers in a small space; make large data sets coherent; encourage the eye to compare different pieces of data; reveal the data at several levels of detail, from a broad overview to the fine structure; serve a reasonably clear purpose: description, exploration, tabulation, or decoration; be closely integrated with the statistical and verbal descriptions of a data set.

The author [19] expresses what would be graphical excellence:

– Graphical excellence is the well-designed presentation of interesting data – a matter of substance, of statistics, and of design
– Graphical excellence consists of complex ideas communicated with clarity, precision, and efficiency.
– Graphical excellence is that which gives to the viewer the greatest number of ideas in the shortest time with the least ink in the smallest space
– Graphical excellence is nearly always multivariate
– And graphical excellence requires telling the truth about the data.

The relation of usability with Information Design urges the recall of usability principles to help guide the proposed investigation. The 10 heuristics of usability of Nielsen and Molich [20] focus primarily on websites through desktop interfaces. As similarly do the 8 golden rules [21] of Schneiderman. We do not intent to present heuristics related other apparatuses, such as Inostrozza's heuristics for mobile, Apted *et al.*'s heuristics for tabletop, Neto and Campos' heuristics for multi-modal environments and Renzi's heuristics for cross-channel interaction [22], as any comparison between these possibilities could defocus from the priority concerns of this research.

The 10 heuristics of Nielsen and Molich [20] are base for the usability evaluation technique (heuristic evaluation) that is still in use today and became foundation to later variations of the technique. The heuristics are consecution to users' needs in a time where the world was moving to the second wave of computing (one computer to one user):

1. Visibility of system status – the system should always keep users informed about what is going on, through appropriate feedback within reasonable time;
2. Match between system and the real world – the system should speak the user's language, with words, phrases and concepts familiar to the user, rather than system-oriented terms. Follow real-world conventions, making information appear in a natural and logical order;
3. User control and freedom – users often choose system functions by mistake and will need a clearly marked "emergency exit" to leave the unwanted state without having to go through an extended dialogue. Support undo and redo;
4. Consistency and standards – users should not have to wonder whether different words, situations, or actions mean the same thing. Follow platform conventions;
5. Error prevention – even better than good error messages is a careful design, which prevents a problem from occurring in the first place.
6. Recognition rather than recall – minimize the user's memory load by making objects, actions, and options visible;
7. Flexibility and efficiency of use – accelerators - unseen by the novice user – may often speed up the interaction for the expert user such that the system can cater to both inexperienced and experienced users. Allow users to tailor frequent actions;
8. Aesthetic and minimalist design – dialogues should not contain irrelevant information nor rarely needed. Every extra unit of information in a dialogue competes with the relevant units of information and diminishes their relative visibility;
9. Help users recognize, diagnose, and recover from errors – error messages should be expressed in plain language (no codes), precisely indicate the problem, and constructively suggest a solution;
10. Help and documentation – even though it is better if the system can be used without documentation, it may be necessary to provide help and documentation. Any such information should be easy to search, focused on the user's task, list concrete steps to be carried out, and not be too large.

These ten heuristics had its foundation on Norman's six principles from 1988:

1. Visibility – the more visible functions are, the more likely users will be able to know what to do next;
2. Feedback – feedback is about sending back information about what action has been done and what has been accomplished, allowing the person to continue with the activity;
3. Constraints – the design concept of constraining refers to determining ways of restricting the kind of user interaction that can take place at a given moment;
4. Mapping – this refers to the relationship between controls and their effects in the world;

5. Consistency – this refers to designing interfaces to have similar operations and use similar elements for achieving similar tasks;

Similarly, Ben Schneiderman's eight golden rules [21] were created based on his research regarding human-computer interaction, in 1987:

6. Objective consistency – similar situations requires consistency of actions, terminologies, prompts, menus, screens and help;
7. Shortcuts for frequent users – with use frequency, users prefer diminish number of interactions to increase the flow of interaction;
8. Offer informative feedback – for each action, should be a feedback;
9. Plan windows that encourage completion – sequence of actions must be organized in groups from start to finish;
10. Offer simple objective error recovery – plan a system that prevents users to make critical errors. If a mistake is made, the system should detect it and offer simple action to solve and recover from it;
11. Reverse actions easily – it relieves users' anxiety when knowing an action can be undone;
12. Sustain control – operators must feel they are in control of systems and that it respond to their actions;
13. Short-term memory load reduction – the human limitation of processing information in short-term memory require that displays be simple.

Although focused on usability, it is relevant to use these principles to guide evaluations and understand users as a base to integrate their needs to Information Design concepts. The integration of HCI, usability and Information Design concepts helped orientate the online questionnaire, applied to frequent users of Booking.com, with digital interaction background experience.

3 Online Questionnaire

In order to understand users' mental model of how a website for hotel reservation should work regarding Information Design, a selected group of users were invited to participate in an online questionnaire. The selection and invitation of participants followed rules where users invited had to have a minimum experience with interaction design, HCI, usability, UX and their respective concepts, in order to fully comprehend the usability references within the questionnaire questions. Participants were invited by e-mail and through the WhatsApp UX community of Rio de Janeiro. A total of 15 people agreed to participate.

A previous questionnaire was sent to a smaller group of UX specialist users to help test and map relevant topics as well as to get an overall view of the subject's ecology. For instance, the previous test confirmed studies that showed preference of using Booking.com, as 80% responded using the referred company in the last year for hotel reservation. The test also pointed a 90% preference to use desktop for searching hotels and making reservations online.

The second and main questionnaire focused on Booking.com following an expected reservation sequential interaction: landing page, search destination, assimilation of information, decision, acquisition of reservation service and terms and conditions agreement. The online questionnaire was built with the help of Typeform (a tool to create online responsive questionnaires and forms), with a total of 14 multiple-choice questions, following suggestions from Moura e Ferreira [23] and Mucchielli [24] in keeping a survey with less than 16 items and to formulate objective questions. Although online surveys have the advantage of reaching participants with no geographical restrains, it is important that the questions are objective and clear for participants, as the interviewer is not near to help with any doubts or misunderstanding [25].

The questionnaire was build with the premise that all participants have knowledge about usability, and therefore, some of the questions points relation to heuristics and HCI. Images and a direct link to each referred page were inserted to help participants investigate further the site and have a more clear analysis for judgment. The options to answer the questions were put together to simulate a descriptive Likert scale.

The descriptive scale intended to help the questionnaire be more objective to the point and bring a better flow to participants and minimize distortion. The first questions relate to general information about participants, their basic preferences and behavior when looking for a hotel. Questions 4 to 10 follows the sequential pattern of gathering information for a reservation decision, while questions 11 to 13 focus on interfaces related to complete the reservation. The last two questions (14–15) are about terms and conditions contracts.

4   Results

The results analysis was based on data tabulation provided by Typeform and presentation of this data follows the purchase motivation sequence interaction: landing page and search tool, search results, hotels' information page, booking procedure and reservation terms and conditions agreement.

4.1   Search and Purchase Motivation

Participants of the questionnaire frequently travel around Brazil, as well as others parts of the world, and the search for hotel reservation services is part of this process. Interestingly, the reservation process is part of the trip planning process in different ways, as 1/3 of respondents choose first the destination city, but start looking for reservation prior to having dates and flight scheduled. Another 1/3 shows that their reservation search is part of the process of planning the trip and helps to decide the best dates and location for staying. The rest of respondents already have their flight tickets purchased before looking for hotel reservation. Despite of the many inspirational options and promotional sales in the homepage, none of the respondents have these as an important step to plan their trip.

4.2   Homepage

When arriving at Booking.com homepage, three major sectors of information are noticeable: the central content space is divided in half, where the left side (occupying the first priority zone of Outing) presents the destination search tool as a big orange rounded square, and the right side offers inspirational destination offers. The top section keeps the logo and global navigation, mostly alternative helpful links, such as promotional sales, destination inspiration, vacation rentals etc.

In this section, most respondents (more than 2/3) affirm they can find easily everything they need. Even those who felt that the information organization could be a little confusing, their requirements could be fulfilled. For the rest of participants, the amount of information could be annoying and intrusive, as half of these declare to need only the destination search tool.

Considering the objective of the company and the expectations of users, the position on priority zone one and the choice of contrast of colors (orange square surrounded by its contrast color – blue) helps the search tool to stand above other sectors of information (Fig. 1).

Fig. 1. Booking.com homepage contrast of colors (Color figure online)

Regarding color and typographic use in the homepage, less than 1/3 of participants think it disturbs the information recognition and cause frustration. Although the majority doesn't think the site's color and typographic choices prevent them from finding relevant information, only 20% of these think they are truly helpful to organize subjects and find easily information of interest.

As opposed to the visibility of destination search pointed by users, the amount of information in the general sense of the landing page can be absorbed as "too much" of irrelevant information competing with their primarily objective: find a hotel.

4.3   Search Results

Almost 2/3 of the participants perceive the options of search filtering as great. From this majority group, 1/3 think the options are perfect and all filters needed are there, exhibited in well distributed information sections, but although the other 2/3 of this group thinks the options are great, they feel the disposition of information could get in the way of finding all possibilities. A minority (20%) found the amount of information too much and the organization confusing, while 13% was indifferent. Participants who inserted opinions, suggested: "not all filtering options need to be open. Analyze which ones are more used and minimize the rest".

Still regarding the results page (Fig. 2), the questionnaire approach the topics of information organization, the use of colors and supporting elements to help hierarchize relevant information – based on Mijksenaar principles of giving form to information (to emphasize or to minimize; to compare or to ordain; to group or to classify; to select or to omit; to choose between immediate or slow recognition; and present it in an interesting way). Although the website shows a concern for the flexibility of need and use (heuristic 7), respondents are divided evenly in their opinions on how these options are presented, as 1/3 considers that information organization, the use of colors and supporting elements adequate and help locate information, 1/3 thinks they do not help (but not interfere) and 1/3 feels they are too much and fight for attention in the page.

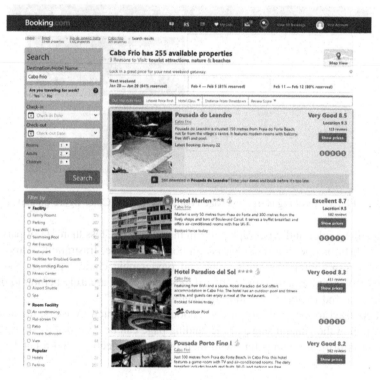

Fig. 2. Booking.com search results page. (Color figure online)

4.4 Hotel's Information Page

When choosing options of hotels from the results page, users can analyze each hotel separately by looking at each hotel specifications, room possibilities, prices, photos of the hotel, map location, rating, reviews by other costumers, description and facilities offered (Fig. 3). The search tool still keeps activated on the top left and an option to search similar properties resides right bellow it. Following the visual hierarchy, almost half of participants show first attention to the pictures of the hotel in order to get the hotel's visual impression – if unsatisfactory, they return to the results page for other options. The location map is the most important information to 1/3 of participants and only 1/5 goes first to price and room availability on the bottom of the page. One person points preference to check consumers' reviews and rating and then goes directly to photos.

Fig. 3. Booking.com hotel page.

Regarding the support elements (arrows, lines, boxes) and icons – to encourage the eye to compare different pieces of data, to reveal the data at several levels of detail, to serve a reasonably clear purpose of description, exploration, tabulation, and decoration – Tufte [19], half of users points that although helpful, the amount of highlights and information can still be overwhelming. A 1/5 of users believe the icons are adequate and fundamental to create areas of topics and help find information, but another 1/5 finds that the although icons help find relevant information, other elements are not significant to the hierarchy of information. A small portion of participants thinks it is all too much.

The page holds a lot of information that could help users analyze options and make decisions, but it seems that the choice of icons and visual elements does not fully creates hierarchy and information sections nor minimizes the sensation of too much information.

4.5   Booking Phase

After choosing the hotel, users reach the reservation page (Fig. 4) in order to finalize the booking procedure. The page holds a reference photo of the chosen hotel and respective basic information (name, location, rating, check-in and check-out dates, total price and basic facilities).

Bellow this quick reference for users self-locate, a box occupies the scroll down section to help users confirm details of the reservation and fill in the blanks with personal information to close the reservation service contract with Booking.com and the hotel. The participants were asked about the organization of the information (from Bonsiepe's use of grouping and arrangements – content must be visualized by means of selection, order, hierarchy, connections and visual distinctions that result in an efficient action). The results showed that almost half (40%) of participants agree that the sections are logical and help to organize content by topics as well as find relevant information easily. A 1/3 of users find that, although the sections do not fully help, they do not hide relevant information. Only 1/5 of participants think the sections are not logical and the amount of information is annoying. One user added a comment: "the organization and sections does make sense, but there is too much information, which brings some confusion to the page. For instance, there are 4–5 warning boxes at the same time, located far apart from each other". Overall, the organization of sections seems to facilitate the locating and understanding of information and proper actions to take. The problems noted by the specialists would be considered minor problems (or even aesthetic problems) in a heuristic evaluation, as they would not disturb the execution of the principal task.

However the pointed problems are minor and doesn't impede the execution of reservation, the amount of information seems to bother as half of the users indicate that they can find everything they need with a little effort, but the organization of sections could be sometimes confusing. Another 1/3 also points out the confusing layout and adds that some information is unnecessary. A commented opinion alerts to layout organization disturbance to him/her: "the information I need, in case of an action, are in opposite sides". Only a small part agrees that all information is well organized and everything needed are right there.

Fig. 4. Booking.com reserve finish page.

4.6   Terms and Conditions

To finalize the hotel reservation (Fig. 5) is necessary to confirm all booking information, include payment information, contact information (if you are not logged in yet) and agree to terms and conditions. The checking box to agree to terms involves three different terms: (1) booking conditions, related to the hotel's conditions; (2) general terms, refering to Booking.com 12 terms for using their service; and (3) privacy policy, which explains about how security, cookies and costumers' privacy work on Booking. com. The hotel terms (booking conditions) are direct and mostly related to rules regarding extra additional beds and cancelation. The Booking.com's general terms involves a long description of 12 terms, from definition and prices rate to disclaimer and intellectual property rights. The how-it-works section (privacy and policy) is long and very detailed. A link "Read me, I'm important" shows as an alternative path to reach the hotel's terms (booking conditions) in a pop up display.

The disposal of the confirmation page brings security issues to half of participants (20% thinks the layout visually intrusive) and only 1/3 are ok with the sense of security and fully understands the hotel reservation policy. One participant points that the unnecessary information does not influence his/her sense of security.

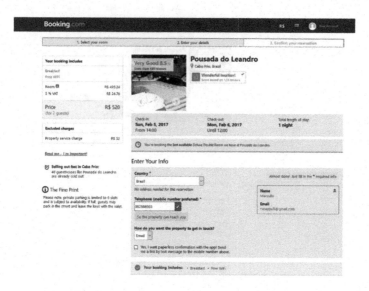

Fig. 5. Booking.com reservation finish page.

The "Read me, I'm important" link brings a pop up (Figs. 6 and 7) with the hotel's terms (booking terms) as an alternative option to reach the information. A 1/3 of the participants showed difficulties to find this link and think the information display can be confusing. Another 1/3 hardly (or never) click on this option and comments resume as: "I never click on it", "oh! I think I have never entered here. Is it new?" and "I couldn't visualize the pop up". The rest of respondents are divided between (1) thinking the hotel's terms could be more objective as it has some unnecessary information, and (2) although a good option of displaying the content, it is hard to find

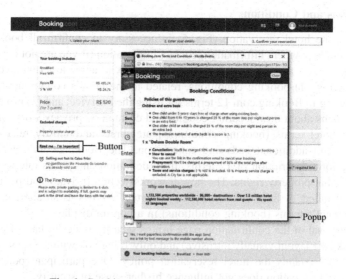

Fig. 6. Booking.com conditions button and popup.

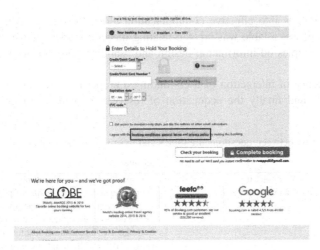

Fig. 7. Booking conditions, general terms and privacy policy buttons.

the link and understand what the information was about. Only one person though the link option was perfect.

Regarding the three terms and conditions that users have to agree (Fig. 7) in order to conclude the hotel reservation, 2/5 of participants declare they never click because they think it is indifferent and will not influence their reservation. A 1/6 of participants also don't click, affirming that the disposition of all the terms is exhausting and unnecessary to have so many buttons and pages of explanation. Almost 1/3 enters the terms links but browse it quickly as the big amount of information and lack of visual elements makes the reading confusing. One of the respondents assumes he/she doesn't click and feels insecure in agreeing to an unread contract. Just 1/6 of the participants clicks and read everything.

It is important to present some of the participants' comments from the last section of the questionnaire, an open box for the possibility of adding any further opinions about Booking.com website. This possibility has upraised interesting information from users: "the website offers a good service, but it has a lot of unnecessary information, bringing visual pollution and distracting from the basic objective", "pages terribly polluted (visually). I prefer Airbnb, as it has solved this in a simple way", "regarding security during the process, some of Booking.com's rules and hotels' rules can be conflicting and confusing".

5 Synthesis

The questionnaire, even applied to a small group, brings attention to a discussion about e-contracts' role in the process of interaction and consumption of a service or product. The idea of just a small percentage of users having the urge to click and read throughout an entire e-contract is an alert to further investigation on how information design and HCI principles could bring positive impact and improvements to potentially transform contracts into effective communication tools. In order to better synthesize this research phase, a table was created relating the topics addressed in the questionnaire with principles od information design and usability, and their respective authors (Table 1):

The sequence of interaction of users finding a proper hotel option, the analysis of characteristics and finally the acquisition of reservation seem to follow an obvious

Table 1. Relation between questionnaire topics and information design and usability principles

#	Questions topics	Principles
1.	Deciding to book a hotel using Booking.com or another web site	- Not specifically related to usability principles, but directly related to the principle of pervasiveness of systems when building a UX journey – Renzi [22] - Related to the description of information design from the The International Institute for Information Design (IIID) with the intention of understand the information needs of the users when decide to book a hotel. – IIID [12]
2.	The Booking.com homepage's display of destinations search tool and inspiration options, insert review and packages	- Nielsen's [20] heuristics 4 and 8 and [17] principles about high contrast and hierarchy of content - Bonsipe's [13] concern with visualization of content by means of selection, order, hierarchy, connections and visual distinctions
3.	The Booking.com homepage's choices of color and typography for hierarchy of information	- Nielsen's [20] heuristics 4 and 8 - Bonsipe's [13] concern with visualization of content by means of selection, order, hierarchy - Mijksenaar's [18] points on to give form to information, to emphasize and to ordain
4.	Presentation and order of choices at the search page	- Nielsen's [20] heuristics 2, 4, 6, 7 and 8 - Bonsipe's [13] concern with visualization of content by means of selection, order, hierarchy - Mijksenaar's [18] points on to give form to information, to emphasize and to ordain
5.	Results page possibilities of reorganizing data	- Nielsen's [20] heuristics 2, 3, 4, 7 and 8 - Bonsipe's [13] concern with visualization of content by means of selection, order, hierarchy - Mijksenaar's [18] points on to give form to information, to emphasize and to ordain
6.	The information differentiation, use of colors and supporting elements at the search results page	- Nielsen's [20] heuristics 4 and 8 - Bonsipe's [13] concern with visualization of content by means of selection, order, hierarchy - Mijksenaar's [18] points on to give form to information, to emphasize and to ordain
7.	Hotel information hierarchy	- Nielsen's [20] heuristics 4 and 8 - Related to the description of information design from the The International Institute for Information Design (IIID) with the intention of understand the information needs of the users when decide to book a hotel. – IIID [12]

(continued)

Table 1. (*continued*)

#	Questions topics	Principles
8.	The use of information differentiation, use of colors and supporting elements at hotel's page	- Nielsen's [20] heuristics 2, 4, 6 and 8 - Tufte's [19] proposed principles to help guide informational projects from a visual point of view to encourage the eye on compare different pieces of data, to reveal the data at several levels of detail, to serve a reasonably clear purpose: description, exploration, tabulation, and decoration
9.	The information organization at the hotel reservation page	- Nielsen's [20] heuristics 2, 4, 6 and 8 - Bonsipe's [13] concern with visualization of content by means of selection, order, hierarchy
10.	Trust elements at the reservation confirmation page	- Nielsen's [20] heuristics 2, 4 and 8 - Frascara's [14] objective of information design in assuring effectiveness of communication through the easiness of perception processes, reading, comprehension, memorization and use of the information, to achieve sense of security and fully understanding - Preece *et al.*'s [16] definition of Interaction Design's primarily objectives as the reduction of negative aspects of user experience, such as frustration, and highlight of positive aspects, building interactive products with easiness, efficiency and pleasant to use
11.	Terms and conditions access	- Nielsen's [20] heuristics 2, 4, 6 and 8
12.	Information understanding and trust at terms and conditions' page	- Nielsen's [20] heuristics 4, 5, 8 and 10 - Tufte's [19] proposed principles to help guide informational projects from a visual point of view to show the data; to induce the viewer to think about the substance rather than others things; avoid distorting what the data have to say; encourage the eye to compare different pieces of data; reveal the data at several levels of detail, from a broad overview to the fine structure; serve a reasonably clear purpose: description, exploration, tabulation, or decoration - Mijksenaar's [18] principles: to emphasize or to minimize; to compare or to ordain; to group or to classify; to select or to omit; to choose between immediate or slow recognition; and present it in an interesting way

pattern where users consider many positive and negative aspects before reaching a decision. The choice of reservation influence not only the fulfilling task of choosing a hotel, but the users' experience of their trip, as a substantial percentage of users considers hotel reservation choices as part of their travel planning.

When considering the user experience as a journey that links short scenes [22], the actions involved in looking for a perfect hotel is a short scene that can relate to users' decision on length of stay, self-location and understanding possibilities of attractions to visit. This short scene (hotel reservation) will affect the experience while the trip is in course and afterwards, in users' analysis of the whole experience.

Specifically regarding the sequence of actions to fulfill the reservation task involving perception of information, click decisions, searches, observation of images, comparison of prices, room availability checks, hotel facilities analysis and payment procedures, in order to users truly finish their reservation, it is mandatory to agree with Booking.com and hotel's conditions. The sequential order of actions can be tiring as it is an important part of users' trip planning and can affect their experience journey. Having the e-contract as a last phase of the process, it is important to consider the time and cognitive consuming actions when projecting e-contracts in order to make this last part with a less cognitive load and easier to understand. After so many clicks, users are no longer willing to spend time with further actions to finalize the reservation, and therefore, expect simpler registrations and forms.

According to Passera [26], "contract drafters too often seem focused exclusively on the contract itself rather than on facilitating successful relationships", resulting in contracts that are unnecessarily complex and difficult to use. It is important to propose information design solutions and bring a new approach to e-contracts. The author adds "that achieving this broader potential for contracting leads in a direction where not many researchers or practitioners have looked before, and where few organizations have invested or innovated: in the human side of contracting and the important role of contract users with non-legal backgrounds. While user-centeredness and simplification have influenced many fields, they have hardly caught the attention of the legal or contracting community".

Results imply the subdued function of the terms and conditions, as many experts, participants of the questionnaire, are indifferent to it. Although a necessary act to finish the process, the e-contract is not perceived as an influence to the reservation and not seen as a communication tool. Even Booking.com's attempt to create a "Read Me. I'm Important" link was not completely effective, as it was considered hard to find and not part of the interaction sequence.

The questionnaire results has brought a better understanding of the whole process of actions, from interaction specialists point of view, and partially map problems in the interaction sequence. The amount of irrelevant information is, throughout the whole experience, pointed as a distraction from users' objectives and sometimes even an annoyance in the relevant information filtering. Although considered not an obstacle to fulfill any sequence actions, its annoyance can increase the cognition load and therefore add to the tiredness at the end of the process. As an example, the website's concern in showing inspirational places and destination good deals does not influence one bit users' objectives, as this information do not take part of users destination decisions or their trip plans. It probably would have an impact only in cases where these inspirations match exactly users' trip plans.

The noticed usability problems seem mostly small and aesthetic (in the heuristic evaluation 0–4 scale) and are not urgent to solve. But considering the accumulative annoyance and cognitive load it provokes throughout interaction sequence, it affects the patience of users and the interest in looking the e-contract in the final phase. A re-planning of the visual information structure and icon adjustments could help minimize distractions and enhance the experience, but a further research with the use of

Think-aloud protocol with users and Heuristic evaluation with usability experts may be needed to better specify solutions accordingly. The appointed problems in information organization and absorption are related mainly to 4 usability heuristics:

- heuristic 4 – Consistency and standards: users should not have to wonder whether different words, situations, or actions mean the same thing. Follow platform conventions;
- heuristic 6 – Recognition rather than recall: minimize the user's memory load by making objects, actions, and options visible;
- heuristic 8 – Aesthetic and minimalist design: dialogues should not contain irrelevant information nor rarely needed. Every extra unit of information in a dialogue competes with the relevant units of information and diminishes their relative visibility;
- heuristic 10 – Help and documentation: even though it is better if the system can be used without documentation, it may be necessary to provide help and documentation. Any such information should be easy to search, focused on the user's task, list concrete steps to be carried out, and not be too large.

The heuristic 10 is directly involved with the e-contracts, as it is related to documentation of information. Although many times disregarded by developers, the 10th heuristic can affect crucial situations for users. In Booking.com case, participants demonstrate difficulties with the detailed information regarding the presented conditions of the chosen hotel and of Booking.com itself. Principles proposed by Mijksenaar [18] and Tufte [19] could help minimize these pointed difficulties: to emphasize or to minimize; to compare or to ordain; to group or to classify; to select or to omit; to choose between immediate or slow recognition; and present it in an interesting way, to show the data; to induce the viewer to think about the substance rather than others things; avoid distorting what the data have to say; encourage the eye to compare different pieces of data; reveal the data at several levels of detail, from a broad overview to the fine structure; serve a reasonably clear purpose: description, exploration, tabulation, or decoration.

As an important section of communication between two (or more) parts involved (service providers and consumers), the terms and condition sections are of great importance in the negotiation and in exposing items to be contracted. It is extremely important the transparency of the information on this screen, and the use of information design resources to ensure a good understanding of the rights related to each part.

6 Conclusion

Results of this research bring the relevance of discussion regarding information design and HCI on e-contracts, as well as, further investigations on the feasibility of using infographics as a tool to enhance e-contracts understanding in hotel reservation processes.

According to Lima [27], the use of infopraphics is revealed as an important graphic language resource, adaptable to the new media and able to cope with the demand of modernization of communication, by unified pictorial elements, schematics and written text. The author emphasizes the use of infographics to increase understanding in situations of complex facts and explanations that need to be communicated and contextualized, as its purpose is to help readers to understand information that, communicated otherwise, could be too complex. Moraes [28] adds that infographics should present information to answer the questions "where", "when", "what", "who" and "why". As similarly, contracts should answer these same questions.

Besides the usability further investigation necessity to map specific problems, it is encouraged the use of infographics as a resource for comparison tests. It is expected that these future results could bring a better understanding of infographics' influence in e-contracts attention and comprehension by users. The continuity of the research can arise further discussion on contractual information translated visually through elements, such as graphs, diagrams, according to facilitate a clear communication, that with new technology and interaction possibilities, endorse the development of electronic contracts containing clauses and conditions open to direct negotiation with users. Such cases, where the consumer would be able to express his will to specific contents of a clause or condition, could change the unilateral nature of the contract and potentially impact the case-law Judicial Courts with adhesion contracts.

Bibliography

1. Passera, P., Pohjonen, S., Koskelainen, K., Anttila, S.: User-friendly contracting tools – a visual guide to facilitate public procurement contracting. In: Proceedings of the IACCM Academic Forum on Contract and Commercial Management 2013, 8th October 2013, Phoenix, USA (2013)
2. de Oliveira Naves, B.T.: Notas sobre a função do contrato na história. Lex, v.3, São Paulo (2006)
3. Smithers, R.: Terms and conditions: not reading the small print can mean big problems. The Guardian. https://www.theguardian.com/money/2011/may/11/terms-conditions-small-print-big-problems
4. Romero, L.: Não li e concordo. Super Interessante magazine. http://super.abril.com.br/tecnologia/nao-li-concordo-contratos-termos-sites-redes-sociais-698482.shtml
5. Alves, G., Araújo, J.: Proteção e defesa do consumidor nos conflitos de comércio eletrônico brasileiro. Revista Científica da Facerb 2(2), 44–65 (2015)
6. Schreiber, A.: Contratos eletrônicos e consumo. Revista Brasileira de Direito Civil. Rio de Janeiro, v.1 (2014)
7. Kim, D.J., Ferrin, D.L., Rao, H.R.: A trust-based consumer decision model in electronic commerce: the role of trust, risk, and their antecedents. Decis. Support Syst. **44**(2), 544–564 (2008). Research Collection Lee Kong Chian School of Business, Singapore
8. Renzi, A.B., Freiras, S.: Usabilidade e fatores de confiança na procura e compra de livros em livrarias on-line. Textos Selecionados de Design 3. PPDESDI UERJ, Rio de Janeiro (2013)
9. Passera, S., Haapio, H., Barton, T.D.: Innovating contract practices: merging contract design with information design. In: Proceedings of the IACCM Academic Forum on Contract and Commercial Management, 8 October 2011, Phoenix: 2013 (2013)
10. Ali, R.: Skift - The Most Popular Online Booking Sites in Travel, 2014 Edition (2014)
11. Shedroff, N.: Information interaction design: a unified field theory of design. In: Jacobson, R. (ed.) Information Design. The MIT Press, Cambridge (2000)

12. IIID. International Institute for Information Design (2007). http://www.iiid.net/home/definitions/. Accessed 2016
13. Bonsiepe, G.: Design, cultura e sociedade. Blucher, São Paulo (2011)
14. Frascara, J.: ¿Qué es el Diseño de Información? Buenos Aires: Ediciones Infinito (2011)
15. Jacobson, R.: Introduction: why information design matters? In: Jacobson, R. (ed.) Information Design. The MIT Press, Cambridge (2000)
16. Preece, J., Rogers, Y., Sharp, H.: Design de Interação: Além da interação homem-computador. Bookman, Porto Alegre (2005)
17. Nielsen, J.: Projetando Websites. Campus, Rio de Janeiro (2000). Trad. Ana Gibson
18. Mijksenaar, P.: Visual function: an introduction to information design. 010 Publishers, Rotterdam (1997)
19. Tufte, E.R.: The Visual Display of Quantitative Information, 2nd edn. Graphics Press, Cheshire (2001)
20. Nielsen, J.: 10 usability heuristics for interface design (1995). www.nngroup.com/articles/ten-usability-heuristics
21. Schneiderman, B., Plaisant, C.: Designing the User Interface. Addison Wesley, Boston (1986)
22. Renzi, A.B.: Experiência do ususário: a jornada de Designers nos processos de gestão de suas empresas de pequeno porte utilizando sistema fantasiado em ecossistema de interação cross-channel. Doctorate thesis, 239 p. Escola Superior de Desenho Industrial. Rio de Janeiro, Brazil (2016)
23. de Moura, M.L.S., Ferreira, M.C.: Projetos de pesquisa: elaboração, redação e apresentação, 144 p. Eduerj, Rio de Janeiro (2005)
24. Mucchielli, R.: O questionário na pesquisa psicosocial. Martins Fontes, São Paulo (1979)
25. Renzi, A.B.: Usabilidade na procura e compra de livros em livrarias online. Dissertation (Master of Science). Esdi – UERJ, Rio de Janeiro (2010)
26. Passera, S., Haapio, H., Barton, T.D.: Innovating contract practices: merging contract design with information design. In: Proceedings of the IACCM Academic Forum on Contract and Commercial Management, 8th October 2011, Phoenix, USA (2013)
27. Lima, R.: O que é infografia jornalística? Revista Brasileira de Design da Informação **12**(1), 111–127 (2015). São Paulo
28. Moraes, A.: Infografia: história e projeto - origens, conceitos e processos do design que modificou a forma da mídia mais tradicional da história. Blücher, São Paulo (2013)

Author Index

Printed in the United States
By Bookmasters

Printed in the United States
By Bookmasters